The Cambridge Handbook of Applied Psychological Ethics

The Cambridge Handbook of Applied Psychological Ethics is a valuable resource for psychologists and graduate students hoping to further develop their ethical decision-making beyond more introductory ethics texts. The book offers real-world ethical vignettes and considerations. Chapters cover a wide range of practice settings, populations, and topics, and are written by scholars in these settings. Chapters focus on the application of ethics to the ethical dilemmas in which mental health and other psychology professionals sometimes find themselves: each chapter introduces a setting and gives readers a brief understanding of some of the potential ethical issues at hand, before delving deeper into the multiple ethical issues that must be addressed and the ethical principles and standards involved. No other book on the market captures the breadth of ethical issues found in daily practice and focuses entirely on applied ethics in psychology.

MARK M. LEACH is Professor and Department Chair in the Department of Counseling and Human Development at the University of Louisville. He has produced over 100 publications, including seven other books, and 120 presentations, many in the area of national and international ethics. He is a Fellow of two American Psychological Association (APA) divisions (17, 52) and was awarded a Presidential Citation from the APA. Dr. Leach was an Associate Member of the APA Ethics Committee and a member of other APA and division committees and boards, has given multiple keynote addresses, and is Associate Editor or reviewer for multiple journals.

ELIZABETH REYNOLDS WELFEL is Professor Emerita in Counseling Psychology at Cleveland State University. Her career spans 36 years in counseling psychology, divided between Boston College and Cleveland State University. She is the author of four books, including the text *Ethics in Counseling and Psychotherapy: Standards, Research, and Emerging Issues*, currently in its sixth edition. In addition, she has published widely in peer-reviewed journals, served on editorial boards of APA journals, and edited several books on ethics. She has presented numerous papers at professional conferences. She is a Fellow in two divisions of the APA

(17, 29) and served on the Board of the Council of Counseling Psychology Training Programs. She earned Cleveland State's Distinguished Faculty Award for her teaching and scholarship in professional ethics. Dr. Welfel is a sought-after speaker for continuing education programs and has offered them across the country for more than two decades.

The Cambridge Handbook of Applied Psychological Ethics

Edited by

Mark M. Leach
University of Louisville

Elizabeth Reynolds Welfel
Cleveland State University

CAMBRIDGE
UNIVERSITY PRESS

CAMBRIDGE
UNIVERSITY PRESS

University Printing House, Cambridge CB2 8BS, United Kingdom

One Liberty Plaza, 20th Floor, New York, NY 10006, USA

477 Williamstown Road, Port Melbourne, VIC 3207, Australia

314–321, 3rd Floor, Plot 3, Splendor Forum, Jasola District Centre,
New Delhi – 110025, India

79 Anson Road, #06–04/06, Singapore 079906

Cambridge University Press is part of the University of Cambridge.

It furthers the University's mission by disseminating knowledge in the pursuit of
education, learning, and research at the highest international levels of excellence.

www.cambridge.org
Information on this title: www.cambridge.org/9781107124547
DOI: 10.1017/9781316417287

First published 2018

Printed in the United States of America by Sheridan Books, Inc.

A catalogue record for this publication is available from the British Library.

Library of Congress Cataloging-in-Publication Data
Names: Leach, Mark M., editor. | Welfel, Elizabeth Reynolds, 1949– editor.
Title: The Cambridge handbook of applied psychological ethics / edited by
Mark M. Leach, University of Louisville, Kentucky, Elizabeth Reynolds
Welfel, Cleveland State University.
Description: Cambridge, United Kingdom ; New York, NY : Cambridge University
Press, 2018. | Includes index.
Identifiers: LCCN 2017043882 | ISBN 9781107124547
Subjects: LCSH: Mental health services – Moral and ethical aspects. | Mental
health counseling – Moral and ethical aspects. | Mental health
personnel – Professional ethics.
Classification: LCC RA790.5 .C3194 2018 | DDC 174.2/9689–dc23
LC record available at https://lccn.loc.gov/2017043882

ISBN 978-1-107-12454-7 Hardback
ISBN 978-1-107-56193-9 Paperback

To Thomas Oakland, one of the most ethical and virtuous people I've ever known

M.M.L.

To Fred and Brandon, the joys of my life

E.R.W.

Contents

List of Contributors   *page* x
Preface   xv
Acknowledgments   xvii

Section I Ethical Issues in Specific Settings and Challenging Populations

1 Ethical Considerations for Working with Military
   Service Personnel   3
   W. BRAD JOHNSON

2 Ethical Issues in Addressing Mental Health Concerns in Schools   20
   HOWARD S. ADELMAN AND LINDA TAYLOR

3 Ethical Issues in Providing Mental Health Services
   to College Students   47
   MARY ANN COVEY AND KARI J. KELLER

4 Ethical Issues When Working in Hospital Settings   70
   KATHLEEN R. ASHTON AND AMY B. SULLIVAN

5 Ethics in a Rural Context   93
   CINDY JUNTUNEN, MELISSA A. QUINCER, AND SINÉAD
   K. P. M. UNSWORTH

6 Ethics and Private Practice   115
   JEAN A. CARTER

7 Ethics on the Edge: Working with Clients Who Are
   Persistently Suicidal   134
   DEREK TRUSCOTT

8 Applied Addiction Ethics   154
   CYNTHIA M. A. GEPPERT AND BRYN S. ESPLIN

9 Ethics and Clients Who Have Experienced Sexual Trauma
   and Intimate Partner Violence   178
   KRISTA M. CHRONISTER, KELSEY SOUTH, ANJULI CHITKARA-BARRY,
   HARPREET NAGRA, ANNA REICHARD, AND SHOSHANA D. KEREWSKY

10 Ethical Issues in the Treatment of Eating Disorders   197
LAURA H. CHOATE

11 Ethical Considerations in Group Psychotherapy   218
MARIA T. RIVA AND JENNIFER A. ERICKSON CORNISH

12 Ethical Issues in Couple and Family Therapy   239
LORNA L. HECKER AND MEGAN J. MURPHY

Section II Ethical Issues in Working with Diverse Populations

13 Ethical Issues in Working with Older Adults   265
ROWENA GOMEZ AND LISA M. BROWN

14 Ethical Issues in Working with Individuals with Disability   285
JENNIFER A. ERICKSON CORNISH AND SAMANTHA
PELICAN MONSON

15 Ethical Issues When Working with People of Color   302
SUZETTE L. SPEIGHT AND MICHAEL C. CADARET

16 Aging: Ethical Issues in Working with Diverse Populations   321
MARY MILLER LEWIS, KATHERINE RAMOS, AND ASHLEY OLIVER

17 Applied Research in Diverse Communities: Ethical Issues and
    Considerations   340
JUSTIN C. PERRY AND ADAM M. VOIGHT

18 Ethical Issues and Challenges Working with Religious
    Individuals and Organizations: Providing Culturally Competent
    Professional Mental Health Services   366
THOMAS G. PLANTE

19 Ethical Issues Associated with Mental Health Interventions for
    Immigrants and Refugees   384
RACHEL R. SINGER AND MILTON A. FUENTES

20 Ethical Issues in Psychotherapy with Lesbian, Gay, Bisexual,
    and Transgender Clients: A Cognitive Developmental Model
    of Ethical Competence   406
RUPERTO M. PEREZ AND JILL S. LEE-BARBER

Section III Legal, Research, and Organizational Issues

21 Major Legal Cases That Have Influenced Mental Health Ethics   429
G. ANDREW H. BENJAMIN AND CONNIE J. BECK

22 Ethical Considerations in Forensic Evaluations in Family Court   452
ROBERT GEFFNER, MORGAN SHAW, AND BRITTANY CROWELL

23 Ethical Issues in Online Research   474
    LYNNE D. ROBERTS AND JESSICA B. A. SIPES

24 Ethical Issues in International Research   493
    MARK M. LEACH AND SHARON G. HORNE

25 Clinical Supervision for Multicultural and Professional
    Competence   511
    ERICA H. WISE AND JENNIFER L. SCHWARTZ

26 Disciplinary Supervision: Ethical Challenges for Supervisors   531
    JANET T. THOMAS AND JOHN H. HUNG

27 Ethical Issues in Psychological Consultation   552
    STEWART E. COOPER AND RODNEY L. LOWMAN

Section IV Emerging Ethical Issues in Professional Practice and Next Steps

28 Genetic Testing and Ethical Considerations: Cases Involving
    Adolescents and Young Adults and Cancer   577
    MARILYN STERN, JENNIFER BLECK, AND GWENDOLYN P. QUINN

29 Ethical Considerations for Behavioral Health Professionals
    in Primary Care Settings   598
    ABBIE O. BEACHAM AND KRISTI S. VAN SICKLE

30 Therapy with Children and Adolescents in an Era of Social
    Media and Instant Electronic Communication   616
    JASON VAN ALLEN, PAIGE L. SEEGAN, BRITTANY LANCASTER,
    AND DEVIN GUNSTREAM-SISOMPHOU

31 Ethics and Ethical Decision-Making in Coaching: Four
    Case Scenarios   637
    SHARON K. ANDERSON AND JUDY B. SMETANA

32 Ethical Issues in Prevention   659
    JONATHAN P. SCHWARTZ, SALLY M. HAGE, AND CHRISTINE PAO

33 Fostering Ethical Mental Health Practice across Diverse Settings
    and Populations: Concluding Thoughts   677
    ELIZABETH REYNOLDS WELFEL AND MARK M. LEACH

    Index   686

Contributors

HOWARD S. ADELMAN, PH.D., Professor and Codirector, School Mental Health Project and Center for MH in Schools, Department of Psychology, UCLA, Los Angeles, CA

SHARON K. ANDERSON, PH.D., Professor, School of Education, Colorado State University, Fort Collins, CO

KATHLEEN R. ASHTON, PH.D., ABPP, Psychologist, Breast Center, Digestive Disease Institute, Cleveland Clinic Foundation; Assistant Clinical Professor of Surgery, Cleveland Clinic Lerner College of Medicine; Cleveland, OH

ABBIE O. BEACHAM, PH.D., University of Colorado Denver, Denver, CO

CONNIE J. BECK, PH.D., Professor of Psychology, University of Arizona, Tempe, AZ

G. ANDREW H. BENJAMIN, J.D., PH.D., Director, Parent Evaluation Training Program, University of Washington, Seattle, WA

JENNIFER BLECK, PH.D., MPH, Department of Child and Family Studies, College of Behavioral & Community Sciences, University of South Florida, Tampa, FL

LISA M. BROWN, PH.D., ABPP, Professor, Director of Trauma Program, Palo Alto University, Palo Alto, CA

MICHAEL C. CADARET, PH.D., Assistant Professor of Psychology, Springfield College, Springfield, MA

JEAN A. CARTER, PH.D., Washington Psychological Center, PC, Washington, DC

ANJULI CHITKARA-BARRY, M.A., University of Oregon, Eugene, OR

LAURA H. CHOATE, ED.D., Professor, Counselor Education, Louisiana State University, Baton Rouge, LA

KRISTA M. CHRONISTER, PH.D., Associate Professor and Assistant Dean for Equity and Inclusion, University of Oregon, Eugene, OR

STEWART E. COOPER, PH.D., Director of Counseling Services; Professor of Psychology, Valparaiso University, Valparaiso, IN

MARY ANN COVEY, PH.D., Associate Director, Student Counseling Service, Texas A&M University, College Station, TX

JENNIFER A. ERICKSON CORNISH, PH.D., Professor and Director of Clinical Training, Graduate School of Professional Psychology, University of Denver, Denver, CO

BRITTANY CROWELL, PSY.D., Institute on Violence, Abuse, and Trauma, San Diego, CA

BRYN S. ESPLIN, JD, Assistant Professor, Department of Humanities in Medicine, Texas A&M University, Health Science Center College of Medicine, College Station, TX

MILTON A. FUENTES, PSY.D., Psychology Department, Montclair State University, Montclair, NJ

ROBERT GEFFNER, PH.D., Institute on Violence, Abuse, and Trauma, San Diego, CA

CYNTHIA M. A. GEPPERT, MD, DPS, Professor of Psychiatry and Director of Ethics Education, University of New Mexico School of Medicine, Albuquerque, NM

ROWENA GOMEZ, PH.D., Director of Clinical Training, Clinical Psychology Program Pacific Graduate School of Psychology, Palo Alto University, Palo Alto, CA

DEVIN GUNSTREAM-SISOMPHOU, B.A., Department of Psychological Sciences, Texas Tech University, Lubbock, TX

SALLY M. HAGE, PH.D., Program Director Counseling Psychology, Springfield College, Springfield, MA

LORNA L. HECKER, PH.D., Professor Emeritus, Marriage and Family Therapy Program, Department of Behavioral Sciences, Purdue University Northwest, Hammond, IN

SHARON G. HORNE, PH.D., Professor and Graduate Program Director of Counseling Psychology, College of Education and Human Development, University of Massachusetts Boston, Boston, MA

JOHN H. HUNG, PH.D., Licensed Psychologist, Independent Practice, Edina, MN

W. BRAD JOHNSON, PH.D., Professor, Department of Leadership, Ethics, Law, United States Naval Academy, Annapolis, MD

CINDY JUNTUNEN, PH.D., Interim Dean/Professor, Counseling Psychology, University of North Dakota, Grand Forks, ND

KARI J. KELLER, PH.D., Psychologist, Student Counseling Service, Texas A&M University, College Station, TX

SHOSHANA D. KEREWSKY, PSY.D., University of Oregon, Eugene, OR

BRITTANY LANCASTER, B.A., Department of Psychological Sciences, Texas Tech University, Lubbock, TX

MARK M. LEACH, PH.D., Professor and Chair, Department of Counseling and Human Development, College of Education and Human Development, University of Louisville, Louisville, KY

JILL S. LEE-BARBER, PH.D., Senior Director, Psychological and Health Services, Counseling and Testing Center, Georgia State University, Atlanta, GA

MARY MILLER LEWIS, PH.D., ABPP, Assistant Professor, Psychology, Columbus State Community College, Columbus, OH

RODNEY L. LOWMAN, PH.D., Distinguished Professor and Program Director, Organizational Psychology Programs, CSPP/Alliant International University, and President, Lowman & Richardson/Consulting Psychologists, San Diego, CA

SAMANTHA PELICAN MONSON, PSY.D., Clinical Psychologist, Integrated Behavioral Health, Denver Health Medical Center, Denver, CO

MEGAN J. MURPHY, PH.D., Associate Professor and Director, Marriage and Family Therapy Program, Department of Behavioral Sciences, Purdue University Northwest, Hammond, IN

HARPREET NAGRA, PH.D., Oregon Health and Sciences University, Portland, OR

ASHLEY OLIVER, M.A., College of Education and Human Services, Cleveland State University, Cleveland, OH

CHRISTINE PAO, B.A., University of Houston, Houston, TX

JUSTIN C. PERRY, PH.D., Dean of the School of Education and Ewing Marion Kauffman/Missouri Endowed Education Chair, Professor, Counseling Psychology, University of Missouri, Kansas City, MO

RUPERTO M. PEREZ, PH.D., Associate Vice President for Student Health and Wellbeing, University of Alabama, Tuscaloosa, AL

THOMAS G. PLANTE, PH.D., ABPP, Augustin Cardinal Bea, S.J. University Professor, Director, Spirituality & Health Institute, Psychology Department, Santa Clara University, Santa Clara, CA; Adjunct Clinical Professor in Psychiatry and Behavioral Sciences at Stanford University Medical School, Stanford, CA

MELISSA A. QUINCER, PH.D., University of North Dakota, Grand Forks, ND

GWENDOLYN P. QUINN, PH.D., Morsani College of Medicine, University of South Florida; Health Outcomes and Behavior, Moffitt Cancer Center, Tampa, FL

KATHERINE RAMOS, PH.D., Geriatric, Research, Education, and Clinical Center (GRECC), Durham VA Medical Center, Center for the Study of Aging and Human Development, Duke University, Durham, NC

ANNA REICHARD, M.S., Department of Psychology, University of Oregon, Eugene, OR

MARIA T. RIVA, PH.D., Professor and Training Director, Department of Counseling Psychology, University of Denver, Denver, CO

LYNNE D. ROBERTS, PH.D., School of Psychology and Speech Pathology, Curtin University, Perth, WA, Australia

JENNIFER L. SCHWARTZ, PH.D., Department of Psychology, Drexel University, Philadelphia, PA

JONATHAN P. SCHWARTZ, PH.D., Associate Dean of Graduate Studies, University of Houston, Houston, TX

PAIGE L. SEEGAN, M.A., Department of Psychological Sciences, Texas Tech University, Lubbock, TX

MORGAN SHAW, PSY.D., Institute on Violence, Abuse, and Trauma, San Diego, CA

RACHEL R. SINGER, PH.D., Assistant Professor Clinical Psy.D. Program, Chicago School of Professional Psychology, Washington, DC

JESSICA B. A. SIPES, PH.D., School of Psychology and Speech Pathology, Curtin University, Bentley, WA, Australia

JUDY B. SMETANA, PH.D., PCC, Assistant Professor, HRD Program, College of Technology, Pittsburg State University, Pittsburg, KS; Affiliate Faculty, EBC Program, Fielding Graduate University, Santa Barbara, CA

KELSEY SOUTH, PH.D., Denver Veterans Administration Hospital Eastern Colorado Health Care System, Denver, CO

SUZETTE L. SPEIGHT, PH.D., Associate Professor Department of Psychology, University of Akron, Akron, OH

MARILYN STERN, PH.D., Professor, Department of Child and Family Studies, Rehabilitation and Mental Health Counseling Program, College of Behavioral and Community Sciences, University of South Florida, Tampa, FL

AMY B. SULLIVAN, PSY.D., ABPP, Director of Behavioral Medicine, Research and Training, Mellen Center for MS, Cleveland Clinic; Assistant Professor of Medicine, Cleveland Clinic Lerner College of Medicine, Cleveland, OH

LINDA TAYLOR, PH.D., Codirector, School Mental Health Project and Center for MH in Schools, Los Angeles, CA

JANET T. THOMAS, PSY.D., Licensed Psychologist, Independent Practice, Saint Paul, MN

DEREK TRUSCOTT, PH.D., Professor, Department of Educational Psychology, University of Alberta, Edmonton, Alberta, Canada

SINÉAD K. P. M. UNSWORTH, PH.D., Student Counseling Services, University of Saskatchewan, Saskatoon, Saskatchewan, CA

JASON VAN ALLEN, PH.D., Assistant Professor of Clinical Psychology, Department of Psychological Sciences, Texas Tech University, Lubbock, TX

KRISTI S. VAN SICKLE, PH.D., Florida Institute of Technology, School of Psychology, Melbourne, FL

ADAM M. VOIGHT, PH.D., Director, Urban Research Center, Cleveland State University, Cleveland, OH

ELIZABETH REYNOLDS WELFEL, PH.D., Professor Emerita, Counseling Psychology, Cleveland State University, Cleveland, OH

ERICA H. WISE, PH.D., Clinical Professor and Director of Psychology Clinic, Department of Psychology and Neuroscience, University of North Carolina at Chapel Hill, Chapel Hill, NC

Preface

Aim of the Handbook

We embarked on this project because we were surprised (and disappointed) by the dearth of ethics scholarship focused on specific settings and the lack of literature about the intersection between specific settings and culturally diverse populations. This gap appeared especially noticeable given the number of excellent books and journal articles published on the broader topic of professional ethics in psychology and mental health. Consequently, we decided to center the chapters in this handbook on those subjects not fully addressed in the existing literature and to give extensive attention to practice with diverse and underserved populations. Our aim was to highlight the variety and complexity of ethical issues confronting practitioners, even seasoned practitioners, in these settings. We sought out authors "in the trenches" who have lived the experience of grappling frequently with complex ethical questions and who can recommend strategies to resolve them that are in keeping with the profession's values. We also strove to broaden the content beyond psychotherapy settings to include research, consultation, and organizational practice, as well as the fundamental activities of applied psychology. As the title of this volume indicates, we asked our authors to avoid abstract discussions of ethical principles and standards. Instead, we directed authors to apply ethical principles and standards to the messy ethical dilemmas practitioners confront, and to acknowledge the stress encountered in these situations. Good ethical decision-making often involves the acknowledgement of emotions and other nonrational processes that can lead to struggles. Plainly put, we sought the kinds of ethical issues that may keep clinicians up at night and that do not often get discussed in graduate ethics courses. In essence, this volume represents a call to mental health professions to expand and enrich the literature that focuses on ethical issues across multiple practice settings and to offer practitioners more guidance about the application of ethical standards and principles to diverse populations. It also represents a call to ethics educators to deepen and broaden ethics training beyond its current scope.

Organization of the Book

The book is delineated into four sections that cover clinical, research, supervision organizational, and legal components of professional work: (I) Ethical Issues in Specific Settings and Challenging Populations; (II) Ethical Issues in

Working with Diverse Populations; (III) Legal, Research, and Organizational Issues; and (IV) Emerging Ethical Issues in Professional Practice and Next Steps. While there may be some periodic overlap among the chapters, these sections were designated to highlight distinct areas of our work.

Within this broader structure, each chapter is organized around complex and realistic cases in order to offer the reader a window into the process of coming to a responsible resolution, including the process of managing the distress inherent in such cases. After all, no mental health professional ever deals with an ethical issue in the abstract. This organization also evolved from the research on the factors that increase the effectiveness of ethics teaching. This research shows that ethics education is more likely to be effective when case analysis and discussion form the basis of instruction than when ethical issues are discussed in the abstract (Welfel, 2012). In short, we hoped to debunk two myths with this structure: first, that resolving ethical questions is a dry, intellectual process; and second, that ethics training either in graduate school or in brief continuing education programs on general topics is sufficient to fully prepare practitioners for responsible practice. Clearly, comprehension of the values, principles, and standards of the profession is an essential foundation for application, but it is not automatically sufficient to ensure ethical action in complex cases in practice settings.

References

Welfel, E. R. (2012). Teaching ethics: Models, methods, and challenges. In S. J. Knapp, M. C. Gottlieb, M. M. Handelsman, & L. D. VandeCreek (Eds.), *APA handbook of ethics in psychology.* (Vol. 2, pp. 277–305). Washington, DC: American Psychological Association.

Acknowledgments

We first wish to thank Fred Leong, who approached us about editing this volume and who encouraged us to structure the book for practitioners and advanced doctoral students. Fred was always available with wise counsel for questions during the preparation of the handbook. We also wish to express our appreciation to the editors and publication staff at Cambridge University Press, including David Repetto, Samantha Town, Bethany Johnson, and Santosh Lami Kota for their assistance in publishing this volume.

Finally, we wish to acknowledge the huge contributions our students and colleagues have made to our understanding of professional ethics and its centrality to effective service with the populations we serve.

SECTION I

Ethical Issues in Specific Settings and Challenging Populations

1 Ethical Considerations for Working with Military Service Personnel

W. Brad Johnson

Military psychologists and psychiatrists have admirably served the nation in support of military forces, military families, and as consultants to the Department of Defense (DoD) since the First World War. More recently, social workers and counselors are employed by the DoD to provide for the needs of service members and their families at military installations around the globe. Psychologists, psychiatrists, and social workers may become commissioned officers in the medical services corps within each branch of the military (Air Force, Army, and Navy), serving simultaneously as military officers and licensed mental health practitioners. Psychologists constitute the largest group of military mental health providers; at present, approximately 500 uniformed (active-duty) clinical psychologists are employed in contexts as varied as service academies, medical centers, outpatient clinics, aircraft carriers, and forward deployed combat stress hospitals (Budd & Kennedy, 2006). An additional 500 civilian psychologists are employed in military clinics, primary care services, and medical centers.

The most prevalent activities of military mental health professionals (MHPs) include candidate screening, counseling and psychotherapy, psychoeducation, and psychological evaluations to discern fitness for duty, fitness for deployment, security clearance, and capacity to stand trial (courts martial). The context of practice for military MHPs is quite unique (Johnson, 2016; Kennedy & McNeil, 2006). Because they are often deployed to combat theaters or isolated military bases as the sole mental health provider, MHPs must be very competent generalists immediately following credentialing and commissioning. Moreover, they must be particularly skilled in treatment triage, crisis intervention, neuropsychological screening, traumatic stress disorders, and rapid screening for psychopathology (Johnson, 2016).

Owing to their unique status as both commissioned officers and mental health service providers, and the not infrequent tension between their licensed practitioner obligations and their obligations to support the military mission, military MHPs sometimes encounter challenging ethical quandaries and conundrums. In this chapter, I discuss those aspects of mental health practice in the military that are likely to create ethical tensions for MHPs. I then focus attention on three specific ethical issues that are most likely to create dilemmas and, at times, significant conflict and personal distress for MHPs. These include multiple relationships, competence and self-care, and conflict between ethical standards and federal laws or regulations. I provide illustrative cases to bring each of the three ethical issues to life for the reader. For consistency, I will rely primarily on the *Ethical Principles of Psychologists and Code of Conduct* of the American Psychological Association (APA, 2010) when referring to specific ethical standards; however, the ethics codes of the allied mental health professions (e.g., ACA, 2014; NASW, 2008) are quite consistent on the ethical issues I discuss. This chapter concludes with a brief set of recommendations for responsible and ethical practice in military settings.

Mixed-Agency Tensions and Embedded Assignments

Various aspects of mental health practice in military settings conspire to create ethical tensions for MHPs. Most fundamentally, ethical issues can be linked to an active-duty provider's dual identity as medical professional and commissioned military officer and his or her embedded status as not only a service provider for a military unit, but also a member of that same unit. Most of the ethical conundrums unique to military contexts can be traced to these two factors (Johnson, 2016).

Mixed-Agency Tensions

Mixed-agency, the simultaneous commitment to two or more entities, is ubiquitous for uniformed MHPs. From the moment psychologists, psychiatrists, and social workers take the oath of office and begin wearing the uniform, they must carefully balance sometimes competing obligations to their clients and the DoD (Kennedy & Johnson, 2009). For the most part, mixed-agency ethical dilemmas occur when the MHP's loyalties or ethical obligations to an individual client create tension or conflict with obligations to the military unit more broadly, the commanding officer, or DoD regulations (Howe, 2003; Johnson & Koocher, 2011).

The role stress created by mixed-agency dilemmas is often exacerbated for MHPs during deployments – particularly in time of war. In this context, providers must make frequent decisions regarding whether to return service members to combat. For instance, in a combat setting, it may be the clinical opinion of an Army psychiatrist that a traumatized soldier's health and well-being would be best served by a period of limited duty away from the front lines. But this professional inclination may be in conflict with the operational reality that the soldier's unique expertise and experience are essential to achieving a critical upcoming mission objective. As a provider, the psychiatrist may wish to arrange a medical evacuation for the soldier; as an officer, the psychiatrist has an acute appreciation of the overarching mission and the necessity of tempering individual interests with those of the unit and even the nation (Johnson, Grasso, & Maslowski, 2010).

Mixed-agency dilemmas for military MHPs are intensified by four facets of the job. First, uniformed MHPs always have *dual identities*; that is, simultaneous identities as military officer and licensed service provider (Jeffery, Rankin, & Jeffery, 1992; Zur & Gonzalez, 2002). There are often moments when one's clinical training – often emphasizing a stringent focus on the needs and best interests of the client – does not mesh well with one's military training and commissioned sensibilities; the needs of the military loom large for an officer. At times, military providers have described feeling like "double agents" who are now and then forced to choose between client-centered therapeutic interests and organization-centered administrative interests (Camp, 1993). One's dual identity may create truly unique tensions for a military MHP who must deploy with clients (e.g., eat, sleep, and travel) while observing boundaries, upholding good order and discipline, and attempting to be "therapeutic" during brief extra-therapy encounters.

Second, there are few mental health contexts in which the provider is obligated to place a superordinate mission first and foremost. Any military officer worth his or her salt will acknowledge that achieving the military mission must at times trump individual interests (Driskell & Olmstead, 1989). Upon commissioning, the military MHP assumes a federally mandated obligation to defend the Constitution and protect the nation first and foremost. Despite genuine concern for the psychological well-being of individual service members – particularly one's own clients – the deployed MHP is committed to promoting the fighting power and combat readiness of both individuals and the military unit generally (Page, 1996).

Third, there are occasional tensions between professional ethical standards and federal laws or DoD regulations, such as the Uniform Code of Military Justice (UCMJ). Although the military MHP is bound to adhere to both ethical and military codes, there are sometimes tensions or conflicts between the two around issues such as confidentiality, multiple relationships, informed consent, and provision of services through a third party (the government; Johnson, 2008; 2016). Jeffery and colleagues (1992) have detailed cases in which military psychologists have been sanctioned by an ethics board for complying with DoD regulations (e.g., client records released to an investigator without consent long after the psychologist had rotated to a different assignment and no longer had any authority to protect records at a previous facility) or, alternatively, have been sanctioned by the government for refusing to comply with a regulation or even a direct order (e.g., to turn over a client's record) when doing so was interpreted by the provider as a clear violation of his or her ethical obligations.

Finally, because military MHPs do not enjoy the luxury and clarity of definitively serving either an individual *or* an organization, it can be vexing to discern who exactly the primary "client" is in any specific situation (APA, 2010; Johnson, 2008). Often, when an evaluation of a service member is requested, there are multiple stakeholders involved, most often the individual client, his or her immediate supervising officer, the commanding officer, and perhaps even an investigative, credentialing, or special operations entity within the DoD.

Embedded Assignments

Military MHPs are increasingly assigned to active combatant military units such as Air Force air wings, Army or Marine Corps brigades, or Navy ships, most often aircraft carriers or helicopter landing ships. Rather than provide services exclusively in traditional clinics and hospitals, professionals embedded with active units become part of the fabric of the unit and the community. Some colleagues and I have defined embedded psychology this way:

> Psychological practice in an environment characterized by the intentional deployment of a psychologist as part of a unit or force when the psychologist is simultaneously a member of the unit and legally obligated or otherwise bound to place the unit's mission foremost. (Johnson, Ralph, & Johnson, 2005, p. 73)

On the upside, embedded MHPs are often seen as more credible and approachable by members of a unit who might benefit from services. On the downside, an MHP's embedded status can easily amplify ethical tensions for providers. Considerable maturity and thoughtful deliberation are required to serve clients' best interests when a practitioner is also a member of a small military community. Embedded assignments amplify tensions in several ways.

First, when an MHP literally lives with his or her clients – eating, exercising, and sleeping in shared berthing units – and encounters clients in all manner of unexpected ways in the course of day-to-day activities, maintaining boundaries and clearly demarcated role contours can be frankly impossible. Embedded MHPs technically have multiple roles with all of their clients. Further, they must often provide services to friends, colleagues, and even superior officers for whom they work (Johnson, 2008). As solo practitioners, they often are unable to refer "clients" to other providers or otherwise avoid multiple relationships that may be uncomfortable for both themselves and their clients (Zur & Gonzalez, 2002).

Second, embedded MHPs often cannot effectively anticipate and prepare colleagues or clients for sudden shifts in professional roles (Johnson et al., 2005). For instance, military clinicians may be asked to conduct a formal evaluation (e.g., fitness for duty, security clearance) with a current or former client, sometimes creating distress for a client and a rupture in a previously helpful clinical relationship. Alternatively, the MHP may find him or herself assuming supervisory duties with clients, or conducting an evaluation with the child or spouse of a close colleague. Embedded practice can easily create distress in a provider when an unexpected role shift appears contrary to the best interests of a client.

I now turn to three of the top ethical challenges facing MHPs who work in the military. These challenges are not presented in any order of significance. The illustrative cases used to introduce each topic are composites; each represents an amalgamation of several cases with critical identifying details masked. Each case is followed by an analysis of the practitioner's essential ethical quandary as well as his or her approach to resolving the issue while keeping the best interests of the client and the exigencies of the military mission in balance.

Multiple Relationships

The Case of CPT Smith

Air Force Captain (CPT) Smith, fresh from a psychiatry residency and newly commissioned, reported to a small Air Force hospital at an air base in rural Japan. Captain

Smith and his wife soon befriended another active-duty couple, John and Marie, both physicians, at the hospital. Located in the same small officer housing area, the two couples became fast friends and shared meals together frequently. Six months into their deepening friendship, Marie appeared at CPT Smith's office one morning before work. She was in tears. With the door closed, she confided that John was having an affair. Although he'd denied it when confronted, Marie had discovered text messages on his phone and receipts in his wallet that clearly indicated he was involved with a younger woman on the base named Rhonda. She confessed that John had done this once before when the two were in medical school. CPT Smith provided empathy and a listening ear. He also felt broadsided. John and Marie were the only close friends he and his wife had made, and he had frequent interaction with both of them around the hospital. In tears, Marie asked that he keep her concerns confidential. Over the next several weeks, Marie began losing weight. In brief, tear-laden conversations with Marie, he learned that she was becoming more depressed, restricting food intake, and even making small lacerations on her body to "punish herself" for being an unsatisfactory spouse. Feeling more distressed himself, CPT Smith wondered how he could possibly begin seeing Marie as a patient in light of their friendship. Still, he recognized that he was the only mental health provider on the base. He expressed serious concern about Marie's mental state and offered to see her in regular therapy sessions. She expressed profound relief and acknowledged that she needed assistance; she admitted that the quality of her work as an Internal Medicine physician at the hospital was slipping. However, she refused to go through formal channels, citing the small hospital community and the potential effects of a psychiatric diagnosis on her fitness for deployment and subsequent career in Air Force medicine. Of course, providing undocumented care would prevent CPT Smith from opening an official client record and documenting Marie's diagnostic intake and subsequent therapy notes. CPT Smith felt trapped. He wanted to be helpful to a friend and fellow healthcare provider. He empathized with her realistic concerns about her career and the disintegrating state of her marriage. He also worried that Marie manifested some personality psychopathology and that her current distress and impairment might be diminishing the quality of her patient care. As an aside, CPT Smith was deeply troubled by the possibility that John was having an affair with the same "Rhonda" that CPT Smith was seeing in therapy; a young medical technician at the hospital who had disclosed to CPT Smith that she had recently become involved with a married man. Meanwhile, CPT Smith felt unable to share any of this information with his own wife, who couldn't understand why John and Marie had become distant and stopped socializing with them. CPT Smith felt caught in a quandary. Should he bring Marie's mental status to the attention of the hospital commander, perhaps forcing her to receive mental health care? Of course, that approach would likely sabotage any therapeutic relationship the two might have. Should he simply do what he could for her informally as a way to help protect her patients by improving her functioning? Providing therapy under the radar carried risks to both his professional standing and the military mission. As he pondered the most appropriate way forward, CPT Smith's anxiety spiked again when it occurred to him that he and his wife had just celebrated the news of their first pregnancy and that John was the only obstetrician available to them.

Discussion

Multiple relationships occur when an MHP is in a professional relationship with a person and then adds a different – potentially conflicting – role with that person, or someone closely associated with that person (e.g., friend, family member, loved one). Multiple relationships are particularly concerning when they place vulnerable clients at risk of exploitation (APA, 2010). Although there are certain bright-line multiple relationships that we would all agree carry the risk of real harm to a client (e.g., sexual or business relationships), other multiple roles are less obviously likely to cause harm. Kitchener (2000) cautioned that the probability of causing harm to a client in the context of multiple roles increases whenever: (a) clients have role expectations of the MHP that go unfulfilled; (b) the behavior or obligations associated with one role conflict with those of another; (c) the MHP's professional obligations conflict with his or her personal interests; or (d) the MHP holds increasing levels of power and prestige vis-à-vis the client.

The case of CPT Smith illustrates in stark terms just how ubiquitous multiple relationships are in military settings (Johnson & Johnson, 2017; Johnson et al., 2005; Staal & King, 2000). Although ethics codes caution MHPs to avoid entering into professional roles with close friends or family members, or to avoid shifting roles with clients without appropriate informed consent, CPT Smith discovered just how quickly the contours between friend, client, and colleague can become blurred. Particularly in embedded contexts or isolated duty stations, MHPs often find themselves assuming clinical roles with colleagues or administrative, supervisory, or evaluative roles with clients without adequate opportunity to anticipate the new roles or provide much in the way of informed consent. When embedded with a deployed unit, the challenge of preserving typical provider–client boundaries is challenging enough, let alone preventing multiple relationships. Consider this description of a typical stroll down the main passageway for a Navy aircraft carrier psychologist:

> One client stops to tell me how the last phone conversation with his wife went. Ten steps later someone who is not a client stops to ask about whether his son has ADHD. Five more steps and I'm having a conversation with a person I've never met about his wife's history of depression and how he "can't even talk to her anymore." Finally, just before arriving at my destination, a sailor whom I've seen for a few appointments stops me to lament about why he can't ever seem to have intimate relationships with women who are not prostitutes. (Johnson et al., 2005, p. 74)

As have other military MHPs before him, CPT Smith has discovered that, as the only mental health provider in a small, isolated unit, he automatically holds a "potential" multiple role with every member of the community should they require mental health care. Unlike other providers in larger communities, he cannot easily refer active-duty members to other colleagues or civilian providers. In the case at hand, all active-duty personnel may be required to receive medical care through formal military channels. There may also be language or cultural barriers were he to try and refer Marie to a provider in the civilian community.

Notice that in this case, the provider must struggle with several competing interests and obligations. Some of those to whom he owes some consideration include Marie (although she has not formally become a client just yet), the medical patients to whom Marie provides services, and the hospital's commanding officer who has a vested interest in the quality of care provided by practitioners as well as the maintenance of good order and discipline among his or her staff (fraternization between John and Rhonda, if this is true, would constitute a serious violation of military law). Moreover, CPT Smith himself has a personal stake in the outcome of this situation. His primary social network and the quality of care his spouse might receive all hang in the balance. This case highlights the fact that military MHPs may often feel pinched both emotionally and ethically by unavoidable multiple relationships with colleagues and clients. Countertransference might easily lead CPT Smith to harbor resentment and anger at Marie and John for costing him a key source of social support while also placing him in an untenable position professionally.

If there is a silver lining in this case, it is the fact that a pre-existing friendship between members of the military can enhance trust and willingness to engage in needed mental health care; it may also stimulate real empathy and genuine care in crafting a treatment plan or disposition recommendation that is most likely to be in the client's best interests. I conclude discussion of this case with several brief recommendations for managing multiple relationships in military settings (Johnson, 2008, 2014; Johnson & Johnson, 2017).

- *Accept that every member of the military unit is a potential client.* Remain aware that any member of the community, including close friends and superior officers, may require your professional services. Adopting such an informed and cautious perspective is likely to help a uniformed practitioner to make wise and informed decisions about levels of self-disclosure as well as engagement in romantic or social relationships within a military community.
- *Increase your own comfort with routine boundary crossings and benign multiple relationships.* While remaining vigilant for boundary *violations* or harmful multiple roles, it is important to accept that not all extra-therapy contact, nor all dual relationships with a person at work, are likely to cause harm (Gutheil & Gabbard, 1993). If you can model calm acceptance of multiple roles while showing you are concerned about protecting your clients' best interests, chances are that your clients will be less anxious about routine role blurring as well. There is something culturally sensitive about appreciating the potential benefits of multiple relationships in the military.
- *Provide informed consent regarding boundary crossings and multiple roles as early in a professional relationship as possible.* It is always wise in military contexts – particularly in embedded units – to discuss upfront the likelihood of extra-treatment interactions and how the client would like to handle them. Similarly, it might be wise to address with friends and colleagues how you handle situations in which you are called upon to provide professional services for them.
- *Carefully document uncomfortable multiple-role relationships.* Particularly when a multiple relationship with a client is unanticipated and difficult – or potentially

harmful – for the client, be careful to document your efforts to discuss and manage the relationship with your client's best interests at the fore.

- *Maintain a strong external consultation relationship.* It is always helpful for a military MHP in an isolated job or deployed unit to maintain a consulting relationship with another MHP who can help him or her troubleshoot prickly boundary issues and develop strategies for minimizing and managing multiple relationships when they occur.

Preserving Competence and Practicing Self-Care

The Case of LT Ridley

Navy Lieutenant (LT) Ridley's story was not unusual. With a recent doctorate in clinical psychology and a commission in the Navy's Medical Services Corps, she had endured a whirlwind officer indoctrination school in Rhode Island, followed by an intense internship year at Walter Reed National Military Medical Center, where she completed rotations with severely wounded warriors rehabilitating from serious injuries suffered in Iraq and Afghanistan. Once assigned to her first duty station, a large medical center in Florida, she managed only nine months before being tabbed for deployment to Iraq. For six months, she provided services to severely traumatized soldiers and marines; she listened to their difficult stories hour after hour, day after day. She was also exposed to disturbing images with some regularity (e.g., severely wounded service members, corpses of enemy combatants when transiting between bases in an armored vehicle). Upon her return to the USA, she had only four months to try to reacclimatize to a noncombat context when she was again tabbed for deployment – this time to Afghanistan – with a forward deployed military surgical hospital. After eight additional months deployed in severe and unpredictable surroundings punctuated by distant explosions and constant sleep deprivation, she found herself sitting across from a Marine Corps Sargent one afternoon. As he described a horrific IED explosion and the carnage he witnessed in the aftermath, LT Ridley felt herself detaching; in her mind's eye, she was bombarded with disturbing images from both deployments, including some of her own clients who had been killed – a few just before their scheduled rotation home. Staring at the patient before her, it occurred to her that she had not heard a word he had said in nearly ten minutes. With two weeks to go before her own rotation back to the USA, she was vaguely aware that she was entirely depleted. Some invisible boundary had been crossed and all her reserves of empathy and compassion were used up. When LT Ridley returned to Florida and attempted to reintegrate into her normal routine, including a full load of clients – primarily young enlisted sailors who had never served in combat – she discovered an emotional barrier between herself and her clients. Showing them genuine compassion and empathy was often a struggle; sometimes, it was impossible. Detachment offered her a sense of self-protection. Most concerning was that she sometimes experienced sudden feelings of intense anger with patients who showed emotional weakness. She was especially irritable with "whiney kids" who had never served in combat and therefore had not – in her honest moments – earned the right to complain about anything. She found it quite distressing that she could no longer muster the empathy needed to feel helpful for these young service members. She also worried about her difficulty sleeping, intrusive images from her deployments, and a slow but steady increase in her use of alcohol. She wondered what to do. She worried that limiting or suspending her clinical work – as recommended by her ethics code if a psychologist was too distressed to provide competent care – would cause serious career repercussions. Seeking care in the hospital would feel uncomfortable for her and cause an awkward dual role for one of her colleagues as well. And besides, none of them had expressed any concern about her work, nor even bothered to check in with her about her readjustment from deployment. Perhaps she was making a mountain out of a molehill. Maybe she should just give it some more time and hope things improved. Sitting in her office at lunch, she mentally calculated the clients standing between her and her first drink of the evening.

Discussion

Thousands of military healthcare providers, including psychiatrists, psychologists, and social workers, have deployed to combat zones in support of the global war on terror during the last decade and a half. Often embedded in military units or stationed at forward casualty/triage clinics and hospitals, these MHPs endure unpredictable living and work environments, extended absences from family, exposure to direct threat, and frequent exposure to traumatic client material (Johnson, Bertschinger, Snell, & Wilson, 2014; McLean et al., 2011). It is rather inevitable that some of these MHPs, like LT Ridley in this case, will become "wounded healers" (Daneault, 2008), professionals who have become so distressed that – at least temporarily – they have become impaired. A few of them have articulated their experiences quite poignantly (e.g., Kraft, 2007).

In the case of LT Ridley, two prominent psychological/emotional syndromes seem to leave her at risk for diminished competence to practice. The first is *secondary traumatic stress*. When an MHP is vicariously or secondarily traumatized by repeated and extended exposure to clients' traumatic disclosures, it is not uncommon for them to report troubling experiences such as intrusive images, generalized fear, sleep disturbances, and persistent affective arousal (Tabor, 2011). The second syndrome – deeply entwined with the first – is *compassion fatigue* (Figley, 2002): a state of emotional exhaustion and diminished emotional resources as a result of empathizing with clients who are in serious pain (Shapiro, Brown, & Biegel, 2007). The greater the empathy in professionals like LT Ridley, the more they are at risk of experiencing helplessness, inefficacy, and emotional detachment following extended periods of working empathically with traumatized clients. Most concerning is that compassion fatigue may portend a state of *empathy failure*, which occurs when a previously competent professional begins to process client experiences and feelings on a purely cognitive level, perhaps no longer being capable of emotional processing and effective mirroring (Johnson et al., 2014). In the case of LT Ridley, we see her distancing from her patients, detaching from her work, and finding it difficult not to feel resentment – sometimes out and out anger – at service members she is supposed to be helping. Were her secondary traumatic stress and compassion fatigue to go unchecked, it is likely she would be at risk for a more general burnout characterized by apathy, exhaustion, and persistent feelings of aversion and hostility toward her clients.

The core ethical concern in the case of LT Ridley is that of *competence*. The APA Ethics Code holds the individual practitioner exclusively responsible for ensuring competence to practice. For instance, in the aspirational section of the Code, Principle A reminds psychologists to "strive to benefit those with whom they work and to take care to do no harm," and "to be aware of the possible effect of their own physical and mental health on their ability to help those with whom they work" (APA, 2010, p. 3). More concerning is enforceable Standard 2.06, "Personal Problems and Conflicts," which details the individual's enforceable duty to continuously self-evaluate competence and to take steps to protect consumers when personal problems or conflicts threaten to reduce competence:

> When psychologists become aware of personal problems that may interfere with their performing work-related duties adequately, they take appropriate measures, such as obtaining professional consultation or assistance, and determining whether they should limit, suspend, or terminate their work-related duties. (APA, 2010, p. 5)

To her credit, it is clear that LT Ridley owns some awareness of her diminished capacity for presence and empathy with her patients. She is not alone. There is good evidence that a significant proportion of MHPs have experienced episodes of depression, emotional exhaustion, and anxiety disturbances (e.g., Sherman & Thelan, 1998). More concerning is that many of these admit seeing clients when too distressed to do so effectively and competently. It is certainly true that the military culture plays a role in her current quandary about how to proceed (Johnson, 2016). Military MHPs often function in solo assignments, far from supervision or consultation, as the only mental health provider; the culture of independence and "making do with less" is palpable in military contexts. Moreover, military MHPs often learn to take pride in their ability to effectively triage and manage "anything that walks through the door." Toughness, heroic independence, self-sufficiency, and resilience in the face of difficult circumstances are all highly valued characteristics in military officers. Still, the ethics code of her profession requires that she self-monitor and address problems of professional competence.

A key question we might have for LT Ridley is, "Why can't you see just how diminished your competence has become?" and a corollary, "Why won't you take steps to seek consultation and limit your practice until such time as your competence is restored?" To be fair, even the most psychologically healthy MHPs are not particularly effective when it comes to accurately assessing their own levels of competence. Comprehensive reviews of social psychological and healthcare education research reveal that human self-assessments of any skill or professional competency are flawed, systematically and consistently (e.g., Davis et al., 2006). Healthcare providers are consistently inaccurate in assessing their own level of competence, and this is exacerbated for the most impaired or least competent providers. Thus, although ethics codes enjoin the individual practitioner to accurately self-assess and then address decrements in professional competence, distressed and impaired providers may actually be the least capable of doing those things reliably and effectively. For these reasons, several colleagues and I have urged some revision of ethics codes in the mental health professions (Johnson, Barnett, Elman, Forest, & Kaslow, 2012). Particularly when an MHP's practice context is *in extremis*, such as during military deployments, it is crucial that he or she is trained to be sensitive to signs of compassion fatigue and empathy problems. But it is equally – perhaps even more – important that the military MHP be surrounded by caring and attuned colleagues who will consistently engage and provide feedback and reflection about an MHP's competence. In a very real sense, sustained competence in military MHPs may "take a village." Closely knit and deliberately constructed communities of engaged and caring colleagues might be the only way to ensure that individual practitioners can consistently adhere to ethical standards bearing on competence.

LT Ridley's case evokes genuine empathy. She has endured very taxing and distressing deployments and now finds herself unable to muster the essential empathy, positive regard, and compassion required of a competent MHP – in the military or any other healthcare context. Although she appears to detect a decline in her own competence, and although she may make the linkage between her ebbing competence and her deployment-induced secondary trauma and compassion fatigue, it is clear that she is probably underestimating her level of professional impairment. Additionally, her identity as a military officer and the culture of independence prevalent in the military may fuel her determination to continue to go it alone and make the best of it. She is also concerned about her own confidentiality and creating an uncomfortable multiple role for a colleague should she seek formal treatment, not to mention the potential impact on her subsequent promotion should she be identified as unable to "stay in the fight" and continue to practice. I conclude discussion of this case with several brief recommendations for effectively managing stress-induced challenges to competence in military practice contexts (Johnson et al., 2014).

- *Vigorously pursue self-care.* Deliberately integrate ongoing personal wellness and stress management strategies into your daily practice, especially during deployments or high-tempo operations. Pursue solid nutrition, sleep, exercise, time for mindful reflection, and some balance between professional work and personal time (even if this means huddling in a remote storage tent, relaxing with an iPod).
- *Nurture self-compassion and normalize distress.* Be as open as possible to your own feelings and accept the normality of periods of exhaustion and compassion fatigue. Whenever possible, refuse to engage in self-stigmatizing attitudes equating symptoms of distress with weakness or failure. Remember that self-criticism and defensiveness will limit capacity for adaptive responses to *in extremis* deployment contexts.
- *Engage with colleagues and construct competence constellations.* Actively combine numerous modalities for collegial support and competence maintenance, such

as friendships with other healthcare professionals, peer consultation arrangements, support groups, phone or videoconference connections with civilian or non-deployed colleagues, and engagement in ongoing professional education. Let some of your closest colleagues know that you are counting on them as key members of your competence constellation (Johnson et al., 2012) to provide you with authentic and frequent feedback about your functioning and your professional work.

- *Model self-care for your clients and colleagues.* In addition to seeking consultation about your ongoing competence to practice, endeavor to be a role model for self-awareness and self-care when feelings of distress and evidence of diminished functioning accrue. Discussing your own experience during deployment, actively taking steps to protect your emotional well-being, and soliciting support and assistance will also serve as powerful and positive exemplars for clients and colleagues.

Conflicts between Ethics and Organizational Demands or Laws

The Case of CDR Ortiz

Navy Commander (CDR) Ortiz accepted orders to Guantanamo Bay Cuba Military Detention Facility (GITMO) with some reluctance and trepidation. A clinical psychologist, his career in the military had been characterized by somewhat routine duty assignments at mental health clinics, military hospitals, and even an aircraft carrier. Like all Americans, he had been inundated with negative news stories related to GITMO in the years immediately following the terrorist attacks of 9/11, claiming harsh interrogations of prisoners and certain detention conditions that appeared to violate various human rights conventions. An active member of the APA and a conscientious psychologist who made ethics consultation a priority in his day-to-day practice, CDR Ortiz had closely followed the slow evolution of the APA's policies related to psychologists' ethics in national security settings. By the summer of 2014, when his orders to GITMO came through, CDR Ortiz was quite clear that APA policy: (1) prohibited torture, cruel, inhumane, and degrading treatment or punishment; (2) prohibited specific interrogation techniques ("enhanced" interrogations); (3) prohibited psychologists from intelligence-gathering activities in unlawful detention facilities; (4) obligated psychologists to report torture and abuse; and (5) commended psychologists who had taken a stand against torture, especially those who had done so in the line of duty. Because he was assigned to the Behavior Health Unit, exclusively for the purpose of providing mental health care to detainees, he felt confident that he could carry out his military clinical duties without running afoul of any element of APA policy or the APA Ethics Code. Long before his arrival at GITMO, the Navy had clearly demarcated healthcare as the only appropriate role for uniformed psychologists at GITMO. CDR Ortiz felt certain that he could steer clear of any form of consultation to intelligence-gathering entities; moreover, he took seriously his obligation to remain vigilant for any sign of prisoner mistreatment. After a full year at the detention facility, CDR Ortiz was frankly astounded at how gratifying and meaningful his work with many of the detainees had been. He had worked diligently to learn about the culture – including religion and traditions – of his clients and, over several months, had begun to establish strong clinical alliances with many of them. In the summer of 2015, the APA amended its policy yet again, this time prohibiting psychologists from serving in any location that the United Nations determined was out of compliance with basic human rights conventions. CDR Ortiz was initially unconcerned; to his eye, it appeared that prisoners were accorded humane treatment, dignity, and respect. He immediately sought consultation regarding the new policy. Four months following the establishment of the new policy, CDR Ortiz received word from the APA that psychologists were banned from providing any service at GITMO, that any service provided in that location would be a violation of association ethics, and that he should depart immediately. He was stunned. It seemed to him that his mission to provide high-quality mental healthcare to detainees in need was filling a critical need. Although threatened by the APA with expulsion from the organization should he decide to continue at GITMO, CDR Ortiz knew that as an officer in the US military, he was bound to serve where ordered by the DoD. Moreover, by suddenly leaving his position, CDR Ortiz concluded that he would be in conflict with the ethical principle of beneficence (pursuing the greatest good on behalf of one's clients) and possibly in violation of ethical standards relating to avoiding harm and abandonment of clients. On the basis of both his legally commissioned obligation to do his job – ethically and professionally – wherever he was called on to serve, CDR Ortiz decided to oppose the APA's policy and continue to provide healthcare services for his detainee clients. In his view, a politically driven association policy could not trump his strong sense of ethical duty to remain loyal to the clients he served and loyal to his oath of office.

Discussion

Inevitably, military MHPs will discover moments of apparent incongruity between professional ethical standards and various legal statutes and DoD regulations (to include lawful orders). For instance, MHPs may find conflicts between ethics and statutes or regulations bearing on confidentiality, multiple relationships, informed consent, and protection of client records, among others (Howe, 2003; Johnson et al., 2010). More often than not, these incongruities are subtle. With a little finesse and creativity on the part of the military provider, they can often be reconciled with the client's best interests as the driving concern. At other times, however, ethical–legal or ethical–organizational policy disparities create genuine conflict; the MHP discovers that fulfilling one obligation will place him or her in direct violation of the other.

For instance, during the last decade, there have been cases of uniformed and civilian military MHPs reporting strong pressure from their immediate commanding officers or supervisors within the DoD to limit the diagnosis of certain clinical disorders, namely post-traumatic stress disorder. The organizational policy in these cases was intended to limit bad press regarding psychiatric casualties or to limit the government's liability for long-term mental healthcare (Moore & Reger, 2006). Whatever the organizational rationale, fabricating or manipulating a clinical diagnosis in any manner would constitute a clear violation of ethical standards bearing on honest, transparent, and evidence-supported statements about one's clients, including formal diagnoses.

When laws, regulations, or organizational policies conflict with one's ethical obligations, ethics codes leave little doubt about the MHP's obligation. The professional has an ethical obligation to clearly articulate the ethical–legal/organizational conflict, continue to adhere to sound ethical practice, and persist in raising concern about the conflict higher up the chain of command until a solution can be found (APA, 2010; NASW, 2008).

In the case of CDR Ortiz, his professional ethics code makes it clear that no law – not even a lawful order from a commanding officer – can ever be used to justify violating human rights (APA, 2010). In fact, CDR Ortiz appears to have little concern about this possibility. Not only is his work limited to the provision of healthcare, he has seen no evidence of any maltreatment of detainees, nor any suppression of human rights. Human rights aside, then, he must decide whether to abide by his lawful commission and designation as a psychologist at GITMO or whether to follow a new organizational stance prohibiting him from service in that location. CDR Ortiz was well aware that the APA Ethics Code does not state that psychologists *must* break the law in order to adhere to an ethical principle or standard. Instead, the Code leaves it to the good judgment of the MHP to deliberately resolve the conflict in the most appropriate manner considering a range of context-specific variables such as obligations to clients and the potential for harm.

It is certainly possible that CDR Ortiz could go to his commanding officer and request immediate reassignment on the basis of the organizational–legal conflict. Were he concerned about maltreatment of detainees or were he asked to participate in any violation of human rights, this would be quite appropriate. Of course, there might be serious career consequences for CDR Ortiz – possibly even adverse legal action within the military – were he to pursue that course of action. But in the case at hand, CDR Ortiz – after careful review of his ethical obligations and good consultation with colleagues – determined that, in this case, complying with the new APA policy would paradoxically be *more* likely to cause harm to his clients. The more he considered his options, the more clearly CDR Ortiz saw that the principle of beneficence and the standards bearing on avoiding harm and abandonment of clients would make it ethically untenable for him to pack up and abruptly leave his clinical responsibilities and shirk his commissioned legal obligation. Moreover, his thorough review of the APA Ethics Code revealed no principle or standard bearing on the *location* in which a psychologist served. Thus, although he could be expelled from the APA for his decision to stay, he could not be found in violation of professional ethics. In the end, he determined that resisting the APA's new policy was the most appropriate course of action both legally and *ethically*.

I conclude discussion of this case with several brief recommendations for effectively managing conflicts between professional ethics and organizational demands or legal statutes in military contexts (Johnson, 2013; Johnson et al., 2010; Kennedy & Johnson, 2009).

- *Avoid elevating tensions to conflicts.* Remember that a discrepancy between your ethical, legal, and organizational obligations does not mean that adhering to ethics is mutually exclusive with adhering to statutes or organizational policies. Quite often, some finesse and good communication about your ethical quandary will lead to a solution that is acceptable to military leaders; middle ground is often achievable.
- *Be familiar with both your ethics code and relevant statutes and regulations.* Military MHPs must be conversant and comfortable with all elements of their professional code of ethics so that they can quickly discern apparent disconnects between ethics and laws or organizational policies. Because disparities between laws and regulations/policies are common in military settings, it is equally imperative to develop a well-formulated approach to ethical decision making.
- *Always seek consultation and communicate transparently with military leaders.* As part of your own competence constellation, maintain strong consulting relationships with one or two colleagues with specific expertise in professional ethics. Before making any seemingly dichotomous decision between adhering to ethics or a lawful order, federal regulation, or organizational policy, seek good consultation and calmly but persistently communicate your quandary to military authorities; in most instances, they will be open to a solution that allows compliance with professional ethics.
- *Always place client best interests first when resolving ethical–legal/organizational conflicts.* When confronted with a genuine conflict between ethical obligations and those imposed by an organization or legal statute, avoid getting mired in the rule-based question, "What shall I do?" Instead, consider ethical virtues and principles before specific standards and first ask the question, "Who shall I be?" By prioritizing clients' best interests and minimization of harm, you will increase the probability of making a decision that honors your most fundamental ethical obligations.

References

American Counseling Association (2014). *Code of Ethics*. Alexandria, VA: American Counseling Association.

American Psychological Association (2010). *Ethical principles of psychologists and code of conduct*. Retrieved from http://www.apa.org/ethics/code/index.aspx

Budd, F. C. & Kennedy, C. H. (2006). Introduction to clinical military psychology. In C. H. Kennedy & E. A. Zillmer (Eds.), *Military psychology: Clinical and operational applications* (pp. 21–34). New York, NY: Guilford.

Camp. N. M. (1993). The Vietnam War and the ethics of combat psychiatry. *American Journal of Psychiatry, 150*, 1000–1010.

Daneault, S. (2008). The wounded healer. *Canadian Family Physician, 54*, 1218–1219.

Davis, D. A., Mazmanian, P. E., Fordis, M., Harrison, R. V., Thorpe, K. E., & Perrier, L. (2006). Accuracy of physician self-assessment compared with observed measures of competence: A systematic review. *JAMA: Journal of the American Medical Association, 296*, 1094–1102.

Driskell, J. E. & Olmstead, B. (1989). Psychology in the military: Research applications and trends. *American Psychologist, 44*, 43–54.

Figley, C. R. (2002). Compassion fatigue and the psychotherapist's chronic lack of self care. *Journal of Clinical Psychology, 58*, 1433–1441.

Gutheil, T. G. & Gabbard, G. O. (1993). The concept of boundaries in clinical practice: Theoretical and risk-management dimensions. *American Journal of Psychiatry, 150*, 188–196.

Howe, E. G. (2003). Mixed agency in military medicine: Ethical roles in conflict. In D. E. Lounsbury & R. F. Bellamy (Eds.), *Military medical ethics: Volume I* (pp. 331–365). Falls Church, VA: Office of the Surgeon General, U. S. Department of the Army.

Jeffery, T. B., Rankin, R. J., & Jeffery, L. K. (1992). In service of two masters: The ethical–legal dilemma faced by military psychologists. *Professional Psychology: Research and Practice, 23*, 91–95.

Johnson, W. B. (2008). Top ethical challenges for military clinical psychologists. *Military Psychology, 20*, 49–62.

Johnson, W. B. (2013). Mixed-agency dilemmas in military psychology. In B. Moore & J. Barnett (Eds.), *The military psychologist's desk reference* (pp. 112–115). New York, NY: Oxford University Press.

Johnson, W. B. (2014). Multiple relationships in military mental health counseling. In B. Herlihy & G. Corey (Eds.), *Boundary issues in counseling: Multiple roles and responsibilities (3rd ed.)* (pp. 254–259). Alexandria, VA: American Counseling Association.

Johnson, W. B. (2016). Military settings. In J. Norcross, G. R. VandenBos, & D. K. Freedheim (Eds.), *APA handbook of clinical psychology: Vol I* (pp. 495–507). Washington, DC: American Psychological Association.

Johnson, W. B., Barnett, J. E., Elman, N. S., Forrest, L., & Kaslow, N. J. (2012). The competent community: Toward a vital reformulation of professional ethics. *American Psychologist, 67*, 557–569.

Johnson, W. B., Bertschinger, M., Foster, A., & Jeter, A. (2014). Secondary trauma and ethical obligations for military psychologists: Preserving compassion and competence in the crucible of combat. *Psychological Services, 11*, 68–74.

Johnson, W. B., Grasso, I., & Maslowski, K. (2010). Conflicts between ethics and law for military mental health providers. *Military Medicine, 175*, 548–553.

Johnson, W. B. & Johnson, S. J. (2017). Unavoidable and mandated multiple relationships in military settings. In O. Zur (Ed.), *Multiple relationships in psychotherapy and counseling: Unavoidable, mandatory, and common relations between therapists and clients* (pp. 49–60). New York, NY: Routledge.

Johnson, W. B. & Koocher, G. P. (2011). Juggling porcupines: Being ethical in challenging work roles and work settings. In W. B. Johnson & G. P. Koocher (Eds.), *Ethical conundrums, quandaries, and predicaments in mental health practice: A casebook from the files of experts* (pp. 1–5). New York, NY: Oxford University Press.

Johnson, W. B., Ralph, J., & Johnson, S. J. (2005). Managing multiple roles in embedded environments: The case of aircraft carrier psychology. *Professional Psychology: Research and Practice, 36*, 73–81.

Kennedy, C. H. & Johnson, W. B. (2009). Mixed agency in military psychology: Applying the American Psychological Association Ethics Code. *Professional Psychology: Research and Practice, 6*, 22–31.

Kennedy, C. H. & McNeil, J. A. (2006). A history of military psychology. In C. H. Kennedy & E. A. Zillmer (Eds.), *Military psychology: Clinical and operational applications* (pp. 1–17). New York, NY: Guilford Press.

Kitchener, K. S. (2000). *Foundations of ethical practice, research, and teaching in psychology.* Mahwah, NJ: Erlbaum.

Kraft, H. S. (2007). *Rule number two: Lessons I learned in a combat hospital.* New York, NY: Little, Brown.

McLean, C. P., Handa, S., Dickstein, B. D., Benson, T. A., Baker, M. T., Isler, W. C., . . . Litz, B. T. (2011). Posttraumatic growth and posttraumatic stress among military medical personnel. *Psychological Trauma: Theory, Research, Practice, and Policy, 5*, 62–68.

Moore, B. A. & Reger, G.M. (2006). Clinician to frontline soldier: A look at the roles and challenges of army clinical psychologists in Iraq. *Journal of Clinical Psychology, 62*, 395–403.

National Association of Social Workers (2008). *Code of Ethics.* Washington, DC: National Association of Social Workers.

Page, G. D. (1996). Clinical psychology in the military: Developments and issues. *Clinical Psychology Review, 16*, 383–396.

Shapiro, S. L., Brown, K. W., & Biegel, G. M. (2007). Teaching self-care to caregivers: Effects of mindfulness-based stress reduction on the mental health of therapists in training. *Training and Education in Professional Psychology, 1*, 105–115.

Sherman, M. D. & Thelen, M. H. (1998). Distress and professional impairment among psychologists in clinical practice. *Professional Psychology: Research and Practice, 29*, 79–85.

Staal, M. A. & King, R. E. (2000). Managing a multiple relationship environment: The ethics of military psychology. *Professional Psychology: Research and Practice, 31*, 698–705.

Tabor, P. D. (2011). Vicarious traumatization: Concept analysis. *Journal of Forensic Nursing, 7*, 203–208.

Zur, O. & Gonzalez, S. (2002). Multiple relationships in military psychology. In A. A. Lazarus & O. Zur (Eds.), *Dual relationships and psychotherapy* (pp. 315–328). New York, NY: Springer.

2 Ethical Issues in Addressing Mental Health Concerns in Schools

Howard S. Adelman and Linda Taylor

The two besetting sins in our prevailing habits of ethical thinking are our ready acquiescence in unclarity and our complacence in ignorance.

William Frankena (1973)

Not long ago, a group in Virginia called for the removal of counselors from their schools. The group's position was that school counselors were discussing inappropriate topics with students – personal and value-laden matters best left to families. In arguing their position, they declared that schools should focus solely on academics and not be involved with "mental health."

A counter-campaign was launched by teachers and counselors. They stressed that students experience many problems that interfere with effective performance and learning, and so support services in schools are essential for enabling school success.

The conflict in Virginia underscores long-standing policy and practice controversies over mental health in schools. It also highlights the central role played by stakeholders' social and moral philosophical commitments.

Anyone who has pursued practices associated with mental health in schools has encountered a wide range of ethical dilemmas. Commonly discussed examples include: when is it appropriate to compel/coerce? How can schools balance privacy and confidentiality and still appropriately share information? How can schools do no harm or at least minimize negative side effects? What is the best way for schools to prevent problems? Fortunately, there is a robust literature on basic ethical principles to aid in addressing such matters (e.g., Beauchamp & Childress, 2012; Raines & Dibble, 2010; Tribe & Morrissey, 2015; Welfel, 2012; also go online and see the ethical guides published by the various school professional associations).

Beyond general principles, however, appreciating specific ethical considerations requires a relatively deep contextual understanding. And it requires going beyond individual cases. Those working in schools must be prepared to deal with ethical concerns about school-wide practices. This rapidly became evident to José in his first year as a school psychologist. He found his training had prepared him well for handling most of the ethical considerations arising from his work with specific students and their families. However, he soon discovered he was ill-prepared for the many system-level concerns he was expected to address.

In this chapter, we highlight the importance of context and the need for preparation in analyzing system-wide school practices. Specifically, we explore major ethical concerns related to: (1) identifying and labeling student problems; (2) the use of social control strategies to manage student behavior; and (3) the call for using evidence-based practices.

Concerns about Labeling and Screening

... consider the American penchant for ignoring the structural causes of problems. We prefer the simplicity and satisfaction of holding individuals responsible for whatever happens: crime, poverty, school failure, what have you. Thus, even when one high school crisis is followed by another, we concentrate on the particular people involved – their values, their character, their personal failings – rather than asking whether something about the system in which these students find themselves might also need to be addressed.

Alfie Kohn

After a school shooting by a student at another school in the state, the principal and teachers turned to José and asked him to set up a screening program to identify potential shooters. And while he was at it, they wanted to screen for potential suicidality. He knew that any first-level screening instrument would produce many false positives and potentially lead to pathological labeling of some students. Clearly, identifying potential problems was a good thing, but did the limitations of available screening procedures make the practice unethical?

Over a school year, many students not only are identified as having problems, they are diagnostically labeled. Sometimes the processes lead to appropriate special assistance; sometimes they contribute to "blaming the victim" – making young people the focus of intervention rather than pursuing system deficiencies that are causing the problem in the first place (Ryan, 1971). Major ethical concerns arise when students are inappropriately assigned diagnostic labels and when systemic deficiencies are not addressed.

Concerns about Labeling

Normality and exceptionally (or deviance) are not absolutes; both are culturally defined by particular societies at particular times for particular purposes.

Ruth Benedict

It is evident that strong images are associated with diagnostic labels, and people act upon these images. Sometimes the images are useful generalizations; sometimes they are harmful stereotypes. In all cases, diagnostic labels can profoundly shape a person's future.

Students manifesting problems at school are commonly and often erroneously assigned labels that were created to categorize internal disorders (e.g., attention deficit hyperactivity disorder [ADHD], depression, autism, learning disabilities [LD]). The diagnoses are made despite the fact that the learning, behavior, and emotional problems manifested by most youngsters are not rooted in internal pathology. Indeed, many of the identified symptoms would not develop if environmental circumstances were appropriately different.

Of major concern to schools is the widespread *misapplication of the terms ADHD and LD* (Center for Mental Health in Schools, 2015; Hinshaw & Scheffler, 2014; Lyon, 2002; Maki, Floyd, & Roberson, 2015). Almost 50% of students currently assigned a special education diagnosis are identified as having LD, and there is widespread agreement that the majority are misdiagnosed "garden variety" learning problems. And, it is likely that similar errors are occurring in diagnosing so many students as having ADHD. Such misdiagnoses contribute to trends of over-pathologizing problems manifested by students.

The many reasons for misdiagnoses include inadequate definitions of disorders, classification schemes that use overlapping symptoms because current assessment procedures cannot identify causation, and the various professional and personal biases that influence decision-making. All of this contributes to false-positive diagnoses of persons with learning, behavior, and/or emotional problems. And this exposes many individuals and subgroups to the negative consequences associated with diagnostic labeling, such as being stigmatized, experiencing self-fulfilling prophecies, and limiting their social relationships and status.

The Dilemma of False-Positive Diagnoses

For schools, a long-standing dilemma stems from the fact that reimbursement for mental health services and special education interventions are only available for youngsters assigned labels that convey significant pathology. This reality is associated with the profound increases in the number of students assigned diagnostic labels and with an escalation in false-positive diagnoses.

Consider these points: a large number of young people are unhappy and emotionally upset; only a small percentage are clinically depressed. A large number of youngsters behave in ways that distress others; only a small percentage have ADHD or a conduct disorder. In some schools, a large number of students have garden variety learning problems; only a small percentage have LD. The constant dilemma for schools is how to minimize inappropriate use of diagnostic labels while still ensuring students receive the help they need.

One aspect of minimizing false positives is to escape the biases built into the institutionalized classification systems used to generate differential diagnoses of students' learning, behavior, and emotional problems (e.g., the *Diagnostic and Statistical Manual of Mental Disorders* [DSM], the set of special education diagnostic labels). These systems predispose the labeling of problems by focusing only on differentiating internal disorders and disabilities from each other. For example, rather than distinguishing subgroups *among the full range of behavior problems*, these classification schemes stress making differential diagnoses *within their defined categories*. The result is that too many students are assigned a pathological label and then are viewed as having problems primarily instigated by internal pathology.

Overemphasis on classifying problems in terms of personal pathology skews theory, research, practice, and public policy. One example is seen in the dearth of comprehensive classification systems for environmentally caused problems or for problems caused by the transaction of internal and environmental factors. There is considerable irony in all this because so many practitioners who use prevailing diagnostic labels understand that most problems in human functioning result from the interplay of person and environment. And this recognition is reflected in efforts to establish multifaceted diagnostic classification systems such as the multiaxial system developed in the latest editions of the DSM. The DSM does include a dimension acknowledging the role of "psychosocial stressors." However, this dimension is used mostly to deal with the environment as a contributing factor to psychopathology, rather than as a possible primary instigating causal factor that leads to severe and pervasive personal symptoms.

In general, most differential diagnoses of children's problems still are made by differentiating among the disorders specified in formal systems dedicated to classifying pathology. Thus, for instance, in evaluating behavior problems, professional diagnosticians generally consider which pathological label to assign (e.g., is it oppositional defiant disorder, ADHD, or an adjustment disorder?), rather than first asking: *is there a disorder?*

Bias toward labeling problems in terms of personal causation also is bolstered by psychological, political, and economic factors and other forces shaping professional practice. For example, research on attributional bias points to the tendency for observers (e.g., professional diagnosticians) to perceive others' problems as rooted in stable personal dispositions. Examples of political and economic influences include government policy priorities and reimbursement decisions by major third-party payers.

Toward Addressing the Above Concerns

Minimizing misdiagnoses and tendencies to over-pathologize are practical and ethical imperatives. For school psychologists and other student support staff to deal with these concerns requires countering nature versus nurture biases and adopting a broad causal paradigm in thinking about student problems. With this in mind, we stress the reciprocal determinist framework illustrated in Exhibit 1 as a useful starting place. The framework is designed to keep the full range of primary causes in perspective when classifying behavioral, emotional, and learning problems.

As illustrated, problems are differentiated along a continuum that separates those caused primarily by external factors (e.g., impoverished and hostile environmental conditions) as contrasted with internal disorders. As a strategy for countering biases that lead to overuse of diagnostic labels in such cases, we find it effective to consider environmental circumstances first in hypothesizing what *initially* caused a student's behavioral, emotional, and learning problems.

The intent is not to ignore internal disorders. The point is that, as a first categorization step, however, it is essential not to limit the diagnostic process to differentiating among categories of disorders. After environmental causes are ruled out, hypotheses about internal pathology become more viable. See Exhibit 2 for details on neighborhood, family, school, and/or peers, which are widely recognized as potential primary instigating causes of commonplace behavior, learning, and emotional problems manifested by students.

Exhibit 1   *A Continuum of Problems Based on a Broad Understanding of Cause**

Primary Source of Cause		
Problems caused by factors in the environment (E)	Problems caused equally by environment and person	Problems caused by factors in the the person (P)
E (E ⟷ p)	E ⟷ P (e ⟷ P)	P
|---|	|--------------------------	--|
Type I problems	Type II problems	Type III problems (e.g., LD, ADHD, other disorders)
• Caused primarily by environments and systems that are deficient and/or hostile	• Caused primarily by a significant *mismatch* between individual differences and vulnerabilities and the nature of that person's environment (not by a person's pathology)	• Caused primarily by person factors of a pathological nature
• Problems are mild to moderately severe and narrow to moderately pervasive	• Problems are mild to moderately severe and pervasive	• Problems are moderate to profoundly severe and moderate to broadly pervasive

* Using a transactional view, the continuum emphasizes the *primary source* of the problem and, in each case, is concerned with problems that are beyond the early stage of onset.

Thankfully, those suffering from true internal pathology (referred to in Exhibit 1 as type III problems) represent a relatively small segment of the population. Ethically, society must never stop providing the best services it can for such individuals. Doing so is aided when great care is taken not to misdiagnose others whose "symptoms" may be similar but are caused to a significant degree by factors other than internal pathology (referred to in Exhibit 1 as type I and II problems). When too many students are misdiagnosed with ADHD and LD, available resources are depleted. As a result, only a relatively small percentage of all the students in need of special assistance are helped effectively (Adelman & Taylor, 2010; Center for Mental Health in Schools, 2015; Hinshaw & Scheffler, 2014; Lyon, 2002; Maki, Floyd, & Roberson, 2015).

While a simple continuum clearly cannot do justice to the complexities associated with labeling and differentiating problems, the framework offered in Exhibit 1 shows the value of starting with a broad causal paradigm. It helps counter the unethical tendency to jump prematurely to the conclusion that a problem is caused by deficiencies or pathology within the individual; this can help combat tendencies toward misdiagnosis and blaming the victim. The framework also helps highlight the notion that improving the way the environment accommodates individual differences often may be a sufficient intervention strategy.

Exhibit 2 *Examples of Risk-Producing Conditions that Can Become Barriers to Healthy Development and Learning*

Environmental	Conditions*		Person Factors*
Neighborhood	*Family*	*School and Peers*	*Individual*
>Extreme economic deprivation	>Chronic poverty	>Poor-quality school	>Medical problems
>Community disorganization, including high levels of mobility	>Conflict/disruptions/ violence	>Negative encounters with teachers	>Low birth weight/ neurodevelopmental delay
>Violence, drugs, etc.	>Substance abuse	>Negative encounters with peers and/or inappropriate peer models	>Psychophysiological problems
>Minority and/or immigrant status	>Models problem behavior		>Difficult temperament and adjustment problems
	>Abusive caretaking >Inadequate provision for quality child care		>Inadequate nutrition

*   A reciprocal determinist view of behavior recognizes the interplay of environment and person variables.

A reciprocal determinist paradigm underscores a significant disconnect between what schools currently do and what is needed. This has immense implications for those concerned with mental health in schools and for the need to transform student and learning supports.

Another strategy many school staff use as a corrective to false-positive labeling is the practice widely referred to in schools as *response to intervention* (RtI). Controversy has arisen over the contrasting ways the process is applied. One form of application mainly views students' problems as deficits in knowledge and skills that can be corrected through better instruction and by analyzing subsequent learning and performance to determine subsequent teaching. The success or failure of the application is used to gauge whether or not a disability may be interfering with learning and performance. In contrast to this limited approach, we have emphasized an expanded RtI strategy that applies a reciprocal determinist causal paradigm (Center for Mental Health in Schools, 2012). The emphasis is on proceeding in stages beginning with personalized instruction to establish a better match with the learner's current motivation and capabilities; then, as necessary, the focus is on special assistance to address barriers to learning and teaching. The special assistance involves a hierarchical sequence of interventions designed to (a) develop missing learning and performance prerequisites and/or (b) provide needed specialized interventions that can address other underlying external and internal barriers to learning.

Approaching the problem of labeling students as discussed above will help José and his colleagues address the ethical and practical concerns that arise. At the same time, we all need to pay greater attention to reforming the policies and processes that contribute to labeling students at schools. With this in mind, we turn to the topic of screening "at-risk" students.

Concerns about Universal, First-Level Screening

Waiting until someone refers a student for special assistance can exacerbate problems. Thus, primary and secondary prevention are essential in keeping problems from worsening. From this perspective, attempts by schools to identify individuals who are "at risk" or who are dangerous commonly are viewed as reasonable ways to intervene early with respect to a variety of health, psychosocial, and educational problems (e.g., violence, drugs, depression, suicide, ADHD, LD, obesity). In schools, the emphasis in identifying such students often is on universal, first-level screening. Unfortunately, this practice often is used injudiciously.

About First-Level Screening of Students

Universal, first-level screening involves using *broad-band* screening procedures. The focus is on all students in order to identify those "at risk" as well as those with existing problems. Because criteria scoring for first-level screens is set low, many false-positive identifications are inevitable. To identify false positives and provide additional data on the rest, first-level screening is supposed to be followed by individual assessments. And the whole enterprise is meant to lead to corrective interventions.

When false positives are identified and corrective interventions follow, first-level screening can be beneficial, albeit with costs (including unintended negative consequences). In such cases, ethical concerns for *schools* mainly arise when the costs to the school outweigh benefits. Ethical concerns about *individuals* involve different cost–benefit analyses and may be downplayed as schools pursue screening.

Arguing Benefits versus Costs

Those in favor of universal, first-level screening emphasize benefits. They state that screening allows for identifying and then preventing potential violent behavior, suicide, and other mental health, psychosocial, and educational problems. Proponents also view school personnel as well situated to screen students and, with training, the presumption is that school staff will screen effectively, using appropriate safeguards for privacy and confidentiality. Advocates clearly believe that positive benefits outweigh any negative effects.

Opponents of universal, first-level screening are not arguing against the value of preventing problems. Rather, they are concerned about research findings that indicate specific universal screening practices are ineffective and therefore are unethical for schools to use.

For example, based on the first major study of drug testing at school (76, 000 students nationwide), Lloyd Johnston and colleagues at the University of Michigan conclude such testing does not deter student drug use any more than doing no screening at all. Johnston states, "It's the kind of intervention that doesn't win the hearts and minds of children. I don't think it brings about any constructive changes in their attitudes about drugs or their belief in the dangers associated with using them." At the same time, he stresses, "One could imagine situations where drug testing could be effective, if you impose it in a sufficiently draconian manner – that is, testing most kids and doing it frequently. We're not in a position to say that wouldn't work." Graham Boyd, director of the American Civil Liberties Union Drug Policy Litigation Project who argued against drug testing before the Supreme Court, said, "In light of these findings, schools should be hard-pressed to implement or continue a policy that is intrusive and even insulting for their students" (quotes are from Winter, 2003). Available research also led the American Academy of Pediatrics to oppose widespread implementation of drug testing in schools (American Academy of Pediatrics, 2015). Other findings indicate inadequate support for efforts to predict who will and will not be violent or commit suicide.

An additional and central ethical argument against universal, first-level screening of students suggests that the practice infringes on the rights of families and students. As one state legislator was heard to say about mental health screening, "We want all of our citizens to have access to mental health services, but the idea that we are going to run everyone through some screening system with who knows what kind of values applied to them is unacceptable."

In considering the adoption of universal, first-level screening practices, the debate requires schools to address the following general questions:

Is such screening an appropriate institutionalized role for schools to play?
If so, what procedures are effective and appropriate?
If so, how will schools avoid doing more harm than good in the process?

Discussions should include exploration of such major ethical concerns as:

- Are the procedures antithetical to the school's education mission?
- How will parental consent and due process considerations be handled?
- How will privacy and confidentiality be protected?
- How will staff become qualified to screen?
- Will the activity distract teachers from teaching?
- Since some of the activity is oriented to policing and monitoring, will it counter efforts to enhance a positive school climate?
- How will the school enhance access and availability of appropriate assistance?
- How will negative consequences be countered?

It is noteworthy that the tendency to implement universal, first-level screening increases after high-visibility press coverage of a student gunning down other students or when there are a series of student suicides. Indeed, legislators at federal and state levels often respond to such events by introducing bills calling for schools to screen. While one school shooting is too many, fortunately few students ever act out in this way. One suicide is too many; fortunately, few students take their own lives. Increasingly, however, such rare events are used as a catalyst for policies that call for screening by schools, and in the responsive rush, ethical concerns are given short shrift.

Before establishing a policy for first-level screening of behavior and emotional problems, in-depth cost–benefit analyses are essential. And where first-level screening is in vogue, greater attention must be paid to minimizing inappropriate assignment of pathological disorder and disability labels to students.

In sum, ethical concerns are a primary consideration and raise fundamental questions with respect to the role of public schools in first-level screening for mental and psychosocial problems. False-positive identifications are one major problem. And, because first-level screens focus mainly on factors residing in the student, another significant problem is that the practice colludes with tendencies to over-pathologize and blame the victim.

There are alternatives. As our research on early-age screening for educational problems found, teachers and parents are a basic and natural early warning system that often can fill the role of first-level screening (Adelman & Feshbach, 1971). Then, what needs to be put in place is a student and learning support system that promotes healthy development, prevents problems, and responds quickly when teachers and parents indicate concerns about students who manifest emotional, behavioral, or learning problems. From this perspective, rather than investing heavily in screening, a better approach for schools is to invest in establishing a unified, comprehensive, and equitable system for (1) addressing barriers that interfere with students performing well at school *and* (2) engaging/re-engaging them in classroom instruction. Note the emphasis on engagement. Engagement is essential to sustaining student involvement, good behavior, effective learning at school, and general well-being.

So José has a growing body of research and practice he can draw on in labeling and screening students ethically. Moreover, he can take a leadership role in helping his school rethink better ways to identify students who need special assistance.

Concerns about Social Control Strategies

Punitive school discipline procedures have increasingly taken hold in America's schools. While they are detrimental to the well-being and to the academic success of all students, they have proven to disproportionately punish minority students, especially African American youth. Such policies feed into wider social issues that, once more, disproportionately affect minority communities: the school-to-prison pipeline, high school dropout rates, the push-out phenomenon, and the criminalization of schools.

David Simpson

José and his student support staff colleagues continuously find themselves in discussions with teachers about how to handle discipline problems. He is distressed that so many school policies and practices emphasize punishing and controlling students and generally ignore what might be *causing* a student to misbehave. While he understands the school's role as a socialization agent, as a psychologist, his ethical and practical beliefs stress that greater attention should be given to preventing rather than waiting for misbehavior and then punishing students. And he is also concerned that some students' misbehavior is the result of stress and frustration at home and at school; he believes that punishing such students simply exacerbates problems for them and the school.

Clearly, misbehavior disrupts schooling. In some forms, such as bullying and intimidating others, it is hurtful. And, observing such behavior may disinhibit others. When a student misbehaves, a natural reaction is to want that youngster to experience and other students to see the consequences of misbehaving. One hope is that public awareness of consequences will deter subsequent problems.

In their efforts to deal with deviant and devious behavior and to create safe environments, schools spend considerable time on discipline and classroom management. A major concern raised is that the emphasis is more on socialization than helping students succeed at school. Also raised are concerns that many of the practices currently in use model behavior that can foster rather than counter development of negative values, and some practices produce other forms of undesired behavior. As a result, the degree to which schools rely on social control strategies is a significant issue practically, ethically, and legally.

Overemphasis on Social Control

In general, teaching involves being able to apply strategies focused on content to be taught and knowledge and skills to be acquired – with some degree of attention given to the process of engaging students. All this usually works fine in schools where most students come each day ready and able to deal with what the teacher is ready and able to teach.

Teachers are indeed fortunate when they have a classroom where the majority of students show up and are receptive to the planned lessons. In schools that are the greatest focus of public criticism, this certainly is not the case. It is evident that teachers in such settings are confronted with an entirely different teaching situation. They encounter many students who not only frequently misbehave, but are not easily intimidated by "authority" figures. Efforts to do something about this state of affairs has escalated the emphasis on social control tactics. We note that a SmartBrief sent out by the Association for Supervision and Curriculum Development (ASCD) reported:

> Southern schools increasingly are requiring students to take "character" classes as part of an effort to combat disrespectful behavior. Louisiana lawmakers, for instance, recently passed "courtesy conduct" legislation that requires elementary students to address their teachers as "ma'am" and "sir."

As teachers and other staff try to cope with those who are disruptive, the main concern usually is "classroom management." At one time, a heavy dose of punishment was the dominant approach. Currently, the call at the policy level is for developing more positive practices designed to provide "behavior support" in and out of the classroom. For the most part, however, even these strategies are applied as a form of *social control* aimed mainly at reducing disruptive behavior rather than engaging and re-engaging students in classroom learning. And ironically, the need to control students has led to coercive and repressive actions that have made some schools look and feel like prisons.

Overemphasis on social control can exacerbate students' emotional, learning, and behavior problems and future well-being. This raises not only ethical but also legal concerns. This is especially the case when schools continue to pursue extreme and failed policies such as enacting zero tolerance and suspension mandates (American Psychological Association, 2008; Losen & Martinez, 2013; Skiba, 2014) and do too little to address the conditions that lead to the need to control student behavior.

Some time ago, the National Coalition of Advocates for Students (1991) expressed concern about the trend toward "predetermined, harsh and immediate consequences for a growing list of infractions resulting in long-term or permanent exclusion from public school, regardless of the circumstances, and often without due process." They cautioned that

> ... such policies are more likely to result in increased drop-out rates and long-term negative consequences for children and communities ... such policies have a disparate impact on children of color, and do not result in safe schools and communities ... alternatives to such policies could more effectively reduce the incidence of violence and disruption in our schools, including but not limited to: (1) creating positive, engaging school environments; (2) provision of positive behavioral supports to students; (3) appropriate pre- and in-service development for teachers; and (4) incorporating social problem-solving skills into the curriculum for all students.

Civil rights researchers estimate that

> ... well over two million students were suspended during the 2009–2010 academic year. This means that one out of every nine secondary school students was suspended at least once during that year ... the vast majority of suspensions are for minor infractions of school rules, such as disrupting class, tardiness, and dress code violations, rather than for serious violent or criminal behavior. (Losen et al., 2015)

Moreover, they report gross disparities in use of out-of-school suspension for students with disabilities and those from historically disadvantaged racial, ethnic, and gender subgroups. They stress that "the egregious disparities ... transform concerns about educational policy that allows frequent disciplinary removal into a profound matter of civil rights and social justice." This is a profound ethical and potentially unlawful example of denying educational opportunity.

It is widely acknowledged that many students who are labeled "dropouts" are actually "pushouts." Increasing pressures for school improvement seem to have the negative consequence of creating policies and practices that, in effect, cleanse the rolls of troubled and troubling students and anyone else who may "compromise" the progress of other students and keep achievement score averages from rising.

To move schools beyond overreliance on control strategies, there is ongoing advocacy for school programs to enhance personal responsibility and positive social interactions (e.g., social skills training, positive behavior support, emotional intelligence training, asset development, and character education). There have also been calls for greater home involvement, with emphasis on enhanced parent responsibility for their children's behavior and learning.

From a motivational perspective, the emphasis is on moving away from overtly coercive strategies and overcontrolling social environments. The call is for autonomy-supportive contexts where teachers "empathize with the learner's perspective, allow opportunities for self-initiation and choice, provide a meaningful rationale if choice is constrained, refrain from the use of pressures and contingencies to motivate, and provide timely positive feedback" (Vansteenkiste, Lens, & Deci, 2006).

Taking a more school organizational view, some reformers are calling for an enhanced focus on school climate. They want to transform schools in ways that create an atmosphere of "caring," "cooperative learning," and a "sense of community." Such advocates usually argue for schools that are holistically oriented and family centered. They call for an emphasis in all curricula and instruction on enhancing values and character, including responsibility (social and moral), integrity, self-regulation (self-discipline), identification with academics, and a work ethic; they also want schools to foster intrinsic motivation, self-efficacy, self-esteem, diverse talents, and emotional well-being.

Social Control and Disengaged Students

Students who misbehave often are the target of egregious social control interventions. Overemphasis on such strategies can disengage students from schooling and interfere with re-engagement. As long as a student is disengaged, misbehavior is likely to occur and re-occur (Deci & Ryan, 2012; Fredricks, Blumenfeld, & Paris, 2004). Unfortunately, strategies for re-engaging such students in classroom *learning* rarely are a prominent part of pre- or in-service preparation and seldom are the focus of interventions pursued by staff whose role is to support teachers and students. The emphasis remains, first and foremost, on implementing social control techniques.

When disengaged students display significant aggressive behavior, one common social control strategy is to place them in a special program. Researchers stress what school staff have long worried about: the increasing levels of deviancy associated with concentrated groupings of aggressive students. As Dishion and Dodge (2005) note: "The influence of deviant peers on youth behavior is of growing concern, both in naturally occurring peer interactions and in interventions that might inadvertently exacerbate deviant development." Such a contagion effect has relevance for student groupings that result from grade retention, alternative school assignments, special education diagnoses and placements, and more. Concerns are that the resulting groupings exacerbate negative outcomes (e.g., increased misbehavior at school, neighborhood delinquency, substance abuse, dropping out of school).

An often-stated assumption about social control is that stopping misbehavior will make a student amenable to teaching. In a few cases, this may be so. However, the assumption ignores all the work on understanding *psychological reactance* and the need for individuals to restore their sense of self-determination (Brehm & Brehm, 1981; Deci & Ryan, 2012). Moreover, it seems to belie two painful realities: the number of students who continue to manifest poor academic achievement and the high dropout rate in too many schools.

Efforts to engage and re-engage students in learning draw on what is known about human motivation, especially intrinsic motivation. What many of us were taught about dealing with student misbehavior and learning problems runs counter to what we intuitively understood about human motivation. Teachers and parents, in particular, often learn to over-depend on reinforcement theory, despite their appreciation about the importance of intrinsic motivation.

An increased understanding of motivation clarifies how essential it is to avoid processes that limit options, make students feel controlled and coerced, and focus mostly on "remedying" problems. Such processes are seen as likely to produce avoidance reactions in the classroom and disengagement from school and, thus, reduce opportunities for positive learning and for development of positive attitudes. Re-engagement depends on use of interventions that help minimize conditions that negatively affect motivation and maximize conditions that have a positive motivational effect.

Fairness in Responding to Troubled and Troublesome Students

It was said of a famous football coach that he treated all his players the same – like dogs! When social control strategies are used in schools, the tendency is to treat everyone the same. This usually is justified as the way to be just and fair. But what does that mean? Fair to whom? Fair according to whom? Fair using what criteria and procedures?

What is fair for one person may cause an inequity for another. Should school personnel respond in ways that consider cultural and individual differences and needs? Should past performance be a consideration?

When students have similar backgrounds and capabilities, the tendency is to argue that an egalitarian principle of distributive justice should guide efforts to be fair. However, when there are significant disparities in background and capability, different principles apply. Students who come from a different culture, students who have significant emotional and/or learning problems, young versus older students, students who have a history of good behavior – all these matters suggest that fairness requires consideration of individual differences, special needs, and specific circumstances.

Sometimes fairness demands that two students who break the same rule be handled differently. For example, to do otherwise with a student who has significant emotional problems may result in worsening the student's problems and eventually "pushing" the student out of school.

Adopting a broad set of principles to guide fairness is an ethical necessity. Moreover, use of the different principles at school provides natural opportunities for social–emotional learning and promoting mental health (Center for Mental Health in Schools, 2003).

When Helping Conflicts with Socialization: A Challenge for Mental Health in Schools

An essential perspective on social control comes from appreciating distinctions between helping and socialization interventions. When interveners focus on deviant behavior, the agenda may be to help or to socialize or both.

Exhibit 3 *Helping and Socialization Interventions*

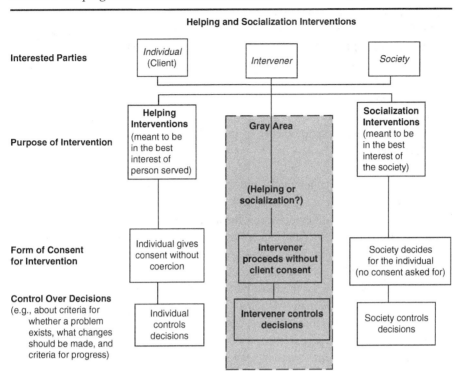

The key to differentiating helping from formal socialization interventions is to determine whose interests are served (see Exhibit 3). Helping interventions are defined in terms of a primary intention to serve what the "client" perceives as his/her interests; socialization interventions primarily seek to serve the interests of the society.

How does one know whose interests are served? The answer is based in the differences in consent and ongoing decision-making. That is, individual interests are defined by the client consenting to intervention without coercion and having control over major intervention decisions. In contrast, socialization agendas usually are implemented under a form of "social contract" that allows society's agents to decide on certain interventions for the individual without asking for consent, and in the process, society maintains control over major intervention decisions.

Situations arise when the intent is to serve the individual's interest but it is not feasible to elicit truly informed consent or ensure the individual has control. Then, one is forced to operate in a gray area. This arises, for example, with legal minors and those with severe and profound problems who are ruled legally incompetent.

In schools, helping and socializing interventions too often come into conflict with each other. Conflict in the form of socialization versus helping can be expected whenever decisions are made about dealing with behavior that the majority of stakeholders find disruptive or view as inappropriate. Such conflicts arise especially in dealing with students who misbehave.

When socialization and helping agenda are in conflict, most school staff find themselves expected to be socializing agents and pursue socialization goals. Helping is not their primary concern. Some school personnel are unclear about their agenda or are forced by circumstances to try to pursue helping and socialization simultaneously, and this adds confusion to an already difficult situation. In contrast, from an ethical perspective, student and learning support staff need to pursue a helping agenda. The goal is to work with consenting individuals to resolve experienced problems. For some students, this includes efforts to make environments more accommodative of individual motivational and developmental differences.

From this perspective, *compulsory* education raises a basic paradox. One major reason for compulsory education is that society wants schools to act as socializing agencies. When a youngster misbehaves at school, one facet of responding involves bringing the deviant and devious behavior under control. Interventions usually are designed mainly to convince the student he or she should conform to the proscribed limits of the social setting. Parents tend to value a school's socializing agenda, but also want their child to receive special help at school when there is an emotionally based problem. Students for the most part do not appreciate efforts to control their behavior, especially since many of their actions are intended to enable them to escape such control. Under the circumstances, not only is there likely to be conflict among the involved parties, it is probable that the intervention efforts actually cause students to experience negative emotional and behavior reactions.

In sum, in institutional settings such as schools and residential treatment centers, interveners often are tasked with both helping individuals overcome underlying problems and controlling misbehavior to maintain social order. At times, the two agenda items are incompatible. And, although interventions may be designated as "counseling," "remediation," or "treatment," the need for social control can overshadow the helping agenda.

It is unfortunate whenever a school's role in socializing the young comes into conflict with the school's role in helping students who have problems. If the aim is to *help* all students have an equal opportunity to succeed at school, then schools must avoid the trap of enforcing rules with such all-too-simple *socialization* solutions as "no exceptions" and "zero tolerance." Concerns about punitive social control practices are compounded when the focus is on students who have emotional problems and when actions are disproportionately aimed at specific subgroups.

The tendency for schools to pursue social control raises ethical dilemmas every day. All school practitioners must personally come to grips with what they view as morally proper in balancing the respective rights and responsibilities of various stakeholders as schools address behavior, learning, and emotional problems. Ultimately, however, the overemphasis on social control needs to give way to addressing conditions that lead to misbehavior and to strategies that fully engage students in learning.

Society's obligation is to do more than exert power to control and punish. Social institutions such as schools must balance socialization with interventions that help individuals in need.

For José, each day means avoiding falling into the trap of just reacting to a student's misbehavior by applying consequences and trying to instill socially appropriate behavior. Ethics calls for working with colleagues on (1) establishing preventive strategies, including helping teachers redesign classrooms to minimize factors that set off misbehavior and (2) moving away from punitive thinking to developing policies and practices that focus on enhancing socialization through helping strategies.

However, José also has to appreciate that the dilemmas that arise related to how a school responds to misbehavior have deep roots. As the following discussion illustrates, his ability to make good ethical decisions requires that he deepen his understanding and that of others at the school about benefits versus costs, distributive justice, coercive interventions, and individual versus societal rights and responsibilities.

About Benefits versus Costs

Those advocating for mental health in schools always stress the benefits of what they propose. However, such benefits usually are acquired at a cost – in several senses of the term. The law of unintended consequences is omnipresent, and negative consequences constantly plague our best intentions. Negative effects encompass a wide range of institutional and individual costs, such as wasted financial resources, system disruption, and personal harm.

Negative effects alone, of course, do not contraindicate practice. Concerns arise when costs clearly outweigh benefits. The problem for schools is that data on effectiveness and negative effects are sparse. This makes it extremely difficult to specify benefits and costs, let alone determine net gains or losses. Thus, decisions about the relative balance between costs and benefits usually involve weighing potential – but unproven – positive and negative effects.

For example, in labeling students, basic questions must be asked, such as: in this instance, is the student really the appropriate focus for intervention or should the emphasis be on systemic changes? Will the label lead to provision of an effective intervention? If so, will the benefits justify the financial expenses to the school and family and the discomfort, stigmatization, and other potential negative effects the student may experience upon being labeled and treated as different from others?

The complexity of cost–benefit analyses is compounded by the realization that one must go beyond consideration of outcomes for a particular person or organization. Persons from *subgroups* whose backgrounds differ from the dominant culture provide a case in point. Such individuals sometimes are classified and treated as deficient primarily because their actions and performance differ markedly from those of the dominant culture. However unintentional, student labeling and corrective intervention practices have colluded with biased attitudes and discriminatory actions against nondominant subgroups in the society.

Over the years, court cases dealing with IQ testing and disproportionate special education placements of minority populations have highlighted this concern. Some litigants argued that minority populations are inappropriately served by most IQ tests and labeling. Court decisions have stressed that intelligence testing should be "culture fair," including use of the individual's "home language," and that tests alone should not be the basis for classifying individuals. The courts even restricted the use of tests because of the costs to persons from minority backgrounds. Such cases highlight that a practice's benefits for an individual may be outweighed by its costs to specific subgroups in the society. Of particular concern are interventions that perpetuate racial injustice in the form of additional discrimination, stigmatization, and restriction of educational and socioeconomic opportunities. Given that harmful effects go beyond specific clients, cost–benefits for subgroups and multiple systems also must be weighed.

An even broader ethical perspective warns that modern societies are manifesting an ever increasing, distressing, and unnecessary overdependence on institutionalized intervention. Some writers suggest that the negative effects of this overreliance on professionals include widespread mystification of the public and a general loss of people's ability to cope with their own affairs.

These effects are illustrated by the unquestioning acceptance by large numbers of people of diagnoses and related special interventions. Illich (1971, 1976) called this state of affairs "cultural iatrogenesis." He argued that professionals must judge the ethics of their activities not only in terms of consequences for specific individuals, subgroups, and institutions, but also with respect to impact on the entire culture. This position, of course, further compounds the complexity of determining whether costs outweigh benefits and goes well beyond what most of us are ready to factor into our ethical analyses.

In sum, every intervention rationale reflects conclusions that the benefits of chosen processes and intended outcomes outweigh costs. At the same time, even when benefits seem to outweigh costs, decisions to intervene must not overemphasize this "utility" principle. Consideration must also be given to the dilemmas of coercive interventions, ensuring fairness (equity and justice), and balancing individual and societal rights and responsibilities.

About Coercive Intervention

Growing awareness of rights has increased attention to the question: *when is coercive intervention appropriate?* A perspective on this question provides an important counterpoint for appreciating informed consent and assent.

Some practitioners argue that any type of involuntary psychoeducational intervention is unjustifiable. Others argue that various forms of majority-disapproved behavior (ranging from illegal acts through immoral and deviant behaviors to compulsive negative habits) produce enough social harm, offense, or nuisance to warrant compulsory intervention.

Examples cited with respect to minors include substance abuse, truancy, aggressive behavior toward adults or peers, and low self-esteem. Even when the focus is on the most dramatic psychosocial problems, serious ethical concerns are raised whenever compulsory treatment is proposed to socialize or "re-socialize" individuals.

When the need for coercive intervention is extrapolated from dramatic cases to less extreme behaviors, such as common misbehavior and attention problems, the ethical concerns seem even more pressing. Ironically, in such instances, the coercive nature of an approach may not even be evident, particularly when the activity is described as in keeping with appropriate socialization goals and as unlikely to be harmful. For behavior that is illegal (or in violation of organizational rules), it is frequently decided to compel or at least "encourage" individuals to enroll in treatment rather than experience usual consequences (e.g., expulsion from school). When treatment is offered as an alternative to punishment, the choice between the lesser of two evils may seem clear and devoid of coercion. For example, many juveniles can be expected to express preference for a "diversion" program of treatment over incarceration. However, given a third nontreatment alternative they see as more desirable, treatment probably would be chosen to a lesser degree.

One moral basis for decisions to allow and pursue involuntary interventions is found in the philosophical grounds for coercion. As Feinberg (1973) suggests, such decisions are informed by principles that address justifications for the restriction of personal liberty. These are: (1) to prevent harm to others, either injury to individual persons (The Private Harm Principle) or impairment of institutional practices that are in the public interest (The Public Harm Principle); (2) to prevent offense to others (The Offense Principle); (3) to prevent harm to self (Legal Paternalism); (4) to prevent or punish sin – that is, to "enforce morality as such" (Legal Moralism); (5) to benefit the self (Extreme Paternalism); and (6) to benefit others (The Welfare Principle).

As Robinson (1974) cogently summarized the matter:

> None of these justifications for coercion is devoid of merit nor is it necessary that any of them exclude the others in attempts to justify actions against the freedoms of an individual. . . . It is one thing to assert each of these justifications enjoys some merit but quite another to suggest that they are equally valid. And it is manifestly the case that they do not share equally in the force of the law. Yet, while not sharing equally, they have all, on one occasion or another, been relied on to validate a legal judgment.

About Fairness

Any discussion of coercive intervention raises concerns about distributive justice and fairness in responding to needs. As discussed, these concerns frequently arise for schools in the context of balancing their role as socialization agents and the need to help students experiencing learning, behavior, and emotional problems.

Legal emphasis on "right to treatment" and "right of all to an education" highlights the moral obligation to ensure fair allocation of society's resources. Given inadequate budgets to underwrite needed programs, many compete for the same resources. Schools vie with social programs. Enrichment interventions compete with treatment programs. Questions arise such as: is it fair to help those who have psychological or educational problems by drawing from the limited resources available for regular educational programs? And, beyond fair resource allocation, the general expectation is that interventions will be carried out in just and fair ways.

In addressing concerns about fairness, a basic problem is: how do we decide what is fair? Decisions about this require dealing with questions such as: fair for whom? Fair according to whom? Fair using what criteria and what procedures for applying the criteria? Should everyone be given an equal share of available resources? Should each be provided for according to specific need? Should we base distribution of resources on their being earned (e.g., through a societal contribution) or because they have been denied previously (e.g., through discrimination)?

Obviously, what is fair for the society or an organization may not be fair for an individual; what is fair for one person may cause inequity for another. To provide special services for one group may deprive another or may raise the taxes of all citizens. To deny services to those who need help is harmful.

Making fair decisions about who should get what and about how rules should be applied requires use of principles of distributive justice. As Beauchamp and Childress (2012) underscore, interveners incorporate different principles of distributive justice into their intervention rationales based on whether they subscribe to (1) egalitarian theories (emphasizing equal access to the goods in life that every rational person desires), (2) Marxist theories (emphasizing need), (3) libertarian theories (emphasizing contribution and merit), or (4) utilitarian theories (emphasizing a mixed use of such criteria in order to maximize public and private utility).

Clearly, interventions based on rationales adopting different views of distributive justice conflict with each other. In addition, confusion may arise when an intervention rationale incorporates more than one fairness principle.

Decisions based on fairness principles often call for unequal allocation and affirmative action with regard to dispensing resources and applying rules. Thus, although justice and fairness are intended, such decisions can be quite controversial, especially when resources are scarce.

Practitioners who see themselves as "helping professionals" lean toward an emphasis on individual need. For instance, they tend to believe that fairness means that those with problems deserve special aid. Indeed, the duty to serve those in need is seen as an ethical reason for diagnostic labeling and other highly intrusive specialized practices.

At the same time, conflicting views exist as to which of many ongoing needs in a society should be assigned highest priority. Are prevention programs more important than treatment programs? Are programs for the gifted more important than programs for students with problems? Should school athletic teams be funded at higher levels than vocational programs?

Beyond resource allocation, interveners consistently are confronted with the problem of fair implementation, especially with regard to applying rules and consequences for infractions. For example, should different consequences be applied for the same offense when those involved differ in terms of needs, problems, stage of development, previous discrimination, potential contribution to society, and so forth?

Some persons try to simplify matters by not making distinctions and treating everyone and every situation alike. For instance, some school administrators insist on enforcing rules without regard to the particulars of the case. They believe standard consequences must be applied without accounting for an individual's social and emotional problems. This is seen with respect to zero tolerance policies. The position taken is that it is unfair to others if the same rule is not applied in the same way to everyone. Unfortunately, while a "no exceptions" approach represents a simple solution, it ignores the possibility that nonpersonalized rule enforcement exacerbates problems not only for the rule breaker but also for society, which is unjust.

In sum, no ethical analysis can ignore concerns about distributive justice. In particular, decisions must be made about what constitutes fair allocation of resources, fair rules, and fair rule enforcement. And these decisions require clarity about which principle of distributive justice is used. They also overlap concerns about individual and societal rights and responsibilities.

About the Individual versus Society

Schools are a societal institution. They are expected to play a role in the socialization of the young, the well-being of the economy, and the maintenance of the country's political system. In pursuing these institutional goals, concerns about individuals often are marginalized.

Discussion of the matter falls into ongoing discussions about the ethics of the common good and the ethics of individual rights and responsibilities. Advocates tend to cite both sets of concerns in proposing agendas for mental health in schools. In doing so, however, they often avoid addressing the problem that maximizing the common good often means increasing limits on individual rights. Our discussions about the need for mental health in schools to promote equity of opportunity and about helping versus socialization highlight the dilemma.

In keeping with the ethics of the common good, schools have a primary responsibility to benefit society. And as societal citizens, we have a responsibility to work in ways that enable schools to succeed. At the same time, our desire and right to pursue personal and subgroup beliefs and interests can conflict with what a school is doing.

There are fundamental disagreements about what is in the best interest of our society and its people. These have been fueled as the voices of marginalized subgroups have found political platforms. The disagreements are seen in conflicts over curricula and instruction, ways to enhance equity of opportunity, strategies for preventing and correcting problems, and so forth.

For all of us who work with schools, there is a constant valuing of individual rights; at the same time, we appreciate that such rights come with societal responsibilities. This, of course, requires moving beyond the ever-pressing desire to do our "own thing" and engaging in a continuous search for feasible ways to minimize harm to individuals and enhance equity of opportunity while maximizing good for society.

Concerns about Science-Based Interventions

Intentional interventions are rationally based. An underlying rationale consists of views derived from philosophical (including ethical), theoretical, empirical, and legal sources. Not all intervention rationales are equal. Some reflect a higher level of scholarly sophistication; some cover a broader range of relevant considerations; some have greater philosophical, theoretical, and empirical consistency. And these are not the only important considerations. Systematic biases that arise from dominating models also are of concern. For instance, prevailing views of intervention for emotional, behavioral, and learning problems tend to (1) attribute cause to factors within the individual, and (2) focus intervention on changing the individual.

Adelman & Taylor (1994)

José was caught off-balance by the demand that school improvement efforts be science-based. Did that mean it was unethical for the school and anyone at the school to use a practice that had not been well-researched? Did not efforts to improve schools often require transformative practices – many of which have not yet been subjected to well-designed studies?

School improvement requires trying new approaches. As a result, schools are continuously introducing new projects, programs, and initiatives (e.g., to improve instruction; address students' behavior, learning, and emotional problems; enhance safety; promote healthy development). Because of the call for schools to use science-based practices, questions arise such as: is there evidence that a proposed new approach works? How good is the evidence? Do benefits outweigh costs?

However, a more fundamental question often is not considered: *will what is proposed reduce or increase inequities and disparities across the student population?* With this ethical concern in mind, cost–benefit analyses must include whether what is proposed will enhance equity of opportunity for success at school and beyond not just for a few students but for the many who are being left behind.

Also, other fundamental matters include: what if there is not an evidence-based approach for effectively addressing the many barriers to learning and teaching that confront schools? Or, with respect to complex problems such as dropout prevention, what if it is necessary to bundle together interventions. *Is it unethical for a district to pursue an unproven approach in such instances?*

Concerns about the Pressure to Use Evidence-Based Interventions

The demand that schools and other public agencies adopt practices that are evidence-based is increasing (Olson & Viadero, 2002; Painter, 2009; Pew-MacArthur Results First Initiative, 2015). As a result, terms such as "science-based" or "empirically supported" are assigned to almost any intervention identified as having research data generated in ways that meet "scientific standards" and that demonstrate a level of *efficacy* deemed worthy of application.

A somewhat higher standard is used for the subgroup of practices referred to as evidence-based *treatments*. This designation usually is reserved for interventions tested in more than one rigorous study (multiple case studies, randomized control trials) and consistently found to be better than a placebo or no treatment.

An even higher standard involves data on *effectiveness*. This involves demonstrating that the practice produces good outcomes under real-world conditions and when replicated widely.

Currently, most evidence-based practices are discrete interventions designed to meet specified needs. A few are complex sets of interventions intended to meet multifaceted needs, and these usually are referred to as programs. Most evidence-based practices are applied using a detailed guide or manual.

No one argues against using the best science available to improve professional expertise. However, as evidence-based practices are increasingly emphasized in school improvement policy, the concerns raised have a variety of ethical overtones (Biesta, 2007; Norcross, Beutler, & Levant, 2005). For example:

(1) *Limited efficacy research, little effectiveness research.* Interventions proposed for schools are mainly based on short-term studies, and these have not included samples representing the range of students with whom the practice is to be used. From a school perspective, until researchers demonstrate that a prototype is effective under real-world conditions, it can only be considered a promising and not a proven practice. At this time, the evidence base continues to consist, as noted by Green and Glasgow (2006), almost entirely of efficacy studies with little effectiveness research.

(2) *Prematurely recommended and adopted practices.* A constant concern is that schools will leap to implement practices with limited evidence and later find that new data show the practice to be not only ineffective, but also harmful. An example was the "research-based" adoption by some schools of single-session psychological debriefing after a crisis with the intent of countering post-traumatic stress. Subsequent research pointed out that such debriefing "appears to be an ineffective intervention to reduce symptoms and prevent PTSD" (Gartlehner et al., 2013) and can be harmful (Van Emmerik et al., 2002).

(3) *Overemphasis on pathology.* The mandate for schools to use science-based practices in addressing student problems brings with it the risk of perpetuating the skewed emphasis on individual pathology found in most approaches to mental health in schools. The movement also contributes to the tendency to prematurely push practices developed under highly controlled laboratory conditions into widespread application.

(4) *Undermining innovation.* Furthermore, as the evidence-based movement gains momentum, an increasing concern is that certain interventions are officially prescribed and others are proscribed by policy makers and funders. This breeds fear that only those professionals who adhere to official lists are sanctioned and rewarded. More generally, there are concerns about the potential "tyranny" of evidence-based practices, and the possibility that an emphasis on such programs can inadvertently undermine rather than enhance school-wide reform efforts necessary for enhancing equity of opportunity for all students to succeed at school and beyond. There is virtually no evidence that evidence-based practices contribute to overall school effectiveness, as data on such an issue are never gathered.

(5) *Increasing inequity of opportunity.* Then there is the concern for equity. *Schools must address the many, not just a few of the students in need.* From a systemic and public policy perspective, introducing any new practice into an organization

such as a school has to be justified not only in terms of its science base, but also on how well it can advance the organization's mission. In the context of school improvement planning, then, each proposal requires cost–benefit analyses that consider need, fit, and the nature and scope of potential outcomes. Just adding a practice because it is evidence-based may not meet a school's needs, especially with respect to addressing the wide range of students manifesting problems and enhancing equity of opportunity. Highly circumscribed practices tend to add little to school improvement; the same is true for practices that are unlikely to be widely implemented. Expending considerable resources on such practices can increase inequities and disparities.

Needed: Equitable and Sustainable System Change and Scale-Up

Efforts to make substantial, sustainable, and equitable improvements to address student problems requires much more than implementing a few science-based demonstrations. From both a practical and ethical perspective, new approaches are only as good as a school district's ability to develop and institutionalize them equitably in all its schools. This process often is called diffusion, replication, roll-out, or scale-up, and it is complex (Adelman & Taylor, 2014).

The complexity is especially evident in making comprehensive, innovative systemic changes to improve how schools deal with factors interfering with learning and teaching. For example, in our work, we stress that addressing such factors requires comprehensive systemic changes – some focused on individuals and some on environmental systems, some focused on mental health and some on physical health, education, and social services, some intended for the short term, but most implemented over extended periods of time (Adelman & Taylor, 2010).

The history of public education is strewn with innovations that were not sustained or replicated to scale. These frequent failures have undermined efforts to enhance equity of opportunity.

Naturally, financial considerations play a role in failures to sustain and replicate, but a widespread "project mentality" also is culpable. We continuously find that new practices – some science-based, some not – are introduced as special projects that usually distract school staff from making transformative systemic changes. New initiatives usually are developed and initially implemented as a pilot demonstration at one or more schools. This is particularly the case when initiatives are specially funded projects. For schools involved in projects or piloting new programs, a common tendency is for personnel to think about their work as a time-limited demonstration. And, other school stakeholders also tend to perceive the work as temporary (e.g., "It will end when the grant runs out," or, "I've seen so many reforms come and go; this too shall pass"). This mindset leads to the view that new activities will be fleeting, and it contributes to fragmented approaches and the marginalization of initiatives. It also works against the type of systemic change needed to sustain and expand major school improvements.

All this underscores the need to increase the understanding and implementation of transformative systemic changes. Elsewhere, we have delineated the nature and scope of what is involved in bringing new prototypes into schools (Adelman & Taylor, 2014).

In sum, the point of improving the science base for school practices is to identify broadly effective and cost-efficient approaches that can be replicated in all schools that can benefit. This goes beyond adopting best practices, because *best* simply denotes that a practice is better than whatever else is currently available and does not indicate that it is a good practice. How good the practice is depends on complex analyses related to costs and benefits, including ethical and practical considerations.

Implicit in the call for schools to use science-based practices is the notion that other practices should be avoided. But what should be done when school improvement requires trying an innovation for which research has not yet been conducted (e.g., innovative approaches to address educational, psychosocial, and mental health concerns; school-wide approaches; comprehensive, multifaceted approaches)? The reality is that many innovative school improvements must go beyond activity for which there is an evidence base. And some proposed science-based practices should not be adopted because they detract from and may undermine efforts to make the type of systemic changes necessary for accomplishing comprehensive school improvements. This is especially so when it comes to *transforming* how schools address inequities and disparities. Enhancing equity of opportunity requires ensuring essential supports for the many students manifesting learning, behavior, and emotional problems.

Clearly, José and all his colleagues at the school understand that ineffective practices should not be adopted and any in use should be dropped. But what should be done when there is a need and there is no evidence-based approach? More broadly, what should be done when transformative approaches to school improvement are needed? José will find that the ethical responsibility in such instances is mainly to analyze rationally how well what is under discussion will:

- Replace an essential, but ineffective practice;
- Fill a high-priority gap in a school's efforts to meet its mission;
- Integrate into school improvement efforts;
- Promote healthy development, prevent problems, respond early after problem onset, or treat chronic problems;
- Help a few or many students;
- Integrate into a comprehensive continuum of interventions rather than become another fragmented approach;
- Be implemented in an effective and sustainable manner and can be replicated to scale.

Concluding Comments

Long ago, Nicholas Hobbs (1975) cautioned: "Society defines what is exceptional or deviant, and appropriate treatments are designed quite as much to protect society as they are to help the child. . . . 'To take care of them' can and should be read with two meanings: to give children help and to exclude them from the community."

Anyone who works in schools must come to grips with the concerns we have discussed in this chapter. There are no simple and straightforward answers. Thus, it is not surprising that discussion about the most ethical and effective ways to pursue mental health in schools is controversial.

The world around us is changing at an exponential rate, and so must the way schools approach behavior, learning, and emotional problems. Our position is that, at present, the agenda for mental health in schools mainly needs to focus on minimizing the barriers to school and student success and helping to develop better systems for enhancing equity of opportunity. This approach is reflected in our efforts to embed mental health into a unified, comprehensive, equitable system of student and learning supports for addressing the needs of all students rather than just focusing on a small segment of students (Adelman &Taylor, 2010).

Now is the time to move forward in ensuring that all youngsters have an equal opportunity to succeed at school and to achieve productive and healthy lives. This is consistent with schools serving the common good and ensuring individual rights. To paraphrase Goethe: not moving forward is a step backward.

References

Adelman, H. S. & Feshbach, S. (1971). Predicting reading failure: beyond the readiness model. *Exceptional Children, 37*, 339–345.

Adelman, H. S. & Taylor, L. (1994). *On understanding intervention in psychology and education*. Westport, CT: Praeger.

Adelman, H. S. & Taylor, L. (2010). *Mental health in schools: Engaging learners, preventing problems, and improving schools*. Thousand Oaks, CA: Corwin Press.

Adelman, H. S. & Taylor, L. (2014). *Bringing new prototypes into practice: Dissemination, implementation, and facilitating transformation*. The F.M. Duffy Reports (epub). Retrieved from http://smhp.psych.ucla.edu/pdfdocs/implrep3.pdf

American Academy of Pediatrics (2015). Adolescent Drug Testing Policies in Schools (AAP Policy Statement). *Pediatrics, 135*, 782–783.

American Psychological Association Zero Tolerance Task Force (2008). Are zero tolerance policies effective in the schools? An evidentiary review and recommendations. *American Psychologist, 63*, 852–862.

Beauchamp, T. L. & Childress, J. F. (2012). *Principles of biomedical ethics* (7th edn.). New York, NY: Oxford University Press.

Biesta, G. (2007). Why "what works" won't work: Evidence-based practice and the democratic deficit in educational research. *Educational Theory, 57*, 1–22.

Brehm, J. W. & Brehm, S. S. (1981). *Psychological reactance: A theory of freedom and control*. San Diego, CA: Academic Press.

Center for Mental Health in Schools (2003). *Natural opportunities to promote social-emotional learning and MH*. Los Angeles, CA: Author at UCLA. Retrieved from http://smhp.psych.ucla.edu/pdfdocs/practicenotes/naturalopportunities.pdf

Center for Mental Health in Schools (2012). *RTI and classroom & schoolwide learning supports*. Los Angeles, CA: Author at UCLA. Retrieved from http://smhp.psych .ucla.edu/pdfdocs/rtii.pdf

Center for Mental Health in Schools (2015). *Arguments about whether overdiagnosis of ADHD is a significant problem*. Los Angeles, CA: Author at UCLA. Retrieved from http://smhp.psych.ucla.edu/pdfdocs/overdiag.pdf

Cornell, D. (2015). Our schools are safe: Challenging the misperception that schools are dangerous places. *American Journal of Orthopsychiatry, 85*, 217–220.

Deci, E. L. & Ryan, R. M. (2012). Motivation, personality, and development within embedded social contexts: An overview of self-determination theory. In R. M. Ryan (Ed.), *Oxford handbook of human motivation* (pp. 85–107). Oxford, UK: Oxford University Press.

Dishion, T. J. & Dodge, K. A. (2005). Peer contagion in interventions for children and adolescents: Moving towards an understanding of the ecology and dynamics of change. *Journal of Abnormal Child Psychology, 33*, 395–400.

Feinberg, J. (1973). *Social philosophy*. Englewood Cliffs, NJ: Prentice-Hall.

Frankena, W. K. (1973). *Ethics* (2nd edn.). Englewood Cliffs, NJ: Prentice-Hall.

Fredricks, J. A., Blumenfeld, P. C., & Paris, A. H. (2004). School engagement: Potential of the concept, state of the evidence. *Review of Educational Research, 74*, 59–109.

Gartlehner, G., Forneris, C. A., Brownley, K. A., et al. (2013). *Interventions for the Prevention of Posttraumatic Stress Disorder (PTSD) in adults after exposure to psychological trauma*. Rockville, MD: AHRQ Comparative Effectiveness Reviews. Report No.: 13-EHC062-EF.

George, J. A. (2015). Stereotype and school pushout: Race, gender and discipline disparities. *Arkansas Law Review, 68*, 101–130.

Green, L. W. & Glasgow, R. E. (2006). Evaluating the relevance, generalization, and applicability of research: Issues in external validation and translation methodology. *Evaluation and the Health Professions*, 29, 126–153.

Hinshaw, S. P. & Scheffler, R. M. (2014). *The ADHD explosion: Myths, medication, money, and today's push for performance*. Oxford, UK: Oxford University Press.

Hobbs, N. (1975). *The future of children: Categories, labels, and their consequences*. San Francisco, CA: Jossey-Bass.

Illich, I. (1971). *Deschooling society*. New York, NY: Marion Boyars Publishers Ltd.

Illich, I. (1976). *Medical nemesis*. New York, NY: Pantheon Books.

Losen, D., Hodson, C., Keith II, M. A., Morrison, K., & Belway, S. (2015). *Are we closing the school discipline gap?* Los Angeles, CA: Civil Rights Project.

Losen, D. J. & Martinez. T. E. (2013). *Out of school and off track: The overuse of suspensions in American middle and high schools*. Los Angeles, CA: Civil Rights Project.

Lyon, G. R. (2002). *Learning disabilities and early intervention strategies*. Testimony to the Subcommittee on Education Reform Committee on Education and the Workforce. Washington, DC: U.S. House of Representatives,.

Maki, K. E., Floyd, R. G., & Roberson, T. (2015). State learning disability eligibility criteria: A comprehensive review. *School Psychology Quarterly, 30*, 457–469.

National Coalition of Advocates for Students (U.S.). Board of Inquiry Project (1991). *Barriers to excellence: Our children at risk*. Boston, MA: Author.

Norcross, J. C., Beutler, L. E., & Levant, R. F. (Eds.) (2005). *Evidence-based practices in mental health: debate and dialogue on the fundamental questions*. Washington, DC: American Psychological Association.

O'Donnell, G. M. & Gersch, I. S. (2015). Professional and ethical issues when working with children and adolescents. In R. Tribe & J. Morrissey (Eds.), *Handbook of professional and ethical practice for psychologists, counsellors and psychotherapists* (pp. 184–196). New York, NY: Routledge.

Olson, L. & Viadero, D. (2002). Law mandates scientific base for research. *Education Week*, *21*, 14–15.

Painter, K. (2009). Legislation of evidence-based treatments in public mental health: Analysis of benefits and costs. *Social Work and Public Health*, *24*, 511–26.

Perfect, M. M. & Morris, R. J. (2011). Delivering school-based mental health services by school psychologists: Education, training, and ethical issues. *Psychology in the Schools*, *48*, 1049–1063.

Pew-MacArthur Results First Initiative (2015). *Legislating evidence-based policymaking.* Retrieved from www.pewtrusts.org/~/media/Assets/2015/03/LegislationResults FirstBriefMarch2015.pdf

Raines, J. C. & Dibble, N. T. (2010). Ethical decision making in school mental health. Oxford Scholarship online.

Rinas, J. & Clyne-Jackson, S. (1988). *Professional conduct and legal concerns in mental health practice.* Norwalk, CT: Appleton & Lange.

Robinson, D. N. (1974). Harm, offense, and nuisance: Some first steps in the establishment of an ethics of treatment. *American Psychologist*, *29*, 233–238.

Ryan, W. (1971). *Blaming the victim.* New York: Random House.

Simpson, D. (2014). Exclusion, punishment, racism, and our schools: A critical race theory perspective on school discipline. *UCLA Law Review*, *61*, 506–563.

Skiba, R. (2014). The failure of zero tolerance. *Reclaiming Children and Youth*, *22*, 27–33.

Skiba, R. (2013). Reaching a critical juncture for our kids: The need to reassess school-justice practices. *Family Court Review*, *51*, 380–387.

Tanenbaum, S. J. (2005). Evidence-based practice as mental health policy: Three controversies and a caveat. *Health Affairs*, *24*, 163–173.

R. Tribe & J. Morrissey (Eds.). *Handbook of professional and ethical practice for psychologists, counsellors and psychotherapists.* New York, NY: Routledge.

Van Emmerik, A. A. P., Kamphuls, J. H., Hulsbosch, A. M., & Emmelkamp, P. M. G. (2002). Single session debriefing after psychological trauma: A meta-analysis. *The Lancet*, *360*, 766–771.

Vansteenkiste, M., Lens, W., & Deci, E. (2006). Intrinsic versus extrinsic goal contents in Self-determination Theory: Another look at the quality of academic motivation. *Educational Psychologist*, *41*, 19–31.

Welfel, E. R. (2012). *Ethics in counseling & psychotherapy* (5th edn.). Belmont, CA: Brooks Cole.

Winter, G. (2003). Study finds no sign that testing deters students' drug use. *The New York Times.* Retrieved from www.nytimes.com/2003/05/17/us/study-finds-no-sign-that-testing-deters-students-drug-use.html

For more on the matters discussed in this chapter, use the Quick Find Online Clearinghouse at our Center at UCLA (http://smhp.psych.ucla.edu/quicksearch.htm). Here are a few examples of relevant documents that are in the Clearinghouse:

>*Behavior Problems and Conduct Disorders* – http://smhp.psych.ucla.edu/qf/p3022_01.htm

>*Assessment and Screening* – http://smhp.psych.ucla.edu/qf/p1405_01.htm

>*Stigma Reduction* – http://smhp.psych.ucla.edu/qf/stigma.htm

>*Ethical/Legal/Consumer Issues* – http://smhp.psych.ucla.edu/qf/p1406_01.htm

3 Ethical Issues in Providing Mental Health Services to College Students

Mary Ann Covey and Kari J. Keller

There has been much publicity regarding many issues that have impacted providing mental health services to college students. In this paper, we will discuss five main ethical dilemmas commonly faced by university mental health professionals: (1) increased demands for services without a concomitant increase in staff; (2) increase in severity of the psychological problems in students; (3) issues related to confidentiality and record-keeping; (4) variable training levels related to serving a diverse population; and (5) technology changes and student expectations (e.g., immediate availability of practitioners via social media).

It is important to understand the changing societal context of universities over the last 25 years that underlies and complicates these ethical dilemmas. Approximately 26 years ago, Stone and Archer (1990) described the problems, issues, and assumptions facing college and university counseling centers. Many of the issues discussed by Stone and Archer (e.g., the increasing number of students that presented with serious psychological problems, training programs that valued diversity and multicultural competence, and providing counseling to an increasingly diverse population) still exist today; however, the changing societal norms and views of universities have changed the way university counseling centers have experienced and dealt with those issues. Those contextual factors include a rise in college enrollment, an increase in the cost of tuition, changing parenting styles, and a decrease in the availability of community mental health resources.

Contextual Factors Impacting Universities

One major contextual variable that has influenced university mental health services is the overall number of students attending college, which has increased dramatically over the past 25 years. According to the U.S. Department of Education, National Center for Education Statistics (2013), the number of college students has increased by over 39 percent between 1992 and 2012. Additionally, it was noted that the diversity of the student body has also changed over the past 25 years, with greater diversity with regards to race/ethnicity, gender, and identified sexual orientation.

Along with an increase in enrollment, another contextual variable impacting university counseling services is the consistent rise in cost of college tuition. Mitchel (2015) reported in the U.S. News and World Report that from 1995 to

2015 the average tuition and fees at private national universities jumped by 179 percent. Furthermore, out-of-state tuition and fees at public universities rose by 226 percent, and in-state tuition and fees at public national universities grew the most by 296 percent. Due to these numbers, Schrecker (2010) argued that the philosophy of higher education has also changed by adopting more of a corporate model where the ultimate payout to the consumer (student) is a high-paid job.

Catering to creating a product (higher-paid jobs) and the incredibly high cost of attending college have impacted parents' expectations of what their child should experience. Parents often feel that rising college tuitions entitle them to protect their investment. Parents make sacrifices to pay tuition, and so their interest in whether their child is using their expensive education wisely is legitimate. However, what may become problematic is when such over involvement leads to the belief that college-age children cannot and should not be responsible for their actions. Many terms and descriptors have been used to illustrate parents' involvement in and expectations of their children's collegiate experience. Marano (2008) wrote the provocative *A Nation of Wimps: The High Cost of Invasive Parenting* and argued that overinvolved parents actually hinder the development of their children. College administrators often use the term "helicopter parents" to describe parents who call to wake their children up for class or email professors to complain about grades. The rise of cell phone usage has often been blamed for the explosion of helicopter parenting – colloquially referred to as "the world's longest umbilical cord." Another popular term that describes the style of parenting experienced by many college students is "bulldozer parenting" (Taylor, 2006). This type of parenting style attempts to remove all obstacles for the child so as to create the highest probability of success. While this type of parenting may be well intended and meant to protect the child, it has been linked to raising children who are more fragile and fearful (Taylor, 2006). As a result, some students come to university counseling centers reporting that their parents are forcing them to seek services and expect to be involved in the treatment process.

The overall decrease of the availability of mental health services is an important context in order to understand related issues in providing mental health services on college campuses. Honberg and colleagues (2011), through the National Alliance on Mental Illness (NAMI), outlined in detail the cuts to funding for mental health, as well as the implications of these cuts. For example, between 2009 and 2012, more than $1.6 billion was cut from state funds for mental health services. NAMI reported the following: "Communities pay a high price for cuts of this magnitude. Rather than saving states and communities money, these cuts to services simply shift financial responsibility to emergency rooms, community hospitals, law enforcement agencies, correctional facilities and homeless shelters" (p.1). It is not a stretch to add university counseling centers to this list of agencies with increased responsibility and decreased resources. Additionally, mental health cuts have also been implicated in public safety concerns on college campuses, especially in high-visibility tragedies such as Virginia Tech and Umpqua Community College.

The significant increase in the demand for mental health services and the severity of mental health concerns on college campuses has been well documented (Center of

Collegiate Mental Health, 2015; Hunt & Eisenburg, 2010; Ibrahim et al., 2013; Novotney, 2014). As the fall semester of 2015 began, *The Chronicle of Higher Education* published an article entitled "An Epidemic of Anguish" by Robin Wilson (2015), which highlighted the unique issues facing college counseling centers related to higher demand for services and the increase in severity of mental health concerns of students. At this time, there are over 100 responses to the article, which certainly illuminates the growing public concern regarding mental health services on college campuses. As a result of this article and increasing public concern, American University and College Counseling Center Directors President Dr. Micky Sharma was interviewed on the PBS NewsHour (2015) in a segment on college student mental health. In the interview, he was asked about both the increase in demand for services and the severity of mental health concerns. For example, the 2014 National Survey of College Counseling Centers (Center for Collegiate Mental Health, 2015) reported that 94 percent of directors indicated an increase in the number of students that presented with severe psychological problems. Sharma explained that the reduced stigma of treatment for mental health has made it more likely for students to seek help and that we live in a fast-paced society that puts additional pressure on college students. Sharma also described strategies that centers have used to cope with the increased demand for services and severity of presenting concerns. In the remainder of this chapter, we will explore how some of these strategies to manage mental health services contribute to five ethical dilemmas commonly experienced by university counseling centers.

Increased Demand for Services

One of the biggest issues faced by many university counseling centers is an increased demand for their services. The percentage of university counseling center clients with severe psychological problems has increased from 44 percent in 2013 to 52 percent in 2014 (Center for Collegiate Mental Health, 2015). Even though staff levels have not changed sufficiently to respond to this demand, it is impossible to provide the level of service each student may request. Each institution of higher learning has the right to determine their level of resources devoted to mental healthcare. Also, each counseling center creates their own service delivery model to adjust to the increase in demand. The issue of supply and demand in and of itself is not an ethical dilemma as long as alternative care is available, but the process of psychologists making the determination of which students receive what type of care can easily become one.

The issues become complicated when counseling centers create guidelines to determine who is appropriate for individual therapy, who can be added to a waitlist, who will be referred to an alternate treatment modality (e.g., biofeedback, group, outreach program, online resources, and workshops), and who will be referred to community resources. Most centers create guidelines that state that they use a "short-term model of care" and often list a maximum number of sessions; however, what is often absent is a list of factors and/or symptoms that warrant outside referral. Specifically, in 2014, 30 percent of centers reported that they limit the number of counseling sessions students are allowed, and 43 percent do not have a specified limit on sessions, but promote their center as a short-term counseling service (Center for Collegiate Mental Health, 2015). The following vignette focuses on the difficulties in balancing agency demands and making appropriate referrals.

The Case of Martha's Dilemma

Martha is an entry-level psychologist at a large university counseling center (approximately 20 full-time employees) in a small college town with limited resources for mental health. Prior to this position, Martha interned at a small counseling center (approximately six full-time employees) in an urban area with adequate resources for mental health. One of the common practices at the previous center was to refer students with insurance to local mental health providers that were affordable and available.

In her new position, Martha was oriented to the clinical procedures by her supervisor for one week before the first day of fall classes. Her supervisor informed Martha of the short-term model of the center, the screening protocol, and typical crisis procedures. Martha has a basic understanding that the center has an eight-session limit and that the schedules of clinicians are typically completely full after the first four weeks of classes. Additionally, the supervisor emphasized to Martha that the dramatic increase in clinical demand has made it difficult for clinicians to keep up, but they "make it work." Martha was also told that the center typically started a waiting list for students after the first month of school, and it was rare that a new student would be seen in the center for therapy after the mid semester mark. Upon the beginning of her clinical work, Martha had trepidation about managing her caseload for the entire semester, since the ambiguity of clinical procedures, lack of resources in the community, and strict eight-session limit were all vastly different from the training she received at her internship. As a new employee, Martha did not feel comfortable in sharing her worries with her supervisor.

On the counseling center's website, services were advertised as welcoming to all students and providing psychological services to those in need. Additionally, there was a statement on inclusivity and definitions of services. Although it briefly stated that the center was a short-term agency, there was not any mention of an eight-session limit.

During the second week of the semester, Martha conducted a screening with a freshman who presented with a low level of depression and homesickness. In the initial appointment, the student told Martha that her parents were willing to pay for her therapy. Martha currently had openings on her schedule and felt competent to offer her services to the student; however, as Martha examined her caseload, she worried that taking on a student with financial resources might not be ethical, given future students who might present to the counseling center without the ability to afford a community referral. Given her concerns about her caseload and the student's apparent resources, Martha refers the student out to the community. Martha gives the student her business card along with three names of local psychologists. Martha does not know any of the names she is sharing with the student, only that another clinician on staff recommended them.

Several days later, the director at the counseling center receives a call from the mother of the student Martha referred out complaining that she did not understand why her daughter was referred out. She questioned the process of offering therapy for "all students" on the counseling center website when her experience is that if you can pay for it you will be referred out to spend over $100 per session. The mother was very angry and frustrated, and she threatened to call the director's boss.

Discussion

There are several ethical questions to address in this vignette. To begin, has the center failed in properly advertising their services? Does leaving out the eight-session limit on their website qualify as a deceptive practice? According to the American Psychological Association (APA) Ethical Principles of Psychologists and Code of Conduct (hereafter referred to as the "Ethics Code") (2010), Standard 5.01 notes that psychologists must not make false or deceptive claims about their services. In this vignette, the counseling center's webpage advertises that their services are for "all students." There is also no statement regarding students' financial support or insurance coverage as a variable warranting a referral out. It is understandable given how the counseling center advertises their services that the mother is angry. It is recommended that counseling centers advertise their services, including referral procedures and session limits, in an honest and straightforward manner that is accessible to all clients.

Next, was Martha's decision to refer out the student in the best interest of the student? Has she been taught by her supervisor that managing her caseload is more important than serving each individual student? It appears that Martha is making a clinical judgement for the greater university student body rather than what is in the best interest of the student in her office. This decision-making process brings up the Justice Principle in the Ethics Code, which encourages psychologists to make an effort to ensure that all people have access to psychological services and to equal quality in the processes, procedures, and services provided by psychologists. In this case, Martha is denying services to a student in the hopes that the student will follow through on her referral. If the student does not follow through on the referral, it can be argued that she was unfairly denied services by Martha. Furthermore, Martha made the referral without having direct information regarding her referral sources, such as whether they were currently taking new patients. If the student is unable to get an appointment with any of the referrals and goes without services, it again could be argued that she was unfairly denied services by Martha. This referral may have been appropriate if Martha believed that she would have been practicing outside her scope of competence; however, in the case it was stated that she did feel competent to work with the student. A more ethical approach to this dilemma would have consisted of Martha consulting with a senior staff member or a supervisor prior to making the referral to ensure it was a beneficial decision for the student as well as the agency. Many centers have addressed this issue directly by hiring case referral coordinators, who have the most up-to-date community resource and availability information. Additionally, managing caseloads is a reality of working in a college counseling center, but the agency should have clearer guidelines regarding the factors to consider when referring to community resources. Factors that contribute to decisions for treatment can include but should not be limited to financial support. Clinicians should be aware of the reality that caseloads vary greatly due to the time of the semester, but their caseload concerns should not dictate clinical judgement at any time of the semester.

Looking closer at Martha's perspective, does she feel responsible for more clients than she could possibly serve? Is Martha more worried about her caseload than meeting the needs of the student? When demand is high, clinicians might feel pressured to see as many clients as possible, which could interfere with clinical judgement. The first principle of the Ethics Code as well as Standard 3.04 state that psychologists should do no harm to their clients, and a component of this practice is for psychologists to be "aware of the possible effect of their own physical and mental health on their ability to help those with whom they work" (p.3). In this vignette, Martha may not have been aware that she was making a clinical judgement based on her fears regarding an excessive caseload. Thus, Martha should have received better training during orientation about personal factors that might influence a decision to refer out, including a clinician's feelings about a client or caseload management. This type of anxiety, which is common, can be addressed directly in orientation and possible solutions discussed with special attention to appropriate referrals. It is clear the supervisor failed to fulfill her ethical duty to protect the best interests of the client and support a new professional. Additionally, for Martha to demonstrate ethical responsibility, she needs to use her supervision to explore her fears regarding managing her caseload. The supervisor should help Martha not only clarify agency procedures, but also engage in self-reflection about the potential impact of her worries on her clinical work.

Increase in Severity of Psychological Problems

As previously mentioned, counseling centers have also been faced with an increase in both the numbers of students seeking services and the severity of psychological problems they present. In 2014, directors reported that 52 percent of center clients have severe psychological problems (up from 44 percent in 2013), including 8 percent that are so serious they cannot remain in school, or can only do so with extensive psychological/psychiatric help (Reetz, Krylowicz, & Mistler, 2014). There was also a significant increase in students reporting to counseling centers on psychiatric medication. Approximately 26 percent of students who presented at counseling centers were on a psychotropic medication, which was up from 20 percent in 2003, 17 percent in 2000, and 9 percent in 1994. Given this increased severity, the case below is not uncommon.

The Case of a Crisis Appointment

Leslie, an 18-year-old freshman majoring in animal science, registers for an initial appointment during the first week of class. In her paperwork she reported that she has been in therapy since she was 11 years old, has had 13 total therapists and received in-patient care for an eating disorder three distinct times. Leslie also indicated that she was currently suicidal, which triggered the associate staff member who reviewed her paperwork to call and offer her a crisis appointment the next day. After receiving the phone call from the counseling center, Leslie came for a crisis appointment within an hour. Before the crisis counselor could begin to introduce himself and discuss the services available at the counseling center, Leslie stated that she had seen 13 therapists and no one had been able to help her. She reported that she had used all of her parents' insurance and cannot pay for any further treatment, so she is glad the university offers free services. Leslie began to complain about all of her previous therapy, and the clinician, Dr. Taylor, was forced to interrupt Leslie to explain the short-term model of the counseling center, as well as the role of the referral coordinator in helping students who need long-term care get connected with community providers. Leslie immediately interrupted him, saying, "I am always suicidal, don't you care?"

Discussion

There are many high-risk indicators in this case that would create ethical concerns for clinicians at a university counseling center. First, has Leslie been informed of and agreed to the terms and conditions of the counseling center policies outlined in the informed consent? According to the Ethics Code regarding informed consent to therapy, "... psychologists inform clients/patients as early as is feasible in the therapeutic relationship about the nature and anticipated course of therapy..." (p.13). It is also stated that there must be time for the client/patient to ask questions of the therapist. It appears in the above vignette that Leslie did not understand the center's short-term model or the possibility of referral. It is our recommendation that eligibility of services be published in a clear and concise manner. Eligibility for services is an essential component of informed consent and an important disclosure to prospective clients. Failure to explain eligibility for services may be interpreted as deceptive. This would ideally occur both on the website and be included in the initial paperwork that needs to be completed for registration. It is also recommended that the clinician begins each initial appointment by discussing the purpose of the initial appointment, which includes assessing for eligibility for services. It seems like Dr. Taylor attempted to start this process, but Leslie interrupted him and did not give him the opportunity to discuss the center's resources and available treatment.

Second, was Dr. Taylor's explanation of the limits of the service poorly timed given Leslie's reaction to him? Was his decision to interrupt her causing her harm? If it is determined that Dr. Taylor, in describing the limits of services, harmed Leslie, then he violated Principle A of the Ethics Code. Although she has a negative reaction, Dr. Taylor has a duty to inform the client of center limitations. Here is an example of the situation being uncomfortable due to Leslie's resistance, but it is not unethical. It is important to note at this time that Dr. Taylor may feel pressure to prematurely want to terminate the session, given Leslie's off-putting presentation. However, Dr. Taylor needs to stay within his role as a clinician when communicating with Leslie. Clinicians must fully explain informed consent, even in situations when the client is demanding.

Third, it is not known from the scenario if Dr. Taylor assessed for suicidality. It is imperative for Dr. Taylor to complete a suicide assessment given her statement that Leslie is "always suicidal." If Dr. Taylor prematurely refers her without assessing for safety, he could be causing Leslie harm. In keeping with good ethical standards regarding "do not harm," a full risk assessment needs to be completed. In accordance with Standard 3.04, it is a fundamental responsibility for Dr. Taylor to assess Leslie's level of suicidal thoughts, behaviors, plans, access to plans, and impulsivity.

Lastly, if Leslie's case was already at the attention of university administrators, it may warrant providing treatment to her as a way for administers to monitor her behavior and safety. It is important to recognize that the counseling center would only share information and records with administrators after the client has agreed to informed consent and signed an authorized release of information. If the clinician feels that the client does not have specific goals that fit within the counseling center role and scope of treatment, then a conflict regarding ethics and organizational demands may occur, as identified in the 2010 amendments to the Ethics Code. Although this case may not fit the role and scope of the center's service-delivery model, administrative concerns may trump that decision. This leads to the topics of confidentiality and record keeping as another ethical issue faced by university counseling centers.

Issues Related to Confidentiality and Record-Keeping

Issues that relate to confidentiality and record keeping on college campuses have also raised public concern. Gorman (2015) reports in *Newsweek* that in the first ten months of 2015, there were 45 school shootings in the U.S. The public perception that colleges are high-risk environments for mass shootings can be seen in the recent campus carry debate at the University of Texas (Morris, 2015). Politicians have argued that college students should have the right to bear arms in the attempt to protect themselves from mass shootings. Often implied in these arguments is that the shooter is mentally ill and did not receive the proper mental health treatment. The public perception that there are mentally ill potential shooters on college campuses places an undue pressure on university counseling centers to prevent such tragedies. In an effort to monitor this, university administrators often hope that counseling centers have information regarding a student that may demonstrate "at-risk" behaviors. The argument presented by university administrators is that they have the right to this confidential information because it might keep the other students safe.

This issue has been at the forefront of news regarding the extent to which a university can legally access a student's clinical file. Recently, the University of Oregon made headlines regarding a lawsuit filed against the university by a student who alleged that she was raped by three of the university's basketball players. According to *Inside Higher Ed*, because the student reported that the assault caused her emotional distress and she utilized university counseling services, university lawyers gained access to her counseling records to prepare for litigation (New, 2015). In defending this move, Oregon's lawyers wrote, "Under Oregon law, a plaintiff who places her psychological state at issue by seeking damages for emotional distress waives any psychotherapist/patient privilege or doctor/patient privilege and is required to disclose counseling records related to her psychological state." This poses a significant concern about the privacy of counseling records within a university.

Additionally, another ethical concern emerges when counseling center administrators must decide what information coming from university professionals should be placed into a student's clinical file. In the wake of the Virginia Tech shootings, many universities have now adopted a behavioral intervention committee to assess the safety of the students brought to their attention. This team often responds to "special reports" and social media posts submitted about students who pose a risk to their own or other students' safety. The counseling center administrators, when in receipt of these kinds of reports, have to make a decision about whether that information should go into the student's clinical chart if he or she is a client of the agency. The following vignette highlights the complexity of balancing confidentiality and student safety on a college campus.

The Case of the Angry Client

Ryan, a 20-year-old sophomore majoring in engineering, originally presents to the university counseling center for help with time management. In the initial appointment, the counselor, Ms. Garland, notes those concerns as well as some unusual paranoia and worrying about not being successful in college. Ms. Garland talks with Ryan about the agency's short-term model, and they agree to an initial treatment plan including a referral to the study skills center on campus and meeting with Ms. Garland every other week to work on anxiety. Ryan and Ms. Garland meet four times, and during the fourth session he reports feeling depressed and failing several exams. He is visibly upset and devastated by his professor's words that he may possibly fail this semester. Ryan and Ms. Garland decide to start meeting weekly. Over the next few sessions, Ryan becomes angrier at his professors and reports experiencing panic and stress daily because of his belief that his professors are purposely trying to fail him. In the eighth session, Ryan describes himself as a lion waiting to pounce on his prey.

Several days after this session, the counseling center receives a report from the university's residence life department about Ryan. The report says that Ryan was found cutting himself in a public lounge in his dorm and telling students about his previous suicide attempts. The police became involved in the situation and described

Ryan as "paranoid and delusional," and other students are documented in the report saying they felt threatened by his angry outbursts. The report indicates that Ryan was taken to the local behavioral health hospital but plans to return to the university counseling center when he is released to continue working with his counselor. He is considered "on watch" by university administrators since his behavior may be a violation of student conduct and a threat to safety.

When he returns to see Ms. Garland, Ryan is noticeably agitated, grandiose, and tangential. It becomes clear to Ms. Garland that Ryan's needs appear to surpass what she and the counseling center are able to provide, especially within their short-term model. Although there is no authorized release of information on file for Ryan, university administers still contact the counseling center director to request that Ryan continues to be seen there so his counselor can "keep them posted" in order to help them better monitor Ryan.

Discussion

Does Ryan's right to privacy and confidential services trump the duty of university administrators to the safety of the university community? At times, this duty comes with requesting access to the clinical information of "concerning students." In these circumstances, university administrators would like to be made aware of all students who are at risk, and they do not always take into consideration whether a student has signed a release of information. Standard 4 of the Ethics Code clearly states that psychologists have a duty to protect confidential information about a client. In the above example, refusal by the counseling center to release confidential information about Ryan may cause friction with university administrators, and it may put other students in harm's way if Ryan continues to deteriorate.

If Ryan signs a release of information regarding services, does this create a trust issue between the client and the counseling center? When the counseling center obtains consent from Ryan to release information to university administrators, he may no longer feel safe in continuing at the counseling center knowing that his private health information may be shared outside the agency. Furthermore, that confidential information could very well be used against him if university administrators felt it violated student conduct and subsequently took punitive action. In this way, releasing the information could conflict with the Ethics Code's first principle to do no harm. As a way to remediate this dilemma, some university counseling centers have tried asking students seeking counseling to sign a waiver upfront allowing some information about their sessions to be shared with administrators in certain circumstances. However, this may discourage students from utilizing the counseling center and receiving the treatment they might really need. In the above illustration, Ryan may have been encouraged to sign a release of information when he began treatment to prevent the dilemma of whether to release confidential information. Nonetheless, Ryan could have refused to sign it or stopped seeking services at the university counseling altogether, which could have continued to pose a risk to himself or others as his mental health deteriorated. It is recommended that clinicians are knowledgeable regarding the state rules and regulations of confidentiality and proper training in ethics occurs yearly.

It is critical to be proactive regarding the importance of confidentiality with other university officials and administrators. Regular meetings should be held with the critical departments on campus (university police, residence life, disability services, conduct offices, health centers, and academic departments). During these meetings, there should be a discussion regarding issues related to confidentiality of psychological services for students. It is pertinent to outline the limits of confidentiality as well as to emphasize that student safety is the first and foremost priority of the counseling center. As a result of the tragedy at Virginia Tech, "special situations" team meetings have been created on campuses in an attempt to share information that is relevant for campus safety. Counseling center administrators need to be members of these groups, which would create another place to discuss limits of confidentiality. It is also common practice to have specific counseling center staff members to be liaisons for other key departments on campus. One of the primary roles of the liaison is to talk about issues related to confidentiality in order to inform departments before there is a conflict.

Should Ms. Garland put the residence life report in Ryan's clinical chart? In keeping consistent with the Ethics Code on record keeping, the information about his self-harm and hospitalization are relevant and clinically useful to Ms. Garland as well as future clinicians. Conversely, some of the other information included is collateral and could be damaging to Ryan should he request to review his records (e.g., that the police referred to him as "delusional"). It is recommended to have a clear policy regarding note keeping for the center. This policy should also be presented to the staff regularly in order to keep staff informed about the issues relevant to record keeping. It is common practice to put in anything that the clinician has direct knowledge of related to the client, such as treatment notes and communications directly to and from the client. If a release of information is signed, any communication with the person that is on the release is legal to share. If there is a university report or other communication where the clinician finds out information about the client, such as the situation presented in the vignette, it would be important to consult with center administrators regarding what is appropriate to add to the file or if a summary would be sufficient. It also may be in the best interest of the client not to put anything in the clinical file. In the case illustration, it might be sufficient to just include a summary of the residence life report. It is also important to note that, as is the case in many of these dilemmas, there is not one clear correct decision.

Given the severity of Ryan's issues, is Ms. Garland competent to work with him? The vignette it is not clear about the training and credentials of Ms. Garland. If she is a licensed professional counselor or social worker, based on her licensure, she would be competent to provide services. If she is a trainee, it would depend on her level of training, experience, and supervision. The stress and emotional impact of working with such a high profile, complicated case may require additional consultation and supervision, even for seasoned professionals.

Training Related to Serving a Diverse Population

Another ethical issue commonly faced at university counseling centers is the training in serving a diverse population, specifically lesbian, gay, bisexual, and transgender (LGBT) clients. In 1989, there were no known gay–straight alliances in any high school or junior high within the United States, and by 2011 there were over 4000 (Hartinger, 2011). Additionally, there were little or no ally groups on university campuses in the late 1980s; however, now they exist at almost every university. College administrative support for LGBT centers on campus is very common, and many institutions of higher learning have classes and/or majors related to sexual orientation. Visibility of LGBT people in the media, political arguments focused on LGBT rights, and the legalization of same-sex marriage has increased awareness of issues related to sexual orientation.

As a result of the increased visibility of LGBT students, counseling centers serve more students who identify as LGBT than ever before. Therefore, it is important to educate staff and trainees on working with sexual and gender minorities. Over the past five years, substantial activity has occurred in the courts and state legislatures addressing the intersection of trainees' religious beliefs and First Amendment Rights (for further reading, see the BEA Virtual Working Group on Restrictions Affecting Diversity Training in Graduate Education, 2015). APA responded with great concern due to the organization's commitment to reducing discrimination of all types and to being able to represent compassionate and competent mental health services. The APA took the stance that the legislation in question directly prevented the ability to train students in fulfilling their ethical obligations regarding nondiscrimination. The APA continues to monitor the legal cases in states where students enrolled in mental health training programs have sued institutions related to refusal to counsel clients on religious grounds.

In addition to the legal cases, the APA also demonstrated a great deal of concern regarding the potential impact of training students regarding diversity and competence. The APA created a working group of the APA Board of Educational Affairs (BEA) to address ways to help those in training negotiate conflicts between religion and serving diverse people. In March 2011, the BEA working group issued the statement *Preparing Professional Psychologists to Serve a Diverse Pubic: A Core Requirement in Doctoral Education Training*. The document was a direct response to recent legal challenges and state legislative efforts to interfere with counseling program training standards for professional competence. The working group has developed additional resources and strategies as well as workshops addressing the focus on professional competence while respecting trainee's religious values and ideals.

Training can be a bit tricky in terms of finding a balance of how to successfully navigate conflicts between trainee beliefs and the profession's commitment to competence. It is critical for those involved in training to be familiar with First Amendment Rights in order to better understand the fundamental constitutional protection for trainees' religious beliefs. It is also very helpful to have a basic understanding of the BEA Pedagogical Statement that outlines psychology's commitment to training competent psychologists. Additionally, the BEA developed a flow chart to assist programs in effectively preparing for and managing these dilemmas when they arise in a training context (see the APA's *Preparing Professional Psychologists to Serve a Diverse Public: Addressing Conflicts between*

Professional Competence and Trainee Beliefs). The case below illustrates the training concerns related to the conscience clause.

The Case of Personal or Professional Attitudes

Bianca is an intern at an APA-accredited university counseling center. A strong training focus of the agency is working with diverse students, including those who identify as LGBT. Bianca is highly motivated, exhibits a lot of energy, and appears to be open to feedback. Bianca and the three other interns receive a four-week orientation to the agency, including several one-on-one meetings with the training director, Dr. Fitzpatrick. In one of the individual meetings, Bianca expresses to Dr. Fitzpatrick a strong desire to work with LGBT students, and she presents herself to him as an advocate for LGBT rights. Shortly after the completion of the orientation, one of Bianca's cohort members, Riley, comes to Dr. Fitzpatrick expressing her concerns about Bianca's rigid religious convictions and the impact they might have on her clinical work. Riley tells Dr. Fitzpatrick that she is friends with Bianca on Facebook and has seen several articles posted by Bianca that are homophobic. Dr. Fitzpatrick encourages Riley to talk directly to Bianca about her concerns, but she returns to him a couple days later saying that, when confronted about the Facebook posts, Bianca was defensive and only said that she separates her personal life from her professional life. Riley also tells Dr. Fitzpatrick that the other two cohort members, one of whom identifies as gay, are also aware of and concerned about Bianca's beliefs.

Discussion

There are several major ethical concerns in this vignette. The first is the navigation of hearing third-party information. How does the training director handle receiving information regarding a trainee from other trainees? From Dr. Fitzpatrick's one-on-one experiences with Bianca, she seems highly motivated and open to feedback. There is no information that suggests Bianca's behavior is concerning or highly rigid. Additionally, Bianca also clearly expressed interest in working with LGBT clients. Dr. Fitzpatrick follows the counseling center's policy for handling conflict by encouraging Riley, the other intern, to directly discuss with Bianca what behavior is concerning her; however, it appears that Bianca does not respond well. At the end of the vignette, it is clear that this situation is going to create a conflict in the cohort if not directly handled. When a cohort does not contain the most basic level of trust among its members, it is nearly impossible to participate in group training activities. Principle E: Respect for People's Rights and Dignity must be maintained by all members of the cohort and the Training Director. If Bianca treats her fellow intern differently due to her knowledge of the intern's sexual orientation or if the cohort/training director treats Bianca different due to her beliefs regarding sexual orientation, then there becomes an ethical dilemma.

It is recommended that counseling centers have an intern grievance policy that follows the rules of their own human resource department in handling such conflicts. In the case example, Dr. Fitzpatrick does follow the center's policy, but the concern remains even after Riley attempts to discuss it directly with Bianca. It would be recommended that the Training Director (TD) engages in a direct conversation with Bianca about her cohort and their potential dynamics, and the conversation should be linked to training. A group intern support meeting or seminar where interns have a space to process their experiences with one another would be an excellent place to talk to one another about this kind of concern. The TD could talk with Bianca briefly about the concerns to prepare her for the group discussion. The TD also needs to talk with the rest of the cohort individually about their possible assumptions regarding Bianca. It is the TD's role to discuss the upcoming Standards of Accreditation on reflective practice, as well as the model of training of the center if use-of-self is highly valued. There would also be a discussion with all of the interns about the separation of personal and professional beliefs.

The second dilemma focuses on information gained from social media. Is it unethical for professionals to post opinions or support behaviors that are in direct contrast to the profession's ethical code? Clearly stating discriminatory opinions or supporting discrimination statements in therapy, research, or educational activities would violate the Ethics Code Principle A: Beneficence and Nonmaleficence, as well as Standard 3: Human Relations, 3.01 Unfair Discrimination, and 3.03 Other Harassment. It is stated multiple times in the APA Ethics Code that in work-related activities, psychologists do not engage in unfair discrimination based on age, gender, gender identity, race, ethnicity, culture, national origin, religion, sexual orientation, disability, socioeconomic status, or any basis proscribed by law; however, it must be reiterated that this behavior has not been seen in "work-related activities," but rather through a personal account on Facebook. This begs the question of whether the personal/professional line has been blurred by the cohort members through the friendship on the social media site. It is understandable that the other cohort members, upon seeing Bianca's display of attitudes that could be considered "discrimination" by the Ethics Code, might feel skeptical that Bianca can truly separate her personal beliefs from her professional activities like she claims. Additionally, the cohort member who identifies as gay might feel especially worried and unsafe at work knowing that his cohort member has such beliefs. As previously discussed, the Ethics Code clearly highlights the importance of respect toward others, and thus should a conflict arise amongst the cohort members, it would be prudent for the training director to step in.

It is recommended that a conversation addressing what to post on Facebook or other social media would need to focus on professionalism. Professionalism should be defined in an evaluation form and clearly linked to the Ethics Code, including the implications of stating beliefs that contradict the Ethics Code. The discussion should emphasize that although making discriminatory comments on any form of social media may not in and of itself be a violation of an ethical code or state law related to the practice of psychology, it may simply be poor judgement that may reflect badly on the individual or profession as a whole. Bianca should be made aware of how future employers may research her history and Internet presence. Depending on how the conversation with Bianca went and how much responsibility she took for the impact of what she posted, the TD may even state that the site would not have selected her as an intern if the training committee had read these posts prior to intern selection. The TD may share several articles that have studied the professionalism of trainees through social media, including Asay and Lal (2014). If it is determined that Bianca has strong religious beliefs that do demonstrably create conflicts with the profession's commitment to training professional psychologists to provide competent care to a diverse public, then the issue will need to be addressed, ideally by the training director. We recommend using the flow chart contained in the APA BEA article *Preparing Professional Psychologists to Serve a Diverse Public: Addressing Conflicts between Professional Competence and Trainee Beliefs* for guidance.

Lastly, if Bianca acknowledged that her religious beliefs were in conflict with serving LGBT students, there would have to be an ongoing conversation and supervision in how she is going to manage the conflict. The TD would contact Bianca's primary clinical supervisor and discuss how they all might work together to help Bianca examine her internal conflicts and the potential clinical implications of the conflicts. A discussion with Bianca could revolve around several of the Ethics Code's principles, including beneficence and nonmaleficence, and justice. Bianca should be reminded that a key aspect of justice includes the practice of examining personal biases and reflecting on the impact of those biases on clinical practice. If Bianca's initial interest in working with LGBT students and wanting to be involved in advocacy work came from her own concerns regarding her religious beliefs, it would be seen as solid start in training and growth in this area.

This case illustrates the need for training programs to effectively manage these dilemmas when they arise in training. The APA 2014 Skill-Building Workshop, which was developed in accordance with the Ethics Code, helps trainers address issues related to the conscience clause by addressing five main points:

1. Do you have an explicit program statement explaining that all trainees are expected to develop competencies to serve diverse clients? Does it address tensions arising from trainee worldviews, beliefs, or religious values that may conflict with professional standards of competent care? How is it consistent with other program policies and descriptions?
2. Is this policy/expectation clear to prospective students? Is it publicly available in program materials and integrated into admissions and orientation? Do students who are offered admission formally agree with program policies?
3. How are these expectations integrated into the curriculum, incorporated into trainee competencies, and included in both formative and summative feedback?
4. Is there faculty and trainer commitment to a developmental process with both pedagogical and practice support to achieve competency? Is it applied consistently across all trainees no matter what their beliefs or values?
5. How do you ensure trainee worldviews, values, and beliefs are treated with dignity and respect in a healthy learning climate?

Technology Changes and Student Expectations

The amount of social media usage amongst the college-age population is an important contextual factor in addressing how social media can raise ethical dilemmas for mental health issues on college campuses. According to Pew Research Center (Perrin, 2010), approximately 65 percent of adults use social networking sites. In 2005, when Pew Research Center began systematically tracking social media usage, only about 7 percent of adults used social networking sites. Prior to 2005, there was not enough known usage to even warrant research of this activity. The largest social media users are adults between the ages of 18 and 29. Currently, 90 percent of young adults use social media, compared with 12 percent in 2005 – a 78 percent increase. The evolution in technology and improvement in high-speed communication channels have grown to be common ethical issues in university counseling centers. The following vignette illustrates one such ethical concern involving the use of technology.

The Case of Social Media Shock

Dr. Katie Smith is providing individual therapy to Luis, a Hispanic sophomore majoring in mathematics. He presents to the counseling center with social isolation, depression, and suicidal ideation. Despite his struggles, Luis does not report his grades to be a concern and is primarily focused on his lack of social connections at the university. Katie has seen Luis for six sessions when they approach spring break, as which point Luis will be traveling out of the country with ten other students for a study trip abroad. During the break, Katie receives a private message on Facebook from Luis. His message reads, "Hi Dr. Smith, the trip's not going well. No one likes me and I'm so alone. I can't take it anymore. Thank you for all you've done to try to help me." Due to the spring break holiday, the university is closed, and Katie receives this message while vacationing in another state.

Discussion

This vignette highlights the ethical considerations found in the easy accessibility of counselors due to technological advancements in communication. In the past, most contact with clients occurred through the office telephone, even for after-hours crisis care. Many universities provided crisis intervention services that allowed students to call a phone number connected to a pager worn by the on-call counselor. Clients who wanted to reach their particular counselor had no viable option to do so (aside from looking up their home information in the White pages). Now, communication between counselor and client commonly occurs through email, which can often be accessed from anywhere at any time of the day. This kind of communication can be complicated, especially with regards to boundaries regarding when a counselor will receive and respond to communication from clients. In the vignette, Luis is able to reach out to Dr. Smith through her personal but public use of social media, even though she may not have directly disclosed that information about herself to him.

Indeed, although Dr. Smith is on vacation in another state, she is able to receive the message and now has an ethical responsibility to determine when and how to respond.

The existence of the Internet alone has created a plethora of ethical concerns for counseling, especially among college students, among whom Internet use is incredibly high. Clients and counselors both have the ability to Google one another and find out information about the other that would otherwise go unknown. Social media profiles have created invisible connections among people – clients may now see that they have "mutual friends" or common interests with their counselor. This brings in the ethical concern about dual relationships and whether private knowledge about the client and/or counselor could impact the therapy experience. From the vignette, it is clear that Luis looked up Dr. Smith on Facebook and was able to message her through this site, and it is possible that he was able to find other information about her from Facebook or other websites.

Many university counseling centers have also begun creating their own social media pages as a way to advertise services to students, but with that comes ethical concerns regarding privacy and immediacy. Centers now have pages on YouTube, Facebook, Twitter, Instagram, and Pinterest. How do administrators respond if a student posts a public message on the counseling center page that they are a client at the agency and considering suicide in the middle of the night? Technology seems to have altered many students' ideas of what is considered "private," and even facilitates the process of making very private information incredibly public. In the illustration, Luis chose to send Dr. Smith a private message. Although that avoids the concern about posting such a message in a public place, it does bring up the issue that Dr. Smith alone will see it and have the responsibility to respond ethically. Had Luis posted his message on the university counseling center's page (and assuming that page is closely monitored), an administrator or another agency clinician may have been able to see the message and reach out to Luis quickly.

In addition to social media complicating communication between counselor and client, technology has expanded university counseling centers' delivery of services and created some unprecedented ethical questions. For example, telepsychology and remote treatment have developed faster than regulatory and ethical practice guidelines have kept up. Clinicians are now finding themselves wondering how they can ensure a client – who is on the other side of a computer screen – is actually alone. How can a clinician ensure confidentiality when the client is not in the same controlled space as the clinician? DeAngelis (2012) pointed out some of the legal and ethical concerns of telepsychology and made some recommendations, including checking with your state licensing board about policies related to telepsychology. In the above case, Dr. Smith is not in the state in which she is licensed, and Luis is in a different country. Which rules apply? Another ethical consideration is that if Dr. Smith replies to Luis's message in a way that confirms that she is his counselor, she may inadvertently breach confidentiality if Luis is not actually the user of the account that sent her the message or if someone else has access to it in addition to Luis.

Lastly, technology has allowed clinicians at many university counseling centers to access confidential information in areas outside the agency. For example, some agencies have "remote access" options on computers, phones, and tablets outside the agency. Although this access facilitates ease of working while not in the office, concerns have arisen regarding the ability of other people (e.g., the counselor's family) to potentially see confidential information. In this case, if Dr. Smith's husband saw the message, she again may have inadvertently breached confidentiality, since he would now know the name and some of the concerns of one of her clients.

Given the issues that this case example raises, the author makes the following recommendations in order to address these ethical concerns: first, it is important for agencies to have clear social media and technology guidelines and rules for both students and staff. This can be advertised on the various websites and should be reminded to clients during the initial informed consent process. In accordance with the Ethical Code's Informed Consent guideline, it is critical to make students aware of the policy (see Appendix A for an example of the University of Utah University Counseling Center's social media guidelines and implications, listed on their website). This policy, however, does not directly address communications that clinicians may receive from clients, which is the issue in the case vignette. Again, a policy regarding communications should be discussed and clear statements regarding expectations should be on the center's website. The following is an example that might be helpful:

> Please do not use SMS (mobile phone text messaging) or messaging on social networking sites such as Twitter, Facebook, or LinkedIn to contact your clinician at the Student Counseling Center. Email may be used, if you have given legal permission, for administrative purposes of scheduling or rescheduling appointments. Email is not completely secure or confidential. Any emails received or sent will become a part of your legal record.

Since Luis has already contacted Dr. Smith, it is imperative that she responds quickly. Because this situation could spark feelings of fear, annoyance, and anxiety, Dr. Smith should consult with one of her supervisors if she is able to get in contact with them quickly. One option Dr. Smith could consider is to respond to Luis's message, asking if they could find a time to talk on the phone. Dr. Smith could use this phone conversation to clarify Luis's message and conduct a safety assessment. If Dr. Smith has reason to believe that Luis is in imminent danger, she (or her supervisor, since she is out of town and may not have access to Luis's chart) may consider getting in contact with the professor on the trip, Luis's parents, or even the police. Above all else, Dr. Smith has a duty to keep Luis safe.

Issues related to telehealth are complicated and create unique ethical dilemmas for counseling centers using this type of service. It is highly encouraged that centers that are engaging in telepsychology services research these unique issues, including state licensing board rules regarding interstate practice and clinician malpractice insurance (see the APA's Guidelines for the Practice of Telepsychology, 2013).

Lastly, the issue of accessing confidential information remotely has become routine for many centers. Great care needs to be taken regarding this process, and discussions regarding keeping information confidential need to occur with staff at regular meetings. Additionally, Information Technology staff needs to explain the technical issues with remote access and stress the importance of password protection and other ways to encrypt the information.

Conclusion

In conclusion, contextual factors such as the rise in college enrollment, the increase in cost of tuition, changing parenting styles, and the decrease in availability of community mental health resources have dramatically impacted university mental health services and the ethical issues they face. While university counseling centers experience many ethical dilemmas in the practice of psychology, in this chapter we explored five common ethical issues: (1) increased demand for services; (2) the increase in severity of psychological problems; (3) issues related to confidentiality and record-keeping; (4) training related to serving a diverse population; and (5) technology changes and expectations.

Appendix A

Sample University Counseling Center Social Media User Terms and Conditions
(Updated April 9, 2014)

Summary

The University Counseling Center (UCC) sponsors a photo sharing, video sharing, and other social media sites to further its mission to meet the cultural, educational, and informational needs of the campus community. Fans, followers, members, likers, and/or friends of our social media pages are encouraged to share, post, like, rate, upload videos and images, and converse with other fans and with content posted on this page. At times, the UCC's sponsored sites are also a place for the public to share opinions about the center, mental health, and related subjects/ issues. Comments are welcome and will be reviewed prior to publishing. The UCC reserves the right not to publish any posting, or to later remove it without notice or explanation.

The UCC offers crisis services M–F 8–5. If you are a U of X student, staff or faculty member and need to talk with someone immediately, a UCC staff member is available to assist. Call us at XXX-XXX-XXXX or walk into the Center at XXXXXXXXXX. For more urgent situations and after hours, please go to the XXXXXXXXXXXXXX. The Crisis Line: XXX-XXX-XXXX offers crisis response 24/7, including: crisis support over the phone, a mobile outreach option that will respond to persons in their home, and the Receiving Center where individuals from Salt Lake County can access a safe and supportive environment to help individuals work through their crisis situation. Individuals may spend up to 23 hours at the Receiving Center, at no cost.

Full policy statement

In keeping with its mission, the UCC may participate in the use of various "social media" sites or applications. The goals of UCC sponsored social media sites are:

- To increase the campus community's knowledge of and use of UCC services;
- To promote the value and importance of the UCC's services among university faculty, students, staff, administrators, and the general public;
- To maintain open, professional, and responsive communications.

The UCC's social media platforms are public sites used for educational purposes only and are not designed as a forum for provision of clinical care. Therefore, becoming a "friend" or "fan" does not indicate you are a client of our services or participating in therapy. If you have questions about your mental or physical health, please consult directly with your physician or other treating provider.

The UCC does not collect, maintain or otherwise use the personal information stored on any third party site in any way other than to communicate with users on that site. Users may remove themselves at any time from the UCC's "friends" or "fan" lists. Users should be aware that third party websites have their own privacy policies and should proceed accordingly.

Comments, posts, and messages are welcome on the UCC social media sites. Users are strongly encouraged to check facts, cite sources, and show respect in expressing their opinions. While the UCC recognizes and respects difference in opinion, all such interactions will be monitored and reviewed for content and relevancy. Having stated that, the UCC is not obligated to take any actions, and will not be responsible or liable for content posted by any subscriber in any forum, message board, or other area within these services.

The UCC offers crisis services M–F 8–5. If you are a University student, staff, or faculty member and need to talk with someone immediately, a UCC staff member is available to assist. Call us at XXX-XXX-XXXX or walk into the Center at XXXXXXX. For more urgent situations and after hours, please go to the Emergency Department at the University Hospital. The Crisis Line: XXX-XXX-XXXX offers crisis response 24/7, including: crisis support over the phone, a mobile outreach option that will respond to persons in their home, and the Receiving Center where individuals from Salt Lake County can access a safe and supportive environment to help individuals work through their crisis situation. Individuals may spend up to 23 hours at the Receiving Center, at no cost.

Code of Conduct

Comments and posts by fans to any of the UCC's social media sites should be relevant to the content posted on the page and its fans. UCC reserves the right not to publish any posting, or to later remove it without notice or explanation. Reasons for removal include, but are not limited to:

- Abusive, defamatory, or hate speech.
- Violations of copyright, trademark, or other intellectual property rights.
- Profanity or racial slurs.
- Illegal activities.
- Threats of violence.
- Pornographic or sexually explicit material.
- Information related to non-university related products or services.
- Spam or commercial advertising.
- Off-topic comments.
- Lack of space.
- Posts that become a nuisance.

In certain situations, the poster, as well as the content, could be blocked from the page or reported to authorities depending on the nature of the content. The UCC reserves the right to remove posts deemed inappropriate.

Posts that contain names (or identifying information) of specific individuals receiving care or working at the UCC may be removed if the individual has not consented to having information shared publically. Names of University of Utah employees identified as part of a complaint, concern, or compliment will be handled on a case-by-case basis. Depending on the circumstances, at the discretion of page administrators, the post or comment may be removed to protect the identity of individuals.

In addition, the UCC reserves the right to edit or modify any postings or comments for space or content (spelling, grammar, etc.), while retaining the intent of the original post. The UCC assumes no liability regarding any event or interaction created or posted by any participant in any UCC sponsored social media service, and does not endorse content outside the "pages" created by UCC staff. Participation in UCC social media services implies agreement with all University of Utah and library policies, including but not limited to University of Utah World Wide Web Resources Policy, Privacy Statement, Disclaimer, Information Resources Policy, and Terms of Service of each individual third-party services. The role and utility of social media will be evaluated periodically by UCC staff, and may be changed or terminated at any time without notice to subscribers.

Adapted from University of Utah Spencer S. Eccles Health Sciences Library Social Media Policy; and the University of Utah Health Care Social Media User Terms and Conditions.

Retrieved from the University of Utah's University Counseling Center website: http://counselingcenter.utah.edu/outreach/social-media-policy.php

References

American Psychological Association (2010). *Ethical principles of psychologists and code of conduct*. Retrieved from http://apa.org/ethics/code/index.aspx

American Psychological Association (2013). *Guidelines for the practice of telepsychology*. Retrieved from www.apapracticecentral.org/ce/guidelines/telepsychology-guidelines.pdf?_ga=1.169376289.1471047140.1451416366

Asay, P. A. & Lal, A. (2014). Who's Googled whom? Trainees' internet and online social networking experiences, behaviors, and attitudes with clients and supervisors. *Training and Education in Professional Psychology, 8*, 105–111.

BEA Virtual Working Group on Restrictions Affecting Diversity Training in Graduate Education (2015). Preparing professional psychologists to serve a diverse public: A core requirement in doctoral education and training a pedagogical statement. *Training and Education in Professional Psychology, 9*, 269–270.

Center for Collegiate Mental Health (2015). *2014 Annual Report* (Publication No. STA 15–30). Retrieved from https://sites.psu.edu/ccmh/files/2017/10/2014-CCMH-Annual-Report-w4xqtb.pdf

DeAngelis, T. (2012). Practicing distance therapy, legally and ethically. *Monitor on Psychology, 43*(3), 52.

Gorman, M. (2015). Another: The 45th school shooting in America in 2015. *Newsweek*. Retrieved from http://www.newsweek.com/45th-mass-shooting-america-2015-378803

Hartinger, J. (2011). Triumphs and setbacks of gay straight alliances. *The Advocate*. Retrieved from www.advocate.com/society/education/2011/08/01/triumphs-and-setbacks-gay-straight-alliances-1

Honberg, R., Kimball, A., Diehl, S., Usher, L., & Fitzpatrick, M. (2011). State mental health cuts: the continuing crisis. *National Alliance for the Mentally Ill (NAMI)*. Retrieved from www.nami.org/getattachment/About-NAMI/Publications/Reports/StateMentalHealthCuts2.pdf

Hunt, J. & Eisenberg, D. (2010). Mental health problems and help-seeking behavior among college students. *Journal of Adolescent Health, 46*, 3–10.

Ibrahim, A. K., Kelly, S. J., Adams, C. E., & Glazebrook, C. (2013). A systematic review of studies of depression prevalence in university students. *Journal of Psychiatric Research, 47*, 391–400.

Marano, H. E. (2008). *A nation of wimps: The high cost of invasive parenting*. New York, NY: Crown Publishing Group.

Morris, J. (2015). Texas figuring out how to handle campus carry law. *CNN*. Retrieved from www.cnn.com/2015/10/09/us/texas-campus-carry-law/index.html

New, J. (2015). Staying confidential. *Inside Higher Ed*. Retrieved from www.insidehighered.com/news/2015/08/03/privacy-loophole-remains-open-after-outrage-over-u-oregons-handling-therapy-records

Novotney, A. (2014). Students under pressure. *Monitor on Psychology, 45*, 36–41.

PBS News Hour (2015). More stress, less stigma drives college students to mental health services. Retrieved from https://www.pbs.org/newshour/show/mental-health

Perrin, A. (2010). Social media usage: 2005–2015. *Pew Research Center*. Retrieved from www.pewinternet.org/2015/10/08/social-networking-usage-2005-2015/

Reetz, D. R., Krylowicz, B., & Mistler, B. (2014). *The Association for University and College Counseling Center Directors Annual Survey*. Association for University and

College Counseling Center Directors. Retrieved from www.aucccd.org/assets/docu ments/2014%20aucccd%20monograph%20-%20public%20pdf.pdf

Schrecker, E. (2010). *The lost soul of higher education: Corporatization, the assault on academic freedom, and the end of the American university.* New York, NY: The New Press.

Stone, G. L. & Archer, J. (1990). College and university counseling centers in the 1990s: Challenges and limits. *The Counseling Psychologist, 18,* 539–607.

Taylor, M. (2006). Helicopters, snowplows, and bulldozers: Managing students' parents. *The Bulletin, 74.* Retrieved from www.taylorprograms.com/images/Bulletin Nov200612-21a.pdf

U.S. Department of Education, National Center for Education Statistics. (2013). *Digest of Education Statistics, 2013* (NCES 2015–011), Chapter 3.

Virginia Department of Criminal Justice Services (2013). *Threat assessment in Virginia public schools: Model policies, procedures, and guidelines.* Retrieved from https://town hall.virginia.gov/l/GetFile.cfm?File=C:%5CTownHall%5Cdocroot%5CGuidance Docs%5C140%5CGDoc_DCJS_5461_v1.pdf

Wilson, R. (2015). An epidemic of anguish. *The Chronicle of Higher Education.* Retrieved from www.chronicle.com/article/An-Epidemic-of-Anguish/232721

4 Ethical Issues When Working in Hospital Settings

Kathleen R. Ashton and Amy B. Sullivan

Increasingly, the delivery of health care is moving toward an integrated model, with mental health and physical health no longer separated by physical and theoretical boundaries. Psychologists are practicing within medical clinics as part of multidisciplinary teams that holistically look at patient issues and work together to provide innovative treatments. Patient care is enhanced by addressing the psychological and behavioral aspects of coping with medical issues. This exciting integrated health movement has opened up opportunities for health psychologists[1] to work directly in hospital settings. The clinical, research, and training possibilities for psychologists in hospital settings are vast. However, psychologists working in hospital settings face unique ethical challenges in this relatively new field. These challenges may include obtaining informed consent in a fast-paced environment, maintaining confidentiality with multidisciplinary teams, providing specialty supervision to high-risk patients, and coping with the ethics of medical tourism. The following cases illustrate potential ethical challenges, consider ethical decision-making, and provide guidelines for best practices in the hospital setting.

The Case of the Psychologically High-Risk Surgery Patient

Working in a multidisciplinary team is one of the hallmarks of the health psychologist. In hospital settings, health psychologists work closely with teams including physicians, surgeons, nurses, physical therapists, dieticians, nursing assistants, and a variety of other professionals. Sharing the psychological perspective regarding patient needs through in-person team meetings, warm hand-offs (physicians or other team members bringing the psychologist into the exam room with the patient for a brief consult), and the electronic medical record are important team communication tools. However, these types of communication can pose difficulties in maintaining appropriate patient confidentiality and privacy (Hodgson, Mendenhall, & Lamson, 2013). Additional issues of informed consent and beneficence versus harm are important to consider in multidisciplinary teams.

---

[1] The term "health psychologist" is used to refer to psychologists practicing in the hospital setting with medical populations and may include clinical, counseling, and child psychologists functioning in this setting.

Consider the high-risk surgery patient, Ms. Bell[2], a 40-year-old Caucasian female seeking weight loss surgery referred for evaluation from a multidisciplinary team including surgery, medicine, nutrition, and psychology. Ms. Bell was a high-risk patient medically, with a body mass index of 68 (approximately 300 pounds above ideal body weight) and medical risks including chronic obstructive pulmonary disease, type II diabetes, obstructive sleep apnea, and hypertension. Ms. Bell expressed interest in gastric bypass surgery. Her understanding of the surgery was fair; however, it was clear she had very high expectations and limited motivation to make behavior changes before the surgery. From a dietary perspective, Ms. Bell showed problematic eating behaviors including binge eating episodes of three to four days each week. Surgically, her medical risks of continued obesity were considered very high.

Ms. Bell met with the psychologist for an evaluation as part of the multidisciplinary team. The purpose of the psychological evaluation was explained to Ms. Bell as "gathering information about habits, mental health, and understanding of surgery to help make recommendations about your weight loss journey." Ms. Bell read and signed an informed consent sheet that detailed the qualifications of the psychologist, the scope of confidentiality, and privacy. The psychologist and Ms. Bell also verbally discussed that her information would be part of her medical record and shared with the multidisciplinary team, as well as other limits to confidentiality (i.e., in the event of abuse, suicidal ideation, etc.).

Ms. Bell's psychological evaluation was significant for many risk factors for bariatric surgery. Ms. Bell had a history of multiple psychiatric hospitalizations and suicide attempts, was on multiple psychotropic medications, and had noted auditory hallucinations. Further, the patient shared that she currently used marijuana daily and had a significant history of alcohol abuse, cocaine abuse, and intravenous drug use. She noted legal problems and custody problems stemming from her abuse. Ms. Bell also presented a history of abuse and trauma as a child and an adult. She noted few social supports and reported her main coping strategy as eating. Ms. Bell was from a low-income background with little education; she was not currently working and received disability benefits related to her obesity and medical issues.

At the conclusion of the psychological evaluation, the psychologist shared her concerns about the patient's risk factors while noting the patient's significant medical problems and risks associated with excess weight. The psychologist made recommendations including establishing substance abuse treatment, re-establishing psychotherapy, consultation with the patient's psychiatrist, a toxicology screen, and binge eating treatment. The psychologist also told the patient that she would consult with the multidisciplinary team regarding the relative psychological and medical risks for the patient and would contact the patient with the team's results.

Ms. Bell was visibly upset and noted no intention to follow through on treatment recommendations. She stated, "That's what I get for being honest with you. I want you

---

[2] Names and key demographic data have been changed to protect anonymity.

to take that all out of the computer. I take it all back. I don't want the surgeon to see your report." The psychologist gently explained the importance of documentation and reminded the patient of their confidentiality discussion at the start of the evaluation, referring the patient to her copy of the informed consent. The patient stated, "I don't think they need to know all the details." The patient and the psychologist reviewed the note together and the patient agreed to leave the note in the electronic chart as it was "pretty factual." The psychologist added some statements per the patient report as requested to clarify her history of legal and substance use. The psychologist agreed to limit discussion in the team meeting to only essential details.

However, upon meeting with the team, many of the members had questions and wanted to discuss the case in detail. They had reviewed the chart and noted the history of sexual abuse and legal problems. Several of the team members were interested in the possible correlation of her history of sexual abuse and her eating pattern and weight gain and asked for more detail, including minute details regarding the identity of the abuser and details of the abuse. Additionally, the team asked for more feedback about the patient's legal history, including whether she was currently on probation and whether she had any felony charges. They noted concerns about adherence and ability to follow up with the bariatric team given the patient's history of antisocial practices. The discussion had the potential to turn into a "voyeurism" exercise. The psychologist worked to comment very briefly on psychological risks (multiple medications, current psychosis, substance abuse, low support, eating disorder) and asked the team to focus on weighing these against the medical risks (300 pounds of excess weight, serious medical comorbidities, risks of weight loss surgery). The team ultimately decided that the psychological and medical risks outweighed the medical benefits of the surgery at the time of the meeting. They recommended that the patient engage in intensive substance abuse and mental health treatment for at least one year prior to reconsidering surgery. They encouraged the patient to consider a more conservative dietary/medical weight loss plan during the next year as she worked toward mental health stabilization.

Ethical Considerations

Psychologists working in similar multidisciplinary care settings may feel pulled in many directions. On one hand, they may feel loyalty to the treatment team. Being part of the team and maintaining good relationships may pressure the psychologist to disclose more than they would normally be comfortable. It can also be uncomfortable for the psychologist acting in the role of evaluator to share difficult news with the patient (such as the patient not being a candidate for a surgery) when they are more typically in a treatment or helping role. The psychologist working with Ms. Bell reported feeling relieved she had clarified informed consent at the outset of the relationship, which made it easier to negotiate when things became more difficult. In addition, although worried about the relationship with the treatment team, Ms. Bell's psychologist felt like she was able to balance the patient's privacy and the team's "need to know."

Confidentiality and Informed Consent with the Electronic Health Record

Obtaining informed consent and discussing confidentiality represent particular challenges in the hospital setting (Hudgins, Rose, Fifield, & Arnault, 2013). For example, as in Ms. Bell's case, the patient is often referred from a medical practice and not actively seeking the services of a psychologist. The patient may not be particularly interested or motivated to seek mental health treatment and may see the referral as a barrier to overcome or have a negative connotation attached to the referral, such as "the doctor thinks it's all in my head." Although the interdisciplinary practice may be explained by the hospital program at the patient's initial medical visit or in written materials, this is a passive form of informed consent (Hodgson et al., 2013). Therefore, it is crucial for psychologists working in the medical setting to clarify the nature of the referral, the role of the psychologist, and the purpose of the visit. Providing this information both in writing and verbally with the patient helps build trust through transparency, and allowing sufficient time to discuss the information ensures attention to the principle of Fidelity and Responsibility outlined in the American Psychological Association's (APA) *Ethical Principles of Psychologists and Code of Conduct*, which notes, "Psychologists establish relationships of trust with those with whom they work ... [and] clarify their professional roles and obligations" (2010, p.3). Similarly, the APA ethical standards suggest that psychologists obtain informed consent and appropriately document services, as well as clarify who will have access to the information (Standards 3.10 and 3.11). Hospital environments can be fast-paced and full of time pressures; hospital psychologists need to be particularly mindful not to gloss over these issues in the interest of being "efficient" (Hudgins et al., 2013).

One important piece of informed consent is making sure the patient is clear about how records will be kept in the medical environment and who has access to these records and patient information. With the rise of electronic health records (EHRs), notes and other chart information are more accessible and searchable. The benefits of the EHR are numerous, such as easing care coordination and communication across disciplines. However, the ease of the EHR comes with misgivings on the parts of both patients and providers as to who will be accessing the records (Clemens, 2012). All EHRs should include an audit system where a record of who has accessed the file can be reviewed (Hodgson et al., 2013).

Many psychologists in hospital systems moving to EHRs have strong concerns about patient privacy and confidentiality (Nielsen, Baum, & Soares, 2013). APA Ethical Standards 4.01 and 4.02 discuss the psychologist's obligation to protect confidential information and discuss limits of confidentiality. Some providers will ask for mental health notes to be kept separately or "hidden" from the rest of the medical record. Other EHR practices include adopting special firewalls and warnings for those accessing mental health notes. In other practices, physical health and mental health are not separated in the EHR, making all notes accessible to all providers. Notably, per Health Insurance Portability and Accountability Act (HIPAA) rules, no provider who does not have a reason to be looking at a patient chart should be accessing their notes (Nielsen et al., 2013). For most health psychologists, it will be essential for their notes to be accessible to the medical team in order to be able to work in a truly integrated manner (Hodgson et al., 2013). For example, in Ms. Bell's case, it would be typical for the psychologist to send a note through the EHR to the dietician in order to discuss concerns about the patient's binge eating behaviors. Health psychologists should take care to write their notes as if the patient were reading the chart, using behavioral terms and quotes when possible and avoiding subjective or judgmental comments. Interestingly, many hospital systems are moving toward making patient notes, diagnoses, and test results fully accessible to the patient online. Psychologists will need to consider the appropriateness of their documentation in light of changing health care norms toward transparency and patient empowerment.

Confidentiality When Working with Multidisciplinary Teams

Further concerns about confidentiality arise in the health care environment when working as part of a multidisciplinary team (Van Liew, 2012) (Table 4.1). It is essential for health psychologists to explain the role of the psychologist as a member of the team and to be clear that the team will discuss the results of the psychological evaluation. Some patients may still see the role of the psychologist like that of a lawyer or clergyperson and assume that "confidential" means that information is not recorded or shared. Educating the patient about the role of the health psychologist is a critical aspect of informed consent. In addition, the psychologist has the responsibility to keep the discussion with the multidisciplinary team relevant to the question at hand, as in the case of Ms. Bell when the potential voyeurism activity ensued. Standard 4.04 notes that psychologists should include "only information germane to the purpose for which the communication is made." Psychologists should consider what level of detail is needed in both written documentation and when consulting with other professionals (Nielsen, 2013). APA Standard 4.06 notes psychologists should disclose "only to the extent necessary to achieve the purposes of the consultations" (2010). Information that is not pertinent to decision-making is not necessary to share with the entire team. Protecting the client's confidential information is part of adhering to APA ethical principles such as Respect for People's Rights and Dignity (APA, 2010). In Ms. Bell's case, the team did ask relevant questions about how her history of legal issues may predict poor adherence after weight loss surgery or affect her access to care. The psychologist appropriately discussed this issue, while limiting discussion to pertinent details or themes. In this case, APA Standard 3.09 is relevant, pointing to psychologists' obligation to cooperate with other professionals. However, the psychologist appropriately set limits under further pressure to share minute details of the patient's history of sexual abuse. The team's interest in the details went beyond their need for information into a form of psychological voyeurism. This is not uncommon in medical settings, where psychological issues are seen as very interesting.

Health psychologists should also be wary of the potential for gallows humor in team discussion situations. Balancing the "need to know" and respecting the dignity

Table 4.1 *Tips for Psychologists Working in a Multidisciplinary Team*

1. **Use team skills.** Get to know the skill sets of the different team members and use them effectively. Psychologists may be able to link patients with community resources, but social workers are typically more effective. If you have unique resources from different team members, do not be afraid to call on them.

2. **Respect each team member** as an equally valuable colleague. Hierarchies only work to a certain extent in teams, and trust is important. You can have a team leader (which in some cases may be you as the psychologist), but teams where each player feels valuable function better.

3. **Communicate, communicate, communicate.** Scheduled team meetings can help to consolidate communication, while informal conversations and good visibility in the clinic can help build relationships.

4. **Share records appropriately.** Using the electronic medical record to securely send information and review team member visits can help to provide a richer picture of the patient and to facilitate better care.

5. **Be available and flexible.** This is not an environment where patients are seen back to back behind closed doors for an hour at a time. Be prepared for warm hand-offs, knocks on the door with questions, and squeezing in patients with emergent issues.

6. **Avoid emotional voyeurism.** Psychological data, especially sensational details, are interesting to the team; however, unless they are relevant, the patient is being exploited. Keep it relevant to the treatment and the patient care.

7. **Be a united front.** Avoid splitting among team members and between patients and the team. Appoint a spokesperson for the team and make sure that patients receive consistent messages from each member of the team.

8. **Include patient voices.** Let patients know when the team members are discussing difficult issues and help to empower patients to provide their perspective.

9. **Be efficient.** This is not the place for a 12-page report detailing every nuance of the patient's issue. Keep it brief and to the point with an action plan.

10. **Maintain relationships with other psychologists.** Many times a psychologist may be the lone person representing the field in a team. It helps to have a good network of psychologists for consultation. Organizations such as the American Psychological Association Practice Organization and your state psychological association are excellent places to reconnect with your roots.

of the patient are important ethical considerations in the multidisciplinary team environment. Psychologists in these settings are likely to encounter mixed feelings, which can be confusing. Their desire to protect confidentiality may be compromised by anxiety that by refusing to disclose information they may damage their relationships with team members, including those who may hold more organizational power, such as surgeons, physician leaders, or department chairs. In the case of Ms. Bell, the psychologist's ethical decision-making process reflected a concern for the dignity of the patient that allowed her to refrain from discussion of the irrelevant parts of the patient's history. In spite of the potential harm to her own status within the team, she placed the patient's welfare and right to privacy as higher concerns.

Beneficence versus Harm – Making Collaborative Treatment Decisions

Psychologists performing evaluations as a part of a medical team may be asked to give input on the potential psychological harm or benefit of a procedure and to help the team weigh these against the medical risks and benefits of a procedure. Ethical considerations include nonmaleficence, beneficence, and the responsible use of power. For example, Ms. Bell had significant medical issues and her severe obesity puts her at risk for serious disease or death; thus, the psychologist in this case must consider the power of her recommendation with the medical team. Bariatric surgery conceivably could help Ms. Bell live longer, reduce medical comorbidity, and improve the quality of her life, providing significant benefit to the patient. However, there are also risks to surgery, including medical risks of death/complications, as well as psychological risks, including increased risk of substance abuse after surgery, weight regain with return of binge eating habits, and increased risk of suicide. Psychologists act as consultants to the team, providing their expertise from the literature as well as their evaluation of the current mental state of the patient. This input, along with that of other team members, is used to help make a team decision for treatment that maximizes patient benefit and minimizes patient risk. Again, it is important that the patient understands that the psychologist will be in communication with the team regarding these issues. In fact, psychologists performing evaluations in medical settings will often be helping the patients themselves weigh the risks and benefits of procedures, which can be important when sharing the patient's own assessment with the multidisciplinary team.

Cultural Considerations in the Hospital Setting

Often, high-risk patients from low-socioeconomic status (SES) backgrounds are seen in academic medical centers given that, as teaching hospitals, they see a wider range of patients, including those on Medicaid or other public assistance plans. Ms. Bell was from a vulnerable population: a low-income background with limited education, a history of abuse, and a difficult environment. Ms. Bell's cultural issues (i.e., low SES, low education, severe mental illness) may have impacted her ability to obtain healthy food choices and feel safe exercising in her neighborhood and exacerbated her mental health and adherence issues. Patients with obesity are more likely to have low SES and have poorer insurance, and patients with less insurance and income are less likely to receive weight loss surgery, resulting in health care disparities with bariatric surgery. In fact, Ms. Bell had travelled several hundred miles to be seen at this academic medical center because she could not find a local hospital that took her insurance.

In addition, patients with obesity are at high risk of facing stigma and prejudice from others, including medical providers. Patients note they are often told that all their problems are due to their weight and receive poorer-quality care from providers. Thus, Ms. Bell may have been predisposed to be concerned as to how she would be talked about by the medical team given her history with other health care providers.

Furthermore, given the patient's limited education, her ability to understand the written informed consent and program materials discussing the multidisciplinary nature of the treatment program may have been limited. Assessing health care literacy and using multiple forms of explanation and ongoing discussion of informed consent are part of cultural competence for the health psychologist. The psychologist in Ms. Bell's case did a fair job in providing the informed consent both in written form and verbally with the client, although ongoing dialogue including patient verbalization of their understanding would have demonstrated even greater competence.

Ethical Decision-Making in the Multidisciplinary Health Care Environment

A principle-based (prima facie) ethics approach (Knapp & VandeCreek, 2012) is recommended for psychologists working in the health care environment. Principle-based ethics attempts to address shortcomings of both deontological ethics (intentions are most important) and utilitarian ethics (outcomes are most important) by weighing various ethical duties such as fidelity, justice, beneficence, and nonmaleficence. Principle-based ethics recognizes that it may be impossible to follow one ethical principle without violating another and encourages the actor to seek morally preferable alternatives or the lowest level of infringement. Knapp and VandeCreek (2012) offer a five-step model for ethical decision-making that includes: (1) identifying the problem, (2) developing alternatives, (3) evaluating options, (4) action, and (5) evaluation.

In Ms. Bell's case, the psychologist weighed the various ethical principles to come to an action. She weighed fidelity (establishing trust/confidentiality) against integrity (removing information from the chart per patient request). She was able to generate an alternative solution (sharing the chart and amending with the patient in session) that was satisfactory in promoting fidelity and adhering to integrity. Further, the psychologist weighed beneficence and nonmaleficence in providing her opinion to the medical team that the patient was not a good candidate for surgery, taking into account justice and respect for people's rights and dignity as she considered the patient's socioeconomic background. In evaluating her ethical decision-making, the psychologist may consider taking steps to enhance her informed consent process and communication with the team. A frank discussion of confidentiality and the sensitivity of psychological information with the multidisciplinary team and the ethical considerations involved may be a good step (Nielsen et al., 2013). In addition, she may want to review her informed consent document for clarity on the EHR, as well as consult with a colleague and role-play about how she verbally discusses this with her patients.

Further Research, Professional Standards, and Guidelines

Further research is needed to assess current practices in obtaining informed consent, confidentiality, and multidisciplinary team decisions in health care settings and to establish guidelines for such in integrated treatment settings.

It is important for health psychologists to have a good network of colleagues to consult regarding ethical issues in the hospital setting. Health psychologists should refer to the APA guidelines, along with their state rules and regulations and state board of psychology. The APA and state psychological associations often offer informal consultation on ethical issues and are great resources. Board certification in Clinical Health Psychology includes a heavy emphasis on ethical decision-making and provides an additional level of evaluation and examination of clinical skills and practice.

It is also important to become familiar with similarities and differences between the APA code and guidelines and other professional ethics codes, such as the American Medical Association, the National Association of Social Workers, etc. Understanding the similarities and differences in ethical guidelines among different professions may help to guide conversations and policies to work toward common understandings of the multidisciplinary practice (Hudgins et al., 2013; Van Liew, 2012). Psychologists may consult with their hospital's legal team regarding policies and informed consent practices. Many hospital systems have a bioethics committee or department that can assist multidisciplinary teams facing difficult ethical decisions.

In conclusion, psychologists working in an integrated health setting must take extra caution when obtaining informed consent by educating the patient about the role of the psychologist in the multidisciplinary team and using EHRs (Table 4.2).

The Case of the Post-Partum Depression Mother with Multiple Sclerosis

Psychologists in academic health care settings are likely to be involved in training, especially postdoctoral fellowships in health, clinical, and counseling specialties. The beginning of a fellowship year is always challenging. There are logistical challenges such as learning a medical record system and getting access to various medical system resources. There are personality challenges such as learning the nuances of new supervisors' or supervisees' work styles or the medical team's preferences. And there are certainly patient issues. These range from transitioning a previous fellow's patients to a new fellow to learning quickly how to handle oneself during a crisis situation, such as in the case below. Fellows typically have advanced training and are entering a program for specialized training in a specific interest area or subspecialty; thus, their clinical judgment is generally sound and their ability to respond under pressure is advanced. Despite advanced skills, encountering the first crisis situation can be challenging.

The case of Mrs. Thomas started as a routine consult to a neurology clinic specializing in the treatment of multiple sclerosis (MS). Notably, it was the fellow's first patient, and as such the supervising psychologist was very involved in teaching. On this morning, the behavioral medicine team received a page from one of the neurology teams stating "stat consult requested for a patient who is here from out of state." The supervising psychologist concluded that this case would make a wonderful teaching experience for the fellow, and so she

Table 4.2 *Recommendations for Best Practices in Integrated Care Settings*

1. Obtain both verbal and written informed consent in the integrated care setting whenever possible.
2. Clarify with whom the information will be shared.
3. Clarify the purpose of the referral and what types of recommendations may be made.
4. Clarify the information that will be included in the electronic health record (EHR).
5. Keep information included in the EHR factual, behavioral, and relevant.
6. Maintain an integrated EHR with both mental health and medical notes to enhance patient care.
7. Encourage other health care providers to understand and respect the sensitivity of psychological information.
8. Use an audit system as part of the EHR to avoid unnecessary viewing of patient records.
9. Limit discussion in multidisciplinary team meetings to relevant details.
10. Consider issues such as cultural competence and health care literacy when obtaining informed consent.
11. Reassess informed consent regularly throughout the patient relationship, making it an ongoing conversation.
12. Clarify the role of supervisees and the level of involvement of supervisors when discussing confidentiality.
13. Clarify the roles of third-parties such as family members, interpreters, or other supports who are part of behavioral health visits.
14. Address confidentiality, EHRs, and working with multidisciplinary teams as part of the training curriculum.
15. Work with multidisciplinary teams to provide psychological perspectives and balance maleficence versus beneficence.
16. Consult with colleagues, relevant ethical guidelines, state rules and regulations, state boards of psychology, state psychological associations, the American Board of Clinical Health Psychology, bioethics teams, and legal counsel regarding ethical concerns.

quickly relayed the information to the fellow and together they headed to the requested exam room. When the behavioral medicine team arrived, they were greeted by the neurology team, the patient (Mrs. Thomas), and her mother (Mrs. Howe). During the discussion of the case, the neurology team informed the behavioral medicine team that the patient with MS was three months post-partum and experiencing severe depression. Mrs. Thomas had expressed depressive symptoms and apathy toward her newborn son. The behavioral medicine team asked the patient if she and her mother would like to come to the behavioral medicine offices to discuss her situation more privately. At that point, Mrs. Thomas began to get very agitated. Her mother intervened, pleading with her daughter to accept an appointment with behavioral medicine, stating that she was concerned for both her daughter's safety and the welfare of her new grandson.

The patient continued to refuse treatment. At this point, her mother called the patient's husband, Mr. Thomas, on the phone to discuss the scenario. While the behavioral medicine team sat in the room, it was clear that the patient was distraught. In addition, her appearance was disheveled and her affect depressed. As the mother continued her phone conversation with Mr. Thomas, she then passed the phone to the psychologist, who spoke to the husband. During this phone call, the husband explained that the patient was not eating and she was not caring for their newborn child. He explained that for the past two weeks he had noticed more apathy toward herself and the baby. Mr. Thomas begged the behavioral medicine team to take care of his wife and stated that his and the patient's mother's only hope for this visit was that the mental health needs of the patient were met. The psychologist and fellow continued to listen and empathize with both the husband and mother, while the patient continued to adamantly deny treatment.

Approximately 20 minutes went by and the Mrs. Thomas asked the psychologist and fellow if she could make a deal with them. She said that she would be willing to come into the psychologist's office if she was allowed to get salad from the cafeteria and eat it during her appointment. They agreed and accompanied the patient and her mother to the cafeteria within the building and then back into the psychologist's office. Once in the office, the patient began slowly eating her salad and telling her story. At this point, the new fellow took over the evaluation. It was noticeable that Mrs. Thomas was becoming agitated. She shared that she and her husband had been trying for a baby for over a year, and when they finally got pregnant they were both ecstatic. She had suffered several miscarriages and so when she was pregnant with their son, she worried constantly about losing the pregnancy. She also reported symptoms of depression since she was a teen and shared that while she was pregnant she had not been depressed and had felt better than she had in years with both her depression and her MS. In an MS population, the pregnancy may serve as a protective factor for MS symptoms, and patients tend to report fewer physical and emotional symptoms. The patient shared that the baby had been born prematurely via emergency C-section and detailed how scared she had been when she went into labor at 29 weeks. The couple coped well with the neonatal intensive care unit (NICU), and the baby made it home after four weeks in the NICU. The patient reported her MS symptoms returned in concurrence with the baby's arrival home, and at the same time she noticed that both her anxiety and depression started increasing. She described thoughts such as, "What if I can't walk? How am I ever going to take care of this baby?" and, "I should have never had this baby in the first place." She felt that her baby and her husband would be "better off without [her]." At this point, the fellow began to exhibit doubt in his clinical skills and evaluation. He began to freeze with his questions and did not ask questions pertaining to her or her son's safety, instead focusing his interview on her clinical issues. The patient's demeanor changed rapidly and within seconds she threw her salad with dressing at the psychology fellow, missing him but spraying salad and dressing all over the wall of the office. She was irate and stormed out of the office.

Ethical Considerations

The Ethics of Supervision for Psychologists in Hospital Settings

The beginning of a training year comes with important responsibilities to a supervisor. Multiple ethical principles and standards from the Code inform and govern the practice of supervision in psychology and provide a basis for the regulations that follow (Education and Training Standard 7; APA, 2010). In the U.S., the ethical and regulatory responsibilities of the supervisory relationship are informed by the Association of State and Provincial Psychology Boards: Supervision Guidelines for Education and Training leading to Licensure as a Health Service Provider (Association of State and Provincial Psychology Boards [ASPPB], 2013) and the APA Code (APA, 2010). In addition, many state boards have regulations that one must understand and follow if s/he is to supervise students. Particularly relevant in this case are competence in both practice and supervision (ASPPB, 2013) and the APA General Principles: Beneficence and Nonmaleficence, Integrity, and Respect for People's Rights and Dignity.

Supervisor Competencies in the Hospital Setting

Supervision is a collaborative, competency-based practice between supervisor and supervisee (Bernard & Goodyear, 2014; Falender & Shafranske, 2004). The goal of supervision is to train the supervisee in an area of specialty, to provide an avenue for the supervisee to gain competence toward independent practice, and, perhaps most important, to protect the public and fragile patient populations (ASPPB, 2015). Relevant ethical standards include Standard 2.05, Delegation of Work to Others. In this guideline, the licensed psychologist/supervisor who delegates work takes reasonable steps to ensure that the supervisee is fully competent and qualified to perform this work. In the case of Mrs. Thomas, it is clear that the trainee has substantial predoctoral education and training; however, it is notable that the trainee was overwhelmed, likely by the new position and this patient. The trainee began to stray from the important questions regarding harm and asked questions pertaining to function. Perhaps the trainee was intimidated with the start of the fellowship year, the supervisor, the situation, etc. The supervisor was either not paying attention to the interview or was hoping that the trainee would start to ask the appropriate questions. Either way, the supervisor did not step in at this point and allowed the interview to digress. At this point, the supervisor should have attended to the interview, but instead the fellow continued and the patient eventually stormed out of the office. The following explains why their actions were ethically problematic.

Supervisors' responsibilities include: (a) supervisor competency in the areas of a supervisees' training; (b) understanding the patient and the care that the student is providing; (c) ensuring the standard and quality of practice, which includes protecting the public; (d) overseeing all aspects of client services; and (e) mentoring the supervisee. However, it is important to note that patient care is never sacrificed based on a student's competency. The supervisor should always become intimately involved in the patient care if a student is not competent to handle a critical case.

In the case above, supervisor competency is important to evaluate. It is essential that the supervisor is competent in both clinical practice and supervision, as past supervision experience does not necessarily guarantee supervisor competence. It is necessary that the individual consistently educates themselves by way of continuing education, relevant readings, and consultation. Supervisor competencies relate to the constructs of knowledge, skills, attitudes, and values (ASPPB, 2015; Table 4.3). The supervisor in the case of Mrs. Thomas had many years of experience in training; however, it was clear that the supervisor did not take over the evaluation when necessary, and in turn put the patient's and her child's welfare at risk. The supervisor may have felt reluctant to interfere with the supervisee's autonomy during the training experience.

APA Ethics and Supervision in the Hospital Setting

Beneficence and Nonmaleficence

According to Principle A of the Code and Standard 3.04 (APA, 2010), psychologists strive to promote the welfare of others and improve the conditions of individuals. Psychologists strive to do no harm. In the case above, the patient was clearly distraught and indeed in need of psychological treatment, which likely would include voluntary or involuntary hospitalization. If the psychologist and fellow had in fact not provided treatment, they would have potentially harmed not only the patient, but also the patient's child. There is no information regarding what happened after the patient stormed out of the office; however, ethically, it was imperative that the psychologist not allow the patient to leave the building and continue the evaluation to determine safety of self and others. Mrs. Thomas was from a different state, which also complicated the nature of the relationship. Even if the psychologist and supervisee were aware of the rules of the hospital's state, if the patient would have gone home, they may have needed to understand the jurisdiction laws of her state. The psychologist should have contacted the hospital's legal team to clarify the rules and law of the patient's state.

Integrity

APA Principle C of Integrity informs our decision on maintaining integrity in all psychological activities. It was clear that in the case of Mrs. Thomas, the trainee/ supervisor relationship was not discussed with the patient and hence the patient's agitation was likely caused by her not understanding why there were two clinicians in the room. Although we are not privy to why this communication did not occur, it is important to think about this. This omission may be the result of a distracted supervisor or a lack of capacity to take the patient's perspective. Either way, the lack of information regarding the relationship was unethical. In looking at Principle C of Integrity, psychologists seek to maintain integrity by way of honest communication and accuracy, in this case of the training relationship. Brief, verbal consent should be obtained by explaining the supervisory role of the trainee and the psychologist and providing an explanation of the role of behavioral health in the MS treatment team, and ideally written consent should be obtained by explaining the above to include multiple clients (the patient and family members). This would have been a more appropriate ethical approach. In addition, when the husband was contacted, there was no mention as to if consent was received.

Table 4.3 *Supervision in the Hospital Setting*

Supervision Knowledge:
1. Understanding of the health specialty area being supervised
2. Research, scientific, and evidence base of the health psychology supervision literature, with specific focus on health psychology
3. Professional/supervisee development
4. Ethics and legal issues specific to supervision in the hospital setting
5. Evaluation and process outcome
6. Diversity in all its forms

Supervision Skills:
1. Providing supervision in multiple modalities
2. Forming a supervisory alliance
3. Providing formative and summative feedback
4. Promoting the supervisee's self-assessment and growth, especially in the health environment
5. Self-assessing by the supervisor
6. Assessing the supervisee's learning needs and developmental level in health psychology
7. Providing direct observation and modeling as needed
8. Ensuring competence and integrity in supervisee work performed
9. Verifying informed consent with supervisee's patients and understanding of the supervisory relationship
10. Eliciting and integrating evaluative feedback from supervisees
11. Teaching and didactics related to specific health psychology literature
12. Setting boundaries
13. Knowing when to seek consultation
14. Flexibility
15. Engaging in scientific thinking and translating theory and research to practice, with a specific focus on the health psychology literature

Supervision Attitudes and Values:
1. Appreciation and responsibility for both clients and supervisees
2. Respect
3. Sensitivity to diversity
4. Balancing between being supportive and challenging
5. Teaching empowerment by modeling and active engagement
6. A commitment to lifelong learning and professional growth in health psychology
7. Balancing obligations to client, agency, and service with training needs
8. Valuing ethical principles
9. Knowing and utilizing psychological science related to supervision
10. A commitment to the use of empirically based supervisor skills
11. A commitment to knowing one's own limitations

Adapted from ASPPB (2015)

Competence

Finally, the APA Standards on competence are relevant to this case. This content ensures that services being provided by supervisees are provided competently (2.01, 2.04, and 2.05). In the case above, the fellow began doubting his skills and, instead of focusing on the patient's psychological symptoms, he began to focus his interview on the functional and physical symptoms. At this point, the supervisor should have stepped in and taken over the interview to focus on the psychological symptoms and the safety of the patient and her baby. This did not happen, and the patient became so frustrated that she first threw her salad and then stormed out of the room. Oftentimes, supervisors can become distracted by multiple job duties and, in this case, what if the supervisor were not focused on the trainee and the interview process? In the same way, the trainee can be distracted or even lack confidence. Either could have happened in this case. In speculating that the supervisor was distracted and the student was not confident, the potential to miss a highly important series of questions arose.

Do No Harm – Challenges for the Psychologist in the Hospital Setting

One of the most anxiety-provoking patient situations for clinicians is the realization that a patient may be at risk of harm to self or harm to others. In the case above, the patient's husband and mother both alluded to the fact that she was at risk of harm to self and of committing neglectful, perhaps harmful behaviors toward their newborn. Her story was incredibly compelling and filled with emotions, and thus the fellow missed an important opportunity to ask questions regarding harm. As above, it is assumed that the student felt overwhelmed by the beginning of the fellowship year, his rotation, and his supervisor and thus missed an opportunity to ask pertinent questions. In many jurisdictions, the duty to protect is a law as well as an ethical responsibility that states that mental health professionals have a legal obligation to protect a patient or a threatened third-party from imminent harm; in this case, harm to the patient's child. In the above example, there was an ethical and legal duty to more clearly explore the risks to the mother (the patient) as well as the child.

Ethical Decision-Making with Supervisees in the Hospital Setting

The APA Code provides broad guidelines for psychologists' ethical decision-making that apply to diverse settings, such as hospitals, where the practice of psychology is conducted. It is important to note that the Code is not a formula for solving ethical issues; rather, it is a set of aspirations and broad rules of conduct that are meant to guide the ethical decision-making processes. Based on the moral dispositions for virtuous professional practice of Beauchamp and Childress (2001), psychologists should focus on the following general virtues of ethical conduct: (1) conscientious-ness, (2) discernment, and (3) prudence. Related to our case above, *conscientious-ness* should have motivated the psychologist to do what was right by understanding the imminent threat to the patient and potentially the baby. The psychologist watched the fellow doubt his skills and the psychologist did not jump in at a critical juncture of care. Regarding the virtue of *discernment*, the psychologist heard a very emo-tionally complex story of the family having failed attempts at pregnancy and the emotional toll that this child being born prematurely took. The providers clearly understood the emotional attachment to the baby and the symptoms of depression, but did not ask about potential harm. From the perspective of this virtue, the providers did not use good judgment in this case to keep others safe. Finally, utilizing *prudent* practice in this case would allow the psychologist to use wisdom to reach the most beneficial solution given the nature of the problem and the individuals involved. Considering the number of individuals involved in this case, it is important to discuss with whom the patient is entering into the treatment relationship. In the case of Mrs. Thomas, it was clear that the patient was Mrs. Thomas, but the providers failed to incorporate the other family members into the complicated family picture or to do what they could to honor the patient's autonomy. In most cases, senior psychologists can also teach by modeling, which enhances the capacity of the trainee to understand the complexity of the Code. Modeling also demonstrates the importance of the commitment of the provider to ethical practice (Beauchamp & Childress, 2001).

Future Research, Professional Standards, and Guidelines

This case was complicated by the fact that the patient came from out of state and she came to a neurology appointment with no intentions of seeing a psychologist. On the other hand, her husband and mother (who accompanied her to the appointment) had the main goal of treating her depression. Thus, both parties had differing goals for the appointment. Should the patient have entered a psychologist's office outside of a neurology clinic, the intentions would have been clearer. Ethical commitment on the psychologist's part is only the first step toward sound ethical practice. Good intentions are insufficient if there is a failure to identify ethical situations in which the principles should be applied. Thus, it is imperative that psychologists continue to critically evaluate the health specialty literature as it relates to the ethical code and conduct. Far too often, psychologists are unaware of the most recent health psychology and specialty research and harm patients. The Code includes both aspirational content in its principles and enforceable standards for practice that require a psychologist to think clearly and soundly and act in accordance with its contents. Psychologists who participate in training should have guidelines in place that include recommendations for responsible conduct, with a particular focus on the specific supervisory roles, activities, and practice setting. It is also important for supervisors to look at their own mental health, especially as it relates to burnout (Standard 2.06). Oftentimes, supervisors have multiple obligations and are focused on those, instead of fully focused on the patient care aspect and, in this case, safety issues. To be a strong supervisor is to look honestly at our strengths and weaknesses and to know ourselves and our patterns well enough to predict mental health needs.

The Case of an International VIP

Hospital settings, especially well-known academic medical centers, may attract high-end patients, including VIPs and international patients. These patients may expect a different level of attention and care from providers, and hospital systems may contribute to different standards based on "self-pay" or special status.

Consider Mr. Isa, a patient referred for psychological evaluation of insomnia at an internationally renowned medical center. Mr. Isa was a 48-year-old male from the Middle East who primarily spoke Arabic and was designated a VIP. As a VIP, it was understood that Mr. Isa was paying out of pocket for specialty services at the hospital facility and was considered a priority patient (i.e., a "medical tourist"). The psychologist was asked by her department chair to add the patient to her schedule the next day, cancelling and rescheduling another patient if necessary. Although the psychologist felt uncomfortable and distressed by this request, she cancelled another local patient to accommodate Mr. Isa. Mr. Isa arrived 45 minutes late to the appointment. The psychologist would have normally asked the patient to reschedule, but given the patient's special status, she went ahead with the interview, feeling pressured to see the patient anyway.

Because they were already running late, the psychologist only minimally reviewed the informed consent document (written in English) with the patient, with the interpreter verbally translating the psychologist's summary. The visit lasted almost two hours due to interpretation services, compared to a typical evaluation lasting 60–75 minutes. Often the interpreter appeared to shorten both the psychologist's speeches and the patient's replies; notably, this interpreter was a "concierge" rather than an interpreter hired by the hospital. Mr. Isa had classic symptoms of primary insomnia, with difficulty falling asleep associated with racing thoughts, muscle tension, and negative thoughts about his ability to sleep. As the psychologist discussed a treatment plan including cognitive behavioral treatment for insomnia, the patient noted that he wanted to be seen on specific days at a specific time. The patient asked for additional accommodations including translations of relaxation exercises, phone therapy once he returned to his country of origin, and on-call services as needed. Increasingly frustrated and irritated, the psychologist stated, "That's just not possible. I certainly can't do therapy over the phone! I can give you two follow-up appointments at 8 AM in the next two weeks, or it just won't work." Mr. Isa nodded and smiled, but did not arrive to either appointment and was lost to follow-up.

Ethical Considerations

Justice When Working with VIPs

Ethical conflicts arise when a clinician provides a different level of care for patients based on their pay status or other types of influence. In this case, the psychologist acted against the principle of "justice" when they cancelled a patient equally in need of services for the international patient if this was motivated solely by the patient's pay status. However, international patients may also have a limited timeline in which to receive treatment, in which case the psychologist may have acted appropriately to provide treatment to Mr. Isa (beneficence). The literature suggests that there is concern that medical tourism has the potential to create health care disparities between local communities and international, high-paying patients (Snyder, Johnston, Crooks, Morgan, & Adams, 2017).

A psychologist in this predicament may have mixed feelings about juggling his/her schedule to accommodate a VIP. On one hand, they may feel flattered that they are receiving a referral for someone "important" and that the department chair respects her/his work. On the other, they may feel frustrated that they are being asked to make special accommodations and upset about cancelling a "regular" patient. Seeking areas of compromise can help psychologists to cope with these emotions; for example, instead of cancelling the local patient, the psychologist may have added a late clinic appointment for the international patient. The psychologist has an ethical obligation to the local patient to do no harm (Standard 3.04), as well as to treat the local patient with fairness (justice). Evaluating the urgency or severity of the local patient's needs versus the international patient's needs may be a factor in decision-making on how to seek a beneficial solution for both patients.

Similarly, providers must examine their own countertransference when working with a VIP, a process that seemed to be absent in this psychologist's actions. Are they providing extra care because they feel flattered? Are they refusing to provide reasonable accommodations because they feel irritated with the patient's "special" status?

Respect for People's Rights and Dignity When Working with International Patients

Some of Mr. Isa's requests, while perhaps unusual for the psychologist in the situation, were reasonable cultural accommodations. Mr. Isa is not likely to benefit from English relaxation training CDs for insomnia that the provider typically used. Working with the international office at the provider's hospital to reasonably translate these exercises was beneficial for Mr. Isa, while not requiring undue effort on the part of the provider. Although the provider in this case made an exception by seeing the patient late because of his status, this could have been a reasonable step out of cultural respect, knowing that Arab patients may have a different orientation to time. Having this cultural knowledge may have helped the provider to work through his/her feelings of irritation and so provide better care to the patient. Knowing the Arab cultural values of respect for authority may have helped the psychologist to realize that the patient was merely being respectful by smiling and nodding agreement to her schedule for appointments. Unfortunately, the lack of cultural competence and the psychologist's irritation likely resulted in early termination of treatment and a likely violation of Standard 2.01b that stipulates that psychologists act with cultural competence. A multicultural approach to ethical decision-making would be reasonable in this situation (Fisher, 2014). Such an approach might include self-assessment, a curious approach to the patient's unique perspective, ongoing learning of cultural values and norms, and the mindful design of culturally appropriate, ethical interventions and actions.

Informed Consent with International Patients

In Mr. Isa's case, it is highly unlikely he understood fully the role of the psychologist in treating his insomnia, how his records would be kept, or how a treatment plan might look. The brief, verbally translated consent does not appear to be consistent with Standard 10.01 (Informed Consent to Therapy) of the Code since Mr. Isa could not be fully informed about entering into a treatment relationship with the psychologist. Psychologists who regularly work with specific international populations are encouraged to have their informed consent forms translated. Spending time with the patient and the interpreter and explaining the role of the psychologist and expectations can also be helpful in setting appropriate limits. Having a frank discussion at the outset of treatment regarding the role of the psychologist may have helped the provider to set appropriate limits.

Working with an interpreter poses its own sets of challenges (Bibla, Pena, & Bruce, 2015). Making sure both the interpreter and the patient understand the limits of this role is important. It is essential to use professional interpreters (rather than family, etc.) as part of the National Standards for Culturally and Linguistically Appropriate Services (NCLAS; U.S. Department of Health & Human Services, 2013). Inviting the patient to share his cultural beliefs and how they would affect treatment would have been a good way to enrich the informed consent discussion, Additionally, APA Standard 9.03 requires psychologists to obtain informed consent to use an interpreter, clarify confidentiality, and discuss limitations of the data obtained from assessments using interpreters.

Ethics of Medical Tourism

Mr. Isa was receiving treatment under a practice typically referred to as "medical tourism." Medical tourism is the practice of traveling internationally for medical care that is paid for out of pocket or by a government (Snyder et al., 2017). Some of the ethical concerns of medical tourism include: (1) health care inequalities (i.e., prioritizing high-paying, international patients at the expense of access for local patients); (2) bypassing a country's regulations/standards on health care (i.e., going to a country that allows payment for organ donations); and (3) concerns about postoperative continuity of care (Snyder et al., 2017). Medical tourism can be profitable, pitting high financial returns against the needs of lower-paying, local/public patients, while on the other hand possibly offering beneficial treatments not available in a patient's home country (Greenfield & Pawsey, 2014). For Mr. Isa, there did appear to be some organizational pressures for profit driving the demand he be seen quickly. It is likely, however, that insomnia treatment (cognitive behavioral therapy for insomnia) offered by the psychologist is not readily available in his own country. Therefore, the patient may benefit from access to this treatment (beneficence, justice). The psychologist may have legitimate concerns about the length of treatment and continuity of care for Mr. Isa. If Mr. Isa is not going to be in the country very long, the psychologist will need to weigh the risks of starting treatment versus the potential benefits of even brief treatment (beneficence versus nonmaleficence). In addition, the psychologist was correct (if not very diplomatic) in pointing out that practicing telemedicine across international boundaries likely would be practicing outside the boundaries of both her license and competence. The psychologist may have considered limiting treatment to the time the patient will be in the U.S., creating a follow-up schedule for when the patient returns to the U.S. for other business, or consulting with a local provider about ongoing treatment.

Ethical Decision-Making Process

Using principle-based ethics, the psychologist in this case could have benefitted from first identifying the problem (Knapp & VandeCreek, 2013). Her emotional reactions (discomfort, irritability) may have been a good indication that she was experiencing an ethical dilemma. The psychologist was struggling with shame, perhaps over cancelling the local patient or her lack of cultural knowledge about the international patient. In addition, she was frustrated with the limits of her ability to help Mr. Isa in such a short time period. Lastly, she was probably experiencing countertransference in reaction to the patient's VIP status, resulting in irritability. Some of the dilemmas included beneficence (helping Mr. Isa with his insomnia by providing care not available in his home country) versus justice (providing care to Mr. Isa over a local patient). The psychologist could have reasonably generated alternatives that would have satisfied both principles (seeing both patients at different times). In addition, she also may have weighed competence (integrity) and respect for people's rights and dignity against beneficence in treating Mr. Isa. Specifically, it appears that the psychologist had less cultural competence in dealing with international (in this case Arab) patients than would be required by the Code. In evaluating her response, she may have decided that she needed to engage in further education and supervision on treating international patients given her role within the hospital. In addition, an evaluation of the ethics involved may have suggested she needed to clarify her ethical obligations with the hospital administration to avoid dilemmas in the future. The psychologist could note her need for additional training to see international patients as well as set limits on such interactions (i.e., ask for hospital interpreters, longer visit lengths, more advanced notice). Psychologists are encouraged to clarify the nature of the conflict when there is a conflict between ethics and organizational demands (Standard 1.03; APA, 2010).

Organizational interventions, such as translations of consent forms, professional interpretation services, and identification of local resources for continuity of care, may also be identified in the evaluation phase of ethical decision-making.

Further Research, Guidelines, and Best Practices

The ethics in the medical tourism field are still nascent. Further research is needed to assess the possible benefits and risks for medical tourists, the possible risks and benefits to the countries from and to which medical tourists travel, and the impact on the institutions providing care. Psychologists providing treatment to international patients and medical tourists are advised to be familiar with the NCLAS, the APA's Guidelines for Working with Culturally Diverse Populations (1990) and the APA's Guidelines on Multicultural Training, Education, Research, Practice, and Organizational Change for Psychologists (2002), as well as culture-specific literature and training. Ongoing self-assessment, education, and supervision for working toward cultural competence are important for any psychologist working with international patients.

Table 4.4 *Best Practices for Psychologists Practicing in a Medical Tourism Facility*

1. Have literature regarding treatment options in the client's preferred language.
2. Use live, professional interpreters when possible who have experience in medical settings.
3. Provide informed consent in the client's preferred language when possible and discuss in detail.
4. Educate the patient about role of the psychologist and elicit the patient's unique understanding of health, mental health, and psychology.
5. Establish the length of stay and set clear treatment plan goals within this length.
6. Arrange for local continuity of care in the patient's country of origin when possible or work with the organization to provide a timeline for expected follow-up at the current facility.
7. Consider boundaries of competence in working with patients from other cultures.
8. Self-assess and engage in continuing education to work toward cultural competence.
9. Consider limits of licensure (i.e., avoid practicing across state lines or international boundaries without a license).
10. Consider limits of telemedicine/telepsychology, as well as competence in providing telehealth.
11. Engage patients in dialogue to better understand how their cultural backgrounds affect their health and treatment planning.

In summary, psychologists working in hospitals with international patients and "medical tourism" need to be mindful of informed consent, cultural competence, continuity of care, and balancing the benefits of treatment for the international patient and organizational demands (Table 4.4).

Conclusions on Ethical Challenges in Hospital Settings

As illustrated above, psychologists practicing in hospital settings are likely to face ethical challenges in areas such as informed consent, confidentiality, balancing beneficence versus nonmaleficence, cultural competence, and justice and respect for all persons. The electronic medical record, working in multidisciplinary teams, providing supervision/training in health psychology specialties, medical tourism/international patients, and balancing organizational demands versus professional ethics are likely areas of challenge for the health psychologist. Health psychologists in hospital settings are encouraged to apply principle-based ethical decision-making, consult with colleagues, and strive toward ongoing self-assessment and the development of ethical best practices in the health care setting. Psychologists in hospitals should be familiar with state rules, the APA Ethics Code, ASPPB guidelines, guild best practices, the emerging research literature, and the national NCLAS standards. Board certification in Clinical Health Psychology may emerge as a standard to provide a higher level of scrutiny regarding competence and ethics in health psychology practice. Future research is needed to establish current ethical practices in hospital settings and to set best practice guidelines for psychologists working in hospitals. The exciting movement toward integrated care brings opportunities for psychologists to continue ethical practice in hospital settings.

References

American Psychological Association (1990). *Guidelines for providers of psychological services to ethnic, linguistic, and culturally diverse populations*. Retrieved from www .apa.org/pi/oema/resources/policy/provider-guidelines.aspx

American Psychological Association (2002). *Guidelines on multicultural training, education, research, practice, and organizational change for psychologists*. Retrieved from www.apa.org/pi/oema/resources/policy/multicultural-guidelines.aspx

American Psychological Association (2010). *Ethical principles of psychologists and code of conduct*. Retrieved from www.apa.org/ethics/code/index.asp

Association of State and Provincial Psychology Boards (2013). *ASPPB code of conduct*. Montgomery, AL: Association of State and Provincial Psychology Boards. Retrieved from https://c.ymcdn.com/sites/asppb.site-ym.com/resource/resmgr/Guidelines/ Code_of_Conduct_Updated_2013.pdf

Association of State and Provincial Psychology Boards (2015). *Supervisory guidelines for education and training leading to licensure as a health service provider*. Montgomery, AL: Association of State and Provincial Psychology Boards. Retrieved from http://c.ymcdn.com/sites/www.asppb.net/resource/resmgr/ Guidelines/Final_Supervision_Guidelines.pdf

Beauchamp, T. L. & Childress J. F. (2001). *Principles of biomedical ethics* (5th edn.). New York, NY: Oxford University Press.

Bernard, J. M. & Goodyear, R. K. (2014). *Fundamentals of clinical supervision* (5th edn.). Uppers Saddle River, NJ: Pearson.

Bibla, T., Pena, A., & Bruce, C. (2015). Consultations across languages. *Hastings Center Report*, *45*, 13–14.

Clemens, N. A. (2012). Privacy, consent, and the electronic health record: The person vs. the system. *Journal of Psychiatry Practice*, *18*, 46–50.

Falender, C. A. & Shafranske, E. P. (2004). *Clinical supervision: A competency–based approach*. Washington, DC: American Psychological Association.

Fisher, C. B. (2014). Multicultural ethics in professional psychology practice, consulting, and training. In F. T. L. Leong, L. Comas-Diaz, G. C. Nagayama-Hall, V. C. McLoyd, & J. E. Trimble (Eds.) *APA handbook of multicultural psychology, vol. 2: Applications and training* (pp. 35–57). Washington, DC: American Psychological Association.

Greenfield, D. & Pawsey, M. (2014). Medical tourism raises questions that highlight the need for care and caution. *Medical Journal of Australia*, *201*, 568–569.

Hodgson, J., Mendenhall, T., & Lamson, A. (2013). Patient and provider relationships: Consent, confidentiality, and managing mistakes in integrated primary care settings. *Families, Systems and Health*, *31*, 28–40.

Hudgins, C., Rose, S., Fifield, P. Y., & Arnault, S. (2013). Navigating the legal and ethical foundations of informed consent and confidentiality in integrated primary care. *Families, Systems, & Health*, *31*, 9–19.

Knapp, S. J. & VandeCreek, L. D. (2012). *Practical ethics for psychologists: A positive approach* (2nd edn.). Washington, DC: American Psychological Association.

Nielsen, B. A., Baum, R. A., & Soares, N. S. (2013). Navigating ethical issues with electronic health records in developmental–behavioral pediatric practice. *Journal of Developmental & Behavioral Pediatrics*, *34*, 45–51.

Snyder, J., Johnston, R., Crooks, V. A., Morgan, J., & Adams, K. (2017). How medical tourism enables preferential access to care: Four patterns from the Canadian context. *Health Care Analysis, 25,* 138–150.

U.S. Department of Health & Human Services, Office of Minority Health (2013). *National standards for culturally and linguistically appropriate services in health and health care: A blueprint for advancing and sustaining CLAS policy and practice.* Retrieved from https://www.thinkculturalhealth.hhs.gov/pdfs/EnhancedCLAS StandardsBlueprint.pdf

Van Liew, J. R. (2012). Balancing confidentiality and collaboration within multidisciplinary health care teams. *Journal of Psychology in Medical Settings, 19,* 411–417.

5 Ethics in a Rural Context

Cindy Juntunen, Melissa A. Quincer, and Sinéad K. P. M. Unsworth

The unique ethical issues of rural psychological practice have received limited attention in the psychological literature, but it is clear that clinicians practicing in rural settings often need to respond to challenges in a culturally informed fashion that may be quite different from the experience of psychologists practice in urban and suburban settings (Malone, 2011; Worth, Hastings, & Riding-Malon, 2010). Small communities often do exist within large urban areas (Schank, Helbok, Haldeman, & Gallardo, 2010; Schank & Skovholt, 2006) and providers in such communities may have similar experiences. However, rural values, geographic isolation, and limited access to other mental or behavioral health care specialists all contribute to rural psychologists experiencing distinctive ethical decision-making demands (Malone & Dyck, 2011; Schank, 1998; Werth, Hastings, & Riding-Malon, 2010).

A full discussion of the diverse definitions and meanings of "rural" and "rurality" is beyond the scope of this chapter. Briefly, we use the term "rural" to describe both a geographical location and a social location (Juntunen & Quincer, 2017). Geographically, there are numerous ways to define "rural," with even various agencies within the U.S. government (Census Bureau, Office of Management and Budget, and the Department of Agriculture) using different definitions. For the purposes of the cases in this chapter, "rural" is defined as communities that are distant from metropolitan areas where services are available, which are identified by the United States Department of Agriculture as Frontier and Remote communities (USDA, 2013). Approximately 35 percent of people in the U.S. live in communities that are sufficiently rural or remote that they need to travel in order to obtain basic necessities such as groceries, fuel, and critical health care (US Bureau of the Census, 2012).

As a social location, rurality includes values of social obligation, social belonging, sharing with others (Greenfield, 2013), independence (Kitayama, Conway, Pietromonaco, Park, & Plaut, 2010), and a preference for seeking help from friends or families rather than professionals (Andren, McKibbin, Wykes, Lee, Carrico, & Bourassa, 2013). In addition to values, rural areas often have the social characteristics of less access to education (Duncan, 2013) and higher levels of poverty (US Bureau of the Census, 2012).

Rural citizens are likely to report higher levels of depression, substance abuse, domestic violence, and child abuse than are nonrural citizens (Smalley, Yancey, Warren, Naufel, Ryan, & Pugh, 2010). In one particularly telling health indicator, rural youth are almost twice as likely to complete suicide as nonrural youth, a disparity that is increasing over time (Fontanella et al., 2015). As even this small number of examples indicates, there is a clear need for psychological services in rural communities, yet there continues to be a critical shortage based at least in part on psychologists' reluctance to work in rural communities. Even among providers satisfied with a rural lifestyle, persistent stress related to professional boundaries and ethics has been identified as a significant concern (Gillespie & Redivo, 2012). In this same study, mental health providers also indicated having insufficient preparation or training for managing ethical boundaries in rural settings (Gillespie & Redivo, 2012).

The primary goal of this chapter is to sensitize psychologists to the unique ethical issues that they may encounter in rural practice. There are several ethical issues that are particularly relevant for rural practice: multiple relationships, boundaries of clinical competence, client confidentiality, bartering as payment, respecting cultural values, working with limited professional support, and protecting the psychologist's privacy (Helbok, Marinelli, & Walls, 2006; Malone, 2010; Werth et al., 2010). In this chapter, we will use case examples to explore issues related to these specific topics and related areas.

Competence: Balancing Expertise with Meeting All Needs

Competence is specifically noted as an ethical obligation by the American Psychological Association (APA) in Standard 2.01(a): "Psychologists provide services, teach, and conduct research with populations and in areas only within the boundaries of their competence, based on their education, training, supervised experience, consultation, study, or professional experience." For rural providers, who are often the only mental or behavioral health care professionals available to address any concern, the boundary of competence can be difficult to assess when weighed against the need to be a generalist who can meet the needs of clients or patients who have no access to other providers.

The Case of If You Can't See Her, Who Will?

Dr. Allison Jones has been practicing as a licensed psychologist for several years and is confident in her generalist clinical skills. She has worked with child, adolescent, and adult client populations on a wide range of mental health issues, including most mood and anxiety disorders, trauma history, adjustment disorders, and psychotic disorders. Dr. Jones recently relocated from an urban city to a rural town to be closer to her family. She now works in an interprofessional primary care setting at a rural health care clinic. In this setting, she has become proficient with behavioral screenings, motivational interviewing, and assisting primary care providers with treatment adherence strategies. She also sees patients referred for specialist mental health care for regular psychotherapy sessions. Although it took some time to fit into the culture of the clinic, she is starting to feel like an integral part of the primary care team.

Dr. Jones has received a patient referral from her colleague, Dr. Otto, a physician and one of the primary care providers working at the rural health care clinic. Dr. Otto has referred Marcia, a 40-year-old, Spanish-speaking, Mexican–American, single, heterosexual mother of two daughters. The patient initially presented to Dr. Otto with symptoms of low energy, fatigue, sleep concerns, and concentration issues. Given her limited fluency in English, Marcia's 10-year-old daughter was present for the physical checkup and acted as an interpreter for communication between her mother and Dr. Otto.

Dr. Otto became concerned that Marcia was exhibiting symptoms of depression. Marcia and her daughter completed the Patient Health Questionnaire (PHQ-9) that is a standard part of each office visit, and Marcia responded to the item of having thoughts about being better off dead or harming herself with the answer "more than half the days." The clinic uses this as a criterion for immediate referral to the psychologist, Dr. Jones. Further, Marcia's daughter told Dr. Otto that her mother is feeling hopeless about life. When he further inquired about suicidality, the daughter indicated that her family is worried that Marcia will hurt herself because of things she has said at home.

Dr. Jones feels confident about her ability to work with Marcia's reported feelings of depression and suicidal ideation, but she does not speak Spanish and she has no previous experience working with Mexican–American patients. She asks Dr. Otto about referrals for Spanish-speaking therapists in the area. Dr. Otto reminds her that the only other mental health provider in town is currently on maternity leave, and the closest Spanish-speaking therapist is two hours away. Dr. Otto also notes that the family has limited financial resources and no vehicle, making commuting to the next nearby city for therapy difficult, if not impossible.

Dr. Otto states that "any treatment is good enough" with Marcia. Dr. Jones shares her concerns about working with the patient, particularly given the language barrier. Dr. Otto suggests that she has Marcia's daughter act as an interpreter in the counseling session, and also makes it clear that he expects Dr. Jones to work with this patient.

Discussion of the Ethical Dilemma and Associated Professional Standards

Dr. Jones recognizes that it is important to connect Marcia to mental health services and is also aware that there are limits to her boundaries of competence that may not optimally serve the client's mental health needs. The initial questions she asks herself are: "Do I have the skills necessary to provide adequate services to Marcia?", "Is it in the client's better interests for me to see her or to refer her to a distant provider?", and "What are the ethical implications of having Marcia's daughter act as an interpreter for her mother in counseling?"

A primary ethical concern is how Dr. Jones's competency limitations regarding the Spanish language and Mexican culture could negatively impact client treatment. In order to understand the ethical dilemma, it is useful to return to the guidelines and standards that psychologists adhere to in their clinical practice. The APA identifies competence as a professional standard that is based on specific guidelines that include the belief that practicing outside one's area of competence is considered unethical. However, the actual definition of competence is open to much interpretation and debate. In addition to knowing how to adhere to and deliver interventions, competence also includes "the judicious application of communication, knowledge, technical skills, clinical reasoning, emotions, values, and contextual understanding for the benefit of the individual and community being served" (Barber, Sharpless, Klostermann, & McCarthy, 2007, p. 494). This statement highlights the importance of the interplay of skills, knowledge, and judgment that serve to determine the level of competency a professional has obtained in their practice. Given the team approach that is commonly practiced in a rural community setting, it is helpful for Dr. Jones to be familiar with the ethical codes of her colleagues. The National Association for Social Workers (NASW) and the American Counseling Association (ACA) echo the standards of competence held by the APA, highlighting the importance of practicing within one's area of competence in order to ensure the highest standards of practice (ACA, 2014; NASW, 2008). All of the associations also emphasize continual professional growth, which can be exemplified by an ongoing commitment to a learning process that extends throughout one's mental health career.

Dr. Jones can with some confidence claim many of the characteristics of competence noted above. However, it can be difficult to decide whether or not one is competent in working with a particular client when even one area of competence (in this case communication) is limited.

It is important to keep in mind that, unlike many mental health professionals in urban settings, rural psychologists (like most rural health care providers) are not usually specialists. They are expected to practice as generalists who can treat clients from varied backgrounds and issues (Schank & Skovholt, 2006). This expectation can create the notion that psychologists should attempt to work with any client. It is very possible that Dr. Otto shares this expectation. As a physician, he may be focused on sharing accurate information, and an interpreter may be able to ensure that goal is achieved. But engaging in therapy and forming a working relationship may be much more difficult to achieve with an interpreter, and this is an aspect of her work that Dr. Jones may need to discuss more fully with her interprofessional colleagues. Further, it is likely that her boundaries of competence will be encountered regularly in this rural environment, given the need to be ready to respond to diverse issues from diverse clients.

Because Dr. Jones is concerned about Marcia's immediate well-being and also because she does want to maintain positive relationships with her new colleagues, she decides that she must consider her options for working at the margins of, if not outside, her current competence. Again, the APA Ethics Code provides some guidance in Standard 2.01(b), which notes that psychologists must either have or obtain appropriate training or make appropriate referrals, unless the situation is an emergency (Standard 2.02). Certainly, Marcia's has indicated some risk of suicidal thought and behavior, but it is not clear that this risk is imminent. Dr. Jones will need to assess this further, and an effective communication strategy needs to be in place in order to do that. However, the consequences of not responding to Marcia could be great, and Dr. Jones decides that there is some leeway in working with her under the emergency clause. However, Standard 2.02 also recommends that "The services are discontinued as soon as the emergency has ended or appropriate services are available." It is not at all clear that appropriate services will become available for Marcia, and so the question of whether Dr. Jones will need to eventually terminate services in an ethical fashion must also be considered.

In addition to emergency situations, psychologists can work with populations or interventions new to them if they "undertake relevant education, training, supervised experience, consultation or study" (Standard 2.01[c]). Further, Standard 2.01(d) explicitly allows psychologists to provide services when other providers are not available, as long as they "make a reasonable effort to obtain the competence required by using relevant research, training, consultation, or study." Both of these caveats are relevant to Dr. Jones's potential work with Marcia, and both will also require that Dr. Jones pursues some additional training or supervision in order to work ethically. She may need to seek out tele-supervision from a Spanish-speaking psychologist, and she may need to talk with her colleagues about methods to cover the expense of such supervision or consultation. She may also seek to learn Spanish, a skill that will take a substantial amount of time and will not be useful to her current work with Marcia, although it may prove useful in the future.

In addition to language, Dr. Jones must also assess her ability to be multiculturally competent in terms of working with Mexican–American culture. Multicultural competence involves having the knowledge, attitude, and skills to work with an individual's cultural background, which can include cultural identities such as gender, age, disability, race, ethnicity, sexual orientation, and socioeconomic status (American Psychological Association, 2002). The NASW and the ACA also highlight the importance of maintaining and developing cultural competence, encouraging an approach that acknowledges client strengths across various cultural backgrounds (ACA, 2014; NASW, 2008).

Although she has not worked with Mexican–American clients before, Dr. Jones has worked with clients from several racial and ethnic backgrounds other than her own. She has also attended training and continuing education events related to diversity during most of her years in practice. She believes that with appropriate consultation, her multicultural competence can generalize to her work with Marcia, and so she focuses on language as the primary potential barrier to their work together.

Reflecting on these considerations, Dr. Jones concludes that although she cannot answer her first question ("Do I have the skills necessary to provide adequate services to Marcia?") fully in the affirmative, she does have sufficient skills to be of assistance. She then moves on to her second question: "Is it in the client's better interests for me to see her or to refer her to a distant provider?"

Unfortunately, rural clinicians do not have referral sources readily accessible compared to their urban counterparts (Schank & Skovholt, 2006). In addition to there being no other local mental health providers available, there is also no transportation service to any surrounding cities. Without a vehicle of her own, Marcia will simply not be able to travel to see another provider. Given these barriers,

Dr. Jones decides that it is in Marcia's better, if not best, interests for her to work with Marcia. Ultimately, she concludes that the benefits of monitoring and evaluating the patient's depressive symptoms, including suicidality, outweigh the risks of providing services to Marcia. Therefore, it is necessary to identify ways to competently communicate with the client.

According to the APA Guidelines for Providers of Psychological Services to Ethnic, Linguistic, and Culturally Diverse Populations, "Psychologists interact in the language requested by the client and, if this is not feasible, make an appropriate referral." Fortunately, these guidelines do recognize that such referrals may not always be possible. In that case, psychologists are to offer an appropriately trained professional translator. In the event that this is not possible, a trained paraprofessional from the client's culture may serve as a translator or cultural broker. This introduces Dr. Otto's suggestion and Dr. Jones third question: "What are the ethical implications of having Marcia's daughter act as an interpreter for her mother in counseling?"

Although having family members serve as interpreters is a common practice in the medical field (Hamerdinger & Karlin, 2010), it is discouraged within both the medical and mental health field. The sensitive information that must be evaluated for Marcia to benefit from psychotherapy is very likely to be emotionally distressing for her daughter, whose welfare and ability to consent as a minor must be fully considered. There is also the potential that the mother may withhold information due to fear of upsetting her daughter (DeAngelis, 2010). The APA Ethics Code addresses the need to avoid dual relationships when working with translators in Standard 2.05. This is further explicated in the APA Guidelines for Providers of Psychological Services to Ethnic, Linguistic, and Culturally Diverse Populations, which specifically state, "If translation is necessary, psychologists do not retain the services of translators/paraprofessionals that may have a dual role with the client to avoid jeopardizing the validity of evaluation or the effectiveness of intervention." Therefore, in order to protect Marcia, her daughter, and the integrity of the psychological services provided, another translator must be identified.

Given the small size of the Spanish-speaking community within the already small rural community, it is very likely that any members of the local community will have a potential dual relationship with Marcia. Therefore, it will be necessary for Dr. Jones to search for other language interpretation services. Hospitals, learning facilities such as schools or universities, and county courts may have interpreter recommendations. Interpreter services may also be available over the telephone or the Internet, although such services can be very expensive. The National Association for the Deaf has a position statement on interpreter services for mental health (available at https://nad.org/issues/health-care/mental-health-services/position-statement-mental-health-interpreting-services-peo), and Hamerdinger and Karlin (2010) provide helpful guidelines on understanding the minimum competence for interpreters in mental health settings. These are resources that may help Dr. Jones make a final decision about using an interpreter to work with Marcia.

Recommendations

In summary, the most suitable action is for Dr. Jones to access interpreter services and to meet with Marcia. In order to reduce the risk of slipping into unethical behaviors, this action must be supported with other recommended actions.

1. Consult with a supervisor and respected colleagues: given that rural clinicians are more prone to being isolated, it will be important for Dr. Jones to identify mentors and colleagues she can consult. This will include consulting by phone or a Health Insurance Portability and Accountability Act-compliant Internet service and can also include interdisciplinary professionals in her workplace, such as Dr. Otto. It is important to be aware not only of providing competent services to clients, but also of interacting in competent communication with interdisciplinary professionals in the rural setting. Forming close ties with colleagues can provide valuable social support, referral sources, and assistance on ethical dilemmas with clients.

2. Engage in informed consent: when meeting with Marcia and the interpreter, it is important that the client is informed of the counselor's areas of expertise and the role of the interpreter. It will be important to assess that Marcia fully understands and can provide truly informed consent. This process is necessary to set clear expectations for the client so that they are aware of what they are committing to in treatment. This also enables the client to be an active participant in decision-making for their treatment. Finally, if Dr. Jones is expecting to transfer Marcia to another provider when the emergency is resolved or when a Spanish-speaking provider becomes available, it will be important to address that as part of informed consent.

3. Clear documentation: carefully documenting the consultation with other professionals is encouraged as part of appropriate treatment protocol, and also to minimize risk and avoid malpractice liability for the counselor. This consultation should also be disclosed to Marcia during the informed consent process.

4. Assess the impact of treatment: it is always important to assess for client improvement, but this will be particularly critical in working with Marcia. Dr. Jones may need to carefully assess behavioral cues, given the potential for verbal information to be lost in translation. Further, given the seriousness of Marcia's initial concern, it will be important to monitor closely that her condition improves or stabilizes. Particularly if Marcia minimizes her concerns because of the presence of the interpreter, it will be necessary to carefully assess suicidal ideation and thoughts at each meeting.

5. Self-care: in order for psychologists to maintain competence in a rural area, it is also important to practice self-care. Not only does self-care help reduce stress, but it can also assist in maintaining a clear head so the professional does not unknowingly fall into unethical behavior. Practicing self-care can also reduce the propensity for burnout, which can increase in response to the stress of working at the edge of competence.

Maintaining Emotional Competence

Attending to self-care brings up the equally important issue of emotional competence. In addition to being able to demonstrate clinical abilities and judgment, it is imperative that psychologists maintain the ability to self-assess and self-monitor their own emotional strengths and weaknesses (Brennan, 2013; Pope & Vasquez, 2007). Doing so will help to manage the distress that can limit one's ability to perform effectively (Welfel, 2013). In addition to self-care, supportive colleagues and continuing professional development can be instrumental in maintaining emotional competence.

Unfortunately, rural mental health professionals receive less opportunity for continuing education in their rural setting (Helbok, 2003). In accordance with the APA, NASW, and ACA codes of ethics, continuing education is an integral aspect for maintaining and honing the competence of a mental health professional. Although some mental health professionals may be able to easily commute to a bigger city for professional workshops, others may have difficulty taking time off, considering that they may be one of the only mental health professionals in the rural setting. Also, because of the pressure of being an often single provider for an isolated community, rural psychologists may sacrifice the time they have available for professional development and consultation because they know taking that time will limit client contact time. This can inadvertently have the effect of negatively impacting client care because of decreased emotional competence.

Dr. Jones may have to monitor the pressure she feels in response to the question, "If you don't see (them), who will?" Given that the client indicated some risk of suicidal thought and behavior in need of further assessment, there is increased urgency to ensure the client receives prompt and appropriate treatment. The potential suicidal risk adds additional pressure for Dr. Jones to work with the client, especially if referrals are difficult to access.

Assuming responsibility for the well-being of everyone in need in a rural community is accompanied by a level of stress that can increase the risk of burnout and vicarious trauma. An important part of maintaining emotional competence in her new rural surroundings will be to set boundaries on her expectations for herself, as well as to clarify the expectations her colleagues and patients have of her. In addition, it will be important for Dr. Jones to seek out opportunities to stay current through continuing education and professional development opportunities in which she can interact with other psychologists and mental health care providers. This will allow her to check on her own ethical decision-making and minimize the likelihood that she will slip into less ethical behavior through the ethical blind spots that can emerge from isolation and reference only to one's own work environment (Bazerman & Tenbrunsel, 2011).

Multiple Relationships

Although there is the potential for multiple relationships in any professional setting, the issue is magnified in rural communities. The limited number of providers, distance from a major metropolitan area, and distrust of "outsiders" in rural populations all contribute to an increased likelihood of multiple relationships. The following vignette explores one such situation.

The Case of the Small-Town Social

Dr. Jason Young is a licensed psychologist working in a rural community. He grew up in this community and returned following completion of his doctorate because he has a passion for serving in underserved areas. He has been able to navigate multiple relationships to this point by referring people he knows to a mental health provider, Dr. Julie Carlson, in another small town about 30 minutes away. This strategy has been mostly successful and individuals have been willing and able to make the short trip. Through this process, he has developed a professional relationship with Dr. Carlson and occasionally consults with her about other cases.

Dr. Young is suddenly presented with a more complicated situation when Dr. Carlson's partner, Shelly, calls and requests an intake. Dr. Young has casually interacted with Shelly socially in the past and recognizes this would be a dual relationship that needs to be managed. However, he is more concerned that he will learn personal information about his colleague through working with Shelly, and that this might become a conflict for his professional relationship.

Shelly reports that she would like to work on her anxiety and expresses no concern about seeing Dr. Young. She also reports that her partner recommended him and did not identify any discomfort because of the situation. Shelly reported that driving to the next nearest mental health provider three hours away would be prohibitive because it would require her to miss too much work.

Discussion of the Ethical Dilemma and Associated Professional Standards

Dr. Young is aware that he is facing a tenuous situation. He recognizes that if he accepted Shelly as a client he would be entering a multiple relationship, which has the potential to impact his practice. He is also aware that if he doesn't see her, there is a very good chance that she will not receive services. Additionally, he must consider how this relationship could isolate him professionally in the area by limiting his relationship with Dr. Carlson.

The main ethical concern highlighted by this vignette is a potential multiple relationship. Multiple relationships, sometimes called dual relationships, are defined by the APA as interacting with a client in more than one role (APA, 2010). Though this case focuses on multiple relationships between a client and a practitioner, the APA codes also cover relationships between supervisors, supervisees, and colleagues. The APA and the ACA do not forbid multiple relationships, but do state they should be avoided if the relationship will impair objectivity or decrease competence or if there is a risk of harming or exploiting the client. The NASW is also in agreement with the APA and the ACA, in that social workers should avoid exploitation and harm to patients and that dual or multiple relationships with clients or former clients are not inherently unethical (NASW, 2008).

In Dr. Young's case, it would be important to consider how knowing Shelly and her partner might impact his objectivity. He may have preconceived notions about Shelly because of his relationship with Dr. Carlson, or he may have difficulty separating what he knows about Shelly's partner or their relationship from what she reveals in therapy. Dr. Young will have to carefully consider if he would in some way risk harming or exploiting Shelly by agreeing to initiate therapy with her. Finally, Dr. Young needs to consider if his competence may decrease if he chooses to discontinue consulting with Shelly's partner because of this relationship.

It is also important to recall that Dr. Young is living in a small community, and by doing so is inherently more likely to encounter multiple relationships. He is likely to interact with clients on a routine basis if he is active in the community. This is less common in urban settings. Helbok and colleagues (2006) explored the number of occurrences of ethical issues across rural and urban settings. They found that psychologists who work in rural areas encountered significantly more multiple relationship behaviors than did urban psychologists. The study explored various types of multiple relationships. Relationships of a concerning nature, such as entering a romantic relationship with a former client, were consistently low, while some multiple relationships, such as interacting with a client at a party, were surprisingly high across rural and urban settings. Overall, in 19 of 34 scenarios described, rural practitioners were more likely to endorse experiencing a multiple relationship. This study highlights the importance for all practitioners to be aware of potential interactions with clients outside the therapy room and emphasizes the increased risks in rural settings. It also suggests that Dr. Young, who grew up in a rural area and returned by choice, has probably had to learn to manage a range of overlapping relationships in order to continue working and being part of the community.

In addition to considering the potential ethical risks that Dr. Young would be exposing himself to if he does take Shelly on as a client, he must also weigh potential ethical violations if he chooses not to see Shelly. Shelly has identified several ways in which seeing another mental health professional would be a hardship. She stated that the distance she would have to drive to the nearest mental health professional would be prohibitive because of the time it would take away from her job.

Rural areas present challenges for access to services even when multiple relationships are not a factor. The U.S. Department of Health and Human Services identified areas that lacked sufficient mental health care access, and over half of these shortage areas were in rural areas (U.S. DHHS, 2013). These shortage areas commonly cause individuals to forgo seeking services because of the inconvenience and expense of taking time off work to travel, on top of paying for the services (Robinson et al., 2012).

The mental health professional associations call on practitioners to provide appropriate services for those who are seeking help. Specifically, the APA's Principle A speaks of beneficence and nonmaleficence, stating that psychologists are to "strive to benefit those with whom they work and take care to do no harm" (APA, 2010). The language of this principle identifies conflicts that can occur in psychologists' obligations. In this case, a conflict has arisen for Dr. Young because providing care for Shelly, and thus benefiting her, would require him to enter into multiple relation-ships with her. Another principle to note is the APA's Principle E, which calls psychologists to respect the dignity, worth, and rights of all people. One such right is the right of self-determination, which is emphasized by the APA, the NASW, and the ACA. In this case, Shelly is choosing a closer provider and accepting the risks of engaging in multiple relationships. Further discussion of how to ensure that Shelly is making an informed choice about these matters can be found later in this chapter.

Beyond access to care, mental health stigma further complicates seeking mental health care in rural communities. Cultural beliefs that value independence make it difficult for some rural individuals to seek help or even recognize that they need help (Elliot & Larson, 2004). Additionally, in rural communities, noncommunity mem-bers are often distrusted and viewed as "outsiders," reducing the likelihood that some will seek services from a practitioner they see as "disconnected" from a community. In fact, in most rural communities, multiple relationships are seen as "normal," and a practitioner who is visible in the community and has interacted with someone may be a more attractive choice when choosing to disclose mental health issues (Campbell & Gordon, 2003). If Shelly is from the rural area she is currently living in, there is a very good chance that she has internalized some of these values. She may be seeking Dr. Young's services because she is aware of his work through her partner. She may actually view this relationship positively because she has reason to believe he is trustworthy.

Before Dr. Young agrees to begin a therapeutic relationship with Shelly, he needs to fully consider the ethical and therapeutic ramifications of doing so. If he does chose to provide therapy for Shelly, there are some steps he can take to minimize the risks inherently associated with the situation. Lamb, Catanzaro, and Moorman (2004) provide a list of five considerations when contemplating entering multiple relationships. First, Dr. Young needs to consider the context of his work with Shelly. What is the nature of her mental health complaint? Is he likely to find out information about her outside of therapy that could complicate their relationship? Does she have information about him that might impact the relationship? Dr. Young carefully considers his previous interactions with Shelly. He's only interacted with her socially a couple of times, in the context of a larger group. Her partner does not make a habit of discussing her personal life with Jason, so he knows little about her at this point. He himself is generally reserved in social situations and he does not believe he has made any disclosures to her or her partner that would impact her view of him.

Second, Dr. Young needs to consider the history of his social relationship with Shelly. How long have they known each other? Given what he does know about Shelly, what characteristics does she possess that would make her a more or less appropriate candidate for this dual relationship (Lamb, Catanzaro, & Moorman, 2004)? Dr. Young has found Shelly to be pleasant in social situations and has seen her gracefully handle her partner being approached by a client. This leads him to believe she understands boundaries and is able to respect them. He does not know of any traits she possesses that would potentially complicate multiple relationships.

Third, it is important for Dr. Young to consider the status of their current relationship. Do they seem to have rapport (Lamb, Cantanzaro, & Moorman, 2004)? Given his previous interactions with Shelly, limited though they have been, Dr. Young believes building therapeutic rapport would be uncomplicated. Shelly seems to harbor no ill feelings toward him and he believes their previous conversations have been natural and unforced.

Fourth, Dr. Young must consider Shelly's reaction to this situation. Does she seem to have strong emotions about the multiple relationship? Does she appear unconcerned (Lamb, Cantanzaro, & Moorman, 2004)? Shelly did not express any concerns about the relationship, and in fact approached Dr. Young knowing that he had a professional relationship with her partner. This leads Dr. Young to believe she is unconcerned with the situation.

Finally, Dr. Young must consider Shelly's reaction to the boundaries he will set in place. How does she feel about his definition of the roles in their relationship? Does she understand the distinction (Lamb, Cantanzaro, & Moorman, 2004)? Dr. Young has not explicitly had this conversation yet, but he thinks he is ready to. After thinking about his current relationship with Shelly, he feels he is ready to begin laying the groundwork for a therapeutic relationship with her.

Recommendations

Though it may not initially seem to be the case, Dr. Young has several options for handling this referral. When considering the factors above, if he was not comfortable seeing Shelly himself, he may politely decline to see her, citing concerns about multiple relationships. He may also refer her to a tele-health option or he may choose to see her following well-researched recommendations.

Tele-health is a viable alternative for Dr. Young to offer to Shelly. Tele-health is an ever-growing field allowing individuals to access medical and mental health care professionals via two-way video conferencing (Becevic, Boren, Mutrux, Shah, & Banerjee, 2015). Tele-health has been suggested as way to combat service deficits in rural areas (Bischoff, Hollist, Smith, & Flack, 2004). Studies have shown high levels of satisfaction for both the consumers and the providers of tele-health services across disciplines (Becevic et al., 2015; Grubaugh, Cain, Elhai, Patrick, & Frueh, 2008). This is a viable resource for Dr. Young to offer Shelly; it removes the distance barrier, as some services may be accessed from the client's home or another health care setting in their area. This option allows Dr. Young to avoid multiple relationships, while Shelly is still able to access the services she needs.

If, after careful consideration, Dr. Young chooses to counsel Shelly, it is important that he closely monitors the relationship. Campbell and Gordon (2003) offer the following recommendations for professionals who find themselves in multiple relationships in rural communities:

1. Consider the worst-case scenario: considering the worst-case scenario, however unlikely, can be very sobering and put the level of risk around multiple relationships into perspective. For Dr. Young, the worst-case scenario would be a rupture

in his relationship with the only other mental health care provider in the area. This would lead to professional isolation and possible referral issues for his practice.

2. Seek consultation: by seeking consultation, professionals can hold each other accountable for their actions and creatively solve problems (Campbell & Gordon, 2003). This is tricky for Dr. Young because he frequently consults with Shelly's partner about rural issues. So in this instance, Dr. Young calls a colleague from graduate school who he knows is in rural practice in a different part of the country. The other professional agrees that the situation is complicated, and she also suggests that he explore tele-health options in case it becomes apparent that Shelly would benefit more from working with another professional. If Dr. Young does agree to counsel Shelly, but finds he is not providing the highest level of care he is capable of because of their multiple relationships, referring to a tele-health provider is still an option.

3. Maintain clear boundaries in as many areas as possible: without exception, the client's needs must take priority over the needs of the psychologist (Campbell & Gordon, 2003). Dr. Young believes he can achieve this. He is willing to give up attending social events he believes Shelly may be attending and will make it clear to Shelly how he will interact if he does run into her.

4. Maintain confidentiality: this can be difficult in multiple relationships because therapists are likely to get information from multiple sources and must monitor where that information comes from. Campbell and Gordon (2003) recommend mastering "appropriate professional vagueness" to assist with this situation. Dr. Young would want to have a careful conversation with Shelly at the beginning of their work together, outlining how they will interact if they meet in another venue. He and Shelly may also want to discuss his relationship with Dr. Carlson. If Shelly is also aware of the possible complications that this relationship could cause, she and Dr. Young can work together to minimize any negative impact.

5. When possible, terminate the multiple relationship as soon as possible: this may mean providing brief therapeutic interventions, terminating social or business relationships, or otherwise discontinuing extraneous relationships. This should always be done with the client's best interests as the first consideration (Campbell & Gordon, 2003). Because of this, Dr. Young plans to consult with a different colleague about rural issues for the duration of his therapeutic relationship with Shelly, and perhaps even afterward. He is also going to choose a time-limited, empirically supported anxiety treatment for Shelly.

Dr. Young will continue to monitor the situation and consult with colleagues to guard against ethical violations or any potential risks to Shelly as the process progresses. He must carefully monitor any tendency to make decisions that would benefit him over the client. Because of his existing relationship with Dr. Carlson, there is a potential for treatment issues with Shelly to impact the existing referring relationship. Dr. Young must make sure that he is not making treatment decisions based on maintaining his referral relationship. For anyone considering entering multiple relationships, it is important to note the thoughtfulness that went into Dr. Young's decision, including research-supported considerations. Above all else, beneficence and nonmaleficence toward the client must be the final considerations.

Confidentiality

The protection of client privacy and the maintenance of confidentiality are primary obligations of ethical mental health practice (ACA, 2014, Section B; APA, 2010, Standard 4.01; NASW Standard 1.07). Further, psychologists must ensure that clients are aware of potential limits to that confidentiality (Standard 4.02). This is standard across all settings, including rural practice. However, the potential threats to confidentiality may be multiplied in rural communities (Mullin & Stenger, 2013), in which people know everyone in the community and much of their personal business and tend to have numerous overlapping relationships (Werth et al., 2010). As one of the authors of this chapter experienced, when growing up in a small town, "people know what you did on Saturday night by Monday morning, whether it really happened or not."

The Case of I'm So Glad Henry Is Coming to See You

Dr. Ruth Liu is a psychologist in a small, rural satellite office for a comprehensive community health agency. Her branch office is located in a small cluster of retail stores and county offices on the outskirts of a town of about 5000 people. The agency has carefully established all of their satellite offices in fairly nondescript and multi-purpose buildings so that clients can park in areas that do not automatically identify them as seeking agency services. This was done in response to a local analysis that indicated that stigma and reluctance to seek help were key deterrents in accessing services in this region, as is true for many rural areas. As such, the agency's commitment to privacy and confidentiality is particularly emphasized. Dr. Liu is also very careful that in her informed consent process she goes over how to handle contacts out of session and how she herself will protect client confidentiality. Dr. Liu herself lives in a neighboring community and this has helped with the management of multiple relationships and avoidance of out-of-session contacts with clients.

As Dr. Liu is leaving the office one afternoon, she stops at the local florist located in her building. She has developed a casual friendship with the owner, Susan, and they often chat at the end of the day. On this day, Susan says, "Oh, Ruth. I saw my nephew, Henry, leave your office today – I am so happy you are working with him. He really needs some help and I hope he starts to get better soon. He has put my sister through a lot of misery with his drug use. The stories I could tell you – ever since he was a teenager, he has been such a problem."

Discussion of the Ethical Dilemma and Associated Professional Standards

Dr. Liu has an immediate and unexpected ethical dilemma to address in the moment in deciding whether or how to respond to this statement. The primary issue facing her is how to maintain the privacy and promise of confidentiality she has made to her client. There is a tension between that obligation and the rural cultural norm of people being involved in and knowing what others in the community are doing. Dr. Liu cannot reveal any information that would confirm that Henry is or is not a client, and she also wants to respond in a way that is consistent with community norms and does not damage her credibility or trustworthiness as a familiar service provider (Malone, 2010).

In addition to this immediate concern, Dr. Liu now has information about Henry from an external source that she did not anticipate receiving. Although this information was not elicited by her, she does have to think about how she might intentionally or unintentionally use it in her future work with Henry. She also needs to examine the pros and cons of sharing this information with Henry. Factors such as his relationship with his family, the extent to which he has shared his concerns with his family, his openness about seeking therapy, and the amount of information he has shared with Dr. Liu about his drug use history will all need to be considered as Dr. Liu decides how she will proceed with sharing this brief conversation with Henry.

Dr. Liu is also cognizant of the reality that whether or not she talks with Henry about this brief conversation with Susan, it is very possible that Henry will learn about it from a family member. Therefore, she must consider the impact this could have on her relationship with Henry and his perception of her integrity and fidelity to him, and must also consider how to best manage any potential damage that may emerge as an unintended consequence of this conversation.

It is important to acknowledge that this brief exchange is not in any way inherently unethical at this point for Dr. Liu and certainly not for Susan. This is a fairly innocuous comment that brings with it a complicated set of sequelae that Dr. Liu now needs to manage as effectively as possible in the best interests of her client, Henry. It is also likely to contribute to some emotional reactions for Dr. Liu, including anxiety about how to respond and perhaps frustration at having to navigate the situation. This situation may also cause Dr. Liu to feel defensive, both for her client and about her own precautions or strategies for managing confidentiality.

Recommendations

Dr. Liu works in an agency that has carefully attended to confidentiality, and so is likely prepared to address random comments about clients in her rural community. Although this may be a novel situation, in that Susan appears to have direct knowledge of Henry's status as a client, Dr. Liu needs to proceed as she would in any similar situation and avoid saying anything that would reveal she has a professional relationship with Henry.

1. Be prepared with deflection strategies: Dr. Liu may feign ignorance of Henry's identity and/or relationship by stating something like, "Oh, people stop in for lots of reasons, to pick up flyers and make donations for community events. I'm

not sure what would have brought your nephew in." She might also opt for a standard response to all such incidents, such as, "Susan, I'm not sure if your nephew came in or not, but you probably know that I never talk about my work outside of my office." Dr. Liu might also try to redirect the conversation quickly to another topic and avoid responding directly, which could work well in some situations. However, that tactic could be risky in this particular situation. The natural thing to focus on in Susan's statement might be to express sympathy about her sister, and that would most likely result in Susan sharing substantially more information about Henry. It could also increase the difficulty that Dr. Liu will have disengaging from this conversation, given Susan's comment about stories to tell. If she changed the topic to something completely unrelated – say a flower display in the shop – this might create feelings of suspicion or distrust for Susan; in this small community, that could have implications for Dr. Liu's credibility. Given the tension between confidentiality as a matter of professional integrity and community pressure (Malone, 2010), Dr. Liu needs to consider this approach carefully.

2. Avoid extending the sharing of information: whether directly or indirectly, it would be very easy for Dr. Liu to give the impression that she is willing to hear more from Susan. It will be important to self-monitor that she does not seek additional information about Henry, even if it might be therapeutically useful. In this and future conversations with Susan, Dr. Liu will want to minimize the possibility of discussing Susan's sister or even her family more generally. It may even become necessary to limit her contact with Susan overall. However, this is the kind of dual relationship that of necessity must be managed in rural communities, because it is almost impossible to avoid. In addition to the immediate conversation, Dr. Liu will also want to be careful not to imply that information is welcome at another time or via another format. If, for example, Susan were to follow-up with a telephone or email conversation about Henry, Dr. Liu will need to have a response ready to deter that communication. Alternatively, she may want to talk with Henry about the incoming information and how it can be useful, or not useful, in their work together.

3. Be transparent with the client: as soon as feasible, Dr. Liu will want to tell Henry about this exchange with his aunt. The amount of detail she shares, such as the specific comments his aunt made or any affective expression connected to those comments, will necessarily be influenced by clinical judgment about the potential risk to Henry. However, sharing that the conversation occurred and that Henry's aunt did notice him leaving the office will be important. It may also be important to let Henry know that his aunt specifically mentioned drug abuse. If this is new information for Dr. Liu, she will want to consider carefully how to communicate this to Henry in a supportive and nonjudgmental way, but letting him know that she has this information will be important to demonstrating respect for him. Dr. Liu will also need to be prepared for Henry to deny the drug use if this has not been addressed previously in therapy. This conversation could have implications for the therapeutic relationship, and Dr. Liu needs to consider in advance how she might respond regardless of Henry's reaction.

4. Examine strategies for preventing future similar circumstances: Dr. Liu and her agency are already employing a number of strategies to protect client confidentiality. They use a shared parking lot and are co-located with other types of offices and the waiting room does not have any windows to the outside or to shared interior spaces. It may be possible to provide separate doors for entrance and exit after sessions, and it may also be useful to examine whether specific unintentional threats to confidentiality can be more fully covered during the informed consent process. However, there really is no way to ensure that clients are not seen entering or exiting a therapist's office. It is also important not to emphasize privacy to the point of implying secrecy or that shame is a reasonable feeling to have about seeking psychological services. Particularly given that stigma can already play a role in limiting help-seeking behavior among rural citizens, it is also important to communicate that seeing a psychologist is no more disgraceful than seeing a primary care provider at the local clinic.

Privacy for the Psychologist

Although there are no particular ethical obligations related to the privacy needs of psychologists, the public role and awareness of psychologists in rural communities are important to recognize as key contextual factors related to rural practice. Health care professionals are easily identifiable in rural communities, and if they live in those communities, they are often expected to be involved in the social activities and welfare of the larger community (Campbell & Gordon, 2003). Community members may therefore hold high expectations for the personal behaviors of psychologists, and knowledge of their personal lives or the lives of their family members can influence local perceptions of their professional integrity and credibility.

The Case of It Could Happen to Anyone

Dr. Richard Sosa has been practicing psychology in a mid-sized rural community with an approximate population of 10 000 for slightly over 20 years. He moved to the area, which is his wife's hometown, and opened a small practice right after getting licensed. Over time, he hired another psychologist and two mental health counselors, and his agency now serves individuals and families from counties throughout the northeastern quadrant of the state. Because there are multiple providers in the agency, Dr. Sosa has been able to avoid working with people with whom he has substantial or close relationships in the community, and he has also been able to strike a good balance between providing services and being an active member of the community. In fact, he was recently elected to the City Council and has been recognized as a key contributor to the recent efforts to establish a health center in town that would serve all of the lower-income youth in the county.

Dr. Sosa is also an active member of the local high school athletic booster club, where his daughter, Rebecca, is a star varsity volleyball player. The local paper has featured her as MVP several times, and Dr. Sosa is regularly congratulated on her accomplishments. Two weeks before regional playoffs – a major event in this small town – Rebecca is caught drinking after school. She is immediately suspended from the volleyball team, and the hopes the team had to travel to the state tournament for the second consecutive year plummet. The news of Rebecca's suspension travels quickly through the local and surrounding schools. Dr. Sosa and his wife discipline Rebecca privately, and he continues to fulfill his duties as a booster parent for the team.

Two separate clients mention Rebecca in the following week. The first is a young father, Paul, who, at the end of their session, says, "Sorry about Rebecca, Doc. You know, that kind of thing can happen to anyone. It's nothing for you to feel bad about." Dr. Sosa replies, a bit surprised and awkwardly, "Ah, thanks, yeah, she's really upset about it," and the session ends. The second client, Suzanne, is a young woman who recently graduated from the same high school as Rebecca and who has been working with Dr. Sosa on substance abuse issues. She starts the session with a comment about Rebecca and then says, "Well, I'm not sure what good it's doing me to talk to you – your own daughter is as messed up as I am."

Discussion of the Ethical Dilemma and Associated Professional Standards

Dr. Sosa has not engaged in any unethical behavior, and certainly his daughter's actions are not a reflection of his professional abilities or ethics. However, in a small town, it is inevitable that most, if not all, of the people who know him as a professional will also know about this (not so) private incident. Although the situation has not emerged because of any ethically difficult circumstances, Dr. Sosa's response to it does involve careful ethical decision-making.

This situation highlights an important area in which ethics codes are often insufficient for rural providers. Professional ethical standards are designed to apply only to the behaviors of an individual in their professional role. However, it might be quite challenging for Dr. Sosa to identify where his professional role ends, given that everyone in town knows him and knows what he does. He could have made the choice to be less visible in the community, and that would theoretically have limited the implications of this situation. However, that could have meant compromising involvement with his family, his own identity as a citizen, or his contributions to the community. Further, being underinvolved in a rural community can limit one's credibility as a caring professional. It is also entirely possible that one of the contributors to his success as a citizen is the respect people have for his profession, such that being a psychologist cannot be fully separated from his role as a City Council Member. The tension between personal autonomy and professional nonmaleficence is central to this dilemma.

In the first exchange, one of Dr. Sosa's clients is essentially expressing sympathy for him. This brings up the question of whether the client's best interests were being served and also introduces some potentially important transference into the session. Dr. Sosa will first need to consider the extent to which this specific session might have been influenced by his external personal factors and identify whether any unintentional harm or lack of benefit may have influenced his work with Paul. He will also want to consider the possibility that Paul is reacting to him as a father of an adolescent, which he himself expects to be, and the impact that this may have on their therapeutic relationship. It will certainly be important for Dr. Sosa to consider whether and/or how he wants to address this subject in an upcoming session, as the timing and unexpected nature of this particular statement did not allow him to assess the impact his personal situation may be having on Paul.

In the second exchange, Dr. Sosa's personal life is being used as a gauge of his professional competency and may diminish the trust his client has in their therapeutic relationship. Depending on Suzanne's relationship with her own father or parents, it is entirely possible that her response represents transference of her own feelings. It will be important for Dr. Sosa to self-assess his reactions for countertransference. This is particularly significant given the fairly close age of his daughter and his client. It is worth noting that mental health care providers in small communities are often placed in situations where they provide services to clients who are known to their children or other family members. Although Dr. Sosa could perhaps have referred Suzanne to one of his colleagues, it is equally possible that he had the least likelihood for dual relationships of anyone in the practice.

Recommendations

In response to the first exchange, Dr. Sosa will benefit from engaging in some self-reflection about whether he might have unwittingly solicited feelings of sympathy. The second exchange highlights the potential for other clients to transfer their concerns about parenting, family issues, or worries about their children onto him.

1. In order to maintain the appropriate focus on client progress and well-being, Dr. Sosa will want to prepare for the variety of ways in which people might evaluate his credibility differently in light of this family event. This preparation will help him be ready to keep the focus on therapeutically relevant issues and stay nondefensive and poised if the topic comes up.
2. For Paul and Suzanne, specifically, Dr. Sosa will want to plan carefully for upcoming sessions to allow the opportunity to discuss this issue further, while being careful not to spend more time on it than would be useful for the clients. These strategies may also be helpful for other clients who broach the subject of Rebecca and her difficulties, either directly or indirectly.
3. It is also important to note that this event is likely distressing to Dr. Sosa, and so assessing his emotional competence is an appropriate action at this time. This is particularly salient if he is working with adolescents or parents of adolescents who might be experiencing parallel issues to himself and Rebecca. Further, the distress for Rebecca could be greater because her father is such a public figure, and being a psychologist's child in a small town may already carry some difficult expectations. In this instance, self-care and caring for his family may be important aspects of maintaining professional competence.

Conclusion

Rural psychologists must deal with the same kinds of ethical dilemmas as nonrural psychologists, and they are held to the same standards of ethicality in their practice. The ways in which they apply those ethics and respond to dilemmas may need to differ somewhat in order to accommodate the realities of rural life. Rather than avoiding or preventing common issues such as dual relationships, rural psychologists need to develop multiple strategies to manage them. The overlapping relationships inherent in rural life complicate the ability to preserve confidentiality and privacy, but they also provide means for psychologists to come to a deeper understanding of how to protect these important principles. Competence must be both broad and deep in order to meet the varied demands of an underserved and isolated population. Clearly, there are challenges in rural practice, but the rewards of providing psychological services to these high-need and drastically underserved communities are also compelling and congruent with the ethical principles of beneficence and justice.

References

American Counseling Association (2014). American Counseling Association code of ethics. Retrieved from www.counseling.org/resources/aca-code-of-ethics.pdf

American Psychological Association (2002). APA guidelines on multicultural education, training, research, practice and organizational change for psychologists. Retrieved from www.apa.org/pi/oema/resources/policy/multicultural-guidelines.aspx

American Psychological Association (2010). American Psychological Association ethical principles of psychologists and code of conduct, including 2010 amendments. Retrieved from www.apa.org/ethics/code/index.aspx

Andren, K., McKibbin, C. L., Wykes, T. L., Lee, A. A., Carrico, C. P., & Bourassa, K. A. (2013). Depression treatment among rural older adults: Preferences and factors influencing future service use. *Clinical Gerontologist: The Journal of Aging and Mental Health, 36,* 241–259.

Barber, J. P., Sharpless, B. A., Klostermann, S., & McCarthy, K. S. (2007). Assessing intervention competence and its relation to therapy outcome: A selected review derived from the outcome literature. *Professional Psychology: Research and Practice, 38,* 493–500.

Bazerman, M. H. & Tenbrunsel, A. E. (2011). *Blind spots.* Princeton, NJ: Princeton University Press.

Becevic, M., Boren, S., Mutrux, R., Shah, Z., & Banerjee, S. (2015). User satisfaction with telehealth: Study of patients, providers, and coordinators. *The Health Care Manager, 34,* 337–349.

Bischoff, R. J., Hollist, C. S., Smith, C. W., & Flack, P. (2004). Addressing the mental health needs of the rural underserved: Findings from a multiple case study of a behavioral telehealth project. *Contemporary Family Therapy: An International Journal, 26,* 179–198.

Brennan, C. (2013). Ensuring ethical practice: Guidelines for mental health counselors in private practice. *Journal of Mental Health Counseling, 35,* 245–261.

Campbell, C. D. & Gordon, M. C. (2003). Acknowledging the inevitable: Understanding multiple relationships in rural practice. *Professional Psychology: Research and Practice, 34,* 430–434.

DeAngelis, T. (2010). Found in translation, *Monitor on Psychology*, *41*(2), 52. Retrieved from www.apa.org/monitor/2010/02/translation.aspx

Duncan, A. (2013). The new narrative of rural education: Remarks of the U.S. Secretary of Education Arne Duncan to the Ohio Department of Education and Battelle for Kids Rural Education National Forum. Retrieved from www.ed.gov/news/speeches/new-narrative-rural-education

Elliott, B. A. & Larson, J. T. (2004). Adolescents in mid-sized and rural communities: Foregone care, perceived barriers, and risk factors. *Journal of Adolescent Health*, *35*, 303–309.

Fontanella, C. A., Hiance-Steelesmith, D. L., Phillips, G. S., et al. (2015). Widening rural–urban disparities in youth suicides, United States, 1996–2010. *JAMA Pediatrics*, *169*, 466–473.

Gillespie, J. & Redivo, R. (2012). Personal–professional boundary issues in the satisfaction of rural clinicians recruited from within the community: Findings from an exploratory study. *The Australian Journal of Rural Health*, *20*, 35–39.

Greenfield, P. M. (2013). The changing psychology of culture from 1800 through 2000. *Psychological Science*, *24*, 1722–1731.

Grubaugh, A. L., Cain, G. D., Elhai, J. D., Patrick, S. L., & Frueh, B. C. (2008). Attitudes toward medical and mental health care delivered via telehealth applications among rural and urban primary care patients. *Journal of Nervous and Mental Disease*, *196*, 166–170.

Hamerdinger, S. & Karlin, B. (2010). Therapy using interpreters: Questions on the use of interpreters in therapeutic setting for monolingual therapists. Retrieved from www .mh.alabama.gov/downloads/MIDS/DS70703_TherapyUsingInterpreters QuestionsUseInterpretersTherapeuticSettingsMonolingualTherapists.pdf

Helbok, C. M. (2003). The practice of psychology in rural communities: Potential ethical dilemmas. *Ethics Behavior*, *13*, 367–384.

Helbok, C. M., Marinelli, R. P., & Walls, R. T. (2006). National survey of ethical practices across rural and urban communities. *Professional Psychology: Research and Practice*, *37*, 36–44.

Juntunen, C. L. & Quincer, M. A. (2017). Underserved rural communities: Challenges and opportunities for improved practice. In J. M. Casas, L. A. Suzuki, C. M. Alexander, & M. A. Jackson (Eds.), *Handbook of multicultural counseling* (4th edn.) (pp. 447–456). Thousand Oaks, CA: Sage Publications.

Kitayama, S., Conway, L., Pietromonaco, P. R., Park, H., & Plaut, V. C. (2010). Ethos of independence across regions in the United States: The production–adoption model of cultural change. *American Psychologist*, *65*, 559–574.

Lamb, D. H., Catanzaro, S. J., & Moorman, A. S. (2004). A preliminary look at how psychologists identify, evaluate, and proceed when faced with possible multiple relationship dilemmas. *Professional Psychology: Research and Practice*, *35*, 248–254.

Malone, J. L. (2010). Reflections of a rural practitioner. *Canadian Journal of Counselling and Psychotherapy*, *44*, 438–440.

Malone, J. L. (2011). Professional practice out of the urban context: Defining Canadian rural psychology. *Canadian Psychology*, *52*, 289–295.

Malone, J. L. & Dyck, K. G. (2011). Professional ethics in rural and northern Canadian psychology. *Canadian Psychology*, *52*, 206–214.

Mullin, D. & Stenger, J. (2013). Ethical matters in rural integrated primary care settings. *Families, Systems, & Health*, *31*, 69–74.

National Association of Social Workers (2008). Code of ethics of the National Association of Social Workers. Retrieved from www.socialworkers.org/About/Ethics/Code-of-Ethics/Code-of-Ethics-English

Osborn, A. (2012). Juggling personal life and professionalism: Ethical implications for rural school psychologists. *Psychology in the Schools*, *49*, 876–882.

Robinson, W., Springer, P. R., Bischoff, R., et al. (2012). Rural experiences with mental illness: Through the eyes of patients and their families. *Families, Systems, & Health*, *30*, 308–321.

Schank, J. A., Helbok, C. M., Haldeman, D. C., & Gallardo, M. E. (2010). Challenges and benefits of ethical small-community practice. *Professional Psychology: Research and Practice*, *41*, 502–510.

Schank, J. (1998). Ethical issues in rural counselling practice. *Canadian Journal of Counselling*, *32*, 270–283.

Schank, J. A. & Skovholt, T. M. (2006). *Ethical practice in small communities: Challenges and rewards for psychologists*. Washington, DC: American Psychological Association.

Smalley, K. B., Yancey, C. T., Warren, J., Naufel, K., Ryan, R., & Pugh, J. (2010). Rural mental health and psychological treatment: A review for practitioners. *Journal of Clinical Psychology*, *66*, 479–489.

United States Bureau of the Census (2012). 2010 census urban and rural classification and urban area criteria. Retrieved from www.census.gov/geo/reference/ua/urban-rural-2010.html

United States Department of Agriculture (2013). Rural–urban continuum codes. Retrieved from www.ers.usda.gov/data-products/rural-urban-continuum-codes/.aspx#.Up9vKuL4Lwc

United States Department of Health and Human Services (2013). Designated health professional shortage area statistics. Retrieved from http://ersrs.hrsa.gov/ReportServer/Pages/ReportViewer.aspx?/HGDW_Reports/BCD_HPSA/BCD_HPSA_SCR50_Smry_HTML

Welfel, E. R. (2013). *Ethics in counseling and psychotherapy* (5th edn.). Belmont, CA: Brooks/Cole.

Werth, J. J., Hastings, S. L., & Riding-Malon, R. (2010). Ethical challenges of practicing in rural areas. *Journal of Clinical Psychology*, *66*, 537–548.

6 Ethics and Private Practice

Jean A. Carter

Psychologists whose professional lives revolve around providing treatment, most commonly psychotherapy, exist in a world filled with ambiguity and uncertainty. Psychotherapy occurs in the context of complex, multifaceted, and frequently shifting relationships and requires continual decisions with often-unclear parameters. Professional ethics offer guidance for decision-making in these nuanced situations and provide grounding when there are compelling but competing courses of action that a psychologist might take (Barnett, Zimmerman, & Walfish, 2014; Bennett, Bricklin, Harris, Knapp, VandeCreek, & Younggren, 2006). The need to make ethically complex decisions occurs frequently, rather than rarely, and clinicians face ethical uncertainties often (Barnett, Behnke, Rosenthal, & Koocher, 2007). While ethical challenges occur for all psychologists, some are more common to psychological practice than they are to other applications of psychology (Pope, Tabachnik, & Keith-Spiegel, 1987; Pope & Vetter, 1992). In addition, there are challenges of particular natures or characteristics that arise more frequently in specific settings or practice opportunities.[1] Although private practice itself does not create more or more significant ethical dilemmas, it creates particular dilemmas that relate to the nature and characteristics of the setting itself.

This chapter addresses some of the ethical challenges that occur with greater frequency in a private practice setting that are specifically related to the characteristics of private practice itself. I will begin with a discussion of the characteristics of private practice that are directly related to this discussion of ethical concerns.

Characteristics of Private Practice

The psychologist in private practice has a big responsibility. She[2] is responsible professionally, financially, and personally for the policies, procedures, and implementation of all aspects of her work. The responsibility for the viability and operation of the business is on her shoulders, as well as the client's and her

---

[1] Although there are numerous settings in which psychological practice occurs, as well as types of practice that can occur within any practice setting, for the purposes of this chapter I refer to private practice as the setting and psychotherapy as the predominant and modal activity. This setting is also understood to mean that the psychologists are self-employed, rather than employed by an agency or organization.

[2] Throughout this chapter, for simplicity of language, I will use the terms "he" and "she" alternately to refer to a psychologist of any gender.

well-being. The primary characteristics that differentiate this kind and setting for practice from other kinds of practice are the *sole professional responsibility*, the *sole financial/business responsibility*, and the *sole responsibility for personal and professional needs and self-care*. While these do not in themselves create higher levels of ethical conflict, each of these heightens the potential for *certain kinds* of ethical challenges. Psychologists are required by the Ethical Principles of Psychologists and Code of Conduct to "strive to benefit . . . and . . . do no harm" (APA, 2010, p. 3), and at the same time be "alert to and guard against *personal* [or] *financial* . . . factors that might lead to misuse of their influence" (p. 3, emphasis added). The inherent tension between the commitment to clients' well-being and the need to maintain a viable business is easy to see. At the same time, other tensions occur around professional and personal responsibility. Such aspects of private practice as fee setting and financial policies, legal and financial contracts with clients and payers, licensure concerns, hiring of staff or other support services, etc., play a role in the concerns that are the focus of this chapter, but I have chosen to emphasize three categories of ethical concern: professional responsibility, financial and business responsibility, and personal and professional needs and self-care.

Responsibility and Competence: It Is All Up to You

Psychologists practice independent of supervision by other professionals and are licensed for practice under their own decision-making authority and their own control. They bear responsibility for the work. Licensure rests on an assumption that the psychologist is competent to provide general psychological services. While essential, this is only a start. Issues of competence arise throughout treatment and at every stage of a psychologist's career, beginning with accepting referrals (or not), making referrals, engaging in and ending treatment appropriately, knowing when to seek additional training or consultation, and balancing clinical decisions with the financial decisions that are required to maintain a business. The individual psychologist is responsible for the treatment itself, oversight of it, and her own professional behavior, including recognizing the boundaries and limits of her competence and the need for continuing professional development and lifelong learning.

The Case of Dr. Crowell and Mr. M

Psychologist John Crowell received a call from Mr. M, a 60-year-old man who was feeling depressed. He had recently started a new job that he was finding quite stressful and wanted to start psychotherapy as soon as possible. He wanted to come before his workday began; to Dr. Crowell's delight, the time matched an opening that Dr. Crowell wanted to fill. Without further discussion, they scheduled the appointment.

At the first of several appointments, Mr. M focused on his work and how challenging he found his boss, who was demanding and difficult. Dr. Crowell, who typically used an insight-oriented approach, explored family history and potential similarities between the boss and Mr. M's also-demanding father. Mr. M had been in psychotherapy with another psychologist, which he said was helpful, but he wanted neither to continue with that psychotherapist nor to allow Dr. Crowell to consult with her. Although Dr. Crowell knew the other psychologist well, he respected the client's wishes. Without a signed release, he also did not have the authority to break the client's confidentiality.

Mr. M continued exploring his family dynamics, and reported beginning to feel some relief. At the same time, however, he began sometimes missing sessions, cancelling at the last minute, sometimes as late as the start time for the session, stating he was not feeling well or "needing to save his energy for a long workday." Exploring the misses was not very productive, although Mr. M's mother's frequently "took to her room in the evening with headaches," which were reminiscent of his frequent low energy and apparent poor health. Dr. Crowell was increasingly curious about the health connection when Mr. M's wife left a voicemail alerting Dr. Crowell to "find out more about his illness." Dr. Crowell was confused by this message. Mr. M also professed to be confused, but he declined to give permission to Dr. Crowell to talk to his wife or to the previous therapist. At the same time, Mr. M was reporting more difficulty with his boss and more conflict with his wife.

Dr. Crowell was concerned about the treatment and suspicious about the early morning misses. Mr. M's insight and improvements in mood seemed to have stalled, although when he came to sessions, he expressed great relief at having Dr. Crowell to talk to.

At a professional conference the next weekend, Dr. Crowell saw the previous therapist and they began to chat about their work. He was tempted to ask the other therapist about her treatment of Mr. M and what she knew about the mysterious illness. He questioned whether the information he might gain, and the possible benefit to Mr. M, would be worth the risks of breaking confidentiality without a release. He considered calling Mrs. M to follow up, and asked himself the same question.

After the conference, which focused on substance abuse – a subject he knew very little about – he had a sudden insight that perhaps Mr. M was an alcoholic who missed his early morning sessions because he was hungover. Mr. M cancelled the following appointment and never returned. Dr. Crowell was unable to reach Mr. M and worried about what he thought of the treatment.

Dr. Crowell continued to wonder about his recent insight and considered calling the previous psychotherapist to discuss the possibility and find out what the other psychotherapist knew. He also realized that, although Mr. M had indicated that he was no longer in treatment with the other psychotherapist, he did not know the nature of the ending; given that Mr. M had left treatment with no defined termination, could that have been the case with the earlier treatment as well? Had he been treating someone who might also be in psychotherapy with another psychologist? He also became concerned that any future psychotherapist who might wish to see Mr. M's records to assist in psychotherapy would judge Dr. Crowell harshly if he had indeed missed possible alcoholism, and he considered inserting comments through the records to cover that.

Understanding Dr. Crowell and Mr. M

The case of Mr. M presents multiple ethical complexities that Dr. Crowell had to navigate. These complexities revolve primarily around Standards 2: Competence; 3: Human Relations; 4: Privacy and Confidentiality; 6: Record Keeping and Fees; and 10: Therapy.

Every time a call comes in from a potential client, the psychologist faces his own competence in treating the problems presented by this particular client; questions of competence are addressed in Standard 2 of the APA Ethics Code (APA, 2010). What do you need to know in order to know if you have the necessary knowledge and skills to treat this person? Can you find those things out before you start treatment, and if not, when and how do you gain what you need in order to provide effective treatment?

Dr. Crowell had very little information about Mr. M when he agreed to the treatment, knowing only that he was depressed and stressed by work. Without more information, Dr. Crowell faced a continual risk in psychotherapy – you do not know yet what you do not know. All psychotherapists face this limitation, which is described in Standard 2.01: Boundaries of Competence, in which psychologists are required to provide services only within their own areas of competence. Although we are licensed for general practice, each of us is obligated to understand the scope of our own competence to provide care, including the knowledge and skills that are relevant to the treatment at hand (Barnett, Doll, Younggren, & Rubin, 2007). Recognizing which referrals are appropriate to accept is an essential skill for ethical practice, as is knowing when and how to send referrals to another, more appropriate practitioner when needed and how to terminate treatment when it is not the appropriate course for a particular client (Bennett et al., 2006). Accepting referrals that we are not adequately prepared to treat because it is outside our areas of competence becomes a potential violation of Standard 2.01.

In private practice, however, there are important nuances to the risk, and it is an ongoing discussion among psychologists in private practice. Gaining sufficient information to be able to make a good decision about the services needed and/or the client characteristics may not be possible in a contact prior to setting up an initial appointment or, frequently, even in early assessments that may take more than one session. How many sessions are appropriate for this assessment and for the concomitant client assessment of the psychotherapist? Should it be the client's responsibility to pay for services that they ultimately will not use? Do the ethical standards require that the psychologist makes the financial commitment of time spent (in economic terms, the opportunity cost) or that the client makes the financial commitment for those services? The investment of time and money by both psychologist and client is potentially significant before the psychologist can make a truly informed decision about competence to treat this client. Private practitioners are also business owners, however, and time and expertise are the stock in trade for practitioners. If the process of accepting a referral is too time-consuming or onerous, the practitioner simply cannot proceed with a successful business.

Dr. Crowell was confronted with another concern around competence, which included Boundaries of Competence (Standard 2.01) and Maintaining Competence (Standard 2.03). He had not received training in alcoholism and substance abuse and therefore did not know what he needed to ask or be aware of. His training, and ongoing practice, was in insight-oriented psychotherapy, and he was diligently applying that model to his work with Mr. M, but without building additional expertise, he may not have been able to assess the additional emphasis that Mr. M may have required. To his credit, Dr. Crowell was in the process of adding to his expertise. His thought of adding to notes in Mr. M's health record as self-protection against the impact of his lack of expertise is a violation of Standard 6.01, Documentation of Professional and Scientific Work and Maintenance of Records, which requires that the record accurately represents the work being done. In private practice, it is the individual psychologist's responsibility to keep abreast of developing areas of knowledge and practice, including maintaining and expanding competence as one of his ethical and professional responsibilities.

It is essential for practitioners to know their areas of competence, as well as to have some understanding of those areas in which they do *not* have the needed training and experience. They continue to hone their skills at diagnosis, assessment, and treatment planning so that they are less likely to be caught off guard by unexpected client problems and risk inappropriate or ineffective treatment. Competence for effective treatment decisions, including emphasis, frequency, and modality, as well as referrals are the responsibility of the treating psychotherapist, and the psychologist's skills must be maintained and expanded in response to the needs of clients and to developments in both the science and practice of psychology. Standard 2.03, while simply stated as "Psychologists undertake ongoing efforts to develop and maintain their competence," is a most essential ethical underpinning to private practice. Since most jurisdictions require continuing education intended to maintain competence for licensure, this is an ethical, a legal, and a professional responsibility for all licensed psychologists. As with the potential financial conflict with incorporating a sufficient assessment period before beginning treatment, the (literal) costs of maintaining and increasing competence rest entirely with the private practitioner and may compete directly with income-producing activities. Recognizing the importance – and ethical imperative – of maintaining competence helps provide the impetus to devote the resources to continuing education.

Barnett et al. (2014) emphasize self-awareness and self-assessment as key to recognizing our own competence and the ongoing responsibilities that rest with those of us in practice. The APA's statement on evidence-based practice in psychology (APA, 2006) included self-reflection as a part of clinical expertise for this very reason. However, self-awareness and self-reflection are limited by the impact of the individual blinders and biases that we all have. They may be moderated by the inclusion of other perspectives and ideas, which can come in the form of consultations and other sources of feedback. For psychologists in private practice, however, those valuable additional perspectives present some particular challenges, which Dr. Crowell was facing in his treatment of Mr. M.

Privacy and confidentiality are cornerstones of ethical practice. Although Principle B of the APA ethical principles promotes "Psychologists consult[ing] with, refer[ring] to, or cooperat[ing] with other professionals and institutions to the extent needed to serve the best interests of those with whom they work," privacy and confidentiality are preeminent. Standards 3: Human Relations and 4: Privacy and Confidentiality provide additional guidance on the relationship between a private practitioner's need for consultation and the preeminent need to respect confidentiality. As Standard 4.01 states, "Psychologists have a primary obligation . . . to protect confidential information. . ." While Standard 4.05 permits disclosure for professional consultation reasons, the client's right to trust in the privacy and confidentiality of what s/he shares with a psychotherapist is an essential component of the therapeutic relationship. This right to the psychotherapist's trustworthiness and to privacy created a challenge for Dr. Crowell. Mr. M was unwilling to sign a release to allow Dr. Crowell to consult with the previous psychotherapist; Standards 3.09: Cooperation with Other Professionals, 4.05: Disclosures, and 4.06: Consultations reflect the conflict that Dr. Crowell faced. He wished to have the benefit of the other psychotherapist's experience with this particular client through a consultation, which could have been quite valuable. Yet without consent to disclose confidential information, he would have violated both Standards 4.05 and 4.06. Particularly in small communities, this can interfere with the private practitioner seeking regular and ongoing consultation, which might have helped Dr. Crowell recognize the potential alcohol abuse earlier in the treatment. Although the limitations that confidentiality concerns raise can affect any treatment, it can be particularly problematic in private practice, in which there are no automatically and perhaps not simply accessible resources for consultation. Professional consultation is an activity that is unpaid, and in fact often bears a cost, which can present a conflict of interest for the psychologist, for whom time is money and for whom the opportunity for independence, autonomy, self-direction, and responsibility may be paramount.

Standard 10: Therapy includes several standards that are relevant to Dr. Crowell's decision, including Standard 10.04: Providing Therapy to Those Served by Others and Standard 10.10: Terminating Therapy. In reviewing the history of this treatment, it appears that Dr. Crowell was unsure whether Mr. M had in fact terminated his treatment with the previous therapist. The ending of psychotherapy may not be as clear and definitive as we would like it to be. In private practice, in which the point of termination may be mutually agreed upon or created by either client or psychotherapist, endings may be less defined. Clients may trail off, come occasionally, or may simply not return, as Mr. M did. While it is helpful and appropriate to ". . .provide pretermination counseling and suggest alternative service providers as appropriate" (APA, 2010, p. 14), a client who does not return makes this impossible. In private practice, in which clients contract and pay for services, their control over the end of treatment is substantial, particularly as private practitioners worry about both abandoning clients and the impact on their financial stability. In addition, since referrals for new clients frequently come from current or former clients who were pleased with the work, a client who simply stops coming or leaves without a proper termination is a source of anxiety for the psychologist. This may lead to concerns like those expressed by Dr. Crowell, who considered contacting Mr. M to try to resume treatment.

The challenges that Dr. Crowell faced demonstrate complex decisions that can be viewed in a variety of ways and as ethical decision points, but not as strictly or clearly ethical violations. This is common in private practice. *Summarizing some of the key factors that are faced in private practice:*

- Psychotherapy in private practice is performed alone, which can lead to loneliness and isolation. While psychotherapy itself can be lonely, psychologists in private practice may not have ready access to colleagues with whom they can share their work.
- Guidance, feedback, and consultation are up to the psychologist himself to find; psychotherapy relies on self-reflection and self-observation to determine what is needed. Decision-making demands include both immediate, in-the-moment responsiveness and choices made through observation, consideration, and thought.
- Responsibility for emergencies rests solely with the psychologist in private practice. Confidentiality and privacy are paramount concerns that must be considered in any arrangement for backup services.
- Boundaries for the treatment and potentially difficult multiple relationships, as well as client privacy, limit the extent to which private practitioners can share their work for both personal and professional reasons. These concerns affect the practitioner on a daily basis, as he needs to be continually alert to the potential to expose clients' confidential concerns through casual conversation with fellow professionals, friends, or family.

Finances: You Own the Business

Significantly, in private practice, the psychologist who provides the treatment also operates a small business. The business remains viable based on fees paid directly by or for clients for services and on the psychologist's ability to provide those services. Private practitioners' financial success rests on maintaining their client load and on being paid by those clients for services. Financial advancement comes only as clients pay higher fees or as clinicians increase their numbers of hours. The financial motive is an inevitable presence in the room. These financial concerns can lead to various risks, including: keeping clients longer than services are truly effective and needed; overprescribing treatment, including adjunctive services; extending the boundaries of competence through accepting referrals for which one is not qualified; and setting and enforcing policies around fees and missed sessions that are in the psychologist's, but not necessarily the client's, best interests. The client–psychologist relationship is both therapeutic and always based on the business owner and customer relationship, which can create inherent multiple relationships and conflicts of interest, with the potential for very complex and challenging outcomes.

The Case of Dr. Adams and Her Maternity Leave

Dr. Suzanne Adams completed her PhD five years ago and she has been licensed for four years. She joined an established group practice at about the same time that she got married and bought a home. Her practice was building slowly but steadily. Her income was sufficient to make payments on her remaining student loans and the costs of regular living while maintaining a practice, although there was little remaining for unusual expenses. She was excited when she became pregnant, but felt gradually building worry about what would happen to her practice and her income during her anticipated maternity leave. Her office expenses, including rent, utilities, phone, and liability insurance, had to be paid even though she would not be working during the leave.

Dr. Adams began processing her upcoming leave with current clients. All of her clients were sorry to see her go for the leave, although of course they understood it. Some of her clients decided they had achieved their desired goals and that this was an appropriate time to stop treatment. Others accepted referrals to other therapists for either emergency or ongoing treatment during her leave, while also expressing their intent to continue their psychotherapy with Dr. Adams on her return.

While Dr. Adams was away, she did not hear from her clients. Although she did not expect to speak with them, she found herself becoming concerned that they might not need her. She felt anxious because her expenses were not insignificant, and she needed these clients to return. She worried that perhaps she should have planned a shorter leave, but was also worried that a shorter leave would have shortchanged herself and her baby. She imagined it would be difficult to pay careful attention to her clients' feelings when she might be preoccupied with her baby. By six months, however, she felt ready to return. She missed her work and her clients, and financially she had reached her limit. As she was preparing to return, she contacted the clients she had been seeing and left messages for them, asking that they call to schedule an appointment to continue psychotherapy.

Marjorie had been in psychotherapy with Dr. Adams for about six months and was one of Dr. Adams favorite clients. She had been depressed about a breakup and had been working on understanding how it related to her mother's death when she was a child. It was difficult for Marjorie to say goodbye to Dr. Adams because it reminded her of her mother and of her recent relationship ending. Dr. Adams gave her a referral to a trusted colleague to see during her six-month absence. They planned to meet on the first Monday after Dr. Adams' return. Dr. Adams left a message for Marjorie reminding her of the meeting time, but Marjorie did not come for the appointment. She did not respond to Dr. Adams' call or email offering time to reschedule. Dr. Adams was unsure how best to proceed, particularly because Marjorie had never missed an appointment even when she had been ill. Had something happened to Marjorie? The release that Marjorie had signed for the two psychotherapists to communicate with each other had expired at six months, just before the point where she was now debating a call to the colleague. Would calling her colleague be a breach of confidentiality? How would she feel if Marjorie did not return? She was counting on her as a reliable cornerstone of her rebuilding practice.

David, a client of Dr. Adams' for over a year, was very dependent, always anxious, and would turn to Dr. Adams for her steadying presence when making decisions for himself. She was helping him trust his own judgment about what he needed and to speak up on his own behalf. He had been doing well in the psychotherapy, but had continued to rely on her, as his anxiety became higher during times of greater stress. Dr. Adams provided the name of a colleague who would be available in case of emergency, although David was pretty sure that what they had already accomplished would help him through the six months until her return. David did not call the colleague, and he did not call Dr. Adams for an appointment as he had said he would. Dr. Adams was puzzled and concerned.

Janelle had been in psychotherapy with Dr. Adams for nine months when Dr. Adams left for her maternity leave. She had been making progress on her difficulties with assertiveness, although it had been slow in the last few months. She accepted a referral to another psychologist for the duration of the leave and expected to return. Dr. Adams contacted Janelle and scheduled an appointment for her return. Janelle arrived for the appointment, but instead of beginning by processing the previous six months as a prelude to the ongoing work on assertiveness, she announced that she had found the other psychotherapy very helpful. She was practicing her assertiveness by making this her final session with Dr. Adams and would return to the new psychotherapist to continue their work. Dr. Adams herself felt increasingly anxious at this latest development in her practice.

Dr. Adams felt worried about the three clients who would not return. The loss was significant to the health of her practice and to her income. As she felt her anxiety rising, she debated what to do. Should she continue trying to reach Marjorie and David? She realized she did not know whether Marjorie had seen her colleague. Dr. Adams was worried about Marjorie, but she was just as worried about how she would pay her expenses. She had budgeted for six months off of work, but these clients not returning to her practice was a significant financial blow. She was angry with them and angry with the other psychologist who would continue with Janelle. She wanted the three clients to return because she really needed the income to pay her bills. At this point, she found that she almost did not care why they had not returned. She began calling them frequently, almost begging them to call her.

Dr. Adams felt considerable anxiety about the financial demands of maintaining her practice, particularly with the uncertainty of her caseload as she was rebuilding it. She considered changing her policies around billing, cancellations, and missed appointments and considered raising fees across the board so that she would have less uncertainty about payments from her clients. She was part of several insurance panels, which paid lower than her desired fee, and she began to consider leaving the panels, which would increase her fees through increasing the payments of clients on those insurance plans. She hired a consultant to provide guidance on how to build businesses, who suggested a variety of ways to advertise her practice, including asking some former clients to provide testimonials. A few clients had built up larger balances or left psychotherapy without paying their final bills, and she considered contracting with a collections agency to get payment from those clients. She determined to use a billing service to increase her income.

Understanding Dr. Adams and Her Maternity Leave

Business practices and financial well-being are inextricably linked in private practice. The ability of the psychologist to maintain a business and provide financial support for her own life depends on her success as a small business owner. This creates ongoing multiple relationships that are unavoidable: the psychotherapist needs to be committed to the well-being of the client and the businessperson needs to be committed to her own financial well-being. While these may be complementary and not inherently harmful, the potential for ethical conflict is obvious and requires careful and thoughtful navigation (Barnett & Walfish, 2011). The general ethical principles offer guidance here.

The general ethical principles of the APA Ethics Code are aspirational. "Their intent is to guide and inspire psychologists toward the very highest ethical ideals of the profession" (APA, 2010, p. 3). As such, they provide a framework for decision-making in situations where conflict is frequent or even inevitable, as in the multiple relationships that occur between client/customer and psychologist/business owner. While the general principles of the Code capture the essential complexities that the business owner faces, specific sections of the Code amplify the principles with specific guidance.

Principle A: Beneficence and Nonmaleficence emphasizes the extent to which the activities of psychologists should focus on benefiting those with whom they work and being careful to do no harm and safeguard the rights of those with whom they work. Psychologists are cautioned to guard against finances (as well as other factors) leading to misuse of their role. Since a financial relationship is inevitably intertwined with the professional relationship in private practice, it is also inevitable that conflicts will occur (Barnett & Walfish, 2011). Principle B: Fidelity and Responsibility calls on psychologists to serve their clients' best interests, which may at times conflict with the psychologist's best interest, particularly financially or in business policies. In addition, Principle B calls on psychologists to contribute professional time without compensation or advantage. Yet, when it is only through performing the professional activities during that professional time that psychologists earn an income, and earning that income has direct costs as well (like rent and utilities), there is an immediate conflict with a direct impact on the psychologist's life. Finally, Principle E: Respect for People's Rights and Dignity is notable because it includes the right to self-determination, which, in the case of Dr. Adams, applies to her clients' right to decide whether to return to psychotherapy with her after her leave, including changing their minds about prior agreements to return.

In the case of Dr. Adams' maternity leave, there are a number of ways in which conflicts between her life as a small business owner intersect with her life as a psychotherapist. Aspects of the role of businessperson are primarily addressed in Standard 3: Human Relations, Standard 5: Advertising and Other Public Statements, Standard 6: Record Keeping and Fees, and Standard 10: Therapy. It is striking, however, how little recognition there is in the Ethics Code (APA, 2010) of this aspect of psychological practice, which carries such high potential for ethical complexity and ethical dilemmas. Additionally, although financial policies and practices have this high potential for ethical dilemmas and pitfalls, they are largely viewed as an aspect of business (and thus a trade or guild issue). Little attention may be paid to their significant role in the realities of psychological practice, the risks private practitioners face, and the needed guidance that helps practitioners avoid pitfalls that are not just financial or business in nature. These pitfalls can have real and dramatic impacts on how psychotherapy unfolds and on the needs of both clients and practitioners in that unfolding.

Standard 3: Human Relations, 3.01 Unfair Discrimination includes unfair discrimination based on socioeconomic status, which is of particular importance for a psychologist in private practice trying to maintain a successful business. Although we do not know about the resources or socioeconomic status of Marjorie, David, or Janelle, we do know that Dr. Adams was considering leaving insurance panels, which could have had a financial impact on her clients and potentially placing psychotherapy outside of their reach. This could even lead to termination of their ongoing psychotherapy if they were unable to afford the fees that Dr. Adams was considering instituting. While termination based on inability to pay for services is addressed in a later code (6.04 Fees and Financial Arrangements), none of the principles or codes address how to handle potential fee increases because of the psychologist's financial need, and, in light of Principle B's (Fidelity and Responsibility) expectation for providing services for little or no compensation, terminating services because a client cannot pay more might be addressed as a conflict of interest and an ethical concern. Similar issues arise if a client loses a job, changes insurance coverage, gets divorced, returns to school, or faces other life changes.

Standards 2.06 Personal Problems and Conflicts, 3.05 Avoiding Harm, and 3.06 Conflict of Interest are also obviously implicated in the case of Dr. Adams. While she was carefully attending to continuity of care through referral and backup resources (Avoiding Harm), Marjorie, David, and Janelle's decisions not to return to psychotherapy with her revealed the risks that personal problems and conflicts of interest raise in private practice. According to 3.06 Conflict of Interest, "Psychologists refrain from taking on a professional role … when financial … interests or relationships could be expected to (1) impair their objectivity, competence, or effectiveness…" (APA 2010, p. 6). When Dr. Adams took on the role of psychotherapist in private practice, she did not predict the conflict that arose; there is little guidance about how to deal with changes in either client or psychologist financial situations. Nor did she recognize the challenge her anxiety about her caseload would present. Conflicts occur frequently, however, as clients' and psychologists' financial and personal situations shift, presenting ethical dilemmas around faithfulness and fidelity (Principle B), fees and financial arrangements (6.04), interruption of therapy (10.09), and terminating therapy (10.10). Code 6.05, which describes when and how bartering for services might occur, may also come into play. As an example, a client chooses to leave a job, thereby losing insurance coverage, to launch a career as an artist at the same time that a psychologist is furnishing her office. Is it appropriate to accept a painting as payment for services? How are relative values determined? What might be the effect on the relationship, and are there privacy concerns if another patient admires the painting and wants to know the artist?

Dr. Adams faced another significant area of potential ethical concern as she considered how to rebuild her practice after her leave. Participating in insurance panels or not is a business/financial decision that also has implications for clients. A decision to leave a panel while continuing to provide psychotherapy for a client who relies on that insurer to pay for the services changes the agreement around fees and financial arrangements (6.04), which requires that psychologists and clients agree on compensation and billing arrangements early in treatment. Although these clients did not have outstanding bills, the use of collections agencies or small claims court to recover unpaid fees presents a similar challenge in which business arrangements that are an expectable part of the operation of a business are not easily reconciled with the confidentiality, fidelity, and trust on which psychotherapy is based.

Another area of concern for Dr. Adams as she rebuilt her business was how to advertise or promote the business while being both honest about her services (5.01 Avoidance of False or Deceptive Statements) and not misusing clients through the use of testimonials (5.05 Testimonials), as her consultant suggested. This is another example of the ways in which standard business procedures and the business aspects of private practice need to be carefully balanced.

Obviously, business-related concerns are wide-ranging and complex for a psychologist in private practice. The psychotherapy relationship includes both business/financial and professional aspects, and the conflicting interests in how the roles and responsibilities are resolved can be substantial. Additionally, when a psychologist's financial well-being is compromised (as Dr. Adams experienced), her objectivity and equanimity can be difficult to maintain. She then needs to take particular care to minimize harm (3.04 Avoiding Harm) and to be judicious and careful around possible exploitation (3.08 Exploitative Relationships).

Summarizing some of the key factors in the implications of being a businessperson and a psychologist in private practice:

- Psychologists in private practice must take great care as they face continuing and dynamic tensions between altruism (which draws most of us into psychotherapy) and the realities of running a business in which clients pay the psychologist directly for time and expertise.
- Business practices, including insurance billing, advertising, use of support services, and collections, must be approached in a responsible and thoughtful way, as they constitute legal agreements and activities that also have clinical and personal implications for both clients and psychologists.
- Psychologists entering private practice should assume there are ethical implications of the business aspects of their practice and should be proactively thoughtful both in how the practices are established and in how financial changes will affect business and clinical decisions from a standpoint of ethics.
- Training programs and continuing education programs that focus on the intersection of business and professional ethics are an important part of ongoing professional success for a psychologist in private practice.

It Is Up to You: Responsibility and Self-Care

Private practitioners work alone, which has a number of implications for the kinds of issues that require careful self-monitoring. Although clients are in the room with them, clients need to be able to rely on the psychologists to provide their best services and should not be responsible for monitoring the psychologist. While the need for self-observation is important for all psychologist practitioners, there are particular concerns for psychologists in private practice. In private practice, it is up to the individual practitioner to take proper steps to maintain their self-care (including their health and well-being) and their effectiveness (including maintaining and developing their skills). Without ongoing opportunities for feedback from others, including the kinds of casual observations colleagues provide each other, the private practitioner herself bears the responsibility for the self-reflection and self-awareness that offer insight into potential problems. This includes attending to negative health concerns and challenging personal situations, coping with difficulties, and performing self-care to enhance well-being through proactive strategies for prevention. It also includes attention to and awareness of gaps in one's skills and the changing state of knowledge about factors that influence treatment and the development of new approaches that maintain effectiveness. The case of Dr. Crowell demonstrated the potential for the deleterious impact on Mr. M that occurred when he had not advanced his own knowledge of alcohol and substance abuse and did not have the opportunity for input from other practitioners. Importantly, the case of Dr. Adams demonstrated the intersection of financial and business matters with clinical practice. The case of Dr. Baker below will demonstrate the impact of health and well-being/ self-care for the private practitioner as it also intersects with both financial and business matters and clinical work.

The Case of Dr. Baker's Health

Psychologist Dr. Alice Baker has had a busy private practice for 35 years. She works alone in her solo office. The clients she sees are often quite troubled, with significant histories of attachment trauma. The psychotherapy is typically intense, relationally demanding, focused more on relationships than on particular target behaviors, and often quite long-term. The psychotherapist needs to be particularly emotionally attuned and available, alert to relational shifts and the interplay between past and present through sharp recall of historic and current events, and Dr. Baker is known for this attunement. She relies on her excellent memory and keen responsiveness, things both she and her clients count on.

Recently, Dr. Baker's energy has been flagging, and she is tiring more than usual. As she prepares for work in the morning, she finds herself not looking forward to the day, which is unusual. Her malaise is unspecific and elusive. Dr. Baker chalks it up to aging, although at 63, Dr. Baker did not feel herself to be anywhere near old. Despite that, she thinks of cutting back in her practice, perhaps even retiring, and this worries her. Financially, she is not ready to retire, and cutting back on her practice would make it difficult to manage her office expenses, as well as the expenses of daily living. Besides, she is important to her clients, and they are not ready for her to leave practice; what would they do without her?

Dr. Baker continues working, but she finds gaps in her usually sharp memory. On several occasions over as many months, she has double-booked appointments, having neglected to write them into her schedule. She has unusual trouble recalling details of previous sessions and mistakes details of one client's life for another. She is unsettled, but she hopes she is doing a good enough job attending to her clients.

After some months like this, Dr. Baker visits her doctor, concerned at her increasing fatigue and problems with both memory and attention. To her surprise, she is diagnosed with a benign tumor that affects her ability to function effectively and will require surgery. The surgeon will not be available for two months, during which time the symptoms are likely to increase. Dr. Baker schedules the surgery and hopes she will be able to manage until then. After all, her clients need her, and she does not want to abandon them. Of course, she also needs the income to pay her bills, but she is just as concerned about the lengthy time she will be unavailable to her clients if she stops work at this point, even temporarily. She deliberates which option is worse: abandoning her clients or remaining available but with increasing limitations on her ability to provide the kind of meaningful therapeutic relationship that they have come to expect. Should she take a medical leave until surgery and for the duration of her recovery? Can she wait out the two months while gradually diminishing in her functioning? What will happen to her clients and to her practice?

Dr. Baker decides to consult with a trusted colleague, who understands her work and may have useful insight into the potential impact on her clients. She has not asked her clients for confidentiality releases, so she is reluctant to give details about them, although she knows it would be more helpful to her colleague and to her if she was able to do so. As she tells her colleague about her diagnosis and projected treatment, and the impact her health is having on her work, he expresses surprise and concern. He then challenges her ability in ethical practice, citing the limitations it imposes on her ability to be responsive and available to her clients. What should she do?

Understanding Dr. Baker and the Impact of Her Health

The ability to be consistently available for clients is an important component of success in private practice, and the kind of self-care that maintains the psychologist's health and well-being is essential to that consistency (Baker, 2003). Self-observation and self-monitoring provide necessary but often insufficient guidance in achieving the careful balance between what the psychologist and the patient need (Barnett & Cooper, 2009). While some of the specific standards are helpful in making decisions in this arena, the aspirational principles are perhaps of even greater utility.

As previously noted, the general ethical principles provide guidance in how to live up to ethical ideals and decision-making in complex situations, such as the one faced by Dr. Baker. Principle A: Beneficence and Nonmaleficence states that "Psychologists strive to be aware of the possible effect of their own physical and mental health on their ability to help those with whom they work." Obviously, we are all subject to life and health circumstances that can affect our well-being (either physical or mental). When our well-being is compromised, however, the impact on clients can be significant and far-reaching, although it will vary based on the extent and the nature of the compromise. For Dr. Baker, the prospect of gradually increasing limitations on her ability to be available and responsive to her clients was troubling. She was trying to find a balance between her own health and well-being (and business/financial needs) and the needs of her clients, but was finding it difficult to determine the tipping point (Johnson & Barnett, 2011). Principle B: Fidelity and Responsibility also emphasizes the importance of trust in the relationship and responsibility for one's own behavior. It also emphasizes consultation as appropriate to assist in serving the best interests of the client. Dr. Baker faced the dilemma as she sought consultation, as Principle B calls for, with maintaining the clients' privacy and confidentiality as called for in Principle E: Respect for People's Rights and Dignity. In addition, "psychologists recognize that fairness and justice entitle all persons to . . . equal quality in the processes, procedures and services being conducted by psychologists" (APA, 2010, Principle D: Justice, p. 3). Dr. Baker's health was compromising her ability to offer the quality of services that her clients were accustomed to and, in fact, both she and her colleague believed they deserved.

When a psychologist is in private practice, the potential impact of aging and attendant decline, more acute health concerns, or personal or social problems are large and complex, as they may have subtle effects that can be difficult to detect or may leave clients confused and uncertain, potentially intersecting with issues such as shame or guilt in ways that compromise the integrity of the psychotherapy or of their growth. It is challenging when one is responsible to and for clients to decide when personal needs supersede client needs, and there is an inherent conflict when impairment or even proactive self-care, like vacation, impedes business while the requirements of business continue (e.g., office costs). Standard 3.06 Conflict of Interest ("Psychologists refrain from taking on a professional role when personal . . . or other interests or relationships could reasonably be expected to (1) impair their objectivity, competence or effectiveness in performing their functions as psychologists or (2) expose the person or organization to whom the professional relationship exists to harm or exploitation" [APA, 2010, p. 6]) also addresses this concern. What Dr. Baker was experiencing, however, was an evolving situation within the context of ongoing relationships.

Standard 2.06 Personal Problems and Conflicts (APA, 2010) addresses Dr. Baker's situation directly, as it states that:

(a) Psychologists refrain from initiating an activity when they know or should know that there is a substantial likelihood that their personal problems will prevent them from performing their work-related activities in a competent manner.

(b) When psychologists become aware of personal problems that may interfere with their performing work-related duties adequately, they take appropriate measures, such as obtaining professional consultation or assistance, and determine whether they should limit, suspend, or terminate their work-related duties (see also Standard 10.10 Terminating Therapy) (APA, 2010, p. 5).

While this standard indeed addresses Dr. Baker's situation directly, it relies on adequacy of self-observation and self-reflection in predicting when personal limitations will present a problem or in knowing when a line has been crossed. In addition to Standard 2.06, Standard 3.04 Avoiding Harm (APA, 2010) bears on Dr. Baker's decision-making, as it calls on psychologists to take steps to minimize and to avoid harm to clients. This standard references harm that is foreseeable and unavoidable. While ongoing self-monitoring is an invaluable part of living up to these ethical standards, it is not always easy to foresee or to avoid difficulties in this area effectively. Without fellow practitioners or other staff with whom one interacts on a regular basis, there may be no one who has the responsibility or depth of knowledge to raise concerns as the Ethics Code calls for in Standard 1: Resolving Ethical Issues (APA, 2010). Additionally, most of us are not experienced in raising those concerns with our colleagues or in making decisions about how to proceed once a concern is raised (O'Connor, 2001).

As Dr. Baker considered how to proceed as she was facing her declining health and the challenge from her colleague, she could turn to Standard 3.12 Interruption of Psychological Services (APA, 2010) to guide her in the ethics of a "plan for facilitating services in the event that psychological services are interrupted by factors such as the psychologist's illness, death..." (p. 7). Alternatively, she could consider Standard 10.10 Terminating Therapy if it became clear that continuing work while her health was failing was harming her clients. For a psychologist like Dr. Baker, however, whose psychotherapy was depth-oriented and attachment-based, interrupting or terminating psychotherapy were decisions that were very difficult to make.

Although the case presented with Dr. Baker focused on a developing health concern, it is also easy to see the importance of self-care and maintaining one's health and well-being for ethical practice. When a psychologist pays careful attention to her own health, she is less likely to find herself in the complex situation of developing problems and can more readily predict and manage her own health. This would suggest the importance of preventive physical and mental health initiatives and careful attention to the health and strength of one's relationships as essential aspects of ethical behavior for psychologists in private practice.

While this section has emphasized health and well-being, the same concepts apply to maintaining competence: Standard 2.03 calls on psychologists to continue in their efforts to build their competence and to ensure that their knowledge is up to date. This is also a version of professional self-care that is an essential responsibility that rests with the individual private practitioner. While most states require continuing education to maintain licensure, the continuous and lifelong learning that continuing education requirements reflect is important for supporting one's professional competence, as well as engaging in ethically responsible treatment. A major challenge faced by all psychologists – but particularly by those who may be isolated in private practice – is taking the personal responsibility of self-monitoring for gaps in one's knowledge, skills, and expertise and devoting the necessary resources to maintaining competence.

Summarizing some of the key factors in the implications of the psychologist as solely responsible for all professional aspects of her career:

- A psychologist in private practice must engage in continuing and deliberate monitoring of her own health, both psychological and physical, as health concerns can have wide-ranging effects on psychotherapy and other psychological interventions and on ethical practice.
- Although private practice is performed alone, it is very helpful to build relationships with colleagues who can offer consultation, observations, and feedback, as self-monitoring is necessarily limited.
- Continuing education and ongoing professional development is a professional, legal, and ethical responsibility to enhance the ability of psychologists in private practice to maintain competence. Although the resources required to do this (both time and money) compete directly with other income-producing activities, the long-term impact is essential.

Conclusion

Like other psychologists, psychologists in private practice derive a strong sense of personal accomplishment and reward from their work. In private practice, however, the sense of accomplishment, the resulting self-esteem, and, importantly, even the ability to support yourself rests directly on success in providing services to clients and on payments from clients for those services. When your full career is in private practice, your professional satisfaction derives from doing what is right because it is the right thing to do and it benefits the clients, but also because it is of personal and financial benefit to you. Difficult choices and ethically challenging decisions are necessary at many points throughout the course of psychotherapy. The private practitioner must demonstrate the good moral character described by virtue ethics, including prudence, integrity, compassion, respectfulness, and trustworthiness (Anderson & Kitchener, 1998; Meara, Schmidt, & Day, 1996). At the same time complex situations arise that may not be so easily resolved by being of good virtue. Conflicts, such as those shown in this chapter, are not so easily resolved when what is right for the client may be clouded or in conflict with what is right for the psychotherapist.

Although this chapter presented three case examples, each of which contained several ethically difficult components, there are a number of other such components that are frequent in practice of all sorts, and some that would become evident in these cases if they were presented in more depth. For example, when considering the case of Dr. Crowell more deeply, complex issues around confidentiality, consultation, and ongoing education arise. Although continuing education is typically a state requirement, meeting that legal minimum does not capture the importance of remaining current in the developing literature and ensuring that both the time and the money are spent to do so. When the case of Dr. Adams is addressed in greater detail, ethical and legal concerns around fee-setting, missed session policies, and contracting with insurance companies become central themes. Barnett, Zimmerman, and Walfish (2014) offer a valuable guide to some of these ethically and legally difficult questions. The case of Dr. Baker raises significant concerns about abandonment and termination and responsibilities for self-care, as addressed in greater detail, for example, by Younggren and Gottlieb (2008) and Baker (2003).

Several Final Recommendations

1. Ethical quandaries and complexities occur daily. The frequency and nature of ethical challenges do not necessarily map neatly onto the specific standards provided in the ethics codes (e.g., Pipes, Holstein, & Aguirre, 2005) or ethical digressions or complaints that are reported by state or national ethics complaint bodies (Wierzbicki, Siderits, & Kuchan, 2012). It is essential for psychologists in private practice to maintain a continually roving attention to ethical challenges, particularly as they are raised in the aspirational principles of APA's code.
2. Financial aspects of private practice are not separable from professional aspects of the practice, and financial management and case management intersect (Barnett, Zimmerman, & Walfish, 2014). The psychologist in private practice must maintain a watchful eye on the conflicts of interest and multiple relationship aspects of being both a psychotherapist and a business owner in order to avoid those aspects of the endeavor becoming harmful (Gottlieb & Younggren, 2009).
3. Psychologists in private practice should devote time, energy, and resources to ongoing professional consultation and skills/knowledge development. That can assist the psychologist with maintaining competence, as required by the ethics code, but it also engages the kinds of resources that can be helpful sources of feedback.
4. As a private practitioner, it is extremely important to attend to issues of psychological, relational, and physical health and well-being. It is easy to delay vacations or medical care when they conflict with income-producing activities, but an essential part of the commitment to the professionalism of the work is to respect the role of self-care in ethical practice.

References

American Psychological Association (2010). *Ethical principles of psychologists and code of conduct*. Retrieved from www.apa.org/ethics

APA Presidential Task Force on Evidence-Based Practice (2006). Evidence-based practice in psychology. *American Psychologist, 61*, 271–285.

Anderson, S. K. & Kitchener, K. S. (1998). Nonsexual posttherapy relationships: A conceptual framework to assess ethical risks. *Professional Psychology: Research and Practice, 29*, 91–99.

Baker, E. K. (2003). *Caring for ourselves: A therapist's guide to personal and professional well-being*. Washington, DC: American Psychological Association.

Barnett, J. D., Behnke, S. B., Rosenthal, S. L., & Koocher G. P. (2007). In case of ethical dilemma, break glass: Commentary on ethical decision making in practice. *Professional Psychology: Research and Practice, 38*, 7–12.

Barnett, J. E. & Cooper, N. (2009). Creating a culture of self-care. *Clinical Psychology: Science and Practice, 16*, 16–20.

Barnett, J. E. & Walfish, S. (2011). *Billing and collecting for your mental health practice: Effective strategies and ethical practice*. Washington, DC: APA Books.

Barnett, J. D., Zimmerman, J., & Walfish, S. (2014). *The ethics of private practice: A practical guide for mental health clinicians*. New York, NY: Oxford.

Barnett, J. E., Doll, B., Younggren, J. N., & Rubin, N. J. (2007). Clinical competence for practicing psychologists: Clearly a work in progress. *Professional Psychology: Research and Practice, 38*, 510–517.

Bennett, B. E., Bricklin, P. M., Harris, E., Knapp, S., VandeCreek, L., & Younggren, J. N. (2006). *Assessing and managing risk in psychological practice: An individualized approach*. Rockville, MD: The Trust.

Gottlieb, M. C. & Younggren, J. N. (2009). Is there a slippery slope? Considerations regarding multiple relationships and risk management. *Professional Psychology: Research and Practice, 40*, 564–571.

Johnson, W. B. & Barnett, J. E. (2011). Preventing problems of professional competence in the face of life-threatening illness. *Professional Psychology: Research and Practice, 42*, 285–293.

Meara, N., Schmidt, L., & Day, J. D. (1996). Principles and virtue: A foundation for ethical decisions, policies and character. *The Counseling Psychologist, 24*, 4–77.

O'Connor, M. F. (2001). On the etiology and effective management of professional distress and impairment among psychologists. *Professional Psychology: Research and Practice, 32*, 345–350.

Pipes, R. B., Holstein, J. E., & Aguirre, M. G. (2005). Examining the personal–professional distinction: Ethics codes and the difficulty of drawing a boundary. *American Psychologist, 60*, 325–334.

Pope, K. S., Tabachnik, B. G., & Keith-Spiegel, P. (1987). Ethics of practice: The beliefs and behaviors of psychologists as therapists. *American Psychologist, 42*, 993–1006.

Pope, K. S. & Vetter, V. A. (1992). Ethical dilemmas encountered by members of the American Psychological Association. *American Psychologist, 47*, 397–411.

Wierzbicki, M., Siderits, M. A., & Kuchan, A. M. (2012). Ethical questions addressed by a state psychological association. *Professional Psychology: Research and Practice, 43*, 80–85.

Younggren, J. N. & Gottlieb, M. C. (2008). Termination and abandonment: History, risk, and risk management. *Professional Psychology: Research and Practice, 39*, 498–504.

7 Ethics on the Edge: Working with Clients Who Are Persistently Suicidal

Derek Truscott

To save a man's life against his will is the same as killing him.

Horace

As I entered the outpatient clinic upon returning from my lunch break, the receptionist stood up nervously and beckoned me over. In hushed, conspiratorial tones she informed me that a group of noon-hour joggers had come upon a young man sitting on the edge of a bridge railing. They called the police, who brought him to us.

Midway through my year-long doctoral internship in clinical psychology, I was comfortable with psychiatric emergencies and the general demands of mental health care delivery. I did not know what challenges this new client would present, but was confident I could figure out what to do. I walked into our waiting area where Brad[1] was looking absently at the floor, flanked by two police officers. I introduced myself, thanked the officers, and confirmed that all necessary paperwork had been completed. They left and I ushered Brad into my office.

Over the next few sessions, Brad told me how he perched on bridges "almost every week." He said that it "just sort of happens" and denied that he particularly wanted to kill himself. He said it was more that he was puzzled by the fact that for most people their life is just an accident of being alive. The immediacy of the possibility of falling to his death fascinated him in "an intellectual sort of way" by bringing the choice to live or die sharply into focus.

I, on the other hand, became quite beside myself with worry that I would be unable to prevent Brad from killing himself. It was obvious to me that such a dramatic threat of ultimate harm required a correspondingly dramatic response and that I should know what to do. The fact that I did not left me frantic. I read everything I could get my hands on and tried one therapeutic intervention after another, seeking desperately to find a way to pull Brad away from death. I was afraid that my supervisor and colleagues would realize the extent of my incompetence and so I withheld from them the seriousness of the risk. This hampered their efforts to advise me and worsened my isolation. During my daily commute to the clinic, I began to daydream about being terminated from my internship after Brad killed himself and what other career I might pursue when I was forced to leave psychology.

---

[1] The case studies presented in this chapter are amalgamations of actual clinical cases and all names are pseudonyms.

Our situation reached its climax when I got a telephone call from Brad, who had never called me before. As usual, he was calm and rational. Unusually, he told me he intended to jump off a particular bridge. I asked why he wanted to. He was noncommittal. I asked him what I could do to help. He said there was nothing anyone needed to do. I encouraged him to come and talk with me in my office straight away. He declined, said goodbye, and hung up.

I was in a state of panic and could think of nothing to do except to call the police. They agreed to have a patrol car drive by the bridge and see if he was there. He was, and they brought him to our clinic. I had an unsettling experience of déjà vu as two police officers brought him into our waiting room. This time, however, Brad responded to my questions with a silent hostility that he had never shown before. He offered no explanation as to why he had decided to jump or why he had called me. It was obvious that he no longer saw me as his ally.

Our sessions continued, but Brad's attendance became sporadic, his mood apathetic, our conversations shallow. He did not offer to tell me about visiting bridges and would change the subject if asked. When I finished my rotation a month later, I referred Brad to another therapist. I told her about his suicide risk, but did not elaborate on his fascination with death or how frightened and ineffective I felt. My relief over no longer having to deal with Brad was spoiled by the nagging feeling that I had avoided disaster through sheer luck and guilt that I had not handled his case at all well.

Near the end of my internship, Brad's new therapist stopped me in the hallway to tell me that Brad had died from a drug overdose. His death was ruled a suicide by the coroner, but my colleague did not agree. Brad had been engaging in increasingly high-risk behaviors, including sexual promiscuity and drug use (this was when AIDS was new and untreatable), while continuing to deny any distress. My colleague felt sure that Brad was naive to the risks of his actions and overdosed accidentally.

I was stunned. I made my way across the hospital grounds to the office of my supervisor. I told him the news and that I felt I had failed Brad. I confessed how I had not told the therapist who took over Brad's care that his risky behavior was in fact intended to bring him close to death. I said I was sure that my fear of being exposed as a fraud had prevented me from seeking appropriate guidance or making a proper referral. I said he might still be alive if I had been more honest with myself and my colleagues about feeling so out of my depth. I began to cry and expressed my embarrassment. Thirty years later, all I remember my supervisor saying in that meeting is, "You should only feel embarrassed if you ever don't cry when a client dies."

Psychologists face few situations that give rise to as much concern as suicide. When a client expresses suicidal intent, we typically feel a range of negative emotions, including anxiety, powerlessness, self-doubt, and anger (Reeve & Mintz, 2001). When a client actually takes their own life, most of us feel some combination of shock, grief, guilt, worry, shame, betrayal, disbelief, and resentment (Hendin, Lipschitz, Maltsberger, Haas, & Wynecoop, 2000). The experience is stressful at best, with common responses being increased vigilance for signs of suicidal intent and avoidance of suicidal clients, and career-threatening at worst, whereby we consider changing professions (Ellis & Patel, 2012).

These concerns are not due to inexperience, however. As many as 90 percent of patients seen in emergency settings for psychiatric reasons report suicidal ideation (Healy, Barry, Blow, Welsh, & Milner, 2006), with 40 percent reporting active ideation and 20 percent a current plan (Encrenaz et al., 2012; Zisook, Goff, Sledge, & Shuchter, 1994). Of those who attempt suicide, about 50 percent sought mental health treatment in the previous year (Han, Compton, Gfroerer, & McKeon, 2014; Pagura, Fotti, Katz, & Sareen, 2009; Stanley, Hom, & Joiner, 2015), with 30 percent of those who kill themselves having received mental health services during the year prior to their deaths and as many as 20 percent within the last month (Booth & Owens, 2000; Luoma, Martin, & Pearson, 2002).

Given such high rates of suicidal ideation, intention, and behavior among those to whom we provide services, it is no surprise that almost all psychologists (i.e., 97 percent) report providing care to at least one client who is suicidal (and often several) before even finishing their professional training (Kleespies, Penk, & Forsyth, 1993). Indeed, with one in four psychologists losing a client to suicide at some point during their careers, it has even been dubbed an "occupational hazard" (Chemtob, Bauer, Hamada, Pelowski, & Muraoka, 1989).

Psychologists are not alone in being concerned about suicide. The belief that suicide is wrong (for various reasons) and that society has a responsibility to prevent it has historically been the norm. The unacceptable nature of suicide is perhaps best evidenced by the fact that ending one's life was for a very long time a criminal offence in most societies. Indeed, it is only in relatively recent times that suicide has been decriminalized in many countries, and it remains a crime in some countries (Leenaars et al., 2002).

Despite this trend among policy-makers, there are those – including psychologists – who maintain that suicide is inherently wrong and that we are obligated to prevent people from ending their own lives. Many who hold such a belief justify it on religious grounds (McCormack, Clifford, & Conroy, 2012). Faith-based arguments are usually some version of the assertion that life is a gift from God and it is an affront to His omniscience for mere mortals to decide when our lives are no longer worth living.

Of course, many secular individuals also feel that suicide is wrong. They tend to argue that taking one's own life has profoundly negative effects on family, friends, community, and society. In fact, research has shown that the family and friends of people who have killed themselves do often experience rather profound physical and psychological problems after the death (Cerel, Jordan, & Duberstein, 2008; Shields, Kavanagh, & Russo, 2015; Sveen & Walby, 2008). Thus, the argument goes, the person who ends his or her pain by suicide causes pain for others, which makes their action immoral. Also usually implied but not stated is that because we have obligations to others, we have a duty to protect our own lives in order that we might continue to be of service.

Sometimes psychologists will defend their feeling that they ought to prevent a client from ending their life by highlighting that those who survive a suicide attempt usually report relief that they failed – a secular version of the "perils of hubris" argument of religious believers. But we know that whenever anyone makes a difficult choice, it is common if not typical that doubts remain, such that regret in itself does not justify us preventing others from acting on their decisions.

The select few who hold that suicide is not necessarily always wrong usually appeal to our freedom to choose the manner and timing of our death and our rational abilities to weigh the evidence for choosing to end – or continue – our own lives. This perspective contains a broad range of beliefs, including suicide as an individual's self-indulgent right to die, a reasonable and calculated strategy for avoiding pain and suffering, or the rational outcome of a contemplated decision that one's life is not worth living. Common to these views is that there exists no *prima facie* obligation to prevent suicide.

Given all of this concern and controversy, many psychologists are surprised to learn that the current professional ethical and legal standards regarding suicide are not really all that complicated. We are expected to do what is reasonable under the circumstances and within the limits of our professional expertise to address whatever mental health issues are prompting our client to contemplate suicide. We are not *required* to intervene in every instance to prevent someone from killing themselves. Indeed, our primary ethical and legal obligation is to respect our clients' autonomy to decide what they want to do with their lives. Preventing someone from killing themselves, provided they are competent to make the decision, is a violation of their autonomy and thus unethical, and in some instances is an assault and thus illegal. If our failing to take all reasonable steps to prevent or reduce a client's risk of suicide contributes to the client's death by suicide, we could be found professionally negligent. However, if we take all reasonable steps and our client still takes his or her own life, their suicide is not the result of our negligence.

Only when someone with whom we have a professional care relationship is incapable of deciding whether or not to end their own life and is at risk of suicide are we expected to intervene to prevent them from doing so. Note that the mere fact that someone wants to end their life does not constitute sufficient evidence that they are incompetent. Competence is decision-specific and not synonymous with mental illness.

The courts recognize that some courses of action undertaken to prevent a suicide, such as involving other people without the client's permission, can be reasonable under some circumstances, while the same action may not be reasonable in circumstances where it will increase the likelihood that a client will kill themselves. This is why in particular we are expected to maintain confidentiality in all but exceptional circumstances. Breaking confidentiality carries a high risk of being experienced as a professional betrayal and thereby increasing the client's risk of suicide. Only when no other option consistent with the client's wishes is likely to reduce their risk of killing themselves do our professional ethics *permit* us to break confidentiality, which would normally take precedence over responsible caring, but do not require us to do so.

Therefore, in some situations, such as when a person wants to kill themselves in response to hallucinations commanding them to do so, doing everything reasonably possible to prevent their death by suicide would be considered right. In most other circumstances, intervening to prevent someone from taking their own life would be wrong to the extent that they are competent to decide that they want to die.

All of this is of course difficult enough in practice, if not in theory, but is made even more difficult when a client repeatedly threatens suicide or is otherwise persistently suicidal. Taking extraordinary steps such as scheduling extra sessions, taking telephone calls in the middle of the night, or arranging involuntary hospitalization is one thing when responding to an emergency, but when a client is in perpetual suicidal crisis, we simply cannot routinely respond in an exceptional manner. So much time and effort ends up being spent responding to suicide that none is left to respond to the distress giving rise to it. Of particular significance in such situations is that our goals for the client are no longer in alignment with the client's for themselves. We want to stop them from taking their own life, while they want to end their emotional pain by means of suicide. What starts out as a lack of collaboration can become working at cross-purposes, and many therapists are left feeling that the client is being manipulative in the service of some goal other than seeking mental health. Such a situation does not bode well for a good outcome.

Of deeper concern for the profession is that our ethical codes and practice guidelines are predicated on suicide as a circumscribed crisis. This has resulted in practices that deny us access to corrective feedback with clients who are persistently suicidal. If we intervene against a client's wishes in a crisis situation they may be grateful, and if not they may deny future suicidal intent in order to be left alone to do as they choose or to discontinue treatment. In any of these situations, it is easy for us to believe that we have done the right thing. Even if the client makes a complaint after we prevent them from killing themselves, our colleagues, the courts, and members of a discipline committee are very likely to be sympathetic toward us for acting to preserve life. If a client is steadfast in their wish to die, however, our assumptions about the rightness of our actions are brought into sharp relief and seriously questioned.

Perhaps most significantly, when a client makes repeated attempts on his or her own life, repeatedly threatens to commit suicide, or is in a state of persistent suicide risk, important issues regarding accepted professional practice are raised. In particular, are we too eager to prevent suicide because we desperately do not want it to happen for reasons of our own self-interest – avoiding the negative emotions aroused by the threat of self-inflicted death – without fully considering what our client wants? Are we subjugating the very person we intend to rescue?

Because I was so afraid of, conflicted about, and categorically opposed to Brad's suicide, I responded unhelpfully to his threat to take his own life. I both over- and under-reacted to his chronic suicidal state, and in so doing acted contrary to my professional obligations as a psychologist. Brad represented an opportunity to learn from the extreme of working with a client who was repeatedly threatening suicide and thereby deepen my understanding of the ethics of suicide prevention. I now know that resolving my feelings, attitudes, and understandings about suicide and a client's wish to die can ultimately improve the ethicality and legality of our practice.

Assessing of Risk versus Providing Care

Caroline and I came to work together by way of a referral from her physician. Of primary concern was that she was frequently cutting herself and threatening suicide. As a former medical student, she knew too well how to bring about death and had made a number of highly lethal attempts to kill herself. It was only the fortuitous intervention of family members that had kept her alive.

From the start of our first session, Caroline manifested extreme distress. Her whole body trembled and she fidgeted constantly in her chair. She was almost always crying or on the verge of tears. Her appearance was unhealthy, with mottled skin, uncombed hair, and disheveled clothing. Whenever I asked how her week had been, she responded in a quivering voice with some variation on "awful," "terrible," or "unbearable." She avoided eye contact or even looking in my direction, as if to do so was more than she could bear.

The intensity of Caroline's distress was such that it was difficult to get a clear picture of her history or current situation. I gradually pieced together that as a child she was unwanted, unloved, and neglected, and had been sexually abused by various men who passed through her parents' home. She told me she had been sexually assaulted on more than one occasion as an adult, but was vague about the details. There was no bright spot in her life that I could find. My attempts to identify personal strengths or interpersonal supports were met with icy disdain.

In fact, Caroline had a palpable anger that simmered beneath the surface of our relationship, never openly expressed. She seemed to be upset with me for failing to understand how badly she was suffering or caring enough to focus all my efforts on her. I found it very difficult to refrain from responding with annoyance given that she did not appear to appreciate how I was spending a disproportionate amount of time and effort on her.

I thought about Caroline so much because I was terrified she would eventually succeed in killing herself and I would be charged with professional incompetence. I worked hard to offer helpful explanations for her distress and to propose interventions to alleviate it. She would guardedly nod her head and then invariably return for our next session saying, "I want to die; I want my life to end." Seeking to protect myself from possible litigation, I diligently devoted the end of each session to assessing her suicide risk. Given that her history could not change and her circumstances were not changed, I inquired about her distress, hopelessness, and suicidal plans. This was not well received – she would answer curtly and leave in a huff.

Caroline was rattling my belief in myself as a good therapist. I felt both irritated with and sad for her. I questioned why she continued to seek therapy and began to suspect that she did so to torment me. Seeing her name on my day's schedule filled me with dread. I found myself wondering if she might actually be better off dead, and worried that my thinking was motivated by feeling that *I* might be better off if she was dead.

Fortunately, I had learned my lesson many years ago and relied on trusted colleagues to help keep me focused on trying to find ways to be effective. Through our consultations, it began to dawn on me that my attempts to protect myself from accusations of malpractice were having a paradoxical effect. The more time I spent assessing Caroline's risk of suicide, the more upset she became with me and the more her risk increased, which intensified my fears and prompted me to be more wary, which intensified her distress, and so on in a vicious cycle.

I therefore decided after much soul-searching to gird my loins, set aside my fear of litigation, and discontinue the risk assessments. For our next few meetings, Caroline appeared suspicious when I did not finish the session with questions about her suicidal intentions, but she soon adapted, and we put the extra time to therapeutic use. By not focusing on protecting myself, I was able to focus on how she could respond to her distress in healthier ways. We collaboratively developed a self-care plan to address her chronic emotional distress and a safety plan for acute suicidal exacerbations. She made gradual progress.

After two and a half years of psychotherapy, including nine months of termination planning, I said goodbye to Caroline. She was still generally unhappy and thought about suicide from time to time, but her rate of self-harming had declined to every other month, and she had not made a suicide attempt for over a year. She contacted me a few years later to tell me that she had married and returned to medical school.

When clients disclose thoughts of suicide, most psychologists consider a risk assessment to be professionally indicated. If asked, however, they typically cannot give a good explanation for doing so. Most assess their suicidal client's risk because they think they are expected to (for unspecified reasons) or because they feel they should be doing something to address the suicidality and can think of nothing else to do. Often they report a vague idea that they are somehow protecting themselves from legal liability. It should be obvious that none of these reasons are based on sound professional reasoning.

The greatest practical challenge with risk assessment is that suicide is a very rare event. Even if we were able to identify those who will take their own life within a small margin of error (an ability we do not have), we would falsely identify a great number of people who would not go on to do so (Large, Ryan, & Nielssen, 2011). Thus, we might think that what suicide risk assessment can do is define a group of people who are more likely to kill themselves than others when, in fact, suicide is highly *unlikely* among those classified as high-risk: less than 1 percent of those classified as high-risk end their own life (Madsen, Agerbo, Mortensen, & Nordentoft, 2012; Steeg et al., 2012), while 40 percent of inpatient suicides (Large, Smith, Sharma, Nielssen, & Singh, 2011) and 60 percent of suicides after discharge (Large, Sharma, Cannon, Ryan, & Nielssen, 2011) occur among patients classified as low-risk.

To make matters worse, while many factors identified as contributing to suicide risk, such as psychiatric diagnosis, previous attempts, hopelessness, and lack of social supports, have a statistically significant (small) relationship with suicide completion (Maris, Berman, & Silverman, 2000), different studies have identified different factors, such that there is no empirical basis for justifying our choosing which factors to assess with any given client (Wang et al., 2015). In fact, those who attempt suicide and those who kill themselves are, by and large, drawn from different populations (Beautrais, 2001), with people who survive a suicide attempt tending to be young women who make multiple attempts and those taking their own life tending to be older men who do so on their first attempt (Encrenaz et al., 2012; Maris et al., 2000).

Most clinicians understandably but naively regard the presence of suicidal ideation as a crucial factor in assessing a client's risk of self-inflicted death, despite the fact that expressed ideation simply does not correspond with completed suicide (Lukaschek, Engelhardt, Baumert, & Ladwig, 2015). Suicidal ideation is only weakly associated with future suicide among psychiatric inpatients (Large, Smith, et al., 2011) and patients recently discharged (Large, Sharma, et al., 2011), while 70 percent of people who kill themselves had not seen a mental health professional in the year prior to their death (Booth & Owens, 2000; Luoma, Martin, & Pearson, 2002). In one study of 67 people who died by suicide within a week of a medical appointment, for example, only seven had disclosed suicidal thoughts to their physician (Britton, Ilgen, Rudd, & Conner, 2012). The combination of thoughts of self-destruction being very common among those who seek our help and the fact that many people intent on suicide do not disclose their desire to do so renders ideation a useless predictor (Large & Ryan, 2014).

Another reason that many psychologists provide for assessing suicide risk is their belief that the vast majority of suicides, if not all, are a symptom of mental illness (Pridmore, 2015). If this were true, we would identify and treat our clients' mental disorders and thereby reduce their risk of killing themselves. Some have argued that it is a "kind of gospel" among mental health professionals that "anyone who contemplates, expresses a desire for, or takes any overt action toward shortening their life must be afflicted with a mental illness" (Rich, 2014, p. 403). Researchers who ascribe to this view have argued that approximately 90 percent of people who kill themselves met the criteria for a mental disorder at the time of their death (Arsenault-Lapierre, Kim, & Turecki, 2004), although others place the rates at closer to 30 percent (Milner, Sveticic, & De Leo, 2012; Owens, Booth, Briscoe, Lawrence, & Lloyd, 2003). Whatever the true rates might be, however, the presence or absence of a mental illness says nothing practically useful about whether a client will kill themselves or not. Most people with a mental illness do not take their own lives and many people who do so are not mentally ill.

Even the fact that suicidality is a manifestation of mental illness for some people does not justify trying to stop them from killing themselves, however, because not every product of mental illness is considered worthy of prevention. The urge of many who produce great works of art, for example, is a manifestation of mental illness, and that does not warrant stopping them from trying. Even the desire to recover from mental illness could be said to be a by-product of the illness, but surely no one would suggest that we are obligated to prevent someone from getting better. So even if all suicidal intent were the product of mental illness (which is certainly not the case), it is not sufficient reason for preventing someone from acting on it. Indeed, the courts have ruled that the only time they would relieve someone with a mental illness of their responsibility for suicide was if they are incapable of voluntary behavior (Appelbaum, 2000).

In some situations, people suffer *from* a mental disorder that restricts their ability to make a rational decision about whether to live or die, as in the case of command hallucinations or psychotic depression. In these situations, suicide is not a voluntary choice of death over life and we are therefore expected on compassionate grounds to intervene against the client's wishes in order to promote their welfare. In other situations, people want to end their lives because they suffer *under* a mental disorder that leaves them feeling demoralized by their inability to overcome it. In these situations, suicide is an autonomous choice and coercive treatment is therefore ethically contraindicated.

Even proponents of risk assessment concede that it has no predictive utility and argue instead that it serves to guide treatment planning (Bryan & Rudd, 2006). The final practical nail in the coffin of suicide risk assessment, however, is that it does not have the necessary discriminating power to distinguish groups of patients at higher and lower risk of suicide in a way that provides a useful guide to treatment. Any therapeutic intervention delivered to those who are categorized as high-risk for suicide can only decrease the likelihood of suicide and not eliminate all risk, and the vast majority of those labeled high-risk would never have killed themselves. Furthermore, given that most suicides occur among people categorized as low-risk, and who are 14 times more likely to take their own life than those in the general population (Steeg et al., 2012), any intervention with a chance of success should surely be applied to low-risk clients as well. Also, assessing the level of a client's risk tells us nothing about how best to respond to their suicidality. Thus, we are left with having to take seriously all clients who express suicidal ideation or intention and applying our energies to addressing their suffering.

Practicalities aside, legal liability has been found for failing to recognize that a client is suicidal and subsequently failing to address the aspects of the client's circumstances that are contributing to their suicidality. If our client is expressing suicidal ideation or intent or we are otherwise worried that a client is suicidal, however, an assessment does nothing to protect us from liability for failing to detect suicide risk because we are already aware of it. Our responsibility is to do something about whatever is motivating our client to want to end their life.

The therapeutic situation with clients who are persistently suicidal, in contrast with clients who are experiencing acute suicidality, highlights how an excessive focus on the illusory goal of preventing a suicide by assessing risk actually interferes with us meeting our ethical obligations. When our goal is to do whatever it takes to prevent a client from killing themselves, we are placing the promotion of their well-being, as we understand it, ahead of respecting their autonomy. Indeed, we are now in a position of trying to outguess the client's true intentions while they are forced to try to outwit us in order to achieve their goal. In such circumstances, we often resort to labeling a client as "manipulative" who is simply trying to further their own interests as they understand them.

Suicidal ideation, intent, and attempt, like any other symptoms, are clinical phenomena that we are expected to address therapeutically. Treating chronically suicidal patients as if they were always in danger reinforces cycles of repeated, exceptional interventions that hinder good therapy. People contemplate or attempt suicide when it seems like their best, and sometimes only, way out of an unbearably difficult situation in which the challenges that confront them overwhelm whatever resources they have to deal with them. Often their resources are depleted, perhaps because the people who usually support them have abandoned them or because their ability to generate a nonfatal solution is impaired by mental illness or intoxication. Always somewhere prominent in the mix of the fatal act is excruciating psychological pain.

By persistently conducting suicide risk assessments with the persistently suicidal Caroline, I took precious time away from responding to her psychological pain. In fact, by making the assessment of her risk the priority in our professional contact, the focus of our therapy shifted from her goals to mine. Ultimately, I was expected to help Caroline deal with her real-life issues, not to protect myself from legal liability. By spending so much time worrying about suicide, the process of good therapy became derailed. From the outset, I should have focused less on responding to her threat of suicide and more on working collaboratively with her to resolve the distress that gave rise to it.

Providing Care versus Respecting Autonomy

Delia presented for psychotherapy stating that she wanted to talk with a therapist to ensure that she "left no stone unturned" before taking her own life. She described her days as "endlessly sad" and couldn't remember ever being happy. She had long ago given up trying to find any reason for living in the face of her "unbearable sadness" and thought about suicide almost constantly. In particular, at night in her apartment she often felt oppressively miserable, which prompted her to actively consider how she might end her life. She said that at those moments the prospect of a life of such pain, stretching out interminably, was more than she could stand. What had prevented her from killing herself was that she did not want anyone to have to deal with her corpse: "I can't imagine how awful it would be for someone to come into my apartment and find my dead body. That would be horrible."

By this point in my career, I had considerable experience with suicide and felt up to the task of helping Delia. I agreed to work with her on the condition that she not kill herself until we had exhausted all therapeutic possibilities. This was not actually too difficult – she was prepared to collaborate with me so long as I was not categorically opposed to her taking her own life. I told her I was not convinced that suicide was the solution to her suffering, but would keep an open mind.

In truth, I felt confident that I could establish a therapeutic alliance strong enough to prevail over her deeply demoralized state. I knew that if I explicitly opposed her wish to die, she wouldn't feel we were collaborating toward a shared goal. But I did not accept that her life was not worth living. The fact that she sought my help and was worried about the effect of her suicide on people she did not even know led me to believe that she was capable of meaningful, satisfying relationships.

The tenuous state of our alliance was tested frequently, however. Delia would call at night feeling desperately sad with an overwhelming urge to die. Many times I intervened to prevent her from killing herself, choosing my words carefully in order to maintain some semblance of working together. More than once I accompanied her to the emergency ward when she was intent on suicide and ambivalent at best about adhering to our safety plan. Twice she was admitted involuntarily after I, without telling Delia, argued with the attending physician that she posed a significant threat to her own life as a result of a mental illness.

After six months of therapy, our work together took a sharp turn. Delia told me that she had been diagnosed with terminal cancer that had started in her breast and metastasized to her bones and internal organs. There was no possibility of cure. She wanted to continue our sessions and within a few short weeks I was providing bedside therapy in her apartment. A nurse visited daily to check on her, but she was otherwise on her own. She told me that the certainty of her death did have an upside: it freed her from having to agonize over whether to go on living. Yet while her physical pain was being kept under control for the time being, it would soon outpace the medication options available. She was very much afraid of the suffering she would have to endure as the end of her life neared.

Then one day Delia asked – pleaded, in fact – to "help me end my life now, on my own terms, before dying an ugly, painful death." I was stunned. When she was dealing with intractable emotional pain, I never lost hope that she would overcome it. I even went against her wishes to keep that possibility alive. Now she faced excruciating physical pain and I had nothing to cling to. I realized that my failure to accept suicide as a reasonable choice was due to my unwillingness to accept that we will all die eventually. Her inescapable death had broken through my denial. I experienced a depth of compassion and sympathy for her that I had not felt before and wanted to help.

The problem Delia – and I – faced was convincing the palliative care physician specialist to help her hasten her death. The specialist was reluctant because of her history of involuntary hospitalization for suicidality, for which I was more than partially responsible. I now found myself arguing that she was competent to decide to kill herself despite still being depressed. I said her desire to die was considered and congruent with her personal values and her death would not negatively impact significant others because she had none. Her physician relented and issued a treatment order for enough pain medication to kill her. Delia died alone a few days later by her own hand.

In response to his own rhetorical question, "Is life so dear or peace so sweet as to be purchased at the price of chains and slavery?" during a rousing speech delivered to the Virginia Convention on May 23, 1775, Patrick Henry famously answered, "I know not what course others may take; but as for me, give me liberty, or give me death!" Although few would take quite so vehement a stance, autonomy is considered by most to be an essential and inviolable right worth dying for. Yet when it comes to suicide – arguably the ultimate expression of autonomy – the only means by which it can be prevented is to curtail personal liberty. This presents us with a dilemma.

Historical trends show that considering personal autonomy as a basic human right is a relatively new concept. Throughout much of recorded history, for example, many people believed they were owned by or belonged to a god, and it was sometimes said that our bodies were "on loan" to us from them. Similarly, many peoples have believed that individuals were owned by their sovereign ruler, king, queen, chief, emperor, or some other. These leaders were entitled to exert ownership under certain circumstances, particularly when human resources were needed, such as the practice of conscription during times of war. And until quite recently, on an historical scale, many members of society, such as slaves, serfs, women, and children, were considered the property of another and could not assert that they owned their own bodies. In fact, if we consider the global population, this is still true for significant numbers of people.

The current consensus among the peoples of democratic countries, as reflected in their laws, is that an individual cannot be said to be truly free who does not have dominion over his or her own life. The view is that all persons own themselves. Our mind and body are not collective resources; they are us and they are ours. In a free society, no one is owned by family, society, or country, or by any other individual.

We might therefore well ask why exercising power over individuals who want to end their own life could be considered justifiable at all. There are many situations where we allow people to engage in activities that can reasonably be expected to result in self-harm. Obvious examples include contact sports such as football and ice hockey. It is very difficult to imagine anyone being forcibly prevented from participating in such sports on the basis that they might seriously injure themselves. In these situations, the individual is clearly considered to have the freedom to subject their body to risk of harm.

Then there are those activities where the chance of serious physical injury, if not death, exists as a very real possibility. Any mistake or error in judgment when engaging in "extreme sports" such as mountaineering, motor racing, and BASE jumping, for example, carries mortal risk by its very nature. Yet as with the relatively milder contact sports, the autonomy of persons engaging in these life-threatening activities is not restricted even though the outcome can be, and often is, their death.

There are also behaviors well-known to hasten a person's death, such as smoking tobacco, consuming excessive amounts of alcoholic beverages, and avoiding physical activity. Despite the entreaties of experts to change our collective unhealthy lifestyle, there does not appear to be any movement toward considering the many self-inflicted deaths resulting from them as suicides. We may introduce "sin" taxes and other methods to make engaging in such behaviors more difficult or to nudge people toward healthier behaviors, but no one is seriously suggesting taking away peoples' liberty to shorten their own lives in this manner.

Current mental health policy and practices with respect to people who are suicidal are thus curiously inconsistent with recognition of self-ownership in other spheres of life. The modal position is that suicide ought to be prevented in most, if not all, cases regardless of the wishes of the suicidal person. Authority to usurp personal autonomy when individuals represent harm to themselves is even enshrined in the mental health laws of numerous countries (O'Brien, McKenna, & Kydd, 2009; Sheehan, 2009).

Of course, the crucial difference between those who risk their lives through dangerous activities or hasten their death through unhealthy lifestyles and those who want to end their lives is intention. High-risk sports have as their goal enjoyment. Participants often say that they feel "more alive" when they risk their necks.

Similarly, smoking, drinking, and loafing on the couch is done for the pleasure of the activity. Death or a shorter life is an unintended consequence. What troubles us so deeply about suicide is that death is not a possible outcome of an activity, it is the goal.

The ethical challenge for most psychologists with respect to a client who is persistently suicidal arises out of our usual desire to work in collaboration with our clients toward the goal of improving their well-being. When faced with a client whose intentions and behavior are, from our perspective, contrary to their welfare, our ethical obligation to provide responsible caring becomes incompatible with our ethical obligation to respect their autonomy. Moreover, the client's persistent suicidal intent calls into question the underlying values of our profession to promote life, well-functioning, bodily integrity, and psychological health. Few of us find such questioning a pleasant experience.

In fact, clients who are persistently suicidal frighten us. Fear of legal sanctions is of course quite common and, on the face of it, understandable given that no one wants to be sued or disciplined. But we are accountable for many actions that could result in a lawsuit or complaint, such as crossing professional boundaries or failing to properly diagnose, and few of us live in fear of these events to anywhere near the extent we do of suicide. Our fears when dealing with someone intent on killing themselves go deeper; they are primal.

All living things are born with biological systems oriented toward self-preservation. Those who lack it would be at a distinct reproductive disadvantage relative to those who would do anything to stay alive. Yet human beings are, as far as anyone knows, unique among all forms of life in being aware of our mortality (Solomon, Greenberg, & Pyszczynski, 2015). We know that sooner or later we will lose the battle against death. In fact, humans are so terrified of death that we go to great lengths in thought and deed to deny it (Becker, 1973). When circumstances conspire to overwhelm our denial and make our mortality salient, death anxiety is aroused and we seek to defend ourselves against it by clinging more tightly to our core beliefs about the nature of the world and our place in it (Pyszczynski, Solomon, & Greenberg, 2015). Working with a client who desires to end their own life is an obvious threat to our denial of death and may arouse awareness of our own mortality.

Belief in the sanctity of life is so fundamental to our worldview that few of us ever stop to even consider its centrality. Beliefs of this kind typically arise without conscious effort such that we rarely question their presence in our minds any more than we question whether something has a particular shape, texture, or taste. That is, we trust our fundamental assumptions as much as we do our perceptions. The *feeling* that we should intervene to save someone from dying, therefore, is usually experienced as a *fact* that we should do so. That dying should be their intention only serves to make it less comprehensible and more worthy of prevention (Liégeois & Eneman, 2012). The net result of this process is that we are at risk of trying to intervene with suicide in ways that seems obviously to be the correct thing to do, yet are inconsistent with society's expectations of us and our professional codes of ethics.

Our human capacity to be aware of our mortality not only provokes existential fear, it also presents us with the choice of whether to live or die. And if the choice exists, there must be some situations where choosing to die is a reasonable alternative. It is illogical to declare people unable to reason logically simply because they consider suicide. Autonomous individuals have the right to behave in any noncriminal way they choose. If suicide can be logically considered, then we are expected to grant mature individuals who are capable of deciding whether to live or die the autonomy to understand their situation from their personal framework.

In fact, most democratic societies have accepted that choosing to hasten one's death can be rational under certain circumstances. Over the last decade, a number of prominent professional organizations have issued policy statements or position papers asserting that the provision of a lethal prescription requested by a terminally ill patient who is competent to decide is just and ethical. This trend reflects a shift in societal attitudes away from the view expressed by the U.S. Supreme Court in the cases of *Washington v. Glucksberg* (1997) and *Vacco v. Quill* (1997) that use of a lethal prescription by a terminally ill patient constitutes suicide, and toward the position taken in the case of *Compassion in Dying v. Washington* (1995) that such action can be the exercise of autonomy in determining the time and manner of one's death.

It is now accepted in most democratic countries (including Canada and the United States) that a person has the right to hasten his or her death following a sound decision-making process when faced with the intolerable suffering associated with a terminal illness (Werth & Holdwick, 2000). Death can be the result of withholding or withdrawing life-supportive technologies or procedures, as well as providing a person with the means to die (usually medication) and having them self-administer it.

Thus, when someone has a high likelihood of severe suffering, as in cases of terminal illness, their decision to die seems understandable. Even if we find it difficult to endorse an individual's death wish, it is comprehensible because they are going to die soon and their remaining quality of life will be poor. Death in this instance is seen as a relief from dying.

This line of reasoning assumes a particular definition of the concept of "quality of life," however. The death wish is acceptable to us because we accept the objective constraints due to a terminal illness as a valid reason. Yet, if we define quality of life objectively, we have to ask why we do not find the *lack* of suicidal intent incomprehensible among those facing a horrible death. Indeed, we tend to consider such stoicism to be admirable. If, on the other hand, quality of life is subjectively defined, it follows that most death wishes must be acceptable, because for a suicidal person their life is unbearable by definition. But we certainly do not consider subjectively experienced suffering as sufficient to make suicide acceptable in every case.

Our inconsistency is the product of the tendency to ask ourselves whether we would feel similarly in the same situation and make the same decision. If someone who is suicidal does not feel or decide as we think we would, then we tend to rely on the implicit norms of our worldview to judge which constraints count as bearable and which do not. We do accept that some people can endure more suffering than most, and indeed venerate them because we hope that we would do likewise if faced with the same challenge. Yet we tend to consider it incomprehensible if someone wants to kill themselves to escape circumstances that we consider tolerable, and typically judge them negatively for showing a weakness of character that we fear we would manifest if similarly tested. If we do not understand or, worse, do not approve, then we do not accept their justification for wanting to die. And our understanding and approval are very much dependent on our comfort with and acceptance of our own mortality (Arndt, Vess Cox, Goldenberg, & Lagle, 2009).

It should be clear, therefore, that we ought neither to judge the validity of an individual's distress by an objective standard nor to make the acceptability of suicide dependent upon imagining ourselves in our client's situation. The fact that suicide can be reasonable, even rational, for some people in some circumstances requires us to accept that an absolute position against suicide is not a tenable one. How, then, do we proceed with the knowledge that there is no ultimate perspective on suicide to which every other viewpoint is subservient? How do we move forward when our fundamental belief that continuing to live under any circumstance is flawed?

My ability to effectively navigate the expectations of our professional ethics and laws when working with Delia in her persistently suicidal state was hampered by my inability to manage my fear of death. If I had a better handle on my existential terror from the outset of our work together, then I could have better met her on her own terms. She was faced with a life that, by her own assessment, was intolerable. My role was not to contradict her about the rightness or wrongness of suicide as a way of ending her suffering. Doing so put me in opposition to her goals when I had no right to do so. I did have an obligation to help her find a way to overcome or find peace with her sad and lonely life. I should have collaborated with her to resolve the despair that was driving her to consider suicide. It may have turned out that, despite my best efforts, her appraisal of her life would have remained unchanged and she may have decided to end it. But interfering with Delia's autonomy to decide whether or not to continue living was an affront to her dignity as a person and, rather than saving her life, only served to diminish it.

Recommendations for Responsible Practice

The overarching ethical issue with respect to suicide is whether, or under what circumstances, we should attempt to prevent it by interfering with an individual's autonomy. As a society, we allow people to act in many other noncriminal ways that are not in their best interests and that even put their life in serious jeopardy. Yet we treat suicide differently. Most of us consider it intrinsically wrong or at least the wrong thing to do under most if not all circumstances. Although it is not logically persuasive to seek to prevent a suicide only because we cannot understand the individual's wish to die – or to allow it because we understand and agree with their intent – our decision to coercively intervene in practice typically does hinge on this very ability.

The greatest barrier for most of us to responding in an ethical manner to the possibility of suicide is that it strikes at the heart of our existential fear of death. Acknowledging that suicide arouses this fear and that our actions may be motivated as much by protecting ourselves from existential anxiety as by protecting our client is a necessary and, for most of us, a very difficult step. We are expected to keep an open mind that suicide can be a rational choice when faced with an unbearable life situation in at least some cases and to respond to each client as an individual facing unique circumstances.

Assessing suicide risk with a client who we know to be suicidal may be an example of our unacknowledged fear of mortality given that it serves no purpose other than to calm our anxiety. While legal liability can be imposed for failing to detect suicide risk, by definition if we are worried about our client's suicidality we have already detected it. Assigning a degree of suicide risk to a suicidal client thus has no legal benefit, and nor does it provide any predictive utility or treatment guidance. Our time and energies are better spent addressing whatever psychological issues are contributing to our client's wish to die.

For many clients presenting with suicidal concerns, the desire to end their life is strongly influenced by a mental illness and may, as a result, be less voluntary or deliberate than those not so afflicted. A mental disorder can result in a diminished capacity to make a rational choice to end one's life, but certainly not completely and not in all instances. Much more typical is that a client suffering from a mental illness loses perspective on their situation and struggles to make a decision one way or another. Under such circumstances, suicide can seem to be the only way to escape the intolerable situation of not knowing how to resolve the overwhelming burden of one's life. Many clients also feel demoralized and desperate as a result of suffering from a mental disorder while retaining the capacity to make a voluntary and deliberate choice of suicide. In such situations, a person can take stock of their life and come to an intentional and thoughtful decision that it is not worth living.

Of course, the client who is unambivalently intent on dying, rare as they are, will find a way to kill him/herself, no matter how hard we try to prevent it. A reasoned choice to end one's life remains an individual's prerogative, however, and only through laborious coercive intervention are we able to orchestrate brief delays. We do so in the hope that time and further treatment might reduce the client's risk of suicide through the ameliorating of a mental illness, strengthening the therapeutic relationship, or inculcating a more positive appraisal of their life and its value. If we cannot realistically anticipate that the client's wish to die will diminish via our intervention within a reasonable period of time, or if in fact it does not do so after a period of treatment even though we expected it to, our ethical position becomes progressively more tenuous. Thus, a coercive intervention that is defensible in many situations of acute suicidality becomes increasingly problematic and unjustified as an obligation to provide care when a client demonstrates a wish to die over an extended period of time or treatment. If we assume perpetual responsibility for protecting a client from their suicidal wishes, we are no longer simply providing treatment, but instead are infantilizing and dehumanizing them.

When working with a client who is persistently suicidal, we are expected to seek to collaborate with them and to find a consensus on goals that we can both agree to work toward. As paradoxical as it may seem, the prevention of suicide is not always furthered by coercive rescuing. The approach that has the best chance of dissuading someone struggling with suicidality begins with empathy because it forms the basis of hope and facilitates problem-solving. Communicating our understanding of just how desperate and hopeless our client feels constitutes a profound intervention by offering the experience of being appreciated rather than coerced. Basing our work together on empathy avoids the trap of having the client view therapy as an oppressive force pressuring them to continue living what they experience as an unbearable life or arguing that their life is worthwhile. Such a domineering stance is very likely to be ineffective and is often actually countertherapeutic. Rather, providing a human encounter that allows us to consider together the struggle and burdens involved in living can in itself decrease the tendency toward compulsive expression of suicidal desires. Empathic understanding allows a chronically suicidal client the freedom to consider whether their expressed intentions are truly a choice to die or, as is very common, an act of desperate defiance in response to overwhelming psychological pain, insoluble personal troubles, and pressure to continue living.

Working with clients who are persistently suicidal requires us to negotiate a delicate balance between respecting autonomy and providing care. People consider their lives worth living only if they enjoy an adequate degree of autonomy to live as they see fit. As psychologists, we are expected to respect our clients' autonomy because it is accepted in our society as a fundamental human right *and* it is a necessary condition for wanting to live. Thus, we are expected to grant our clients as much autonomy as possible, which in practical terms means restricting their autonomy as little as possible. On the other hand, we are also expected to assume responsibility for providing effective psychological care, including limiting our clients' autonomy when necessary, if their risk of suicide is a product of an involuntarily, irrational decision-making process. However, we must be careful to avoid the mistake of considering someone presenting with mental health concerns to be irrational until proven otherwise. All in all, this represents a very difficult practice situation, but hopefully one in which the relevant parameters are now more clearly articulated.

References

Appelbaum, P. S. (2000). Patients' responsibility for their suicidal behavior. *Psychiatric Services, 51*, 15–16.

Arndt, J., Vess, M., Cox, C. R., Goldenberg, J. L., & Lagle, S. (2009). The psychosocial effect of thoughts of personal mortality on cardiac risk assessment. *Medical Decision Making, 29*, 175–181.

Arsenault-Lapierre, G., Kim, C., & Turecki, G. (2004). Psychiatric diagnoses in 3275 suicides: A meta-analysis. *BMC Psychiatry, 4*, 37.

Beautrais, A. L. (2001). Suicides and serious suicide attempts: Two populations or one? *Psychological Medicine, 31,* 837–845.

Becker, E. (1973). *The denial of death.* New York, NY: Simon & Schuster.

Booth, N. & Owens, C. (2000). Silent suicide: Suicide among people not in contact with mental health services. *International Review of Psychiatry, 12,* 27–30.

Britton, P. C., Ilgen, M. A., Rudd, M. D., & Conner, K. R. (2012). Warning signs for suicide within a week of healthcare contact in veteran decedents. *Psychiatry Research, 200,* 395–399.

Bryan, C. J. & Rudd, M. D. (2006). Advances in the assessment of suicide risk. *Journal of Clinical Psychology, 62,* 185–200.

Cerel, J., Jordan, J. R., & Duberstein, P. R. (2008). The impact of suicide on the family. *Crisis: Journal of Crisis Intervention & Suicide, 29,* 38–44.

Chemtob, C. M., Bauer, G. B., Hamada, R. S., Pelowski, S. R., & Muraoka, M. Y. (1989). Patient suicide: Occupational hazard for psychologists and psychiatrists. *Professional Psychology: Research and Practice, 20,* 294–300.

Compassion in Dying v. Washington, 79 F. 3d 586 (9th Cir. 1995).

Ellis, T. E. & Patel, A. B. (2012). Client suicide: What now? *Cognitive and Behavioral Practice, 19,* 277–287.

Encrenaz, G., Kovess-Masféty, V., Gilbert, F., Galéra, C., Lagarde, E., Mishara, B., & Messiah, A. (2012). Lifetime risk of suicidal behaviors and communication to a health professional about suicidal ideation. *Crisis, 33,* 127–136.

Han, B., Compton, W. M., Gfroerer, J., & McKeon, R. (2014). Mental health treatment patterns among adults with recent suicide attempts in the United States. *American Journal of Public Health, 104,* 2359–2368.

Healy, D. J., Barry, K., Blow, F., Welsh, D., & Milner, K. K. (2006). Routine use of the Beck Scale for Suicide Ideation in a psychiatric emergency department. *General Hospital Psychiatry, 28,* 323–329.

Hendin, H., Lipschitz, A., Maltsberger, J. T., Haas, A. P., & Wynecoop, S. (2000). Therapists' reactions to patients' suicides. *American Journal of Psychiatry, 157,* 2022–2027.

Kleespies, P. M., Penk, W. E., & Forsyth, J. P. (1993). The stress of patient suicidal behavior during clinical training: Incidence, impact, and recovery. *Professional Psychology: Research and Practice, 24,* 293–303.

Large, M. & Ryan, C. (2014). Suicide risk assessment: Myth and reality. *International Journal of Clinical Practice, 68,* 679–681.

Large, M., Ryan, C., & Nielssen, O. (2011). The validity and utility of risk assessment for inpatient suicide. *Australasian Psychiatry, 19,* 507–512.

Large, M., Sharma, S., Cannon, E., Ryan, C., & Nielssen, O. (2011). Risk factors for suicide within a year of discharge from psychiatric hospital: A systematic meta-analysis. *Australian and New Zealand Journal of Psychiatry, 45,* 619–628.

Large, M., Smith, G., Sharma, S., Nielssen, O., & Singh, S. P. (2011). Systematic review and meta-analysis of the clinical factors associated with the suicide of psychiatric in-patients. *Acta Psychiatrica Scandinavica, 124,* 18–19.

Leenaars, A., Cantor, C., Connolly, J., et al. (2002). Ethical & legal issues in suicidology: International perspectives. *Archives of Suicide Research, 6,* 185–197.

Liégeois, A. & Eneman, M. (2012). Ethical aspects of the prevention of suicide in psychiatry. *Ethical Human Psychology and Psychiatry, 14,* 140–149.

Lukaschek, K., Engelhardt, H., Baumert, J., & Ladwig, K. H. (2015). No correlation between rates of suicidal ideation and completed suicides in Europe. *European Psychiatry, 30*, 874–879.

Luoma, J. B., Martin, C. E., & Pearson, J. L. (2002). Contact with mental health and primary care providers before suicide: A review of the evidence. *The American Journal of Psychiatry, 159*, 909–916.

Madsen, T., Agerbo, E., Mortensen, P. B., & Nordentoft, M. (2012). Predictors of psychiatric inpatient suicide: A national prospective register-based study. *The Journal of Clinical Psychiatry, 73*, 144–151.

Maris, R., Berman, A., & Silverman, M. (2000). *Comprehensive textbook of suicidology.* New York, NY: Guilford.

McCormack, R., Clifford, M., & Conroy, M. (2012). Attitudes of UK doctors towards euthanasia and physician-assisted suicide: A systematic literature review. *Palliative Medicine, 26*, 23–33.

Milner, A., Sveticic, J., & De Leo, D. (2012). Suicide in the absence of mental disorder? A review of psychological autopsy studies across countries. *International Journal of Social Psychiatry, 59*, 545–554.

O'Brien, A. J., McKenna, B. G., & Kydd, R. R. (2009). Compulsory community mental health treatment: Literature review. *International Journal of Nursing Studies, 46*, 1245–1255.

Owens, C., Booth, N., Briscoe, M., Lawrence, C., & Lloyd, K. (2003). Suicide outside the care of mental health services: A case-controlled psychological autopsy study. *Crisis: The Journal of Crisis Intervention and Suicide Prevention, 24*, 113–121.

Pagura, J., Fotti, S., Katz, L. Y., & Sareen, J. (2009). Help seeking and perceived need for mental health care among individuals in Canada with suicidal behaviors. *Psychiatric Services, 60*, 943–949.

Pridmore, S. (2015). Mental disorder and suicide: A faulty connection. *Australian and New Zealand Journal of Psychiatry, 49*, 18–20.

Pyszczynski, T., Solomon, S., & Greenberg, J. (2015). Thirty years of Terror Management Theory: From genesis to revelation. *Advances in Experimental Social Psychology, 52*, 1–70.

Reeves, A. & Mintz, R. (2001). Counsellors' experiences of working with suicidal clients: An exploratory study. *Counselling and Psychotherapy Research, 1*, 172–176.

Rich, B. A. (2014). Pathologizing suffering and the pursuit of a peaceful death. *Cambridge Quarterly of Healthcare Ethics, 23*, 403–416.

Sheehan, K. A. (2009). Compulsory treatment in psychiatry. *Current Opinion in Psychiatry, 22*, 582–586.

Shields, C., Kavanagh, M., & Russo, K. (2015). A qualitative systematic review of the bereavement process following suicide. *OMEGA – Journal of Death and Dying, 72*, 1–29.

Solomon, S., Greenberg, J., & Pyszczynski, T. (2015). *The worm at the core: The role of death in life.* New York, NY: Random House.

Stanley, I. H., Hom, M. A., & Joiner, T. E. (2015). Mental health service use among adults with suicide ideation, plans, or attempts: Results from a national survey. *Psychiatric Services, 66*, 1296–1302.

Steeg, S., Kapur, N., Webb, R., et al. (2012). The development of a population-level clinical screening tool for self-harm repetition and suicide. *Psychological Medicine, 42*, 2383–2394.

Sveen, C. A., & Walby, F. A. (2008). Suicide survivors' mental health and grief reactions: A systematic review of controlled studies. *Suicide & Life-Threatening Behavior, 38,* 13–29.

Vacco v. Quill, 521 U.S. 793 (1997).

Wang, Y., Bhaskaran, J., Sareen, J., Wang, J., Spiwak, R., & Bolton, J. M. (2015). Predictors of future suicide attempts among individuals referred to psychiatric services in the emergency department: A longitudinal study. *The Journal of Nervous and Mental Disease, 203,* 507–513.

Washington v. Glucksberg, 521 U.S. 702 (1997).

Werth, J. L. & Holdwick, D. J. (2000). A primer on rational suicide and other forms of hastened death. *The Counseling Psychologist, 28,* 511–539.

Zisook, S., Goff, A., Sledge, P., & Shuchter, S. R. (1994). Reported suicidal behavior and current suicidal ideation in a psychiatric outpatient clinic. *Annals of Clinical Psychiatry, 6,* 27–31.

8 Applied Addiction Ethics

Cynthia M. A. Geppert and Bryn S. Esplin

The 2014 National Survey on Drug Use and Health (NSDUH) offers an annual picture of one of the most significant public health problems in the United States: addiction. A review of the survey's highlights raises a number of abstract ethical concerns that are concretized every day in private offices, community hospitals, and the very streets of the nation. The NSDUH found that 10.2 percent of the population above the age of 12 had used an illicit drug in the month before the survey. This is the highest percentage in 11 years and reflects higher rates of marijuana use and the nonmedical use of prescription pain medications. Thirty-nine percent of adults were given both a mental health and a substance use diagnosis in the past year compared to 16 percent without a drug or alcohol problem. In the year before the survey, 914 000 people were current heroin users, an increase from the prior decade, and 2.6 million had both a drug and alcohol use disorder (Center for Behavioral Statistics and Quality, 2015).

Addiction affects all ages, genders, ethnicities, and socioeconomic strata, with some of the most poignant and perplexing ethical dilemmas encountered in youth and the elderly. In the age group of young adults aged 18–25, nearly a third engaged in binge drinking and more than 10% were heavy drinkers. The 2013 NSDUH found that as baby boomers age, they continue to use substances at a higher rate than previous cohorts; for example, illicit drug use among adults aged 50–64 increased from 2.7 percent in 2002 to 6.0 percent in 2013. Despite the passage of the Affordable Care Act and governmental efforts toward parity in physical and mental health care, 22 million people needed specialty addiction treatment in 2013, but only 4.5 percent acknowledged their need for treatment. Of the 34.8 percent who attempted to obtain treatment, inability to afford care was the primary reason for not receiving care (Center for Behavioral Health Statistics and Quality, 2015). Perhaps no area of applied ethics is more complex than dilemmas involving patients with addiction. Several distinct scientific, clinical, professional, legal, and social factors contribute to this complexity, making ethical resolution of these conflicts more challenging for even experienced and highly trained mental health professionals (Taleff, 2010).

Scientifically, the twenty-first century has witnessed unparalleled discoveries in the basic science of addiction. Yet, despite the progress of neurobiology, the ghosts of past ages continue to haunt the diagnosis, and the question of whether addiction is a brain disease, a medical condition, a personality flaw, a sin against God, or a social problem remains the topic of intense debate. The reigning brain disease model is the object of recent criticism (Hall, Carter, & Forlini, 2015). This controversy is especially significant for addiction ethics, as each of the various models has a different position regarding the agency of the individual with a substance use disorder and the relative contributions of genes, environment, culture, and character to the development of addiction. Importantly, these various positions continue to inform public health policy and law. Neuroscience is now revisiting the profound philosophical question of free will and determinism in the choices of persons with addiction with profound legal, social, and political implications (Hyman, 2007; Morse, 2007).

Clinically, there is a dearth of general education about substance use disorders in almost all health professional training, including mental health. This lack of contemporary and practical knowledge reinforces negative social attitudes toward addiction, which in turn leads to lost opportunities to screen, diagnose, and treat addiction in a variety of health care settings. As the NSDUH data show, it is likely that the majority of health care practitioners – whether psychologists, physicians, or nurses – will be involved in the care of persons with addiction. When clinicians do not attain a level of competence and comfort in managing these often-difficult clinician–patient relationships during their training, they are left to confront them in practice, where lack of experience may unwittingly lead to therapeutic nihilism (Rasyidi, Wilkins, & Danovitch, 2012). This is particularly tragic given that addictive disorders are at least as treatable as other chronic diseases like hypertension and diabetes and that caring for these patients provides a professional opportunity that can be fulfilling and rewarding (McLellan, Lewis, O'Brien, & Kleber, 2000).

Socially, despite the very real medical progress in treating addiction, the condition continues to be stigmatized. A recent web-based survey of over 700 individuals found that stigma was more strongly associated with addiction than mental illness, and many of the respondents would have discriminated against persons with addiction in work and family relationships (Barry, McGinty, Pescosolido, & Goldman, 2014).

Professionally, the normative stances toward core ethical dilemmas in addiction are not yet established, and with the notable exception of licensed addiction counselors (The Association for Addiction Professionals, 2004), there is less definitive guidance available for clinicians in traditional authoritative sources of ethics knowledge such as codes of ethics, position statements, or published literature. This is nowhere more apparent than in contemporary views of medical marijuana. While still illegal at the federal level and in some states, as of this writing, 25 states and the District of Columbia have legalized the use of medical marijuana and four states and the District of Columbia permit the recreational use of marijuana (Cohen, 2009a, 2009b).

As the example of medical marijuana suggests, the law plays a more prominent role in addiction ethics than in many other areas of bioethics, but the legal approaches to addiction issues range from harsh criminal penalties in some jurisdictions to the use of drug courts as a mechanism of rehabilitation and leniency in others. The legal frame restricts practitioners confronting addiction ethics dilemmas in two main and important areas: confidentiality and coercion. The federal regulations regarding disclosure of protected health information contained in 45 Code of

Federal Regulations (CFR) Part 160, as well as Subparts A and E of Part 164 of the Health Insurance and Portability and Accountability Act (HIPAA) Privacy Rule, are the most stringent in health care (Confidentiality of Alcohol and Drug Abuse Patient Records, 1987; Health Insurance and Portability and Accountability Act, 1996). Conversely, the law regarding involuntary commitment for persons even with acute and chronic substance use disorders is both inchoate and inconsistent, limiting the choices patients, families, and clinicians have when faced with crises that endanger patients and third-parties directly or if severe addiction makes patients unable to meet their own basic needs.

In this chapter, we will explore these factors as they interact in complicated – yet all too common – cases, examining the arguments and counterarguments relevant to the decision-making process and offering the most ethically justifiable recommendations for practitioners confronted with issues related to the treatment of persons with substance use disorders. The case-based analysis will focus on five major ethical dilemmas encountered in addiction ethics: confidentiality, decisional capacity, informed consent, psychosocial stigmatization, and the misuse of prescription stimulant medication.

A Case of Confidentiality

Pam is a 45-year-old nurse working in the intensive care unit of a hospital. She suffers from fibromyalgia and anxious depression for which she frequently calls in sick to work. Pam is being seen in a complex care pain clinic where she insists only opioids and benzodiazepines effectively manage her conditions and without them she will lose her job. She is also the mother of two teenage sons, one of whom she tells the clinic social worker also suffers from depression. Pam has mentioned to the nurses in the clinic that her husband is a computer technician and the couple has experienced some marital strain over finances, but she has always portrayed her husband as supportive and the more stable of the two of them.

Pam increasingly exhibits aberrant behavior such as coming to the emergency department at night demanding intravenous opioids, running out of her prescriptions early, doctor shopping, and requesting the clinic staff complete paperwork so she does not have to go to work. During the first years of her treatment, the staff advocated for Pam and provided documentation to her employer that her headaches required the use of controlled substances in order to explain her abnormal workplace toxicology screens. Clinic nursing staff approached the clinic director, Dr. Ogden, a psychiatric nurse practitioner with a doctorate in nursing practice, expressing their concern that Pam is an impaired health professional who may be placing the critically ill patients under her care at risk. They tell Dr. Ogden that they feel they have an ethical obligation to report Pam to the nursing board or her supervisor.

When looking up Pam's contact information in order to call her to come in to discuss these issues, the nurse practitioner inadvertently discovers that Pam is married to another patient in the clinic, Cliff, who receives opioids for back pain and headaches and who has also been misusing his medications. Neither Pam nor

Cliff has ever mentioned to the clinic staff that they are married. The clinic team is now worried about the couple's ability to care for their two children and wonders if they should also call child protective services.

The director feels that before she or anyone in the clinic reports the couple to state authorities, she should try to speak to Pam and strongly encourage her to voluntarily seek addiction treatment. If she does not admit she has a problem and agree to get help, then Dr. Ogden will have to decide whether or not to report.

Confidentiality Case Analysis

Dr. Ogden was not searching for this information; she just happened to notice that both patients had the same address and then saw that each had named the other as their spouse in their contact information. But now that Dr. Ogden is in possession of the knowledge, she must decide whether to act upon it and how. This is a question of truth-telling, and she struggles to know whether withholding the information or disclosing it will cause more damage to the therapeutic alliance. As part of her doctoral work, she studied feminist ethical theory and her personal affinity is for the ethics of care, which she feels most closely articulates the traditional virtues of nursing, to which she is professionally committed (Bowden, 1995). While she believes there is a way to share the information with Pam that can promote Pam's own attention to self-care and choice for a healthier life, she also can foresee that Pam's fear and shame might end the treatment relationship, further isolating Pam from a trusted helper.

An ethically defensible option then would be to choose not to disclose the information, even should Pam not admit she has a problem and agree to get help. Substance use information carries strong confidentiality protections precisely because it is so stigmatizing. However, there is a provision in the federal privacy regulations allowing health care professionals to report a suspicion of child abuse (Brooks, 2005). As there is no evidence that the children are being neglected or abused and it is only a presumption that the two are inadequate parents, it is not clear in this scenario that the concern actually rises to a level that requires reporting. Dr. Ogden could well ruin Pam's career without any real evidence that she is an impaired mother. In addition, reporting may only further alienate the couple, sacrificing any chance to engage them in treatment, which, if successful, could benefit the entire family.

Yet as a mother herself, Dr. Ogden is mindful of the chaotic home situation and how this may be adversely affecting the welfare of the teens. If something happened – say, the depressed son attempted suicide – Dr. Ogden would never be able to forgive herself. In addition, Dr. Ogden respects and trusts her nurses, who are experiencing moral distress about the situation and who could potentially report on their own if Dr. Ogden does not do so. She feels it is up to her to provide ethical leadership for the staff facing this dilemma.

There is no such provision in the federal confidentiality regulations for reporting impaired health professionals, but Dr. Ogden believes the questions involved are far more ethical than legal (Brooks, 2005). She is sensitive to the ethical issues her nursing staff have raised regarding the fact that this woman is taking high doses of psychoactive drugs that impair judgment and is caring for critically ill human beings. But again, it is only an assumption that she is impaired. The clinic staff have no objective indication she is not competent as a nursing professional. It can also be argued that identifying Pam as an impaired nurse is the responsibility of her employer and clinical supervisor and that if her performance in such a demanding arena were unsafe, it would have been detected long before. Yet, Dr. Ogden knows she must assume some responsibility for providing documentation to Pam's employers that the use of controlled substances was clinically indicated for Pam's conditions. She is painfully aware that this may have led Pam's supervisors to believe she can safely function while taking the medications since she is under medical supervision or to feel that they have no administrative recourse since a physician has provided the prescriptions.

Turning to the newly revised Code of Ethics for Nurses, Dr. Ogden finds support for her moral intuition not to report at this time. Statement 3.6 on Patient Protection and Impaired Practice states: "Nurses must protect the patient, and the public, and the profession from potential harm when practice appears to be impaired. The nurse's duty is to take action to protect patients and to ensure the impaired individual receives assistance" (Lachman, Swanson, & Winland-Brown, 2015; Winland-Brown, Lachman, & Swanson, 2015). Dr. Ogden feels she can best accomplish both these goals through taking a more therapeutic approach, as she has successfully done with Pam so many times in the past.

Dr. Ogden decides to try and persuade Pam as a fellow nurse to enter treatment voluntarily or to self-report to the professional health monitoring programs that exist in almost every state. Previously when other health care practitioners such as the emergency department social worker documented their belief that Pam was addicted, the clinic team called her in, and she seemed to always have a plausible explanation and denied she had a problem. Dr. Ogden takes this approach because she feels that an appeal as a fellow parent and health professional may be able to break through Pam's denial and, if constructive, would have the fewest adverse consequences on Pam's career and family life, as well as perhaps preserving the treatment alliance. She discusses her plan with Dr. Reed, the clinic psychologist. In retrospect, the clinic psychologist Dr. Reed realizes the entire staff has likely overidentified with Pam as a fellow health care professional and working mother, and this only intensifies their feeling of responsibility. Dr. Reed must also manage the resentment and anger that are the natural human reactions of the staff at being deceived and manipulated.

Dr. Reed believes that if Dr. Ogden meets with Pam and takes a harder line about the need for substance use treatment, Pam will likely resort to denial and defensiveness. Dr. Ogden as clinic director will still be left with the decision of whether to disclose the information about the marriage or report Pam, but agrees that from a humanistic perspective it is worth trying, especially as it does not prevent them from reporting Pam later if she rejects help. Further, now robbed of the comforting illusion that Cliff is a stable parent and partner, Dr. Reed recognizes she may need to disclose to Pam that she knows that Cliff is not only a patient at the clinic, but also one with his own substance use disorder. Such a disclosure clearly violates the privacy of each individual, even though they are married, and could be actionable in court, resulting in professional sanctions adversely impacting Dr. Reed's career and ability to help similar patients in the future.

Dr. Ogden can humanely taper the medications, but she knows Pam has insurance and can go elsewhere for care, thereby only transferring the problem to another practitioner who does not know Pam's history or circumstances. The only real leverage Drs. Ogden and Reed have is to tell Pam she must enter addiction treatment or they will report her to the nursing board. Such an ultimatum smacks of the discredited confrontational interventions of old and will likely disrupt, if not terminate, the treatment alliance.

But failing to disclose will leave Drs. Reed and Ogden with the ethical awareness that they have not done all they could possibly do to prevent harm to the children in Pam's care at home and the seriously ill individuals she looks after at the hospital. Even worse for them as clinicians is that if they take this approach, they may have missed a chance to engage the couple in treatment, which would be the most beneficial outcome for all involved.

The rules-based resolution of this conundrum is for the director to "forget" what she knows and to continue to care for the two patients as individuals. This is a legally defensible and even ethically justifiable option, but is not likely to relieve the staff's moral sense of responsibility or the fundamental clinical commitment to the virtues of veracity and fidelity. While not reporting seems the safer course, if one of the boys took their parents' medications and was hospitalized with an overdose, or one of the intensive care patients under Pam's care died due to her oversedation or inattention, the documentation would show Drs. Ogden and Reed knew about these risks and did nothing to prevent the harm to third-parties. In contrast, a values-based solution risks disclosing the information and requires moral courage in that the disclosure may end the treatment relationship and ironically result in the director or nurse practitioner themselves being reported.

However, it is not the fear of legal sanctions but her primary ethical orientation that persuades the nurse practitioner not to report Pam to any authority, but rather to disclose the information to her face to face. Early in her doctoral studies, Dr. Ogden was drawn to the ethics of care because it recognizes the importance of emotions and relationships, which she believes were neglected in many theories that overemphasize rule-based reasoning. Her compassion for Pam and empathy with her situation as a mother and a nurse led Dr. Ogden to feel that preserving her role as a healer in Pam's life was paramount, which meant not reporting her to either child protective services or the nursing board at this time (Lachman, 2012). But not disclosing what she knows does give Pam the opportunity for self-improvement. It may be that only a person Pam trusts and respects can break through her defenses and enable her to take positive action to heal herself. The ethics of care affirms the strength of human relationships to endure trials and the resilience of the person in the face of shared difficulty.

Dr. Ogden, after talking it over with the entire team and a mentor who is a nurse ethicist, decides to disclose to Pam that she knows she is married to another clinic patient and that the entire staff is worried the couple have serious substance use problems that could endanger their children, and also that Pam's addiction could jeopardize her career. As she anticipated, the meeting with Pam does not go well, and when a frustrated Dr. Ogden mentions that she has considered reporting Pam to the nursing board, the patient becomes enraged and threatens to report Dr. Ogden for a breach of confidentiality. Pam storms out of the office and both she and her husband transfer their care to a provider in the community, and Dr. Reed later learns the couple has moved to Florida. Drs. Ogden and Reed decide not to proceed with any reporting to external authorities, hoping that Pam may in time be able to accept that Dr. Ogden truly cared about her welfare. Reporting would harm Pam's marriage, her career, and her sons without any reliable promise that good would emerge. Her response might well be greater denial and regression, rather than self-realization and growth, the benefits Dr. Ogden felt ethically justified truth-telling even at the risk of rupturing the relationship with Pam. Ethically, if Dr. Ogden reports, Pam might never again feel safe seeking treatment, which is ultimately what Dr. Ogden hoped to accomplish in disclosing the information. For several months after the encounter, Dr. Ogden is apprehensive about a lawsuit against her, but still feels she did the right thing according to her own conscience in trying to reason with Pam.

The Case of Decisional Capacity

Bernice is a 65-year-old woman diagnosed with rheumatoid arthritis, diabetes, borderline personality disorder, and major depression. She takes numerous medications for her mental and physical conditions. Her long-time partner who handled all the household and financial matters dies unexpectedly, leaving her with a young adult daughter who herself has a history of drug addiction. Since they never married, Bernice loses the house, leading to a downward spiral where she is frequently homeless despite having adequate income to afford a decent apartment. The lawyer representing her in the probate hearing, Ms. Jane Jackson, realizes that Bernice is unable to care for herself and successfully petitions the court for a conservator to handle Bernice's modest assets.

Soon after the house is sold, Bernice has the first of what will be many admissions to the intensive care unit with "accidents" and unintentional overdoses. Her toxicology screen shows dozens of substances, some illicit like methamphetamine, other prescribed like muscle relaxants and sleeping pills. When the consulting psychologist, Dr. Antonio, interviews Bernice, she denies she was trying to kill herself. When asked how all the drugs got into her system, Bernice provides extremely dubious explanations such as her daughter injected her or someone put it in her drink. These stories are so improbable that the psychologist comes to believe Bernice is exhibiting the most profound denial regarding her substance use he has ever seen. Bernice has received little benefit from several acute, voluntary psychiatric hospitalizations and refuses substance use treatment, stating she does not have a problem.

The police have been called to the home several times because the intoxicated daughter is verbally abusive to her mother, but they consider these altercations to be domestic disputes between adults and have no interest in or time for prosecution, recommending that Bernice obtain a restraining order against her daughter.

After an intensive care stay for a multidrug overdose in which Bernice is on a ventilator and dialysis for weeks with a guarded chance for survival, the attorney and the psychiatrist decide to petition the court for guardianship. As part of the evaluation, Bernice undergoes neuropsychological testing, which finds she has slightly below normal intelligence but sufficient cognitive ability to make her own decisions. When this is presented to the judge along with Bernice's own appearance before him, he rejects the petition, ruling that she can handle her own affairs. Dr. Antonio testifies at the hearing that, in his professional judgment, Bernice has such poor insight and judgment that she lacks the mental acuity necessary to keep herself safe. Under cross-examination, he is forced to admit he has no objective evidence to support this contention other than his years of experience and clinical judgment. The neuropsychologist continues to insist that Dr. Antonio's claims are subjective and that Bernice may be exercising judgment in a way that is risky and contrary to what a prudent person may choose, but that it is her right to make these choices, even if they are bad ones. Dr. Antonio's many interactions with Bernice have persuaded him to conclude that she functions like a child, frequently crying if he raises his voice or says anything remotely critical about her substance use, and begging him for more medications with a plaintive exclamation that if he liked her he would give her more medications so she does not have to feel bad.

Bernice is in the process of having the conservator dismissed on the basis of the judge's ruling when in a single month she is admitted three times with drug misadventures, including an insulin overdose that almost kills her. At this juncture, the hospital's consulting psychologist is once more called in to determine if Bernice has decision-making capacity and to make recommendations regarding disposition. The psychologist administers the Montreal Cognitive Assessment at the bedside and conducts a thorough psychological assessment (Nasreddine et al., 2005). Bernice is cooperative with the cognitive screen and scores 26, which for her educational level is in the normal range. She is childlike and passive during the assessment, which identifies no delirium, major depression, severe anxiety disorder, or psychotic symptoms that would render Bernice incapable of making a decision to return home. The psychologist finds on the basis of his assessment that Bernice possesses adequate intellectual ability to refuse placement in a higher level of care.

Decisional Capacity Case Analysis

This case underscores the medical and legal netherworld where many patients and practitioners facing addiction ethical dilemmas dwell. If these overdoses were truly suicide attempts borne of depression and desperation, under most state mental health codes Bernice could meet criteria for involuntary admission to an inpatient psychiatric unit. A mental health court would likely concur with Dr. Antonio that Bernice is a danger to herself and needs involuntary commitment to receive aggressive psychiatric treatment with the goal of restoring her decisional capacity. In fact, some state laws would also permit involuntary hospitalization of Bernice on the basis of severe self-neglect, as her decisions have resulted in situations that deprive her of essential services necessary to maintain minimal mental, emotional, or physical health and safety. Dr. Antonio has not been very successful in the local mental health court with these cases in the past, but feels he may need to try again if for no other reason than to keep Bernice safe for a few days and to give Dr. Antonio time to consult with Ms. Jackson.

In discussing the dire situation with the attorney, Ms. Jackson suggests to Dr. Antonio that she could make an argument for involuntary commitment on the basis that Bernice is indirectly suicidal, and that on a not completely conscious level Bernice wants to die. Dr. Antonio thinks this could work as the courts worry about having a patient's death on their hands. Yet he does not honestly believe Bernice is truly suicidal, and Dr. Antonio worries about setting a precedent of deception before the court, as well as compromising his own professional integrity. Yet if Dr. Antonio prevailed in court, it would be the judge who made the decision for commitment. Once on the inpatient unit for an extended period, Dr. Antonio could seek a second opinion from another neuropsychologist regarding Bernice's capacity.

Dr. Antonio is having difficulty sorting out the many competing value claims and so requests an ethics consultation from the hospital ethics committee. The committee's written response opines that attempting to hospitalize a patient that a court has determined to be competent against her will is a violation of her autonomy and the law. Hospital counsel learns of the case from the risk manager who serves on the ethics committee. The hospital counsel pressures Dr. Antonio to respect the judge's decision, since contradicting the ruling of the district court could be a real liability for the hospital. Hospital counsel reminds Dr. Antonio that in a similar case a few years ago where a patient with schizophrenia had been involuntarily committed despite not being declared a danger to himself nor incompetent, mental health advocates and the state Protection and Advocacy Office had threatened their own lawsuits and also gone to the media. The attorney insinuates that the hospital might not be able to represent Dr. Antonio in court should he disregard this advice about dropping the entire Bernice matter, but then quickly adds the subtle qualifier, "I am not telling you what clinical decision to make."

Dr. Antonio knows that Bernice is not acutely or directly suicidal as the law in his state requires, and he realizes that to present the patient as such is a softly paternalistic act that, despite good intentions, borders on dishonesty. Based on long experience with patients like Bernice, Dr. Antonio also knows that if bending the truth results in Bernice being admitted, she will cooperate with inpatient treatment while continuing to deny she has a substance use problem. Bernice's cooperation and continued denial of any abuse of substances will eventually lead the treatment team to legally be required to convert her to voluntary status. Once voluntary, Bernice will soon request discharge. The team would of course offer and strongly encourage Bernice to remain on the ward for stabilization and then consider a residential addiction program, but she will likely refuse. Moreover, the hospital's utilization reviewers will demand discharge, as will Bernice's insurance company, contending that she does not require this acute level of care. Bernice is street-smart and could also contact protection and advocacy or disability rights organizations and would have a valid complaint that keeping her as an inpatient is coercive and a violation of her autonomous rights. Bernice may or may not attend outpatient appointments depending on whether the clinicians are prescribing medications she abuses, but she will certainly tell the judge and the advocates she will be adherent to any outpatient treatment regimen in order to avoid commitment or any restriction on her personal liberty.

In the vast majority of states, even severe substance use apart from other mental health disorders like depression or psychosis is not grounds for involuntary psychiatric admission. In those jurisdictions where mental health treatment can be forced, it is primarily for acute intoxication and agitation and/or on a short-term basis (Gendel, 2006). There is currently no judicial mechanism for handling a person with mental health needs like Bernice who has such a chronic and severe addiction. This is a source of anguish for families begging for help for their loved ones and a source of frustration for health care professionals unable to obligate a patient to enter substance use treatment against their will outside of a forensic context.

The psychiatrist on Dr. Antonio's consultation team checks the prescription monitoring program and sees that most of the drugs found in her urine are not prescribed. For those that are he posts an alert identifying Bernice as a high-risk patient abusing her prescriptions. But he accepts this will not dry up the illegal sources, nor deter harried emergency room practitioners or less knowledgeable practitioners from giving prescriptions when confronted with this woman who looks like their grandmother crying about her pain and who, after all, has very real medical problems.

Dr. Antonio and Ms. Jackson are convinced that Bernice is incapable, yet that incapacity lies in a volitional and affective dimension, the nuances of which the law has yet to recognize (Roberts, 2002). Using the more objective cognitive standard used in most guardianship hearings (Gutheil & Bursztajn, 1986), the court would likely be constrained to find Bernice competent to continue to make bad choices or "have bad luck."

In making their case, the doctor and lawyer can draw upon a growing body of neurobiological literature suggesting that patients with heavy and prolonged drug use may eventually reach a point where they are unable to choose anything other than to use. In some persons like Bernice, the rewards of addiction have eclipsed and subsumed every other value, including relationships and quality of life. A person who finds salient motivation, pleasure, and satisfaction only in addiction is likely deficient in the higher-order faculties of appreciation and reasoning, even if these cannot be parsed out in conventional assessments of executive functioning.

In his heart, Dr. Antonio does not believe that Bernice is capable in any functional sense, but he also does not think that the patient meets current legal criteria for incompetence or involuntary hospitalization. Ms. Jackson wants to go back to court and try to persuade the judge that without a guardian of person, Bernice will eventually die, albeit unintentionally. Ms. Jackson feels that she as an attorney and Dr. Antonio as a health care professional both have a fiduciary duty and ethical obligation to protect Bernice from the dire consequences of her own functional incapacity, even if the court will not declare her incompetent. Dr. Antonio is tired and afraid; he has two children in college and, as a single father, needs his job to pay for their education. He cannot muster the courage to act on his own deepest integrity and so tells the attorney that he will not go to court, but that the next time Bernice is in the hospital he will transfer her involuntarily to the psychiatric unit and let the inpatient team decide whether to file for commitment. Dr. Antonio does agree to provide a written statement in support of keeping the conservator. He rationalizes that without having control of her funds, Bernice will not have as easy access to drugs and may keep a roof over her head.

Despite her strong commitment to civil rights, the attorney believes that both the court and the neuropsychologist are placing too much emphasis on a reflexive and unreflective view of autonomy, one that runs contrary to Bernice's best interests and that fails to take into account the complexities of addiction. Dr. Antonio reviews the Ethical Principles and Code of Conduct of the American Psychological Association Principle E on Respect for People's Rights and Dignity, which reads, "Psychologists are aware that special safeguards may be necessary to protect the rights and welfare of persons or communities whose vulnerabilities impair autonomous decision-making" (APA, 2010). This also strongly accords with 3.04 of the APA's Code of Conduct, obliging the practitioner to take reasonable steps to avoid, mitigate, and minimize foreseeable harm to patients (APA, 2010). In this instance, taking necessary precautions, including those that risk disclosing confidential information without consent, works to safeguard patient well-being and help preserve patient autonomy and dignity. This concept is further elaborated in 4.05 of the APA Code of Conduct, which provides: "Psychologists disclose confidential information without the consent of the individual only as mandated by law, or where permitted by law for a valid purpose such as to (1) provide needed professional services; (2) obtain appropriate professional consultations; (3) protect the client/patient, psychologist, or others from harm" (APA, 2010).

These intertwining imperatives resonate with Dr. Antonio's own deepest moral commitment to place the well-being of the patient above all other considerations. He is dejected about his own inaction and reflects that he is likely suffering from burnout due to the highly stressful work on the consultation service. He calls a former trusted supervisor and, after several meetings, asks the Chair – who is quite happy with Dr. Antonio's decision about Bernice – to assign him to an outpatient clinic.

The Case of Informed Consent

Jose is a 70-year-old married man who retired five years earlier from his longtime job as a state transportation worker. He belongs to a large Hispanic family and is proud of his six successful children. Jose had always drunk heavily on holidays and weekends, but his drinking has never resulted in legal or employment trouble. However, he did experience medical complications from his alcohol use, including hypertension and several brief hospitalizations for gastritis. Recent screening found mild cognitive impairment, likely from alcohol, but Jose remained capable of making his own decisions.

Jose never had hobbies and had few friends outside work. His wife, Maria, was often out of the house caring for other relatives, so that once he retired he became bored and lonely. Frequently left alone, Jose began to drink daily and was often intoxicated or passed out when Maria returned home. Jose had lapses of memory and once left the grandchildren unattended in a backyard pool. Although no one was injured, the adult children had reached their limit and demanded Jose get help for his drinking. Maria spoke only Spanish, and although under state law she was his default legal surrogate, she was completely passive in any discussion about Jose's alcohol problem, saying, "My husband has always done this."

The eldest son, a well-respected businessman on the city council, made an appointment for his father at a community residential treatment program without his father's knowledge or agreement. At the intake, the son answered most of the questions and Jose gave vague, apathetic responses when asked if he wanted to stop drinking or was interested in the program. Jose never explicitly refused treatment and, with his son pressuring him, he agreed to sign the consent to admission. The son intimated that the family could pay for the entire treatment and would, in their gratitude, likely make a generous contribution to the program. The nurse conducting the intake was uncomfortable with the interaction and told Jose's son that his father still had the ability to make his own decisions and would need to express his desire for help with his drinking and make an informed decision about entering the program. The son indignantly replied that his father was not saying no and that she could not expect an elder Hispanic man to tell an Anglo nurse about his private business. The son accused the nurse of being culturally insensitive and demanded to speak to the director immediately. The nurse said she would discuss the case with her entire treatment team later in the day and would call the son to inform him of the decision.

At the team meeting, the social worker, Miguel, who was from the local community, objected strongly to what he felt was the nurse's lack of cultural sensitivity. He contended that the kind of individual autonomy she was asking of Jose is a distinctly Anglo-American perspective that did not take into account the value of family and communal autonomy in Hispanic culture and the cultural view that doctors are respected authorities who should act beneficently (Bedolla, 1995). In addition, he pointed out that, from a systems perspective, addiction is inherently a family problem and it was not the treatment team's right to make a value judgment about how this family handled threats to its solidarity.

Informed Consent Case Analysis

The treatment team was sharply divided, mainly along discipline lines, about whether it was ethically appropriate to admit Jose. At the admissions meeting, the psychologist directing the clinic argues that Jose was acquiescing to family pressure, not authentically consenting to treatment. Without such autonomous engagement, the treatment team is colluding with the family to compel a capable patient into a program he does not wish to enter. Moreover, the treatment team would be relying on consent that is invalid given the coercive circumstances. Motivational interviewing and other psychotherapeutic modalities employed in the program, as well as the recovery-oriented philosophy of the facility and the integrity of the addiction professionals, would all be compromised if Jose is accepted.

The medical director, an internist, cited the literature showing coercion can be effective in addiction treatment (Sullivan et al., 2008), adding that a period of supervised sobriety would confer mental and physical health benefits for Jose and there were no real medical risks of treatment. She did not see the family as forcing the patient into treatment as much as strongly persuading him to live up to his family obligations as a husband and father. The physician contended that this sort of soft paternalism was compatible with respect for the patient.

The addiction therapist expressed a consequentialist perspective that how or why Jose entered treatment was not nearly as important as what he did once he got there and his family was no longer pushing him. Jose's indifference was less troubling to him than the potential to obtain additional funding for the program. It was rare that the not-for-profit group had a patient with insurance who could pay the full fee. And the money made from Jose's treatment, not to mention the possibility of family philanthropy, could fund substance use treatment for several indigent patients.

The administrator of the program, a nonclinician, was apprehensive about the son's political power and that, should the clinic refuse to admit Jose, the son could launch an investigation of the program on some regulatory pretense that could shut them down.

The director was a utilitarian who believed that the goal of public policy is to provide help to the most people possible. If this meant that the rights of one individual were not completely respected, she was willing to live with that on her conscience. In the team meeting, she argued that Jose would be treated well and no harm would come to him if he was admitted without actually consenting to treatment.

Miguel pointed out that this was a manifest conflict of interest and that they all needed to remember as health care professionals to reach a decision that was best for Jose *and* for his family. The social worker eloquently told the team that his profession was about social justice and patient advocacy, not risk management or securing the financial future of the program. He rejected the physician's use of a medical model as failing to honor social work values in ethical decision-making. The "Dignity and Worth of the Person" and the "Importance of Relationships" are two of the core ethical principles of the National Association of Social Workers Code of Ethics, which Miguel felt should be central to the resolution of the dilemma (National Association of Social Workers, 2008).

Miguel explained his ethical reasoning to the team. Jose was not actively refusing treatment or insisting he did not have a problem. Jose he argued was providing "informed consent" within his own historical and cultural context in that he was allowing his family, specifically his eldest son as the leader of the family, to make decisions on his behalf for the good of the extended family and Jose. From Miguel's perspective, justice and beneficence for the family system trump pure individualistic autonomy. Were the team to refuse Jose's admission, they would be sacrificing perhaps the only chance the family had of regaining stability and peace. Miguel insisted that this was a question of fairness and that what was most respectful of all involved would be to admit Jose to the program on a trial basis to see if, through participation in the programming and working with staff, he can develop internal motivations to continue in treatment. If at two weeks Jose was still not able to make a commitment to recovery, he would be asked to leave the program. Because their treatment program is voluntary, all agreed that if Jose persistently stated he did not wish to be there and asked to leave, he would be discharged with appropriate referral to outpatient services.

The Case of Stigmatization

Nora is a 46-year-old stay-at-home wife who presented to the emergency department in respiratory distress, with chest tightness and stomach pain. Because of her difficulty breathing, she looked to her husband, Patrick, to answer the medical team's questions. Although it was standard practice to obtain a patient's explicit consent before discussing his or her health information with another party present, a confluence of factors, including Nora's reliance on Patrick to provide past medical information, as well as the emergent nature of her admission, created a presumption that her health information could be discussed with him in the room. Patrick explained that Nora always suffered from allergies around this time of year and that she had a history of moderate asthma, but her chest discomfort and stomach pain were new. The team decided to admit her as an inpatient for diagnostic workup. This made Nora nervous, but with Patrick's assurance, she agreed.

During the times Patrick was away, Nora began to share stories about her life with her bedside nurse, Carol. Nora said she and Patrick had been high-school sweethearts and happily married for 27 years. Their life together had not been without tragedy, however, as they had lost their only son in a motor vehicle accident four years ago. Since then, Nora had not been the same. She became withdrawn, stopped seeing friends, and her normal day-to-day routine became excruciating. During this difficult period, Nora began to experience panic attacks. They would seize her without warning, leaving her paralyzed with fear and doubt. The only way she could get through them was by drinking, which she explained she hid from Patrick. Having grown up with a drunken father who took his rage out on his family, Patrick vowed never to touch alcohol and did not allow it in the house.

When Nora's laboratory results came back, the team concluded that there was no indication of an acute coronary syndrome and that her respiratory distress and chest pain seemed most likely to be attributable to anxiety. The lab work did reveal that Nora had severely compromised liver function that was likely alcohol-induced. Nora begged Carol and the rest of the care team not to tell Patrick that her medical condition had anything to do with drinking, insisting he would be devastated. She implored them instead to tell Patrick that her respiratory distress and stomach pain were the result of her asthma, not anxiety, as she felt ashamed that she could not gain control over her overwhelming emotions without alcohol.

Wanting to do everything to respect Nora's autonomy and honor her request, the team was caught between their duty to her as their patient and their professional obligation for transparency and truthfulness while acting in her best interest. Relying on her past implied consent to include Patrick, they had already shared so much of her medical information with him, both upon admission and over the phone when he called for updates. Although the team knew that it was squarely within Nora's ethical and legal right to revoke or limit her consent regarding medical information, withholding information now seemed both difficult and awkward. In addition, attributing her symptoms to false causes obscured her mental health needs, which could prohibit Nora from following the medical recommendation regarding mental health care and treatment. In other words, the team felt caught between the ethical imperatives to respect a patient's autonomy while fulfilling their professional obligation for beneficence.

Stigmatization Case Analysis

Nora's case presents intertwined ethical and logistical dilemmas. Nurses – and health care providers more broadly – have an ethical as well as legal obligation to respect a patient's autonomous decision to restrict with whom medical information is shared. This obligation stems from a "fundamental and universal moral truth . . . that humans are owed respect for their ability to make reasoned choices that are their own and that others may or may not share" (Pellegrino & Thomasma, 1993). Additionally, this is codified in the American Nurses Association's Position Statement on Privacy and Confidentiality, which states that privacy and confidentiality are essential to maintaining a trusting relationship, a component of treatment that is indispensable, particularly in addiction recovery (American Nurses Association Center for Ethics and Human Rights, 2015). Despite these imperatives, obtaining a patient's explicit consent presupposes there is always a seamless opportunity to ask a patient in advance whom, and to what extent, he or she wishes for others – even spouses who are present at admission – to be involved. In hindsight, the emergent nature and circumstances of Nora's admission prevented the team from obtaining explicit consent, even though Nora did not object to Patrick's involvement until now. While the law provides that, as long as a patient does not object, health care providers may rely on implied consent to communicate with family members, friends, or other persons involved in providing or paying for a patient's health care ("Security and Privacy"), this does not resolve the ethical dilemma.

Another consideration here is that Nora not only begged the team to withhold information from Patrick, she also requested the team make false statements to him about the nature of her condition. From a practical standpoint, even if a health care provider were to agree to Nora's request, it is impossible to guarantee that every other person involved in her care would know about her request for deception and also agree to abide by it. Such an endeavor becomes even more impractical in a large academic institution, where patients may have many different services and teams involved in their care. No matter how altruistic the motivation for engaging in deception, this request causes the health professionals on the team to breach their professional and ethical obligation of truth-telling and perhaps even acting in a patient's best interest. For example, if Nora suffers a true medical emergency that leaves her unable to speak for herself in the future, Patrick's understanding that her previous episode was secondary to asthma may mislead medical providers, delaying accurate diagnosis and treatment.

The American Nurses Association's Code of Ethics has nine provisions that assist in guiding ethically optimal decision-making and professional conduct, many of which are useful here (ANA, 2015). For example, Provision Two states that "(t)he nurse's primary commitment is to the patient, whether an individual, family, group, community, or population" (ANA, 2015). This helps focus on the nurse's obligation to ensure the primacy of the patient's interests, regardless of conflicts that arise between clinicians or patient and family. Refusing to divulge any more information regarding Nora's condition could confuse Patrick and even evoke his suspicion. The consequences of this conflict should not interfere with putting Nora's request to restrict information first. However, Nora's request to deceive him is ethically impermissible and carries both immediate and far-reaching consequences that could erode trust in the medical profession at large (Palmieri & Stern, 2009). It is important, therefore, to appreciate the difference between respecting a patient's autonomous control over his or her own health information and drawing an ethical boundary against acquiescing to a patient's unfair request to engage in deception, no matter how sympathetic or seemingly innocuous it may appear.

It would be ideal for the team to engage in an empathetic dialogue with Nora regarding her requests, explaining all the potential benefits of pursuing mental health treatment and the long-term harm of continuing to suffer in silence. But if this proves unsuccessful and she continues to refuse Patrick's involvement, the team should discuss the practical ramifications of ceasing to share information with him at this time, which could foreseeably cause him bewilderment and frustration with her.

As Paul Ramsey elegantly stated, "Act always so as not to abuse trust; act always so as to exhibit faithfulness, to deserve and inspire trust" (Ramsey, 1970). Although the team risks angering Nora by setting a professional boundary against deception, they should take time to discuss the reasoning behind this action. Providing justifications in this way may guard against a sense of betrayal or abandonment and help preserve the therapeutic alliance and closeness with the team.

Finally, although the health care team may feel frustrated when patients reject interventions or seem to self-sabotage, it is important to keep in mind the correlation between a strong therapeutic alliance and substance use disorder recovery in order to fight off compassion fatigue (Meier, Donmall, McElduff, Barrowclough, & Heller, 2006). Ultimately, although patients like Nora may not be receptive to treatment recommendations at one time, this does not mean they discount the team's expertise or will always refuse recommendations. Although it may be difficult, taking the long view can help providers renew their commitment to patients like Nora, which, in turn, makes recovery all the more possible.

The Case of Misuse of Prescription Stimulants

Amir is a bright, first-generation American in the midst of his second year of law school. Always an overachiever, his admission to a top-tier law school has brought heretofore unexperienced competition, and he is no longer receiving the A's to which he and his parents have grown accustomed during college. He received his first C in Administrative Law, which was distressing on a personal level, but when compounded with his parents' disappointment, was absolutely devastating. His mother and father had sacrificed so much to give him the opportunities that were now in front of him, and though he was studying harder than ever before, the demanding material made him question his natural ability and undermined his confidence. This self-doubt left him unable to concentrate, but strengthened his resolve to improve his performance by any means necessary.

Although he had encountered classmates abusing stimulants during college, it paled in comparison to the rampant use by his law school colleagues. In fact, one of his best friends, Jules, who was in the top ten percent of their class, even casually bragged about how easy it was to feign symptoms of ADHD to get an Adderall prescription. Amir felt he had no other option but to pursue the same course of action or else he would fall further and further behind. He asked Jules for the contact information of her prescribing psychologist, Dr. Sarra Wylder. She coached him about what to say to Dr. Wylder, including which symptoms to exaggerate and which to deny. Soon, Amir was sitting in Dr. Wylder's examination room, making his case for the diagnosis, and, if he pulled it off, ultimately for a prescription.

Dr. Wylder listened while Amir recounted his symptoms and the degree to which they impacted his studies. Because Amir was a new patient, Dr. Wylder did not have any personal knowledge of his past medical or psychiatric history, but she found it curious that Amir was able to achieve such academic success despite what he painted as a lifetime struggle with ADHD. With such a level of disability, Dr. Wylder wondered why he had never sought treatment in the past. She was always hesitant to discredit patients' accounts, especially since they were the only ones who could quantify their quality of life, but something in Amir's account made her skeptical.

Dr. Wylder's first inclination was always to trust her patients and to do everything to appropriately alleviate their suffering. As she listened to Amir describe the demands of his daily life, there was no doubt he was distressed, but Dr. Wylder grew more and more inclined to attribute this to the intense pressure of academia and external expectations, not undiagnosed ADHD. However fatalistically, Dr. Wylder could not help but think that even if she refused to write a prescription, it was almost inevitable that Amir would go from provider to provider until he found one who would, or, worse, buy it off the street. Another troubling dimension was that Dr. Wylder had other patients, both adolescents and adults alike, whom she had watched endure the disabling effects of ADHD before receiving treatment.

She felt as though prescribing this medication to someone without these struggles would provide an unfair cognitive advancement and widen the disparity between populations with higher socioeconomic status and those without. Instead of taking the time to delve deeper while holding firm to professional boundaries, writing a prescription could save time and appease Amir. However, doing so would sacrifice ethical and professional responsibilities, risking irreparable damage to Amir's well-being, as well as her professional reputation.

Misuse of Prescription Stimulants Case Analysis

In this case, Amir is not simply asking Dr. Wylder to consider a request for cognitive enhancement – he is delivering a well-rehearsed speech in order to deceive Dr. Wylder into treating a nonexistent disorder with a substance of abuse. Amir may be tempted to deny other preexisting health needs if he suspects they could prevent obtaining the prescription. This kind of deception, resulting from desperation, threatens the therapeutic relationship and prevents Dr. Wylder from acting in Amir's best interest; worse, it may even result in grave harm to Amir.

Principle A of the American Psychological Association's (APA) Ethical Principles of Psychologists and Code of Conduct states that psychologists must strive to benefit those with whom they work and take care to do no harm (APA, 2010). Prescribing these medications without an appropriate clinical indication is not a benign action; as with any other medication, prescription amphetamines like Adderall carry the risk of adverse events. Because of their effects on the catecholamine system, these medications increase executive functions in patients and most other healthy people, improving their ability to focus their attention, manipulate information in working memory, and flexibly control their responses (Sahakian & Morein-Zamir, 2007). However, if Amir were to obtain a prescription and not use it responsibly by taking a higher dosage than prescribed, he could face more severe physical and mental side effects, such as cardiovascular complications, seizures, aggressive behavior, and mania (Brown, 2002). He may also be vulnerable to severe psychological or physical dependence.

Dr. Wylder must be mindful of both the immediate and far-reaching consequences of treatment decisions. As stated in Standard 3.04 in the APA Code of Conduct, psychologists must take reasonable steps to avoid harming their clients/patients, students, supervisees, research participants, organizational clients, and others with whom they work, as well as to minimize harm where it is foreseeable and unavoidable (APA, 2010). It is reasonably to predict that the health of the general public may also be harmed if Amir either gives or sells his stimulants to other students. Finally, Dr. Wylder must also consider whether prescribing amphetamines for Amir provides him with an unfair advantage in classroom competition, which could lead to a different kind of social harm and perpetuate health care disparities.

In addition, Dr. Wylder also wants to uphold her ethical obligation to practice with integrity; according to her assessment, these medications are not indicated for Amir. She knows that under the APA Ethics Code, psychologists must promote accuracy, honesty, and truthfulness in the practice of psychology (APA Principle C); therefore, writing a prescription would put both her patient and her reputation in jeopardy (APA, 2010). Also of concern is that prescribing this medication would abrogate Dr. Wylder's ability to attend to Amir's larger health needs, keeping him from developing tools to help mitigate life's unavoidable stressors. While stimulant medication may seem optimal in terms of efficacy and immediacy of enhancing cognition, other interventions that do not carry the same level of risk may be even more potent. For example, recent research has identified beneficial neural changes engendered by exercise, nutrition, and sleep, which do not pose the kinds of long-term risks these medications may indeed present. Similarly, psychological interventions such as cognitive behavioral therapy have consistently been shown to be effective for treating myriad mental health needs, especially anxiety and depression (Butler, Chapman, Forman, & Beck, 2006).

The ethical analysis of prescription cognitive enhancement is complex and evolving, and many well-respected authors have advocated the availability of cognition-enhancing pharmaceuticals for healthy individuals (Greely et al., 2008). Recently, the U.S. Bioethics Commission released the second volume of its report on neuroscience and ethics entitled *Gray Matters: Topics at the Intersection of Neuroscience, Ethics, and Society*, which took up the debate (Allhoff, Lin, & Steinberg, 2011; Presidential Commission for the Study of Bioethical Issues, 2015). Needless to say, there are conflicting views. Physicians who view medicine as devoted to healing may view such prescribing as unethical, whereas those who view medicine more broadly as helping patients live better or achieve their personal goals may be open to considering such a request. The difference between these two views lies in the physician–patient encounter.

Dr. Wylder recognizes that her duty to nonmaleficence and her commitment to professional integrity will not permit her to prescribe medications with considerable risks to a patient who shows no clinical indication he could benefit from them. She also recognizes her obligation to uphold the principle of justice to other patients and society at large, which includes maximizing the accessibility of mental health treatment and a fair distribution of services to those truly in need. Dr. Wylder knows Amir is truly distressed, so she takes care to explain with empathy that the young man does not meet the diagnostic criteria for medications and that taking them without indication exposes him to serious side effects.

She offers instead to see him for therapy or to make a referral to a counselor at the student health center who can help recalibrate his goals and mitigate his stressors. Dr. Wylder also recommends a learning assessment to ascertain whether other study habits or strategies could improve his concentration.

While it is true that another health care professional may prescribe these medications for Amir, it is important to emphasize that Dr. Wylder had the moral courage to let the ethical principles and professional values guide her through the analysis and ultimate treatment decision. She also took care not to simply turn Amir away, recognizing that his distress was real and deserving of compassion and care. By offering different treatment modalities and brainstorming alternative strategies for success apart from medication, she did not abandon a patient in need, but instead upheld personal and professional commitments.

Recommendations for Ethically Responsible Practice in Addiction Treatment

1. Understand and internalize professional ethics, especially regarding emerging ethical issues. Know and apply in practice the respective codes of the mental health professions. Undertake self-study in ethical theory and principles to develop a deeper understanding of moral reasoning. Take advantage of continuing education in professional ethics such as local and regional conferences and electronic offerings. Adopt and regularly employ an ethical decision-making model that can be used to deliberately work through particularly difficult ethical dilemmas. Engage in moral reflection to identify personal values and anticipate potential conflicts with professional norms. Arrange to meet regularly with a morally serious person to obtain trusted counsel regarding challenging ethical questions. Dr. Ogden in the case presented benefitted both from her study of ethical theory and from the ability to seek expert advice from an ethics mentor.

2. Know the available resources: the Joint Commission requires hospitals and other health care institutions to have a mechanism available to staff and patients and families for resolving ethical disputes (Joint Commission for Accreditation of Healthcare Organizations, 1993). Universities and law and medical schools increasingly have bioethicists among their faculty who can serve as subject matter experts. Most professional societies such as the APA and the National Association of Social Workers have national and often local chapter ethics committees or officers who can provide discipline-specific guidance. These organizations also produce more general ethics codes, opinions on current or debated ethical issues, and position statements such as those cited in this chapter on core ethical questions significant to the profession. State licensing boards are invaluable references for the regulations governing practice. In the age of the Internet, even the health care professional in a remote rural area or small community instantly has access to continuing education, webinars, e-ethics consultations, blogs, and message boards, with the caveat that practitioners should rely only on reputable sites for information. Finally, we recommend that health care professionals study the burgeoning scholarly literature in addiction ethics and read a text on addition ethics to provide a solid foundation and to address gaps in knowledge in this rapidly growing area of applied ethics (Bissell & Royce, 1994; Geppert & Roberts, 2008; Taleff, 2010).

3. Consult, consult, consult: Jose's case emphasizes the advantages of having a variety of different perspectives on complicated ethical issues. No one practitioner or ethicist, no matter how self-reflective or skilled, is without bias and limitations. The best practitioners have ongoing supervision for their most challenging patients and develop relationships with respected supervisors with whom they can process not just their ethical reasoning when making hard decisions, but also their emotional reactions to what are often stressful, even tragic situations.

Having such "wise persons" to consult can prevent burnout and reduce the burden of making tough and often risky ethical decisions. Often, busy clinicians obtain outside expert opinions, but fail to document the consultation. Such documentation can be protective not only psychologically, but also legally if the decisions made come under institutional review, professional scrutiny, or even legal action. Consulting shows that a practitioner possesses, and exercises, the key professional virtues of humility, discernment, and prudence.

4. Explain your thinking: clinicians often may arrive at a sound and defensible ethical resolution of a complex case, but neglect to explain how they arrived at the decision. We have attempted to provide examples of such ethical explication in these cases. The standard of responsible clinical practice is not omniscience or perfection, but that the practitioner establishes the clinical facts, clarifies the ethical questions, analyzes the issues, reflectively deliberates about the relative the benefits and risks of the ethically justifiable options, and then provides a rationale for choosing among them. Particularly when the decision is not the safest institutionally or the outcome is unfavorable, demonstrating that the health care professional exercised the due diligence expected of a reasonable practitioner is strong evidence that the standard of care was upheld.

5. Think prospectively: the unfortunate truth about addiction is that the disease compromises individuals' cognitive abilities and, consequently, deprives them of autonomy. When patients lack capacity, even temporarily, medical professionals must rely on surrogates, whether appointed legally or through state hierarchies listing those persons that may make medical decisions on behalf of the patient. In some situations, default surrogates are able to exercise substituted judgment and can speak to what the patient him or herself would have wanted. But in many cases, surrogates are unable to meet this higher standard and must resort to the less patient-centered best interest criteria. Substance use disorders are fueled by isolation and thrive in secrecy. It is therefore important to keep in mind that this disease may, by its very nature, subvert open communication with family and friends and rupture relationships. Practitioners should thus encourage all patients, especially those who struggle with a substance use disorder, to designate a person to speak on his or her behalf in order to safeguard autonomy and help that individual feel more empowered and respected. It is hoped that this will also serve as a catalyst to having difficult but crucial conversations that illuminate an individual's values and long-term goals, including recovery.

Conclusion

Ethical theory can draw sharp lines about abstract situations where caricatures of one-dimensional people behave according to clear rules. In practice, the multilayered relationships and multidetermined events that constitute clinical ethical reality require the dynamism and richness of an applied ethics approach. Nowhere are boundaries more blurred, values more nuanced, or humanity messier than in the area of addiction ethics. In this chapter, we have tried to set up some guideposts for those courageous and compassionate health professionals who have chosen to navigate the rough terrain of caring for patients with substance use disorders.

Informed consent, confidentiality, and decisional capacity – foundational in any aspect of mental health ethics – assume an even greater weight in addiction treatment, where the accountability and responsibility of both the practitioner and the patient have legal import. The men and women who are characters in these case stories display internal vulnerabilities that are intensified in a culture that has long equated addiction with failure, casting individuals as criminals. Perhaps the most formidable obstacle to treatment is stigma, which too often prevents those who need help from being honest with themselves, their health care providers, their employers, and their loved ones.

Caring for this population and ensuring best ethical practice therefore entails a unique magnanimity to take the challenges and dilemmas in stride, knowing recovery is indeed always still possible. Where practitioners face less-than-ideal options, it is even more crucial to consult wise colleagues and to clearly document reasoning and decisions. Most importantly, the addiction practitioner must learn to trust his or her own moral awareness. Practitioners must rely on their own clinical and ethical judgment regarding the primacy of the choices of capacitated patients, even when these may harm them while also fulfilling the duty to protect the safety and well-being of patients who can no longer choose for themselves.

References

Allhoff, F., Lin, P., & Steinberg, J. (2011). Ethics of human enhancement: An executive summary. *Science and Engineering Ethics*, *17*, 201–212.

American Nurses Association Center for Ethics and Human Rights (2015). *Privacy and confidentiality: Revised position statement*. Retrieved from www.nursingworld.org/DocumentVault/Position-Statements/Ethics-and-Human-Rights/Position-Statement-Privacy-and-Confidentiality.pdf

American Psychological Association (2010). *Ethical principles of psychologists and code of conduct including 2010 amendments*. Retrieved from www.apa.org/ethics

Barry, C. L., McGinty, E. E., Pescosolido, B. A., & Goldman, H. H. (2014). Stigma, discrimination, treatment effectiveness, and policy: Public views about drug addiction and mental illness. *Psychiatric Services*, *65*, 1269–1272.

Bedolla, M. A. (1995). The principles of medical ethics and their application to Mexican–American elderly patients. *Clinics in Geriatric Medicine*, *11*, 131–137.

Bissell, L. C. & Royce, J. E. (1994). *Ethics for addiction professionals* (2nd edn.). Center City, MN: Hazelden.

Bowden, P. L. (1995). The ethics of nursing care and "the ethic of care." *Nursing Inquiry*, *2*, 10–21.

Brooks, M. K. (2005). Legal aspects of confidentiality and patient information. In J. H. Lowinson, P. Ruiz, R. B. Millman, & J. G. Langrod (Eds.), *Substance abuse: A comprehensive textbook* (4th edn., pp. 1361–1382). Philadelphia, PA: Lippincott Williams & Wilkins.

Brown, T. (2002). *Attention deficit disorders and comorbidities in children, adolescents and adults*. Washington, DC: American Psychiatric Press.

Butler, A. C., Chapman, J. E., Forman, E. M., & Beck, A. T. (2006). The empirical status of cognitive-behavioral therapy: A review of meta-analyses. *Clinical Psychology Review, 26,* 17–31.

Center for Behavioral Statistics and Quality (2015). *Behavioral health trends in the United States: Results from the 2014 National Survey on Drug Use and Health.* Retrieved from www.samhsa.gov/data/sites/default/files/NSDUH-FRR1-2014/NSDUH-FRR1-2014.pdf

Cohen, P. J. (2009a). Medical marijuana: the conflict between scientific evidence and political ideology. Part one of two. *Journal of Pain and Palliative Care Pharmacotherapy, 23,* 4–25.

Cohen, P. J. (2009b). Medical marijuana: The conflict between scientific evidence and political ideology. Part two of two. *Journal of Pain and Palliative Care Pharmacotherapy, 23,* 120–140.

Confidentiality of Alcohol and Drug Abuse Patient Records, 42 Part 2 (1987).

Gendel, M. H. (2006). Substance misuse and substance-related disorders in forensic psychiatry. *Psychiatric Clinics of North America, 29,* 649–673.

Geppert, C. M. A. & Roberts, L. W. (2008). *The book of ethics: Expert guidance for professionals who treat addiction.* Center City, MN: Hazelden.

Greely, H., Sahakian, B., Harris, J., Kessler, R. C., Gazzaniga, M., Campbell, P., & Farah, M. J. (2008). Towards responsible use of cognitive-enhancing drugs by the healthy. *Nature, 456,* 702–705.

Gutheil, T. G. & Bursztajn, H. (1986). Clinicians' guidelines for assessing and presenting subtle forms of patient incompetence in legal settings. *American Journal of Psychiatry, 143,* 1020–1023.

Hall, W., Carter, A., & Forlini, C. (2015). The brain disease model of addiction: Is it supported by the evidence and has it delivered on its promises? *Lancet Psychiatry, 2,* 105–110.

Health Insurance and Portability and Accountability Act, § Parts 160 and 164 of Title 45 (1996).

Hyman, S. E. (2007). The neurobiology of addiction: Implications for voluntary control of behavior. *American Journal of Bioethics, 7,* 8–11.

Joint Commission for Accreditation of Healthcare Organizations (1993). *Patient Rights 1992 Accreditation Manual for Hospitals.* Chicago, IL: Joint Commission Resources.

Lachman, V. D. (2012). Applying the ethics of care to your nursing practice. *Medsurg Nursing, 21,* 112–114, 116.

Lachman, V. D., Swanson, E. O., & Winland-Brown, J. (2015). The new "code of ethics for nurses with interpretative statements" (2015): Practical clinical application, part II. *Medsurg Nursing, 24,* 363–366, 368.

McLellan, A. T., Lewis, D. C., O'Brien, C. P., & Kleber, H. D. (2000). Drug dependence, a chronic medical illness: Implications for treatment, insurance, and outcomes evaluation. *Journal of the American Medical Association, 284,* 1689–1695.

Meier, P. S., Donmall, M. C., McElduff, P., Barrowclough, C., & Heller, R. F. (2006). The role of the early therapeutic alliance in predicting drug treatment dropout. *Drug and Alcohol Dependence, 83,* 57–64.

Morse, S. J. (2007). Voluntary control of behavior and responsibility. *American Journal of Bioethics, 7,* 12–13.

Nasreddine, Z. S., Phillips, N. A., Bedirian, V., et al. (2005). The Montreal Cognitive Assessment, MoCA: A brief screening tool for mild cognitive impairment. *Journal of the American Geriatrics Society, 53*, 695–699.

National Association of Social Workers (2008). *Code of ethics of the National Association of Social Workers*. Retrieved from www.socialworkers.org/About/Ethics/Code-of-Ethics/Code-of-Ethics-English

Palmieri, J. J. & Stern, T. A. (2009). Lies in the doctor–patient relationship. *Primary Care Companion to the Journal of Clinical Psychiatry, 11*, 163–168.

Pellegrino, E. D. & Pellegrino, D. C. (1993). *The virtues in medical practice*. New York, NY: Oxford University.

Presidential Commission for the Study of Bioethical Issues (2015). *Gray matters: Topics at the intersection of neuroscience, ethics, and society*. Retrieved from http://bioethics .gov/sites/default/files/GrayMatter_V2_508.pdf

Ramsey, P. (1970). *The patient as person*. New Haven, CT: Yale University Press.

Rasyidi, E., Wilkins, J. N., & Danovitch, I. (2012). Training the next generation of providers in addiction medicine. *Psychiatric Clinics of North America, 35*, 461–480.

Roberts, L. W. (2002). Informed consent and the capacity for voluntarism. *American Journal of Psychiatry, 159*, 705–712.

Sahakian, B. & Morein-Zamir, S. (2007). Professor's little helper. *Nature, 450*, 1157–1159.

Sullivan, M. A., Birkmayer, F., Boyarsky, B. K., et al. (2008). Uses of coercion in addiction treatment: clinical aspects. *American Journal of addictions, 17*, 36–47.

Taleff, M. H. (2010). *Advanced ethics for addiction professionals*. New York, NY: Springer.

The Association for Addiction Professionals (2004). *NAADAC code of ethics*. Retrieved from www.naadac.org/code-of-ethics

Winland-Brown, J., Lachman, V. D., & Swanson, E. O. (2015). The new "code of ethics for nurses with interpretive statements" (2015): Practical clinical application, part I. *Medsurg Nursing, 24*, 268–271.

9 Ethics and Clients Who Have Experienced Sexual Trauma and Intimate Partner Violence

Krista M. Chronister, Kelsey South,
Anjuli Chitkara-Barry, Harpreet Nagra,
Anna Reichard, and Shoshana D. Kerewsky

Sexual violence and intimate partner violence (IPV) are serious public health issues in the United States and around the world. Such violence substantively compromises the health and well-being of children, adults, families, and communities. The aim of this chapter is to identify central ethical questions that often arise when working with clients who have experienced sexual trauma and IPV. We use a broad, inclusive ethical decision-making heuristic and two case studies to frame the consideration of various ethical dilemmas. We devote particular attention to understanding the intersections of clients' identities and contexts and ethical decision-making.

Definitions and Scope

We use the terms *survivor* and *victim* interchangeably throughout this chapter to identify an individual who has experienced sexual or IPV. Extant research suggests the utility of using the term *survivor* to describe the recipient of violence because it seems more empowering than *victim* and highlights an individual's agency (e.g., Hockett, McGraw, & Saucier, 2014; Parker & Mahlstedt, 2010; Thompson, 2000). Alternatively, other studies highlight the importance of the term *victim* to acknowledge the violence and lasting effects of victimization that many believe the term *survivor* does not capture (e.g., Thompson, 2000; Young & Maguire, 2003). To recognize the importance of both terms, we use the terms *victim* and *survivor* interchangeably.

Sexual violence comprises a specific group of crimes including sexual harassment, sexual assault, stalking, and rape. A stranger, acquaintance, friend, family member, or intimate partner may perpetrate sexual violence (Black et al., 2011). In the majority of sexual violence occurrences, victims know the perpetrator or the violence occurs in the context of a dating relationship (Shorey, Cornelius, & Bell, 2008). National lifetime prevalence data indicate that in the United States, an estimated 19.3 percent of women and 1.7 percent of men have been raped and an estimated 43.9 percent of women and 23.4 percent of men have experienced sexual violence other than rape (e.g., sexual coercion, unwanted sexual contact, and noncontact unwanted sexual experiences) (Black et al., 2011). Young adult women experience higher rates of rape and sexual assault than females in any other age group (Department of Justice, 2014).

IPV is a term used to describe a pattern of coercive control committed by a current or former partner. IPV includes a continuum of abusive behavior comprising physical abuse, sexual abuse, threat of physical or sexual abuse, sexual coercion, psychological/emotional abuse, denial of economic and vocational resources, spiritual abuse, harassment, or torture (e.g., APA, 2002; Chronister & McWhirter, 2003). IPV is experienced and perpetrated by individuals of all genders and occurs between couples who are dating, cohabitating, or married. National estimates show that more than one in three women (35.6 percent) and more than one in four men (28.5 percent) have experienced rape, physical violence, and/or stalking by an intimate partner during their lifetime (Black et al., 2011). It is important to note that IPV and sexual violence are the most underreported crimes in the United States (Bureau of Justice Statistics, 2003). Moreover, national IPV prevalence rates rarely include nonphysical forms of IPV and the experiences of individuals who are serving in the military, undocumented, incarcerated, or without a home.

Researchers have studied stalking victimization primarily within the context of intimate relationships (Black et al., 2011); more recently, scholars are examining stalking and sexual harassment victimization outside of abusive intimate partnerships. Stalking is a pattern of harassing or threatening acts, used by a perpetrator, that is unwanted and causes the victim fear or safety concerns (Black et al., 2011; Tjaden & Thoennes, 1998). National estimates indicate that approximately 1 in 6 women and 1 in 19 men experience stalking during their lifetime (Black et al., 2011). Sexual harassment is defined as unwelcome sexual advances, requests for sexual favors, and other verbal or physical conduct of a sexual nature that creates a hostile or offensive work environment (Equal Employment Opportunity Commission, 2016), with sexual harassment in the workplace receiving the most national attention.

Individuals of all racial, ethnic, disability, gender, sexual orientation, religious, economic, national, and other cultural backgrounds experience sexual violence and IPV (Chronister & Aldarondo, 2012; Chronister, Knoble, & Bahia, 2013; Tjaden & Thoennes, 2000). These forms of violence, however, disproportionately affect women and members of marginalized groups. Communities that experience social and economic marginalization are at greatest risk for sexual violence and IPV, and in particular women, ethnic minority women, adolescents, and young adults (e.g., Aldarondo & Mederos, 2002; Hampton, LaTaillade, Dacey, & Marghi, 2008). It is essential that this disproportionality is considered along with the social and economic marginalization and oppression that specific communities experience (Benson & Fox, 2004a, 2004b). Disproportionality in rates across ethnic groups is less pronounced when access to employment and other economic resources and the impact of acculturation and other contextual factors are considered (e.g., Heise & Garcia-Moreno, 2002; Wilson & Brooks-Gunn, 2001).

The aims of this chapter are to use an ethnical decision-making heuristic and two case studies: (a) to illuminate the important, multifaceted intersections between sexual violence and IPV, context, and ethics; and (b) to consider the diverse range of ethical dilemmas that psychologists frequently encounter when working with victims of sexual trauma and IPV.

Applying an Ethical Decision-Making Model

Therapists working with clients who have experienced sexual trauma and IPV hear the painful details of clients' violence experiences. Caring providers will react emotionally to such content, and most often with feelings of stress, anxiety, fear, or confusion about the type and number of ethical dilemmas that arise when working with survivors of sexual violence and IPV. We encourage psychologists to apply an ethical decision-making model to their clinical work to most effectually manage and use their strong emotional reactions and to anticipate, evaluate, and respond successfully to the ethical and legal challenges that arise.

Many scholars have published frameworks for conceptualizing and working through ethical problems that are relevant to research and practice. These models tend to focus narrowly on ethics or ethics and the law. There are additional factors and processes involved in ethical decision-making. The Oregon Psychological Association's Ethics Committee (2008) presented a summary heuristic that we find helpful for identifying the broad factors involved with ethical dilemmas (cf. APA, 1990). A psychologist may ask:

1. What are my personal values related to this situation?
2. What are the professional ethics related to this situation?
3. What are the laws related to this situation?
4. What are the agency policies related to this situation?
5. What is clarified or may change based on diversity considerations?

A psychologist may answer these questions by constructing a set of four overlapping circles to show points of overlap or disjunction between these factors with a "diversity" circle superimposed on the others (see Figure 9.1). After exploring the relationship between these factors, the care provider may move on to an ethical decision-making process. Corey, Corey, and Callanan (2011, pp. 22–27) provide a useful overview and a model that includes these steps:

1. Identify the problem or dilemma.
2. Identify the potential issues involved.
3. Review the relevant ethics codes.
4. Know the applicable laws and regulations.
5. Obtain consultation.
6. Consider possible and probable courses of action.
7. Enumerate the consequences of various decisions.
8. Choose what appears to be the best course of action.

Given the complexity of the situations presented in this chapter, and especially the likelihood of multiple decision-makers and stakeholders, it is prudent to incorporate

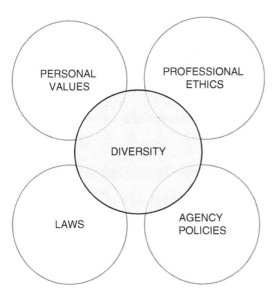

Figure 9.1 *Original figure for Oregon Psychological Association's Ethics Committee summary heuristic (2008)*

the issues of "personal biases, stresses, or self-interest" that the Canadian Psychological Association's Code of Ethics includes:

> . . .assume responsibility for the consequences of the action, including correction of negative consequences, if any, or re-engaging in the decision-making process if the ethical issue is not resolved, and . . . take appropriate action, as warranted and feasible, to prevent future occurrences of the dilemma. (Canadian Psychological Association, 2000, p. 5)

Applying these models and sequence of decision-making techniques helps to decrease the negative influence of psychologists' strong emotional responses to personal history, the client, and the systems involved, and to increase the likelihood that psychologists' actions are the most ethical, sensitive, and inclusive. The remainder of this chapter includes application of these ethical decision-making frameworks to two case examples involving therapeutic work and research with clients who have experienced sexual trauma or IPV.

Client Safety and Confidentiality

Beneficence and nonmaleficence, justice, and respect for people's rights and dignity are three fundamental ethical principles outlined by the American Psychological Association's (APA) Ethical Principles of Psychologists and Code of Conduct (APA, 2010). Psychologists are obligated ethically to "take reasonable steps to avoid harming their clients/patients, students, supervisees, research participants, organizational clients, and others with whom they work, and to minimize harm when it is foreseeable and unavoidable" (APA Ethics Code, Standard 3.04). Psychologists also facilitate equitable access to psychological care and respect and guard the dignity and worth of all persons. Psychologists who work with victims of sexual trauma and IPV face unique challenges with safeguarding clients' and others' safety, rights, and dignity; protecting confidentiality; and ensuring individuals' access to care.

Clients may continue to live in an abusive situation, for example, while seeking psychological services, or have recently left an abusive partner – a time of high risk for retaliatory violence from perpetrators (Browne, 1987). In addition to assessing the threat that a perpetrator poses the client, psychologists must assess if the perpetrator poses a threat to others, including the client's children, other family members, and community members. We consider potential ethical dilemmas for psychologists to consider in the following two case studies.

The Case of Amy

Laura was hired recently as a postdoctoral fellow at a large university counseling center (UCC). She identifies as European–American, heterosexual, cisgender female, and as a feminist multicultural therapist who uses primarily interpersonal approaches to facilitate client healing. During her first week on the job, Laura conducts an intake assessment with Amy. Amy shares that she suffers from migraines and muscle tension that sometime interfere with her ability to sleep, concentrate in class, and complete schoolwork. She is a first-year university student, 22 years old, and self-identifies as a queer Pacific Islander woman who is able-bodied, although her current physical symptoms are sometimes debilitating. Amy shared that she is seeking counseling for the first time to improve her stress level and interpersonal relationships.

At the beginning of the intake, Laura talked with Amy about her role as a postdoctoral employee and the university's informed consent policies and limits of confidentiality. Specifically, most university employees are responsible for reporting all forms of gender-based discrimination (i.e., sexual assault and harassment, gender-based bullying and stalking, and IPV). Laura highlights that within the therapy context she is not mandated to report, but rather she must provide de-identified aggregate information to the university about gender-based discrimination that her clients report. Amy does not ask any questions and consents.

For the remainder of the intake meeting, Amy elaborates on her presenting concerns and therapy goals. She shares that she is struggling financially to pay rising tuition costs because her family abruptly ended contact with her last month and withdrew their financial support after she shared with them that she is dating a woman and identifies as queer. Amy reported that her increased stress, migraines, and muscle tension began after her family withdrew their support. Amy is also experiencing stress in her romantic relationship; her partner is her only current source of support. Amy is eager to gain relationship skills that will help her strengthen her relationship with her partner, reduce her stress, and feel happier. Laura and Amy work together for several weeks and the alliance develops well. Amy shares one day that she experienced sexual abuse during childhood and more recently experienced a sexual assault. As Amy shares more, Laura suspects that Amy's current partner perpetrated the recent sexual assault.

Case Analysis

Laura has two principal ethical concerns to consider at this point in her work with Amy: (a) assessing Amy's and others' current safety; and (b) identifying her reporting responsibilities. Fortunately, Laura has worked with child survivors of abuse and has notable experience creating therapeutic contexts that facilitate clients' healing from trauma experienced during childhood. She has less knowledge about IPV and working with clients who are experiencing IPV. Laura may ask herself, "Am I competent to work with Amy as a potential IPV survivor?" How do my values as a woman and as a feminist multicultural therapist influence my identification of clinical and ethical dilemmas and subsequent decision-making? How do I ask Amy about who perpetrated the childhood abuse and who assaulted her most recently in order to assess her safety and others' safety? If Amy's current romantic partner assaulted her, what do I do with that information? What are the laws, agency policies, and ethical issues influencing my reporting obligations and limits of confidentiality? How does my role as a trainee affect my decision-making? What other contextual and cultural factors influence my decision-making?" To consider these questions, we use the ethical decision-making models identified previously.

Personal Values

Laura adheres most closely to interpersonal theories of human change and feminist and multicultural approaches to psychotherapy. She values thinking critically with clients about how people, institutions, and societies reinforce power dynamics, oppression, marginalization, and gender roles, as well as how different gender role assignments and expressions decrease well-being. Laura also believes that the therapeutic relationship is a key mechanism by which to foster clients' critical thinking and to challenge, and respond differently to, societal messages and norms that clients receive. Laura values working collaboratively with Amy to identify therapeutic goals. She asks questions that help Amy evaluate how her interpersonal relationships contribute to her well-being and uses the therapeutic relationship to provide a corrective experience that promotes Amy's agency and well-being.

Amy's current therapeutic disclosures, however, have left Laura feeling anxious about assessing Amy's safety. Laura is uncertain about how to determine whether Amy's current romantic partner assaulted her and whether she is experiencing other forms of IPV in this relationship. Laura is concerned about being more directive than she prefers in order to conduct a thorough safety assessment. She also feels pulled to provide more psychoeducation than she prefers to do with clients; that is, talking with Amy about positive as well as abusive relationship dynamics and how abuse perpetrators use power and control. Laura understands how experiences of childhood abuse increase violence revictimization risk, and she feels eager to help Amy leave this potentially abusive romantic relationship and end the cycle of violence.

These are human reactions, and they underscore the importance of Laura identifying her values and how her values influence the therapy agenda and therapeutic relationship. For example, scholars have documented more gender symmetry in young adults' experiences of IPV; that is, victimization and perpetration rates reported by young adult males and females are more similar than rates reported by males and females of other ages (Capaldi & Kim, 2007; Melander et al., 2010; Renner & Whitney, 2012; Sabina & Straus, 2008; Straus, 2008). Gender symmetry between women in same-sex partnerships is similar, although significantly fewer data have been collected (Linville, Chronister, Marsiglio, & Brown, 2012). Laura may not know about the risks associated with greater gender symmetry in violent intimate partnerships or understand the unique tactics that abusers use in same-sex relationships. Moreover, if Laura discovers that Amy has used violence toward her partner or others, she will need to assess the context of the violence; that is, it will be important for Laura to assess if Amy used violence as self-defense or not, what injuries were incurred and their severity, and whether there was an imminent threat to someone's safety. This kind of contextual information influences the ethical and legal issues that Laura will need to consider and what she does with the information that Amy shares.

Professional Ethics

The professional ethics that are most relevant to Laura's work with Amy are the APA's ethical obligations of practicing within boundaries of competence (APA Ethics Code, Standard 2.01), avoiding harm (Standard 3.04), obtaining informed consent (Standard 3.10), and discussing limits of confidentiality (Standard 4.02). It is of utmost importance that Laura understands young adult IPV relationship dynamics and the development, cultural, and contextual factors associated with this violence risk.

The National Survey of Children's Health (NSCH, 2011, 2012) revealed that approximately 35 million children in the U.S. have experienced one or more of these childhood traumas, which translates to roughly half of the nation's children. Current estimates for young adults in college indicate that 80 percent have endured psychological aggression, 20–30 percent have been recipients of physical assault, and 15–25 percent have experienced sexual abuse (Bell & Naugle, 2007; Shorey, Cornelius, & Bell, 2008). Considering these violence victimization rates, most practicing psychologists will work with clients who have experienced IPV. It is essential, therefore, for psychologists to obtain education and training related to working with IPV victims in order to build their competence when working with violence survivors.

Very few psychologist training programs, however, offer coursework and supervised practical or research experiences involving working with victims of adult sexual violence and IPV. Consequently, few psychologists know about typologies of sexual violence and IPV, relationship dynamics and larger contextual factors that sustain violence perpetration and victimization, violence and safety assessment methods, and individual psychotherapeutic approaches to working with victims. State psychologist licensing boards recognize the need for such formal education and training, and consequently many boards require psychologists to obtain education on IPV assessment and intervention and childhood abuse assessment and reporting (e.g., State of California, 2015). Such state laws underscore how important it is for psychologists to gain competencies necessary to work with sexual trauma and IPV survivors. Laura has not had much training in the etiology of IPV risk or violence risk assessments. Laura will want to consider carefully how to increase her competence in these areas.

Amy has several developmental and contextual factors and demographic and socio-cultural identities that place her at higher risk for sexual violence and IPV victimiza-tion. First, experiences of abuse during childhood increase individuals' risk for violence revictimization and injury across the lifespan (Fergusson, McLeod, & Horwood, 2013; Koenig, Doll, O'Leary, Pequegnat, 2004). Second, young adult females, and young adult female college students in particular, are the most common victims of sexual assault and rape in the U.S. (Black et al., 2011; Renner & Whitney, 2012). IPV rates begin to increase during adolescence and peak during early adulthood (Kim, Laurent, Capaldi, & Feingold, 2008), similar to how rates of crime and arrest, alcohol and other drug use, and risky sexual behavior increase and peak during this same time period (Johnston, O'Malley, Bachman, & Schulenberg, 2004; Centers for Disease Control and Prevention, 2013; Uniform Crime Reports, 2009). Each of these risk behaviors is linked directly with IPV (Campbell, Alhusen, Draughon, Kub, & Walton-Moss, 2011). Third, women with marginalized identities, including racial/ethnic and sexual minorities, experience markedly higher rates of violence victimiza-tion (Chronister, Knoble, & Bahia, 2013). For example, women who identify as bisexual and lesbian report distinctly higher rates of emotional abuse from intimate partners than do their heterosexual peers and experience greater difficulty finding people who believe their experiences (Walters, Chen, & Breiding, 2013).

Confidentiality and trust are of concern for most clients, but especially for clients who have experienced sexual violence and IPV. It will likely be difficult for Amy to talk about her abuse experiences. Her emotional and physical distress and overall well-being may ebb and flow during the course of therapy, and so may her under-standing of the therapy process, privileged communication, and Laura's ethical reporting obligations. A key consideration for psychologists working with victims of sexual assault and IPV is to obtain ongoing informed consent and to regularly talk with clients about the limits of confidentiality. It is challenging to balance building rapport so that survivors are able to share painful experiences while also ensuring that clients understand what information and concerns may need to be reported. To communicate clearly about the limits of confidentiality, Laura must also under-stand the legal and agency policies that affect her reporting obligations, the reporting process, and what happens to aggregate data that are collected (i.e., who sees it, for what purpose are the data used, etc.).

Laws and Agency Policies

As Laura investigates the laws and agency policies that influence her work as a postdoctoral trainee, she will likely discover a multitude of laws and policies to negotiate. Differing state laws complicate these responsibilities (e.g., some states require reporting of past abuse, while others do not). Psychologists must take time to gather clear, consistent information about their legal and agency obligations, especially obligations to report abuse experiences and concerns about client safety. These obligations can be even more difficult for trainees to understand and communicate to their clients because they have the added complexity of practicing under a supervisor's license, and potentially different statutes or rules.

According to the Office of Civil Rights (OCR) and the Clery Act, licensed professional counselors, or those under the supervision of a licensed professional counselor, are not obligated to report incidents of sexual violence to the school without the student's consent in a way that identifies the student (U.S. Department of Education, 2014). Professional counselors are exempt from helping foster a sense of safety and security with the services that they provide to students. Title IX is the most significant federal law that affects Laura's reporting obligations. It protects people from discrimination based on sex in education programs or activities that receive federal financial assistance (U.S. Department of Education, 2014). The UCC that Laura works for is mandated federally, under Title IX, to collect aggregate data about sexual violence incidents that university students experience in a way that does not identify any one student. At the state and agency level, it is common for psychologists' obligations to report past child abuse and IPV to vary by state and agency, and as noted above, agency policies may conflict with state laws and professional ethical obligations. Laura should consult with her supervisor, under whose license she is practicing, to talk about ethical decision-making processes and to include resources such as secondary supervisors and consultants as part of the process, especially if Laura and her supervisor disagree or are uncertain about how to proceed.

Diversity Considerations

Amy self-identifies as a queer Pacific Islander woman, identities too often marginalized and underrepresented in our society and institutions of higher education. Laura will want to consider several cultural factors as she engages in an ethical decision-making process. First, Amy's ethnic and cultural identification and acculturation may influence her relationship with Laura and her perception of the therapeutic process. Amy is seeking counseling services for the first time in her life, and so she may not know how therapists and clients work together. Although Laura prefers to use a collaborative, more client-centered feminist approach to therapy, Amy may not feel comfortable with talking a lot or sharing many private details about others. She may think of Laura as the expert and seek her advice and instruction (Iwamasa, 2003; Lewis, 2003). These preferences may significantly impact how Laura engages in the therapy process, assesses Amy's and others' safety, and talks about limits of confidentiality.

A second cultural consideration is how to include Amy in the reporting process if confidentiality needs to be breached. If Amy's or others' safety is threatened, it may be very difficult for Laura to involve Amy in the reporting process and in ways that feel emotionally and culturally congruent for both of them. Although Laura may want to empower Amy to take the lead with reporting her abuse experiences if necessary, Amy may see Laura as the authority figure who is responsible for the reporting process and may see her own participation in therapy and the reporting process as a cultural, racial, or familial betrayal to others. Violations of racial and familial loyalties and cultural privacy values (Iwamasa, 2003; Nadal, 2011) may make it difficult for Amy to stay engaged in therapy and access resources that are culturally relevant.

Differences between Laura's therapeutic approach and Amy's spiritual or religious values are a third diversity consideration. If Amy believes that she is to accept her suffering or to forgive without reparation or reconciliation, Laura may fear that Amy will not follow a safety plan more typical of the majority culture or seek available resources (e.g., campus police, residence hall advisor) that are not particularly culturally inclusive. Amy also may not seek resources because she does not want many people to know that she is dating a woman and she fears that others will not believe her report of abuse. Laura will need to think critically about her own conceptualization of IPV in same-sex relationships. Too often, care providers do not consider IPV between same-sex partners to be as serious as violence between male and female partners. It is important for psychologists to understand dynamics of IPV in same-sex partnerships and how emotional, physical, sexual, economic, and spiritual abuse tactics are used to threaten a partner's well-being. Ultimately, each of these diversity factors may influence Amy's access to and engagement in therapy and the culturally relevant and inclusive resources available to her.

Another critical diversity consideration requires Laura to engage in critical self-reflection about her own cultural identification, knowledge, and experiences, and how each of these factors influence her therapeutic approach and ethical decision-making. Laura's different life experiences, cultural values, and identities will influence how she conceptualizes Amy's presenting concerns and safety, the resources that she encourages Amy to access, and how she evaluates the effectiveness of their therapeutic work.

Recommendations

Safety is a primary concern for psychologists working with clients who have experienced, or who are experiencing, violence. Client safety can be threatened by perpetrators of violence, serious declines in mental health and well-being (e.g., suicidality, eating disturbances), and environmental risk factors that result from, or are associated with, violence (e.g., homelessness, poverty, presence of weapons). We recommend that psychologists talk about the therapeutic process and obtain clients' informed consent regularly. Obtaining ongoing consent gives Laura more opportunities to provide Amy with clear, accurate information about her reporting obligations and limits of confidentiality and increases the likelihood that Amy will make more informed, autonomous, and empowering therapy decisions. Ongoing consent also provides Amy with more opportunities to ask questions about the therapy process and for Laura to assess how much Amy understands, as well as to clarify any misinformation.

We also recommend that psychologists stay informed about best practices for childhood abuse screening and IPV screening across the lifespan, in diverse relationship contexts (e.g., married, cohabiting, hooking up), and for partners of different genders and cultural groups (Ard & Makadon, 2011; Chitkara-Barry & Chronister, 2015; Chronister & Aldarondo, 2012; Linville, Chronister, Marsiglio, & Brown, 2012). Scholars have identified several inclusive violence assessment practices that may help foster a strong therapeutic alliance while trying to learn from their clients' very sensitive information about their abuse experiences (e.g., Stith, McCollum, & Rosen, 2011; Todahl & Walters, 2011). Professional development activities allow psychologists to learn to stay relevant as well as to reflect critically on the strengths, limitations, and biases of their training. Finally, we recommend that psychologists frequently clarify their federal, state, and agency laws and policies that impact their client safety assessment strategies, limits of confidentiality, and reporting obligations and procedures. Similarly, we recommend that psychologists consult proactively with colleagues and supervisors to talk about these laws and policies and to determine an ethical decision-making process that maximizes the resources available to themselves as well as their clients (Pope & Vasquez, 2011).

The Case of John

John is a 30-year-old, cisgender male student who is enrolled in the Women and Gender Studies doctoral program at a major university. He is in the fourth year of the program and is conceptualizing his dissertation topic. Recently, John was the victim of a sexual assault off campus and reported the incident to the university's Title IX officer. John's reporting experience increased his academic and research interests regarding sexual violence, as he experienced both helpful and unhelpful responses from his peers, colleagues, and the university upon his report. In addition, as a teaching assistant in the Women and Gender Studies doctoral program, John has spoken with many students and heard positive and negative feedback about their sexual violence reporting experiences. He believes that the university could benefit from research on students' experiences of the university reporting process.

John contacts the university's Title IX officer to inquire about the opportunity to evaluate the institution's response to students who report sexual misconduct. He shares that he would like this project to culminate in his dissertation. The Title IX officer is excited about John's research and how it may help the university improve survivor services. The officer briefly mentions the importance of protecting study participants' identities and refers to the need to comply with existing federal and university policies. The Title IX officer also shares that the Title IX office has not yet evaluated the services they offer, so there is no precedent for how John should proceed with his project, but University administration would like to see the full data reports.

Case Analysis

Personal experiences inform some of our finest research. John's sexual assault and reporting experiences motivated him to investigate others' assault and reporting experiences and to identify ways to promote healing and just services for survivors.

As John and the institution consider his proposed dissertation project, it is important to contemplate several ethical issues in order to maximize the fidelity and responsibility with which he conducts his research, the integrity of his findings, and the potential contributions of his research. The primary ethical concerns include the misuse of John's work, conflicts between ethics and organizational demands, multiple relationships, conflicts of interest, cooperation with other professionals, maintaining confidentiality, and discussing reporting obligations and limits of confidentiality.

Personal Values

John has several personal experiences, values, and roles within the university that influence the fidelity, responsibility, and integrity with which he conducts his dissertation research. John is a sexual assault victim who reported the incident to his university's Title IX office. Title IX office staff were charged with responding to his needs as a victim; consequently, staff know very personal information about John and have worked with him after an especially difficult experience. There are potential challenges for John and the Title IX office staff as he studies staff practices and students' reporting experiences. John may ask, "How will my assault and reporting experiences influence my larger research questions and specific participant survey questions? How will my experience of reading other students' assault and reporting experiences influence my reflections on the assault that I experienced, my healing, and my relationships with Title IX office staff and university officials? What if the data reflect negatively on the Title IX office staff? How might my desire to improve the reporting experience for survivors influence my work?" John's awareness of his personal and professional values, strengths, weaknesses, needs, and resources is essential to his ethical decision-making.

Professional Ethics

John's multiple roles within the institution present unique opportunities to learn from survivors and unique challenges regarding communicating with survivors and protecting their data. To manage conflicts of interest and facilitate cooperation with others, it will be critical that John clarifies all stakeholders' roles and involvement with his study. This clarification reduces the likelihood that stakeholders will bias the study with their agendas and interactions, exploit and harm research participants, misuse participant data, and undermine the rigor and validity of the dissertation study (McClain et al., 2007).

Researchers seek to generate knowledge and provide benefits to research participants. Similarly, an institution that permits the conduct of a particular research study may have specific hopes or expectations for their research involvement. Is it possible that John and the university have divergent goals about how the data will be used? What will John and the university do with the study results, especially if the results reflect negatively on the university? How much control does John have over how the data are interpreted and used? Will data be censored? How will John and the university protect participants' anonymity and confidentiality when the final dissertation results are publicly available?

John also must consider how his role as a student and male survivor may influence solicitation, interpretation, and use of participant data. How will he explain his affiliation with the university and the Title IX office in the informed consent document? How does his gender identification influence his perspective and credibility as a researcher investigating gender-based violence? Participants will have their own questions: "How did John identify me as someone who reported a Title IX offense when he does not work in the Title IX office? How does John's affiliation with the university influence his trustworthiness?" Federal laws, university policies, and his interpersonal competence will affect John's responses to these questions.

Laws and Agency Policies

To protect study participants and their data, it is critical that stakeholders talk openly about legal and ethical obligations and make collaborative decisions about how to proceed when legal, university, or ethical obligations are in conflict (Wooten & Mitchell, 2015). John and all research partners, for example, will need to comply with federal laws such as Health Insurance Portability and Accountability Act of 1996 (HIPAA), Family Educational Rights and Privacy Act of 1974 (FERPA), and Title IX, in addition to the policies of the university's Institutional Review Board (DeMatteo, Galloway, Arnold, & Patel, 2015). John's ability to understand the legal, university, and ethical contexts and complications associated with his research is essential. There also will be study procedures, like data collection methods, that laws and university policies do not restrict, though they may be subject to ethical constraints.

To protect victims' privilege and comply with all legal protections for victims, it is likely that Title IX staff will contact victims about the research study rather than provide John with information that will identify individual victims. If John needs to communicate about his study (e.g., email, phone call) via the Title IX office staff, he will want to consider participants' reactions to his study invitation. How will John communicate information about himself and his relationship to the university and Title IX office? How will he address participants' questions about whether he knows their name, contact information, or violence experience? Also, some victims may not have been the direct reporters of their gender-based violence experiences, and so they may not know of or remember the experience about which John is asking. How will John communicate which incident he is asking about and answer participants' additional questions? What survey questions and study procedures will John choose to reduce the risk that study participants are negatively triggered and to increase participants' opportunity to debrief their study participation and access resources?

Any study method that John chooses will have benefits and drawbacks related to protecting participants' confidentiality, rights, and dignity. Participants may feel a greater sense of anonymity and confidentiality with an online survey and experience less shame and distress (Buchanan & William, 2010). In contrast, an in-person interview may allow John to answer participants' questions more thoroughly and to help debrief the survey questions more effectively. John also will want to consider how he will obtain informed consent, how much detail he will solicit from participants about their violence experiences, and how he will solicit that information. If John's university requires him to report all identifying information that is gathered about an incident (e.g., a study participant discloses the perpetrator's name in one of the survey's open-ended questions), then he will want to decide how to communicate this mandate explicitly in the informed consent and throughout the course of the study. Alternatively, John may decide to construct survey questions that solicit minimal information about students' violence experiences and add notes that inform participants of the mandated reporting process so that they can make informed decisions about what to disclose.

Diversity Considerations

Several considerations regarding culture, equity, and inclusion are important for John to consider. First, it is essential for John to think about how his and participants' gender identification may influence the research process. John's name will appear on all study materials, and participants will most likely assume that he identifies as male. Females continue to comprise the vast majority of sexual assault and IPV victims on college campuses (Fisher, Cullen, & Turner, 2000). At the same time, individuals who identify as men and transgender experience intense stigma about coming forward as victims of sexual violence or IPV. John's assumed gender identification may encourage some students to participate, and it may also elicit doubt, fear, and caution from other students. Second, it may be difficult to protect the anonymity and confidentiality of students from underrepresented groups, particularly if the university is small or specific violence incidents have received notable attention. Third, John will want to ensure that survivors with certain disabilities can access the survey, such as ensuring that online surveys are accessible to readers and paper–pencil copy surveys are provided in large print.

Recommendations

Conducting research with sexual violence and IPV survivors is important because such research can enrich our understanding of survivors' experiences and needs and lead practitioners and scholars to prevention and intervention efforts that are more effective. Research with survivors of sexual violence within an institutional setting presents an array of opportunities and ethical challenges. We encourage researchers working with survivors of sexual violence to consider several key ethical issues. First, researchers must identify the multiple relationships that exist when conducting research within an institution and outline as clearly as possible how they will navigate those relationships to reduce client harm and maximize benefits. Second, we encourage researchers working with sexual violence survivors to articulate how all stakeholders will use participants' data prior to participant contact. Third, we recommend that researchers consider the costs and benefits of including university stakeholders and survivors at each phase of the research design and implementation process. Inclusion of multiple stakeholders may help reduce research bias and inform the methods used to protect participant confidentiality or anonymity, for example. Fourth, we recommend that researchers learn about research with vulnerable populations, and in particular the specific vulnerabilities of sexual violence survivors (e.g., Becker-Blease & Freyd, 2006; DePrince, Chu, & Combs, 2008). Fifth, we recommend that stakeholders clarify in all communications with study participants who the stakeholders are and their responsibilities, policies related to maintaining participant confidentiality and protecting anonymity, participant resources, and research debriefing opportunities. Finally, we recommend that researchers understand the relationship between federal government, university, and Institutional Review Board policies in order to make informed research decisions when these policies are in conflict or to provide ambiguous information about how to proceed.

Conclusion

The vast majority of psychologists will work with clients who have experienced sexual trauma or IPV. Working with clients or research participants who have survived such harm is rewarding and provides numerous opportunities for the client and provider to learn and grow. These types of work also present important ethical considerations. We encourage practitioners and researchers to honor and capitalize on clients' resiliencies and involve survivors in collaborative decision-making throughout the course of treatment and research. We also recommend that psychologists use an ethical decision-making model that considers ethics in the context of other pertinent factors. Specific ethical foci include seeking ongoing informed consent, repeatedly providing information about the limits of confidentiality, and engaging in professional development that promotes clinical competence and lifelong learning about violence victimization risk, assessment, impact, and evidence-based prevention and treatment options that foster individuals' safety and well-being in the long-term.

References

Aldarondo, E. & Mederos, F. (Eds.) (2002). *Programs for men who batter: Intervention and prevention strategies in a diverse society.* Princeton, NJ: Civic Research Institute.

American Psychological Association (1990). Guidelines for providers of psychological services to ethnic, linguistic, and culturally diverse populations. Retrieved from www.apa.org/pi/oema/resources/policy/provider-guidelines.aspx

American Psychological Association (2002). Intimate partner abuse and relationship violence. Booklet developed by the Intimate Partner Abuse and Relationship Violence workgroup. Retrieved from www.apa.org/topics/violence/intimate-partner-violence.pdf

American Psychological Association (2010). Ethical principles of psychologists and code of conduct. Retrieved from www.apa.org/ethics/code/principles.pdf

Ard, K. L. & Makadon, H. J. (2011). Addressing intimate partner violence in lesbian, gay, bisexual, and transgender patients. *Journal of General Internal Medicine, 26,* 930–933.

Becker-Blease, K. A. & Freyd, J. J. (2006). Research participants telling the truth about their lives: the ethics of asking and not asking about abuse. *American Psychologist, 61*, 218.

Bell, K. M. & Naugle, A. E. (2007). Effects of social desirability on students' self-reporting of partner abuse perpetration and victimization. *Violence and Victims, 22*, 243–256.

Benson, M. L. & Fox, G. L. (2004a). *When violence hits home: How economics and neighborhood play a role. Research in brief.* Washington, DC: National Institute of Justice.

Benson, M. L. & Fox, G. L. (2004b). *Concentrated disadvantage, economic distress, and violence against women in intimate relationships.* Washington, DC: U.S. Department of Justice.

Black, M. C., Basile, K. C., Breiding, M. J., et al. (2011). *The National Intimate Partner and Sexual Violence Survey (NISVS): 2010 summary report.* Retrieved from www.cdc.gov/violenceprevention/pdf/nisvs_report2010-a.pdf

Breiding, M. J., Smith, S. G., Basile, K. C., Walters, M. L., Chen, J., & Merrick, M. T. (2015). Prevalence and characteristics of sexual violence, stalking, and intimate partner violence victimization – National Intimate Partner and Sexual Violence Survey, United States, 2011. *American Journal of Public Health, 105*, E11.

Browne, A. & Williams, K. R. (1993). Gender, intimacy, and lethal violence: Trends from 1976 through 1987. *Gender and Society, 7*, 78–98.

Buchanan, T. & William, J. E. (2010). Ethical issues in psychological research on the Internet. In S. D. Gosling & J. A. Johnson (Eds.), *Advanced methods for conducting online behavioral research* (pp. 255–271). Washington, DC: American Psychological Association.

Bureau of Justice Statistics (2003). Crime data brief: Intimate partner violence, 1993–2001. https://www.bjs.gov/content/pub/pdf/ipv01.pdf

Canadian Psychological Association (2000). Canadian code of ethics for psychologists (3rd edn.). Retrieved from www.cpa.ca/cpasite/UserFiles/Documents/Canadian%20Code%20of%20Ethics%20for%20Psycho.pdf

Campbell, J. C., Alhusen, J., Draughon, J., Kub, J., & Walton-Moss, B. (2011). Vulnerability and protective factors for intimate partner violence. In J. W. White, M. P. Koss, & A. E. Kazdin (Eds.), *Violence against women and children, Vol. 1: Mapping the terrain* (pp. 243–263). Washington, DC: American Psychological Association.

Capaldi, D. M., & Kim, H. K. (2007). Typological approaches to violence in couples: A critique and alternative conceptual approach. *Clinical Psychology Review, 27(3)*, 253–265.

Catalano, S., Smith, E., Snyder, H., & Rand, M. (2009). *Female victims of violence.* Washington, DC: Department of Justice Publications and Materials.

Centers for Disease Control and Prevention (2013). National Vital Statistics Report, 61(4), 1–118. Author: U.S. Department of Health and Human Services.

Chitkara-Barry, A. & Chronister, K. M. (2015). Identifying male victims of partner abuse: A review and critique of screening instruments. *Partner Abuse, 6*, 442–460.

Chronister, K. M. & Aldarondo, E. (2012). Partner violence victimization and perpetration: Developmental and contextual implications for effective practice. In N. A. Fouad, J. A. Carter, & L. M. Subich (Eds.), *APA handbook of counseling psychology, Vol. 2: Practice, interventions, and applications* (pp. 125–151). Washington, DC: American Psychological Association.

Chronister, K. M., Knoble, N., & Bahia, H. (2013). Community interventions for domestic violence. In F. Leong (Ed.), *Handbook of multicultural psychology, Vol. 1.* (pp. 561–576). Washington, DC: American Psychological Association.

Chronister, K. M. & McWhirter, E. H. (2003). Applying social cognitive career theory to the empowerment of battered women. *Journal of Counseling and Development, 81,* 418–424.

Corey, G., Corey, M. S., & Callanan, P. (2011). *Issues and ethics in the helping professions* (8th edn.). Pacific Grove, CA: Brooks.

DeMatteo, D., Galloway, M., Arnold, S., & Patel, U. (2015). Sexual assault on college campuses: A 50-state survey of criminal sexual assault statutes and their relevance to campus sexual assault. *Psychology, Public Policy, and Law, 21,* 227.

DePrince, A. P., Chu, A. T., & Combs, M. D. (2008). Trauma-related predictors of deontic reasoning: A pilot study in a community sample of children. *Child Abuse & Neglect, 32,* 732–737.

Department of Justice (2014). *National crime victimization survey [NCVS].* Bethesda, MD: Office of Justice Programs. Retrieved from www.bjs.gov/content/pub/pdf/cv14.pdf

Equal Employment Opportunity Commission (2016). Policy guidance on current issues of sexual harassment. Retrieved from www.eeoc.gov/policy/docs/currentissues.html

Fergusson, D. M., McLeod, G. F. H., & Horwood, L. J. (2013). Childhood sexual abuse and adult developmental outcomes: Findings from a 30-year longitudinal study in New Zealand. *Child Abuse & Neglect, 37,* 664–674.

Fisher, B. S., Cullen, F. T., & Turner, M. G. (2000). *The sexual victimization of college women.* Washington, DC: U.S. Department of Justice, and Bureau of Justice Statistics.

Halpern, C. T., Spriggs, A. L., Martin, S. L., & Kupper, L. L. (2009). Patterns of intimate partner violence victimization from adolescence to young adulthood in a nationally representative sample. *Journal of Adolescent Health, 45,* 508–516.

Hampton, R. L., LaTaillade, J. J., Dacey, A., & Marghi, J. R. (2008). Evaluating domestic violence interventions for black women. *Journal of Aggression, Maltreatment & Trauma, 16,* 330–353.

Heise, L. & Garcia-Moreno, C. (2002). Violence by intimate partners. In E. G. Krugs (Ed.), *World report on violence and health* (pp. 87–121). Geneva, Switzerland: World Health Organization.

Hockett, J. M. & Saucier, D. A. (2015). A systematic literature review of "rape victims" versus "rape survivors": Implications for theory, research, and practice. *Aggression and Violent Behavior, 25,* 1–14.

Hockett, J. M., McGraw, L. K., & Saucier, D. A. (2014). A "rape victim" by any other name: The effects of labels on individuals' rape-related perceptions. In H. Pishwa & R. Schulze (Eds.), *Expression of inequality in interaction: Power, dominance, and status* (pp. 81–104). Amsterdam, The Netherlands: John Benjamins Publishing Company.

Iwamasa, G. Y. (2003). Recommendations for the treatment of Asian American/Pacific Islander populations. American Psychological Association. Retrieved from www.apa.org/pi/oema/resources/ethnicity-health/asian-american/psychological-treatment.pdf

Johnston, L. D., O'Malley, P. M., Bachman, J. G., & Schulenberg, J. E. (2004). *Monitoring the future national survey results on drug use, 1975–2003. Volume II: College students and adults ages 19–45* (NIH Publication No. 04-5508). Bethesda, MD: National Institute on Drug Abuse.

Kim, H. K., Laurent, H. K., Capaldi, D. M., & Feingold, A. (2008). Men's aggression toward women: A 10-year panel study. *Journal of Marriage and Family, 70,* 1169–1187.

Koenig, L. J., Doll, L., O'Leary, A. E., & Pequegnat, W. E. (2004). From child sexual abuse to adult sexual risk: Trauma, revictimization, and intervention. Washington, DC: American Psychological Association.

Lewis, N. K. (2003). Balancing the dictates of law and ethical practice: Empowerment of female survivors of domestic violence in the presence of overlapping child abuse. *Ethics and Behavior, 12*, 353–366.

Linville, D., Chronister, K. M., Marsiglio, M. C., & Brown, L. (2012). Treatment of partner violence in gay and lesbian relationships. In *Handbook of LGBT-affirmative couple & family therapy* (pp. 327–342). New York, NY: Routledge.

Martin, S. L., Ray, N., Sotres-Alvarez, D., et al. (2006). Physical and sexual assault of women with disabilities. *Violence against Women, 12*, 823–837.

McClain, N., Laughon, K., Steeves, R., & Parker, B. (2007). Balancing the needs of the scientist and the subject in trauma research. *Western Journal of Nursing Research, 29*, 121–128.

Nadal, K. L., Issa, M. A., Leon, J., Meterko, V., Wideman, M., & Wong, Y. (2011). Sexual orientation microaggressions: "Death by a thousand cuts" for lesbian, gay, and bisexual youth. *Journal of LGBT Youth, 8*, 234–259.

National Survey of Children's Health (2011, 2012). Data query from the Child and Adolescent Health Measurement Initiative Data Resource Center for Child and Adolescent Health. Retrieved from www.childhealthdata.org

O'Leary, K. D., Slep, A. M. S., Avery-Leaf, S., & Cascardi, M. (2008). Gender differences in dating aggression among multiethnic high school students. *Journal of Adolescent Health, 42*, 473–479.

Oregon Psychological Association Ethics Committee (2008). *A process approach to ethical dilemmas*. Portland, OR: Oregon Psychological Association Conference.

Parker, J. A. & Mahlstedt, D. (2010). Language, power, and sexual assault: Women's voices on rape and social change. In S. J. Behrens & J. A. Parker (Eds.), *Language in the real world: An introduction to linguistics* (pp. 139–163). New York, NY: Routledge.

Pope, K. S. & Vasquez, M. J. T. (2011). Ethics in psychotherapy and counseling: A practical guide (5th edn.). New Jersey, NJ: Wiley.

Renner, L. M. & Whitney, S. D. (2012). Risk factors for unidirectional and bidirectional intimate partner violence among young adults. *Child Abuse & Neglect, 36*, 40–52.

Shorey, R. C., Cornelius, T. L., & Bell, K. M. (2008). A critical review of theoretical frameworks for dating violence: Comparing the dating and marital fields. *Aggression and Violent Behavior, 13*, 185–194.

Shorey, R. C., Zucosky, H., Brasfield, H., Febres, J., Cornelius, T. L., Sage, C., & Stuart, G. L. (2012). Dating violence prevention programming: Directions for future interventions. *Aggression and Violent Behavior, 17*, 289–293.

State of California (2015). Application for licensure as a psychologist. Retrieved from www.psychology.ca.gov/applicants/instructions.shtml

Stith, S. M., McCollum, E. E., & Rosen, K. H. (2011). *Couples therapy for domestic violence: Finding safe solutions*. Washington, DC: American Psychological Association.

Styles, K. (2015). Dear colleague letter. Washington, DC: Department of Education.

Thompson, M. (2000). Life after rape: A chance to speak? *Sexual and Relationship Therapy, 15*, 325–343.

Tjaden, P. & Thoennes, N. (1998). Prevalence, incidence, and consequences of violence against women: Findings from the national violence against women survey. Research in brief. Washington, DC: National Institutes of Justice.

Tjaden, P. & Thoennes, N. (2000). Full report of prevalence, incidence, and consequences of violence against women: Findings from the national violence against women survey. Washington, DC: National Institutes of Justice.

Todahl, J. & Walters, E. (2011). Universal screening for intimate partner violence: A systematic review. *Journal of Marital and Family Therapy, 37*, 355–369.

Uniform Crime Reports (2009). *Crime in the United States 2008*. Washington, DC: Federal Bureau of Investigation, U.S. Department of Justice.

U.S. Department of Education, Office of Civil Rights (2014). Questions and answersabout Title IX and sexual violence. Retrieved from www2.ed.gov/about/offices/list/ocr/docs/qa-201404-title-ix.pdf

Walters, M. L., Chen, J., & Breiding, M. J. (2013). National Intimate Partner and Sexual Violence Survey (NISVS): 2010 findings on victimization by sexual orientation. Retrieved from www.cdc.gov/ViolencePrevention/pdf/NISVS_SOfindings.pdf

Wilson, M. & Brooks-Gunn, J. (2001). Health status and behaviors of unwed fathers. *Children and Youth Services Review, 23*, 377–401.

Wooten, S. C. & Mitchell, R. W. (Eds.) (2015) *The crisis of campus sexual violence: Critical perspectives on prevention and response*. New York, NY: Routledge.

Young, S. L. & Maguire, K. C. (2003). Talking about sexual violence. *Women and Language, 26*, 40–52.

10 Ethical Issues in the Treatment of Eating Disorders

Laura H. Choate

Eating disorders (EDs) are mental disorders with significant biopsychosocial consequences, including potentially lethal medical complications. They follow a chronic course, with poor treatment outcomes, high rates of remission, and high mortality rates (American Psychiatric Association [APA], 2006). Anorexia nervosa (AN) in particular is associated with the highest mortality rate of all psychiatric disorders (between 10 and 19 percent). Further, suicidality is associated with AN and bulimia nervosa; these two conditions have suicide attempt rates that are considerably higher than for the general population (Arcelus, Mitchell, Wales, & Nielsen, 2011; Swanson, Crow, LeGrange, Swendsen, & Merikangas, 2011) and suicide is the cause of death for one out of every five individuals who die from AN (Arcelus et al., 2011).

Despite the serious consequences associated with EDs, in many cases clients do not seek treatment, and even when they do, they are not motivated to change their disordered eating patterns. In contrast with many other psychiatric disorders, EDs are ego-syntonic in nature, resulting in poor client insight into the problems associated with their symptoms (APA, 2013). Because the disorder is an important aspect of the client's identity, eating behaviors such as restriction, bingeing, and purging serve an important function in the client's life and are not easily stopped just by willpower or force (Sigman, 2005). Further, because of the medical consequences that come from extreme weight loss and malnourishment, EDs in general and AN in particular can result in neuropsychological impairments that greatly impact a client's capacity to make rational and reasoned decisions about his or her health and need for treatment, even when treatment is needed to save the client's life (Bodell et al., 2014).

Due to their complexity, the treatment of EDs is often fraught with ethical challenges for the practitioner. Relatively few therapists receive specialized training in the treatment of EDs, yet all mental health professionals will work with clients who experience problems related to eating, weight, and shape at some point in their practice (Berg & Petersen, 2013). In this chapter, I will highlight three of the most challenging ethical conflicts that a nonspecializing therapist might face in practice: (a) issues related to one's scope of competence when treating complex EDs with potential medical complications; (b) tensions in upholding client confidentiality versus parental legal rights when working with minor clients who disclose disordered eating symptoms; and (c) deciding when to prioritize a client's right to make his or her own treatment decisions (and even to refuse treatment) versus upholding one's duty to protect clients from imminent harm in cases when medical intervention is deemed necessary.

To frame the discussion of these three dilemmas, I draw upon the principles of biomedical ethics as presented by Beauchamp and Childress (2013) and as also highlighted in the American Psychological Association Code of Ethics (2010). Throughout the case examples, I emphasize the aspects of these principles that are most relevant to ethical decision making in ED treatment:

Respect for autonomy: when respecting client autonomy, the therapist allows the client the freedom to make informed choices and to take action based upon his or her own beliefs and values.

Nonmaleficence: this principle refers to the therapist's obligation to refrain from any action that might bring harm to his or her client.

Beneficence: this principle refers to a therapist's obligation to do what is best for the client and to take active steps to provide the best care possible.

Justice: this principle refers to fairness and justice for each client and respecting a client's dignity, including the provision of care in the least restrictive setting.

In addition to the four major principles of biomedical ethics, there are principles that apply specifically to the therapist–client relationship that are relevant to this discussion (Beauchamp & Childress, 2013): respecting the client's privacy (not disclosing information about the client to anyone outside of their wishes); upholding confidentiality (the promise that the therapist will not disclose information to anyone else without the client's authorization); veracity (telling the truth to clients, remaining transparent, and providing accurate, objective information in language that the client can understand); and fidelity (carrying out your promises to the client that you favor the client's interests over your own interests or over third-party interests).

In addition to considering relevant biomedical ethical principles, I use an ethical decision-making model to guide the discussion for each case. Using the model posited by Remley and Herlihy (2015), the following steps are conducted: (a) the problem and associated ethical challenges are evaluated; (b) relevant professional literature and ethical principles are considered in terms of how they apply and take priority in the case; (c) the client's cultural context is examined along with a discussion of how the client can be involved in the decision-making process; (d) the counselor's feelings and emotions and how they might influence the decision-making process are also considered; (e) the importance of consultation with other mental health and medical professionals is highlighted; and (f) the desired outcomes, the courses of action the therapist might potentially take in achieving the ideal outcome, and the benefits and risks involved in each course of action are described.

The Case of Maggie

Kathy, age 45, is a Caucasian therapist with ten years of counseling experience. She is currently working in a solo private practice in a rural community. Her practice is thriving, primarily because there are few mental health professionals in her small town. She maintains a generalized practice, seeing a full caseload of children, adolescents, and adults. During her graduate training, she completed an internship at an inpatient psychiatric facility and worked on the ED treatment unit for several weeks, but during her career, she has never sought out an area of expertise, nor gained any type of specialized training. She sometimes feels isolated while working in her solo practice, but does not feel that she has the time to reach out to other professionals in surrounding communities for consultation or collaboration.

She agrees to meet with a 24-year-old Caucasian female client, Maggie, who says she is seeking treatment for depression due to the recent breakup of a romantic relationship. Kathy feels prepared to help her with this issue. She is surprised, however, when Maggie arrives for her first appointment. Not only is Maggie quite thin in appearance, she is dressed in a large sweatshirt and sweatpants even though it is the middle of summer. Kathy feels extremely uncomfortable with the way Maggie stares at her and seems to be judging her physical appearance. Kathy, who has always felt dissatisfied with her weight and has been on and off diets most of her adult life, feels scrutinized and evaluated by Maggie: *What must she thinking about me and my weight? Does she think I am incompetent because I am overweight?*

Because Kathy is distracted by these thoughts, she misses some key opportunities for forming a therapeutic alliance during the first session. Because of her discomfort, she also fails to conduct an assessment of Maggie's weight and eating behaviors. By the time Maggie comes back for her second session, however, Kathy has recomposed herself enough to assess for a potential ED. She finds out that Maggie has intentionally lost 25 pounds during the past year, but that she believes she needs to lose at least 10 more in order to look her best. Kathy is shocked to hear this, as Maggie appears to be medically underweight and she shows initial signs of malnourishment (e.g., she has not had a menstrual cycle in 6 months, she is always cold in her extremities, and she has fainting spells). When Kathy asks if she would like to work on changing her attitudes toward weight and eating during therapy, Maggie initially refuses, stating that she wants to continue to lose weight and that her real problem is depression. However, after some further discussion, Maggie reveals that her food restriction is greatly interfering with her life, and in fact is the main reason her romantic partner ended their relationship. She admits that her weight and eating are the predominating thoughts in her life right now and that she is having trouble maintaining her work schedule and limited social life. She admits she needs help and she thinks Kathy is the one to help her. When Kathy asks if she has talked to any other professionals about her eating concerns, she adamantly refuses, stating that her physician is a male who would not understand and that she only wants Kathy to help her. "After all," she states, "you are the only one I trust." Kathy feels flattered that Maggie has such confidence in her, and is even excited to work with a client with an ED after so many years since her training on the inpatient unit. She also knows that Maggie would need to travel quite a distance to find another qualified therapist with training in EDs. Kathy reasons that she can certainly help Maggie gain some weight and she believes that working with Maggie might even help her to become more disciplined in her own attempts at weight loss. Because she knows it has been over ten years since she had any work in the area of EDs, she decides to reread her graduate school textbook on EDs to refresh herself on her knowledge of treatment. She agrees to start Maggie's treatment on a once-per-week basis.

Ethical Concerns

The ethical codes of all mental health professions state that therapists must know their scope of competence and practice within their area of training and experience (e.g., American Psychological Association Code of Ethics Standard 2.01). Therefore, the ethical issues in this case stem from Kathy's lack of awareness of her own scope of competence in providing treatment for this client. Also relevant to this case is the consideration of nonmaleficence; there are questions as to whether Kathy's lack of current knowledge and reluctance to collaborate might actually cause her client further harm if she provides Maggie with limited and inadequate treatment. Kathy seems unaware that the treatment of clients with EDs is highly complex and requires specialized training and advanced levels of supervised experience beyond what a typical therapist might have received during graduate preparation (Williams & Haverkamp, 2010). While she does have some experience, her training was limited to a brief graduate internship and her skills have not been updated in over ten years. Her lack of current knowledge is particularly relevant in the treatment of AN, which can involve intensive medical intervention in addition to psychological treatment. Current practice guidelines state that effective treatment for AN should involve a treatment team consisting of, at minimum, a psychotherapist, a medical provider, and a dietician (APA, 2006). Therapists should have knowledge in the area of basic nutrition and an understanding of the medical consequences of AN and the effects that nutritional deficiencies can have on a client's cognitive functioning. Further, because of the ego-syntonic nature of the disorder, the therapist should have skill in managing client resistance to change, in engaging client motivation for treatment, in making proper referrals to medical professionals, and in working effectively with an interdisciplinary team (Williams & Haverkamp, 2010).

The guidelines also state that the initial treatment goal for AN should be to provide nutritional rehabilitation in the hopes of restoring the client to a healthy weight. Only once the client is at a medically stable weight will she then benefit from psychotherapy. When the client is renourished, she can benefit from therapeutic work that typically involves an examination of cognitive distortions about the importance of weight and shape, of developmental themes about identity and family relationships, of the role that AN played in the client's life, and of how to develop more effective coping skills (APA, 2006; 2012).

In this case, Kathy is taking a simplistic approach to treatment that reflects her lack of awareness of the seriousness of AN, despite the fact that she did have some brief past experience in working with clients who were hospitalized for an ED. By focusing on only one aspect of treatment, she is withholding other aspects (nutrition and medical monitoring) that are essential to a comprehensive approach to treatment (Andersen, 2008). With this sole focus on the client's psychological concerns and a neglect of the medical complications of AN, she has the potential to cause passive, unintentional harm to the client (Andersen, 2008; Long, 2014). Because Maggie is already experiencing some of the consequences of self-starvation (amenorrhea and fainting spells), Kathy's inattention to the medical details of the case is particularly concerning. Further, engagement in therapy without first paying attention to Maggie's medical condition will render the overall treatment ineffective, as she is not likely to be able to "just gain weight" on her own as Kathy wants her to do. Finally, Kathy's reluctance to refer or even collaborate on this case is also an indicator of her lack of knowledge or awareness of effective ED treatment.

Client Context and Therapist Feelings

Kathy and Maggie are both Caucasian women living in a rural community where there are few mental health professionals. The client is young and very thin, while Kathy is 45 and struggles with a desire to lose weight. Being immersed in a culture in which being young and thin is held up as an ideal standard for women, Kathy seems unaware that she is experiencing strong countertransference reactions regarding her own weight, shape, and appearance while working with Maggie (Jacobs & Nye, 2010). She feels self-conscious and judged by the client, believing that Maggie has a negative view of her because of her weight. These reactions are not uncommon; in one study of therapists working with clients experiencing EDs, 83 percent said they felt they were being monitored, examined, or evaluated and that they were self-conscious about their appearance throughout the treatment process with these clients (Warren, Crowley, Olivardia, & Schoen, 2009). It is likely that Kathy is not prepared for this scrutiny and that she has not examined the importance she places on her own weight, shape, and appearance. The fact that she is flattered by Maggie's trust and willingness to work only with her also indicates Kathy's lack of self-awareness in this case, and these countertransference reactions are preventing Kathy from prioritizing the client's treatment needs over her own needs and feelings. Overall, Kathy clearly needs to spend some time learning to manage her personal values and biases in this area (Choate, Hermann, Pottle, & Manton, 2013).

Client Involvement

Kathy is honored that Maggie trusts her so much; she enjoys Maggie's respect and her wish to work with her on an exclusive basis. Her own needs for importance and acceptance seem to be clouding her judgment in making ethical decisions in this case. Instead of working with her in isolation, Kathy should build Maggie's motivation to work with a treatment team and to understand that comprehensive treatment is in her best interest. This will take skill on the part of Kathy, as Maggie is currently adamant that she only wants to work on her depression and is not interested in change related to her weight or AN symptoms.

Consultation and Collaboration

As is clear from the previous discussion, Kathy needs to be in consultation with medical professionals who can conduct a thorough assessment of Maggie's condition. It is an ethical imperative that she should involve a physician and a knowledgeable nutritionist who can assist with weight restoration and renourishment (APA, 2006; 2012). In addition, not only would Kathy benefit from collaboration with medical professionals, she should seek supervision from a seasoned clinician (particularly to help her manage her countertransference reactions) and seek out advanced professional development training in the area of ED treatment. This would enable her to make efforts to adhere to standard 2.01(d) in the APA Code of Ethics:

> (d) When psychologists are asked to provide services to individuals for whom appropriate mental health services are not available and for which psychologists have not obtained the competence necessary, psychologists with closely related prior training or experience may provide such services in order to ensure that services are not denied if they make a reasonable effort to obtain the competence required by using relevant research, training, consultation or study.

Desired Outcome and Possible Courses of Action

The desired outcome in this case is that Maggie will receive effective treatment for the psychological aspects of AN and that she will also be able to maintain a healthy weight. The courses of action could include:

- *Honor the client's wishes and continue to work with her once per week in private practice*. The obvious benefit to this option is that client autonomy is respected and Maggie will likely continue in treatment for depressive symptoms. The consequence, however, is that she would not receive effective treatment for her AN symptoms, her medical condition could deteriorate, and her health could become jeopardized.
- *Continue to honor Maggie's wishes by working with her alone, but seek out additional training, consultation, and supervision to improve the provision of services*. There are clear benefits to Kathy seeking out support while working with Maggie, but the likelihood is that these consultants would recommend that she refer to a treatment team. Further, this would take time, and the client's condition may deteriorate during this period.
- *Refer to another mental health professional who specializes in the treatment of EDs*. The benefit is that the client has a better chance of receiving adequate services, but a potential consequence is that the client might not follow through on the referral and will subsequently receive no treatment at all. In addition, they both live in a small community where there are few mental health professionals, so an adequate referral may be difficult to obtain.
- *Require that she work in collaboration with a treatment team in order for their treatment to continue*. This option would be in compliance with practice guidelines, yet this path is in opposition to the client's current wishes. An alternative to this option would be to use motivational enhancement to empower the client to actively participate in seeking out members of her own treatment team.

The best outcome would likely involve a combination of the last three options. The first option is unethical because Maggie is already experiencing symptoms of AN that indicate medical risk; it would be negligent for Kathy not to refer her to a medical professional and nutritionist. This is inconsistent with the ethical principle of nonmaleficence (General Principle A) and with Standards 2.01 (Boundaries of Competence) and 3.04 (Avoiding Harm) of the APA Code of Ethics. The most ethical approach would involve a comprehensive direction for treatment as described in the practice guidelines (APA, 2006; 2012). If Maggie does agree to work with a medical professional and nutritionist while in treatment, Kathy would still be ethically required to seek out ongoing supervision to manage her countertransference issues. Further, she would require collaboration with seasoned ED specialists, perhaps consulting weekly during her initial work with Maggie (see American Psychological Association Code Standard 2.01.d). However, if Maggie's health deteriorates at any point, Kathy will need to conduct additional assessment and make a referral to a higher level of care.

The Case of Sasha

Nancy, a Caucasian therapist who works with children and adolescents in a community mental health clinic, is counseling a 14-year-old African–American girl named Sasha. Sasha is in counseling at her mother's request because of concerns that Sasha is less social than she used to be and is spending too much time alone in her room at home. During their first session, Sasha says that she is tired of her mother "being so pushy, being in my business, and treating me like a baby." She says that she spends a lot of time in her room because it is the only way she can have any privacy. In response to her mother's concerns that she has become less social, she says that it is because her mother will not let her spend time with her friends outside of school because she fears they will be "bad influences" and "she doesn't approve of them." They agree to work together to help Sasha establish some autonomy at home while also improving her relationship with her mother. Nancy's mother agrees with these treatment goals, but says she wants to be regularly updated on their progress.

After the fifth session, Nancy notices that Sasha seems to have lost some weight over the last several weeks, and notices some swelling in her neck area and a large scrape on the fingers of one hand. Sasha seems weak and lethargic. After Nancy asks specific questions about her weight and eating patterns, Sasha admits to being on a diet since the school year started, but that sometimes she "just can't stick to it" and ends up "losing control" and engaging in binge eating. She says this usually occurs after she has eaten a "dessert that my mom made me eat because she is just trying to fatten me up." She says that she also binges on junk food after she has a "stressed-out day" at school. When this happens, she takes cookies and chips from the pantry and eats them in her room as quickly as possible. She hides the wrappers in her book sack and then throws them away on the way to school the next day. She says that her mom has not said anything about the missing food, but she wonders why her mom has not questioned her about it. During the past two weeks, she has started feeling guilty and "disgusted with myself" after these binge eating episodes, so she has started purging. She learned on the Internet the best way to stick her fingers down her throat to make herself vomit; she has also stolen laxatives from her mom's medicine cabinet. She assures Nancy that she only binges and purges "once in a while," that she has it "under control," and that "it is not a big deal."

Sasha begs for Nancy not to tell her mother about these behaviors because her mother is already overly intrusive in her life. She believes that if her mother finds out she is bingeing and purging, she will become even more controlling, wanting to watch her every move. Sasha promises her that she can stop on her own without her mother's help. Nancy is perplexed as to whether or not to alert Sasha's mom to these newly emerging behaviors.

Ethical Concerns

The ethical dilemma for Nancy in this case is which principle takes priority: the parent's legal right to knowledge of what is disclosed in her daughter's counseling sessions versus the minor client's ethical right to privacy and autonomy, and how these decisions will influence Nancy's duty to provide effective treatment and to protect her client from future harm. Because the client in this case is only 14 years of age, her legal rights belong to her mother. This means that her mother was the one who provided consent to treatment and who has the right to knowledge of the content of the sessions.

Therapists, however, must balance parental legal rights with the ethical rights of minor clients to autonomy, confidentiality, and privacy (Boldt, 2012). These tensions are particularly difficult when working with adolescent clients for whom independence and privacy are increasingly important as part of the developmental pull toward separation and individuation from parents or guardians. If the therapist errs too far on the side of disclosure to the parent, there will be little trust in the therapist–client relationship and the therapy will have a poor chance for success, particularly for older adolescents (ages 14 and up) who are legally considered minors but who also may be cognitively capable of understanding treatment decisions and the implications of confidentiality (Gustafson & McNamara, 1987). However, if the therapist errs too far on the side of protecting the minor client's ethical rights, then the therapist is not respecting the parent's legal right to protect her child and make important decisions on her behalf (Remley & Herlihy, 2015).

Nancy is facing a difficult decision about when and what to disclose to Sasha's mother at the same time that her client is asking for privacy. Clearly, adolescent clients the age of Sasha (14) do have ethical rights to confidentiality and privacy (Gustafson & McNamara, 1987). Adolescent clients often request that their therapists refrain from telling parents about certain behaviors and actions, often when they fear such disclosures will result in parental disapproval or enforcement of negative consequences. A general agreement in the literature is that a parent's right to knowledge of what is discussed in sessions will take priority over a minor client's right to privacy in those cases when the client is engaging in behavior that puts him or her at risk and that could result in future harm (Remley & Herlihy, 2015). While determining risk might be clear when the client is actively suicidal or homicidal, determining which behaviors rise to the level of "risk" or "future harm" is often a difficult judgment call (Behnke & Warner, 2002). If therapists break confidentiality and disclose to parents every time an adolescent client shares a high-risk behavior like smoking, drinking, or sexual activity, then it would be difficult to ever build rapport with an adolescent. Therefore, decisions to disclose risky behaviors that do not rise to the level of suicide or homicide should be weighed on a case-by-case basis, with careful consideration to the client's developmental growth, the therapist's duty to inform parents so that they can protect their children (see Standard 4.05 a and b in the American Psychological Association Code of Ethics), and the therapist's obligation to promote the well-being of the client. To that end, while adolescent clients do have a right to have their wishes respected, therapists should consider that "anytime they decide to withhold information from a parent, they assume responsibility for harm caused if that information later leads to injuries for the client" (Remley & Herlihy, 2015, p. 268).

In this case, Sasha's initial symptoms of bulimia are not life-threatening, nor is she suicidal or homicidal. However, in determining her next steps, Nancy needs to be knowledgeable about the serious and potentially lethal nature of EDs, the chronic and compulsive nature of the diet/binge/purge cycle, and the medical and psychological consequences of the disorder. While Sasha currently displays symptoms of bulimia, diagnostic migration is common in those with EDs, so that there is a real concern that her restrictive dieting could result in the development of AN over time. At her age, Sasha's health could deteriorate quickly, with symptoms resulting in permanent medical consequences such as stunted growth, osteoporosis, and infertility (Matusek & Wright, 2010). Therefore, while Sasha's symptoms are not currently life-threatening, it is possible that they might become so in the near future.

Nancy will also have to consider whether or not disclosing Sasha's behavior to the mother is necessary for her to fulfill her duty to promote Sasha's best interests and to provide the most effective treatment for Sasha. Most pressing is that Sasha will need a medical evaluation, particularly due to her purging behaviors, which can cause serious complications due to electrolyte imbalances (Berg & Petersen, 2013). In addition to a medical professional, if Nancy determines that other treatment team members are needed in order to provide optimal care, the mother must be involved to schedule the medical evaluation and additional treatment providers (Matusek & Wright, 2010). Finally, practice guidelines call for family interventions with children and adolescents who experience EDs (APA, 2006; 2012), and this component would not be possible if Sasha's mother is not aware of the need for this aspect of treatment.

Client Context and Therapist Feelings

Sasha is an African–American girl of normal weight. Many therapists might have overlooked Sasha's symptoms and failed to ask essential assessment questions due to the common perception that EDs only occur in Caucasian, middle-class girls who are extremely thin (Tallyrand, 2013). Because of her knowledge and skill, however, Nancy was able to assess for these problems early in Sasha's treatment. Nancy is also mindful of the client's developmental status. At age 14, Nancy is sensitive to Sasha's concerns over the need for independence and privacy from her mother and the fact that she is feeling powerless because of her mother's unwillingness to respond to her increased need for autonomy. These developmental needs should be taken into consideration when and if Nancy discloses information to the mother and in how she involves the client in tailoring a treatment plan.

Overall, Nancy is torn because she is unsure whether or not telling the mother about Sasha's bulimic symptoms will actually make the situation worse for Sasha. How can she uphold her ethical duty to protect Sasha's best interests? Telling Sasha's mother about the behaviors might cause the mother to increase her control over Sasha. If she perceives that she is being scrutinized by her mother, Sasha's level of distress might escalate, potentially leading to an increase in binge/purge episodes or other self-harming behavior. Further, if Nancy does disclose this information to Sasha's mother, Sasha might lose trust in Nancy and begin to hide her behaviors even from her therapist, thereby impeding effective treatment. If she feels betrayed by Nancy, she might want to drop out of treatment altogether.

Client Involvement

At the outset of treatment, Nancy first upheld her ethical duty to Sasha by informing Sasha of her rights as well as the limitations to confidentiality. While Sasha could not give legal consent, she was able to give her assent to treatment; she had agreed to the course that her treatment would take and she indicated her understanding of the limitations to confidentiality. Additionally, in upholding her ethical duty to Sasha's mother, Nancy also had a conversation with the mother to review informed consent documents and to explain when and how she would disclose information about Sasha. Nancy had emphasized the need for confidentiality with Sasha so that Sasha would feel safe in the relationship, but Nancy had also reassured the mother that she would share information with her if she ever felt that Sasha was in any way at risk of harm. However, these discussions had occurred prior to her knowledge of Sasha's disordered eating behaviors.

Nancy's Next Steps

Now several weeks into therapy, Nancy reminds Sasha of the limitations to confidentiality that she reviewed with her during the first session. Nancy emphasizes her concerns about Sasha's emerging bulimia symptoms and the consequences to her physical health. She also takes the time to validate Sasha's fears about her mother's possible reaction to the news about her daughter's eating and purging behavior. She then asks Sasha for her cooperation in determining when, where, and what specific information they will share with her mother. Because she is aware that it is rarely beneficial to speak to a parent without a minor client's prior knowledge (Remley & Herlihy, 2015), Nancy proposes that the mother come to the next session so that Sasha can be the one to tell her about her problems related to dieting, bingeing, and purging. Sasha does not agree with this decision.

Consultation and Collaboration

Before disclosing any information to Sasha's mother, Nancy consults with colleagues who have experience in ED treatment. They agree with her concerns for Sasha and that the mother should be informed. Nancy recognizes that without the mother's support she will not be able to enlist the expertise of medical providers who are skilled in the assessment of EDs. This limitation weighs heavily in her decision to tell the mother even when such disclosure is against Sasha's wishes.

Desired Outcome and Possible Courses of Action

The ideal outcome in this case is to honor Sasha's initial treatment goal for increased independence while also providing effective treatment for her emerging symptoms of bulimia before they escalate into an entrenched, full-syndrome ED. Some options Nancy could consider are as follows:

- *Continue to work with Sasha and help develop a list of positive coping skills to replace binge eating.* The benefits to this option are continued privacy and independence for Sasha, an important goal for treatment. However, her health could quickly deteriorate, and Nancy would be withholding knowledge from the parent that might have prevented this harm from occurring.
- *Tell her mother about the symptoms, but ask the mother not to disclose this conversation to Sasha.* This could potentially be helpful in that the mother might recognize the need to give Sasha increased independence and to encourage Sasha to socialize with others instead of isolating herself in her room (seemingly a trigger for binge eating). However, if Sasha finds out about this disclosure, she will feel betrayed and therapy progress will be sabotaged.
- *Invite the mother to the next session and have Sasha share her symptoms, fears, and concerns.* While Sasha currently refuses this option, Nancy can let Sasha know that she will still invite the mother to the session due to her concerns about Sasha's health. She can give Sasha an opportunity to speak during the session, but if she declines to share, then Nancy will go ahead and tell the mother about her concerns. Even though Sasha might be upset that Nancy told her mother about her secret behaviors, Sasha will know exactly what was shared and can provide input if she decides to do so. This might also increase the likelihood that Sasha will continue to trust Nancy during subsequent therapy sessions.

This last option seems to be the most ethical action because of the potential medical risks that could result from Sasha's bulimia-related behaviors and Sasha's inability to give consent for the medical care that she needs. Further, if the mother is aware of Sasha's mental health problems, she is in a better position to provide support and to become involved in family treatment. However, this decision does involve violating Sasha's right to privacy and autonomy. Nancy should do everything she can to ameliorate this violation by involving Sasha as much as possible in the process of discussing these issues with her mother. Because Sasha will be in the session when this information is disclosed, she is less likely to feel betrayed by

Nancy and it is hoped that the therapeutic relationship can be repaired. In accordance with the American Psychological Association Code of Ethics (see Principle A, Beneficence and Nonmaleficence, Standard 3.04, and Standard 4.05), Nancy's ethical duty to protect Sasha and promote her well-being is a higher priority than Sasha's right to autonomy at this point in the case.

The Case of Marcus

Marcus is a 19-year-old Asian–American male, living alone in an apartment near a large state university where he is a part-time student. He seeks counseling from Sydney, a therapist in private practice whose office is near the university. She regularly works with college students and has had some limited but positive experience in working with clients experiencing disordered eating. Marcus was referred to Sydney by one of his friends, a former client of Sydney's who had received treatment for bulimia. The friend was quite worried about Marcus because of his extremely low weight. Further, she was concerned that he had started to skip most of his classes and had recently declined any invitations to socialize. He only agreed to come to therapy after his friend scheduled the appointment and drove him to his first session.

At the first session, Marcus told Sydney that he felt in control of his body and weight, but that he was "nowhere close" to reaching the weight where he would look his best. He stated that he was at his lowest weight since high school. He had no awareness that he was underweight and even saw himself as "slightly overweight" for his frame. According to Marcus, it was important to him to continue on his "quest" to "weigh the right amount" and he wanted Sydney to know that he was highly committed to his current eating routine (roughly 500 calories or less per day).

He stated that he had been in and out of counseling for depression and EDs since he was in middle school, when his parents first "forced" him to go to counseling, even though counseling was seen as a last resort for them because they did not want other people to know about private family problems. He said that he was socially isolated and withdrawn from his family throughout middle and high school and felt they were ashamed of him. He reported that he was happy to move away from them to go to college. When asked about his current relationship with his parents, he stated that they are paying for him to be in college, but they keep their distance because they are tired of trying to convince him to eat, to gain weight, and to "be normal." Instead of being concerned about his unstable relationship with them, Marcus said he was relieved that they were finally "off his back" about his weight and about his decisions in life.

Because Marcus was not concerned about his low weight or the distance from his parents, Sydney asked him whether or not there were things in his life that he might want to change. He admitted that he was a bit concerned about his declining grades, so he agreed that this could be their focus in treatment. He also admitted that he was frequently tired and did not feel like doing much lately, but he had experienced this before and was not concerned; he was sure that his energy would return if he could just make himself exercise more. Overall, he told Sydney that he would agree to meet with her to help him "pull myself out of this slump" and do better in school. He stated that he absolutely did not want to pursue any type of treatment that would require him to gain weight.

Sydney quickly recognized that, despite his denial, Marcus was at medical risk due to his extreme dietary restriction and low weight. At the same time, she also recognized that he would be reluctant to seek medical assistance. Since she knew that he wanted to increase his energy level, she asked Marcus if he would be willing to meet with a physician who might be able to help him evaluate his overall health and energy. Marcus reluctantly agreed to the appointment and signed a release so that Sydney could exchange information with the physician. After a thorough medical assessment, it was determined that Marcus was severely underweight; at 101 pounds, he was 75% below his ideal body weight for his height and age. His examination and lab work showed an electrolyte imbalance including low blood potassium, anemia, low heart rate, and an abnormal heart rhythm. The physician shared this information and her serious concerns about his health with Sydney prior to Marcus's next appointment.

When he returned for a second appointment, Marcus had lost additional weight, had missed all of his midterms, and had not left the apartment for several days before coming to the session. When Sydney shared her concerns about the doctor's evaluation and his continued weight loss, Marcus became angry that she had tricked him to go see the doctor for his "health" when actually she was sending him for an ED evaluation. He told her that he knew she would "be like all of the others, just conspiring to get me to gain weight, the one thing I don't want to do!" Sydney felt compelled to tell Marcus that she strongly recommended an evaluation for hospitalization, as the outpatient services she could provide would not be sufficient for his needs. Marcus became even more infuriated, stormed out of the session, and did not return. At this point, Sydney was unsure of the next steps she needed to take in order to uphold her ethical duty to protect her client's life.

Ethical Concerns

Sydney's ethical dilemma in this case is an extremely difficult one: at what point should she override this adult client's right to autonomy and take action to restrict his personal freedoms? Should she go against Marcus's wishes and work with his family or physician to enforce possible hospitalization? When does the duty to act on a client's behalf and protect him from harm outweigh his right to determine the goals of treatment (Matusek & Wright, 2010)? In this case, Marcus does not want to gain weight and refuses any medical intervention that would require him to do so. If he is to reach a medically stable weight, however, coercive and often intrusive measures (e.g., nasogastric feeding, mandatory bed rest and movement restriction, surveillance at meals and in the bathroom, and admission to a locked treatment unit) may be required and would have to be enforced against his will.

To take away a client's fundamental right to make his own decision about undergoing such drastic medical intervention is a serious ethical decision for any mental health professional. Ultimately, Sydney must balance Marcus's right to confidentiality and autonomy with her own duty to protect him from harm and to prolong his life. The question of whether or not a person should ever be forced into treatment for a potentially life-threatening ED has been debated extensively in the literature, with arguments on both sides; some scholars view involuntary treatment as unethical, while others claim it is a therapist's best chance at providing compassionate care (Carney, Tait, Richardson, & Touyz, 2008; Elzakkers, Danner, Hoek, Schmidt, & Van Elburg, 2014; Guarda, Pinto, Coughlin, Hussain, Haug, & Heinberg, 2007; Kendall, 2014; Matusek & Wright, 2010; Tan, Hope, Stewart, & Fitzpatrick, 2006).

On the one hand, those who argue against involuntary treatment for AN state that compulsory treatment strips away a client's dignity and autonomy and is therefore fundamentally unethical, stigmatizing, paternalistic, and discriminatory and is an infringement on the client's civil liberties (Charland, 2013; Giordano, 2005). According to critics, it may not be effective in treating the core of the disorder. Because clients feel violated and out of control, they may take even more drastic measures to regain that control by quickly returning to their former weight after discharge. Further, if a therapist breaks confidentiality and pursues involuntary treatment, there will be obvious ruptures in the therapeutic alliance and little progress in therapy or willingness to seek out care in the future.

On the other side of the argument, other scholars claim that if a client is hospitalized and is able to gain weight, his or her life can be saved and prolonged. AN has the highest mortality rate of all psychiatric conditions (Arcelus et al., 2011; Keel & Brown, 2014). Werth, Wright, Archambault & Bardash, (2003) emphasize that when the course of AN is uninterrupted, it leads to medical jeopardy and death, and they assert that a therapist's duty to protect clients may call for hospitalization in order to prolong life. Further, studies indicate that treatment outcomes are similar for both voluntary and involuntary clients after discharge (Clausen & Jones, 2014), showing that involuntary treatment can and often does serve as a life-saving measure for clients with AN (Elzakkers et al., 2014).

Another reason relevant to Sydney's decision regarding involuntary hospitalization is that refeeding and proper nourishment are both needed for a client to be able to recognize the necessity of treatment and to eventually benefit from psychotherapy. In one study, clients with AN who denied the need for treatment upon their admission to the hospital were interviewed two weeks into treatment. After only two weeks in the hospital, roughly half of them admitted that they did need the treatment, despite their initial denial about their need for weight gain or renourishment (Guarda et al., 2007). Interestingly, other studies also indicate that compulsory treatment is not significantly related to a worsening of the therapeutic relationship, and clients tend to stay in therapy after being discharged from the hospital setting (Elzakkers et al., 2014).

Overall, treatment guidelines indicate that involuntary treatment can be justified when: (a) the treatment is in the client's best interest; (b) there is a reasonable chance for recovery; and (c) the client lacks the capacity to make his or her own informed treatment decisions (APA, 2006). One of the most difficult aspects of these decisions is related to this third justification: client capacity to make treatment decisions. In this case, Sydney will have to answer the following questions: does Marcus actually possess the insight needed to make reasoned decisions about whether or not he needs medical intervention and weight restoration? Is he thinking clearly and rationally enough to understand the seriousness of the disorder and to foresee the consequences of his actions if he decides not to seek treatment?

Sydney's decision about possible involuntary hospitalization and making judgments about Marcus's capacity for rational decision-making is further complicated because, for many clients with AN, there exists a discrepancy between an individual's ability to understand the nature of the disorder and its associated health risks as compared with the client's ability to apply that understanding to him or herself specifically. Marcus seems quite knowledgeable about nutrition and the impact of starvation, but he does not believe that it applies to him and his own condition (Tan et al., 2006). Further, clients with AN often maintain global competence (the ability to function and make rational decisions in other domains of their lives), but lack specific competence to make decisions about their own health, eating, activity level, and treatment (Bodell et al., 2014).

Marcus's ability to understand yet not apply health information to himself, along with the discrepancy between global and disorder-specific competence, can be understood in part as a result of the physical effects of self-starvation. Studies of individuals who are in a state of starvation (no matter what the cause) show that they are no longer able to make rational decisions and process information clearly due to chemical changes in the body that occur as a result of starvation (Douzenis & Michopoulos, 2015; Matusek & Wright, 2010; Vitousek, Watson, & Wilson, 1998; Werth et al., 2003). Sydney needs to consider whether or not Marcus is below the weight threshold at which functional changes to the central nervous system begin to appear, resulting in poor concentration, deficits in information processing, disruption of emotion regulation, and difficulty engaging in rational judgments and decision-making processes (Adoue et al., 2015; Bodell et al., 2014; Turrell, Peterson-Badali, & Katzman, 2011).

In addition to the cognitive effects of starvation, the nature of the disorder itself leads to significant body image distortions and overvalued beliefs about the importance of thinness (APA, 2013). AN is ego-syntonic, and AN symptoms help individuals to feel in control of their lives. They may even claim that they would rather die than gain weight (Douzenis & Michopoulos, 2015). Therefore, individuals like Marcus are highly threatened and fearful of anyone who claims to want to force them to gain weight. Given the cognitive effects of starvation paired with the ego-syntonic nature of AN, Sydney must decide: would my client make this same decision regarding treatment refusal if he was not in a state of starvation and in the throes of this chronic mental disorder (Andersen, 2008; Matusek & Wright, 2010)?

Client Context and Therapist Feelings

Marcus is a 19-year-old Asian–American male. Sydney will have to ask herself if her decision about compulsory treatment might be different if this client were Caucasian or female. She wonders if her client will receive appropriate, gender-sensitive treatment if he is in an inpatient treatment unit. She questions: *Is it harder for him to open up and share with me because I am a female therapist? Will it be difficult to collaborate with his family because of their traditional Asian beliefs about the shaming nature of therapy?*

Another relevant client characteristic is that Marcus is a college student. If Sydney worked for his university, she would have to grapple with decisions about his rights under the Family Educational Rights and Privacy Act (FERPA) and how to balance those with her obligation to the university (to inform them if his life is in jeopardy) as well as to his parents (to honor their right to information about their son because he is still their dependent). As a community practitioner, she is governed by the Health Insurance Portability and Accountability Act (HIPAA) and is not legally obligated to notify his parents or his university due to his age. Because of his ethical and legal rights to confidentiality, Sydney must carefully weigh any decisions about parental notification and involvement and determine whether or not the family will be influential in obtaining the most effective care for Marcus.

Sydney's feelings are mixed: she is angry at Marcus for storming out of the session and for refusing all of her efforts to help him when his life is at risk. On the other hand, she has empathy for him in understanding his resistance to the compulsory weight gain that will undoubtedly be forced upon him if he enters a hospital setting. She understands what a loss it will be for him to give up power, control, and a large aspect of his identity. However, because he appears to be so fragile and frail, she is fearful that his life is at serious risk. Because she is aware of the high mortality rate for AN, she is also highly concerned about Marcus's level of suicide risk. Despite her mixed feelings, Sydney firmly believes that it is her obligation to promote Marcus's well-being and to prolong his life, even when her actions to do so might go against his current wishes. Because she is invested in her legal duty to protect Marcus as well as her ethical duty to ensure nonmaleficence and promote beneficence (see General Principle A as well as Standard 3.04, American Psychological Association Code of Ethics), she wants to do all she can to help him stay alive.

Client Involvement

Sydney could have done more to involve and prepare her client at the outset of treatment. She could have expanded her informed consent document to require Marcus to sign a safety plan that included the lowest weight possible he could maintain in order to stay out of the hospital and remain in outpatient treatment. With this type of signed agreement, if his weight drops below a certain level and hospitalization is needed, he might be less likely to feel that treatment is being forced upon him (Matusek & Wright, 2010). Because she did not take this step, Marcus felt betrayed and abandoned therapy when she suggested hospitalization.

In addition, during the first session, Sydney should have shared her grave concerns about his poor health and low weight. In addition, she should have been more transparent about her reasons for the medical referral. The client felt betrayed by her intentions to send him for an ED evaluation when he thought he was only receiving a general health checkup. Sydney should have carefully considered her decision through balancing the ethical principle of veracity (to always tell the truth to her client) versus her duty to protect her client and have him actually follow through with the medical evaluation. She would need to weigh the risks associated with the possibility that he would not have kept the appointment had he known the truth versus his feelings of betrayal that contributed to his ultimate treatment refusal. Another final way she could have involved the client more would have been to call Marcus prior to informing his parents to make sure he was fully aware of the information she was about to share and the actions she was preparing to take.

Consultation and Collaboration

In following APA practice guidelines regarding consultation with medical professionals (APA 2006; 2012), Sydney knew to collaborate with a physician who then provided a medical evaluation. Their plan was for Sydney to coordinate care and to have Marcus see the physician on a regular basis for medical monitoring. However, because Marcus's health deteriorated so rapidly between the first and second sessions, this plan was abandoned in favor of seeking inpatient admission for Marcus.

Desired Outcome and Possible Courses of Action

The desired outcome in this case is first and foremost to prolong Marcus's life and restore his weight. This goal is best accomplished in a medically supervised inpatient treatment setting. Options for Sydney are as follows:

- *Call Marcus and ask him to return for individual sessions to work on his grades in college; she would not break confidentiality at this point.* A benefit is that he might continue in counseling and become invested in the process because this is his desired treatment goal. When he regains trust in his therapist, he might be more agreeable to working with a nutritionist and physician as part of his treatment team. An obvious downside to this option is that he is currently in medical danger due to starvation and his status could worsen quickly.
- *Call the police to pick him up to take him to the hospital because he poses a danger to himself.* A benefit is that this is the quickest method for him to receive medical intervention. His life could be prolonged. A major consequence of this action, however, is that Marcus would feel violated and stripped of dignity, and his family's rights to make decisions about their son's health would be ignored as well.
- *Call Marcus, tell him about her concerns and the action she is about to take, and then call his family with the recommendation that they come immediately to take their son for medical evaluation and possible hospitalization. Explain to them that he might need to be hospitalized against his will, but also provide a rationale for why this decision is medically necessary to save their son's life.*

The first option is unethical because it would require Sydney to neglect her obligations under the American Psychological Association Code of Ethics (see General Principle A [beneficence and nonmaleficence], Standard 2.01 [boundaries of competence], and Standard 3.04 [avoiding harm]), as well as her legal duty to protect Marcus from serious harm. Conversely, the second option is not a beneficent decision because it is overly intrusive and paternalistic; it would not make sense to call the police without first calling a family member or a friend to take him to the hospital for the evaluation. The third option is the least intrusive and causes Marcus the least harm at this point in the situation. It is a major decision any time a therapist has to break confidentiality and require involuntary treatment; therefore, his family or a significant other should ideally be involved and take the lead in making these decisions instead of the therapist working in isolation. Once at the hospital, they can collaborate with a medical treatment team and take the steps necessary to authorize medical intervention to save his life, even if this is against Marcus's wishes.

Recommendations for Ethical Practice

- Ethical decision-making related to EDs is a complex process. Refer to relevant practice guidelines (APA, 2006; 2012), codes of ethics (e.g., American Psychological Association Code of Ethics, 2010), as well as decision-making models (e.g., Remley & Herlihy, 2015) to guide the process.
- In making treatment decisions, remain mindful of the serious and even lethal medical complications that can result from EDs, particularly in children and adolescents whose health can deteriorate quickly. Remain aware of the high suicide risk associated with AN and always include a thorough suicide assessment when working with these clients. These are requirements of ethically competent care.
- Act consistently with APA practice guidelines (2006; 2012) that call for a multi-disciplinary treatment team composed of a therapist, physician, and nutritionist. Other medical professionals such as a psychiatrist might also need to be included. When working with children and adolescents, family therapy is also a recommended component of treatment.
- Acknowledge the boundaries of your competence and the value of consulting and collaborating with both medical and mental health professionals in the treatment of EDs; maintain referral sources in your community at various levels of care and in multiple medical and mental health disciplines.
- Seek supervision and/or consultation to avoid placing your own interests and values ahead of the clients'. This action can assist in the management of counter-transference reactions that arise when working with clients experiencing EDs. Take the time to examine your attitudes toward the importance of weight, shape, and appearance in determining your own identity and worth.
- When working with adolescent clients, be careful to balance the parents' legal right to knowledge of what is disclosed in the counseling sessions, the minor client's ethical right to privacy and autonomy, and your duty to provide effective treatment and to protect your client from future harm.
- Seek extensive supervision and consultation regarding decisions related to involuntary hospitalization for clients whose low weight and malnourishment call for immediate medical assessment and intervention.

References

Adoue, C., Jaussent, I., Olié, E., Beziat, S., Van den Eynde, F., Courtet, P., & Guillaume, S. (2015). A further assessment of decision-making in anorexia nervosa. *European Psychiatry, 30*, 121–127.

American Psychiatric Association (2006). Part A: Treatment recommendations for patients with eating disorders. In *Treatment of patients with eating disorders* (3rd edn.). Washington, DC: American Psychiatric Publishing. Retrieved from http://psychia tryonline.org/pb/assets/raw/sitewide/practice_guidelines/guidelines/eatingdisor ders.pdf

American Psychiatric Association (2012). Guideline watch: Practice guideline for the treatment of patients with eating disorders (3rd edn.). Retrieved from http://psychiatryon line.org/pb/assets/raw/sitewide/practice_guidelines/guidelines/eatingdisorders-watch.pdf

American Psychiatric Association (2013). *Diagnostic and statistical manual of mental disorders* (5th edn.). Arlington, VA: American Psychiatric Publishing.

American Psychological Association (2010). *Ethical principles of psychologists and code of conduct.* Washington, DC: American Psychological Association. Retrieved from www.apa.org/ethics/code/principles.pdf

Andersen, A. E. (2008). Ethical conflicts in the care of anorexia nervosa patients. *Eating Disorders Review, 19*, 1–3, 11.

Arcelus, J., Mitchell, A. J., Wales, J., & Nielsen, S. (2011). Mortality rates in patients with anorexia nervosa and other eating disorders: A meta-analysis of 36 studies. *Archives of General Psychiatry, 68*, 724–731.

Beauchamp, T. L. & Childress, J. F. (2013). *Principles of biomedical ethics* (7th edn.). New York, NY: Oxford University Press.

Behnke, S. H. & Warner, E. (2002). Confidentiality in the treatment of adolescents. *American Psychological Association Monitor, 33*, 44.

Berg, K. C. & Petersen, C. B. (2013). Assessment and diagnosis of eating disorders. In L. Choate (Ed.), *Eating disorders and obesity: A counselor's guide to prevention and treatment* (pp. 91–118). Alexandria, VA: American Counseling Association.

Bodell, L. P., Keel, P. K., Brumm, M. C., et al. (2014). Longitudinal examination of decision-making performance in anorexia nervosa: Before and after weight restoration. *Journal of Psychiatric Research, 56*, 150–157.

Boldt, R. C. (2012). Adolescent decision making: Legal issues with respect to treatment for substance misuse and mental illness. *Journal of Health Care Law & Policy, 15*, 75–115.

Brown, T. A. & Keel, P. K. (2012). Current and emerging directions in the treatment of eating disorders. *Substance Abuse: Research and Treatment, 6*, 33–61.

Clausen, L. & Jones, A. (2014). A systematic review of the frequency, duration, type, and effect of involuntary treatment for people with anorexia nervosa, and an analysis of patient characteristics. *Journal of Eating Disorders, 2*, 29.

Carney, T., Tait, D., Richardson, A., & Touyz, S. (2008). Why (and when) clinicians compel treatment of anorexia nervosa patients. *European Eating Disorders Review, 16*, 199–206.

Charland, L. C. (2013). Ethical and conceptual issues in eating disorders. *Current Opinion in Psychiatry, 26*, 562–565.

Choate, L. H., Hermann, M. A., Pottle, L., & Manton, J. (2013). Ethical and legal issues in counseling clients with eating disorders. In L. H. Choate (Ed.), *Eating disorders and obesity: A counselor's guide to prevention and treatment* (pp. 69–88). Alexandria, VA: American Counseling Association.

Douzenis, A. & Michopoulos, I. (2015). Involuntary admission: The case of anorexia nervosa. *International Journal of Law and Psychiatry, 39,* 31–35.

Elzakkers, I. F., Danner, U. N., Hoek, H. W., Schmidt, U., & van Elburg, A. A. (2014). Compulsory treatment in anorexia nervosa: A review. *International Journal of Eating Disorders, 47,* 845–852.

Giordano, S. (2005). *Understanding eating disorders: Conceptual and ethical issues in the treatment of anorexia and bulimia nervosa.* New York, NY: Oxford University Press.

Guarda, A. S., Pinto, A. M., Coughlin, J. W., Hussain, S., Haug, N. A., & Heinberg, L. J. (2007). Perceived coercion and change in perceived need for admission in patients hospitalized for eating disorders. *American Journal of Psychiatry, 164,* 108–114.

Gustafson, K. E. & McNamara, J. R. (1987). Confidentiality with minor clients: Issues and guidelines for therapists. *Professional Psychology: Research and Practice, 18,* 503–508.

Jacobs, M. J. & Nye, S. (2010). The therapist's appearance and recovery: Perspectives on treatment, supervision, and ethical implications. *Eating Disorders, 18,* 165–175.

Keel and Brown Kendall, S. (2014). Anorexia nervosa: The diagnosis: A postmodern ethics contribution to the bioethics debate on involuntary treatment for anorexia nervosa. *Bioethical Inquiry, 11,* 31–40.

Long, S. (2014). Potential ethical dilemmas in the treatment of eating disorders. *Psychotherapy Bulletin, 41,* 37–44.

Matusek, J. A. & Wright, M. O. (2010). Ethical dilemmas in treating clients with eating disorders: A review and application of an integrative ethical decision-making model. *European Eating Disorders Review, 18,* 434–452.

Remley, T. P. & Herlihy, B. (2015). *Ethical, legal, and professional issues in counseling* (5th edn.). Boston, MA: Pearson Publishing.

Sigman, G. (2005). An adolescent with an eating disorder. *The Virtual Mentor, 7,* 3.

Swanson, S. A., Crow, S. J., LeGrange, D., Swendsen, J., & Merikangas, K. R. (2011). Prevalence and correlates of eating disorders in adolescents: Results from the National Comorbidity Survey Replication Adolescent Supplement. *Archives of General Psychiatry, 68,* 714–723.

Tallyrand, R. (2013). Clients of color and eating disorders: Cultural considerations. In L. Choate (Ed.), *Eating disorders and obesity: A counselor's guide to prevention and treatment* (pp. 45–68). Alexandra, VA: American Counseling Association.

Tan, J. O. A., Hope, T., Stewart, A., & Fitzpatrick, R. (2006). Competence to make treatment decisions in anorexia nervosa: Thinking processes and values. *Philosophy in Psychiatry & Psychology, 13,* 267–282.

Turrell, S. L., Peterson-Badali, M., & Katzman, D. K. (2011). Consent to treatment in adolescents with anorexia nervosa. *International Journal of Eating Disorders, 44,* 703–707.

Vitousek, K., Watson, S., & Wilson, G. T. (1998). Enhancing motivation for change in treatment-resistant eating disorders. *Clinical Psychology Review, 18,* 391–420.

Warren, C. S., Crowley, M., Olivardia, R., & Schoen, A. (2009). Treating patients with eating disorders: An examination of treatment providers' experiences. *Eating Disorders, 17,* 27–45.

Werth, J. J., Wright, K. S., Archambault, R. J., & Bardash, R. J. (2003). When does the "duty to protect" apply with a client who has anorexia nervosa? *Counseling Psychologist, 31,* 427–450.

Williams, M. & Haverkamp, B. E. (2010). Identifying critical competencies for psychotherapeutic practice with eating disordered clients: A Delphi study. *Eating Disorders, 18,* 19–109.

11 Ethical Considerations in Group Psychotherapy

Maria T. Riva and Jennifer A. Erickson Cornish

Group psychotherapy is a commonly practiced, complex, and effective format of treating a wide range of presenting problems and client populations. In fact, in many situations, group therapy has been found to be as effective, and sometimes more effective, than individual therapy (Burlingame, Strauss, & Joyce, 2013). However, even with the large number of groups that are currently conducted in many treatment settings (e.g., Veterans Administration Hospitals, mental health agencies, schools, residential facilities for adolescents, and so on), resulting in a need for a large number of skilled group facilitators, training of group leaders is much less a focus of training programs compared to that directed toward individual therapists. The unique characteristics of group psychotherapy require knowledge and skill in group methods and group ethics. Certainly, attempting to generalize treatment methods and ethical consideration from individual to group therapy can open up the possibility of ethical dilemmas for group leaders and for the ethical practice of group therapy. This chapter will address some of the more challenging ethical considerations in group psychotherapy and group psychotherapy leadership.

The primary focus of this chapter will be on psychotherapy groups specifically and not on psychoeducational or more didactic types of groups. Just like all groups, ethical dilemmas can occur in didactic and psychoeducational groups, although these types of groups tend to be less process-oriented, often have less deep self-disclosures, and most typically are brief treatment groups. For these reasons, the ethical decisions in such groups can be less complicated. Group therapy is a therapeutic format that typically includes several group members and one or two group leaders. There are many terms that are used for group psychotherapy. In this chapter, the following terms will be used interchangeably: group counseling, group psychotherapy, group therapy, group work, therapeutic groups, and group treatment. This chapter primarily discusses groups of adults since most of the research and theories address this age group. It is important to mention, though, that working with children and adolescents in groups adds additional layers of ethical decision-making given that, for a minor, a parent or guardian needs to provide consent to treat, and several group methods that are typical for adults need to be adapted for children and adolescents such as the session length, group methods, number of sessions, language, and cognitive level of material presented just for starters.

This chapter begins with a brief literature review of group therapy ethics, including a discussion of the relevant ethics codes that address group psychotherapy specifically and more generally. The second section will present four ethical dilemmas that occur frequently in group treatment. Although the complexities of group psychotherapy can (and do) result in numerous potential ethical decisions for group leaders, this chapter will focus on the following four areas: (a) confidentiality, (b) dual and multiple relationships, (c) voluntary participation, and (d) group leader competence. For each of these four areas, a short vignette will be presented highlighting an ethical dilemma. After each vignette, there will be a discussion that illuminates ethical choice points and provides recommendations for resolving them based on ethical codes, principles, and best practices. The chapter will conclude with overall recommendations related to the ethical practice of group psychotherapy.

Brief Literature Review on the Ethical Considerations in Group Therapy

Group therapy ethics are considerably more complex than are the ethical concerns for individual psychotherapy, yet the amount of information on the ethics of group work is startlingly small. Rather, much of the focus on psychotherapy ethics is on individual therapy, with some additional attention given to the ethics involved in treating families and couples. Although there are some relevant overlaps in these ethical discussions, with limited consideration for multiple persons in therapy, group counseling is generally composed of members who are unrelated to each other and most often do not even know each other prior to the beginning of group sessions. Working in group psychotherapy with people who have no prior relationship poses some additional dilemmas, such as the need for a careful discussion of confidentiality and its limits and the development of trust within the group. Typically group members are working on their own goals that are separate from those goals of the other group members, even though there might be a shared group theme (i.e., communication, anger management, development of interpersonal relationships, etc.).

The limits of confidentiality are quite different from those for individual therapy, and confidentiality is generally considered to be one of the most common areas that result in the need for ethical decision-making by group leaders. Confidentiality in groups is briefly addressed in most ethical principles and codes, yet this chapter will describe in more depth the multiple areas that group leaders need to understand in order to address this area effectively. Along with a vignette that underscores the complexities of confidentiality that regularly arise in groups, other ethical quagmires that are not addressed or only minimally addressed in professional ethics writings but are salient for group psychotherapy include dual and multiple relationships, voluntary participation, and group leader competence. Each of these will be discussed in more depth in the following sections.

Most ethics documents from major associations such as the American Psychological Association (APA) and the American Counseling Association (ACA) are broad in scope and only provide limited information that is specific to the ethics of group psychotherapy, most notably confidentiality. For example, Standard 10.03 in the APA Ethical Principles of Psychologists and Code of

Conduct (APA, 2010) states, "When psychologists provide services to several persons in a group setting, they describe at the outset the roles and responsibilities of all parties and the limits of confidentiality." B.4.a of the ACA Code of Ethics (2014) states, "In group work, counselors clearly explain the importance and parameters of confidentiality for the specific group." Besides confidentiality, the ACA Code of Ethics does address groups in two other specific areas. It states that "counselors screen prospective group counseling/therapy participants. To the extent possible, counselors select members whose needs and goals are compatible with the goals of the group, who will not impede the group process, and whose well-being will not be jeopardized by the group experience" (A.9.a). This code continues in A.9. b with, "In a group setting, counselors take reasonable precautions to protect clients from physical, emotional, or psychological trauma."

The general codes of ethics for the APA and ACA are helpful in providing direction for treatment yet there are many areas in conducting groups where much more detailed information is needed for group leaders. Thankfully, there are some ethical standards and best practice guidelines that are specifically related to group therapy and provide additional guidance. Several documents to help direct group leaders to ethical decisions and best practices have been published by the Association for Specialists in Group Work (ASGW). These documents include the ASGW Best Practice Guidelines (2007), the ASGW Professional Standards for Training Group Workers (2000), and the ASGW Multicultural and Social Justice Competence Principles for Group Workers (Singh, Merchant, Skudrzyk, & Ingene, 2012). Also, the American Group Psychotherapy Association (AGPA) has the Clinical Practice Guidelines for Group Psychotherapy, the AGPA and the International Board for Certification of Group Psychotherapists (IBCGP) provide the Guidelines for Ethics (AGPA & IBCGP, 2002), and the Association for the Advancement of Social Work with Groups (AASWG) published the Standard for Social Work Practice with Groups (2005). Both the general and more specific codes and best practice guidelines will be used to address the vignettes that follow.

The Case of Confidentiality and Its Limits

Dr. Janice Strong is a staff psychologist working in a university counseling center at a small, private university. Recently, the center has experienced a rapidly expanding caseload along with pressure from upper administration related to reducing financial costs. Thus, the center director has decided to place more clients in groups and has asked Dr. Strong to start a coed interpersonal process group for seven undergraduates presenting mostly with relationship problems. Due to the need to assign clients quickly, Dr. Strong has only had time to meet briefly with each potential client prior to the start of the group, mainly to determine obvious rule-outs such as apparent personality disorders. Generally, Dr. Strong has preferred to co-lead process groups and to take more time to interview potential candidates so that she and her co-leader could get to know candidates better while also discussing group purposes and norms with them in more detail. Nevertheless, understanding the current context and wishing to support her director, she has forged ahead with the new group. The first session focused mostly on introductions, and Dr. Strong was pleased to see that the group members all seemed highly motivated, although a few expressed their confusion at being put in a group rather than in individual psychotherapy. Halfway through the second session, when the group was starting to focus on shared goals, a group member revealed that a Facebook friend had "liked" a description of the group posted by another group member. Several group members expressed their confusion with the post, asking the member why she did that. The group member said she did not see any harm in it and is glad to be in this group. One other member stated that she was angry, no longer trusted the group member, and did not want to continue in this group. She stated, "I really did not want group therapy from the beginning but was willing to give it a try because of Dr. Strong's initial statements to me about keeping things private within the group." She then demanded individual therapy. Dr. Strong is clear that the Facebook post has increased the group members' anxiety, caused a lack of trust among group members, and increased their concern about being in group therapy. She wonders if this group will be able to recover from this breach of confidentiality and she is distressed that two areas of omission – not competently providing enough feedback about confidentiality and the truncated screening process – are at the heart of the current problems.

Clearly, Dr. Strong has considerable work to do in establishing norms for this new group, including the importance of addressing confidentiality in more depth. She is worried that she put her group members at risk for breaches of private information, even though there is no guarantee that group members will not reveal information that is shared in the group. Yet, Dr. Strong did not even consider the dangers of members posting descriptions online. APA Ethics Code Principle E: Respect of People's Rights and Dignity applies here as it states "psychologists respect the dignity and worth of all people and the rights of individuals to privacy, confidentiality, and self-determination." Dr. Strong also will want to take responsibility for her error in not discussing the harm that can arise from sharing personal information with others outside of the group, including in online formats. APA Ethics Code Principle B: Fidelity and Responsibility is key for Dr. Strong as it states "psychologists . . . accept appropriate responsibility for their behavior and seek to manage conflicts of interest that could lead to exploitation or harm." Unlike individual psychotherapy, where she would be solely responsible for holding client privilege, she cannot promise member confidentiality in a group setting. This situation has driven home the point that there can be many more threats to confidentiality in group than in individual therapy (Klontz, 2004). When multiple members are involved in group therapy, communication related to multiple interactions of group members becomes available (Anderson, 1996; Lasky & Riva, 2006). Thus, as the group leader, Dr. Strong has the challenge of helping her clients understand that it is imperative that they not share privileged information outside of the group setting while she also obtains their informed consent that confidentiality cannot be guaranteed.

As noted earlier, Standards 10.03 (Group Therapy) in the APA Ethics Code and B.4 in the ACA Ethics Code both prescribe discussing confidentiality in group settings. In addition, the APA Ethics Code Standard 4.02 (Discussing the Limits of Confidentiality) requires psychologists to clearly communicate the limits of confidentiality. The ACA Ethics Code further asks counselors to deliberately select group members who will be compatible with the group and not pose any threat of harm. The importance of carefully selecting group members and taking adequate time to plan for group therapy also has been underscored by Rapin (2014) and others. In reflecting back on the screening and selection process, Dr. Strong now sees that she was likely acting unethically when she responded more to the self-interest of the Director's request than to the group members' best interests. She also is unsettled because she did not perform a thorough screening process and provide enough information about how group therapy works and what the potential group members could expect. Without a complete picture of group psychotherapy, there is no way for the potential members to consent to participate in this therapeutic format.

Particularly since this is an interpersonal process group that is in the early stages of development, it will be crucial for Dr. Strong to develop trust among group members. Yet she is challenged in this endeavor due to multiple factors, including the quick formation of the group and the lack of a co-leader who might have helped her with pregroup interviews and planning, including setting norms. The ACA Code of Ethics (2014) includes a helpful statement in H.6.b: "Counselors clearly explain to their clients, as part of the informed consent procedure, the benefits, limitations, and boundaries of the use of social media." Given the brief discussion with group members prior to beginning the group and the focus in the first session on introductions and discussing group members' concerns about being in a therapy group instead of individual therapy, Dr. Strong provided only a superficial discussion of the limits of confidentiality and the detrimental effects that can occur from breaches of private group discussions with persons outside of the group in general. She omitted entirely information on how the use of social media can exponentially exacerbate this damage. The speed at which Dr. Strong felt she needed to start the group sessions resulted in her not making ample time to address confidentiality or the consent process. These omissions were ethical lapses in her judgment.

Besides more thoroughly reading the APA and ACA Ethics Codes and the various group psychotherapy guidelines, what else might be helpful for Dr. Strong who is now in this difficult situation? To begin, we would recommend that Dr. Strong directly address the issue of confidentiality in the group. It is entirely possible that the group member who described the group on Facebook had no idea this would potentially compromise the confidentiality of other group members, since the discussion of norms, including confidentiality and its limits, had not previously been broached by Dr. Strong either in the pregroup interviews or in the first session. The use of social media is ubiquitous among most undergraduates and privacy considerations are generally not thoroughly considered by this population. This breach suggests the need for a very early discussion of confidentiality by the group leader during the screening process and then again in the first group session, and at other times during the life of the group.

In this scenario, it is Dr. Strong's ethical duty to avoid being judgmental, and instead to focus on educating the group members about norms, including confidentiality, in a way that will encourage their active involvement in both setting and upholding those norms. This discussion will need to include consideration of group members' autonomy and rights to privacy. Dr. Strong will want to highlight the respect she has for the dignity of the individuals in the group and the importance that all group members understand the concept of dignity and how it plays out with each other member in the group (APA Ethics Code Principle E). Group members benefit from clear norms related to how in-group information is discussed. For instance, it is common for group members to agree to share information only about themselves and not share any information about what other group members reveal in the group with anyone outside of the group. It is also important to discuss what information the leader can share with group members about members who do not attend a specific group session. For example, if a group member is in the hospital, it seems beneficial for the group leader to inform group members of this, since group members often will feel quite anxious about not knowing the status of a group member, especially if that group member has attended regularly and has been a valued member of the group and the group has become cohesive. The group leader could ask the member how much he or she wants the leader to share, but without some ability to say that the group member will be away for several weeks due to a serious injury, for example, group members will worry and make assumptions that are often not helpful for the progress of the group.

A possible approach to setting norms, including those related to confidentiality, could be through the use of a group therapy contract. Group contracts have been described (e.g., MacColl, 2014) and can be a helpful addendum to standard informed consent (or professional disclosure statements; e.g., Thomas & Pender, 2008) as they may help avoid confusion by clarifying the purpose and processes of the group while also outlining the roles and responsibilities of the group leader and the group members. A written contract is consistent with APA Ethics Code Principle C: Integrity, which discusses the need to promote accuracy and truthfulness in the practice of psychology. Some of the group members, for example, have expressed confusion about why they were assigned to a group rather than to individual therapy. Dr. Strong failed to make this clear in the screening and initial group sessions, which was an ethical lapse on her part and will require her to provide them with a truthful discussion of why they were selected for group instead of individual psychotherapy.

As Dr. Strong leads the group members through a discussion of norms, including confidentiality, and the group develops a shared contract together, she can work on explaining the need for confidentiality and also can actively begin to use the group process to discuss relationship issues. She should try to help the group members talk directly to each other about their feelings related to the Facebook incident and to use this as an example of how challenging situations can be processed in the group. She could also help the group members learn that by explicitly practicing new behaviors within the safe confines of the group, they may learn healthy approaches that can generalize to other relationships and thus lead to more satisfying relationships outside of the group. Of course, developing ground rules and presenting confidentiality are dynamic processes and should not only be discussed in the initial group sessions, but at several points throughout the group sessions. Unfortunately, even if

Dr. Strong is able to have group members participate in a deep discussion about their feelings, it is possible that one or more group members will choose to leave group therapy. If this occurs, Dr. Strong will be obligated to help with a referral to individual therapy for those who decide to leave, and for the remaining group members, Dr. Strong will need to begin again to build a strong, positive group climate based on trust where group members are motivated to work on their goals.

The Case of Dual and Multiple Relationships

Drs. Beverly and George Tillman, longtime co-owners of a small group private practice, primarily provide individual psychotherapy for adolescents and adults. In addition, they have co-led several different types of groups with adults ranging from a six-session anger management group and an eight-session couples counseling group to longer-term groups for eating disorders and communication skills. The Tillmans met at graduate school where they both took a course in ethics that only briefly covered issues related to group counseling. At present, they have started a new coed anger management group. Of the five clients in the group, two are currently being seen by George for individual therapy, while Beverly ended individual treatment with two others prior to referring them to the new group. The fifth member has not been in any type of counseling in the past. One of the clients who terminated individual sessions with Beverly has become quite angry in the group session. He wants to know why he had to stop seeing her individually and states "this is totally unfair." Another member that George continues to see individually becomes anxious about whether some sensitive information that she shared with George in an individual session has been discussed with Beverly. This client asks, "Have you talked about me with your wife?" The co-leaders are aware and very distressed that the group is now questioning whether the two of them are competent and trustworthy and if certain members have been given special treatment. Reflecting on this situation, Beverly realizes that although she was very intentional about discussing the benefits of group psychotherapy, encouraging her individual clients to enter group treatment and doing an effective job with them of terminating individual psychotherapy, she is frustrated that she and George did not talk specifically about decisions and criteria surrounding member inclusion in this group. She looks to George to address this current dual relationship problem since she sees it as his clients who are the source of this current quandary.

Clearly, this vignette illustrates potential problems with multiple relationships (APA Ethics Code Standard 3.05). Here, the Ethics Code states, "(a) A multiple relationship occurs when a psychologist is in a professional role with a person and at the same time is in another role with the same person, (b) at the same time is in a relationship with a person closely associated with or related to the person with whom the psychologist has the professional relationship, or (c) promises to enter into another relationship in the future with the person or a person closely associated with or related to the person." In this scenario, there are two major dual relationship considerations. The first point (a) is most relevant for George, who is seeing two clients individually who are also in the group. The second point (b) may not specifically address George and Beverly's co-leadership relationship as one that is a dual relationship, yet it is important to address George's role with Beverly given that he is seeing clients in both treatment formats and she is providing treatment with him in the group. This also is made more complex by their personal relationship.

To address the first dual relationship mentioned above (a), it may be useful to begin by considering the problems that often occur when clients are seen simultaneously in individual and group therapy by the same therapist. Yalom and Leszcz (2005) point out difficulties that may impede group cohesion and the ability of a group to engage in meaningful work if favoritism is perceived (even if the intent were different from the impact) by group members. This ethical dilemma may be considered not only within Standard 3.05 of the APA Ethics Code, but also as it relates to the ethical principle of justice in which the Ethics Code prescribes "equal quality in the processes, procedures and services being conducted by psychologists." Since George is currently treating two of the group clients in individual therapy, other group members are questioning whether he might show preference to those clients (and those clients may actually expect some sort of preference). Conducting both group and individual treatment with the same clients is not an uncommon practice and it is not clearly unethical, yet whenever possible, dual relationships should be avoided. Additionally, this situation is particularly problematic because two members are receiving both types of treatments, two members were seen individually but then transferred to the group, one member is seen in the group but was never seen in any previous treatment, and George and Beverly are in a personal and professional relationship. Due to these multilayered multiple relationships and how these relationships have interfered with the progress of the group, it certainly is not best clinical practice and verges on being unethical.

Also, it is important to focus on the second dual relationship issue related to Beverly and George's role of co-leadership and who have varying relationships with the group members. Since George and Beverly are partners, their relationship could immediately provoke feelings in their individual and group clients, including whether they talk to each other about clients and whether they uphold confidentiality and/or use informed consent from clients for consultation within their practice. Beverly terminated individual therapy with two clients before referring them to the group, and at least one of these clients is questioning why he was not allowed to continue with her, especially considering that George's clients are still seeing him individually. The fifth client was never in individual therapy with either George or Beverly and may be wondering if she is not as interesting as a client, or whether she is healthier and does not need individual treatment. The APA Ethics Code Principle D (Justice) states that "psychologists recognize that fairness and justice entitle all persons to access to and benefit from the contributions of psychology and to equal quality in the processes, procedures and services being conducted by psychologists."

Although ethical dilemmas involved in multiple relationships are more apparent in this vignette when it comes to the multitude of roles between the clients and the group leaders, confidentiality (APA Ethics Code Standards 4.01 Maintaining

Confidentiality and 4.02 Discussing the Limits of Confidentiality) between George and Beverly is also important for the Tillmans to consider. Although the APA Code is not explicit with regard to the dual relationship for two group leaders who are in different roles, the second prong states, "(a) A multiple relationship occurs when a psychologist is in a professional role with a person . . . [and] (b) at the same time is in a relationship with a person closely associated with or related to the person with whom the psychologist has the professional relationship." Since the co-facilitators may routinely co-lead couples counseling groups in which their marital status could . be perceived as an asset, they may not realize that their relationship may be seen differently by clients in other types of groups. For instance, group members may wonder whether the Tillmans share information about individual clients with each other, which is a clear violation of confidentiality.

In order to help the Tillmans begin to resolve some of these ethical dilemmas related to multiple relationships, the group leaders need to state directly that information concerning individual sessions is not shared between them because they are ethically obliged to follow APA Ethical Principle E that states that "psychologists respect the dignity and worth of all people and the rights of individuals to privacy, confidentiality, and self-determination." They will want to revisit a deep discussion of confidentiality and also set clear norms for the group. There are many difficult choice points for these leaders. For example, what if one of George's individual clients talks about suicidal feelings and then this client does not come to the next group session? It might be tempting to discuss his concerns with Beverly. These are the types of ethical dilemmas that these leaders will need to address in order to make this arrangement consistent with ethical standards. It is essential, for instance, for George to clarify with his individual clients what will or will not be shared in the group. It is also at times difficult for a psychotherapist who sees clients in individual and in group treatment to remember in which format the client information was revealed. In this case, this can be extended to what he talks about with Beverly. If George confuses material that was presented in his individual sessions when his clients reveal something very personal with material presented in group, it is also possible that George may talk to Beverly about it assuming that she was already privy to this information. Therefore, it is possible for George to reveal information learned in individual treatment that was assumed to be confidential by the client and not something that the client wanted shared with group members. Since this is clearly a complex and multileveled situation, the current informed consent and group contract templates would be in need of modification and clarification.

Finally, Ethics Code Standard 2.01 (Boundaries of Competence) may be an underemphasized issue for the Tillmans. Neither of them had much training in the ethics of group therapy in their graduate training, so they would be well-advised to seek continuing education in this area through readings, workshops, and consultation with their state and national ethics committees. Their lack of forethought about including this mix of group members and not anticipating all of the potential problems that can and did arise in this group show their lack of competence at least in this area of group selection. The Tillmans need to talk to the group members about their therapy options; none of them are without problems. Some to consider would include George referring his two clients to another individual psychotherapist, terminating his two clients from individual therapy altogether, or possibly having Beverly lead the group without George.

The Case of Voluntary Participation

Two female co-leaders, who identify as African-American, Caucasian, and heterosexual, are conducting a group for persons who were sexually abused as children by a male family member. The group members are eight unrelated women who are between ages 18 and 32. Many of the women have not had previous therapy and this is the first time that any of them are participating in group psychotherapy. The women are diverse in their cultural background and race (two African–American, three Latina, and three Caucasian women) and in their sexual orientation (there are two lesbian and six heterosexual women). Several of the women were quite hesitant to join the group for fear that there would be men in the group or that one of the co-leaders would be a male, even though they were assured several times that the group members and the leaders would all be women. The group leaders spent considerable time talking about confidentiality and its limits, goals and group norms, and how group therapy works, yet as anticipated the group members were reluctant to discuss their abuse history for several weeks. The group leaders were very intentional about helping the group develop safety and trust. They provided low-risk exercises and ways for the members to connect with each other in a safe and positive way. One group member, Anjelica, who is Latina, was silent for most of the sessions, and as the group sessions continued, all but this member began to discuss their difficulties in relationships and their distrust of others. At the sixth session, one Caucasian member, Francine, said to Anjelica in an angry voice, "You need to start working on your stuff. Just sitting there will not fix your problems. I am not sure why you are in this group if you are not going to talk." Anjelica appeared scared, looked down at the floor, glanced at the leaders, and did not reply. The leaders looked at each other and one of them stated, "This seems important, but we have a lot to cover today, so Francine, let's discuss your concerns next week." The group leaders completed the last 15 minutes of the session on communication skills and ended the session. Anjelica did not show up for the next session.

Knowing that active participation by group members is typically associated with more positive outcomes, this vignette demonstrates the fine balance between voluntary participation and pressure/coercion of group members to participate. This is a complexity related to autonomy, which assumes that the group members have the ability to make good decisions and that they have the freedom to choose if, when, and how much they will participate. A strength of group psychotherapy is that group clients can:

> ... interact with group members from different backgrounds, cultures, sexual orientations, and those who have diverse views on such areas as religion and politics. This is an asset when group members are working on interpersonal relationships or when, for instance, they are working on being more tolerant, or less judgmental. With a multicultural and diverse group membership, members can

address their biases, begin to understand the roadblocks in their relationships, or learn to appreciate their own diverse views and gain confidence in expressing their own views assertively and with respect. (Riva, 2014, p. 151)

Yet, it is important for group facilitators to appreciate individual differences in how group members participate and to know how to encourage group members who are more reluctant to participate safely.

Corey, Corey, and Corey (2014) stated that having silent members in a group is a situation often encountered by group leaders and "if the quiet members go unnoticed, their pattern of silence could hide a problem that may need to be addressed in the group" (p. 235). These authors outline several reasons why a group member may be silent, such as "showing respect and waiting to be called on by the leader," "feeling that one does not have anything worthwhile to say," "fear of being rejected," and "lack of trust in the group." Silence can be a result of cultural values, fear of taking risks, or not feeling comfortable with the group, among others. The longer the silence occurs, the harder it may be for Anjelica to participate. Corey et al. (2014) find it beneficial to invite the quiet member to explore the meaning of her silence. Understanding the reason for silence will help the group leaders know how to move forward. Corey et al. suggested "approaching such members by expressing concern rather than judgments about their silence" (p. 236).

Coercing, pressuring, or cajoling Anjelica by the leader or the group members is not ethically acceptable because it will very likely cause harm. It is clear that Anjelica does not see the group as a safe place yet to speak about her trauma history, and after this confrontation, it is likely that she may feel again like she is being forced to do something against her will. Competent and ethical leadership requires group leaders to do no harm. The leaders should have done much more, and earlier, to invite Anjelica to participate. The APA Ethics Code Standard 3.04 (Avoiding Harm) says emphatically that "psychologists take reasonable steps to avoid harming their clients/ patients . . . and to minimize harm where it is foreseeable and unavoidable."

The vignette highlights the vital role of the leader in keeping the group members safe. In all group ethics standards and guidelines, safety of group members is a consistent mandate (Rapin, 2014). In this situation, nonmaleficence or do no harm is key (Kitchener, 1984; Posthuma, 2002). Specifically discussing group work, Gazda, Ginter, and Horne (2001) stated that nonmaleficence incorporates both "acts of omission or commission" (p. 98). For a group leader to stop the situation (or not to stop the situation) and not address it would be cause for much concern for the quiet group member, for all other members, and also for the group functioning. In this vignette, the leaders did not address the situation and seemed to underestimate the distress of both Anjelica and Francine.

This situation most often escalates if there is no leader intervention. Typically, this is a difficult scenario for inexperienced group leaders due to the speed at which the interactions between members can occur and the intensity of the interactions. This vignette also demonstrates that group members may be pressured to participate before they are ready and willing, blurring the ability for group members to participate voluntarily or to the degree that they choose to participate. An important aspect of this dilemma is that group members who have a history of trauma and were coerced by those in power may lack trust in others to keep them safe and they may respond by protecting themselves even more by remaining silent, potentially dropping out of the group, and feeling violated once again. Yalom and Leszcz (2005) stated that "silence is never silent" (p. 399), and in this scenario, it may be that for at least Anjelica, the group does not yet feel like a safe place to share very personal information.

There are many directions that these group leaders could have chosen after the fact that are ethically unacceptable. For example, they may be tempted to agree with Francine that Anjelica did not want to work in the group. They also could rationalize this situation so as not to admit their part in this confrontation. They could get angry with Anjelica for not returning to the group. They also could take an ethical stance while the situation is occurring. For example, one group leader strategy for addressing this member exchange is to use the modification method described by Clark (1995). In this method, the group leader needs to stop the interaction and say something to the verbal group member such as, "I can tell that you have something important to say, yet I can tell by the way Anjelica is responding that she will not be able to hear it. Can you say it in a way that she can hear what you are saying to her?" In this statement, the leader is assuming that Francine has something of worth to say but that it needs to be modified so that it is beneficial to the other member. For example, the group leader may hypothesize that the vocal member wants to hear more from the silent group member and that she is concerned that if the person does not talk, she will not be able to improve her relationships. The group leader can encourage Francine to make a statement such as, "You are an important part of the group and I want you to let us know what you are thinking." The group leader may also guess from the silent member's reaction that she does not feel safe yet in the group and so could say to Anjelica, "How can we help you feel more safe in the group so that you can participate?" With this type of dialogue, the group leader conveys that it is critical for members to participate, but it is equally important for them to feel safe. This is the sticky dilemma around voluntary participation. It is certainly possible for a group member to learn new skills vicariously by watching others, yet group members will eventually find a silent member to be problematic. In this group, cultural values such as waiting for others to speak, listening more than talking, and not sharing intimate family information also may be at play for several members. Because the group members and the group leaders are not hearing directly from Anjelica, they may make inaccurate assumptions that she is unmotivated or dislikes other group members or they may wonder what this member will do with the private information shared by others.

In this group, as in all groups, multicultural competence is essential for group leaders in order for them to understand their members and to help their members feel heard and safe. All aspects of group psychotherapy are diverse. The most extensive directives on group leader multicultural competence are in the ASGW's Multicultural and Social Justice Competence Principles for Group Workers (Singh et al., 2012). It has three principles, each with multiple parts, which are "intended to guide group workers in the ongoing development of multicultural and social justice competence" (p. 315). One of these principles (Principle 1.2) discusses the importance that group leaders demonstrate movement toward being increasingly aware of and sensitive to the multiple dimensions of the multicultural and multi-layered identities of group members (p. 315). It will be important for the group leaders to attend to the diversity in the group and to consider whether Angelica is quiet because she perceives any implicit racism toward her and/or the other Latina group members. It will also be necessary for the group leaders to reflect on their own leadership skills and look at areas where they can be more culturally and diversity sensitive and knowledgeable in their group facilitation, as stated in these guidelines.

This vignette also underscores the critical need for group preparation prior to beginning the first session. Preparation of group members is one area that has considerable empirical research showing its beneficial aspects, including promoting member comfort and satisfaction and group cohesion (e.g., Burlingame, Fuhriman, & Johnson, 2004). Members who have not been in group psychotherapy before will need a deeper discussion of the therapeutic aspects of groups, including the benefits of participation. In this vignette, the group leaders seemed to cover many important aspects of group, yet they may not have addressed voluntary participation in enough depth. The interaction between Francine and Anjelica could have provided them with an excellent opportunity to intervene at that moment in a way that highlighted the norms of safety, participation, learning to address member differences, and interacting in ways that allow members to be heard and supported. In this particular situation, the leaders did not help Anjelica feel safe, and therefore she did not come to the next session. The leaders also failed to acknowledge Francine's concerns about the meaning of Anjelica's silence, and as often happens, responses like Francine's leave group members feeling guilty and responsible for Anjelica's absence in the group. With a primary goal of nonmaleficence in group therapy, as in all therapy, the leaders need to reach out to Anjelica to provide support and to see if she wants to return to the group or to some other therapeutic option. Failure to do so would be inconsistent with APA Ethics Code Standard 3.04 (Avoid Harm). They will also want to address their errors in not encouraging participation earlier and then not handling the situation competently when it arose. It will take considerable work to reset norms, especially around helpful member interactions.

The Case of Group Leader Competence

A newly hired psychotherapist, Aisha Wells, who has a year of experience after her MA degree, has been hired at an outpatient mental health facility. She has been asked by her supervisor to conduct a psychotherapy group for clients who have major depression. Ms. Wells has taken one course in group counseling and has co-led a group with her previous supervisor. Her current supervisor, Norman Fine, PhD, is familiar with the research on group treatment with major depression and he knows that recent studies have shown that it is effective for this presenting diagnosis (Burlingame, Strauss, & Joyce, 2013). Most studies showing positive gains have used cognitive behavioral group therapy (CBGT). Ms. Wells has read material to help her prepare for this group. She recognizes the need to screen and select members carefully. She knows that she is not very confident in her leadership skills and wonders if she is competent to conduct this group. She also realizes she will need to rely on the guidance of her supervisor to help. In the third session, two members are discussing their depression and past suicidal attempts. Another member becomes visibly agitated and says that her problems are obviously not as serious as the other members since she has never considered suicide and thinks it is "an easy way out." Ms. Wells is shaken by the revelation of past suicidal behaviors, and although she did assess current suicidality in her group screening, she wonders what else she may have missed and again is concerned about whether she can lead this group. She decides to conduct a brief suicide assessment of all group members during the group session, and feels confident that no members are currently experiencing any suicidal thoughts or behaviors, although three group members barely say anything more than "no" to her question on suicidal ideation. Feeling relieved, she ends the group without considering the importance of the statement about suicide being "an easy way out." She does not connect how this statement could silence other members from reporting any current suicidal thinking or behavior now or in later sessions. The group member that made the statement feels unsure about whether to continue in the group.

This vignette relates to the competence of a psychotherapist who appears to lack the training and experience to offer effective treatment to severely depressed clients in a group format. She is aware that she did not thoroughly assess for past suicidal ideation and behavior in the individual screening meetings with potential members. Typically, most psychotherapists have received much more training in individual psychotherapy than in group treatment, and the coverage of ethics in group treatment is often very limited, even though the ethical considerations in groups are much more complicated. It will benefit Ms. Wells to be familiar with the ASGW Best Practice Guidelines (2007) that provide guidance on planning, performing, and processing in group work. Although these are not specifically ethical principles, they do include detailed best practices for group leadership. The ACA Ethics Code states clearly that "counselors screen prospective group counseling/therapy participants" (A.9.a). This mandate is important, yet it is not clear how to screen members or what characteristics to focus on when screening members. Corey et al. (2014) stated that:

> . . . it is essential to consider including potentially difficult individuals as they may well be the very ones who could most benefit from a group experience. Sometimes leaders screen out individuals due to their own personal dislike or countertransference issues even though these individuals might be appropriate clients for the group . . . The goal of screening is to prevent potential harm to clients, not to make the leader's job easier by setting up a group of homogeneous members. (p. 151)

After recognizing that her initial omission in the screening process when she did not ask about past suicidal attempts was ethically problematic, Ms. Wells did attempt to assess suicide risk for the group members, but her brief assessment again was not thorough enough to determine whether any of her members are currently considering suicide. In addition, it could be perceived as upsetting to the group members that she assessed for suicide after the group had already begun. With more clear information, she would be able to assess risk of suicide, talk to members about their feelings, and determine whether a group member(s) might need an individual session to process risk more deeply. Ms. Wells also would be able to contact clients' individual therapists if any group members are being seen individually (with the required consent as described in APA Ethics Code Standard 4.04 [Disclosures]) or, if appropriate, consider voluntary or involuntary hospitalization if the severity warrants it. Ms. Wells needs to work extremely closely with her supervisor in all dimensions of this situation and acknowledge that she feels very anxious about dealing with suicidal behavior.

It is Dr. Fine's duty in supervision to oversee Ms. Wells' work and provide the necessary support needed. Dr. Fine will need to review the Guidelines for Clinical Supervision in Health Service Psychology Domain F: Professional Competence Problems (APA, 2015, pp. 40–41). Several guidelines apply here, including, "Supervisors strive to address performance problems directly" (Guideline 1), "Supervisors strived to identify potential performance problems promptly, communicate these to the supervisee, and take steps to address these in a timely manner allowing for opportunities to effect change" (Guideline 2), "Supervisors are competent in developing and implementing plans to remediate performance problems" (Guideline 3), and "Supervisors strive to closely monitor and document the progress of supervisees who are taking steps to address problems of competence."

Screening clients for group therapy is directly related to group member selection. The ACA Ethics Code continues in A.9.a by stating, "To the extent possible, counselors select members whose needs and goals are compatible with the goals of the group, who will not impede the group process, and whose well-being will not be jeopardized by the group experience." From our experience, there is little clarity on how to select members, what variables to use, and how to decide which members will be best for which groups. Yalom and Leszcz (2005) suggested that group leaders typically deselect members on certain variables (e.g., current suicidal behavior, extreme anxiety, psychotic behavior) instead of selecting them on what characteristics of value they will bring to the group. Two variables that are regularly suggested as positive selection criteria are motivation and expectations that the group treatment will be effective (Yalom & Leszcz, 2005).

In her future screening meetings, Ms. Wells will want to consider asking questions that address more about the clients' group behavior than what is usually covered in an intake interview. She will want to consider specific questions such as, "'What types of groups have you joined in the past?', 'What was your specific role in these groups?', 'What did you enjoy/dislike about the groups?', and 'How did you address problems when they occurred in the group?' These questions do not need to be exclusively about the client's experience in group therapy, since participation in other types of groups (e.g., group projects, sports teams, task/work groups) also will provide beneficial information about the client's experience, behavior, and perceptions of his or her participation in a group" (Riva & Lange, 2014, p. 20). These strategies will provide additional information about the potential clients' behavior in a group setting so that leaders can make more informed decisions about doing good and who will potentially benefit from a group format (APA Ethics Code Principle A: Beneficence and Nonmaleficence).

In a study that looked at selection practices used by group leaders, the most common selection method was not about group member characteristics, but rather whether the person fit the group theme (Riva, Lippert, & Tackett, 2000). In this study, experienced group leaders also were asked to look back at their groups and describe a selection error. Two categories of behaviors that group leaders overlooked in the selection process that ultimately affected their group in a major way were hostile clients and persons who continued to abuse substances. Descriptions of hostile behaviors that frightened other group members and the group leaders and of group members coming to group sessions inebriated were examples of these two areas. Ms. Wells needs to take extra precautions in her group selection methods to tease out these behaviors along with others, such as actively suicidal behavior, as well as past suicidal ideation and attempts.

It is a positive sign that Ms. Wells knows that she needs to rely on supervision to guide her on her leadership of her group of depressed persons. Yalom and Leszcz (2005) stated that "a supervised clinical experience is a sine qua non in the education of the group therapist" (p. 548). In this situation, where the group will be led by a new group leader who has had one course in group counseling that briefly discussed ethics and has conducted one previous group, it is vital that the group leader receives close supervision on the group dynamics, as well as on the individual members of the group. Riva (2014) underscored the need for supervisors to have a deep understanding of both supervision and group psychotherapy. Supervision also will be key given that research suggests that novice group leaders think differently about their groups and group members than do experienced group leaders. For example, Kivlighan and Kivlighan (2009) found that early group leaders have knowledge structures that are more linear and simplistic compared to experienced group leaders. Early group leaders often get lost in the content of the group and have much more difficulty seeing themes and the group process. In this vignette, Ms. Wells' anxiety and relatively early development as a group leader may have resulted in her inability to deal with or even be aware of the entirety of the group process beyond assessing for current suicidal considerations. Underlining supervision as a vital component in gaining competence, the Boundaries of Competence section of the ACA Ethics Code (2014) states, "Counselors practice only within the boundaries of their competence, based on their education, training, supervised experience, state and national professional credentials, and appropriate professional experience" (C.2.a). The APA Ethics Code also references boundaries of competence in Standard 2.01. In order to support Ms. Wells, Dr. Fine should, for example, provide additional supervision, co-lead the group with her, and observe Ms. Wells' videotapes of group sessions.

Although membership characteristics in this vignette are not specified, group counseling is always diverse. The ACA Code also points to the need for all counselors to be multiculturally competent or working toward this essential goal. Again in C.2.a, the Ethics Code states that "whereas multicultural competency is required across all counseling specialties, counselors gain knowledge, personal awareness, dispositions, and skills pertinent to being a culturally competent counselor working with diverse people." The group leader and the supervisor will want to be familiar with the ASGW Multicultural and Social Justice Competence Principles for Group Workers (2012).

Barlow (2012) outlined the suggested competencies for group leaders that are expected in the areas of knowledge, skill, and experience by a doctoral-level graduate when they enter their first job. These are great aspirational goals, yet many programs offer little training in group psychotherapy, and on the other hand, many group facilitators are at the bachelor's or master's level. In our consultation with community facilities that provide group treatment as a primary treatment choice, training new employees to work in a group format is often limited. Also, research on group leadership is sorely lacking, and there often is calls for more training and research. Burlingame, Fuhriman, and Johnson (2001) outlined six leader skills that encourage cohesion and relationships between members. They include: (a) pregroup preparation; (b) clarifying the dynamics that occur within the group across the group sessions; (c) promoting relationship development and modeling here-and-now communication; (d) tailoring the timing of feedback; (e) demonstrating appropriate emotional expression; and (f) facilitating the process of member disclosures and helping members make meaning of their self-disclosures. When considering even these six leader skills mentioned by Burlingame et al., it is clear that group leadership is multileveled and considerably complex, having many of its own unique characteristics. In the sixth leadership skill (f) above, facilitating the process of member disclosure *and* helping the members make meaning of these self-disclosures is particularly pertinent to Ms. Wells in this vignette. Ms. Wells will benefit from reading the many theoretical and clinical discussions of group work, participating in regular supervision, reviewing the research and evidence-supported treatments with depression such as CBGT (Burlingame et al., 2013), and possibly adding a co-therapist that has expertise in this area. As with most critical incidents that occur in group treatment, they can be extremely beneficial if managed well by the leader. For instance, Ms. Wells could use the opportunity to have members learn more about their self-disclosures, find new coping skills when they are depressed, aid others in sharing coping strategies that work for them, and gain empathy for other group members who have made choices that they do not understand or find disagreeable.

Another prong of this vignette addresses at least one client's feelings that she does not belong because her problems are not big enough. This is a serious and common problem for group members as they compare themselves with others in the group. Ms. Wells should address this conversation directly because without doing so it is very likely that the group member will not benefit from the group and may drop out altogether, potentially resulting in harm. One method would be to say that the purpose of the group is to help members learn beneficial ways to respond when they are feeling depressed. She could say something like, "Depression is a struggle for all of you and we will learn new ways to cope and respond. We will focus on strategies that can help you live a healthier life." Without an immediate intervention, the one member concerned about her fit with the group may drop out and the other members may agree that she should not be in the group. Ms. Wells will need to address the impasse with the help of her supervisor, who may want to role-play options for the next session with her and carefully oversee her work.

Conclusions and Recommendations

This chapter provides ethical dilemmas for some of the most common and difficult group psychotherapy conundrums: confidentiality, dual and multiple relationships, voluntary participation, and group leader competence. Ethical codes such as those provided for psychologists, those belonging to the APA, and those for counselors outlined by the ACA are important documents that provide general ethical principles for members of their respective organizations and do include group-level ethics information in a few of the principles and sections. They are necessary as foundational documents, but they clearly are not sufficient in providing enough information for group leaders to navigate many of the multidimensional ethical dilemmas that occur in group psychotherapy. Depending on what organization group leaders belong to, they should be familiar with materials such as those specifically addressing ethical decisions and best practices in group counseling such as the ASGW Best Practice Guidelines (2007), the ASGW Professional Standards for Training Group Workers (2000), the ASGW Multicultural and Social Justice Competence Principles for Group Workers (Singh, Merchant, Skudrzyk, & Ingene, 2012), the AGPA and the IBCGP Guidelines for Ethics (AGPA & IBCGP, 2002), and the AASWG Standard for Social Work Practice with Groups (Advancement of Social Work in Groups, 2005).

Although group psychotherapy consistently has been found to be effective, often is used as the primary treatment format, and frequently has been shown to be equally effective as individual therapy, and at times even more effective than individual therapy, group counseling continues to receive much less attention than it deserves. There are many additional vignettes that could have been highlighted in this chapter. It is recommended that those interested in group leadership also become familiar with the many sources that discuss group psychotherapy practice. A few recent guides include: *Groups: Process and practice* (Corey et al., 2014), *The handbook of group counseling and psychotherapy* (DeLucia-Waack, Kalodner, & Riva, 2014), *The Oxford handbook of group counseling* (Conyne, 2011), and the older but pivotal book on group psychotherapy, *The theory and practice of group psychotherapy* (Yalom & Leszcz, 2005). The following are some recommendations from several sources (Conyne, 2011; Corey et al., 2014; DeLucia-Waack, Kalodner, & Riva, 2014; Lasky & Riva, 2006; Yalom & Leszcz, 2005) that address group psychotherapy specifically:

• The complexities of group psychotherapy require a comprehensive understanding of the basic ethics codes along with an understanding of how to put the ethical expectations into practice. Group leaders need to be cognizant of the unique features of group psychotherapy and that information learned about individual, couples, and family counseling does not easily generalize to group psychotherapy.

- Confidentiality is a common sticking point for group leaders. It is important to develop a safe and cohesive group, and at the same time autonomy requires that the group members know and understand the limits to confidentiality and the potential risks involved in order to make a decision about if, how much, and when to disclose personal information. Being aware of the group stage will often guide decisions about confidentiality. The early group sessions should be focused on developing a safe space for later self-disclosures.

- Group leaders need to address confidentiality throughout the group sessions and not only during the screening session and at the first meeting. At the beginning, group members are often anxious about being in the group and may have a hard time hearing the information and feeling comfortable asking questions if they do not understand. Likewise, discussions about privileged communication, informed consent, and confidentiality take on different meanings at various points in the group process. It is helpful to remind people about the norms and expectations of refraining from revealing information and that what happens in group stays in group when members begin to feel more cohesive and share deeper self-disclosures.

- Multiple relationships, especially those related to group members, are important to consider. Although there are many dual relationships resulting from group leaders who see the same clients in both individual and group counseling, it continues to be a too common treatment method. There are other dual and multiple relationship concerns that occur among group leaders and their group members, such as differential fees, group members who get an inordinate amount of attention and time during sessions, and special relationships between leaders and certain members (neighbors, a friend of a friend, etc.). Although it is almost impossible to avoid all dual and multiple relationships, when group members have a sense of favoritism within the group, group psychotherapy generally suffers.

- Voluntary participation is important, but is especially complex within groups with diverse participants. It is helpful for group leaders to screen and select members carefully for the group. If a member is extremely anxious or shy and does not think he or she will participate in the group, it may be better for this client to receive individual counseling prior to joining a group. After selection, preparation of members for what group treatment entails is beneficial for members, as well as the functioning of the group as a whole. Silence or lack of participation is one end of the continuum. Some clients participate too much. Yalom and Leszcz (2005) states that too much or too little participation are both problematic. Clients who monopolize group sessions often interfere with the group process. Voluntary participation does not mean that group members can volunteer to participate whenever they want to. Group norms are essential in encouraging group participation and at the same time allowing all group members to be heard. The ethical consideration here is one of harm, which can be a result of coercion by other members or the leader.

- Competence as a group leader does not come after one group course or after conducting one psychotherapy group. Group leaders are encouraged to obtain supervision from a supervisor who is competent in group facilitation. There are workshops, conferences, and other forms of continuing education that can augment group leader skills. For example, the AGPA has a yearly conference that focuses on group practice. The ASGW provides training at the annual ACA conference and has a specialty conference every two years. The annual APA convention has offerings on group leadership practice from its Division 49, Group Psychology and Group Psychotherapy. There are many other opportunities to seek additional professional development in group leadership. To become competent group leaders takes familiarity with group theory, specific skills, multicultural and diversity knowledge and awareness, ethical codes, principles, and best practices, as well as the experience of conducting many groups. We do not consider expertise to be the same as experience, and therefore it seems necessary to do more than conduct several groups to be a competent group psychotherapist.

References

American Counseling Association (2014). *ACA code of ethics*. Alexandria, VA: American Counseling Association.

American Psychological Association (2015). Guidelines for clinical supervision in health service psychology. *American Psychologist, 70*, 33–46.

Anderson, B. S. (1996). *The counselor and the law* (4th edn.). Alexandria, VA: American Counseling Association.

Association for Specialists in Group Work (2000). Association for Specialists in Group Work: Professional standards for training group workers. *Journal for Specialists in Group Work, 25*, 327–342.

Association for Specialists in Group Work (2007). Association for Specialists in Group Work best practice guidelines. *Journal of Specialists in Group Work, 33*, 111–117.

American Group Psychotherapy Association (AGPA) & International Board for Certification of Group Psychotherapists (IBCGP) (2002). *AGPA and IBCGP guidelines for ethics*. New York, NY: American Group Psychotherapy Association and International Board for Certification of Group Psychotherapists.

Association for the Advancement of Social Work with Groups (2005). *Standards for social work practice with groups* (2nd edn.) Alexandria, VA: Association for the Advancement of Social Work with Groups.

American Psychological Association (2010). Ethical principles of psychologists and code of Conduct (2002, Amended June 2, 2010). Retrieved from www.apa.org/ethics/code

Barlow, S. H. (2012). *Specialist competencies in group psychology*. New York, NY: Oxford University Press.

Burlingame, G. M., Fuhriman, A. J., & Johnson, J. E. (2001). Cohesion in group psychotherapy. *Psychotherapy: Theory, Research, and Training, 38*, 373–379.

Burlingame, G. M., Fuhriman, A. J., & Johnson, J. E. (2004). Process and outcome in group counseling and psychotherapy: A perspective. In J. L. Delucia-Waack, D. A. Gerrity, C. R. Kalodner, & M. T. Riva (Eds.), *Handbook of group counseling and psychotherapy* (pp. 49–61). Thousand Oaks, CA: Sage.

Burlingame, G. M., Strauss, B., & Joyce, A. S. (2013). Change mechanisms and effectiveness of small group treatments. In M. J. Lambert (Ed.), *Bergin and Garfield's handbook of psychotherapy and behavior change* (6th edn., pp. 640–689). Hoboken, NJ: Wiley.

Clark, A. J. (1995). Modification: A leader skill in group work. *Journal for Specialists in Group work*, *20*, 14–17.

Conyne, R. K. (Ed.) (2011). *The Oxford handbook of group counseling*, New York, NY: Oxford University Press.

Corey, M. S., Corey, G., & Corey, C. (2014). *Groups: Process and practice* (9th edn.). Belmont, CA: Brooks/Cole.

DeLucia-Waak, J. L., Kalodner, C. R., & Riva, M. T. (Eds.) (2014). *Handbook of group counseling and psychotherapy* (2nd edn.). Thousand Oaks, CA: Sage.

Gazda, G. M., Ginter, E. J., & Horne, A. M. (2001). *Group counseling and group psychotherapy: Theory and application*. Needham Heights, MA: Allyn & Bacon.

Kitchener, K. S. (1984). Intuition, critical evaluations and ethical principles: The foundations of ethical decision-making in counseling psychology. *The Counseling Psychologist*, *24*, 92–97.

Kivlighan, D. M., Jr. & Kivlighan, D. M., III (2009). Training related changes in the ways that group trainees structure their knowledge of group counseling leader interventions. *Group Dynamics: Theory, Research, and Practice*, *13*, 190–204.

Klontz, B. T. (2004). Ethical practice of group experiential psychotherapy. *Psychotherapy: Theory, Research, Practice, Training*, *41*, 172–179.

Lasky, G. G. & Riva, M. T. (2006). Confidentiality and privileged communication in group psychotherapy. *International Journal of Group Psychotherapy*, *73*, 284–292.

MacColl, G. J. (2014). The group contract revisited. *Group*, *38*, 103–113.

Posthuma, B. W. (2002). *Small groups in counseling and therapy: Process and leadership* (4th edn.). Boston, MA: Allyn & Bacon.

Rapin, L. S. (2014). Guidelines for ethical and legal practice in counseling and psychotherapy groups. In J. L. DeLucia-Waack, C. R. Kalodner, & M. T. Riva (Eds.). *Handbook of group counseling and psychotherapy* (pp. 71–83). Thousand Oaks, CA: Sage.

Riva, M. T. (2014). Supervision of group leaders. In J. L. DeLucia-Waack, C. R. Kalodner, & M. T. Riva (Eds.). *Handbook of group counseling and psychotherapy* (pp. 146–158). Thousand Oaks, CA: Sage.

Riva, M. T. & Lange, R. E. (2014). *How leaders can assess group counseling*. Thousand Oaks, CA: Sage.

Riva, M. T., Lippert, L., & Tackett, M. J. (2000). Selection practice of group leaders: A national survey. *Journal for Specialists in Group Work*, *25*, 157–169.

Singh, A. A., Merchant, N., Skudrzyk, B., & Ingene, D. (2012). Association for specialists in group work: Multicultural and social justice competence principles for group workers. *Journal for Specialists in Group Work*, *37*, 312–325.

Thomas, V. & Pender, D. A. (2008). Association for Specialists in Group Work: Best Practice Guidelines 2007 Revisions. *The Journal for Specialists in Group Work*, *33*, 111–117.

Yalom, I. D. & Leszcz, M. (2005). *The theory and practice of group psychotherapy* (5th edn.). New York, NY: Basic Books.

12 Ethical Issues in Couple and Family Therapy

Lorna L. Hecker and Megan J. Murphy

Ethical issues that arise when working with couples and families are both similar to and different from those issues that emerge when working with individuals. First, given that therapists are working with more than one person, there are multiple viewpoints to consider. Simply having more than one client in the room changes the relational dynamics within the therapeutic system, providing more complex and nuanced ethical dilemmas to the therapist. In addition, therapists who work with couples and families typically do so from a systemic perspective, which includes considerations for multiple levels and layers of interactions. Issues of power, for example, become multiplied when one considers the relationships between members of the therapeutic system. In working with one client, the therapist must consider the relationship between oneself and the client. In working with a couple, the therapist must consider the relationships between oneself and each of the two clients, the relationship the clients have with each other, and the relationship between the therapist and the couple's relationship – for a total of four direct relational considerations. The picture gets further complicated when working with families, where the number of relationships for the therapist to consider multiplies substantially. Issues of multiple relationships abound. In these situations, professional codes of ethics caution therapists to be aware of this influential position, avoid conditions that may increase the risk of exploitation, monitor their objectivity, and resolve issues of multiple relationships with the best interests of the clients in mind. Additionally, therapists should take precautions to avoid multiple relationships whenever possible (Section 1.3, AAMFT, 2015; Standard 3.05, APA, 2010).

The systemic frame used in working with more than one person necessitates consideration of context, relationships, and power (Murphy & Hecker, 2016). Power considerations are extraordinarily complex, even when working with one client, as a therapist and client hold different types of power. The therapist, by virtue of their professional role, is said to have power in the professional relationship by their ability to guide the conversation, decide on matters of normalcy and health in relation to the client, and receive payment by clients, their insurers, or other third-parties. Other power considerations include differences in age, sex, ethnicity/race, gender expression, sexual orientation, religious beliefs, etc., which may combine in various ways to give the client and the therapist differing levels of influence in the relationship. The picture is multidimensional even with one client, yet increases exponentially when adding another client (or five!) to the therapeutic system. The parent/parents in a family system are typically expected to hold power in relation to their children. This presents itself in terms of the laws and rights parents have in relation to their children, such as the ability to compel treatment of a minor or have access to therapy information (depending upon state statute). The power of the parental subsystem can vary greatly depending upon implicit and accepted gender roles, financial influence, or involvement of outside parties such as child protective services. These are just a few considerations that illustrate the complex relational dynamics that couples and families can present in therapy, which can quickly and greatly complicate ethical considerations when they arise in therapy. The major mental health codes of ethics (i.e., the American Association for Marriage and Family Therapy [2015], American Psychological Association [2010], National Association of Social Workers [2017], and the American Counseling Association [2014]) address relational dynamics only in the limited contexts of confidentiality and multiple relationships, leaving therapists to navigate further relational complexities on their own.

The ethical challenges faced by therapists working with couples and families are similar in content to those faced by therapists working with individuals, yet they differ in process due to multiple vantage points and needs. In this chapter, we explore specific ethical considerations for couple and family therapists (CFTs): determining who is considered the client (individual, couple, family, or outside entity); examining how confidentiality is managed; examining who holds the power in therapy; evaluating who defines reality; and evaluating who defines normalcy/health. We present ethical scenarios common to CFTs and explore these five processes within these scenarios.

Who Is the Client?

One of the most central decisions a therapist makes when working with couples and families is determining who the client is. Ideally, this decision is made very early in the course of therapy and the decision is maintained through to the end of therapy. Once again, the situations get complicated with more than one client in therapy, and issues get further muddied when minors are involved or there is a possibility of relationship dissolution (divorce). When seeing people who have a relationship, CFTs should "take reasonable steps to clarify at the outset (1) which of the individuals are clients/patients" and what relationship the therapist will have with each person (Standard 10.02, APA, 2010). In addition, the relationship status may change at any moment, posing further challenges to the therapist.

A number of ethical responsibilities may contribute to a CFT's treatment decisions when defining the client (individual or system). One consideration is the autonomy of the client to make decisions for themselves and/or their family and allowing clients to decide who needs to attend therapy. CFTs are to respect the rights of clients to make decisions and help them understand the consequences of these decisions. Specifically, CFTs should "respect the rights of clients to make decisions and help them to understand the consequences of these decisions. Therapists clearly advise clients that clients have the responsibility to make decisions about relationships such as cohabitation, marriage, divorce, separation, reconciliation, custody, and visitation" (Section 1.8, AAMFT, 2015), and we need to be "aware that special safeguards may be necessary to protect the rights and welfare of persons or communities whose vulnerabilities impair autonomous decision making" (Principle E, APA, 2010). For example, if a family insists on scapegoating a particular child as the "identified patient" (IP), insisting that they are bad or the cause of family problems, CFTs must help the family decide who will be involved in therapy while protecting the scapegoated family member.

In some cases, there are clients (consumers of services) and payers for services (customers). These may be the same or different entities. This concern may be a challenge in working with individuals; for example, the therapist may need to determine that, indeed, the state is a customer when clients are mandated for therapy. In spite of competing needs, the CFT must ensure that a therapeutic relationship is beneficial to a client. CFTs must be clear that "clients are benefiting from the relationship" (Section 1.9, AAMFT, 2015) while they "cooperate with other professionals in order to serve their clients/patients effectively and appropriately" (Standard 3.09, APA, 2010).

Training of the therapist also comes to bear in making decisions about the definition of the client. If a therapist is not relationally trained, they may not be competent to handle complex family dynamics. Therapists should "provide services, teach, and conduct research with populations and in areas only within the boundaries of their competence, based on their education, training, supervised experience, consultation, study, or professional experience" (Standard 2.01, APA, 2010). Conversely, a CFT may not have the skills to work with mentally ill individuals. Again, scope of competence is an important consideration: "Marriage and family therapists do not diagnose, treat, or advise on problems outside the recognized boundaries of their competencies" (Section 3.10, AAMFT, 2015).

How Is Confidentiality Managed?

Assurances of confidentiality are central to therapy, whether for individuals or for couples and families. Confidentiality concerns are relatively straightforward for individuals; challenges to confidentiality involve harm to self, harm to others (at times including harm to property), child or dependent adult abuse, matters of the court, and others depending upon other state or federal regulations. Our intention is not to minimize confidentiality concerns for the individual, as these instances in themselves can pose difficult ethical dilemmas for therapists, but rather to explore confidentiality of relational clients. When working with couples, confidentiality may be viewed as within the "couple domain" or may relate to maintaining confidentiality for each member of the couple. The major mental health ethical codes may allow the therapist to work with family members to determine confidentiality or designate that written releases be provided by all family members in order to share information (cf. Section 2.2, AAMFT, 2015).

Another ethical conundrum when seeing multiple clients is record-keeping. When CFTs see the system as the client, individual information may be combined into a couple or family file. It is not unusual that a couple may divorce and wish to have access to their file in the advent of a divorce. This type of situation requires written authorization from each individual competent to sign a release of information. Alternatively, a CFT may redact information of other involved family members should a client insist on the records.

Who Holds the Power in Therapy?

This may seem like a strange or unusual question. Perhaps one would assume that the therapist has the power in therapy, and in many ways this is true. Yet, even if the therapist embraces the idea that they are in charge of therapy, they will likely wrestle with conflict between subsystems in a family or partners of a couple. In couples therapy, one member of a couple may have decided to end the relationship, whereas the other partner wants to remain in the relationship. It may be argued that the partner with the least interest in maintaining the relationship holds the most power in the relationship, for without that partner's investment and participation, couples therapy – at least therapy aimed at maintaining or improving the relationship – will not proceed. In a similar vein, for families with minor children, parents may hold the power in determining the goals of therapy for a minor child. Therapists may be more or less bound by parents' wishes in this regard. A child who is acting out may gain power over both the parents and the CFT as they scramble to gain control of the child's behavior. The CFT must have competence in power dynamics to be able to manage these multifarious dynamics; if not, they may cause harm to the family system. Avoiding harm to clients – nonmaleficence – is paramount to practicing therapy (Standard 3.04, APA, 2010), as is beneficence, whereby CFTs provide therapy only as long as it is benefitting the client(s) (Section 1.9, AAMFT, 2015).

Power disparities between family members and between the family and the CFT can be managed in part by the informed consent process. Therapists must "inform clients/patients as early as feasible in the therapeutic relationship about the nature and anticipated course of therapy, fees, involvement of third parties, and limits of confidentiality and provide sufficient opportunity for the client/patient to ask questions and receive answers" (Standard 10.01, APA, 2010). Informed consent generally necessitates that the client: (a) has the capacity to consent; (b) has been adequately informed of significant information concerning treatment processes and procedures; (c) has been adequately informed of potential risks and benefits of treatments for which generally recognized standards do not yet exist; (d) has freely and without undue influence expressed consent; and (e) has provided consent that is appropriately documented. Additionally, uses and disclosures of protected health information are required by federal Health Insurance Portability and Accountability Act (HIPAA) regulations to be included in the HIPAA Notice of Privacy Practices, which include applicable state law (Hecker, 2016). CFTs must have knowledge of laws, ethics, and professional standards, which they should accurately present to clients. All of these educational endeavors can increase client power over the therapeutic process.

Who Defines Reality?

Therapists typically enter the profession to help people; they believe in the inherent "good" of the client. Although no one would argue with these noble intentions in deciding to enter the field, this belief in clients can pose challenges when working with multiple clients who are telling different versions of the same event. It could be reasoned that negotiating these differences is part and parcel of therapy. Yet differences in perspective may have a very large impact on clients' lives, particularly when issues of safety and abuse are in question. The therapist must tread carefully when exploring different versions of powerful and/or painful events in family life. The therapist's responsibility to gather information from multiple parties and objectively and competently evaluate that information is tantamount to working through difficult issues and helping families come to some sort of resolution.

Who Decides Normalcy/Health?

The role and power of the therapist to decide the normalcy or health of individuals or relationships is enormous – and with it comes great responsibility. Therapists also need to consider the larger world of mental health, including the use of established labels found in the Diagnostic and Statistical Manual of Mental Disorders (DSM), in order for insurance companies to reimburse therapeutic services. Relational therapists view problems as typically located within the relationship between people, not as a disorder centered on one person, as is currently the discourse regarding payment for therapeutic services. At times, CFTs can feel torn between the needs of the family system and the individual medical model in which families are embedded.

Therapists often must assign a code from the DSM, which may or may not fit the therapist's understanding of the concern (an ethical issue in and of itself). Yet, CFTs must be truthful in their representation to both clients and third-party payers (Section 8.4, AAMFT, 2015; Standard 6.04(c), APA, 2010). This can create an ethical dilemma for the CFT when they believe that diagnosis lies within the family system, but clients may not be able to access therapy without the benefit of individually driven diagnosis for reimbursement purposes; they erroneously believe that they are helping their clients, when in fact they are committing insurance fraud (i.e., theft by deception) and can be prosecuted for these actions. While the larger medical model system defines pathology, CFTs must learn to operate within the system ethically and legally.

Below, we will describe several likely scenarios in working with couples or families. In these scenarios, we will explicate how therapists grapple with these five ethical challenges that intersect in unique ways.

Children and Family Therapy

Bob and Sandy Jones brought their teenage daughter, Brandy, age 16, to Dr. Shindell for individual therapy as Brandy had recently been arrested for shoplifting. The intake process was started for individual therapy for Brandy. Brandy's parents signed the informed consent; Dr. Shindell also had Brandy sign the form as a sign of assent to therapy. Dr. Shindell listened to Bob and Sandy describe how Brandy was the model child, yet as soon as she became a teenager she began to defy them. When Brandy started acting out, Bob would restrict privileges or ground Brandy. Sandy, however, would grant Brandy reprieve and tell her she could go out with her friends or drive the family car, in spite of Bob's move to discipline Brandy for misbehaving. Additionally, Bob recently learned that Brandy was smoking pot.

It was clear to Dr. Shindell that Bob blamed Sandy for Brandy getting into trouble, and he was also worried about the effect of the arrest on Brandy's life and college prospects. Sandy believed that Brandy was a "good kid," but occasionally fell in with the wrong crowd. While the parents were describing their concerns about Brandy, Brandy kept her eyes on the floor. When Dr. Shindell asked her a question, Brandy would repeatedly respond with "I don't know," continuing to look downward. Brandy did not appear angry, but instead she seemed sad.

Bob and Sandy also have an 11-year-old son, Brett, who was left at home by himself. Dr. Shindell insists that all family members attend therapy in the subsequent session, but the parents decline, stating Brett was adamant about not attending for "Brandy's stupid problems." Dr. Shindell does not push the issue, being concerned that the parents will abandon therapy altogether. While Bob was paying Dr. Shindell, Sandy and Brandy had already left the therapy room together. At this point, Bob revealed to Dr. Shindell that Sandy has smoked pot most of her adulthood, and he worries Brandy may do the same.

Ethical Analysis

Who Is the Client?

Because CFTs see the family system as the client, it can be difficult to ascertain which stakeholders are the actual client(s). In this scenario, we would likely consider Brandy our client, as she is the one who got arrested and is being mandated to therapy by her parents and has signed the informed consent. However, systems therapists believe that problems reside in the family system, and seeing only one client in that system risks that person being the IP as the symptom bearer in that family (in this case, the IP is Brandy). Should Dr. Shindell see the family as a unit given the information obtained in the initial session? If so, does Brett need to attend therapy?

Another difficulty with seeing Brandy individually is that, from a systems perspective, treating Brandy by herself may keep the family in homeostasis, thus curtailing the ability of the system to change its structure, where the problem resides. In this case, it seems clear that there are structural issues in the family; Bob and Sandy do not agree on discipline and have different views of Brandy's problem. While some of the founders of family therapy insisted on seeing all members of the family (e.g., Minuchin, 1974), others believed that family structure can be shifted by seeing one member of the system (e.g., Bowen, 1978). Since client autonomy must be respected (Section 1.8, AAMFT, 2015), should Brandy make this decision? Or should the parents make this decision because Brandy is not yet an adult? Does Brett, the little brother, have any voice in this decision?

Alternatively, if Brandy is not seen alone, the therapist will have less of a chance to establish rapport with her and assess her substance use. In one study, 84 percent of suicidal ideation or intentions were revealed when the parent was not present (Heflinger, Nixon, & Hamner, 1999). Might Brandy be at risk given that the therapist notices that she appears sad? Has the therapist erred in not seeing Brandy alone in this first session, with potentially serious results? Dr. Shindell must consider potential consequences of her path forward to help ensure the dictate to "do no harm" (Standard 3.05, APA, 2010) is upheld. Should Dr. Shindell have insisted on a "no secrets" policy, even though the parents wanted Brandy seen individually? Dr. Shindell should definitely "inform clients/patients as early as is feasible in the therapeutic relationship about the nature and anticipated course of therapy, fees, involvement of third parties, and limits of confidentiality" (Standard 10.01, APA, 2010) and "disclose to clients . . . at the outset of services the nature of confidentiality and possible limitations of the client's right to confidentiality" (Section 2.1, AAMFT, 2015).

How Is Confidentiality Managed?

If Brandy is seen individually, how is her confidentiality managed? CFTs must "disclose to clients and other interested parties at the outset of services the nature of confidentiality and the possible limitations of the clients' right to confidentiality. Therapists review with clients the circumstances where confidential information may be requested and where disclosure of confidential information may be legally required" (Section 2.1, AAMFT, 2015). Likewise, CFTs must discuss "(1) the relevant limits of confidentiality and (2) the foreseeable uses of the information generated through their psychological activities" (Standard 4.02, APA, 2010). Brandy's rights as a minor will vary by state. Since her parents were legally required to give consent to her treatment instead of Brandy herself, it is fair to assume her right to confidentiality will be limited based on her status as a minor. Her parents will likely have legal access to her treatment information. Any deviations to that would need to be established with the parents and Brandy: ". . . in the context of couple, family, or group treatment, the therapist may not reveal individual confidences to others in the client unit without the prior written permission of that individual" (Section 2.2, AAMFT, 2015).

However, if the family agrees that Brandy should have confidentiality of her sessions, what happens if she relates that she is engaged in risky or dangerous behavior (e.g., drug use, drinking and driving, etc.)? Dr. Shindell could benefit from a "no secrets" policy (Hecker & Sori, 2017) that outlines limitations to Brandy's confidentiality.

Additionally, as the session wraps up and Bob is paying, he alerts the therapist to Sandy's substance abuse history. The therapist is now triangled into an unwitting alliance with Bob without Sandy's knowledge he has shared this information. Should the therapist share this information with Sandy, ask Bob to share this information, or ignore it until Bob brings it up in therapy? Because Dr. Shindell has not introduced the "no-secrets" policy, she has been therapeutically thwarted by this information. If she brings up the topic with the couple or family sans a signed release, she is betraying Sandy's confidentiality, which is an ethical violation (and potentially a legal violation as well, depending upon state law).

Who Holds the Power in Therapy?

Bob and Sandy have requested therapy for their minor daughter, but based on her training, the therapist believes that she should see the family as a unit. Should Brandy have been able to assert a request for individual treatment or should Dr. Shindell have the decision-making power regarding the format of treatment, assuming an expert role? Might the family curtail getting help for Brandy if all members of the family are required to attend therapy? Should Brandy be mandated to treatment? Do the parents' concerns for her well-being supersede her autonomy to make decisions for herself?

The therapist also holds power in deciding to see Brandy alone or only within the context of her family. The therapist may believe that the most efficacious treatment is to see the parents due to their conflicting parenting styles and views. Alternatively, the therapist may insist that all family members attend therapy, including Brandy's brother, Brett. The therapist has the power to set the structure for treatment, yet if the family retreats from therapy, it will have been an exercise in futility and therefore an action that fails to provide any benefit at all. The therapist wishes to aid the parents in gaining their power back in their executive subsystem, but must first teach the parents how to re-establish their rightful place in the executive subsystem of the family. Thus, the more ethical approach, at least at this point, is to share power with the family and avoid refusing them treatment because one member of the family will not agree to attend.

Who Decides Reality?

In this case, Bob believes that Brandy is defiant, Sandy believes that Brandy has just fallen in with the wrong crowd, and Brandy's reality remains unrevealed, which is probably quite different from those of her parents. Additionally, the therapist may hypothesize Brandy is suffering from depression based on her downward gaze and sad expression. The parents are paying, but Brandy is suffering, and the therapist must also present the case accurately to the third-party reimburser (Section 8.4, AAMFT, 2015; Standard 6.04(c), APA, 2010).

Who Decides Normalcy/Health?

The therapist in this case is in the role of expert. Systemically, she may believe that the child is the IP of a dysfunctional family system. She may ask the parents to therapy to work on their parenting relationship (which she believes rests with marital problems). Alternately, she may decide that Brandy is indeed depressed and opt to see her individually in order help her cope with her relational environment (e.g., her parents' marital issues). The parents do not believe that Brandy is acting "normally," but we have little information on what Brandy and her brother believe is normal.

Finally, Sandy's use of marijuana may be seen as normal if the family lives in a state where marijuana has been legalized and consequently normalized versus living in a state where marijuana is still illegal. The therapist, however, is concerned about the effect of marijuana on Brandy's developing brain, given the latest research on the issue. In this situation, both state law and the therapist's views and professional acumen can strongly influence what is normal and healthy.

Summary

When seeing multiple members of a family, there are multiple ethical and legal issues that need to be evaluated. Defining who the client is, managing decision-making power with multiple stakeholders, and defining individual members' levels of confidentiality are important and must all be addressed. In this case, the needs of all stakeholders must be taken into account, with particular attention paid to those family members who hold less power, such as Brandy.

This scenario speaks to the importance of having conversations with family members about expectations and thorough informed consent, with potential reframes on Brandy's behavior in order to move her out of the role of the IP, thus empowering her in a system where she holds little authority. Additionally, issues of safety must be kept at the forefront of therapy; one option is to have a written agreement that details Brandy's confidentiality with agreements as to what can or must be shared with her parents.

Developmental issues must also be weighed when considering power in the system, as curtailing Brandy's power to make therapeutic decisions for her own well-being may negatively affect her developmental needs to differentiate herself from her parents. Brandy's ability to garner this power will also be impacted by state laws regarding the treatment of minors, as well as therapeutic conversations between the parents and their daughter. As with many ethical issues, there is no absolutely right way to treat this case; there are many ways one could treat this situation, all depending upon the information revealed in therapy and the interactions between the therapist, the family system, the family subsystems, state and federal laws, ethical codes, etc.

Dr. Shindell will likely need to come to a collaborative solution with the parents and Brandy about how to treat Brandy, taking into account the parents' roles in the executive subsystem, as well as Dr. Shindell's own therapeutic expertise. As part of the family system and because she is the impetus for the family seeking treatment and is in some distress, Brandy should be included in the decision-making to the greatest extent possible. Brett's inclusion in therapy will also need to be considered, and if there are varying ideas between family members and the therapist, collaboration can be established that best meets the needs of all family members, though this outcome may not be clear at the outset of therapy. The AAMFT Code and the APA Code both emphasize the requirement for informed consent from individuals receiving couples and family services (APA 10.02; AAMFT 1.2) and assent from minors for services (APA 3.10b) as soon as is feasible in the process. What would be ethically problematic is for Dr. Shindell to make a unilateral decision about what happens next.

Intimate Partner Violence in Couples Therapy

Shelly and Dan attend their first session for communication issues and conflict in their relationship. They have been married for three years, yet have been together for seven years. They have a four-year-old daughter, Shenille, who is staying with her grandmother during sessions. At the start of the intake session, the therapist, Mr. Aaron, reviews confidentiality as a part of the informed consent process. Mr. Aaron indicates that he adheres to a no secrets policy, meaning that whatever is said in individual sessions can be shared by Mr. Aaron with the other member of the couple, as he believes, based on his training, that secrets are harmful to couples' relationships. The couple agrees to this policy. During the intake session, both partners describe being unhappy in the marriage. Shelly says she wishes they could communicate better, but is vague when asked further about this by Mr. Aaron. Dan agrees that communication could improve, and he wants to spend more time together as a couple. Both report that their arguments get heated at times, but they say that no one has hurt the other during these arguments.

At the second session, Mr. Aaron decides to spend half of the session with each partner individually, per agency protocol when working with couples. Mr. Aaron first meets with Shelly alone, who immediately starts crying and saying she is very fearful of her husband, stating that Dan is a "master manipulator" and has threatened her and Shenille if they ever leave. Shelly says that Dan occasionally hits her during arguments. She adds that there are times when he actually says nothing during an argument; he will simply get his handgun out and lay it on the kitchen table. Shelly tells the therapist that she wants to leave the marriage, but is frightened about leaving. Shelly's parents have never liked Dan, and now she is isolated from her parents to the point where Shelly is cut off from them. Shelly begs Mr. Aaron not to tell Dan any of this information, saying she does not know what will happen if he knows about her thoughts and feelings.

During the second half of the session, Mr. Aaron meets with Dan and asks him further about communication difficulties and conflict in the marriage. Dan says he has tried to communicate clearly with Shelly, but that she just will not listen to him. He says that there are times when their arguments get loud – there is screaming and yelling, and he says that they have thrown things at each other. Dan says he loves Shelly and cannot imagine life without her. During the course of the session, Mr. Aaron does not hear anything close to Shelly's account of abuse in their relationship. Paper-and-pencil assessments of marital satisfaction and violence indicate that Shelly is much more dissatisfied in the relationship than Dan, although both are above the clinical cutoff for marital satisfaction on the measure used by the agency; they also indicate that no violence is present in the relationship.

At the third session, the therapist sees the couple jointly to discuss goals. Shelly continues to be very vague and quiet, minimally participating in the discussion of goals. Dan is taking leadership in setting goals for the relationship, which include increased intimacy, more time spent together, and improved communication. Mr. Aaron had dreaded this session, wondering what the best approach would be given his safety concerns for Shelly and Shenille, the disparate goals shared by the couple individually, and the dilemma about whether to honor the no secrets policy established in the first session.

Ethical Analysis

Who Is the Client?

Mr. Aaron has several options here in considering who the client is: the wife, the husband, or the couple/family. In terms of surface-level presentation, it is clear that the couple is the client. Both partners came in for therapy, or at least discussed being dissatisfied with the relationship. In terms of the case scenario, at the end of the second session, safety issues may move the focus from the couple to the wife in terms of determining who the client is. Safety issues need to be addressed prior to commencement of couples therapy. It is possible that the husband has a covert agenda (if indeed he is violent) that has not been shared with the therapist (or even his wife). Moreover, the wife has suggested that if the husband learns of her plan to leave, he may become more angry or violent. The question arises as to how to ensure the safety of all parties, including the therapist. Moving forward with viewing the wife as the client in terms of safety, steps could be made for her to contact a battered women's shelter and to enact a safety plan for her and her daughter. However, this direction of therapy is counter to that which was originally presented – the couple being the client. Ethically, does the therapist need to do additional assessment prior to taking action? Does the husband lose his autonomy in making treatment decisions if his wife suggests that he has been or could be violent? Ethically, what should the therapist do if he is unclear whether the wife is being honest?

How Is Confidentiality Managed?

Issues of confidentiality are related in this case to safety concerns. Mr. Aaron indicated his "no secrets" policy at the start of therapy with this couple. Does the "no secrets" policy still apply when safety concerns are present? After all, the "no secrets" policy is intended for use with couples in which affairs are or could be present. Yet in this case, the "no secrets" policy could be harmful, because sharing Shelly's intentions of leaving the relationship may prove harmful or fatal to her and/or her daughter. Research indicates that the most dangerous time for women in abusive relationships is when they are trying to leave the relationship (Campbell et al., 2003). Moreover, the wife's report of abuse suggests that the form of violence present is patriarchal terrorism (Johnson, 1995). Given this research, there is compelling reason to maintain the wife's confidentiality in this scenario, at least for a time, if she is amenable to taking steps to leave the relationship. If Mr. Aaron proceeds in this direction, it is apparent that keeping the wife's plans to leave the relationship confidential would be time limited; that is, at some point, the information divulged by the wife would need to be shared with the husband and supports offered and made available to him as necessary.

Some may say that supporting the wife in her plans to leave her husband is a bold step and depends on the therapist's evaluation of risk, given current research on intimate partner violence (IPV). Some therapists place more emphasis on maintaining and improving the relationship, above and beyond any indications of abuse from either partner. In this case, if the decision is made that the couple is the client and confidentiality is not guaranteed or held in terms of what either partner says in individual sessions, then the goal could be to deal with the violence. From this perspective, the couple could be seen in order to work through their experiences of violence in the relationship. Some research has supported the idea that couples in which violence is present can be treated successfully in couples therapy (Stith, McCollum, Amanor-Boadu, & Smith, 2012). It is important to know if this couple is experiencing patriarchal terrorism or common couple violence. Patriarchal terrorism is "a product of patriarchal traditions of men's right to control 'their' women, is a form of terroristic control of wives by their husbands that involves the systematic use of not only violence, but economic subordination, threats, isolation, and other control tactics" (Johnson, 1995, p. 284). Common couple violence is a less gendered conflict where the conflict "occasionally gets 'out of hand,' leading usually to 'minor' forms of violence, and more rarely escalating into serious, sometimes even life-threatening, forms of violence" (Johnson, 1995, p. 285).

Couples therapy may be indicated only for couples experiencing common couple violence (Johnson, 1995), not patriarchal terrorism, which may be represented in the case scenario with Shelly and Dan. The therapist is ethically bound to practice competently (i.e., to do a thorough assessment and understand the type of violence dynamics at play) prior to prescribing couples therapy (AAMFT Standard 3; APA Standards 2.01 and 10.03).

Who Holds the Power in Therapy?

A frequent debate relates to how much power the therapist and client hold, respectively, and how this is negotiated in the session and in the moment. In regard to this case scenario, a collaborative therapist who gives the couple power to define the future/outcome of their relationship may be more likely to work with the information the couple has presented as a couple and may interpret assessment results as confirmation that the couple wants to improve their relationship. Mr. Aaron may take the information shared by the wife and help the couple improve their communication (and help her share her thoughts and feelings with her husband) and help them spend more time together. By privileging the couple's view of the goals of therapy, the therapist may be inadvertently (or intentionally) siding with the husband's perspective of the marriage; that is, the therapist may align with a destructive side of the marriage and put the wife in danger as a result of his treatment decision. Because of the potential for harm, Mr. Aaron would be wise to consult with a more seasoned therapist, being careful to not share identifying information, or obtaining a release of information for both clients (Standard 4.06, APA, 2010). It may be that the case is beyond his scope of practice and a referral is in order (Section 1.10, AAMFT, 2015, Code 2.01, APA, 2010).

Who Defines Reality?

Many times in working with more than one client, the therapist is faced with the question of determining the reality of the couple so that therapy can move forward. Therapists learn early on that reality is often found within a combination of perspectives provided by the clients in the room. Clients can be influential in their contributions to defining reality. Sometimes this is influenced by the client who is most articulate, persuasive, charming, loud, etc.; all of these factors may be tied to gender, race and culture and can be difficult for therapists to navigate. Yet, when the stakes are particularly high – as in the case of violence, abuse, or neglect – the therapist must often make a quick determination of which reality is most accurate, or which is most concerning under a worst-case scenario, because inaction may lead to harm or death. In an IPV scenario between members of the couple, the perpetrator of abuse is typically the person who defines reality. The victim's decision to leave a relationship can so utterly disrupt the assumptions about who defines reality that are embedded within the relationship that perpetrators may attempt to exert more control as a reaction to losing the ability to define reality. If the therapist believes the reality of the victim, then that may add to the perpetrator's humiliation and decrease willingness to continue engaging in therapy. On the other hand, if the therapist chooses to believe the reality of the victim when – unbeknownst to the therapist – the "perpetrator" has not engaged in any abusive behaviors, then the unbalancing does not bode well for the couple to return. It is clear from this scenario that when working with IPV, competence in treating the nuances of violent relationships is imperative. The therapist may have to weigh client autonomy – their right to make decisions about their relationship – against the need to ensure client safety. This stance derives both from the principle of nonmaleficence and from APA 3.04, the ethical duty to avoid harm to those we serve.

Who Decides Normalcy/Health?

With any and all decisions a therapist makes, they are contributing to the discourse of normalcy/health. Therapists need to consider cultural influences in determining the normalcy or health of behaviors (and of relationships). Gender roles vary across cultures; religious values may also impact the values the couple holds, which may be quite different from the values familiar to the therapist. However, in this scenario, the therapist must take a stand against violence, thereby disapproving of violence to the extent that perhaps the therapist does not advocate for the continuance of the relationship. This seems to go against the ethical dictate that clients have autonomy in their decision-making (Section 1.8, AAMFT, 2015), but that dictate does not override the duty to protect patients from avoidable harm. It seems the therapist making the decision to extricate the wife to safety is making a statement about what is normal and healthy.

Summary

The possibility of abuse raises the stakes for therapists working with couples and families. Ethical quandaries emerge that erase the therapist's luxury of time when making decisions about how to respond. The therapist in this scenario, Mr. Aaron, must ensure the safety of all participants before proceeding; that may involve continuing to see the partners individually for a time to allow for further assessment, preparing a safety plan, and providing perhaps quite different supports to each partner. While CFTs view the system as the client, in cases where safety is at risk, individual therapy is more ethical in the sense that safety is more privileged than the perceived needs of the couple to be seen together. It is an ethical imperative to avoid harm, and therapists need to "take steps to avoid harming their clients/patients" and "minimize harm where it is foreseeable and unavoidable" (Standard 3.04, APA, 2010). Mr. Aaron felt stressed and torn by this dilemma, as there were multiple possible directions to go with this case.

Immigration, Language, and Coming Out Issues

Rosa called for therapy for her teenage son, José, aged 15, who is having school problems. José has been truant, his grades have dropped below passing, and he is seldom home on the weekends, spending time with friends and refusing to tell his family where he goes. Rosa's husband, Roberto, refuses to come to therapy. In addition to José, Rosa and Roberto have two other sons, Miguel, aged 21, who no longer lives at home, and Juan, aged 8, who is in elementary school. At the first session, the therapist, Dr. Corso, learns that the family is originally from Mexico and that Rosa is an undocumented immigrant who knows just enough English to get by.

José is translating for Rosa in the session, as Rosa feels most comfortable speaking Spanish. When Dr. Corso enquires about the use of a translator, José says that Rosa is uncomfortable with having an unknown person in the therapy room, being fearful that a translator may be a member of the community. Dr. Corso learns that both parents are undocumented immigrants, although Juan was born in the United States. When Dr. Corso talks with José individually, José reveals that has come out as gay to a few close friends, but not to his family. José expresses to the therapist in English that he fears his parents' reactions to his sexual orientation, although he thinks his mother is more likely to be accepting of his orientation.

Dr. Corso really wants to help this family, knowing that there are very few, if any, resources in the community for immigrant families. The therapist feels comfortable and competent working with the family on LGBT issues, yet is not as familiar with Mexican culture or immigrant issues. While Rosa verbally consents to therapy, José must translate the informed consent for her verbally, as Dr. Corso does not have a copy of it available in Spanish and nor does she speak Spanish. José himself assents to therapy. Dr. Corso feels torn in her desire to help this family, but she wonders about how her inability to speak Spanish and her lack of cultural knowledge will impact therapy. Dr. Corso worries about the position José is placed in as translator, and she knows that the therapeutic process will be slowed down considerably as everything that Rosa and the therapist say will need to be translated.

Ethical Analysis

Who Is the Client?

At first glance, José appears to be the IP, as he is the one who is having difficulties at school. However, family therapists think systemically, so the therapist may need to know about other family members' involvement in the presenting problem, yet must do so in this case with limited information. In order to get a full picture of family dynamics, some family therapists insist on seeing the entire family. CFTs typically endorse this stance as it avoids the potential harm of alliances or coalitions that may be formed at another member's expense if they are not in attendance. In fact, there seems to already be a strong alliance between José and his mother, forged in part by her need to have José translate for her. Additionally, Roberto's absence may be a significant problem in understanding the family. Did he actually refuse to come to therapy or is Rosa trying to take on the role of family caregiver, as might be common in Mexican families? Is José's identifying as gay impacting Roberto's absence? Dr. Corso faces a dilemma around the importance of bringing in Roberto for family therapy, highlighted by the ethical duty to be sensitive to cultural factors in this case (Principle E, APA, 2010). The likelihood of bringing Roberto in may quickly diminish as therapy progresses. The same question can be raised for bringing in Miguel and Juan; although they may be more likely to attend family sessions. Dr. Corso is likely to work with the family to shift the focus of the problem from José to the family. Out of respect for the family and in an effort to work collaboratively, the therapist decides to begin therapy with Rosa and José only, respecting their autonomy, but keeping open the possibility for other family members to join later. The therapist wants to be sensitive to the roles of the family members and wants to learn more about the family dynamics and family culture before proceeding. She is concerned that a lack of assessment around the cultural and familial factors about José's sexual orientation may place him in harm's way if she moves too quickly to inclusive family work.

How Is Confidentiality Managed?

Whenever minors are in therapy, *as part of the consent and assent process*, the therapist needs to talk about the limitations of confidentiality *with both the minor and the parent* in the event that the minor is seen individually. In this case, the therapist might foresee that there may be times to share with Rosa what is learned in José's individual sessions and times to keep José's disclosures confidential. *Both José and Rosa need to understand and agree to this.* José's unexplained time away from home may involve activities such as alcohol/drug use, theft, vandalism, etc. The therapist is wise to talk with both Rosa and José together about the types of information that will be shared with Rosa (and perhaps Roberto) as a result of individual sessions. Depending upon the limits of privilege in the jurisdiction in which therapy is taking place, activities that are of potential or actual harm to José or others may need to be reportable not just to José's parents, but also to law enforcement.

Therapists must be prepared for minors to reveal any kind of concern, which may raise ethical questions about the extent of confidentiality. Wise therapists are prepared and anticipate working with minors engaged in criminal behavior. Secretive behavior may also be related to issues such as sexual identity. Instead of engaging in criminal activity, José has found a group of friends who support him in his identity as a gay teenager. Dr. Corso may eventually want to discuss with José the possibility of coming out to Rosa, but then an ethical dilemma is presented in terms of José's autonomy. Does Dr. Corso work with Rosa and Jose to decide whether to open up the possibility of a disclosure to José's father about José's sexual orientation? What if José's fears are founded that his father would be extremely upset to the point of disowning José if he knew his son is gay? Dr. Corso may decide to work with José to determine to whom – if anyone – in his family he may consider coming out. If José identifies Rosa as the family member with the greatest potential to be supportive, then Dr. Corso would likely work with José to eventually come out to Rosa. In the event that José comes out to Rosa, the next step may be to help Rosa and José decide together whether and if so how to approach Roberto with information about José's sexual orientation. Clearly, Dr. Corso's decision must be grounded in concern for the welfare and safety of the teen based on the most fundamental ethical principle of maleficence articulated in both the AAMFT and APA codes.

Who Holds the Power in Therapy?

Even if Roberto never attends therapy, he could be considered to hold a great deal of power as the husband/father in a Mexican family. José himself holds quite a bit of power in therapy if he is serving as a translator. There are many cultural nuances embedded in language that, even under the most ideal circumstances, may not be adequately conveyed to the therapist. José would naturally filter his translation through his own lens of reality. The therapist ultimately cannot be sure that what is said in session is what is being received. Rosa and the therapist are connected only through José. Unless an outside translator is brought in, José must be present in session to translate for Rosa. The therapist would be unable to have a direct and confidential conversation with Rosa, and there is a *role complication* when José is put in a parental position.

Dr. Corso also holds a tremendous amount of power in this scenario: the clients may be concerned about the possibility of deportation as reported by the therapist or other professionals who get involved in the case. Clients place great trust in their therapists to appropriately use the power that comes with the role of therapist. Ethically, the therapist must avoid harm (Standard 3.04, APA, 2010), and given her inability to speak Spanish and the resulting harmful family dynamic of José becoming parentified by being Rosa's translator, a referral to a Spanish-speaking therapist is in order (Section 1.10, AAMFT, 2015).

Who Decides Reality?

In this case, who decides reality is closely aligned with who holds the power. Dr. Corso can never know the extent to which Rosa understands what the therapist is saying, and likewise Rosa can never know how much the therapist is understanding her. José holds more power due to his English skills, but at the cost of a position that catapults him into a parental role.

Who Decides Normalcy/Health?

Dr. Corso is in an influential position to define normalcy and health for this family. How should an immigrant Mexican family function? Perhaps the family adheres to traditional gender roles, in which case Rosa is responsible for the family. In respecting the family's culture, Dr. Corso has decided to make an ethical decision to conduct therapy with only Rosa and José because Dr. Corso believes that this approach has the best chance of helping the family and avoiding harm to José. Given her systems training, Dr. Corso realizes that this may uphold a family alliance or coalition that is harmful to the family. Ethically, she must evaluate the family dynamics therapy to avoid harm to the family system (Standard 3.04, APA, 2015). Alternatively, Dr. Corso could still respect the hierarchy and roles in the family, yet request that Roberto attends therapy so that the bond between the parents can be strengthened.

In this case, Dr. Corso feels competent in working with LGBT concerns; however, she will need to learn more about or revisit training on issues specific to Mexican immigrant families if a referral is not possible or if the family agrees to a translator other than José. Both the APA Code (Principle E and Standard 2.0.1) and the AAMFT Code (Aspirational Values and Standard 1.1) emphasize the importance of cultural competence. When cultural values emphasize the importance of family over the needs of the individual, then clients such as José may decide not to come out to any family members out of fear of losing their family connections. Although Dr. Corso may feel disappointed in the client's decision in this case, she must respect the autonomy of the client to decide what is best for himself.

Summary

Upon learning José's sexual orientation, Dr. Corso can support José's understanding of himself and work with him to share this part of himself with Rosa, the person he has identified in the family as most amenable to his coming out. From there, Dr. Corso could work with José and Rosa together to approach Roberto with this information about José, supporting them both in growing together as a family. However, Dr. Corso could also respect José's decision to keep his sexual orientation confidential out of consideration for the client's safety and cultural context.

Non-Normative Divorce and Parent Alienation from a Child

Robert and Kelly had been married for ten years with two small daughters, Kaley and Rose, aged 5 and 7, respectively, and while there was strife in the marriage, there was no violence. Both parents had good relationships with Kaley and Rose. However, after several years of struggling to right their relationship, Robert said he wanted a divorce. Kelly immediately found her way to a domestic violence shelter, where she took the children, leaving Robert unable to locate them for some time.

At the shelter, Kelly engaged in therapy with a volunteer therapist who was a CFT, Mr. Skrags, who, for personal reasons, was very invested in the recovery of women who had been abused. Mr. Skrags saw Kelly for several months. Mr. Skrags supported Kelly in her efforts to break free of what she told the therapist was an emotionally abusive husband. As the divorce proceeded, Kelly related to Mr. Skrags that Robert had physically and sexually abused her. When it became clear that Robert was allowed to have parenting time with the girls, Kelly revealed to the therapist that she had an "epiphany" that Rose had been sexually abused by Robert when she was 18 months old. Mr. Skrags did not report the alleged abuse to authorities as legally required. Instead, Kelly and Mr. Skrags pursued an extensive campaign to limit Robert's access to the children. Mr. Skrags continued treatment with Kelly, which revealed numerous contradictions in Kelly's stories of abuse; Mr. Skrags also learned from Kelly herself that she had a habit of lying in several areas of her life. Additionally, Mr. Skrags discovered Kelly had an extensive history of mental illness, and even in the current therapy had made several statements that indicated she was not completely in touch with reality. For example, Kelly asserted Robert starved the children and that he prostituted her and the eldest daughter. In addition, Kelly was banned from the local mental health center as, when she took the girls there for treatment, she had accused both of their therapists of being inappropriate with the children. Yet Mr. Skrags felt compelled to testify on Kelly's behalf in the divorce proceedings. The therapist testified that he believed Robert to be a danger to the children, though he had never met Robert, nor evaluated Kaley and Rose regarding the abuse allegations.

Because of Kelly's allegations and Mr. Skrags' testimony, Robert was forced to have supervised visitation until the court had access to parenting evaluations, which were extensively delayed because Kelly refused to cooperate. Kelly even refused to allow the guardian ad litem to have contact with Kaley and Rose. Finally, the evaluation was completed, whereby the parental evaluator reported on evaluations of both parents, including in-depth psychological assessments. The evaluator noted Robert's parenting strengths and stated that Kelly was unable to separate her needs from those of her children, and stated that the alienation Kelly engaged in was abusive to Kaley and Rose. The guardian ad litem also advocated for Robert. After two years, the court gradually returned parenting time to Robert. Even after the court had ruled for parenting time for Robert based on the parenting evaluation results, Mr. Skrags continued to work with Kelly's attorney to limit Robert's access to the girls.

Ethical Analysis

Who Is the Client?

In this case, Kelly is the client of Mr. Skrags, who is advocating for her with the court system. Mr. Skrags may also believe that the children are his clients because of his extreme efforts to "protect them" from Robert. CFTs as well as other therapists are often unfamiliar with these extreme dynamics and fall into the belief that this is a systemic "couple" issue between the parents (Kelly and Robert's relationship), with less understanding of how the individual pathology of one or both parents may be fueling the alienation process (Friedman, 2004). With non-normative divorces becoming more prominent in caseloads, therapists have an obligation to become competent in discerning case dynamics, which include the parents, the children, and various factions of the court system. Because extreme conflict often developmentally affects the child/children, CFTs have an obligation to understand how to intervene in these complex systems.

In this case, Mr. Skrags did not diagnose the mental illness from which Kelly was suffering, but instead joined in her reality without checking out the validity of her claims. He has little basis for his opinion, forgoing assessment before advocating to limit Robert's rights. CFTs who "provide forensic evaluations avoid offering professional opinions about persons they have not directly interviewed" (Section 7.8, AAMFT, 2010). Indeed, Mr. Skrags had never even met Robert. He also should have been able to diagnose Kelly's prominent mental illness, and it appears he is operating outside of his scope of competence (Section 3.10, AAMFT, 2015; Standard 2.01, APA, 2010). Likewise, Mr. Skrags could have received supervision and learned new skills with which to deal with a complex case (Section 3.6, AAMFT, 2015) or taken additional training to maintain his competence (Standard 2.03, APA, 2010). There is also evidence Mr. Skrags may not be unbiased due to his history with IPV. At the very least, when the case entered the legal arena, Mr. Skrags had a responsibility to clarify his role with Kelly, the children, and Robert. Specifically, "If it becomes apparent that psychologists may be called upon to perform conflicting roles (such as a family therapist and then a witness for one party in divorce proceedings), psychologists take reasonable steps to clarify or modify, or withdraw from, roles appropriately" (Section 10.02, APA, 2010).

Mr. Skrags failed to check for any evidence of Kelly's claims of abuse, and instead formed a coalition with Kelly against Robert, presenting a conflict of interest for him due to his relationship with Kelly appearing to impair his objectivity (Section 3.4, AAMFT, 2015; Standard 3.06, APA, 2010). His lack of training in parent alienation left him with his unethical action of engaging in the alienation process and harming the children through his actions by inappropriately advocating for them to have restricted access to their father. Mr. Skrags' alignment with Kelly and subsequent coalition against Robert are abuses of his therapeutic power; his abuse of power is an ethical violation (Section 1.7, AAMFT, 2010), and his advocating for Kelly in the court system is both a dual relationship of therapist and legal advocate (Section 1.3, AAMFT, 2010; Standard 3.05, APA, 2010) and continued evidence of his conflict of interest in the case (Section 3.4, AAMFT, 2015; Standard 3.06, APA, 2010). His clients appear to be Kelly and the children, with little attention paid to the family system or Robert's parental rights, thereby continuing to engage in unethical role conflicts. Section 7.5 of the AAMFT Code of Ethics states, "Marriage and family therapists avoid conflict in roles in legal proceedings wherever possible and disclose potential conflicts." His testimony is misleading, based on his limited expertise of the family system. "Marriage and family therapists who provide expert or fact witness testimony in legal proceedings avoid misleading judgements, base conclusions and opinions on appropriate data, and avoid inaccuracies insofar as possible. When offering testimony, as marriage and family therapy experts, they shall strive to be accurate, objective, fair, and independent" (Section 7.2, AAMFT, 2015).

How Is Confidentiality Managed?

Because of court involvement, there is little to no confidentiality for any involved party – not for Kelly, nor Robert, nor the children. While Kelly may hold some degree of confidentiality regarding her treatment with the CFT, the judge can easily override that (depending upon state statute). *This reality must be made clear to the family at the onset of services.*

Who Holds the Power?

All therapists encounter clients who are divorcing. Fewer encounter cases that have such severe polarizations that they are willingly or unwillingly drawn into the conflict. In alienation cases, typically there is one parent who is engaged in turning a child against a parent, the latter of whom Kelly and Johnston (2001) have termed the "target" parent. Alienation strategies can include both covert strategies, such as subtle messages that the other parent is dangerous, uninvolved or absent, and overt strategies, such as open belittling of the target parent or continued returns to court in attempts to limit contact. While it may look like "couple conflict," in these cases one parent is taking active steps to curtail the parenting rights of the target parent. In this case, the court and its appointees have little influence. Kelly appears to have power in that she seems to be able to manipulate others in the system to do her bidding. Robert seems to hold little power in that his access to his daughters is limited by Kelly, her supporters, and the court. In this case, Mr. Skrags holds significant power through his court testimony advocating for Kelly, and he abuses that power (Section 1.7, AAMFT, 2015), harming the family in the process (Standard 3.04, APA, 2010).

Who Defines Reality?

Mr. Skrags lacked education on parental alienation, instead assisting Kelly with her campaign to denigrate Robert and curb his parenting rights, propelling Kelly's reality to be the dominant one inside and outside of court. The domestic violence shelter also upholds Kelly's view of reality. While therapists are typically taught to accept and validate clients, in cases of non-normative divorce, it can be damaging to not explore all potential hypotheses as to what the family is experiencing. In this case, there was evidence Kelly may not be a reliable source due to her admitted history of lying and false accusations. There was also evidence that Robert had not abused the girls, evidenced by the parent evaluation, psychological evaluation, and highly questionable reports and actions on the part of Kelly. Mr. Skrags unethically attempts to define reality for the court based on his limited training, expertise, and knowledge of the actual dynamics at play in the divorce. "Psychologists base the opinions contained in their recommendations, reports, and diagnostic or evaluative statements, including forensic testimony, on information and techniques sufficient to substantiate their findings" (Standard 9.01, APA, 2010). Mr. Skrags did not have comprehensive information from which to make his allegations. "Psychologists provide opinions of the psychological characteristics of individuals only after they have conducted an examination of the individuals adequate to support their statement or conclusions" (Standard 9.01, APA, 2010).

Alienation cases differ from families transitioning in normative divorce experiences. Alienation leaves children with altered realities during their formative years, and they are also denied a loving relationship with the target parent, which can have significant long-term implications for them. In initial research on the long-term effects of divorce, the greater the number and frequency of alienating strategies that children were exposed to, the more both their self-esteem and self-sufficiency suffered. These children also suffer high rates of depression (Baker & Ben-Ami, 2011). While courts often view protracted conflict as a "couple's issue," in alienation cases, one reality that is not identified is abuse of children caused by the alienating parent. In this case, Kelly is abusing both Robert and the children. CFTs may inadvertently play into this dynamic as Mr. Skrags did, unethically assuming Kelly's reality is accurate, further aiding in defining a false reality to the court.

Who Decides Normalcy/Health?

For Robert and Kelly's divorce, Mr. Skrags initially had considerable influence in defining what was normal and healthy for the children, and even fabricated information to support his view. CFTs and other therapists have an ethical edict to have sufficient evidence to substantiate their findings, as well as to avoid offering professional opinions about people they have neither met nor interviewed. Special care must be exercised when making public statements as this CFT did, especially considering the potential effects of biased information on the family members, as well as not having interviewed Kaley and Rose, nor ever meeting Robert or seeking information about the alleged abuse (e.g., police reports). Mr. Skrags also has decided to diagnose sexual abuse himself, failing to notify authorities of potential abuse as his state law mandated. An evaluation by authorities may have garnered a very different view of the health of this family, and Mr. Skrags has abused his power as a therapist (Section 1.7, AAMFT, 2015).

Who Holds the Power in Therapy?

Kelly's therapy with Mr. Skrags was voluntary. However, due to the CFT's poor judgments and unfamiliarity with alienation dynamics, Kelly held significant power in the therapy. As additional information eventually became available, Robert regained some power, though not without him and the children suffering significant emotional damage. The court was manipulated into a reality created by both Kelly and Mr. Skrags. Mr. Skrags holds significant power in his position as a licensed, treating professional within the court. This power is maligned due to his over-involvement; we know that he himself has some personal reason to advocate for abused women. Because Mr. Skrags' responses aimed at rescuing Kelly are so strong, it appears he has personal issues about abuse that have not been addressed. By not addressing them, he allows his personal values and feelings to erroneously dictate his treatment and his testimony, unethically leaving this family in harm's way. Even when he has the parenting evaluation results, Mr. Skrags continues to advocate against Robert, at this point seeming to have a personal vendetta against Robert. "When psychologists become aware of personal problems that may be interfering with their work performing work-related duties adequately, they take appropriate measures, such as obtaining professional consultation or assistance, and determine whether they should limit, suspend, or terminate their work-related duties" (Standard 2.06, APA, 2010). When Mr. Skrags continues to work to limit Robert's parenting time, even after the court has ruled to the contrary, he should reflect on his extreme position and seek outside consultation to discuss the discrepancy between the courtroom evidence and his deeply held beliefs.

Summary

Non-normative divorces can bring unique ethical challenges of which many therapists are unfamiliar. The CFT should remember that the family system is a client in these situations and that the children are most certainly clients in that the CFT should advocate for their well-being. Forming coalitions or alliances with one parent over the other can cause harm to the family. Because CFTs can hold significant power in these situations, an educated stance is imperative and ultimately ethically needed.

Conclusion

CFTs see ethical issues that are the same as those encountered by individual therapists; differences arise, however, when having to take multiple viewpoints, needs, expectations, and relational dynamics into account as the numbers of clients rise. When working with family systems, the therapist must consider who the client actually is from potential individual and relationship configurations and how to manage confidentiality with multiple stakeholders involved. The CFT will encounter power issues in couple relationships, between family members, and with the larger systems in which families function. Within these relational systems, there are power considerations with regard to age, sex, ethnicity/race, gender expression, sexual orientation, religious beliefs, and many more.

Context must be considered when making ethical decisions in therapy. The therapist holds considerable power in defining reality for families and is typically in charge of what is considered normal individual and family functioning. Given this power, the CFT must consider the client system's needs, larger systems that impinge upon those needs, and what is needed by the therapist to provide effective treatment. Continued education is required to stay abreast of changes in the field; both education and personal reflection are required to be good stewards of ethical practice.

References

American Association for Marriage and Family Therapy (2015). AAMFT code of ethics. Retrieved from www.aamft.org/iMIS15/AAMFT/Content/legal_ethics/code_of_ethics.aspx

American Counseling Association (2014). ACA code of ethics. Retrieved from www.counseling.org/resources/aca-code-of-ethics.pdf

American Psychological Association (2010). Ethical principles of psychologists and code of conduct (2002, Amended June 1, 2010). Retrieved from www.apa.org/ethics/code

Baker, A. J. L. & Ben-Ami, N. (2011). To turn a child against a parent is to turn a child against himself: The direct and indirect effects of exposure to parental alienation strategies on self-esteem and well-being. *Journal of Divorce & Remarriage*, *52*, 472–489.

Bowen, M. (1978). *Family therapy in clinical practice*. New York, NY: Aronson.

Campbell, J. C., Webster, D., Koziol-McLain, J., et al. (2003). Risk factors for femicide in abusive relationships: Results from a multisite case control study. *American Journal of Public Health*, *93*, 1089–1097.

Friedman, M. (2004). The so-called high-conflict couple: A closer look. *The American Journal of Family Therapy*, *32*, 101–117.

Green, R. J. (2012). Gay and lesbian family life: Risk, resilience, and rising expectations. In F. Walsh (Ed.), *Normal family processes: Growing diversity and complexity* (4th edn., pp. 172–195). New York, NY: Guilford.

Hecker, L. (2016). *HIPAA demystified: HIPAA compliance for mental health professionals*. Crown Point, IN: Loger Press.

Hecker, L. & Sori, C. F. (2017). Ethics in therapy with children in families. In M. J. Murphy & L. Hecker (Eds.), *Ethics and professional issues in couple and family therapy* (2nd edn. pp. 183–203). New York, NY: Taylor Francis.

Heflinger, C. A., Nixon, C. T., & Hamner, K. (1999). Handling confidentiality and disclosure in the evaluation of client outcomes in managed mental health services for children and adolescents. *Education and Program Planning, 19,* 175–182

Johnson, M. P. (1995). Patriarchal terrorism and common couple violence: Two forms of violence against women. *Journal of Marriage and the Family, 57,* 283–294.

Kelly, J. B. & Johnston, J. R. (2001). The alienated children: A reformulation of parental alienation syndrome. *Family Court Review, 39,* 249–266.

Minuchin, S. (1974). *Families and family therapy*. Boston, MA: Harvard University Press.

Murphy, M. J. & Hecker, L. (2017). Power, privilege, and ethics in couple and family therapy. In M. J. Murphy & L. Hecker (Eds.), *Ethics and professional issues in couple and family therapy* (2nd edn., pp. 99–119). New York, NY: Taylor & Francis.

National Association of Social Workers (2017). NASW Code of Ethics. Retrieved from www .socialworkers.org/About/Ethics/Code-of-Ethics/Code-of-Ethics-English

Stith, S. M., McCollum, E. E., Amanor-Boadu, Y., & Smith, D. (2012). Systemic perspectives on intimate partner treatment. *Journal of Marital and Family Therapy, 38,* 220–240.

SECTION II

Ethical Issues in Working with Diverse Populations

13 Ethical Issues in Working with Older Adults

Rowena Gomez and Lisa M. Brown

Older adults are the fastest-growing age group in the United States (Colby & Ortman, 2015) and in most countries around the world (United Nations, Department of Economic and Social Affairs, Population Division, 2015). Although this age group has a relatively low prevalence for most psychiatric disorders compared to younger age groups (Kessler et al., 2005), older adults have the largest prevalence rate for cognitive disorders, which increases with advanced age (Ferri et al., 2005). Older adults are a culturally and ethnically diverse subgroup. For many their long-held religious beliefs, cultural practices, and worldviews may not be aligned with the values of their children or healthcare staff. Thus, issues of competency and independence commonly occur in settings that treat or provide care to older adults. Medical, mental health, and long-term care providers should be prepared to encounter challenging situations where an older adult, their family members, or healthcare staff do not share the same perspective about the best and most ethical way to proceed. In some settings, an ethics board may be in place to help resolve conflicts. In instances where an ethics board is not available, a psychologist may be called in to facilitate these difficult conversations and to negotiate elements of a care plan when opinions about the best course may be varied and strongly held.

To highlight the complexity of common ethical issues and aging, this chapter focuses on four areas that have recently received national media coverage or have engendered considerable discussion in the field of geropsychology. These four areas are: dementia and suicide risk; race, ethnicity, and end of life medical decision-making; lesbian, gay, bisexual, and transgender (LGBT) adults in long-term care settings; and dementia and sexuality. The common ethical theme across these four areas, is the vulnerability of older adults. The aging process, whether normal or abnormal that results in increased vulnerability due to loss of cognitive or physical functioning, can raise concerns and challenges regarding an older person's right to independently behave, choose, and do what they please without question. A guide for applying core ethical principles to difficult and often evolving situations is offered as one method that can be used to facilitate decision-making. The core ethical principles are reviewed and then applied to each of the four case vignettes presented below.

Core Ethical Principles

The American Psychological Association (APA) Ethics Code identifies five core values or principles for psychologists: (a) beneficence (i.e., to protect) and nonmaleficence (i.e., not to harm); (b) fidelity and responsibility; (c) integrity; (d) justice; and (e) respect

for rights and dignity (APA, 2010). Although each of these principles informs professional conduct, many ethical dilemmas are not choices between right and wrong, but
among competing ethical principles with the goal of doing good. This chapter will focus
on three of the five ethical principles that are shared by a majority of health care
professionals who work in clinical settings: (1) beneficence (Principle A); (2) fidelity
(Principle B); and (3) respect for rights and dignity in regard to autonomy (Principle E)
(Schwiebert, Myers, & Dice, 2000). Beneficence is the concept of providing protection
and producing a positive outcome or benefit. Fidelity is concerned with the quality of
the relationship between the psychologist and the older adult. Ideally, it is one that is
based on trust and the confidence that the psychologist will act in their best interest.
Autonomy is self-determination and includes the right to make life-affecting decisions
and choices. The overarching goal is to promote dignity and take appropriate action that
is in the best interest of the older adult. This chapter also includes APA Ethics Code
standards that are applicable.

Given that most treatment teams are composed of a variety of disciplines and are
now standard in many health care settings, using shared common ethical principles
as a way to consider complex ethical dilemmas is helpful. However, there are often
challenges encountered in reconciling or prioritizing the competing demands of the
principles. For example, the desire to support self-determination (i.e., autonomy)
may have to be tempered by the need for beneficence (i.e., protection). In real life,
how does a psychologist proceed when an older adult has a progressive dementia or
begins to behave in a way that is inconsistent with long-held beliefs or past behaviors? When is it best to step in and protect an older adult when that person wants to
be autonomous and rejects your offer of help?

Several models have been developed that describe steps and use a deductive
reasoning process for making ethical decisions (Kaldjian, Weir, & Duffy, 2005).
The steps are not necessarily sequential, but are intended to serve as a guide when
addressing difficult issues where no optimal solution is evident. Steps proposed in
a variety of models include identifying the problem, reviewing the ethical codes,
knowing the laws and regulations, obtaining consultation with peers or supervisor,
identifying how the problem might be resolved, considering the potential outcomes
and consequences of decisions and actions, and taking action or making the decision.
Within each of these steps is a series of smaller steps or considerations. For example,
when carrying out the first step – *identify the problem* – sub-steps could include
determining the nature of the problem (i.e., moral, professional, legal, clinical, or
a combination), identifying who could provide consultation, and understanding what
are the beliefs and preferences of your patient and their family members.
The following vignettes demonstrate how ethical principles could be used to inform
clinical decisions when addressing complex situations.

Dementia and Suicide Risk

As more people live longer with chronic conditions and progressive neurological diseases, a growing number of patients want to talk about their options for

living and dying. At present, health care proxy forms and living wills are routinely offered to patients in health care settings. However, end-of-life planning is rapidly expanding beyond choices about where a person wants to die (e.g., home, nursing home, hospital) and under what circumstances (e.g., hospice, pain management, life-sustaining treatment) to include discussions about the right to make death-hastening decisions and how to end one's life. From media reports, it appears that an increasing number of people are exploring options for ending their life with dignity. How dignity is defined varies by person. For some, it consists of decisions about feeding tubes and comfort care. For others, it involves a plan to end their life when their mind and body reach a stage where planned and organized activity becomes increasingly difficult to initiate and carry out. As the detection of cognitive decline at ever-earlier stages of dementia continues to improve with the advent of new screening tools and neuroimaging techniques, but the disease remains incurable, psychologists should be prepared to talk with patients who are struggling with difficult life and death decisions.

The Case of Balancing Beneficence, Fidelity, and Dignity

Tom is a 76-year-old, married Caucasian male with three adult children who was referred by his physician for neuropsychological assessment as part of a memory disorders clinic comprehensive evaluation. Tom, with the assistance of his wife, reported a four- to five-year history of worsening memory that included problems with recalling planned activities for the day, mild name-finding and concentration difficulties, getting lost while driving, and increased repetitiveness. Tom currently manages the household finances. However, several months ago, his wife started to review their monthly banking statements to ensure accuracy. She noted that her husband was slower when reconciling their monthly statements and was making computational errors.

During his evaluation, Tom interacted appropriately with the neuropsychologist and was alert, fully oriented to person and location, and mostly oriented to date; he inaccurately stated the day of the week. His comprehension appeared grossly intact, memory for remote events was mostly intact, and recent memory was fair. Tom accurately reported his morning meal, but was unable to recall what he had eaten for dinner the previous evening.

He currently denied feeling depressed or anxious, although he reported low but adequate energy, poor sleep, and less than usual appetite. Compared to premorbid abilities in the high average range, results of his neuropsychological evaluation indicated impairments in verbal memory. Given his high level of premorbid functioning, Tom reported that he had been able to compensate for his memory difficulties for quite some time. He disclosed that he planned to take his life should his memory problems worsen or if he is diagnosed with Alzheimer's disease. He owns a handgun and intends to use it when "the time is right." He is concerned about becoming a burden on his wife and does not want the psychologist to share his suicide plan with his wife or the memory disorder clinic treatment team.

One week later during the feedback session, Tom learned he had been diagnosed with a mild neurocognitive disorder and was again assessed for suicide risk. Once more, he admitted to having a plan to end his life, but refused to allow the psychologist to disclose any of this information to his family, including his wife. Although the neuropsychologist has a limited role in the clinical care of Tom, he feels very conflicted, as he wants to tell Tom's wife about her husband's suicidal thoughts and plan. He really believes that doing so is in the best interest of Tom to keep him safe and to obtain the necessary support to help him cope with his diagnosis and feelings of depression, anxiety, and suicidal ideation.

Discussion

On the basis of the core ethical principles presented above, what are your first considerations? First and foremost, Tom's safety and his best interest must be maintained. Based on a variety of assessments, the treatment team's opinion is that it is highly likely that Tom has a progressive neurological disorder that will worsen in time. Their goal is to maintain beneficence (i.e., take action in the best interest of Tom), fidelity (i.e., trust in the relationship with the psychologist and treatment team members), and Tom's dignity while protecting him from harm.

At the start of the evaluation, the neuropsychologist should have described the limits of confidentiality (see APA Standards 4.01 Maintaining Confidentiality and 4.02 Discussing the Limits of Confidentiality) and explained to Tom that the treatment team members would have access to all his records (6.02 Documentation of Professional and Scientific Work and Maintenance of Records), because they are integral in diagnosis and treatment planning. The neuropsychologist should remind Tom of their earlier discussion about the limits of confidentiality as it pertains to sharing information with the treatment team and his wife. It would be optimal to have Tom independently decide to share this information with his wife and his children. Because this can be a difficult discussion to have with a loved one, the neuropsychologist should offer to meet with Tom, his wife, and family members together to discuss his prognosis and begin to develop a care plan for the future. Although the neuropsychologist should strive to preserve the rights and dignity of Tom, the best course of action is one that creates the best outcomes for the greatest number of people. Tom, his wife, and his children are involved and each will be directly affected by his decision to end his life.

It is useful to compare the two options the neuropsychologist has to consider: the choice of keeping Tom's suicidal ideation a secret or sharing that he is at risk with others. Keeping his suicide plan a secret from others may eventually result in Tom's death. Keeping in confidence his suicidal thoughts is technically in line with the ethical Principle E of respect for the rights and dignity to autonomy. Currently, there does not seem to be an imminent threat for harm to self. Thus, the limits of confidentiality would not apply. But in the future, if Tom takes his life, it would only benefit him because this action satisfies his desire to die on his own terms.

However, research suggests that suicide has both short- and long-term negative effects on family and medical staff alike (Cerel, Jordan, & Duberstein, 2008; Cvinar,

2005; Hendin, Lipschitz, Maltsberger, Haas, & Wynecoop, 2000). In the aftermath of a suicide, clinicians and family members are likely to feel upset, as well as feelings of guilt, shame, and grief (Brown, Bongar, & Cleary, 2004). Notably, Tom may feel conflicted about taking his life because he did share this information with the neuropsychologist. At minimum, this disclosure would indicate a cry for help.

The neuropsychologist should refer Tom to a psychologist for therapy to further discuss these issues. The possible outcomes from sharing his plan with others is that Tom's suicide would be prevented, his death delayed, and his wife and family provided an opportunity to enjoy his company as well as plan for the future. Although protection prolongs Tom's life and maintains his safety, which benefits both his family and his treatment team, his autonomy and dignity will be compromised if this information is shared against his will (see also Standard 4.05 Disclosures). Consulting with the members of the memory disorder clinic team can help identify next steps, address ethical issues, and enhance the quality of care received by Tom.

Recommendations

1. The neuropsychologist should, as part of the informed consent process, describe the limits of confidentiality and fully explain to Tom that treatment team members would have access to his records because they are integral in diagnosis and treatment planning. If memory problems are an issue, Tom should be consistently reminded.

2. When weighing confidentiality and safety, seek the consultation of the treatment team or a supervisor. When conflicting ethics make decision-making difficult, especially when there is a threat to safety, it is best to discuss with colleagues even if it means asking for advice in a hypothetical situation. It is difficult for any psychologist to comfortably arrive at a reasoned decision alone. Consultation can verify if the intended course of action is the better choice or provide another perspective or alternative solutions.

3. The neuropsychologist should suggest therapy to Tom and his wife. Even if the psychologist decides not to share Tom's suicidal thoughts as the reason for this referral, the therapy may help both Tom and his wife cope with the diagnosis and cognitive decline. It would also hopefully provide an opportunity for Tom to better cope with his memory difficulties and work though his feelings of depression and anxiety. Therapy may help bring Tom's suicidal thoughts into the open and reduce his desire to die by suicide.

Racial, Ethnic, and Cultural Considerations with End-of-Life Discussions and Advanced Care Planning

Knowledge of research-informed strategies (Standard 2.04 Bases for Scientific and Professional Judgments) for engaging in end-of-life discussions, understanding of state laws that pertain to advanced care directives, and awareness of commonly encountered ethical issues are critical when working with older adults who are close to the end of their lives. It is also crucial to consider religious, cultural, and ethnic differences that can influence medical decision-making. For some older adults, the value of personal autonomy may not be as important as the family's opinion of what to do. This next case illustrates the dilemma of divergent family opinions complicating the older adult's right to deny treatment with or without family consensus.

The Case of Questioning the Right to Choose to Not Pursue Treatment

Juana is a 79-year-old woman who emigrated from Mexico with her husband and two small children when she was in her late 20s. When her husband died three years ago, she moved into an assisted living facility. She is close to her two married daughters who visit her several times a week. Juana has worked most of her life cleaning homes to help support her family in the United States and in Mexico. Her ability to speak English is fair and she is not literate in Spanish or in English. She also has limited vision as a complication of poorly controlled diabetes mellitus and peripheral vascular disease.

A surgical consultant recently recommended a right-side below-the-knee amputation for nonhealing ulcers and wet gangrene of the right leg. Juana not only refuses to consent to the surgery – she is also unwilling to discuss her need for the surgery with the surgeon or staff. She repeatedly tells the surgeon that she has had a good life and that her health is in the "hands of God." The surgeon wonders if Juana has the capacity to make medical decisions and expresses concern about her choice not to accept treatment. He refers her for psychological evaluation to determine her capacity for medical decision-making.

The psychologist conducting the capacity evaluation speaks fluent Spanish and is able to converse with Juana in her preferred language. She reviews Juana's medical chart, conducts an intake interview, and learns about her history and beliefs. Juana confides that she feels sad and lonely most of the day. She reports that she has stopped attending church services and is eating more meals alone in her room. She also notes that her daughters do not agree with her decision about the amputation surgery. Both daughters advocate for the surgery and argue that their mother should use all available life-sustaining interventions. The psychologist listens attentively to her history and administers the Aid to Capacity Evaluation. When the therapist is alone with the patient, Juana talks about the difficulty in standing up to her daughters because of her choice not to have surgery. She talks about how much she wants her daughters to understand and support her decision.

As the psychologist writes her report, she struggles with writing the conclusion section. She is keenly aware that her recommendations will strongly influence Juana's ability to refuse treatment, despite the pleas of her daughters and her physician. The psychologist recently went through a similar situation with her own mother, who refused bypass surgery and passed away about two years ago. She is aware of her "emotional tug" in this case, but wants to make sure that she maintains her objectivity as she writes her report.

Discussion

Older Mexican–Americans are more likely to rely on family and professional opinion for end-of-life decisions (e.g., Blackhall et al., 1995). In this instance, it may be challenging to elicit an autonomous decision about treatment from Juana. Although psychologists strive to work collaboratively with their patients to foster independent decision-making to the greatest degree possible, each older adult will want to participate in their care in their own way. However, regardless of cultural differences, some patients may be more passive than desired.

It is not unusual for people who are close to death to want to defer to others to make decisions because it is too effortful to make a choice, because they feel pressured by divergent family opinions, or because they are in pain, feel ill, or are fatigued. In contrast to Juana, other older adult minority subgroups may desire an aggressive treatment approach because of their fear of abandonment, worries about receiving suboptimal medical care, or limited understanding of palliative options despite strong evidence of poor outcomes. Taking time to discuss various options along with a description of the risks and benefits associated with each is a respectful way to proceed. Trust influences the ability to have a meaningful dialogue about advance directives, end-of-life considerations, and palliative care.

At minimum, a capacity assessment for medical decision-making and an evaluation for depression should be conducted by the psychologist. If Juana no longer has capacity to make medical decisions (Standard 3.10 Informed Consent), in order to uphold the ethical principle of beneficence, a surrogate should be selected to make medical decisions and advocate for the benefit of Juana. In this instance, serving as a surrogate might be particularly challenging because Juana's daughters strongly oppose their mother's choice to forgo surgery. The belief that withdrawing life support is a sin or the desire not to lose a parent can result in children keeping their parents alive even when an advance directive is available that clearly states their choices. However, artificial nutrition and hydration are medical treatments and may be withheld or withdrawn under the same conditions as any other form of medical treatment.

In end-stage disease, when the number and intensity of life-sustaining interventions are likely to increase, patients will often decide to discontinue treatment or nourishment. Not surprisingly, this can be disturbing and distressing to some family members, as well as to treating physicians and psychologists. For patients, their families, and clinicians, the proximity to death in a medical setting intensifies the encounter. Treatment no longer offers hope and the possibility of a cure. The discussion shifts to comfort care and when to limit or forgo life-sustaining support. Adult children have different abilities to provide for the needs of their parents. Yet adult children are often placed in precarious situations because they are limited in their understanding of the implications of the treatment choices they are being asked to consider (Standard 3.10 Informed Consent), distressed at being unable to provide comfort and care to a dying parent, and contending with siblings who may disagree and fight regarding end-of-life choices. Moreover, many health care settings providing care to dying people lack the resources necessary to adequately address and manage an array of emotional, social, spiritual, and clinical issues.

Recommendations

1. The psychologist should have ongoing discussions to highlight changes in medical status, explain the trajectory of the illness, and describe possible interventions. These should take place with Juana and her children at regular intervals. Patients and family members need sufficient information to make informed choices.

2. Many states have reached agreements that competent patients have a constitutional and common-law right to refuse treatment. However, there is variability in state laws. It is advantageous to be familiar with your state's legal requirements before a situation arises. Legal, ethical, and moral choices may be different, and those affected may place a priority on one aspect over another.

3. In the case of Juana, the psychologist's responsibility is to support and maximize the autonomy of Juana while recognizing the emotional distress of her children. The psychologist should make ethical decisions *with* Juana, not *for* Juana.

4. Finally, the psychologist should be keenly aware of personal bias due to her experiences with her own mother. Her objectivity is in question. Alternatively, even if she is aware of her bias and appreciates the need for her to remain objective, she could be at risk of overcompensating in favor of Juana. To help mitigate this type of response, the psychologist could first look at the data and the Aid to Capacity Evaluation score (Etchells et al., 1999). The psychologist should also consult with her colleagues about the issues between Juana and her daughters, as well as with her own experience with her mother. If the psychologist and her colleagues or supervisor can arrive at a shared conclusion regarding the patient's capacity to refuse treatment, it would offer reassurance of objectivity.

LGBT Adults in Long-Term Care Settings

The Case of Choosing to Be Open or Not About Who You Are

Abbey is a 75-year-old Asian–American woman whose health has been steadily worsening due to Parkinson's disease (PD). Professionally, she worked as a librarian at her local public library. Although she retired at age 67, she continued to volunteer at the library for a few hours per week until she developed significant symptoms of PD. She has lived with her partner, Carol, a 72-year-old white woman, for 15 years in a small apartment. Carol has been struggling to take care of Abbey for the past five months. Due to the high costs and unreliability of employing an in-home caregiver coupled with the increased physical demands of helping Abbey with her daily activities, they both decided that Abbey should move to a nearby nursing home. The facility is conveniently located within walking distance from their home.

When going through the application process of being admitted, they consciously decided not to disclose their relationship, fearing that Abbey would not be accepted. For the first few weeks, all went well and no one suspected that they were partners in a significant and enduring relationship. As Carol visited almost every day, within a couple of months, the residents and staff soon realized that the women were partners. Abbey and Carol started noticing passing whispers about them and some stares from staff and residents. They began to feel uncomfortable. A couple of weeks later, one of the male residents began making ongoing rude and hostile comments in a loud voice, such as, "Their kind is not welcome here," and that their relationship "is a sin." The male resident has been at the nursing home for over five years, and until now has not been a problem for staff or with other residents. The administrator and director of nursing spoke to the staff and the resident about his remarks to Abbey, but not much changed as a result. Carol wants Abbey to stay in the nursing home because it is only a few blocks from her home and she believes that the physical care provided to Abbey is relatively good. Carol is increasingly frustrated that more has not been done in the nursing home to improve Abbey's social environment. Although Carol feels bullied by the male resident, she is also worried that if she makes too many complaints, Abbey would not be treated as well as the other residents when Carol is not around. Neither Abbey nor Carol feel safe to openly admit to the importance of their relationship.

A psychologist is called in by the nursing home administrator to help Abbey adjust to the nursing home. The nursing home staff feel that they are faced with an ethical dilemma of wanting to be fair to Abbey and Carol, but also giving consideration to the strong religious beliefs of the long-term male resident who does not approve of same-sex relationships. Abbey is open to working with the psychologist as she is struggling to fit in at her new home environment, but also feels anxious and fearful of discrimination. Because of her fears, she states that she does not want to disclose that she is lesbian.

Discussion

All three APA principles – beneficence, fidelity, and respect for rights and dignity in regard to autonomy – need to be addressed in this situation. Consider what is in the best interest of Abbey. The psychologist's responsibility and respect toward Abbey are what help guide her decisions regarding her desire for privacy in terms of receiving treatment, as well as her relationship with Carol. Fidelity and respect of rights are also the basis of advocacy. To address that issue, providing in-service training to enhance the cultural competency of nursing home staff caring for older LGBT adults and, if possible, offering education to the residents and the larger nursing home community could be beneficial.

There are legal regulations that prevent discrimination based on sexual orientation and identity. The Fair Housing Act of the federal Department of Housing and Urban Development prohibits discrimination of residents in long-term care institutions (Department of Housing and Urban Development, 2010). However, despite these regulations, there are still reports of perceived or actual incidences of discrimination of older LGBT adults in nursing homes and other long-term care institutions. A survey conducted by several community organizations examined experiences of discrimination of older LGBT adults living or wanting access to long-term care facilities in 284 older LGBT adult and 485 social support persons (e.g., family, friends, social service providers) (Barrington, 2011). Part of the survey asked if "[they], a loved one or a patient ever experienced any of the following because of actual or perceived sexual orientation and/or gender identity." The three most frequently reported experiences were "verbal or physical harassment from other residents" (23 percent), "refused admission, readmission, or attempted abrupt discharge" (20 percent), and "verbal or physical harassment from staff" (14 percent). When asked whether older LGBT adults could be open with facility staff, only 22 percent of LGBT respondents answered "yes." Another question asked, "Has the staff of a long-term care facility that you, a loved one or a patient has lived in ever done any of the following because of actual or perceived sexual orientation or gender identity?" The most common reported incidences were "attempted discharges" (58 percent) and "admission refusal" (50 percent).

As mental health providers, we have to consider the ethical issues that we may face in this situation. First is the privacy issue. What if the older LGBT adult preferred to "stay in the closet" and not disclose his or her sexual orientation? In the vignette, Abbey is very hesitant to disclose her relationship with Carol to the staff and residents of her nursing home. Being back in the closet can be isolating and anxiety-provoking, and the psychologist should help Abbey work through these issues. If Abbey decides to continue to not disclose her sexual orientation, the psychologist must be keenly mindful to also withhold any information and not make any reference to this to the staff and other residents. However, if advocacy and education is needed or asked of the psychologist, one has to deal with the topic in a very broad sense of individual differences and diversity without referring in any way to Abbey.

Another related issue is the problem of confidentiality in patients seeking or receiving treatment in a long-term care facility. Lichtenberg and colleagues (1998) wrote an article on the "Standards for Psychological Services in Long-Term Care Facilities." Similar to the ethics of confidentiality (4.01 Maintaining Confidentiality), they stated that psychologists should "try to ensure that psychological services are provided in the most private manner possible" (p. 126). The authors mentioned that this is more difficult in long-term care facilities, especially because many facilities do not have a separate room for private sessions and the patient may be sharing their room with another patient. Thus, creativity may be needed to provide as much privacy and confidentiality as possible. For instance, we could ask the roommate if they would be willing to leave the room and then conduct the session with the door closed. We could also notify the staff so that the session is not interrupted. As always, psychologists must be aware of and follow the regulations of the facility and government regulations concerning privacy of treatment. They also recommended that, before treatment starts, the patient be consulted about privacy accommodations and their requests be honored as best as possible.

Other activities that the psychologist can do at the nursing home involve advocacy and education. As psychologists, we can educate the staff and residents. We can also help monitor the emotions and beliefs that are expressed by the residents and staff of long-term care facilities. However, in Abbey's situation, there is a conflict of interest between her and at least one of the residents and possibly with the staff. Thus, the psychologist must be aware of and sensitive to these conflicts. A question can be asked as to whether a psychologist should offer education or other psychological services to residents and staff in general if that has not been directly asked of them. Lichtenberg and colleagues (1998) stated that self-referral is acceptable if staff perceive a need for such services. In the case of Abbey and Carol, there is a need, as tensions between residents can create a negative social environment. Since the nursing home administrator requested that the psychologist help Abbey, the psychologist is better able to extend the scope of that help to include advocacy and education. Lichtenberg et al. (1998) also talked about the ethics of advocacy to "improve the quality of life" (p.126). Educating staff and residents should include how to work through conflict and to recommit to respect for all residents, no matter their background. In psychology, "cultural competency" is a term used as a training goal to help providers understand and integrate cultural considerations in the treatment of their patients. In this case, the cultural competency of older sexual minorities involves understanding the discrimination fears of older LGBT adults in long-term care settings (e.g., Jackson et al., 2008). Education approaches to enhancing cultural competency in the nursing home staff can include efforts to increase knowledge of health disparities in LGBT communities, facilitate lectures or small group discussions on LGBT terminology, and offer case presentations involving LGBT patients (Rutherford, McIntyre, Daley, & Ross, 2012).

However, if the patient wishes for her sexual orientation to remain private, the psychologist should respect that decision. This does not mean that the psychologist cannot work to improve the social environment of the facility. The psychologist can still advocate for mutual respect for all residents and staff. Educational offerings can focus on cultural diversity and differences in general. They can also include teaching the staff and residents practical ways to resolve conflict in their facility, whether it be between residents or between residents and staff.

Recommendations

1. The psychologist should address the issues of privacy of sexual orientation with the patient and also acknowledge the potential issues of isolation and fear of not being accepted by other residents and staff. If the patient continues to keep her sexual orientation private, the psychologist must respect this decision, whether or not she agrees with this decision.
2. The psychologist should try her best to maintain the confidentiality of conducting therapy in a long-term care facility. Any special accommodations to procedures or space that may limit confidentiality (reserving a room with staff to meet with a patient) should be openly addressed with the patient, but assurances and efforts should be made to keep the content of therapy confidential. Use of a noise machine is often helpful.
3. If possible, the psychologist should advocate for the rights of her patient and educate staff and residents to work through conflict and to recommit to respect for all residents, no matter their background. But if the patient wants to keep the issue

private, the psychologist is encouraged to still help and think about advocacy and education more broadly to deal with issues of mutual respect and find practical ways to address or resolve conflicts within the long-term care facility.

Dementia and Sexuality: Capacity to Consent to Continued Sexual Relations

The Case of Sex and Dementia

Steven, a 75-year-old Hispanic man, has been married for 35 years to his wife, Christina, a 74-years-old woman. They have two grown children and three grand-children. They have lived happily together in their home for most of their marriage. Five years ago, when Christina was developing memory problems, she was diagnosed with Alzheimer's disease. Although her symptoms have been steadily progressing, she still lives at home with help from her husband and paid caregivers.

A multidisciplinary treatment team is conducting their annual assessment of Christina to develop a treatment plan for providing medical care and support at home. As a psychologist, you conducted a Mini-Mental State Examination on Christina. She scores 5 out of 30 points. She is not oriented to person, place, or time, no longer recognizes her family or caregivers, and rarely speaks. When her husband is asked if she verbally or non verbally consents to sexual activity, he states, "Of course, she is my wife!" When you try to talk with Christina about it, she simply nods and says "yes" softly, no matter the question. When she is with her husband, you notice that she is relaxed and seems to be happy when he is near her.

Discussion

This situation is similar to the 2015 case of Senator Henry Rayhons, who was charged with sexual assault of his wife, Donna Lou Rayhons. Donna had severe dementia and was engaging in sexual relations with her husband in the nursing home despite ongoing concerns raised by staff (Pishko, 2015). In the end, this legal case was dismissed. But the dismissal did not provide clear insight into the ethical decision-making of whether a sexual relationship with a patient with dementia should be allowed or not. Clearly, his wife did not have the competency to consent. What is less clear is if lack of capacity to consent constitutes a possible abuse that health providers are mandated to protect against.

The current scenario is complicated by the fact that Christina still lives at home and has had a long and happy marriage. The husband, Steven, is still in charge of her care with the help of full-time caregivers. Since the husband is the caregiver with legal guardianship, do the issues of need for consent and the safety of Christina become even more salient? Since her everyday well-being is monitored by the husband, should the criteria be more or less strict?

His wife also seems to be more responsive that Senator Henry's wife. Thus, the issue of competency can be perceived to be more uncertain as the issue of ability to provide sexual consent is put more into question. There have been several comments about the guidelines to determine competency to consent to sexual relations (e.g., Lyden, 2007; Metzger & Gillick, 2002; Wilkins, 2015). At the same time, although there is cognitive decline in dementia in the long run, cognitive functioning can fluctuate over time.

Another ethical issue involves the concepts of independence, autonomy, and intrusiveness. How much and when should the psychologist or interdisciplinary team intrude in the privacy of this married couple? Some would say it starts when competency to consent in general is called into question. As cognition declines, the need for oversight, assessment, and intervention increases (Wilkins, 2015).

On a related note, at what point does competency play a role in a married couple's ability to continue sexual relations? One approach to answering this question is to talk about the issues of safety and competency as early possible, hopefully before Christina's dementia is so severe that the she cannot meaningfully engage in the discussion and disclose her preferences. By addressing it earlier, it would plant the seed for the husband to process the situation, understand the limitations of his wife to consent to sexual activity, and have time to prepare for the time when they would need to stop. Unfortunately, it seems too late for this to be addressed with Christina, but it is not too late with the husband.

So, then, how does one assess capacity to consent to sexual activity in patients with dementia? What level of capacity is needed? Should it be set at as high a capacity standard as medical or legal decisions? There is some debate about the strictness or conservativeness of the standard for this issue (e.g., Casta-Kaufteil, 2004; Wilkins, 2015). Nevertheless, some have tried to create a model or guidelines for capacity assessment. Wilkins (2015) integrates several assessment models by stating six criteria for sexual consent: (1) voluntariness, (2) safety, (3) no exploitation, (4) no physical or psychological abuse, (5) ability to say no either verbally or nonverbally, and (6) socially appropriate time and place (p. 719).

Once competency is in serious question or if the person with dementia is deemed incapable to provide consent, are there alternative decision-making procedures that are ethical to enable a couple to continue sexual relations? It has been suggested that people with dementia who are living in a long-term care facility should not make the decision alone, but have a team or committee to advocate on behalf of the person regarding the appropriateness to continue sexual relations with their spouse (Wilkins, 2015). This committee would consist of health providers and family members. In the case of Steven and Christina, the committee would consist of the treatment team and family members, such as adult children. Wilkins recommended that the biases of both types of members be openly acknowledged and for them to remain mindful of these biases when making decisions regarding continued sexual expression. For the family, while they may know or think they know what is best for the person with dementia (Christina), they may struggle with acknowledging or accepting sexual behaviors expressed by their parents. Moreover, adult children may not make decisions that accurately reflect their mother's wishes or preferences. As for the treatment team, although they may have the medical and formal experience of working with patients with dementia who are "obligated to provide for the patient's autonomy and best interests," they may still be persuaded by the family opinions due to fears of liability (p. 721).

Wilkins also stressed the importance of clarifying the reasons or factors upon which the advocacy decision should be based. Harvey (2006) wrote a paper on advance directives of patients with dementia and suggested that substituted judgment (advanced directives) and the best interest standard should both be simultaneously considered with advocacy decision-making. If we apply this approach to this vignette, then the advocacy committee for Christina already likely has a general understanding of the need for substitutive judgment. What is more questionable, however, is the determination of "best interest standard." Harvey defined this as "the 'uniqueness' of dementia and worries over unwarranted medical risk" (p. 56). He clarified that the "Best Interest Standard is agent neutral: what matters most is securing the best medical outcome possible for the incompetent patient in question" (p. 57).

In conclusion, we can draw from past articles about ethical recommendations of setting procedures to determine capacity to consent in the engagement of sexual relations, monitor that capacity periodically, and make recommends with the family members to continue or discontinue sexual relations. These recommendations keep in mind the APA principles of what is in the best interest of the patient (beneficence), the responsibility to keep the patient safe (fidelity), and respecting the rights and dignity of married older couples to engage in sexual relations. However, these recommendations are usually meant for nursing homes or other long-term care facilities, where the activities of the patients are well-monitored and are better monitored by formal health providers compared to the people with dementia living at home.

Recommendations

1. If the patient with dementia is still being taken care of at home, a proactive and diligent stance is needed to address the issue of competency to consent to sexual relations and safety concerns openly with the patient, caregivers, and family members regularly and as early as possible. The psychologist should talk openly to Steven and Christina about sexual activity and the increased need for some oversight if sexual activity will continue so that the respect and dignity of both spouses would always be represented, even as the dementia progresses.

2. As cognition declines, the need for more consistent assessment increases. This assessment for continued sexual activity and safety should also involve reminders to Steven and Christina about why the assessment is being conducted.

3. As part of that oversight, the psychologist should identify a team or committee to advocate on behalf of the person with dementia regarding the appropriateness to continue sexual relations. The team can involve other family members such as the adult children if this is acceptable to the married couple.

Dementia and Sexuality: Dementia and Aggressive Sexual Behavior

The prior ethical case presented the ethical issue of cognitive competency to consent to sexual relations. But what if we flip the scenario? What happens if the patient with dementia is the sexual aggressor? The vignette below describes such a situation and explores what considerations might inform ethical decision-making.

The Case of Partner Disputes

A 74-year-old white male patient, Travis, is referred to you by his physician for possible cognitive issues. He has been with his partner, Greg, who is 63 years old, for 17 years. They are not married. They live in a metropolitan city where most of their close friends ("family") are located. According to Travis, their relationship, for the most part, has been fairly happy. Sometimes, however, their age difference has caused them not to see "eye to eye" on all issues. Travis has had health issues including chronic cardiovascular disease that his doctor suspects is affecting his cognition and behavior. Travis recently lost his driver's license for driving the wrong way on a one-way street, which resulted in a car accident and caused injury to himself as well as the other driver. Travis also reports that he has been forgetting things more often, but notes he has been able to deal with it fine. Travis says that he does not worry about these issues because Greg has always been helpful in "getting [him] through any problems."

When talking with his partner, Greg, the psychologists finds out that Travis is having more memory problems and confusion than what Travis reported. He now has to help Travis with managing his medication and driving him to his appointments. Greg also mentions changes in Travis's personality. He reports that Travis more easily loses his temper and can be aggressive. When the psychologist asks for more information about this, Greg states that Travis does not hit or kick, but that he can be verbally aggressive and sometimes sexually aggressive. Greg states that although he still loves Travis, he sometimes does not feel safe or respected by him. Greg states that they are still having sexual relations.

Greg asks if the medications can be adjusted to help with some of Travis's behavioral problems. He asks the psychologist to talk with Travis to get his advice about seeking medication adjustments. In her initial interview with Travis, he admits to memory problems and that his anxiety and fears about it have made him increasingly "moody" and "edgy." When the psychologist talks about Greg's concerns to better understand Travis's awareness of the issue, Travis verbally lashes out at him about sexual discrimination. The psychologist is caught off guard and apologizes for causing Travis distress.

Discussion

Elder abuse has been defined as a deliberate act that can cause physical, emotional, or psychological harm to an older adult (APA, 2012). At this point, Greg's situation does not seem to be as serious as elder abuse. However, proactive steps are needed to prevent the situation from becoming worse. In this vignette, the person with dementia, Travis, seems to be the aggressor. We know that as dementia progresses there is increased risk for changes in executive functioning that can affect judgment, psychosocial behaviors, or personality (Duke & Kaszniak, 2000). But at what point do these changes warrant reevaluation of medications? Furthermore, how much does the threat of discrimination affect our decision to recommend or not recommend a medication evaluation?

Adjustments to treatment, such as medication, to manage behaviors can be perceived by the patient as a threat, and in Travis's case was perceived as discrimination. For older gay men who have spent a great deal of their life facing discrimination due to their sexual orientation (Balsam & D'Augelli, 2006), they may perceive negative comments or questions about their sexual activity as discrimination, even in medical or mental health settings (e.g., Malebranche, Peterson, Fullilove, & Stackhouse, 2004; Stein, 2001). In this vignette, Travis, due to his cognitive decline, is less likely to be aware of how his behavior affects Greg. Furthermore, he would have significant difficulties in understanding that the psychologist's questions about his behaviors, including sexual behaviors, toward Greg were with the intention to understand Travis's perceptions of recent events, rather than to question or judge his sexual orientation.

Building trust may not be sufficient if the dementia has progressed to more negative thinking or negative delusions. Again, the issue of competency of the person can compromise the psychologist's ability to help Travis and Greg without medication. But this is also complicated by the perceptions of discrimination due to sexual orientation (see 3.04 Avoiding Harm). What are some of the ethical principles to help the psychologist ensure that he is indeed not biased, especially if he identifies as heterosexual? APA (2012) reminds us of Principle E to reduce bias and provides the guideline to recognize how a psychologist's "attitudes and knowledge about lesbian, gay, and bisexual issues may be relevant to assessment and treatment and seek consultation or make appropriate referrals when indicated" (APA, 2012, p. 15). Being accused of discrimination can be perceived by the psychologist as a professional and personal threat. To help keep this "threat" and potential bias in check, the APA guideline reiterates the importance of understanding the "effects of stigma (i.e., prejudice, discrimination, and violence) and its various contextual manifestations in the lives of lesbian, gay, and bisexual people" (APA, 2012, p. 12). This is especially true when there is an intersection of multiple minority statuses, including ethnicity and age. Older lesbian, gay, and bisexual persons are more likely to have more visits to medical doctors (age effect), but are also more likely to conceal their sexual orientation (cohort effect), resulting in less-than-optimal health care (Fassinger & Arseneau, 2007).

In the case of Travis and Greg, age-related declines in mental health, including cognitive functioning, have resulted in dysfunction in their relationship. Although they are not concealing their romantic relationship, their past personal history of sexual orientation discrimination and even ageism may make them more sensitive and less trusting. Psychologists should strive to understand cohort and age differences in older LGBT persons (see 2.03 Maintaining Competence). The psychologist then needs to properly balance the issues related to aging, sexual orientation, and cognitive functioning with the needs and safety of both Travis and Greg. If Travis does become more aggressive, including more sexually aggressive, the psychologist should help intervene with recommendations to Travis's medical doctor for medication adjustment. But in this intervention the psychologist must be mindful of the diversity of characteristics. Special care should be taken to build trust with both Travis and Greg. Part of building that trust is not just understanding the history and issues of older LGBT adults, but also being able to genuinely connect with them by acknowledging these issues with them and providing unconditional respect. In addition, as much as Travis is cognitively able, the psychologist should help Travis understand the possible need for medication intervention to protect the person he loves, Greg, and to strengthen their relationship as much as possible.

Fortunately, there are many papers on the ethics of working with LGBT patients, including APA guidelines from 2012. Unfortunately, there is less discussion about how to work with LGBT patients, especially if the patient has declining cognitive abilities. Thus, approaching this case to include the APA principles of beneficence, fidelity, and respect for rights and dignity in regard to autonomy, in addition to multiple standards, should continue to guide the psychologist in understanding, respecting, and treating Travis.

Recommendations

1. If a psychologist is accused of discrimination, be mindful that this can be perceived as a professional and personal threat, and this "threat" and potential bias must be in check. Thus, seek consultation or supervision with colleagues or supervisors and openly talk about reactions to the accusations, ability to continue to work affectively with the patient, and making decisions about approaches to address discrimination concerns with the patient.
2. The psychologist should build trust and understanding before taking action or making decisions, and should actively and genuinely connect with the patient by acknowledging sensitive issues of LGBT discrimination, competency, and safety while providing unconditional respect.
3. The psychologist should strive to understand cohort and age differences in older LGBT persons and balance the issues related to aging, sexual orientation, and cognitive functioning with the needs and safety of the patient and relevant family members. As part of obtaining that knowledge, the psychologist should seek consultation of professionals with experience or expertise in working with older LGBT adults if possible.
4. The psychologist should talk as openly as possible about the potential need for medication to help with mood and/or behavioral issues. The psychologist should try to help Travis understand that medication intervention may help with his mood and "edginess" and that it may also help strengthen his relationship with Greg.

Conclusion

Vulnerability in late life is related to issues of health, functioning (e.g., ability to perform instrumental and basic activities of daily living), and competence to make independent decisions. Psychologists frequently encounter difficult choices concerning what is best for their patients. What older adults choose for themselves may not always be in unison with what family members or the treatment team believe is the best course of action. Even among culturally similar older adults, cultural values and belief systems may be radically different. Use of an ethical decision-making process can provide guidance when a good or optimal action is not readily evident.

References

American Psychological Association (2010). American Psychological Association Ethical Principles of Psychologists and Code of Conduct. Retrieved from www.apa.org/ethics/code/index.aspx

American Psychological Association (2012). Elder abuse and neglect: In search of solutions. Retrieved from www.apa.org/pi/aging/resources/guides/elder-abuse.aspx

American Psychological Association (2012). Guidelines for psychological practice with lesbian, gay, and bisexual clients. *American Psychologist, 67,* 10–42.

Balsam, K. F. & D'Augelli, A. R. (2006). The victimization of older LGBT adults: Patterns, impact, and implications for intervention. In D. Kimmel, T. Rose, S. David, D. Kimmel, T. Rose, & S. David (Eds.), *Lesbian, gay, bisexual, and transgender aging: Research and clinical perspectives* (pp. 110–130). New York, NY: Columbia University Press.

Barrington, V. (2011). LGBT older adults in long-term care facilities: Stories from the field. Health disparities, Nursing homes. Retrieved from www.justiceinaging.org/lgbt-older-adults-in-long-term-care-facilities-stories-from-the-field

Blackhall, L. J., Murphy, S. T., Frank, G., Michel, V., & Azen, S. (1995). Ethnicity and attitudes toward patient autonomy. *JAMA: Journal of the American Medical Association, 274,* 820–825.

Brown, L. M., Bongar, B., & Cleary, K. M. (2004). A profile of psychologists' views of critical risk factors for completed suicide in older adults. *Professional Psychology: Research and Practice, 35,* 90.

Casta-Kaufteil, A. (2004). The old & the restless: Mediating rights to intimacy for nursing home residents with cognitive impairments. Michigan State University College of Law: *The Journal of Medicine and Law, 8,* 69–86.

Cerel, J., Jordan, J. R., & Duberstein, P. R. (2008). The impact of suicide on the family. *Crisis: The Journal of Crisis Intervention and Suicide Prevention, 29,* 38–44.

Colby, S. L. & Ortman, J. M. (2015). *Projections of the size and composition of the U.S. population: 2014 to 2060, Current Population Reports, P25-1143.* Washington, DC: U.S. Census Bureau.

Cvinar, J. G. (2005). Do suicide survivors suffer social stigma: A review of the literature. *Perspectives in Psychiatric Care, 41,* 14–21.

Department of Housing and Urban Development (2010). HUD issues guidance on LGBT housing, discrimination complaints, HUD press release no. 10-139. Retrieved from https://archives.hud.gov/news/2010/pr10-139.cfm

Doll, G. M. (2013). Sexuality in nursing homes: Practice and policy. *Journal of Gerontological Nursing, 39*, 30–37.

Duke, L. M. & Kaszniak, A. W. (2000). Executive control functions in degenerative dementias: A comparative review. *Neuropsychology Review, 10*, 75–99.

Etchells, E., Darzins, P., Silberfeld, M., et al. (1999). Assessment of patient capacity to consent to treatment. *Journal of General Internal Medicine, 14*, 27–34.

Fassinger, R. E. & Arseneau, J. R. (2007). *"I'd rather get wet than be under that umbrella": Differentiating among lesbian, gay, bisexual, and transgender people.* Washington, DC: American Psychological Association.

Ferri, C.P., Prince, M., Brayne, C., et al. (2005). Global prevalence of dementia: A Delphi consensus study. *The Lancet, 366*, 2112–2117.

Gary, L., Stein, K. A., & Bonuck, K. (2001). Original research: Physician–patient relationships among the lesbian and gay community. *Journal of the Gay and Lesbian Medical Association, 5*, 87–93.

Harvey, M. (2006). Advance directives and the severely demented. *The Journal of Medicine and Philosophy, 31*, 47–64.

Hendin, H., Lipschitz, A., Maltsberger, J. T., Haas, A. P., & Wynecoop, S. (2000). Therapists' reactions to patients' suicides. *American Journal of Psychiatry, 157*, 2022–2027.

Jackson, G. L., Johnson, M. J., & Roberts, R. (2008). The potential impact of discrimination fears of older gays, lesbians, bisexuals and transgender individuals living in small- to moderate-sized cities on long-term health care. *Journal of Homosexuality, 54*, 325–339.

Johnson, M. J. & Roberts, R. (2008). The potential impact of discrimination fears of older gays, lesbians, bisexuals and transgender individuals living in small- to moderate-sized cities on long-term health care. *Journal of Homosexuality, 54*, 325–339.

Kaldjian, L. C., Weir, R. F., & Duffy, T. P. (2005). A clinician's approach to clinical ethical reasoning. *Journal of General Internal Medicine, 20*, 306–311.

Kessler, R. C., Berglund, P., Demler, O., Jin, R., Merikangas, K. R., & Walters, E. E. (2005). Lifetime prevalence and age-of-onset distributions of DSM-IV disorders in the National Comorbidity Survey Replication. *Archives of General Psychiatry, 62*, 593–602.

Lichtenberg, P. A., Smith, M., Frazer, D., et al. (1998). Standards for psychological services in long-term care facilities. *The Gerontologist, 38*, 122–127.

Lyden, R. E. (2007). Assessment of sexual consent capacity. *Sexuality and Disability, 25*, 3–20.

Malebranche, D. J., Peterson, L., Fullilove, R. E., & Stackhouse, R. W. (2004). Race and sexual identity: Perceptions about medical culture and healthcare among black men who have sex with men. *Journal of the National Medical Association, 96*, 97–107.

Metzger, E. D. & Gillick, M. R. (2002). Ethics corner: Cases from the Hebrew Rehabilitation Center for Aged – Sex in the facility. *Journal of the American Medical Directors Association, 3*, 390–392.

National Senior Citizens Law Center (2011). LGBT older adults in long-term care facilities. Retrieved from www.lgbtlongtermcare.org

Pishko, J. (2015). *Pacific Standard.* To have and to hold: Consent and intimacy for people with Alzheimer's. Retrieved from www.psmag.com/health-and-behavior/to-have-and-to-hold-consent-and-intimacy-for-people-with-alzheimers

Rutherford, K., McIntyre, J., Daley, A., & Ross, L. E. (2012). Development of expertise in mental health service provision for lesbian, gay, bisexual and transgender communities. *Medical Education, 46,* 903–913.

SAGE (Services and Advocacy for Gay, Lesbian, Bisexual & Transgender Elders) and Movement Advancement Project (2010). Improving the lives of LGBT older adults. Retrieved from www.sageusa.org and www.lgbtmap.org

Schwiebert, V. L., Myers, J. E., & Dice, C. (2000). Ethical guidelines for counselors working with older adults. *Journal of Counseling & Development, 78,* 123–129.

Stein, K. A. & Bonuck, K. (2001). Original research: Physician–patient relationships among the lesbian and gay community. *Journal of the Gay and Lesbian Medical Association, 5,* 87–93.

United Nations, Department of Economic and Social Affairs, Population Division (2015). World population prospects: The 2015 revision, Volume I: Comprehensive tables. ST/ESA/SER.A/379. Retrieved from www.un.org/en/development/desa/publica tions/world-population-prospects-2015-revision.html

Whitfield, K. & Baker, T. (2013). *Handbook of minority aging.* New York, NY: Springer Publishing Company.

Wilkins, J. M. (2015). More than capacity: Alternatives for sexual decision making for individuals with dementia. *The Gerontologist, 55,* 716–723.

14 Ethical Issues in Working with Individuals with Disability

Jennifer A. Erickson Cornish and Samantha
Pelican Monson

Approximately 57.8 million (18.7 percent) people in the U.S. live with one or more disabilities (U.S. Census, 2010), representing what has been called the largest minority group (Andrews & Lund, 2015). In addition, around 45 percent of people around the globe are living with a chronic health condition that includes disabling features (World Health Organization, 2001). Particularly as the population ages, people may experience disability not only in themselves, but in their friends and relatives (Erickson Cornish, Gorgens, & Pelican Monson, 2008). Clearly, health service psychologists are increasingly likely to be called upon to work with this population (Olkin & Pledger, 2003).

Yet, disability is underrepresented in psychologists and, unlike most other minority groups, has not increased in recent years (Andrews & Lund, 2015). Graduate students with disabilities appear to lack sufficient supervisors/role models with disabilities, and in a recent study (Andrews et al., 2013), 43 percent of students with disabilities reported significant discrimination during their internship or the internship selection process. In combination, a scarcity of mentorship and fear of prejudice may lead students to withhold information about their own disability status, causing further marginalization and limiting opportunities to advance self-awareness in this area. Perhaps because of this, Lund, Andrews, and Holt (2014) found that trainees with disabilities tend to specialize in areas related to disability, such as rehabilitation psychology, where there may be more perceived safety and support.

Education and training for health service psychologists in disability issues has generally focused on "client (vs. community) populations, and intrapsychic (vs. systemic or political) phenomena" within the rehabilitation branch of psychology (Olkin & Pledger, 2003, p. 303). In fact, a 1999 study revealed that the numbers of courses related to disability issues in clinical/counseling psychology programs had decreased from 1989, with only 11 percent of such programs even offering a class, of which only 3 percent included a psychosocial (rather than medical model) focus (Olkin & Pledger, 2003).

Although resources exist on working with those with disabilities, it is unclear whether health psychologists are aware of or use them. For instance, the American Psychological Association (APA) Policy and Planning Board recently considered awareness and utilization of APA guidelines, including those related to disability (e.g., the Guidelines for Multicultural Education, Training, Research, Practice, and Organizational Change for Psychologists [APA, 2003] in which disability is mentioned, the Guidelines for the

Assessment and Intervention with Persons with Disabilities [APA, 2012a], the Guidelines for the Evaluation of Dementia and Age-Related Cognitive Change [APA, 2012b], and the Guidelines for Psychological Practice with Older Adults [APA, 2014]). Unique web page views were considered, along with a survey of employed psychologists and students. The multicultural guidelines and the guidelines for working with persons with disabilities were among the more widely recognized (endorsed by 60 percent or more of the sample), yet they were used by fewer than 50 percent of those who were aware of them (APA Policy and Planning Board, 2005).

Disability has been defined in a variety of ways, including physical or mental impairment that substantially limits one or more major life activities, a record of such impairment, or being regarded as having such an impairment (Americans with Disabilities Act – United States Department of Justice, Civil Rights Division, 2010). However, we consider disability to be an evolving concept that includes "physical, mental, intellectual or sensory impairments that, in the face of negative attitudes or physical obstacles, may prevent those persons from participating fully in society" (United Nations Enable, 2006, Defining Disability section, para. 1). This latter definition seems more in line with the new paradigm of disability as a diversity issue as described by Olkin and Pledger (2003) and their explanation of disability studies as an interdisciplinary field seeking to "legitimize the study of disability as a universal human condition" (p. 296).

July 26, 2015 marked the 25th anniversary of the Americans with Disabilities Act. Although the Act prohibits discrimination in employment and with regard to access, clearly social and attitudinal barriers remain (Puryear Keita, 2015). We earlier focused on the importance of developing and enhancing ethical treatment for persons with disabilities (Erickson Cornish, Gorgens, & Pelican Monson, 2008). In this chapter, we further describe ethical issues related to disability within clinical practice, illustrate these dilemmas with vignettes, comment on emotional/social dimensions, offer some suggestions for dealing with such dilemmas, and conclude with recommendations for the field.

Ethical Issues

The APA Ethical Principles of Psychologists and Code of Conduct (APA, 2010) specifically include disability in four places. In Principle E (Respect for People's Rights and Dignity), disability is listed among 12 diversity statuses ("age, gender, gender identity, race, ethnicity, culture, national origin, religion, sexual orientation, disability, language, and socioeconomic status"). Disability is also mentioned in Standard 2.01b (Boundaries of Competence), where psychologists are required to have or obtain competence related to diversity statuses or to make referrals to those with such competence (except in emergency situations). Standard 3.01 (Unfair Discrimination) prohibits psychologists from engaging in discrimination in their work activities, including discrimination related to disability, while Standard 3.03 (Other Harassment) also specifically mentions disability.

Of course, the entire Ethics Code may be useful in supporting health service psychologists in their work with persons with disabilities. In addition to the Principles and the Standards mentioned above, Standards 2.06 (Personal Problems and Relationships), 3.05 (Multiple Relationships), 3.08 (Exploitative Relationships), 3.10 (Informed Consent), and 4.02 (Discussing the Limits of Confidentiality) may be particularly relevant when treating this population.

Considering the scant graduate training in disability issues and the apparent low use of existing APA resources, we wonder "what if we don't know what we don't know about disability?" (Olkin, 2008, p. 492). If competence includes knowledge, skills, and attitudes, achieving basic competence to serve a disabled population as described in Standard 2.01(b) may currently be only aspirational for many health service psychologists.

Ethics Code Standard 2.06 (Personal Problems and Conflicts) could potentially be relevant to attitudes held by psychologists related to disability issues, whether conscious or implicit. For instance, if a psychologist is overtly accepting of a client with diabetes but flinches internally when the client needs to check his blood sugar in session, the psychologist may be internally conflicted in a variety of ways, including her or his own feelings about medical procedures. Unfair Discrimination (Ethics Code Standard 3.01) could apply in more obvious circumstances, such as when a psychologist simply refuses to treat people with disabilities.

Standard 3.05 (Multiple Relationships) might include potential conflicts when a psychologist is asked to serve in dual roles, potentially due to the dearth of adequate referral sources and community resources with disability competence. For example, a psychologist may be compelled to provide both psychotherapy and psychological assessment for a given client, or a psychologist may feel they need to advocate for a therapy client in their social or employment relationships if the client is experiencing discrimination and is unable to fill this role for themselves, in some cases due to their disability.

The parameters of the therapeutic relationship are also vulnerable if ability status is not appropriately incorporated. Informed consent (Standard 3.10) may be particularly important yet problematic with persons experiencing neurocognitive disabilities. A psychologist may be the first person to identify the extent of this disability, so they may find themselves in a double bind of needing to help the client secure an appropriate legal representative who can provide informed consent, but until such a person is identified, the psychologist may need to support the client in understanding what is occurring and to ensure acute mental health needs are appropriately managed. Similarly, Standard 4.02 (Discussing the Limits of Confidentiality) becomes important with clients who are incapable of giving their own informed consent. In this case, it is crucial to discuss confidentiality not only with the client, but also his/her legal representative. Involvement of another person in an individual client's therapeutic process can alter the treatment course, so the legal representative's role needs to be clarified at the outset and incorporated into the treatment plan. Because persons with disabilities may be at risk of violence and abuse (Hassouneh-Phillips & Curry, 2002; Horner-Johnson & Drum, 2006; Hughes, 2005; Sullivan & Knutson, 2000), Standard 3.08 (Exploitative Relationships) should also be considered. This can occur within or outside the therapeutic context. Exemplifying the former, a psychologist needing income could inadvertently (or purposely) take financial advantage of a client with a cognitive disability by recommending a longer course of therapy than is actually needed. One example of the latter would be a psychologist remaining particularly vigilant when a client with a disability describes an unhealthy relationship, ensuring that dynamics on the spectrum of abuse are identified and appropriately addressed.

The Case of Dr. Kind and Changing Competencies

Dr. Beth Kind is a 40-year-old licensed psychologist in private practice. She has been widowed for several years and is the single parent and sole support for her two young sons. She wrote her dissertation on couples counseling, which became her focus area both during and after graduate school. In fact, her practice consists mainly of couples work, and she meets regularly in a consultation group with colleagues who also mostly treat couples. Despite her busy schedule, Dr. Kind also makes a point of attending continuing education offered by her state psychological association, and particularly tries to attend conferences and workshops related to couples therapy. She has also received some training during and after graduate school related to incorporating diversity (specifically race, ethnicity, and national origin, but not disability issues) into clinical practice.

Jim and Irena Smith had been working with Dr. Kind for about eight months following the revelation that Mr. Smith had been having an affair with another woman. The couple had made considerable progress in counseling, with Mr. Smith ending the affair and expressing considerable remorse and Mrs. Smith learning to trust him again. Since Mrs. Smith had emigrated to the U.S. from Russia five years prior to meeting her husband, Dr. Kind also worked to include cultural issues in counseling in a way to help each member of the couple understand each other better.

Last week, Mr. Smith was hit by a truck while riding his motorcycle. He has been hospitalized since then with a diagnosis of spinal cord injury, and all indications are that he is now quadriplegic. Dr. Kind has focused on providing crisis stabilization for the couple and helping Mrs. Smith maneuver the inpatient and insurance systems. Although disability issues were never explicitly included in Dr. Kind's graduate training or subsequent continuing education, her cousin is quadriplegic and her husband died from a heart attack. Through her own experience dealing with grief and loss, she hopes that she has the competence to help the Smiths deal with their current situation.

Response to the Case of Dr. Kind and Changing Competencies

Ethics Code Standards 2.01 (Competence) and 2.06 (Personal Problems and Conflicts) may be particularly helpful in beginning to understand Dr. Kind's ethical dilemmas with Mr. and Mrs. Smith. In fact, in this vignette, the two standards may be intertwined.

Beginning with Standard 2.01, Dr. Kind's training and expertise as a couples counselor may give her the initial competence needed to help the Smiths deal with the initial crisis, but since issues related to disability were apparently not included in her graduate or subsequent training, Dr. Kind likely lacks the competence to help the couple deal with the new disability issues in their relationship. Having a cousin with quadriplegia is clearly insufficient to provide her even with basic knowledge of spinal cord injuries. For instance, the location of the injury, whether the quadriplegia is incomplete or complete, and the nature of rehabilitation therapy would be preliminary information necessary to even beginning to achieve the knowledge needed for competence. Since Mr. and Mrs. Smith come from different cultural backgrounds, it would be especially important to understand how disabilities are considered within their individual cultural histories. In addition to considering the effects of disability on the Smiths individually and as a couple, it would be crucial for Dr. Kind to understand the way their current community and social environment might respond, including potential bias and discrimination.

Standard 2.06 (Personal Problems and Conflicts) may also be a factor in this vignette. Dr. Kind's own trauma related to her husband's death, her financial needs as sole support for her family and possible reluctance to refer out cases, together with her initial feelings of expertise in treating this couple, may unconsciously lead her to overestimate her competence in this case. Thus, she may be at risk of "not knowing what she doesn't know" (Olkin, 2008) about Mr. Smith's disability and its effect on the couple.

Lacking basic competence, especially in the presence of possible unconscious personal conflicts, could lead Dr. Kind to inadvertently harm the couple. She could, for instance, project her own experiences of grief and loss onto the couple, without even realizing she is doing so. Since her training during and after graduate school did not include disability as a diversity consideration, she could miss or minimize the discrimination Mr. Smith may face in everyday life. She could fail to understand the Americans with Disabilities Act implications related to his job. She may not even realize that her office is inaccessible by wheelchair. She could assume that spinal cord injuries lead to sexual problems, unnecessarily inducing anxiety about sexual performance in this couple. Perhaps her list of referral sources does not include local therapists with expertise in disability issues. False confidence in herself as a treatment provider could, therefore, prove to be unhelpful at best and, at worst, could be harmful.

Dr. Kind's ethical dilemmas could be approached in several ways. First, of course, she should become aware of her potential blind spots with this case. She should recognize some tension she likely has between wanting to be competent and realizing that she is not fully competent. This anxiety may be the motivation to help her seek consultation and recognize the limits of her current knowledge. Since she is in a consultation group, with her clients' consent to share information, her colleagues could help her understand her lack of competence in disability issues, as well as the personal triggers this case may involve for her. She might want to seek psychotherapy for herself, particularly since Mr. Smith's accident may prompt additional feelings of grief related to her husband's death.

A caring therapist and/or consultation group might be able to assist Dr. Kind in becoming more aware of her emotional reactions to the Smiths and how her personal issues could interfere with competent treatment of this couple. As an example, since her own husband only died a few years ago and she has been the sole support of their children since then, Dr. Kind may not have worked through her own sense of grief and loss, leading her to perhaps deny the Smiths' reactions while moving too quickly to problem-solving in the case.

Assuming that Dr. Kind does become aware of her own personal reactions to the accident and her probable lack of competence, she could refer the couple to a different psychologist who does have expertise with the type of disability issues they now face. However, the Smiths may not want such a referral, since they have worked successfully with Dr. Kind around the affair, they trust her, and they may not want to transfer to someone else, especially in a time of crisis. In addition, it may not be possible to identify a psychologist in the area with competence in both couples therapy and disability issues. Dr. Kind could openly discuss her lack of competence related to disability issues with the Smiths and ask their permission to seek consultation and/or supervision with psychologists with competence in disability issues. With Mr. Smith's informed consent, she could work with his inpatient and rehabilitation treatment teams, gaining knowledge herself while also enabling continuity of care. She could also complete reading in this area and enroll in conferences and workshops to help her start gaining the competence needed to successfully work with the couple. If she continues to provide couples therapy, she may also want to refer Mr. and/or Mrs. Smith to individual psychologists with expertise in spinal cord injuries.

Consulting the Guidelines for the Assessment and Intervention with Persons with Disabilities (APA, 2012) would be an excellent way for Dr. Kind to start increasing her knowledge base. These guidelines were written to help psychologists provide more effective, fair, and ethical psychological testing and treatment of persons with disabilities. They include ways to make practices more accessible and information on how psychologists can develop productive therapeutic relationships with this population. The guidelines also include many helpful resources and references, including for various divisions within the APA (e.g., 22 Rehabilitation, 40 Clinical Neuropsychology, 43 Family).

This document includes 12 general, 5 assessment, and 5 intervention guidelines. Guidelines 1–12 (general) and 18–22 (intervention) could be particularly helpful for Dr. Kind. For instance, Guideline 5 relates to providing physical environments that are barrier-free; once Mr. Smith is released from the hospital and returns to couples counseling in her office, Dr. Kind must ensure accessibility. Guideline 18 notes that psychologists should strive to recognize the wide range of individual responses to disability and should collaborate with clients who have disabilities and with their family members (Mrs. Smith, in this case) to develop and implement appropriate interventions.

In addition to the guidelines, Dr. Kind might want to consider other resources, including, for instance, the section of Kenneth Pope's website related to accessibility (http://kpope.com). And most importantly, she should consult with APA's

Committee on Disability Issues in Psychology, who could provide her with additional resources as well as potential consultants and/or supervisors.

The Case of Dr. Mark and the Multicultural Disability Evaluation Request

Dr. Sandra Mark is a 39-year-old licensed psychologist who works as part of an interdisciplinary team in a primary care medical clinic. A large portion of the clients seen in this clinic are refugees from around the world. Dr. Mark has worked in refugee mental health for over a decade and has deliberately developed her expertise with this population through attending continuing education trainings, engaging in ongoing peer consultation, and reading professional publications. Dr. Mark only recently started her position at the medical clinic. Previously she provided psychotherapy through a nonprofit agency specializing in meeting the myriad needs of the refugee community.

Shortly after starting at the medical clinic, Dr. Mark was referred Mr. Adan Gurung, a 66-year-old male who was a refugee from Bhutan. He had spent 17 years in a camp in Nepal before being resettled with his son, daughter-in-law, and three grandchildren in the United States five years ago. For as long as anyone in the family could remember, Mr. Gurung had exhibited problems with his memory. At first, they noticed him struggling to find his way around the camp and forgetting where he had placed items. Over the years, it gradually progressed so they now had to provide 24/7 supervision to ensure he did not leave the stove on or get lost walking outside the home. Mr. Gurung and his daughter-in-law attributed these changes to him "thinking too much" about all he had endured as a result of being displaced. Although Mr. Gurung was conversational with Dr. Mark using a Nepali interpreter, his daughter-in-law often had to clarify questions or provide information he could not recall.

Dr. Mark was familiar with presentations similar to Mr. Gurung's. Knowing his cognitive limitations, she knew psychotherapy would be reliant upon the involvement of family members who could help provide structure for some of the recommended behavioral modifications that could decrease anxiety. Additionally, Dr. Mark planned to help Mr. Gurung's family enroll him in an adult day program for Bhutanese elders, providing the family with much-needed respite and Mr. Gurung with culturally congruent socialization outside the home. As Dr. Mark was discussing this treatment plan with Mr. Gurung and his daughter-in-law at the end of the first session, they asked Dr. Mark if she could help Mr. Gurung's primary care provider complete paperwork stating Mr. Gurung was cognitively impaired such that he could not take the United States citizenship examination. Dr. Mark was surprised by the timing of this request. By their attendance at an initial psychotherapy appointment, she was under the impression the priority was decreasing his distress (i.e., "thinking too much") and improving his functioning (i.e., "memory problems"). The question of disability felt counter to these therapeutic goals.

Dr. Mark verbalized her concerns to Mr. Gurung and his daughter-in-law. Both explained that he had never been able to learn English or civics, despite taking several language and citizenship classes and practicing one-on-one at home with his son. They reasserted their request, asking that Dr. Mark work with Mr. Gurung's primary care provider to help them ensure the exam was not a barrier to Mr. Gurung securing citizenship. They also agreed with Dr. Mark that they wanted her to help Mr. Gurung's "thinking too much" and "memory problems."

Response to the Case of Dr. Mark and the Multicultural Disability Evaluation Request

Dr. Mark's ethical dilemma in this case is complex, but centers on the question of whether her role as psychotherapist conflicts with her role as assessor regarding Mr. Gurung's capacity for new learning (Ethics Code Standard 3.05 Multiple Relationships). This question must be considered in the context of Mr. Gurung's culture's conceptualization of disability and how a label of disability may enable equality in some circumstances.

Psychotherapy is based on the premise that a client is striving for health, including decreasing distress and improving functioning. Evaluating a client for a disability amidst this process introduces a potentially disruptive variable. For example, how will the client's treatment engagement be impacted by their expectations of the outcome of the disability assessment? How will the therapeutic relationship be differently affected by an affirmative or negative disability finding? Similar role conflict is discussed in the forensic literature when a treating psychologist is asked to shift into the role of assessor or expert witness. A common recommendation is that while some circumstances may call for the psychologist to assume this dual role, it should be avoided whenever possible (Strasburger, Gutheil, & Brodsky, 1997). Suspending judgment on whether this case presents one of the aforementioned exception circumstances would be necessary while the other salient factors of this case are explored.

Mr. Gurung's multicultural context must be considered alongside his request to be assigned a disability designation. As is the case with 60 percent of Bhutanese refugees, Mr. Gurung is Hindu (Ranard, 2007). According to this doctrine, disability can be linked to *karma*, sins committed during past lives. However, the direct Nepali translation of the word "disability" (i.e., *apanga*) is more akin to visible congenital physical disability. This opens the possibility that Mr. Gurung's and his family's suggestion that Mr. Gurung is too cognitively disabled to complete the citizenship examination carries different meaning than the general and more widespread concept of disability (i.e., *apanga*). The fact that he requires 24/7 supervision may not be as disruptive to his family system when compared to more individualistic cultures where multigenerational cohabitation occurs less frequently. On the contrary, the average household size of a Bhutanese refugee family in the United States is eight, and it is common for a daughter-in-law to move in with her husband's parents after marriage and to assume some caregiving for these aging members of the family (Ranard, 2007). Developmental phases should be adjusted for the different age anchors of an individual born in Bhutan. According to the World Health Organization (2012), the life expectancy for a person born in the United States is over a decade longer than for someone born in Bhutan. Thus, quantification of age-related cognitive decline must be recalibrated for this population.

Although disability across cultures can trigger prejudice and discrimination, there can also be social justice advantages to this descriptor. When indicated, correct identification of disability can ensure a person receives accommodations to equalize their life experiences. For example, if an employee's job is put in jeopardy when they must take time off for medical appointments during a rigid schedule, then this could be corrected with a disability accommodation to increase the flexibility of their schedule in order to ensure their health can be maintained without sacrificing total work hours. In this way, the employee's ability status can be viewed as a difference instead of a deficit, which is consistent with the movement toward disability as a multicultural descriptor (Gilson & Depoy, 2000). The request by Mr. Gurung and his family that his medical team provide documentation of a disabling cognitive deficit runs parallel to this employment example. They are asserting Mr. Gurung's right to become a United States citizen and asking that the examination requirement, which poses an insurmountable barrier in his case, be waived. By doing so, the path to citizenship is not a discriminatory one.

After clarifying the ethical complexities inherent in this case, Dr. Mark would be best advised to consult the relevant ethical guidelines to help shape her plan. As noted earlier, the dilemma of whether to simultaneously occupy the role of therapist and assessor relates to Standard 3.05 (Multiple Relationships) of the Ethics Code. Although this standard is often thought of as related to a psychologist performing a professional service in conflict with a personal role, the essence of it is still informative, as two different professional roles can also clash. Objectivity and effectiveness are best maintained when only a single role is carried out at a time. In this specific case, the therapist could focus on the pursuit of wellness, while the assessor could evaluate whether the extent of functional impairment exceeds the threshold of disability. Separating these two roles is also clearer from the client perspective. Although Dr. Mark may feel pulled to occupy both roles to decrease Mr. Gurung's number of appointments, which could also de-burden the family members who accompany him, she is best advised to proceed with the course of action that is most clinically beneficial.

When informed consent in keeping with Standard 3.10 (Informed Consent) is provided, each psychologist can explain their unique role and align with the client around reaching the associated goal. Particularly for a client like Mr. Gurung, who has multiple factors potentially compromising his ability to provide informed consent (i.e., compromised cognitive functioning, low health literacy, minority ethnic status, and a cultural framework of healthcare that is different from the one in which he is receiving care), keeping this as simple as possible is essential. As should be the case with any informed consent process, the psychologists should create bidirectional processes. They should provide information, elicit questions, and solicit feedback from the client sufficient to demonstrate that they understand to what they are agreeing. The psychologists should bear in mind the position of power they hold and empower the client to raise concerns. For clients who speak a language other than their psychologist, the use of a trained medical interpreter throughout is imperative. Regarding Mr. Gurung's case, and assuming there are no issues with the informed consent process, there is nothing to suggest his cultural framework of disability would preclude these two roles from being separated. Although a referral to another psychologist might in some cases lead a client to feel stigmatized, as if their level of pathology exceeds the scope of the initial practitioner, the Bhutanese general conceptualization of disability as congenital, physical, and visible may in this case be protective. Mr. Gurung and his family likely think of his decline in functioning differently from this definition of disability and therefore do not attach the same stigma to it.

If Dr. Mark's role is ultimately defined as the assessor and she possesses the necessary competency based on her prior experience in refugee mental health, there are several relevant ethical considerations to inform her practice. Although Mr. Gurung has not yet been confirmed to be a person with a neurocognitive disability, his presentation during his initial session with Dr. Mark suggests this may be the case. If this possibility exists, a comprehensive assessment approach ensures the most accurate evaluation. Guideline 16 of the Guidelines for the Assessment and Intervention with Persons with Disabilities (APA, 2012) asserts the need to include ecological and functional assessment. The former could be obtained by talking with Mr. Gurung's primary care provider or reviewing their documentation in the medical record about his longitudinal presentation during medical visits (e.g., his ability to remember and apply information discussed and his ability to provide independent history). The latter could come from collateral sources who have had the opportunity to observe Mr. Gurung in his day-to-day life (e.g., his daughter-in-law and English instructor). The onus would be on Dr. Mark to report the sources of this information and to consider possible biases present from their individual perspectives. This is also aligned with Guideline 17 of this same document, which touts the value of multiple sources being included in assessments of persons with disabilities. This guideline also cautions against neglecting to consider how personal bias around disability may influence the assessment outcome.

Mr. Gurung's age may trigger inaccurate assumptions about what would be expected of his cognitive functioning; Dr. Mark needs to bear in mind the life expectancy of Bhutanese refugees and factor that into her comparisons of his functioning. Talking with Mr. Gurung may prompt Dr. Mark to reflect on other individuals in her personal life who are of similar age. Considering their age difference, Mr. Gurung may be of similar age to Dr. Mark's parents. Her relationship with her parents and their functioning level may create an emotional reaction in Dr. Mark that would need to be managed. For example, if Dr. Mark's parents are highly functional, she may inadvertently judge Mr. Gurung against this, suspecting malingering or downplaying his deficits to decrease her cognitive dissonance. Conversely, if Dr. Mark's mother is experiencing early-onset dementia, Dr. Mark may feel particularly sympathetic to Mr. Gurung, and her desire to help may over-shadow her clinical decision-making. Such countertransference reactions are potentially present in any client–psychologist interaction, but with a person experiencing the hardship of disability, the pull for empathy may be especially strong.

Dr. Mark also needs to be aware of how her political views on a person with disability acquiring citizenship and accessing the associated benefits of this designation may influence her assessment; if these are not appropriately accounted for, she may perpetuate this type of discrimination. For example, some political perspectives purport that immigrants are burdensome for the United States and their numbers should be more strictly limited. An immigrant who may require disability-associated services from government agencies could be viewed as a larger financial liability in this regard. If Dr. Mark either holds these beliefs herself or is located in a community where this perspective is omnipresent, she needs to enact extra safeguards (e.g., professional consultation) to ensure bias does not alter her evaluation. The converse could also be true if the political perspectives at play hold that the United States should more freely welcome immigrants into the United States. Owning and setting aside strong proclivities in either direction will ensure the most objective evaluation. Finally, with Mr. Gurung's permission, Dr. Mark could communicate the outcome of the assessment with his therapist so that his therapy could incorporate necessary accommodations.

Summary

This case represents the intersection of culture and disability, even in cases where the disability status is yet to be confirmed. Like all multicultural descriptors, the context in which a given variable arises determines its meaning. In the case of disability, the culture(s) with which a person identifies and the culture(s) that comprise his/her environment define how ability is conceptualized. The cause of a given disability is differently attributed across cultures, with some believing in a spiritual origin while others solely ascribing a biologic factor. The extent to which a given disability impacts an individual's functioning is culturally embedded. For more individualistic cultures, a minor disability may prove disruptive to everyday functioning, while in more collectivities cultures, the same disability may be more easily managed with natural supports from an individual's community. Type and extent of stigma of disability are culturally determined, and an individual may experience variability in stigma as they move throughout the different cultural environments that comprise their life. Considering such complexities while navigating a case like this, Dr. Mark should continue all her previous good practice of attending continuing education trainings, engaging in ongoing peer consultation, and reading professional publications to ensure her competence is robust.

The Case of Dr. Robbins and Consideration of Disability through Multiple Lenses

Dr. Richard Robbins is a 60-year-old licensed psychologist in practice at a community mental health center. He has worked in the same agency for the majority of his 30-year career and he frequently publishes and presents about approaches to recovery for people with severe and persistent mental illness. His treatment team is composed of a psychiatrist, a psychiatric nurse, and several case managers. They meet frequently to coordinate care on complex cases and to discuss the evolving literature on best treatment practices.

Dr. Robbins had recently started psychotherapy with Marla Johnson, a 32-year-old woman who was diagnosed with bipolar disorder in her late teens. Dr. Robbins has had significant experience managing his own bipolar disorder. Ms. Johnson had not experienced a significant mood episode since starting mood-stabilizing medication many years before. However, her last manic episode required psychiatric hospitalization, which caused a prolonged absence from her work as a nurse assistant. Her employer at the time was not aware of her diagnosis of bipolar disorder and she chose not to disclose it to him. As a result, her nonattendance was misunderstood and resulted in termination.

Following her hospitalization, Ms. Johnson had been adherent to her medication regimen and had actively engaged in a community-based support group for persons with bipolar disorder. She described the relief she felt at prolonged mood stability for the first time in her adult life, and she attributed this to the insight she now had into her illness and ongoing need for treatment. However, she had been unable to secure a new job. When asked about her thoughts on this, Ms. Johnson explained that she now told any potential employer the story about how her bipolar disorder had been the reason for the loss of her last job. She asked Dr. Robbins to provide her with a letter explaining this, because she was tired of telling her story over and over again. When Dr. Robbins started discussing bipolar disorder as a disability and Ms. Johnson's rights as a person with a disability, Ms. Johnson interrupted him. She rejected the idea that she was disabled and asserted that withholding "the real reason" for the loss of her last job was dishonest. She told Dr. Robbins that if he did not provide the letter she desired, she would request her treatment records to provide to future potential employers. She explained that she was starting to feel hopeless and worthless in the setting of her unemployment and that she wanted to secure a job as soon as possible.

Response to the Case of Dr. Robbins and Consideration of Disability through Multiple Lenses

Dr. Robbins' ethical dilemma essentially weighs two of the Ethics Code principles against one another. Principle A: Beneficence and Nonmaleficence cautions psychologists to do no harm to their clients. Dr. Robbins could reasonably worry that providing Ms. Johnson with her requested letter or not doing so and leaving her to request her treatment records could negatively impact her by continuing to make it difficult for her to secure employment. Principle E: Respect for People's Rights and Dignity reminds psychologists of their clients' right to self-determination. Dr. Robbins could make the argument that it is within Ms. Johnson's rights to utilize her diagnosis as she chooses, including during the course of a job search.

To clarify the nuances of each of these perspectives, the Guidelines for the Assessment and Intervention with Persons with Disabilities (APA, 2012) are useful. Dr. Robbins obligation to do no harm is supported by Guidelines 4 and 9. Guideline 4 states that psychologists should be knowledgeable about laws that protect people with disabilities (see also 2.01 [Boundaries of Competence] and 2.03 [Maintaining Competence] of the APA Code). Dr. Robbins should refamiliarize himself with the Americans with Disabilities Act, including its provisions that prohibit discrimination in employment for qualified persons based on the presence of a disability. Knowing that the mere presence of this law does not mean prejudicial hiring practices do not exist is also an important context to bear in mind. Dr. Robbins should consider how a letter from him or Ms. Johnson's treatment records could potentially put her at risk during the hiring process. The level of knowledge about mental health and its associated legal protections of the hiring individuals means they may operate with inaccurate information about Ms. Johnson and her application. Additionally, if they are unaware of societal – and potentially their own – biases around the dependability/employability of individuals with bipolar disorder, they are at risk of incorporating these into their decision-making. Knowing this, as well as Ms. Johnson's seeming naïveté to it, may trigger a protective impulse in Dr. Robbins. He may find himself arguing with Ms. Johnson or expressing his own associated emotions to try to convince her of his perspective on the risks. Although this reaction is understandable, it deviates from the client-centered perspective that is core to all therapeutic processes.

Guideline 9 declares that psychologists should be aware of how the social environment and the nature of a person's disability combine to impact the trajectory of their development. In this case, Dr. Robbins should consider how the timing of the onset of Ms. Johnson's bipolar disorder may shape her understanding of this condition as a disability and the attitudes society holds about it. As Ms. Johnson was diagnosed in her late teens but did not experience prolonged stability until her late twenties, Dr. Robbins should be aware that her adjustment to the diagnosis and understanding of the implications of it may have been truncated, and perhaps are not similar to his own experiences. During the time when most young adults are entering the workforce and acquiring associated career development skills, Ms. Johnson was struggling to manage her disruptive mood symptoms. The fact that she was early in her career and also new to her diagnosis at the same time might have caused bidirectional problems in both areas. Dr. Robbins should hold this in mind when deciding how to proceed and should also be aware of his own emotional response. For example, he may feel the vicarious loss she experienced by having a portion of her early adulthood consumed by dysregulated mood. If she is not ready to consider this, Dr. Robbins will need to ensure his sadness on her behalf does not cause him to act in an overprotective fashion.

Dr. Robbins' responsibility to respect Ms. Johnson's right to self-determination is supported by Guidelines 2 and 7. Guideline 2 cautions against allowing personal beliefs to influence treatment. Included in this is the "spread effect" – the erroneous assumption that any person with a disability has certain stereotypical characteristics (Olkin, 1999). In this case, Dr. Robbins could be at risk of assuming Ms. Johnson is not capable of thoughtful decisions due to the presence of impulsivity followed by later remorse during some manic episodes of bipolar disorder. Unless there is evidence of this during her recent period of mood stability, this would be an incorrect prejudice. Guideline 2 also reminds psychologists to inventory their biases about people with disabilities in general. In this case, if Dr. Robbins holds the unconscious belief that people with disabilities need special protection and care, he could inadvertently behave in a paternalistic fashion. This could have the unintended consequence of disempowering Ms. Johnson in a way similar to the societal tendency to do the same. Although potentially dangerous, the impulse to protect Ms. Johnson in this case is understandable, especially considering the way she links her unemployment to what could be early symptoms of a depressive episode. This may be compounded by the long-standing experience Dr. Robbins has with bipolar disorder. He has likely seen very severe cases of bipolar disorder in his community mental health population. He may overestimate Ms. Johnson's need to have someone "fix things" for her. Awareness of this professional liability is essential to ensuring it does not become problematic.

Guideline 7 asks that psychologists recognize the common group experiences of people with disabilities alongside the factors that shape a person's individual identity as a unique person with a disability. It asserts that although someone may possess the criteria of a disability, they may not identify as being disabled. Their self-understanding is shaped by their personal history, and neglecting this could lead to grouping them with a category they do no own. In this case, Dr. Robbins must recognize that simply carrying the diagnosis of bipolar disorder does not mean that Ms. Johnson identifies as having a disability. He should work to understand how her life experiences have shaped the way she defines this aspect of herself.

Although Dr. Robbins initially appeared to be put in a difficult position by Ms. Johnson's assertion that she would use her diagnostic information during her job search, through careful consideration of the Ethics Code and the Guidelines for the Assessment and Intervention with Persons with Disabilities, it becomes clear that Dr. Robbins' obligation is to arm himself with correct, unbiased information and to ask – but not demand – that Ms. Johnson incorporate it into her decision-making. In this way, he can simultaneously minimize the risk of harm to Ms. Johnson while supporting her autonomy.

Summary and Recommendations

Clearly, the ethical issues involved in psychological practice related to disability are numerous and complex. Despite the prevalence of disability in the U.S. (U.S. Census, 2010), leading people with disabilities to be called the largest minority group (Andrews & Lund, 2015), many health service psychologists may lack sufficient education and training in this area and may be at subsequent risk for diminished (or nonexistent) competence, and thus may be prone to ethical mistakes with this population. Without awareness, such mistakes may even include a basic lack of sensitivity (Leigh, Powers, Vash, & Nettles, 2004).

In this chapter, we have barely scratched the surface of the many potential ethical dilemmas involved in working with disability. The case of Mr. Gurung highlights multiple diversity statuses within a single individual, and may be increasingly common.

Other scenarios could include less obvious disabilities, such as learning disabilities (e.g., Foster & Tribe, 2015), or disabilities that are even more highly stigmatized, including mental illness in psychologists themselves.

The field would be well served by better incorporating disability into diversity descriptions (Gibson & Depoy, 2000; Olkin & Pledger, 2003) and by increasing education and training related to this important minority group. The APA Standards of Accreditation for Health Service Psychology (APA, 2015) mention disability in sections related to commitment to cultural individual differences and diversity, an improvement from the previous Guidelines and Principles for Accreditation of Programs in Professional Psychology (APA, 2006), which only reference diversity in general. Of course, it remains to be seen whether this results in any positive changes.

Currently practicing psychologists are encouraged to actively seek competence in diversity by consulting the references noted in this chapter, including the Americans with Disabilities Act, the World Health Organization, the APA Ethics Code, the various APA guidelines, relevant APA divisions including 22 (Rehabilitation), and the APA's Committee on Disability Issues in Psychology. Only then may we be less likely to not know "what we don't know about disability" (Olkin, 2008, p. 492).

References

American Psychological Association (2003). Guidelines for multicultural training, research, practice, and organizational change. *American Psychologist*, *58*, 377–402.

American Psychological Association (2006). Guidelines and principles for accreditation of programs in professional psychology (G&P). Retrieved from www.apa.org/ed/ accreditation/about/policies/guiding-principles.pdf

American Psychological Association (2010). Ethical principles of psychologists and code of conduct (2002, Amended June 1, 2010). Retrieved from www.apa.org/ethics/code/ index.aspx

American Psychological Association (2012a). Guidelines for the assessment and intervention with disabilities. *American Psychologist*, *67*, 43–62.

American Psychological Association (2012b). Guidelines for the evaluation of dementia and age-related cognitive change. *American Psychologist*, *67*, 1–9.

American Psychological Association (2013). Guidelines for psychological practice in health care delivery systems. *American Psychologist*, *68*, 1–6.

American Psychological Association (2014). Guidelines for psychological practice with older adults. *American Psychologist*, *68*, 34–65.

American Psychological Association (2015).The standards of accreditation for health service psychology. Retrieved from www.apa.org/ed/accreditation/about/policies/standards-of-accreditation.pdf

American Psychological Association Policy and Planning Board (2005). APA guidelines awareness and utilization: A first look. *American Psychologist, 70*, 431–443.

Andrews, E. E. & Lund, E. M. (2015). Disability in psychology training: Where are we? *Training and Education in Professional Psychology, 9*, 210–216.

Andrews, E. E., Kuemmel, A., Williams, J. L., Pilarski, C. R., Dunn, M., & Lund, E. M. (2013). Providing culturally competent supervision to trainees with disabilities in rehabilitation settings. *Rehabilitation Psychology, 58*, 233–244.

Erickson Cornish, J., Gorgens, K. A., & Pelican Monson, S. (2008). Perspectives on ethical practice with people who have disabilities. *Professional Psychology: Research and Practice, 39*, 488–491.

Forster, P. & Tribe, R. (2015). Professional and ethical issues when working with learning disabled clients. In R. Tribe & J. Morrisey (Eds.), *Handbook of professional and ethical practice for psychologists, counselors, and psychotherapists*. New York, NY: Routledge/Taylor & Francis Group.

Gilson, S. F. & Depoy, E. (2000). Multiculturalism and disability: A critical perspective. *Disability & Society, 15*, 207–218.

Hassouneh-Phillips, D. & Curry, M. A. (2002). Abuse of women with disabilities: State of the science. *Rehabilitation Counseling Bulletin, 45*, 96–104.

Horner-Johnson, W. & Drum, C. E. (2006). Prevalence of maltreatment of people with intellectual disabilities: A review of recently published research. *Mental Retardation and Developmental Disabilities Research Reviews, 12*, 57–69.

Hughes, R. B. (2005). Violence against women with disabilities: Urgent call for action. *The Community Psychologist, 38*, 28–30.

Leigh, I., Powers, L., Vash, C., & Nettles, R. (2004). Survey of psychological services to clients with disabilities: The need for awareness. *Rehabilitation Psychology, 49*, 48–54.

Lund, E. M., Andrews, E. E., & Holt, J. M. (2014). How we treat our own: The experiences and characteristics of psychology trainees with disability. *Rehabilitation Psychology, 59*, 367–375.

Olkin, R. (2008). Social warrior or unwitting bigot? *Professional Psychology: Research and Practice, 39*, 492.

Olkin, R. (1999). *What psychotherapists should know about disability*. New York, NY: Guilford Press.

Olkin, R. & Pledger, C. (2003). Can disability studies and psychology join hands? *American Psychologist, 58*, 296–304.

Pope, K. Accessibility and disability resources for psychology training and practice. Retrieved from http://kpope.com

Puryear Keita, G. (2015). The ADA: Improving lives for 25 years. *Monitor on Psychology, 46*, 42.

Ranard, D. (2007). Bhutanese refugees in Nepal. Center for Applied Linguistics. Retrieved from www.hplct.org/assets/uploads/files/backgrounder_bhutanese.pdf

Strasburger, L. H., Gutheil, T. G., & Brodsky, A. (1997). On wearing two hats: Role conflict in serving as both psychotherapist and expert witness. *American Journal of Psychiatry, 154*, 448–456.

Sullivan, P. M. & Knutson, J. F. (2000). Maltreatment and disabilities: A population-based epidemiological study. *Child Abuse & Neglect, 24*, 1257–1273.

United Nations Enable (2006). Convention on the rights of persons with disabilities. Retrieved from www.un.org/development/desa/disabilities/convention-on-the-rights-of-persons-with-disabilities/convention-on-the-rights-of-persons-with-disabilities-2.html

United States Census (2010). Americans with Disabilities 2010. Retrieved from www.census
.gov/people/disability/publications/sipp2010.html

United States Department of Justice, Civil Rights Division (2010). Americans with
Disabilities Act. Retrieved from www.ada.gov

World Health Organization (2001). *International classification of functioning, disability, and
health*. Geneva, Switzerland: World Health Organization.

World Health Organization (2012). Global Health Observatory data repository. Retrieved
from http://apps.who.int/gho/data/node.main.688

15 Ethical Issues When Working with People of Color

Suzette L. Speight and Michael C. Cadaret

This chapter will engage some of the ethical issues that may arise when conducting therapy with people of color. We will utilize the term "people of color" to reference those of Asian, African, Latina/o, Native American, North African, and Middle Eastern descent. "People of color" does not represent a distinct group of people, but rather refers to communities of people who, by nature of their phenotypic pigmentation of skin color, have been subjugated to practices of exclusion and oppression throughout history. While all forms of discrimination and oppression are horrific and objectionable, the history and conditions of oppression differ across racial and ethnic groups. Even within racial categories, one's experiences of oppression and socialization may be different given sexuality, gender, class, and religion, and thus shape how individuals from these communities negotiate issues of race and ethnicity in U.S. society. Through the lens of cultural competence, this chapter will focus on several topics relevant to ethical practice, including the fluidity of identity, addressing racial/ethnic differences, the utility of an exclusively intrapsychic framework, and understanding the community setting.

Defining Race and Ethnicity

Many practitioners may question where and when racial and ethnic categories are useful and when do they become stereotypes and, therefore, harmful in our conceptualization of persons in clinical work. Markus (2008) argues that for us to understand race and ethnicity in psychology, we must understand history and context. The dominant discourse in psychology is largely influenced by northern European and Western thought, which gives primacy to the individual often to the exclusion of one's existence as a social being. Thus, Markus maintains, to truly understand race and ethnicity, psychology needs to reform its model of the person, seeing people not as self-determined, agentic, and stable, but instead as shaped by their relationships with others, their values, and their judgments about the self in relation to society. The definitions of race and ethnicity have a long, hotly contested history within the field of psychology. Ethnicity commonly refers to "a characterization of a group of people who see themselves and are seen by others as having a common ancestry, shared history, shared traditions, and shared cultural traits such as language, beliefs, values, music, dress, and food" (Cokley, 2007, p. 225). Ethnic identity, then, is one's subjective sense of belonging to an ethnic group. Ethnic groups are not fixed but flexible, and ethnic cultural traits are learned and transmitted to others and across generations. Markus (2008) maintains that race and ethnicity are human inventions. Race is often used as a way to uphold social power and does not often typify the groups that it is purported to define. Race refers to a characterization of a group of people believed to share physical characteristics such as skin color, facial features, and other hereditary traits (Cokley, 2007, p. 225). Smedley and Smedley (2005), in their review of the origins of the concept of race, outline how race does not have biological or genetic meaning, but rather represents an ideology, "an invented conception about human differences" (p. 22). Smedley and Smedley claim that race and ethnicity are often used in a sociopolitical context to control or abuse other groups: "Race became an important mechanism for limiting and restring access to privilege, power, and wealth" (p. 22).

The social construction of race results in the differing opportunities arising from the inequities perpetrated by society's racial ideology. Thus, it is imperative that we view the impact of racial stratification on individuals' daily experiences. The effects of race and racism can be manifest at different levels, from the microsocial to the macrosocial. For instance, individuals may believe the stereotypes about their race (i.e., internalized racism) while also having restricted access to quality public education, employment opportunities, and health care (i.e., institutionalized racism). Consequently, decades of research have documented significant disparities in health care and mental health care between people of color and whites. With regard to mental health care, the Surgeon General's report (U.S. Department of Health and Human Services, 2001) concluded: "Racial and ethnic minorities have less access to mental health services than do whites. They are less likely to receive needed care. When they receive care, it is more likely to be poor in quality" (p. 3). The report identified barriers such as the cost of care, stigma, clinicians' lack of awareness of cultural issues, biases, clients' mistrust, and the effects of racism and discrimination.

Culturally competent mental health care is seen as one key remedy to these mental health disparities. The Surgeon General's report defines culturally competent care as "the delivery of services responsive to the cultural concerns of racial and ethnic minority groups, including their languages, histories, traditions, beliefs, and values" (U.S. Department of Health and Human Services, 2001, p. 36). The delivery of culturally competent services to people of color is, in a word, complex. This complexity is reflected in Lynn Weber's work on intersectionality, she writes:

> If we are to understand race, class, gender, and sexuality systems, we must be willing to have our stereotypes of subordinate groups challenged and to make the social privilege of dominant groups visible. To do so we must be open to learning information and ways of thinking that may not have been included or validated in our education. We must also be aware that everyone holds stereotypes – that we may even have them about our own groups – and that we can challenge and change them. And because all of these systems operate in our lives at all times, recognizing the complexity in our own multiple statuses helps us to consider the complexity in the lived experiences of others. (p. 218)

Mental health professionals are obliged to deliver services that are responsive to the needs of racial and ethnic minority clients. The Ethical Principles of Psychologists and Code of Conduct (APA, 2010) assert that psychologists should practice within areas of their competence, including scientific and professional knowledge that is related to race, ethnicity, and culture (Principle E – Standard 2.01). The overarching principle of "Respect for People's Rights and Dignity" (Principle E) includes special knowledge that takes into considerations the vulnerability of certain communities and practices that are inclusive of awareness and respect for diversity. Furthermore, the Code suggests that psychologists work to eliminate biases that could be harmful to their work (Principle E – Standards 3.01 and 3.03).

Direct guidance for upholding these principles and standards is given within the APA Guidelines on Multicultural Education, Training, Research, Practice, and Organizational Change for Psychologists (APA, 2003). The guidelines are organized into six areas that explain the infusion of multicultural practice in several areas of psychology. The first two guidelines discuss the knowledge of the role of culture within psychology and psychologists themselves (Guideline 1) and the necessity for recognizing race, ethnicity, and culture in the persons that psychologists serve (Guideline 2). Guideline 3 addresses the inclusion of diversity issues in education, while Guideline 4 addresses culturally sensitive research. Guideline 5 directly addresses the application of culturally appropriate skills in clinical practice. The guideline suggests that practitioners be aware of their "client in context"; that is, recognizing that clients (and psychologists) are socialized to understand themselves as racial, ethnic, and cultural beings. Thus, practitioners should appropriately assess for the social, political, and historical factors that may influence a client. In situations involving assessment, psychologists should be aware of the limitations and the cultural validity of such instruments and ensure that their value is adequately explained. Finally, psychologists should be informed in their use of psychological interventions. Specifically, practitioners should take special consideration when conceptualizing clients, especially in cross-cultural encounters. Interventions should be carefully chosen and applied so that they incorporate culture-specific elements. Guideline 6 encourages psychologists to support institutional and organizational change.

Providing mental health services in a culturally informed manner is an ethical imperative (Gallardo, 2009; Ridley, 1985). Ethical practice must extend beyond knowledge and awareness of diversity issues regarding culturally informed practice and be free of bias in order to provide culturally responsive interventions. Such practice seeks to infuse ethical principles of practice (Kitchener, 1984) and multi-cultural competence, along with responding to the needs of the individual within their community.

(Cultural) Competence

Cultural competence is relevant at the level of the clinician and his/her clinical interactions, to the supervision provided to the clinician-in-training, and at the institutional level of the mental health agency and service delivery system.

The widely accepted framework for delineating the components of cultural competence come from Sue et al. (1982, 1992), who identified cultural awareness and beliefs, cultural knowledge, and cultural skills as the overarching characteristics of a culturally competent therapist. Sue et al. (1998) adds that competence on the clinical level involves being scientifically minded and appropriately and flexibly applying generalized understandings of cultural components with any individual client who may present with a myriad of culturally relevant identities. Competent clinicians utilize culturally specific resources to meet the needs of their clients. Utilizing culture-specific resources may take the form of adding culturally appropriate interventions to existing therapy or, what we will advance later, having knowledge of the cultural practices and resources of the community.

The Council of National Psychological Associations for the Advancement of Ethnic Minority Interests in their brochure titled *Psychological treatment of ethnic minority populations* (2003) cautioned that awareness or knowledge alone are not enough. Clinicians believing that the knowledge gained by reading "is sufficient to make one culturally competent would be the height of naïveté" (p. 3). Competence with people of color requires responsiveness, not just sensitivity and awareness. Thus, as will been seen in the upcoming case of Rachelle, the therapist, Dr. Louis, *asked* about the client's identity and experiences with racism within the predominantly white university. Knowing that in our racialized society an Asian–American woman is likely to have experiences with gendered racism that are detrimental to her self-concept and well-being, a competent therapist would inquire about the client's social context.

"Treatment as usual" can have a deleterious result for those with whom it is intended to serve, as traditional ethnocentric treatments have rarely taken into account the cultural values of people of color. Sue (2003) states that "rather than feeling that they have been provided benefits, clients often feel invalidated, abused, misunderstood, and oppressed by their providers" (p. 5). Cultural competence, therefore, demands that clinicians have knowledge of general applications of treatment, along with those that are specific to the cultures and communities within which they work. Clinicians are socialized into the worldview of the dominant groups; bringing this unchallenged worldview into practice, with its assumptions about treatment processes, goals, boundaries, and expectations, can hinder the development of an effective working relationship.

Sue (2003) suggests that for clinicians to become culturally competent they must be aware of their own culture and worldview and the cultures and worldviews of their clients and become flexible in their helping role in order to meet the goals and needs of culturally diverse populations. Perhaps fundamental to cultural competence is the therapist's "way of being" with the client or their general perspective on issues of diversity (Hook, Davis, Owen, Worthington, & Utsey, 2013). Cultural humility is a lifelong commitment to self-evaluation and self-critique, to redressing power imbalances within helping relationships, and to developing partnerships with communities to advocate for system change (Tervalon & Murray-Garcia, 1998). Beyond the ability to perform a task, clinicians must possess an attitude of openness and curiosity about their clients. Culturally humble therapists are motivated to understand their clients' cultural backgrounds (Hook et al., 2013). Consequently, cultural humility as a philosophy or a virtue represents an essential quality that enables clinicians to be other-oriented and to approach the client's cultural background with respect.

The conversation surrounding how to best deliver mental health services to people of color has a rich history that is beyond the scope of this chapter. Therefore, the following case examples seek to illustrate the importance of various aspects of cultural competence in terms of knowledge, awareness, and skills built on a foundation of cultural humility. It is our hope that these cases and their analysis represent some key concerns of ethical practice with people of color and help the reader to discern the best course of ethical practice.

The Case of Dr. Louis, Cultural Knowledge, and Boundary Crossing

Rachelle is a 20-year-old Filipino–American woman who is attending her second year at college. Rachelle has stopped attending classes and has become distracted from school work, and last semester was put on academic probation. Her roommates encouraged Rachelle to attend counseling after she became very upset and ran out of their residence hall. The roommates were concerned and called campus safety. Rachelle was found walking alone, crying, and talking to herself. The campus police took her to psychiatric emergency services, fearing she may harm herself. She was released with no follow-up other than a verbal agreement to attend counseling. At intake, Rachelle requested a male counselor, indicating that she did not have any racial or ethnic preferences. She was assigned to Dr. Louis, a multiracial male licensed psychologist in his thirties. Rachelle was not forthcoming with her difficulties and appeared embarrassed to discuss the incident that led to her hospitalization. She minimized the reaction of her roommates and believed that her academic performance would no longer suffer, as she had addressed this with her parents and has "recommitted" to attending classes and doing her work. Rachelle readily agreed to a safety plan.

Dr. Louis was curious about the impact of Rachelle's race and gender on her experiences at a predominantly white campus. Rachelle shared that she had grown up in a predominantly white, middle-class, suburban community and attended predominantly white schools. Rachelle said that she was "used to" being a "minority" at school and that "it really didn't bother me too much anymore." Rachelle said that she gets along well with white males, but often feels "snubbed" by white women peers. This is why she requested a male counselor because she was fearful of being paired with a "blonde, blue-eyed female" counselor who she would have resentment toward. Rachelle connected her struggles in school to her anxiety about her relationship with Gabe, a white male student. Rachelle was "terrified" of losing him, although they seemed to really like each other and had been dating for almost six months. Rachelle had seen pictures of his previous girlfriends, most of whom were "skinny, white, blonde-haired cheerleader types," and that compared to them she was not attractive. Rachelle felt that others were always looking at her and judging her, questioning, "Why would he even be with someone like me?"

Dr. Louis and Rachelle discussed the socialization process by which she developed her standards of beauty. Dr. Louis did some reading on colorism and gendered racism among Asian–American women in preparation (Hall, 1995; Lee & Thai, 2015). Rachelle explored her own stereotypes of Asian women as they discussed internalized standards of beauty, body type, facial and physical features, and skin color. Rachelle and Dr. Louis processed topics that Rachelle said she had "never talked about out loud before," even though she did write poetry about this in her journal. In fact, after about four months of therapy, Rachelle invites Dr. Louis to attend a poetry slam at an off-campus coffeehouse to hear her read a few pieces. Dr. Louis' first instinct is not to attend, but he tells Rachelle that he will think more about it.

Discussion of the Ethical Dilemmas and Associated Professional Standards

Dr. Louis effectively utilized his cultural knowledge about race, racism, and racial identity in his work with Rachelle. The American Psychological Association (APA) Multicultural Guideline 1 (2003) addresses the need for culturally specific knowledge: "Psychologists are encouraged to recognize the importance of multicultural sensitivity/responsiveness to, knowledge of, and understanding about ethnically and racially different individuals" (p. 385). Dr. Louis demonstrated cultural competence due to his facility in processing Rachelle's multiple identities in light of her minority status in the predominantly white social contexts where she grew up and now attends university. The hegemony of the dominant society's standards of beauty was internalized by Rachelle and accepted as true. Thus, Rachelle saw herself as unattractive, inferior, and unworthy of her white partner, Gabe. Dr. Louis is upholding Principle E: Respect for People's Rights and Dignity (APA, 2010). It is critical that clinicians understand the social construction of race, the meaning of race, and racial identity within society. Race, as we know, is not biologically significant; rather, it is socially meaningful. Due to racism and white privilege, people of color often experience marginalization, discrimination, and violence in our society. The case of Rachelle and Dr. Louis represents the importance of cultural humility. Dr. Louis recognized that Rachelle was an expert on her own experience and was open to helping her to explore her cultural background and experiences.

Now, Dr. Louis has to consider if he should cross a boundary and attend the poetry slam. According to the APA Codes (2010), 3.05 Multiple Relationships encourages psychologists to refrain from entering into a multiple relationship if it could impair one's objectivity, competence, or effectiveness, but on the other hand, it indicates that those multiple relationships that are not expected "to cause impairment or risk exploitation or harm are not unethical" (p. 6). Would attending the poetry slam create a potentially harmful multiple relationship? It appears that attending the poetry slam would not be a harmful or exploitative multiple relationship. Speight (2012) urged a culturally attuned approach to the placement and management of therapy boundaries rather than the predominant risk-avoidance approach to boundaries. Dr. Louis could make a good argument that attending the poetry slam would be a positive boundary crossing that would enhance the therapy relationship and even extend the therapy gains that Rachelle has made (e.g., Glass, 2003). Dr. Louis would be able to support his client as she ventures out and shares her experiences with her community. This is precisely the type of culturally responsive treatment that a culturally competent therapist should consider. A key determination is the appropriateness of the therapist's behavior in light of the client's best interest. The best service Dr. Louis can provide to Rachelle might be to attend her social event and witness her public self-expression. This boundary crossing moves beyond the "therapeutic status quo" to provide Rachelle with culturally competent care (Gallardo, 2009).

Recommendations

1. Like Dr. Louis, clinicians must have knowledge of racial and ethnic groups' histories and experiences, within-group differences, and the intersection of multiple identities in our stratified society, and they must possess the cultural humility to enter into open dialogue about clients' experiences surrounding their cultural identity.
2. Race and ethnicity are but two aspects of identity, and in this case Rachelle's experience as a Filipino–American female was key. Age, sex, sexual/affectional orientation, visible and invisible disabilities, socioeconomic status, gender identity and expression, and religious and spiritual orientation are all important aspects of identity that frame experience within a nation, a region, and a community and shape worldview.
3. Therapists can establish culturally congruent boundaries that are flexible and provide opportunities to personalize the therapeutic relationship based on the needs of the client in a manner that is culturally congruent.

The Case of Sarah and Self-Awareness

Sarah is a practicum student at a college counseling center, her first external practicum. On her caseload she has Ignacio, a Latino male who is struggling with the stress of being a senior accounting major (honors student), is about to graduate, and is looking for a job. Ignacio has talked about being disappointed in not getting any job offers after having what he thought were some good interviews. He is seeking counseling for help with stress management and career options. In their initial few sessions, Sarah has given Ignacio several stress management techniques and she feels he has shown some engagement, but he still reports high stress. Sarah feels somewhat helpless as to what to do next and is considering giving Ignacio some career inventories.

Sarah brings this case to her group supervision, where her peers and practicum instructor ask about the dynamic between Sarah and her client in regard to diversity. Sarah is a 25-year-old, white, upper-middle-class, feminist, heterosexual woman who identifies as atheist. Her client, Ignacio, is a 22-year-old, Puerto Rican, working-class, heterosexual male who identifies as a practicing Catholic. Unfortunately, Sarah did not have many answers to her peers' questions about Ignacio's ethnicity. In fact, Sarah said, "I didn't really even notice that Ignacio was different except for his name and a slight accent." Her classmates and faculty supervisor challenged her color-blind statement and Sarah became tearful and defensive – she wanted to run out of the classroom. Later that evening, Sarah posted some negative comments on social media about being "so tired" and "confused" by all of the controversy around race and ethnicity. Sarah said she was furious at being unfairly accused of being racist when she is "not being prejudiced at all." Several of her classmates read her posts and are wondering if they should mention Sarah's comments to their faculty instructor.

Discussion of the Ethical Dilemmas and Associated Professional Considerations

A key ethical issue here is Sarah's lack of competence in discussing race and ethnicity, apparently due to her own anxiety owing to a lack of self-awareness and experience in discussing race, ethnicity, and culture. As Sue (2013) described, racial dialogue can be difficult for some whites due to fears about appearing racist or realizing their own racism and reluctance to combat racism. Sarah's white privilege has insulated her from engaging in issues of race and ethnicity, and thus she has had very little experience of discussing such topics. The APA Multicultural Guideline 1 (2003) speaks directly to Sarah's difficulty: "Psychologists are encouraged to recognize that, as cultural beings, they may hold attitudes and beliefs that can detrimentally influence their perceptions of and interaction with individuals who are ethnically and racially different from themselves" (p. 382). Sarah seems to have difficulty examining her own biases, assumptions, and worldview. Sarah could be jeopardizing the quality of the clinical services she offers by not being open to reflect on her own background and biases. In research with counselors-in-training, Knox et al. (2003) found that white students feel they are not given opportunities or instruction to explore bias and involve themselves in cross-cultural dialogues. Even so, there is the possibility that it is fear that inhibits action toward multicultural competence. Research has shown that clinicians who attend to issues concerning clients' cultural identity, appreciate clients' cultures, and understand how clients' presenting concerns can be framed in a cultural context demonstrate better outcomes with clients of color (Atkinson, Casas, & Abreu, 1992). Sue et al. (2007) state that clinicians need to be aware of their biases, seek to involve themselves in situations where their empathy will increase for others, and move toward becoming allies. Yet, even if well-intentioned persons who view themselves as egalitarian have this knowledge, there can still be resistance to engaging in issues of diversity.

For instance, Shelton, West, and Trail (2010) studied a group of roommate pairs to examine the relationships between white students and students of color. Due to the fear of being perceived as prejudiced, white students reported increased anxiety on a daily basis. This increased anxiety resulted in participants of color viewing their white roommates in a less favorable light. The implications for clinicians is that the fear of appearing prejudiced could decrease the likelihood of addressing aspects of a racial/ethnic minority client's identity. This fear is often manifested as avoiding such awkward and uncomfortable conversations. Thus, clinicians' anxieties over saying the wrong thing or appearing racist may actually fracture the client's trust in the relationship and hinder the development of a therapeutic alliance.

Sarah's unwillingness to engage in issues of race and ethnicity seems fueled by a lack of self-reflection of her own positionality, privilege, and cultural identity. Sarah appears to be operating within a color-blind racial ideology where she utilizes color evasion and emphasizes sameness. According to the APA (1997), "treating different people differently and celebrating their cultural uniqueness appears to be a more equitable way to achieve social justice than attempting to adopt a colorblind stance" (p. 8). Sarah's color-blind approach is antithetical to multicultural competence. It is surprising and disappointing that Sarah has reached such a point in her training that she is working with clients from a color-blind perspective. Sarah's supervisor at the counseling center (and at her academic program prior to her beginning practicum) have not adequately prepared her to explore her own social identities or those of her clients. Sarah needs a supervisor who is open, aware, discusses culture, and focuses on race and ethnicity in case conceptualization to facilitate her development (Inman & Ladany, 2014).

Given Sarah's negative social media statements, should her peers "report" Sarah to the faculty supervisor? Often, other students have greater knowledge about their peers' inappropriate behaviors than do faculty. Tirpak and Lee (2012) discuss the importance of navigating the multiple relationships that doctoral students experience with their peers and the need for programs to prepare students to ethically manage these relationships. At what point would Sarah's posts alarm her peers enough for them to inform the faculty? The APA Ethics Codes (2010) 1.04 Informal Resolution of Ethical Violation suggests that psychologists should first bring their concerns directly to their colleague. Sarah has not committed an ethical violation, so there is no need for her peers to unduly escalate the situation by "reporting" her to the faculty. However, engaging Sarah to help her to continue dialoging about her positionality with her practicum classmates and faculty supervisor would be very helpful to her own growth. Becoming a culturally competent psychologist will require Sarah to examine her attitudes and biases, which can be a painful process. Sarah's program must provide a learning environment that will both support and challenge her (BEA Virtual Working Group, 2015). Cultural competence is the obligation of all clinicians and is the responsibility of the trainee, the supervisor, and the training program (Inman & Ladany, 2014).

Recommendations

1. Within a therapy encounter between the clinician and the client, each participant comes with separate worldviews, identities, values, and experiences that necessarily shape the process and outcome of that encounter. Thus, clinicians must be willing and able to explore their own social identities, worldviews, and

positionalities in the larger social hierarchy in order to be culturally competent. Sarah needs to access supervision in order to challenge and support her awareness of her own cultural identity and privilege.

2. Sarah must learn about color-blind racial ideology and her own racial privilege.

3. Sarah should make efforts personally and through the support of her program to examine her emotional responses to this and similar incidents. Sarah is likely feeling distress related to white guilt and as a result is distancing herself from engagement in understanding her own privilege (Iyer, Leach, & Pedersen, 2004; Todd, Spainerman, & Aber, 2010).

4. Interaction and discussion from persons of color with Sarah can serve to increase her empathy and broaden her understanding of how racism harms individuals (Spanierman, Todd, & Anderson, 2009).

The Case of Dr. Avery and the Intrapsychic Model

Dr. Nina Avery, an African–American postdoctoral fellow, is in her first job at a local community mental health center. Nina is working for the first time with an urban, poor, primarily African–American clientele. Dr. Avery has been seeing Mia, a 27-year-old, African–American single mother of four- and two-year-old daughters, for six months for issues of depression and a history of significant childhood trauma, including abandonment, physical abuse, and sexual abuse. Prior to beginning therapy, Mia gave temporary custody of her children to their paternal grandmother because she was homeless, had lost her low-wage job, and felt overwhelmed. Consequently, Mia's depression has increased as her financial resources depleted. She feels defeated, frustrated, agitated, and hopeless, with passive suicidal ideation, but her children are good reasons for living. Dr. Avery has been processing her internal reactions to Mia including anger, guilt, and caretaking feelings on her own, but not with her supervisor. Given her caseload of 25 clients, Dr. Avery spends time in supervision talking about her other clients and has avoided talking about Mia.

Mia has been staying with friends and living in her car and does not have money for her basic needs. For instance, Mia recently did not have food, laundry detergent, or feminine hygiene products. Christmas is approaching and Mia does not have money to purchase gifts for her children. Given that her children are not currently in her custody, she is not eligible for toy assistance from local charities. Dr. Avery is struggling with the point of therapy given Mia's circumstances and is wondering what good therapy is really doing. Mia expressed the same sentiment in her last therapy session. Dr. Avery wants to help Mia and intends to purchase some items for Mia and her children without discussing this with her supervisor.

Discussion of the Ethical Dilemmas and Associated Professional Considerations

Dr. Avery is feeling discouraged and pessimistic about her ability to aid her client, Mia, through individual psychotherapy. Mia's psychological symptoms have

increased while her circumstances have not improved; in fact, they have deteriorated. Dr. Avery has apparently defined her role as a mental health provider in
a narrow manner. Moreover, Dr. Avery is withholding her feelings, reactions, and
plan about her client from her supervisor. The APA Multicultural Guideline 4
states, "Psychologists are encouraged to apply culturally appropriate skills in
clinical and other applied psychological practices" (2003, p. 390). This guideline
asks clinicians to develop skills, practices, and interventions that are consistent
with their clients' worldviews and needs, including "nontraditional interventions" (p. 292). Dr. Avery appears to be trapped in a box of her own making.
Vera and Speight (2003) encouraged clinicians to "expand their role" in order to
provide culturally competent care. Intrapsychic explanations for psychological
distress result in interventions that are intrapsychic in nature. Dr. Avery's exclusive focus on Mia's internal issues has not been effective and, in fact, leaves Mia
(and Dr. Avery) feeling hopeless and helpless. As Greenleaf and Bryant (2012)
explained, "The resultant perception that clients' problems are internally-based
or self-caused, and the not result of chronic, environmentally-caused stress, leads
individuals to think that their own mental health problems are a result of their own
psychological and biological deficiencies" (p. 22). Dr. Avery's purchasing of
a few items for Mia might meet a short-term need but does not address the
environmental problems contributing to Mia's distress. The gift giving seems
motivated predominantly by Dr. Avery's internal feelings. Moreover, giving gifts
to the client might set up a relationship dynamic that could prove awkward or
even damaging to the therapeutic relationship. Dr. Avery could benefit from the
experience of her supervisor, who has been working in community mental health
for several years. The supervisor would likely help Dr. Avery to access a range of
community resources to aid the client. Unfortunately, Dr. Avery has been avoiding talking with her supervisor, which leaves both of them at risk of providing
poor client care.

Recommendations

1. Dr. Avery is not meeting her client, Mia, at her need. Simply talking about
   feeling depressed does not help Mia to find housing, search for a job, find
   steady income, and regain stability so that she can parent her children
   again.
2. What resources are available within Mia's community? More importantly, why
   does Dr. Avery not know about these resources and how to activate the relevant
   ones? Mia might benefit from shelter care, job readiness training, temporary cash
   and/or food assistance, and family supportive services through the Department of
   Children Services or local charities and churches.
3. Dr. Avery must avail herself of the support and experience of her supervisor to help her to navigate this difficult situation. Not talking to her
   supervisor is potentially putting both of them at risk of providing poor care
   to the client.

The Case of Rules of Group Therapy at the Arch Street Center

Several clients at the Arch Street Center are on the verge of being terminated from the treatment program due to noncompliance.[1] The clients live on the city's east side and the Arch Street Center in downtown. The mandatory group therapy sessions are held on Tuesday and Thursday mornings from 9:00 a.m. to 11:00 a.m. According to the group therapist, three clients in particular – Maria, a Mexican–American woman; Nadine, a biracial woman; and Tyson, an African–American man – have inconsistent attendance. Each has arrived late three times (sometimes 45 minutes late) to group "without good excuses," which is seen as an indicator of their resistance and lack of commitment. The center director, Ms. Williams, asked to speak with Maria after the group to warn her that she was in danger of being terminated. Maria attempted to explain that they had difficulty getting to the center due to the unpredictable bus schedule – some days the two buses the clients ride run on time, and other days either one or both of the buses is late. Ms. Williams listened impatiently and told Maria, "You, Nadine, and Tyson just need to put more effort in or decide if you really want to be here or not. I would suggest that you work on your time management and organize your kids and your mornings much better. Probably you should get up earlier to give yourself enough time to get here. You have been late too many times, Maria, and it is up to you to do better. I hope you can pull it together!" Maria quietly said, "OK," and left the building. While walking to the bus stop, Maria started to cry, feeling frustrated, misunderstood, and hurt.

Discussion of the Ethical Dilemma and Associated Professional Considerations

The group therapy rules of the Arch Street Center illustrate a lack of cultural competence at the institutional level enacted by the therapists and center director to the detriment of the agency's clients. The attendance policy of the Arch Street Center does not appear to consider the environmental barriers that might hinder clients' ability to access mental health services. The APA Code (2010) 3.01 Unfair Discrimination indicates that psychologists must not discriminate provision of services on the basis of age, race, gender, socioeconomic status, or national origin which are legally protected social identities. Moreover, APA (2003) Guideline 6 – "Psychologists are encouraged to use organizational change processes to support culturally informed organizational (policy) development and practices" (p. 392) – is particularly germane. The mental health professionals at the Arch Street Center, in setting and implementing the attendance policy, apparently lack knowledge of the communities that they serve. Knowing the bus routes and bus schedules would allow the clinicians to develop an attendance policy that better fits the daily lives of their clients. In this situation, the clinicians have not considered the actual barriers that their client's encounter. (Our assumption is that the clinicians lack knowledge. We are loathe to consider a situation where the professionals do have this knowledge but do not care.)

---

[1] Greenleaf and Bryant (2012) briefly mention a similar situation about bus transportation, rush hour, and agency policy. We utilized our own experiences with client transportation difficulties, expanded the Greenleaf and Bryant example, and added details for our purposes.

Maria explained what the obstacle was, but Ms. Williams did not believe Maria and instead implied that Maria was not dedicated and was unorganized and lazy. Ms. Williams added insult to Maria's injury and committed a so-called microaggression with monumental impact. The APA guideline calls for clinicians to utilize "culturally informed organizational policy." Clearly, the Arch Street Center's policy is not culturally informed. Apparently, Ms. Williams and her staff are not aware that the bus route begins at 8:00 a.m. and that if both buses are on time, Maria, Nadine, and Tyson would arrive at the Center at 8:55 a.m. However, as all regular riders of public transportation know, buses can be unreliable. Maria can do everything right and still be 20 minutes late through no fault of her own. It is surprising and disconcerting that the center's staff and director do not know this. Moreover, Ms. Williams' dismissive, patronizing, and disrespectful behavior toward Maria at best indicates a lack of awareness and at worst might indicate a prevailing set of assumptions and biases that the professional staff hold against their clients. Ms. Williams' comments blame Maria for her circumstances. Wrenn (1962) would say that the professionals at the Arch Street Center are culturally encapsulated, being unaware of the social conditions around them. The consequence of this encapsulation has erected a barrier that makes access to mental health services difficult for some clients. This situation could be easily remedied if the staff modified the start time of the group to 9:30 a.m., which would provide a needed cushion for the clients who rely on public transportation. Empathy from the clinicians at the Arch Street Center would be a good first step toward making the necessary changes.

The American Counseling Association's Advocacy Competencies (Lewis, Arnold, House, & Toporek, 2002) might even propel the clinicians to collaborate with existing community organizations in order to address the inequitable distribution of reductions in public transportation whereby certain communities bear the brunt of budget cuts resulting in fewer public transportation options. "When counselors identify systemic factors that act as barriers to their students' or clients' development, they often wish that they could change the environment and prevent some of the problems that they see every day" (Lewis et al., 2002, p. 2). In order to be effective advocates, clinicians must identify those impinging environmental factors, develop community alliances, and listen effectively in order to change the system. "Change is a process that requires vision, persistence, leadership, collaboration, systems analysis, and strong data" (p. 2). Ms. Williams and the staff can begin by changing the time of the group session in order to be more responsive (and less discriminatory) to the needs of the community they serve. In fact, connecting with the local community is a key element of cultural humility (Tervalon & Murry-Garcia, 1998).

Recommendations

1. The staff at the Arch Street Center must learn more about the communities that they serve, perhaps by leaving the office to forge alliances and to gain familiarity with resources and community leaders.

2. The voices of the clients appear to not be heard at the Arch Street Center. Perhaps the center could develop a consumer advisory board that could participate in developing policy, conducting a needs assessment, and advising on programming.

3. The staff might need additional diversity training to explore their own biases, particularly their positionality and privileges. In particular, Ms. Williams made some assumptions about Maria and committed a microaggression against Maria. The staff might benefit from exploring the stereotypes they hold about various racial and ethnic groups.

Ethical Principles for Culturally Competent Practice

Following the framework of awareness, knowledge, and skills, ethical practice with persons of color can intersect with the ethical principles that guide psychological practice generally. Kitchener (1984) outlined ethical principles for practice: autonomy, nonmaleficence, beneficence, justice, and fidelity. Kitchener explains that the principle of autonomy includes more than respect for individuality. Rather, it is expressed as mutual respect. In our framework, we underscore the importance of recognizing that cultural differences may lead to differences in values and differences in motivations for decisions from clients. Therefore, awareness of how one's biases, stereotypes, and experiences shape reactions can be helpful to ensuring that clinicians are not inadvertently making judgments that do not respect culture, language, and values. Clinicians must understand how institutional and cultural racism impacts people of color. For instance, in the case example at the Arch Street Center, Ms. Williams failed to recognize how her reaction and the center's policy unintentionally disregarded their clients' contextual barriers to treatment, thereby creating an institutional constraint on their access to treatment. It may be unrealistic to expect clients of color to make decisions or to initiate action within social and institutional systems where they do not hold status or power and instead may feel alienated and marginalized. White privilege may enhance a clinician's feeling of entitlement within a given system, which does not necessarily translate to people of color who have been marginalized and discriminated against in these same institutions. From the perspective of cultural humility, autonomy serves both as a process of mutuality in providing care, whereby the clinician recognizes the standpoint of the client and their assessment of institutional and structural influence; as well as the attribute of egoless (Foronda et al., 2016).

Nonmaleficence, the principle that guides "do no harm," is directly relevant to ethical practice with people of color. Certainly there are guiding practices, such as the decisions that may infringe on one's civil rights or misuse of assessment (as cited by Kitchener), but we would argue that the very nature of addressing racial and cultural differences is part of the ethical responsibility of practitioners. Given the literature reviewed above surrounding the degree of cultural mistrust, as well as the pernicious impact of practice-as-usual that does not attend to the culture-specific worldviews and experiences of clients of color, it may follow that when clinicians avoid certain topics due to their own discomfort or their lack of awareness, clients are harmed by what goes unsaid. This was evident in the case of

Sarah and Ignacio. Due to Sarah's discomfort with addressing cultural differences, she neglected to attend to a vital part of Ignacio's identity. By not addressing the complexity of clients' multiple identities, clinicians may reinforce a client's assumption that therapy (like the larger society) is not a safe space to discuss racial or other cultural experiences. This inadvertent silencing would certainly make the development of a working alliance more difficult. Additionally, as Sue (2003) has stated, the incorrect assumptions we can draw based on our worldviews and assumptions of what constitutes "normal" behavior as opposed to abnormality may bias us toward an incorrect diagnosis and labeling of a client of color. This label may then inform treatment and other professional opinions, which may inadvertently harm the client's well-being. Conversely, the case of Dr. Louis and Rachelle illustrates that when clinicians attend to clients' cultural identities, they validate and affirm their experiences as cultural beings. Dr. Louis acted in a manner that involved not only taking care to do no harm, but also creating a positive and supportive interaction with Rachelle, his client.

Beneficence can be seen to extend beyond the conventional individual treatment model to examine the person in relation to their community, as well as the social and political systems in which the practitioner and client both exist. As an ethical principle, beneficence obviously demands that the clinician works toward the ultimate benefit for the client. In the utilitarian sense (the greatest good), a clinician motivated by beneficence might devote time and energy to working toward policy change in order to increase criminal penalties for domestic violence. This advocacy work might not impact a current client who is leaving an abusive situation, but can serve the overall good of the community. This example may seem to overlap with the notion of justice, but Kitchener's (1984) original justice question, posed over 30 years ago, is particularly relevant to psychology today: "To what extent do we have an ethical obligation to insure equal access to mental health services?" (p. 50). Communities of color experience inequities in access to mental health care services and are given treatments that are inadequate. Thus, it follows that justice is not being upheld generally in clinical practice. Did the response of Ms. Williams and the staff of the Arch Street Center uphold the spirit of beneficence? In short, no. Alternatively, if they had taken Maria's concerns seriously and changed their policy to adapt to and meet the needs of the people they serve, they would then be upholding the ethical principle of beneficence. As an overarching principle, it is imperative that ethical services with persons of color remove barriers to access and are delivered in a way that is culturally competent and aware of the individual and community needs. As another example, in the case of Dr. Avery and Mia, Dr. Avery's desire to do good did not serve the ultimate benefit of the client, Mia. Instead, as suggested, Dr. Avery should work to advocate and connect Mia to services and the support of her community, thereby creating a sustained, positive contribution to Mia's well-being.

Finally, the principle of fidelity asks that clinicians are truthful and loyal to their clients. Here it is recommended that clinicians be truthful about the nature and limitations of practice and about their competency, and in this way work to create a strong alliance between themselves and their clients. Loyalty asks clinicians to go beyond what may be a standard obligation of services, extending loyalty to the clinician's investment in the community in which they work. Faithfulness to the community represents a principle of mutuality or solidarity with communities of color. While the clinician may not be from the community and may be able to be differentiated by a myriad of identity dynamics, they may strive toward being a strong ally and seek to understand the community they serve, including knowledge of the history, leaders, cultural institutions, and social services that exist in a community. Sue (2003) suggests that culturally competent therapists "do not live in isolation from a diverse world. They are involved with culturally diverse groups outside of their work role – community events, celebrations, neighbors, and so forth. They realize that becoming culturally competent comes best through lived experience" (p. 6). This approach may challenge some clinicians' views of appropriate boundaries. Boundaries are themselves a cultural enterprise. We must be flexible and creative when working within communities of color. Dr. Louis, in the case example above, acted in a manner that served to strengthen his fidelity to the therapeutic relationship with his client. By attending her poetry reading, he relinquished the power and authority of the therapeutic office and moved into a shared space that required vulnerability on his part, as well as from Rachelle.

Conclusion

Cultural competence is an ethical imperative. Effective service to racial and ethnic communities requires clinicians to have cultural knowledge, to be aware of their own biases, privileges, assumptions, and positionality, to apply their skill set appropriately to meet clients' needs, and to utilize advocacy skills to challenge policies, practices, and barriers to their clients' well-being. Cultural competence requires a holistic appraisal of the person and their environment, as well as the ability to design a range of interventions to address clients' needs. Furthering competence, cultural humility is the manifestation of ethical practice that is culturally informed. Cultural humility is not only aspirational – by its very nature, it outlines the attributes befitting of culturally competent practice. With cultural competence and cultural humility as the foundation, mental health professionals should be equipped to provide ethical and efficacious services.

References

American Psychological Association (1997). *Can – or should – Americans be colorblind? Psychological research reveals fallacies in a colorblind response to racism.* Washington, DC: American Psychological Association.

American Psychological Association (2003). Guidelines on multicultural education, training, research, practice, and organizational change for psychologists. *American Psychologist, 58*, 377–402.

American Psychological Association (2010). Amendments to the 2002 "Ethical principles of psychologists and code of conduct". (2010). *American Psychologist, 65(5)*, 493.

Atkinson, D. R., Casas, A., & Abreu, J. (1992). Mexican–American acculturation, counselor ethnicity and cultural sensitivity, and perceived counselor competence. *Journal of Counseling Psychology, 39*, 515–520.

BEA Virtual Working Group (2015). Preparing psychologists to serve a diverse public: A core requirement in doctoral education and training a pedagogical statement. *Training and Education in Professional Psychology, 9,* 269–270.

Cokley, K. (2007). Critical issues in the measurement of ethnic and racial identity: A referendum on the state of the field. *Journal of Counseling Psychology, 54(3),* 224–234.

Council of National Psychological Associations for the Advancement of Ethnic Minority Interests (2003). *Psychological treatment of ethnic minority populations.* Washington, DC: Association of Black Psychologists.

Foronda, C., Baptiste, D. L., Reinholdt, M. M., & Ousman, K. (2016). Cultural humility: A concept analysis. *Journal of Transcultural Nursing, 27,* 210–217.

Gallardo, M. E. (2009). Ethics and multiculturalism: Where the rubber hits the road. *Professional Psychology: Research & Practice, 40,* 426–430.

Glass, L. L. (2003). The gray areas of boundary crossings and violations. *American Journal of Psychotherapy, 57,* 429–444.

Greenleaf, A. T. & Bryant, R. M. (2012). Perpetuating oppression: Does the current counseling discourse neutralize social action? *Journal for Social Action in Counseling and Psychology, 4,* 18–29.

Hall, C. C. I. (1995). Asian eyes: Body image and eating disorders of Asian and Asian American women. *Eating Disorders: The Journal of Treatment & Prevention, 3,* 8–19.

Hook, J. N., Davis, D. E., Owen, J., Worthington, E. L., Jr., & Utsey, S. O. (2013). Cultural humility: Measuring openness to culturally diverse clients. *Journal of Counseling Psychology, 60,* 353–366.

Inman, A. G. & Ladany, N. (2014). Multicultural competencies in psychotherapy supervision. In F. T. L. Leong (Ed.), *American Psychological Association's handbook of multicultural psychology* (pp. 643–658). Washington, DC: American Psychological Association.

Iyer, A, Leach, C. W., & Pedersen, A. (2004). Racial wrongs and restitutions: The role of guilt and other group-based emotions. In M. Fine, L. Weis, L. P. Pruitt, & A. Burns (Eds.), *Off white: Readings on power, privilege, and resistance* (2nd edn.) (pp. 345–361). New York, NY: Routledge.

Kitchener, K. S. (1984). Intuition, critical evaluation and ethical principles: The foundation for ethical decisions in counseling psychology. *The Counseling Psychologist, 12,* 43–55.

Knox, S., Burkard, A. W., Johnson, A. J., Suzuki, L. A., & Ponterotto, J. G. (2003). African American and European American therapists' experience of addressing race in cross-racial psychotherapy dyads. *Journal of Counseling Psychology, 50,* 466–481.

Lee, M. R. & Thai, C. J. (2015). Asian American phenotypicality and experiences of psychological distress: More than meets the eyes. *Asian American Journal of Psychology, 6,* 242–251.

Lewis, J., Arnold, M. S., House, R., & Toporek, R. L. (2002). ACA Advocacy competencies. Advocacy Task Force, American Counseling Association. Retrieved from http://www.counseling.org/resources/html

Markus, H. R. (2008). Pride, prejudice, and ambivalence: Toward a unified theory of race and ethnicity. *American Psychologist, 63(8),* 651–670.

Ridley, C. R. (1985). Imperatives for ethnic and cultural relevance in psychology training programs. *Professional Psychology: Research and Practice, 16,* 611–622.

Shelton, J. N., West, T. V., & Trail, T. E. (2010). Concerns about appearing prejudice: Implications for anxiety during daily interracial interactions. *Group Processes & Intergroup Relations, 13,* 329–344.

Shin, S.-M., Chow, C., Camacho-Gonsalves, T., Levy, R. J., Allen, I. E., & Leff, H. S. (2005). A meta-analytic review of racial–ethnic matching for African American and Caucasian American clients and clinicians. *Journal of Counseling Psychology, 52,* 45–56.

Smedley, A., & Smedley, B. D. (2005). Race as biology is fiction, racism as a social problem is real: Anthropological and historical perspectives on the social construction of race. *American Psychologist, 60(1),* 16–26.

Spanierman L. B., Todd N. R., & Anderson, C. J. (2009). Psychosocial costs of racism to whites: Understanding patterns among university students. *Journal of Counseling Psychology, 56,* 239–252.

Speight, S. L. (2012). An exploration of boundaries and solidarity in counseling relationships. *The Counseling Psychologist, 40,* 133–157.

Sue, D. W., Arredondo, P., & McDavis, R. J. (1992). Multicultural counseling competencies and standards: A call to the profession. *Journal of Counseling & Development, 70(4),* 477–486.

Sue, D. W., Bernier, J. E., Durran, A., Feinberg, L., Pedersen, P., Smith, E. J., & Vasquez-Nuttall, E. (1982). Position paper: Cross-cultural counseling competencies. *The Counseling Psychologist, 10(2),* 45–52.

Sue, D. W., Capodilupo, C. M., Torino, G. C., Bucceri, J. M., Holder, A. M. B., Nadal, K. L., & Esquilin, M. (2007). Racial microaggressions in everyday life: Implications for clinical practice. *American Psychologist, 62(4),* 271–286.

Sue, D. W., Carter, R. T., Casas, J. M., Fouad, N. A., Ivey, A. E., Jensen, M., Vazquez-Nutall, E. (1998). Multicultural aspects of counseling, Vol. 11. *Multicultural Counseling Competencies: Individual and Organizational Development.* Thousand Oaks, CA: Sage Publications.

Sue, S. (2003). In defense of cultural competency in psychotherapy and treatment. *American Psychologist, 58(11),* 964–970.

Tervalon, M. & Murray-Garcia, J. (1998). Cultural humility versus cultural competence: A critical distinction in defining physician training outcomes in multicultural education. *Journal of Health Care for the Poor and Unserved, 9,* 117–125.

Tirpak, D. M., & Lee, S. S. (2012). Navigating peer-to-peer multiple relationships in professional psychology programs. *Training and Education in Professional Psychology, 6(3),* 135–141.

Todd, N. R., Spanierman, L. B., & Aber, M. S. (2010). White students reflecting on whiteness: Understanding emotional responses. *Journal of Diversity in Higher Education, 3,* 97–110.

U.S. Department of Health and Human Services (2001). *Mental health: Culture, race, and ethnicity. A supplement to mental health: A report of the Surgeon General.* Washington, DC: U.S. Department of Health and Human Services.

Vera, E. M. & Speight, S. L. (2003). Multicultural competence, social justice and counseling psychology: Expanding our roles. *The Counseling Psychologist, 31*, 253–272.

Weber, L. (2009). Understanding race, class, gender, and sexuality. *A Conceptual Framework* (2nd ed.). New York, NY: Oxford University Press.

Wrenn, G. (1962). The culturally encapsulated counselor. *Harvard Educational Review, 32*, 444–449.

16 Aging: Ethical Issues in Working with Diverse Populations

Mary Miller Lewis, Katherine Ramos, and Ashley Oliver

Most psychologists are aware that the aging population is one of the fastest-growing demographic groups in the United States, consisting of an increasingly complex and diverse population of individuals (Karel, Gatz, & Smyer, 2012). The current prevalence of mental health disorders, including dementia, is estimated to be over 20 percent in this population (Karel et al., 2012). Beyond diagnosable mental health disorders, older adults experiencing developmental changes in late life (e.g., retirement, changes in health status, modification in social structures) can also benefit from psychological interventions that offer emotional and psychological support (Qualls, 2011). The increasing number of older adults needing psychological services underscores a significant need in the workforce expansion for geropsychologists and geriatric providers. Workforce surveys indicate that approximately 39 percent of psychologists provided psychological care to an adult over the age of 65; however, only 4.2 percent indicated having specific training in the unique physical, cognitive, social, and psychological concerns that face older adults (Hoge, Karel, Zeiss, Alegria, & Moye, 2015). Further, the treatment of older adults requires specialized training, knowledge, skills, and ability competencies (APA, 2014; Karel et al., 2012; Molinari, 2011). The discrepancy between the expanding number of older adults needing psychological care and the number of practitioners that specialize in the treatment of older adults is a concern, especially given the unique ethical and legal issues that can occur.

Specifically, the ethical issues that arise when working with older adults relate to the unique physical and emotional health status that can occur with this group, as well as and the complexities of intersections of identity with cohort, culture, race and ethnicity, sex and gender, socioeconomic status, sexual orientation, ability status, and religion. In addition, the top ethical issues encountered by psychologists working with older adults can vary based on whether the presenting concern is assessment, treatment, or consultation. Location of service (e.g., home, outpatient clinic, hospital, Veterans Affairs [VA], assisted living, skilled nursing facility [SNF], or long-term care [LTC] facility) also plays a role, highlighting additional factors that come from working with interdisciplinary treatment teams, site-specific policies, and Health Insurance Portability and Accountability Act (HIPAA) regulations.

The primary ethical issues in geriatric care include a range of issues: professional competence, confidentiality, informed consent, capacity versus competency, and conflict between autonomy and safety (Bush, 2009, 2012; Karel, 2009; Molinari, 2011). Within these broad categories, there may be distinct ethical issues that arise depending on end-of-life concerns, elder abuse, substance use/abuse, family dynamics, cognitive impairment, and treatment setting (Bush, 2009; Karel, 2009). Unique ethical issues also exist for older adults regarding driving competency, finances, relocation, advance directives, and treatment decisions around medication or electroconvulsive therapy (Hays & Jennings, 2015). Complicating these ethical issues may be legal concerns that may arise when working with older adults, such as those related to elder abuse and neglect or issues around capacity and competency. Particularly in LTC, prevalent ethical issues include topics such as informed consent, confidentiality, privacy, conflict of interest, and advocacy (Karel, 2009; Lichtenberg et al., 1998). Although this chapter is not exhaustive or specific to all of these issues, they are critical factors to consider when working with older adults.

The cases of Mrs. T, Mr. O and Mr. L presented below are not necessarily "standard" ethical cases seen in the aging population; however, they are presented as complex ethical issues that can arise when working with older adults. Further, all three cases reflect Karel's (2009) framework for ethical decision-making, which includes the following five steps: (1) clarify what ethical dilemma is; (2) clarify the relevant stakeholders and each of their values, goals, and interests; (3) clarify the decision-making authority, who has the right to make the decision in a particular situation; (4) consider all ethically justifiable options and their pros and cons for each stakeholder; and (5) implement a plan, evaluate, and reevaluate.

The Case of Mrs. T – Safety versus Autonomy

Mrs. T was 77 years old, African–American, female, heterosexual, and Christian. She was initially seen in a SNF due to Type II diabetes complications and a nonhealing wound resulting in a below-the-knee amputation. Mrs. T was married and had no biological children. She was initially referred for symptoms of depression and "noncompliance with diabetes management." Mrs. T was agreeable to the initial assessment and provided consent. She scored 7/15 on the Geriatric Depression Scale (Sheikh & Yesavage, 1986), which indicated moderate depression. Mrs. T reported symptoms of difficulty with falling asleep, low energy, irritability, low mood and feeling "blue," difficulty concentrating, and feelings of worthlessness. She demonstrated psychomotor retardation during interview. Notably, Mrs. T also reported discontinued participation and disinterest in enjoyable activities (e.g., reading). Mrs. T stated she had not previously been depressed, although "there were plenty of times where I was down" in the past, which she attributed to her spouse's declining health and caregiver stress.

During the initial assessment, Mrs. T's score on the Mini-Mental Status Exam (Folstein, Folstein, & McHugh, 1975) was 24/30, indicating mild cognitive impairment. Specific concerns included impairments in the areas of short-term memory and orientation and naming errors, in addition to attention difficulties. She participated in treatment planning and identified goals related to adjusting to her amputation and prosthesis, loss of independence, and sadness about the change in her role as a spouse. She was diagnosed with major depressive disorder, single episode, moderate, per the Diagnostic and Statistical Manual of Mental Disorders (5th edn.; DSM-5; American Psychiatric Association, 2013).

Exploring Ethical Decision-Making

There were a number of ethical issues that arose almost immediately with Mrs. T's case. For the purposes of this chapter, the focus will be on the conflict between Mrs. T's right to autonomy versus protection of her safety, APA General Principle A, Beneficence and Nonmaleficence and APA General Principle E, Respect for People's Rights and Dignity. Specifically, Mrs. T had a strong desire to return home to her spouse and be fully autonomous in her role as a wife. She was her husband's primary caregiver, and due to her religious and cultural identity, felt a strong need to be the sole caregiver for him, refusing the offer of home health or assistance by family. However, there were several concerns about her safety and ability to function independently at home that were brought up by the treatment team.

First, Mrs. T demonstrated some mild cognitive impairments specifically in the areas of short-term memory and appropriate decision-making. For example, she often forgot her physical therapy appointments and whether she had taken her diabetes medication. She was impulsive at times, standing without her walker even when asked to do so or going to the bathroom without assistance. Second, she also was "noncompliant" (per staff reports) with her diet, choosing to eat sweet foods that spiked her blood sugar instead of low-sugar foods. Mrs. T was aware that her diet was negatively impacting her health, but informed all the SNF staff and this psychologist that she had the "right to eat the foods I enjoy" because she had been eating these foods her entire life and "wasn't going to stop now." She clearly identified her eating habits as her "only pleasure" at this time in her life. Further, Mrs. T was reluctant to take the antidepressant medication prescribed by the hospital after her surgery, stating, "I'm not crazy."

Third, as her treatment for depression progressed and Mrs. T began to disclose more freely to the psychologist, she revealed that her spouse was also demonstrating some memory decline and she was fearful that he was taking the wrong medication at home, or worse, not taking his medication at all. Mrs. T's had limited insight into her own slight memory loss, so it was unclear whether her reports were accurate or due to her own memory difficulties. There was significant concern on the part of the psychologist, as well as the SNF staff, as to whether Mrs. T or her husband were safe in their home.

Using Karel's (2009) framework for ethical decision-making, the therapist considered multiple ethical dilemmas. First, the safety of the client and her right to autonomy were concerns. There were potential concerns related to a number of APA Ethics Code standards (2002, 2010) including 3.04 Avoiding Harm, 3.09 Cooperation with Other Professionals, 3.10 Informed Consent, 4.01 Maintaining Confidentiality, and 9.06 Interpreting Test Results. While the psychologist wanted to respect Mrs. T's cultural values and desire to return to be the primary caregiver, she was also concerned about the neglect within the home as well as the client's lack of self-care. While Mrs. T was in the SNF and was safe in that environment, the psychologist also wanted to focus on using therapy to explore the safety issues at home, address self-care issues, clarify cognitive issues, and also explore the physician's recommendation of antidepressant use. These discussions also focused on Mrs. T's spouse and his health and memory issues. Due to Mr. T's failing health and inability to be come in for interview, it was challenging to verify Mrs. T's reports of his cognitive issues. Further, Mrs. T was upset at staff for "trying to control" her diet choices and felt pressured to make decisions that were inconsistent with her life values (e.g., stay in the SNF versus going home to her spouse), resulting in her resistance to complying with requests. During therapy sessions, she clearly admitted that this worsened her depression as well as contributed to her lack of participation in physical and occupational therapy sessions. All of these factors were taken into consideration when identifying the ethical concerns at hand.

Second, identifying the relevant stakeholders was important. The primary stakeholder here was the client and her desire to return home as healthy and functional as possible. Her values included her self-worth as a caregiver, concern for her spouse, and her belief that she would be a negligent caregiver if she failed to care for her spouse and herself versus asking others for assistance. Secondary stakeholders included the client's spouse, family, the facility staff, the physician, and the psychologist. The psychologist discussed the stakeholders' values with the client and explored with her whether these values conflicted or were in sync with her own values and goals. It was clear that while the client's spouse and family did support her return home, their goals was focused less on caregiving and more on being emotional and spiritually supportive figures. During the therapy process, it became clear that Mrs. T's church also was a stakeholder, as she had been a member for a number of years. Her pastor frequently visited her in the SNF and often expressed his desire to see her healthy and offer her support.

In order to clarify who the decision-maker was in this case, it was important to explore the client's cognitive deficits and severity of impairment. At the request of the physician and physical therapy staff, and with the client's consent, the psychologist conducted an in-depth neuropsychological screening to explore competency. Although the client continued to demonstrate cognitive deficits that met the criteria of mild cognitive impairment, she exhibited mostly intact decision-making abilities. It was necessary to use age- and race-adjusted norms for this client in order to conduct an accurate assessment of her cognition, which anticipated and resolved any potential ethical issue for APA Ethics Code Standard 9.06 Interpreting Test Results.

For Mrs. T., even though she was the primary decision-maker and was cognitively able to do so, due to her cultural and religious beliefs, she also wanted the input of her family. Mrs. T also highly valued her privacy when it came to the therapy sessions and how much information was shared with SNF staff, but she wanted "everything" shared with her spouse and family. In this case, it was crucial to discuss the role of confidentiality in the therapy process and have her sign the appropriate forms so that the psychologist could communicate with her family to discuss the issues around her emotional well-being. She did sign the release of information forms so that the psychologist could speak first to her nieces and then to her spouse. Mrs. T's nieces confirmed that Mr. T did have some cognitive deficits, but they were unsure how much those deficits were due to actual cognitive decline versus poor physical condition since Mrs. T had been at the SNF. A plan was discussed with the nieces to take Mr. T to his primary care physician not only as a way to start a plan of care for him regarding physical and cognitive care, but also to help alleviate Mrs. T's concerns related to his medication and health.

The next step in the decision-making process was to explore all the ethically justifiable options. The ethically justifiable options included: (1) the psychologist supporting the client's return home with full-time home health care, which the client could not afford; (2) the client staying within the SNF and moving to an LTC status until she regained strength, so that she could have the health care support she medically required; or (3) if the client returned home against medical advice, the psychologist would contact Adult Protective Services (APS) so that they could assist her in identifying safe ways to stay at home. One additional ethically justifiable option was for Mrs. T to allow the psychologist to talk in more specific detail to the therapy staff about how her depression was impacting her ability to fully participate in rehabilitation sessions. This would also allow the psychologist to observe sessions in order to make "in-time" recommendations and reduce the conflict between Mrs. T and staff while also facilitating better engagement by Mrs. T. The psychologist discussed how the antidepressant medication prescribed by the physician may also assist her with energy, concentration, and mood so that she would be able to more fully participate in the rehabilitation process. In this way, Mrs. T could see the pros and cons of each treatment and identify her choices accordingly.

Ultimately, Mrs. T decided to stay in the rehabilitation facility for an extra week beyond her Medicare-approved stay to start taking her antidepressant medication, to continue therapy, and to allow the psychologist to speak with staff regarding how her depression was impacting her rehabilitation. As previously mentioned, Mrs. T signed a consent form for the psychologist to speak with her nieces and spouse regarding safety issues at home, as well as emotional concerns specific to caregiving and how this might impact Mrs. T's healing process and ability to function. Mrs. T was part of most of these phone conversations, held on speakerphone during her sessions, and was able to verbalize her feelings and needs with her family.

Mrs. T also worked out a plan in collaboration with therapy staff to work specifically on three top safety issues, including transfers in and out of the bathtub and on/off the toilet, precautions with standing in the kitchen, and the development of an alternate diet plan to help manage her diabetes. By collaborating on the safety plan, Mrs. T had a sense of control over the process and felt a sense of personal autonomy. Finally, Mrs. T agreed to have a one-month "trial" of daily nurses' visits from a faith-based home health agency that she selected with assistance from the facility social worker. All of these interventions allowed Mrs. T to have supervision and assistance in her own home for physical, emotional, and spiritual support and gave the home health social worker an opportunity to observe the potential neglect that was occurring in the home, while at the same time allowing Mrs. T the autonomy to go home and live "a happy life." Mrs. T chose not to follow-up with psychological counseling, but agreed to her antidepressant medication continuing to be monitored by her primary care physician.

Professional and Personal Difficulties in Ethical Decision-Making

This case ended well; however, this may not always hold true in cases involving the autonomy versus the safety of older adults, particularly in LTC or rehabilitation settings. Clients who are independent in decision-making can still make and have the right to make unhealthy choices, and therefore it is up to the psychologist to make clients aware of their options and follow the most ethical course of action. If Mrs. T had chosen to leave the facility against medical advice, the psychologist would have to explore options regarding reporting the client's situation to APS and informing Mrs. T of that decision. It may also have been critical to also consult with another psychologist regarding the case to ensure that the psychologist was seeing the full range of ethical issues and options in order to act in fully ethical manner. Mrs. T had an extensive support system that rallied behind her when they realized how much she had been hiding from them, and they found a way to get her the support she needed. Not every older adult has a supportive network of family, friends, or faith-based communities that can assist with this process. In those cases, it is challenging to find the balance between autonomy and safety for older adults having medical and emotional needs.

The treating psychologist had a number of conflicting concerns with this case. In this particular LTC facility, the therapy staff and psychologist work closely together and rely on each other as a team. However, Mrs. T clearly had a negative relationship with a number of the therapists; had she felt that the psychologist was colluding with the therapists (e.g., "you're part of them"), even with the goal of helping her, it would have adversely impacted the therapeutic alliance and undermined the outcome. The struggle to openly address the client's self-care and possible neglect issues without alienating the client or the staff was a theme throughout the treatment, as staff often felt that the psychologist was minimizing the client's cognitive impairment. Additionally, the psychologist also had to look internally at her own bias regarding older adults and how they are treated within a mostly paternalistic health care system. Mrs. T was quite frail, and there was an underlying desire not to just keep her safe, but to "take care of her," despite her assertions that she could function independently. Internalized stereotypes of older adults, when not openly acknowledged and addressed, can contribute to unethical treatment. Further, as Mrs. T was African–American and the psychologist was Caucasian, the psychologist had concerns that implicit bias could impact her care of the client. It was clear that Mrs. T had negative experiences with the medical field, likely due to her ethnicity, gender, and socioeconomic status, and therefore the psychologist's inclusion "with those people" was a constant threat to the therapeutic alliance. There were no easy answers to these concerns, and while during treatment the psychologist openly addressed ethnicity and gender with the client, she minimized these concerns in session. This is a reminder to constantly evaluate the therapeutic alliance and address threats to ethical treatment, particularly with underserved groups.

The Case of Mr. O – Abuse and Confidentiality

Mr. O was a 68-year-old Caucasian heterosexual male with no known religious affiliation. He was widowed and had two adult children. He lived independently in his home and as of six months ago has been residing in an LTC unit of a hospital. Last year, Mr. O suffered a cerebrovascular accident on the left side of his brain, leading to severe right-side immobility and impaired speech, specifically language apraxia. He was considered physically disabled and was issued an electric wheelchair for mobility. Prior to being admitted to the hospital, he lived with his daughter at his home for a period six months. She served as his primary caregiver. As Mr. O's physical needs became increasingly demanding, his daughter sought and admitted her father to a hospital offering LTC and rehabilitation services. Since his time in LTC, Mr. O had become increasingly socially isolated, rarely desiring to be helped out of bed and onto his electric wheelchair. He made minimal eye contact with others. Thereafter, he was referred for psychology services as his nurse practitioner grew increasingly concerned over his decompensating disposition that seemed consistent with depressive symptoms. He also presented with loss of interest in participating in previously attended recreational activities as hosted by the facility.

Once agreeable to treatment, he worked with a male psychology clinical intern. Mr. O displayed symptoms consistent with other specified anxiety disorder, limited symptom attacks, and major depressive disorder, moderate, recurrent episode (per DSM-5; American Psychiatric Association, 2013). Mr. O indicated his symptoms were a result of his loss of strength and independence and were further worsened by feeling helpless and lonely while living in an LTC residence with infrequent visitations from his daughter. Mr. O, in collaboration with his therapist, set goals of becoming more self-reliant and autonomous and wanted to learn coping strategies to improve his mood. As Mr. O made progress throughout the sessions, he disclosed having a tumultuous relationship with his daughter, though he desired a better relationship. He further noted having no relationship or contact with other family members. In these later sessions, he self-described as an "absent father" for the majority of his life who also struggled with substance use, though currently he has been sober. As of late, he had become upset and frustrated by the decline in visits from his daughter, though he expressed excitement to go home on pass.

Upon Mr. O's return, and during a scheduled therapy session, Mr. O was melancholy, visibly upset, and in tears. When checking in, Mr. O disclosed he and his daughter had had a serious verbal altercation. Mr. O cried loudly and shook his head, but said "yes" when asked if he was aggressed by his daughter. He then looked at the therapist and verbalized that he could "trust only him" and did not want to make an issue of this matter. Mr. O further stated that "it's not a big deal." Mr. O subsequently pleaded with the therapist not to disclose this matter to any other provider, threatening to discontinue therapy treatment altogether. The intern is unsure how to proceed regarding breaking confidentiality and trust with this patient, while also striving to protect and maintain Mr. O's safety.

Exploring Ethical Decision-Making

This case presents difficult ethical dilemmas that necessitate careful considerations in order to ensure both the safety and the psychological well-being of Mr. O. To begin, this older adult represents two vulnerable populations: one that is elderly and another that is based on his disability status. Given Mr. O's disclosure to the therapist, there is concern about abuse, neglect, and possible negligence, which he appears resistant to fully disclosing. Safety is also a concern that may involve informing an interdisciplinary team under Mr. O's care, including discussions of contacting APS.

The ethical issues highlighted in this case and the decision-making process thereafter were primarily guided by the APA's General Principles: Principle A, Beneficence and Nonmaleficence; Principle B, Fidelity and Responsibility; and Principle E, Respect for People's Rights and Dignity. For this case, the ethical decision-making process occurred according to Karel's (2009) and Celia Fisher's (2009) models. Using these two models, the therapist processed the case in the following way: in order to work through Step 1, the therapist, who was also a supervised intern, was committed to doing right by his client, Mr. O. Therefore, in considering his role as a therapist and a trainee, the therapist viewed himself as a person of integrity, compassion, and honesty. He was currently struggling with his desire not to betray Mr. O's trust while also maintaining confidentiality. During this step, the therapist came to a decision regarding the extent that "limits of confidentiality" applied to this case.

There were numerous ethical considerations to work through in Step 2. The therapist disclosed to Mr. O that he first must assess his current distress and, given the content shared in the session, the therapist must contact and discuss this matter with his supervisor. The therapist underscored his care for Mr. O, but unfortunately the patient said he may never trust the therapist again. Prior to adjourning the session, the therapist addressed Mr. O's immediate distress and reviewed emotion regulation strategies to mitigate concerns and anxiety. The therapist further reviewed the ethics code standards and met immediately with his supervisor to discuss the complexity of Mr. O's case and needed follow-up. In discussion and consultation with his supervisor, the therapist and the supervisor, Dr. A, discussed the most applicable ethical standards involved in this case as highlighted earlier.

Under Principle A, the trainee considered his own understanding of how this case was influenced by Mr. O's age and disability status and the additional supervision he needed (e.g., based on experience, needed referrals, working with the interdisciplinary team). The therapist then also processed how Principle B, Fidelity and Responsibility, 3.09 Cooperation with Other Professionals, and 3.11 Psychological Services Delivered to or Through Organizations played a role in this case. In his efforts to uphold such standards of conduct, he realized consulting with his supervisor and specific interdisciplinary team members (e.g., facility director, nurse practitioner, and social worker) was important. Finally, Principle E, Respect for People's Rights and Dignity, 4.01 Maintaining Confidentiality, 4.02 Discussing the

Limits of Confidentiality, 4.05 Disclosures, and 4.06 Consultations were considered. It was important to the trainee that he maintained Mr. O's dignity, privacy, and confidentiality. However, given the circumstances and after consulting with other professionals, it appeared that a full review of Mr. O's medical records when coming home from weekend passes was needed. Such additional investigation would help further address whether any changes in mood or physical appearance were noted by the admitting nurse. His medical records revealed a history of bruising upon returns from weekend passes, though Mr. O would be dismissive and attribute them to bruising easily when clumsily bumping into household items with his chair. Such new evidence raised further concern in protecting Mr. O. The trainee also realized that in breaking confidentiality he must also abide by hospital and state policies including regulations in reporting a case of elder abuse.

In following Step 3 (Fisher, 2009), the trainee gathered additional information regarding state and county law when reporting elder abuse. He also consulted with the hospital ethics committee to notify them of the matter, in addition to speaking directly with the facility director. He then scheduled a meeting with Mr. O, the attending nurse, the social worker, the trainee and Dr. A, the supervisor. Step 4 included a scheduled meeting with Mr. O's interdisciplinary team without Mr. O present in order to understand their concerns and perspectives. The rationale for this a priori meeting was twofold: (a) it allowed the interdisciplinary staff to discuss the current case (in its entirety) as a team, which also allowed everyone to fill in any ambiguity about vague details, misunderstandings, etc.; and (b) it offered an opportunity for the team to be in agreement and to offer a united front with the primary purpose of protecting the health and safety of Mr. O.

At this point in the case, Step 5 involved applying Steps 1–4. Therefore, ethical alternatives were discussed with the trainee's supervisor and interdisciplinary team, such as: not reporting elder abuse; the impact that such reporting would have with his daughter's relationship; and the likelihood that Mr. O would discontinue receiving therapy services and completely mistrust his providers. The trainee and supervisor, with the team's input, decided that a report needed to be made, as not reporting would cause more harm than good (e.g., 3.04 Avoiding Harm), and that such a report superseded complete confidentiality and aligned with ethical standard 4.02 (Limits of Confidentiality). Moreover, such a decision not only protected Mr. O, but also as psychology professionals, it is within the ethical scope of practice to report (e.g., Principle B, Fidelity and Responsibility). This consideration also involved keeping in mind that every decision made was also relayed to Mr. O as a sign of respect for his rights and concerns (e.g., Principle E, Respect for People's Rights and Dignity).

Upon identifying the ethical dilemmas present, followed by extensive review and consultation, the trainee selected a course of action (Step 6; Fisher, 2009). After consultation and treatment team meetings, the therapist followed up with Mr. O and discussed the need to break confidentiality, the reasons for this, and with whom his case was being discussed. Third, the interdisciplinary team and ethics committee met privately and agreed to a nursing report addressing Mr. O's bruises. Fourth, the therapist contacted APS directly and followed up with Mr. O. Finally, once APS was contacted, Mr. O was alerted and given support through this difficult time. Upon completion of the nursing report, APS was subsequently contacted. An APS worker was identified and communicated that Mr. O's evaluation would be initiated within 72 hours and a thorough evaluation completed within 30 days. Given that Mr. O has capacity, no consent by power of attorney or medical power of attorney was necessary. For this case, no additional modifications were needed for the ethical plan.

After the plan was implemented (Step 7; Fisher, 2009), Mr. O was frustrated and angry toward his therapist, though he agreed to having a nurse examine him. Mr. O was also against APS being contacted and expressed fear and anxiety about what may transpire. The therapist offered to alert Mr. O when the APS worker would contact him, and he was agreeable. Per the APS report, not enough evidence was found to indicate abuse. However, Mr. O would have supervised visits (as decided by APS) with his daughter until further notice.

At this time, Mr. O discontinued with psychology services, as he felt betrayed and hurt. The therapist processed this with him, discussing the possible harmful effects of prematurely terminating therapy, but ultimately respected his wishes. Four weeks later, Mr. O stopped by the therapist's office. He reported that he missed his time with the therapist and now understood his intentions. Mr. O and the trainee scheduled a session to discuss updates with each other. The session provided a unique opportunity in modeling how a ruptured therapeutic relationship could be repaired. It allowed Mr. O and the therapist to also continue their work. Mr. O benefitted from future sessions and engaged in additional behavioral activation strategies to improve his mood. He also decorated his room in order to feel more at home and began to foster new relationships with other members in the facility. He continued to have chaperoned visits with his daughter and happily reported that they are mending their relationship. Mr. O expressed his appreciation for the trainee's time and care at the end of termination.

Professional and Personal Difficulties in Ethical Decision-Making

For the trainee, the ethical decision-making process was both emotionally and socially taxing. Not only was this the trainee's first experience of elder abuse, he also genuinely cared for the safety of Mr. O. The trainee became aware of his own self-imposed pressure to ensure that he appropriately advocated for his vulnerable client. Furthermore, given Mr. O's isolation, his ability to emotionally connect and trust another individual was quite significant for the trainee. Unfortunately, the therapeutic relationship ruptured. This was a risk that the trainee needed to take in order to ensure Mr. O's best interests were at heart. However, this was a difficult risk to take, particularly because of the rapport and trust that was established in the therapeutic relationship. It also made the therapist question himself and whether he "could have done more" or approached the ethical dilemma differently. Another struggle the therapist experienced included involving APS. Mr. O potentially could have lost his family and succumbed to even worse depression. These additional dimensions weighed heavily on the trainee, as his efforts to ensure Mr. O's well-being in the long-term meant he had to jeopardize the therapeutic bond they had fostered in the short-term.

The trainee made significant attempts to also understand the present ethical dilemmas and how he personally felt from an ethical, contextualist perspective. He understood the universal value of autonomy and Mr. O's own struggle to care for himself and to be independent. He also understood that as a younger man and a minority, such statuses may have placed him in a position of being a gatekeeper to Mr. O's only source of family. From personal experience, the trainee had known and lived through the imposition of privilege from a majority group and consequently how the exertion of privilege in different circumstances had made him feel. For example, he had been made to feel "less than," incapable of succeeding, and alone. This was an experience that the trainee paralleled with his experience of Mr. O, and so (in this self-analysis) wanted to safeguard Mr. O from personal hurt.

The trainee also extensively reviewed the APA Guidelines for Practice with Older Adults (2014) to address whether his own attitudes and beliefs about aging (e.g., believing that Mr. O could not make his own decisions) may have colored his personal perspectives of Mr. O's needs and influenced his professional decisions in adopting and implementing an ethical plan. It benefited the trainee to have continuous supervision throughout this process and to consider how his position of privilege needed to be evaluated in order to make decisions in the best interests of Mr. O's safety and well-being. Though the relationship between Mr. O and the therapist ended well, such outcomes may not always occur. The self-exploration process and resolve to make just decisions that are in the best interests of a client are important. Equally important is how therapists can psychologically "ready" themselves (e.g., seeking consultation, participating in self-care, or engaging in self-exploration) to move forward with their own work when client cases go awry or feel personally disappointing.

The Case of Mr. L – Competency to Treat versus Not Treat and Confidentiality

Mr. L is a 72-year-old transgender (female to male) Latino who lived independently in the community. He began his gender transition journey when he was 26 years old after several severe bouts of depression due to feeling unhappy with trying to fit in with societal gender norms. Identifying as transgender was difficult for Mr. L as his family and Hispanic community did not support his transition. Five years later, Mr. L made the decision to begin hormone therapy, which significantly improved his mood. He finally began to feel like himself. While receiving hormone injections, Mr. L experienced negative side effects such as mood swings and headaches. Doctors reassured Mr. L that the side effects were normal and would gradually subside. When he was 35 years old, Mr. L decided to undergo both top and bottom reassignment surgery. After the surgery, he began dating and fully immersed himself in male gender norms. However, Mr. L was not able to maintain long-term relationships and never had any children of his own due to relationship difficulties.

Mr. L came to therapy to explore interpersonal struggles that he had been experiencing in his new relationship with Elsa, a cisgender Latina. During the initial interview, Mr. L disclosed to his psychologist that he is transgender. Mr. L had been dating Elsa for four months. He explained that he thoroughly enjoyed her company and hoped that they would be together for a long time. He was concerned about the longevity of their relationship, as Elsa recently disclosed that she does not support individuals who identify as LGBTQ due to personal religious beliefs. Mr. L was concerned because he wants to continue his relationship with Elsa. Thereafter, he began debating whether or not to tell Elsa that he was assigned female at birth. Part of him felt that he was obligated to tell her, as he had such discussions with women from his previous relationships. The therapist suggested to Mr. L that he should tell Elsa that he was assigned female at birth due to concern for Elsa's religious beliefs and for honesty in the relationship.

In this discussion, Mr. L also explained to the psychologist that he had been experiencing negative side effects possibly due to hormone intake for 36 years. He had been feeling ill and sick to his stomach and had even fainted on several occasions. On one occasion, he was found unconscious by Elsa, which led to a 911 call. He confided in his psychologist that he did not alert the emergency medical service or doctors at the emergency department that he was taking hormones. He requested further education about the long-term effects of hormone therapy. He also requested his therapist not tell Elsa or any doctors about his hormone therapy use, even though the therapist verbalized concern that Mr. L could be putting his life in danger. In this particular case, the therapist was uncertain how to conceptualize Mr. L's case as he had no prior experience in working with individuals who identify as transgender.

Exploring Ethical Decision-Making

There are several ethical issues that are present in Mr. L's case. By way of explanation, this case will focus on issues of competency to treat versus not treat (APA General Principle A, Beneficence and Nonmaleficence; Standard 2.01, Boundaries of Competence), confidentiality (APA General Principle E, Respect for People's Rights and Dignity, Standard 4.01), and disclosures (APA General Principle E, Respect for People's Rights and Dignity, Standard 4.05). Specifically, Mr. L was the first transgender client that the psychologist had served and the psychologist had little knowledge of the needs of older adult individuals who identify as transgender. Additionally, Mr. L was seeking clarity as to whether or not he should tell Elsa that he is transgender. Mr. L was deeply concerned about how Elsa would react to the news and was resistant to jeopardizing the current status of his happy relationship. The psychologist suggested that Mr. L tell Elsa that he is transgender, as the psychologist believed Elsa's religious beliefs should be honored and that honesty is an important value in relationships. However, given prior conversations, it seemed Elsa would likely end the relationship, which would ultimately negatively impact Mr. L. Next, Mr. L was concerned about the long-term effects of hormone therapy and asked the psychologist to provide hormone use education. The psychologist, however, knew very little about the effects of hormone therapy. Finally, Mr. L did not want the psychologist to tell Elsa or medical personnel about his hormone treatment, though the therapist feared that Mr. L might be putting his life in great danger.

To better understand the ethical concerns and decision-making processes that should be explored, it is important to review the APA Guidelines for Psychological Practice with Transgender and Gender Nonconforming People (2015) and the APA Ethics Code (2010). Specifically, the APA Ethics Code (2010) advises that psychologists should only practice in areas of competency (Standard 2.01). In regard to the case of Mr. L, the psychologist had no prior experience of working with clients who identify as transgender and had no knowledge of the effects associated with long-term hormone therapy in the older adult population. A self-report survey completed by transgender and gender-nonconforming individuals reported that mental health care providers lack the training, knowledge, and skills needed to care for transgender and gender-nonconforming individuals (Bradford, Xavier, Hendricks, Rives, & Honnold, 2007).

The Guidelines for Psychological Practice with Transgender and Gender Nonconforming People (Guideline 4) specify that the "assumptions, biases, and attitudes" that govern a therapist's interactions with transgender and gender-nonconforming people can ultimately affect the therapeutic relationship (p. 837). For example, Mr. L requested support from the therapist as to whether or not he should tell Elsa that he is a transgender male. The therapist had a prior assumption that Mr. L should disclose to Elsa without processing the potential effects of such a disclosure: the psychologist assumed it was the right thing to do for Elsa's religious values and to maintain honesty in the relationship. However, the psychologist failed to assess how the disclosure could negatively affect Mr. L. Elsa could terminate their relationship, resulting in harm to Mr. L, which does not follow APA General Principle A, Beneficence and Nonmaleficence. Additionally, the psychologist may be unaware that older transgender adults are at an increased risk for depression, suicidal ideation, and loneliness compared to gay, lesbian, and bisexual elders (Auldrige, Tamar-Mattis, Kennedy, Ames, & Tobin, 2012). As such, the psychologist needed to educate himself in order to better process the potential negative effects for Mr. L if he did disclose as transgender. Furthermore, that psychologist should consider continued evaluation and monitoring of Mr. L after such a disclosure.

To provide Mr. L with ethically sound and culturally competent therapy, the psychologist needed to be aware of his own biases due to a lack of exposure and knowledge. In regard to being culturally incompetent, Karel's (2009) framework for ethical decision-making was used. Using this framework, the therapist first needed to be aware of his own competencies and lack of experience in working with individuals who identify as transgender. Little research has been conducted examining the specific experiences of older adults who identify as transgender (Auldridge et al., 2012), making their needs potentially more sensitive compared to younger transgender populations. Taken together, it is pertinent that the attending psychologist be competent to treat individuals who identify as transgender or be willing to educate himself and seek consultation on the needs and barriers of individuals who identify as transgender.

Next, the therapist should acknowledge that his lack of training could also negatively impact Mr. L. The psychologist should consider whether or not he should refer Mr. L to a different provider, and if not, the psychologist should be willing to educate himself on the special needs of transgender and gender-nonconforming people. Though referring Mr. L to a different provider may not be ideal, it could be beneficial to Mr. L's presenting concerns. For instance, the psychologist could select a transgender-competent therapist to provide Mr. L with more sensitive care. A negative consequence of referring Mr. L to a different provider would be the loss to an already established trusting relationship and a referral may be contraindicated (Wampold, 2001). Further, Mr. L may have difficulty transitioning to another therapist if he has trust issues or is apprehensive of telling his life story for a second time. Furthermore, this was a great opportunity for the psychologist to educate himself and become more culturally competent. In the case of Mr. L, the attending psychologist decided to continue treatment and not refer Mr. L. To better serve transgender and gender-nonconforming people, the psychologist formulated a plan to help him develop cultural competency though several activities, including education, supervised experience, consultation, and training (APA, 2015).

Issues of confidentially needed to be discussed as they related to Mr. L. He was engaging in behaviors that were potentially putting his life in great risk due to the long-term side effects associated with hormone use. Though the psychologist's concerns may be relevant, the APA encourages client–therapist collaboration when making clinical decisions with potential benefits or negative consequences and when offering resources related to treatment (APA Presidential Task Force on Evidence-Based Practice, 2006). The Guidelines for Psychological Practice with Transgender and Gender Nonconforming People (Guideline 6) specify that therapists should be familiar with the institutional barriers that affect transgender or gender-nonconforming people. In the case of Mr. L, he did not want other care providers to know of his transgender status out of fear of institutional discrimination. The APA Code of Ethics (2010) specifies that a therapist may break confidentially to protect the client from harm (4.05 Disclosures). However, more exploration is needed to determine whether this case is a scenario where confidentiality should be broken.

In order to fully understand the necessity for a potential breach of confidentiality, first, the psychologist clarified the reasons for such a breech, including the belief that Mr. L was putting his life at great risk. Second, the psychologist then explored Mr. L's values, goals, and interests. Third, the psychologist determined if he had the decision-making authority in this scenario or if Mr. L's request discredited an opportunity for such decision-making. Additionally, the psychologist considered all ethically justifiable options and the pros and cons of particular decisions. For example, if the psychologist breached confidentially, Mr. L might receive more appropriate health care and be closely monitored to ensure safety. However, Mr. L may be subject to discrimination and prejudice resulting in poor health care, the loss of his relationship with Elsa, and a loss of trust with the psychologist. Finally, the psychologist then implemented a plan, evaluated it, and continued to reevaluate it throughout the course of treatment. Specifically, with Mr. L, the psychologist decided not to breech confidentiality. Instead, he and Mr. L had a frank conversation about the importance of transparency in the therapeutic relationship, including continued openness about his hormone use and changes in side effects.

Studying the ethical concerns regarding the case of Mr. L is important because more individuals are openly identifying as transgender and gender-nonconforming. It is estimated that 70 000 people (or more) identify as transgender, and that number will continue to rise due to political reforms for the LGBTQ population (Gates, 2011). It is likely that psychologists working with older adults will experience individuals who identify as transgender or gender-nonconforming. Coupled with ageism, transphobia fosters additional barriers for the older adult population. Sensitivity to potential ethical issues for competency to treat and breeches of confidentiality need to be discussed beginning in graduate training programs and through continuing education.

Professional and Personal Difficulties in Ethical Decision-Making

This particular case was difficult for the attending psychologist. Mr. L was potentially experiencing negative side effects due to prolonged hormone therapy. However, Mr. L told the psychologist that he did not desire medical providers to know about his hormone treatment. The psychologist was concerned for Mr. L's overall health and safety if he continued to use hormone therapy without proper medical attention. The psychologist spent time looking over research and the side effects of prolonged hormone therapy use to try to determine just how at risk Mr. L was. This put the psychologist in a difficult position because he is not a medical provider nor an expert in working with transgender clients. He also sought medical guidance from physicians about the potential long-term effects of hormone therapy.

Furthermore, the psychologist battled his own bias regarding advising Mr. L that he should tell his girlfriend, Elsa, that he is transgender. The psychologist believed that Elsa should know, as it could later cause problems in their relationship. The attending psychologist had to put his beliefs aside and spend time processing Mr. L's reluctance to confide in Elsa. To help manage his own bias, the psychologist participated in professional consultation in order to process why he thought it was important for Mr. L to tell Elsa that he is transgender. Professional consultation created an environment where the psychologist could talk about his concerns and struggles with another professional in order to ensure his own biases were not affecting or influencing treatment.

The psychologist also worried that his cisgender identity could result in a lack of understanding for Mr. L's personal struggles. He personally acknowledged his cisgender identity and acknowledged the gender role stereotype that he himself uses to govern society. Acknowledging and addressing these concerns was a challenge; however, it allowed the psychologist to recognize the limitation present in gender roles.

Conclusion

In reviewing the cases of Mrs. T, Mr. O, and Mr. L, there are similar themes throughout that are critical for the ethical and competent psychological treatment of older adults. It is clear that APA General Principle A, Beneficence and Nonmaleficence and APA General Principle E, Respect for People's Rights and Dignity are the key overarching principles to consider in many cases with older adults, as well as a number of standards. The subtle nuances of geropsychology within those general principles can lie within concerns about competency, elder abuse, consultation with others, confidentiality, and, at times, conflicts of interest (Karel, 2009). Further, the treating psychologist (or psychology trainee, intern, or postdoctoral fellow) may need to advocate for the older adult client in ways that are unique from younger adult populations. All of the clinical cases presented here provide only a small glimpse into the complex world of geriatric mental health care.

For practitioners working with older adults, competent care begins with familiarity of the unique physical, cognitive, emotional, and spiritual concerns of older adults. Ideally, psychologists who are working with older adults would have received training in graduate school and internship and postdoctoral training with older adults, or at least with supervision by psychologists who have expertise with older adult populations. However, for those psychologists without such a background, one starting place is to read seminal articles and books such as the APA's (2014) Guidelines for Psychological Practice with Older Adults, Bush's (2012) book chapter on ethical considerations in the psychological evaluation and treatment of older adults, Duffy's (1999) *Handbook of counseling and therapy with older adults*, or Molinari's (2011) *Specialty competencies in geropsychology*. It is recommended that psychologists interested in working with older adults understand the attitude, knowledge, and skill competencies outlined in Molinari's (2011) book, and as also detailed in articles by Karel, Knight, Duffy, Hinrichsen, and Zeiss (2010) and Karel et al. (2012). Psychologists working with older adults are also encouraged to complete the geropsychology competency tool discussed by Karel, Emery, and Molinari (2010).

Understanding multicultural issues in older adults is equally essential, as discussed in the cases above. Therefore, additional essential readings includes the APA Committee on Aging's (2009) multicultural competency in geropsychology working group paper, the APA's Guidelines for Psychological Practice with Transgender and Gender Nonconforming People, and the *Handbook of minority aging* (Whitfield & Baker, 2013), to name a few. The APA's *Handbook of clinical geropsychology* (Lichtenberg & Mast, 2015) has useful chapters on diversity in aging, including gender, religion and spirituality, LGBT concerns, and international trends in aging. An excellent list of resources for diversity in aging can also be found at the APA Office on Aging Multicultural Aging and Mental Health Resource Guide (www.apa .org/pi/aging/resources/guides/multicultural.aspx).

Second, attending workshops and continuing education events on topics specific to older adults is crucial, particularly as health care information changes quite rapidly. This can include topics such as medication, evidence-based treatments, dementia care, and end-of-life concerns such as advance care planning, as well as information about Medicare rules and appropriate billing practices, all of which can impact the ethical treatment of older adults (but were not discussed in this chapter). Membership in aging-related organizations, such as the Society for Clinical Geropsychology (APA Division 12 Section II), Psychologists in Long-Term Care (PLTC), the Older Adult Special Interest Group (APA Division 17), and the Gerontological Society of America (GSA) allows access to up-to-date research and information about aging, as well as to knowledgeable colleagues who can be available for consultation. Websites such as GeroCentral (http://gerocentral.org) and the APA's Office on Aging (www.apa.org/pi/aging) provide psychologist-specific, valuable, and timely resources for practice with older adults. Additionally, following national health-related websites with information relevant to geriatric care, such as the Center for Medicare and Medicaid Services (www.cms.gov), the National Institutes of Health (www.nih.gov), the National Institute on Aging (www.nia.nih.gov), the National Institute of Mental Health (www.nimh.nih.gov), and the Centers for Disease Control and Prevention (www.cdc.gov/aging) may be useful.

Finally, all psychologists, in addition to becoming familiar with the most current edition of the APA Ethics Code (2010), should also have a working model for ethical practice. Karel's (2009) and Fisher's (2009) were the two models presented in this chapter, but there are numerous others that psychologists may use in clinical work. In particular, Bush's (2009) four A's of ethical practice and decision-making (i.e., anticipate, avoid, address, and aspire) is one model that allow psychologists working with older adults to adhere to higher practice standards. This model encourages psychologists to be mindful of the numerous ethical pitfalls that can exist and to be proactive, rather than reactive, in managing those ethical concerns.

The cases of Mrs. T, Mr. O, and Mr. L are only glimpses into the geropsychology practice world that address ethics solely within the context individual therapy. Psychologists who work with older adults will also need to consider ethical issues encountered in assessment, consultation, family therapy, group therapy, couples counseling, and work with caregivers. In sum, psychologists who have the knowledge, skills, and ability to work with older adults, in addition to support and consultation from colleagues, will find that while working with older adults can be complex and challenging, it can also be immensely rewarding.

References

American Psychiatric Association (2013). *Diagnostic and statistical manual of mental disorders* (5th edn.). Arlington, VA: American Psychiatric Publishing.

American Psychological Association (2010). Ethical principles of psychologists and code of conduct (2002, amended June 1, 2010). Retrieved from www.apa.org/ethics/code/principles.pdf

American Psychological Association (2015). Guidelines for psychological practice with transgender and gender nonconforming people. *American Psychologist, 70,* 832–864.

American Psychological Association (2002). Ethical principles of psychologists and code of conduct. *American Psychologist, 57*, 1060–1073.

American Psychological Association (2014). Guidelines for psychological practice with older adults. *American Psychologist, 69*, 34–65.

American Psychological Association, Committee on Aging (2009). *Multicultural competency in geropsychology.* Washington, DC: American Psychological Association.

American Psychological Association Presidential Task Force on Evidence-Based Practice (2006). Evidence-based practice in psychology. *American Psychologist, 61*, 21–285.

Auldridge, A., Tamar-Mattis, A., Kennedy, S., Ames, E., & Tobin, H. J. (2012). *Improving the lives of transgender older adults services and advocacy.* New York, NY: Services and Advocacy for LGBT Elders & Washington, DC: National Center for Transgender Equality. Retrieved from www.lgbtagingcenter.org/resources/resource.cfm?r=520

Bradford, J., Xavier, J., Hendricks, M., Rivers, M. E., & Honnold, J. A. (2007). The health, health-related needs, and lifecourse experiences of transgender Virginians. Virginia Transgender Health Initiative Study Statewide Survey Report. Retrieved from www.vdh.state.va.us/epidemiology/DiseasePrevention/documents/pdf/THISFINALREPORTVol1.pdf

Bush, S. S. (2009). *Geriatric mental health ethics: A casebook.* New York, NY: Springer Publishing Company.

Bush, S. S. (2012). Ethical considerations in the psychological evaluation and treatment of older adults. In S. J. Knapp, M. C. Gottlieb, M. M. Handelsman, & L. D. VandeCreek (Eds.), *APA handbook of ethics in psychology, Vol 2: Practice, teaching, and research. APA handbooks in psychology* (pp. 15–28). Washington, DC: American Psychological Association.

Duffy, M. (1999). *Handbook of counseling and therapy with older adults.* New York, NY: John Wiley.

Fisher, C. B. (2009). *Decoding the ethics code: A practical guide for psychologists.* Los Angeles, CA: Sage Publications.

Folstein, M. F., Folstein, S. E., & McHugh, P. R. (1975). "Mini-mental state": A practical method for grading the cognitive state of patients for the clinician. *Journal of Psychiatric Research, 12*, 189–198.

Gates, G. (2011). How many people are lesbian, gay, bisexual, and transgender? The Williams Institute. Retrieved from http://williamsinstitute.law.ucla.edu/wp-content/uploads/Gates-How-Many-People-LGBT-Apr-2011.pdf

Hays, J. & Jennings, F. L. (2015). Ethics in geropsychology: Status and challenges. In P. A. Lichtenberg, B. Mast, B. Carpenter, & J. L. Wetherell (Eds.), *APA handbook of clinical geropsychology, Vol. 1: History and status of the field and perspectives on aging* (pp. 177–192). Washington, DC: American Psychological Association.

Hoge, M. A., Karel, M. J., Zeiss, A. M., Alegria, M., & Moye, J. (2015). Strengthening psychology's workforce for older adults: Implications of the Institute of Medicine's report to Congress. *American Psychologist, 70*, 265–278.

Karel, M. J. (2009). Ethical issues in long-term care. In E. Rosowsky, J. M. Casciani, & M. Arnold (Eds.), *Geropsychology and long term care: A practitioner's guide* (pp. 111–123). New York, NY: Springer Publishing Company.

Karel, M. J., Emery, E. E., & Molinari, V. (2010). Development of a tool to evaluate geropsychology knowledge and skill competencies. *International Psychogeriatrics, 22*, 886–896.

Karel, M. J., Gatz, M., & Smyer, M. A. (2012). Aging and mental health in the decade ahead: What psychologists need to know. *American Psychologist, 67*, 184–198.

Karel, M. J., Knight, B. G., Duffy, M., Hinrichson, G. A., & Zeiss, A. M. (2010). Attitude, knowledge, and skill competencies for practice in professional geropsychology: Implications for training and building a geropsychology workforce. *Training and Education in Professional Psychology, 4*, 75–84.

Lichtenberg, P. A. & Mast, B. T. (2015). *APA handbook of clinical geropsychology: Vol 1. History and status of the field and perspectives on aging.* Washington, DC: American Psychological Association.

Lichtenberg, P. A., Smith, M., Frazer, D., et al. (1998). Standards for psychological services in long-term care facilities. *The Gerontologist, 38*, 122–127.

Molinari, V. (2011). *Specialty competencies in geropsychology.* New York, NY: Oxford University Press.

Qualls, S. H. (2011). The field of geropsychology. In V. Molinari (Ed.), *Specialty competencies in geropsychology* (pp. 14–20). New York, NY: Oxford University Press.

Sheikh, J. I. & Yesavage, J. A. (1986). Geriatric Depression Scale (GDS). Recent evidence and development of a shorter version. In T.L. Brink (Ed.), *Clinical gerontology: A guide to assessment and intervention* (pp. 165–173). New York, NY: The Haworth Press, Inc.

Wampold, B. E. (2001). *The great psychotherapy debate: Models, methods, and findings.* Mahwah, NJ: Erlbaum.

Whitfield, K. & Baker, T. (2013). *Handbook of minority aging.* New York, NY: Springer Publishing Company.

17 Applied Research in Diverse Communities: Ethical Issues and Considerations

Justin C. Perry and Adam M. Voight

When asked what it means to conduct applied research, images of running studies on the services and approaches to treatment covered in the first section of this handbook would likely come to many psychologists' minds. In contrast to conducting applied research among *clients, communities* are composed of people who share something in common outside of a clinical setting, and may therefore not be "treated" or "served" in the conventional sense. In fact, they may actually be mutual partners in the research process and play an equal role in deciding how the research is run and disseminated (Shore, 2006). This is an important distinction to make when engaging in applied research with communities that have been marginalized, oppressed, or disadvantaged. Compared to dominant or mainstream culture, minority groups may not trust the authoritative researcher from the ivory towers, regardless of the good nature of his/her intentions. Further, the goals and methods of the research may not be relevant or useful to addressing the needs of the community. When we talk about diverse communities, we must recognize that with the notion of diversity are the inseparable ethical issues related to justice, fairness, and equity.

Interestingly, the literature from which we draw is virtually nonexistent in fields of psychology, with the notable exception of community psychology (Roos, Visser, Pistorius, & Nefale, 2007; Serrano-Garcia, 1994); much of our discussion is based on prior scholarship in public health (e.g., Flicker, Travers, Guta, McDonald, & Meagher, 2007; Israel, Schulz, Parker, & Becker, 1998; Minkler, 2004). As psychological specializations like counseling psychology continue to evolve with the changing landscape of health care access and delivery, while trying to establish their relevance in broader social and economic spheres of influence like education or criminal justice, the need to cross-fertilize our psychological theories, methods of research, and practices with those in other disciplines will become even more imperative and commonplace (Bond & Hauf, 2007; Buki, 2014). The time is ripe for psychologists to expand their scope of work into the more complex, fluid world of applied community-based research, even though it is still a marginal activity rarely adopted in the normal work activities of academic psychologists (Perry, Wallace, & Pickett, 2017). To this end, we seek to meld our practical experiences and knowledge with work that tends to be found in public health. The ethical issues emphasized here are thus framed within a community-based participatory action (CBPA) research approach.

Consistent with the goals of the handbook, this chapter presents and analyzes a set of complex case examples that elucidate in realistic detail the ethical processes, dimensions, and outcomes commonly involved when trying to reconcile the ideals of applied CBPA research with the realities of working in higher education. Specifically, we draw from the present climate and expectations in research universities across the nation for faculty to pursue grants or extramural research funding, which is often applied in nature and is typically designed to support endeavors in communities that can partner with institutions of higher education, especially institutions whose missions are based in part on serving their local communities through faculty research and service. Before turning to the case examples, a clarification of pertinent terms is warranted, as well as an overview of the ethical issues and dilemmas that typically arise in applied CBPA research.

Clarifying Our Terms: Basic versus Applied Research

The fundamental differences between *basic* and *applied* research can be captured in their purposes and consequences. With respect to the former term, advancing scholarly knowledge through a scientific or public outlet is the over-arching purpose of the research activity; hence, the aims of basic research are not meant to directly benefit "human research subjects" or improve some aspect of their lives. On the other hand, the latter refers to research in a naturalistic setting designed to directly benefit people who participate in the study; investigating the processes or testing the impact of an intervention are the reasons why the research is performed. Although basic research may eventually "translate" into services that have the potential to contribute to knowledge about "what works" in a given profession or field, it does not involve the study of actual interventions.

Basic research may involve the collection of data from participants in a natural setting, such as collecting surveys among youth in a school building or adults in a homeless shelter; yet, the people in the community from whom that very data were collected continue to face the same problems after the study is completed: their lives will go on essentially as if nothing happened. All too often, community members who are recruited as sources of data in basic research never hear back from the researcher again. Applied CPBA research brings the question of "so what and who cares?" into critical light when assessing the ultimate worth of basic research, or its capacity to be used for solving critical problems that matter to public stakeholders and taxpayers. Flicker, Travers, Guta, McDonald, and Meagher (2007) argue that academics who follow the "helicopter research" paradigm – that is, flying into a community with surveys and then flying back out, but giving little back in return – may be doing harm to those communities that granted them access to investigate some aspect of their experience or problems. With these points in mind, we turn to the CBPA literature and how its practices intersect with ethical issues in applied research.

Applied CBPA Research: An Overview of Ethical Issues

Researchers who obtain approval from an institutional review board (IRB) must meet certain requirements related to the protection of human subjects. The Belmont Report (1979) serves as the dominant framework of principle-based ethics that informs the regulations found in IRB policies. From a CBPA perspective, Shore (2006) reviewed criticisms leveled against the Belmont Report for its Western cultural bias favoring primarily individual rights and autonomy. In CPBA research, ensuring that vulnerable groups are not exploited or that certain groups in society are included in a study is important, but falls well short of its broader purposes in which building trustful partnerships with multiple constituencies is the primary aim, and is therefore as important as investigating the hypotheses/questions of the study. This paradigm thus requires an expansion of how ethics scholars think about, in particular, concepts of beneficence and justice, which must be interpreted from the standpoint of assessing how a study ensures that it will lead toward social or systemic change while enacting inclusive, mutual decision-making among all participants in the study. These considerations pose unique criteria against which researchers are judged to be ethical.

Based on a content analysis of forms and guidelines used by 30 IRBs located in the U.S. and Canada, Flicker et al. (2007) found that none of the IRB protocols evaluated whether or not a procedure existed for the following questions: (a) is there community involvement in identifying the study's rationale? (b) Is staff training or community capacity building involved? (c) Is there a justification for expenses related to the study, such as minimizing costs for transportation? (d) Is the equitable distribution of resources between community and institutional partners included? (e) Is obtaining consent from the "community" required? (f) Is there a process for vetoing publication or ending the study based on community concerns? All of these questions stand in clear contrast to the biomedical framework that dominates basic and applied research. Other procedures coded in only a handful of these 30 IRBs (e.g., commitment to follow-up, role of advisory boards, addressing power differences) speak to the general absence of issues pertaining to sustainability, collaboration, and action that defines CBPA research. Not surprisingly, the authors concluded that an alternative framework is needed that is consistent with the principles and values of CBPA research, including: (a) engagement with community partners in a mutual, collaborative manner throughout all phases of the study; (b) answering questions that are relevant and useful to the community, not just for the researcher or for scientific discovery; (c) building capacity to have the intervention diffused into a community's structures or routines; and (d) empowering community members with a greater sense of control and a critical awareness of barriers in society (Israel et al., 1998; Maiter, Simich, Jacobson, & Wise, 2008; Minkler, 2004).

Historically, the emphases of CBPA research ethics that contribute to the dissolution of traditional "neutral" or "objective" boundaries held between the researcher and the researched have their roots in the exploitative studies conducted among Indigenous communities, First Nations, and Aboriginal tribes in Canada (Schnarch,

2004). Ball and Janyst (2008), for example, described how Indigenous peoples have become exhausted and mistrustful of outside researchers who take up their time collecting data and documenting their problems, but give no tangible benefit in return. Similarly, trust is the lynchpin of ethical conduct with any diverse community that has been oppressed. In their research, Ball and Janyst worked toward gaining an Indigenous community's trust through a memorandum of understanding, whereby the community would have authority to approve all aspects of the research process, from the design to recruitment, overhead costs, and reporting of findings. In the impoverished, predominantly Latino town of Lawrence, Massachusetts, Silka, Cleghorn, Grullon, and Tellez (2008) described a case study reflective of the sort of actions taken by Ball and Janyst. After years of mistrust due to researchers conducting studies of gang violence and pollution with very few attempts at collaboration, Silka et al. came together with community members and civic leaders to form a group known as the Mayor's Health Research Initiative Working Group. Under the mayor's task force, this group reached a consensus on how CBPA principles could be promoted on behalf of the community.

Ball and Janyst (2008) argue that if trust is the foundation of ethical conduct in CPBA, it is easier to talk about than to actually forge, especially in the context of being held accountable by an external funder. The dilemma between endorsing ethical principles of CBPA while adhering to the scientific rigor of applied research presents an unavoidable tension. This tension should not be construed, however, as an irreconcilable conflict. Rigorous standards do not need to be compromised in order to gain a community's trust, but to balance both prerequisites does require interpersonal, organizational, and political skills that one might not have to use in traditional applied research. The ability to enlist the support and cooperation of various stakeholders and constituencies, where boundaries between research *subjects* and the *partners* become blurred, defies traditional procedures of research participation. Nonetheless, CBPA research should not be viewed as favoring one method over another, but as an approach to using the tools of inquiry as a vehicle for change – or, as some scholars argue, a philosophical attitude akin to feminist ethics (Minkler, 2004).

To summarize, the paradigm of research we propose here is founded on the tenet of using the fruits of inquiry on behalf of the community, not just as an intellectual exercise to serve the academic interests of the researcher. So long as its principles of empowerment are governed by a disposition toward openness to ideas, respect for community members and leaders, and an inherent appreciation for patience and humility, applied CBPA research will be "based" in the community rather than conveniently "placed" in it. In the case examples, the issue of trying to advance science (and benefit research agendas) relative to benefiting the community (and making a meaningful difference) is a recurrent theme. Although certain issues are featured in order to coincide with each case example, this central concept is consistently manifested.

In the first three cases, we discuss salient ethical issues that arise across different phases of the research process based on the same hypothetical scenario of "Rockville." In the fourth case, a different scenario is presented to highlight other unique ethical issues. Taken together, these cases offer thought-provoking material to grapple with when considering the unorthodox, nonlinear approach to applied research in community settings. It should be noted that while each case is fictitious, they are based on an amalgamation of real-life projects we have worked on in collaboration with a wide range of K–12 communities through the years.

The Case of the Big Research Grant at Rockville City School District

The city of Rockville is located in a diverse urban metropolitan area that enrolls approximately 30 000 students in its public schools, with a racial composition of 65 percent black/African–American, 10 percent Hispanic/Latino, 20 percent white, and 5 percent multiracial, an even distribution of males and females (50 percent each), and 95 percent of students eligible for free/reduced-price lunch. As typifies urban school districts, Rockville has struggled with poor academic achievement and graduation rates for several decades. Its last performance index report card was an F. Now more than ever, Rockville is looking for solutions that can help improve its schools' and students' performance.

One day in the middle of the summer, a federal research grant competition is announced, designed to promote innovative partnerships between schools and university researchers in the service of improving K–12 academic achievement with evidence-based strategies that can be replicated and brought to scale. A key requirement is to employ an experimental or quasi-experimental research design. Another requirement is to evaluate outcomes that are both academic and nonacademic. Applicants can request up to a maximum of $1.5 million.

After Rockville administrators learn about the grant, they contact a researcher at a local university who has previously worked with the district, Dr. Haywood. Over the past five years, he has worked with them on several projects, such as facilitating parent focus groups on bullying, applying for grants related to physical health, evaluating a professional development program, or coming in as a guest speaker to talk about college. Dr. Haywood agrees to work with them. In fact, he was thinking of the same idea. He will serve as the principal investigator and the school district's director of curriculum, Dr. West, will serve as the co-principal investigator. They have worked together in the past. The grant will be submitted through the university.

With only two months before the deadline, there is little time for them to brainstorm or consult with other people or community stakeholders. Among the topics they can choose from, Drs. West and Haywood select school dropout prevention, focusing on developing innovative middle school interventions. They prioritize programs that can promote an effective transition to high school in Rockville's strategic plan as one strategy to reduce dropout rates of students in high school, given that the ninth grade is when they are most at risk. This grant presents a win–win situation. To make their proposal more competitive, Dr. Haywood solicits a colleague at another university to serve as the external evaluator on the grant,

Table 17.1 *Research Design of the Evaluation*

Grade 8 Students	First Quarter Health	Second Quarter PE	Third Quarter Health	Fourth Quarter PE
Program A (j = 8)	X	X	X	X
Program B (j = 8)				X
Control (j = 8)	–	–	–	–

Note: "j" denotes number of classrooms to be randomized to each condition in each school; "X" denotes implementation of the intervention; "PE" denotes physical education; "Health" denotes health education.

Dr. DeGroot. In turn, Dr. DeGroot recommends that a colleague of hers, Dr. Lavel, could serve as a consultant, to which Dr. Haywood agrees. Dr. West is supportive of these decisions, though in a more deferential than invested manner.

The next eight weeks fly by in a flurry of activity and communication. In between the planned vacations, rescheduled meetings, and late cancellations among the four individuals involved in the grant writing, they manage to pull together two meetings, along with several teleconference calls. During this time, the district superintendent is notified about the grant, but is not involved in the "heavy lifting" of the writing itself. In a similar vein, principals in K–8 schools and 9–12 schools are notified; only a few of them, however, reply back confirming their interest, to ask questions, or to decline to participate. Because of the short timetable, no effort is made in reaching out to parents, teachers, school staff, partnering organizations, or the district board.

Ultimately, the research team proposes that the purpose of the project will be to implement, evaluate, and refine two universal school dropout prevention programs across six K–8 buildings. These programs are to be delivered to eighth-grade students during regular school hours. The two interventions were identified by Drs. Haywood and Lavel based on their knowledge of the existing evidence base: (a) a life skills/social skills curriculum (Program A), delivered during the whole school year; and (b) a "growth mindset" activity (Program B), designed to be completed in five sequential one-hour sessions. There are 35 K–8 schools in the district; only six are chosen for the goals of the grant competition, which emphasizes innovation in new or existing approaches and the establishment of their preliminary efficacy. However, which six schools would participate is left open; for the proposal, six candidates are identified based on Dr. West's insight concerning which principals would be more receptive than others to participate. By randomizing classrooms in each school, the basic evaluation design is summarized in Table 17.1, according to each quarter of the school year.

The classes that made the most sense content-wise were health and physical education (PE) classes, which all students are required to take in alternating quarters. The same students in each health class take the same PE class throughout the school year.

The core team of grant writers agree that the appropriate timeframe would be three calendar years. Because of the CBPA emphasis, they decide that the two interventions would not occur until the second year. In the third year, the same interventions would be delivered to a new cohort, while the first cohort would be tracked in ninth grade. In the first year, activities would involve planning, development, and organization of the programs with the input and buy-in of stakeholders. Hence, the plan for the first year involves a series of milestones that include the following: (a) completing a needs assessment; (b) engaging parents and seeking feedback; (c) integrating the program curricula into health/PE curricula; (d) designing and planning implementation; (e) designing fidelity measures; (f) assigning classes to conditions; and (g) conducting professional development workshops and an orientation day.

As the core team get into the weeds of the budget, Dr. West urges Dr. Haywood to consider including a large subcontract for Rockville to fund a district coordinator that includes a full-time salary and benefits, as well as generous stipends for each teacher who agrees to participate in delivering the interventions. At the same time, Dr. DeGroot requests that at least 20 percent of the total direct costs be allocated to the evaluation, whereas Dr. Lavel insists she be compensated almost as much as the costs for the evaluation. It is not clear what the scope of work is for Dr. Lavel, or how much effort will be required of Dr. DeGroot and her staff. Dr. West's requests are hard to assess when it is not clear what the coordinator will do. Moreover, these costs do not include funds needed for Dr. Haywood, graduate assistants, and incentives for participants – not to mention the indirect cost rate of 48 percent at the university.

In the final analysis, Dr. Haywood must ask his colleagues to reduce their costs. Specifically, when Dr. Lavel is told she can only be paid half of what she requested, she withdraws from the project. Dr. West is not pleased when told that the coordinator position can only be allocated half the amount requested, but nonetheless agrees. Dr. DeGroot concedes to getting 14 percent of total direct costs, yet indicates that certain analyses may not be performed. Similar to grants of this nature, a formative and summative evaluation is required. Dr. Haywood will be responsible for the formative evaluation, whereas Dr. West will be responsible for the summative evaluation.

In the midst of final deliberations, Dr. Haywood changes the budget. Instead of compensating teachers, he decides it is not a wise idea insofar as it may induce views of unequal treatment, though Dr. West assures him that it would not violate the teachers' contracts. He also believes that it is not affordable, even if stipends were cut significantly. Furthermore, it would not be fair to the school social workers and counselors delivering interventions if they were not compensated. A final reason is that Programs A and B are part of daily classroom instruction, and thus constitute a normal part of teachers' duties. Dr. Haywood reallocates such monies to hiring another graduate assistant to cover indirect costs and to pay for the costs of principals to hire substitute teachers during days for planning and curriculum training, as well as focus groups. He informs Dr. West of his rationale for this decision, to which she reluctantly agrees.

Another stipulation of the grant is that there is a product (e.g., curriculum) made accessible to the public as a deliverable, aside from annual reports and journal articles. In addition, the funding agency wants to know how the activities that are tested during the course of the project are made sustainable. These requirements do not need a lengthy explanation in the proposal, but it is not clear how they will be addressed. The proposal is submitted on time.

Introductory Comments

In this first case, the circumstances that give rise to the core ethical issues of justice are typical in applied CBPA research with K–12 schools. What is also representative is the fact that the project was triggered by a grant. If such a grant never existed, it is extremely unlikely that the university and district would have undertaken this research since there would not have been resources available to galvanize and maintain the work. Hence, the thorny issue of money enters the balance of the partnership. Even before they know whether the grant is awarded, ethical concerns already form at the center with respect to the fair, transparent distribution of fiscal resources. We can also see at the periphery of the proposal other critical issues that will come into play later on, namely the role of various stakeholders and constituencies in decision-making about the proposed interventions and how they will or will not benefit from them in an equitable manner.

With respect to the budget, at the root of the ethical dilemma are the conflicting agendas and financial motivations of the key personnel. Dr. Lavel's decision to abruptly withdraw from the grant clearly illustrates the sensitive nature of tying a specific role on a project to an amount of money; it is evident that Dr. Lavel is somewhat driven by monetary gain. Although Dr. West and Dr. DeGroot are not completely satisfied, they seem willing to compromise, presumably because their motives are not as strongly influenced by money. We can see in the beginning stages of the process the seeds of conflict brewing with regard to the time demands on the various constituencies in the design and writing of the project. Preparing the grant among the core team enables the proposal to be written and submitted on time; the drawback of this course of action, however, is not having an adequate opportunity to secure buy-in from key stakeholders ahead of time, especially among the teachers who will be expected to deliver the interventions.

Analysis of Decision-Making Processes

First and foremost, it is critical to understand that large research grants such as these are double-edged swords. When these opportunities are announced by outside funders (e.g., federal agencies), they tend to elicit a mix of emotions that can be experienced in fairly intense ways. On the one hand, they create feelings of excitement about being able to achieve something that has never been done before; yet, on the other hand, they can elicit strong doubts or anxiety, including how one's life might change if the grant is awarded and he/she is expected to deliver. Coupled with such worries are natural fears about embarking into the unknown or going outside of one's usual comfort zones.

The process of preparing and submitting a large grant proposal can strain the boundaries and patience of all parties. Indeed, it often constitutes a project unto itself that can test levels of trust and collegiality, sometimes between old friends and sometimes between strangers who have just met. This process is only exacerbated with tight deadlines. It is not unusual to witness the last-minute efforts portrayed in this case. The other source of ethical tension and work-related stress resides in the budget that is needed in order to carry out the grant. Compared to basic research, applied CBPA research is often hard to accomplish on a large scale without external dollars for university faculty, which often means that their time and effort in teaching courses is paid for by the grant. Money is further needed to hire other personnel such as graduate assistants, co-principal investigators, evaluators, and consultants. These costs tend to be part of a bigger, more complex budget to manage. When addressing such budgets under short windows of time, the concomitant pressures of pulling together a competitive grant proposal may tempt key parties to take advantage of the situation by requesting more money than what is justified or needed. In this case, Dr. Haywood shows a disciplined sense of restraint and fairness in budget-related decisions. Other individuals, however, may be so overwhelmed by the demands of the situation that the tough decisions of monetary allocations may be overlooked in order to get the proposal done and thus avoid potential conflicts that could interfere with its timely submission. Because Dr. Haywood is efficient in his decision-making, he does not hesitate to resolve these conflicts before they could potentially implode if the grant is awarded.

With these considerations in mind, the process that quickly unfolds during the pre-award phase of Rockville's big research grant is not uncommon. In an ideal situation, the expenditures associated with each line item in the budget are deliberated and consensually agreed upon among all personnel; but in reality, this rarely happens. In this case, the K–8 schools are not identified yet, so teachers, school counselors, and social workers cannot be consulted, let alone parents and students. There is also a significant amount of conflict among the few people involved in writing the grant. What complicates matters are the multiple agendas; as such, it is almost expected that various stakeholders will have different interests and priorities that influence what they want to varying degrees. In public school districts, there are many layers of interests represented at many levels of influence that must be recognized; if they are minimized or ignored, potential divisions in the community may not be well anticipated or effectively resolved when they emerge.

Perhaps the best way to keep the budget "well-lit" for open scrutiny is to ensure that the roles and responsibilities (scope of work) for each of the personnel/parties involved is as clear and quantifiable as possible. For example, the request by Dr. West to have a coordinator lacks a job description that justifies a time commitment of 40 hours per week. Parenthetically, Dr. West may have had duties in mind that branch out into work that should not be compensated. This drifting of duties is a potential risk. It would not be fair to pay the coordinator full-time when it is not clear that the duties require 40 hours, even at the risk of losing the cooperation of Dr. West. The same dilemma is illustrated through Dr. DeGroot's and Dr. Lavel's requests. Once again, these areas of ethical concern, motivated primarily by financial interests, can undermine the goal of CBPA, which is to actively involve and include all relevant stakeholders as partners who also benefit from the work that is done. When such self-interests overtake the decision-making process of a few people in the absence of consulting with the community as a whole, there is the risk of losing the trust of the very people one wishes to empower.

Until the grant begins, it is hard to project how much time and effort will be required of consultants such as Dr. Lavel. In this case, suppose that she wants to work for 125 hours per year on the project; this would translate into roughly 16 days of consultation (eight hours per day). While Dr. Lavel would be useful for professional development and perhaps other activities (e.g., assessment, curriculum design), 16 days per year is a very liberal estimate. Generally speaking, the costs of a consultant should not be the same amount, and certainly should not exceed, the costs of key personnel; in this case, the consultant would be getting paid about as much as the principal investigator and about 70 percent of the entire evaluation budget. Dr. Haywood's decision incites Dr. Lavel to withdraw on a sour note, but the action is well-justified. Our analysis of these decisions should be tempered by the understanding that the designated principal investigator, Dr. Haywood, has some power over the other core team members because of his fiduciary control over the grant. Had Dr. West been the principal investigator, it would have presented the same power differential, but most likely resulted in a different budget with different decisions. Regardless of who makes the final decisions, the principles of beneficence and nonmaleficence are of central importance in this case because of a psychologist's duty to protect against financial, personal, and political factors that could potentially lead to misuse of power.

Ethical dimensions in this case can also be analyzed based on the planning activities. In this situation, the core team of personnel crafts a plan that adheres to principles of sharing power and decision-making throughout the research process. Despite their good intentions, they are based on assumptions that "put the cart before the horse." In other words, will the community agree to implement Program A and B? Given that most grants require proposed strategies with concrete objectives, the nature of this work poses a conundrum. Fortunately, this case was built on a positive existing relationship. Adopting an idea from the ivory towers and absorbing it into a school system is not unrealistic when it is supported by staff and school leaders and/or has the power to address their needs in a practical way (Minkler, 2004; Perry, Cusner, & Pickett, 2015). Nonetheless, the core team faces the risks associated with proposing ideas on paper but winding up with very different solutions once the needs assessment, feedback, and other challenges are completed. By virtue of the grant, this risk cannot be avoided because not all aspects of the research can be identified up-front. As Israel et al. (1998) observe, "...there is the challenge of selling a process without completely specifying all the outcomes beforehand..." (p. 188). In the end, the risks of "selling" such ideas are worth the effort because of the long-lasting benefits that can be gained. This approach is consistent with the principle of fidelity and responsibility, as psychologists are acting in the best interests of the community they are trying to serve, even in the face of uncertainty. They are trying to make a difference when given the opportunities and the resources to enact change in ways that extend beyond the four walls of the therapy office.

The Case of the First Year of Planning at Rockville City School District

The grant was awarded. After a brief period of joy and disbelief, the news starts to sink in. One of the first obstacles to be overcome is securing the participation of principals and health/PE teachers from six K–8 middle schools. As Dr. West works with the superintendent on this matter, the needs assessment survey is distributed online to all teachers and staff in middle school grades, jointly constructed between Drs. Haywood and West. The findings reveal a pattern of ideas to improve resilience by providing mentoring, social skills programs, leadership activities, career exploration, cultural enrichment activities, or some combination of these services.

As word gets out to health/PE teachers that the intent is to focus only on eighth-grade students in their classes, some express their interest, but others become immediately resistant. Meanwhile, the principals implore Dr. West to offer their teaching staff an incentive. After consulting with Dr. West, Dr. Haywood agrees to set aside funds to cover a professional development workshop for each teacher. To free up this money, he reallocates funds assigned for a graduate assistant. The vast majority of health/PE teachers approached agree to participate. The few teachers who do not agree are informed that they can serve in the control group. The rest of the teachers agree to random assignment in spite of not knowing what the interventions are.

As participation from teachers is getting secured, the core team has to resolve the issue of obtaining active consent from parents versus passive consent. In one camp, Dr. DeGroot wants to bypass active consent; she argues that since the activities involve normal classroom practice, parents only need to be notified about the study. Dr. Haywood opposes passive consent because the research involves survey, focus group, and observational data that fall outside the normal assessments routinely administered. As innocuous as the methods are, they are utilized for the purposes of original data, not just for the analysis of secondary data. Dr. Haywood further adds that to bypass parental consent runs the risk of not being approved by his university's IRB, which has a precedent for requiring active consent for studies with minors. Dr. West and other administrators in the district seem to be relatively neutral about the issue. In addition, a formal data-sharing agreement for using student data to evaluate the project is signed.

During program implementation, the proposal contained a formative evaluation plan whereby the two programs would be continuously assessed for making improvements or modifications based on iterative cycles of ongoing feedback, consultation, and supervision. In short, the tasks involve an infrastructure of meetings among all key constituents, program staff fidelity logs/lists, student satisfaction questionnaires, student focus groups, and program staff observations. While nicely laid out on paper, once the principals are informed about this plan, they question its feasibility. In particular, they are worried that the teachers involved in Program A would not comply with filling out a fidelity measure or activity log. They are further concerned that observations of the teachers will be negatively viewed as part of their evaluations. It is thus incumbent on the core research team to clearly communicate that in no way will these observations be used as part of their evaluation.

By the time they get around to addressing these issues, a part-time coordinator has been hired by Dr. West, Mr. Holder. Although Mr. Holder will devote 50 percent full-time equivalent to the project, what he will do requires greater clarity. Mr. Holder will coordinate the meetings, take minutes, and facilitate communication. It is not clear what role he will have in the tasks associated with assessment of implementation. After several core team meetings, it is agreed that Dr. Haywood will oversee the formative evaluation; Dr. DeGroot will be responsible for the summative evaluation and writing an evaluation report each year. Dr. Haywood agrees to provide Dr. DeGroot program attendance records, as well as implementation data. The data-sharing agreement includes Drs. DeGroot and Haywood as partners.

The formative evaluation proves easier to sort out compared to agreeing on which nonacademic measures to use for the student self-report surveys. These measures are essentially designed to assess constructs referred to as "noncognitive" factors or skills. When the proposal was written, Dr. DeGroot was not involved in crafting this section. Based on her opinion, Dr. DeGroot feels that alternative measures should be used. Not surprisingly, Dr. Haywood disagrees. They reach a compromise in which some measures are retained and some are replaced. Dr. West asks if it would be a good idea to show the teachers, principals, parents, and students these measures. It crosses her mind that perhaps a more basic question of what outcomes they should in fact be measuring should be first addressed. The professors concur, but say it is not feasible given the timetable.

Based on the needs assessment, parent focus groups, and feedback offered by principals, social workers, and guidance counselors, it is decided that an innovative approach to mentoring should be "Program B," replacing the "growth mindset" activity that would have been delivered as a web-based computer program. Drs. West and Haywood are amenable with mentoring, but they struggle with how to implement mentoring in health/PE classes, assuming that it would still be for regular school hours. If so, would the teachers, the social workers, or perhaps students from the university be mentors? The core team eventually figures this issue out by agreeing to the following: (a) the mentoring program will be delivered in health/PE classes using a group format; (b) mentoring will be based on academic, health-related, and career-related topics; and (c) the frequency of delivery will be twice per month. The frequency of the social skills–life skills program (Program A) is planned to be delivered once per week in health/PE classes, or four times per month. As planned, the health/PE teachers, school counselors, and school social workers meet with the core team throughout the second, third, and fourth quarters to flesh out the details of what the programs will look like and how they will be delivered. Dr. Haywood and his graduate assistant are intensely involved in this process.

When the teachers and school support staff agreed to participate in one of the two programs, they did not have a clear idea (and perhaps nor did the core team) about the amount of time and effort required of them in the planning stages. This naturally created some degree of friction. In some of the meetings, all of which occurred after school, either a teacher(s) did not show up or one of the counselors/social workers did not attend. Some program personnel did not make substantial contributions, while others did the lion's share of the work in between meetings. All of these events led some to resent their peers who did not put in a good faith effort, while others complained about not getting paid for their time. Drs. Haywood and West sense that declining morale and building resentment could jeopardize the project, and so decide to address the issue by providing each school staff member who participates in the planning a stipend. Dr. Haywood uses revenues generated by indirect costs to achieve this end. This assuages the climate of dissatisfaction, but it is not clear after the PD workshops and summer kickoff how committed staff are, or how much money will be available to pay stipends in the second and third years.

Introductory Comments

In the pre-award stage, we described how a seemingly large amount of money ($1.5 million) can quickly dwindle, introducing an array of challenges. With this second case, the best-laid plans go awry in the post-award phase. Despite having nearly an entire year to plan, build consensus, and organize the school-based interventions, the researchers run up against a host of ethical concerns. Before discussing these issues, it is important to note that the research team embraces the principles of CBPA. Consistent with recommendations made by other scholars (e.g., Zins & Elias, 2007), the first phase of "diffusing" new interventions into Rockville's middle schools is dedicated to an inclusive planning process (i.e., program adoption) with all stakeholders providing their input and voicing their concerns. As part of the process of creating a sense of ownership, the core team strengthens organizational support at all levels. These actions occur in a methodical way to maximize stakeholder feedback, exchange ideas meaningfully, and make timely decisions about design, implementation, and evaluation.

In this case, quality programming depends on gaining staff buy-in in order for programs to be institutionalized and sustainable (Meyers, Durlak, & Wandersman, 2012). It also depends on professional development and training systems undergirded by a robust system of supervision and monitoring (Durlak & DuPre, 2008). The milestones and activities in the first year illustrate how collaboration and communication are critical for laying these important foundations. The system of meetings among the core team and personnel is intensified as the project moves into the implementation stage. The question that is left open is how committed personnel will be to even more meetings and following through on their ensuing roles and responsibilities.

Analysis of Ethical Decision-Making Processes

The underlying principles of beneficence and justice play out in a variety of ways. From the standpoint of empowering the whole community, beneficence is illustrated through the process of bringing people together and collectively trying to solve a common problem. This does not mean that the process is going to be conflict-free.

One of the most pressing ethical issues pertains to whether or not parents need to "actively" provide their consent. The difference in perspectives between Drs. DeGroot and Haywood is interesting; in many cases, the conflict arises between the researcher and the school district, but here we have two researchers debating the merits. With passive consent, all students can take a survey; with active consent, if only 60 percent of students return a signed form, then only 60 percent of them can take it, thus reducing the sample size and threatening a study's findings. If we apply this to Dr. DeGroot's motives as the evaluator, it is plausible that she wanted passive consent because of how "publishable" the results might be. In other words, the motive of wanting to obtain as high a sample size as possible – presumably so that threats to internal and external validity are not viewed as "fatal flaws" to the research design – appears to be at odds with the principle of the researchers to place the value and meaning of the CBPA project within the community as the overriding ethical concern, rather than how likely it would be for the results to be published in a journal one prefers. Alternatively, Dr. DeGroot might believe that active parent consent is not required, or she has never had to obtain active consent in her own research with minors at her own institution. In this scenario, Dr. Haywood's decision respects the autonomy of parents and minors.

As a general rule, interventions not integrated into regular instruction cannot be provided to students without signed parent consent. Under Dispensing Informed Consent with Research, this principle is consistent with the specifications of Standard 8.05 of the American Psychological Association (APA, 2010) Ethical Principles and Code of Conduct. In this particular situation, psychologists may only dispense with informed consent when the research would not reasonably be assumed to cause distress or harm and involves the study of "normal educational practices, curricula, or classroom management methods conducted in educational settings. . ." This may conflict with the personal motives, however, which seem to have driven Dr. DeGroot. Fortunately, Rockville chooses to implement them as part of "normal classroom instruction" or educational curricula in health/PE classes; that is, even if students did not return a consent form, they would still participate in the intervention. They would not be allowed to be surveyed or interviewed, though, as part of an approved research study. This situation becomes more critical if the identities of minors are videotaped or photographed for various purposes, such as wanting to use photographs of real students in the manual of the program/intervention or using them for training and orientation activities. Though the argument could be made that a media release/hold harmless form that parents sign in school districts will automatically protect the researchers, such a rationale is tenuous given that the data are still considered data for research purposes.

In basic research, "cognitive interviewing" can be employed to improve the validity of a measure for diverse populations (Desimone & Le Floch, 2004). Perhaps Dr. Haywood does not think he has the personnel to undertake such steps while trying to accomplish the other tasks. Even so, he could have asked community members what they would like to see measured based on the goals of the project. Whether or not the community gets to choose which measures are used may be trivial compared to the broader feelings of collaboration experienced. This is powerfully displayed in the decision to change Program B. However, this introduces a host of new challenges related to the delivery of the program and how to make adjustments in the budget.

Comment on Alternative Courses of Action

Because of the relationship between the distribution of funds and benefiting the community, a different course of action taken by Dr. Haywood with respect to paying teachers and school staff stipends might have altered the course of the project. Specifically, what if he decided to not give a stipend? The answer depends on how it is judged from a management perspective and a moral perspective. Since the staff are devoting labor that goes beyond their normal duties, it arguably merits additional compensation. On the other hand, the decision to not pay them a stipend may prevent an even bigger ordeal that could fester later on. Even if he continued to direct the overhead revenue to the stipends, he still may not have enough funds to pay them each the amount he desires since, proportionately, they would be doing at least twice the amount of work. Another argument could be made that to give them stipends in the first year, but not during the implementation stage, is setting up even greater resentment that could result in failure to meet the project's goals. In the end, Dr. Haywood takes a risk that he believes outweighs the greater risk of withholding the stipends.

Examining Dr. Haywood's dilemma from a social and emotional perspective warrants further attention. When acting as the principal investigator on a grant of this magnitude, the interpersonal demands of the work, combined with the ultimate goal of meeting the project's expectations, can naturally turn into a high-pressured situation that introduces unanticipated barriers and problems. For Dr. Haywood, it is reasonable to assume that he is "feeling the heat" when the overall morale starts to decline among the program personnel and school support staff. Without their buy-in and commitment, it is easy to see how Dr. Haywood might be worried that the project will fail because the programs will be delivered with poor quality, or might not be delivered at all. To remedy the situation, then, his decision to pay the school staff involved in the planning stages is justifiable, even at the potential risk of other staff feeling resentful for not being paid. The alternative outcome of dedicated staff simply withdrawing from the project, in his view, would prove to be even more disastrous. From this vantage point, Dr. Haywood is acting in a way that is consistent with ethical standards of beneficence, fidelity, and justice.

For applied research grants, a formative evaluation plan is typically required. In studies like the one at Rockville, standards of "implementation science" are increasingly imperative (Durlak & DuPre, 2008), albeit a recent review of mental health intervention studies in the community showed that the assessment of fidelity of implementation is inconsistent (Perry, Wallace, & Pickett, 2017). What if a formative evaluation was not done or significantly curtailed in its scope? Dr. Haywood would have run into the same limitations found by Perry, Wallace, and Pickett (2017) with respect to not having useful data that could help explain the program's impact while helping to make program improvements. The tension between wanting to achieve rigor and wanting to not overwhelm school staff is clearly evidenced by this question. It is understandable that Dr. Haywood might feel pressured to not require staff to complete activity logs, participate in focus groups, or be observed. In this case, the two choices cannot be completely pulled apart.

The Case of the Implementation and Evaluation at Rockville City School District

During program implementation and evaluation, new challenges are presented. One of the first issues is that one school is heavily concentrated with Hispanic/Latino students (90 percent). At this school, students respond to the interventions in different ways compared to other schools, even though both programs have a basis among diverse urban youth. In particular, the formative evaluation data indicate that Program A overlooks salient issues of acculturation. For example, life skills activities do not address the roles of language brokering, coping with anti-immigrant sentiment, or family members unable to find jobs due to their illegal status. Students and staff from other schools that primarily enroll African–Americans describe some activities as boring or not useful. When talking about managing stress in Program A, students and staff mention that racism and community violence are not acknowledged or addressed, including ways of coping. When it comes to talking about their personal lives, many students want to discuss the Black Lives Matter movement and recent events in the law enforcement and criminal justice system.

With continued feedback and anecdotal observations, it becomes more evident that there are not only issues with cultural congruence in lesson content, but improvements can be made in terms of delivery. It is recommended, for example, that technology be more frequently used, such as YouTube. At a deeper level, the core team realizes that while some teachers, social workers, and counselors genuinely buy-in to the project, they are not well-trained in counseling issues related to multicultural competence. The interventions stretch personnel beyond their traditional roles. Even the social workers and school counselors feel that the material is new; most of the time, they are used to dealing with classroom management or individualized education programs or managing crises. Dr. Haywood comes to recognize that more time should have been spent on role-playing and skill development in the planning and professional development phases.

Carrying out the formative evaluation and structure of meetings as they were intended proves to be unrealistic. Whereas some program staff are reliable in completing their fidelity measures and attending meetings, others are more sporadic; some teachers refuse to complete fidelity measures and do not attend meetings. Meanwhile, some school social workers and counselors are unreliable in showing up to their classes. This is detrimental to the mentoring program, as teachers have to cancel these sessions. Throughout the second year, other obstacles arise that interfere with exposure to the programs, including snow days, fire drills, and testing days. At the end of the fourth quarter, Dr. Haywood finds that about 50 percent of the teachers and staff complete their fidelity measures, while about 85 percent provide student program attendance data. There was a 35 percent attrition rate in survey data on average. The attrition rate is attributable, in part, to poor follow-through among some teachers; in other instances, students simply did not return consent forms.

Based on formative evaluation data gathered from stakeholders over the course of the second year, it becomes clear that modifications to programs as well as the training and professional development sequence must be made. In the middle of the second year, Mr. Holder also abruptly resigns from his position, announcing that he has found a new job in California. His announcement is fortuitous insofar as it frees up funds that can be reallocated toward program modification and professional development. Still, Drs. Haywood and West know that even with this money, they cannot afford to compensate all staff if they want to organize a two-week retreat over the summer. They decide to invite ten staff (six teachers and four social workers/ school counselors) who they believe to have been the most dedicated and who can make the greatest contributions. They are asked to not divulge this information to coworkers; they get paid a stipend as compensation for two weeks of labor during their summer, devoting eight hours per day each week. As justified as this stipend is, Dr. West fears that it might create resentment. Be that as it may, Dr. Haywood believes it is necessary for the project's success. His predictions are confirmed, for the retreat turns out to be highly productive, with the bulk of the curricula fully revised. The best way to approach the PD sessions in August is also discussed during the retreat. On this issue, they decide to devote PD sessions to role-playing and multicultural competence, while building those key topics into staff meetings throughout the year. During the third year, the major investment in the summer retreat proves to pay dividends. Because of the improvements and a new approach to staff meetings, personnel experience a greater sense of clarity, autonomy, and control. The completion of fidelity measures and meeting attendance rates in turn substantially improve.

In terms of the final summative evaluation conducted by Dr. DeGroot and her team, the results failed to detect any significant differences between the two treatment groups and the control group in promotion rates to the tenth grade among the first cohort. When examining the impact of dosage, however, a few significant effects are detected; specifically, students in Programs A and B have higher intrinsic academic motivation and a greater sense of belongingness in school when they participate in at least ten sessions. Dr. DeGroot suggests that if the second cohort were to be tracked next year, a main significant effect may be revealed because of the higher program quality in the second year. Dr. West is invested in following up the second cohort. Before the final year ends, she and Dr. Haywood sign a memorandum specifying the university's role in tracking the second cohort. Perhaps more importantly, it lays out an agreement for the Rockville staff to supervise master's students enrolled in counseling programs during their practicums, and also to work with doctoral students in counseling psychology for the mutual purpose of sustaining the project and growing it through combining training needs with CBPA.

When discussing how the results will be disseminated, Dr. West wants the marketing department to see the report written by Dr. DeGroot, reserving the right to authorize what is disseminated to external audiences. Off the record, Dr. West shares with Dr. Haywood the district's concerns about white students not doing as well as other races and the lack of improvement in promotion to the tenth grade among the first cohort. She wonders if Rockville should continue with Program A since Program B did better, or at least it seems to have done, and requires less time. Dr. Haywood makes sure to convey the fact that some if not all of these findings could be the product of the pilot testing nature of the first year and the various problems with buy-in, performance, and research procedures that occurred. These precautions will be shared with relevant audiences when the time comes to discuss such decisions. In any case, Dr. Haywood is pleased to inform Dr. West that he has a no-cost extension to complete the production of the program manuals. The core team will hold meetings in August with all Rockville constituents about the next steps in the project and to discuss the future goals of the partnership between the district and the university.

Introductory Comments

In this third case, the tensions between meeting the aspirational ideals of justice and beneficence at the same time are brought to life, which involve benefits to the students. Fiscal decisions regarding the budget are influenced by a confluence of events, some of which are controllable and some of which are not; a chain of consequences play out as a result of those decisions. As the grant approaches its final phase, we also see how findings of the programs' impacts – which are used to judge the value or worth of an intervention – must take into account what happens inside that mysterious "black box" between pre-test and post-test, for without a rendering of processes related to program implementation and fidelity, the results may distort a community's decision to support, reject, or expand the interventions. In most journal articles, readers never know about the contextual processes that occur because they are either viewed as trivial or are not considered to be conducive to the format of an empirical study. At Rockville, the social, emotional, and politically laden processes of the research and evolving relationships are anything but sources of "nuisance variance" or "white noise"; instead, they are essential to understanding the findings and for conducting future CPBA studies (for a review of best practices in reporting CBPA research, see Smith, Rosenzweig, & Schmidt, 2010).

Analysis of Decision-Making Processes

At first glance, perhaps the thorniest ethical dilemma is Dr. Haywood's decision to invite ten staff to the summer retreat and to pay them each a stipend, while discretely asking them to not divulge such information to their coworkers. Like other situations, the core team is faced with a decision that must reconcile principles of being transparent and inclusive with doing what is best for the project. If Dr. Haywood does not pay, then he may not have a summer retreat and thus may not achieve the positive results we see. If he does pay, there is a risk that others may find out, which could lead to a host of problems related to perceptions of inequality. Dr. Haywood is willing to take that risk. A third option is to lower the stipend, which may in turn force him to lower the amount of time at the retreat, thereby reducing the amount of work that can get done. Yet, even so, the same conflict of principles apply. From his view, paying retreat members a reasonable amount of money is more than well-justified, especially when compared to, say, psychologists who charge two to even three times as much for their consultation fees. Dr. Haywood thus believes that the stipend serves the best interests of the community.

Given all of the positive changes that transpire in the third year, do the so-called ends justify the means? From a pragmatic and scientific standpoint of achieving positive results in the project, there is a strong rationale that they do. From a purely ethical perspective, however, the best course of action that should have been taken is much more ambiguous. If a retreat would have never happened because of concerns of equity that not every teacher and school staff could be invited or paid for their labor, then it is highly likely that improvements in the programs and the research process would not have occurred. In fact, the project might have failed completely. Therefore, it could be argued that the unethical course of action would have been to do nothing at all with regard to a retreat because the success of the overall CBPA process would have been clearly jeopardized. The merits of each alternative decision, including their many variations, are ultimately left to readers to hypothetically consider for themselves. As it so happened in this case, the success of the project – and the future sustainability of the partnership – was strongly supported by the decision to provide stipends to a select group of staff for a strategic objective.

When psychologists think of ethical standards of competence in counseling diverse client populations, as operationalized by Sue, Arredondo, and McDavis (1992), it is the role of providing one-to-one counseling services that tends to be the working assumption. In applied CBPA research, this prevailing schema transforms into viewing the role of the psychologist as a catalyst of organizational change, leadership, and consultation. In this case, the goal is to diffuse these new approaches into the norms and practices of Rockville. This work lies not in the hands of the psychologist alone, but in all of the teachers and master's-level school staff who, for the most part, probably did not receive intense training in these areas. Because the project entails a curriculum being provided during regular school hours, as opposed to a clinical treatment that occurs outside of education, a tension is set up between wanting educators to implement these programs as pseudo-therapists versus respecting their ideas and advice as "experts" in their own right. To not engage in a dialogue about what are (or are not) the correct approaches to use in the teachers' own classes and subject matters would contradict the principles of collaboration in CBPA research. That is why the psychologist must be careful in not being too eager to inject his/her solutions.

The formative evaluation data play a crucial role in allowing Dr. Haywood to have the leverage that he needs to bring attention to what is a problem of competence. In the planning phase, one can assume that such matters are addressed, but given the other milestones that also need to be accomplished, it is likely that cultural competencies are not regularly discussed and processed at the deep, intense level that they should be under ideal conditions. In a way, perhaps this works out for the best as the school staff come to realize this concern after listening to student feedback and seeing how some activities can be improved. Although these experiences are necessary for individual awareness to occur, the critical factor is to have a solid infrastructure of supervision and consultation in place to support these areas of systematic professional development. With the inclusion of students in counseling psychology in Program B – psychologists-in-training who have a solid background in multicultural counseling – a relevant question to ask relates to the extent to which the impact of the results is a product of these new personnel versus the progression made in the teachers, school staff, and the content of the curriculum. Only future studies can tease out these rival explanations. It is quite plausible that both explanations may account for the findings. If so, it would provide greater leverage for the memorandum of understanding that is established.

Lastly, ethical issues concerning dissemination of the project's findings warrants brief discussion. The evaluation conducted by Dr. DeGroot, as in many CBPA applied studies, is contingent on decisions that have little to do with the merit or rationale of the proposed programs, but instead are directly tied to matters related to training, supervision, and the budget, including events that happen to unexpectedly favor the gradual success of the project, such as Mr. Holder's decision to resign. With this point in mind, the evaluation yields mixed results, which can be interpreted in different ways depending on the interests of the stakeholder. Dr. West's concerns reflects a common source of tension in this phase of program diffusion; it is in the interests of the scientific community to report such findings, but they may clash with the interests of the local community who want to ensure that its parents, media, the board, and school staff do not interpret these results in the "wrong way." It is a conflict that tests the core value of shared authority and decision-making over the dissemination of results.

At the end of the day, it is plausible that Rockville representatives may not care if Drs. Haywood and DeGroot, for example, publish all of the results from the evaluation in a journal that does not disclose the district's identity. One issue that is left unresolved in this case is whether the district partners, such as Dr. West and teachers and staff, should be authors on a journal article or co-presenters at conferences. Consistent with the ideals of CBPA research, the university partners should not only ask them to be coauthors, but should request their input in manuscript writing (Israel et al., 1998). When actually faced with putting this principle into practice, many researchers may have a difficult time granting nonacademics such power. To not abide by this principle, however, would not only contradict ethical standards of justice, but also lead to the risk of compromising the integrity of the partnership, which seems to be headed in the right direction with the memorandum of understanding and agreement to sustain the project. Of course, such an agreement may have never materialized had the results been different, bringing us back full circle to that one fateful summer day when the grant competition was announced.

The Case of Finding a Local High School for a Pilot Field Experiment

Dr. Holt, a 28-year-old, white assistant professor at a university, spent the first several years in her position conducting basic research to examine how aspects of schools' social environments are associated with students' behavior. During that time, she developed a model explaining how making changes to school social processes can lead students to be more engaged in class, reduce bullying, and increase prosocial behavior. Eventually, Dr. Holt determined that she was ready to put her ideas to the test at a local high school. The intervention that Dr. Holt had in mind was creating a committee of about ten students that would meet weekly, learn critical thinking and leadership skills, and recommend school improvement strategies to the administration.

Dr. Holt identified a high school in the large city school district adjacent to her university with a new principal, Mr. Taylor, who by all accounts was very energetic and open to new ideas. The school had experienced significant turnover in leadership in the preceding years, due in part to failure to make progress in student performance. Dr. Holt was determined to make her intervention consonant with the values of the school community. Working with Mr. Taylor, Dr. Holt arranged short presentations at the beginning of the school year to each homeroom, at a staff meeting after school, and at a meeting after school to which all parents would be invited to attend. During these meetings, Dr. Holt planned to solicit input from participants on how the intervention might be implemented. Dr. Holt intended these meetings to be a means to engage the community in the conceptualization of the study, to empower them with a sense of control, and to make the intervention fit into the existing culture of the school.

Dr. Holt's homeroom and staff meeting presentations went well enough, but students and staff offered very few ideas and mostly went along with what Dr. Holt proposed. One teacher requested that the intervention not interfere with her English class, as she was feeling pressure to improve her students' reading standardized test scores due to a new evaluation system that emphasized student growth. To Dr. Holt's disappointment, only two parents attended the scheduled parent meeting, but they seemed mostly supportive of her idea. In discussing the outcomes of these meetings, Dr. Holt and Mr. Taylor made most of the decisions regarding details of how the intervention would be implemented.

Considerations of the Ethics of Power

In this fourth case, a typical scenario of CBPA research that emanates from circumstances different from those portrayed in Rockville is brought to life, for here the study is initiated by the researcher, not the community. In other words, the intervention has already been significantly developed by Dr. Holt prior to her initiating contact with the school, and thus she has already made a number of important decisions related to the research. In theory, the principal, Mr. Taylor, has the power to say "no" to Dr. Holt's request, but he may be in a position of vulnerability due to being new and under pressure to quickly improve school performance. Dr. Holt should consider this vulnerability when selecting a school site in terms of whether the principal may be feel compelled, in a way, to say "yes." Furthermore, Mr. Taylor may perceive Dr. Holt as an "expert" and be reluctant during the first meeting to suggest changes to the proposed intervention that may bring it into better alignment with his goals for the school.

The lead authority figure in the school (i.e., the principal) is the researcher's initial point of contact and, subsequently, the de facto institutional champion of the intervention at the time it is presented to students and school staff. Whether or not Mr. Taylor vocalizes his support for the intervention, his tacit endorsement may be communicated to the school community simply by Dr. Holt being granted permission to present in classrooms and at a staff meeting. Students and staff may therefore be fearful of voicing concern of disapproval of the intervention due to the potential for administrative censure. To allay this concern, Dr. Holt could make it very clear to students and staff that participation is voluntary and that they stand to experience no negative repercussions by refusing involvement.

Dr. Holt convenes one-time meetings for students, school staff, and parents to take part in making decisions about how the intervention will look. Are these important stakeholder groups truly "listened to" in this context? Somewhat perfunctory gestures of collaboration may not make possible authentic shared decision-making and may even disaffect and disempower stakeholders by presenting them with an already-developed idea that may appear to be on an inevitable course to implementation. Dr. Holt could have considered engaging the school community at the very earliest stages of developing the intervention to avoid this problem. This, of course, leaves open the chance that the community will choose a course of action that is not consonant with what the research literature suggests are "best practices" (Nation et al., 2011).

Democracy, Values, and Benefits

Serrano-Garcia (1994) argues that ethics in CPBA are a function of the composite values of the community. The researcher should earnestly seek to understand these values prior to embarking on a study. Some explicit values communicated through Dr. Holt's study are that classroom engagement and prosocial behavior are important goals, potentially more important than the content that students are exposed to in elective courses (since they will be pulled from these courses to participate). More implicitly, the study – with its emphasis on the student voice – suggests that students can and should challenge the assumptions of school staff regarding how to best structure the environment. Do the students, school staff, and parents share this value? Following from the previous point, Dr. Holt's limited exposure to these groups may make it difficult to know this. Complicating this issue is the reality that "communities" are not always homogenous entities with shared values. For example, students may think that they should have a voice in changing their schools, whereas parents may feel that their children should simply focus on improving their standardized test performance to better navigate the system as it exists, and teachers may balk at reduced classroom time for music and art. These latter values are not reflected in the study. Finally, the question of values relates directly to the question of the benefits of the study; namely, the benefits a stakeholder perceives stem directly from what he or she values.

Competence

An important consideration in any applied study is the ethical standard of competence (APA Code 2.01). Applied research typically involves disrupting systems, structures, and communities in some fashion, and it is imperative that the researcher is adequately qualified to justify these disruptions. In the example, Dr. Holt is causing a disruption to the school by creating a new in-school program, pulling some students out of their elective classes, and changing the way in which students and school staff interact with one another. Dr. Holt likely believes that she has done her due diligence by rooting the intervention in the research literature, and it is critical that interventions like hers have sufficient evidence to suggest they will benefit the community. The trick, so to speak, is not becoming so technical and esoteric in the communication of these ideas that researchers like Dr. Holt are unable to connect with the school's representatives on a social, emotional, or practical level where the community feels as if she "gets who I am and what I am going through." Once a community senses that the outsider is not able to connect or genuinely care about their experience, it is unlikely that they will want him/her to stick around long-term.

Conclusion and Future Directions

The four case examples in this chapter represent the core ethical dilemmas and conflicts that arise in applied CBPA research. They also speak to broader aspirations of justice. Although the APA (2010) does not mandate psychologists to engage in work that is presented here, making the services we provide accessible to the public, regardless of one's ability to pay, is a noble cause that is implicitly captured by its underlying standards. Indeed, it can be powerfully argued that applied community-based research ought to be the wave of the future in psychological science, for it naturally aligns with movements toward prevention, equal access to mental health services, and the elimination of health disparities in communities facing significant barriers to high-quality treatment in hospitals and clinics. As illustrated in this chapter, such a radical transformation of how psychologists think about the true value or currency of the research they conduct would require preparation for having to wrestle with all sorts of ethical quandaries and complex decisions that one does not have to deal with in an experimental lab or in the isolated comforts of the campus.

According to Perry, Wallace, and Pickett (2017), conducting applied research on interventions that are delivered in high-need communities, like the cases we present, is more of an art than a science in the sense that it involves the forging and negotiation of relationships that bring together multiple entities with different motives, interests, and agendas. As they put it, "...the relationship-building does not conveniently follow a set of laws or patterns of behavior that can dictate real-life decision-making and practices" (p. 467). Insofar as this precept of CBPA research is true, especially in the context of grant-funded research, then any recommendation in this domain of ethics has to be relatively generic so that it can be flexibly applied to a seemingly infinite range of situations. In this chapter, we based our case examples on the fabric of our own experiences working with diverse communities in K–12 schools. To be sure, we could have presented four different cases that focused on entirely separate communities, such as LGBT adults, the homeless, or survivors of domestic violence. Rather than viewing this as a limitation, we believe that the consistency of our examples offers a rare insiders' glimpse into the messiness of decision-making processes that so often transpire in studies of this nature, but never get reported. To fully appreciate such issues, the approach we took in this chapter was the best learning strategy to achieve these goals. Nonetheless, the many issues discussed across the four cases, and there natural variations, can be applied to considerations of the CBPA research that psychologists may conduct in other communities.

We encourage psychologists who wish to undertake similar research to consult models and various lists of recommended practices that have been described by scholars in public health and community psychology (e.g., Ball & Janyst, 2008; Israel, 1998; Nation et al., 2011; Shore, 2006). These resources contain rich information that can be transferred to virtually any situation and set of ethical issues that researchers will likely encounter in their own work. The purpose of this chapter was to illustrate such issues with an intense level of candor and complexity that can serve as a practical guide and a realistic frame of reference. In the final analysis, psychologists who engage in this type of research will ultimately need to answer a simple question: "Why am I doing this?" If the answer is to serve the community, rather than just to serve one's self-interests, then it is likely that the research will become something much more rewarding than what anyone ever anticipated, long after the initial effect sizes from the inaugural study have been calculated.

References

American Psychological Association (2010). *Ethical principles of psychologists and code of conduct*. Washington, DC: American Psychological Association.

Ball, J. & Janyst, P. (2008). Enacting research ethics in partnerships with indigenous communities in Canada: "Do it in a good way." *Journal of Empirical Research on Human Research Ethics*, *3*, 33–51.

Bond, L. A. & Hauf, A. M. C. (2007). Community-based collaboration: An overarching best practice in prevention. *The Counseling Psychologist*, *35*, 567–575.

Buki, L. P. (2014). The relevance of counseling psychology in addressing major social issues. *The Counseling Psychologist*, *42*, 6–12.

Desimone, L M. & Le Floch, K. C. (2004). Are we asking the right questions? Using cognitive interviews to improve surveys in education research. *Educational Evaluation and Policy Analysis*, *26*, 1–22.

Durlak, J. A. & DuPre, E. P. (2008). Implementation matters: A review of research on the influence of implementation on program outcomes and the factors affecting implementation. *American Journal of Community Psychology, 41*, 327–350.

Flicker, S., Travers, R., Guta, A., McDonald, S., & Meagher, A. (2007). Ethical dilemmas in community-based participatory research: Recommendations for institutional review boards. *Journal of Urban Health: Bulletin of the New York Academy of Medicine, 84*, 478–493.

Israel, B. A., Schulz, A. J., Parker, E. A., & Becker, A. B. (1998). Review of community-based research: Assessing partnership approaches to improve public health. *Annual Review of Public Health, 19*, 173–202.

Maiter, S., Simich, L., Jacobson, N., & Wise, J. (2008). Reciprocity: An ethic for community-based participatory action research. *Action Research, 6*, 305–325.

Meyers, D. C., Durlak, J. A., & Wandersman, A. (2012). The quality implementation framework: A synthesis of critical steps in the implementation process. *American Journal of Community Psychology, 50*, 462–480.

Minkler, M. (2004). Ethical challenges for the "outside" researcher in community-based participatory research. *Health Education & Behavior, 31*, 684–697.

Nation, M., Bess, K., Voight, A., Perkins, D. D., & Juarez, P. (2011). Levels of community engagement in youth violence prevention: The role of power in sustaining successful university-community partnerships. *American Journal of Community Psychology, 48*, 89–96.

Perry, J. C., Cusner, A., & Pickett, L. L. (2015). Fostering adolescent work and career readiness. In C. Juntunen & J. Schwartz (Eds.), *Counseling across the lifespan: Prevention and treatment* (2nd edn., pp. 147–164). Thousand Oaks, CA: SAGE.

Perry, J. C., Wallace, E. W., & Pickett, L. L. (2017). Underserved urban community interventions. In M. Jackson, M. Casas, L. Suzuki, & C. Alexander (Eds.), *Handbook of multicultural counseling* (4th edn., pp. 456–471). Thousand Oaks, CA: SAGE.

Roos, V., Visser, M., Pistorius, A., & Nefale, M. (2007). Ethics and community psychology. In N. Duncan, B. Bowman, V. Roos, J. Pillay, & A. Naidoo (Eds.), *Community psychology: Analysis, context, and action* (pp. 392–407). Cape Town, South Africa: University of Cape Town Press.

Schnarch, B. (2004). Ownership, control, access, and possession (OCAP) or self-determination applied to research. *Journal of Aboriginal Health, 1*, 80–95.

Serrano-Garcia, I. (1994). The ethics of the powerful and the power of ethics. *American Journal of Community Psychology, 22*, 1–20.

Shore, N. (2006). Re-conceptualizing the Belmont Report: A community-based participatory research perspective. *Journal of Community Practice, 14*, 5–26.

Silka, L., Cleghorn, G. D., Grullón, M., & Tellez, T. (2008). Creating community-based participatory research in a diverse community: A case study. *Journal of Empirical Research on Human Research Ethics, 3*, 5–16.

Smith, L., Rosenzweig, L., & Schmidt, M. (2010). Best practices in the reporting of participatory action research: Embracing both the forest and the trees. *The Counseling Psychologist, 38*, 1115–1138.

Sue, D. W., Arredondo, P., & McDavis, R. J. (1992). Multicultural counseling competencies and standards: A call to the profession. *Journal of Counseling & Development, 70*, 477–486.

The National Commission for the Protection of Human Subjects of Biomedical and Behavioral Research (1979). *The Belmont Report: Ethical principles and guidelines for the protection of human subjects of research.* Washington, DC: U.S. Department of Health and Human Services. Retrieved from www.hhs.gov/ohrp/humansubjects/guidance/belmont.html

Zins, J. & Elias, M. (2007). Social and emotional learning: Promoting the development of all students. *Journal of Educational and Psychological Consultation, 17,* 233–255.

18 Ethical Issues and Challenges Working with Religious Individuals and Organizations

Providing Culturally Competent Professional Mental Health Services

Thomas G. Plante

All mental health professionals are required to provide competent, evidence-based, professional services in an ethical manner (American Association for Marriage and Family Therapy, 2015; American Psychiatric Association, 2013; American Psychological Association, 2002, 2003; National Association of Social Workers, 2008). Years of quality graduate school, practicum, internship, and postgraduate training are needed to ensure that those who are entrusted with the health and mental health care of others are thoughtful and state-of-the-art professionals. The national and international professional organizations such as the American Psychological Association, the National Association of Social Workers, the American Association of Marriage and Family Therapists, the American Psychiatric Association, and others have also carefully drafted aspirational and practical ethical guidelines for their members. A careful reading of these documents along with those from many international organizations such as the Canadian Psychological Association (2000), the British Psychological Society (2009), and others suggests that there is generally excellent agreement about guiding ethical principles for mental health care professionals. These include a focus on the importance of respect, responsibility, integrity, competence, and concern for others (Plante, 2004). Special attention is given to the importance of maintaining confidentiality, avoiding dual relationships and thus the exploitation of others, continuing quality improvement through ongoing engagement with peer consultation and formalized continuing education opportunities, and always working for the benefit of others.

Although great care and attention are directed to the training of mental health professionals, ethical challenges and dilemmas are frequent occurrences even under the very best of circumstances (Koocher & Keith-Speigal, 2007; Pope, 2007). In fact, it is likely that all mental health professionals confront ethical challenges almost daily in their professional work (Plante, 2004, 2007a). These dilemmas may be subtle or dramatic, but if one is thoughtful and reflective about one's work, they will likely see that ethical issues and challenges need to be confronted more often than not and on a very regular basis.

These ethical difficulties are certainly more likely when dealing with high-risk groups. Although not an exhaustive list, these include cases that involve high-conflict divorce, child custody conflicts, homicidal and suicidal clients, and certain personality disorder cases such as borderline and antisocial clients, among others (Koocher & Keith-Speigal, 2007; Pope, 2007). Additionally, clinical work with organizations such as law enforcement, the military, school-based mental health services, and consultation liaison work within hospital settings are just a few of the organizations that offer special and often complex ethical challenges.

Religious organizations offer a very special type of unique ethical challenge for the mental health professional for a variety of reasons. First, the vast majority of graduate training and internship programs offer little if any training on religious issues and organizations. Although almost every training program supports training in cultural competence, these offerings focus on ethnic, gender, sexual orientation, and racial diversity, usually leaving religious diversity out (Plante, 2007a, 2012, 2013). Although professional ethics codes call for training and respect toward religious diversity, most training programs tend to simply ignore this important element of human diversity (Russell & Yarhouse, 2006).

Second, few mental health professionals are interested in religion themselves (Delaney, Miller, & Bisonó, 2007; Ellis, 1971; Freud, 1961; Hage, 2006; Russell & Yarhouse, 2006). For example, while most Americans and people throughout the world are affiliated with and engaged by a religious tradition, most psychologists are not (Delaney et al., 2007; Gallup & Lindsay, 1999). The only exception to this trend is when several religiously based clinical or therapeutic approaches are greatly secularized, with both yoga and mindfulness-based stress reduction being perhaps the best current examples (e.g., Kabat-Zinn, 1990, 2003). While yoga originated and is rooted in the Hindu tradition and mindfulness is rooted within the Buddhist tradition, the versions that are often practiced and endorsed by mental health professionals today in clinical practice are so secular that their religious roots are difficult if not impossible to appreciate (Plante, 2009, 2012).

Third, religious organizations have their own and long-established rules, traditions, languages, and approaches that likely are quite foreign to most mental health professionals. Additionally, they are often exempt from or allowed as an exception from many state and federal mandates, laws, and customs. For example, the Roman Catholic Church can limit their priest roles to single, celibate, heterosexual men and prohibit those who differ from this demographic from pursuing ordained ministry in the Church. Thus, employment laws and other familiar rules that apply to other organizations such as hospitals, schools, and corporations simply do not apply to most Church and other faith-based organizations.

Finally, religious organizations are especially ripe for transference reactions and strong opinions even from generally level-headed, evidence-based mental health professionals (Ellis, 1971; Freud, 1961). Since most mental health professionals have little interest in or minimal experience with religious organizations and get little or no training on this subject during graduate and postgraduate training, they typically get whatever information they can secure from popular press news reporting. For example, the Roman Catholic Church most often gets news attention around sexual abuse perpetrated by their clerics or perhaps on their typically unpopular stance on matters related to sexual ethics (e.g., abortion, homosexuality, contraception use). Jewish groups often get press attention regarding anti-Semitic violence, their conflicts with Arab groups, and many issues related to their ultra-orthodox communities (e.g., sexually abusive rabbis, refusing to sit near women while using public transportation). Protestant groups often receive press attention when pastors find themselves in sexual, financial, or other scandals. Rarely does the popular press report on the best that religious organizations have to offer (e.g., hosting soup kitchens and food pantries, providing free counseling and day care services, offering service trips and youth programs, providing a wide range of services and products to the poor, marginalized, and traumatized). Therefore, a casual and religiously nonaffiliated person – even a highly educated, empirically minded mental health professional – likely maintains a warped and biased view of the major religious traditions and those who are devoted to them (Plante, 2009).

In this chapter, I hope to highlight some of the most common and most challenging ethical dilemmas and concerns for mental health professionals who work closely with religious organizations. Since my almost 30 years of clinical experience with religious groups have been conducted primarily with the Roman Catholic Church, I will focus my attention in this chapter on Catholics. However, many of the challenges discussed in this chapter could also be applied to other religious organizations. In the spirit of the adage "write what you know," I will limit my observations to these groups. Additionally, in accordance with the spirit of the other chapters in this edited volume, I will highlight several complex and unique case studies that provide rich material for ethical reflection and discernment. All of the cases discussed in this chapter are actual cases that I have worked with, but in order to carefully respect and protect confidentiality, names and minor details have been changed.

The RRICC Model: A Universal and Practical Ethical Frame of Reference

Before addressing the ethical cases for discussion, it is important to present and highlight an ethical frame of reference that can be used to organize our thinking about ethical dilemmas. While all of the mental health professional organizations offer detailed and thoughtful ethical codes of conduct (American Association for Marriage and Family Therapy, 2015; American Psychiatric Association, 2013; American Psychological Association, 2002, 2003; National Association of Social Workers, 2008), I would like to highlight an easy to use and understand five-word value approach to ethics model that is consistent with all of the professional mental health codes at both the national and international level. This is called the RRICC model, with each letter representing a critical ethical value (Plante, 2004, 2007a). These values include *respect, responsibility, integrity, competence*, and *concern* for others. A careful review of all of the mental health professional codes of ethics highlights these five important and overarching virtues (Koocher & Keith-Speigal, 2007; Plante, 2004, 2007a; Pope, 2007). While they are certainly not an exhaustive list of the values and virtues needed within professional mental health practice, they do represent a common way of proceeding when it comes to ethical reflection and decision-making and will be used here to think through the ethical cases presented in this chapter.

Let us briefly unpack these five virtues before proceeding to use them with common ethical challenges. "Respect" refers to respecting the rights, dignity, and self-determination of individuals and groups. For example, regardless of the offenses committed (e.g., clergy sexual offending of children) or religiously inspired asocial behavior (e.g., violence), clients are respected and treated with human dignity. "Responsibility" refers to keeping promises and acting in professional ways at all times. "Integrity" means wholeness, completeness, and truthfulness. Being honest and sincere without deceit or deception is what integrity underscores. "Competence" refers to the needed education, training, certification, and consultation to provide clients with evidence-based, state-of-the-art, second-to-none quality professional service. Finally, "concern" for others refers to working in the best interest of and benefit to the client at all times. Using this RRICC framework can help us to engage in effective problem-solving strategies and reflections on ethical concerns in a straightforward and easy to use and remember manner. The five principles act as a helpful filter or set of organizing principles for considering all ethical challenges confronted by professionals. When these five words are considered when considering ethical challenges, good decisions are more readily available (Plante, 2004).

Four Typical Ethical Dilemmas with Religious Organizations

Confidentiality

While confidentiality is often difficult to secure in any professional clinical practice, it is even more challenging in organizations such as schools, clinics, hospitals, and, perhaps most especially, religious organizations. First, religious organizations often have very different standards, norms, and practices about confidentiality. For example, in the Roman Catholic, Episcopal, and several other religious groups, clerics take a vow of obedience to their religious superior such as a bishop, provincial, mother superior, rector, or other religious leader. In this way, the individual cleric does not retain their rights to confidentiality and often are thus treated, like minor children, as an extension or ward of the religious superior. Even laypersons that are not ordained ministers or clerics may have different perspectives, views, and rules about confidentiality as well within their religious groups. Often mental health professionals who have little experience with religious organizations have challenges understanding and working with these different views about confidentiality, as well as the fact that, like in the military, clerics sometimes have to take orders form religious superiors even when it involves mental health evaluations and treatment against their will.

Sexual Ethics

Typically individuals, including children and teens, are free to explore and use their bodies as they wish for sexual/sensual pleasure without interference from others (as long as they do not seriously harm themselves or others or commit a crime such as engaging in child pornography, sexual victimization of minors, or human trafficking). In secular and Western culture, sexual expression, even among youth, is not only respected but even celebrated. For example, public displays and expressions of sexual affection are commonplace, as are sensual and sexually highlighted clothing and behavior. Television shows, movies, and advertisements for everything from cars to pizza and beer features scantily clad, youthful bodies to promote their products and services. This freedom and emphasis on sexual expression is not enjoyed among most in religious life, and most especially among clerics or the devout in traditionally conservative religious organizations. For example, within the Roman Catholic tradition, priests, brothers, and religious sisters (or nuns) take a sacred vow of chastity and celibacy such that they cannot engage in any sexual behavior with others and are also forbidden to participate in sensual or sexual behaviors on their own, such as engaging in masturbation. Roman Catholic deacons can be married when they are ordained to the permanent diaconate, but if their spouse passes away after ordination they are not allowed to remarry. Homosexuals, whether actively engaged with a partner or not, are not allowed to be ordained clerics (i.e., priests or deacons) in the Roman Catholic Church. They are also not allowed to marry within the Church or have their sexual orientation or partnerships with others supported in any formalized manner. Using the example of a different religious tradition, Jewish rabbis typically cannot be married to non-Jews. Additionally, some of the more conservative Jewish groups such as the orthodox and conservative traditions forbid homosexual unions among clerics and nonclerics alike. Therefore, sexual freedom of expression and behavior is uniquely managed in many religious communities that would be illegal to control within most secular organizations. Thus, religious leaders can forbid even private sexual behavior among their rank-and-file clerics and congregants.

Conflict with Values

The mental health community and religious communities may not always agree on certain values and virtues, which can create tensions and ethical challenges when working with religious organizations as well as the devout. For example, most mental health professionals, reflecting secular culture, tend to value individual freedoms, equality, self-care, and assertiveness to get needs met. Yet, many religious organizations and the devout may take issue with values and virtues that are endorsed and highlighted by the secular community, including among mental health professionals. For example, women often do not receive equal treatment or have equal opportunities in many religious organizations. This is especially true of those religious traditions that lean toward a more conservative approach to their faith tradition. For example, women cannot be ordained ministers (i.e., deacons or priests) in the Roman Catholic

Church or in many of the more conservative dioceses of the Episcopal Church. Additionally, women cannot be rabbis in the orthodox Jewish traditions. In fact, women are not allowed even to pray at the sacred Western Wall in Jerusalem and often get physically attacked when they try to do so. Many religious groups recognize men, but not women, as household leaders, which is commonly found in highly conservative and evangelical Protestant, orthodox Jewish, and conservative Muslim communities. Thus, secular and mental health professionals' emphasis on gender equality is not shared among many diverse religious groups and traditions.

Many religious rituals and practices can also cause significant conflicts in values between religious groups and mental health professionals. For example, religious rituals such as male or female circumcision, arranged marriages, and strict fasting demands may cause tension and ethical conflicts. While some behaviors and values may be supported by religious groups, they may be considered offensive or unethical to secular mental health professionals. Perhaps female circumcision within some conservative Muslim groups is a good example. What is normal and expected within some religious groups is considered barbaric and abusive in secular society.

Many religious organizations and groups also support virtues and values such as humility, self-sacrifice, restraint, and other qualities (Plante, 2012) that may not be viewed as favorably among the mental health community. While a mental health professional may wish to support a client's assertiveness and self-care, their religious leaders and community may expect humility and self-sacrifice, perhaps especially from women and children. Humility is a quality that is often highly supported among many diverse religious groups but tends not to be supported within secular society or among many mental health professionals (Plante, 2012).

Cultural Competence

Ethical issues regarding cultural competence frequently emerge while working with religious organizations and with their clerics and layperson devotees (Plante, 2007a, 2009). Since mental health professionals very rarely receive any training with these religious groups and tend not to be actively engaged within religious communities themselves, their ability to understand their unique cultures, traditions, languages, and rules may be poor (Plante, 2009; Russell & Yarhouse, 2006). Without quality training and experience, religiously based bias and prejudice can occur easily among mental health professionals. Additionally, many of our standard clinical treatments and perspectives may be contraindicated with religious populations (e.g., assertiveness training, acceptance of sexual orientation and expression). For example, while our professions and codes of ethics typically support self-expression, freedom, and self-determination, many religious communities highlight vows of obedience, poverty, chastity, and restraint in many areas of life that are taken for granted in secular society. This is true when working with both clerics as well as devout laypersons. Reasonable and appropriate ways of proceeding and working with secular clients may not be reasonable and appropriate with clerics or the devout. In fact, they may be insulting and humiliating to the highly religious.

Clinical Case Illustrations

In order to enliven the presentation of ethical challenges when working with religious organizations and groups, it is important to highlight some typical examples with case illustrations. These are provided below for reflection and further elaboration. Some involve particular work with clerics themselves while others focus on issues among devout laypersons.

The Case of Homosexual Applicants to Ordained Ministry

A psychological screening evaluation that includes standard psychological testing instruments as well as a clinical interview is routinely used as part of the application process for ordained ministry in most religious organizations (Plante, 2010; Plante & Boccaccini, 1998). The purpose of these evaluations is to try and determine if applicants to ministry are psychologically "fit for duty" and generally free of indices of psychopathology. This includes evidence of a major mood or thought disorder, impulse control disorder, personality disorder, or substance abuse disorder. Additionally, a review of their medical, psychiatric, substance abuse, sexual, legal, educational, work, and family histories is conducted as well. Finally, having some understanding of the reasons why they feel called to religious life and ordained ministry is important to include in these evaluations. These psychological screening evaluations are unlike secular employment evaluations. For example, detailed questions about sexual orientation and behavior, psychological and psychiatric history, and other questions can be asked in ways that would be illegal if the person was applying for most secular employment opportunities. The evaluations are highly personal and the results are shared with the religious superior such as a vocations director, bishop, or seminary rector or president. Applicants are advised as to the nature of these evaluations as well as who will get to read the final evaluation report. They waive their rights to privacy and confidentiality in order to complete the evaluation and apply to ordained ministry.

According to Roman Catholic tradition and policy, homosexual men are not allowed to pursue ordination as a priest or deacon in the Church. Reinforced by a fairly recent 2005 Vatican Instruction (Congregation for Catholic Education, 2005), men with "deep seated homosexual" tendencies are considered "inherently disordered" and not allowed to become priests or deacons. Yet, quality available research suggests that the percentage of homosexual men in the Roman Catholic priesthood far exceeds expected percentages within the general population of men, with up to a third to almost a half of American priests being homosexual (Plante, 2007b; Plante, Aldridge, & Louie, 2005). Yet, since the Roman Catholic Church requires a vow of chastity and celibacy, sexual orientation seems moot if they are not allowed to be sexually active with anyone, male or female.

The ethical dilemma occurs since the ethics codes for all of the major mental health organizations emphatically state that we do not support or condone discrimination based on sexual orientation and that sexual orientation is not evidence of a psychiatric disorder or disturbance of any kind. Mental health professionals conducting these psychological screening evaluations are then put in a position of "outing" homosexuals so that the Church can then reject their candidacy (Congregation for Catholic Education, 2008). It is important to mention that this dilemma is not only found within the Roman Catholic tradition. It is also an important and similar issue for some, but not all, Episcopal dioceses in the United States, in several more conservative Protestant traditions, as well as in conservative and orthodox Jewish groups as well.

Perhaps a case illustration can help with bringing these issues and challenges to life.

Mr. X is a devoted Catholic interested in becoming a priest after several years of careful reflection, discernment, and spiritual direction. He has attended several vocational discernment retreats during the past few years and feels called to a life of parish ministry. However, he considers himself homosexual in orientation, but as an engaged and devoted lifelong Catholic he has not acted on his homosexual impulses and desires, never dating or sexually engaging with men. He considers himself a virgin and is proud that he has shown great restraint with sexual expression over the years. Mr. X reports that he went on a few dates in high school and in college, attending proms and other special events with females, before his sexual orientation was clearer to him. He admits to some masturbation experiences, but proudly reports that he has been able to control these sexual impulses and temptations over the past few years. He is well aware of the Roman Catholic Church's position on homosexual priests, but he feels that his feelings and impulses are under excellent control and that he has felt especially inspired to pursue religious life as a priest after Pope Francis's famous quote during an important interview about homosexual priests in the Vatican: "Who am I to judge?" Some of Mr. X's friends and his clerical spiritual director have wondered if switching to a different Church organization that is more welcoming of homosexual men as clerics, pastors, and spiritual leaders might be a good idea. For example, in his area, the Episcopal Church welcomes former Catholics who are homosexual men looking to become ordained clerics, including both priests and deacons. Mr. X rejects this suggestion outright, saying that "being Catholic is in my DNA," and that he just cannot imagine leaving the religious tradition that is such an integral part of who he is both inside and out. He says, "It's is like asking someone who is Mexican to not be Mexican anymore . . . it just doesn't make sense to change religious traditions."

Using the RRICC model described earlier in the chapter, it is important for psychological evaluators to respect the rights and dignity of the applicant and thus thoughtfully provide informed consent, highlighting the potential consequences of disclosing sexual orientation. Responsibility to both the applicant and to the Church organization is needed as well, so that they clearly understand the ethical obligations of the evaluator. Concern for all parties is needed, too, as is integrity to conduct these evaluations for a Church organization that the evaluator might respectfully disagree with when it comes to views and rules about sexual orientation among their clerics. The evaluator must make very clear what their role is within the evaluation and what will and will not be mentioned in a written report about sexual behavior and orientation. Some mental health professionals may choose to not conduct these evaluations due to their difficulty accepting church teachings about homosexuality and policies about homosexual clerics. Others, although respectfully disagreeing with church policy and traditions, may feel ethically comfortable with the evaluation requirements and processes as long as full and informed consent is obtained from all parties.

In reality, religious organizations do not really need a licensed mental health professional to determine the sexual orientation of their clerical applicants. They can ask these questions to applicants on their own. Rather, the mental health professional can use their professional competence to screen for psychiatric disturbance and both psychological and behavioral risk factors that should be thoughtfully considered by the religious organization prior to accepting the applicant for seminary training or ordination. This can be done regardless of what information they secure about the sexual orientation of the applicants.

Personal Reflection

As an active and engaged Catholic employed by a Catholic (and Jesuit) university as well as working very closely with local, national, and international Church authorities regarding clinical work with clerics and having many friends and colleagues who are priests, I find it challenging that the Church denies openly homosexual applicants admission to seminary. Since I know many highly effective clerics who are identified as homosexual (but remain private in their orientation), I personally find that religious orientation should not matter at all, but that sexual behavior should matter a great deal. In other words, chastity and celibacy is the behavioral goal that is desired by the Church and not sexual orientation for Catholic priests in my view. Yet, regardless of my personal views, it is critical for me to stay within my professional area of expertise as a psychologist and thoughtfully follow the American Psychological Association Code of Ethics of not allowing personal views or potential biases to interfere with the work that I am hired to do for the Church. The Church is not interested in my personal views on this matter, but rather employs me to screen and treat their clerics and clerical applicants in a professional manner as a psychologist. While I must act with integrity as a psychologist, I also must respect the rules and doctrine of the religious institution I work so closely with as well.

The Case of Evaluations and Treatment without Consent

Due to the nature of many religious organizations that use a vow of obedience for their clerics, it is common to have seminarians and ordained ministers present themselves for evaluation or treatment solely due to the insistence of their religious superior. To remain in the religious organization, even as a seminarian in training prior to ordination, they must follow the orders of their religious superior and present themselves for evaluation and treatment with or without their individual and personal consent. Typically, this occurs when seminarians or clerics have found themselves in some trouble with pornography (either adult or child pornography), alcohol and substances of abuse, sexual engagement with either consenting adults or illegally with minors, or when they have personality conflicts with important others in the church such as religious superiors. Even contradicting the established doctrines of the church or challenging the authority of a religious superior such as a formation director, seminary rector, or bishop can result in a referral for psychological intervention that could include an evaluation, treatment, or both. These services can and often are ordered for inpatient services as well.

Using the RRICC model, it is important to respect the policies and procedures, rules, regulations, and traditions of the religious organization, yet also respect the needs, desires, and feelings of the referred person. Again, informed consent is crucial so that the referred cleric knows the terms of engagement with the mental health professional. Limits of confidentiality and freedom to attend or not attend scheduled sessions need to be made clear to the client, for example. The mental health professional must be responsible to the religious organization, making clear what can and cannot be expected from vow of obedience-driven evaluations and treatment. As in court-ordered evaluations and treatment within forensic settings, one can "lead a horse to water but you cannot make them drink." Integrity requires that the mental health professional is honest about the terms of engagement in working with vow of obedience cases and discusses the limits of working together under these conditions (e.g., that case material from evaluation or treatment sessions will be reported back to the religious superior and that sessions will be scheduled regardless of willingness to participate in the evaluation or treatment process). Concern for the well-being and interests of the client is especially needed since they often are highly resistant to the evaluation and treatment process and often experience the mental health professional as a mere extension of the will and power of the religious superior.

Perhaps a few specific examples can help illustrate these ethical issues and potential conflicts.

Fr. K was accused of sexually violating several children 30 years ago. He adamantly denies any wrongdoing and claims that he never sexually violated anyone at any time. Since the accusations appeared credible to the religious superior as well as to the lay review board of prominent Catholics who serve as a consultative body to the Church, law enforcement was contacted and an investigation was conducted. The investigation was ruled inconclusive and no charges were filed in the case. However, due to the intense media attention clergy sexual abuse has received since 2002 in the United States (Boston Globe Investigative Staff, 2002), the Church in their efforts to be "better safe than sorry" ruled that Fr. K is now a "chartered priest," named after the famous Dallas Charter for the Protection of Children and Vulnerable Adults (United States Conference of Catholic Bishops, 2002a, 2002b) that provided agreed-upon policies and procedures for any Catholic cleric in the United States who has credible, even if unproven, accusations against them regarding sexual engagement with minors or dependent adults. These policies mean that Fr. K must now be retired from all public ministry, cannot present himself as a priest to the public, must maintain a life of "prayer and penance" (United States Conference of Catholic Bishops, 2002a, 2002b), and cannot leave his Church-run living facility without a fellow cleric to supervise him at all times. Fr. K cannot thus travel along or even conduct simple errands without someone to accompany him and he can no longer wear a clerical collar in public. Fr. K is devastated, depressed, and angry at his religious superior for not believing him when he says that he never engaged in sexual abuse of minors. While he could leave his religious community and essentially quit religious life to be free to live and work as he pleases (again, no criminal charges were filed), he feels that at his now advanced age he would not know how to manage his life as a defrocked priest without work skills that could be used outside of the religious or church community setting. He feels that he has no choice but to "swallow a very bitter pill."

Fr. A provides another similar case but without sexual abuse and potential legal risks as in the Fr. K case.

Fr. A lives at a retreat center managed by a religious order of men. Complaints have been made by fellow priests that Fr. A is a "hothead," getting frustrated and angry quickly and sometimes unexpectedly. Members of his religious community have provided Fr. A with corrective feedback about their concerns, which they feel he dismisses or minimizes. The religious superior of the religious community gets involved and, under the vow of obedience, orders Fr. A to submit to a psychological evaluation with a psychologist who works closely with the Church. Fr. A feels like this request is ridiculous and initially refuses to comply, claiming that he is not the problem in the community, but rather that a community dynamic has unfolded in a way that victimizes him as the problem. Yet, Fr. A's superior insists that the evaluation be conducted and uses the vow of obedience to reinforce his demand. Fr. A feels that he has no option but to participate and cooperate with the evaluation request, stating that he has to "grin and bear it."

In both cases, Fr. K and Fr. A were asked to receive professional psychological services against their will. The RRICC model is used in both cases to help these priests and their religious superiors to be respected and treated with concern under very challenging and conflictual circumstances. Additionally, the psychologist maintains integrity by being honest and forthright and managing the case with informed consent and care in a responsible manner. These clerics understand that their vow of obedience to their religious superior may mean that they will be asked to do things that they prefer not to do. This includes psychological evaluations and treatment. The ethical mental health professional often has to remind all parties of the terms of informed consent in these circumstances. Being clear about the limit of confidentiality and respecting the rules and procedures of the church need to be underscored and discussed.

Personal Reflection

Working with clerics under the vow of obedience can be challenging when our culture and the American Psychological Association Ethics Code respects and highlights autonomy and self-determination. There are times when I believe that the religious superior is wrong in his judgment and that those clerics under his charge are being harmed. Regardless of my personal views, I must work within the framework and rules of the Church, acknowledging the role and responsibilities of the religious superior, and yet also help the clerical clients to understand and appreciate their options to respond to the vow of obedience in a thoughtful manner. On occasion, I must disagree with the views of a religious superior, yet must know that my place is to act as a consulting psychologist, not letting personal views and perspectives impact my professional work.

The Case of Cultural Competence in Treatment

Religious organizations clearly have their own traditions, rules, languages, perspectives, and ways of proceeding, often based on centuries of history, wisdom, and reflective foundations. Mental health professionals, wishing to provide culturally competent and ethical services to these organizations and those who are closely associated with them, must be very familiar with these traditions and perspectives and get adequate ongoing consultation to ensure that they are doing so in an evidence-based and professional manner. Cultural competence associated with religious organizations also interfaces with ethnic cultural competence as well. For example, many Roman Catholic devotees (either laypersons or clerics) are from outside of the United State, with the majority being from the southern hemisphere. Latin America, the Philippines, Vietnam, and parts of Africa are frequent places where Catholics reside and where clerics and the most devout come from in contemporary times.

Religious perspectives as well as multicultural factors interface to create unique clinical and ethical challenges needing careful and thoughtful assessment and intervention. Again, perhaps a few examples can be informative.

Mrs. N was referred to a psychologist by her local parish priest due to her worries about being possessed by the devil. She had experienced a range of stressful, disturbing, and uncomfortable impulses as well as upsetting dreams that she concluded were the devil's work. Her priest wondered if Mrs. N could be psychotic and hoped that a referral to a mental health professional might be informative. Within her African community, her worries were reinforced by her peer group and several clerics. She recently presented herself to a priest who was trained as an exorcist by the Vatican in Rome. After a careful psychological evaluation and consultation, it was determined that Mrs. N was not psychotic or experiencing any kind of delusion or hallucination at all, but rather used the language of devil possession and influence to understand and deal with her upsetting impulses and dreams. Her language and approach were consistent with her African subgroup and were normal within that cultural context.

Using religious language as well as psychological understanding of impulse control management reduced her fears and improved her functioning. Ongoing consultation with her local parish priest also helped to bridge the gap between the religious community and the professional mental health community as well. Being mindful of cultural differences was especially helpful in this case to ensure that the patient was not diagnosed or treated for a psychotic illness when none existed. Respecting her language and traditions was important and in fact critical in order to gain the trust of both her and her cleric.

In another example, Mrs. D is a very engaged and devout Catholic who suffers from panic disorder and agoraphobia. She comes from a highly conservative Filipino background. She attends daily Mass and participates in a variety of devotional prayer practices and rituals. Since she suffers from panic disorder and agoraphobia, she often skips the crowded Sunday Mass, preferring to attend the smaller early-morning daily Mass during the workweek. She believes that she is committing a grave sin by failing to attend services on these holy days of obligation, often providing excuses such as sickness to her friends, family, and fellow parishioners. She feels especially guilty and in fact mortified that she has actually lied to her parish priest about her reasons for missing Sunday Mass. She is fearful that her deception is a terrible mortal sin and that she will be punished by God with eternal damnation after she dies. These beliefs and fears make her panic symptoms worse. She problematically copes with these feelings by abusing her prescription of Xanax and drinking too much alcohol on occasion, as well as having a short temper with her husband, resulting in further guilt, shame, and fears. She frequently asks her psychologist if she is a sinner and is doomed to hell for her many weaknesses.

Using the RRICC model, her religious views and perspective, although causing her great distress, are respected and appreciated. Consulting regularly with her parish priest assists the psychotherapy process and helps her to feel that her faith and traditions are taken seriously. With integrity the psychologist cannot weigh in on what is or is not a sin or the will of God, being clear that he must stay within the limits of his professional license to practice as a mental health and not clerical professional. Ongoing consultation with clerical and peer experts assists with providing a competent service and supports efforts to express concern for her welfare.

The Case of Conflict with Values – Helping the Devout with Managing their Religiously Inspired Beliefs and Practices

Strongly held religious beliefs and practices can sometimes contradict best clinical practices and evidence-based treatment that tend to be supported by the secular mental health community. Often religious traditions, groups, and individuals may hold near and dear certain values, virtues, and perspectives that very much contradict those of mental health professionals. While mental health professionals must respect the beliefs, practices, virtues, and values of people from a wide range of religious traditions and persuasions, they also must follow their own ethical principles and codes of ethics and maintain competence and integrity in doing so. In the end, mental health professionals must provide evidence-based and state-of-the-art professional practice, yet be culturally competent to work with those from a variety of religious beliefs, practices, and traditions. Several case examples involving ego-dystonic homosexuality resulting in conversion therapy as well as strongly held, religiously based views about sexual expression among consenting adults are excellent examples.

Mr. B works as a social worker for an agency providing case management of adults with significant physical and mental disabilities. He is a very conservative Roman Catholic, following the beliefs, practices, and traditions of Opus Dei, a highly conservative wing or branch of the Roman Catholic tradition. Mr. B is homosexual in orientation, which is highly disturbing and distressing to him. He believes that his sexual orientation is a great sin and he is very disturbed by his attractions to men. He periodically engages in masturbation using homosexual images and he has had homosexual encounters in the past, including anonymous meetings with men that he finds in public parks, bathrooms, and so forth. To cope with his homosexual impulses and behaviors, he engages in extreme self-mortification behaviors. He uses devices, approved by his spiritual director and Opus Dei peers, for ongoing self-punishment of his sexual impulses and behaviors. Additionally, he desires conversion treatment to try and channel his sexual attractions and desires into heterosexual, rather than homosexual, outlets.

Using the RRICC model, his beliefs and conservative religious perspective are respected. However, it is the responsibility of the psychologist to inform him that conversion therapy is not approved or supported in any way by professional mental health organizations such as the American Psychological Association or the American Psychiatric Association. Integrity and competence are supported by offering Mr. B only evidence-based professional services that assist him in managing and coping with his homosexual behavior and impulses in ways that respect him but also highlight the professional stance that sexual orientation is not a psychiatric disturbance of any kind. Concern is expressed for his use of religiously inspired self-mortification activities and other ways that he physically and emotionally harms himself with his views and behavior. Ongoing consultation with his conservative spiritual director helps with working in a collaborative manner even when disagreements occur between the psychological and theological perspectives at times. Mutual respect and mutual concern for Mr. B's welfare are paramount.

Although conversion therapy is not endorsed by any of the professional mental health organizations, Mr. B decided to attend a week-long conversion therapy workshop and treatment program as an adjunct to his professional psychotherapy services. The psychologist respected his freedom to choose this type of treatment and helped him to understand the pros and cons of engaging in this intensive yet not evidence-based experience.

In another example, Ms. L is a very devout 65-year-old retired secretary from a Catholic university. Her husband died suddenly from a heart condition when she was in her late twenties and she never remarried and never had children. She has recently started dating a fellow Catholic man who is interested in having sexual intimacy with her. Since they are not married and do not plan to marry due to financial and tax issues, she feels that it would be sinful for her to engage in any kind of sexual activities outside of marriage. She consults with her highly conservative Catholic priest at her local parish who instructs her to break up with the man immediately and that all sexual activity outside of marriage is a "grave sin." This advice upsets and unsettles her, especially given her age, and she consults a Catholic psychologist to try and get another point of view about her challenging dilemma.

Using the RRICC model, Ms. L's beliefs and religious viewpoints are respected, as are the views of her parish priest. However, the psychologist has some responsibility to help Ms. L develop a plan that helps her cope with her feelings as well as come to a decision about her relationship in a way that makes good sense to her. The psychologist encourages her to secure a second opinion from another priest, who may offer a different and more nuanced point of view. The psychologist maintains integrity by stating that sexual mores may differ based on the times and age differences as well. For example, expectations of sexual behavior may differ for the elderly than for young adults or teens. Concern for her welfare is expressed since she very much enjoys having a companion and a relationship and worries about being isolated and lonely if she is too rigid in her religious beliefs and practices. The psychologist discusses the research on intimacy and companionship, trying to help her integrate her religious perspectives with best research findings on relationship satisfaction and engagement, especially during the elderly years.

Personal Reflection

When working with clients within my religious tradition it is easy to fall into a potential trap when I am asked to comment on Church or theological matters. Patients will ask for my views on Church doctrine and rules and ask me to weigh in on comments made by the Pope, a local bishop, or what their parish priest has said. The American Psychological Association Code of Ethics makes clear that psychologists must stay within their area of expertise. A license to practice psychology is a license to practice state-of-the-art psychological assessment and interventions, not to offer theological advice or consultations. So, although I am tempted to weigh in on questions about Church matters, I must bite my tongue, behave as a secular psychologist with a license and code of ethics to maintain, and refer theological and other Church questions to appropriate authorities and experts in these fields.

Ethical Lessons Learned from Working with Religious Organizations and the Devout

These case examples provide some flavor of the kinds of clinical issues and ethical challenges encountered when mental health professionals work closely with religious organizations, groups, and the highly devout, in terms of both clerics and laypersons. The examples have been limited to mostly Roman Catholic individuals based on the experiences and skills of the chapter author. In reviewing overarching ethical principles while working in this important area of professional service, it is important to keep the RRICC model, as well as the full code of ethics of the relevant professional mental health discipline, in clear view.

The need to respect religious traditions, cultures, languages, and perspectives is obvious and is expected and demanded by our professional codes of ethics. Yet it is also challenging for many mental health professionals who are much more comfortable living and working in secular environments. Religious engagement and devotional behavior and thinking can be off-putting to many secular mental health professionals who typically have little or no training and interest in the world of the religiously devout and engaged (Delaney et. al., 2007; Plante, 2009; Russell &

Yarhouse, 2006). When mental health professionals do engage in these wisdom traditions they tend to strip them of their religiousness (e.g., Kabat-Zinn, 2003), preferring to use a secular version of their techniques (e.g., yoga as a stress-reducing exercise class, mindfulness meditation as a way to cope with anxiety). Personal bias and ultimately disrespect is too easy to come by when it comes to the relationship between the mental health community and religious traditions (Ellis, 1971). Yet, we as ethical mental health professionals are expected to respect diversity, including religious diversity (e.g., American Psychological Association, 2002).

Mental health professionals also have a responsibility to provide professional, competent, state-of-the-art, and evidence-based services that are culturally competent, including religiously based cultural competence (Falender, Shafranske, & Falicov, 2014; Frederick & Leong, 2013; Plante, 2007a, 2009). They need not be an expert on all of the religious traditions in the world, but they do need adequate training, supervision, and consultation to provide adequate and well-informed, culturally competent, professional services (Pargament, 2007, 2013; Plante, 2009; Vieten, Scammell, Pilato, Ammondson, Pargament, & Lukoff, 2013). Clearly, their respect for and training in multiculturalism that includes issues related to gender, gender identity, sexual orientation, race, ethnicity, and so forth must also include religion as well. Lack of interest in or experience with religion are simply not reasonable and appropriate excuses, just as lack of interest in or experience with matters related to gender, race, and ethnicity are not excuses as well.

Mental health professionals must work to maintain integrity, being thoughtful about their professional activities with people from different religious traditions. They must know their limits of practice, avoid potentially exploitative dual relationships, and find ways to be honest with themselves and others at all times. Ongoing consultation with appropriate experts is one of many ways to ensure that integrity, as well as the other ethical principles discussed, are more closely followed while working with religious organizations and religiously minded people.

Our increasingly connected and multicultural world provides challenges to all mental health professionals to maintain the highest standards of professional practice informed by the most up-to-date evidence-based approaches available for use in our practices. Our increasingly multicultural world is also one that includes religious diversity that can have a deep influence on those who we are privileged to work with in our professional roles. This chapter has tried to stimulate thoughtful reflection on some of the ethical challenges in working with the religiously devout, especially within the Roman Catholic tradition. Much more research and reflection is still needed, of course. While religious traditions and organizations have been with us for centuries and even millennia, our thoughtful integration of these traditions within our professional mental health services is surprisingly in its infancy. There is still much to learn.

References

American Association for Marriage and Family (2015). Code of Ethics, 1–10. Retrieved from www.aamft.org/iMIS15/AAMFT/Content/Legal_Ethics/code_of_ethics.aspx

American Psychological Association (2002). Ethical principles of psychologists and code of conduct. *American Psychologist, 57,* 1060–1073.

American Psychological Association (2003). Guidelines on multicultural education, training, research, practice, and organizational change for psychologists. *American Psychologist, 58,* 377–402.

American Psychiatric Association (2013). The principles of medical ethics with annotations especially applicable to psychiatry. Retrieved from www.psychiatry.org/practice/ethics

Boston Globe Investigative Staff (2002). *Betrayal: The crisis in the Catholic Church.* New York, NY: Little Brown.

British Psychological Society (2009). *Code of ethics and conduct.* London, UK: British Psychological Society. Retrieved from https://www.ed.ac.uk/files/atoms/files/bps_code_of_ethics_and_conduct.pdf

Canadian Psychological Association (2000). *Canadian code of ethics for psychologists* (3rd edn.). Toronto, Ottawa: Canadian Psychological Association. Retrieved from www.cpa.ca/aboutcpa/committees/ethics/codeofethics

Congregation for Catholic Education (2005). Concerning the criteria for the discernment of vocations with regard to persons with homosexual tendencies in view of their admission to the seminary and to holy orders. Retrieved from www.vatican.va/roman_curia/congregations/ccatheduc/documents/rc_con_ccatheduc_doc_20051104_istruzione_en.html

Congregation for Catholic Education (2008). Guidelines for the use of psychology in the admission and formation of candidates for the priesthood. Retrieved from www.vatican.va/roman_curia/congregations/ccatheduc/documents/rc_con_ccatheduc_doc_20080628_orientamenti_en.html

Delaney, H. D., Miller, W. R., & Bisonó, A. M. (2007). Religiosity and spirituality among psychologists: A survey of clinician members of the American Psychological Association. *Professional Psychology: Research and Practice, 38,* 538–546.

Ellis, A. (1971). *The case against religion: A psychotherapist's view.* New York, NY: Institute for Rational Living.

Falender, C. A., Shafranske, E. P., & Falicov, C. J. (2014). *Multiculturalism and diversity in clinical supervision: A competency-based approach.* Washington, DC: American Psychological Association.

Leong, F. T. L. (2013). *APA handbook of multicultural psychology.* Washington, DC: American Psychological Association.

Freud, S. (1961). *The future of an illusion* (J. Strachey, Ed. and Trans.). New York, NY: Norton.

Gallup, G., Jr. & Jones, T. (2000). *The next American spirituality: Finding God in the twenty-first century.* Colorado Springs, CO: Cook Communications.

Gallup, G., Jr. & Lindsay, D.M. (1999). *Surveying the religious landscape: Trends in U.S. beliefs.* Harrisburg, PA: Morehouse.

Hage, S. (2006). A closer look at the role of spirituality in psychology training programs. *Professional Psychology: Research and Practice, 37,* 303–310.

Kabat-Zinn, J. (1990). *Full catastrophe living.* New York, NY: Delacourte Press.

Kabat-Zinn, J. (2003). Mindfulness-based interventions in context: Past, present, and future. *Clinical Psychology: Research and Practice, 10,* 144–156.

Koocher, G. & Keith-Speigal, P. (2007). *Ethics in psychology,* (3rd edn.). New York, NY: Oxford University Press.

National Association of Social Workers (2008). Code of ethics. Retrieved from www
.socialworkers.org/About/Ethics/Code-of-Ethics/Code-of-Ethics-English

Pargament, K. I. (2007). *Spiritually integrated psychotherapy: Understanding and addressing the sacred.* New York, NY: Guilford Press.

Pargament, K. I. (Ed.). (2013). *APA handbook of psychology, religion, and spirituality.* Washington, DC: American Psychological Association.

Plante, T. G. (2004). *Do the right thing: Living ethically in an unethical world.* Oakland, CA: New Harbinger.

Plante, T. G. (2007a). Integrating spirituality and psychotherapy: Ethical issues and principles to consider. *Journal of Clinical Psychology, 63,* 891–902.

Plante, T. G. (2007b). Homosexual applicants to the priesthood: How many and are they psychologically healthy? *Pastoral Psychology, 55,* 495–498.

Plante, T. G. (2009). *Spiritual practices in psychotherapy: Thirteen tools for enhancing psychological health.* Washington, DC: American Psychological Association.

Plante, T. G. (2010). Assessment of men and women entering religious life. In S. Walfish (Ed.). *Earning a living outside of managed mental health care: Fifty ways to expand your practice* (pp. 127–129). Washington, DC: American Psychological Association.

Plante, T. G. (Ed.). (2012). *Religion, spirituality, and positive psychology: Understanding the psychological fruits of faith.* Santa Barbara, CA: Praeger/ABC-CLIO.

Plante, T. G. (2013). Consultation with religious institutions. In K. Pargament (Ed.-in-Chief), J. Exline, J. Jones, A., Mahoney, & E. Shafranske (Assoc. Eds.). *APA handbooks in psychology: APA handbook of psychology, religion, and spirituality* (pp. 511–526). Washington, DC: American Psychological Association.

Plante, T. G., Aldridge, A., & Louie, C. (2005). Are successful applicants to the priesthood psychologically healthy? *Pastoral Psychology, 54,* 81–89.

Plante, T. G. & Boccaccini, M. (1998). A proposed psychological assessment protocol for applicants to religious life in the Roman Catholic Church. *Pastoral Psychology, 46,* 363–372.

Pope, K. S. (2007). *Ethics in psychotherapy and counseling: A practical guide.* San Francisco, CA: Jossey-Bass.

Russell, S. R. & Yarhouse, M. A. (2006). Religion/spirituality within APA-accredited psychology predoctoral internships. *Professional Psychology: Research and Practice, 37,* 430–436.

United States Conference of Catholic Bishops (2002a). *Charter for the protection of children and young people.* Washington, DC: United States Conference of Catholic Bishops.

United States Conference of Catholic Bishops (2002b). *Essential norms for diocesan/eparchial policies dealing with allegations of sexual abuse of minors by priests or deacons.* Washington, DC: United States Conference of Catholic Bishops.

Vieten, C., Scammell, S., Pilato, R., Ammondson, I., Pargament, K. I., & Lukoff, D. (2013). Spiritual and religious competencies for psychologists. *Psychology of Religion and Spirituality, 5,* 129–144.

19 Ethical Issues Associated with Mental Health Interventions for Immigrants and Refugees

Rachel R. Singer and Milton A. Fuentes

In 2015, there were an estimated 45 million immigrants living in the United States, with 14 percent of the country's population being individuals who are foreign-born (Pew Research Center, 2015). Of the immigrant population, 11.4 million undocumented individuals reside in the United States (Baker & Rytina, 2013). Research suggests that between 2015 and 2065, immigrants will account for 88 percent of the population growth (Pew Research Center, 2015). Immigrants are defined as those individuals who are foreign-born and move to the United States (APA, 2012). Individuals who themselves migrate are identified as first-generation immigrants, whereas those whose parents migrated to the United States are defined as second-generation immigrants (APA, 2012). Refugees and asylum seekers represent individuals "who have been persecuted or fear they will be persecuted on account of race, religion, nationality, and/or membership in a particular social group or political opinion ... [they] are unable or unwilling to return home because they fear serious harm" (U.S. Citizenship and Immigration Services, 2015). Those individuals who qualify for refugee status may apply for asylum in the United States.

Individuals may immigrate for a variety of reasons, such as striving to gain access to new work or educational opportunities, reunifying with families, or seeking refuge or asylum from unsafe circumstances (APA, 2012). A variety of factors may impact immigrants' and refugees' experiences of migration and their subsequent acculturative experience in the United States. The present chapter will explore these factors through identifying potential ethical issues that may arise in treating immigrants and refugees in the United States. After providing an overview of the main theoretical lenses and contextual factors that affect care provision for immigrants, the present chapter will highlight common ethical issues that might impact this population through case studies.

Ethical Aspirations and Obligations

Professional clinicians have a mandate to provide ethical services to protect the health and well-being of the intended recipients of treatment. The American Psychological Association (APA) revised its Ethical Principles and Code of Conduct of Psychologists in 2010, and in their present form they represent aspirational goals and enforceable ethical standards (APA, 2010). General guiding principles include the aspirational goals of A: Beneficence and Nonmaleficence; B: Fidelity and Responsibility; C: Integrity; D: Justice; and E: Respect for People's Dignity. *Beneficence* and *nonmaleficence* represent obligations to protect the welfare and minimize harm to one's clients. Maintaining *fidelity* and *responsibility* entails fulfilling professional obligations and clinical relationships. Clinicians promote *integrity* through honesty and limiting unscrupulous behavior. Establishing *justice* includes facilitating access to appropriate and effective interventions, addressing bias, and maintaining boundaries of competence. *Respecting people's rights and dignity* entails identifying and valuing individual differences in identity as well as protecting vulnerable populations. These general principles, combined with specific ethical standards, are intended to guide clinicians' actions. Utilizing these standards in practice with immigrants and refugees involves eliminating barriers to treatment, recognizing and addressing complex aspects of identity, and utilizing culturally competent interventions (APA, 2012; Remy, 1995). Further, the APA Guidelines on Multicultural Education, Training, Research, Practice, and Organizational Change for Psychologists highlight the ethical importance of clinicians' self-awareness of their own identities as well as knowledge other cultures (APA, 2003a).

Lenses of Treatment

Given the complexity of the individual and environmental factors surrounding the process of immigration, providing ethical and effective mental health treatment for immigrant, refugee, and asylum-seeking populations necessitates using a comprehensive conceptual and systemic perspective, regardless of the therapist's underlying theoretical orientation. Bronfenbrenner's (1977) systemic perspective, Berry's (2005) model of acculturation, and Falicov's (2012) multidimensional ecosystemic comparative approach (MECA) provide deeper understanding of the contextual factors that impact treatment for immigrants and refugees. These lenses further promote APA Principles D and E, Justice and Respect for People's Rights and Dignity (APA, 2010), as well as Multicultural Guidelines 2, "recognizing the importance of multicultural sensitivity," and 5, "[applying] apply culturally appropriate skills" (APA, 2003a, p. 9).

Bronfenbrenner's Ecological Model

Bronfenbrenner's (1977) ecological model highlights the nested systems that impact one's experiences. The intersecting *micro, meso, exo*, and *macro* systems represent external forces that impact individual functioning. According to this theory, individuals exist within a complex web of intersecting aspects of identity and experiences that may shape their health outcomes and impact goals for therapy. The larger macrosystem entails larger forces, such as cultural context and xenophobia (APA, 2012). This ecosystemic lens is particularly salient when working with immigrant and refugee populations whose life experiences and contextual conditions can vastly impact their experiences of acculturation, health, and stressors (APA, 2012, p. 8). Utilizing a systemic perspective allows mental health professionals to build on immigrant clients' existing resources while effectively addressing external factors that may contribute to negative mental health outcomes.

Berry's Model of Acculturation

One critical systemic influence for all immigrants and refugees is the complex experience of acculturation. Berry (2005) defines acculturation as "the dual process of cultural and psychological change that takes place as a result of contact between two or more cultural groups and their individual members" (p. 698). Depending on immigrants' maintenance or rejection of the culture of their country of origin and host culture, they may fall into one of four categories: *assimilation, separation, integration*, or *marginalization*. Integrating aspects of the two cultures may yield less stress and more effective adaptation than separation or assimilation, which in turn result in better outcomes than marginalizing both cultures (Berry, 2005). Schwartz, Unger, Zamboanga, and Szapocznik (2010) noted in their expanded multidimensionality model that cultural practices, cultural values, and cultural identification all influence the acculturation process.

Falicov's MECA

Falicov's MECA provides context for understanding acculturation. Falicov (2012) describes the process of migration as being "in constant flux" (p. 297). The experience of migration may result in new opportunities or "gains," as well as key stressors or "losses" (Falicov, 2012, p. 301). Aspects of identity may include rituals or cultural ideals as well as the subsequent impact of migration on cultural identity. Falicov (2012) further suggests that family structure, composed of relational experiences, stressors, separations, and transitions, is a key component in understanding the potential experiences of each individual within a family.

Contextual Factors

The theories of Bronfenbrenner, Berry, and Falicov highlight the potential impact of systemic and interactional experiences as they shape individual immigrants and refugees. Factors that provide a context for treatment may include stressors, strengths, and aspects of an immigrant client's identity (Singer & Tummala-Narra, 2013). Immigrants' and refugees' experiences may also depend on their developmental stage, reason for immigration, experience of migration, and status as a first-, second-, or later-generation immigrant (Morales, Lara, Kington, Valdez, & Escarce, 2002; Suárez-Orozco & Suárez-Orozco, 2001; Zhou, 2001). It is important to recognize that while individuals may emigrate from the same country or culture, their unique experiences may be different. Potential systemic stressors, such as documentation status, history of trauma, conflict between value systems, and exposure to racism or microaggressions, may lead to additional problems for immigrant clients (APA, 2003b, 2012; Remy, 1995). Further challenges may include limited access to interpreters (Remy, 1995), differing manifestations of distress that are not recognized by clinicians (Nicolas et al., 2007; Tummala-Narra, 2011), lack of availability of appropriate or culturally competent services (Wu, Kviz, & Miller, 2009), and cultural stigma for help-seeking behavior (Hong & Domokos-Cheng Ham, 2001).

Conversely, both internal resilience and external resources, such as social support from the community (Singer & Tummala-Narra, 2013; Yeh, Arora, & Wu, 2006), may improve outcomes for immigrant populations. The APA's Taskforce on Immigration recently proposed that utilizing a strengths-based perspective that also identifies key factors of resilience is essential to providing comprehensive and ethical care for this unique and multifaceted population (APA, 2012).

The cases that follow will focus on key ethical issues that may arise within immigrant and refugee populations using an ecological framework. Each case will include a summary of the client, a history of clinical treatment, guiding discussion questions, and an analysis of underlying factors that may impact ethical considerations. It is important to note that these cases represent an overview of potential ethical concerns and related clinical issues that may arise in working with immigrant and refugee clients, but may not address all the ethical issues that impact all clients.

The Case of Diego

Diego Madrigal is a 13-year-old boy from the Dominican Republic who was referred for individual therapy by his teacher due to concerns regarding auditory hallucinations. Diego reports that "el diablo" (the devil) talks to him during class and tells him that he is sinful and bad. He describes these experiences as very scary and distracting. Diego's teacher reports that he frequently appears lost in thought during class and is unable to participate in most social interactions and academic assignments.

Diego is bilingual, though he speaks primarily Spanish at home with his parents and three siblings. Diego's parents do not speak any English. Diego's therapist, Michael, has taken two years of a Spanish for mental health workers course and conducts the therapy in Spanish. While the therapy is conducted in Spanish, all school meetings are conducted in English without an interpreter present, and the psychiatrist does not speak any Spanish. At present, no interpreter is available in the school, though one of the secretaries in the main office will translate some of the letters that get sent to Diego's parents into Spanish. A recent letter was sent to the family's home, but it was returned due to a change of address. Ms. Madrigal, Diego's mother, was unable to provide a new address for the family, though she informed the school secretary that they are staying with a friend from church. Michael observes that the school officials do not include Ms. Madrigal in conversations about treatment during meetings, but rather will discuss interventions and progress with each other. The school secretary will occasionally participate in school meetings to interpret, when scheduling allows. Michael does not intervene during the school meetings, despite Ms. Madrigal's expressions of frustration during parent-only clinical sessions, because he is worried this will compromise his relationship with the school and thereby limit his ability to be of service to other students.

Michael has met with Ms. Madrigal for several parent consultation sessions. Ms. Madrigal reported that she has taken Diego to get exorcised numerous times at the family's church, but the problem of "hallucinations" persists. Ms. Madrigal reported that the family has received much emotional support from the members of their church throughout this process. Ms. Madrigal also states that she does not trust Diego's psychiatrist because he is adamantly encouraging her to give her son pills that she believes are poisonous. Michael finds his anxiety increasing as he feels uncertain how his ethical responsibilities intersect with his clinical obligations and multiple roles within the treatment. In meetings with the school and the family, Michael finds himself feeling torn between wanting to advocate for the family and wanting to present the school's concerns to Ms. Madrigal in a way that will encourage her to comply with treatment.

Guiding Questions

1. What steps should Michael take to ensure that Ms. Madrigal is able to give valid consent for treatment?
2. What are the conflicting goals for treatment between the school, the therapist, and the family? What are Michael's ethical obligations in order to address these divergent objectives?
3. Do Michael's concerns about negatively impacting his availability to other students in the future and the staff's good feelings about him carry any ethical weight?
4. How might language barriers contribute to challenges in competent and responsible treatment? What therapist strategies might be ethically acceptable?

Ethical Issues

Language Barriers and Consent

One of the biggest challenges for providing ethical treatment for immigrants, refugees, and asylees is ensuring that services are available in the appropriate language for the client or family (Remy, 1995). Often children may develop language skills in the host country before their parents, and parents' language barriers may impede effective communication with schools (Grolnick, Benjet, Kurowski, & Apostoleris, 1997). In the case of Diego, there are multiple ethical concerns regarding language. Diego's family will not be able to provide consent for academic decisions or for informed decisions about treatment if they are not provided comprehensive information with appropriate interpretation and translation. Per APA Standard 10.1, this entails providing comprehensive information regarding treatment and ample opportunities for individuals receiving treatment to receive answers to any questions they may have (APA, 2010).

It is the school's responsibility to ensure a professional interpreter is present for all school meetings and it is the patient's right to have a trained interpreter present for psychiatry appointments. If a Spanish-speaking psychiatrist were available, this might also increase the family's comfort in seeking psychiatric support to ensure appropriate treatment, diagnosis, and understanding of treatment recommendations. Additionally, while the therapist has taken two years of Spanish, it is unknown whether these training opportunities were sufficient to provide effective clinical treatment in Spanish. APA Ethical Standard 2.01 dictates that therapists are responsible for identifying the boundaries of their own competence and taking adequate steps to ensure that their clients are not harmed as a result of gaps in competence (APA, 2010). Michael should both recognize the limits of his own competence and potentially bolster his skills by seeking supervision and consultation with a colleague who is fluent in Spanish.

Power Dynamics

The barriers in language and the school's exclusion of Ms. Madrigal from conversations regarding treatment also highlight ethical concerns regarding power dynamics in treatment. Mental health providers, as well as other individuals in a multidisciplinary treatment team, may possess a fundamentally higher level of power than those whom they treat. Michael has multiple roles to balance in this scenario: advocating on behalf of the Madrigal family; maintaining a working relationship with the school; assessing his ethical and clinical responsibilities; and protecting his own professional responsibilities. Indeed, psychologists are often asked to navigate complex and conflicting roles, and therefore the therapist must be able to prioritize in terms of importance. Michael's primary responsibility is to the client and the family. While he may want to maintain a positive relationship with the school, this is secondary to the needs of Diego and his family.

In this case, an existing power imbalance between the family and the school may lead to discomfort, errors in communication, or more grave consequences for the clients themselves (Goodman et al., 2004; Singer & Tummala-Narra, 2013). These dynamics fall within the aspirational ethical goal of nonmaleficence, or doing no harm to clients (APA, 2010), and within the enforceable Standard 3.04 (Avoiding Harm). Indeed, the identified "pathology" may ultimately be a normative response to an unhealthy or problematic situation. Perhaps Diego's family has chosen not to support him in taking the medication because of past violations of trust in medical relationships. Addressing this inequity involves committing to making changes within the therapeutic alliance and with an eye for social justice interventions.

Michael can further address this conflict by focusing on principles of empowerment and facilitating opportunities for the family to express their own needs and preferences (Goodman et al., 2004). In the case of Diego, this might involve his therapist providing opportunities for the family to advocate for their preferred modality of treatment interventions, drawing attention to ineffective or unethical practices within the school, treating Diego's parents as equal partners in the decision-making process, and building in opportunities for future empowerment. This experience may be a challenging one for Michael to maintain and may lead to potential strain within the school. However, the family's well-being is paramount and trumps concerns about professional relationships with other providers. Indeed, putting the family's needs first may fundamentally alter the outcomes of treatment. It is also essential to recognize that the family may have encountered these types of experiences before and may have limited trust for the school, psychiatrist, or social worker. As noted by Boyd-Franklin (2003), black families may engage in "healthy cultural suspicion," as some of their experiences with the majority culture or formal institutions (e.g., schools, mental or medical settings, or Child Protective Services) are problematic, leading these families to be distrustful of and not as amenable to the provision of services. Essentially, building these relationships may take time and effort, but may ultimately provide a greater chance of positive treatment outcomes.

Integrating Treatment

Clinicians need to work to "eliminate bias" and cultivate "awareness and respect" of individual differences, as dictated by the APA ethical principle of Respect for People's Rights and Dignity (APA, 2010). Further, Standards 3.01 and 3.04 call for elimination of discrimination based on identity and avoidance of causing harm to clients, respectively. These combined goals may entail fostering an understanding of the role that cultural factors play in shaping the manifestation of symptoms, as well as a subsequent integration of treatment modalities. As the APA's Multicultural Guideline 1 suggests, awareness of one's own attitudes toward others' identities is essential for limiting harm toward clients (APA, 2003a).

Diego's concerns regarding his reported visions of "el diablo" might be classified as psychosis using a Westernized model of diagnosis, but might be identified as more culturally normative for Diego and his family. Culture-bound syndromes represent manifestations of symptoms that are linked to specific underlying cultures (Balhara, 2011). Michael has an ethical obligation to further explore the potential underlying etiology of Diego's symptoms to determine whether they are developmentally and culturally normative or an indication of an underlying mental disorder, and to use his assessment to assist the school in responding appropriately to Diego's needs. Providing ethical treatment involves using appropriate interventions based on this analysis as well as an accurate and dynamic assessment of culturally relevant factors and interventions (Hays, 2008). The present approach of using a solely Westernized approach in the case of Diego may limit access to readily available community supports and the opportunity to integrate care.

The APA's report on Psychological Treatment of Ethnic Minority Populations suggests that "traditional" or Westernized systems of mental health care essentially fail when they ignore the subjective worldviews of the populations they are designed to treat (APA, 2003b). This recommendation is further bolstered by the APA's Multicultural Guidelines that call for cultural sensitivity, clinician self-awareness, and a thorough understanding of the unique needs of diverse populations (APA, 2003a). Rather than selecting one approach over the other, a more holistic, comprehensive treatment model might incorporate elements of the family's religious and cultural interventions with therapy and psychiatric support (APA, 2003b). In practice, this might mean that Michael should both utilize conventional therapy and also incorporate the family's preference for interventions at their church.

Family Transience

While it was not explicitly stated by Diego or by his family, it appears as though they are currently without a home. Homelessness for immigrant clients may enhance feelings of powerlessness and limit feelings of consistency, stability, and predictability, particularly for families with children. This may also lead to gaps in treatment, which may inhibit ethically and clinically coherent interventions. Given that Ms. Madrigal did not openly address this issue, it would also be critical to provide an opportunity for the family to indicate whether they would like to address it in treatment or not. From an ethical standpoint, this experience may also be a critical part of maintaining confidentiality related to issues that are nonessential for the school or other providers to know. Standard 4.05 provides more in-depth guidelines on the circumstances in which clinicians may disclose confidential information. Lastly, Boyd-Franklin's (2008) multisystems model suggests helpful strategies for competently serving the treatment needs of low-income families.

The Case of Yasamin

A school psychologist referred Yasamin Al-Khatib, a 16-year-old Syrian refugee, for therapy due to concerns regarding truancy and possible depression. Yasamin's family fled Syria six months ago due to sectarian violence in the region. Yasamin's teachers reported that they have observed classmates teasing Yasamin about wearing a headscarf and calling her a terrorist. Yasamin presents as very quiet and polite in therapy sessions. Ms. Al-Khatib, Yasamin's mother, has only attended the first therapy session. In the initial intake, the interpreter arrives and reports that he knows Ms. Al-Khatib because the family worships at his same mosque. Ms. Al-Khatib indicates that she is worried the interpreter will discuss her family's information with others in the community and requests that her daughter interpret for her instead. Yasamin's therapist, Sylvia, assures the family that confidentiality will be maintained with the present interpreter and that the family should not have any concerns regarding this issue. Ms. Al-Khatib does not attend subsequent sessions, which Ms. Al-Khatib attributes to the fact that she works three different jobs to support Yasamin and her five younger siblings. When she is unable to reach Ms. Al-Khatib by phone, Sylvia focuses subsequent sessions on Yasamin's experiences. Yasamin reports that while she enjoys school, her family relies on her to take charge of her younger siblings while her mother and father are at work.

During treatment, Yasamin further reports a significant history of trauma related to spending four months in refugee camps in Lebanon. Yasamin tells her therapist, Sylvia, that she witnessed violence and discrimination against her mother and other family members during their migration experience and in the refugee camp. Once in the camps, Yasamin reported that she had to restrict her own eating to ensure that her siblings had enough food to eat. She reports that she feels sad when she thinks about her migration experience. Yasamin discloses in therapy that these memories intrude on her daily functioning.

Sylvia is an experienced psychologist with 24 years of practice. During treatment, she provides an opportunity for Yasamin to reflect on her negative experiences with peers, including discussing actions that Yasamin can implement in school. Sylvia attends a monthly consultation group with therapists who work with refugees and asylees. Sylvia tells her peer group that she has been having nightmares about Yasamin's stories of refugee camps and finds it difficult to focus in scheduled sessions after she meets with Yasamin. Sylvia describes herself as more distractible and irritable when she is home with her family. Additionally, Sylvia has limited experience in working with Syrian and Muslim clients as most of her previous work with immigrants has been with individuals from Central and South America. While Sylvia has worked with victims of trauma, Yasamin's experiences far exceed the stressors of Sylvia's previous clients.

Guiding Questions

1. How should Yasamin's therapist address the family's concerns related to the interpreter? What ethical alternatives does Sylvia have for ensuring adequate interpretation of sessions for the family?
2. How should Sylvia balance Yasamin's needs versus the needs of the family? What ethical responsibility (if any) does the therapist have to address family or systemic concerns in addition to Yasamin's needs?
3. What responsibility does Sylvia have to address Yasamin's experiences of discrimination within the school?
4. What potential ethical concerns might arise if Sylvia does not address her own response to Yasamin's trauma? What resources or strategies should Sylvia use to address these concerns?

Ethical Issues

Interpreters

Lack of access to interpreters is a potential barrier that can prohibit effective assessment and therapy (Remy, 1995; Searight & Searight, 2009; Wright, 2014). Even when interpreters are present, clinicians typically do not receive training to effectively utilize interpreters. At times, working with an interpreter can alter the dynamics of treatment, either serving as a seeming impediment to forming a therapeutic alliance or causing potential rifts in communication, and clients may express a preference for clinicians who themselves are bilingual (Villalobos et al., 2016). Further, per APA Standard 2.05, clinicians are responsible for taking reasonable steps to monitor delegation of work to others and to assess for multiple relationships, as well as ensuring interpreters do not have multiple roles with families, impaired objectivity, or limited competence (APA, 2010). In the case of Yasamin and her mother, finding another interpreter with whom the family does not have a relationship may reduce concerns regarding Ms. Al-Khatib's ability to disclose her concerns. If an on-site interpreter is not available, using an interpreter through a call-in service is likely to be more beneficial than having an on-site interpreter whose skills are hindered due to impaired objectivity. Specifically, The APA's Standard 4.01 highlights the obligation to maintain client confidentiality, and Standard 2.05 calls for ensuring adequate training and supervision of interpreters. Using the same interpreter throughout treatment can also facilitate a good working relationship and allow the interpreter to become familiar with the client's particular style of communication. Furthermore, given ethical concerns regarding the use of interpreters who may play multiple roles, family members are not acceptable interpreters because they may have their own lenses or experiences, and they themselves have need of a clinical intervention (Tribe & Morrisey, 2004; Wright, 2014). Hays (2008) and Wright (2014) also provide additional helpful strategies for integrating interpreters in treatment.

Client and Family Trauma

Refugees and asylum seekers may emigrate from their respective countries due to humanitarian concerns or persecution. The process of migration itself can add to a complex web of trauma for individuals who are detained in refugee camps. Numerous researchers have highlighted the potential impact of this trauma, including a greater predisposition for a variety of mental health outcomes (APA, 2012). Refugee children may be particularly vulnerable to these stressors, which can lead to elevated risk for post-traumatic stress disorder, anxiety, depression, dissociation, and psychosis (Keyes, 2000).

Treating individuals who have experienced trauma necessitates obtaining adequate training regarding appropriate interventions for this population. Therapists must recognize the boundaries of their competence and either obtain necessary additional training or make appropriate referrals where necessary (APA, 2010; Welfel, 2016). Sylvia's lack of experience with Syrian and Muslim clients and her limited experience with complex trauma pose serious ethical concerns for providing competent interventions. In order to adhere to Standard 2.03, Maintaining Professional Competence, Sylvia needs to obtain additional supervision, explore evidence-based treatment options for trauma, and seek culturally sensitive interventions for this population. Sylvia should further explore whether this client would be better suited by working with a clinician who may be able to provide more comprehensive care. Consideration of a referral to another clinician with more skill and experience with this population would be in order even if Sylvia were not experiencing her current level of stress.

Additionally, it is important to recognize that while Yasamin describes her own experiences of trauma, she also refers to trauma experienced by her other family members. While recognizing that Yasamin is the identified patient in the family, it is important to identify whether family factors impact Yasamin's health. Complex trauma often impacts multiple family members, and responses to these experiences may be contingent on individual and developmental factors. Reaching out to Yasamin's parents can create opportunities to discuss additional resources for the family and to further ascertain whether supports are needed to assist other family members. Further, it is essential establish the boundaries of treatment as highlighted by Standard 2.01 (APA, 2010). The therapist would need to either possess or obtain appropriate training to fully understand the distress and experiences of victims of violence, as well as expertise in family systemic interventions.

Sylvia's impulse to address Yasamin's teasing at school is a start toward protecting the well-being of the client and acting beneficently with the client, as well as attending to the immediate environmental causes of her stress. Further interventions might also include advocating on Yasamin's behalf in the school to encourage more proactive and preventive measures to decrease psychological distress. These efforts may entail sharing information regarding culturally sensitive approaches for interventions, providing psychoeducation about the psychological impact of discrimination, and providing recommendations for teacher- or student-based interventions to decrease hostility, with parental consent and client assent per APA Standards 3.10 and 10.01.

Secondary Trauma

Clinicians who work with high-stress populations such as refugees and survivors of trauma are highly vulnerable to secondary trauma. This condition, also known as compassion fatigue or burnout, leads to feelings of emotional, psychological, or spiritual distress (Wise, Hersh, & Gibson, 2012). Like Sylvia, clinicians may find themselves perseverating on a particular trauma or client, experiencing heightened distractibility and exhibiting emotional distress. Seeking consultation and support from colleagues can serve as an important step to assessing clinical strategies and enhancing self-awareness. Reflexivity about one's responses to clients is also an essential component for ethical care, particularly if care is compromised as a result of the clinician's response to treatment. Engaging in self-care is essential to providing ethical care for clients with trauma (Newell & MacNeil, 2010). If peer support is not sufficient, Sylvia might also seek her own mental health supports to supplement professional consultation.

Further, Sylvia's strategy of attending a peer consultation group might provide opportunities for her to process her own experiences, though it is also ethically essential to consult with colleagues who have worked with Syrian clients as well. Technological advances may assist with connecting to helpful supervisory or consultative resources across the country and world. Cultural responses to trauma may impact treatment and may further enable Sylvia to utilize the most culturally salient interventions for Yasamin and her family. It is critical for Sylvia to consider her ethical responsibilities to both Yasamin and her other clients. If providing effective treatment is undermined by Sylvia's own symptoms of secondary trauma, she may consider the benefits of providing a more effective referral. Providing impaired or subpar treatment may violate Sylvia's responsibility to avoid harm per Standard 3.04 (APA, 2010).

Family Resources

The case of Yasamin highlights many family and systemic dynamics. In working with families, Standard 10.02 mandates that the therapist is ethically responsible for clarifying who the client is at the outset of therapy (APA, 2010). Beyond these basic ethical roles, it is also essential to recognize the potential impact of family functioning on the well-being and experience of the individual client. Yasamin's therapist can play an active role in assessing present needs and serving as a conduit for additional resources and supports. Cultural expectations for children may differ, as in Yasamin's case, in which older children may become secondary supports for parents. Indeed, parentification of immigrant children may be more common than for those individuals who are native-born. This role may provide some positive experiences, such as feelings of self-efficacy among the parentified adolescent (Titzmann, 2012). Recognizing specific family roles related to culture and further integrating family and systemic influences in individual therapy are essential to providing ethical care of diverse clients, as emphasized in the Multicultural Guidelines (APA, 2003b).

The therapist can provide additional supports by helping the family identify alternative support systems that may be more effective as a resource for childcare, such as consulting with Yasamin's parents regarding community support. Doing so may serve as an acknowledgment of the boundaries of competence of the role of the clinician highlighted in Standard 2.01 (APA, 2010) and also mobilize necessary external supports. Establishing these supports may help ensure that there is adequate supervision of the younger siblings and that Yasamin is able to attend her school as well. Further, the family may experience additional systemic stressors, including financial constraints, as evidenced by Ms. Al-Khatib's multiple jobs, as well as interpersonal discord between Yasamin and her classmates. Discrimination due to cultural differences may compound existing acculturative stress (Berry & Sabatier, 2010). Providing space to address these concerns in the context of treatment can be helpful for normalizing frustrations and identifying effective and culturally sensitive interventions. Additionally, external resources, such as a case worker or social worker, may reduce overall stressors and provide instrumental support.

The Case of Noor

Noor Khoury is a 42-year-old woman from Iraq. Noor's primary care doctor referred her to therapy due to concerns regarding mood dysregulation and difficulty sleeping. She moved to the United States with her husband and two teenaged children two years ago. Noor and her family are currently seeking asylum due to religious persecution. Noor's husband was recently deported when authorities discovered that his visa had expired. Noor reports that she has very vivid dreams about her family's migration experience in which they had to hide in a hidden compartment in a friend's van to escape. Noor indicates that at times she is unable to concentrate at her job because she feels like she is reliving the migration experience. Furthermore, Noor's teenaged son and daughter told her that they are afraid to walk home after school because they have been receiving racial slurs and threats from gang members in their area. Noor tells her therapist that she feels pulled between the stresses of raising her children on her own, fears about her husband's safety, and worries about the future.

Since her husband's deportation, Noor reports that her daughter has started wearing more Westernized clothing that Noor characterizes as "indecent" and staying out past her curfew with friends. Noor is concerned that she does not know the parents of her children's friends and that her children are losing respect for her. Noor reports that she thinks that physical punishment may be the only way to teach her children about the importance of respecting her authority.

Noor's therapist, Vladimir ("Vlad"), is a psychology intern. Vlad's family emigrated from Russia to escape persecution. Vlad reports to his supervisor that he feels very connected to Noor's story, but that it also triggers memories about immigrating when he was seven years old. He requests help from his supervisor in disentangling his own feelings of loss and memories of immigration from his clinical interventions. Vlad also tells his supervisor that given Noor's level of emotional distress in the first session, he secured an abbreviated verbal consent to dedicate the session time to starting the clinical intervention. Further, Vlad indicated that he did not address any of Noor's concerns regarding her daughter or her husband's deportation, as he felt this was outside the purview of therapy. Vlad also reports to his supervisor that he finds himself feeling very angry with Noor's response toward her children, stating that he thinks that they will have better health outcomes if Noor just lets them be themselves rather than her restricting them.

Guiding Questions

1. What ethical responsibility does Vlad have to address his reactions to Noor in this session? Should Vlad's supervisor suggest transferring this case to a more qualified therapist?
2. Is there currently a duty to explore whether there is child abuse or neglect? How might Vlad and his supervisor balance this responsibility with potential cultural drives that may impact Noor's actions?
3. Has Vlad acted unethically by ignoring some of Noor's comments, or was he reasonable in avoiding these topics because of his concerns regarding his own competence?
4. How might deportation impact the family system? What role could Vlad play in advocating for the family?
5. What are the ethical concerns associated with securing abbreviated verbal consent?

Ethical Issues

Intersecting Identities in Therapy

Identifying one's own issues and concerns falls under Standard 2.06 of addressing personal problems and conflicts (APA, 2010). Therapists and clients may have intersecting aspects of identity, also known as "cultural borderlands" (Falicov, 2013, p. 24). Falicov (2013) suggests that supervisees and supervisors should regularly discuss these aspects of their own identities, as well as exploring potential intersections between their identities and those of their clients. Fuentes and Adames' (2011) Socio-Cultural Profile is a useful tool for assessing these intersecting identities and identifying the power, privilege, or oppression associated with these varying identities. In the present case, Vlad identifies numerous aspects of Noor's experience that trigger his own emotional response. This dynamic will likely impact Vlad's therapeutic interventions and therefore should be addressed and discussed in supervision. Indeed, his supervisor should further address the ethical concern that Vlad did not obtain adequate consent for treatment. Vlad's own response to Noor's story may have impaired his clinical judgment. Vlad's supervisor should assess whether his personal experiences pose an ethical concern per Standard 2.05. As previously noted, it is also critical to address potential effects of secondary trauma on therapists working with a multistress population (Newell & MacNeil, 2010).

Generational Differences in Acculturation

Vlad's responses to this family in part reflect his values regarding acculturation. Indeed, some clinician's may identify assimilation with positive functioning (Singer & Tummala-Narra, 2013), although there is conflicting research that links the duration of time in the United States with poorer health outcomes (APA, 2012). In order to address the APA's Multicultural Guidelines regarding addressing bias and utilizing culturally competent skills (APA, 2003), Vlad must recognize his own biases and understand the underlying family dynamics. Vlad's supervisor can play a pivotal role in providing a forum for reflexive discussions about Vlad's reactions and provide guidance about appropriate interventions based on level of acculturation and psychoeducation about the intergenerational experiences of migration and acculturation experiences. For example, Falicov (2012) suggests younger generations may experience more social pressure to assimilate or to give up cultural influences that diverge from those of their new host culture. Conflicting cultural expectations may lead to clients feeling "strung between cultures, strung between identities" and unless Vlad recognizes this client tension he may not be able to offer the competent care this client needs (Singer & Tummala-Narra, 2013, p. 294). As in the case of Noor's family, these differing pressures and rates of acculturation may cause strife within the family (APA, 2012). Noor may see this as a rejection not just of the culture, but also of herself.

Safety and Cultural Values

Vlad's decision to ignore Noor's responses to her daughter may prove problematic, as Vlad is also a mandated reporter. The therapist's ethical responsibility extends beyond the welfare of the identified client to also include other vulnerable populations, such as minors or elderly individuals. Mandated reporting laws may vary between states, but typically include a legal mandate to inform appropriate agencies within a 24-hour window of receiving the information (Welfel, 2016). While it is unclear whether Noor is using excessive physical punishment, it is essential for Vlad to assess this matter and further to provide Noor with an outlet for her own frustrations. It is also important for Vlad to curtail potential cultural bias by not making assumptions about Noor's actions without engaging in an accurate assessment. Vlad should also address potential limits to confidentiality as indicated by Standard 4.02 (APA, 2012). It is also important to recognize that individual state licensing boards may have different regulations regarding mandated reporting.

Impact of Deportation

While it was Noor's husband who was deported, the systemic impact of deportation can have profound ramifications on the entire family system. Vlad's decision to ignore this concern represents a problematic ethical concern. Deportation or the threat of deportation can increase feelings of instability among immigrant and refugee families (APA, 2012). Additionally, navigating the bureaucratic process of immigration can be stressful on its own (Singer & Tummala-Narra, 2013), and concerns about deportation can lead to a heightened sense of loss and trauma (Falicov, 2013). Depending on the role that Vlad chooses to take, he will face different ethical challenges. The APA's aspirational ethical goal of fidelity and responsibility (Principle B) indicates that psychologists must "clarify their professional roles and obligations" (APA, 2010). For example, if Vlad decides to engage in advocacy he will need to resolve any potential dual role dilemmas. Conversely, if he opts to secure an external advocate, he will need to clarify and resolve any related confidentially conflicts (Standard 4.01, APA 2010). Further, as the APA's ethical Principle D denotes, Vlad will need to address his own personal biases associated with the deportation and the family's acculturation to ensure the provision of a sound treatment plan that is in the best interests of the client and the family (APA, 2010).

To assist in identifying which role best promotes the client's well-being, Atkinson, Thompson, and Grant (1993) propose a three-dimensional model for establishing the role of the therapist when providing mental health support to minority clients. The specific interventions and roles of the therapists depend upon the locus of the problem (internal vs. external), the client's level of acculturation (low vs. high), and the specific goals of counseling (remediation vs. prevention). Further, Vlad may determine that outside supports are necessary to address specific needs related to immigration outside his realm of competence and link Noor with appropriate services.

Racism and Xenophobia

Exposure to racism, bias, and xenophobia may have profound ramifications for immigrants' and refugees' "sense of well-being and belonging" (APA, 2012, p. 65). Providing comprehensive and ethically responsible care includes an assessment of individual and systemic factors. This new stressor may compound existing feelings of loss related to the process of immigration or acculturation (Falicov,

2012). The pervasive and multifaceted impact of racism may include psychological, emotional, and physical health effects (Carter, 2007). Immigrants and refugees may be perceived as the "other" due to fear, xenophobia, or underlying bias (Falicov, 2012). For Noor and her children, these threats may also come with concerns regarding physical safety. Vlad should consider establishing a safety plan for the family, which may serve as a protective factor. Additionally, it is unclear whether Noor or her family has established any external social or community supports. The ethical responsibility to provide culturally competent care may also include facilitating connections with community supports. Specifically, connecting clients with interpersonal resources with whom they may have a shared identity or culture may serve as a protective factor to alleviate some of the negative and isolating effects of encountered bias (APA, 2012).

Ensuring Adequate Consent

Obtaining informed consent from clients is an ethical obligation, regardless of the particular presentation of a client or possible language barriers. Both Vlad and his supervisor have a responsibility to ensure that this process takes place. While this process may be an ongoing discussion (Welfel, 2016), Standard 10.01 outlines the requirement to obtain consent "as early as is feasible in the therapeutic relationship" (APA, 2010). In working with immigrant populations, it is also important to ensure that adequate translations of documents are available for clients who may speak a language other than English.

The Case of Francisco

Francisco Martínez, a 36-year-old first-generation immigrant from Mexico, was referred to individual therapy by his primary care doctor after he fell off a ladder at his construction job. Francisco informed his therapist, Ann, that he nearly died in the incident and vividly remembers every moment of his trip to the emergency room. Now Francisco experiences symptoms of panic whenever he has to cross a bridge, climb stairs, or look out of a window. He also describes vivid flashbacks on a daily basis and feelings of panic whenever he thinks about falling. Francisco reported that he occasionally experiences pains in his chest and difficulty breathing, but he is afraid to go to the hospital because he does not have insurance. Francisco has been unable to work because he has to drive over a bridge to get from his apartment to his various jobs.

Francisco cites a broken rung on his employer's ladder as the reason for his fall, but he does not want to press charges because he is undocumented and afraid that he will get deported. Ann places a call to an immigration office to obtain more information regarding the path to citizenship. Francisco tells his therapist that he feels like he is letting his wife down by not being able to work outside of the home and support the family. He also tells Ann that he will not be able to pay for services because he does not have any insurance. Due to concerns regarding Francisco's current symptomatology and his ability to obtain adequate care at another facility, Ann offers to see him on a pro bono basis. While he expresses gratitude, he also reports that he is ashamed he will not be able to pay for these services. Francisco's wife, Rosalita, has started working in a home-cleaning agency to cover the family's daily expenses and costs of food and clothes for their daughter.

Ann asks about Francisco's preferred language for treatment, as she has received training in using Spanish in mental health services. Francisco speaks English with Ann, but requests that his monolingual, Spanish-speaking wife be present as well. Rosalita tells Ann in Spanish that her husband has healed physically, but has not been the same emotionally since his accident. Rosalita reports that Francisco is a loving husband and a caring father, but that he has started withdrawing from the family after the incident.

Guiding Questions

1. How should the therapist address Francisco's documentation status? What are the ethical implications of contacting immigration services regarding undocumented clients?
2. What strategies can therapists utilize to address changing gender or family roles for immigrants? How is addressing these dynamics a clinical and ethical responsibility?
3. What role should clinicians play in mobilizing resources for immigrant clients who are uninsured?
4. What strategies should a therapist utilize to effectively implement and address barriers to accessing care for clients with limited resources?

Ethical Issues

Documentation Status

Fears about deportation may severely impact immigrants' abilities to seek restitution from unsafe work conditions, as there are few protections in place for individuals who are not naturalized citizens. Those undocumented individuals who do live in the United States may be plagued by fear or uncertainty. This experience may also include stressors related to unpredictability and feelings of marginality (Falicov, 2013). Living as an undocumented individual may also result in experiences of isolation or concerns of persecution. Ann's decision to contact immigration may represent an attempt to connect Francisco with resources, but may also lead to deportation and additional strain on the family (APA, 2012). Further, this action marks a violation of Standard 4.05 as Ann disclosed confidential information regarding her client without appropriate consent, contributing to potential harm toward her client (APA, 2010).

Addressing Gender Roles

For many families who immigrate to the United States, immersion in a new culture means changes to gender roles and family dynamics (Curran & Saguy, 2001).

Cultural phenomena of prescribed gender roles for Latino clients and divisions in labor between men and women may dictate that the father in a family is the primary provider. However, many immigrant families face the experience of loss of status with immigration and potential restrictions in opportunities. Additionally, Rosalita's new employment may provide financial relief, but may also elevate Francisco's feelings of shame about not being able to provide for his family. Clinicians have a duty to ensure continuity of care, whether it be through providing adequate referrals or offering reduced-fee services. While Ann's offer to provide pro bono services represents a positive ethical decision, there may also be clinical implications to address in therapy that result from this changing financial relationship. Addressing these changing dynamics is an integral part of ensuring that clinicians adequately integrate multiculturally competent strategies in practice and respect clients' cultural traditions, which may be very divergent from those of the therapist (Welfel, 2016).

Language and Family Responsibilities

Ann's offer to conduct therapy in Spanish and further impetus to seek training in utilizing Spanish in therapy represent positive ethical steps toward providing adequate care. This situation is complicated by the family's divergent preferences for the chosen language in session. While Ann may be able to provide treatment in Spanish, her intervention skills may be compromised by serving as both interpreter and clinician. In this instance, using an official interpreter may allow the therapist to focus more effectively on clinical interventions and limit dual roles as noted in Standard 2.05 (APA 2010). Utilizing a culturally competent approach for treatment may also allow the therapist to build upon familial and community resources as valuable external supports (Singer & Tummala-Narra, 2013). Instrumental resources are those that address basic needs – shelter, food, and financial resources – while interpersonal supports may include emotional support and relational connections. Rosalita provides both instrumental and interpersonal support through her financial contributions to the family and her presence in treatment. Ensuring that these multifaceted needs are met in tandem represents an ethical mandate to "safeguard [clients'] welfare" (APA, 2010).

Continuity of Care

Maintaining necessary clinical interventions for clients extends to ensuring that continuous care is provided, despite potential financial barriers or limitations. For immigrants and refugees, stability of income and resources may prove to be problematic (APA, 2002). Clinicians are expected to discuss issues of payment as early as feasible in treatment per Standard 6.04, but ethical recommendations also encourage professionals to provide pro bono services to clients who cannot afford full-fee therapy (Welfel, 2016). This act further focuses on the welfare or beneficence of the client (APA, 2010). Specific states may also have options for linking uninsured clients to potential resources. Connecting clients to resources may represent a nontraditional role for therapy, but may leave clients with valuable tools to ensure adequate access to care (Goodman et al., 2004).

Conclusion

Immigrants, refugees, and asylum seekers may experience a unique constellation of stressors, acculturative processes, and adaptive coping mechanisms. Clinicians have ethical and clinical obligations to address the needs of these clients through utilizing evidence-based and culturally salient strategies. Ethical guidelines provide overarching, aspirational goals as well as specific standards for guiding clinicians' decisions (APA, 2010). Achieving these tenets entails interweaving knowledge of existing ethical standards and guidelines for effective clinical interventions and culturally competent strategies.

As illustrated in the various case studies, addressing these intersecting factors builds upon the ethical tenets of beneficence, justice, integrity, fidelity, responsibility, and respect for clients' rights and dignity (APA, 2010), as well as on ethical standards for competence, privacy and confidentiality, and therapy per Standards 2, 4, and 10, respectively. Refugees' and immigrants' complex identities may increase their risk for exploitation due to their potentially disempowered status (APA, 2012). Further, while involving interpreters and other community supports may bolster treatment and clinicians' cultural competence, they are also fraught with a host of potential ethical pitfalls, especially regarding confidentiality and consent, if not handled responsibly (Wright, 2014). Consultation, continuing education, and appropriate referrals may further serve as critical resources when clinicians are not equipped to ethically address the current needs of immigrant and refugee clients.

Tailoring clinical approaches for immigrants and refugees necessitates maintaining familiarity with current research in order to assess boundaries to competence per Standard 2.01 (APA, 2010). Interventions that blend culturally appropriate methods of healing and conventional forms of clinical interventions may be adaptable to the immigrant and refugee client's unique presentations and preferences (Atkinson, Thompson, & Grant, 1993). While individuals from shared cultural backgrounds may exhibit commonalities, it is also critical to recognize the unique experiences of each individual. Various individual, experiential, and systemic factors may shape the unique needs, strengths, and clinical goals of treatment (Berry, 2005; Bronfenbrenner, 1977; Falicov, 2012). Balancing the focus on stressors with internal and community resilience will allow for more comprehensive intervention and more responsible care (APA, 2012).

It is also critical for therapists to examine and explore their own roles, skills, and intervention strategies in treating immigrant clients. Therapist reflexivity and awareness of their own identities as clinicians will provide further information regarding factors that might impact ethical nuances and concerns (Singer & Tummala-Narra, 2013). Power dynamics are often an issue in clinical settings and may be of particular concern given immigrant and refugee populations' potentially restricted access to resources or opportunities to obtain documented status (APA, 2012). Creating opportunities to share power and transferring tools to clients themselves ensures the performance of ethical practices while imparting lasting change (Goodman et al., 2004).

To further promote ethically adherent practices and provide culturally competent care, mental health clinicians are encouraged to provide interventions that extend beyond traditional clinical models. Specifically, clinicians should build upon the particular needs and strengths of their clients and consider clients' levels of acculturation as they develop the goals of treatment (Atkinson, Thompson, & Grant, 1993). Clinical interventions need to be developed in concert with the clients' preferences and objectives. Additionally, beyond providing clients with tools for responding to challenging situations, clinicians can also monitor legislative efforts and advocate for systemic changes to oppressive or challenging policies, as well as create opportunities for interdisciplinary collaboration (APA, 2012). Doing so may expand upon existing services to promote justice, safeguard clients' welfare, and reduce vulnerabilities through fostering dignity (APA, 2010). Through comprehensive, strategic, culturally informed, and ethically grounded efforts, mental health professionals can successfully address the unique needs of immigrants and refugees.

References

American Psychological Association (2003a). Guidelines on multicultural education, training, research, practice, and organizational change for psychologists. *American Psychologist, 58*, 377–402.

American Psychological Association (2003b). *Psychological treatment of ethnic minority populations*. Washington, DC: Association of Black Psychologists. Retrieved from www.apa.org/pi/oema/resources/brochures/treatment-minority.pdf

American Psychological Association (2010). *Ethical principles of psychologists and code of conduct* (2002, Amended June 1, 2010). Retrieved from www.apa.org/ethics/code/index.aspx

American Psychological Association (2012). Crossroads: The psychology of immigration in the new century. Retrieved from www.apa.org/topics/immigration/report.aspx

Atkinson, D. R., Thompson, C. E., & Grant, S. K. (1993). A three-dimensional model for counseling racial/ethnic minorities. *The Counseling Psychologist, 21*, 257–277.

Baker, B. & Rytina, N. (2013). Emigration of the unauthorized immigration population residing in the United States: January 2012. Washington, DC: Office of Immigration Statistics, Policy Directorate, Department of Homeland Security. Retrieved from www.dhs.gov/publication/estimates-lawful-permanent-resident-population-2013

Balhara, Y. P. S. (2011). Culture-bound syndrome: Has it found its right niche? *Indian Journal of Psychological Medicine, 33*, 210–215.

Berry, J. W. (1980). Acculturation as varieties of adaptation. In A. M. Padilla (Ed.), *Acculturation: Theory, models, and some new findings* (pp. 9–25). Boulder, CO: Westview Press.

Berry, J. W. (2005). Acculturation: Living successfully in two cultures. *International Journal of Intercultural Relations, 29*, 697–712.

Berry, J. W. & Sabatier, C. (2010). Acculturation, discrimination and adaptation among second generation immigrant youth in Montreal and Paris. *International Journal of Intercultural Relations, 34*, 191–207.

Boyd-Franklin, N. (2003). *Black families in therapy: Understanding the African–American experience*. New York, NY: Guilford Press.

Bronfenbrenner, U. (1977). Toward an experimental ecology of human development. *American Psychologist, 32*, 513–531.

Carter, R. T. (2007). Racism and psychological and emotional injury: Recognizing and assessing race-based traumatic stress. *The Counseling Psychologist, 35*, 13–105.

Curran, S. R. & Saguy, A. C. (2001). Migration and cultural change: A role for gender and social networks? *Journal of International Women's Studies, 2*, 54–77.

Hong, G. K. & Domokos-Cheng Ham, M. (2001). *Psychotherapy and counseling with Asian American clients: A practical guide*. Thousand Oaks, CA: Sage.

Falicov, C. J. (2012). Immigrant family processes: A multidimensional framework (MECA). In F. Walsh (Ed.), *Normal family processes* (4th edn., pp. 297–323). New York, NY: Guilford Press.

Falicov, C. J. (2013). *Latino families in therapy* (2nd edn.). New York, NY: Guilford Press.

Fuentes, M. A. & Adams, H. Y. (2011). The social cultural profile. In M. Pope, J. Pangelinan, & A. Coker (Eds.), *Experiential activities for teaching multicultural counseling classes and infusing cultural diversity into core classes* (pp. 153–155). Alexandria, VA: American Counseling Association Press.

Goodman, L. A., Liang, B., Helms, J. E., Latta, R. E. Sparks, E., & Weintraub, S. (2004). Major contribution: Training counseling psychologists as social justice agents: Feminist and multicultural theories in action. *The Counseling Psychologist, 32*, 793–837.

Grolnick, W. S., Benjet, C., Kurowski, C. O., & Apostoleris, N. H. (1997). *Predictors of parent involvement in children's schooling. Journal of Educational Psychology, 89*, 538–548.

Hays, P. A. (2008). *Addressing cultural complexities in practice: Assessment, diagnosis, and therapy* (2nd edn.). Washington, DC: American Psychological Association.

Keyes, E. F. (2000). Mental health status in refugees: An integrative review of current research. *Issues in Mental Health Nursing, 21*, 397–410.

Morales, L. S., Lara, M., Kington, R., Valdez, R., & Escarce, J. (2002). Socioeconomic, cultural and behavioral factors affecting Hispanic health outcomes. *Journal of Healthcare for the Poor and Underserved, 13*, 477–503.

Newell, J. M. & MacNeil, G. A. (2010). Secondary traumatic stress, and compassion fatigue: A review of theoretical terms, risk factors, and preventative methods for clinicians and researchers. *Best Practices in Mental Health, 6*, 57–68.

Nicolas, G., DeSilva, A. M., Subrebost, K. L., et al. (2007). Expression and treatment of depression among Haitian immigrant women in the United States: Clinical observations. *American Journal of Psychotherapy, 61*, 83–98.

Pew Research Center (2015). Modern immigration wave brings 59 million to U.S., driving population growth and change through 2065. Retrieved from www.pewhispanic.org /2015/09/28/modern-immigration-wave-brings-59-million-to-u-s-driving-popula tion-growth-and-change-through-2065/#fn-22980-1

Remy, G. M. (1995). Ethnic minorities and mental health: Ethical concerns in counseling immigrants and culturally diverse clients. *Trotter Review, 9*, 13–16.

Schwartz, S. J., Unger, J. B., Zamboanga, B. L., & Szapocznik, J. (2010). Rethinking the concept of acculturation: Implications for theory and research. *American Psychologist, 65*, 237–251.

Searight, H. R. & Searight, B. K. (2009). Working with foreign language interpreters: Recommendations for psychological practice. *Professional Psychology: Research and Practice, 40*, 444–451.

Singer, R. R. & Tummala-Narra, P. (2013). White clinicians' perspectives on working with racial minority immigrant clients. *Professional Psychology: Research and Practice, 44*, 290–298.

Suárez-Orozco, C. & Suárez-Orozco, M. (2001). *Children of immigration*. Cambridge, MA: Harvard University Press.

Titzmann, P. F. (2012). Growing up too soon? Parentification among immigrant and native adolescents in Germany. *Journal of Youth and Adolescence, 41*, 880–893.

Tribe, R. & Morrisey, J. (2004). Good practice issues in working with interpreters in mental health. *Intervention, 2*, 129–142.

Tummala-Narra, P. (2011). A psychodynamic perspective on the negotiation of prejudice among immigrant women. *Women & Therapy, 34*, 429–446.

U.S. Citizenship and Immigration Services (2015). Refugees and asylum. Retrieved from www.uscis.gov/humanitarian/refugees-asylum

Villalobos, B. T., Bridges, A. J., Anastasia, E. A., Ojeda, C. A., Hernandez R. J., & Gomez, D. (2016). Effects of language concordance and interpreter use on therapeutic alliance in Spanish-speaking integrated behavioral health care patients. *Psychological Services, 13*, 49–59.

Welfel, E. R. (2016). *Ethics in counseling and psychotherapy: Standards, research, and emerging issues* (5th edn.). Belmont, CA: Brooks/Cole.

Wise, E. H., Hersh, M. A., & Gibson, C. M. (2012). Ethics, self-care and well-being for psychologists: Reenvisioning the stress-distress continuum. *Professional Psychology: Research and Practice, 43*, 487–494.

Wright, C. L. (2014). Ethical issues and potential solutions surrounding the use of spoken language interpreters in psychology. *Ethics & Behavior, 24*, 215–228.

Wu, M. C., Kviz, F. J., & Miller, A. M. 2009). Identifying individual and contextual barriers to seeking mental health services among Korean American immigrant women. *Issues in Mental Health Nursing, 30*, 78–85.

Yeh, C. J., Arora, A. K., & Wu, K. A. (2006). A new theoretical model of collectivist coping. In P. Wong & L. Wong (Eds.), *Handbook of multicultural perspectives on stress and coping* (pp. 55–72). New York, NY: Springer.

Zhou, M. (2001). Contemporary migration and the dynamics of race and ethnicity. In N. J. Smelser, W. W. Wilson, & F. Mitchell (Eds.), *America becoming: Racial trends and their consequences* (pp. 200–242). Washington, DC: National Academies Press.

20 Ethical Issues in Psychotherapy with Lesbian, Gay, Bisexual, and Transgender Clients

A Cognitive Developmental Model of Ethical Competence

Ruperto M. Perez and Jill S. Lee-Barber

Professional ethics is at the core of providing competent and affirmative therapy and it is the obligation of all psychologists to be keenly aware of the impacts of their own beliefs and attitudes in their work with clients (APA, 2010; Morrow, 2000). For psychologists working with lesbian, gay, bisexual, and transgender (LGBT) or sexual minority and gender diverse clients, this awareness is crucial. Barón (1991) identified professional ethics as "the cutting-edge challenge" for therapists working with sexual minority individuals. While significant gains have been made toward understanding the needs of and developing clinical competence in providing therapy to LGB clients (APA, 2012), therapist antigay bias continues to exist (Greene, 2007). Moreover, significant therapist bias against transgender individuals exists that stifles and hinders the provision of affirmative psychotherapy for transgender clients (APA, 2015; Bess & Stabb, 2009; Rachlin, 2001). With the existence of professional guidelines that address the competent and ethical provision of psychotherapy to LGBT persons (APA, 2012, 2015), it is incumbent upon all psychologists to be knowledgeable of these guidelines in order to provide skilled and affirmative psychotherapy.

Ethical dilemmas are likely to arise in psychotherapy, and knowledge of various models and approaches to addressing and resolving ethical dilemmas is essential to providing competent therapy. For psychologists working with LGBT clients, addressing and resolving ethical dilemmas are paramount to providing affirmative therapy. Therapists' knowledge of how to identify and resolve ethical dilemmas is integral to providing competent care for any client. A number of models and processes exist that may reflect an intuitive or critical-evaluative style of ethical reasoning (Kitchener, 1984; Welfel, 2013) and that outline ways in which therapists can effectively identify and navigate through questionable ethical situations as they arise in therapy (e.g., Hill, Glaser, & Harden, 1998; Kitchener, 2000; Knapp, Gottlieb, & Handelsman, 2015; Welfel, 2013). While a number of these models call on the therapist to be aware of values, beliefs, and attitudes that might affect their work with clients, few models define the process of the therapist's development of awareness of bias. That is, while various models of ethical decision-making call for the therapist's own initial self-awareness, psychologists may not be cognizant of the process of becoming aware of their own biases and prejudices to begin with. Therapist biases in the therapeutic process are many (Morrow, 2000). Without knowledge of the process of developing and acquiring self-awareness, successful implementation of ethical decision-making is precluded, adversely affecting both the psychotherapy process and the likelihood of a positive therapy outcome with clients.

The purpose of this chapter is to describe a cognitive developmental model of ethical competence that outlines a process of preawareness to awareness of ethical conflicts and dilemmas that arise when working with LGBT clients. While much of the literature in ethical decision-making has focused on various forms and iterations of ethical decision-making models and the implementation of these models through various case examples, what has been lacking to date is an overall conceptualization of how ethical competence is defined and developed from a cognitive developmental perspective. We believe that insight into a cognitive developmental model of ethical competence can shed light on the processes that may impact ethical decision-making when working with LGBT clients. Moreover, we propose that this model is foundational to ethical decision-making and may also be extended to all ethical situations in the practice of affirmative psychotherapy, regardless of sexual orientation or gender identity status. Our goal is to provide a developmental model of ethical competence that takes into account a process of gaining awareness of potential biases held in unawareness by therapists. In this way, this model aims to make conscious what may be unconscious for many therapists in their efforts to successfully identify and resolve ethical dilemmas.

In the first section of this chapter, we provide an introduction to our concept of ethical competence by defining it in the context of a cognitive developmental model that describes a process of gaining awareness of the underlying biases that pose an ethical dilemma and that affect the provision of affirmative psychotherapy to LGBT clients. We then proceed to describe the cognitive developmental model of ethical competence by outlining and describing the three key stages of (1) preawareness, (2) exploration and awareness, and (3) enactment and self-evaluation. The basic premise of the model will be discussed as well as the fundamental process of developing awareness and developing ethical competence. In addition, we attempt to illustrate each stage of the model with case examples (names and identifying information changed) that are intended to provide scenarios and ways in which ethical conflicts can arise based on biases held in unawareness by the therapist and how these scenarios may be successfully resolved through the developmental process of gaining ethical competence. The importance of developing ethical competence through supervision and training is also discussed. Finally, we conclude this chapter with a discussion and recommendations on how therapists can overcome and engage in undoing heterosexist and anti-LGBT bias.

Cognitive Developmental Model of Ethical Competence

Affirmative psychotherapy is, by its very nature, ethical psychotherapy and is rooted in the ethical principles of beneficence, fidelity, justice, and respect for the rights and uniqueness of individuals (APA, 2010). LGBT-affirmative therapy recognizes and validates the key developmental, contextual, and cultural factors that are critical to providing therapy. It is only with a full comprehension and understanding

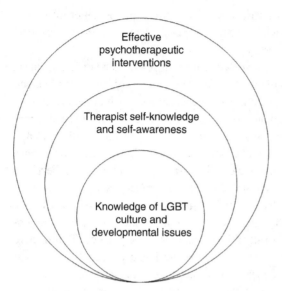

Figure 20.1 *Fundamental Elements of Affirmative Psychotherapy*

of these aspects that LGBT-affirmative therapy can be effectively provided (Bieschke, Perez, & DeBord, 2007). Providing affirmative psychotherapy to LGBT clients, therefore, rests in the three areas: (1) the integration of the therapist's knowledge and awareness of the unique and distinct cultural and developmental aspects of sexual minority and gender-diverse individuals; (2) the therapist's own self-knowledge and awareness; and (3) the translation of knowledge and awareness into effective therapeutic interventions (Figure 20.1) (Perez, 2007).

Therapist self-knowledge and awareness are critical in the provision of affirmative psychotherapy to LGBT clients. In the absence of therapist self-knowledge, the insidious effects of anti-LGBT sociocultural and personal biases and prejudices remain unchecked and prohibit the delivery of affirmative therapeutic services to LGBT clients (Greene, 2007; Perez, 2007). Moreover, therapist self-knowledge is fundamental to developing ethical competence. For the purposes of our discussion, we define ethical competence as the psychologist's ability to engage in effective self-reflection and awareness that leads to effective self-appraisal and eventual successful resolution of ethical conflicts. Ethical competence requires knowledge of various models of ethical decision-making in navigating through ethical dilemmas and resolving them successfully in accordance with existing ethics codes and professional codes of conduct. At its core is the therapist's process of developing self-awareness to become conscious of internal biases and prejudices that can affect judgment and the ability of the therapist to provide affirmative psychotherapy.

Cognitive development of ethical competence is based on Hill et al.'s (1998) feminist model of ethical decision-making, which suggests that internal dissonance (i.e., a felt sense that a dilemma exists) or uncertainty are the first signs of awareness that a problem exists and must be examined and addressed. A recent application of this feminist model of ethical decision-making was presented by Fischer and

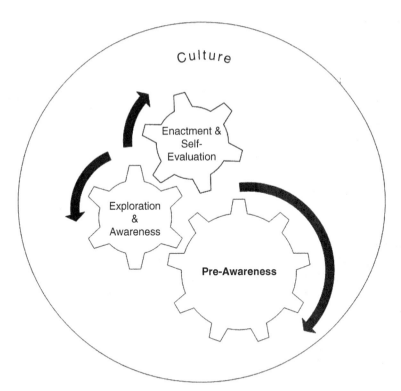

Figure 20.2 *Cognitive Developmental Model of Ethical Competence*

DeBord (2007) in an examination of how therapists can utilize Hill et al.'s model to reconcile the perceived conflicts of sexual and religious diversity. Our cognitive developmental model of ethical competence further elaborates on Hill et al.'s model by describing a model that is based on three main cognitive processes: (1) preawareness, (2) exploration and awareness, and (3) enactment and self-evaluation (Figure 20.2). It is developmental in nature as it assumes that inevitable enactment of an ethical decision-making process cannot effectively occur without the therapist's successful development of preawareness and awareness of their internal bias that is at the heart of an ethical dilemma. In describing this process of ethical competence, we also identify salient factors that may impact various stages of development.

Furthermore, we acknowledge the importance of recognizing that ethical competence and the developmental process also occurs within a cultural context. Culture, broadly defined, serves to inform us of how we can understand our client's experiences as well as our own. Culture also influences our values and behaviors as well as our beliefs and our biases. We believe that the influence of cultural factors on the cognitive developmental process of ethical competence plays a significant and vital role in developing an awareness of internalized hidden biases and how a therapist may then choose to act in addressing and resolving the ethical dilemma. It therefore becomes crucial that psychologists recognize the significant role of culture in the process of developing ethical competence, and we therefore believe that the development of ethical competence underlies all other practice competencies in the delivery of psychotherapy.

Stage 1: Preawareness

Case Example

C. J. is a gay male who emigrated from Malaysia to the U.S. to accept a soccer scholarship at a large public university. He was specifically interested in attending college in the U.S. to escape the pressures coming from his Muslim family to marry. C. J. enrolled at the university and, by the first spring semester, he was experiencing symptoms of depression and problematic alcohol use. C. J. was concerned that he might lose his soccer scholarship and have to return home to Malaysia if he did not do something immediately to improve his concentration and academic motivation. He was referred to the university counseling center by his athletic trainer and began therapy with Josie, a U.S.-born daughter of Nigerian immigrants who identified as heterosexual and Christian. Josie read the demographic information in C. J.'s file and reviewed his scores on intake assessment instruments; she met with C. J. for the first time and spent the majority of the session exploring his fears about what would happen if he did not get his concentration and motivation back. She explored C. J.'s schema about performance and began to provide some challenges to thought distortions in that area. She tasked C. J. to complete a thought log. As therapy progressed, Josie explored C. J.'s relationships with his parents and siblings and how these may have contributed to his distorted beliefs about what it means to come to the U.S. and succeed. She explored C. J.'s problematic substance use and his feelings about its contradiction with his Muslim values. Josie was unaware of the role of substances in socialization experiences within sexual minority communities.

From her perspective, both substance use and same-sex attraction equated to sins she did not want to challenge. Josie never asked C. J. anything specific about his sexual orientation, relationships, or struggles with family and culture around those issues. She focused on addressing the solution for the "presenting problem" of depression and, when asked by her supervisor if she considered C. J.'s sexual minority status in her conceptualization and intervention, she replied, "I didn't ask him anything about that. I felt if he wanted to discuss it, he would have." Josie demonstrated little awareness at first of her "color-blind" stance toward C. J.'s sexual minority status.

With the process of supervision, Josie was able to identify that she believed she knew why C. J. would not want to come out to her or anyone else. She stated that she knew that homosexuality had to be forbidden in his culture as it was in hers and did not want to make him ashamed of himself while he was seeking help. Josie's rationalization about not acknowledging or exploring C. J.'s sexual identity brought to light unconscious biases about LGBT individuals probably rooted in her Nigerian Christian culture. The discomfort that was underlying Josie's clinical decision not to acknowledge or explore sexual identity was manifested as a hesitancy to ask questions about relationships that would have seemed natural for her to ask with sexual majority group clients. By not acknowledging or exploring C. J.'s sexual minority status, Josie's lack of awareness inadvertently perpetuated heterosexism in the therapy relationship. The supervision relationship, in which there was a trusting connection and a stated goal of increasing cultural competency, allowed this therapist to move from the preawareness stage to exploration and awareness (see Figure 20.2). Josie's supervisor became increasingly aware of an ethical dilemma: she realized she had an ethical responsibility to ensure that the client, C. J., received competent care and that she had a duty to help the trainee develop clinical skills. While it was an uncomfortable issue to address, not doing so would have not only jeopardized the client's care, but also allowed a trainee to pass practicum without the benefit of the knowledge needed to provide competent care. Based on her assessment of Josie's work thus far, the supervisor knew she could not guarantee the quality of care that Josie was able to provide the client based on her trainee's newly discovered bias. The supervisor also realized that removing the client from this trainee's caseload would take a much-needed opportunity for development and professional skill building from the trainee.

The supervisor decided to directly challenge Josie about this issue, sharing her concerns that because Josie had just become aware of her biases with sexual minority clients and had not had adequate time yet to address them, the quality of care she provided to C. J. may be suboptimal. The supervisor was aware that the ethics code requires that psychologists and counselors provide services, teach, and conduct research with populations and in areas only within the boundaries of their competence, based on their education, training, supervised experience, consultation, study, or professional experience (Standard 2.01; APA, 2010). Further, where scientific or professional knowledge in the discipline of psychology establishes that an understanding of factors associated with age, gender, gender identity, race, ethnicity, culture, national origin, religion, sexual orientation, disability, language, or socioeconomic status is essential for effective implementation of their services or research, psychologists must have or obtain the training, experience, consultation, or supervision necessary to ensure the competence of their services or they must make appropriate referrals (Standard 2.01; APA, 2010). The supervisor decided that it was her ethical responsibility to address Josie's competence to provide care and to assist her, if possible, in gaining the training and supervision to expand her competence.

Josie was visibly stressed by being challenged about the quality of care she could provide. She initially felt defensive and argued with her supervisor that she felt perfectly comfortable and capable of working effectively with C. J. She seemed to be more invested in defending herself as a "good trainee" than in learning the cultural competency skills needed to provide affirmative care to C. J. Given that the stress Josie demonstrated was related to being challenged rather than owning her bias and beginning to invest in providing the most competent care possible, the supervisor made the difficult decision to transfer C. J.'s care to a therapist on staff who was more experienced with LGBT individuals. It is important to note that transferring the client does not end the supervisor's ethical responsibility for Josie's training. Her supervisor should work directly with Josie to identify the gaps in her knowledge, awareness, and skills with LGBT individuals and to provide not only didactic instruction in those areas, but also a context for more in-depth exploration of how her biases can be addressed and the quality of care she can provide clients can be improved (see Figure 20.1).

All therapists are subject to their own internal biases and assumptions that can blind the therapist to an ethical concern. While some therapists may be prone to believing in their consistent adherence to ethical principles and codes of conduct and in their full awareness of their internalized anti-LGBT biases, the reality is contrary to this. In reality, a number of ethical dilemmas may reside outside the bounds of conscious awareness and may not be recognized as conflicts or dilemmas, in which case the probability of unethical practice is likely (Welfel, 2013). Moreover, it may also be likely that many consciously well-intentioned and consciously ethical therapists may hold anti-LGBT biased beliefs of which they are unaware, similar in principle to well-meaning white persons who hold racist beliefs and perspectives of which they may be unaware but that manifest as aversive racism (Dovidio, 2001; Pearson, Dovidio, & Gaertner, 2009).

In much the same way, we propose that anti-LGBT bias that is not held in conscious awareness may result in erroneous understanding and application of ethical principles and codes of conduct. This ultimately can result in the delivery of psychological care that may be at the very least unhelpful and at the very worst harmful to the client, as Josie's case illustrates. It is important, therefore, that as therapists we must first be open to being aware of those biases that obstruct our clear understanding and self-awareness, which may signal an ethical dilemma that has the potential to result in unethical practice; in other words, gaining awareness of our "ethical blind spots." As noted by Bazerman and Tenbrunsel (2011), "Without an awareness of blind spots, traditional approaches to ethics won't be particularly useful in improving behavior" (p. 37). As others may do, therapists may also suppress their anti-LGBT biases, thereby creating false justification of therapeutic interventions (Crandall & Eshleman, 2003). This suppression of prejudice and anti-LGBT bias may also produce an intuitive, internal dissonance for the therapist. This intuitive sense of dissonance may be affectively experienced as a discomfort or a sense of uneasiness about a specific situation.

In this preawareness stage, existence of anti-LGBT bias is characterized by personal discomfort or a sense of uncertainty (see Figure 20.2). In this regard, the preawareness stage is similar to Hill et al.'s initial stage of recognition of a problem, where "the first indication that there is an ethical dilemma is the therapist's feeling of discomfort. It may be as simple as uncertainty concerning how to proceed in a given situation or may be complicated by other feelings" (p. 111). However, in our cognitive developmental model of ethical competence, we contend that this intuitive sense of dissonance, which may be affective, behavioral, or cognitive, exists at a level at which the therapist is not yet aware and that, in fact, an ethical problem has not yet been identified. That is, it is this intuitive discomfort that acts as the catalyst to bring the bias and potential ethical conflict to conscious awareness. Whereas Hill et al. suggest that recognition of an ethical problem exists followed by or along with the therapist's feeling of discomfort, we posit that the discomfort is actually the signal that an ethical problem may exist prior to recognition of that problem.

This stage is characterized by a feeling that something is not quite right or of dissonance. The experience of uneasiness can be behavioral (e.g., lateness in meeting with a particular client), affective (e.g., feeling annoyed with a client during a session), cognitive (e.g., ascribing to beliefs that may stereotype a client), and interactional. Signals of bias may be present; that is, finding oneself responding or feeling pulled to respond in a biased manner, or hoping that one's internal response will be undetected by the client or one's colleagues. Therefore, the first task of the ethical therapist in response to these signals is to pause to self-reflect on the dissonance and then to identify those elements of dissonance. These initial steps are necessary and foundational so that the therapist's central task of naming and owning the bias can occur. During this stage of preawareness, it may also become possible and likely that the intuitive, behavioral, affective, or other indicators that an anti-LGBT bias exists are shunned or dismissed. It is our belief that denial of the dissonance and bias prevents full awareness, which prevents further development of ethical competence and ethical practice. However, the preawareness state, once successfully navigated, promotes and generates the next stage of ethical competence: exploration and awareness.

Stage 2: Exploration and Awareness

Case Example

Sarah identifies as a married, Caucasian, Christian, cisgender (i.e., an individual whose experiences of their own gender agree with the sex they were assigned at birth) female. Her presenting counseling concerns are related to balancing the demands of parenthood, marital stress, and completing her law degree at the university. She describes having a history of previous therapy with a Christian counselor who helped her address her extensive sexual trauma history. Sarah reported that she does not want therapy to address her sexual trauma history as she feels that this work has been completed, but rather she would like assistance with intense symptoms of anxiety and panic that paralyze her at times. Sarah described that she has lost weight while not dieting, has never "had any libido," and that she has difficulty concentrating, which is causing her to wonder if she can finish law school. During the course of therapy, Sarah described that she longed for sexual intimacy with a partner and has never had this with anyone. She wondered aloud if she might be bisexual since all of her emotional intimacy is with women.

Tom, her therapist, a married, heterosexual, Christian, cisgender male, did not comment or explore this idea. He found himself wanting to "rescue" Sarah by creating a trusting relational experience with a male that could model what is possible. Sarah's anxiety and panic symptoms continued and she seemed to be stuck, even after Tom's best efforts to create a safe space for her to experience intimacy with a male, himself. Tom began to have a nagging feeling that Sarah just was not going to get better and he sought consultation from a trusted peer. Through the process of the peer consultation, Tom's bias about Sarah's sexual identity having been formed as a result of traumatic experience was challenged. Tom's peer questioned the source of his bias and how it was being manifested in his case conceptualization and treatment plan. Tom was able to realize that his heterosexist bias was influencing his work with Sarah as he had been assuming that restoring her to heterosexuality was the goal. Part of his assumption was Tom's idea that Sarah's sexual abuse had caused her to question her sexual orientation.

Additionally, Tom had not considered the idea that Sarah might be bisexual or lesbian and also married. In challenging these assumptions, his peer suggested that Tom should reconstruct his treatment goals in order that Sarah may benefit from further exploration of her sexuality in an open and affirming context. In order to reinforce his commitment to ongoing exploration and awareness, Tom engaged weekly peer consultation with an experienced mentor; it should be noted that the choice of a peer consultant, supervisor, or mentor is a critical one that requires investigation into that individual's training and expertise. It would be counterproductive, for example, to consult with a peer supervisor or mentor who actually shared similar biases or lack of professional education. In Tom's case, the specific purpose of his consultation with a mentor was to continue to check his biases so that he could ethically provide Sarah with an open and affirming context for treatment. Additionally, Tom improved his fundamental knowledge of LGB issues through familiarizing himself with the American Psychological Association Guidelines for Affirmative Psychotherapy with LGB Individuals (www.apa.org/pi/lgbt/resources/guidelines.aspx) and by attending a continuing education workshop offered by his state professional organization.

This stage – exploration and awareness – is characterized by active exploration of the bias and a conscious acknowledgment of the bias (see Figure 20.2). In this stage, the therapist identifies the bias through personal and active exploration and examination of their prejudice. Some important and key self-reflection questions to pose might be, "What is the source of my bias?", "How is my bias guiding my perceptions and potential actions?", and, "In what ways am I attempting to justify my bias?" Once made aware, it is the psychologist's ethical obligation to recognize the bias and ensure that it does not lead to unjust practices or disregard of the rights and dignity of the client (APA, 2010). Like many prejudices, a therapist's anti-LGBT bias may be regarded as prejudice that has been internalized through exposure and adoption of societal heterosexism. As such, anti-LGBT bias may be seen as a type of genuine prejudice that, according to Crandall and Eshleman's justification-suppression model of prejudice (2003), "...is an authentically negative reaction that is usually not directly accessible but that is primary and powerful. The genuine prejudice is an affective reaction that has motivational force" (pp. 416–417). This motivational force may serve to provide continued suppression of anti-LGBT bias and provide justification for its eventual expression in a manner that, either implicitly or explicitly, justifies the bias (e.g., a therapist who, based on religious beliefs, rejects providing services to an LGBT client).

The ethical therapist's task at this point is to hold and explore the dialectic, recognizing the bias and the temptation to deny it (i.e., suppress) and to also potentially justify the bias. At this point, it may be tempting for some psychologists to believe that they have thoroughly acknowledged the bias to themselves and can move forward with its resolution. However, because genuine prejudice and bias have motivational force for either their suppression or justified expression, it becomes crucial that psychologists aware of their prejudices or biases seek out peer consultation or supervision to assist them in openly discussing and processing their awareness of these. It is also critical for the trusted colleague or supervisor to resist their own potential joining with the potential justification of the bias, but to instead offer support to the process and to continue successful exploration and awareness into the bias.

Successful resolution of the dialectic is the realization that anti-LGBT bias exists and is socialized, as well as personal ownership of the bias. Effective and ethical movement toward resolving the dialectic involves the awareness of a higher good in a desire to "do no harm" and to provide therapy that is effective for the client (see Figure 20.1). Successful navigation of the ambivalence toward change in the awareness stage generates awareness and personal ownership of the bias. It is also important to note that there are many other obstacles to reaching awareness. For example, ethical therapists must ask themselves how their internalized prejudices against LGBT persons and how their experiences with privilege across multiple identity statuses affect their ethical awareness and oppression of others. In addition, consistent with the ethical principle of competence, ethical therapists must go beyond asking themselves about their biases to engaging in training and supervision so that these can be unlearned (Principle D and Principle E; APA, 2010). The case example of Tom's work with Sarah highlights how active exploration can lead to awareness and how holding the dialectic and seeking peer consultation can facilitate exploration and awareness.

Stage 3: Enactment and Self-Evaluation

Case Example

Chase, a trans man (i.e., an individual whose sex assigned at birth was female, but who identifies as male; APA, 2015), came to therapy at the university counseling center with concerns about his relationship with his family. Chase's parents have been contacting him regularly to try to "help" him with his "problem," and they have let him know directly that he is not a man and never will be and is "Christy" to them. Chase was feeling stressed, lonely, and depressed about the thought of losing his parents now that he has come out to them as transgender. Sue, a married, cisgender, lesbian therapist, wondered aloud with Chase about his identity and offered suggestions about the grief his parents must have felt. Chase seemed to become angry and withdrew in the therapy session. He did not show up for his session the following week. Sue became uncomfortably aware that she would not have empathized aloud with a client's parents under most other circumstances. She asked herself what made this session with Chase different and realized that she held unconscious bias toward transgender individuals. This was evidenced by her internal questioning of whether or not Chase's identity was a phase and her open empathy with his parents within the session. These thoughts and behaviors reminded Sue of ways that others responded to her own coming out years ago. Sue's countertransference with Chase was useful to her in deepening her empathic understanding of a sexual minority client who was different from herself. Importantly, Sue became aware of ethical challenges;

specifically, she was concerned about beneficence and nonmaleficence (Principle A; APA, 2010) and wanted to ensure that her own newly conscious bias did not inadvertently cause harm to her client (Standard 3.04 Avoiding Harm). Further, Sue was concerned about ensuring that she respected her client's rights and dignity and that she could gain enough knowledge to provide competent care to her client.

Sue reached out to Chase following the missed appointment and asked him if he would consider coming in for a session that week. Chase initially was noncommittal. Sue told Chase that she had thought a lot about their discussion in the last session and wanted to talk with him about how he experienced her. She told him she felt that she had disappointed him or hurt him in some way and that she wanted to talk about it if he was willing. Chase agreed to come in for his next scheduled session. When they met, Sue stated aloud that Chase had seemed angry the last time they met and then had not come back. She told Chase that in her experience anger is a sincere wish for something to be different and that she wondered about what should have been different for Chase, especially with regard to her comments. Sue told Chase that she wondered what his experience of her remarks was. He shared that he had felt angry and that she just "didn't get it." He said he realized she was too different from himself to understand. Sue was able to empathize with Chase and apologized to him. She asked Chase if he felt that it would be worthwhile to continue working together or if he would like a referral to a therapist with greater expertise in transgender care. Sue acknowledged that as a sexual minority she understood what it was like to have majority group members empathize with one's family and she had not intended to repeat this offense toward Chase. Chase told Sue that for the most part no one in authority had ever acknowledged hurting him or had ever apologized. He said he wanted to continue in therapy with Sue and the two agreed on direct communication about experiences of misunderstanding or harm. This case was successfully and ethically resolved as Sue engaged in self-evaluation, recognized her bias, and made a commitment to engage in seeking out peer consultation to process her counter-transference and continuing education about ethical practice with transgender individuals. Importantly, she acknowledged her error to her client and empowered the client to describe his experience with the mistake and his needs going forward. Welfel (2013) states that "virtuous professionals believe so strongly in the ethical values of their profession, that they hold themselves accountable when others do not." In this case, Sue became aware of her own ethical challenges and chose to hold herself accountable, though it is doubtful that any ethics board would have ever learned about her conflicts with beneficence, malfeasance, and competence in her treatment of a transgender client. Welfel (2013) further outlines a questioning process with which an ethical professional should engage when we confront our own mistakes: (1) "Have I really acknowledged that I violated professional standards?", (2) "What damage have I done? And how can I ameliorate that damage?", and (3) "What steps should I take to make sure I don't repeat this mistake?" (p. 330). Sue clearly recognized that she had violated professional standards and connected with Chase to both learn about the damage she had done and to take steps to make amends. She engaged in peer consultation and continuing education to ensure that she did not repeat her mistake.

The final stage of enactment and self-evaluation is defined as the commitment of the therapist to act affirmatively on the new awareness gained as well as engaging in a process of self-reflection and self-appraisal of the therapist's efficacy in successfully engaging in the overall process (see Figure 20.2). This newly gained insight allows the therapist to more clearly and accurately define the ethical dilemma based on an awareness and ownership of anti-LGBT bias and other prejudicial beliefs and attitudes. We strongly contend that it is impossible to act affirmatively upon a new awareness of bias that one has gained *and* to simultaneously deny to oneself the existence of the bias or to rationalize to oneself the reasons that the biased beliefs are justified. To do so would be to perpetuate a justification-suppression of anti-LGBT bias rather than to disrupt this process. Once biases and the existence of an ethical dilemma are defined and anti-LGBT biases personally accepted by the therapist, ethical decision-making can occur. Continued successful enactment involves the successful resolution of the dissonance and the implementation of an ethical decision-making model. Successful resolution of dissonance is defined as full awareness and understanding of the dialectic followed by honest exploration of the role of personal bias in the conflict. This full awareness and honest exploration of one's personal bias serves to disrupt the justification-suppression of LGBT bias and aids movement toward successful enactment. In addition, it is also crucial that the therapist engages in the process of self-evaluation. Engaging in a self-reflective, self-appraisal process provides ongoing learning and awareness of one's biases and the potential to suppress or justify the expression of bias. During this process of self-evaluation, it is important for the therapist to ask themselves, "What were the internal cues/signs/triggers that a bias existed for me?", "How accurately did I recognize and identify my bias?", "What were my justifications for continuing or suppressing my bias?", "What was helpful to me in acknowledging and owning my bias?", and "How can I continue to be aware of my bias in the future?" These and other self-evaluative questions can facilitate the process of self-exploration and continued awareness. In addition, the self-evaluation process can be made even more meaningful and effective by involving peer-consultation or supervision, which facilitates self-appraisal and insight into one's biases that interfere with providing competent, affirmative psychotherapy to LGBT clients. In addition, we believe that the integration of peer consultation or supervision can enhance and strengthen the cognitive developmental process in developing ethical competence. It should be noted, however, that professional development of a more didactic nature is also essential in providing ethical care to clients. Reading the professional literature and attendance at continuing education training are strongly recommended.

Developing Ethical Competence in Supervision and Training

Case Example

Peter is a predoctoral psychology intern who identifies as a cisgender, Asian, heterosexual male and whose training objective is to gain additional experience of working with sexual minority and gender-diverse clients. Among his clients, Peter has been working with a white, cisgender, gay, male graduate student, Andrew. Andrew presented in counseling with concerns regarding his difficulty in establishing meaningful and emotionally fulfilling relationships. Through the course of individual counseling, Peter and Andrew worked together to understand Andrew's interpersonal dynamics and the unmet relationship needs that were underlying Andrew's relationship difficulties. As counseling progressed, a healthy and trusting working alliance developed between Peter and Andrew. During one particular session, Andrew began the session by stating that he saw Peter with his other intern colleagues walking through campus one day and expressed that he had thoughts of what it would be like to be a part of Peter's group. In exploring the underlying wish, Andrew related his fantasy of what it would be like for him not only to be a part of Peter's intern group, but to be in a relationship with Peter. As Peter continued to explore Andrew's fantasy, Peter became aware of Andrew's emotional and sexual attraction toward him. This awareness of Andrew's emotional and sexual attraction created significant discomfort and uneasiness for Peter because his discomfort was noticeably different from what he had previously experienced when a female client was attracted to him. After the disclosure, Peter explained to Andrew the professional boundaries and ethics to which he was bound and then abruptly changed the focus from exploring Andrew's feelings toward him to a discussion of Andrew's potential difficulties in maintaining boundaries in relationships. This discussion confused Andrew and he expressed his confusion to Peter, at which point Peter interpreted the confusion as resistance. Peter then ended the session ten minutes early, adding to Andrew's confusion. Peter explained to Andrew that he suddenly remembered that he had to prepare for an upcoming staff meeting.

After the session, Peter reviewed the session video and it became apparent to him that his discomfort and uneasiness were noticeable. Peter became concerned that he had created a possible rupture in the therapeutic relationship and was worried that he had ultimately acted incompetently because of his uneasiness. As he was reviewing the session video, Peter's anxiety rose to a significant level, such that he also began to have thoughts of not sharing the session with his supervisor for fear of criticism from his supervisor since, understandably, Peter wanted to be perceived as a competent intern by his supervisor. Peter also realized that processing his countertransference reactions in supervision would also be scary since Peter knew that an exploration of his own biases as well as his own sexual orientation and potential attraction to Andrew would likely be a part of the supervision.

Peter met for his regularly scheduled supervision meeting with his supervisor, Richard, a white, cisgender, heterosexual male who possessed extensive experience and knowledge of working with LGBT clients. Peter sought out Richard as his individual supervisor during internship for his known expertise in providing affirmative psychotherapy to LGBT clients and providing effective supervision to trainees working with sexual minority and gender-diverse clients. Peter realized that while he would be uncomfortable processing any client attraction, the attraction of his male client to him was especially challenging due to internalized biases of which he was now aware. During the supervision session, Peter initially did not disclose his session with Andrew during his review of clients with Richard. However, after some inquiry from Richard as to the progress of Peter's work with Andrew, Peter eventually chose to review the session with his supervisor. During the supervision session, Peter disclosed his discomfort to Richard and, in doing so, also expressed his concern that he may have created a rupture in his therapeutic alliance with Andrew and that he also may have acted unethically (Principle A and Principle E, Standard 3.04; APA, 2010). After openly acknowledging his discomfort with the session, Peter openly wondered whether or not he should continue his work with Andrew to avoid any further perceived harm. Richard seized on this as a valuable supervisory and training opportunity to explore Peter's worries, consistent with ethical guidelines and guidelines for working with LGBT clients (Standard 2.01 Boundaries of Competence, Standard 7.06 Assessing Student and Supervisee Performance; APA, 2010; Guideline 1, Psychologists strive to understand the effects of stigma and its various contextual manifestations in the lives of lesbian, gay, and bisexual people; APA, 2012). Richard skillfully navigated the issues regarding Peter's countertransference by engaging Peter in a discussion on the role of Peter's sexual orientation and internal biases and how to best address and repair the rupture of the therapeutic alliance with the client.

In addition, Richard and Peter also discussed the question of whether or not to refer Andrew to another intern or senior staff therapist. During supervision, Richard provided an effective balance of support and challenge to successfully guide Peter through an exploration of his internalized homophobia and of his apprehensions regarding same-sex attraction and his own sexual orientation. Richard recognized that these areas of discomfort were underlying Peter's question of whether to continue his work with his client or to refer his client to another therapist. Through thoughtful and intentional dialogue with Peter, Richard upheld the ethical responsibility that he had to Peter as his supervisee through timely assessment of Peter's performance (Standard 7.06 Assessing Student and Supervisee Performance; APA, 2010) and also reminded Peter of his ongoing ethical responsibility to maintain his competence (Standard 2.01 Boundaries of Competence, Standard 2.03 Maintaining Competence; APA, 2010). As part of providing competent therapy, Richard emphasized the importance of becoming aware and maintaining awareness of biases that would negatively impact the competent provision of affirmative therapy (Standard 3.01 Unfair Discrimination, Principle A Beneficence and Nonmaleficence, Principle E Respect for People's Rights and Dignity; APA, 2010; Guideline 4, Psychologists are encouraged to recognize how their attitudes and knowledge about lesbian, gay, and bisexual issues may be relevant to assessment and treatment and seek consultation or make appropriate referrals when indicated; APA, 2012). Supervision was successful in navigating Peter through to an awareness of his discomfort, the related unconscious biases, the unintended consequence of a disruption in the working alliance, and other potential pitfalls that could occur and that Peter needed to be aware of in order to avoid (e.g., perpetuating heterosexist and anti-LGBT beliefs) in subsequent individual counseling sessions with Andrew. As a result of supervision, Peter was able to directly and successfully address the transference reactions that

Andrew was experiencing as well as managing his own countertransference feelings that were hindering effective, affirmative psychotherapy in his continuing work with Andrew (see Figure 20.1). Richard was successful in providing effective and affirming supervision that resulted in a greater awareness of bias on the part of his supervisee and the provision of affirmative psychotherapy for the client, consistent with ethical guidelines and guidelines for working with LGBT clients (Principle A Beneficence and Nonmaleficence, Principle E Respect for People's Rights and Dignity, Standard 2.01 Boundaries of Competence, Standard 7.06, Guideline 1, Psychologists strive to understand the effects of stigma and its various contextual manifestations in the lives of lesbian, gay, and bisexual people; APA, 2012).

We believe that the need for ethical competence also extends to the supervisory relationship. As illustrated in the previous case examples, supervision and peer consultation can be key to fostering ethical competence for therapists. The importance of acknowledging sexual identity and sexual orientation status is core to the provision of ethical supervision for sexual minority and gender-diverse clients and therapists. Various models of supervision exist to address sexual identity status in supervision. The Integrative Affirmative Supervision (ISA) model (Halpert, Reinhardt, & Toohey, 2007) provides a model and approach to affirmative supervision that addresses supervisor and supervisee sexual identity status. Together with the cognitive developmental model of ethical competence (see Figure 20.2), the IAS model of supervision can be a useful way to explore hidden prejudices in a manner that affirms all gender identities and sexual orientations, thus creating a safe context to explore and raise to awareness underlying anti-LGBT prejudices, navigate ethical dilemmas, and reach resolution within a supervisory relationship.

The period of training and education of therapists in training is a particularly important developmental period during which supervisors can instill and model ethical behavior and nurture ethical competence. It can also often be the case that graduate students and therapists in training may not always be aware of ethical conflicts as they occur and may not, then, be fully aware of their internalized biases. While ethical sensitivity may be a critical element in developing ethical competence (Moffett et al., 2014), we believe that, without an understanding of a cognitive model of ethical competence, graduate students and trainees may lack development of ethical sensitivity and full ethical competence. As such, the indispensable value of supervision and peer consultation must be strongly encouraged and reinforced throughout the formative training and education curricula of therapists during graduate studies. In addition, peer consultation and supervision should be regarded as professional obligations and educational opportunities in order to continue one's ongoing exploration of bias and therapist development through awareness. Developing ethical competence for graduate students and trainees relies on the openness of students and trainees to honestly explore their unexplored biases and assumptions as well as skilled supervisors who are aware of their own biases (and who themselves engage in peer consultation and supervision) to guide graduate students and trainees through the cognitive development process.

Recommendations

Anti-LGBT bias remains a strongly socialized and internalized prejudice to which all persons are subject. As a result, psychologists are just as prone to experiencing anti-LGBT bias in their work with LGBT clients. These biases and prejudices can pervade and affect a therapist's judgment and interactions with LGBT clients. In this chapter, we have chosen to specifically focus on an aspect of ethics with LGBT clients that illustrates an intuitive form of ethical judgment and reasoning by further exploring and expanding Hill et al.'s model of ethical decision-making. The cognitive developmental model of ethical competence attempts to outline and delineate for psychologists and therapists the underlying cognitive processes that are involved in bias awareness and ethical action. The utility of the model for therapists working with LGBT clients is that it provides a deeper, more nuanced understanding of the effect that anti-LGBT bias may have on the therapeutic process. Our hope is that, through this model, therapists can further understand how to be aware of anti-LGBT bias and how to make conscious those prejudices that may be unconscious.

As this chapter has emphasized, it is necessary for therapists to be knowledgeable about models of ethical decision-making and to develop ethical competence in gaining an awareness of internal biases. However, such knowledge and competence may not be fully sufficient, and awareness of anti-LGBT biases alone may not be fully sufficient if therapists truly desire to provide affirmative psychotherapy to LGBT clients. We believe that it is critical for therapists to make active, continued efforts toward understanding and unlearning internalized negative LGBT bias. Just as Sue (2003) outlined fundamental principles and recommendations for individuals to unlearn the oppressive forces of racism, we conclude with an outline of our core principles and recommendations for mental health professionals to unlearn the oppressive forces of heterosexism and anti-LGBT bias, as adapted from Sue (2003).

Overcoming Heterosexist and Anti-LGBT Bias

Overcoming heterosexist and anti-LGBT bias calls on therapists to: (1) take personal responsibility for gaining awareness and knowledge and enacting in affirmative ways; (2) actively work to unlearn heterosexist and anti-LGBT assumptions that manifest in both cognitive and affective ways; and (3) obtain continued education, peer consultation, experience, and support. These core therapist responsibilities underlie the following five principles for overcoming and unlearning heterosexist and anti-LGBT bias.

Knowing Culture and Community

The first fundamental to overcoming heterosexist and anti-LGBT bias is for the therapist to gain knowledge and experience about LGBT individuals, communities, and culture. Acquiring knowledge and personal experience about LGBT communities serves to challenge assumptions and internalized biases and provides a broader as well as a deeper understanding of the lived experiences of LGBT individuals and LGBT communities. Attending LGBT community events (e.g., community Pride Parade, movies, book discussions, theater), engaging in readings on LGBT sociocultural literature and history, and attending professional educational conferences (e.g., Southern Comfort Conference, American Psychological Association Division 44 presentations) are direct avenues for obtaining fundamental knowledge of and education regarding the LGBT community. Additional helpful resources can also be found on various professional websites, such as the American Psychological Association's Society for the Psychological Study of Lesbian, Gay, Bisexual, and Transgender Issues (www.apadivisions.org/division-44/resources/index.aspx).

Connecting and Learning

Make individual personal social and professional connections in order to know and understand the lived and direct experiences of sexual minority and gender-diverse individuals whose identities differ from your own. Acquiring experiences in this way may be more challenging than it first appears due to the realization and confrontation of one's own unconscious biases and within-group assumptions. However, establishing personal connections and relationships is essential to gaining the continued understanding and awareness and having a context within which challenging privilege can occur. That is, it is difficult to challenge one's own biases without the inclination to suppress those same biases. Volunteering in an organization serving LGBT communities, attending services and programs that encompass the spiritual and religious lives of LGBT people, and joining groups or organizations that serve the LGBT community can provide valuable connections to an LGBT community and promote learning.

One's intentions in establishing personal connections are selfless rather than self-serving. Personal and professional connections are aimed at continued self-insight and continued vigilance of internal biases and motivations. Valuable and constructive challenging of assumptions occurs when personal connections and relationships are established to assist and facilitate the understanding of the lived and direct experiences of sexual minority and gender-diverse communities and individuals.

Experience and Awareness

Personal social and professional connections are integral to gaining the in-depth experience and awareness needed for ethical practice. As Sue (2003) stated, "...you must supplement your factual understanding with the experiential reality of the groups you hope to understand" (p. 212). Cultural understanding and sensitivity cannot take place without an experiential understanding of lived experience. Personal connections can facilitate this lived experience, and continued engagements in communities other than one's own can facilitate the continued awareness and unlearning of anti-LGBT bias and assumptions. Some avenues for pursuing personal and professional connections in this manner might be to identify a friend or colleague to serve as a mentor or guide in order to better understand members of the group and to obtain accurate information about LGBT community and culture. As important is a relationship with a mentor or guide to engage in processing reactions and emerging awareness in a safe and validating way. Mentors can challenge and assist in unlearning biases, assumptions, and misinformation. As such, this mentoring relationship is key to encouraging and supporting continued experience and awareness.

Ongoing Education and Awareness

Making a personal commitment to ongoing education and awareness involves more than just an intellectual exercise and experience. The task is to remain open, vulnerable, and curious to a process of continued introspective exploration as well as continued education from engaging in communities that are different from one's own. This process allows for engaging with others who can provide unabating challenge and support for the discovery of unseen biases and their integration into conscious awareness. A useful way to facilitate this process is to engage in continued dialogue and scrutiny of unlearned biases, regardless of personal discomfort or resistance. Again, it is the discomfort that signals the existence of a potential ethical dilemma, as well as an opportunity for growth.

Making a Personal Commitment

Engagement in social justice for LGBT individuals and communities is the natural fruit of a deeply rooted personal commitment to sustained self-awareness. The work to sustain self-awareness is echoed in the ethical principles of beneficence, fidelity, justice, and respect for the rights and uniqueness of individuals (APA, 2010). Sustaining self-awareness and making a personal commitment to engage in social justice for LGBT people and communities can take many forms, such as membership in groups and organizations that advocate for sexual minority and gender-diverse people. Another pathway to engaging in social justice for LGBT people is to educate others, either through didactic and experiential teaching or through research and scholarship, in how to recognize, address, and unlearn anti-LGBT bias.

There are several other opportunities for therapists to make a personal commitment to social justice and sustained self-awareness. However, engaging in sustained self-awareness requires therapists to continue to be honestly open to the discomfort of recognizing internalized bias, to be invested in the work of dismantling heterosexist privilege, and to be willing to be an ally in joining sexual minority and gender-diverse communities in advocacy for equitable, all-around opportunities.

Conclusion

Ethical practice is the cornerstone for providing effective and affirmative therapy for LGBT clients. We believe that at the core of providing ethical and affirmative therapy for LGBT clients is the therapist's awareness of and vigilance for personal biases that hinder affirmative therapy.

> Psychologists exercise reasonable judgment and take precautions to ensure that their potential biases, the boundaries of their competence, and the limitations of their expertise do not lead to or condone unjust practices. (Principle D; APA, 2010)

> Psychologists are aware that special safeguards may be necessary to protect the rights and welfare of persons or communities whose vulnerabilities impair autonomous decision making. Psychologists are aware of and respect cultural, individual, and role differences, including those based on age, gender, gender identity, race, ethnicity, culture, national origin, religion, sexual orientation, disability, language, and socioeconomic status, and consider these factors when working with members of such groups. Psychologists try to eliminate the effect on their work of biases based on those factors, and they do not knowingly participate in or condone activities of others based upon such prejudices. (Principle E; APA, 2010)

Ethical competence calls for familiarity and knowledge of ethical principles and codes of professional behavior and knowledge of ethical decision-making models in order to successfully address and resolve ethical dilemmas. Successful cognitive development of ethical competence also integrates an understanding and awareness of cultural contexts. While it is beyond the scope of this chapter to explore all the iterations and intersections of cultural contexts and the development of ethical competence, we are hopeful that this chapter has provided some additional understanding to the complex nature of developing one's awareness of internalized anti-LGBT bias through a cognitive developmental model of ethical competence (see Figure 20.2).

In conclusion, we believe it is incumbent upon the ethical therapist to be fully cognizant and aware of internalized biases that cloud and obstruct ethical, affirmative psychotherapy and to eliminate the effects of bias and prejudice in their work with all clients. This obligation necessitates the ongoing education and personal efforts of therapists to engage in developing ethical competence and in social justice action in order to overcome the costly and deleterious effects of anti-LGBT bias and oppression upon sexual minority and gender-diverse people and communities.

Author Note

We thank Matthew D. Brown, M.A., University of Tennessee-Chattanooga, for his valuable comments on an earlier draft of this chapter.

References

American Psychological Association (2010). Ethical principles of psychologists and code of conduct. Retrieved from www.apa.org/ethics/code/principles.pdf

American Psychological Association (2012). Guidelines for psychological practice with lesbian, gay, and bisexual clients. *American Psychologist, 67*, 10–42.

American Psychological Association (2015). Guidelines for psychological practice with transgender and gender nonconforming people. Retrieved from www.apa.org/prac tice/guidelines/transgender.pdf

Barón, A. (1991). The challenge: To make homosexuality boring. *The Counseling Psychologist 19*, 239–244.

Bazerman, M. H. & Tenbrunsel, A. E. (2011). *Blind spots*. Princeton, NJ: Princeton University Press.

Bess, J. A. & Stabb, S. D. (2009). The experiences of transgendered persons in psychother- apy: Voices and recommendations. *Journal of Mental Health Counseling, 31*, 264–282.

Bieschke, K. J., Perez, R. M., & DeBord, K. A. (2007). Introduction: The challenge of providing affirmative psychotherapy while honoring diverse contexts. In K. J., Bieschke, R. M. Perez, & K. A. DeBord (Eds.), *Handbook of counseling and psychotherapy with lesbian, gay, and bisexual clients* (2nd edn., pp. 3–11). Washington, DC: American Psychological Association.

Crandall, C. S. & Eshleman, A. (2003). A justification-suppression model of the expression and experience of prejudice. *Psychological Bulletin, 129*, 414–446.

Dovidio, J. F. (2001). On the nature of contemporary prejudice: The third wave. *Journal of Social Issues, 57*, 829–849.

Fischer, A. R. & DeBord, K. A. (2007). Perceived conflicts between affirmation of religious diversity and affirmation of sexual diversity: That's perceived. In K. J., Bieschke, R. M. Perez, & K. A. DeBord (Eds.), *Handbook of counseling and psychotherapy with lesbian, gay, and bisexual clients* (2nd edn,. pp. 317–339). Washington, DC: American Psychological Association.

Greene, B. (2007). Delivering ethical psychological services to lesbian, gay, and bisexual clients. In K. J., Bieschke, R. M. Perez, & K. A. DeBord (Eds.), *Handbook of counseling and psychotherapy with lesbian, gay, and bisexual clients* (2nd edn., pp. 181–199). Washington, DC: American Psychological Association.

Halpert, S. C., Reinhardt, B., & Toohey, M. J. (2007). Affirmative clinical supervision. In K. J., Bieschke, R. M. Perez, & K. A. DeBord (Eds.), *Handbook of counseling and psychotherapy with lesbian, gay, and bisexual clients* (2nd edn., pp. 341–358). Washington, DC: American Psychological Association.

Hill, M., Glaser, K., & Harden, J. (1998). A feminist model for ethical decision-making. *Women in Therapy, 21*, 101–121.

Kitchener, K. S. (1984). Intuition, critical evaluation and ethical principles: The foundation for ethical decisions in counseling psychology. *The Counseling Psychologist, 12*, 43–55.

Kitchener, K. S. (2000). *Foundations of ethical practice, research, and teaching in psychol- ogy*. Mahwah, NJ: Erlbaum.

Knapp, S. J., Gottlieb, M. C., & Handelsman, M. M. (2015). *Ethical dilemmas in psychother- apy*. Washington, DC: American Psychological Association.

Moffett, L. A., Becker, C. J., & Patton, R. G. (2014). Fostering the ethical sensitivity of beginning clinicians. *Training and Education in Professional Psychology, 8*, 229–235.

Morrow, S. L. (2000). First, do no harm: Therapist issues in psychotherapy with lesbian, gay, and bisexual clients. In R. M. Perez, K. A. DeBord, & K. J. Bieshcke (Eds.), *Handbook of counseling and psychotherapy with lesbian, gay, and bisexual clients* (pp. 137–156). Washington, DC: American Psychological Association.

Pearson, A. R., Dovidio, J. F., & Gaertner, S. L. (2009). The nature of contemporary prejudice: Insights from aversive racism. *Social and Personality Psychology Compass*, *3*, 314–338.

Perez, R. M. (2007). The "boring" state of research and psychotherapy with lesbian, gay, bisexual, and transgender clients: Revisiting Barón (1991). In K. J., Bieschke, R. M. Perez, & K. A. DeBord (Eds.), *Handbook of counseling and psychotherapy with lesbian, gay, and bisexual clients* (2nd edn., pp. 399–418). Washington, DC: American Psychological Association.

Rachlin, K. (2001). *Transgender individuals' experience of psychotherapy.* Paper presented at the American Psychological Association 109th Annual Convention, San Francisco, CA.

Sue, D. W. (2003). *Overcoming our racism: The journey to liberation.* New York, NY: Wiley.

Welfel, E. R. (2013). *Ethics in counseling and psychotherapy* (6th edn.). Boston, MA: Cengage Learning.

Legal, Research, and Organizational Issues

21 Major Legal Cases That Have Influenced Mental Health Ethics

G. Andrew H. Benjamin and Connie J. Beck

During the twentieth century, several courts struggled with the tension of protecting the inviolability of psychotherapist–client confidentiality and the encroachment upon confidentiality. Many mental health professionals (MHPs) suffered through lawsuits in cases involving confidentiality where they were held accountable for their actions in court. The judicial decisions in these cases led to the formation of "common law" findings that shaped the practice of psychotherapy as these the issues had not yet come before that court or at least not in that jurisdiction. These judicial decisions changed how MHPs managed confidential information. Reacting to common law, legislatures created statutes and agencies promulgated administrative rules to modify the various rulings in these cases. The judicial decisions – common law findings – often required modification because the decisions established legal liability that affected practice standards egregiously.

The dynamic growth of these duties and the direction of the changes of psychotherapeutic practices are unpredictable because judges have tremendous authority and, motivated by the shocking facts of individual cases, create common law findings that are often impractical. Their decisions represent judicial activism that usurps the function of our state legislatures and administrative bodies that regulate practice. Generally, legislative statutes and administrative rules are justified by testimony from representatives from broader interest groups and are created or promulgated through the judgments of many public and private servants. Such laws regulating mental health practice lead to more informed and useful standards compared to those based on the common law founded upon the limited facts of individual cases.

The chapter discusses three major cases that have changed the direction of MHPs' duties in the practice of psychotherapy with abusive or dangerous clients. It also provides ethical approaches to managing the risks of such clients, particularly in light of an unsettled climate in which to treat such dangerous clients. The courts will continue to engage in judicial activism; therefore, it is critical that MHPs stay up to date concerning legal cases creating common law or subsequent legislative or administrative law changes in their respective jurisdictions.

Duty to Report Child Abuse: In the Case of Mary Ellen

Mary Ellen was born in 1864 and was orphaned as a baby. In 1866, she was adopted by Thomas and Mary McCormack. Within months, Mary McCormack began severely beating Mary Ellen. Neighbors heard the beatings and the crying of Mary Ellen. In late 1873, the landlord (Margaret Bingham) became concerned and asked a missionary from St. Luke's Mission (Etta Wheeler) to check on Mary Ellen.[1] Ms. Wheeler was eventually able to see Mary Ellen in her home. What she saw was a pale, thin, barefoot child in a dirty, tattered, thin dress with multiple scars on her arms and legs from beatings with a twisted leather whip that lay on the table.

At this time, there were no laws against child abuse or governmental agencies to protect the rights of children. Ms. Wheeler approached the founder of the American Society for the Prevention of Cruelty to Animals (ASPCA), Henry Bergh, to help her in advocating for Mary Ellen in court. Mr. Bergh directed his lawyer, Elbridge Gerry, to determine a legal argument to make on Mary Ellen's behalf. In April 1874, Mary Ellen's case came before the New York Supreme Court and is widely thought to be the first child abuse case in the United States where a child was successfully removed from her guardians for child abuse (Shelman & Lazoritz, 2005). From this case, other courts and eventually legislatures created laws that mandated reporting child abuse and neglect to state or provincial Child Protection Services.[2] Currently, most of the professionals involved with parents and their children (including many other professionals in addition to MHPs) must meet the duty to report abused or neglected children to Child Protective Services.

Liability for failing to report child abuse and neglect exists in all jurisdictions (Children's Bureau, 2014), and three major ethical issues have arisen from the duty to report[3]:

- When and how to breach confidentiality;
- How to sustain the therapeutic relationship in light of making the report (Kalichman, 1999);
- How to avoid multiple relationships in cases with court involvement.

When and How to Breach Confidentiality

Mandatory reporting duties fall under the general professional obligation of the duty to protect (Kalichman, 1999). First the courts and now the legislatures imposed laws to report clients or the child(ren) of clients who may potentially be harmed or have been harmed (Kalichman, 1999). All jurisdictions created statutes adding greater specificity about when to make a report of child abuse or neglect. Nevertheless, it is

---

[1] For an extensive review of this case, including original legal documents, see Shelman, E. A. & Lazoritz, S. (2005). *The Mary Ellen Wilson child abuse case and the beginning of children's rights in 19th century America.* Jefferson, NC: McFarland & Company.

[2] An example of this was *L. A. R. v Ludwig, 821 P.2d 291* in Arizona. The case was decided in 1991 and created "common law" in the state that modified the state mandatory reporting statutes and required MHPs to report child abuse even if they had not observed or examined the child prior to reporting. It was several years before the state reporting statute was modified to reflect this change.

[3] Although somewhat dated, for an extended review of ethical issues that arise in child abuse and neglect cases, see Kalichman, S. C. (1999). *Mandated reporting of suspected child abuse: Ethics, law, and policy* (2nd edn.). Washington, DC: American Psychological Association.

at times difficult to determine under some circumstances when the clinician should breach confidentiality and make a report.

For example, a mother who is divorced brings her seven-year-old son to his treatment session and the boy reports to the treating MHP that he was afraid because his dad smelled like beer when driving. The MHP should follow up this disclosure with invitational questions ("Please say more about what happened when. . ."), cued invitational questions ("You said that you were scared, please say more about. . ."), and cued recall prompts ("When did your father smell like beer?") to elicit more information in order to determine whether a Child Protective Services report was required. The form of these questions will help prevent the son from being influenced by suggestive or leading questions (Lamb, Orbach, Hershkowitz, Esplin, & Horowitz, 2007). Assume that the statements made by the son and the follow-up questions did not rise to the level of suspicion required by the law or professional ethics (APA, 2010, Standard 1.02) to make a report to Child Protective Services. In this context, the MHP avoids harm (APA, 2010, Standard 3.04) by not arriving at a finding about the son's concerns because the MHP has never personally evaluated the father (APA, 2010, Standard 9.01[b]) and the statements made by the son do not meet the threshold of reasonable suspicion.

Therapeutic Relationship in Light of a Report

Second, making a report can affect the therapeutic relationship and put at risk the ongoing relationship. Informed consent is required (APA, 2010, Standard 10.01) before entering a professional relationship with a client. A critical part of informed consent is engaging in the process of clearly stating the limits of confidentiality (e.g., harm to self/others, child abuse, abuse of an elder or vulnerable adult) at the initiation of therapy and when necessary later during the therapy. As therapy progresses, clients may forget these limits or the limits can severely constrain important issues that could be addressed in therapy. Making a report can result in a client feeling betrayed and the client leaving or being pulled from treatment. Handled sensitively, it may also strengthen the therapeutic relationship by refocusing the therapy on ending the abusive behavior and increasing access to additional needed services for the family or refocusing the therapy on the unresolved issues (Kalichman, 1999).

Following on the case example above (a child alleged his father drove while smelling like beer), from the onset of the case, the MHP should be aware of the possibility that a problematic custody relationship between the parents may lead to a request for records or testimony in court. In any case of a divorced adult client seeking services for a child or for both parent and child, the MHP is advised to obtain a copy of the last custody order and determine who has decision-making authority for the child. Assume for this case that the mother and father had joint health care decision-making authority. With the mother's permission, the MHP and the mother should conduct a phone conversation with the father about joining family therapy. Assume for this case example that the father reported that he thought that the mother and son had a good relationship that would become much better if he stayed out of it.

Next, the MHP is also advised to attempt to limit who could obtain any information from the family psychotherapy. To do so, the MHP should also ask both parents to stipulate that no information disclosed during the psychotherapy with the mother and son be later released for any legal proceeding, either during discovery or trial, unless one of the mandatory reporting duties required release of information.[i] A good practice is to send the practice agreement and the stipulation by e-mail for both of the parents to review and confirm before meeting a second time with the mother and the son. Obtain signed copies of this stipulation before proceeding in therapy.

If a lawyer calls to discuss why no report was filed with Child Protective Services concerning the son's allegation, the MHP should first obtain a release from the mother to send a response to the lawyer's message. MHPs should expect such a call. It probably would involve the lawyer reminding the MHP that she is mandated to report possible abuse or neglect if there is reason to believe that the father's driving placed the child in physical danger. In a written response to the lawyer and both parents, the MHP should then describe for the lawyer that the son reported only that he felt fearful because his father smelled like beer and that evidence-based follow-up questions did not reveal additional information that rose to the level of reasonable suspicion.

If the lawyer responds to the MHP's written response that she will be called as a witness at a family court hearing, the MPH is advised to remind the lawyer in writing about the stipulation and urge the lawyer to reconsider her request based upon the probable outcome that the son would not want to continue psychotherapy and the relationships in the family would be further strained. If the lawyer remains insistent that the MHP provides testimony, the MHP should forward to the clerk of the judge in the case and the lawyers of both parties the stipulation and a clear statement declining any further involvement in the legal part of the case. Also, the MHP should advise the lawyer that if one of them is considering sending a subpoena to testify to the MHP, the response would recite the facts of the stipulation and no recommendations would be made.

The MHP is strongly advised to then put in the client's chart the facts that were conveyed to the lawyer and the mother and the responses of the lawyer. The dated record would show that the MHP attempted to meet ethical and legal standards of care. The MHP should forward the notes to the lawyer for her file. Such an action serves to reinforce the resolutions. It also serves as a record that will likely prevent a later complaint from the lawyer. The key is transparency for all parties and documentation in complex cases where mandated reporting is at issue and where court involvement is likely.[4]

A subsequent frank discussion with the mother should ensue to address her concern about the father's relationship with their child.

---

[4] Transparency is a key protective factor for the therapeutic alliance. When a report of abuse or neglect is made, the MHP is urged to make the report with their client present so that processing of the event can occur before and after the report is made.

Multiple Relationships in Cases with Court Involvement

Note that the mother's lawyer was attempting to shift the MHP from a treating role within the case to a forensic role. As a therapist and mandatory reporter, the MHP is not a forensic evaluator. Briefly, the role of the forensic evaluator must be independent from treatment and no previous relationship should exist with any of the parties. The forensic evaluator responds to the specific questions or concerns of the parties, lawyers, and the court. The evaluator would then conduct a thorough examination of the necessary parties, including interviews, observations, testing, and obtaining collateral information where appropriate. Only after these steps would the evaluator render an opinion for the court. Lawyers in family law often attempt to blur the lines between being a treating therapist (fact witness) and a forensic evaluator (expert witness). They request or subpoena the MHP's records and testimony or may obtain a court order to mandate the MHP's involvement in the litigation. The lawyers mistakenly want to force the MHP to offer opinions concerning the entire family as opposed to restating the facts of the case only (e.g., diagnosis, treatment plan, dates of service). The release of the records or testimony is likely to not only rupture the therapeutic alliance for at least one of the parties involved in the case, but also it would likely lead to an ethics complaint from one of the parties involved in the case – the father in the example above.

Ethics complaints are quite common in cases with court involvement because MHPs unwittingly engage in multiple relationships under such circumstances (e.g., the MHP started in a treatment role but then provided forensic opinions in the second role during discovery or in testimony before the court, even though that role occurred because of the bullying of a lawyer). Violations of state and provincial laws and the American Psychological Association (APA) Code of Conduct regarding multiple relationships (APA Ethical Principles of Psychologists and Code of Conduct, 2010, Standard 3.05) continue to occur as some MHPs, when pressed by such circumstances, struggle with how to protect the confidences of their clients (Fisher, 2008). Treating MHPs can hold to the role in which they agreed to serve by clarifying the boundaries of the role from the beginning of the treating relationship. The best protection is to stay within that role throughout the case whenever lawyers become involved with the person that is being treated.

Careful, in-depth discussions regarding the need to erect prohibitions against MHPs becoming involved in any court proceeding ensures that no client, the domestic partner, nor a family member will attempt to soil the therapeutic alliance. The surest way to remain faithful (APA, 2010, Principle B: Fidelity and Responsibility) to your clients is by upholding their confidentiality (APA, 2010, Standard 4.01: Maintaining Confidentiality) while adhering to the requirements of the law (APA, 2010, Standard 1.02: Conflict between Ethics and Law, Regulations, or Other Governing Legal Authority), all the while avoiding harm (APA, 2010, Principle A: Nonmaleficence and Standard 3.04: Avoiding Harm) and remaining true to the principle of beneficence (APA, 2010, Principle A).

Who Needs to Report What and When

Mandatory reporting laws include several key features that are important for MHPs to know (Kalichman, 1999):

- Definition of child abuse
- Age limits of children covered by the law
- Circumstances under which a mandated reporter must report
- Degree of certainty that reporters must have that abuse occurred
- Definitions about who are considered mandated reporters
- Rules about sanctions for failing to report
- Immunity standards for civil and criminal actions

During the years following the Mary Ellen case, state statutes broadened from first only including physicians to including other professionals who work with children (e.g., chiropractors, day care providers, dentists, nurses, school personnel, teachers, etc.). At this time, all MHPs are considered mandatory reporters.

Definitions of abuse and neglect across the 50 states and American Territories were recently reviewed in one monograph (Children's Bureau, 2014). These definitions commonly include physical abuse, sexual abuse/exploitation, neglect, and emotional abuse. In some states and American Territories, parental substance abuse and abandonment are also included in the definition of child abuse (Children's Bureau, 2014). The definitions of what is considered reportable abuse also expanded over time (Weithorn, 2001). In the 1960s and 1970s, the focus was on physical abuse. In the 1980s and 1990s, attention focused upon sexual abuse. Currently, we are experiencing again an expansion of what is reported and acted upon. In recent years, some state laws have mandated reports when children are exposed to domestic violence (Weithorn, 2001).

The expansion of definitions of neglect to include exposure to domestic violence is beginning to occur in some states, while in other states it is specifically excluded. This type of mandatory reporting is extremely controversial and was determined to be unconstitutional in the New York case of *Nicholson v Williams, 203 F. Supp 2d 153*. In 2001, a class action was filed on behalf of mothers who had been charged with neglect and had their child(ren) removed by the New York State child welfare agency for the sole reason that they were victims of domestic violence and that their child(ren) had witnessed domestic violence (*203 F. Supp. 2d 153*). The court issued a preliminary injunction to protect mothers against this agency policy. In a sweeping condemnation of the agency policy, Judge Weinstein in 2002 ruled that a mother's victimization by an abuser and her children witnessing this domestic violence cannot in and of itself be charged as neglect against the victim mother and cannot be the sole basis for removing the children from the mother's home.

In the years following the Judge's ruling, the Nicholson Review Committee, a body of the legislature, determined that changing agency culture was difficult (Stark, 2005). Even with significant training there remained a deep divide between the focus of workers in child welfare agencies on protecting children from abuse and an understanding of the dynamics of domestic violence. There was still an unwillingness to treat the adult victims of domestic violence with respect and care. Offers of referrals to advocacy agencies so that adult victims could obtain the assistance needed to improve their lives and the lives of their children were not occurring consistently. Instead, child welfare agencies continued to remove child(ren) from a mother's care without a clear reason to do so (Stark, 2005). Although there are several jurisdictions in the United States where mandatory reporting includes children exposed to domestic violence, Australian and American experts concluded that to be effective these mandatory reporting laws must be coupled with: adequate training of reporters to comply with the expanded duty; cross-training of child welfare and victim advocates so that they can work together to serve all family members; and significant additional resources, personnel, and programs to adequately respond to the reports (Cross et al., 2012).

In summary, a report must be made when a mandated reporter knows or has reason to believe or reason to suspect that a child has been abused or neglected (Kalichman, 1999). The definitions of these terms remain ambiguous under many laws. Differentiating abuse under these circumstances from hunches, impressions, and intuitions is difficult (Kalichman, 1999). It is important to remember that MHPs are not to function as investigators or evaluators for law enforcement or child welfare. Coupled with the duty to provide clear, informed consent at the beginning of the professional relationship detailing the limits of confidentiality, MHPs must follow the duty to make a report if reason exists to believe a child is or has been abused or neglected. Such reports must be conducted as sensitively as possible to preserve the therapeutic relationship with our clients and to avoid a later charge of engaging in a multiple relationship.

The Duty to Protect/Warn, Tarasoff v. Regents of University of California

In 1974, the California Supreme Court in *Tarasoff v. Regents of University of California* (551 P.2d 334 [1976]) ruled that MHPs had a *duty to warn an identifiable victim.* In a reconsideration of the first ruling, the Court held that MHPs must "protect" a third party when a client is judged to be dangerous and threatens that third party by either warning the victim, notifying the police, or taking "whatever steps are reasonable necessary under the circumstances" (p. 340).[5]

---

[5] "When a therapist determines, or pursuant to the standards of his [or her] profession should determine, that his [or her] patient presents a serious danger of violence to another, he [or she] incurs an obligation to use reasonable care to protect the intended victim against such danger. The discharge of this duty may require the therapist to take one or more of various steps, depending on the nature of the case. Thus it may call for him [or her] to warn the intended victim or others likely to apprise the victim of the danger, to notify the police, or to take whatever steps are reasonably necessary under the circumstances" (p. 340). Later (p. 345, footnote omitted), the court indicated, "While the discharge of this duty of due care will necessarily vary with the facts of each case, in each instance the adequacy of the psychologist's conduct must be measured against the traditional negligence standard of the rendition of reasonable care under the circumstances."

In August 1969, Tatiana Tarasoff rejected Prosenjit Poddar's attempts to continue to date her. Poddar disclosed to his psychologist Moore in a psychotherapy session that he intended to purchase a gun. Moore believed Poddar was dangerous in light of his obsessive attachment to Tarasoff (who was identifiable but not known by name to Moore). Moore consulted with colleagues about his conclusion, decided that he should contact police, and gave police oral and written notice that he believed Poddar to be dangerous. Moore asked that Poddar be evaluated for civil commitment under California law. After interviewing Poddar, the police determined that he was rational and not truly dangerous, and they reported securing a promise from Poddar not to harm Tarasoff. He was released. Moore's clinical supervisor, psychiatrist Powelson, asked the police to return Moore's letter, directed that copies of the letter and notes Moore had taken be destroyed, and ordered that no action be taken to involuntarily hospitalize Poddar. Soon thereafter, Poddar ended psychotherapy.

Two months later, Poddar shot and stabbed Tarasoff to death. Tarasoff's family sued University of California, Berkeley, the campus police, and Moore and Powelson. Both the trial court and the appeals court ruled that the family had no legal basis under California law for the claim. No statute existed that identified therapists as having any duties to people who were not their clients. The family appealed to the California Supreme Court, asserting that the defendants had a duty to warn the victim and her family of the danger. The record showed Tarasoff was unaware of Poddar's violent feelings toward her. The 1974 California Supreme Court ruling overturned the lower courts' decisions and ruled that therapists had a duty to warn the identifiable victim. In 1976, a number of groups, including MHP state associations, urged the Supreme Court to reconsider the 1974 ruling. In 1976, the California Supreme Court issued a second ruling and released the police from liability without comment. It also modified the duty of therapists to only when a client is judged to be dangerous to third parties. It created a duty to protect that an MHP could discharge by engaging in actions other than warning the victim. It found that MHPs had a responsibility to use reasonable care to protect third parties against a dangerous client. The Court recognized the difficulty in reliably predicting whether a client will act violently, but asserted the responsibility under two conditions:

1. The therapist uses professional knowledge and makes a reasonable judgment that the client is dangerous to a third party; or
2. The therapist should have known that the client posed a serious risk to a third party (e.g., a competent assessment would have revealed that likelihood).

University of California, Berkeley, Dr. Moore, and Dr. Powelson from the University of California, Berkeley, health service settled the civil case for an undisclosed sum. Both continued to practice and no disciplinary action was taken against either professional. Poddar was convicted of second-degree murder, but his conviction was overturned on appeal because of faulty jury instructions. He was subsequently convicted of voluntary manslaughter and served five years in prison. He then returned to India, his home country. A thorough analysis of the case history is discussed elsewhere (Monahan, 2006; Welfel, Werth, & Benjamin, 2012).

Prompted by this seminal decision, during the last 40 years, standards of professional associations, laws enacted by many state and provincial legislatures, and decisions of state and federal courts have limited the confidentiality for mental health clients when they disclosed threatening behavior directed at a third party. There are substantial variations in interpretation of this legal issue and most jurisdictions do not apply the *Tarasoff* standards literally. At the last count, only seven states and six provinces have not enacted a statutory duty to protect or created a duty to protect as a result of judicial activism (a duty imposed upon the people of the state because of a judicial decision as a result of a court case). In fact, no two states or provinces have created the same law related to the duty to protect/warn (Benjamin, Kent, & Sirikantraporn, 2009).

In a thorough review of the laws for each state and province, Benjamin et al. (2009) found the following:

- Some jurisdictions mandate disclosures while other jurisdictions permit disclosures.
- A majority of the jurisdictions do not specify warning as the only option for carrying out the duty.
- Most allow hospitalization (voluntary or involuntary) and some allow intensification of outpatient treatment or other actions that appear appropriate to the treating MHPs.
- Even when a duty to protect or warn is identified, laws vary substantially in defining when a duty is present (e.g., threats against person versus threats against property) and what an MHP is obligated to do in that situation (e.g., several different types of warning or protective actions have been specified by the various jurisdictions).
- State and provincial statutory laws and court rulings are not static and from time to time are modified by statutory changes and case law. In addition, the direction of change is unpredictable;many jurisdictions have narrowed the types of circumstances that provoke the duty while others have widened it (Walcott, Cerundolo, & Beck, 2001).

The case law generated by *Tarasoff* is only binding in California and does not apply in other states or provinces. Any duty to protect/warn within each state and province must originate through legislation or administrative rules or in subsequent court rulings.[6]

The changing face of the duty to warn or protect is not the only challenge that MHPs face when clients threaten third parties. Every state has passed privileged communication and confidentiality statutes or administrative rules in which client disclosures in psychotherapy cannot be revealed without client consent or legal authority (Caudill & Kaplan, 2005). Unauthorized disclosure leaves MHPs vulnerable to being sued for negligence, having a licensing board complaint filed, or both. Sometimes state laws are clear about whether a breach of confidentiality to

---

[6] A complete review of the duty to protect/warn law (legislative, administrative, or judicially mandated) for each state and province is within Benjamin et al. (2009).

implement a duty to protect a third party is protected from civil liability and sometimes the laws are silent (Benjamin et al., 2009). Many jurisdictions with duties to protect or to warn include protection against liability claims, but this protection exists only when the breach meets the standard in the statute for triggering a duty (Benjamin et al., 2009). If MHPs breach confidentiality against client wishes and without sufficient legal justification, they are not protected under the immunity provisions of these statutes.

A study of 300 psychologists in four states with varying legal requirements regarding duty to protect/warn in cases with dangerous clients found that most psychologists (76.4 percent) were misinformed about their state laws (Pabian, Welfel, & Beebe, 2009). The findings included:

- In states where no legal duty existed, many psychologists mistakenly believed that they were legally mandated to warn, and in states where there were legal options other than warning the potential victim, most psychologists assumed that warning was their only legal option.
- Most of the psychologists involved in this research would have breached confidentiality without client permission and risked a civil suit from their client for negligence and/or a disciplinary action by their licensing board for failing to understand their jurisdiction's approach to the duty to protect/warn.
- Even more alarmingly, 89 percent of the participant psychologists expressed confidence that they were very up to date or somewhat up to date in their knowledge about their jurisdiction's duty.

Practical Approaches to Meeting the Duty

Ambiguity about how to fulfill the duty to protect/warn can arise because of a lack of clarity about the laws of many jurisdictions, the conflict between the duty to protect and the duty of confidentiality to the client, and the inexact science of predicting violence. How can you act as a prudent and practical MHP?

- Know the legal and ethical standards for the duty to protect/warn in your jurisdiction.
- Provide disclosure and informed consent before evaluation and treatment begin and at points during the evaluation and treatment as needed.
- Conduct a brief risk assessment at the onset of each case.
- Build and maintain a strong therapeutic alliance.

When your client makes statements that lead you to believe that she or he might be dangerous or pose an imminent threat to others, the MHP can engage in the following additional practices to establish a reasonable course of action whenever a duty to protect and/or warn emerges within a case:

- Conduct a thorough risk assessment based on current facts.
- Obtain peer consultation.
- Implement a plan to reduce the risk of violence.
- Maintain thorough documentation.

What is the Law about the Duty to Protect/Warn?

Preparation begins with knowing the law about the duty to protect/warn and what constitutes the standard of care within your jurisdiction (Benjamin et al., 1995). Regarding dangerous threats of your client against someone, in most jurisdictions, legal standards for negligence and ethical conduct require that MHPs conduct an assessment and intervention (Benjamin et al., 2009). MHPs can check with their state and provincial/territorial professional associations (SPAs) to determine if current recommendations for meeting the duty to protect have been developed. In addition, SPAs can refer MHPs to lawyers specializing in legal practices focused on mental health practices for individual consultation. Professional liability carriers also provide free legal and professional consultation.

Disclosure and Informed Consent

A therapeutic alliance is founded on the informed consent process (Fischer & Orlandky, 2008; Waitzkin, 1984). One of the linchpins of successful evaluation and intervention in a duty-to-protect case is full disclosure with the client about the limitations of protecting confidences before any dangerous ideation has been expressed (Glosoff et al., 1997). The laws related to all mandatory reporting duties and the duty to protect should be delineated clearly to the client by the MHP verbally and in writing before therapy begins. Forewarning the client about these duties can prevent the client from feeling surprised and betrayed. Later, if a threat of violence emerges, the MHP has a solid foundation on which to launch an active collaboration with the client to determine what precipitating and inhibiting factors exist.

Therapeutic Alliance

The therapeutic alliance remains a significant factor in reducing the risk of a client behaving in a violent manner (Pope, Simpson, & Weiner, 1978). Clients who have difficulty forming a therapeutic alliance are more likely to object to the legal and ethical limitations about protecting confidences during the informed consent process (Benjamin et al., 2009). This interaction can provide the MHP with data about whether a meaningful therapeutic alliance can be formed. If a healthy alliance does not begin to emerge early in the therapeutic relationship and before any duty to protect/warn issue might arise, carefully discuss your concerns with the client, document reasons for termination, and refer the client to other service providers. The client may form an effective, working clinical relationship with one of the referrals. Without a therapeutic alliance, it is unlikely the client will actively engage in the interventions and there is a greater chance that the client will feel a sense of abandonment or betrayal. When clients feel abandoned or betrayed, they are more likely to file ethics complaints to licensing boards and/or professional organizations and/or malpractice actions in civil courts (Benjamin et al., 1995).

Risk Assessment

The process of identifying and influencing the precipitating and inhibiting factors related to threats of violence will not work as well without the client's active engagement. If the therapeutic alliance is strong, when a client raises a threat of violence, the client more easily accepts the risk assessment process, provides releases to obtain additional data, and collaboratively engages in the necessary interventions.

Researchers have concluded that the "inexact science" of predicting violence should occur through structured risk assessments that reduce clinical judgment errors and increase the accuracy of the findings and include (Monahan, 2006; Scott & Resnick, 2006):

• A detailed, structured interview;
• An actuarial risk assessment instrument.[7]

During the session in which the threat emerges, the MHP collaborates with the client to begin to understand the possible impact of factors associated with potential violence and to determine the specific risk and how to mediate that risk. Recent literature has clustered the variables related to violence into four domains (Monahan et al., 2001). A structured interview includes specific questions about the precipitating and inhibiting data within each of the domains:

• *Dispositional variables*, including age, age of first criminal conviction, sex, personality variables involving impulsivity or those involving long-range planning abilities, and neurological factors such as closed-head injury;
• *Historical variables*, including educational level, childhood and adolescent anti-social behavior, prior convictions for violence, comparable circumstances of prior violence, pattern of unstable conflictual interpersonal relationships, substance abuse history, and history of mental hospitalization;
• *Contextual variables*, including family stability, dangerous or criminal social network, quality of social support, level of occupational responsibilities, financial resources, access and presence of weapons, and availability of victim(s); and
• *Clinical variables*, including types and symptoms of mental disorder, whether alcohol/drug use is occurring, physical warning signs, level of functioning to cope with stressors, recent changes in mood states (anger, anxiety, and sadness), day-dreams or thoughts about physically hurting or injuring someone, specificity of violent thoughts or plans, and level of intention to act on violent thoughts.

Look for corroboration between the findings of an actuarial assessment instrument and the standardized clinical interview and collateral information about the various relevant precipitating and inhibiting factors that will produce effective

---

[7] A very accessible actuarial instrument to evaluate a threat of violence against another person is the Iterative Classification Tree (Monahan et al., 2000, 2001; see the measure at http://bjp.rcpsych.org/cgi/reprint/176/4/312). It is viewed as the "instrument of choice for nonforensic" (i.e., non-criminal) clients (Harris, Rice, & Camilleri, 2004, p. 1071). Software (Classification of Violence Risk [COVR™]) also is available for processing a ten-minute structured interview and the data from a chart review (Monahan, 2006).

interventions.[8] Also obtain collateral information from key respondents or sources (e.g., prior spouses/partners, prior treatment professionals, hospital records) to better inform clinical judgments; such data will provide further multiple-measure corroboration about findings (Benjamin et al., 2009). The collateral discussions should occur with the client present so that the therapeutic alliance will not be compromised. The effective processing of any client concerns will more likely occur if the client witnesses the MHP's good faith efforts at providing help and the airing of the concerns among the people who know the client best.

Scott and Resnick (2006) recommended detailing the likely impact of each known risk variable and the management or treatment strategy to implement the violence prevention plan. On the basis of corroboration of findings from the risk assessment, the psychologist can justify the violence prevention interventions to the client as part of the assessment process in order to obtain consent to proceed and to continue to build the therapeutic alliance.

Peer Consultation

A consultation with a knowledgeable colleague is recommended for all serious ethical questions (Benjamin et al., 1995). This consultant must understand violence risk assessment in clinical practice to be useful in this context. The psychologist would convey to the consultant the salient facts about the case to corroborate whether sufficient assessment has occurred and whether the planned interventions are adequate. Once the peer consultation is obtained, the MHP should send a dated written communication to the peer that memorializes the facts relied upon by the peer, the opinions provided by the peer about the process, and the agreed approach that emerged at the time of the consultation (Benjamin et al., 2009). The peer consultation with dated documentation shows a transparent decision-making process that has taken into account the facts while meeting the standard of care at the time the threat emerged. If the complaint is filed or the psychologist is sued, this process will assist the psychologist's contention that she or he acted within the standard of care of the community. A consultation also ensures that all relevant facts of the case have been explored and helps to eliminate any missed information or blind spots the psychologist may be experiencing because of the stress of the situation.

Implement a Plan to Reduce the Risk of Violence

Link the specific interventions to precipitating and inhibiting variables and continue to assess whether each intervention works. Ongoing assessment will also allow the

---

[8] Though no instrument can be used blindly or considered infallible, combined with data from a detailed structured interview, clinical judgment errors may be more likely to be detected. On the other hand, false positives from an actuarial instrument may occur as a result of the client not being typical of the population used in the norm group. Clinical judgment about the details of precipitating factors and inhibiting factors can temper being misled by a lack of an instrument's generalizability to the particular client.

MHP and client to refocus on how to ameliorate variables that may trigger future violence. If progress has not occurred in reducing the impact of a particular precipitating variable, a midcourse correction to the original plan can result in more efficacious treatment. On the other hand, if a particular inhibiting variable seems to be working well, the MHP can focus on increasing its impact. For example, if the client reports that a definite reduction in anger and tension follows each psychotherapy session, then maintaining or increasing the number of psychotherapeutic sessions per week would be a reasonable next step.

In some cases in which the therapeutic alliance is waning and the precipitating variables appear to be escalating, more intrusive interventions must occur. A useful approach in this context is for the MHP to suggest that an objective evaluation for involuntary treatment occurs. In some jurisdictions, such an evaluation will be conducted within the MHP's office. In other jurisdictions, a police officer can take both the MHP and the client to the facility where such evaluations are conducted. In both instances, no abandonment of the client occurs and a new treatment plan can be developed. Such a formal approach can lead to involuntary outpatient treatment with allied intensive case management being ordered. For other cases, a period of voluntary admission to the hospital or even involuntary inpatient treatment might be ordered. Both types of interventions will lead to a treatment team and the client addressing whether continued treatment of the client by the MHP should occur subsequent to the hospitalization or commitment. The use of such a process can insulate the MHP from liability in many jurisdictions and end the need for the MHP to manage the legal risk.

Documentation

Documenting the rationale and procedures of the evaluation and treatment of the client must be thorough. The extraordinary event of disclosing a threat of violence to appropriate authorities requires this level of documentation to show what kind of threat prompted the MHP's disclosure, how that threat was assessed, and that the MHP acted in a prudent manner (Benjamin et al., 1995). The documentation about the evaluation and intervention is strengthened by the inclusion of the dated peer consultation notes. Documentation could include direct quotes from the client about the threat, the results from the structured risk assessment, a listing of the precipitating and inhibiting factors about the threatened violence, and an analysis about how to manage the risk in light of all those factors. Every subsequent action related to the management plan requires dated documentation. For example, documentation of the written releases to talk with collateral witnesses and their views about the context can bolster the reliability of the data collected from the client directly. Forwarding brief, written narratives to the collaterals and asking whether they have any other facts to add can also increase the reliability of the data. As the risk is lowered, the evidence establishing the diminution of the risk should also be documented and dated.

Psychotherapist–Client Privilege, Jaffee v. Redmond

In 1991, on-duty police officer Redmond responded to a call regarding a fight in progress at an apartment complex in suburban Chicago. Officer Redmond repeatedly ordered Mr. Allen to drop the butcher knife he was wielding, but Mr. Allen did not do so. Believing Mr. Allen was about to stab another man with the butcher knife, Officer Redmond shot Mr. Allen, who died at the scene. The administrator of Mr. Allen's estate, Ms. Jaffee, sued Officer Redmond in Federal District Court, alleging Officer Redmond violated Mr. Allen's constitutional rights by using excessive force. As part of the pretrial process, Ms. Jaffee learned that Officer Redmond received 50 counseling sessions from a licensed clinical social worker, Ms. Beyer, and requested copies of the notes taken during those sessions. Officer Redmond refused to provide the necessary consents for Ms. Beyer to provide the notes to Ms. Jaffee, arguing psychotherapist–patient privilege, which she asserted Ms. Beyer had to uphold. The District Court judge allowed the request by Ms. Jaffee, but Officer Redmond and Ms. Beyer did not comply. The District Court judge advised the jury that Officer Redmond's refusal to allow Ms. Beyer's notes to be disclosed could be used against her and the jury should presume that the content of the notes would have been unfavorable to Officer Redmond. The jury then awarded Ms. Jaffee $545 000 in damages. Officer Redmond appealed the case and the Court of Appeals for the Seventh Circuit reversed and remanded for a new trial, concluding that the psychotherapist–patient privilege should be recognized.

This decision is important for both substantive and symbolic reasons (Mosher & Swire, 2002). It is substantive in that it is an absolute privilege, meaning that it is not subject to any balancing by trial court judges of the needs of the justice system against the privilege afforded psychotherapy clients. It is symbolic in that this case served as a turning point in the expression of a societal understanding that confidentiality in psychotherapy is so important that other compelling considerations should give way (Mosher & Swire, 2002).

In *Jaffee v. Redmond* (*518 U.S. 1* [1996]), the U.S. Supreme Court emphasized the crucial nature of maintaining a high degree of psychotherapy–client confidentiality within treatment cases and found that within federal cases privilege existed in psychotherapy–client relationships. In *Jaffee*, the question arose as to whether the confidential treatment records and testimony of the clinician were discoverable. The Court held that "confidential communications between a licensed psychotherapist and her patients in the course of diagnosis or treatment are protected from compelled disclosure. . ." (*Jaffee, 518 U.S. at 15*).

In *Jaffee*, the plaintiff (the administrator of the estate of the person killed) sought disclosures about the contents of the client police officer's psychotherapy sessions, the defendant in the case. The social worker that was treating the defendant relied upon her ethical standards and refused either to submit treatment records or to answer questions during a deposition. The lower court judge found that the clinician's refusals to provide records or testimony had no "legal justification."

The Supreme Court upheld the Court of Appeals' reversal of the lower court's ruling after a thorough review of the long history of privilege in other types of relationships. It also was influenced by several compelling empirical research studies that were discussed within *amicus* briefs submitted by the APA and the American Psychiatric Association. The Supreme Court clearly embraced the research findings that:

- Psychotherapy clients had a strong expectation of confidentiality;
- Confidentiality is essential for the success of psychotherapy;
- Society has a strong interest in fostering psychotherapeutic relationships and in protecting client privacy;
- The benefits of psychotherapeutic privilege outweigh its costs.

The Supreme Court noted that some form of psychotherapist–patient privilege existed within all 50 states. It also recognized that variations for protecting the confidences of mental health treatment existed within several jurisdictions, but ultimately concluded that such "limited" variations did not eviscerate the need for such protection. Indeed, every jurisdiction has delineated the extent of confidentiality and when and how third parties, such as lawyers, engaged in legal actions involving psychotherapy clients can obtain treatment records and testimony from MHPs (Benjamin, Luini, & Younggren, 2013).

The Supreme Court did not want to deter the purposes of state legislation and the enactments of confidentiality protections. Instead, the Supreme Court recognized that such protections served numerous important purposes, including:

> Effective psychotherapy, by contrast, depends upon an atmosphere of confidence and trust in which the patient is willing to make a frank and complete disclosure of facts, emotions, memories, and fears. Because of the sensitive nature of the problems for which individuals consult psychotherapists, disclosure of confidential communications made during counseling sessions may cause embarrassment or disgrace. For this reason, the mere possibility of disclosure may impede development of the confidential relationship necessary for successful treatment. (*Jaffee, 518 U.S. at 10*)

Not only in the federal courts but also within most state and provincial jurisdictions of North America are MHPs obligated to protect the privileges of their clients (Glosoff, Herlihy, Herlihy, & Spence, 1997). Unless a release is provided or a court has issued an order requiring the MHP to release information, MHPs must protect their client's privilege. It is becoming increasing common in many different types of cases for MHPs to be pressed by lawyers to protect the privileges of their clients. These cases include those involving:

- Child evaluation and treatment cases;
- Couples' evaluation and psychotherapy cases;
- Adult evaluation and psychotherapy cases related to job issues;
- Elder adult evaluation and psychotherapy cases; and
- Criminal cases.

The MHP is both obligated to protect the client by not releasing the requested information and simultaneously obligated to respond to the lawyer's *subpoena duces tecum*.

Practical Approach to Meeting the Duty

Any subpoena requires a timely answer. Typically, a lawyer will send a subpoena to obtain information related to the litigation. Although many subpoenas are written in a manner that strikes MHPs as threatening, it is merely a legal notice that information is being sought and is expected to be delivered within a certain time period. In most instances, the client has alerted the MHP about the litigation and a release has been provided. When a sufficient release is provided, records should be released. However, in some cases, the MHP's client has not provided a release to the information and wants the privilege protected.

Psychologists establish relationships of trust with those with whom they work (APA, 2010, Principle B). Maintaining client confidentiality is one way in which psychologists enact the principle of fidelity. As directed by the Code of Conduct (APA, 2010, Standards 4.01 and 4.05), psychologists protect client information and do not release information unless the client has provided the psychologist with the appropriate consent to release confidential information. The MHP should contact the client regarding the lawyer's request for information and document the effort at making contact and how the client responded.

In contacting the client, the MHP should take the opportunity to clarify the reasons for confidentiality, the treatment rational behind privilege, and the possible harm that might arise from an unspecified authorization to release confidential information. Informed consent to all aspects of the treatment relationship is best maintained through repeated review of each treatment activity as it occurs. Most clients are not fully aware of the amount of information an MHP holds and the extent to which confidential information might travel should such privilege not be asserted. The MHP should discuss with the client alternatives to compliance with a subpoena.

If a court order directs the release of the records, respond by releasing the records as directed by the court order signed by the judge in the case. If the document is a subpoena, treat it as a notice, and always reply. Subpoenas have a timeline within which the MHPs must respond. Though it is imperative that the MHP provides a response to the lawyer within the time limit, their response does not require releasing the information as requested in the subpoena. The MHP may refuse to comply with the subpoena based upon the laws regulating the MHP within the state or provincial jurisdiction. The MHP also may specify a course of action for the lawyer to follow rather than following any of the directives within the subpoena. The MHP would do so by preparing a written response to the subpoena in the form of an affidavit or declaration. Using the appropriate legal form of the MHP's jurisdiction would protect against perjury or contempt being charged. The affidavit or declaration would convey the rationale for not releasing the records.[ii] This course of action should be sent to all of the lawyers in the case and the clerk of the judge. It shows that the MHP is acting in good faith and serves as an inexpensive option to moving to quash the subpoena. This latter option requires appearing at a hearing and should occur with a lawyer representing the MHP. Often the approach of submitting the affidavit or declaration will satisfy the judge and the MHP will not have to personally appear.

Obtain consultation to review the affidavit or declaration before sending it to all of the lawyers involved in the case and the clerk of the judge. Do not consider any lawyer or any psychologist as equally knowledgeable when obtaining consultation. Call the volunteer specialists who serve in your state, provincial, and territorial association ethics committees, or a J.D./Ph.D.-trained clinical psychologist in your jurisdiction who know the nuances of the laws related to psychological practice in your jurisdiction. Often the MHP's malpractice carrier will provide consultation.

Put in the chart the facts relied upon by the consultant and the opinions provided and forward the consultation note to the consultant. The consultation shows a transparent decision-making process while attempting to meet the ethical and the legal standards of care. Such an action seems to decrease the risk of ethics complaints or lawsuits, and if a complaint is filed or the MHP is sued, it can help to bolster the MHP's contention that she or he acted prudently at the time. If your client is not reachable, make a note in the chart. MHPs still are obligated to protect their clients' privileges, whether or not the client can be found.

Practice Tips from the Three Cases

The three cases above demonstrate how judicial decisions in a court create common law, which then cascades into significant changes in law governing how MHPs practice. From the three cases there are several practice tips that span the three types of scenarios with dangerous or abusive clinical contexts. The major ethical issues in all of the cases revolve around duties of confidentiality, sustaining a therapeutic relationship, adequate assessment of the issue at hand, and avoiding multiple relationships in cases likely involving court actions. Confidentiality in all cases is based on the foundation of informed consent, essentially providing the client with information concerning when and under what conditions a therapist will and will not be able to maintain confidentiality. First, within the informed consent process, an MHP should clearly state both in writing and orally the limits of confidentiality. This information then provides the basis of trust for a client in therapy. The client can then determine what to discuss based on this information. Clients who are surprised by their therapists' actions are more likely to feel abandoned and betrayed. At the least, the therapeutic alliance becomes sullied, and at the worst, such strong feelings can drive ethics complaints or negligence charges. Second, a therapist should maintain the confidentiality of a client and protect disclosures even if pressured by lawyers or a court.

If early in the therapeutic process a strong therapeutic alliance does not develop, the MHP is advised to discuss this with the client and refer them to other professionals. Without a strong therapeutic alliance, the client will likely not make progress and the MHP will be vulnerable to complaints. If a strong therapeutic alliance is developed, later in therapy if a client discloses information that triggers either a mandatory report to Child Protective Services or further action to protect a potential victim, the MHP can remind the client of the limits discussed and work therapeutically with the client in making the report or determining the best course of action. A strong therapeutic alliance will provide the basis in trust for the MHP and client to move forward.

Clients can be involved in a variety of legal matters, some of which may then involve the MHP's records and/or require testimony in court. There are several steps an MHP can take to protect their client and themselves from intrusion into the therapeutic relationship. First, it is imperative that MHPs know their professional ethics codes and that they stay up to date with laws in their jurisdiction. These include state statutes and administrative rules and the common law that apply to an MHP's practice. Statutes, rules, and common law are difficult to find for an MHP; therefore, it is advised that the MHP accesses resources through their state or province licensing board, malpractice insurance provider, their professional associations, and/or a knowledgeable lawyer with training in mental health issues in your jurisdiction.

In addition, it is important that an MHP understands their role and stays within it if lawyers contact the MHP. Treating MHPs are not forensic evaluators, and knowing the difference between these roles will provide the basis for declining involvement in litigation.

Finally, transparency in decision-making processes with dated memorialization to all parties involved will provide the necessary documentation if a court pressures an MHP to testify or a licensing board or criminal complaint is filed by one of the parties. Documentation of a thoughtful, careful decision-making process will impress a judge who may be asked to order the release of records and force testimony from a treating clinician. Both a stipulation and the declaration (or affidavit) that describes the therapist's practice standards will lead to most judges protecting the confidentiality of the treatment process.

Notes

i. An example of such a stipulation follows:

STIPULATION OF (Names of the couple)

THIS STIPULATION is entered into between (Names of any adults who may likely seek your testimony or your records), and they declare and agree to the following:

1) All communications among the parties, their child, and the Psychologist (insert your name here) will be confidential and privileged from disclosure;

2) Both parties agree that (insert your name here) will not be required to testify at or to produce for any proceeding or in any court, opinions, records, documents, or recordings formed or created as part of the psychotherapy process;

3) It is in the best interests of the child and the parties that no one feels influenced by any impending legal action when involved in psychotherapy;

4) Without the parties entering into this type of stipulation, it is quite likely that the therapeutic alliance would be affected detrimentally;

5) Empirical research has demonstrated that if clients of mental health services are assured of confidentiality, they are more willing to respond to personal inquiries

and are more honest in their responses during psychotherapeutic evaluation and treatment;

6) As a society we want our mental health professionals to protect the confidences of our clients unless a few very specific limitations should arise. Destroying the privileged communication protection for psychologist and client communications would prevent effective therapeutic interventions from occurring;

7) This stipulation does not preclude obeying the statutory requirements to report information about: child, adult dependent person or elder abuse, neglect or exploitation; an actual threat of violence against a reasonably identifiable victim(s); or mental illness that requires involuntary commitment because of danger to self or others or grave disability;

8) These stipulations have been explained to us and we agree to abide by them. We have been provided ample opportunity to inquire into the experience and credentials of the Psychologist and have consulted with our lawyers or other Psychotherapists about these stipulations. We are fully satisfied with the proposed approach to protecting our confidences from disclosure for the purposes of any legal process.

We certify under penalty of perjury under the laws of Washington that the foregoing is true and correct, and mutually agreed upon.

_____   _____
One parent   The other parent

Date_____   Date_____

ii. An example of such a declaration follows:

IN THE SUPERIOR COURT OF THE STATE OF WASHINGTON

FOR KING COUNTY

Whoever,	)
	)
	)
Plaintiff,	)
	)
v.	) No. cause number here
	)
	) DECLARATION OF
	) your name, your degree
Whoever	)
	)
Defendant.	)
	)

Your name declares the following:

1. I am licensed to practice as a psychologist in the State of Washington;

2. My practice involves evaluating and treating children with mental health problems at_____;

3. RCW 71.05.630(2) establishes a clear duty on the part of mental health professionals to not release confidential records unless a court order compels disclosure because of certain narrow exceptions;

4. Ms. LAWYER apparently is seeking disclosure of clinical records by applying the Health Care Information Act (Chapter 70.02 RCW);

5. RCW 70.02.900(2) specifically states that the act does not modify the terms or conditions of disclosure when Chapter 71.05 RCW applies;

6. To permit the statements made to a psychologist to be disclosed without careful consideration by a judge would be detrimental to the purposes of mental health services;

7. If mental health professionals were obligated to disclose the confidences of those seeking mental health services in all types of civil litigation without judicial review, such an obligation would violate the basic value of confidentiality that promotes psychotherapeutic evaluation and treatment;

8. The concept of privileged communications is based on the theory that the release of confidential information will restrict the open and necessary communication between the professional and the client. Without a court order directing the release of records, the value of full disclosure between mental health professionals and their clients outweighs the potential benefit to justice that might occur if testimony or the release of confidential information was required;

9. Empirical research has demonstrated that if clients of mental health services were assured of confidentiality, they were more willing to respond to personal inquiries and were more honest in their responses;

10. As a society we want our mental health professionals to protect the confidences of our clients unless a few very specific limitations should arise. Destroying the privileged communication protection for mental health professional and client communications would prevent effective therapeutic intervention from occurring in many cases;

11. Ms. LAWYER has not sought a court order, nor has she proven that the records she seeks should be disclosed because of the narrow exceptions created under the law.

I declare under penalty of the laws of the State of Washington that the foregoing is true and correct.

DATED at Seattle, Washington, whenever, 20XX

Your name, degree

References

American Psychological Association (2010). Ethical principles of psychologists and code of conduct. Retrieved from www.apa.org/ethics/code/principles.pdf

Benjamin, G. A. H., Rosenwald, L., Overcast, T., & Feldman, S. B. (1995). *Law and mental health professionals: Washington*. Washington, DC: American Psychological Association.

Benjamin, G. A. H., Kent, L., & Sirikantraporn, S. (2009). Duty to protect statutes. In J. L. Werth, E. R. Welfel, & G. A. H. Benjamin (Eds.), *The duty to protect:*

Ethical, legal, and professional responsibilities of mental health professionals (pp. 9–28). Washington, DC: American Psychological Association.

Benjamin, G. A. H., Luini, C., & Younggren, J.N. (2013). The duty to record: Ethical, legal, and professional considerations. Retrieved from www.apadivisions.org/division-31/publications/index.aspx

Caudill, O. B. & Kaplan, A. I. (2005). Protecting privacy and confidentiality. In S. F. Bucky, J. E. Callan, & G. Stricker (Eds.), *Ethical and legal issues for mental health professionals: A comprehensive handbook of principles and standards* (pp. 117–134). Binghamton, NY: Haworth Maltreatment and Trauma Press/The Haworth Press.

Children's Bureau (2014). *Definitions of child abuse and neglect.* Child Welfare Information Gateway. Retrieved from www.acf.hhs.gov/cb/resource/child-maltreatment-2014

Cross, T. P., Mathews, B., Tonmyr, L., Scott, D., & Quimet, C. (2012). Child welfare policy and practice on children's exposure to domestic violence. *Child Abuse & Neglect, 36*, 210–216.

Fischer, C. B. & Orlandky, M. (2008). Informed consent to psychotherapy: Protecting the dignity and respecting the autonomy of patients. *Journal of Clinical Psychology, 64*, 576–588.

Glosoff, H. L., Herlihy, S. B., Herlihy, B., & Spence, E. B. (1997). Privileged communication in the psychologist client relationship. *Professional Psychology: Research and Practice, 28*, 573–581.

Harris, G. T., Rice, M. E., & Camilleri, J. A. (2004). Applying a forensic actuarial assessment (the violence risk appraisal guide to nonforensic patients). *Journal of Interpersonal Violence, 19*, 1063–1074.

Kalichman, S. C. (1999). *Mandated reporting of suspected child abuse: Ethics, law, and policy* (2nd edn.). Washington, DC: American Psychological Association.

Lamb, M. E., Orbach, Y., Hershkowitz, I., Esplin, P. W., & Horowitz, D. (2007). A structured forensic interview protocol improves the quality and informativeness of investigative interviews with children: A review of research using the NICHD Investigative Interview Protocol. *Child Abuse & Neglect, 31*, 1201–1231.

L. A. R. v. Marie Rose Ludwig, 821 P.2d 291.

Monahan, J. (2006). *Tarasoff* at thirty: How developments in science and policy shape the common law. *University of Cincinnati Law Review, 75*, 497–521.

Monahan, J., Steadman, H., Appelbaum, P., et al. (2000). Developing a clinically useful actuarial tool for assessing violence risk. *British Journal of Psychiatry, 176*, 312–319. [See Iterative Classification Tree at http://bjp.rcpsych.org/cgi/reprint/176/4/312]

Monahan, J., Steadman, H., Silver, E., et al. (2001). *Rethinking risk assessment: The MacArthur Study of Mental Disorder and Violence.* New York, NY: Oxford University Press.

Mosher, P. W. & Swire, P. P. (2002). The ethical and legal implications of *Jaffee v Redmond* and the HIPAA medical privacy rule for psychotherapy and general psychiatry. *Psychiatric Clinics of North America, 25*, 575–584.

Pabian, Y., Welfel, E. R., & Beebe, R. S. (2009). Psychologists' knowledge of their state laws pertaining to Tarasoff-type situations. *Professional Psychology: Research and Practice, 40*, 8–14.

Pope, K. S., Simpson, M. H., & Weiner, N. F. (1978). Malpractice in outpatient psychotherapy. *American Journal of Psychotherapy, 32*, 593–602.

Scott, C. L. & Resnick, P. J. (2006). Violence risk assessment in persons with mental illness. *Aggression and Violent Behavior, 11*, 598–611.

Shelman, E. A. & Lazoritz, S. (2005). *The Mary Ellen Wilson child abuse case and the beginning of children's rights in 19th century America.* Jefferson, NC: McFarland & Company.

Stark, E. (2005). Nicholson V. Williams revisited: When good people do bad things. *Denver Law Review, 82*, 691.

Tarasoff v. Regents of the University of California, 13 Cal.3d 117, 529 P.2d 553 (1974).

Tarasoff v. Regents of University of California. 551 P.2d 334 (1976).

Waitzkin, H. (1984). Doctor–patient communication: Clinical implications of social scientific research. *JAMA, 252*, 2441–2446.

Walcott, D. M., Cerundolo, P., & Beck, J. C. (2001). Current analysis of the Tarasoff duty: An evolution towards the limitation of the duty to protect. *Behavioral Sciences and the Law, 19*, 325–343.

Weithorn, L. A. (2001). Protecting children from exposure to domestic violence: The use and abuse of child maltreatment. *Hastings Law Journal, 53*, 1–156.

Welfel, E. R., Werth, J. L., & Benjamin, G. A. H. (2012). Clients who threaten others or themselves. In S. Knapp, M. M. Gottlieb, & L. VandeCreek (Eds.), *APA handbook of ethics in psychology* (Vol. 2, pp. 377–400). Washington, DC: American Psychological Association.

22 Ethical Considerations in Forensic Evaluations in Family Court

Robert Geffner, Morgan Shaw, and Brittany Crowell

A growing number of child protection and family law cases require that a mental health professional conducts some type of psychological evaluation for the court in order to make a determination and/or recommendation regarding the best interests of a child. These mental health professionals should have extensive training and specific expertise in the areas of child and adult psychopathology, child development, attachment, trauma, forensic, and family psychology, as well as in the relevant legal and ethical standards and guidelines. Psychologists who work as forensic evaluators should also have training and expertise in psychological assessment including, but not limited to, personality measures, parenting measures, measures of emotional functioning, trauma assessment, and risk assessment. All of this training and expertise should be used appropriately to provide valuable sources of information and perspectives that may not otherwise be available to the court. As such, these types of forensic evaluations can help guide legal decision-making and have a profound impact on a child's life and the welfare of a family.

Forensic psychological evaluations regarding child protection matters are usually ordered by the court or a child protection agency and, depending on the jurisdiction, typically take place in either the family court system or the juvenile dependency system. Most often in child protection matters, mental health professionals are asked to evaluate parties to assess their psychological, emotional, and/or cognitive functioning in order to help answer specific referral questions. Most commonly, mental health professionals are asked to make specific custody recommendations, assess abuse allegations, provide removal or placement recommendations, and/or recommend appropriate intervention options for either parents or children.

Child protection matters, particularly in child custody evaluations, are the fastest-growing source of ethics complaints made against mental health professionals (Bucky & Callan, 2014; Greenberg, Martindale, Gould, & Gould-Saltman, 2004). In these types of cases, it is not difficult to imagine why one or more parties would be upset with the results and recommendations of an evaluator. While a percentage of the ethics complaints are likely made by a disgruntled parent or family member hoping to discredit the evaluator and the evaluation determinations, a likely larger percentage results from professionals possibly exceeding the boundaries of their competence, making determinations outside of the scope of their data points and information base, violating role boundaries, and/or using inappropriate evaluation procedures or techniques (Bucky & Callan, 2014). There are a number of professional organizations that have established standards or guidelines for child protection evaluations including the American Psychological Association's (APA; 2002, 2010) Ethical Principles of Psychologists and Code of Conduct, the Specialty Guidelines for Forensic Psychology (American Psychological Association, 2013b), and the Guidelines for Psychological Evaluations in Child Protection Matters (APA, 2013a). Furthermore, other important guidelines have been authored by various organizations, including the American Professional Society on the Abuse of Children's (APSAC) Guidelines for Psychosocial Evaluation of Suspected Sexual Abuse in Young Children (1990) and the Association of Family and Conciliation Courts' (AFCC) Model Standards of Practice for Child Custody Evaluation (2006). There are also standards for other mental health professionals that govern ethical conduct when in practice, regardless of the role, such as the National Association of Social Workers' (2008) Code of Ethics and the American Psychiatric Association's (2013) Principles of Medical Ethics of the American Medical Association. While the guidelines can help provide guidance to evaluators as to the appropriate evaluation procedures, they are often not exhaustive or adequately regulated. Further, guidelines are aspirational in nature, and thus are not required practice.

Mental health professionals who use inappropriate evaluation procedures can end up generating unreliable or biased information about the functioning of individuals. If the court then relies on this distorted information in their legal decision-making, serious harm can be caused to the children and the families. As such, evaluators critiquing the work of other evaluators, particularly in the case of child custody evaluations, has become increasingly common within the forensic field (Kirkpatrick, Austin, & Flens, 2011; Pepiton, Zelgowski, Geffner, & Pegolo de Albuquerque, 2014). The authors of this chapter regularly review other professionals' evaluations and reports and too often come across serious and blatant ethical violations. These individuals are oftentimes well respected in one of the mental health fields and hold impressive credentials and positions of authority. The severity of the ethical violations we have come across range from minor negligence to much more serious offenses such as misrepresenting one's credentials or experience, dismissing abuse allegations without a thorough investigation, basing opinions and conclusions on discredited myths that are not well accepted in the field, distorting or misrepresenting test data, or being blatantly biased toward one party. We are hoping that with this chapter we can bring awareness to these types of ethical violations we come across around the country in order to bring attention to the significant negative impacts they are having on the lives of families, as well as provide more sufficient training to new and practicing evaluators.

In this chapter, some of the more common ethical mistakes we have come across are outlined in various vignettes. This is by no means an exhaustive list of all the different types of ethical violations that are possible and prevalent, but instead is meant to draw attention to some of the overarching areas that are commonly seen. APA Ethics Code standards will be included when appropriate, as well as guidelines from other ethics documents. The major areas that we will discuss include practicing outside the scope of one's competency, role conflicts and boundary violations, preconceived or inaccurate notions and beliefs, and lastly misrepresentation of test data and biased evaluation procedures. The underlying theme throughout the entire list of ethical violations that we will discuss is how those violations can, and typically do, lead to biased evaluation determinations and inappropriate recommendations about child custody and/or visitation arrangements. These biased opinions and conclusions then inevitably leave the legal decision-maker with distorted or inaccurate information when assigning dispositions that significantly affect the lives of children and families. We will conclude this chapter with specific guidelines and recommendations for best practices in conducting forensic evaluations in child protection or family law matters.

Exceeding the Boundaries of Competence

Presumably, few mental health professionals would knowingly practice in an area with full awareness that they lacked competence or ability. However, with the ever-growing involvement of mental health in court-related matters, often clinicians find themselves working on multidimensional forensic cases. They may begin their work with the best of intentions, but quickly find themselves stretching the scope of their expertise, working in areas they *believe* they are *adequately* knowledgeable in. Quickly, they may find themselves practicing beyond their scope of competence, being that there are many aspects of forensic cases involved with the court system that differ from those of traditional mental health training.

Being competent in such areas of practice is exceptionally important when the court relies on mental health professionals' opinions in making life-changing determinations. Due to such increased potential for causing harm in court-related matters, some authors have argued that psychologists who practice in the realm of forensic work should be expected to demonstrate and hold the "highest level" of professional competence and ethical practice (Greenberg & Gould, 2001). Arguably, work in the forensic realm does require a broader knowledge base, as professionals must be familiar with: (1) state law and applicable court rules for the type of proceeding in which they are providing services; (2) research relevant to the population and issues of concern; and (3) ethical and professional standards relevant to forensic psychology, in addition to knowledge of the specific psychological issues at hand (Greenberg & Gould, 2001).

In order to better guide court-related practice regarding family law or child protection matters, the APA has produced Guidelines for Psychological Evaluations in Child Protection Matters (APA, 2013a), as noted above. Such guidelines are self-described as "aspirational in intent" (APA, 2013a) and are intended to facilitate the continued development of professional work in this field. Strategically, the APA has depicted various guidelines to adequately direct care. Guideline 5 deals particularly with the topic of competence and will be stressed throughout this section of the chapter. APA Ethics Code, Standard 2.01 states: "psychologists provide services ... in areas only within the boundaries of their competence." However, it is permissible for one who is not yet competent to conduct the evaluation under the supervision of or in a consulting relationship with a colleague who is competent. To better illustrate the importance of being competent in child protection matters, we will turn to a case example.

The Case of Dr. Doowrong

Dr. Doowrong has been in private practice for 20 years, specializing in child development and attachment. She has been involved in a number of forensic cases, most often testifying on the dynamics of child development and parent–child attachment in child protection matters. Early in her career, she underwent the state-required training for child custody evaluators and has stayed current on general research and guidelines for custody evaluators. She has also consulted and participated in a number of custody evaluations within her practice, most often speaking to the attachment dynamics at play. A partner in her practice whose primary focus was child custody evaluations recently retired, and Dr. Doowrong has started expanding her practice to take on more referrals for independent comprehensive child custody evaluations.

One day, Dr. Doowrong receives a call from Ms. Carter, a mother in need of a child custody evaluation. Dr. Doowrong took on the Carters' case, believing she would be able to assist the family in conducting the custody evaluation. Unfortunately, Dr. Doowrong did not complete a thorough initial screening of the case and the issues of concern in order to gather basic information about referral questions to determine if she was competent in all aspects of this particular case. This case was much more complex than the ones she had successfully completed in the past, including allegations of domestic violence perpetrated by the husband, as well as allegations of methamphetamine use by Ms. Carter. Dr. Doowrong is an experienced clinician; however, her experience and up-to-date knowledge is limited in the realm of substance abuse and domestic violence dynamics.

After hearing about the domestic violence and substance abuse allegations, Dr. Doowrong revisited her decision to take on the case. She felt conflicted because she was obviously experienced in child custody evaluations and has extensive training in areas that are particularly relevant for custody determinations that are in line with the best interest of the child standard. While she recognized that there were several confounding factors that she was not as well versed in regarding the Carter case that made it more complex, she still trusted her own clinical judgment and expertise to not refer the case out. She was also reminded of an article she recently read that depicted the prevalence of these types of allegations in "high-conflict" cases. She decided (without corroborating evidence) that such accusations conveyed by Ms. Carter and Mr. Carter were likely mere allegations and possible attempts to sully their ex-spouse's appearance. When Dr. Doowrong asked Ms. Carter about the allegations of abuse perpetrated by Mr. Carter, she denied having reported the abuse to anyone else and she stated she did not leave the house until her bruises had healed. Ms. Carter also dismissed Mr. Carter's allegations of methamphetamine use and denied having ever experimented with drugs. Ms. Carter claimed that Mr. Carter was only making such allegations to keep her children away from her. Likewise, when confronted about the domestic violence allegations, Mr. Carter denied ever "laying a hand" on Ms. Carter and asserted that he also did not have any evidence to support his claims of substance abuse by Ms. Carter.

Dr. Doowrong decided to dismiss the claims made by both parties and only included a small section in her report titled "Unsubstantiated Allegations," where she mentioned the allegations of domestic violence and substance abuse. Dr. Doowrong noted that research suggests high prevalence rates for such allegations in child custody matters, but did not address how she further investigated either party's claims or the underlying dynamics at play in cases of domestic violence. Additionally, Dr. Doowrong did not address such allegations in her collateral interviews. Dr. Doowrong's role in this case is not necessarily that of an investigator, but it is her role to look for corroboration of such allegations if they exist in the records or interviews. If such corroboration does not exist, she must document the lack thereof. It is also important to note that she administered no questionnaires or psychological tests regarding substance abuse, trauma, or domestic violence. She also did not ask the children any questions related to the allegations, directly or indirectly, even though they may have been witnesses to either or both behaviors.

Upon submitting her final report recommending joint custody that did not really deal with the domestic violence allegations nor the substance abuse issues, Dr. Doowrong was called to testify in family court regarding her findings. Dr. Doowrong was slightly nervous, but was confident in her report and her experience. Upon taking the stand, Ms. Carter's attorney (Mr. Blindsided) goes through Dr. Doowrong's experience as a licensed psychologist, particularly her work with children and attachment. Dr. Doowrong is feeling more confident, until Mr. Blindsided begins asking more specific questions about her experience assessing for domestic violence in custody cases. He further asks her very specific questions about her knowledge on the research related to domestic violence, as well as the names of key experts in the field. Unfortunately, Dr. Doowrong is able to provide only minimal references and no up-to-date research in her answers, which leads to Mr. Blindsided becoming more aggressive in his approach with her. He then begins asking her about specific documentation and corroboration of the domestic violence allegations that are not included in her report. While Dr. Doowrong is working to remain calm in her demeanor, she is becoming obviously flustered as Mr. Blindsided begins highlighting corroborating evidence that Dr. Doowrong did not have knowledge of, or did not review, as he continues to assert that she did not conduct a thorough evaluation and repeatedly draws attention to her lack of experience in domestic violence. Mr. Blindsided is very well versed in the research on domestic violence as it relates to custody matters, and within 20 minutes has artfully picked apart Dr. Doowrong's whole report and recommendations and demonstrated her bias and lack of expertise in these specific areas. By the end, Dr. Doowrong is feeling incredibly overwhelmed and frustrated by the whole experience. The judge then calls for a recess as Mr. Blindsided makes a motion to have Dr. Doowrong's report excluded from the custody proceedings due to what he states is a lack of experience in these types of matters and an incomplete evaluation of the key issues at hand.

While we know that Dr. Doowrong had no intention of behaving unethically when she took on the Carter evaluation, it should have become clear to her that the dynamics in the case were likely outside of her scope of expertise (2.01, Boundaries of Competence). It is not uncommon for professionals, particularly those who have been in practice for a long time and have a wealth of experience, to take on these types of cases believing that they have a sufficiently solid foundation of clinical experience to manage them appropriately. In addition, it is easy for those not adequately trained to develop biases and not be current on the research. While Dr. Doowrong was more than qualified to render a professional opinion about some of the dynamics in the Carter case, contested custody cases are often very complex and require that the professionals involved have training and knowledge on all of the major factors. Dr. Doowrong was well versed and adequately trained in all of the assessment measures she administered, but she was not trained on measures outside her customary ones that were needed in this case. Her report was well written and some of her recommendations were supported by some of the facts of the case. However, she lacked the expertise on matters that dealt specifically with the dynamics of complex custody cases, domestic violence, and substance abuse.

In Dr. Doowrong's defense, such allegations of abuse, neglect, and substance abuse can occur in contested custody matters, making the role of evaluator extremely challenging. She was not wrong in initially taking the case, as conducting a custody evaluation is within her scope of expertise. The ethical concern arose as new information became available to Dr. Doowrong related to areas in which her knowledge base was more limited, and at that time she did not seek consultation nor refer the case to others with needed expertise in these issues (see also 2.04, Bases for Scientific and Professional Judgments). Because of her lack of training in these areas, she also decided not to thoroughly investigate the abuse allegations based on the assertion that these types of allegations are often false in custody cases (see 9.01, Bases for Assessments). Had Dr. Doowrong thoroughly investigated such claims, administered appropriates tests and questionnaires, asked the appropriate questions, reviewed the records carefully, and then found no substantial support, she could have included her findings (or lack thereof) in her report and would have done her due diligence in an ethical manner.

The above example focused on the traditionally assumed role of mental health professionals involved with the court, specifically one who is considered a forensic expert and conducts evaluations and/or provides expert testimony to assist the court. Although not all psychologists conduct child custody evaluations, more and more are finding themselves involved in court-related matters. Much of the literature draws a clear distinction between "forensic" and "clinical" roles, but there are areas of forensic work in which there is more of a clinical component than before. Mental health professionals are being called on to serve as mediators, parent coordinators, reunification therapists, and treating therapists for parents and children alike who are involved with the court. Authors have coined the term "hybrid treatment roles" for such professionals who find themselves requiring higher levels of competence than before in both clinical and forensic areas in order to ethically practice (Greenberg & Gould, 2001).

In fulfilling such roles ethically, the mental health professional should have education, training, experience, and/or supervision in various areas as mentioned above, as well as specific expertise in the assessment and dynamics of alleged child abuse and domestic violence, substance abuse, the impact of divorce on children, and the complex dynamics of custody evaluations. While it appears that Dr. Doowrong may have read articles that outline such topics, it is a far stretch from being deemed an expert equipped to handle such complex cases. Such knowledge and experience is not only recommended, but necessary in order to work effectively in forensic cases (Association of Family and Conciliation Courts [AFCC], 2006; Kelly & Lamb, 2000). Experts are generally assumed to have extensive experience in these areas and do more than merely read articles. Some states, like California, have additional appointment requirements for child custody evaluators, and it is the evaluator's responsibility to be aware of and meet such criteria. The mental health professional should always conduct an initial screening prior to accepting child custody or other forensic cases to ensure they are competent to complete the evaluation (AFCC, 2006; APA, 2002, 2010; Pepiton et al., 2014). If unable to gain the required experience/ knowledge or seek consultation or supervision in the timeframe for the expected evaluation, it is imperative for the evaluator to refer the case to someone with the appropriate credentials and experience (Pepiton et al., 2014). Mental health professionals should also be well read and familiar with *current* research on the above-mentioned topics.

Role Confusion/Role Conflict

More frequently, ethical complaints result from a role boundary violation (3.05, Multiple Relationships). When mental health professionals become involved in the realm of forensic work, their role is understandably more confusing than if they were to work in one domain. Given the guidelines and albeit limited structure mentioned in prior sections above, there are quite a few ways in which roles can become blurred. One example that we have seen is that of an evaluator acting more in a therapist or advocate role at the same time as conducting the forensic evaluation. Arguably, mental health is a profession that appeals to compassionate individuals who want to help. When court appointed as an evaluator, there is no "compassion switch" to just turn off, allowing one to merely focus on assessments. We are not suggesting that mental health professionals who primarily work with assessments should lack compassion, but it is a different approach one takes in forensic evaluations from when one is working clinically. To better illustrate the importance of role awareness and proper boundaries in child protection matters, we will turn to a case example.

The Case of Dr. Blurr

Dr. Blurr is a well-known and widely respected social worker who owns a private clinical practice where he works primarily with families and frequently conducts court-appointed child custody evaluations. Having worked in the realm of forensics for many years, Dr. Blurr is a provider who often offers competent and impartial opinions with direct relevance to the best interests of the child. When he is called by Ms. Conflikt with a referral for a child custody evaluation, he does not hesitate to accept and begin his initial screening with the parents to ensure he would be a good fit. Dr. Blurr schedules evaluation days for both parents separately and then schedules a day to see the family together. Child custody evaluations require a great deal of time and hours with both parties, as well as collateral sources, to fully understand the family dynamic and the best possible resolution for the child. After numerous sessions with Mr. Conflikt, Dr. Blurr soon finds himself being able to relate to Mr. Conflikt's description of his tumultuous relationship with his ex-wife and her "continual nagging." Dr. Blurr has recently undergone a similar divorce with his ex-wife.

Appropriately, Dr. Blurr seeks consultation and goes to one session to process his countertransference so that he may proceed to work with the Conflikts and provide the court with a neutral report. Despite Dr. Blurr's insight and due diligence in seeking consultation, he has spent roughly 15 more hours with Mr. Conflikt than he has with Ms. Conflikt, and also had a couple of additional conversations with his attorney that were not divulged to the other attorney or court. Dr. Blurr rationalizes that Mr. Conflikt was in a great deal of turmoil and required more attention than did Ms. Conflikt, and he needed to help his attorney understand this. Dr. Blurr did attempt to refer Mr. Conflikt to a therapist and stated that would be a recommendation he made in his evaluation, but Mr. Conflikt stated he "didn't have time for therapy and was much more comfortable talking to Dr. Blurr." More appropriately, Dr. Blurr should have reiterated his role as evaluator and not therapist to Mr. Conflikt and encouraged him to see a therapist to help him navigate through this difficult time in his life. Having two roles is a violation of accepted practice, and Dr. Blurr's typical protocol as his standard assessment procedure is to spend about the same amount of time with both parents. If, in fact, he finds himself having spent more time with one parent, he usually will explain the disparity to the other parent and offer them the same amount of time to discuss any material relevant to the case. However, he did not do so in this case and he made this decision without consultation.

Dr. Blurr allowed his role as a child custody evaluator to become blurred when he took more of a therapeutic or advocate approach while working with the father. This behavior was likely well intentioned, although quite inappropriate. When Dr. Blurr's evaluation was critiqued, which as noted above has become increasingly common within the forensic field (Kirkpatrick, Austin, & Flens, 2011; Pepiton et al., 2014), the subtle bias toward the father was noted in his report. In this case, Dr. Blurr's billing sheets were not requested by the party critiquing the evaluation he conducted. However, such would be acceptable and is an encouraged practice by good attorneys due to the necessity to ensure equality and rule out biases. Had they obtained the billing, it would have been quite clear that Dr. Blurr was spending significantly more time with Mr. Conflikt as well as his attorney and had not disclosed this to the other attorney or court. In reviewing the actual notes of each session (which could be subpoenaed), it was clear that Dr. Blurr was talking to Mr. Conflikt regularly about his situation with his wife and his frustrations in dealing with the divorce and court process. It also appeared that no additional information relevant to the child custody evaluation was obtained, and that Dr. Blurr was providing information to the husband about his court case and divorce that would be much more appropriate from an advocate or possibly from a therapist. Dr. Blurr billed for $3000 more for his additional time with Mr. Conflikt and his attorney. This information leads to the conclusion of a dual relationship and bias.

While Dr. Blurr initially recognized some of his own countertransference issues and how these were likely impacting his ability to remain objective, his brief consultation was not enough to manage the conflict. A motion to exclude his report could have been made by Ms. Conflikt's attorney had the critiquing party been thorough in their evaluation of Dr. Blurr's report and billing. Additionally, based on the practices of Dr. Blurr, an ethics complaint could have easily been filed with the state board and his credibility could have been called in question. While it is not uncommon to notice oneself beginning to align with one party in these types of cases, particularly when one party appears to be poorly suited to parent or is exhibiting some of their own pathology during the evaluation, it is paramount that evaluators remain objective in rendering their professional opinion and not let their own personal biases cloud their recommendations. Further, it is necessary that child custody evaluators keep track of the hours they spend with each parent and their respective attorneys and use their data as a way to monitor their own interactions to ensure equality (6.01, Documentation of Professional and Scientific Work and Maintenance of Records; 6.04, Fees and Financial Arrangements). Another critical aspect to monitor in an ongoing manner is one's own family-of-origin issues, personality biases, and personal interests (2.06, Personal Problems and Conflicts), as well as the importance of having a stable current family situation in order to avoid undue countertransference issues (Zimmerman et al., 2009). Much like Dr. Blurr's case, his own issues and so being able to relate to a tumultuous divorce and the current situation of Mr. Conflikt quickly became a court and ethical issue. This type of dual relationship can lead to potentially disastrous results professionally (Pipes, Holstein, & Aguirre, 2005). Being aware of one's own blind spots and countertransference issues when a client does not meet our expectations or behaves in a manner that does not fit our stereotypes is easier said than done. Thus, there is a need for securing consultation and having others review procedures and possibly our reports to see if a neutral professional might spot such a bias. It is also very important for evaluators to clearly state their role and responsibility to all parties at the outset and maintain the same role with a particular case. Later becoming a therapist for one of the parties, a parent coordinator, or taking on a new role can be quite problematic, especially without the informed consent of all parties and their attorneys.

Additionally, this example illustrates the need for third parties to pay attention to all details that could affect the case. If hours are properly documented, which typically is due to the fact that professionals want to get paid for their work, invoices are a fairly simple way to check how much time is spent with each party during an evaluation. Oftentimes, it is easy to overlook these type of details if the finalized report seems straightforward and does not overtly appear to be biased. Unfortunately, many professionals are exceptional report writers and are able to disguise overt bias despite their multiple relationships with or biased opinions of evaluated parties.

One of the most valuable aspects of our forensic work is the team approach we take in working on cases. Regardless of who takes the lead on cases, we discuss weekly any changes in the cases or overarching issues in conceptualizing. Differing perspectives are welcomed and all conclusions are challenged in an atmosphere that leads to critical self-observation and professional growth. This double check helps avoid dual relationships and points out possible countertransference and biased assumptions. Often, discussing a case has allowed the lead evaluator to approach issues and interpret the case from various perspectives, leading to the most thorough and unbiased report possible.

Preconceived Notions Leading to Biased Evaluations

Let us now turn to what can likely be considered a more blatant example of ethical misconduct. Unfortunately, in our work, we often come across evaluators who allow their own preconceived notions or biases to affect their ability to conduct an objective and thorough evaluation. Further, in line with previous sections, these same evaluators often allow their lack of knowledge and training to affect their ability to make accurate and research-driven determinations. The following case example will better illustrate these ethical considerations.

The Case of Dr. Swayd

Dr. Swayd is an early-career psychologist who has been trying to build a forensic practice specializing in the evaluation of child protection matters. She has done most of her training under a psychologist who focuses solely on child custody evaluations, parental alienation, and "false child sexual abuse allegations." Because of her mentor's limited interactions with groups outside of those who promote specific research, Dr. Swayd has only attended training and conferences hosted by very specific groups and agencies who have been known to promote an agenda of parental alienation to minimize abuse allegations. As such, Dr. Swayd has been trained to discount or disregard research or professional opinions that differ in their approach to these types of cases.

She was recently appointed by the court to assess allegations of sexual abuse within the Smith household as part of a child custody evaluation. Kerry Smith, an eight-year-old girl, has made a disclosure of sexual abuse by her father, Carl, to her school teacher and the school counselor. Carl Smith and his ex-wife, Sharon, divorced two years prior, and the parties had a contested child custody case in which both parties made derogatory allegations against the other party, including claims of domestic violence by Ms. Smith against Mr. Smith. At the time, the child custody evaluator determined that joint custody was in the best interest of the child, despite the allegations of domestic violence, and the judge so ordered this.

Upon learning of the contested custody dispute that took place two years prior and realizing that the past evaluation was conducted by a psychologist who she had seen present at a past training she attended, Dr. Swayd immediately appeared to discount the recent sexual abuse allegations made by Kerry. Her first thought was that it "just appears to be another high-conflict custody case and possibly one of alienation by the mother." She further felt as though since the previous evaluator believed that joint custody was in the best interest of the child, there was likely no basis for the claims of domestic violence, as this was in line with her past training. However, she did not review any of these records or allegations and she was not familiar with the research that showed an overlap and a higher correlation of child abuse in domestic violence cases (Geffner, Griffin, & Lewis, 2009). She did agree to assess the sexual abuse allegations by reviewing the videotape of the forensic interview of Kerry at her local child advocacy center, interviewing the parties involved, and reviewing the records regarding the previous custody hearings. However, because of her already formed belief that the abuse likely did not take place, Dr. Swayd had a difficult time remaining objective and did not appear to actively seek out data points that were not already in line with her preconceived notions.

In her evaluation report, in which she concluded that no sexual abuse had taken place and that it was clear that Kerry had made these statements at the urging of her mother, Dr. Swayd reported that the disclosures made in the forensic interview were not credible. Dr. Swayd also reported that when the forensic interviewer asked Kerry if "anyone had told her what to say here today," Kerry reported, "Yes, my mommy did . . . She told me to tell the truth." Dr. Swayd opined from watching this not only that was Kerry not credible in her disclosures, but that it appeared likely that Ms. Smith had "coached" or "programmed" Kerry into making these disclosures, as she remembered similar accounts in the training that she attended. She also commented that the interviewer had not followed accepted standards of practice in conducting her forensic interview of Kerry, so it too was not reliable.

To support her conclusions, Dr. Swayd cited articles regarding "parental alienation syndrome" (PAS), as well as articles on how highly suggestible children can be, which she was well versed in because of her training. She used these citations to opine that the abuse had not occurred and that Ms. Smith was coaching the child to make the abuse disclosures because of her resentment and dislike of her ex-husband. This is an example of how her limited training impacted her knowledge base in these types of cases, but it also speaks to the fact that child sexual abuse is not an easy thing for individuals, including evaluators, to believe is happening. Dr. Swayd has learned to discount allegations because of her training, but also because of her own personal desire to want to believe that these types of disclosures are more the result of a vindictive parent than a child who is being abused by a parent or loved one.

Dr. Swayd also did not mention the domestic violence allegations made by Ms. Smith against Mr. Smith in her report, nor did she include the possibility that it could have occurred or what impact that might have had in any of her opinions or conclusions. She also suggested that the mother made negative statements about the father, which is what caused Kerry to make these statements about the abuse. However, this conclusion was based solely on the report of the father and was not endorsed by any other collateral information, for which Dr. Swayd did not seem to account.

There are a number of areas in the above illustrated vignette of Dr. Swayd that highlight how her preconceived notions impacted her ability to conduct a thorough and objective evaluation of the sexual abuse allegations and biased her overall findings and opinions. In addition, Dr. Swayd engaged in a number of inappropriate behaviors, such as practicing outside her areas of expertise (2.01, Boundaries of Competence), not staying abreast of current literature (2.03, Maintaining Competence), misrepresenting research (9.06, Interpreting Assessment Results), and not conducting a thorough, independent evaluation (9.01, Bases for Assessment). Her actions and statements are in conflict with a number of ethical standards and forensic guidelines. For one, it was clear from the beginning of the evaluation that Dr. Swayd had preconceived notions or biases as soon as she found out that the case involved what she considered a "high-conflict custody case," and that domestic violence allegations were made previously by the mother but not confirmed in the prior evaluation. Ethical standards of psychologists (APA, 2002, 2010) require that evaluators strive to maintain impartiality throughout the evaluation process and advise them to withhold conclusions as best as possible until all the data are collected. This is important because oftentimes, once an initial impression is formed, information that could discount or combat this impression may be overlooked or minimized (Pepiton et al., 2014). As evaluators, one should always be mindful of confirmatory bias and actively seek out data that could possibly disconfirm initial impressions or beliefs. Countertransference often plays a role in developing preconceived notions or opinions. Evaluators, just like therapists, should be particularly aware of these feelings.

Additionally, in the Specialty Guidelines for Forensic Psychology (American Psychological Association, 2013b), Guideline 1.01, Integrity specifically states that forensic practitioners strive for accuracy and to resist partisan pressures to provide services in any ways that might tend to be misleading or inaccurate. Furthermore, Guideline 1.02, Impartiality and Fairness states that forensic practitioners should recognize the adversarial nature of the legal system and strive to treat all participants and weigh all data, opinions, and rival hypotheses impartially. It was clear in this case that the evaluator had negative views of the mother and did not pay much attention to the child. Also, when conducting forensic examinations, forensic practitioners strive to be unbiased and impartial and to avoid partisan presentation of unrepresentative, incomplete, or inaccurate evidence that might mislead finders of fact. Finally, Guideline 2.05, Knowledge of the Scientific Foundation for Opinions and Testimony states that forensic practitioners should seek to provide opinions and testimony that are sufficiently based upon adequate scientific foundation and reliable and valid principles and methods that have been applied appropriately to the facts of the case.

Additionally, Dr. Swayd appeared to take the previous child custody evaluator's conclusions and recommendations at face value, without examining or critiquing any of the evidence herself. She did not really interview collateral sources from the mother who heard the allegations and observed the sexualized behavior of Kerry

(Everson & Faller, 2012; Faller & Everson, 2012; Friedrich et al., 2001). We often come across evaluators who simply use past evaluation results to guide their current determinations without reviewing original evidence. Past opinions and determinations should be used as important data points, but should always be reviewed with a critical eye, as one never knows if that previous evaluator had their own preconceived notions that biased their own findings, and then the use of their conclusions will just be perpetuating the cycle.

Further, in order to adhere to the ethical guidelines and to help counter preconceived biases, evaluators should always stay abreast of current, peer-reviewed research on specialty topics in which they claim expertise. We have seen many evaluators, like Dr. Swayd, who hold misinformed beliefs and assumptions about research because of a workshop by someone else who may not be adequately trained in that field. They also appear to have the mistaken belief that all articles published in journals are peer-reviewed research when many journals do not publish such articles. One of the concepts that we come across quite frequently, though it oftentimes can take different forms and various names, is the notion of PAS, a view developed by Dr. Richard Gardner in the 1980s. This assumes that children who show a dislike for one parent or demonstrate an unwillingness to live with him or her are frequently the victims of "programming" by the other parent, usually the mother, who is trying to alienate the child against the other parent (Gardner, 1998; see review of this by Pepiton et al., 2014). PAS is not based on any scientific or peer-reviewed research or theory (Bond, 2007; Kelly & Johnston, 2001; Meier, 2009; Walker & Shapiro, 2010), though it is often touted as such by special interest groups such as the one whose training Dr. Swayd attends. The concept has also been excluded from the newest edition of the Diagnostic and Statistical Manual of Mental Disorders, Fifth edition (DSM-5; APA, 2013) as well as all previous editions, and has been considered inadmissible now in a number of courts (Hoult, 2006) as it does not meet the established legal standard for the admissibility of expert testimony (Bond, 2007). While we have noticed that the actual term "parental alienation syndrome" is not used as frequently now in evaluations and court cases for the above-mentioned reasons, the exact same conclusions, opinions, and recommendations that match what Gardner (1998) had proposed are still being used under different names and terms, such as in the example of Dr. Swayd. Again, the framework, no matter what label is used, is not supported by any research or theory of child development, trauma, forensic, or family psychology.

With regard to suggestibility research, we often hear of experts throughout the country using dated or misconstrued research to support their opinions that young children are not accurate historians who often cannot provide credible information about abuse. Similarly, they use this same research to maintain that children can be highly suggestible and are easily "coached" or "programmed" by an alienating parent. The current state of the research actually does not support these assertions (Faller & Everson, 2012), as studies have shown that children as young as three years old can provide useful and factually accurate information regarding traumatic experiences such as abuse (Leander, Christianson, & Granhag, 2007), intrusive medical procedures (Melinder & Gilstrap, 2009), and having witnessed the murder of a loved one (McWilliams, Narr, Goodman, Ruiz, & Mendoza, 2013). There is also other research that has focused on ways that forensic interviewers can reduce suggestibility by implementing specific interview protocols (Cronch, Viljoen, & Hansen, 2006; Crossman, Powell, Pincipe, & Ceci, 2002; Lamb, Sternberg, Orbach, Esplin, Stewart, & Mitchell, 2003; London, 2001; Newlin et al., 2015; Saywitz, Camparo, & Romanoff, 2010). Research like this does not support the assertions that children are highly suggestible and coachable, the process in which such inadvertent programming supposedly takes place has not been elucidated in articles, and too many custody evaluators make inaccurate assumptions when assessing abuse allegations.

Unfortunately, we have also actually come across well-respected professionals in the field who have made comments very similar to those of Dr. Swayd. While assessing allegations of sexual abuse, particularly in young children, can be difficult and complex, one who is not well trained or who does not have sufficient experience in the areas of child development, sexual victimology, or sexual offending should not be conducting these types of evaluations. Further, evaluators who wish to work in this area should frequently examine their own views related to child sexual abuse, since it is a very difficult topic area, and how those views impact one's ability to provide an objective evaluation of the issues. In addition, stating that a child was not abused or that a person is not an offender based upon an interview or testing is beyond the scope of what a mental health professional can do. We do not have the expertise or technology to make such absolute statements. An ethical statement that can be made would be focused on probabilities and likelihood and based upon the evidence and data in conjunction with what we know in the research. There can be no such expertise in assessing *false* allegations of sexual abuse, especially if the individual does not hold specific expertise in the abovementioned areas.

Inappropriate Evaluation Procedures/Misinterpretation of Testing Results

In our last case example, we will highlight the importance of utilizing appropriate evaluation procedures that are in line with ethical guidelines. Further, we will discuss the common mistakes that we see evaluators make in their use of psychological test measures and their subsequent interpretations. For those professionals who conduct evaluations with the use of psychological testing, these are important areas of concern to be aware of. Let us now turn to the case illustration of Dr. Toobias to better highlight these areas.

The Case of Dr. Toobias

Dr. Toobias has a private forensic practice in which most of his evaluation referrals come through the family court system. He has been doing these types of evaluations for the past ten years and has become more rigid in his approach to the testing. He feels comfortable with his standard evaluation procedures and has gotten into the habit of not seeking out new or differing approaches. He was appointed by the court to conduct a child custody evaluation for Mr. and Ms. Conner regarding their two children, Jack, aged eight, and John, aged six. This is a particularly contested custody case with allegations that the mother committed physical abuse against both sons. During his child custody evaluation, Dr. Toobias administers only two psychological measures to both parents: the Minnesota Multiphasic Personality Inventory – 2nd version (MMPI-2) and the Rorschach. Dr. Toobias did not administer any psychological measures to either child. Again, this is the standard battery that Dr. Toobias has become accustomed to, and since he has been following this approach for so long with little contention, he does not feel the need to broaden his practice to include different testing procedures that could give him additional information to strengthen his formulation of the case.

In his 95-page custody evaluation report, Dr. Toobias concluded that based on Ms. Conner's MMPI-2 results, there is no chance that she is at risk for abusing her children. He bases this claim on the MMPI-2 interpretive report generated by the Caldwell Interpretive System. He further goes on to report that the father's testing results demonstrate serious psychological concerns, including hysteria and paranoia. He concluded that in the best interests of the children, joint custody should be maintained between both parties, or if this is not possible because the father is not facilitating a positive relationship between the mother and her children, the mother should then obtain sole managing conservatorship.

Dr. Toobias is a good example of a child custody evaluator who did not follow appropriate evaluation guidelines or procedures and later used the testing results in an inappropriate manner (9.01, Bases for Assessments; 9.02, Use of Assessments). For example, he did not assess all of the appropriate areas in a child custody evaluation, did not interpret or report the testing results appropriately (9.06, Interpreting Assessment Results), and did not take the context of the situation into account in his determinations, as described in Standard 9 of the APA's (2002, 2010) Code of Conduct. Additionally, the APA's Guidelines for Child Custody Evaluations in Family Law Proceedings (2010) state that evaluators should evaluate the parenting attributes of both parents, the child's psychological needs, and the resulting fit. Further, in the Specialty Guidelines for Forensic Psychology (American Psychological Association, 2013b), Guidelines 9.01 through 10.04 specifically discuss the need for evaluators to use appropriate assessment methods and to select and use appropriate assessment procedures.

More often than not, psychological testing can be used as a useful evaluation tool to provide information regarding an individual's strengths and weaknesses psychologically as well as information on family dynamics and parenting, which is why it is used frequently in child custody evaluations (Bow & Quinnell, 2002). Unfortunately, we have come across many child custody evaluators who use psychological testing inadequately or inappropriately, such as in the case of Dr. Toobias. For example, Dr. Toobias's use of two test instruments in his evaluation would be considered inadequate testing given the seriousness of the issues and allegations. We see this often in evaluators who are only comfortable with tests that they learned early in their careers in graduate school and who do not stay abreast of new and relevant test instruments. While there is nothing inherently wrong in using either the MMPI-2 or the Rorschach in an evaluation, assuming the evaluator is trained in the administration and interpretations of them, the guidelines for custody evaluations state that evaluators should also be assessing parenting attributes, the child's psychological needs, and the resulting combination of the two. Geffner and colleagues (2009) suggested that psychological testing in custody evaluations should assess for not just personality, but also anxiety, depression, trauma, parenting stress, and parenting attitudes. Also, if there are other specific concerns involved in the case, such as substance abuse or family violence, then specific testing instruments should be used for those as well. There are now standardized measures that can be utilized in evaluations to address all of these factors for both adults and children (e.g., Children's Depression Inventory – 2nd edition, Trauma Symptom Checklist for Children, Children's Inventory of Anger, Parenting Stress Index – 4th edition, Personality Assessment Inventory, etc.). A comprehensive battery of inventories and questionnaires provides important information regarding the functioning of the parties in various contexts, and also their strengths and weaknesses that may be relevant to the referral questions. By giving a battery of measures, it is more difficult for the parent to fake the results, be coached on ways to respond to them, or prepare ahead of time for the test.

As outlined in the Guidelines for Child Custody Evaluations in Family Law Proceedings (APA, 2010), it is important for evaluators to choose assessment measures that fit the needs of their specific referral questions, in this case specific custody-related concerns and child abuse allegations. In only using the MMPI-2 and the Rorschach, Dr. Toobias is not fully addressing the psycho-legal issues relevant to a child custody matter, and unfortunately, this is all too common in custody evaluations, especially if extensive interviews and observation sessions are not conducted. Research on this topic has found that parenting inventories, which can provide very useful information about an individual's parenting abilities and the parent–child relationship, are used in only about 45–66 percent of child custody evaluations (Ackerman & Pritzl, 2011; Bow & Quinnell, 2002). Similarly, Bow and Quinnell (2002) also found that psychological measures for children were used in only 39–61 percent of cases. Often, administering psychological measures to children who are old enough is useful in getting, for example, a child's perspective and information regarding their current psychological needs, their self-concept, and their levels of trauma, if any (Geffner et al., 2009; Pepiton et al., 2014).

In addition to the concerns regarding Dr. Toobias's evaluation procedures, there are also significant ethical concerns noted in his representation of the test data. For one, the MMPI-2 was not created with the intention of identifying child abuse offenders, or intimate partner violence (IPV) offenders for that matter. Furthermore, there is no current research that indicates that any of the scales produced by the measure can be used to accurately identify offenders. As such, Dr. Toobias's claim that there is no chance that Ms. Conner could be abusing her children based on his testing results is far outside the scope of what the test instrument is intended to measure. Unfortunately, in a similar case that we had, a court-appointed child custody evaluator made the exact same absolute statement that the parent could not have committed incest with his child based upon an interview (of the child in the alleged offending parent's home with the parent there), observations, and the two tests noted above. An ethics complaint was filed with the evaluator's state board, and the ethics committee found that the procedures, report/testimony, and statements were unethical and recommended that the mental health professional lose her license.

With regard to the use of interpretive systems for test interpretation, in line with the Specialty Guidelines for Forensic Psychology (American Psychological Association, 2013b) Guidelines 9.01 through 10.04, one must take the context of the evaluation and the individual's situation into account. This can be difficult when strictly basing interpretations on an interpretive system. Further, we have come across many child custody evaluators who use the Alex Caldwell Interpretive System or Caldwell Custody Evaluation reports for MMPIs. Unfortunately, there is little independent research on the Caldwell Interpretive System, nor does Dr. Caldwell provide any research or data upon which he bases his claims and some of his scales. As such, it is difficult to contest some of the claims and interpretations made on the basis of the Caldwell reports. What is interesting is that in our experience, many of the evaluators who are not trained adequately on psychological testing, child abuse, and/or IPV tend to more often use this interpretive system for the MMPI-2 than the research-based, accepted one by Pearson (Butcher, Graham, Ben-Porath, Tellegen, & Dahlstrom, 2001).

Additionally, when speaking about the necessity of including the context of the situation into testing results and conclusions, as outlined by the APA (2010) in Guideline 11, given what we know of Dr. Toobias, he seems to have made this ethical misstep with regard to Mr. Conner as well. Dr. Toobias reported that the father's testing results demonstrated significant concerns related to his psychological functioning, including demonstrations of hysteria and paranoia. When considering the importance of recognizing context in an evaluation, it is necessary to keep in mind that for parents who are claiming fear of abuse, signs of paranoia, distrust, or hysteria coming through in the assessment results may be explained by acknowledging the framework of fear that this individual is likely living in. This holds true for parents who are claiming fear of abuse of themselves or their children, and especially in the context of an evaluator, court, or other parent who denies, minimizes, or does not believe their allegations. In fact, this would be a normal reaction and behavior to finding out that your child has been abused (Pepiton et al., 2014). Misconstruing the test results without reporting situational or contextual factors that are likely related can lead to significant negative outcomes for that parent or child and a misrepresentation of information to the court, which would be an ethical violation.

Dr. Toobias did not intend to be malicious in his evaluation findings, but unfortunately because of his unwillingness to incorporate new testing procedures and his overreliance on certain interpretive systems, his findings were not the most reliable or helpful in this case. While it can be easier for an evaluator to only administer psychological tests with which he or she is familiar or to simply base their conclusions on computer-generated interpretive systems, this is not the best ethical practice for forensic evaluators. Evaluators should instead keep up to date on new and relevant test measures that can assist in answering the specific psycho-legal questions that they have been asked to address. Further, evaluators who use psychological testing should understand the limitations of the testing measures that they utilize in their evaluations, and should never make claims or absolute determinations based on those instruments if that is not what they were designed to measure. In addition, it is important for evaluators to take a step back from the test results to think critically about the information that they acquired and how it makes sense considering situational and contextual factors (i.e., looking at the big picture to come to the best conclusion that fits all of the data).

Conclusions and Best Practice Standards

In sum, it is easy to see how many forensic evaluators can intentionally or unintentionally engage in unethical or inappropriate conduct that can have a significant impact on the lives of individuals and families. As illustrated through our four case examples, the types of violations of ethical standards and accepted guidelines of practice can vary from more minor acts reflecting a general lack of knowledge or insight to more blatantly harmful behaviors. It is important for any professional who is going to work within the forensic realm to be aware of and stay up to date on changing standards and guidelines for their profession. Our hope in writing this chapter is to highlight what types of actions to avoid while also giving you some guidelines for best accepted standards of practice.

All clinicians who are conducting forensic evaluations in child protection or family law matters should not only stay up to date on the ever-changing practice guidelines and standards in their area, but also on research relevant to their specialty areas. Again, as highlighted in several of the case examples, staying abreast of current research regarding child development, family systems and dynamics, psychopathology, trauma, child abuse and domestic abuse concerns, and psychological assessment is paramount. Similarly, it is important as a professional to ensure that the training and research is obtained from a range of knowledgeable experts in the field, and not just one group or organization that may have special interests or an ideological agenda, such as in the case of Dr. Swayd above. Attending a workshop for a day does not mean the evaluator has sufficient expertise in such complex areas as substance abuse, child maltreatment, IPV, attachment, family psychology, or trauma. Workshops in each of these areas and specialized conferences through continuing education would be the minimum necessary to work on such child custody cases, especially with consultation or supervision initially.

It is also very helpful to somehow consult or work in a team whenever possible to help address any underlying biases, countertransference issues, or preconceived notions that might be affecting your work. As was seen in multiple case examples, we as professionals are not immune from becoming overinvolved in a case or allowing some of our life occurrences to affect our ability to remain neutral or objective. Similarly, it can also be easy to allow oneself to develop specific patterns as evaluators, such as only testifying for one side or always seeking out information to confirm "false" allegations of sexual abuse. Each case must be evaluated on its own merits and conclusions and recommendations must be based upon the data that make sense toward the overall picture. However, knowing prevalence rates of the various situations under evaluation can help the evaluator to be aware of possible biases in their practice. For example, knowing that the research indicates that allegations of IPV or child abuse in child custody cases are no more likely to be false or misinterpreted than in noncustody cases (e.g., Everson & Faller, 2012; Thoennes & Tjaden, 1990; Trocme & Bala, 2005) and that such allegations are as likely to be accurate as not can highlight bias in evaluators. In one case we reviewed, the evaluator stated that he had conducted 300 child custody evaluations and there were abuse allegations in at least 100 of them. That percentage is not unreasonable. However, when asked how many of those 100 or so cases with allegations of abuse that he had supported with his findings, he testified that only four were validated by him. We know from substantial studies by federal agencies and researchers over many years that none have come close to only 4 percent of alleged cases being validated (Lyon, Ahern, & Scurich, 2012). In fact, the most likely percentage of validation would be 30–50 percent true, so the evaluator who was not familiar with the research clearly had a bias just based upon his substantiation rates in his own cases.

Finally, it is important for evaluators to make sure that they are following ethical standards and guidelines for appropriate evaluation protocols and procedures. For those who utilize psychological testing in their evaluations, it is important to stay up to date on current and relevant measures that can help better address the specific psycho-legal questions at hand, as well as to be aware of the limitations of test interpretations and the importance of including context in the overall results and conclusions. When evaluators do not follow accepted standards of practice, practice outside their areas of competence and expertise, do not conduct a comprehensive evaluation, or misrepresent data due to bias, the damage can be severely traumatizing to children for many years. We sometimes do not take our work sufficiently seriously when drawing conclusions or making recommendations that can affect parents' and children's lives for many years to come.

References

Ackerman, M. J. & Pritzl, T. B. (2011). Child custody evaluation practices: A 20-year follow up. *Family Court Review, 49*, 618–628.

American Professional Society on the Abuse of Children (1990). *Guidelines for psychosocial evaluation of suspected sexual abuse in young children*. Chicago, IL: American Professional Society on the Abuse of Children.

American Psychiatric Association (2013). *The diagnostic and statistical manual of mental disorders* (5th edn.). Washington, DC: American Psychiatric Publishing.

American Psychological Association (2002). Ethical principles of psychologists and code of conduct. *American Psychologist, 57*, 1060–1073.

American Psychological Association (2010). Guidelines for child custody evaluations in family law proceedings. *American Psychologist, 65*, 863–867.

American Psychological Association (2013a). Guidelines for psychological evaluations in child protection matters. *American Psychologist, 68*, 20–31.

American Psychological Association (2013b). The specialty guidelines for forensic psychologists. *American Psychologist, 68*, 7–19.

Association of Family and Conciliation Courts (2006). Model standards of practice for child custody evaluation. Retrieved from www.afccnet.org

Bond, R. (2007). The lingering debate over the parental alienation syndrome phenomenon. *Journal of Child Custody, 4*, 37–54.

Bow, J. & Quinnell, F. (2002). A critical review of child custody evaluation reports. *Family Court Review, 40*, 164–176.

Bucky, S. F. & Callan, J. E. (2014). Anger as a frequent factor in custody evaluation complaints to boards of psychology. *Journal of Child Custody, 11*, 128–138.

Butcher, J. N., Graham, J. R., Ben-Porath, Y. S., Tellegen, A., & Dahlstrom, W. G. (2001). *Minnesota Multiphasic Personality Inventory-2 (MMPI-2): Manual for administration and scoring* (rev. edn.). Minneapolis, MN: University of Minnesota Press.

Cronch, L., Viljoen, J., & Hansen, D. (2006). Forensic interviewing in child sexual abuse cases: Current techniques and future directions. *Aggression and Violent Behavior, 11*, 195–207.

Crossman, A., Powell, M., Principe, G., & Ceci, S. (2002). Child testimony in custody cases: A review. *Journal of Forensic Psychology, 2*, 1–31.

Everson, M. D. & Faller, K. (2012). Base rates, multiple indicators, and comprehensive forensic evaluations: Why sexualized behavior still counts in assessments of child sexual abuse allegations. *Journal of Child Sexual Abuse, 21*, 45–71.

Faller, K. & Everson, M. D. (2012). Contested issues in the evaluation of child sexual abuse allegations: Why consensus on best practice remains elusive. *Journal of Child Sexual Abuse: Research, Treatment, & Program Innovations for Victims, Survivors, & Offenders, 21*, 3–18.

Friedrich, W. N., Fisher, J. L., Dittner, C., et al. (2001). Child Sexual Behavior Inventory: Normative, psychiatric, and sexual abuse comparisons. *Child Maltreatment, 6*, 37–49.

Gardner, R. A. (1998). The parental alienation syndrome: A guide for mental health and legal professionals (2nd edn.). Cresskill, NJ: Creative Therapeutics.

Geffner, R., Griffin, D. A., & Lewis, J., III (Eds.) (2009). *Children exposed to violence: Current issues, interventions and research*. Philadelphia, PA: Taylor & Francis Publishers.

Geffner, R., Igelman, R. S., & Zellner, J. (Eds.) (2003). *Effects of intimate partner violence on children*. New York, NY: Haworth Maltreatment & Trauma Press.

Greenberg, L., Martindale, D., Gould, J., & Gould-Saltman, D. J. (2004). Ethical issues in child custody and dependency cases: Enduring principles and emerging challenges. *Journal of Child Custody, 1*, 7–30.

Greenberg, L. & Gould, J. (2001). The treating expert: A hybrid role with firm boundaries. *Professional Psychology, Research and Practice, 32*, 469–478.

Hoult, J. (2006). The evidentiary admissibility of parental alienation syndrome: Science, law, and policy. *Children's Legal Rights Journal, 26*, 1–61.

Jaffe, P. G., Baker, L. L., & Cunningham, A. J. (2004). *Protecting children from domestic violence: Strategies for community intervention*. New York, NY: Guilford.

Kelly, J. B. & Johnston, J. R. (2001). The alienated child: A reformulation of parental alienation syndrome. *Family Court Review, 39,* 249–266.

Kelly, J. B. & Lamb, M. E. (2000). Using child development research to make appropriate custody and access decisions for young children. *Family and Conciliation Courts Review, 38,* 297–311.

Kirkpatrick, H. D., Austin, W. G., & Flens, J. R. (2011). Psychological and legal considerations in reviewing the work product of a colleague in child custody evaluations. *Journal of Child Custody, 8,* 103–123.

Lamb, M. E., Orbach, Y., Hershkowitz, I., Esplin, P. W., & Horowitz, D. (2007). A structured forensic interview protocol improves the quality and informativeness of investigative interviews with children: A review of research using the NICHD Investigative Interview Protocol. *Child Abuse & Neglect, 31,* 1201–1231.

Lamb, M., Orbach, Y., Sternberg, K., Aldridge, J., Pearson, S., & Stewart, H. (2009). Use of structured investigative protocol enhances the quality of investigative interviews with alleged victims of child sexual abuse in Britain. *Applied Cognitive Psychology, 23,* 449–467.

Lamb, M. E., Sternberg, K. J., Orbach, Y., Esplin, P. W., Stewart, H., & Mitchell, S. (2003). Age differences in young children's responses to open-ended invitations in the course of forensic interviews. *Journal of Consulting and Clinical Psychology, 71,* 926–934.

Leander, L., Christianson, S., & Granhag, P. (2007). Internet-initiated sexual abuse: Adolescent victims' reports about on- and off-line sexual abuse. *Applied Cognitive Psychology, 22,* 1260–1274.

London, K. (2001). Investigative interviews of children: A review of psychological research and implications for police practices. *Police Quarterly, 4,* 123–144.

Lyon, T. D., Ahern, E. C., & Scurich, N. (2012). Interviewing children versus tossing coins: Accurately assessing the diagnosticity of children's disclosures of abuse. *Journal of Child Sexual Abuse, 21,* 19–44.

McWilliams, K., Narr, R., Goodman, G., Ruiz, S., & Mendoza, M. (2013). Children's memory for their mother's murder: Accuracy, suggestibility, and resistance to suggestion. *Memory, 21,* 591–598.

Meier, J. S. A. (2009). A historical perspective on parental alienation syndrome and parental alienation. *Journal of Child Custody, 6,* 232–257.

Melinder, A. & Gilstrap, L.L. (2009). The relationships between child and forensic interviewer behaviours and individual differences in interviews about a medical examination. *European Journal of Developmental Psychology, 6,* 365–395.

Newlin, C., Steele, L.C., Chamberlin, A., et al. (2015). *Child forensic interviewing: Best practices*. Washington, DC: Juvenile Justice Bulletin, Office of Juvenile Justice and Delinquency Prevention.

Pepiton, M., Zelgowski, B., Geffner, R., & Pegolo de Albuquerque, P. (2014). Ethical violations: What can and does go wrong in child custody evaluations? *Journal of Child Custody, 11,* 81–100.

Pipes, R., Holstein, J., & Aguirre, M. (2005). Examining the personal–professional distinction: Ethics codes and the difficulty of drawing a boundary. *American Psychologist, 60,* 325–334.

Saywitz, K., Camparo, L., & Romanoff, A. (2010). Interviewing children in custody cases: Implications of research and policy for practice. *Behavioral Sciences & the Law, 28,* 542–562.

Thoennes, N. & Tjaden, P. J. (1990). The extent, nature, and validity of sexual abuse allegations in custody/divorce disputes. *Child Abuse & Neglect, 151,* 153–154.

Trocme, N. & Bala, N. (2005). False allegations of abuse and neglect when parents separate. *Child Abuse & Neglect, 29,* 1333–1345.

U.S. Department of Justice (2015). Office of Juvenile Justice and Delinquency Prevention. Retrieved from www.ojjdp.gov

Walker, L. E. & Shapiro, D. L. (2010). Parental alienation disorder: Why label children with a mental diagnosis? *Journal of Child Custody, 7,* 266–286.

Zimmerman, J., Hess, A., McGarrah, N., Benjamin, G., Ally, G., Gollan, J., & Kaser-Boyd, N. (2009). Ethical and professional considerations in divorce and child custody cases. *Professional Psychology: Research and Practice, 40,* 539–549.

23 Ethical Issues in Online Research

Lynne D. Roberts and Jessica B. A. Sipes

The rapid adoption of the Internet by the general public over the past two decades has been accompanied by new ways of communicating, seeking, and sharing information. The proportion of the global population with Internet access has increased from less than 1 percent in 1995 to approximately 40 percent by the end of 2015 (see www .internetlivestats.com/internet-users/). Accompanying this growth has been interest in using the Internet for research, with the first psychology online research studies recorded in the 1990s and the number of studies rapidly expanding since that time (Gosling & Mason, 2015). The advantages of conducting research online, including access to specialized and hidden populations, potential savings in time and resources, and reduced demand characteristics (Roberts, 2007), have resulted in a proliferation of online psychological studies employing quantitative, qualitative, and mixed methodologies.

Three broad domains of psychological research online have been identified: "translational" research, which applies existing methodologies, such as surveys or interviews, within the online context; "phenomenological" research that has as the topic of interest an aspect of Internet activity; and "novel" research where the capabilities of the Internet are used to develop new methodologies (Gosling & Mason, 2015). We take the stance that regardless of the broad domain of online psychological research, the ethical principles governing psychological research offline apply. What is required is consideration of how these principles can best be addressed in the widely varying online research contexts.

National psychological associations provide guidelines for the conduct of ethical research, and some have now provided specific guidelines for ethical research online. Key amongst these are the British Psychological Society's (2013) Ethics Guidelines for Internet-Mediated Research and the American Psychological Association's Report of Board of Scientific Affairs Advisory Group on the Conduct of Research on the Internet (Kraut, Olson, Banaji, Bruckman, Cohen, & Couper, 2004). Further, nondisciplinary-specific recommendations for conducting research online are offered by the Association of Internet Researchers (AoIR, 2012). Each of these documents provides a useful starting point for researchers planning to undertake ethical psychological research online.

The British Psychological Society's (2013) Ethics Guidelines for Internet-Mediated Research maps key ethical considerations in online research against ethical principles. Key considerations when addressing the principle of "respect for the autonomy and dignity of persons" in online research are distinguishing between private and public domains online, assessing risks to confidentiality, addressing copyright issues, and implementing robust consent, withdrawal, and debriefing procedures. The key consideration when addressing the principle of "scientific value" is maximizing the level of control over the study. To address the principle of "social responsibility" requires consideration of the potential impact of the research and research dissemination procedures on groups and communities. Finally, consideration is required of how each of these issues impact upon "maximizing benefits and minimizing harm." When ethics principles and standards are included below, they originate from the American Psychological Association's Ethical Principles of Psychologists and Code of Conduct (2010) in order to maintain consistency with the rest of the handbook.

Ethical psychological research online requires ongoing reflection and action throughout the research process. It is useful to distinguish between *procedural* ethics and *process* ethics. Procedural ethics – the formal process of applying for, and receiving, ethics approval prior to commencing research (Guillemin & Gillam, 2004) – requires careful consideration of potential foreseen ethical issues. Process ethics (also known as "ethics in practice," Guillemin & Gillam, 2004; "situated ethics," Calvey, 2008; or "embedded ethics," Whiteman, 2012) requires researcher reflexivity throughout the research process to attend to "ethically important moments" resulting from new events or information that arise following procedural ethics (Guillemin & Gillam, 2004). While procedural ethics (or obtaining a waiver) is a requirement for all online and offline psychological research involving human subjects, we argue that process ethics assumes greater importance when researching in new or unfamiliar settings, such as some online environments, where there is greater potential for issues to arise that were not foreseen and therefore not considered in the research planning process.

In this chapter, we provide four case studies designed to work through some of the ethical considerations previously outlined in preparing for and conducting psychological research in online contexts. The first case study, presenting a counseling psychologist preparing to undertake his first qualitative online study using passive data collection methods, focuses on distinguishing between private and public domains online and the resulting considerations on whether consent or copyright should be prioritized. The ethical issues in this first case study relate to the principle of respect for the autonomy and dignity of persons. The second case study, presenting a postdoctoral researcher engaging in qualitative, covert active data collection in online communities, explores issues related to researcher (non)identification, covert data collection methods and deception, and the potential impacts of these on groups and communities, addressing the principle of social responsibility. The third case study, presenting an academic planning to conduct an online quantitative survey using a commercial survey provider, explores ethical considerations when recruiting online and using commercial survey providers. Potential threats to survey respondents' anonymity, privacy, and consent processes, data protection, and scientific value are discussed. The final case study, presenting a Ph.D. student seeking supervisory advice on the protection of both the researcher and research participants for a planned online mixed methods research project on a sensitive topic, addresses the principle of maximizing benefits and minimizing harm. After each of the case studies, consideration of procedural ethics will be followed by an exploration of process ethics – potential issues during the research process that may require researcher reflexivity and further ethical consideration.

The Case of Online Qualitative Research with Passive Data Collection

Abdul is a counseling psychologist with an adjunct position at a major university. His practice and research focus on psychosocial support for men following the diagnosis of major illness. Abdul has a new male client who has been recently diagnosed with breast cancer. His client is reluctant to attend local "mainstream" breast cancer support groups and services as they largely cater for women. Unable to locate a local breast cancer support group for men and aware of the significantly lower prevalence of breast cancer in men than women, Abdul is interested in whether online support groups might help meet the psychosocial needs of men with breast cancer, such as his current client. After conducting a thorough literature search, Abdul has not been able to locate any studies that focus on online breast cancer support groups for men and decides to conduct his own research.

After exploring methodologies appropriate for studying online support groups, Abdul narrows down his design choices to three options: a content analysis of postings to existing support groups for men with breast cancer, setting up an online support group specifically for the research, or interviewing men who have been involved in online support groups for men with cancer. Having limited available research funds and research time, Abdul decides to conduct a content analysis of postings to existing support groups for men with breast cancer (or if he cannot locate enough male-specific support groups, men's involvement in nongender-specific breast cancer support groups). He plans to use this as a precursor to applying for funding to conduct a study where he will create and facilitate an online support group. His initial plan is to locate as many online discussion board support groups for men with breast cancer as he can, "scrape" the data, and analyze the types of support offered using content analysis. He does not believe ethical approval is necessary as "it's all public – the equivalent to analyzing letters to the editor from newspapers," and expects to be able to complete the study quickly. However, when he talks this idea over with a colleague from the university, she expresses concern over his plan, questioning the possible impact on the continuing functioning of groups if members find out their interactions have been the subject of research unbeknown to them. The discussion has left Abdul torn between his desire to conduct a "quick" study and the need to consider the possible effects of a quick study on the groups he studies.

The discussion with his colleague has left Abdul questioning his original decision to scrape and analyze the data. What initially seemed straightforward and unproblematic, viewed from the perspective of the proposed "data" being in the public domain, has now been recast in terms of considering the impact on participants and groups. Abdul will need to decide if the online sites he plans to use for his data collection are likely to be perceived by group members as public or private domains. The defining of public versus private space online is a contested area. While at first glance, online sites that are accessible to all (such as the newsgroups Abdul proposes to use in his research) appear to be public while those that have membership requirements (e.g., password-protected sites) appear to be private, there is increasing recognition that other factors might impact on this perception. People participating in freely accessible online communities may view their communication as private or intended for community members only, and not view researchers as part of their intended audience (Principle E, Respect for People's Rights and Dignity; Bromseth, 2002).

As part of the consideration of whether an online group should be regarded as public or private, it will be helpful for Abdul to consider the equivalent offline context to the online context of interest. Support groups exist both on- and offline. An offline equivalent to scraping data from an online support group might be analyzing the recording of a support group that meets in a coffee shop without alerting the group to the presence of the researcher or seeking group members' informed consent. The sensitivity of the topic and the process of support groups arguably demands greater consideration of privacy than other types of groups on less sensitive topics such as social interest groups (Holtz, Kronberger, & Wagner, 2012).

Key considerations in determining whether a particular online setting should be regarded as private or public are the accessibility of the site to the general public, the perceptions of members and their expectations of privacy, statements about use that may be posted on the site, the sensitivity of the topic and setting, the permanence of the records, and the intended audience (Roberts, 2015). Abdul will need to consider these factors and the potential impact of the dissemination of research findings on the group members of the discussion boards he plans to include in his research. There are documented examples of the detrimental effects on community functioning in online groups where members have discovered postpublication they were "researched" without their knowledge or consent (see King, 1996). Thus, Abdul might want to consider whether this falls within the Standard 8.07, Deception in Research.

The determination as to whether a particular online setting is public or private has ramifications for procedural ethics, data collection, consent procedures, and whether the aim should be complying with copyright requirements or protecting identities. If the decision is made that the setting is public, then rather than being conceptualized as human subject research requiring ethical consideration, the project may be considered a secondary textual analysis (Bradley & Carter, 2012). If working from this perspective, Abdul may view the postings as produced by authors, rather than research participants (Beaulieu & Estalella, 2012), negating the need for ethics approval or consent procedures, with a resultant focus on meeting copyright obligations when direct quotes are used. Copyright issues online are complex, and it is often unclear who owns a newsgroup posting and holds the copyright: the author, the community, or the owner of the site on which it is posted (see Roberts, Smith, &

Pollock, 2004). Alternatively, if the online setting is determined not to be fully public, if the topic is of a sensitive nature, or if the group members have a reasonable expectation of privacy, formal ethical approval for the research needs to be sought (8.01, Institutional Approval). In this case, Abdul would need to carefully consider consent procedures (8.02, Informed Consent to Research) and protection of participants and research settings as part of the procedural ethics process. Having thought through the sensitivity of the topic, the likelihood that at least some group members will view their groups as being in the personal domain, and the potential impact on group function, Abdul decides to view the research settings as being in the private domain.

Abdul's next consideration is whether informed consent (Standard 8.02) for the use of postings should be obtained. Hewson (2015) recommends that researchers contact group moderators prior to conducting online observation studies to seek their advice on the likely impact on the group of disclosing the study. Previous research has indicated that even in publicly accessible discussion boards some individuals want their permission sought before their quotes are used (Bond, Ahmed, Hind, Thomas, & Hewitt-Taylor, 2013). However, if a decision is made to seek consent before including postings, difficulties in obtaining consent may reduce the body of postings that can be used. Not all individuals posting to a discussion board may be contactable, especially if they no longer use the discussion board. Not all those contacted may consent to the use of their postings. The reduced body of postings for analysis may adversely affect the scientific value of the study and this needs to be taken into account when weighing the potential risks and benefits of the proposed research. Considering these possible effects, Abdul elects to follow a two-stage process of gaining consent. Initially, he will contact the gatekeepers of each community, explain his planned research, and seek consent to collect postings. He will follow the gatekeepers' advice on whether or not to seek consent. Where seeking consent is recommended, he will use "opt-out" consent, contacting posters, advising them of his research, and asking them to contact him within 14 days if they do not want their postings used in his research. He believes this method will result in a near-complete data set, while also alerting potential participants to his research and providing them with the opportunity to decline to participate.

Now that Abdul has clearly identified his research as human rather than textual research, he will need to prepare an application for ethics approval that clearly sets out his position on the private nature of the newsgroups, how he will be seeking informed consent, and how the results from the proposed research will be presented to protect the anonymity of the posters and their online groups. Assuming his ethics application is approved, as part of process ethics, Abdul will need to remain alert to any unforeseen ethical issues that might arise during the research process. This may include keeping track of any new members to the group and making sure that he sends them information and a chance to opt out of the study if he might use their postings. Additionally, because the group he is researching involves people with cancer, it is possible that some members may have passed away since posting and do not opt out because they are unable to do so. If this situation comes to Abdul's attention, possibly through notification by group monitors or memorial postings by group members, he will have to consider whether or not it is ethical to use the postings without the ability to get consent. Monitoring postings to the selected groups during the period of data collection will alert Abdul to any postings relating to his research that might indicate concern.

Abdul successfully completes his first study and elects to continue with his proposed second study, creating and facilitating an online support group for men with breast cancer. He is now faced with a new range of ethical issues related to his professional responsibilities as a psychologist working with group members from a range of jurisdictions. These include the dual and potentially conflicting roles of researcher and facilitator (3.05, Multiple Relationships), the potential misinterpretation of public advice as a personal therapeutic relationship, and balancing confidentiality (4.01, Maintaining Confidentiality) against the need to report threats of harm to self or others. While a full discussion is outside the scope of this chapter, Humphreys, Winzelberg, and Klaw (2000) provide a useful discussion of recommended strategies for psychologists participating in online groups in a professional capacity.

The Case of Online Qualitative Research with Covert Active Data Collection

Anya is a postdoctoral researcher attached to a psychology research group within a university. Her broad area of research is stigma associated with non-suicidal self-injury (NSSI). She is interested in how people with NSSI engage with others online and the impact this might have on increasing or counteracting stigma. Existing research suggests there may be both benefits (increased social support and validation) and risks (in terms of enabling behavior through normalization, reinforcement, sharing of strategies, and triggering) associated with online engagement for people with NSSI (Lewis & Arbuthnott, 2014; Lewis & Seko, 2016). However, online research to date has largely focused on publicly accessible material, such as websites and social media, or interviews and surveys. Due to the stigma associated with self-injury, much of the online interaction between people engaging in NSSI occurs in password-protected sites. These sites generally do not welcome researchers and, to date, no direct observational or ethnographic studies in this area have been conducted.

Anya plans to conduct research within three NSSI groups as a participant-observer. The groups provide a variety of modes of communication, including "live" chat, discussion boards, and personal messaging. She is currently a "lurker" (watching but not participating) on the three groups, but plans to start actively engaging with group members once her study commences. Anya wants to obtain meaningful data and believes she will not be able to do this if she enters the groups as a researcher. Instead, she is considering creating a profile as an 18-year-old university student who engages in NSSI sporadically. She has noticed that people seem to share more in-depth information on message boards than she believes they do with researchers. Anya thinks conducting covert and interactive research will allow her to get more details from members of the community than she otherwise would. However, Anya is uncertain whether this is sufficient to offset the deception involved.

Motivated by the desire to collect what she sees as more meaningful data, Anya decides to apply to the university's ethics body to conduct the research using a "fake" identity. She reasons that ultimately it is the university's decision whether or not she can use this approach and decides to focus her attention on preparing an application for ethics that demonstrates she has thought through the issues.

Anya's plan for data collection goes far beyond the scraping of existing data on publicly accessible online sites proposed by Abdul. By using a fake identity and interacting with online group members, Anya will be actively creating "data" through her interactions within private online settings. Key ethical considerations are (non)identification as a researcher, the use of covert deceptive data collection methods (8.07, Deception in Research), and the potential impact of these on the online groups and individuals (3.04, Avoiding Harm).

Anya is electing not to identify as a researcher in her proposed research in order to be able to obtain richer data. There are a range of levels of identification as a researcher that can be adopted in online communities, enabled by the technical affordances of the digital environment. Within an online community, full "overt" identification involves both identification as a researcher and linking to any social identities used within the community (Roberts, 2015). Researcher-only overt identification requires identification as a researcher, but without linking to social identities (if any) used within the community (Roberts, 2015). Covert research occurs when the researcher elects not to identify as a researcher, the position Anya is proposing to adopt in her research.

A common justification for covert research is that it does not intrude on participants or discussions (e.g., Rier, 2007). While this justification may apply when a researcher situates him/herself as an observer (a "lurker"), such as Abdul's proposed research in the previous case study, it fails to hold when the researcher plans to actively engage with (unknowing) participants in order to create data, as proposed by Anya. Other justifications used in online situations that involve active engagement with participants in order to create data are that covert research prevents nonresponse bias and biases in responding (Glaser, Dixit, & Green, 2002) and is justified in situations where the potential benefits from the research are viewed as outweighing the risks (Brotsky & Giles, 2007). Anya bases her ethics application on the notion that the knowledge she will gain can be used to inform approaches to reducing the stigma associated with NSSI and that this outweighs potential risk (consider Principle A, Beneficence and Nonmaleficence). However, Anya's argument that her covert engagement is justified by the "better data" she will be able to collect ignores the rich data on NSSI that have been previously obtained through observational research online (e.g., Whitlock, Powers, & Eckenrode, 2006).

A key concern with covert research is that it does not provide the opportunity for potential participants to make an informed decision (3.10, Informed Consent) as to whether or not they wish to participate in the research. Debriefing is recommended following covert research, especially as informed consent has not been obtained (van

Deventer, 2009). The absence of informed consent is further compounded in research where "participants" are not advised of the research at the end of the project, debriefed, or provided with the opportunity to withdraw their "data" from the study. Interestingly, at least one study has used the argument that because retrospective consent would be unlikely to be obtained, it would not be sought! Brotsky and Giles (2007) justified not debriefing participants of their study involving covert research in pro-anorexia online communities on the basis that "it was believed that, since site users were unaware they were taking part in a study at any time, they would be extremely unlikely to give retrospective consent" (p. 96). Anya plans not to debrief research participants following her study, reasoning that "what they don't know can't harm them." This means her participants will not have provided consent and are unlikely to know that they have been participants in a research project unless either Anya's identity is inadvertently exposed or a member of one of the communities studied recognizes their community/their words in resultant publications or presentations. To minimize discovery, Anya plans to exit the groups by stating she is going overseas and will only have sporadic Internet access in the future. However, despite the precautions she may take, Anya does not have complete control over whether or not her identity will be revealed. If revealed, group members who believe they have formed a genuine personal relationship with Anya may feel particularly violated. This violation could have negative mental health effects for the participants and reduce their trust in others within the group. As part of procedural ethics, Anya will need to decide how she will respond if her identity is exposed during or after conducting the research.

Arguably, covert research that moves beyond passive observation to interacting with participants via a created persona that does not reflect the researcher is deceptive research. Spicker (2011) noted that covert research becomes deceptive when researchers' actions are misrepresented to participants; that is, they "say they are doing one thing when they are actually doing another" (p. 2). In this case study, Anya, presenting herself as an 18-year-old university student who engages in NSSI when communicating in a private setting with other young people who engage in NSSI, is deceptive (8.07, Deception in Research), as her actions will be perceived as private peer conversations when her intention is to collect research data. This places the researcher's desire to collect data above the research participants' rights to privacy, anonymity, and confidentiality in their private lives (Principles A, Beneficence and Nonmaleficence; B, Fidelity and Responsibility; and E, Respect for People's Rights and Dignity) and has been equated to surveillance (van Deventer, 2009). In summarizing the literature on objections to covert, deceptive research, Parker and Crabtree (2014) further highlight the breach of trust with research participants, the potential for harm to research participants and potential damage to the reputation of the research community. The concerns about covert, deceptive research mean that it should only be conducted after careful consideration of the potential risks and benefits of the proposed research and where other possible research methods are deemed not feasible. While there are precedents for using covert, deceptive methods online (e.g., Brotsky and Giles' [2007] research using similar methods within online pro-anorexia sites and Glaser, Dixit, and Green's

[2002] chatroom research on hate crimes), it seems likely that Anya will find it difficult to gain ethics approval for her study, as she will have difficulty demonstrating that suitable data could not be obtained using less intrusive methods (e.g., observation) that carry a lower risk of harm to participants and the community.

If Anya's research was to go ahead, process ethics would be of greater importance than in the previous case study where Abdul was using passive data collection methods. Anya will need to carefully reflect on how she is interacting with group members and how they are responding. Any number of issues may arise, from forming attachments, becoming aware of suicidal activity, or being exposed as a "fake." In preparation, Anya might establish regular meetings with colleagues to discuss issues as they arise.

The Case of Online Quantitative Survey Research

Jonathan is a teaching academic working within a psychology department in a large university and has experience in survey research using pen-and-paper surveys. Having heard a lot about the advantages of online surveys in terms of access to large samples and ease of recruitment, Jonathan would like to use an online survey for his latest research project on how parents make decisions about food choices for children. He assumes it will be a simple matter of taking the pen-and-paper version of the survey he has already created and cutting and pasting it into one of the commercial online survey sites, such as SurveyMonkey. He plans to recruit parents online and has heard he can obtain a sample quickly and cheaply through Amazon's Mechanical Turk (www.MTurk.com), or alternatively through parenting websites and forums. However, knowing little about any of these options, he is seeking advice on whether recruiting and hosting his survey online may pose risks to participants' anonymity and privacy.

While Jonathan may have ethics approval for conducting his pen-and-paper survey, there are additional ethical considerations associated with conducting the same survey online. These considerations relate to recruitment processes online, the functionality of online survey systems, the loss of control when using a commercial online survey site, potential threats to respondent anonymity, privacy, and consent processes, and protection of data and scientific value related to these.

Working on a budget, Jonathan first considers posting requests for participants on websites, online forums, and Facebook pages. To uphold the principle of social responsibility, Jonathan needs to ensure that his actions are not seen as socially disruptive (BPS, 2013). Many forums have rules regarding what can be posted and may ask that research participant requests are posted on specific topic boards. Jonathan will need to be aware of where he can post requests for participants and if permission from a forum moderator is required. Posting too often, in the wrong spot, or without permission could result in his posts being removed and Jonathan being banned from further postings. Beyond seeking permission, Jonathan will need to consider how each group may react to his posting, as there is the potential for negative reactions (Alessi & Martin, 2010). Looking through previous posts to see responses to other research participant requests will help Jonathan determine if group members might be willing to participate in his study (see Alessi & Martin [2010] for further information on recruitment location considerations).

Another ethical consideration when recruiting through online forums or Facebook group pages is the circumstances under which research participants' comments about the survey made in these forums may be used. Typical comments in these forums relate to study questions, why particular questions might have been asked, and additional thoughts on the research question. Jonathan may find some of this additional information interesting and useful for his research, in addition to providing insight into how his survey is being received. However, Jonathan will not be able to use these comments as further "data" for research purposes without obtaining specific consent (see 8.02, Informed Consent to Research and 8.05, Dispensing with Informed Consent for Research). If someone comments on the content of the survey, it could reasonably be concluded that they have participated in the survey and provided consent for their responses to be used by the researcher. However, this consent applies to the survey only and does not extend to information provided by the participant in other domains, even if it is about the survey. Ensuring valid consent procedures is an important component of the ethical principle of respect for the autonomy and dignity of participants (Principle E, Respect for People's Rights and Dignity).

Jonathan also explores the possibility of using Mechanical Turk to recruit research participants who will complete online surveys for a fee. Mechanical Turk acts as an online labor market connecting jobs and workers. An ethical issue associated with recruitment through these sites, as with other online recruitment methods, is the possibility of minors or other people who do not meet the inclusion criteria participating in the research (Mason & Suri, 2012; see also Emma's case study below). Privacy concerns have also been raised over the potential for participants' e-mail addresses to be inadvertently exposed to researchers during payment queries, even if they participate anonymously (Mason & Suri, 2012). Further, Amazon is able to collect sensitive information about research participants from their participation in such studies (Mason & Suri, 2012). Jonathan is particularly concerned when he realizes that the "independent contractors" accessed through Mechanical Turk generally receive only small payments for their labor. He weighs up whether it is more ethical to recruit survey participants who participate voluntarily and do not receive any payment or to pay a low rate (below minimum wage) to Mechanical Turk workers for the same activity. He decides that as Mechanical Turk contractors are free to choose the projects they work on and do so knowing the payment offered, inviting Mechanical Turk contractors to participate in his research is no more coercive than inviting other online users. He decides to recruit through Mechanical Turk as the monetary cost will outweigh the time commitment required to recruit more generally online.

Jonathan turns next to find out whether he can safely use commercial online survey providers for his research. A colleague with expertise in the area points out that the increasing functionality of commercial online survey systems can provide threats to survey respondents' anonymity and privacy. Internet protocol (IP) addresses are automatically collected by many online survey systems and provide geographical information that, in combination with time and date stamps, may aid in identifying survey respondents. His colleague advised that he should treat IP addresses as potential identifiers and either not collect them or strip them from his data set once received. His colleague also warns him that unique tracking links also threaten anonymity through providing a link between survey responses and the e-mail address of the survey respondent. Increasingly, Institutional Review Boards do not allow collection of IP addresses in online surveys, or only allow for collection of IP addresses and use of tracking links with conditions (Baker, 2012). Cookies may also be used and can track individuals' use of the system and collect personal information (Alessi & Martin, 2010). Jonathan's colleague recommends he should check the procedures in place with the commercial online survey provider he selected to ensure confidentiality protections are present.

A further functionality of commercial online survey systems is the ability to enforce responding. Researchers have the option to stop a survey respondent moving onto the next question until the current question has been answered. This is viewed by most Institutional Review Boards as violating research participants' rights not to answer individual questions, an important component of informed consent (Baker, 2012; Mahon, 2013). Jonathan elects to use "prompts" or "reminders" to alert participants, without requiring a response before continuing onto the next question.

Jonathan also considers how he can protect the survey data collected. Traditional methods of protecting data collected in offline research (such as storing completed questionnaires in locked cabinets) are not adequate when data is collected online. In any online survey system, there is the potential for breaches of anonymity and privacy through hacking and other malicious activity, despite the widespread use of industry-standard data protection methods. When a commercial (rather than in-house) online survey system is used, further concerns relate to the researcher's loss of control over who has access to the research data and the security of the transmission of data from the survey host to the researcher (Allen & Roberts, 2010). Jonathan decides to seek expert advice on how to best protect his survey data (see Emma's case study).

Jonathan then turns his attention to the likely quality of the data he may obtain through using online surveys. His search of the literature suggests that factors that may limit the quality of data collected include the (non)representativeness of the sample, low response rates, careless responding, and the potential for individuals to respond multiple times. Jonathan will need to take steps to maximize response rates and screen completed questionnaires for multiple responders and careless responses (for a review, see Roberts & Allen, 2015). Compounding these issues, potential research participants may experience difficulties in differentiating between academic and commercial surveys, particularly when banner advertisements appear on survey pages. This has the potential to affect credibility, potential research participants' willingness to participate, and the candidness of responding (Allen & Roberts, 2010), impacting upon the scientific value of the research. To counteract these issues,

Jonathan notes he will need to clearly brand his survey as academic research through the use of university logos.

Although Jonathan already has ethics approval for the pen-and-paper version of his survey research project, he will need to submit an ethics amendment for approval prior to conducting the survey online. Procedural ethics is important, but it also needs to be acknowledged that not all ethics review committees have current knowledge of the issues associated with conducting surveys online using commercial providers or consider evaluation of privacy and security policies of commercial online survey providers to be part of their remit (Buchanan & Hvizdak, 2009). Once data collection commences, issues requiring ethical consideration that may arise include actual threats to data security and participant anonymity resulting from hacking or data breaches and responding to participants' concerns. Jonathan will need to respond to any such issues as they arise in order to minimize the potential for harm to research participants and others.

The Case of Online Mixed Methods Research on a Sensitive Topic

Emma is a 29-year-old Ph.D. student in psychology at a major Australian university. She is in the first year of her program and is in the process of designing her research prior to candidacy. She is planning on conducting mixed methods research into the different ways that people express their sexuality on the Internet. This will involve both online surveys and interviews conducted online through a chat program. As sexuality is a sensitive topic and the legality of certain sexual acts varies across jurisdictions, Emma and her supervisors are concerned not only about protecting the research participants and protecting the data collected, but also about protecting Emma from personal harm and legal issues. Emma's supervisors are researchers who have some but limited experience in conducting sexuality studies online.

Emma's supervisors are concerned that in the process of her research, Emma may be exposed to material or situations that will cause emotional distress. As Emma's research is about sexuality, the concern is that she will come across disturbing, sexually explicit materials. These could be in the form of images, video, text descriptions, or disclosures and comments from participants of a sexual nature unwarranted by the research questions. Disclosures regarding abuse and sexually explicit talk from participants is particularly concerning due to their more personal nature.

Emma's supervisors are also aware that in determining a target geographic participant population for Emma's research, legal issues regarding the questions being asked become concerns. Not all sexual behaviors are legal in all countries, and legality can even vary by jurisdiction within a country. Further, there is the potential for participants to disclose information on illegal sexual activities even where these are not asked about. Emma's supervisors need to be sure that Emma's responses to such disclosures, disclosure of abuse, or her inadvertent viewing of illegal, sexually explicit materials is appropriate and both ethically and legally defensible.

All of Emma's data are being collected online and there are particular concerns about appropriately protecting the data. Emma and her supervisors want to make sure that her data are being collected using the securest means possible and that they will be appropriately backed up and stored.

When conducting research on human behavior, one of the primary concerns is – rightly so – protecting the research participant. It is hard to predict what type of questions or investigations will lead to a participant feeling distress and it is particularly important to have precautions in place when asking about sensitive subjects such as sexuality. There are many precautions and checks that should occur in the procedural ethics process to make sure this is managed, such as Human Research Ethics Committee and peer-review processes that take place before the research is conducted. While these steps work to protect the participant, they do not always consider the potential harm to the researcher. It is possible in the course of asking sensitive questions or working with and listening to people who are recalling distressing or sensitive issues that this will have an impact on the researcher. Some researchers have reported feelings of distress and burnout when working with sensitive populations, such as those who experienced a traumatic medical proce-dure (Elmir, Schmied, Jackson, & Wilkes, 2011). More researchers are beginning to highlight a need to make sure that protections for researchers are in place, as a lack of preparedness or support can make managing the distress more difficult (Dickson-Swift, James, Kippen, & Liamputtong, 2008; Poole, Giles, & Moore, 2004). Legal issues also become a concern, especially when conducting research online, as it is important not to inadvertently participate in or uncover an illegal activity, which may be more difficult when research is being conducted across different legal systems and laws. Data protection is important in online research as well. With online surveys there is no hard copy original, so digital backups or hard copies need to be made to avoid loss of data. Additionally, making sure that the data are protected from being hacked and are securely stored are important for protecting participant anonymity and data integrity.

It is the supervisors' responsibility to ensure that Emma has worked through the possible ethical and legal issues relating to her research prior to applying for ethics approval and that ongoing support and debriefing is available for the duration of Emma's dissertation project as issues arise. It is likely most supervisors will not have the level of knowledge required of technical and legal systems to be able to fully advise Emma (2.01, Boundaries of Competence) and will need to refer Emma on for expert advice.

Emma and her supervisors will need to develop strategies for how Emma will handle disclosures of abuse and sexually explicit communication from participants and how she will manage self-care during the course of research. These concerns come from the sensitive nature of the topic and the inclusion of interviews as parts of some of the studies. While participants are not being asked directly about specific sexual behaviors or inclinations, they are being asked to discuss other elements of their sexuality. Due to the topic, some participants may be drawn to participate because they believe they can talk about their sexual desires or they may try to engage Emma in sexually explicit talk, as has been encountered by other sexuality researchers (Zurbriggen, 2002). Further, participants may disclose they have been abused, have been sexually abusive toward another, or are sexually attracted to children.

In order to develop a plan to address responding to these types of disclosures, Emma's supervisors have referred Emma to a university counselor for advice. Emma has worked with the counselor to develop a plan on how to deal with disclosures when they occur and what follow-up actions may be required. The counselor has provided information on relaxation techniques and planned written responses that Emma can reference during the event and offered debriefing, all of which will help mitigate the impacts of these potential experiences.

As Emma has had some experience volunteering at a telephone crisis line, there is some concern that she could want to go into a counseling role. In researching sensitive topics, such as illness or abuse, researchers have reported difficulty in not switching to a counseling role when confronted with disclosures or a distressed client (Coles & Mudaly, 2010). Using counseling skills to either reframe the distressing events or offer support and advice to the participant would be appropriate in a counseling setting, but not within a research interview. Offering this support may mislead the participant about the role of the researcher, possibly ending with the participant feeling that they received counseling instead of having participated in an interview. Keeping within the researcher role will protect both the participant and researcher. A counselor has helped Emma develop a plan that stops her from switching to a counseling role if a disclosure should occur. She has a script to follow that will appropriately end the interview and contact details for appropriate resources, such as national counseling hotlines, for the participant to contact. An additional concern in this area is how Emma will cope with not being able to offer more assistance than providing information for support services. The counselor's suggestions include focusing on her role as a researcher and recognizing that providing information for appropriate services is a form of helping. Focusing on her role as researcher will help both Emma and the participants; it will protect Emma from feeling like she should have done more and it will protect the participants by providing them with appropriate resources and services to aid with their distress.

One of the benefits to conducting Emma's research online is the increased anonymity for the participant. People can answer surveys and participate in discussions in a place of their choosing and without having to ever meet or directly interact with anyone who is part of the study. This can make people more comfortable and more likely to respond honestly, but it can also increase their comfort with being more sexually explicit. Some qualitative researchers have reported inappropriate behavior from participants, which results in feelings of distress (Dickson-Swift et al., 2008). Due to the nature of the study, it may be that participants feel comfortable sexualizing the researcher and believing that Emma is open to or interested in sexual experiences with them and not just interested in conducting research. In order to prevent this and protect Emma from potential harm, Emma and her supervisors have decided that all interviews will be conducted as voice-only chat using a program that can block incoming video feeds (consider 8.03, Informed Consent for Recording Voices and Images in Research). This gives Emma some control over what she is exposed to and will help protect her from participants behaving in a visually sexually explicit manner. Additionally, the counselor has helped Emma come up with a prewritten response for use with participants who are behaving sexually inappropriately. If this does not stop the behavior then the interviews can be ended. Emma will need to debrief with either her supervisors and/or a counselor should this occur. Putting these protections in place will work toward protecting Emma.

One potential difficulty with voice-only chat, which can also be found in interviews conducted over the phone, is the inability to read body language or facial expressions during the course of the interview. This can make gauging the level of distress of the participant difficult. It may be that a participant will disclose past abuse, and while this is distressing, it may be something that they are stating merely as a fact of their history and not as a disclosure in need of immediate attention. Decisions on whether or not to end the interview will have to be based on the context of the disclosure and tone of voice. Emma will need to be prepared to make that judgment call while managing both her own and the participant's risk of harm from further discussion. Practicing the breathing techniques and other self-care practices prior to the interviews will help Emma use them more naturally during the interviews and will help keep overall stress levels low. Debriefing with her supervisors after interviews, keeping a journal of the research process and her thoughts throughout it, and seeing the counselor again when necessary will also help Emma avoid personal harm.

Conducting research online can mean that research participants may be located in areas with different legal systems and laws than the research. Emma's supervisors need to make sure the research does not cross any known legal boundaries. One way of doing this is to restrict the area from which participants will be recruited. For example, the research could be restricted to individuals who reside in Australia or, given the differing laws between states and territories within Australia, restricted to a particular jurisdiction within Australia. As Emma's supervisors have insufficient legal expertise to advise Emma within this area, they have referred Emma to the university's legal team in an effort to mitigate risk for the participants, researchers, and university.

The primary concern is that a participant will inadvertently disclose participation in an activity that is illegal within their jurisdiction. The legal team may request to review the questions Emma is going to be asking in order to assess the likelihood that they will expose illegal activities. This will allow for the questions to either be altered or appropriate protections to be put into place. Even if the questions are unlikely to elicit a disclosure, Emma will need to know what her legal obligations are if they do. As the goal of this research is not to discuss specific sexual behaviors or illegal sexual activities, it is unlikely that these behaviors will be reported by participants; however, the sensitive nature of the topic and the possibility of disclosure mean that this needs to be considered. With online data collection and the use of participant-generated usernames, there will be no simple way to identify participants in the event of a disclosure of illegal activity. However, Emma will need to keep a record of the interview, a written log of the disclosure, and the location and storage precautions made for the data after the interview in case a copy is needed at a later date.

A further legal concern is ensuring that participants are adults. Conducting research online can make verifying the age of participants difficult. In each of her studies, Emma will need to include a step at the beginning that asks participants if they are aged 18 or older to avoid including any underage participants. Those who state that they are under 18 will not be able to complete the survey or participate in the interview. While this is not a foolproof system, it is a widely used measure for assessing age of participants in online settings.

Collecting and storing data on computer systems comes with the risk of data being hacked, deleted, or altered (see previous case study). Emma's supervisors are responsible for ensuring data are properly protected from the start of data collection using secure software and that they are securely stored. Emma has consulted the university's Information Technology Securities team on the best ways to protect the data and online security practices. This requires consideration of access to secure servers and where and how the data will be stored and backed-up. Emma has been encouraged to use an ad blocker as, in searching for and engaging with sexually related topics online, it is possible she will receive targeted advertising for unrelated sexual services. There is also a concern that pop-up advertisements may link to viruses that could infect her computer. Being aware of what programs she can use or has access to at both the university and at home will help Emma protect both her data and her computer.

One final consideration with online research is Emma's online presence. It is likely that participants or people interested in her studies will look her up online and look at any social media presence that she has. Being aware of and using privacy filters on social media sites will help Emma control what people see and what they can learn about her. Emma has created a separate research username to use in interviews to prevent participants from being able to contact her on her personal username after the interviews are over.

As many of the potential risks to the researcher in online research can be foreseen, plans to counteract these can be developed as part of the procedural ethics process. However, there is still the potential for unforeseen issues to arise during the conduct of the research that will require ethical consideration. In combination with her supervisors, the contacts Emma has made with legal, information technology, and counseling services in preparing for her research will provide a support network should any difficulties arise.

Recommendations for Responsible Practice

In this chapter, we have presented four cases studies that raise a range of ethical issues associated with conducting psychological research online. Rather than promoting a prescriptive approach to dealing with these ethical issues, we recommend a case-by-case examination that takes into account ethical principles and standards, the research purpose, the research context, and the identification and careful weighing of potential risks and benefits. As part of this, we view it as essential that researchers are familiar with the ethical guidance documents provided by psychological bodies within their own jurisdictions. Further, we encourage researchers to contact experienced online researchers and the Human Research Ethics Committees/Institutional Review Boards within their own institutions to discuss possible ethical issues associated with their proposed methodologies.

Human Research Ethics Committees/Institutional Review Boards play an important role in the procedural ethics process through ensuring ethical consideration of the overall research project and foreseeable issues. In this chapter, we have highlighted the need for researchers to consider issues such as the public versus private distinction in online settings, obtaining informed consent, covert and deceptive online research, and protecting the researcher within the online environment prior to applying for ethical approval. Each of these issues requires consideration as part of the weighing of potential risks and benefits. However, researchers' ethical considerations need to continue beyond the point of study approval to ensure that unforeseen issues are also appropriately addressed. This attention to process ethics complements procedural ethics.

References

Alessi, E. J. & Martin, J. I. (2010). Conducting an Internet-based survey: Benefits, pitfalls, and lessons learned. *Social Work Research, 34,* 122–128.

Allen, P. J. & Roberts, L. D. (2010). The ethics of outsourcing online survey research. *International Journal of Technoethics, 1,* 35–48.

American Psychological Association (2010). *Ethical principles of psychologists and code of conduct.* Washington, DC: American Psychological Association.

Association of Internet Researchers (2012). Ethical decision-making and Internet research: Recommendations from the AoIR ethics working committee (Version 2.0). Retrieved from http://aoir.org/reports/ethics2.pdf

Baker, T. D. (2012). Confidentiality and electronic surveys: How IRBs address ethical and technical issues. *IRB: Ethics & Human Research, 34,* 8–15. Retrieved from www .thehastingscenter.org/Publications/IRB

Beaulieu, A. & Estalella, A. (2012). Rethinking research ethics for mediated settings. *Information, Communication & Society, 15,* 23–42.

Bond, C. S., Ahmed, O. H., Hind, M., Thomas, B. & Hewitt-Taylor, J. (2013). The conceptual and practical ethical dilemmas of using health discussion board posts as research data. *Journal of Medical Internet Research, 15,* e112.

Bradley, S. K. & Carter, B. (2012). Reflections on the ethics of Internet newsgroup research. *International Journal of Nursing Studies, 49,* 625–630.

British Psychological Society (2013). *Ethics guidelines for Internet-mediated research.* INF206/1.2013. Leicester, UK: British Psychological Society. Retrieved from www .bps.org.uk/system/files/Public%20files/inf206-guidelines-for-internet-mediated -research.pdf

Bromseth, J. C. H. (2002). Public places: public activities? Methodological approaches and ethical dilemmas in research on computer-mediated communication contexts. In A. Morrison (Ed.), *Researching ICTs in context* (pp. 31–61). Oslo, Norway: University of Oslo.

Brotsky, S. R. & Giles, D. (2007). Inside the "pro-ana" community: A covert online participant observation. *Eating Disorders, 15,* 93–109.

Buchanan, E. A. & Hvizdak, E. E. (2009). Online survey tools: Ethical and methodological concerns of Human Research Ethics Committees. *Journal of Empirical Research on Human Research Ethics, 4,* 37–48.

Calvey, D. (2008). The art and politics of covert research: Doing "situated ethics" in the field. *Sociology, 42,* 905–918.

Coles, J. & Mudaly, N. (2010). Staying safe: Strategies for qualitative child abuse researchers. *Child Abuse Review, 19,* 56–69.

Dickson-Swift, V., James, E. L., Kippen, S., & Liamputtong, P. (2008). Risk to researchers in qualitative research on sensitive topics: Issues and strategies. *Qualitative Health Research, 18,* 133–144.

Elmir, R., Schmied, V., Jackson, D., & Wilkes, L. (2011). Interviewing people about potentially sensitive topics. *Nurse Researcher, 19,* 12–16.

Glaser, J., Dixit, J., & Green, D. P. (2002). Studying hate crime with the Internet: What makes racists advocate racial violence? *Journal of Social Issues, 58,* 177–193.

Gosling, S. D. & Mason, W. (2015). Internet research in psychology. *Annual Review of Psychology, 66,* 877–902.

Guillemin, M. & Gillam, L. (2004). Ethics, reflexivity and ethically important moments in research. *Qualitative Inquiry, 10,* 261–280.

Hewson, C. (2015). Ethics issues in digital methods research. In H. Snee, C. Hine, Y. Morey, S. Roberts, & H. Watson (Eds.), *Digital methods for social science: An interdisciplinary guide to research innovation* (pp. 206–221). Basingstoke, UK: Palgrave Macmillan.

Holtz, P., Kronberger, N., & Wagner, W. (2012). Analyzing internet forums. *Journal of Media Psychology, 24,* 55–66.

Humphreys, K., Winzelberg, A., & Klaw, E. (2000). Psychologists' ethical responsibilities in the Internet-based groups: Issues, strategies, and a call for dialogue. *Professional Psychology: Research and Practice, 31,* 493–496.

King, S. (1996). Researching Internet communities: Proposed ethical guidelines for the reporting of the results. *The Information Society, 12,* 119–127.

Kraut, R., Olson, J., Banaji, M., Bruckman, A., Cohen, J. & Couper, M. (2004). Psychological research online: Report of Board of Scientific Affairs Advisory Group on the conduct of research on the Internet. *American Psychologist, 59,* 105–17.

Lewis, S. P. & Arbuthnott, A. E. (2014). Non-suicidal self-injury, eating disorders, and the Internet. In *Non-suicidal self-injury in eating disorders* (pp. 273–293). Heidelberg: Springer Berlin.

Lewis, S. P. & Seko, Y. (2016). A double-edged sword: A review of benefits and risks of online nonsuicidal self-injury activities. *Journal of Clinical Psychology, 72,* 249–262.

Mahon, P. Y. (2013). Internet research and ethics: Transformative issues in nursing education research. *Journal of Professional Nursing, 30,* 124–129.

Malik, S. H. & Coulson, N. S. (2013). Coming to terms with permanent involuntary childlessness: A phenomenological analysis of bulletin board postings. *Europe's Journal of Psychology, 9,* 77–92.

Markham, A. (2012). Fabrication as ethical practice: Qualitative inquiry in ambiguous internet contexts. *Information, Communication & Society, 15,* 334–353.

Mason, W. & Suri, S. (2012). Conducting behavioral research on Amazon's Mechanical Turk. *Behavior Research Methods, 44,* 1–23.

Parker, J. & Crabtree, A. S. (2014). Covert research and adult protection and safeguarding: An ethical dilemma? *The Journal of Adult Protection, 16,* 29–40.

Poole, H., Giles, D. C., & Moore, K. (2004). Researching sexuality and sexual issues: Implications for the researcher? *Sexual and Relationship Therapy, 19*, 79–86.

Rier, D. A. (2007). Internet social support groups as moral agents: The ethical dynamics of HIV+ status disclosure. *Sociology of Health & Illness, 29*, 1043–1058.

Roberts, L. D. (2007). Opportunities and constraints of electronic research. In R. A. Reynolds, R. Woods, & J. D. Baker (Eds.), *Handbook of research on electronic surveys and measurements* (pp. 19–27). Hershey, PA: Idea Reference Group.

Roberts, L. D. (2015). Ethical issues in conducting qualitative research in online communities. *Qualitative Research in Psychology, 12*, 314–325.

Roberts, L. D. & Allen, P. J. (2015). Exploring ethical issues associated with using online surveys in educational research. *Educational Research and Evaluation, 21*, 95–108.

Roberts, L., Smith, L., & Pollock, C. (2004). Conducting ethical research online: Respect for individuals, identities and the ownership of words. In E. A. Buchanan (Ed.), *Readings in virtual research ethics: Issues and controversies* (pp. 156–173). Hershey, PA: Information Science Publishing.

Spicker, P. (2011). Ethical covert research. *Sociology, 45*, 118–133.

van Deventer, J. P. (2009). Ethical considerations during human centred overt and covert research. *Quality & Quantity, 43*(1), 45–57.

Whiteman, N. (2012). Ethical stances in (Internet) research. In N. Whiteman (Ed.), *Undoing ethics* (pp. 1–23). New York, NY: Springer.

Whitlock, J. L., Powers, J. L., & Eckenrode, J. (2006). The virtual cutting edge: The Internet and adolescent self-injury. *Developmental Psychology, 42*, 407–417.

Zurbriggen, E. L. (2002). II. Sexual objectification by research participants: Recent experiences and strategies for coping. *Feminism & Psychology, 12*, 261–268.

24 Ethical Issues in International Research

Mark M. Leach and Sharon G. Horne

The globalization of psychology has increased over the past two decades, with improved communications and international collaborations, easier travel, increased international exchanges (Lyons & Leong, 2012), and greater access to international journals, all of which have assisted psychology in becoming more internationally diverse. In many respects, formal psychology has always had global foundations because national psychological associations, indigenous psychologies, and research departments around the world have existed for decades, and psychologists in these countries have contributed to the psychological literature (Pickren & Rutherford, 2010). Most of this literature has historically been constrained to national or regional journals, though there has been increased recognition of the need to further internationalize psychology. As greater numbers of psychologists become more involved globally, the psychology profession benefits, as there is improved dialogue, broader thinking, and a better understanding of the influence of cultural context on psychological constructs.

Within this global expansion, there have been increased efforts to better understand research ethics from an international perspective. The historical background leading to contemporary psychology ethics codes is well known to U.S. psychologists. The Nuremberg Code was the direct result of the medical experimentation atrocities of World War II, and the interest in research ethics has been maintained because of multiple examples of unethical research in many countries and the proliferation of ethics documents (Benatar, 2004). The Universal Declaration of Human Rights (www .un.org/Overview/rights.html) adopted in 1948 as well as the principles within the World Medical Association Declaration of Helsinki (www.wma.net/policies-post/ wma-declaration-of-helsinki-ethical-principles-for-medical-research-involving- human-subjects) adopted in 1964 and last revised in 2013 are considered foundational to good human ethical research. In the U.S. in 1974, the National Research Act was signed into law, creating the National Commission for the Protection of Human Subjects of Biomedical and Behavioral Research (Department of Health, Education, and Welfare, 1979), which is generally considered the first national bioethics commission. This commission created the Belmont Report, which is a set of ethical principles and guidelines for the protection of human subjects in biomedical and behavioral research fields. These broad and aspirational principles served to set the foundation for future rules and standards to be developed. The report included three ethical principles (Respect for Persons, Beneficence, and Justice), as well as three applications that are based on the principles (Informed Consent, Assessment of Risks and Benefits, and

Selection of Subjects). The American Psychological Association (APA) Ethical Principles of Psychologists and Code of Conduct (APA, 2017) draws much of its research areas from the Belmont Report, including specific research standards.

Briefly, there are three types of ethics documents, national, regional, and international (see Leach, 2016). Nationally, codes of ethics are found in over 50 psychological organizations. They are structured differently, have different emphases, and include cultural components specific to their countries. Regional codes include those of the Scandinavian countries, each of which shares a common code of ethics. The Meta-Code of Ethics of the European Federation of Psychologists' Associations (EFPA, 2005) is a principle-based document that offers guidance for the content of each member country's ethics code. Each European member country can still have its own ethics code, but should be consonant with the Meta-Code's principles. In the 1990s, South America's Mercosur countries (Argentina, Brazil, Paraguay, and Uruguay) developed an economic trade agreement, and the resultant openness across countries also occurred within psychology. They created the Ethical Framework for Professional Practice of Psychology in the Mercosur and Associated Countries, a regional document of ethical principles. Finally, there are international ethics documents. The Universal Declaration of Ethical Principles for Psychologists (Gauthier, Pettifor, & Ferrero, 2010) is the culmination of years of development, and approved by the three international psychological organizations consisting of the International Union of Psychological Sciences, the International Association of Applied Psychology, and the International Association for Cross-Cultural Psychology. This document does not prescribe or proscribe specific behaviors, but offers a common moral framework and a generic set of ethical principles for global psychology organizations.

Questions arise as to which ethics documents are most appropriate for international research given that there is no standard ethics document in psychology from which to derive guidance. U.S. psychologists are obliged to follow the APA Code regardless of where their work is conducted, though other countries have their own ethics codes and documents that have ethical expectations that may differ from the APA Code of Ethics. Research ethics can become more complicated with the increasing numbers of international research teams. Leach, Jeppsen, and Discont (2012) conducted a content analysis of research standards found in 43 countries' code of ethics and determined that 17 ethics research standards were found in multiple countries; 8 or 9 (depending on criteria) were found in over 50 percent of the countries. Thus, there does seem to be some overlap among countries on the inclusion of research standards in ethics codes, but no consensus. Of course, ethics codes are developed within cultural systems, so the interpretation and implementation of these standards from an international perspective has yet to be determined.

These issues present ethical challenges to U.S. as well as other national researchers. As indicated above, ethics codes are developed within cultural contexts, and very little is known about handling ethical concerns cross-culturally when specific ethics codes are utilized (Leong & Lyons, 2010). Differences in the understanding of informed consent within individualist and collectivist countries is one example.

Approaching consent from an individualistic perspective can often lead to dissent among community leaders, who expect to be approached about the research project itself prior to requesting consent from individual participants. Benatar (2004) has argued that international research ethics disputes often occur at two levels. Though not completely orthogonal, there are researchers who wish to advance knowledge for knowledge's sake and those who are sensitive to the possible exploitation of individuals and communities, particularly in developing countries.

Even the latter type of study can become muddied. As an example of possible though unintentional exploitation, Karim, Qurraishi, Coovadia, and Susser (1998) conducted a study to determine participants' understanding of informed consent for HIV testing in South Africa. Though the researchers followed standard informed consent procedures, including voluntary participation and the right to withdraw, the authors found that 84 percent of participants still considered participation mandatory (see also Bardsdorf & Wassenaar, 2005). Molyneaux, Wassenaar, Peshu, and Marsh (2005) found that obtaining true informed consent for medical research in rural Kenya was extremely difficult given participants' education levels, medical access, values, and differing understandings of health and illness. Bhutta (2004) examined global guidelines on informed consent across organizations, found disparities, and made compelling arguments about our need for a deeper understanding of informed consent given the complexities in international research.

Informed consent is only one of the myriad of ethical issues that can arise when conducting international research. Though by no means exhaustive, others may include multiple relationships, testing (e.g., measurement equivalence), participant remuneration, confidentiality, competence, data, and authorship expectations, as well as many others. When discussing international research, many ethical issues are consistent regardless of the region of the world. However, there are additional complexities when considering language, dissimilar cultures, and local expectations, ethics, and laws. Below are two cases that have multiple ethical issues to consider. These are written in a way that is different from other chapters in this handbook, as they are presented from a "developmental" perspective, in that one ethical issue led, though nonlinearly, to another. They are also less formal.

The Case of a Rwandan Experience Cut Short

I (M.M.L.) contributed a small piece of my research time to a center at my university, and this center was asked to conduct outcome research of workshops in Rwanda directed toward teachers and community leaders acquiring training in counseling skills. The goal was for these individuals to help their community recover from the aftermath of the 1994 genocide by working with those still experiencing emotional, familial, and cognitive turmoil. The outcome of the evaluation might help the instructor garner grant money from the Rwandan government to further develop the program and assist more individuals and families. Issues of post-traumatic stress, anxiety, depression, substance abuse, and a variety of other mental health concerns are common. These problems are also common not just for the adults who survived, but also the generation of children who have largely grown up without parents and support.

No one in the university center had previously visited Rwanda with the exception of one individual who did not conduct research; thus, questions about the validity of the research and ethics of my going to Rwanda and conducting such a project immediately came to mind. I have studied cultural influences on a variety of psychological variables, including ethics, and wanted to be sensitive to being perceived as a "helicopter researcher," where an individual, generally from a well-resourced country, drops in and conducts research in a less-resourced country and then leaves. I first consulted the APA Code and immediately identified the Standard of Exploitative Relationships (3.08), as well as the principle of Respect for People's Rights and Dignity (Principle E), particularly if there was no follow-up postevaluation. Rather than discuss one or two ethical issues that arose from a dilemma that occurred, I have decided to discuss the multiple ethical issues that arose throughout the process of considering, developing, and implementing the project.

Prior to accepting the task I considered my previous professional work in different countries and the difficulties and joys I had encountered working with different cultural groups. I have engaged in many cultural missteps and, being totally unfamiliar with Rwandan culture, became anxious. I wanted to be thoughtful about conducting the research, but how could I avoid being a helicopter researcher, particularly compounded by the fact that I am a U.S. citizen? I recalled the 1994 genocide and how the U.S., along with NATO and other countries, failed to significantly intervene, and wondered at the extent to which I would be welcomed in Rwanda. The intersection of politics and research initially began to merge. Weighing the APA principles and standard with my concerns over the brief intervention, I decided to proceed to collect more information before a decision was made. There was no way to avoid being a helicopter researcher in this case, which still caused me some concern, but the center was asked to develop the project and it was expected by my Rwandan colleague to be a short-term project. I also recognized the possible significance of the project and the number of people who could potentially be helped. Principle A was a primary motivator in the decision-making process.

I met with the Rwandan instructor while she was on a visit with her sister in the U.S. in order to determine her goals. During our discussion, I realized that she wanted an evaluation of her program, but within a research frame in order to show positive (implied) outcomes to the Rwandan government. She expressed minimal research background and little idea about what such a project might entail. We had a very brief amount of time together prior to her departure. Due to her research inexperience, she essentially allowed me carte blanche to determine the best method to evaluate her program. The following includes some of the ethical issues that arose, from pretrip research development and ethical thinking through my time in Rwanda.

The first ethical concern that arose was one of competence (APA Standard 2.01, Boundaries of Competence), in that while I had previously engaged in international work, I knew virtually nothing about Rwanda and its cultures. Additionally, a literature search on Rwandan mental health was interesting but very limited, and was primarily written by researchers from countries other than Rwanda. Questions regarding whether I was the appropriate person for the task lingered, though I was chosen by the center because of previous international research experience. When considering my competence, I also considered Principle A of the APA Code of Ethics, Beneficence and Nonmaleficence. Because of the limits to my competence, I knew it was critical to at least strive to do no harm. The question remained, though: was I sufficiently competent to engage in this project? However, I was well versed in research, had been involved in international work in various capacities, and had thought about the tremendous national need. More importantly, Principle A was again the primary motivator in that there were very few mental health resources in Rwanda and this was a way to benefit, albeit indirectly, those in need. Principles D (Justice) and E (Respect for People's Rights and Dignity) must also be considered, as understanding potential biases, boundaries of competence, fairness, self-determination, and respect for cultural, individual, and role differences is critical when engaging in international research.

I also considered a decision-making model (see Barnett & Johnson, 2008). First, it was important to define the situation clearly. The situation as I saw it was whether I was the most qualified and competent individual to conduct the research. Second, who would be impacted by my decision? My response was not only the Rwandan participants, but also the Rwandan people, given that the intent of the study was to assess a program designed for participants to provide basic services in their communities to help others. My professional obligations included providing the best possible services, being sensitive to potential harm, and considering my obligation to promote the interests of those involved. I also considered the reputation and the mission of the center, as this project was directly related to their mission of anti-violence and equality at both national and international levels. I was already considering the APA ethical principles and standards as well as other professional guidelines. Next, I began to reflect on my personal feelings and competence. My primary feelings were anxiety and perhaps fear, because I was unfamiliar with the Rwandan culture and saw the significance of this study given the horrific events of the genocide and its possible aftermath. I also felt eager because of my interest in travel. I had never visited Rwanda before and was excited about the possibilities. However, there is growing evidence of the role of emotions in ethical decision-making and I needed to be cognizant of the influence of my excitement on making a good, ethical decision. It was from this intentional assessment of feelings that I thought if I moved forward with the project then I would have to read about the genocide and include the history leading up to it, as well as any relevant research. I consulted with a colleague familiar with my previous work. From there, I considered alternative courses of action. I had considered searching for colleagues nationally with more familiarity with Rwanda and weighed the possible benefits and risks for all parties.

A primary issue was that the instructor who requested the research assistance was unfamiliar with anyone else who could complete the project. When I earlier suggested contacting others who may have more experience with the culture, she quickly dismissed the idea because she did not have an existing relationship with them and did not trust them. Additionally, to hand the project to another individual or university negated the purpose of the center and would not have fulfilled its mission. Taking all of the information together, I decided to move forward with the project.

Development of the research project was the next consideration. The instructor's workshops included basic counseling and group counseling skills as well as information on mental health issues commonly reported by survivors of the genocide. International researchers are well aware that constructs such as PTSD, depression, anxiety, and substance abuse may not have conceptual equivalence, or be defined or assessed in a similar manner across cultures. Additionally, assessment instruments are valid in some cultures and not in others, and a literature review of these constructs and previously included instruments to measure mental health outcomes in Rwanda was not useful. Ethical questions arose such as, "Will I be forcing responses into Western concepts from participants?", "What are my Bases for Assessment and Uses of Assessment?" (9.01), and "What are my Bases for Scientific and Professional Judgment? (9.02). For example, how confident am I that the instruments I want to use are appropriate given that they have not been normed on a Rwandan sample. My initial thought was that, while there are some common features of depression, anxiety, and PTSD internationally, the instruments I considered including had not been normed in Rwanda. I then reviewed sections of The Standards for Educational and Psychological Testing, which offers guidance on testing standards and is jointly published by the American Educational Research Association, the APA, and the National Council on Measurement in Education (1999).

Simultaneously, there were also ethical concerns about qualifications and supervision. The project was supposed to be introduced to the on-site instructor who would administer it over different time periods during the year. The instructor has a master's degree in counseling but very limited research knowledge and experience, raising a concern about 9.07, Assessment by Unqualified Persons and 2.05, Delegation of Work to Others. The instructor would need to be trained in a short amount of time regarding how to use the instruments and answer specific questions, and it would not be possible to adequately supervise her work. Fortunately, the instruments were not complicated, but unforeseen issues could arise given that the extent to which the participants had previous experiences with Likert-type scales was unclear.

Unfortunately, at that moment, I was not convinced that the instruments were fully appropriate and relied on Principle A. I decided that there was enough evidence for me to seriously consider using instruments not previously published on Rwandan mental health topics. Weighing the issues related to accurate assessment with the principle of beneficence, I decided that the potential moral and ethical gain outweighed the potential methodological and additional ethical concerns. My reasoning was that there is a potential to make a positive impact on real people in need, and that p-values were not as important as the potential clinical benefits.

During the selection of instruments, I questioned the method itself. How likely is it that the participants had been exposed to a Likert-type instrument that we take for granted in many industrialized countries and cultures? The expectation (which turned out to be accurate) was that practically all participants would be unfamiliar with a Likert-type scale and would be unsure how to respond to questions using this scale. From a professional perspective, Principle C (Integrity) could be considered because of its emphasis on promoting "accuracy, honesty, and truthfulness" and because it can easily be considered within a research realm. Additionally, can I expect participants to understand what I am asking of them, and even if a description of a Likert-type scale is presented, how are the stems and anchors presented, how do these translate into Kinyarwanda (the national language), and what is the likelihood that they have a similar meaning to English? Those reading this chapter can briefly engage themselves in an example. Develop one question that includes a Likert-type scale, place the anchors on the end, and complete the rest of it. For example, 1 = highly unlikely, 2 = somewhat unlikely, 3 = neither likely nor unlikely, 4 = somewhat likely, 5 = highly likely. Explain precisely the differences among these categories to a friend. Now, explain it through a translator into another language.

The next issue included receiving institutional approval from my university's Institutional Review Board (IRB; 8.01, Institutional Approval). Difficulties resulted from seeking approval, as many university IRBs are structured with expectations of formal informed consent (8.02) that includes information for participants regarding contact information and other important data. IRBs are designed to protect research participants as well as the institutions to which they belong. Multiple issues surrounding the IRB occurred given that the instructor was not associated with a university, agency, institution, or organization, and she acknowledged that the local university did not have a structure in place to evaluate the project.

Basic issues such as the location in which the research would take place caused initial concerns given that the actual setting would be a room in a local school/community building in a village, with no address or phone. The instructor would have a phone, but many participants had no phone. Many universities have standard language for whom to contact at the university should research concerns arise among participants. While wishing to be in compliance ethically, there were difficulties explaining to members of the IRB that participants in Rwanda could not make a long-distance phone call or e-mail should concerns arise. First, not all Rwandans have cell phones and e-mail access. If a research concern arose, issues such as the cost of an international call and the expense of e-mail rental time, language and translation concerns, and navigating an unknown system all precluded this language from becoming part of the informed consent information. It could be argued that offering information to participants without a reasonable means of actually following through is unethical.

Informed consent is included four times in the APA Ethics Code, attesting to its role as a cornerstone to good and ethical practices. There are differences regarding what constitutes *informed* consent, and much has been written about areas of content related to consent and what constitutes true understanding of consent (e.g., Bhutta, 2004; Fitzpatrick, Martiniuk, D'Antoine, Oscar, Carter, & Elliott, 2016; Molyneux et al., 2005). Unlike in other sections of the APA Code, in the Research and Publication section, Informed Consent to Research (8.02) lists eight specific areas that must be included, including the purpose of the research, the participant's right to decline, foreseeable consequences of declining or withdrawing, foreseeable factors that may influence their willingness to participate, research benefits, confidentiality limits, incentives, and whom to contact for questions about the research and participant rights. A couple of initial ethical issues immediately came to mind. Assuming written informed consent was necessary for this research project, questions about whether participants would truly understand the right to withdraw without consequences may occur in this project, similar to many other studies (Bhutta, 2004). Additionally, given that the topic of participants' own trauma histories could become more prominent, this could result in a need to have local mental health resources available (overall, keep in mind that I could not adequately supervise her). The instructor was a respected member of the community and could act as a counselor, yet that could place her in a position leading to a boundary violation (3.04, Multiple Relationship). However, multiple relationships are considered differently in collectivistic cultures and I had to question my assumptions of multiple relationships based on Western thinking.

In keeping with ethical compliance, I could not make the argument to the IRB that Dispensing with Informed Consent for Research (8.05) would apply as the research could create harm, though the questionnaires were anonymous and would not place participants at risk for any damage or confidentiality breaches. That said, the university IRB required a translated application prior to acceptance. The statement of contacting the university if issues arose was included, even though I knew well that it was unlikely anyone from Rwanda would call the university IRB number if needed. The response from the IRB appeared to be a clash between perceived legal and ethical, if not moral (financial) responsibilities. As a means to find a reasonable solution, the contact number of the local researcher was also included on the final document, and she was instructed to contact me should an issue arise. Prior to the meeting with the participants in Rwanda, paper copies of the instruments were made and paid for by me and not the instructor who asked for the study to be completed, in accordance with Principle D: Justice. Incurring additional costs was not appropriate given the economic and power differential between me and the instructor and participants.

A meeting in Rwanda was arranged with the instructor to discuss the research project with participants. Upon meeting with the participants the instructor, speaking in native Kinyarwanda, began explaining the project, followed by a question-and-answer period. She clarified its purpose as well as stating that the results may help assist with future funding from the government in order to expand the amount of assistance that could be offered to Rwandan citizens. A number of questions were raised, and both she and I (through the instructor as translator) did our best to respond. During a long interchange in Kinyarwanda I heard "American" interjected, followed by a third of the 20 participants in the room turning to look at me. After the meeting, the instructor noted that they were concerned about an American, and a white American at that, conducting a research project when they did not know me or my intentions. There was also a concern expressed about whether their responses would be held anonymously and whether the U.S. or Rwandan governments would have access to their responses. Though the instructor attempted to allay their concerns, the project was eventually cancelled upon my return to the U.S., as the trust necessary for an international research project did not arise.

This project reminded me of an ethics proposal years ago that also failed to materialize. I was working with an Iranian colleague and trying to replicate a well-known ethics study by Pope and Vetter (1992), who asked clinicians to describe an incident encountered over the past year that was ethically troubling. This type of study had been conducted in seven Western countries, which limited its generalizability, but never in a country such as Iran. The project was developed and needed the approval of the Iranian government rather than a university IRB. The government stated that Iranian clinicians do not have ethical dilemmas and halted the project. These failed projects helped me to consider more fully the relationship of global politics with my own research projects and that more scholarship in this area is needed. Going forward, I may have to discuss more prominently with international colleagues the potential political issues surrounding a particular research project and how the proposed project will be received prior to its development.

These projects were disappointing and frustrating, though informative. Most of the research I had previously conducted in my career had personal meaning, yet few projects such as that in Rwanda had direct application possibilities. It was disappointing and frustrating on multiple levels, including the inability to help ensure quality training to participants to help their communities, using much time and resources with no substantive outcome, and not previously considering the possible political ramifications. However, this experience has helped me grow as an international researcher and I hope to have another opportunity to make a significant impact on communities in the future.

The Case of Engaging in Culturally Sensitive Research Topics

For many years, I (S.G.H.) have conducted transnational research in post-communist countries, including Romania, Hungary, Russia, Uzbekistan, and Kyrgyzstan. My work is primarily focused on topics that carry a great deal of cultural salience; for example, on violence against women and lesbian, gay, bisexual, and transgender (LGBT) concerns. During Soviet-era communism, prevalence and incidence rates of domestic violence were not collected, and violence against women was characterized as a product of the instability of capitalism; the official government position was that it was unnecessary to keep statistics since this issue was largely nonexistent (Horne, 1999). In a similar way, homosexuality was considered an import from the West and not a natural expression of human sexuality. For example, until 1993, same-sex behavior was criminalized in Russia; many gay men were imprisoned during the Soviet era, and lesbian and bisexual women were often subjected to mandatory medical treatment to address their same-sex desires, and LGB men and women served terms in labor camps (Essig, 1999).

This vignette is centered on a research study my colleagues and I embarked upon in the mid-2000s to explore the experiences of Russian LGBT people related to mental health treatment. In the relative openness that occurred in Russia following the decriminalization of homosexuality in the mid-1990s, as well as the development of social services during this period, I was inspired to conduct research to learn more about the burgeoning openness. In terms of ethical principles, I was primarily motivated for this research due to Principle E, Respect for People's Rights and Dignity. Principle E indicates that psychologists respect all people as well as their rights of "privacy, confidentiality, and self-determination, the necessity to protect vulnerable individuals, as well being aware of cultural and individual differences" (APA Code of Ethics, 2017).

In the advent of increasing support for the rights of LGBT people in Russia, I wished to explore the ways that LGBT individuals were navigating the new atmosphere of openness and expansion of rights. My partner, who is a Canadian–U. S. researcher who also focuses on LGBT issues, as well as a dear friend who is also a U.S. citizen but has many years of experience working in the former Soviet Union and wrote a book on LGBT issues in Siberia, formed our team. We decided to conduct a qualitative research study with LGBT people in three different cities in Russia (Moscow, St. Petersburg, and Novosibirsk in Siberia) and draw upon our contacts and resources to reach participants who could speak to their experiences. We considered our research project and its alignment with Principle A, Beneficence and Nonmaleficence; our research was likely to provide benefit by increasing awareness and understanding of the experiences of LGBT individuals, could potentially advocate for needed mental health resources, and would likely not cause harm to those who participated in the research. Principle A is associated with benefitting others and doing no harm. However, it is also related to safeguarding the welfare and rights of individuals, as well as understanding how psychologists' actions may influence others and guarding against factors "that may lead to misuse of their influence."

In light of these principles, we consulted the Code of Ethics and, in particular, Standard 2.01, Competence. This standard states, "Psychologists provide services, teach, and conduct research with populations and in areas only within the boundaries of their competence, based on their education, training, supervised experiences, consultation, study, or professional experience" (APA Code of Ethics, 2017). We thought that our research team was composed of individuals with competence in the area of study. My undergraduate education was in Slavic languages and literature, I had studied in the Soviet Union, and I had made nearly yearly trips to Russia since it had become an independent nation in 1991. With our combined expertise in LGBT issues and with our collaborator who had documented LGBT issues in Siberia in the 1990s, we thought we met the standards of competence. Still, in order to address any potential barriers to communication, we decided to have native Russian speakers serve as interpreters. In utilizing interpreters, we had to consider Standard 2.05, Delegation of Work to Others, and whether using interpreters would compromise the project by introducing potential multiple relationships. The interpreters would need to have familiarity with LGBT issues (so were likely to be LGBT themselves), feel comfortable discussing various themes related to LGBT experience, and not interject their own experiences into the interviews. At the same time, we would not want the participants to feel inhibited in what they might share due to having a local interpreter involved in the interviews. We elected to include a screening questionnaire to ask about comfort with interpreters and whether participants wished to provide their own interpreter. My collaborator and I would need to be present for all the interviews, listen to both the participant and the interpretation to ensure that the interviewee's experience was not altered through the interpretation, and carefully review all the tapes for any instances of multiple relationships influencing the interviews.

As we developed the protocol and research methods, we consulted the APA Ethics Code and also considered Principle D, Justice, and whether our study would be accessible to and provide benefit to our participants. We needed to exercise reasonable judgment and take precautionary steps to limit our potential biases from influencing the study and to not allow our limitations in expertise in the area to lead to or support unjust practices. The observance of Principle D, Justice, is particularly important for international research because of the inevitable differences in equity, geopolitics, and purported valence of research in different contexts (Sultana, 2007). In particular, we wanted to represent the experiences of LGBT individuals through their experiences and through the historical context; such pursuit of justice required us to represent the history and literature of LGBT lives with accuracy and in-depth study. We embarked upon a thorough exploration of LGBT lives and experiences from pre-Revolutionary Russia, through the Soviet era, to the present time. Using qualitative methods allowed us to bracket out many of our biases and discuss expectations that we predicted we would hear in the narratives.

Next, we needed to procure institutional approval from our university's IRB (8.01, Institutional Approval). Like most IRBs that review research with human subjects, the issue of informed consent was of primary consideration. As the former vignette described, we were expected to protect research participants and provide contact information for our university's IRB. We were able to provide the phone number on our informed consent forms; however, we knew that it was unlikely that participants would follow-up and consult with our IRB due to the distance. Therefore, the responsibility was on us to ensure that we would be taking precautions to protect human subjects during the research. Our study was on mental health concerns of LGBT individuals and we were proposing to conduct this research in a country at a time when there were practically no LGBT-affirmative mental health services. If our participants described suicidal ideation or severe depression, we would not be able to provide a national hotline or suicide crisis line to provide them with support. Fortunately, we were working closely with a volunteer LGBT clinic that had been established in Moscow and we were able to provide assurance that two psychologists with whom we were acquainted would be willing to be consulted if such cases were to arise. This consideration was related to Standard 2.02, Providing Services in Emergencies, which states that psychologists may provide such services in order to ensure that services are not denied. Had we had any incidents that would have required mental health services, we would have worked with this emerging clinic to adequately provide short-term services until a long-term support plan could be identified. We added questions to our protocol about self-harm and mental health status to further protect our participants and as an added check.

Of utmost concern to us as the research team as well as the university's IRB was Standard 4, Privacy and Confidentiality. At this time, the LGBT community was relatively small and many of our participants were associated with nonprofit organizations that provided services for HIV or sexual health, which could easily compromise confidentiality. In this small-world phenomenon, many of our participants had familiarity with other LGBT participants, even in different cities. We had to determine what steps would need to be taken to protect confidentiality (4.01) and minimize intrusions on privacy (4.04). We decided to utilize pseudonyms and not to identify any place or agency names. Once we began the research, we were asked often in our interviews if we would be publishing the names of the nongovernmental organizations (NGOs) that they worked for. I recall one participant saying, "Feel free to use my name, I have nothing to hide." Many of these participants were proud of the work they were doing and wished to highlight some of the positive contributions of their organizations. These interviews were conducted in a time of a general thawing of LGBT rights; it seemed by all measures that LGBT rights were following a similar trajectory to what was occurring in other European countries and in the U.S. Homosexuality had been decriminalized and was removed from the formal designation of Russian mental disorders in 1999. In the major cities, there were now LGBT-themed bookstores, magazines, and cafes, and although most LGBT people could not be out at work for risk of losing their jobs, more people were writing openly about being LGBT and sharing and identifying as LGBT to friends and family.

In 2013, under an increasingly repressive and anti-LGBT government headed by Vladimir Putin, Article 6.21 of the Code of the Russian Federation on Administrative Offenses was passed. The law deemed the following as a punishable offense: propaganda of nontraditional sexual relations among minors, manifested in the distribution of information aimed at forming nontraditional sexual orientations, the attraction of nontraditional sexual relations, distorted conceptions of the social equality of traditional and nontraditional sexual relations among minors, or imposing information on nontraditional sexual relations that evokes interest in these kinds of relations (Legislation Bulletin of the Russian Federation, 2011, p. 1). Immediately, LGBT resources were found to be suspect, especially if they were accessible to minors in any way. Deti-404, a website for LGBT teens, was blacklisted and blocked by government regulators, and the founder, Elena Klimova, was fined and brought before a court (*Washington Times*, 2016). In 2013, the Russian foreign agent bill was put into effect (*The Guardian*, 2012); this law mandates that nonprofit organizations that receive foreign donations and engage in "political activity" are required to register and declare themselves as foreign agents. The combination of these bills has effectively shut down any of the forward progress for LGBT rights, and organizations that have depended upon support from international funding agencies, including HIV organizations, have been severely impacted in the face of the foreign agents bill.

During the publication process, a new ethical concern arose. In 2005, the Uzbek Government issued a process of re-registration for NGOs, which led to increased scrutiny of NGOs, including counseling centers, and in particular those that had received international funding or support. Our participants raised concern about the manuscript that was due to be published in a Western journal, suggesting that showing they had participated in Western research might add to the persistent bias against the centers as imports of Western influence and therefore not really addressing local needs. Informed consent (8.02) includes informing participants about "reasonably foresee-able factors that may be expected to influence their willingness to participate such as potential risks, discomfort, or adverse effects" (p. 10). Although we titled our manu-script "Leaving the herd: The lingering threat of difference for same-sex identities in post-communist Russia" (Horne, Ovrebo, Levitt, & Franeta, 2009), we could not have anticipated the sharp curbing of LGBT rights. Had we not followed our protocol of removing place-names and using pseudonyms, our research might have placed our participants in great risk years after the study was completed. When asked by partici-pants to publish their names or organizations, we were conflicted between principles of beneficence (psychologists strive to benefit those with whom they work) through our desire to highlight the good work that was occurring on behalf of LGBT rights and respect for people's rights and dignity (psychologists are aware that special safeguards may be necessary to protect the rights and welfare of persons or communities whose vulnerabilities impair autonomous decision-making) by protecting the privacy of our participants. We did not anticipate the propaganda bill and our participants could not have predicted such a measure; however, we knew that we were working with sensitive issues that had only recently been decriminalized; we took precautions in protecting our participants and safeguarding their identities and organizations.

This scenario is an example of the need for ethics codes to be applicable across a diverse range of activities; a research study that may seem ethical and fitting with particular principles at one time (e.g., prizing beneficence and justice in order to highlight emerging LGBT rights) may morph into the importance of emphasizing other principles (e.g., fidelity and responsibility and respect for people's rights and dignity) when those same participants may warrant safeguarding and enhanced privacy. Indeed, this was not the only time that political movements shaped the context of the informed consent our participants were providing; another example is interviews with crisis counselors in Uzbekistan, whose crisis centers were suddenly bound by the passage of a law requiring a process of registration for NGOs by the Uzbek Government, which led to increased scrutiny of NGOs, including counseling centers, and in particular those that had received international funding or support (Horne, Mathews, Brown, & DeGroff, 2009). Our participants were entitled to raise concerns about the manuscript that was due to be published in a Western journal, and were reassured only after we shared that no identifying information was included (e.g., even the names of cities were changed due to the fact that many regions had only one counseling center). Informed consent is not a static, one-time event when one is engaged in international research in complex, transnational contexts.

Currently, I am in the process of concluding a research study on LGBT activists living in medium- and high-risk countries for repression and criminalization of LGBT rights. Several of the participants have asked that their organizations be cited or that they be listed in the publication. Given my experience thus far of navigating ethical concerns related to research and publication and ethical principles,

I will maintain the privacy and use of pseudonyms for my participants. There is no guarantee that participants' need for privacy and confidentiality will stay static. Our obligation is to protecting our participants and we may need to explain that informed consent is something that needs to be revisited depending on the sociopolitical situations; therefore, we will side with the principles of nonmaleficence and respect for people's rights and dignity. Our participants have other mechanisms to highlight their activities and the positive outcomes of their engagement in LGBT rights that do not compromise the integrity of the research process. Even if it appears that such recognition of an organization's work could be beneficial in the short-run, there is no guarantee that sociopolitical changes may not put the LGBT activists at greater risk or compromise the goals of the organization. These are serious considerations when engaging in cross-cultural research, bringing beneficence and nonmaleficence, justice, and people's rights and dignity to bear. In particular, standards related to informed consent and confidentiality are vital to consider in the context of the research project that includes consideration of the sociopolitical environment and potential for harm.

The Case of Japanese School Children

I (M.M.L.) was approached by a doctoral student interested in collecting data in Japan from adolescent students in a school. His sister would be able to assist in the collection of these data as a result of her employment as a teacher at the school. The project was developed, implemented, and completed. For this study, three classrooms of only eighth-grade students would be evaluated using questionnaires based on theoretical constructs and norms from the U.S.

At this point, let us consider the early possible ethical concerns that should be addressed. First, the culture of Japan is considered collectivistic, and with that there is a hierarchical system in which adolescent students do not question their teachers. Individualistic societies might consider that ethical standard 3.08, Exploitative Relationships should be considered prior to moving forward with the research project. While the teacher, with the permission of the principal, held local responsibility, the psychologist conducting the study also has the responsibility not to exploit students. Thus, this issue needed to be addressed. The principal and teacher are held in high regard and hold authoritative positions, and given the teacher's familial ties with the student investigator, the project could easily feel manipulative for the students. Completed instruments given back to this teacher also could feel manipulative. The doctoral student and I weighed the amount of potential felt manipulation against the anonymity of the completed instruments and the degree to which these students would likely believe that they could withdraw without penalty (8.02, Informed Consent). The doctoral student was raised in this culture and believed that an unusual amount of exploitation would not occur given that students complete questionnaires on a variety of topics throughout the year.

The parents and children were given consent and assent forms, respectively. Not only was this related to 8.02 (Informed Consent), but we considered whether we could dispense with informed consent (8.05). This standard indicates that dispensing with consent is reasonable if, among other areas, the study would not cause distress or harm and uses anonymous questionnaires. However, given that the study occurred in a different country, I wanted to be conservative with my ethical thinking.

There was also a concern about 4.01 (Maintaining Confidentiality). In essence, how will students know that their teacher will not review their responses? In addition to information supplied in the assent form, we wanted to take an additional precaution given that teachers have a strong authoritative role in Japan. Ultimately, we decided to ask a different teacher to collect the responses without the actual teacher in the room to mitigate any uncomfortable feelings or confidentiality concerns. This teacher was given the means by which to submit the responses and send the responses directly back to the U.S. for analysis.

The IRB at the university wanted translated documents, including the instruments and assent form, and they were translated and back-translated. There was no IRB at the Japanese school. The university student acknowledged early in the study development process that some of the language from the instruments did not easily translate into Japanese (especially emotion-laden terms), and word or theme approximations were instead included. Standard 9.01 (Bases for Assessment) was considered, as well as 9.02 (Use of Assessments). The latter states that instruments should have known validity and reliability for the group assessed. Unfortunately, these instruments had not been included in previous studies in the research area. The consideration to move forward was determined because results would include clarifications of the limited information of the instruments in the culture, and the decision was made that results should be tentatively held, thus maintaining consistency with ethical reporting responsibilities (see 9.06, Interpreting Assessment Results). We were also in alignment with 9.02, in that we conducted the research in a manner appropriate to the students' language and competence.

Standard 9.08 (Assessment by Unqualified Persons) was a standard that we considered, though it was unclear as to the extent it would apply in this study. Technically, if there are questions from the students, then psychologists are responsible for the responses by the teachers in the rooms. We wanted to make sure that they understood the purpose of the study and could answer any questions by the students. My doctoral student and I decided to construct an FAQ sheet for the teachers. Questions included, "How should I respond if I cannot adequately answer a question from a student?" and "If they don't want to complete all of the questions how do I respond to them?" The purpose of the FAQ sheet was, as best we could, to make sure that teachers received consistent information for their students and were qualified to administer the questionnaires. A questionnaire study may not seem as critical when considering that psychologists should not allow the use of psychological assessments by those not qualified (9.07, Assessment by Unqualified Persons), but we wanted to hold ourselves to the highest ethical standards. A question we asked ourselves prior to putting together the FAQ was, "What is an assessment technique?" We determined that we would be conservative with our thinking. The concern about teacher competence also fell under 2.05 (Delegation of Work to Others) in that our responsibility is to ensure that they competently perform their work.

We considered 9.10 (Explaining Assessment Results), which essentially states that psychologists should make certain that steps are taken to ensure that appropriate explanations of results are given. While participants in many questionnaire studies never receive a summary of the results, and some are not even given the opportunity to request results, we decided that in order to uphold the highest ethical standards, we would offer the school a summary at the end of the project. This summary was in language that was easily understandable and offered some ideas about how the results may fit with enhancing eighth-grade student experiences.

Summary

Conducting international research, much like in other areas, implies that there will likely be multiple ethical issues that need to be addressed. The addition of cultural and linguistic variables, for example, adds layers of complexity that have to be considered in order to engage in good, ethical research. International research is much more theoretically, ethically, and practically complex than research conducted within a home country. Because of this complexity, familiarity with other ethical and legal documents is often needed in order to best navigate the cultures and present psychology in the best ethical light.

Ethical issues are often hidden from others and require personal accountability and responsibility. They also require a more complex, continual examination than the ethical analysis found in most graduate-level ethics courses and personal and professional accountability. Unfortunately, ethical issues should also lead psychologists to consider nonrational areas that can influence ethical behaviors. Recently, there has been increased understanding of the role that emotions, and nonrational factors in general, have in decision-making (see Rogerson, Gottlieb, Handelsman, Knapp, & Younggren, 2011). These can both interfere with or enhance optimal ethical decision-making. However, they are rarely discussed when ethical issues arise and are typically not taught in graduate ethics courses. Because of their importance, in addition to the blind spots that frequently occur during ethical processes (see Bazerman & Tenbrunsel, 2011), it is important that psychologists seek consultation with trusted and honest colleagues.

References

American Educational Research Association, American Psychological Association, National Council on Measurement in Education (1999). *Standards for educational and psychological testing*. Washington, DC: American Educational Research Association.

American Psychological Association (2017). *Ethical principles of psychologists and code of conduct* (2002, Amended June 1, 2010 and January 1, 2017). Retrieved from www.apa.org/ethics/code/index.aspx

Bardsdorf, N. W. & Wassenaar, D. R. (2005). Racial differences in public perceptions of voluntariness of medical research participants in South Africa. *Social Science & Medicine*, *60*, 1087–1098.

Barnett, J. E. & Johnson, W. B. (2008). *Ethics desk reference for psychologists*. Washington, DC: American Psychological Association.

Bazerman, M. H. & Tenbrunsel, A. E. (2011). *Blind spots: Why we fail to do what's right and what to do about it*. Princeton, NJ: Princeton University Press.

Benatar, S. R. (2004). Toward progress in resolving dilemmas in international research ethics. *Journal of Law, Medicine, & Ethics*, *32*, 574–582.

Benatar, S. R. (2004). Towards progress in resolving dilemmas in international research ethics. International and comparative health law and ethics: A 25-year retrospective. *Journal of Law, Medicine & Ethics*, *32*, 574–582.

Bhutta, V. A. (2004). Beyond informed consent. *Bulletin of the World Health Organization*, *82*, 771–777.

Department of Health, Education, and Welfare (1979). *The National Commission for the Protection of Human Subjects of Biomedical and Behavioral Research*. Washington, DC: Department of Health, Education, and Welfare.

Essig, L. (1999). *Queer in Russia: A story of sex, self, and the other*. Durham, NC: Duke University Press.

European Federation of Psychologists' Associations (2005). Meta-code of ethics. Retrieved from http://ethics.efpa.eu/meta-code

Fitzpatrick, E. F. M., Martiniuk, A. L. C., D'Antoine, H., Oscar, J., Carter, M., & Elliott, E. J. (2016). Seeking consent for research with indigenous communities: A systematic review. *BMC Medical Ethics*, *17*, 65.

Gauthier, J., Pettifor, J., & Ferrero, A. (2010). The Universal Declaration of Ethical Principles for Psychologists: A culture-sensitive model for creating and reviewing a code of ethics. *Ethics & Behavior*, *20*, 179–196.

The Guardian (2012). Russia plans to register "foreign agent" NGOs. Retrieved from www.theguardian.com/world/2012/jul/02/russia-register-foreign-agent-ngos

Horne, S. (1999). Domestic violence in Russia. *American Psychologist*, *54*, 55–61.

Horne, S. G., Mathews, S. S., Brown, D., & DeGroff, S. H. (2009). Not staying home: The experience of Uzbek women crisis counselors and therapists. *Women & Therapy*, *32*, 317–337.

Horne, S. G., Ovrebo, E., Levitt, H. M., & Franeta, S. (2009). Leaving the herd: The lingering threat of difference for same-sex identities in post-communist Russia. *Sexuality Research and Social Policy*, *6*, 108–122.

Karim, A., Qurraishi, S. S., Coovadia, H. M., & Susser, M. (1998). Consent for HIV testing in a South African hospital: Is it truly informed or truly voluntary. *American Journal of Public Health*, *88*, 637–640.

Leach, M. M. (2016). Professional ethics around the world. In J. C. Norcross, G. R. Vandenboss, & D. K. Freedheim (Eds.), *APA handbook of clinical psychology* (Vol. 5, pp. 339–354). Washington, DC: American Psychological Association.

Leach, M. M., Jeppsen, B., & Discont, S. (2012). The search for common standards: A case of research standards. In M. M. Leach, M. J. Stevens, G. Lindsay, A. Ferrero, & Y. Korkut (Eds.), *The Oxford handbook of international psychological ethics* (pp. 134–148). New York, NY: Oxford University Press.

Leong, F. T. L. & Lyons, B. (2010). Ethical challenges for cross-cultural research conducted by psychologists from the United States. *Ethics & Behavior*, *20*, 250–264.

Lyons, B. J. & Leong, F. T. L. (2012). A call for ethical standards and guidelines for cross-cultural research conducted by American psychologists. In M. M. Leach, M. J. Stevens, G. Lindsay, A. Ferrero, & Y. Korkut (Eds.), *The Oxford handbook of international psychological ethics* (pp. 149–160). New York, NY: Oxford University Press.

Molyneux, C., Wassenaar, D., Peshu, N., & Marsh, K. (2005). Community voices on the notion and practice of informed consent for biomedical research. *Social Science & Medicine, 61*, 443–454.

Mullings, B. (1999). Insider or outsider, both or neither: Some dilemmas of interviewing in a cross-cultural setting. *Geoforum, 30*, 337–350.

Nagar, R. (2002). Footloose researchers, "traveling" theories, and the politics of transnational feminist praxis. *Gender, Place and Culture, 9*, 179–186.

Legislation Bulletin of the Russian Federation (2011). Article 5 of the Federal Law on Protecting Children from Information Harmful to their Health and Development and other legislative acts of the Russian Federation aimed at protecting children from information propagating the rejection of traditional family values. N 1, Article 48; 2013, N 14, Article 1658).

Pickren, W. E. & Rutherford, A. (2010). *A history of modern psychology in context*. Hoboken, NJ: John Wiley & Sons Inc.

Pope, K. S. & Vetter, V. A. (1992). Ethical dilemmas encountered by members of the American Psychological Association: A national survey. *American Psychologist, 47*, 397–411.

Rogerson, M. D., Gottlieb, M. C., Handelsman, M. M., Knapp, S., & Younggren, J. (2011). Nonrational processes in ethical decision making. *American Psychologist, 66*, 614–623.

Sultana, F. (2007). Reflexivity, positionality and participatory ethics: Negotiating fieldwork dilemmas. *ACME: An International E-Journal for Critical Geographies, 6*, 374–385.

Washington Times (2016). Russia blacklists Deti-404, a website for LGBT teens. Retrieved from www.washingtontimes.com/news/2016/oct/11/russia-blacklists-deti-404-a-website-for-lgbt-teen

25 Clinical Supervision for Multicultural and Professional Competence

Erica H. Wise and Jennifer L. Schwartz

There are many complex technical skills that must be developed and maintained by health service psychologists as they move through training and into independent practice. In doctoral programs, the theory and research that underpin technical clinical skills are learned in academic courses, whereas the experiential practice that is essential to attaining the competence to use these skills effectively and safely with members of the public generally occurs in applied settings under the clinical supervision of faculty and community supervisors. Contemporary competency-based models (e.g., Hatcher et al., 2013) define technical clinical skills, such as psychological assessment or intervention, as the *functional* competencies, or the "what" of practice. Although these technical skills are essential to training and practice, additional attributes and capabilities, termed *foundational* competencies, are considered central to the development and maintenance of competence. In contrast to the functional competencies, these foundational competencies reflect the "how" of practice, as in how we do what we do. This chapter is devoted to conceptualizing and providing examples through vignettes of how clinical supervision can be used to foster selected foundational competencies as we move from early training into independent practice. In the competence-based model referenced earlier, ethics is identified as a foundational competency under the broader category of *professionalism*. Under this rubric, professionalism includes: professional values and attitudes; individual and cultural diversity (ICD); ethical and legal standards and policy; and reflective practice/self-assessment/self-care. These foundational competencies are at the heart of clinical training and practice. We believe that they are best developed by supervisees and maintained as professional psychologists via academic course work that is reinforced by high-quality clinical supervision in applied practice settings, through active participation in high-quality continuing education, and through dedication to lifelong learning. Using ethics as our overarching framework, this chapter will focus on the role of clinical supervision in fostering multicultural and professional competence.

Defining Clinical Supervision

Clinical supervision is essential to training in the foundational competencies of professionalism, ethics, and multicultural practice. Despite the fact that most practicing psychologists believe that they know what supervision is and what it means to be a supervisor, these terms can be surprisingly difficult to define in a comprehensive manner. What follows is a classic and broadly accepted definition of supervision:

> Supervision is an intervention provided by a more senior member of a profession to a more junior colleague or colleagues who typically (but not always) are members of that same profession. This relationship
>
> - is evaluative and hierarchical,
> - extends over time, and
> - has the simultaneous purposes of enhancing the professional functioning of the more junior person(s); monitoring the quality of professional services offered to the clients that she, he, or they see; and serving as a gatekeeper for the particular profession the supervisee seeks to enter. (Bernard & Goodyear, 2014, p. 9)

It is important to understand this definition since it captures the central functions of supervision (from the Latin for *oversight*) and the roles of the supervisor in contemporary professional psychology. The first sentence of the definition states that supervision is an *intervention*. The notion that supervision is an intervention in its own right is somewhat counterintuitive, but makes sense as we consider the meaning of the term *intervention*. It is derived from the Latin word *intervenire* or *inter* (between) *venire* (come) – to come between. Psychological treatment interventions are, at their essence, intended to alter a negative course or process in order to improve psychological functioning or other outcomes. If supervision is properly considered to be an intervention, then it must also involve some aspect of *coming between*. In considering the definition provided above, supervision as an intervention involves striving to alter the behavior of the supervisee who is, in turn, attempting to intervene with the client. Of course, all interventions (whether they are treatments or supervisions) must articulate an expected outcome. In this spirit, we believe that for psychologists to ethically enact their supervision role, they must articulate expected training outcomes. The definition provided above further clarifies that there is an ongoing and evaluative component to supervision that includes overseeing the quality of what is being provided to the client(s) and *serving as a gatekeeper* for the profession. This last statement reminds us that supervision is not only intended to ensure training to the supervisees and high-quality treatment for current clients, but for future clients as well. In training programs, it is common to differentiate between *formative evaluations*, which are designed to support the growth and development of the psychotherapy supervisee, versus *summative evaluations*, which are designed to assess competencies, determine if adequate progress is being made, and provide a gatekeeping function for the academic program or internship site and the profession (Bender & Goodyear, 2014). Many of the common ethical considerations and dilemmas embedded in clinical supervision relate to the complexity of these myriad roles and functions.

Ethical and Legal Considerations

Supervision occurs within an ethical and legal context. While state laws vary, it is likely that supervision is addressed in the Psychology Practice Act in each jurisdiction. The American Psychological Association (APA) Ethics Code (APA, 2010) applies to all psychologists and it provides parameters, guidance, and standards regarding the practice of clinical supervision. The major ethical issues related to clinical supervision are generally considered to include competence and client welfare, informed consent, supervisee rights, the relationship between supervisor and supervisee, evaluation, and confidentiality. Several of these issues will be considered here; these and other ethical considerations will also be interwoven into our discussion and analysis of vignettes. We will start our discussion of ethical standards by highlighting the ethical expectations for competence. Standard 2 (Competence), 2.01 Boundaries of Competence (a) reminds us, "Psychologists provide services, teach, and conduct research with populations and in areas only within the boundaries of their competence, based on their education, training, supervised experience, consultation, study, or professional experience" (APA, 2010, p. 4). Consistent with this standard, we believe that it is rarely sound practice to supervise a psychological treatment or assessment that the faculty supervisor is not himself/herself competent to provide. This standard also reminds us that we must become and remain competent as supervisors since this is a critical professional function for many psychologists.

Our responsibility to the public is addressed in Standard 2.05 Delegation of Work to Others, and it is interesting to consider the implication for training programs related to the importance of supervisory oversight: "Psychologists who *delegate work to … supervisees … take* reasonable steps to … authorize only those responsibilities that *such persons can be expected to perform competently* on the basis of their education, training and experience … with the level of supervision being provided" (APA, 2010, p. 5, emphasis added). What does this mean and why is it important? If our supervisees were already fully competent, they would not need to learn how to do it, they would not need to be in a training program, and they would not need supervision. The faculty or community supervisors in your doctoral program, practicum settings, or internships are responsible for ensuring that supervisees receive sufficient preparation and oversight so that competent service is provided to the client. A term that reflects this delicate balance in the learning of new skills in practice settings is considered by many trainers to be the *learning edge* (e.g., Freyer-Edwards et al., 2006). Navigating the learning process with real clients requires careful assessment and communication to ensure that the supervisee is being challenged to learn necessary clinical skills, but not overwhelmed in a manner that might cause harm. The learning needs of the supervisee must always be balanced with the needs of the client. The ethical standards related to informed consent (10.01) remind supervisees to inform clients that they are being supervised and to provide the name of the supervisor when legal responsibility for the treatment resides with the supervisor. The multiple relationship standard (3.05) reminds us to be careful about potential conflicts in roles that could impair objectivity or judgment. There is significant potential for complex multiple relationships to occur, especially for training clinics that are embedded in an academic training program.

Ethical Dilemmas and Decision-Making

Before we move to discussing clinical supervision vignettes, we provide an overview of the essential elements of an ethical dilemma and provide a suggested approach to ethical decision-making.

Defining Ethical Dilemmas

Ethical dilemmas tend to involve competing pulls or mandates, a potential risk of harm, emotional intensity, and, most commonly, as we attempt to find a path forward, the uncomfortable realization that there is no perfect solution. The vignettes in this chapter vary as to which of these elements is involved and in their emotional or risk intensity. In order to make ethical decisions when facing dilemmas, it is important to have a clear understanding of the ethics code and the codes related to practice in the local jurisdiction. Many of the most complex dilemmas occur when situations lead to conflicts within and/or between codes or with other values or duties. In these situations, and ones in which a preferred course is not apparent, it may be helpful to implement a structured ethical decision-making process that allows for a systematic approach to examining the situation and a full consideration of the factors that will influence the professional decision-making.

Ethical Decision-Making Model

Several different models for ethical decision-making have been proposed (for a review, see Cotton & Claus, 2000). Regardless of the one chosen, an overarching aim of decision-making models is to give practitioners a methodology to evaluate their response options at times when a definitive course is not evident. Often, the need to take action, when such situations arise, is accompanied by a sense of urgency or an emotionally intense reaction to the situation at hand. It is at those times that having a methodology for a systematic examination of the issues and potential courses of action can be especially valuable (Bricklin, 2001). One of the most widely used models is that of Keith-Spiegel and Koocher (1998). Their model includes nine steps:

1. Determine that the problem is an ethical one.
2. Consult the guidelines already available that might apply to a specific identification and possible mechanism for resolution.
3. Consider, as best as possible, all sources that might influence the kind of decision you will make.
4. Locate a trusted colleague with whom you can consult.
5. Evaluate the rights, responsibilities, and vulnerabilities of all affected parties.
6. Generate alternative decisions.
7. Enumerate the consequences of making each decision.
8. Make the decision.
9. Implement the decision.

We ask that you keep these ethical decision-making steps in mind as you read the vignettes and work through the discussion questions and analysis that we provide.

Clinical Supervision Vignettes

The Case of the Long-Time Supervisor

Dr. Jacobson, the director of a large community mental health center in an urban setting, has been providing supervision for over 30 years. Over the years, he has regularly supervised practicum students, doctoral interns, and postdoctoral supervisees. Dr. Jacobson is white and he grew up in an affluent professional family in the diverse urban community in which the center is located. He attended racially diverse public schools, studied sociology as an undergraduate, and generally prides himself on his sensitivity to cultural issues. In fact, he has led sensitivity training groups in the local community and he frequently volunteers at a local homeless shelter. He and his wife love to travel internationally and his office is decorated with items he has accrued from multiple trips to destinations all over Africa and Asia. A current supervisee is treating a Nigerian woman who wears modest clothing and a head covering and who has been living in the United States for the past year. The client describes feelings of hopelessness and a sense of failure as she has had great difficulty finding adequate employment despite her level of education in her country of origin. The client describes experiencing high levels of discrimination based on her racial and religious identity. In supervision, Dr. Jacobson advises his supervisee to consider that the client might be contributing to her own problems. He coaches the supervisee to say the following in the next session: "Perhaps the problem is that you're not blending in. Have you ever thought about shopping for some less identifying clothing so that you don't make potential employers uncomfortable?"

The supervisee is taken aback by the advice and voices this to Dr. Jacobson. He counters with the fact that he knows his community and understands what it takes to get a job and to be successful. He then goes on to say that the supervisee is not being helpful to this client if she refrains from providing this critical feedback to her.

Questions to Consider

What are the ethical issues at play? What should the student do in this situation? Do you see any potential risks to the client if the supervisee were to follow Dr. Jacobson's advice? Would your response differ based on the student's level of training?

Case Analysis

Unfortunately, the dilemma now faced by Dr. Jacobson's student is not an unusual one that supervisees encounter when their supervisors have received less training related to multicultural and diversity competence than they have received. Many supervisors who trained before the mid-1990s, when accreditation standards began to require training in ICD, typically did not have course work or supervision focused on multicultural competence as part of their training programs. Therefore, they often are not as well versed in multicultural topics such as microaggressions, implicit bias, gender, oppression, and power differentials as their supervisees. Students then find themselves in the awkward position of being more informed in appropriate and competent practice than their supervisor(s).

This vignette brings into question several areas of ethical practice. We will first question whether or not Dr. Jacobson and his student are practicing within the boundaries of their competence (APA, 2010, Standard 2.01) and whether or not Dr. Jacobson is sufficiently maintaining his competence as a supervisor (APA, 2010, Standard 2.03). We believe that Dr. Jacobson has made an untenable assumption based on his understanding of culture. In addition, in his instructions to the supervisee, he has failed to adequately consider level of acculturation, socioeconomic status, sexual identity, age, and religion. Additionally, Standard 2.04 reminds us that work should be based on established scientific knowledge of the field. Dr. Jacobson's suggestion for how to help the client is not grounded on a knowledge base, but rather on his well-established personal beliefs and on his general worldviews, failing to consider how growing up as an educated and affluent white male has impacted his development and status. The APA Guidelines on Multicultural Education, Training, Research, Practice, and Organizational Change for Psychologists suggest that psychologists be aware of their "attitudes and beliefs" that can negatively influence how they view and act with clients different from themselves, that they recognize the importance of being knowledgeable about the differences their clients have, that they educate their students about multiculturalism and diversity, and that they use "culturally appropriate skills" when working with such clients (APA, 2010, Guidelines 1, 2, 3, and 5).

We will next consider the path Dr. Jacobson might take to move toward practicing in a more multiculturally competent manner, the ethical dilemma now faced by Dr. Jacobson's supervisee given her concern that she is not being given appropriate advice (but is under Dr. Jacobson's supervision), and the issues related to the interaction of Dr. Jacobson and his supervisee.

What Are the Supervisee's Options?

The student has to decide how to proceed in this situation. She is aware of the ethical issues described above and also the standard to avoid harming clients (APA, 2010, Standard 3.04), which she might very well perceive she would be doing if she were to follow Dr. Jacobson's advice. There are many considerations that would factor into how this student might proceed, some of which might hinge on her level of training or the nature of the training setting. A student who is further along in training or especially confident might independently investigate Nigerian culture, learn about the common experiences of recent immigrants from Nigeria, consider relevant religious variables, or seek out alternate consultation. The nature of the supervisory alliance is a key factor in how the student might respond. The student might consider options such as ignoring her supervisor's advice or speaking with another supervisor or the training director in her setting or program about her concerns. She might also consider consulting with the faculty member who taught her in relevant coursework. She could opt to speak directly with the supervisor regarding multicultural competence issues as she sees them, although his initial response to her raising the concern might make this a daunting option for her. If the student decides to raise the issue directly with Dr. Jacobson, she might seek emotional support from a trusted faculty mentor and gain confidence by role-playing the conversation in advance. Finally, if the leadership of the training program is made aware of the issue, they may need to consider approaching Dr. Jacobson in a formal manner to suggest or require additional training. This last consideration raises an ethical issue for the program in that they are expected to ensure that students receive competent education and training (APA, 2010, Standard 7.03, Accuracy in Teaching).

The ethics code suggests that, when possible, psychologists should attempt to resolve ethical problems that involve other psychologists informally (APA, 2010, Standard 1.04). Even though Dr. Jacobson might not have committed an ethical violation per se, he is teetering on the edge of practicing in an area where he is not demonstrating competence in a situation that involves a vulnerable client. In addition, he is potentially passing along his limitations to an impressionable supervisee. Finally, this situation creates a valuable professional development opportunity for the student to develop the skill of discussing difficult topics with another psychologist. However, she is also in the position of being evaluated by this individual and it would be understandable if she does not feel empowered or safe to confront Dr. Jacobson, especially given his initial dismissive response to her concerns.

What Might Dr. Jacobson Have Done?

Dr. Jacobson, having trained in a time period in which multicultural competence was not typically taught didactically or experientially, should have pursued ongoing education, consultation, and/or supervision in order to be aware of and competent to address the issues faced by individuals of underserved, marginalized, and/or minority groups. He should also be aware of the relevant sections of the APA Ethics Code (2010), APA Guidelines on Multicultural Education, Training, Research, Practice, and Organizational Change (2002), and Domain B: Diversity from the Guidelines for Clinical Supervision in Health Service Psychology (HSPC; APA, 2014).

The HSPC guidelines (APA, 2014) suggest that "supervisors are encouraged to infuse diversity into all aspects of clinical practice and supervision, including attention to oppression and privilege, and the impact of those on the supervisory power differential, relationship, and on the client and supervisee interactions and supervision interactions." Therefore, Dr. Jacobson should have considered the oppression faced by the client, the privilege he and his student have received, and how those impact the power differential he has over his supervisee and how his supervisee impacts the client. Dr. Jacobson should have noted that his privilege of being born in the country in which he is working and privy to the cultural norms and expectations places him in a different position from the client in question. In addition to his status as a white male, he has also had the opportunity to receive higher education, travel extensively, and benefit from growing up in an affluent family. This is presumably different from the life experiences of the client, at least since she came to the United States. Therefore, Dr. Jacobson could have used this situation as an opportunity to praise his student for being aware of and bringing to his attention the concerns she has in working with this client. He also could have used it as an opportunity to model how to gain competence in treating a client from an unfamiliar population. Dr. Jacobson could have encouraged his supervisee to read about Nigerian culture and the experiences of recent immigrants from there, educated her about models of acculturation and identity development, and discussed the impact of racism, religious discrimination, privilege, and microaggressions with his student. The supervisee would likely have also benefited from developing a plan to increase her awareness of these issues and her ability to respond compassionately to the concerns of the client and to validate the very real stressors faced by her client. She also could have been encouraged to seek out consultation from providers who have experience treating individuals who recently moved to the United States or who have specific expertise with Nigerian culture. In contrast, as described in this vignette, Dr. Jacobson is recommending that his supervisee conveys a potentially harmful message to the client – that she must change her identity in order to survive. In addition, he is missing an important training opportunity for the supervisee.

Supervisee Religious Conflict

In order to set the stage for this next vignette, we will provide a definition of "conscience clause" and an overview of the implications that cases and legislation have for clinical supervision in training programs. Per standard definition ("Conscience Clause," n.d., para. 1), a "conscience clause is a legislative provision that relieves a person from compliance on religious grounds. It permits pharmacists, physicians, and other health care providers not to provide certain medical services for reasons of religion or conscience." These legislative provisions can also be framed as a "right to refusal" based on the First Amendment right to religious freedom. As conscience clauses relate to psychology education and training programs, several legal cases and a series of legislative initiatives have involved conservatively religious graduate students who decline to treat or to provide affirmative psychological treatment to LGBTQ clients. Although the two legal cases to date have involved graduate students in master's counseling programs, the legislative initiatives that followed have much broader implications for education and training programs in health service psychology (see Wise et al., 2015). Generally, these dilemmas involve a conflict between competent practice as defined by the profession and the supervisee's religious beliefs and values.

The Case of the Conflicted Counselor

You are the primary clinical supervisor of a second-year graduate student who is just starting to see clients in the doctoral program training clinic. Her second client is a 19-year-old male college sophomore who came to the clinic because he was experiencing anxiety, dysphoric mood, and intense social anxiety. He shared on the screening that he never felt that he fit in growing up in a rural southern community in his conservatively religious family. He reported that his interests were "different" and that he always felt like "an outsider" in his family and hometown. He reported that he was an excellent student in high school, but that most of his relationships were limited to the school-based clubs that he had joined; he socialized very little outside of these structured settings. Since coming to a university in a relatively liberal and progressive college town, he has been relieved to find himself in a more diverse community. He has especially enjoyed meeting students who came from different places and from different backgrounds. During the first three sessions in the clinic, he provided general information about his background and upbringing to his supervisee therapist and a positive therapeutic alliance seemed to be developing. At the fourth session, the client very hesitantly shared with the supervisee that he has feared for some time that there might be something "wrong" with him. With great hesitance and anxiety, he shared that he had always felt more comfortable with girls, was "maybe attracted to boys," and that he did not fit in with the other boys and their interests or activities when he was growing up. He also shared that there had been several incidents of bullying by his high school classmates because he did not fit in. He was so ashamed and scared to call further attention to himself that he never told his parents or school officials about these incidents. He has done some research on the Internet and understands that he might be questioning his gender identity and sexual orientation. He signed up for a first-year seminar on human sexuality when he came to the university and reported that he was experiencing a very frightening sense of being flooded by the awareness that he "might not be normal." He has always been aware at some level that this might be the case, but is just now truly coming to acknowledge it for the first time. He shared with the supervisee that he wanted to take this slowly, but hoped that therapy would be a safe space to explore his thoughts and feelings. He has also been contemplating several additional steps, including joining a support group for "questioning" students at the campus LGBTQ center, so that he might experience a sense of community on campus. He was also able to talk more openly in the session about his fears of being rejected by his family. He shares that he is certain that, because of negative comments that they have made in response to news stories about marriage equality, his parents would disapprove of what they would call his "lifestyle" if he were ever to really explore his sexuality openly.

After this fourth session, your supervisee comes to find you in a bit of a panic to tell you that she is not sure that she can continue to work with this client. The supervisee tells you that she "believes intellectually" that sexual orientation and gender identity are not a choice and that "everyone has a right to be who they are." However, she also continues to be influenced by the beliefs she grew up with in her family and her childhood church "that homosexuality is a sin against God and nature." She shares with you that she grew up attending an evangelical church that is opposed to same-sex marriage and that she is still trying to sort out how she can reconcile her religious beliefs with the "values of the profession." She tells you that she is aware of the doctoral program's publicly stated commitment to multicultural competence. She also tells you that she is aware that the training clinic explicitly encourages clients from traditionally marginalized and underserved groups to come in for psychological services. In fact, as a supervisor, you are pleased that the training clinic has a particularly strong reputation in the community for providing affirmative psychological services to members of the LGBTQ community. Your supervisee tells you that she had been feeling very comfortable working with this client until he revealed this information about his gender identity and sexual orientation questioning. Now she is feeling extremely uncomfortable. In particular, she "dreads" hearing more about his thoughts and experiences and she is not sure that she can be fully supportive of his choices if they work together. She asks you to quietly transfer the client to another graduate student and to not tell the other faculty members since she is convinced that the "liberal faculty members" would respond to her dilemma in a negative or discriminatory manner. She promises to work on this issue, but does not want to have to face her discomfort about this issue so early in training when she is already anxious about learning to become a therapist.

Questions to Consider

What would your personal/internal reaction be? What additional questions might you want to ask or what information might you want to gather from the supervisee? How would you balance the clinical needs of the client and the training needs of the supervisee? How would you decide whether (or not) to reassign the client? How would you handle the supervisee's request to not discuss this situation with your faculty colleagues? What other steps would you take (or not take)?

Case Analysis

This is clearly a challenging clinical supervision vignette that is likely to create uncertainty for many clinical supervisors. As reported in a recent article (Wise et al., 2015), participants at the 2013 Education Leadership Conference were provided with the following prompt: "I believe that faculty are prepared to effectively engage students in discussions when their religious beliefs conflict with their ability to provide client care." Among the psychology education leaders who responded, 86 percent reported that they either "strongly disagreed" or "disagreed" with the statement. Clearly, this is a common area of discomfort for supervisors. There are many reasons that clinical supervisors may struggle with how to respond. At a systemic level, "conscience clause" dilemmas reflect broader cultural struggles related to religious freedom and the historical marginalization and discrimination of LGBTQ individuals. In the wake of highly publicized federal legislation that has resulted in marriage equality laws in many states, there has been cultural backlash. In addition, supervisors and training programs may experience heightened concern since religious conflict situations are potentially fraught with legal challenges in the wake of highly publicized legal cases and legislative initiatives. It has also been noted (e.g., Campbell & Kim, 2015) that psychologists tend to be less religious than the general population. These factors, among others, can help us to appreciate why it is that the majority of supervisors feel poorly prepared to address these conflicts when they arise.

Let us now return our attention to the specifics of this vignette. It is likely that both the supervisor and the supervisee are feeling quite uncomfortable after the supervisee has shared her thoughts and feelings. The feelings experienced by supervisor and supervisee can influence the paths taken by the parties involved. Both general findings from the area of positive psychology and several series of lab-based studies have confirmed that when people experience positive emotions, they tend to cope better with stressors, experience a greater sense of well-being that continues to improve, and show greater resiliency as compared to those who are experiencing negative emotions (e.g., Fredrickson, 2001). After taking a deep breath himself/ herself, we would encourage the supervisor to consider taking an important first step: to express appreciation to the supervisee for bringing forth these concerns so directly since it likely feels risky to do so. With regard to ethics, the supervisor could point out that according to Standard 2.06 (APA, 2010), when there is a personal issue that might interfere with professional judgment, it is incumbent upon the psychologist to seek consultation. The student did just this. The disclosure of the supervisee may indicate that the supervisor has established a strong supervisory alliance that has enabled the supervisee to feel safe enough to raise the concerns at all. However, there is a risk that the conversation may quickly become polarized and adversarial, especially if the intense emotions of both the supervisor and supervisee are not explicitly recognized and addressed. In fact, current thinking about conscience clause dilemmas would advise just the opposite; we strongly recommend that the supervisor makes every attempt to take a calm, open, compassionate, and developmental approach to conscience clause issues that arise in training. Wise et al. (2015) have proposed five "core tenets" in responding to conscience clause dilemmas. Most relevant here is the notion that conflicts with religious beliefs be responded to in a manner consistent with how the supervisor might respond to other value or religious conflicts (e.g., a supervisee's discomfort with a couple that decides to divorce or discomfort with a client who admits to racist or homophobic beliefs). Another critical core tenet is that trainers respect supervisees' developmental process and foster cognitive complexity. In applying this tenet, the supervisor might consider the notion of "integration" as articulated by Handelsman, Gottlieb, and Knapp (2005), in which they would encourage supervisees to maintain their own core values and beliefs while learning to meaningfully integrate the values and beliefs of the profession. In this situation, the supervisee might be encouraged to find ways to navigate the intersection of her religious upbringing and the profession's expectation of providing competent care to diverse clients. Discussion of perspective-taking (i.e., truly understanding the experience of the other) and a genuine consideration of the many ways in which another person's core identity may make us uncomfortable can help to broaden the conversation. Some aspects of the supervisee's statements indicate a willingness to work on these issues, which can be taken as a positive sign. The supervisor might ask the supervisee to reflect on what it is that the client is truly asking of her and remind the supervisee that it is not generally the psychologist's role to make personal life choice decisions for the client. Stated differently, clients make many choices that we may not agree with or wish them to make throughout the course of therapy.

Several recent articles suggest strategies for approaching conscience clause dilemmas in training (e.g., Cohen-Filipic & Flores, 2014). In particular, these authors recommend a balance between a developmental approach (that is sensitive to supervisee's learning curve) and a more contemporary competency-based approach that specifies required end points to training. In discussing the tensions between respecting a supervisee's values and beliefs and expectations for competence, these authors make the following suggestion:

> It is important to note that issues of "changing" or "taking away" a supervisee's belief system arise frequently in discussions of values conflicts. Although supervisors are not in the business of questioning a student's deeply held beliefs, supervisors are responsible for challenging and exploring a supervisee's preconceptions about human nature. To expect to proceed through a graduate program that focuses on the broad range of human behavior without reflecting upon one's own preconceptions would be misguided at best. (Cohen-Filipic & Flores, 2014, pp. 304–305)

If the supervisor does decide to reassign the case, it would be important to articulate a plan for the supervisee. It might not be a formal remediation plan unless the supervisor believes that this is necessary to attain training goals. In addition, the manner in which the care of the client is handled in a case transfer will have to be very carefully considered in order to minimize harm. Ethical principles 3.04 (Avoiding Harm) and 10.10c (Terminating Therapy) are key here. Conversely, if the supervisor decides to have the student proceed with treatment, it would be important to carefully monitor treatment sessions (ideally via video recording or another direct observation method) in order to ensure that the client is being provided with competent treatment that incorporates validation, acceptance, and compassion. Competence is an ethical standard and particularly Standard 2.05 (Delegation of Work to Others) would be important to consider, as the supervisor would need to ensure that the student is acting in a competent manner. It is important to remember that while it may be ethical to refer if we believe we are truly not competent to treat a particular client, a case transfer or reassignment can be discriminatory if it is based on core aspects of client identity (Shiles, 2009), unless it is determined to be essential for the welfare of the client.

Overall, there is surprisingly little written about how supervisees experience what clients share with them when they are early in training. In a qualitative analysis of doctoral students' responses to a conscience clause vignette similar to the one described here (Paprocki, 2014), it was instructive to learn that many of the issues discussed by clients make supervisees uncomfortable. In characterizing supervisee responses to the vignette, the following was noted:

> Discomfort was repeatedly described as simply part of the training experience for therapists, especially when learning to treat a new presenting issue, or a client from a very different background for the first time. One therapist early in training explained, "When you are first starting, you're building your confidence and learning at the same time, you're going to go in feeling unprepared no matter how much you prepare . . . it feels a little bit like jumping off a cliff." (Paprocki, 2014, p. 286)

This response captures some of the emotional intensity of early clinical training experiences, which is heightened when a supervisee is also faced with the added complexity of a value conflict. In relation to value conflicts more specifically, graduate students in the Paprocki (2014) study cited the distinction between "incompetence" and "discomfort" when considering whether or not a client should be reassigned. This distinction may prove useful to supervisors as they navigate supervisee value conflicts.

What about the supervisee's request to not tell other faculty members about her religious beliefs that are creating conflict? Depending on how the program is set up, the supervisor may decide to discuss the situation with a training committee, other supervisors, and/or the program director. It is not uncommon for supervisees to mistakenly believe that training and competence issues are confidential matters in a training program. This is an important issue to clarify prior to entering into clinical training (suggestions for informed consent and supervision contracts can be found in the HSPC Guidelines; APA, 2014). Not specifically addressed in the vignette is the possibility that the supervisor may himself/herself be a member of the LGBTQ community (as might the supervisee). These factors would add to the complexity of the discussion and how the situation is handled. Effective supervision strategies for addressing supervisee conflicts is an emerging area for supervisors and for academic training programs. Among other resources, the promulgation of a Pedagogical Statement (BEA Working Group, 2015) and associated resources provides a useful conceptual framework for training programs. As a field, we are just beginning to articulate how to effectively and compassionately approach these dilemmas in a manner that also ensures competence and public welfare.

The Case of the Bicultural Couple

You are a supervisor in a doctoral program training clinic that provides individual and couples counseling. Recently, a Euro-American, white, female client "Julia," who self-identifies as "nonreligious," has contacted the clinic and was assigned to a supervisee for individual therapy. Her presenting concern relates to stress in her five-year relationship. Her romantic partner is a Latina female, "Estella," who came to the United States as an undocumented immigrant with her family from rural Mexico when she was four years old. The client is an academic researcher and her partner works in a local publishing firm. They are very committed to each other; the central area of conflict for them revolves around their different cultural backgrounds and family contexts. The client grew up in a small town with her siblings, her parents, and a large extended family in the mid-western U.S. Her parents are both employed as philosophy professors at a small liberal arts college. They are upper-middle-class, identify as "secular humanists," and have worked hard to be supportive of their daughter's sexual orientation ever since she came out to them in early high school. They invite the partner, Estella, on all of their family vacations and include her in much the same way as they do the heterosexual partner of the client's brother (more on this later). The partner's family still lives in a poor, rural area of Mexico where her father is unemployed (he is on disability from a farming accident) and her mother works on the cleaning crew of a local tourist hotel. They are devout Catholics and Estella has never come out to them. It is reported by Julia that Estella lives a life that is "completely separate" from her family, even though she loves them deeply. The issue that has now come to a head is that Julia would like to get married, but Estella will not tell her family that she has a female partner or that she self-identifies as lesbian, nor will she agree to get married without their blessing. The supervisor recommends individual therapy (for Estella) and couples therapy. Julia will continue with her individual therapy. Both individual therapists and the couples co-therapists are Euro-American and identify as nonreligious.

In a collaborative case conference, they discuss their case plan, which includes suggesting to Estella that she simply tells her parents about the relationship with Julia and their plan to get married. They also encourage informing Estella that her parents will in all likelihood eventually come to accept this news (difficult though it may be for them). They could mention to Estella that she should "let the cards fall where they may" after telling her parents the news. Alternatively, they will suggest that Estella considers getting married without telling them so that the couple can go forward with their marriage plans unimpeded by her parent's disapproval. They note that her family has never come to the United States, so it may not be essential for them to know. The couples co-therapists introduce this basic approach to the couple at their next session. After this session, Estella e-mails her individual therapist and the couples co-therapists that "nobody understands how difficult this is for me" and tells them that she plans to discontinue treatment.

Questions to Consider

What is it that has gone awry in this treatment situation? What are the multicultural and ethical considerations? How might the treatment team proceed?

Case Analysis

The treatment team, including the clinical supervisor, decides to consult with the faculty member who teaches the program's multiculturalism course. This faculty member is also known to be a skilled multicultural supervisor. They understand that there is a problem in the treatment and they all want to provide the best treatment that they can, consistent with the APA Ethics Code (2010) and the multicultural practice guidelines cited earlier. The consulting supervisor listens carefully to the course of events and then gently suggests that the treatment context may be recreating (unintentionally) the dislocation already experienced by Estella as a Latina living in a college town in the United States. The consulting supervisor makes a number of suggestions, including that the individual therapist reaches out to Estella to encourage her to return to discuss her concerns. Further, the consulting supervisor encourages the individual therapist to own that there has been a failure to adequately understand Estella's experiences. The individual therapist is encouraged to learn more about the "voyage" of Estella's family to the United States since there may be a narrative of trauma located in the experience. More information on how the family came to the United States would also allow the individual therapist and the team to better understand and appreciate the sacrifices that Estella's parents made for her and her siblings to come to the United States for a better life. The consulting supervisor hopes to thereby increase the team's empathy to the dilemma that Estella is experiencing. The consulting supervisor also suggests that Estella may benefit from considering the heretofore unaddressed loss of her childhood engagement with Catholicism, which was a source of joy and solace to her as a young child. The consulting supervisor also suggests that the treatment team might explore more carefully the portrayal of Julia's family as totally accepting of the relationship, which has contributed to a conceptualization of the "good parents" and the "bad parents." As mentioned in the Long-Time Supervisor (Dr. Jacobson) vignette, the HSPC guidelines (APA, 2014) are important to consider here as well. The treatment team and the faculty supervisors can be reminded that "supervisors are encouraged to infuse diversity into all aspects of clinical practice and supervision, including attention to oppression and privilege, and the impact of those on the supervisory power differential, relationship, and on the client and supervisee interactions and supervision interactions."

Incorporating the Multicultural Feedback

Estella's individual therapist meets with her and presents a more multiculturally sensitive case conceptualization based on the consultation. This allows Estella to share her guilt, sense of loss, and conflict about having to choose between Julia and "everything else." As treatment proceeds, Estella decides to talk with a campus minister who is a liberal Catholic priest. He helps her to begin to consider how she might reconcile her religious beliefs and her core identity. In couples sessions, the co-therapists gently probe more into how Julia's parents treat the couple. It turns out that there have been multiple microaggressions, for example, referring to Estella as Julia's "friend" to extended family, and in other ways treating Estella differently from how they treat Julia's brother's opposite-sex romantic partner. This results in a more balanced conceptualization that allows Estella to own parts of herself that have felt cut off and Julia to acknowledge their shared experience of familial distance.

In summary, the multicultural consultation allows the treatment team to better appreciate Estella's experience and the often invisible power of being a member of the dominant culture. This recognition helped create a more accepting context for both members of the couple to benefit from treatment. The treatment team's case consultation and the beneficial modifications made to the treatment approach are consistent with the APA Ethics Code (2010) Standards 2.01 (Boundaries of Competence), 3.04 (Avoiding Harm), and 4.06 (Consultations).

The Case of the Complaint about a Supervisee

Dr. Myers, the director of a mental health facility, contacts Dr. Rosenberg, the supervisor of a graduate student, and reports that a client has called the clinic to complain about services provided by the supervisee. According to the client, twice in a row, the supervisee, Ms. Perkins, has nodded off during the session. The client was understandably upset by this and he questioned whether or not this was something to be expected in therapy, expressed hopelessness at getting anyone to care about him and his problems, and said he is not sure if he wishes to continue being seen at the clinic. He was not interested in a referral to another facility.

When questioned by Dr. Myers about the supervisee and whether or not Dr. Rosenberg had observed this behavior in Ms. Perkins' sessions, what her affect had been recently, or if any other problems with Ms. Perkins had been noted, Dr. Rosenberg reported that he had not met with Ms. Perkins in the last few weeks due to scheduling problems and was unaware of what might have led up to this problem. Dr. Rosenberg reported that since Ms. Perkins had been seeing her cases as usual and had not contacted him with any questions or concerns, he was not able to comment at the time on what had happened.

Angry that he looked uninformed in front of his colleague, Dr. Rosenberg contacted Ms. Perkins and made clear that she needed to come meet with him immediately to discuss clinical work. The supervisee complied, but cited that this was difficult as she was in the middle of collecting data for her thesis. When she arrived, Dr. Rosenberg said to Ms. Perkins, "How come you've blown off supervision for the past two weeks and then did something that made me look really bad? I trusted you to come to me if there were problems, but instead you didn't tell me." Ms. Perkins was confused, and then Dr. Rosenberg explained the nature of the complaint that was made. With that, Ms. Perkins started to cry. Between sobs, she said, "Oh no! I didn't realize that was such a big deal. I couldn't help it. I've been doing so much work between my classes, research, and clinical work. On top of that, I have bipolar disorder and my psychiatrist just changed my medication. The dosage was a bit off and it made me extremely tired. I'm getting used to it and it shouldn't be a problem anymore. This happens sometimes when my medications are changed." After she relayed this information, she then had a horrified look on her face and said, "Please don't tell anyone that I have bipolar disorder. It's under control and not a problem as far as training goes. I don't want people here to know and talk about me. There's a lot of stigma that goes with having mental health problems and I don't need the added stress of people talking about me here."

Questions to Consider

What is your reaction regarding the supervisor of this case? What do you see as his role in the problems that have arisen? What do you think about how he handled the situation? How should he proceed from this point forward? What about the role of Dr. Myers? Are there steps that you might suggest Dr. Myers might take to address the situation? What foundational competencies appear deficient for this supervisee? What form of remediation would you propose?

Case Analysis

This case brings up many ethical issues related to supervision (APA, 2010, Standard 2.05 Delegation of Work to Others), client care (3.04 Avoiding Harm, 10.01 Informed Consent to Therapy), and privacy of supervisees (2.06 Personal Problems and Conflicts, 7.04 Student Disclosure of Personal Information). The story illustrates the harm that can come when supervisees do not receive adequate and ongoing supervision.

Supervision

A competent supervisor provides both oversight and intervention, yet in this case, the supervisor has done neither. The lack of involvement in the day-to-day responsibilities toward clients/supervisees and the failure to adhere to a regular meeting schedule contributed to poor client care by the supervisee. Supervisees can have a difficult time prioritizing all of the demands of a graduate program and as such it is up to the supervisor to assist the supervisee in understanding the importance of attending supervision, or at the very least communicating with the supervisor, particularly when she is not fulfilling the obligations associated with beginning clinical work. Given Dr. Rosenberg's responses to Dr. Myers' questions, we can also assume that he has not been reviewing the content of Ms. Perkins' sessions with any regularity. Supervisors have the ethical responsibility to ensure that the work done by supervisees is done competently (APA, 2010). Furthermore, review of several areas of the HSPC guidelines (APA, 2014) supports the aforementioned concerns and leads us to worry about Dr. Rosenberg competence as a supervisor. Specifically, according to the HSPC guidelines (APA, 2014), Dr. Rosenberg should have articulated clearly to his supervisee the expectations for her performance and been clear about her duties as a supervisee and his as a supervisor. He should have provided timely feedback about her performance and ideally should have reviewed her sessions or observed them live.

Had Dr. Rosenberg created an environment in supervision where his supervisee felt comfortable disclosing the mistake she made in session and/or that she was struggling with personal issues at the time, this problem might have been prevented or at least identified prior to problems occurring in treatment. Even if the supervisee had been unaware herself of the magnitude of the problem of falling asleep during a client's session, Dr. Rosenberg might have identified this through a systematic review of sessions and addressed the lack of self-reflection as a foundational competency concern for the supervisee. This would have been an ideal time for Dr. Rosenberg to discuss Standard 2.06 (Personal Problems and Conflict) with his supervisee, as he could have made her aware of her duty related to self-care while protecting the client. Hopefully, Dr. Rosenberg has created a supervision contract at the outset of this relationship and incorporated the limits of confidentiality related to supervisee disclosures (APA, 2014). He is in a bind otherwise as he has an obligation as a gatekeeper to the profession and to create a remediation plan, all of which would be difficult should he not believe that he can discuss these steps with the necessary personnel in the supervisee's program. In fact, even if Dr. Rosenberg has failed to communicate to the supervisee that he will give feedback on the program, we believe that he will still need to do so in order to fulfill his primary obligation as a supervisor.

Client Care

The vignette also raises concerns related to the care of the client. It is suggested that the client is understandably disenchanted with the therapy thus far. This has turned the client off therapy and the client is unwilling to accept a referral elsewhere. When harm is done by a practitioner to an individual client, harm can also be done to the field as a whole. While other explanations are possible, we can also be concerned that the client called the clinic director as opposed to the supervisor of the case. As an ethical provider, the supervisor should have been sure to instruct the supervisee to provide his information to the client at the outset of therapy so that the client knows of the person responsible for his/her care while undergoing treatment.

Remediation

Remediation plans would be beneficial for both the supervisor and supervisee in this vignette. Of all those involved, Dr. Myers appears to have handled the situation most appropriately. The concerns were brought to the supervisor immediately and attempts were made to gather data about the potential problems that may be impacting the supervisee, the supervisor, and, most importantly, the client. Dr. Myers' behavior was consistent with the HSPC guidelines (APA, 2014) when attempting to work with the supervisor to ascertain and address the supervisee's training needs.

Ideally, Dr. Myers will address the deficits in supervisor competence with Dr. Rosenberg and create a remediation plan that includes education about supervision models, supervisor responsibilities, and benchmarks for demonstrated competence as a supervisor. Just as a supervisor must monitor closely his/her supervisees, the director will likely have to monitor supervisors in his/her facility to ensure competence in this domain.

Dr. Rosenberg will also need to create a remediation plan with his supervisee. This will need to incorporate a plan for attending supervision regularly, discussion of the importance of openness with the supervisor when therapy goes well and when it does not, and a coherent plan for self-care, including but not limited to time management and ongoing medical and mental health support. The ethics code (see excerpt below) allows for the training program to request information regarding the supervisee's mental health treatment, as this would be essential to determining whether or not the supervisee is able to fulfill competently her clinical obligations. Dr. Rosenberg might need to discuss the student's mental health concerns with other program personnel, despite the student's objections, as there are concerns related to client care and the status of the supervisee in the program (should she not pass practicum). Dr. Rosenberg and the faculty members who need to be made aware of the issues could ideally be discrete with the information about the supervisee's health; however, there is no confidentiality related to disclosures made to supervisors in the supervision context.

Since it is so relevant to this vignette, Standard 7.04 (Student Disclosure of Personal Information) is included below:

> Psychologists do not require students or supervisees to disclose personal information in course- or program-related activities, either orally or in writing, regarding sexual history, history of abuse and neglect, psychological treatment, and relationships with parents, peers, and spouses or significant others except if (1) the program or training facility has clearly identified this requirement in its admissions and program materials or (2) the information is necessary to evaluate or obtain assistance for students whose personal problems could reasonably be judged to be preventing them from performing their training or professionally related activities in a competent manner or posing a threat to the students or others. (APA, 2010, p. 10)

The supervisee should also be made aware of the literature on alliance ruptures in psychological treatment and might be asked to reach out the client, apologize profusely, and attempt to repair the therapeutic relationship. The appropriateness of this call would depend on the nature of what was said when the client and Dr. Myers spoke. The supervisee could also be asked to review the literature on self-disclosure and make an informed decision about how much information to give or not give to the client as a rationale for her behavior during the sessions. Overall, this vignette demonstrates the many teaching moments that are possible based on this mistake made by the supervisee.

Conclusions

The vignettes presented in this chapter represent just a few of the complex ways that multicultural and professional competence issues are embedded in clinical training and supervision. An ethical framework serves to remind us that we need to continue to strive to provide psychological services and supervision that is multi-culturally competent. This can involve learning new skills and gaining the ability to genuinely recognize our blind spots. Some of these blind spots are personal and others are more commonly held in our profession and our culture. An openness to these issues is our best hope of meeting our ethical obligations to our supervisees and the clients they treat now and in the future. We further recommend that training programs and the profession consider incorporating opportunities for experienced supervisors to maintain their multicultural and professional competence so that they can best serve the training needs of their supervisees as they learn to serve the public, both now and in the future.

References

American Psychological Association (2002). APA guidelines on multicultural education, training, research, practice and organizational change for psychologists. Retrieved from www.apa.org/pi/oema/resources/policy/multicultural-guidelines.aspx

American Psychological Association (2010). *Ethical principles of psychologists and code of conduct*. Retrieved from http://apa.org/ethics/code/index.aspx

American Psychological Association (2014). Guidelines for clinical supervision in health service psychology. Retrieved from www.apa.org/about/policy/guidelines-supervision.pdf

BEA Virtual Working Group on Restrictions Affecting Diversity Training in Graduate Education (2015). Preparing professional psychologists to serve a diverse public; a core requirement in doctoral education and training. A pedagogical statement. *Training and Education in Professional Psychology, 9*, 269–270.

Bernard, J. M. & Goodyear, R. K. (2014). *Fundamentals of clinical supervision* (5th edn.). Upper Saddle River, NJ: Pearson.

Bricklin, P. (2001). Being ethical: More than obeying the law and avoiding harm. *Journal of Personality Assessment, 77*, 195–202.

Campbell, C. D. & Kim, C. L. (2015). The conscience clause in religious-distinctive programs. *Training and Education in Professional Psychology, 9*, 279–285.

Cohen-Filipic, J. & Flores, L. Y. (2014). Best practices in providing effective supervision to students with values conflicts. *Psychology of Sexual Orientation and Gender Diversity, 1*, 302–309.

Conscience Clause (n.d.) In *U.S. Legal*. Retrieved from http://definitions.uslegal.com/c/conscience-clause

Cottone, R. & Claus, R. (2000). Ethical decision-making models: A review of the literature. *Journal of Counseling and Development, 78*, 275–283.

Fredrickson, B. (2001). The role of positive emotions in positive psychology. *American Psychologist, 56*, 218–226.

Fryer-Edwards, K., Arnold, R. M., Baile, W., Tulsky, J. A., Petracca, F., & Back, A. (2006). Reflective teaching practices: An approach to teaching communication skills in a small-group setting. *Academic Medicine, 7*, 638–644.

Handelsman, M. M., Gottlieb, M. C., & Knapp, S. (2005). Training ethical psychologists: An acculturation model. *Professional Psychology: Research and Practice, 36*, 59–65.

Hatcher, R. L., Fouad, N. A., Grus, C. L., Campbell, L. F., McCutcheon, S. R., & Leahy, K. L. (2013). Competency benchmarks: Practical steps toward a culture of competence. *Training and Education in Professional Psychology, 7*, 84–91.

Koocher, G. P. & Keith-Spiegel, P. (1998). *Ethics in psychology: Professional standards and cases* (2nd edn.). New York, NY: Oxford.

Paprocki, C. M. (2014). When personal and professional values conflict: Supervisee perspectives on tensions between religious beliefs and affirming treatment of LGBT clients. *Ethics and Behavior, 24*, 279–292.

Shiles, M. (2009). Discriminatory referrals: Uncovering a potential ethical dilemma facing practitioners. *Ethics & Behavior, 19*, 142–155.

Wise, E. H., Bieschke, K. J., Forrest, L., Cohen-Filipic, J., Hathaway, L. A., & Douce, L. A. (2015). Psychology's proactive approach to conscience clause court cases and legislation. *Training and Education in Professional Psychology, 9*, 259–268.

26 Disciplinary Supervision: Ethical Challenges for Supervisors

Janet T. Thomas and John H. Hung

Clinical supervision has been a fundamental component of the training of psychotherapists since the time of Freud (Jacobs, David, & Meyer, 1995), and as such it has become a required element of psychology graduate practicums, internships, postdoctoral training, and prelicensure employment. More recently, supervision has become recognized as a subspecialty requiring specific knowledge, a unique skill set acquired through specialized training and education (Falender & Shafranske, 2004). This recognition has led to a proliferation of literature offering guidance for supervisors providing developmental supervision for students and postdoctoral supervisees.

Complementing this body of literature, the American Psychological Association's (APA, 2017) Ethical Principles of Psychologists and Code of Conduct include sections applicable to the practice of supervision. Pertinent ethical standards address issues such as confidentiality, competence, informed consent, and multiple relationships. The APA Guidelines for Clinical Supervision in Health Service Psychology [Supervision Guidelines] (2014) offer detailed guidance, as do the Supervision Guidelines for Education and Training Leading to Licensure as a Health Service Provider (Association of State and Provincial Psychology Boards [ASPPB], 2015). Both documents delineate supervisory issues including diversity, assessment of supervisee progress, and professionalism. Literature on the ethical dimensions of supervision further illuminates considerations for supervisors (Goodyear & Rodolfa, 2012; Thomas, 2015).

Familiarity with the professional literature, ethical standards, and practice guidelines is important for any supervisor, yet more specialized guidance is essential for supervisors agreeing to oversee the work of another psychologist or mental health professional as part of a disciplinary action taken by a licensing board, ethics committee, employer, or academic institution following a finding of an ethical violation (Thomas, 2010). This chapter focuses primarily on the supervision of psychologists as mandated by licensing boards. Nevertheless, its information may be applicable to the supervision of other mental health professionals and to the supervision required by any entity with the authority to mandate the remediation of identified deficits in clinical skills or ethical practice.

Ethical Violations Precipitating Disciplinary Action

Psychologists at all stages of professional development are vulnerable to making ethical errors and, in fact, minor mistakes are virtually inevitable.

Psychologists may not be aware of these mistakes and most do not rise to the level of licensing board complaints. The ASPPB compiles data regarding those errors that do result in actions by licensing boards. These data indicate that the most common categories of violation in licensing board complaints in the United States and Canada are unprofessional conduct, sexual misconduct, nonsexual dual relationships, negligence, and criminal conviction (ASPPB, 2012). When violations are severe and the public is considered in imminent danger, a regulatory board may decide that license revocation or suspension is necessary. Less serious violations may result in sanctions such as financial penalties, board-ordered tutorials, graduate coursework, practice monitoring, and consultation. In some cases, supervision is deemed necessary for a disciplined psychologist to continue clinical work or to resume work after a period of suspension.

Factors Contributing to Violations

Several factors may contribute to a psychologist's violation of ethical standards. Failure to stay current with practice standards, deficits in education or training, and practicing outside one's area of competence are common examples. Often triggering or perpetuating these violations are concomitant physical illnesses, mental health problems, and cognitive impairments that may compromise professional judgment and lead to ethical violations.

The stage of a psychologist's professional development also may be a factor in the types of errors to which he or she is most vulnerable (Thomas, 2010). Graduate students and early-career psychologists are more likely to make ethical mistakes based on ignorance, inexperience, or naïveté, but such mistakes can also be made by more experienced psychologists, particularly when they are attempting to practice in new specialty areas for which they are just beginning to develop skills. Conversely, mistakes made by experienced psychologists are more likely born of arrogance, complacency, or, again, difficult life circumstances or compromised physical or mental conditions. Each of these factors has the potential to affect psychologists at any point in their careers.

Link between Contributing Factors and Disciplinary Action

Regardless of the genesis of an individual's ethical error, licensing boards, like employers and graduate programs, must make disciplinary decisions on the basis of the individual's behavior (Elman & Forrest, 2007; Gilfoyle, 2008). Psychologists cannot be disciplined for having a medical or mental health diagnosis. Generally, disciplinary decisions are based on some failure to properly execute professional responsibilities in compliance with established ethics codes, statutes, regulations, or policies, not on the conditions that may have contributed to these failures. Boards in some jurisdictions also may be authorized to act where there is reasonable expectation that a psychologist is unable to practice with skill and safety, regardless of cause.

Although the cause of an ethical misstep alone is not the basis for disciplinary action, its identification may be critical to devising an appropriate remedy. When a licensee's behavior suggests that some medical or mental health condition may have contributed to compromised competence or poor professional judgment, the licensing board may require the individual to undergo assessment to identify or rule out such factors. Such assessment helps ensure that the plan for remediation addresses the problems or conditions that have led to the violation (Cobia & Pipes, 2002; Thomas, 2014).

With contributing factors accurately identified, an effective formula for resolution may be devised. Possible remedies include psychotherapy, medical care, treatment for alcohol or drug abuse, psychiatric intervention, individualized tutorials, practice monitoring, and other specified education or training. In addition to these strategies, clinical supervision is among the most common requirements resulting from such assessment (Celenza, 2007).

Distinctions between Developmental and Disciplinary Supervision

All supervision involves multiple levels of responsibility. Supervisors must be continually mindful of the welfare of the supervisee, the supervisee's current clients, and the public, thus serving as gatekeepers for the profession (Behnke, 2005; Bernard & Goodyear, 2014). Disciplinary supervision includes these elements and others as well.

Disciplinary Supervision Defined

Disciplinary supervision has been described as that "mandated for psychologists [or other mental health professionals] following a determination by a licensing board that they have violated ethical or practice standards or relevant laws. The primary objectives of such supervision include the rehabilitation of the professional and the protection of the supervisee's clients and the public" (Thomas, 2014, p. 1105).

Disciplinary supervision has been likened to overseeing the behavior of someone who is on parole or probation (Adams, 2001), and thus is distinct from other types of supervision. It requires expertise as well as a willingness to assume the clinical, ethical, and legal responsibilities commensurate with this position (Thomas, 2010, 2014).

Experienced supervisors are accustomed to managing ethical challenges in their work (Sarnat, 2016). Such experience is necessary but not sufficient preparation for supervising clinicians with histories of compromised professional judgment, ethical violations, lawsuits, or criminal behavior. This feature of disciplinary supervision has significant ramifications for competence, informed consent, boundaries and multiple relationships, documentation, and confidentiality. Further, the power differential fundamental to disciplinary supervision underlies the importance of these ethical issues.

Power Dynamics and Diversity

The supervisory relationship is one of unequal power. Supervisors have an ethical responsibility to understand that power and use it responsibly for the benefit of supervisees and their clients. The seminal work of social psychologists John French and Bertram Raven (1959) on the bases of power in relationships is relevant (Thomas, 2010). Applied to supervisory relationships, their theory suggests that supervisors' power relative to supervisees' is a function of five factors: their ability to compel compliance (coercive power); authority to offer or deny privileges or tangible rewards (reward power); position in a hierarchy (legitimate power); influence relative to their associations (referent power); and their special expertise (expert power). Each type of power may influence the supervisory relationship and, to that extent, supervisees are vulnerable to misuse by supervisors.

Such power dynamics, present in any supervisory relationship, are amplified by the significant power inherent in supervision conducted in disciplinary cases. Supervisors' reports to licensing boards may determine whether supervisees are able to resume practice and whether they will be allowed to do so with or without conditions. Such conditions may affect the individual's ability to secure employment, obtain malpractice insurance or credentialing, and attract clients.

Another factor affecting power in supervisory relationships involves diversity, particularly as related to the identities of the supervisor and supervisee and to the status and privilege ascribed to each by the dominant culture. A large body of evidence indicates that such bias is pervasive and most often unconscious (Banaji & Greenwald, 2013). Discriminatory behavior on the part of well-meaning supervisors may occur; thus, supervisors must be informed about and sensitive to all aspects of diversity, including the potential impact of the gender, ethnicity, race, social class, culture, and so forth of each member of the supervisory triad (APA, 2002, 2014; Gatmon et al., 2001).

When there is a history of exploitation or discrimination in broader society and the supervisor is a member of the historically dominant group, the risk of error increases and the supervisor's responsibility for vigilance and self-reflection is heightened. Ignorance of cultural and other aspects of diversity implies greater risk for impaired objectivity and compromised effectiveness as well as harm to supervisees and clients. Soliciting feedback from knowledgeable colleagues and studying relevant publications will illuminate a supervisor's vulnerabilities and may minimize the likelihood of exploiting privileged status to the detriment of supervisees (Garcia & Tehee, 2014).

Attention to Themes from the Complaint Case

Disciplinary supervision by definition involves a finding of ethical violation. Therefore, its primary objectives include helping supervisees develop a grasp of the nature and significance of their errors, an understanding of the factors contributing to them, and a comprehensive and viable plan to prevent future mistakes. The achievement of these objectives requires supervisors to focus on themes evident in the complaint case and on the ways these themes reverberate through the supervision. Thus, the function of the supervisor is not only to monitor clinical work, but also to provide ethics education and scrutinize attitudes, beliefs, and practices to prevent further error.

Enhanced Need for Modeling Ethical Behavior

The supervisor's modeling of ethically sound professional behavior is a critical component of any supervision. In disciplinary supervision, the risks created when this is absent are magnified. Psychologists mandated to supervision are acutely attuned to the ethical practices and behaviors of their supervisors. Even minor errors of omission – much more so overt mistakes – detected by the supervisee may precipitate anger and indignation. More perilous is the possibility of a supervisee assuming ill-considered behavior to be correct and incorporating it unexamined into his or her subsequent practice.

Clearly, disciplinary supervisors must ensure that their behavior with supervisees conforms to applicable ethics codes, rules, and civil and criminal statutes. Supervisees benefit from watching their supervisors routinely refer to those standards, as well as to professional guidelines, during discussion of clinical cases and ethical dilemmas. Demonstrating self-reflection, highlighting ethical issues, discussing clients and colleagues respectfully, maintaining boundaries, and inviting supervisees to do so are examples of modeling ethical practice.

Legal Liability

Another category of responsibility for disciplinary supervisors relates to legal liability. The ASPPB guidelines assert that supervisors "assume professional and legal responsibility for the work of supervisees" (2015, p. 10). All clinical supervisors incur legal liability at two levels: first, liability for their own actions (direct liability); and second, liability for the actions of their supervisees (vicarious liability) (Falvey, 2002). Those under disciplinary supervision have histories of ethical violation, and thus the risk of ethical and legal problems increases for both the supervisor and supervisee.

Case Vignettes

Many types of licensing board cases result in mandated supervision. Despite commonalities, licensees who commit ethical violations are not a homogenous group (Gabbard, 1995b; Gonsiorek, 1995) and supervision must be tailored to the unique needs and circumstances of the supervisee. Two cases illustrate different supervisee presentations and the commensurate ethical challenges confronting their supervisors.

Dr. Rebecca Gray's Supervision of Dr. Dan Shaw's Complaint Case

Dr. Dan Shaw practiced psychology independently in a rural community for seven years after leaving his position at a community mental health center. Burdened by the clinic's onerous requirements, Dr. Shaw wanted the chance to operate his own business. His plan seemed to be working well until Maria, one party in a now-divorced couple he had seen for therapy, called to request a copy of their marital treatment record. Maria had decided to challenge the joint child custody agreement she had with her ex-husband, Brian, and she indicated that her lawyer had advised her to obtain a copy of the record to support her case. Dr. Shaw tried to dissuade her from this action, noting that Brian was always a good father and would be distressed by it. Maria became angry and demanded the record. Dr. Shaw told her that without a court order he could not release it. She hung up on him.

Remembering his responsibility for protecting confidentiality, Dr. Shaw refrained from disclosing that, after the marital therapy ended, he began seeing Brian for individual therapy. Dr. Shaw continued using the same file he had created for the couple. He had not thought to discuss the transition to individual therapy with either party and he had not considered *who* under *what conditions* had the right to *which* records.

Dr. Shaw felt protective of his current client and texted Brian to alert him about his ex-wife's call. Grateful for the heads-up but furious with Maria, Brian contacted his lawyer to launch a preemptive attack. Dr. Shaw agreed to write a letter to the court and to testify that it was in the best interests of the children for Brian to be the primary custodial parent. Dr. Shaw had minimal experience with the legal system, but he welcomed the opportunity to broaden his areas of expertise.

Several months later, the licensing board notified Dr. Shaw of a complaint and cited him for engaging in a multiple relationship that compromised his objectivity, for practicing outside his competence, for neglecting to obtain informed consent, and for failing to follow record-keeping standards. The board mandated an individualized tutorial focused on appropriate professional boundaries as well as a minimum of one year of weekly supervision with a board-approved supervisor.

Overview of the Supervision

Dr. Shaw discovered that the few supervisors preapproved by the board were at least 150 miles away. Hoping to avoid a long trip, he contacted Dr. Rebecca Gray, a psychologist practicing in a nearby town. Sympathetic to Dr. Shaw's circumstances, she considered his request for disciplinary supervision.

Dr. Gray recalled supervising several practicum students and one postgraduate therapist about 25 years earlier. She had no formal course work in supervision, but she had attended a related workshop at some point. Although she had not previously supervised anyone under board order, this sounded like an opportunity to help a colleague and expand her skills. Dr. Gray wrote to the board, declaring her qualifications and willingness to provide Dr. Shaw's supervision, and the board approved her. Dr. Shaw presented as cooperative and amiable. He expressed remorse for his mistakes, willingness to learn, and the desire to do whatever was necessary to remove conditions from his license. Dr. Gray structured the supervision by suggesting that Dr. Shaw choose a couple of cases to discuss during each supervision session, and he readily agreed. Dr. Gray felt they were off to a good start.

Dr. Shaw came to subsequent sessions with no clinical records to which he might refer during discussion. He offered brief case presentations, recalled minimal information about the clients, and typically said he had no questions. Despite Dr. Gray's encouragement to do so, he failed to record the feedback provided. He assured her his memory was intact; he saw no need to record her comments. She decided to let it go.

Dr. Gray became increasingly uncomfortable about the progress of the supervision as she observed Dr. Shaw's enthusiasm give way to defensiveness and what appeared to be resentment. She decided to consult a colleague in another state who she knew had a great deal of expertise in supervision. That individual expressed alarm about her liability and concern that she had proceeded without much experience or training in supervision. He recommended relevant publications and suggested Dr. Gray consider withdrawing from the case. She began to reconsider her plans for moving forward. Dr. Gray had assumed that, given her supervisee's expressed regret, he had worked through the issues in the complaint before beginning the supervision. Based on the advice of her colleague, she decided that reviewing the case with him could be beneficial. She was surprised when Dr. Shaw was unable to identify his mistakes. He said, "Apparently, going out of your way to help a client is no longer considered ethical." He presented a seemingly well-rehearsed rationale for the decisions flagged by the board: "I agreed to help this man after his marriage broke up because he already knew me and he didn't want to have to start over with a new therapist. I wrote a letter supporting his bid for custody because I knew them both and he was clearly the better parent. I guess I figured that after 14 months of treatment I would know a bit more about the situation than some evaluator who would meet them for a couple of hours. But that's just me." He didn't see how going over this again was a good use of his money and time.

Taken aback, Dr. Gray shared her observation that, through the supervision, Dr. Shaw had not seemed to take responsibility for his professional behavior. He vehemently disagreed and demanded examples to substantiate her claim. At that moment, Dr. Gray regretted that her records included only the dates of supervisory service and a list of payments. Unable to produce specific examples and feeling intimidated, she agreed to drop the subject, though her consternation persisted.

Reflecting on the supervision, Dr. Gray considered that her supervisee was indeed following her only clear instruction – to present cases during supervision. Yet his responses had been increasingly perfunctory, and periodically his tone conveyed aggravation, if not contempt. He often alluded to financial hardship caused by the supervision and once noted how expensive her attractive furniture must have been.

Dr. Gray decided to confront Dr. Shaw about his apparent irritation. He responded defensively, noting that this was not therapy and her speculative interpretation of his feelings felt intrusive and inappropriate. Dr. Gray was confused and not confident in her approach, so she quickly pivoted to talking about his cases.

Dr. Gray's misgivings about having accepted the supervisory case intensified. The conversation with her colleague raised her awareness of how little she actually knew of Dr. Shaw's clinical work. She was not convinced his clients were being well served. Too embarrassed to contact her colleague for further consultation, she decided that the best course of action was to terminate the supervision.

At the next session, Dr. Gray announced that the supervision was not working out and recommended that Dr. Shaw continue his work with another supervisor.

Dr. Shaw was incredulous. He pointed out that she had made a commitment to supervise and that he had done exactly what she had asked. His career would be devastated should she terminate with five months of the mandatory supervision remaining. Feeling threatened, she agreed to table the discussion. The next day, Dr. Shaw left her a message indicating that his attorney concurred that termination would be a breach of contract and could result in financial damages.

Possible Courses of Action

Examination of the supervision of Dr. Shaw reveals an array of technical errors and problematic ethical decisions. First, Dr. Gray agreed to provide the supervision with minimal forethought. Its difficulties may have been prevented had they been anticipated and appropriate measures taken. Without them, she has no clear, problem-free path out.

Second, the supervisor's lack of confidence has led to a pattern of deferring to her supervisee's judgment about how she should conduct the supervision. Dr. Shaw's apparent resistance to Dr. Gray's efforts to direct the process and his minimal participation represent serious limitations to the effectiveness of the supervision. The supervision appears to have reached an intractable impasse.

Alternative A: Stay the Course

If Dr. Gray continues the supervision without substantially modifying its structure, dynamic, and method, its potency will be severely compromised, and the likelihood of Dr. Shaw's problem being remediated will be minimal. Further, Dr. Gray may be legally culpable should Dr. Shaw make clinical or ethical errors while under her supervision. Dr. Shaw's recent comments suggest he lacks appreciation for the problems in his behavior at issue in the complaint. This alone makes the risk of violation considerable and increases the exposure to vicarious legal liability for Dr. Gray.

Continuing the supervision without addressing its problems will create an additional dilemma relative to the board. Boards typically require progress reports from supervisors throughout the supervision, as well as a final report evaluating the supervisee's ability to practice ethically and competently. Dr. Gray, fearing retribution, might report adequate progress and verify Dr. Shaw's ability to practice ethically.

Opting for this course, however, would be antithetical to the APA ethical principles (2017). Although not enforceable as minimum standards, the principles encourage psychologists to "establish relationships of trust with those with whom they work" (Principle B: Fidelity and Responsibility) and to "promote accuracy, honesty, and truthfulness" (Principle C: Integrity) (APA, 2016, p. 2). Endorsing a supervisee who is clearly not rehabilitated and who has been told as much models and reinforces unethical behavior for the supervisee.

Alternative B: Continue but Convey Concerns to the Board

Dr. Gray could complete the supervision and inform Dr. Shaw that she is dissatisfied with his progress and intends to apprise the board. This revelation will likely arouse his resentment and anger, but conveying this assessment without telling him in advance is inconsistent with APA Ethical Principle C, Integrity (2017). Doing so also risks alerting her own licensing board to her questionable management of the case. Further, she increases the probability of incurring direct legal liability for errors in her supervision of Dr. Shaw should he decide to initiate legal action against her.

Alternative C: Work to Rectify the Supervision
Alternatively, Dr. Gray might try to repair the supervision with Dr. Shaw, which may or may not be achievable. Dr. Gray will certainly benefit from thinking the case through, in consultation with a knowledgeable colleague, before proceeding.

Minimally, she must devise a plan to educate herself about both the fundamentals of clinical supervision and, more specifically, about the nuances of disciplinary supervision. Enrolling in related trainings and reviewing relevant publications would be a beginning. She should also arrange for continuing consultation with an expert as she attempts to redirect the supervision. Suspending the supervision for some period would allow her time to implement this plan, but this would also necessitate the addition of a temporary supervisor or the temporary suspension of Dr. Shaw's practice.

This trajectory is complicated and not without its risks. Dr. Gray's announced change of course will necessarily represent a substantial increase in the demands of Dr. Shaw. He may be assigned a variety of tasks such as the completion of outside readings and the presentation of case notes, reports, or recorded sessions for the supervisor's critique. Such demands may fuel the acrimony between supervisee and supervisor.

One of their many difficult and unavoidable conversations will involve some admission of error on her part for her previous neglect of these responsibilities. This concession will highlight her decision to practice in an area in which she lacked competence. Her failure to obtain Dr. Shaw's informed consent to supervision will become obvious and her inability to provide examples to support her contention that he has "not been taking responsibility" will illuminate deficits in her supervisory record-keeping. Finally, Dr. Gray's anxiety and intimidation will be difficult to conceal and the likelihood that these emotions will continue to compromise her objectivity is substantial.

Analysis

The very ethical issues evident in the complaint case recur in varying forms in Dr. Gray's supervision of Dr. Shaw. Her ethical errors in supervision are related to informed consent, record-keeping, competence, and compromised objectivity.

In the complaint case, Dr. Shaw agreed to provide a service – a child custody evaluation – for which he had no training or experience but about which he wanted to learn. He did not obtain informed consent from his clients for the marital and individual counseling or for the custody evaluation, and he engaged in multiple roles (couples therapist, individual therapist, and forensic evaluator), compromising his objectivity and effectiveness. His records of service failed to meet accepted standards and his rationale for changing roles was the convenience of his clients.

Like her supervisee, Dr. Gray practiced outside her areas of competence when she assumed the role of supervisor, a decision she rationalized as a way to help a colleague and an opportunity to develop new skills. She failed to obtain her supervisee's informed consent and she kept inadequate records. Her objectivity was corrupted by her lack of confidence and feelings of intimidation relative to her supervisee. Dr. Gray's realization that she has painted herself into a proverbial corner and her concomitant emotional distress are palpable and add a layer of complexity to the prudent ethical decision-making that this situation requires.

Prevention Strategies

Although rectifying the situation at this juncture is fraught with difficulty, retrospectively examining the case will illuminate strategies that, if implemented from the outset, would likely have allowed Dr. Gray to avoid the quagmire she is currently facing. Had Dr. Gray been properly prepared to provide disciplinary supervision, she would have approached the case very differently. For example, when she received Dr. Shaw's request to provide supervision, she would have carefully evaluated the situation not only in terms of her availability and desire to help a colleague, but also, more fundamentally, in light of her competence. At that point, she may have declined. However, she did not do so because of a combination of a mistaken belief that her training and competency were adequate to engage in this supervision and her sympathy for Dr. Shaw's circumstances.

A decision to go forward would have required a delay before starting to allow training and education and arrangement for continuing consultation with a knowledgeable colleague as Dr. Gray developed her competence in disciplinary supervision. Such specialized skills may require her to arrange for consultation outside of her immediate area, perhaps by telephone or another confidential technology, with due consideration for jurisdictional regulations. Unfortunately, she decided to move forward rather than judiciously consider the possible outcomes of her decision.

Her lack of competence with this type of supervision was manifested in multiple ways. Obtaining the supervisee's informed consent to supervision and devising a supervisory plan or contract are recommended for beginning a supervisory relationship (Cobia & Boes, 2000; Thomas, 2007). This procedure affords the opportunity to discuss all relevant aspects of the supervision, including the risks and benefits, limits to confidentiality, emergency procedures, duration, grounds for termination, and expectations of the supervisee (Thomas, 2010). Such a discussion should also delineate supervisory methods.

Dr. Gray should have a system for routinely examining work samples such as Dr. Shaw's informed consent materials, privacy statement, billing system, reports, case notes, and recordings of sessions. She might want to require completion of assigned readings, preparation of documents, and an agreement to follow supervisory directives. Dr. Gray should be clear that failure to meet these established expectations could result in termination of supervision and/or an unfavorable report to the licensing board (for a more complete discussion of these issues, see Thomas, 2007, 2014).

Soon after this initial agreement, Dr. Gray should consider arranging a site visit to evaluate Dr. Shaw's work setting. Such visits may reveal problems such as inadequate soundproofing, unprofessional decor, insecure storage of confidential information, and factors reflecting ethical compromise that might otherwise go unidentified (Thomas, 2011). If the supervisee is employed, the visit not only allows the supervisor to assess the environment, but also affords an opportunity for the off-site and on-site supervisors to meet and thus facilitate the collaboration and coordination of the supervision. The supervisee's authorization of their communication must be obtained.

Dr. Gray also must assert her authority. Ideally, the supervision will be a collaborative process, but she must clarify that when there is a difference of opinion about a matter she considers critical, her decisions will prevail. Dr. Shaw may or may not agree to supervision given these parameters, but the informed consent process at the outset is the best time for this to be decided. The criteria used to evaluate his progress must also be discussed in advance.

Dr. Jane Ross's Supervision of Dr. Sharon Cohen

Complaint Case

Sharon Cohen, Ph.D., has practiced independently as a psychologist for 12 years. A generalist, she has provided assessment and treatment services to adults of all ages. Her licensing board has notified her of a complaint regarding a case involving her sister-in-law, whom Dr. Cohen had agreed to treat for anxiety. The board alleged that Dr. Cohen engaged in a multiple relationship by agreeing to provide psychotherapy to a family member, which compromised her objectivity. Relying on the recommendation of an independent evaluator, the board has ordered individual psychotherapy and clinical supervision for Dr. Cohen.

Overview of the Supervision

Dr. Jane Ross was listed as a board-approved psychologist who could provide disciplinary supervision. In addition to her skills as a generalist, she has expertise in substance abuse, mood disorders, post-traumatic stress disorder, and supervision. Dr. Ross held an exploratory meeting with Dr. Cohen and concluded that her areas of competence were a good fit with Dr. Cohen's remedial needs. In a second meeting, they reviewed informed consent and developed a supervision contract. Consistent with the board's order, they planned weekly, one-hour meetings. Dr. Ross agreed to monitor Dr. Cohen's continuing cases for case management and identified the following issues to address in supervision: professional boundaries, multiple relationships, scope of practice, countertransference and impaired objectivity, and setting limits with clients.

The first three months of supervision went well. Dr. Cohen maintained perfect attendance and came prepared for each meeting. Initially, she was cautious and appeared reluctant to disclose anything that might reflect negatively on her capabilities. Recognizing her reticence, Dr. Ross took a gentle and supportive approach, emphasizing rapport-building and avoiding confrontation. That approach appeared to pay off, as Dr. Cohen seemed increasingly willing to disclose her struggles with challenging cases. She seemed to respect Dr. Ross's clinical acumen and rarely disagreed, but for on one occasion.

The one instance of disagreement involved Nate, a prospective client discussed at their sixth session. Nate attended the same synagogue as Dr. Cohen. Their rabbi had provided spiritual counseling, but he thought Nate needed more specialized help and referred him to Dr. Cohen. She was proud of the rabbi's vote of confidence and excited to share the news with her supervisor.

Dr. Cohen was deflated and angry after Dr. Ross expressed reservations about her accepting the referral. Without exploring the issue, Dr. Ross lectured Dr. Cohen about the risks of multiple relationships and potential complications in treating a fellow congregant. Dr. Cohen disagreed, saying her previous interactions with Nate were minimal enough so as not to cause difficulty. Dr. Ross concluded, "Well, I still don't think you should accept this referral."

During one session about five months into the supervision, Dr. Cohen was unusually quiet and noticeably ill at ease. After much prodding, she told Dr. Ross, "There is something my therapist said I should tell you, but I am afraid you'll be mad at me." Dr. Ross responded with reassurance, promising she would not be angry or punitive. Eventually, Dr. Cohen disclosed that she had accepted the referral from her rabbi and she had been counseling with Nate for two months without mentioning him in supervision.

Nate's problems included a history of violence with his ex-partner and dependence on opiate pain medications obtained from multiple physicians and through illegal purchase. He declined to give Dr. Cohen authorization to communicate with his doctors and rejected her suggestion of a substance abuse assessment. Nate did agree to a gradual tapering of his opiate use and Dr. Cohen had become involved in monitoring these efforts by counting his pills.

Dr. Cohen reported that Nate had come to a session two weeks earlier in possession of a large supply of hydrocodone. Dr. Cohen convinced him to leave the pills with her for "safekeeping." She regretted the arrangement almost immediately and flushed the pills down the toilet. Nate subsequently demanded return of the pills or reimbursement of the $200 he had spent on them. He showed up at her office without an appointment and told her he had complained of her "incompetence" to their rabbi. He threatened to report her to the licensing board if his demand was not met.

Through her tears, Dr. Cohen said, "I don't know what to do. Will you talk to Nate? I am afraid the board will take my license if they find out."

Ethical Considerations for Dr. Ross

Dr. Ross endeavored to build a solid foundation for her supervision, in sharp contrast to Dr. Cohen's inauspicious beginning with Nate. She exercised due diligence in determining that she had the necessary skills, engaged in a thorough informed consent process, and developed a supervisory contract. These measures helped Dr. Ross to avoid many of the technical and ethical difficulties befalling Dr. Cohen. Nevertheless, Dr. Ross neglected to address adequately the themes and dynamics of Dr. Cohen's disciplinary case, which contributed to the development of the ethical problems described below.

Maintaining Role Boundaries

Ethical dilemmas may arise when a supervisor is not sufficiently vigilant about challenges to boundaries and unintentionally assumes another role. This role shift may occur when a supervisee presents with emotional distress, when a supervisee's shame interferes with the constructive review of cases, or when a supervisee's behavior indicates underlying psychopathology. In response, supervisors may inadvertently default to the role of a friend, colleague, or therapist.

Dr. Ross's "gentle and supportive" approach with Dr. Cohen may have helped to establish rapport, but it also could cultivate inappropriate expectations in the supervisee. The shift into another role undermined Dr. Ross's objectivity and effectiveness as a supervisor and runs contrary to APA Ethical Principle A: Beneficence and Nonmaleficence, as well as to Principle B: Fidelity and Responsibility (2017).

Dr. Cohen came to supervision as the result of a board complaint concerning her over-involvement with a client who was also a family member. Similar dynamics of over-involvement and impaired objectivity are manifest in her relationship with Nate. Dr. Ross might reasonably address this reenactment, but she must do so without slipping into the role of therapist. She might provide feedback and identify problem areas (e.g., "It seems to me you are repeating the pattern that got you into trouble in the first place"). She might help the supervisee identify warning signs of problems and strategies for managing them (e.g., "When you feel the pull to 'rescue' a client, that may be a warning signaling the need for extra vigilance in your effort to maintain professional boundaries"). Still, it is potentially problematic for the supervisor to engage the supervisee in an in-depth exploration of the origins of the behavior (e.g., "Let's explore why you keep repeating this pattern, even when you recognize that it can get you into trouble"). Remaining in the supervisor role may mean encouraging Dr. Cohen to pursue such exploration with her psychotherapist, who would be in a better position to help her examine related emotional issues and personality dynamics.

Dr. Cohen's request for Dr. Ross to intervene directly with Nate reflects a "parallel process" in which the dynamics of the client–therapist relationship are reflected in the supervisory relationship (Frawley-O'Dea & Sarnat, 2001). Dr. Cohen became overly involved with her client by confiscating his pills and assuming responsibility for preventing his drug use. Now she requests over-involvement by her supervisor.

Although highlighting the parallel process may facilitate self-awareness, Dr. Ross must do so in a way that is consistent with the boundaries of supervision. Role-playing may improve Dr. Cohen' skills and confidence in setting limits with Nate, but at this point, it would inappropriate for Dr. Ross to usurp her responsibility and intercede directly with the client.

Managing Disagreements

Differences of opinion about clinical approaches and practice management are inevitable, and they may lead to beneficial discussion. When addressing such disagreements, the supervisor should be mindful of the amplified power differential in disciplinary supervision. Some supervisors, uncomfortable with this power difference, may attempt to divest themselves of it by adopting a collegial, conflict-avoidant style. This can be problematic because avoiding issues that may provoke conflict will likely convey approval when the supervisor is, in reality, concerned about the supervisee's behavior.

Dr. Ross was anxious and so expressed reservations about the referral during the initial discussion. She ended that discourse by saying that she was not persuaded and still did not think Dr. Cohen should work with Nate. Dr. Ross was unclear as to whether this was a suggestion or a directive. The ambiguity likely reflected her discomfort and reluctance to assert her authority, an aspect of competence as a supervisor. But her duty requires that she provide guidance in an unambiguous manner that minimizes the likelihood of misunderstanding.

The supervisor's use of authority must be tempered with sensitivity to diversity as well as recognition of the ultimate supervisory goal of facilitating increasing autonomy in the supervisee. Dr. Ross seems to have overlooked the potential role of Dr. Cohen's faith in her inclination to help her fellow congregant. Because of her respect for the rabbi, Dr. Cohen may have assigned more weight to his request than to the objection of her supervisor. Dr. Ross also did not take time in supervision to reflect on variables such as the size of the congregation, the nature of Dr. Cohen's history with Nate, her desire to please her rabbi, and any theological foundation that may have contributed to her determination to accept the referral.

Rather than unilaterally issuing a veto, she might have provided a safe and respectful environment in which Dr. Cohen could have explored these factors and arrived at a sound decision taking into account her religious values and the meaning she ascribed to her membership in a faith community. Further Dr. Cohen's concern about her relationship with referral sources should have been taken into account.

After further discussion, Dr. Ross might have changed her mind and supported acceptance of the referral. Dr. Cohen would not have felt the need to conceal the treatment and may have received sufficient guidance to avoid the missteps that unfolded. Conversely, a more nuanced exploration of potential pitfalls may have led Dr. Cohen to decline the referral. As it was, Dr. Cohen was deprived of a potentially valuable opportunity to practice contemplating the complexities of such ethical decisions – an experience that could have served her well in the future.

Countertransference and Self-Interest

Even had Dr. Ross navigated the above issues in an ethically responsible way, Dr. Cohen's situation with Nate would present its own set of challenges. Dr. Ross may have her own, perhaps unconscious, emotional responses beyond those pertaining directly to Dr. Cohen's predicament. These may cover a range of feelings including disappointment with the supervisee for "failing," anger with the supervisee for ignoring her advice and concealing important information, or resentment for her having created a conundrum that Dr. Ross now has to address. She may also feel compassion for Dr. Cohen, who is obviously distressed, or guilt over not having done a better job as supervisor.

These countertransference reactions may compromise Dr. Ross's judgment going forward. For example, disappointment or anger may lead to distancing and rejection. Anger and resentment may prompt a punitive response. Compassion and guilt may lead to over-identification and over-involvement.

A dynamic of self-interest might also be considered. Dr. Ross may be concerned about how her handling of the supervision will affect her professional stature. If she worries that the licensing board will view her as too soft, she may take an unnecessarily harsh stance. Conversely, if she is concerned about avoiding a reputation as rigid or authoritarian, she may overcompensate in the opposite direction. Another possibility is that Dr. Ross could become excessively concerned about legal exposure should Nate sue Dr. Cohen and name her as a codefendant.

Each of these responses is understandable. Yet, allowing personal feelings or self-interest to eclipse her focus on Dr. Cohen's supervision and the client's welfare will likely lead to technical errors, if not ethical transgressions on the part of Dr. Ross as she attempts to discern the next steps in this complicated case. Analyzing these responses in consultation with knowledgeable colleagues may illuminate the pitfalls and possible courses of action.

Potentially Conflicting Obligations

Dr. Ross has obligations to several parties: the supervisee's client, the supervisee, and the board. Ideally, these responsibilities will align. Should her obligations conflict, however, ethical challenges will emerge. The supervisee in a disciplinary case must be informed at the outset and reminded as needed that the supervisor's responsibilities include fulfilling reporting conditions established by the licensing board.

Courses of Action

Two issues in the current supervision situation require action by Dr. Ross: Dr. Cohen's mismanagement of Nate's therapy and her concealment of critical information in the supervision. Her primary concern is the best interests of Nate and Dr. Cohen's other current and future clients, followed by her obligations to the board and to her supervisee. Guided by these considerations, Dr. Ross's course of action should include taking the following steps.

Rectify Errors in the Treatment

Dr. Ross must determine whether and to what extent Dr. Cohen's compromised objectivity with Nate generalizes to her work with other clients. Assuming a determination that the deficiencies pertain to Nate's case only, Dr. Ross and Dr. Cohen could develop a plan of action. The resulting plan may be for Dr. Cohen to do one or more of the following:

- Decline to yield to Nate's demands and inform him of such.
- Acknowledge and accept responsibility for her therapeutic error.
- Inform Nate about his right to file a complaint with the licensing board.
- Issue a clear recommendation that Nate undergoes a substance abuse assessment.
- Discuss and facilitate the transfer of Nate's care to another psychotherapist.
- Enforce professional boundaries with Nate, taking reasonable precautions to protect Dr. Cohen from harassment and physical harm.

Dr. Ross also may decide to temporarily increase the length of their weekly meetings to allow time for oversight of Dr. Cohen's implementation of the plan and for intensified supervision of her other cases. Such a collaborative case analysis exemplifies the type of process in which supervisors should engage with supervisees.

Recalibrate the Supervision

Dr. Cohen's concealment of her treatment of Nate represents a breach of trust in the supervisory relationship and its impact must be thoroughly examined. Dr. Ross may consider whether or not to continue the supervision. That determination should not be based solely on Dr. Cohen's breach of the supervision contract, but rather include an examination of Dr. Ross's obligation to different parties, evaluation of the benefit of enforcing a previously established boundary versus potential harm to her supervisee, and honest self-examination of her own ability to remain objective and effective.

Formulate Steps with the Licensing Board

Dr. Ross also must consider her obligation to keep the licensing board informed about significant events in the supervision. Dr. Cohen's ethical and clinical errors in the management of Nate's treatment, her failure to follow her supervisor's direction, and the concealment of her work are relevant. Her responsibility to disclose such information to the board must be transparent from the beginning. At this point, she must remind Dr. Cohen of her responsibility and inform her of the planned action, discuss with her the likely consequences, and provide her with a copy of all communications with the board.

Transparency is consistent with APA Ethical Principle C: Integrity, and so models ethical behavior. Dr. Ross should model appropriate boundaries by declining any request to withhold pertinent information from the board.

Suggestions for Effective Disciplinary Supervision

Best practices for disciplinary supervision are similar to those for any supervision, though the risk of errors and repercussions may be greater. The effective and ethical practice of disciplinary supervision will be enhanced by attention to the following guides.

Maintain Clear Boundaries

Supervisees will benefit when supervisors are clear about the boundaries of their roles; thus, they can ensure behavior consistent with that role. Although congeniality may facilitate the development of the supervisory connection, being overly friendly, confiding in the supervisee about personal matters, or consulting the individual about the supervisor's cases may result in a sense of betrayal should the supervisor find she must exert her authority or deliver challenging feedback.

Obtain Informed Consent

Securing the informed consent of supervisees at the outset of and throughout supervision clarifies the expectations of supervisors and supervisees (Thomas, 2007, 2010, 2014). For example, supervisees will benefit from understanding the goals of the supervision, the methods that will be employed, the structure of supervision sessions, and how they will be evaluated. Limits to supervisees' privacy must be explained in any supervision, but in disciplinary supervision, supervisees must understand that information they disclose may be included in reports to the board. Further, supervisors' assessment of supervisees' progress may or may not be favorable to their cases. Supervisees also must be given a clear explanation of what they are expected to report and discuss with their supervisors. Allegations of unethical behavior by clients or colleagues, departures from standard practice, and disputes with clients are some examples.

Explicating such expectations contributes to supervisees' sense of security. It enhances their ability to use supervision to help clients and it minimizes misunderstanding that could derail the supervision and result in harm to supervisees and clients. The use of a thorough informed consent process in supervision provides the supervisor with an opportunity to teach supervisees how to conduct such a process with their clients and to model the importance of doing so.

Employ Multiple Methods for Oversight

The presentation of cases is a common strategy for monitoring a supervisee's work. Other methods should be considered in light of their feasibility and appropriateness for the particular clinical setting and circumstance and for deficits identified in the complaint case. Examples include establishing a procedure for tracking cases and caseload management, examining clinical records, and critiquing psychological reports. Reviewing recordings of sessions may be illuminating, but is not always possible or appropriate to the setting. Supervisees conducting court-ordered forensic evaluations or crisis intervention services, for example, may not be permitted to record encounters. Still, some type of work sample generally may be made available for the supervisor's examination. In short, making use of diverse methods will increase the supervisor's ability to detect clinical and ethical problems that may arise.

Maintain Competence

Maintenance of professional competence in supervision is essential. Unlike developmental or training supervision with a novice clinician, however, in which the supervisor must have competence in the areas in which the supervisee is practicing, the focus of disciplinary supervision may be elsewhere. If identified violations are specifically related to a supervisee's technical competence (such as in the interpretation of a particular psychological test), the supervisor's expertise must map closely with the technical aspects of providing that psychological service. Conversely, if violations primarily involve inappropriate boundaries or billing irregularities, the supervisor must be competent in those aspects without need for advanced skills in the area of practice of the supervisee, such as the facilitation of grief groups.

Attend to the Supervisory Relationship

Respect and some degree of empathy are important in every supervisory relationship, perhaps being even more critical in disciplinary supervision. The supervisees are likely to present with more trepidation than most. Embarrassment, shame, and fear are not uncommon (Thomas, 2005). Conveying empathy for the difficulty inherent in disciplinary supervision may diminish defensiveness that may otherwise interfere with learning. Familiarity with a supervisee's previous accomplishments and attention to evidence of continuing proficiency will allow the supervisor to highlight strengths – at least as important to learning as noting deficiencies.

When problems related to the supervisee's attitude, compliance, competence, or ethics are detected, the supervisor must address them as soon as possible. Doing so will enable correction, protect client welfare, and avoid the consequences of a failed supervision for both supervisor and supervisee.

As discussed, attention to the diversity of dimensions in each supervisory triad is essential (APA, 2002, 2014; ASPPB, 2015). Encouraging supervisees to discuss concerns they have about how the supervision is progressing will help to foster openness and minimize the likelihood of important issues going unaddressed.

Document Supervision

The documentation of disciplinary supervision serves multiple purposes. Perhaps most importantly, it allows supervisors to monitor clinical cases over time, observe and track supervisees' progress, and prepare more accurate reports to licensing boards about what has transpired. Supervisees should also be required to keep records of the supervision. Doing so facilitates a more effective integration of feedback into subsequent clinical work and provides documentation of their compliance with the board order.

In the event of a board complaint or lawsuit regarding the supervisee's clinical work or the supervision, a written account of supervisory discussions will supplement the supervisor's memory and provide evidence of what has occurred (Falvey, 2002).

Seek Consultation about Supervision

Disciplinary supervision requires vigilance. Beyond the responsibilities described, supervisors must monitor any interpersonal aspects of the supervisory relationship – including their own countertransference – that might jeopardize their effectiveness (Gabbard, 1995a). Continuing consultation affords opportunities for routine exposure of a psychologist's work to the scrutiny of others. Knowledgeable and trustworthy colleagues committed to sharing candid feedback will supplement supervisors' self-reflection and serve to monitor their objectivity and effectiveness, thus mitigating the likelihood of technical and ethical errors.

Final Comments

Supervision requires a unique skill set including clinical expertise; disciplinary supervisors have significant ethical and legal responsibilities and therefore require specialized training and expertise. The decision to offer disciplinary supervision is not to be made lightly. The potential supervisor must contemplate a multitude of potential clinical and ethical challenges, including legal exposure.

The rewards of offering disciplinary supervision also deserve consideration. Helping colleagues recover from a significant and potentially devastating interruption of their careers and seeing them regain and, in many cases, exceed previous levels of competence can be tremendously gratifying.

Further, the supervisor's own work is inevitably informed by the comprehensive examination of the mistakes of colleagues. Opportunities for supervisors to reflect on and improve their own work are substantial, as are the incentives for ensuring that their clinical and supervisory practices are consistent with current clinical, ethical, and professional standards. The experience is similar to the ways in which teaching a graduate course or preparing a publication provides an opportunity to expand and deepen knowledge of a particular subject area.

No psychologist's work is flawless, and we must lean on one another when we falter – for our own benefit, as well as that of the profession and the public we serve.

References

Adams, J. M. (2001). *On your side: Protecting your mental health practice from litigation.* East Hampton, NY: Mimesis.

American Psychological Association. (2002). *APA guidelines on multicultural education, training, research, practice, and organizational change for psychologists.* Washington, DC: American Psychological Association.

American Psychological Association. (2014). *Guidelines for clinical supervision in health service psychology.* Washington, DC: American Psychological Association.

American Psychological Association. (2017). *Ethical principles of psychologists and code of conduct.* Washington, DC: American Psychological Association.

Association of State and Provincial Psychology Boards. (2012). ASPPB disciplinary data system: Historical discipline report. Peachtree City, GA: Association of State and Provincial Psychology Boards. Retrieved from www.asppb.net/?page=DiscStats

Association of State and Provincial Psychology Boards. (2015). *Supervision guidelines for education and training leading to licensure as a health service provider.* Peachtree City, GA: Association of State and Provincial Psychology Boards.

Banaji, M. R. & Greenwald, A. G. (2013). *Blindspot: Hidden biases of good people.* New York, NY: Random House.

Behnke, S. H. (2005). The supervisor as gatekeeper: Reflections on Ethical Standards 7.02, 7.04, 7.05, 7.06, and 10.10. *Monitor on Psychology, 36,* 90.

Bernard, J. M. & Goodyear, R. K. (2014). *Fundamentals of clinical supervision* (5th ed.). Upper Saddle River, NJ: Pearson Education.

Celenza, A. (2007). *Sexual boundary violations: Therapeutic, supervisory, and academic contexts.* Lanhan, MD: Jason Aronson.

Cobia, D. C. & Boes, S. R. (2000). Professional disclosure statements and formal plans for supervision: Two strategies for minimizing the risk of ethical conflicts in post-master's supervision. *Journal of Counseling and Development, 78,* 293–296.

Cobia, D. C. & Pipes, R. B. (2002). Mandated supervision: An intervention for disciplined professionals. *Journal of Counseling and Development, 80,* 140–144.

Elman, N. S. & Forrest, L. M. (2007). From trainee impairment to professional competence problems: Seeking new terminology that facilitates effective action. *Professional Psychology: Research and Practice, 38,* 501–509.

Falender, C. A. & Shafranske, E. P. (2004). *Clinical supervision: A competency-based approach.* Washington, DC: American Psychological Association.

Falvey, J. E. (2002). *Managing clinical supervision: Ethical practice and legal risk management.* Pacific Grove, CA: Brooks/Cole.

Frawley-O'Dea, M. G. & Sarnat, J. E. (2001). *The supervisory relationship: A contemporary psychodynamic approach.* New York: Guilford Press.

French, J. R. P., Jr. & Raven, B. (1959). Bases of social power. In D. Cartwright (Ed.), *Studies in social power.* Ann Arbor, MI: University of Michigan.

Gabbard, G. O. (1995a). Transference and countertransference in the psychotherapy of therapists charged with sexual misconduct. *Psychiatric Annals, 25,* 100–105.

Gabbard, G. O. (1995b). Psychotherapists who transgress sexual boundaries with patients. In J. C. Gonsiorek (Ed.), *Breach of trust: Sexual exploitation by health care professionals and clergy* (pp. 133–144). Thousand Oaks, CA: Sage.

Garcia, M. A. & Tehee, M. (2014). *Society of Indian Psychologists Commentary on the American Psychological Association's Ethical Principles of Psychologists and Code of Conduct.* Retrieved from www.aiansip.org

Gatmon, D., Jackson, D., Koshkarian, L., Martos-Perry, N., Molina, A., Patel, N., & Rodolfa, E. (2001). Exploring ethnic, gender, and sexual orientation variables in supervision: Do they really matter? *Journal of Multicultural Counseling and Development, 29,* 102–112.

Gilfoyle, N. (2008). The legal exosystem: Risk management in addressing student competence problems in professional psychology training. *Training & Education in Professional Psychology, 2,* 202–209.

Gonsiorek, J. C. (1995). Assessment for rehabilitation of exploitative health care professionals and clergy. In J. C. Gonsiorek (Ed.), *Breach of trust: Sexual exploitation by health care professionals and clergy* (pp. 145–162). Thousand Oaks, CA: Sage.

Goodyear, R. K. & Rodolfa, E. (2012). Negotiating the complex ethical terrain of clinical supervision. In S. J. Knapp (Ed.), *APA handbook of ethics in psychology: Vol. 2, Practice, teaching, and research* (pp. 261–275). Washington, DC: American Psychological Association.

Jacobs, D., David, P., & Meyer, D. J. (1995). *The supervisory encounter: A guide for teachers of psychotherapy and psychoanalysis.* New Haven, CT: Yale University Press.

Sarnat, J. E. (2016). *Supervision essentials for psychodynamic psychotherapies.* Washington, DC: American Psychological Association.

Thomas, J. T. (2005). Licensing board complaints: Minimizing the impact on the psychologist's defense and clinical practice. *Professional Psychology: Research and Practice, 36,* 426–433.

Thomas, J. T. (2007). Informed consent through contracting for supervision: Minimizing risks, enhancing benefits. *Professional Psychology: Research and Practice, 38,* 221–231.

Thomas, J. T. (2010). *The ethics of supervision and consultation: Practical guidance for mental health professionals.* Washington, DC: American Psychological Association.

Thomas, J. T. (2011). Knocked off kilter: Supervising in the wake of sexual boundary violations. In W. G. Johnson & G. P. Koocher (Eds.), *Ethical conundrums, quandaries and predicaments in mental health practice: A casebook from the files of the experts* (pp. 297–305). New York, NY: Oxford University Press.

Thomas, J. T. (2014). Disciplinary supervision following ethics complaints: Goals, tasks, and ethical dimensions. *Journal of Clinical Psychology: In Session, 70,* 1–11.

Thomas, J. T. (2015). Ethical considerations for clinical supervisors. *The National Psychologist, 24,* 11.

27 Ethical Issues in Psychological Consultation

Stewart E. Cooper and Rodney L. Lowman

This chapter focuses on some of the ethical issues likely to be encountered when professionals are engaged in consultation as a mode of general applied or mental health/health services delivery to achieve goals with individuals, groups, organizations, or communities. Having an understanding of some basic issues about consultation provides a helpful context for considering ethical risks and approaches.

Consultation is a primary professional activity important in many areas of professional psychological practice both in general applied and health/mental health services content areas of psychology. Nearly 50 years ago, Gerald Caplan's (1970) *The Theory and Practice of Mental Health Consultation* was published and for many years was the major work in the area. The consulting skill set was particularly relevant to the then-emerging field of community psychology (Lewis, Lewis, Daniels, & D'Andrea, 2011). Morrill, Oetting, and Hurst (1974) subsequently developed a three-dimensional model for categorizing counseling-related interventions, including consultation, by target, purpose, and method. Atkinson, Thompson, and Grant (1993) later included consultation as one of eight roles for psychologists working with racial/ethnic minorities. In the same era, organizational psychological consulting was emerging as a focal area (see Argyris, 1970; Levinson, with Molinari & Spohn, 1972).

More recently, Rodolfa et al. (2005), in a seminal piece of education in professional psychology, included consultation as one of the six functional competency development domains of health/mental health services provision. The other core competencies identified by these authors were: assessment, diagnosis, and conceptualization; intervention; research and evaluation; supervision and teaching; and management and supervision. In their model, Rodolfa et al. (2005) suggested that professionals develop consultation competencies across the professional lifespan through a variety of educational and applied learning and supervised experiences.

Dougherty (2014) provided a more specific definition of consultation, especially as used to assist individuals, groups/teams, organizations, or communities. In his view, "Consultation is an indirect process in which a human service professional (consultant) assists a consultee with a work-related (or caretaking-related) problem with a client system, with the goal of helping both the consultee and the client system in some specified way" (p. 8).

Consultation in this model is typically triadic, with the consultant providing direct assistance to the consultee, who in turn provides direct services to the client system.

In the case of organizational consultation, it is not uncommon for the consultant either to work directly with the client system or to focus almost exclusively on the consultee with the expectation that an improved consultee will lead to an improved client system. The latter is equally valid for much mental health consultation. Consultants typically provide their services using one or more of six roles – advocate, expert, trainer/educator, collaborator, fact finder, or process specialist – ranging on a continuum of more to fewer directives, with advocate being the most directive (Lippit & Lippit, 1986). How consulting is conceptualized or implemented has implications for the ethical issues to be considered.

A number of publications about psychological consultation have appeared in recent years aimed at providing an introduction to or overview of the field. Sources that provide succinct overviews focusing on psychologists engaged in consultation include the book, *An Introduction to Consulting Psychology: Working with Individuals, Groups, and Organizations* (Lowman, 2016), and the book chapters "Counseling psychologists as consultants" (Cooper & Shullman, 2012), and "Counseling psychologists as consultants" (Cooper, Newman, & Fuqua, 2012). All of these resources include material on the particular ethical dilemmas that more commonly arise in the practice of consultation. These include informed consent, confidentiality, multiple relationships, conflicts of interest, and competence (Lowman & Cooper, 2017).

In this chapter, we focus on common ethical issues that arise in the practice of psychologically based consultation. The material is divided into two main sections. The first part starts with a brief overview of the main mental health consultation and organizational psychological consultation approaches with identification of some of the likely ethical issues of each. It then continues with a brief description of the differences between consultation and therapy and between consultation and collaboration, along with the ethical implications of each of these differences. This is presented because many readers may have limited exposure to formal course work or study in psychological consultation and the understanding basics about it sets a requisite context for the ethical challenges and dilemmas that emerge in its practice. The second part of the chapter then introduces and expounds upon five typical psychological consultation ethical concerns areas.

Consultation Elaborated and Differentiated

Mental Health Consultation

Understanding more about the specific approaches nested within the mental health consultation model will help contextualize the ethical issues likely to arise from it. Psychiatrist Gerald Caplan is rightfully considered the founder of mental health consultation. His first article on this topic, "Types of mental health consultation," was published in the *American Journal of Orthopsychiatry* in 1963. As an update to his original 1970 book mentioned previously, he co-wrote *Mental Health Consultation and Collaboration* in 1993. In this edition, he added in and contrasted the newly developing field of mental health collaboration and he revised several of his original concepts in line with criticisms and feedback received subsequent to the original release. While older, this book remains an excellent resource. Brief summaries of mental health consultation are available that may be useful to the reader (see Caplan, Caplan, & Erchul, 1994; Mendoza, 1993). Publications on mental health consultation continue yearly (e.g., Allen & Green, 2012; Carney & Jefferson, 2014).

Caplan (1970) defined mental health consultation "as a process of interaction between two professional persons – the consultant, who is a specialist, and the consultee, who invokes the consultant's help in regard to a current work problem with which he [or she] is having difficulty and which he [or she] has decided is within the other's area of specialized competence" (p. 19). There are five principal forms mental health consultation can take depending on the need of the consultee and the client system (Dougherty, 2014). Client-centered case consultation (Caplan & Caplan, 1993) focuses on helping a consultee with a client (with minimal contact with the consultee and the major focus being on the client). Consultee-centered case consultation (Caplan & Caplan, 1993) considers caregiving, work-related problems to reside in the consultee; it emphasizes helping the consultee by focusing on the consultee's feelings, thoughts, and actions with the case. Program-centered administrative consultation (Caplan & Caplan, 1993) seeks to help an administrator fix a program-related problem or meet a new goal. Consultee-centered administrative consultation (Caplan & Caplan, 1993) aims to help an administrator and other consultees develop their skills to improve the mental health aspects of the organization and its programs. It involves close parallels to executive or managerial coaching. More recently, the ecological approach (Dougherty, 2014), often used when addressing programs or system's needs, focuses on changing the human–environment interface. The ecological approach represents a decrease of emphasizing internal dynamics only. Through the years, ethical concerns raised about the mental health consultation approach have particularly focused on the deliberate use of fictitious stories and lack of informed consent as manipulations of consultees. These concerns are less relevant at present as consultants more straightforwardly deal with the underlying cognitive and belief systems of consultees.

Organizational Consultation

Understanding the basics about organizational consultation is likewise important as a foundation for understanding likely emerging ethical issues in the practice of consultation. A number of psychologists helped create the specialty area of organizational consulting psychology. Among these were Chris Argyris (see *Intervention Theory and Method*, 1970), Harry Levinson (*Organizational diagnosis*, first published in 1972), and Edgar Schein's (1987, 1988) *Process consultation*. Schein's 1999 book, *Process consultation revisited: Building the helping relationship*, is an excellent resource.

Organizational consultation can vary as to its method and approach (Agyris and Schein, for example, used more of a process approach, whereas Levinson used more of psychoanalytical one). Lowman (2002, 2016) writes that organizational consultation seeks to improve the functioning of the organization by improving the functioning of individuals, teams, and the overall organization. Schein posits four sub-approaches to organizational consultation. In educational/training consultation, the consultant provides training or education to consultees to be more effective in some area. Program-focused organizational consultation aims to assist an organization with some aspect of a program, frequently evaluation. Doctor–patient consultation involves the consultant entering an organization, diagnosing a problem, and prescribing a solution. In Schein's preferred form of organizational consultation – process consultation – efforts focus on assisting consultees in becoming better decision-makers and problem-solvers in the future (Gladding & Newsome, 2017). Ethical issues that arise in organizational consultation are usually associated with multiple roles, failing to identify the client, and not working through all the parameters of the contracting phase.

Psychological Consultation Differentiated from Psychotherapy

Although consultation and therapy are both "helping relationships," they also differ in important ways. Consultation almost always takes place within an organizational context, is typically delivered to persons who do not have significant psychopathology, and is performance enhancement based (Dougherty, 2014). The focus is on helping the consultee in his or her work or caregiving role. When the level of mental health impairment is higher, then the consultant has the options of referring out, referring in, or integrating into the consultation (Murphy, 2012). Referring out is the cleanest but misses out on the possible beneficence of addressing psychological issues, which is key to increasing work performance for many consultees. The ethical issue of conflicts of interest may exist when referring in (though the consultee may pressure for this due to personal comfort with the consultant and if the consultant is licensed as a Health Service Provider in Psychology (HSPP)), as well as the ethical issue of a potentially harmful multiple relationship (when attempting to integrate both therapy and consultation).

As an additional comment, it is noteworthy that the power differentials are typically less in the practice of consultation than they are in therapy, teaching, or supervision due to a number of factors. The consultee is typically not being evaluated by the consultant, nor is their work the consultant's responsibility. Consequently, the consultee is freer to disregard the recommendations of the consultant without as much fear of repercussion (Gladding & Newsom, 2017). This lessens the probability of the ethical issue of exploitation manifesting.

Consultation as Differentiated from Intra- and Inter-Professional Collaboration

The differences between consultation and collaboration can lead to some confusion because consultation, to be successful, usually requires a high level of collaboration and being a collaborator may be the dominant role the consultant is employing. *Collaboration*, particularly intra-professional or inter-professional collaboration, is a type of helping relationship in which a human services professional cooperates with other professionals to both offer consultation to them and receive consultation from them (Lake, Baerg, & Paslawski, 2015). In such a type of collaboration, each of the members of the team provides direct services to the client system in their respective area of expertise – psychologists would provide psychologically related services (Arredondo, Shealy, Neale, & Winfrey, 2004). Choices of engaging in consultation or collaboration are particularly prevalent for those doing such work internally to an organization. Collaboration is a typical mode of service that is becoming more prevalent among those working internally to an organization (Dougherty, 2014; Gladding & Newsome, 2017).

As an additional source of confusion, the historic, more medically oriented view of consultation involving referral to an expert who then takes over the case also leads to confusion in advancing the study and practice of consultation. This is easily seen if one conducts a psychology journal article search using the term "consultation." Many examples of single or brief direct services immediately emerge. That consultants sometimes do have direct contact with the client system for assessment or intervention aspects adds to the conceptual ambiguity (Lowman & Cooper, 2017). A significant difference in ethical considerations is that in intra- and inter-professional collaboration the professional maintains direct ethical obligations to the client, as well as to his or her fellow collaborator consultees. So, all ethical issues associated with direct practice with clients are also operative.

Ethical Issues in the Practice of Psychological Consultation

Common ethical dilemmas that arise in the practice of mental health and organizational consultation as well as with coaching and collaboration were mentioned in the preceding pages. Also mentioned were the five most common ethical issues likely to emerge in the practice of psychologically based consultation regardless of the particular model or approach employed – informed consent, confidentiality, multiple relationships, conflicts of interest, and competence. In this section, elements of these five common ethical issues will be illustrated by hypothetical cases based on typical situations that arise when consultants use either a mental health or an organizational consultation approach. Ethics are often complicated and each of these cases involves several elements. *Note that all names of the consultants, consultees, companies, and assessment instruments in these cases are fictitious but are derived from syntheses of aspects of actual cases.* The case material will be followed by an analysis of applicable ethical standards that are useful in determining the best course of action to address the case. When appropriate, aspects of the ethical decision-making process, cultural context, and emotional/social dimensions of the issue will be discussed. A final section of each case will discuss the case's implications and recommendations.

Although primary attention is given to the applicable, enforceable ethical standards of the American Psychological Association (APA) Code of Ethics (APA, 2017a), applicable aspirational principles will also be mentioned. Additionally, several other ethical codes have relevance for consulting, but any relevant standards from these will not be included. Some of these other relevant codes include the British Psychological Society Code of Ethics (BPS, 2009), the Canadian Psychological Association Code of Ethics (CPA, 2000), the 2014 American Counseling Association Code of Ethics (ACA, 2014), and the 2010 National Association of School Psychologists Principles for Professional Ethics (NASP, 2010). Each of these was developed by psychologically oriented and related disciplines. Other codes, such as the Society for Human Resource Management Code of Ethics and Business Contact (SHRM, 2014) and the 2015 International Coach Federation Code of Ethics (ICF, 2015), emerged from professional groups whose more narrow or alternative focuses on facilitating change within organizational contexts may inform ethical and competent consultation practice.

The Case of Confidentiality, Informed Consent, and Misuse of Work

Self and collateral information about several members of the management team of a large multicounty mental health services organization was collected and used for coaching purposes. This consultee-centered administrative coaching arrangement had been approved by the board of directors of the organization upon strong recommendations from its CEO and COO. The main goal of the coaching was to assist these nine manager-level staff, all of whom were trained in mental health but not in managing others, to enhance their administrative and organizational work. Individual targets of improvement or of concern with each manager were identified. Based on his understanding from the head of HR who discussed the coaching engagement, Joe, the consulting psychologist, and an external consultant, ensured confidentiality of the coaching information to the nine upper-level managers who were being coached.

Nine months into the contract, the agency faced significant unexpected financial challenges and the strategy that was then being considered was letting go of two to three members of this leadership team. The CEO and COO called Joe on a conference call and pressured him to make a recommendation of who to retain and who to fire based upon the knowledge he had gained from the developmentally oriented coaching. Joe pushed back, saying confidentiality was assumed by all the managers involved and he had specifically covered this with them at the beginning of the engagement. The CEO stated that the situation had drastically changed and that Joe was hired by the organization, not those receiving the coaching. The COO commented that there was nothing in writing about not using the information gained from the coaching for other purposes and made it clear that Joe's continuing to receive contracts with the organization was contingent upon his "cooperation." Joe had a history of several consultation engagements with the organization and was concerned not to lose future options.

Discussion of This Case

Misuse of data occurs when information gathered in the consultation process is used for purposes not agreed upon by the consultees. This problem is more likely when working with managers and executives employed in organizations with multiple levels of administration. Moreover, the likelihood of misuse of sensitive information is higher when inadequate discussion and agreements have been reached up front as to the scope of the work and the use of the information produced. In this case, Joe moved too quickly into the work itself without setting out in writing with a formal contract the particulars of confidentiality to individuals and information to be or not to be shared with others. Had Joe done so, this might have lessened the pressure to which he was ultimately subjected or at least made it easier to respond to the pressure. Having a written contract is not ethically or legally required, but is typically a very good step to take and does not have downsides. Use of Standard 3.11(a) may have been very helpful here as Joe would have had an agreement – best in writing, but not required to be so – that he could have used to bolster his response.

Additionally, Standard 1.03 (Conflicts between Ethics and Organizational Demands) also has some relevance in this situation were Joe to make the error of complying with this request, as it would violate ethics for him to do so. It states:

> If the demands of an organization with which psychologists are affiliated or for whom they are working are in conflict with this Ethics Code, psychologists clarify the nature of the conflict, make known their commitment to the Ethics Code and take reasonable steps to resolve the conflict consistent with the General Principles and Ethical Standards of the Ethics Code. Under no circumstances may this standard be used to justify or defend violating human rights. (APA, 2017a, p. 5)

In this case, the line of keeping impressions gained from the coaching confidential seems pretty clear. Joe's sharing information may have caused harm (3.04, Avoiding Harm) to those who were fired and had a subsequent loss of livelihood should that step have happened. That is not always the situation in other consultations, which are often more messy or unclear or where the stakes involved in complying with requests from upper-level administrators create greater pressures.

Recommendations Emerging from This Case

We conclude discussion of this case with two brief recommendations for managing the issues that emerged in the practice of consultation.

- *Do clear contracting for the consultation work.* To minimize the likelihood of such misuse of information, consultants should obtain a clear agreement at the front end as to uses of the information obtained and the limits of confidentiality, as well as the details of the planned consultancy.
- *Work from a written contract.* While not required by law, having a written contract can not only help alignment of the consultation work, but also be helpful if the consultee or others push for drifting away from it.

The Case Regarding Defining the Client, Informed Consent/Coercion, and Confidentiality

Nancy, a consulting psychologist, was contacted by a hospital as there was reportedly a good deal of tension between several units on the medical services side of the organization. In her initial organizational assessment it appeared that most problems were with the Respiratory Therapy (RT) unit. Further information demonstrated that the issues were not those only of the leadership of the unit, but more that the way it functioned created challenges and difficulties for many of the other medical units. Nancy recommended organizational mirroring (French & Bell, 1999), a technique in which members of related units provide feedback to all the members of the unit for them to benefit from the feedback. Organizational mirroring is recommended for inter-group conflict when the tensions are primarily group focused rather than emerging from a group leader or only one to two members of the group (Schein, 1999). Nancy first worked with the members of the RT unit to explain the benefits and risks of the organizational mirroring intervention in order to get buy-in for the value of this intervention. Organizational mirroring involves a process of the members of the target team receiving feedback from members or representatives of other teams with whom there is frequent work collaboration needed. If size permits, to promote inter-team collaboration and cooperation, it is best to have all members of all the teams be involved (Dougherty, 2014).

Nancy then sent an e-mail to all the personnel of the other units giving some information on the process and some suggestions on the best ways to deliver feedback. She set up three open meetings for anyone who had questions. In these open sessions with employees from these other medical units, she learned that several employees were not happy about not having a choice about participating in this process. They voiced the fear of retributions of various sorts from some of the staff in the RT unit with whom they had trust issues. As a result of this feedback, Nancy decided to adjust strategies and argued with her contact in the organization that rather than forcing all to participate, she needed to solicit volunteer representatives from these other departments that work closely with this unit and to then train these volunteers in the feedback process. She worked with the contracting person in the organization to communicate clearly that no retributions would be tolerated. This was needed because retaliation in such circumstances, both to those that were involved as part of the client system and the direct consultees, is less likely to take place if it is clearly prohibited. Her advocacy was accepted and the intervention was productive.

Discussion of This Case

Informed consent addresses issues associated with making clear in advance of participation in psychological activities what is entailed and having the right to choose to or not to participate in such activities and to discontinue participation at will. One of the earliest issues to address in consultation as part of contracting that can raise ethical issues is the question of the definition of the client. For those working in mental health contexts, this issue may seem straightforward enough. Within that context, the client is usually one person, or at most a family or small group. In the case of consulting to organizations, the client is often an entire organization or its leadership, while the psychologist simultaneously has responsibilities to others (e.g., those they coach or subordinates of leaders). The single word "client" does not capture this complexity. An informative article in this topic is "Who is the client in organizational consultation?" (Fuqua, Newman, Simpson, & Choi, 2012). In this case, the primary client was the entire RT unit, with the hospital overall as the secondary client. The ultimate beneficiaries would be the patients. Specifically, the improved functioning of the unit would likely lead to enhanced services and interventions with the patients it serves. Such indirect benefits to the client system are a typical goal of most consultations.

In this case, Nancy did not well define the client or get appropriate consent up front. In defining one of the units as being the "problem" on the basis of limited information, it was not clear that the client was appropriately defined. By implying participation was mandated without considering that some individuals or even units might decline to participate, the psychologist did not engage in an appropriate informed consent process. It might be argued that consent was implied in organizational development (OD) work and employees do not have the option not to participate. However, in this case, people were asked to provide feedback to another unit. At the least, participants should have been assured that their comments would be anonymous. The consulting psychologist should also have dealt with the issue of confidentiality. Since the information was going to be provided to the defined problematic unit, confidentiality could not be ensured, even if it were asked of those receiving the information. The consultant should assume that anything shared about the identified problematic unit might be shared with others.

Coercion is the antithesis of voluntary informed consent but, in reality, consultation in organizational contexts takes place on a coercion–voluntary continuum. Seldom is the situation completely at one pole or the other. With that in mind, coercion takes place when members of a team or teams are forced to participate in the intervention. Such coercion can be direct or subtle. As an example of direct coercion, employees may have it made clear that they will be terminated from employment if they do not agree to a coaching engagement. As an example of more subtle, less blatant coercion, members of a team may be informed that participation is essential for the team to meet its goals.

Given the investment of time and energy required of consultees, coaching and consultation more likely lead to better outcomes when participation is voluntary and all can see that the end results may be worth the work to identify problems and goals, the efforts to change, and the vulnerability of disclosure that may be part of this (Grant, 2016). Work with consultants can help them mitigate the inherent power differentials coercion between those in various layers of an organization. In specific, the consultant can help the consultee develop strategies that provide more even voice to those with whom they are working across the hierarchical positions in the organization. Additionally coercion can also involve manipulation or dependency – manipulation on the part of the consultant to get the consultee to engage in a particular course of action the consultant feels strongly about and dependency of the consultee on the consultant to determine a proper course of change and to provide the majority of efforts to get these achieved. Standard 3.07 (Third-Party Requests for Services) may be applicable to this case. Standard 3.07 states:

When psychologists agree to provide services to a person or entity at the request of a third party, psychologists attempt to clarify at the outset of the service the nature of the relationship with all individuals or organizations involved. This clarification includes the role of the psychologist (e.g., therapist, consultant, diagnostician, or expert witness), an identification of who is the client, the probable uses of the services provided or the information obtained, and the fact that there may be limits to confidentiality. (See also Standards 3.05, Multiple Relationships, and 4.02, Discussing the Limits of Confidentiality.) (APA, 2017a, p. 6)

Recommendations Emerging from This Case

- *Identify the client and others to whom one has ethical obligations up front.* In general, definitions of the client in a consultation and of the others to whom one has collateral ethical obligations should be made at the start of the consulting engagement. This will lessen the likelihood of situations arising later in which it becomes necessary to sort out responsibilities to various parties involved in the consultation.
- *Confidentiality cannot always be ensured, nor can it be promised when it is not likely to happen. Anonymity may be a sufficient basis for protecting some information.* Newman, Robinson-Kurpius, and Fuqua (2002) suggested four steps in their chapter on issues in the ethical practice of consulting psychology: (1) openly recognize and acknowledge the limits to which confidentiality can be ensured; (2) work to maximize the extent to which confidentiality becomes a norm; (3) discuss issues of confidentiality early and often with participants; and (4) communicate shared, collaborative responsibility for confidentiality when sensitive data exist or when harm to individual members is possible (Newman et al., 2002).
- *Work out the details of the consultation up front.* Three of the APA Code of Ethics standards provide helpful guidance relevant to this recommendation. The first is 3.07 (Third-Party Requests for Services). Standard 3.04 (Avoiding Harm) is also applicable. Finally, attending to the details of Standard 3.11 can be helpful. This standard focuses on the contracting phase of consultation. Attending to all parts of it will assist in addressing issues of informed consent, confidentiality, multiple relationships, and identification of the client. Even if done carefully, however, contracting will not guarantee that an ethical dilemma or situation will not arise subsequently, but it makes that likelihood much lower. In the case example, Nancy needed to make midcourse adjustments to reduce the likelihood of coercion being involved and to ensure safety for participation.
- *Develop consultee buy-in to the change process.* In addition to the ethical standards, the general principles of the code, which are aspirational rather than enforceable, may also provide guidance. In this case, the general principle of beneficence and nonmaleficence would indicate that going with volunteers for the organizational mirroring intervention rather than mandating participation by all was likely superior to forcing their participation. Nancy's making midcourse adjustments to obtain individual and team engagement with the consultation was essential to reducing organizational and individual resistance and to supporting the work involved in making productive change (Dougherty, 2014).

The Case of Multiple Relationships and Confidentiality

Jon is an experienced counseling psychologist who has been hired by the local mental health association to provide case-centered mental health counseling for therapists with challenging clients. He works with a number of the clinical staff and does so using different formats. Specifically, he works as a supervisor of some of the participants individually and a consultant to a group of people, including those directly supervised, on cases. Additionally, he is providing some executive coaching for the head of clinical services.

After some months, an opening for an assistant director in the clinical services area appears and the head of that service approaches Jon and asks who he thinks would be good in the role. She adds that she believes that Jon would have a unique perspective because he knows how all the therapists have worked with their clients. The consultation Jon had provided to these therapists had been promised to be confidential. Jon has an extensive consultancy with the agency and feels a loyalty to it. Moreover, he does have a decided opinion about who would be best for the opening, plus he has developed some significant concerns about the ethical behavior of one of the individual consultees and the professionalism of one of the group consultees with whom he has worked. He cares deeply about the success of the agency. The head of the service tells John she wants the opinion only for herself as an additional piece of information in making her hiring decision. John informs her who he thinks would make for an excellent assistant director.

Discussion of This Case

> A multiple relationship occurs when a psychologist is in a professional role with a person and (1) at the same time is in another role with the same person, (2) at the same time is in a relationship with a person closely associated with or related to the person with whom the psychologist has the professional relationship, or (3) promises to enter into another relationship in the future with the person or a person closely associated with or related to the person.
>
> (3.05, Multiple Relationships; APA, 2017a, p. 7)

Professional writings by Cooper, Newman, and Fuqua (2012), Cummings and Worley (2015), Dougherty (2014), and many others have discussed the complications of multiple relationships in consultation work. There can be different sources of these complications. Level of intervention is one such factor. It is not uncommon to blend interventions at the individual, dyad, triad, team, and/or systems levels, with work at any of these levels likely effecting some or all of the other levels. For example, if a consultant is working on structural change, such change may have a large impact on individuals. In this case, Jon was hired by the agency to improve the work of a number of therapists through individual and group consultation. His primary obligation was to these individuals. Moreover, his commitment to confidentiality should have been honored. He should have refused to share his opinion. As an alternative, he could have worked with the head of the service to identify additional means of assessing the applicants for the position.

Recommendations Emerging from This Case

- *Expect the existence or emergence of multiple relationships.* Multiple relationships are very common in consultation. The central focus needs to shift to that of making sure they represent either a productive boundary crossing or at least are not damaging or exploitative to any parties.
- *Carefully contract the work.* Use of Standard 3.11 (Consulting to and Through Organizations) assists the consultant and consultee to identify likely multiple roles and to develop processes and make decisions to avoid these being destructive.

The Case of Conflicts of Interest, Multiple Relationships, and Legal Practice

Brenda was a consulting psychologist whose coaching work had involved performance enhancement with high-level performers in the sports industry. Brenda has received some recognition for her specialty practice. She has been working with Janice, a basketball player who was the star player for her nationally ranked team for some time. Given Janice's heavy travel schedule with her team, a good deal of the coaching contact was by technology since they resided in different states. Their work up until several months ago was focused on improving Janice's skills and performance, especially at away games. They would converse before the game to review strategies Janice planned to execute and then talk the next day to review how this implementation went. In recent times, Janice had experienced a number of losses and challenges had emerged in her personal life. Her mother passed away after a long illness and her marriage ended. Further, she developed an injury that had taken her out for part of the season. She returned to play but she was not performing at the expected levels.

Janice began shifting the focus during their sessions to these personal issues as these losses took place. Since Brenda was a licensed psychologist and had been engaged in psychotherapy earlier in her professional life, she moved into this mode rather than referring Janice for therapy and maintaining the focus of the coaching contract. Such role-switching, to some degree, is normative among athletics coaches (Murphy, 2012). It was only in the last few weeks that Brenda recognized that what was now occurring between her and Janice was no longer coaching-related, but she felt trapped, in that making a referral now would be experienced as a betrayal. Also in the mix was that the work with Janice had become an important revenue source for Brenda. She currently had some large unexpected bills and needed to maintain her income to cover these.

Discussion of This Case

Coaching and executive coaching have received attention as areas of work expansion for those trained in counseling or clinical work to move into. This is due to interest, to working with often well persons, and because coaching to leaders in organizations is often more lucrative, particularly as compensation rates for managed care decrease and competition from other mental health service providers increases (International Coaching Federation, 2013). There is a growing body of literature available on coaching (see Passmore, Peterson, & Freire, 2013).

Work on the ethics of coaching has also been appearing in recent years. Lowman (2013a) synthesized much of the writing on the topic of ethics in coaching that had been published up to that time. Specifically, Lowman (2013a) addressed whether ethics codes that were not developed specifically for coaching work were sufficient for coaching. He examined several different ethics codes, including those of the APA Code of Ethics, the International Federation Code of Ethics, the British Psychological Society Code of Ethics, and the CPA Code of Ethics. He concluded, "Because most ethical codes in professions whose members practice coaching were not developed with coaching in mind (the exception is the ICF code) we cannot at this time point to one particular code of ethics that would universally be accepted as providing the ethical ground rules for the practice of coaching" (Lowman, 2013a, pp. 71–72). He did, however, outline what he viewed as the eight main general ethical principles for this practice. Using these would be helpful for those engaging in coaching consultation.

In this case, his fifth principle is avoiding or effectively managing multiple relationships (3.05, Multiple Relationships). The working relationship between Brenda and Janice, as in much of coaching, does not allow for so much of a clean dividing line between performance enhancement work and dealing with personal issues, as it is a continuum. Lowman's taxonomy of work dysfunctions (Lowman, 1993) is useful here, as an assessment that the issues are primarily personal would be the basis for referral to therapy, whereas a mixed focus on performance and personal, but where performance remains the priority would likely remain within the purview of athletics-oriented coaching.

Equally important in this case was the undue influence of Brenda's need for income from the consultation with Janice. This need may have influenced her decision to change the focus of their work together to an area that involved much greater role ambiguity Standard 3.06 (Conflict of Interest) is relevant. It states, "Psychologists refrain from taking on a professional role when personal, scientific, professional, legal, financial, or other interests or relationships could reasonably be expected to (1) impair their objectivity, competence or effectiveness in performing their functions as psychologists or (2) expose the person or organization with whom the professional relationship exists to harm or exploitation" (APA, 2017a, p. 7).

The other issue in this case scenario is not ethical but legal. Brenda and Janice live in different states. Without being licensed in the state in which Janice lives, Brenda's provision of what could be construed to be therapy might be challenged, even though the work was delivered electronically from the state in which she was licensed. That would depend on the regulations for out-of-state practice in that particular jurisdiction. Harris (2015), one of the three main consultants for APAIT (the insurance trust that most psychologists use for their malpractice coverage), wrote that no legal cases on the provision of coaching across state lines have yet arisen to his or his colleagues' awareness. It is uncertain whether this will be viewed as a different service and not under regulation. That each state has its own regulations makes this a challenge because a few, like Colorado, include coaching as a psychological practice (Harris, 2015). Harris has written an ethical and legal risk-informed article on coaching. In it, he suggests the main factor to consider in such cross-jurisdictional practice is the distinctness versus the similarity of the coaching to therapy.

Recommendations Emerging from This Case

- *Be mindful of situations involving conflicts of interest.* Being mindful of the APA's and other relevant codes can enhance good practice. Reading about ethics in the practice of consultation can raise professional awareness. Building in a practice of monitoring consultancies for the emergence of ethical issues is also useful. Additionally, seeking consultation from other professionals to get feedback about whether a conflict of interest is involved can often be a helpful step in preventing such occurrences.
- *Deal with destructive multiple roles if they emerge.* If a multiple role emerges and it does or will cross the threshold of the standard, a consultation to develop and take steps to address this can be very helpful.
- *Become educated on the legal aspects of practice.* Lack of awareness of the legal restrictions of practicing across state lines is not a protection from liability if one does so. Currently, efforts are underway with an interstate compact and with the Association of State and Provincial Psychology Boards (ASPPB) to enable some levels of cross-jurisdictional practice, but practice is far exceeding these needed legislative initiatives.

The Case of Competence, Deceptive Statements, and Avoiding Harm

Colby was an up-and-coming multinational company in the highly competitive heart health treatment pharmaceutical industry. The sales branch of a psychological consulting firm contacted the HR department at Colby. They suggested that the use of the EQA™ (name assumed), a well-known emotional intelligence (EI) assessment, coupled with individual feedback sessions and publicly shared among all the members of the executive leadership team, was guaranteed to lead to improved performance of the organization. These outcomes were prominently listed on the consulting agency's website. Jayne, a psychologist and consultant who had taken a continuing education (CE) workshop on EI, proposed use of a two-hour education/training experience to expose members of the leadership team to the dimensions assessed by the EQA with a follow-up of an individualized one-hour session with each participant to discuss the person's assessment results. Jayne produced an aggregate chart where the individual scores of all the members of the leadership team on the EQA were displayed together with the names being revealed. Several of the members had one or more scores that were very low on the various scales. Some members of the leadership team who had scored high on many of the scales began to advocate for a pay increase on the basis that they were differentially adding value to the organization by dint of their higher EI. Several members of the team who had low scores on some of the scales were very upset about the results being public to so many. To make matters worse, the vice-president (VP) for the unit then used the assessment results as the primary basis for making recommendations for promotions within the company. He did so without discussing this with Jayne as she was no longer involved. Two members of the leadership team who were not promoted filed both an ethics grievance against Jayne and a lawsuit against the company.

Discussion of This Case

Incompetence/technical ineptness can result when the consulting psychologist lacks either the expertise or training or when the client is not ready or able to execute the implementation. Although this may also play out at the individual or the organizational level of consultation, the strong pull of interpersonal dynamics in group-level interventions makes consultation interventions at this level particularly vulnerable to technical ineptness. Selection of an appropriate intervention is critical, but so are the knowledge and skills needed by both the consultant and the consultees to execute it well. Because so little graduate education and supervised practicum and internship experience focuses on psychological consultation, the majority who engage in it are forced to find other means of obtaining the requisite attitudes, knowledge, and skills (Lowman, 2016).

This particular case of Jayne using a standardized assessment inventory involves misrepresentation. Misrepresentation results when consultants promise results that are unlikely for the team change program or the organizational situation. Such misrepresentation can occur when the benefits of a particular consulting intervention are oversold or when the needs and goals of the consultees have not been made clear. Misrepresentation is more likely to take place during the early phases of a consultancy.

Several ethical problems are illustrated by the above case. First, Jayne, the consulting psychologist, and the psychologist-led consulting firm, overpromised positive results without having any basis to do so. Section 5 of the APA Code of Ethics covers Advertising and Other Public Statements (e.g., see 5.01, Avoidance of False of Deceptive Statements). Second, Jayne, the psychologist–consultant, had not received adequate education or supervised experience in use of the EQA (2.01, Boundaries of Competence). Moreover, Jayne appears to have violated several of the standards in the assessment section of the Code (Standard 9; minimally 9.02, Use of Assessments; 9.04, Release of Test Data; 9.06, Interpreting Assessment Results; 9.07, Assessment by Unqualified Persons).

Additionally, Jayne did not obtain informed consent from the members of the team to have their individual results made public in aggregate form. This would constitute a violation of 9.03(a). Finally, Jayne did not engage in careful contracting as specified in APA Ethics Standard 3.11 (Psychological Services Delivered to or Through Organizations). Jayne following Standard 3.11 might have protected participants and the organization from some of the misuse of the EQA results that took place subsequent to the individual feedback sessions. In employing it, issues of the consultation that had not yet been worked through may have been made more apparent.

Recommendations Emerging from This Case

- *Be careful in following the regulations considering advertising of services.* Psychologists are allowed to advertise but not to falsely represent their products, services, or outcomes. Standard 5.01(b) states, "Psychologists do not make false, deceptive or fraudulent statements concerning (1) their training, experience or competence; (2) their academic degrees; (3) their credentials; (4) their institutional or association affiliations; (5) their services; (6) the scientific or clinical basis for or results or degree of success of, their services; (7) their fees; or (8) their publications or research findings" (APA, 2017a, p. 10).
- *Practice only in areas of competence.* Standard 2.01(a) states, "Psychologists provide services, teach and conduct research with populations and in areas only within the boundaries of their competence, based on their education, training, supervised experience, consultation, study or professional experience" (APA, 2017a, p. 5). Standard 2.01(c) stipulates, "Psychologists planning to provide services, teach or conduct research involving populations, areas, techniques or technologies new to them undertake relevant education, training, supervised experience, consultation or study" (APA, 2017a, p. 6).
- *Follow good assessment processes and procedures for assessment-focused consultations.* The assessment section of the APA Code of Ethics and the recently revised Standards for Educational and Psychological Testing jointly published by the American Educational Research Association, the American Psychological Association, and the National Council on Measurement in Education (AERA, APA, & NCME, 2014) provide very helpful guidance on best ethical and applied practice of assessment. Jayne's work would have been enhanced had she followed this guidance.

Cultural Incompetency

Understanding of multicultural issues, important in any practice area, assumes new dimensions when practicing consultation. Lowman (2013b, 2013c) addressed some of these issues, especially with respect to the cultural issues emerging from the large numbers of international immigrants. In his chapter in the APA Handbook of Multicultural Psychology, Lowman (2013c) showed the relevance of culturally based diversity differences to some aspects of organizational development and consulting. His 2013 book, *Internationalizing multiculturalism*, demonstrated how international issues constitute an important part of work in these areas. Cooper and Leong (2008) coedited a special issue of *Consulting Psychology Journal: Practice and Research* on the topic of culture, race, and ethnicity in organizational consulting psychology. The cultural issues that emerge in dyadic health services practice are inherently more complex in triadic, generally applied practice due to the multiple parties involved (Cooper & Leong, 2008). Specifically, the cultural factors of the consultant differ from those of the consultee, which in turn are likely to differ from those of the client system (Dougherty, 2014). As an example, culturally related issues are more likely to arise with a black, female, middle-aged consultant working with an older, male consultee of Middle Eastern descent who supervises a diverse global team versus a client and therapist of like ethnic background, age, and gender.

Perhaps the best current work available is written by Gloveman and Friedman (2015). Their book, *Transcultural competence: Navigating cultural differences in the global community*, presents applications, assessments, and intervention approaches that are prerequisites for gaining transcultural competence, whether as a consultant, organizational leader, or professional in any number of fields dealing with diversity and globalization. Many case examples as well as helpful hints to avoid cultural encapsulation are included. The research from Hofstede and others (see Hofstede, Hofstede, & Minkov, 2010) and the GLOBE Studies from the Center for Creative Leadership are also useful resources.

The cross-cultural concepts from these sources not only can but should be applied by consultants in their work with individuals, teams, organizations, or communities (Cooper & Leong, 2008). Given the large power of culture, effective work often requires that adjustments be made to best meet the needs of the consultee(s) and the client system, whether that is an individual, a group, or a larger collective. Particular areas where such adjustments are made are the preferred roles of the consultant, choices among diverse methods or organizational assessment, selection of interventions, amount of involvement from the consultant in the implementation process, and the nature and length of the disengagement process. The proportion of time spent on relationship development versus task focus is particularly influenced by cultural variables (Cooper & Leong, 2008).

The Case of Cross-Cultural Competency and Maintaining Competency

Jerry was a white/Caucasian consulting psychologist who grew up in an upper-middle-class home in the western part of the United States. He identified as a Christian, heterosexual man. He prided himself on being a self-made man and a goal achiever. His consulting firm was active in seeking contracts with multinational corporations in the education business, seeking to assist the performance of overseas offices. Jerry felt most comfortable using the "doctor–patient" organizational development approach. He believed that through conversation and observation he could see what an organization needed and could then make helpful suggestions for its improvement. This approach had seemed to work well in several countries in Asia where Jerry had done the majority of his work. His consultees were always complimentary of how helpful he had been. Jerry then took on a consultancy with a branch office in France. Too late in the process, he realized that he had not taken the time to learn about the culture of the operation and this western European office. His approach had offended a number of the consultees, who saw him as arrogant and not taking their experience and knowledge into consideration and as not taking enough time to develop a good working relationship prior to focusing on the tasks of assessment and intervention development. He also recognized that his education and training were deficient in cultural competency and began to take some steps to remedy his lack of knowledge and competency.

Discussion of This Case

Standard 2.01 (Boundaries of Competence) and Standard 2.01 (Maintaining Competence) are relevant here. Jerry was woefully unprepared to do this consultation work that required much greater cultural preparation in working in a very different culture than he had obtained though his previous consultation experience. Many professionals, especially those trained a number of years ago before issues of culture were receiving as much attention, would be in a similar boat of not having had educational or supervised experiences where cultural competence was required (Imoh, 2012).

Recommendations Emerging from This Case

Of particular utility to consultants are the APA Guidelines on Multicultural Education, Training, Research, Practice and Organizational Change for Psychologists originally approved in 2002 and recently revised (APA, 2017b). Each of its guidelines is a source of rich information and suggestions for competent practice when working with culturally diverse consultees and client systems.

Enhancing the Ethical Practice of Psychological Consultation

This final section of the chapter will focus on additional considerations that consultants may want to consider to enhance their practicing ethically. Two areas will be addressed: ethical skills competencies and steps to making better decisions when matters involve ethics.

Ethical Skills Competencies

Dougherty's book (2014), *Psychological consultation and collaboration in school and community settings*, described key competencies that consultants should possess, not to perfection, but at least adequately and with ongoing efforts to develop further. He listed eight of these, two of which are pertinent to this chapter: skills in consulting working within organizations and ethical and professional behavior skills. These skill sets rest on a foundation of the professional and personal development of the consultant. Genuineness of the consultant and having positive regard and acceptance of the consultee are needed as much in consultation as they are in counseling. The consultant functioning at a high level personally may be more important in consultation than in therapy given the growth aspired to by consultation (Gladdings & Newsome, 2017).

Since most mental health and organizational consultation happens within organizational contexts, practicing ethically requires skills in working with an organization and contextualizing the consultation issue to the environment within which it is taking place. Skills in working in organizations involve steps such as creating productive working relationships with consultees, understanding ecological variables as they affect the consultancy, using organizational analysis and systems theory, determining the culture of the organization and its cultural competency, and using the human resources within the organization.

Good ethical practice contributes to good applied practice (Cooper et al., 2012). This connection is additionally present because such professional and ethical behavior leads to the expertise and social influence needed to facilitate the consultees engaging in the change process. Ethical consultants must act with integrity and be informed by relevant codes of conduct and ethics. They should use their influence for legitimate purposes only. Ethical consultants must know and practice within the limitations of their education and training and must demonstrate their intent to help by the thoroughness of their work. On the personal side, ethical consultants make efforts to maintain their professional and individual growth and they must cope effectively with the sometimes high stress of consulting. Doing all the above at a high level is a tall order!

Making Better Ethics Decisions

Practicing ethically means having a process by which ethical issues are considered and resolved. A number of authors of psychological ethics books and book chapters have made suggestions on steps to follow to increase the likelihood of making good ethical decisions and lessening the likelihood of bad ones and the consequential malpractice suits that can follow (e.g., Fisher, 2013; Pope & Vasquez, 2016). Of the available ethics codes, the Canadian Psychological Association Code of Ethics stands out due to its formal incorporation of sections to assist psychologists facing ethical dilemmas. Specifically, one of the sections in the Preamble presents a hierarchically based list of four fundamental principles, roughly parallel to the general principles of the APA Code of Ethics, applicable when ethics principles of a particular case compete with each other. The subsequent section lists the ten basic steps consultants should attend to in order to make better decisions when ethical issues are involved.

We offer several suggestions for the ethical practice of consultation. First is the need to be familiar with the various applicable ethics codes. Because consultation and coaching are somewhat unique, looking at the related codes is also helpful. Second, is the need to be aware of higher-risk situations, including awareness of personal interests and bias. Such higher-risk situations could be associated with pathology of the individuals or the systems involved. Third is the need to consult with knowledgeable colleagues. Such discussions can be valuable for help in making ethically sound decisions. Fourth is the need to document situations and decisions. Current practice in psychology is to document more rather than less, and this would be as relevant for consultation as it is for therapy. Absence of documentation makes a defense more difficult. Fifth is the need to generate alternative courses of action and to weigh the consequences of each on all parties involved. As consultation involves the consultees and the client system, such analysis is typically more challenging than in individual therapy. Sixth is to consult with specialized expertise when needed. This could include APAIT or the state ethics committee. Seventh is acceptance of responsibility for the choices made and an evaluation of their outcomes. The latter should be a deliberate process. The above steps, when combined with considerations of any laws applicable to the situation, client risk factors, and evidence concerning best practices, are not only likely to reduce the chances of ethics problems spiraling badly, but also will likely have the effect of improving the quality of the consultation work being delivered.

Summary

This chapter on the ethics of consulting commenced with an explanation of the practice of consultation and its context, followed by brief descriptions of the various models of mental health consultation and organizational consultation. Areas of ethical concern were then discussed in detail. This was followed by a final section that included a description of key skills related to practicing ethically along with suggested strategies for making ethically informed decisions.

References

Allen, M. D. & Green, B. L. (2012). A multilevel analysis of consultant attributes that contribute to effective mental health consultation services. *Infant Mental Health Journal, 33*, 234–245.

American Counseling Association (2014). ACA code of ethics. Retrieved from http://www .ncblpc.org/LawsAndCodes

American Educational Research Association (AERA), American Psychological Association (APA), & National Council on Measurement in Education (NCME) (2014). *The standards for educational and psychological testing.* Washington, DC: APA Press.

American Psychological Association (2017a). American Psychological Association ethical principles of psychologists and code of conduct. Retrieved from www.apa.org/ ethics/code/ethics-code-2017.pdf

American Psychological Association (2017b). APA Guidelines on Multicultural Education, Training, Research, Practice and Organizational Change for Psychologists. Retrieved from http://www.apa.org/pi/oema/resources/policy/multicultural-guidelines.aspx

Argyris, C. (1970). *Intervention theory and method. A behavioral sciences view.* Reading, MA: Addison-Wesley.

Arredondo, P., Shealy, C., Neale, M., & Winfrey, L. L. (2004). Consultation and interprofessional collaboration: Modeling for the future. *Journal of Clinical Psychology, 60*, 787–800.

Atkinson, D. R., Thompson, C. E., & Grant, S. K. (1993). A three-dimensional model for counseling racial/ethnic minorities. *The Counseling Psychologist, 21*, 257–277.

British Psychological Society (2009). *Code of ethics and conduct: Guidance published by the Ethics Committee of the British Psychological Society.* Leicester, UK: British Psychological Society.

Canadian Psychological Association (2000). *Canadian code of ethics for psychologists* (3rd edn.). Retrieved from www.cpa.ca/cpasite/UserFiles/Documents/Canadian%20Code%20of%20Ethics%20for%20Psycho.pdf

Caplan, G. (1970). *The theory and practice of mental health consultation.* New York, NY: Basic Books.

Caplan, G. & Caplan, R. B. (1993). *Mental health consultation and collaboration.* San Francisco, CA: Jossey-Bass.

Caplan, G. C., Caplan, R. B., & Erchul, W. P. (1994). Caplanian mental health consultation: Historical background and current status. *Consulting Psychology Journal: Practice and Research, 46,* 4061–4087.

Carney, J. M. & Jefferson, J. F. (2014). Consultation for mental health counselors: Opportunities and guidelines for private practice. *Journal of Mental Health Counseling, 36,* 302–314.

Center for Creative Leadership (2014). Leadership effectiveness and culture: The GLOBE Study. Retrieved from http://www.inspireimagineinnovate.com/pdf/globesummary-by-michael-h-hoppe.pdf

Cooper, S. E. & Leong, F. L. (2008). *Consulting Psychology Journal: Practice and Research, 6.*

Cooper, S. E. & Shullman, S. L. (2012). Counseling psychologists as consultants. In E. M. Altmaier & J. C. Hansen (Eds.), *The Oxford handbook of counseling psychology* (pp. 837–855). New York, NY: Oxford University Press.

Cooper, S. E., Newman, J. L., & Fuqua, D. R. (2012). Counseling psychologists as consultants. In N. A. Fouad (Ed.), *APA handbook of counseling psychology* (Vol. 2, Ch. 21). Washington, DC: APA Books.

Cummings. T. G. & Worley, C. G. (2015). *Organizational development & change* (10th edn.). Stamford, CT: Cengage Learning.

Dougherty, A. M. (2014). *Casebook of psychological consultation and collaboration in school and community settings* (6th edn.). Belmont, CA: Brooks/Cole, Cengage Learning.

Fisher, C. B. (2013). *Decoding the ethics code: A practical guide for psychologists* (3rd edn.). Thousand Oaks, CA: Sage Publications, Inc.

French, W. L. & Bell, C. H., Jr. (1999). *Organization development: Behavioral science interventions for organizational improvement* (6th edn.). Englewood Cliffs, NJ: Prentice-Hall.

Fuqua, D. R., Newman, J. L., Simpson, D. B., & Choi, N. (2012). Who is the client in organizational consultation? *Consulting Psychology Journal: Practice and Research, 64,* 108–118.

Gladding, S. T. & Newsome, D. W. (2017). *Clinical mental health counseling in community and agency settings* (5th edn.). Merill, WI: Merrill Counseling.

Glover, J. & Friedman, H. L. (2015). *Transcultural competence: Navigating cultural differences in the global community.* Washington, DC: APA Books.

Grant, A. M. (2013). The efficacy of coaching. In *The Wiley-Blackwell handbook of the psychology of coaching and mentoring* (pp. 15–39). West Sussex, UK: Wiley-Blackwell.

Grant, A. M. (2016). What can Sydney tell us about coaching? Research with implications for practice from down under. *Consulting Psychology Journal: Practice and Research, 68,* 105–117.

Harris, E. (2015) Coaching: A new frontier some questions and answers. APAIT Resources. Retrieved from http://apait.com/resources/articles

Hofstede, G., Hofstede, G. T., & Minkov, M. (2010). *Cultures and organizations: Software of the mind* (3rd edn.). New York, NY: McGraw-Hill.

Imoh, C. (2012). *Cultural competence for global management.* Houston, TX: Heritage Publishing Company.

International Coach Federation (2013). 2013 ICF organizational coaching study. Retrieved from http://coachfederation.org/orgstudy

International Coach Federation (ICF) (2015). Code of Ethics. Retrieved from https://coachfe deration.org/about/ethics.aspx?ItemNumber=854

Lacey, M. (1995). Internal consulting: Perspectives on the process of planned change. *Journal of Organizational Change Management, 8,* 76.

Lake, D., Baerg, K., & Paslawski, T. (2015). *Teamwork, leadership, and communication: Collaboration basics for health professionals.* Edmonton, Canada: Brush Education, Inc.

Levinson, H., with Molinari, J. & Spohn, A. G. (1972). *Organizational diagnosis.* Boston, MA: Harvard University Press.

Lewis, J. A., Lewis, M. D., Daniels, J. A., D'Andrea, M. J. (2011). *Community counseling: A multicultural–social justice perspective* (4th edn.). Boston, MA: Cengage Learning.

Lippit, G. L. & Lippit, R. (1986). *The consulting process in practice* (2nd edn.). La Jolla, CA: University Associates.

Lowman, R. L. (1993). *Counseling and psychotherapy of work dysfunctions.* Washington, DC: American Psychological Association.

Lowman, R. L. (Ed.) (2002). *Handbook of organizational consulting psychology. A comprehensive guide to theories, skills, and techniques.* San Francisco, CA: Jossey-Bass.

Lowman, R. L. (2013a). Coaching ethics. In J. Passmore, D. B. Peterson, & T. Freire (Eds.), *The Wiley-Blackwell handbook of the psychology of coaching and mentoring* (pp. 68–88). Hoboken, NJ: John Wiley & Sons, Ltd.

Lowman, R. L. (Ed.) (2013b). *Internationalizing multiculturalism: Expanding professional competencies in a globalized world.* Washington, DC: American Psychological Association.

Lowman, R. L. (2013c). Multicultural and international issues in organizational change and development. In F. T. L. Leong (Ed.), *APA handbook of multicultural psychology* (pp. 627–639). Washington, DC: American Psychological Association.

Lowman, R. L. (2016). *An introduction to consulting psychology: Working with individuals, groups, and organizations.* Washington, DC: American Psychological Association.

Lowman, R. L. & Cooper, S. E. (2017). *The ethical practice of consulting psychology.* Washington, DC: American Psychological Association.

Mendoza, G. W. (1993). A review of Gerald Caplan's Theory and practice of mental health consultation. *Journal of Counseling & Development, 71,* 629–635.

Morrill, W. H., Oetting, E. U., & Hurst, J. C. (1974). Dimensions of counselor functioning. *The Personnel and Guidance Journal, 52,* 354–359.

Murphy, S. M. (2012). *The Oxford handbook of sport and performance psychology.* New York, NY: Oxford University Press.

National Association of School Psychologists (2010). Principles for professional ethics 2010. Retrieved from www.nasponline.org/Documents/Standards%20and% 20Certification/Standards/1_%20Ethical%20Principles.pdf

Newman, J. L., Robinson-Kurpius, S. E., & Fuqua, D. R. (2002). Issues in the ethical practice of consulting psychology. In R. L. Lowman (Ed.), *The California School of Organizational Studies: Handbook of organizational consulting psychology: A comprehensive guide to theory, skills, and techniques* (pp. 733–758). San Francisco, CA: Jossey-Bass.

Passmore, J., Peterson, D. B., & Freire, T. (Eds.) (2013). *The Wiley-Blackwell handbook of the psychology of coaching and mentoring.* Hoboken, NJ: John Wiley & Sons, Ltd.

Pope, K. S. & Vasquez, M. J. T. (2016). *Ethics in psychotherapy and counseling: A practical guide* (5th edn.). San Francisco, CA: John Wiley & Sons.

Rodolfa, E., Bent, D.R., Eisman, E., Nelson, P., Rehm, L., & Richie, P. (2005). A cube model for competency development: Implications for psychology educators. *Professional Psychology, 36,* 347–354.

Schein, E. H. (1978). The role of the consultant: Content expert or process facilitator? *Personnel and Guidance Journal, 56,* 339–343.

Schein, E. H. (1988). *Process consultation: Its role in organization development.* Vol. 1 (2nd edn.). Reading, MA: Addison-Wesley.

Schein, E. H. (1999). *Process consultation revisited: Building the helping relationship.* Reading, MA: Addison-Wesley.

Society for Human Resource Management (SHRM) (2014). Code of Ethics and Business Contact. Retrieved from www.shrm.org/search/pages/default.aspx?k=ethics%20code

Emerging Ethical Issues in Professional Practice and Next Steps

28 Genetic Testing and Ethical Considerations

Cases Involving Adolescents and Young Adults and Cancer

Marilyn Stern, Jennifer Bleck, and Gwendolyn P. Quinn

Genetic Testing

The use of genetic testing has increased due to advances in technology, awareness, and greater social acceptance. Genetic testing can be either *diagnostic* (testing for the presence or absence of a disease), *carrier* (testing for the existence of a specific genetic trait), or *predictive* (testing for the risk of getting a disease in the future) (Fulda & Lykens, 2006; Nyrhinen, Hietala, Puukka, & Leino-Kilpi, 2007; Ross, Saal, David, & Anderson, 2013). Diagnostic testing is used to establish the cause of disease symptoms as well as guide clinical management for a patient, including drug selection and dosing decisions (Nyrhinen et al., 2007), while carrier testing can identify recessive genetic traits and is commonly used for reproduction-related decision-making (Ross et al., 2013). Finally, predictive testing can guide the development of risk reduction plans, including interventions to modify behavioral and environmental risk factors and continued monitoring plans (Collins, 2010). While diagnostic testing is conducted with patients who have active symptoms or an existing diagnosis, patients seeking carrier or predictive testing are healthy individuals who either will not develop the condition of interest or who have not yet experienced symptom manifestation (Nyrhinen et al., 2007).

Genetic Testing and Cancer

Increases in genetic testing are particularly evident in cancer-related cases, as cancer is caused by a complex combination of behavioral, environmental, and genetic risk factors (Burke & Press, 2006; Manolio et al., 2009). There are approximately 45 identified heritable cancers, with genetic mutations accounting for 5–10 percent of cases (Riley et al., 2012). Genetic testing for hereditary cancers can be used for both predictive and diagnostic purposes.

Predictive genetic testing can identify an individual's predisposition for hereditary cancers such as breast, ovarian, colorectal, prostate, pancreatic, skin, and endometrial cancers (Riley et al., 2012). A genetic predisposition for a hereditary cancer is often associated with early age of onset and increased risk for multiple cancers (Riley et al., 2012). Findings from predictive genetic testing can be used for preventive purposes, including increased screenings and symptom surveillance, reduction of behavioral and environmental risk factors, and pharmaceutical or surgical options (Ross et al., 2013). However, there is a potential for negative effects if the patient resorts to ineffective or harmful prevention methods (Ross et al., 2013). Accordingly, post-testing prevention decisions should be discussed with both a genetic counselor and a mental health professional, such as a psychologist. Although a range of mental health professionals might be appropriately trained to work with such patients, we refer hereafter to psychologists in this role. Consultation with a psychologist may be critical as the identification of an increased risk for cancer may be associated with significant emotional distress. In this context, psychologists can therefore have a great impact on the psychosocial functioning of the patient.

Diagnostic genetic testing is used for confirmation of a clinical diagnosis or clinical management decisions. For example, a diagnostic test is often used to confirm a diagnosis of Huntington's disease once symptoms manifest (Nance et al., 2003). Within oncology, diagnostic testing is typically used to determine if a cancer diagnosis was partially due to inherited traits. As previously stated, only a portion of cancer cases result from genetic risk factors. With many known carcinogens, it may be difficult to determine if a family history of cancer is genetically inherited or resulting from an environmental risk factor that multiple family members were exposed to, such as an environmental toxin or tobacco smoke. Diagnostic testing investigates the potential cause of the cancer, which can then be used to inform family members of their risk and guide the patient's treatment regimen.

The advancement of genetic testing technology has led to an increase in availability of direct-to-consumer genetic testing (American Psychiatric Association, 2013). In the case of direct-to-consumer testing, the consumer (i.e., patient) does not consult with a genetic counselor or health care provider and is left to interpret the results and implications on his or her own. Additionally, direct-to-consumer tests only analyze common genetic mutations, providing information for only a portion of the individual's risk for only the most common cancers. This is likely to amplify the confusion and emotional turmoil associated with genetic testing by resulting in either unnecessary distress or unfounded reassurance (Spencer et al., 2011). Additionally, due to the direct-to-consumer genetic testing procedures, there may be an increased likelihood of a lack of informed consent and breeches in confidentiality.

Adolescents and Young Adults and Cancer

Adolescents and young adults (AYAs) are a unique group characterized by a set of qualities associated with their age, disease biology, and psychosocial needs (Bleyer, 2005; Bleyer et al., 2008; Soliman & Agresta, 2008; Thomas, Seymour, O'Brien, Sawyer, & Ashley, 2006). In oncology, adolescence and young adulthood is defined as 15–39 years of age. Population-based data indicate a consistent increase of cancer diagnoses among AYAs, and although worse than pediatric and older adult outcomes, overall survivorship has increased with the advent of new treatments (Bleyer, O'Leary, Barr, & Ries, 2006). These rates of survivorship are encouraging; however, the life-saving treatments leave greater numbers of AYA cancer survivors facing difficult long-term effects, including psychosocial, physical, and fertility complications.

AYAs at risk for a hereditary cancer may benefit from genetic counseling and testing to increase their health awareness and initiate early cancer screenings. AYAs with an inherited cancer may benefit from genetic testing for clinical management purposes (Ross et al., 2013). Furthermore, AYA cancer patients and survivors may be concerned about the genetic risk for future offspring (Quinn et al., 2015). Concerns for the possibility of transmitting a mutation to a child might affect their decisions about future childbearing.

Given the sensitive nature of cancer among AYAs, awareness of ethical considerations is needed to help AYA patients navigate the decision-making processes associated with genetic testing. Genetic testing among underage AYA patients may have implications for consent related to conceding decision-making authority to the parent or guardian (Ross et al., 2013). Due to potential risks, the American Academy of Pediatrics' position is that genetic testing for adult-onset conditions should be deferred until adulthood or until the adolescent has mature decision-making capabilities (American Academy of Pediatrics, 2001). Harmful psychosocial effects may develop if early testing among young patients is associated with misunderstanding of the distinction between carrier status and affected status (Ross et al., 2013).

Ethical Considerations of Genetic Testing

Although there is significant potential to improve patient outcomes and overall well-being, there are many ethical concerns associated with genetic testing. Concerns include informed consent, privacy, confidentiality, respect for autonomy, beneficence and nonmaleficence, and conflicts of interest (Burgess, 2001; Fulda & Lykens, 2006; Nyrhinen et al., 2007). In 1968, the World Health Organization published ten criteria for disease screening that aimed to reduce the potential for unethical use or consequences of genetic testing (Table 28.1). Among the list is that the condition being investigated should be an important health problem, there should be an accepted treatment plan, and the cost of diagnosis and treatment should be balanced with the expenditure of medical care as a whole (Wilson & Jungner, 1968). Each criterion should be carefully evaluated when considering genetic testing.

Role of the Psychologist

Decisions pertaining to genetic testing are typically discussed with a genetic counselor, as they are responsible for providing information and support for genetic syndromes both pre- and post-testing. Their main responsibilities include identifying families at risk for genetic disorders, gathering and analyzing family histories, and providing education on genetic screening options and risk assessment calculations (Genetic Alliance, 2010). Moreover, genetic counselors communicate test results and provide basic supportive counseling services to help families cope with the

Table 28.1 *World Health Organization's Criteria for Disease Screening*

1. The condition sought should be an important health problem
2. There should be an accepted treatment for patients with recognized disease
3. Facilities for diagnosis and treatment should be available
4. There should be a recognizable latent or early symptomatic stage
5. There should be a suitable test or examination
6. The test should be acceptable to the population
7. The natural history of the condition, including development from latent to declared disease, should be adequately understood
8. There should be an agreed policy on whom to treat as patients
9. The cost of case funding (including diagnosis and treatment of patients diagnosed) should be economically balanced in relation to possible expenditure on medical care as a whole
10. Case finding should be a continuing process and not a "once and for all" project

Note: Taken from Wilson and Jungner (1968)

consequences of testing results (Genetic Alliance, 2010). However, patients typically only have a few sessions with a genetic counselor (Richmond-Rakerd, 2013), and with increased use of genetic testing there is a shortage of genetic counselors (Ross et al., 2013). The relative shortage of trained oncology genetic counselors is even greater, despite the fact that the AYA cancer population is increasing (Quinn et al., 2015).

Another key role of the genetic counselor is that of a resource person who provides referrals to community resources and support groups when more in-depth psychological issues arise (Genetic Alliance, 2010). Given the shortage of genetic counselors and their limited psychological training, a psychologist, particularly ones with psycho-oncology experience, may take an active role in working with individuals both pre- and post-testing. For patients seeking both genetic and psychological counseling, the psychologist acts as a valued source of support. To provide such support, the psychologist should work collaboratively with the genetic counselor in a team-based approach to ensure the highest level of care for the patient and family. A collaborative approach will enhance care as it will allow the patient to gain a clearer understanding of what the testing results can tell them and how they can impact their assessment of cancer risk, as well as providing an opportunity to evaluate objective information within the context of their personal views, experiences, and expectations (American Psychiatric Association, 2013).

A psychologist working with patients on cases specifically related to both cancer and genetic testing is likely to encounter a range of ethical challenges in clinical practice. These ethical dilemmas are expected when working with patients facing a life-threatening illness and needing to make important medical decisions. Working with such patients is multifaceted and often emotionally laden due to the difficult subject matter; however, the psychologist can have a significant influence on the ability of the patient to process these difficult decisions and reduce decisional uncertainty.

When working with issues related to genetic testing and cancer, psychologists could be faced with a range of patients in varying stages of the testing process. It is just as important to work with individuals post-screening as those who are struggling with the initial decision of seeking the test. Moreover, it is equally important to work with patients who found that they have a genetic risk factor for cancer as those who found no risk factors, as both face differing yet significant emotional situations. For example, women who had genetic testing to investigate a predisposition for breast cancer have similar levels of depression and anxiety at a year post-screening regardless of the test findings (Bosch et al., 2012). Also, some women who test negative for a genetic predisposition when their siblings test positive may experience survivor's guilt (American College of Medical Genetics, 1999).

Historically, when working with patients considering genetic testing, counselors were strictly neutral in the conversation. The counselor would provide patients with information to use to make their own decision. More recently, this norm has been phased out in replacement of shared physician or counselor decision-making and consultation with a psychologist (Caplan, 2015). The shared decision-making process allows for a greater influence of professional support to help the patient navigate the dilemmas they face (American Psychiatric Association, 2013). To facilitate the decision-making process, psychologists should be aware of the possible implications of testing on the individual's psychological and social health, as well as on the individual's family and the individual's perspective and role within the larger community or society (Nyrhinen et al., 2007).

Psychologists need to be informed of the specific considerations for working with an AYA patient and his or her family when they are making decisions related to genetic testing. Moreover, additional attention is needed to guarantee age-appropriate care for AYA patients facing decisions related to both cancer and genetic testing. Prior to predictive testing, it is essential the psychologist ensures that the patient and parent fully understand the limits of testing and treatment or prevention options post-testing, as well as the potential psychological risks (3.10 Informed Consent; 9.03 Informed Consent in Assessments), Providing this guidance and counseling is crucial to guaranteeing that the family understands the capacity and consequences of the testing and thus can be fully informed when providing consent (Nyrhinen et al., 2007).

This chapter examines a range of ethical dilemmas pertinent to mental health professionals engaged in working with patients struggling with genetic testing issues related to cancer. Three scenarios based on real-life issues are provided to illustrate foreseeable ethical challenges. The scenarios include a woman with breast cancer facing life-altering treatment decisions, a young man facing the decision-making process to seek genetic testing for colorectal cancer (CRC) in light of social and cultural barriers, and a conflict between an adolescent in treatment for cancer and his parents regarding fertility preservation. A review following each scenario describes the ethical dilemma at hand and offers recommendations for responsible clinical practice.

The Case of Diagnostic Genetic Testing for Breast Cancer

Rachel is a 35-year-old breast cancer survivor and had a lumpectomy as part of her treatment. She knows that breast cancer can be caused by genetic risk factors, specifically mutations in the *BRCA1* and *BRCA2* genes. While approximately 12 percent of all women will develop breast cancer during their lifetime, mutations in the *BRCA* genes are associated with a 26–85 percent risk of breast cancer (Lea, Williams, & Donahue, 2005; Sarata, 2015). On average, *BRCA1* carriers develop cancer more often and *BRCA2* carriers develop cancer at a younger age (Skytte et al., 2011). Based on her age at diagnosis, Rachel was worried about her risk of reoccurrence as well as the risk to any future offspring, and so she met with a genetic counselor to have a diagnostic genetic test. The genetic counselor informed her that she did in fact have a genetic predisposition for breast cancer. The counselor explained her risk and her preventive options. It can be difficult for a patient to face these life-altering decisions alone, so her genetic counselor suggested involving a psychologist in the discussion.

Beneficence and Nonmaleficence (Principle A)

Prior to discussing Rachel's options, the psychologist needs to assess her emotional state to make sure not to cause any additional emotional harm when discussing risks and prevention. Rachel may be facing several different emotions, potentially including confusion, denial, anger, and fear (Nelson et al., 2014). She also may be experiencing intrusive thoughts, sleep disturbance, and impairments in daily functioning (Metcalfe, Esplen, Goel, & Narod, 2004). She may benefit from discussing her anxiety about the results as well as her fear related to the impact on her health and future fertility options.

Rachel's pre-test anxiety related to the uncertainty may be reduced and, with the help of a psychologist, replaced with acceptance and adjustment, followed by the ability to make rational decisions related to test results (Ross et al., 2013). On the other hand, based on the available predictive technology, she has to consider what the results mean in terms of probability as opposed to a diagnostic guarantee. As findings only provide a level of risk assessment, not certainty, Rachel may be facing increased anxiety over her preventive decisions. The psychologist in this case plays a crucial role in helping to evaluate her perceptions of the results and the consequences of the results in her life (Burgess, 2001).

Informed Decision-Making (3.10 Informed Consent; 9.03 Informed Consent in Assessments)

It may be difficult for a patient to comprehend the risks and benefits of genetic testing based solely on the information provided by a physician or a genetic counselor. There is a wide range of estimates for the association between mutations in the *BRCA* genes and risk of breast cancer. With the decision of what preventive measures to take, the psychologist can discuss the potential risks and benefits in order to evaluate the meaning of the statistics and consider all options.

In some cases, the patient may react by doubting the trustworthiness of the results. The psychologist does not take the place of the genetic counselor in this case, but helps the patient understand the meaning behind the results and risk assessments and evaluate each preventive option and the perceptions of the resulting consequences on her life (Burgess, 2001).

One of the key guidelines for ethical genetic testing is that the condition being screened should have a suitable treatment or prevention option (Wilson & Jungner, 1968). There are several preventive options for women with a genetic predisposition for breast cancer (Payne & Payne, 2013). To avoid a reoccurrence, Rachel works with her psychologist to discuss the possible preventive measures. The patient's preferences in the decision-making process may be based on varying psychosocial characteristics, including the patient's emotional state and perception of risk. Interventions that may reduce risk for reoccurrence include earlier, more frequent, or intensive screening; risk-reducing medications (e.g., tamoxifen, raloxifene); and risk-reducing prophylactic surgery (e.g., mastectomy, salpingo-oophorectomy). However, the strength of evidence varies across the types of interventions (Heemskerk-Gerritsen et al., 2013).

The surgical option of risk-reducing bilateral mastectomy can be fraught with psychological implications. Surgery is an irreversible and aggressive option for risk reduction. While bilateral mastectomy significantly reduces the risk of breast cancer, it does not eliminate the risk completely (Skytte et al., 2011). As with any surgery, there is accompanied risk of negative physical health effects and surgical complications (Moyer, 2014). Bilateral mastectomy is associated with a significant reduction in anxiety and depression (van Oostrom et al., 2003); however, it is also associated with reduced sexual pleasure and body image and can negatively impact romantic relationships (Gahm, Wickman, & Brandberg, 2010; Metcalfe et al., 2004; Moyer, 2014; Nelson et al., 2014; Wasteson, Sandelin, Brandberg, Wickman, & Arver, 2011). On average, women who have had surgery report being satisfied with their decision; however, less satisfaction has been reported among younger women (Gahm, Wickman, & Brandberg, 2010). Combined with the decision to pursue mastectomy is the consideration of reconstructive surgery, which also has the potential for medical complications. Young women such as Rachel do typically opt for breast reconstruction as it improves positive body image and quality of life. Women often select surgical options for "peace of mind" (Rosenberg et al., 2015). Electing for a surgical measure is life-altering and requires significant support during the decision-making process. Several issues must be considered before electing for a specific option. For some women, and as may be the case for Rachel, the decision to elect for surgery is associated with decreasing mortality risk and ensuring health for raising children (American Psychiatric Association, 2013). Other issues to be considered include the psychological and psychosexual consequences of surgery and breast reconstruction (American Psychiatric Association, 2013).

As a less irreversible option, some women seek prevention through medications. There are several medication risk reduction options using tamoxifen, tibolone, or raloxifene, all of which have been effective at decreasing the risk for breast cancer, particularly *BRCA*-related cancer. However, there are potential harmful consequences of each, including increased risks for thromboembolic events, endometrial cancer, cataracts, and stroke (Fisher et al., 2005; Moyer, 2014; Nelson et al., 2009). In an attempt to avoid medical intervention or irreversible surgery, Rachel could choose to remain with her current remission screening protocol, which consists of regular self-examination, clinical breast exams, mammography, and magnetic resonance imaging scans. Regular screenings would reduce the psychosocial implications of more intensive options; however, there will still be significant uncertainty regarding future development of breast cancer. Moreover, screening will not prevent recurrence; it will simply lead to earlier identification and thus increased odds of treatment success. Intensive screening is sometimes associated with discomfort, pain, and anxiety (Nelson et al., 2014).

It is essential to focus on the individual patient's psychological and physical concerns when discussing her best options. Most importantly, as these are life-altering decisions, these concerns must be thoroughly evaluated prior to any action. Maintaining strong communication, management of anxiety, and encouragement of a shared patient–physician decision may be beneficial in order to ease the process (Rosenberg et al., 2015).

Duty to Warn

As mutations in the *BRCA* genes are inherited, results of genetic testing extend beyond the individual patient and impact other family members. Rachel's test results may mean that her first-degree relatives could be at significant risk for breast cancer. There has been debate about a provider's duty to warn the at-risk relatives since genetic testing was first made available for preventive screening purposes. The provider has a responsibility to encourage the patent to share genetic information with the family; however, the provider should be sure to avoid any form of coercion (Nyrhinen et al., 2007). Prior to initial screening, a psychologist might have Rachel consider what she would do with the genetic testing information before she agreed to the testing. Best practice would include documenting the patient's agreement for disclosure prior to genetic testing (Storm, Agarwal, & Offit, 2008). Ideally, Rachel would speak with her family members in advance of her testing (Nance et al., 2003). It is essential that issues related to disclosing results to the family be addressed with the patient prior to testing in order to avoid or at least reduce conflict once results are obtained. It is widely suggested that the provider discusses disclosure of testing results and provides support and encouragement for the patient to discuss risks with family members. Genetic information is considered protected health information and regulations require the provider to maintain confidentiality regarding any results (Lea, Williams, & Donahue, 2005).

Although less likely in this case, it is conceivable that Rachel might choose to keep the genetic testing information to herself. Some have argued that if the provider is unsuccessful in persuading the patient to disclose his or her testing results, the provider should provide warning to the relatives if it is the case that the relatives face serious harm that could be prevented by giving them the information (Ross et al., 2013). Confidentiality (4.02 Discussing the Limits of Confidentiality) is not absolute, as there are some scenarios that would require a physician to disclose patient information to health officials or law enforcement (Guttmacher, Collins, & Clayton, 2003); however, these are unique scenarios for which the provider is held liable. In terms of genetic testing, as confidentiality is established with the individual patient and not the entire family (Burgess, 2001), there are very few cases where disclosing such information would be urgent enough to justify breach of confidentiality (Ross et al., 2013).

The Case of Predictive Genetic Testing for CRC

Paul is a 27-year-old Latino man. His father was diagnosed with CRC at 48 years old. CRC is responsible for 8 percent of all cancer deaths (Bleyer, 2005) as there are limited curative therapeutic options (Bleyer et al., 2008). While CRC is the second most commonly diagnosed cancer among Latinos, Latinos are less likely to have preventive screening tests, and on average present with later-stage CRC at younger ages (Goldman, Diaz, & Kim, 2009). As a result, early detection is crucial, especially among the Latino population, as prognosis is heavily based on the stage at which the cancer is detected (Bleyer et al., 2008). Although CRC typically occurs in older patients, there has been a significant increase in its incidence in young adults (Liang, Kalady, & Church, 2015). Routine screening through colonoscopies among patients 50 years and older has helped decrease the number of CRC deaths. Based on the increase in AYA cases and the success of regular screening, it is recommended that young adults with specific genetic risks get colonoscopies every one to two years starting at age 20–25, or ten years younger than the age of the youngest person diagnosed in the family (Lindor et al., 2006). Based on how young his father was when diagnosed, Paul's doctor talks to him about the risk for CRC and suggests that he gets tested for a possible genetic predisposition. The doctor explains that if a genetic syndrome were detected, annual colonoscopies would be recommended. Upon hearing this, Paul declares that he is not going to get CRC and does not need the test. Knowing the importance of early detection, Paul's father gets him to agree to talk to a psychologist about the decision before refusing the test.

Beneficence and Patient Autonomy (Principles A and E)

There is no direct or immediate benefit of predictive genetic testing; rather, the test provides information that can be used to reduce the likelihood of developing cancer or to identify it at an earlier stage (Nance et al., 2003). With a lack of direct benefits, it is important to help the patient balance the immediate risks with the hypothetical future benefits. Risks of predictive testing are typically emotionally based, including changes in the perception of self, stresses in relationships with friends or family, and increased anxiety, denial, and cancer worry. While a result suggesting no genetic predisposition could have several psychological benefits, including relief and anxiety reduction, the existence of a genetic predisposition for CRC may impact self-image and trigger adverse psychological responses (American Academy of

Pediatrics, 2001). Common responses include feelings of shame and fear of stigma (Ross et al., 2013); one in four men with CRC report self-blame and associated depression (McCann et al., 2009).

On the other hand, identification of a predisposition may lead to acceptance and integration of a prevention plan into his life. The patient also may avoid the shock and depression associated with late-stage diagnosis (Ross et al., 2013). Addressing these issues with the patient requires significant consideration as psychological responses of genetic screening can vary widely. While someone may feel a sense of anxiety relief by having definitive information about their risk and may benefit from a carefully determined prevention and screening plan, others, especially in Paul's case of regular colonoscopies, may be faced with increased anxiety associated with repeated screenings.

As previously stated, the psychologist should be informative and encouraging, not coercive. Before declining the test, it may help to have the patient plan out how he would behave given the different possible predictive results. If the proposed long-term benefit outweighs the current emotional burden, helping the patient overcome the anxiety toward testing may also increase the patient's self-determination (Nyrhinen et al., 2007). Despite the benefits, Paul ultimately has a right to not know if he has a genetic predisposition to CRC. Given the immediate emotional consequences and lack of limited immediate benefit, it is important to recognize and respect the patient's right to decline testing. As CRC genetic screening may have life-altering implications, some people may prefer not to know (Fulda & Lykens, 2006).

Genetic Discrimination

Privacy and confidentiality (4.01 Maintaining Confidentiality) are key concerns with predictive testing. As opposed to diagnostic and carrier testing, where the individual either already has the illness or is not expected to develop it, the individual with an identified predisposition via a predictive test is at increased risk, but it is unknown if or when the condition will manifest. Based on the impending possibility of developing a life-threatening illness at any time, there is a commonly expressed fear that genetic information will be used to deny access to health insurance, education, and employment (Guttmacher et al., 2003; Nance et al., 2003; Richmond-Rakerd, 2013). Fear of discrimination (see 3.04 Avoiding Harm) is a deterrent to genetic testing and of particular concern among younger patients (Nance et al., 2003).

Historically, health insurance companies could refuse to offer coverage, decrease benefits, or increase premiums based on results of genetic testing (Fulda & Lykens, 2006). Beginning in the mid-1990s, legislation was passed to protect individuals from being discriminated against based on genetic predispositions (Fulda & Lykens, 2006). The two main pieces of legislation aimed at correcting this abuse were the Health Information Portability and Accountability Act (HIPAA) of 1996 and the Genetic Information Nondiscrimination Act (GINA) of 2008. HIPAA includes the Privacy Rule, which requires health care providers and facilities to protect the privacy of health information and empowers patients to maintain control over the use and sharing of their genetic and medical records. Similarly, GINA directly bans genetic discrimination for health insurance eligibility, health insurance rates, and employment suitability (Guttmacher et al., 2003; Nyrhinen et al., 2007).

Despite legal protection, many patients who undergo genetic testing still do not bill their insurance companies for fear of subsequent discriminatory action against them or their children (Fulda & Lykens, 2006). The Patient Protection and Affordable Care Act (ACA) of 2010 provided additional protection for the confidentiality of genetic information. Specifically, insurance companies can no longer deny coverage based on preexisting conditions, including a genetic predisposition. Moreover, premiums cannot be changed based on health status. However, as it is not considered a basic health need, not all companies cover the costs of genetic testing. As this fear is very common, a working knowledge of state health coverage and employment policies related to genetic discrimination could help the psychologist reassure the patient of his or her rights. Moreover, it can help guide the patient during post-testing sessions if he or she experiences any form of discrimination.

Cultural Sensitivity and Stigma

The burden of CRC varies widely across ethnic minorities as well as within ethnic groups worldwide (Siegel, DeSantis, & Jemal, 2014). While the incidence of CRC is slightly lower compared to non-Latinos, Latinos are more likely to be diagnosed at a later stage, significantly lowering their survival rate (Pollack, Blackman, Wilson, Seeff, & Nadel, 2006). Additionally, regardless of socioeconomic status, rates of screening for CRC are significantly lower among the Latino population (Anderson & May, 1995; Goldman et al., 2009; Pollack et al., 2006; Winterich et al., 2008). Moreover, genetic tests vary in their ability to predict risk for different ethnic groups (Lee et al., 2006). The majority of genetic testing research has been conducted with non-Latinos, leaving uncertainty about the influence of Paul's ethnicity on his test results.

Racial differences in genetic testing for CRC may be due to differing perspectives of CRC and colonoscopies. Paul refused testing upon hearing about annual colonoscopies. Within the Latino community, there is significant stigma associated with CRC and, by extension, colonoscopies and genetic testing stemming from the perception of an association of CRC and colonoscopies with anal sex and homosexuality. Moreover, on average, Latinos are more likely to report being embarrassed, humiliated, or uncomfortable about colonoscopies, and men view them as a threat to their masculinity and sense of machismo (Christy, Mosher, & Rawl, 2014; Goldman et al., 2009; Winterich et al., 2008).

There are also noted differences in knowledge and beliefs regarding CRC and screening in the Latino population. Studies have found that, on average, Latinos have more misperceptions and misunderstandings about CRC and are less likely to get screening if they feel healthy. Ethnic-specific attitudes and beliefs may also impact one's decision to seek genetic testing. Latinos also report more negative beliefs about the consequences of genetic testing (Singer, Antonucci, & Van Hoewyk, 2004; Sussner, Thompson, Valdimarsdottir, Redd, & Jandorf, 2009). Specifically, perceptions related to the predictive ability of genetic testing and the perceived severity and worry related to the illness are ethnically linked (Kaphingst et al., 2015; Singer et al., 2004). However, these disparities can be addressed by increasing awareness. Latinos who report believing that CRC can be prevented and that they are at risk of CRC are more likely to seek screening (Christy et al., 2014; Goldman et al., 2009; Winterich et al., 2008). Similarly, Latinos report facing additional barriers such as a lack of time, a lack of insurance, and financial difficulty (Sussner et al., 2009; Thompson, Valdimarsdottir, Jandorf, & Redd, 2003). Psychologists can help by addressing stereotypes and promoting normalization of CRC and CRC screenings. Normalization would mean that CRC and its risk factors are generally understood in the community and that screening is regularly completed without stigmatization (Goldman et al., 2009).

Generally speaking, the Latino population puts a high value on family. Distress associated with genetic testing is moderated by social support. People who have fewer social contacts and lack satisfactory social support experience higher genetic testing-related emotional distress (Bleiker et al., 2007). Involving family in the genetic testing decision-making process may provide the needed support to motivate at-risk patients (Koehly et al., 2003). Being part of a cohesive family with supportive relatives can help the patient when considering genetic testing (McCann et al., 2009).

The Case of Carrier Genetic Testing for Fertility Preservation

Javier is a 15-year-old who has been diagnosed with leukemia. He is very active in the conversation about his treatment and asks many questions about both the disease and treatment. The recommended treatment – a stem cell transplant – has a high risk for permanent sterility. Javier hopes to be a parent one day and wants to have sperm cryopreservation in a fertility preservation attempt. Based on their experience with the emotional struggle of caring for a child with a severe illness, his parents worry about the risks of any future offspring having a genetic condition. Additionally, based on treatments to date, his parents worry that he may already be suffering from sterility. Given the high cost of sperm cryopreservation, his parents want him to have genetic testing to investigate the potential risks for his future offspring to help with making an informed decision before consenting to any fertility preservation. However, Javier wants to have the procedure regardless of the genetic risk and does not feel that he needs any testing. Although a minor, Javier is considered developmentally mature for his age and demonstrates insight into the reasons for sperm banking as well as the benefits and potential risks. The psychologist is faced with helping the family manage the conflicting preferences between Javier and his parent.

Beneficence and Nonmaleficence (Principle A)

The current guidelines set by the American Cancer Society for Clinical Oncology advocate that fertility options be discussed with each patient at risk for fertility impairment related to their cancer treatment (Lee et al., 2006; Loren et al., 2013). A number of options for fertility preservation exist (Levine & Stern, 2010). Routes for postpubertal male cancer patients include sperm cryopreservation. Experimental options for prepubertal males include cryopreservation of testicular tissue. Discussions about these methods of preservation are multifaceted and include full disclosure of both the positive and negative outcomes related to the treatment. In addition to the goal of ensuring future fertility, a range of potentially negative health effects (e.g., late effects), long-term financial costs, and personal responsibilities accompany the treatment/preservation. Further, these discussions often occur shortly after diagnosis, and decisions for fertility preservation can be pressured by the time sensitivity of starting cancer treatment.

Considering the potential psychosocial ramifications and the rising trends in survivorship status, conversations regarding fertility preservation should be considered standard treatment for AYAs with cancer (Bleyer, 2005; Bleyer et al., 2006; Ishibashi, 2001; Murphy, Klosky, Termuhlen, Sawczyn, & Quinn, 2013; Quinn & Vadaparampil, 2012; Soliman & Agresta, 2008; Thomas et al., 2006), and the team psychologist is uniquely qualified to facilitate this discussion with the oncologist, patient, and family caregivers. The team psychologist has an opportunity to facilitate the overall communication and empower the group to make a decision in the child's best interest. Critical topics include the patient's reasons for wanting fertility preservation and distinguishing parental values from those of the child. In addition to these personal reasons related to the procedure, the psychologist should examine the practical dilemma of the financial burden. This is clearly a major concern for the parents and it is valuable to examine their reasons for concern and brainstorm alternative solutions for financial assistance. If the psychologist is not aware of available resources, consultations with social workers or other allied health professionals may aid in helping families identify financial assistance. It is not uncommon for a patient or family to immediately reject consideration of fertility due to finances, so it is important to provide families with all available information regarding support. Throughout this conversation, it will be important for the psychologist to promote perspective-taking, process the difficult emotions related to this dilemma, and maintain a central focus on the child's best interest.

An emotional benefit of fertility preservation is the symbolic reassurance of survivorship (Aubard, Piver, Pech, Galinat, & Teissier, 2001; Grundy et al., 2001; Wallace, Anderson, & Irvine, 2005). Hopefulness and future thinking can be protective features that can moderate distress related to the difficulties of the cancer experience (Nieman et al., 2007; Quinn et al., 2010; Schover, 1999; Schover, Rybicki, Martin, & Bringelsen, 1999). For Javier, the future hope of becoming a father might enhance his resiliency and offer some protection against the negative emotions associated with having a life-threatening illness.

On the other hand, Javier faces many long-term negative consequences. There is a range of potentially negative health outcomes as well as infertility for AYA cancer survivors. These consequences include anxiety, depression, decreased quality of life, and lowered self-esteem (Benedict, Shuk, & Ford, 2015; Green, Galvin, & Horne, 2003; Lee et al., 2006; Wenzel et al., 2005). Fertility preservation also comes with the long-term financial costs of sperm banking, as insurance rarely covers the procedure or the annual costs to store cryopreserved sperm (Campo-Engelstein, 2010).

Nonmaleficence describes a clinician's responsibility to prevent harm to a patient. Although most forms of fertility preservation do not increase the risk of harm, concerns can arise when a preservation procedure delays life-saving treatment or the rare potential for reintroducing cancer cells through transplantation of spermatogonia, testicular tissue, or ovarian tissue (Oktay, 2001; Seshadri et al., 2006; Shaw, Bowles, Koopman, Wood, & Trounson, 1996; Shin, Lo, & Lipshultz, 2005).

If resources are inadequate, it could be argued that the parents are ethically making the right decision to forego preservation. The cost-effectiveness of genetic testing should be considered within the context of the anticipated impact of the findings. In addition to financial concerns, it can be argued that although Javier desires fertility preservation, it is not a medically required procedure. However, this latter argument does not take into account the long-term emotional impact of infertility (Nieman et al., 2007; Schover, 1999).

Issues of Consent and Confidentiality (3.10 Informed Consent; 9.03 Informed Consent in Assessment; 4.01 Confidentiality)

Genetic testing of children is common; however, after early childhood, genetic testing among adolescents is much less common (Ross et al., 2013). Parental decisions about genetic testing of minors should be based on the child's best interest (Ross et al., 2013). In this case, carrier genetic testing is an elective procedure. Elective procedures on minors generally require both parent consent and child assent. If the adolescent is considered developmentally mature and the testing is elective in nature, the adolescent's assent should drive the final consent decision (Ross et al., 2013).

Confidentiality concerns may be heightened when genetic testing is predictive as opposed to diagnostic (Sarata, 2015). While confidentiality is established with the individual patient, predictive testing reveals information pertaining to the entire family (Burgess, 2001). In this case, confidentiality is established between the provider, Javier, and his parents pertaining to Javier's health information. However, the results of his screening may reveal sensitive information about the parents' genetic composition as well. While consent and confidentiality are not required for the parents, information regarding the meaning of the possible results and implications of the results on the parents should be made clear before testing.

Patient Autonomy (Principle E)

Javier is a minor as a function of his age; therefore, his parents have legal authorization to consent or refuse to consent (Litton, 2008). As a minor, there is a "right in trust" that the parents are asked to uphold until the child is of adult status (Jadoul, Dolmans, & Donnez, 2010). Until that time, medical decisions should be based on Javier's best interest. Based on minors' lack of legal and cognitive decision-making ability and limited understanding of the results, children and adolescents should not have genetic testing unless medically necessary. Javier's parents' concerns about carrier status do not constitute a medical necessity (Nance et al., 2003) and might not have a direct benefit (Dudzinski, 2004; Sugarman & Rosoff, 2001).

Carrier genetic testing and subsequent decisions with minors can significantly impact the adolescent's current and future autonomy. In this case, if Javier's parents do not consent while he is a minor, he will not have the opportunity to make his own reproductive decisions when he comes of age (and so become a biological father). On the other hand, even though Javier does not legally have the right to individual autonomy, if his parents consent to the procedure with his best interests in mind, Javier will eventually be able to make his own reproductive decisions. His parents would not be making his reproductive choices for him, but rather would provide the opportunity for Javier to take control of his reproductive decisions later in life. Consistent and clear communication is needed in order to preserve the future autonomy of the minor to make reproductive choices and to prevent future infertility-related distress. Bearing in mind Javier's maturity, his decision should be honored due to the principle of respect for persons and his right to autonomy (Beauchamp & Childress, 2001; Kohrman et al., 1995).

Selective Reproduction

Carrier testing to aid in fertility preservation may be considered a form of selective reproduction. Most commonly, selective reproduction consists of prenatal genetic screening in which results regarding devastating genetic conditions inform decisions to terminate the pregnancy. In Javier's case, unless his cancer is inherited, there is no evidence to suggest an increased risk of congenital abnormalities or cancer in his offspring. It is difficult to know if his parents' desire for carrier testing is motivated by the financial concerns of sperm banking – the motivation should be discussed prior to testing. If results suggest a possible risk for a genetic condition in Javier's offspring, the next decision is whether they should still proceed with the fertility preservation. This is an ethically laden decision that should be discussed as a family while keeping Javier's desires in focus. The decision would involve the best interests of his future offspring and deciding whether sperm banking is a worthwhile endeavor given the potential complications for the offspring.

Although there is no evidence for passing on risks for cancer or congenital abnormalities, recent evidence has suggested that the sperm of untreated men with cancer may have poor DNA integrity (Lee et al., 2006). There is a possible risk of genetic damage in sperm stored after diagnosis of cancer even before initiation of cancer therapy. Damage to sperm DNA may adversely affect reproductive outcomes. If this is the case for Javier, there may be concerns about the health of the offspring (Lee et al., 2006). As opposed to preservation decisions based on carrier testing results, the conflicting opinions between Javier and his parents may best be initially directed at determining the existing DNA damage and preparing for potential emotional responses if Javier is found to already be suffering from cancer-related DNA damage.

Discussion

While the price of genetic testing remains high and insurance coverage remains inconsistent, the procedure may not yet be readily available. This may have consequences on the patient's awareness of the benefits, harms, and additional ethical concerns related to genetic services. Future considerations may include cases of individuals with significant anxiety and worry about cancer who utilize excessive screening (Hadley et al., 2004) and cases of genome-wide testing among individuals with no evidence of increased risk.

There is a wide range of potential scenarios and ethical concerns that a psychologist might face when working with AYAs, cancer, and genetic testing. While no one patient will be the same as any other, the psychologist must evaluate the individual's needs within the context of his or her larger sociocultural community. The individual may be facing confusion, fear, denial, and emotional distress related to his or her own health and well-being. They will also be dealing with the others directly in their lives, whether it is the influence of a parent or responsibility to other family members. Finally, the patient might be facing concerns about his or her place in society and the possible repercussions of their genetic results with regard to work, insurance, and discrimination. Ultimately, it is the psychologists (and other mental health professionals) who need to be prepared to provide comprehensive and supportive care to any AYA cancer patients considering genetic testing that they may encounter.

References

American Academy of Pediatrics (2001). Ethical issues with genetic testing in pediatrics. *Pediatrics*, *107*, 1451–1455.

American College of Medical Genetics (1999). *Genetic susceptibility to breast and ovarian cancer: assessment, counseling, and testing guidelines*. Bethesda, MD: American College of Medical Genetics.

American Psychiatric Association (2013). Addressing psychological impacts of genetic testing on patients, families: Six questions for psychologist Andrea Farkas Patenaude, PhD. Retrieved from www.apa.org/news/press/releases/2013/05/genetic-testing.aspx

American Psychological Association (2010). *Ethical principles of psychologists and code of conduct*. Washington, DC: American Psychological Association.

Anderson, L. M. & May, D. S. (1995). Has the use of cervical, breast, and colorectal cancer screening increased in the United States? *American Journal of Public Health*, *85*, 840–842.

Aubard, Y., Piver, P., Pech, J. C., Galinat, S., & Teissier, M. P. (2001). Ovarian tissue cryopreservation and gynecologic oncology: A review. *European Journal of Obstetrics & Gynecology and Reproductive Biology*, *97*, 5–14.

Beauchamp, T. L. & Childress, J. F. (2001). *Principles of biomedical ethics*. New York, NY: Oxford University Press.

Benedict, C., Shuk, E., & Ford, J. S. (2015). Fertility issues in adolescent and young adult cancer survivors. *Journal of Adolescent and Young Adult Oncology*, *5*, 48–57.

Bleiker, E., Menko, F. H., Kluijt, I., Taal, B. G., Gerritsma, M. A., Wever, L., & Aaronson, N. K. (2007). Colorectal cancer in the family: Psychosocial distress and social issues in the years following genetic counselling. *Hereditary Cancer Clinical Practice, 5*, 59–66.

Bleyer, A. (2005). The adolescent and young adult gap in cancer care and outcome. *Current Problems in Pediatric and Adolescent Health Care, 35*, 182–217.

Bleyer, A., Barr, R., Hayes-Lattin, B., Thomas, D., Ellis, C., & Anderson, B. (2008). The distinctive biology of cancer in adolescents and young adults. *Nature Reviews Cancer, 8*, 288–298.

Bleyer, A., O'Leary, M., Barr, R., & Ries, L. A. G. (Eds.) (2006). *Cancer epidemiology in older adolescents and young adults 15 to 29 years of age, including SEER incidence and survival: 1975–2000. National Cancer Institute, NIH Pub. No. 06-5767.* Bethesda, MD: National Cancer Institute.

Bosch, N., Junyent, N., Gadea, N., et al. (2012). What factors may influence psychological well being at three months and one year post *BRCA* genetic result disclosure? *The Breast, 21*, 755–760.

Burgess, M. M. (2001). Beyond consent: Ethical and social issues in genetic testing. *Nature Reviews Genetics, 2*, 147–151.

Burke, W. & Press, N. (2006). Genetics as a tool to improve cancer outcomes: Ethics and policy. *Nature Reviews Cancer, 6*, 476–482.

Campo-Engelstein, L. (2010). Consistency in insurance coverage for iatrogenic conditions resulting from cancer treatment including fertility preservation. *Journal of Clinical Oncology, 28*, 1284–1286.

Caplan, A. L. (2015). Chloe's Law: A powerful legislative movement challenging a core ethical norm of genetic testing. *PLOS Biology, 13*, 1–4.

Christy, S. M., Mosher, C. E., & Rawl, S. M. (2014). Integrating men's health and masculinity theories to explain colorectal cancer screening behavior. *American Journal of Men's Health, 8*, 54–65.

Collins, F. S. (2010). Opportunities for research and NIH. *Science, 327*, 36–37.

Dudzinski, D. M. (2004). Ethical issues in fertility preservation for adolescent cancer survivors: Oocyte and ovarian tissue cryopreservation. *Journal of Pediatric and Adolescent Gynecology, 17*, 97–102.

Fisher, B., Costantino, J. P., Wickerham, D. L., et al. (2005). Tamoxifen for the prevention of breast cancer: current status of the National Surgical Adjuvant Breast and Bowel Project P-1 study. *Journal of the National Cancer Institute, 97*, 1652–1662.

Fulda, K. G. & Lykens, K. (2006). Ethical issues in predictive genetic testing: A public health perspective. *Journal of Medical Ethics, 32*, 143–147.

Gahm, J., Wickman, M., & Brandberg, Y. (2010). Bilateral prophylactic mastectomy in women with inherited risk of breast cancer – Prevalence of pain and discomfort, impact on sexuality, quality of life and feelings of regret two years after surgery. *The Breast, 19*, 462–469.

Genetic Alliance (2010). *Understanding genetics: A District of Columbia guide for patients and health professionals.* Washington, DC: District of Columbia Department of Health.

Goldman, R. E., Diaz, J. A., & Kim, I. (2009). Perspectives of colorectal cancer risk and screening among Dominicans and Puerto Ricans: Stigma and misperceptions. *Qualitative Health Research, 19*, 1559–1568.

Green, D., Galvin, H., & Horne, B. (2003). The psycho-social impact of infertility on young male cancer survivors: A qualitative investigation. *Psycho-Oncology, 12*, 141–152.

Grundy, R., Larcher, V., Gosden, R., et al. (2001). Fertility preservation for children treated for cancer (2): Ethics of consent for gamete storage and experimentation. *Archives of Disease in Childhood, 84,* 360–362.

Guttmacher, A. E., Collins, F. S., & Clayton, E. W. (2003). Ethical, legal, and social implications of genomic medicine. *New England Journal of Medicine, 349,* 562–569.

Hadley, D. W., Jenkins, J. F., Dimond, E., de Carvalho, M., Kirsch, I., & Palmer, C. G. (2004). Colon cancer screening practices after genetic counseling and testing for hereditary nonpolyposis colorectal cancer. *Journal of Clinical Oncology, 22,* 39–44.

Heemskerk-Gerritsen, B., Menke-Pluijmers, M., Jager, A., et al. (2013). Substantial breast cancer risk reduction and potential survival benefit after bilateral mastectomy when compared with surveillance in healthy *BRCA1* and *BRCA2* mutation carriers: a prospective analysis. *Annals of Oncology, 24,* 2029–2035.

Ishibashi, A. (2001). The needs of children and adolescents with cancer for information and social support. *Cancer Nursing, 24,* 61–67.

Jadoul, P., Dolmans, M. M., & Donnez, J. (2010). Fertility preservation in girls during childhood: is it feasible, efficient and safe and to whom should it be proposed? *Human Reproduction Update, 16,* 617–630.

Kaphingst, K. A., Stafford, J. D., McGowan, L. D. A., Seo, J., Lachance, C. R., & Goodman, M. S. (2015). Effects of racial and ethnic group and health literacy on responses to genomic risk information in a medically underserved population. *Health Psychology, 34,* 101–110.

Koehly, L. M., Peterson, S. K., Watts, B. G., Kempf, K. K., Vernon, S. W., & Gritz, E. R. (2003). A social network analysis of communication about hereditary nonpolyposis colorectal cancer genetic testing and family functioning. *Cancer Epidemiology Biomarkers & Prevention, 12,* 304–313.

Kohrman, A., Clayton, E. W., Frader, J. E., Grodin, M. A., Moseley, K. L., Porter, I. H., & Wagner, V. M. (1995). Informed consent, parental permission, and assent in pediatric practice. *Pediatrics, 95,* 314–317.

Lea, D. H., Williams, J., & Donahue M. P. (2005). Ethical issues in genetic testing. *Journal of Midwifery & Women's Health, 50,* 234–240.

Lee, S. J., Schover, L. R., Partridge, A. H., et al. (2006). American Society of Clinical Oncology recommendations on fertility preservation in cancer patients. *Journal of Clinical Oncology, 24,* 2917–2931.

Levine, J. & Stern, C. J. (2010). Fertility preservation in adolescents and young adults with cancer. *Journal of Clinical Oncology, 28,* 4831–4841.

Liang, J., Kalady, M. F., & Church, J. (2015). Young age of onset colorectal cancers. *International Journal of Colorectal Disease, 30,* 1653–1657.

Lindor, N. M., Petersen, G. M., Hadley, D. W., et al. (2006). Recommendations for the care of individuals with an inherited predisposition to Lynch syndrome: A systematic review. *JAMA, 296,* 1507–1517.

Litton, P. (2008). Non-beneficial pediatric research and the best interests standard: A legal and ethical reconciliation. *Yale Journal of Health Policy, Law, and Ethics, 8,* 361–420.

Loren, A. W., Mangu, P. B., Beck, L. N., et al. (2013). Fertility preservation for patients with cancer: American Society of Clinical Oncology clinical practice guideline update. *Journal of Clinical Oncology, 31,* 2500–2510.

Manolio, T. A., Collins, F. S., Cox, N. J., et al. (2009). Finding the missing heritability of complex diseases. *Nature, 461,* 747–753.

McCann, S., MacAuley, D., Barnett, Y., Bunting, B., Bradley, A., Jeffers, L., & Morrison, P. J. (2009). Family communication, genetic testing and colonoscopy screening in hereditary non-polyposis colon cancer: A qualitative study. *Psycho-Oncology, 18,* 1208–1215.

Metcalfe, K. A., Esplen, M. J., Goel, V., & Narod, S. A. (2004). Psychosocial functioning in women who have undergone bilateral prophylactic mastectomy. *Psycho-Oncology, 13,* 14–25.

Moyer, V. A. (2014). Risk assessment, genetic counseling, and genetic testing for *BRCA*-related cancer in women: US Preventive Services Task Force recommendation statement. *Annals of Internal Medicine, 160,* 271–281.

Murphy, D., Klosky, J. L., Termuhlen, A., Sawczyn, K. K., & Quinn, G. P. (2013). The need for reproductive and sexual health discussions with adolescent and young adult cancer patients. *Contraception, 88,* 215–220.

Nance, M., Myers, R., Wexler, A., et al. (2003). *Genetic testing for Huntington's disease: It's relevance and implications (revised).* Washington, DC: United States Huntington's Disease Genetics Testing Group.

Nelson, H. D., Fu, R., Griffin, J. C., Nygren, P., Smith, M. B., & Humphrey, L. (2009). Systematic review: comparative effectiveness of medications to reduce risk for primary breast cancer. *Annals of Internal Medicine, 151,* 703–715.

Nelson, H. D., Pappas, M., Zakher, B., Mitchell, J. P., Okinaka-Hu, L., & Fu, R. (2014). Risk assessment, genetic counseling, and genetic testing for *BRCA*-related cancer in women: A systematic review to update the US Preventive Services Task Force recommendation. *Annals of Internal Medicine, 160,* 255–266.

Nieman, C. L., Kinahan, K. E., Yount, S. E., et al. (2007). Fertility preservation and adolescent cancer patients: Lessons from adult survivors of childhood cancer and their parents. *Cancer Treatment and Research, 138,* 201–217.

Nyrhinen, T., Hietala, M., Puukka, P., & Leino-Kilpi, H. (2007). Consequences as ethical issues in diagnostic genetic testing – A comparison of the perceptions of patients/parents and personnel. *New Genetics and Society, 26,* 47–63.

Oktay, K. (2001). Ovarian tissue cryopreservation and transplantation: Preliminary findings and implications for cancer patients. *Human Reproduction Update, 7,* 526–534.

Payne, J. D. & Payne, T. (2013). Implications of *BRCA* testing in a 27-year-old breast-feeding mother with a strong family history of malignancy. *Journal of Medical Cases, 4,* 372–375.

Pollack, L. A., Blackman, D. K., Wilson, K. M., Seeff, L. C., & Nadel, M. R. (2006). Colorectal cancer test use among Latino and non-Latino U.S. population. *Preventing Chronic Disease: Public Health Research, Practice, and Policy, 3,* 1–12.

Quinn, G. P., Pal, T., Murphy, D., Vadaparampil, S. T., & Kumar, A. (2012). High-risk consumers' perceptions of preimplantation genetic diagnosis for hereditary cancers: A systematic review and meta-analysis. *Genetics in Medicine, 14,* 191–200.

Quinn, G. P., Peshkin, B. N., Sehovic, I., Bowman, M., Tamargo, C., & Vadaparampil, S. T. (2015). Oncofertility in adolescent and young adult hereditary cancer: Considerations for genetics professionals. *World Journal of Medical Genetics, 5,* 52–59.

Quinn, G. P., Vadaparampil, S. T., Jacobsen, P. B., Knapp, C., Keefe, D. L., & Bell, G. E. (2010). Frozen hope: Fertility preservation for women with cancer. *Journal of Midwifery & Women's Health, 55,* 175–180.

Richmond-Rakerd, L. S. (2013). Modern advances in genetic testing: Ethical challenges and training implications for current and future psychologists. *Ethics & Behavior, 23*, 31–43.

Riley, B. D., Culver, J. O., Skrzynia, C., et al. (2012). Essential elements of genetic cancer risk assessment, counseling, and testing: Updated recommendations of the National Society of Genetic Counselors. *Journal of Genetic Counseling, 21*, 151–161.

Rosenberg, S. M., Sepucha, K., Ruddy, K. J., et al. (2015). Local therapy decision-making and contralateral prophylactic mastectomy in young women with early-stage breast cancer. *Annals of Surgical Oncology, 22*, 3809–3815.

Ross, L. F., Saal, H. M., David, K. L., & Anderson, R. R. (2013). Technical report: Ethical and policy issues in genetic testing and screening of children. *Genetics in Medicine, 15*, 234–245.

Sarata, A. K. (2015). *Genetic testing: Background and policy issues*. Washington, DC: Congressional Research Service.

Schover, L. R. (1999). Psychosocial aspects of infertility and decisions about reproduction in young cancer survivors: A review. *Medical and Pediatric Oncology, 33*, 53–59.

Schover, L. R., Rybicki, L. A., Martin, B. A., & Bringelsen, K. A. (1999). Having children after cancer. *Cancer, 86*, 697–709.

Seshadri, T., Gook, D., Lade, S., et al. (2006). Lack of evidence of disease contamination in ovarian tissue harvested for cryopreservation from patients with Hodgkin lymphoma and analysis of factors predictive of oocyte yield. *British Journal of Cancer, 94*, 1007–1010.

Shaw, J., Bowles, J., Koopman, P., Wood, E., & Trounson, A. (1996). Ovary and ovulation: Fresh and cryopreserved ovarian tissue samples from donors with lymphoma transmit the cancer to graft recipients. *Human Reproduction, 11*, 1668–1673.

Shin, D., Lo, K. C., & Lipshultz, L. I. (2005). Treatment options for the infertile male with cancer. *Journal of the National Cancer Institute monographs, 34*, 48–50.

Siegel, R., DeSantis, C., & Jemal, A. (2014). Colorectal cancer statistics, 2014. *CA: A Cancer Journal for Clinicians, 64*, 104–117.

Singer, E., Antonucci, T., & Van Hoewyk, J. (2004). Racial and ethnic variations in knowledge and attitudes about genetic testing. *Genetic Testing, 8*, 31–43.

Skytte, A. B., Crüger, D., Gerster, M., et al. (2011). Breast cancer after bilateral risk-reducing mastectomy. *Clinical Genetics, 79*, 431–437.

Soliman, H. & Agresta, S. V. (2008). Current issues in adolescent and young adult cancer survivorship. *Cancer Control: Journal of the Moffitt Cancer Center, 15*, 55–62.

Spencer, D. H., Lockwood, C., Topol, E., Evans, J. P., Green, R. C., Mansfield, E., & Tezak, Z. (2011). Direct-to-consumer genetic testing: reliable or risky? *Clinical Chemistry, 57*, 1641–1644.

Storm, C., Agarwal, R., & Offit, K. (2008). Ethical and legal implications of cancer genetic testing: Do physicians have a duty to warn patients' relatives about possible genetic risks? *Journal of Oncology Practice, 4*, 229–230.

Sugarman, J. & Rosoff, P. M. (2001). Ethical issues in gamete preservation for children undergoing treatment for cancer. *Journal of Andrology, 22*, 732–737.

Sussner, K. M., Thompson, H. S., Valdimarsdottir, H. B., Redd, W. H., & Jandorf, L. (2009). Acculturation and familiarity with, attitudes towards and beliefs about genetic testing for cancer risk within Latinas in East Harlem, New York City. *Journal of Genetic Counseling, 18*, 60–71.

Thomas, D. M., Seymour, J. F., O'Brien, T., Sawyer, S. M., & Ashley, D. M. (2006). Adolescent and young adult cancer: A revolution in evolution? *Internal Medicine Journal, 36,* 302–307.

Thompson, H. S., Valdimarsdottir, H. B., Jandorf, L., & Redd, W. (2003). Perceived disadvantages and concerns about abuses of genetic testing for cancer risk: Differences across African American, Latina and Caucasian women. *Patient Education and Counseling, 51,* 217–227.

van Oostrom, I., Meijers-Heijboer, H., Lodder, L. N., et al. (2003). Long-term psychological impact of carrying a *BRCA1/2* mutation and prophylactic surgery: A 5-year follow-up study. *Journal of Clinical Oncology, 21,* 3867–3874.

Wallace, W. H. B., Anderson, R. A., & Irvine, D. S. (2005). Fertility preservation for young patients with cancer: Who is at risk and what can be offered? *The Lancet Oncology, 6,* 209–218.

Wasteson, E., Sandelin, K., Brandberg, Y., Wickman, M., & Arver, B. (2011). High satisfaction rate ten years after bilateral prophylactic mastectomy – A longitudinal study. *European Journal of Cancer Care, 20,* 508–513.

Wenzel, L., Dogan-Ates, A., Habbal, R., et al. (2005). Defining and measuring reproductive concerns of female cancer survivors. *Journal of the National Cancer Institute monographs, 34,* 94–98.

Wilson, J. M. G. & Jungner, G. (1968). *Principles and practice of screening for disease.* Geneva: World Health Organization.

Winterich, J. A., Quandt, S. A., Grzywacz, J. G., Clark, P. E., Miller, D. P., Acuña, J., & Arcury, T. A. (2008). Masculinity and the body: How African American and white men experience cancer screening exams involving the rectum. *American Journal of Men's Health, 3,* 300–309.

29 Ethical Considerations for Behavioral Health Professionals in Primary Care Settings

Abbie O. Beacham and Kristi S. Van Sickle

Over the past three decades, it has become generally accepted that primary care is the "de facto" mental health system (McDaniel et al., 2014). Consequently, the prevalence of and need for behavioral health professionals (i.e., psychologists, social workers, and counselors) integrated into primary care clinics are growing at unprecedented rates (Beacham, Kinman, Harris, & Masters, 2012; Health Service Psychology Education Collaborative [HSPEC], 2013). Recent trends suggest that the demand is far out-weighing the supply of qualified professionals to work in these settings (Blount & Miller, 2009; HSPEC, 2013). Furthermore, the increasing need for clinics to achieve designation as patient-centered medical homes (National Committee for Quality Assurance [NCQA], 2016) increases demand for adequately trained and competent professionals in these settings, as *behavioral health* is a required element for this recognition (Beacham et al., 2017; Nash, Khatri, Cubic, & Baird, 2013). As a result of the changes in health care service delivery, the knowledge, skills, and attitudes of behavioral health professionals must likewise adapt to proficiently meet the need of patients and systems (Beacham & Van Sickle, 2014; Van Sickle & Beacham, 2014). Accordingly, behavioral health providers' knowledge, skills, and attitudes regarding the ethical considerations inherent to these settings must shift to accommodate the broadening and changing landscape (Cubic & Beacham, 2014; HSPEC, 2013).

In general, psychology training has been slow to adapt to a changing market and systems. First, with some exceptions, the training of psychologists and other mental health professionals continues to focus on traditional models of care, financial support, and modes of care delivery (HSPEC, 2013). Second, psychology's discipline-specific professional ethical principles and codes of conduct likewise remain focused on the traditional roles and activities of professionals (APA, 2010; Runyan, Robinson, & Gould, 2013). The overarching effect of these two slow-to-evolve areas is that the professional wanting to enter into primary care may be woefully unaware of the differences in culture, modes and mores of operation, and policies that seem to directly conflict with traditional training. Moreover, the result of an ethics code directed primarily at traditional practice may lead to an inordinately large gray area with respect to ethical problem-solving and decision-making in nontraditional settings such as primary care.

We assume that the reader of this chapter is seeking to garner entry-level knowledge and awareness regarding important ethical questions that commonly arise for psychologists in primary care settings. The chapter authors have over two decades of experience working in and training behavioral health professionals in primary care. We first provide a very basic overview of the primary care model of care with important concepts, terms, and resources. Second, we present case examples of commonly encountered ethical and professional dilemmas in primary care settings, based heavily on both our own experiences and issues that arise from leaders in the field (e.g., Hodgsen, Mendenhall, & Lamson, 2013; Hudgins, Rose, Fifield, & Arnault, 2013; Reiter & Runyan, 2013; Runyan, Robinson, & Gould, 2013). More recently, case examples illustrating the unique ethical and legal issues faced by behavioral health providers in pediatric primary care have been offered as well (Williamson et al., 2017). Each of the case examples provided in this chapter is followed by a brief discussion of the primary ethical and professional considerations. As the reader will note, few of the most common ethical and professional dilemmas inherent to primary care and medical settings fall neatly into the ethics code and guidelines. Many of the most common dilemmas encountered in primary care are actually reflective of "cultural" and professional differences between medical and psychological service provision ethics and tradition. Therefore, the commentary we provide may not point the reader to one clear, irrefutable solution to a problem or dilemma; in fact, there are surely many more than we can outline here. However, we share a recommended framework (Kanzler, Goodie, Hunter, Glotfelter, & Bodart, 2013) for working through ethical dilemmas in integrated primary care (IPC).

Because the authors are psychologists, we will refer the reader of this chapter to the resources that are psychology discipline-specific. It is especially important to note that in primary care settings the "behavioral health consultants (BHCs)/professionals" are composed of a number of disciplines, including psychiatry, social work, counseling, and coaching. In light of this, throughout the chapter, we utilize the widely used term "BHC" in referring to these professionals – including psychologists – who provide these services in primary care settings. We would be remiss if we did not offer some warning to readers who have not been exposed to primary care psychology training. The dilemmas and the possible solutions offered may run counter to your own training and experience. In fact, you may find that you disagree quite strongly with us. Primary care is an exciting and very different way of practicing psychology. The challenge is what makes it so alluring to those of us who work in the area. We invite you to explore your own reactions, thoughts, and impressions.

The Primary Care Model

In order to understand and identify common ethical dilemmas and approaches to problem-solving, it is essential that the reader is familiar with the differences between traditional "psychological" care provision and how care is often delivered in primary care settings. Although a full review of this topic is beyond the scope of this chapter, we provide a working example and structure of an integrated model of care and contrast the model to traditional models of care to provide a context and common language for the reader. There are excellent reviews and texts that offer more comprehensive descriptions of models of primary care behavioral health service delivery to which the reader may wish to refer (see Gatchel & Oordt, 2003; Hunter, Goodie, Oordt, & Dobmeyer, 2009; Robinson & Reiter, 2016).

Behavioral Health Extends Beyond "Just" Mental Health

One crucial concept in understanding the scope of behavioral health in primary care is that care extends well beyond mental health problems and symptoms. Primary care clinics – especially those that seek patient-centered medical home recognition – define behavioral health as addressing three domains: mental health, alcohol and other drug use, and health-enhancing or -compromising behaviors. Therefore, behavioral health professional should have requisite levels of competence to be able to address each of these three areas.

Population-Based Care

In fully integrated clinics, behavioral health services are delivered very differently from traditional clinic or private practice settings. The basic premise of care in these settings is "Population Based Care: A population health perspective encompasses the ability to assess the health needs of a specific population; implement and evaluate interventions to improve the health of that population; and provide care for individual patients in the context of the culture, health status, and health needs of the populations of which that patient is a member" (Association of American Medical Colleges, 1999, p. 138). A population may be an entire community, a clinic population, or a population within a clinic such as all persons who have been diagnosed with type 2 diabetes. Generally speaking, if a small amount of care were distributed widely in a population, it would result in an incremental improvement in the health of the population. We like to use cardiovascular disease (CVD) as a parallel example. Common risk factors for CVD such as hypertension, high cholesterol, and health behaviors such as diet, exercise, and smoking can be effectively assessed and managed in primary care. However, if a patient is having chest pain and requires more extensive assessment and evaluation and ultimately surgical intervention, this would be routinely (and, hopefully, immediately) referred to emergent/comprehensive and specialty care (i.e., emergency room and cardiology). The primary medical provider would not attempt to intervene with surgery in the primary care clinic. The primary care clinic can, however, have an appreciable impact on the health of the clinic population through CVD risk factor modification such as management of hypertension, cholesterol, and obesity and assisting with smoking cessation. The same is true for behavioral health symptoms and concerns. For example, if all clinic patients who have elevated levels of symptoms of depression are assessed sooner, they may respond favorably to small "doses" of intervention such that their symptoms can be addressed and managed before they become debilitating and severely affect the health of the patient.

Table 29.1 *Stepped-Care Conceptualization of Integrated Primary Care (Pruitt, Klapow, Epping-Jordan, & Dresselhaus, 1998)*

Level III – comprehensive/specialty care Emergency consult and referral Comprehensive mental health service/referral (possible comprehensive individual treatment) Specialty pathways of care (e.g., chronic illness management, depression management)
Level II – brief "targeted" interventions Addresses needs of all members of patient population through screening and referral May offer brief, problem-focused intervention in the form of one to five abbreviated visits (e.g., 20–30 minutes) after initial patient contact
Level I – population-based screening/targeted consultation Patient screen and collaborative consultation

Stepped-Care Conceptualization of IPC

There are a number of models of primary care psychology collaboration. In this chapter, we refer exclusively to a fully integrated model of care. A "stepped-care" conceptualization of IPC depicts a way to think about levels of care in order to most efficiently address the needs of patients within available primary care clinic resources (see Table 29.1; Pruitt, Klapow, Epping-Jordan, & Dresselhaus, 1998). We present this model as a way of helping the reader acquire a working visual schematic of structure and an understanding of the concepts and common language. In this model, there are three levels of care: I – screening/targeted consultation; II – brief targeted intervention; and III – comprehensive/specialty care. Levels I and II are levels of care that are most consistent with population-based care and are expected to be used liberally and moderately, respectively. At these levels of care, BHCs provide brief assessment, referral, and intervention with the capacity to provide access to care to a larger proportion of the target population. Level III care is most consistent with traditional models of psychological care. This level of care is typically characterized by comprehensive batteries of assessment, case conceptualization, and intervention or psychotherapy and in primary care should be used sparingly or in emergent cases. Chances are, most of us reading (or writing) this chapter were trained in this traditional mode of service delivery.

In a clinic that relies primarily or exclusively on "co-location" of behavioral health service provision that is characterized by traditional-length, 50-minute sessions, the greatest proportion of patient contacts occurs at Level III – comprehensive or specialty services. In this model of care, the highest concentration of resources and effort is extended to fewer numbers of patients. This is the opposite of population-based care; that is, fewer numbers of patients have access to behavioral health services and the population-based impact becomes negligible.

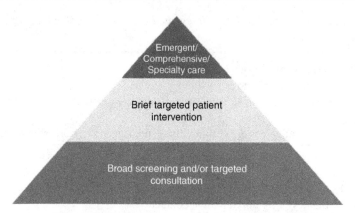

Figure 29.1 *Proportional Pyramid Schematic of Number of Direct and Indirect Patient Contacts in "Stepped-Care" Integrated Primary Care Conceptualization*

Figure 29.1 depicts a fully IPC clinic configuration with the highest proportion of patient contacts occurring in Level I, thus extending program reach and maximizing opportunities for access to behavioral health care. This proportional pyramid model offers a more stable depiction of the behavioral health service delivery and sustainability. Although there are many approaches to assessing the degree to which integration of care is achieved, we find a useful metric to apply as a way of assessing adherence to an integrated model of primary care is that approximately 80 percent of all behavioral health patient contacts should occur at Levels I and II (Pruitt et al., 1998).

Behavioral health professionals must be able to provide brief assessment/ screening and referral across the three behavioral health domains and within each of the three levels of care. Ideally, they should be able to provide appropriate and suitable assessment and intervention for the degree of severity/complexity of the presenting problem and the resources and setting in which they work. For example, if upon initial brief assessment it is apparent that a patient presents with significant symptoms of post-traumatic stress disorder, it may not be appropriate to offer intervention in the primary care clinic for two reasons. First, if the behavioral health service in the clinic follows a model of brief visits (15–30 minutes) and/or is limited to few numbers of visits (i.e., Levels I or II), it may be in the best interest of the patient to refer them elsewhere for necessary and appropriate treatment. The patient may be in need of Level III comprehensive and/or specialty care. Second, if a patient's symptom severity and constellation show that they require treatment in an area of practice that extends beyond the behavioral health professional's area(s) of competency or resources, then the patient may be better served elsewhere. Balancing patients' needs with available resources is one common ethical professional and cultural dilemma in primary care. We will now illustrate ethical dilemmas frequently encountered by primary care behavioral health providers.

Ethics Codes and Competencies

As a starting point, we suggest readers refer not only to their respective ethical codes and guidelines (e.g., American Counseling Association, 2014; American Medical Association, 2015; American Psychological Association, 2010; National Association of Social Workers, 2008), but also to the specific competencies for general and specialty areas of practice of other health care disciplines.

In addition to general training competencies, the American Psychological Association (APA) published an extensive overview of Competencies for Psychology Practice in Primary Care (McDaniel et al., 2014). In this document, the competencies are organized into the following categories: science, systems, professionalism, relationships, application, and education. Competence and competencies as they apply to primary care psychology are defined as follows:

> Competence in [primary care] psychology refers to the knowledge, skills, and attitudes – and their integration – that allow an individual to perform tasks and roles as a [primary care] psychologist regardless of service delivery model (Kaslow, Dunn, & Smith, 2008). (Cited in McDaniel et al., 2014, p. 413)

> Competencies are distinctive elements necessary for competence; they correlate with performance and can be evaluated against agreed-upon standards (Kaslow, 2004). (Cited in McDaniel et al., 2014, p. 413)

While all of the outlined primary care competencies are important and can have implications for/interactions with each other, those in the professional cluster are particularly pertinent here and include a specific competency (3 C) for ethics in primary care. The first essential component of this competency (3 C.1) requires the psychologist to identify and address ethical issues unique to primary care "with particular attention to dual relationship matters, confidentiality, informed consent, boundary issues, team functioning, and business practices" (McDaniel et al., 2014, p. 418). The second essential component (3 C.2) provides that psychologists demonstrate knowledge of health care legal practices, including documentation, billing, and reimbursement, as well as state mandatory reporting requirements. Finally, essential component 3 C.3 emphasizes understanding of policies that regulate health care service delivery, such as those set by health care organizations themselves and standards promulgated by national accrediting bodies.

Framework for Resolving Ethical Dilemmas in IPC

Kanzler et al. (2013) suggest an eight-step process that can be used for ethical decision-making in primary care settings (see Figure 29.2). They emphasize that these steps are to be used as a guide and do not have to be applied in a linear fashion.

Considering one's context requires understanding the setting you work in, its norms, and your role in it. Consulting one's ethics code, as previously discussed, is paramount, particularly with respect to adhering to the laws of your licensing state. Determining risks and benefits involves reviewing possible options to better

Recommended Steps for Resolving Ethical Dilemmas in Integrated Primary Care
1. Consider your context
2. Consult your ethics code
3. Determine risks/benefits
4. Critically interpret/implement your code
5. Consider different perspectives
6. Identify others' expectations
7. Clarify your role
8. Discuss your concerns

Figure 29.2 *Recommended steps from Kanzler et al. (2013, p. 45)*

understand the implications of each. Critically interpreting and implementing one's ethics code demands a closer look at how the ethics code would be operationalized with respect to your specific ethical dilemma. Considering different perspectives in an IPC setting may include examining the ethics codes of other professions involved in or effected by the ethical decision being considered. Identifying others' expectations suggests establishing an explicit understanding of how others view the situation and any outcomes they may be seeking. Clarifying one's role with respect to the issue at hand is also critical and may involve securing informed consent from involved parties. Finally, discussing one's concerns is helpful in creating honest, productive dialogue and may even help parties anticipate and avoid possible pitfalls.

Case Examples of Ethical Dilemmas

The following are offered as examples of some commonly encountered ethical dilemmas in primary care.

Dilemmas Due to Differences in Culture

Perhaps the most frequent reason that behavioral health professionals (e.g., psychologists) do not succeed in primary care settings is their lack of necessary core competencies in the form of knowledge, skills, and attitudes specific to these settings and systems. McDaniel et al. (2014) emphasize that primary care is an entirely new practice environment for many psychologists. In fact, for those who elect to transition from traditional mental health treatment settings into primary medical care, they may be completely unaware of the differences that exist. One might assume that it is a matter of bringing an intact mental health/psychology practice into a clinic. This assumption could not be further from the truth.

Practicing psychologists and other mental health providers may be entirely unaware of the need for them to make dramatic shifts in how they practice in order to meet the needs of a primary care clinic structure and culture. The BHC must be keenly aware of the space configurations and use, pace of the clinic, clinical treatment outcome goals, referral procedures, documentation requirements, and billing structures (Brown Levey, Miller, & deGruy, 2012; Runyan, Fonseca, Meyer, Oordt,

& Talcott, 2003). The following case example illustrates the complexities and pitfalls of transitioning from the traditional practice of psychology into a primary care setting without adequate training and preparation.

Case Example: Dr. Penny

Dr. Penny has been practicing psychology in a mental health clinic for the majority of her 25-year career. During her time in the clinic, she was afforded the luxury of being able to see her clients for an unlimited number of psychotherapy visits.

The clients she saw often had rather complex and severe symptom presentations and few resources and were long-standing clients of the clinic. Dr. Penny was proud of the long-term relationships, which she believed fostered the success of her clients over time. After meeting a nurse practitioner at a recent social event, she became intrigued by the complexity of mental health presentations that were being managed solely through primary care. The nurse practitioner exclaimed, "Boy, do we ever need you on our clinic staff! We have an opening for a part-time BHC. You should apply!"

Dr. Penny thought about this recent conversation quite a bit. Ultimately, she decided to follow-up on the nurse practitioner's recommendation and apply for the part-time position. To her delight, Dr. Penny was offered the position and was welcomed into a team of experienced BHCs. On her first day, the behavioral health director shared that one of the biggest selling points of Dr. Penny's application was her expertise in conceptualizing and treating complex patients. One of her first referrals was a 32-year-old man who had been diagnosed with bipolar disorder by his previous physician. The consult request today was for a differential diagnosis to assist the provider in writing a medication prescription. Dr. Penny requested to see the "client" for three more extended appointments to conduct a thorough diagnostic assessment and begin psychotherapy sessions. Exasperated, the provider stressed that she really needed the consult today and that the patient would be unable to return to the clinic for at least three weeks.

The medical provider subsequently complained to the behavioral health director about the interaction with Dr. Penny, as well as several other aspects of Dr. Penny's practice. For one, Dr. Penny hung a "Do Not Disturb – In Session" sign on her office door when she was seeing patients, making her largely unavailable for most of the day. In addition, her recent chart notes in the electronic health record were quite long, with many very personal patient details.

The director was sympathetic regarding the adjustment to the difference between this type of service provision and the model of Dr. Penny's previous clinic. Nonetheless, he scheduled a meeting with Dr. Penny and gently shared the provider's feedback and reinforced the primary care model under which the clinic operates. While Dr. Penny understood this information in theory, she had difficulty with it in application and began to wonder if this model of care was for her.

At first glance, one might assume that the primary dilemma is a work mismatch. However, this case illustrates the complexities of entering into a new and different professional culture. Dr. Penny made an assumption that practicing as she had always practiced would be appropriate for her new primary care position. Her training and experience probably led her to operate within her practice at what would be considered Level III in our stepped-care model. In doing so, she risked isolating herself from her team and rapidly filling her schedule with longer appointments for assessment and traditional psychotherapy. Although this type of practice has great utility, it does not fit within a primary care context.

Primary care providers expect that the behavioral health provider will be readily accessible to them and will respond to their patients' needs. Thus, Dr. Penny may have failed both of her "customers" in this setting – the patient, who did not receive needed services, and the referring primary care medical provider (PCP), who did not receive a response to the referral request in a timely fashion. Additionally, an argument could be made that APA Ethics Standard 2.03 (Maintaining Competence) could be considered, as Dr. Penny does not appear to be providing appropriate service given the care model (i.e., unavailability much of the day, inappropriate notes).

In this situation, Dr. Penny had a responsibility to clarify her role in the new setting and to seek education and training about her position and the system within which she would be working. It may have been ideal for her to seek supervision and mentorship if it was not explicitly offered to her. Regardless, simply learning the day-to-day tasks of her position would not be adequate for Dr. Penny to be a competent BHC. Rather, she must understand her role in the context of primary care and be an active and contributing team player. To this end, she will need to achieve both primary care psychology competencies (McDaniel et al., 2014) and become acquainted with interprofessional competencies (Interprofessional Education Collaborative [IPEC], 2016). The latter have been endorsed by numerous health care professional organizations, including the APA, and underscore the importance of developing a common knowledge base and skill set to function optimally in team-based care.

Dr. Penny's situation also highlights another issue that can create discomfort for behavioral health providers in primary care: that of confidentiality. Confidentiality is held sacrosanct by psychology and our ethics code, as is its close relative, informed consent. There are frequent misunderstandings regarding what information can and should be shared among team members, especially due to the complexities of discipline-specific professional ethics codes and state and federal laws and regulations. This confusion can result in behavioral health providers being reluctant to share information with others or, as in Dr. Penny's case, providing others with unnecessarily detailed information (see 4.01 Maintaining Confidentiality, 4.05 Disclosures, and 4.06 Consultations). Several resources provide excellent guidance on confidentiality and informed consent issues in primary care (Hodgson et al., 2013; Hudgins et al., 2013; SAMHSA-HRSA Center for Integrated Studies, 2015). With careful planning and attention, it is our experience that IPC teams can manage confidentiality and informed consent in a legal and ethical manner that honors patients' rights and autonomy and facilitates whole-person care without perpetuating the myth and stigma of mind–body separation.

One common pitfall in behavioral health arises because we are, by nature, helpers. We strive to accommodate everyone's needs and desires whenever possible, including extensive and comprehensive patient and medical provider needs. Despite our best intentions, however, this may not be advisable when working within a primary care model. Ultimately, our desire to be helpful can actually hinder the good that can be accomplished by adhering to a population-based model of care. In some cases, the medical providers may want their patients to be treated in the clinic because they have an established trusting relationship with the BHC and, from a purely pragmatic standpoint, it is the most convenient for all parties. This can introduce a wide array of complex ethical and professional dilemmas. Some of these multiple dilemmas are illustrated by the case example of "Dr. Giselle."

Case Example: Dr. Giselle

Since early in her graduate training when she took a course in primary care psychology, Dr. Giselle wanted to make it her career. She was thrilled that she had been able to land a BHC position at a family medicine clinic where she completed her postdoctoral fellowship hours. She had always enjoyed a positive relationship with all of the clinic providers. She was conscious of making a shift to being an autonomous BHC – no longer in need of supervisory oversight. As part of the shift, she was responsible for making decisions that affected her status in the clinic. One of the most positive aspects of the clinic is the close relationship among the providers and staff. Dr. Giselle has, however, been very aware of different discipline-specific variability boundaries regarding providers treating friends and family members. On one occasion, the medical director (Dr. Q) of the clinic asked Dr. Giselle for a consult about her daughter's difficulty in school and recent attention deficit/hyperactivity disorder (ADHD) diagnosis. Dr. Q was concerned about her daughter's upcoming move to middle school. She was worried about her difficulty making friends and getting along with teachers. Dr. Q believes that a significant contributor to her daughter's difficulties is that she is quite bright and is bored and unchallenged in her current classes. Given the upcoming move to middle school, she believes that her daughter would be better off with regular therapy and advanced placement classes. She asked if Dr. Giselle would please conduct a full assessment battery for giftedness as well as ADHD/learning disability. Dr. Q would also like for Dr. Giselle to see her daughter for ongoing therapy to assist in her daughter's transition.

In a recent conversation with Dr. Q, Dr. Giselle offered to find an appropriate referral for the assessment and treatment. She conveyed to Dr. Q that this was not her area of expertise and, ethically, she was not comfortable with this arrangement. She suggested that someone who had expertise in children and these presenting problems would be much better suited to serve them. Dr. Q seemed to become frustrated and said, "I have seen you with kids. You're great with them and I'm sure that you will be wonderful. Besides, my daughter is comfortable here with you and in the clinic. I can't imagine finding the time to take her somewhere else. My schedule is too crazy and we trust you. I'm not sure I understand why you are so resistant to this. My daughter gets her primary medical care here – why are your services any different?"

In this case example, there are multiple "dilemma" areas to consider. In terms of context, the full ADHD/learning disability/advanced placement assessment and subsequent services requested by Dr. Q comprise a full assessment battery followed by intervention based on treatment recommendations. This comprehensive level of care is not appropriate for the primary care setting and model of care. This level of care would be considered a resource- and time-intensive Level III assessment and intervention, which should be referred out for specialty and/or comprehensive intervention.

Another consideration with respect to the APA Ethics Code was astutely pointed out by Dr. Giselle in her conversation with Dr. Q. Dr. Giselle refers to her level of expertise as it pertains to practicing within the boundaries of her competence (see Standard 2.01, Boundaries of Competence). Given that this is not an emergency situation, Dr. Giselle is attempting to resolve the ethical conflict appropriately (see Standard 1.03, Conflicts between Ethics and Organizational Demands). Dr. Giselle attempts to provide appropriate referral to specialty services that can provide the necessary level of expertise to best serve the needs of Dr. Q's daughter.

Determining the risks and benefits, considering different perspectives, and identifying others' expectations all lead to one of the most complex issues for Dr. Giselle – maintaining her relationship with Dr. Q. One of the major tenets of successful primary care integration is the development and maintenance of positive working relationships among health care team members (Gatchel & Oordt, 2003; Hunter et al., 2009). Based on the APA Ethics Code (2010), the solution to Dr. Giselle's dilemma is clear. She should be concerned with the potential for a multiple relationship (Standard 3.05). However, one commonly encountered dilemma is that other health care professionals' ethical codes and guidelines may not preclude them from entering into multiple relationships of various types. In fact, it is our experience that medical professionals consult each other regarding personal/family health issues on a fairly routine basis and, if their relationships with the clinic's behavioral health providers are positive ones, they have no qualms with doing the same with psychologists. Therefore, Dr. Q may not understand the dilemma presented by her request of Dr. Giselle and likely does not experience Dr. Giselle's role and being a service provider to her daughter as mutually exclusive.

Dr. Giselle finds herself in an ethical and a relationship dilemma. In this case, it may be that following the recommended procedure as outlined in the APA Code (2010) could rectify the situation. Standard 1.03, Conflicts between Ethics and Organizational Demands requires that when such conflicts exist, psychologists clarify the nature of the conflict, communicate their commitment to the APA Ethics Code, and take reasonable steps to resolve the conflict consistent with the general principles and ethical standards of the Code. Dr. Giselle may also find that once Dr. Q is made aware of how the APA Ethical Code restricts Dr. Giselle's ability to agree to provide such services, it will be helpful when similar situations arise in the future. The other part of Dr. Giselle's dilemma is how she can resolve the ethical conflict while preserving the positive working relationship. It behooves Dr. Giselle to discuss her concerns with Dr. Q. Dr. Giselle may find it helpful to acknowledge that it is flattering that Dr. Q would entrust her daughter's care to her. Although there are no guarantees, perhaps assisting in providing Dr. Q with qualified experts to provide these services will foster continued trust.

Dilemmas Related to Roles and Expertise in Interprofessional Team-Based Care

In primary care settings, patient care is frequently delivered by teams of professionals consisting of representatives of different health care disciplines. More often than not, the head of the team is the medical doctor or nurse practitioner who serves as the patient's PCP. The PCP determines the course of action for a patient's care in collaboration with other health care team members including the BHC. It is noteworthy that the ultimate responsibility for a patient is the PCP's. As experts in primary care psychology underscore, in most primary care settings, patients are not the behavioral consultant's patients; rather, they are the PCP's patients (Gatchel & Oordt, 2003; Hunter et al., 2009; Robinson & Reiter, 2016). The PCP, therefore, may determine if, and for what reason, behavioral health is consulted. When a patient is referred to behavioral health for a specific reason, it is imperative that the BHC addresses that referral reason. In some cases, it becomes apparent that the initial referral reason may not fully capture the presenting problem as assessed by the BHC. This may present a dilemma for the behavioral health provider. The following case example of Dr. Manuel illustrates this dilemma, along with several others.

> **Case Example: Dr. Manuel**
>
> Dr. Manuel, a psychologist, has been working in a small primary care clinic for four years. Overall, he enjoys his work immensely. From time to time, however, he receives referrals for reasons that, upon further assessment, he finds do not fit his conceptualization of the patient's problem. Last week, Dr. Manuel received a referral from a PCP requesting brief intervention with a 48-year-old woman for depression. When Dr. Manuel met with the patient, it became clear that one of the biggest challenges for the patient was sleep. The patient reported in the previous six-month period she been having difficulty with nighttime awakenings, early-morning awakenings, and excessive daytime sleepiness. The patient described awakening with excessive "pounding of my heart" and being "covered in sweat." This happened on an average of twice per night. She also noted that it was happening during the day. The "sweaty, heart pounding" episodes were accompanied by feelings of what the patient was describing as "panic" and racing thoughts about everything she worried about in her life.
>
> Dr. Manuel inquired more about anything else she had been noticing over the past six months. She mentioned that the only thing that was different was that she thought she might be going through menopause as her menstrual periods had changed and she wondered if what she was experiencing were actually hot flashes. When Dr. Manuel asked if she thought she was depressed, she said, "No. Although the form I filled out had a lot of the same experiences I'm having, I don't really feel depressed." She added, "I am tired of not feeling rested and of having these panicky feelings!" Dr. Manuel inquired about whether the patient had discussed her thoughts about the link between possible menopause and her panicky and sleep symptoms with her PCP and she said that it really had not occurred to her until this conversation.

In this case, the patient was referred for symptoms of depression. However, Dr. Manuel has identified two other plausible explanations for the symptoms that often resemble depression: sleep difficulties and symptoms related to hormonal changes inherent to menopausal status. He may not be comfortable assigning a depression diagnosis if another diagnosis might better account for the depressive symptoms endorsed by the patient on the standardized depression questionnaire. Moreover, the patient denies feeling "depressed."

The following ethical considerations emerge. Contextually, given that Dr. Manuel has been working in this small clinic for four years, it is likely that he has developed a positive relationship with the PCPs in the clinic. The PCP has an expectation that Dr. Manuel will respond to the referral and Dr. Manuel has a responsibility to address the reason for which this patient was referred. If his relationship with the patient's PCP is especially positive, the conversation about the patient's care may be an easy one. If Dr. Manuel and the PCP do not know each other well, it may be more challenging and he will need to be more sensitive in the manner in which he communicates his hypotheses about the basis of the patient's difficulties to the PCP, as the PCP's expectation may be that Dr. Manuel will support his/her diagnosis and treatment (see 1.03, Conflicts between Ethics and Organizational Demands). Either way, the issue of depressive symptoms is likely best addressed by the providers working together to help her achieve better sleep while discussing any concerns they might have and considering next steps should this focus not improve her discomfort.

In addition, although Dr. Manuel is demonstrating a desired knowledge competency in the biological underpinnings of health and diversity (i.e., women's health) across the lifespan, this is certainly a health-related conversation that the patient should have with her PCP. Dr. Manuel was correct in enquiring about whether that topic had been discussed with her PCP and asserting his role as a behavioral health provider who consults with the PCP. The next step may be for him to help the patient initiate the conversation with her PCP so that options for assessment of her menopausal status and subsequent medical and behavioral management can be discussed further; if the patient is uncomfortable doing so for whatever reason, Dr. Manuel would raise this issue directly with the PCP as discussed above. In another scenario, if Dr. Manuel were to engage in recommendations about how to *medically* manage her menopausal symptoms, he would clearly step outside the bounds of his own expertise. Such an action would constitute a violation of Standard 2.01, Boundaries of Competence. Thus, Dr. Manuel should consider his own ethics code and critically examine its implications with respect to his patient's treatment.

As part of working in a health care team, BHCs may also encounter situations in which they are explicitly requested to engage in an activity that they believe is outside their scope of practice or area of expertise. One common experience among most BHCs is being asked to provide psychotropic medication recommendations. If a PCP asks for specific input regarding medications for their patients, we typically regard this as sign that the PCP trusts our opinion and seeks our input. Regardless of the impetus, unless we reside in a state that allows psychologists to prescribe medications and have the appropriate training, making medication decisions would be outside of our level of competence and training. The following case example illustrates this very common scenario. In this case, it should be assumed that the psychologist does not have prescription privileges.

Case example: Dr. Findlay

Dr. Findlay ("Fin") received his doctorate in psychology and license to practice in his state approximately 20 years ago. Since that time, he has worked in community mental health and, later, his own private practice. In his practice, Fin provided some assessment and psychotherapy primarily to adults in a fee-for-service model that provided him with a financially and professionally comfortable position. However, upon learning about changes in the health care system, billing, and service delivery trends, he decided to pursue a new experience in primary care. He was welcomed as a BHC into a fast-paced primary care clinic with numerous health care providers. Fin was provided with an office that he shares occasionally with other team members. The standard behavioral health protocol of the primary care clinic adheres to a stepped-care model approach to care, which requires that he is able to offer Level I and II rapid assessment, differential diagnosis assistance, and consultation (typically 15–20 minutes). He also regularly needs to be prepared to consult with PCPs on an as-needed basis, be interruptible, and be responsive to team needs. In some cases, he is asked to provide on-the-fly clinical input on patients whom he never actually sees or speaks with – referred to as "curbside" consultations. With some consultations, the PCP asks about a particular diagnosis. Other consultations are inquiries about how best to proceed with a patient. Fin finds the pace of the clinic and the different ways of practicing exhilarating. He also enjoys the team camaraderie and finds his interactions to be more stimulating than traditional psychology practice. On this particular day, Fin was waiting in the central area of the clinic where various providers and medical assistants gather to review cases and enter chart notes.

One of the physicians stopped in to ask Fin for a "curbside" consult. "Hey, Fin, I have a patient who is presenting with depression. I'd refer her to see you but she doesn't have a lot of time today. She isn't suicidal or anything, but I want her to leave with a prescription for an antidepressant and check in with her in about a month. I've narrowed the choices down to two – which of these do you think would be the best to go with? I have used the first with a fair amount of success with patients, but the second one is newer. Any recommendations?"

Given that the PCPs and other clinic staff refer to Dr. Findlay as "Fin," we might regard that as evidence that he enjoys a positive working relationship with them. However, the request may indicate that the psychologist's role within the primary care setting, his training in psychotropic medications, and the limitations placed upon him by state law and the APA Ethics Code (2010) may need to be clarified. If Fin were to recommend a specific medication, he would be in violation of Standard 2.01 (Boundaries of Competence). Regardless of how congenial the relationships may be in a clinic, this could be construed as "practicing medicine without a license." In this case, it is likely that Fin understands the culture and his role within the team as one that is valued. First and foremost, it is advisable to restate to or remind the PCP (in a friendly way) of his role from the outset – primarily that he is not a prescribing professional. He might say something like, "Gosh, given that I'm not a prescribing professional, I can help with behavioral interventions, but when it comes to medica- tion, you would know better than I would!" In some cases, psychologists (who cannot prescribe medications) can be confused with psychiatrists (who can prescribe medications) and so such a reminder may be all that is required. In some cases, the PCP may simply want to walk through their own thought processes. In that case, a Socratic approach to help refine decision-making may be useful. If the PCP has it narrowed to two alternatives, Fin may inquire about what were the decision points regarding the patient and medication characteristics that led to selecting (or not selecting) the medication previously in order to explore risks and benefits of various choices. "What are the attributes of the newer medication that might make it a good choice for this particular patient?" Fin may also suggest consulting with available psychiatric providers who may be able to provide guidance. Regardless, adopting a solid strategy ahead of time for navigating such requests is recommended for every BHC.

The authors have had numerous personal experiences of, when reviewing a patient's medical record, they find that patients were prescribed a starting dose of a medication but never returned for follow-up to determine if the medication was well tolerated and could be increased. This can lead to patients believing that such medications are not effective when they have never truly received a therapeutic dose upon which to make an informed decision. In such cases, we have been inclined to inform our medical colleagues of the situation and ask if they would consider adjusting the dose in order for the patient to determine whether the medication is in fact helpful or not. Again, this relies on strong communication between medical and behavioral health providers and interprofessional team-based care.

Another medication-related issue that occurs with some regularity is adult patients presenting with histories of ADHD and requesting stimulant medications to manage it. Because many of these medications can be drugs of abuse and have street value, primary care physicians may be appropriately wary of prescribing them. Unfortunately, patients who rely on safety net clinics, such as federally qualified health centers, may have limited availability to psychiatric services and therefore cannot access these medications other than through primary care. This is an excellent point of intervention for psychologists. Using clinical interviews, retrospective and current symptom screening tools, and assessment of the patient's current functioning (Post & Kurlansik, 2012), psychologists can provide PCPs with valuable information that increases their comfort with making such medication decisions. Further, psychologists can offer cognitive behavioral health interventions that help manage ADHD.

Regardless, there will be circumstances when PCPs request guidance in which the psychologist is well trained in psychotropic medications and consulting psychiatric providers are unavailable. In those cases, psychologists may be able to provide more concrete input regarding psychotropic medications, as long as they adhere to ethical/legal considerations of their state licensure laws, the APA Ethics Code (2010), and the APA Practice Guidelines Regarding Psychologists' Involvement in Pharmacological Issues (APA, 2011).

Summary

In this chapter, we have attempted to introduce some important concepts and commonly encountered dilemmas for the BHC. We cannot adequately cover all of the information necessary for the reader to become well informed in this area; however, through the case examples and related text, we have attempted to illustrate some important "take-home" topics. First, behavioral health services in primary care are delivered very differently from in more traditional psychology or mental health settings; thus, it is incumbent on the behavioral health provider to learn both the primary care model and the competencies necessary to work within it. Second, the BHC typically functions as one member of an interprofessional team, of which the PCP is typically the "captain." Although some behavioral health providers may rightfully be wary of the professional hierarchy implicit in this arrangement, particularly given the many years they have undertaken to establish their own professional expertise and identities, it is our experience that they have a tremendous amount to offer in these settings and often become leaders in their own right because of the value they add to clinic functioning, health outcomes, and patient and provider satisfaction. Third, most dilemmas encountered by the BHC do not fall neatly into a category of traditionally focused ethical codes. In fact, as clinical practice continues to become more interprofessional in nature, it may be necessary to consider how the APA Ethics Code (2010) might better accommodate dilemmas that frequently occur in health care practice.

It is our hope that by reading and considering the main points and case examples in this chapter, the reader has developed an appreciation of the complexities of working in primary care. As we mentioned from the outset, the challenge of the dilemmas commonly encountered in primary care are part of what makes it exciting and rewarding to work in these settings. We readily acknowledge that working in primary care does not suit everyone's professional identity. If, however, you have become more interested in this area of practice, we encourage you to obtain some of the resources cited throughout this chapter. Additionally, the APA (www.APA.org) and the Society for Health Psychology (https://societyforhealthpsychology.org) have produced excellent training materials and resources for training in primary care psychology.

References

American Counseling Association (2014). ACA Code of Ethics. Retrieved from www .counseling.org/resources/aca-code-of-ethics.pdf

American Medical Association (2015). AMA's Code of Medical Ethics. Retrieved from www .ama-assn.org/ama/pub/physician-resources/medical-ethics/code-medical-ethics.page

American Psychological Association (2010). Ethical principles of psychologists and code of conduct: Including 2010 amendments. Retrieved from www.apa.org/ethics/code

American Psychological Association (2011). Practice Guidelines Regarding Psychologists' Involvement in Pharmacological Issues. *American Psychologist, 66*, 835–849.

Association of American Medical Colleges (1999). Contemporary issues in medicine – Medical informatics and population health: Report II of the Medical School Objectives Project. *Academic Medicine, 74*, 130–141.

Beacham, A. O., Van Sickle, K. S., Khatri, P., Ali, M., Reimer, D., Farber, E., & Kaslow, N. (2017). Meeting rapidly evolving workforce needs: Preparing psychologists for the Patient Centered Medical Home. *American Psychologist, 72*, 42–54.

Beacham, A. O. & Van Sickle, K. S. (2014). *Catching a speeding train: Creating a workforce pipeline for psychology in the patient-centered medical home. Panel 1 [Part 1]: Perspectives from the pipeline: What you need to know when.* Washington, DC: Annual Meeting of the American Psychological Association.

Beacham, A. O., Kinman, C., Harris, J. G., & Masters, K. S. (2012). The patient-centered medical home: Unprecedented workforce and leadership growth potential for professional psychology. *Professional Psychology Research and Practice, 43*, 17–23.

Blount, A. & Miller, B. F. (2009). Addressing the workforce crisis in integrated primary care. *Journal of Clinical Psychology in Medical Settings, 16*, 113–119.

Brown Levey, S. M., Miller, B. F., & deGruy, F. V. (2012). Behavioral health integration: An essential element of population-based healthcare redesign. *Translational Behavioral Medicine, 2*, 364–371.

Cubic, B. A. & Beacham, A. O. (2014). Creating educational and training opportunities for psychology trainees in medical settings: Training in primary care as a foundation. In C. L. Hunter, C. Hunter, & R. Kessler (Eds.), *Handbook of clinical health psychology in medical settings* (pp. 41–76). New York, NY: Springer Publishers.

Gatchel, R. J. & Oordt, M. S. (2003). *Clinical health psychology and primary care.* Washington, DC: American Psychological Association.

Health Service Psychology Education Collaborative (2013). Professional psychology in health care services: A blueprint for education and training. *American Psychologist, 68*, 411–426.

Hodgson, J., Mendenhall, T., & Lamson, A. (2013). Patient and provider relationships: Consent, confidentiality, and managing mistakes in integrated primary care settings. *Families, Systems & Health, 31*, 28–40.

Hudgins, C., Rose, S., Fifield, P. Y., & Arnault, S. (2013). Navigating the legal and ethical foundations of informed consent and confidentiality in integrated primary care. *Families, Systems & Health, 31*, 9–19.

Hunter, C. L., Goodie, J., Oordt, M., & Dobmeyer, A. (2009) *Integrated behavioral health in primary care: Step-by-step guidance for assessment and intervention.* Washington, DC: American Psychological Association.

Interprofessional Education Collaborative (2016). *Core competencies for interprofessional collaborative practice: 2016 update.* Washington, DC: Interprofessional Education Collaborative.

Kanzler, K. E., Goodie, J. L., Hunter, C. L., Glotfelter, M. A., & Bodart, J. J. (2013). From colleague to patient: Ethical challenges in integrated primary care. *Families, Systems, & Health, 31*, 41–48.

McDaniel, S., Grus, C., Cubic, B., et al. (2014) Competencies for psychology practice in primary care. *American Psychologist, 69*, 409–429.

Nash, J. A., Khatri, P., Cubic, B., & Baird, M. A. (2013). Essential competencies for psychologists in patient-centered medical homes. *Professional Psychology: Research and Practice, 44*, 331–342.

National Association of Social Workers (2008). Code of Ethics of the National Association of Social Workers. Retrieved from www.socialworkers.org/About/Ethics/Code-of-Ethics/Code-of-Ethics-English

National Committee for Quality Assurance (2016). Patient-centered medical home (PCMH) recognition. Retrieved from www.ncqa.org/programs/recognition/practices/patient-centered-medical-home-pcmh

Post, R. E. & Kurlansik, S. L. (2012). Diagnosis and management of attention-deficit/hyperactivity disorder in adults. *American Family Physician, 85*, 890–896.

Pruitt, S. D., Klapow, J. C., Epping-Jordan, J. E., & Dresselhaus, T. R. (1998). Moving behavioral medicine to the front line: A model for the integration of behavioral and medical sciences in primary care. *Professional Psychology: Research and Practice, 29*, 230–236.

Reiter, J. & Runyan, C. (2013). The ethics of complex relationships in primary care behavioral health. *Families, Systems, & Health, 31*, 20–27.

Robinson, P. & Reiter, J. (2016). *Behavioral consultation and primary care: A guide to integrating services* (2nd edn.). New York, NY: Springer Publishers.

Runyan, C. N., Fonseca, V. P., Meyer, J. G., Oordt, M. S., & Talcott, G. W. (2003). A novel approach for mental health disease management: The Air Force Medical Service's interdisciplinary model. *Disease Management, 6,* 179–188.

Runyan, C., Robinson, P., & Gould, D. A. (2013). Ethical issues facing providers in collaborative primary care settings: Do current guidelines suffice to guide the future of team-based primary care? *Families, Systems & Health, 31,* 1–8.

SAMHSA-HRSA Center for Integrated Health Studies (2015). Confidentiality. Retrieved from www.integration.samhsa.gov/operations-administration/confidentiality

Van Sickle, K. S. & Beacham, A. O. (2014). *Catching a speeding train: Creating a workforce pipeline for psychology in the patient-centered medical home. Panel 2 [Part 2]: Tips for trainers: Fostering knowledge, skills and opportunities in your setting.* Washington, DC: Annual Meeting of the American Psychological Association.

Williamson, A. A., Raglin Bignall, W. J., Swift, L. E., Hung, A. H., Power, T. J., Robins, P. M., & Mautone, J. A. (2017). Ethical and legal issues in integrated care settings: Case examples from pediatric primary care. *Clinical Practice in Pediatric Psychology, 5,* 196–208.

30 Therapy with Children and Adolescents in an Era of Social Media and Instant Electronic Communication

Jason Van Allen, Paige L. Seegan, Brittany Lancaster, and Devin Gunstream-Sisomphou

A topic of increasing interest among psychologists treating children and adolescents surrounds the use of social media (e.g., Facebook, Instagram, Twitter, and Snapchat) and instant electronic communication. As the use of cell phones and social media expands, youths are learning at increasingly younger ages how to utilize related technology. In 2006, 55 percent of adolescents in the United States who utilized the Internet also reported using at least one form of social media. In 2015, this number increased to 76 percent, indicating an increasing trend in the number of youths using social media sites (Lenhart, 2015; Lenhart, Purcell, Smith, & Zickuhr, 2010). In addition to the rising rates of social media use, Lenhart (2015) found that 88 percent of adolescents (aged 13–17) have access to a cell phone, making social media easily accessible. Moreover, 91 percent of adolescents (aged 13–17) who own phones use text messaging at least occasionally, with a median of 30 text messages sent per day (Lenhart, 2015). These high rates of use are important to consider within professional settings that work closely with children and adolescents, as they indicate such use is an important feature in their lives.

In regard to psychology, youths are in constant communication with their peers and are often consumed with checking their social media pages, which can ultimately have important repercussions on a variety of psychosocial outcomes (e.g., self-esteem, depressive symptoms, peer relationship quality). Not only are the repercussions of technology utilization important for professionals who work with youths, it is particularly important for professions in which ethical dilemmas may arise. Specifically, a high rate of electronic communication and social media use among children and adolescents ensures that issues related to use will arise in the course of psychological treatments. Electronic communication and social media use can potentially be seen as an advantageous tool for therapists or as a significant detractor from the therapeutic process. While text messaging and social media could be valuable assets through which therapists could gain information, send reminders, and obtain immediate assessments, these outlets of communication also bring up ethical quandaries for therapists to consider.

A variety of studies have documented the potential ethical dilemmas relating to social media that may arise within the context of psychotherapy. For example, Van Allen and Roberts (2011) reviewed a variety of ways in which text-based communications can set the stage for ethical dilemmas. Moreover, McMinn, Bearse, Heyne, Smithberger, and Erb (2011) found that approximately 80 percent of psychologists agreed that providing services through a social media site would be unethical. Although the majority of psychologists sampled viewed social media use as unethical, between 35 and 45 percent of psychologists were uncertain if the following issues were ethical: allowing a client limited access to their social media profile; providing services through instant communication (either e-mail, instant messaging, or text messaging); and researching clients' social media pages. Thus, there is little consensus among psychology professionals regarding whether the use of social media and the Internet within a psychology setting should be embraced or rejected.

The American Psychological Association's (APA) Ethical Principles of Psychologists and Code of Conduct (2010) provide some guidance related to technology and psychological services, including Standards 3.10, 4.01, and 4.02, in addition to the Guidelines for the Practice of Telepsychology (2013). Nonetheless, many difficult issues and decisions related to technology present unique challenges that are not addressed by specific codes or guidelines, and new issues related to technology are being introduced at a rapid pace. Overall, the breadth and depth of issues related to technology can be overwhelming. Although some psychologists incorporate detailed policies regarding social media and instant electronic communication into their practice to safeguard against ethical dilemmas, the uncertainty psychologists express with regard to social media use and electronic forms of communication warrants further discussion among professionals, as well as the potential implementation of updated ethical guidelines.

The goal of this chapter will be to examine a variety of scenarios in which ethical issues may arise in regard to youths' electronic communication and social media usage. In addition, recommendations related to the implementation of new policies and education related to social media and Internet use with clients will be provided. Case examples will be used as a springboard to discuss ethical issues in various psychological settings that could arise, including issues related to text messaging, social media posts, blogging, and the clinician's policies regarding technology use in the course of therapy. Ethical concerns that arise in regard to social media and Internet use include violations of confidentiality, intrusions of privacy, multiple relationships, boundary concerns, and appropriateness of communication. In youth populations specifically, considerations regarding social media use and therapeutic relationships with parents will also be examined.

The Case of Social Media Policies and Group Therapy

Dr. Mitchell, a licensed psychologist, has chosen to use a specific social media policy with his clients and their families. In the policy, it is stated that sharing information regarding group therapy sessions on social media sites is prohibited and any evidence of this type of behavior will result in termination of therapy services for that client. Dr. Mitchell believes that by informing his clients about the limitations and potential violations to confidentiality, as well as consequences related to intentional violations, his clients' privacy will be better protected. Last week, Dr. Mitchell began an anger management skills therapy group for youths diagnosed with attention deficit/hyperactivity disorder (ADHD). The group specifically focuses on social skills development, as well as helping his clients build positive coping and problem-solving skills. Joey, a 13-year-old group member, often complains that he feels singled out as a "troublemaker" when issues arise in group sessions. Upset after one of the group sessions, Joey went on Twitter to complain about his group members. Although he did not use any identifying information, he did mention session content. The next day, another group member found the post and brought it to Dr. Mitchell's attention. According to the social media policy, Joey's services should be terminated. When researching referrals for the family, Dr. Mitchell realizes that the client's family cannot afford other community therapy providers.

What should Dr. Mitchell do? Should he terminate services with his client? Should he ignore his policy and make an exception to the rule? Notable ethical dilemmas presented in this case concern issues related to confidentiality, as well as an issue related to absence of referral sources within the context of termination of services. The example above illustrates the benefit of setting expectations prior to treatment and developing clear consent and assent processes; however, it also illustrates the potential problems that may arise from having strict guidelines related to social media and Internet use. As we will see in this case example, as well as in the examples that follow, issues of confidentiality are often complex.

In the era before social media and instant electronic communication, members attending therapy groups may have violated confidentiality expectations, but it would have been hard to compile evidence to suggest a violation had been made. Social media and its use by youths presents new issues related to violations of confidentiality, as there are now multiple forums in which violations can be directly seen by other group members, the treating clinician, and the general public. Psychologists may find it more difficult to maintain their professional and ethical duty to protect the confidentiality and general well-being of clients, especially in a time in which a common way to disclose thoughts and feelings is by making them publicly available online. This may be especially true in group settings, where issues of confidentiality are likely to arise simply due to the increased number of individuals in attendance. Within a group therapy setting, information is not just being revealed to the psychologist alone – it is also revealed to the other group members, with no guarantee that these members will maintain confidentiality. Moreover, while it is encouraged that therapists take precautions to protect their personal information and be aware of various privacy settings, etc., is it reasonable to expect that the same level of attention to social media privacy will be shared by clients, especially children and adolescents? Should there be specific consequences applicable to all clients who violate social media policies agreed upon prior to beginning treatment?

Psychologists are beginning to utilize social media policies as part of their informed consent process to communicate with clients about social media and Internet use within the context of psychological treatment. A notable benefit of having social media policies is that the psychologist is able to provide clear expectations for what will happen when clients enter into a therapeutic relationship. While there are potential benefits to having such a policy, caution should be placed on the content and potential ramifications of having detailed guidelines.

The ethical issue of confidentiality, specifically within the context of group therapy, is clearly illustrated by the case example above. There may not be a simple solution to the problems highlighted in this case example. Instead, focus should be placed on educating clients about confidentiality and how it can differ depending on whether clients are seen individually or in a group setting. For example, psychologists may be guilty of oversimplifying confidentiality statements, which may lead group members to believe that confidentiality within a group setting is guaranteed. In regard to this case example, Dr. Mitchell failed to thoroughly explain limits related to confidentiality to group members and their guardians prior to the start of treatment. Simply providing the policy to clients without discussion is not sufficient and could open the door to future ethical issues. Dr. Mitchell may have been able to avoid this ethical dilemma had he made explicit the limits to confidentiality and what constitutes grounds for termination of therapy services. To avoid similar ethical dilemmas, providers should discuss potential ethical issues related to group therapy services (e.g., limits to confidentiality, social media practices, multiple relationships inside and outside of therapy, etc.) prior to the start of treatment. Given that Dr. Mitchell failed to consider the potential ramifications of his social media policy, he is now faced with the choice of whether or not to continue providing services to Joey.

Although psychologists can ensure confidentiality between the therapist and client in individual services, they could not promise that other group members will maintain confidentiality even before the advent of electronic communication. Group members may expect complete confidentiality because they do not fully understand how confidentiality in group settings differs from confidentiality in individual therapy. Therefore, it is the responsibility of the psychologist to address such issues prior to the start of treatment. Specifically, Standards 3.10 and 10.03 of the APA Ethical Principles note that psychologists must provide education regarding confidentiality to clients before they decide to enter into group therapy. Moreover, psychologists are required to discuss with group members how confidentiality can be violated by other group members.

As per APA standards, group members should be informed that the group psychologist is legally mandated to break confidentiality in certain circumstances; however, additional limitations to confidentiality among group members should be discussed. Although APA standards include some discussion of confidentiality within the context of electronic transmission (and the APA's Guidelines for the Practice of Telepsychology [2013] provide additional information), there are no guidelines specific to violations of confidentiality via social media sites or to what clinicians should do to protect themselves and their clients. Therefore, psychologists should also rely on the general APA ethics principles (e.g., beneficence and non-maleficence) and standards, as well as their ethical decision-making skills, to solve potential ethical dilemmas.

Ethical decision-making processes should involve both the psychologists' values and the APA's ethical principles and code of conduct. The first step in the ethical decision-making process is to determine a course of action. Referring back to the case example, the psychologist may decide to follow his policy and terminate therapy services with Joey. It is important to also consider the emotional impact making such a decision will have on the treating psychologist. For example, Dr. Mitchell likely feels an obligation to provide much-needed services to Joey and his family. This sense of moral obligation in the context of following business policies would likely cause Dr. Mitchell to experience psychological and emotional distress. In addition to Dr. Mitchell feeling very conflicted, he may also feel pressured by group members to terminate Joey for breaking therapy rules. It is important for psychologists to consider all potential outcomes and reach out to colleagues for emotional support when handling such cases. Moreover, to avoid overreliance on subjective judgment, psychologists should seek out professional consultation with colleagues regarding their decision-making processes.

Once a course of action has been decided, the psychologist must reference ethical principles and standards to ensure there is support for their decision. Outlined in the general principles of the APA's Code and Standard 3.04 (APA, 2010), it is the ethical duty of the psychologist to minimize harm to their client. In the case of Joey, would discontinuing therapeutic services due to a violation of policy be considered a form of potential harm, especially when the clinician has no viable referral sources for the client? On the other hand, Joey and his family were aware of the potential consequences of violating the social media policy. Should an exception be made to the social media policy? In the case of Joey, the psychologist may not have the ability to strictly enforce his social media policy guidelines, as it appears Joey's family are not located in a community with other low-cost mental health resources. Therefore, Dr. Mitchell is setting himself up for future challenges with regard to ethical decision-making unless he revises his policy to reflect the needs of individual clients. In addition, promising this level of confidentiality for group therapy members is often unrealistic; therefore, making strict guidelines may be inappropriate and will likely open the door to additional ethical issues in the future.

Finally, it is important to consider the age of the client. When creating treatment policies, it is necessary for providers to create policies that are written in age-appropriate language. Given that Joey is 13 years old, it is likely that he understood the instruction to protect his group members' privacy; however, it is unlikely that he fully understood the ramifications of his actions. Prior to treatment, the therapist should provide each client and guardian(s) with informed consent details that explicitly state the potential ramifications of violating treatment policies. The therapist should also discuss the informed consent and assent forms with the client and guardian(s) to preemptively answer any questions regarding information that could be unclear to youths varying in age (e.g., issues related to breaking confidentiality).

Recommendations

When constructing a social media and/or Internet policy for clinical practice and research, many recommendations may be appropriate and beneficial. Clinical and counseling psychology training programs, as well as licensed practicing clinicians, should decide whether policies should be included within the context of informed consent. If included, social media policies should be explained to the client(s) prior to the start of treatment. By explaining such policies at the beginning of treatment, psychologists gain the opportunity to set expectations regarding social media and Internet use prior to treatment and can educate clients on limitations to confidentiality, specifically with regard to social media and Internet use. As it relates to this case, the social media policy adopted by each psychologist should also be discussed with the caregivers of each child and adolescent client, particularly as it may influence a parent's consent to their child's treatment. This will ensure that the parents are aware of the policy, the potential consequences of their child violating the policy, and ways in which they might also violate the social media policy themselves. The child's age should also be taken into account when implementing a social media policy, especially if it is part of the assent process for them. Younger children may have a harder time understanding the policy and its consequences or the reasons for the policy, and therapists may need to ensure that the client is educated enough to make an informed decision about their own assent as outlined in Ethical Standard 3.10.

In addition, psychologists should provide some education regarding privacy settings for online communications in order to encourage clients to become active in protecting their own confidentiality. Even if a psychologist does not have extensive personal experience with social media and other online communication media, it is important for the psychologist to be familiar with these topics, because many of their youth clients may consider them to be a significant part of their lives. Moreover, psychologists should help clients understand that interactions via text-based or Internet communications can be included in a client's medical record.

Kolmes (2010a) has developed a social media policy that she has made available for adoption and editing to other professionals. Her policy outlines what clients can expect from electronic communications with their therapist, which she believes helps clients understand boundaries and limitations with regard to receiving electronic responses and services from their psychologist. For example, social media policies may include information related to the therapist's expectations regarding what information is safe to share online, how to protect oneself from potential harm when sharing information on social media forums, and text-based communication between the therapist and client. For specific examples and recommendations, psychologists are encouraged to visit Dr. Kolmes' online blog (http://drkkolmes.com/clinician-articles), where she addresses various issues and challenges associated with Internet blogs and social networking profiles within the context of psychotherapy.

Providing a consent document that details expectations among group members and the potential pitfalls of using social media forums to talk about therapeutic experiences may be helpful in educating individuals that the use of social media compromises not only the client's individual confidentiality, but also the confidentiality of the other group members. If a psychologist does not have a social media policy in place, it is recommended that the psychologist talks with the group members, both individually and together, about the importance of protecting member confidentiality, as well as educates members on what is considered to be "identifying information." All of the aforementioned information is likely to help minimize confusion, but how and when should this information be disseminated to group members?

Psychologists should provide informed consent about confidentiality not just at the beginning of treatment, but throughout. This allows for the discussion of confidentiality and its limits to be an ongoing process. Keeping confidentiality issues at the forefront may decrease the likelihood of breaches of confidentiality among group members. By continuing to educate group members on the potential limitations of confidentiality and social media within a group setting, the psychologist is able to put into practice the general ethical principles upon which psychological services should be based.

In general, we recommend that psychologists view their social media policies as live documents that can be changed over time; however, clinicians should be prepared to make difficult ethical decisions depending on how strict they make their policies. In the case of Joey, Dr. Mitchell should consider modifying his social media policy, or at the very least adding that the policy is subject to change. Modifications to his policy are necessary, as he clearly works in an environment where affordable services may be limited for families, thus increasing the probability of a similar event happening again in the future. As the APA Code requires, Dr. Mitchell should also explain the limits to confidentiality again to Joey, his parents, and the group therapy members and their families. In an effort to minimize harm to Joey and his parents, Dr. Mitchell would be encouraged to continue to provide Joey and his family therapeutic services. Dr. Mitchell should also discuss what happened in session with the group members to cause minimal harm to the group members and to provide an explanation of limitations to the social media policy. Since Joey did not disclose any identifying information about fellow group members, Dr. Mitchell should try to help the group members understand the limitations to group therapy, especially in the context of social media. Dr. Mitchell should encourage Joey, as well as his fellow group members, to bring their grievances into therapy sessions instead of the Internet. If the psychologist remains uncertain of how to proceed or if unforeseen problems arise, appropriate consultation with colleagues or even the APA Ethics Committee is encouraged.

The Case of the Blog

Amelia is a third-year clinical psychology doctoral student who currently sees clients in her university's psychology clinic. Her clinical interests include eating disorders and addiction problems related to adolescent mental health. Three weeks ago, Amelia began seeing a new adolescent client, a 14-year-old named Josie. Prior to beginning treatment, Amelia discussed limitations to confidentiality with Josie and her parents as well as Amelia's preference for keeping general session information confidential between Josie and Amelia. Josie's parents agreed to keep sessions confidential unless Josie disclosed any risk-related behaviors. Throughout the intake process, Amelia learned that Josie struggles with problems related to her body image and eating, as well as her family environment. At the end of the fourth session, Josie's parents asked to speak privately with Amelia and Amelia agreed to the conversation without telling Josie about it in advance. During the meeting, Josie's parents disclosed to Amelia that Josie posts on a private blog about her battles with food and anxiety, as well as her experiences in therapy. Josie's parents have told Amelia that they monitor the blog and proceeded to give Amelia information so that she could access the blog. Amelia believes that Josie is unaware that her parents monitor her blog. Although Amelia acknowledges that the blog may provide additional information that could be helpful to future treatment plans, she is also aware of the trust issues surrounding Josie and her parents, as well as how looking at Josie's blog could impair the way the therapist responds to Josie in future sessions. Amelia is now faced with the dilemma of whether or not she should look at the blog and whether or not she should inform Josie that her parents monitor the blog.

Should the therapist read the blog? How should the therapist respond to the parents? Should the therapist tell the client what the client's parents are doing? This case illustrates not only the potential difficulties that can arise when working with youths and their families, but also problems related to the way in which youths may disclose too much personal information via public social media forums.

As previously mentioned, psychologists are encouraged to choose a course of action when faced with a difficult decision. In this case, one potential approach is for the therapist to tell the parents that she will not look at Josie's blog without direct permission from Josie. By not accessing the client's information without the client's permission, the therapist is able to retain rapport, as well as the client's trust. On the other hand, by not accessing the information, the therapist may be missing out on information on the blog that may be particularly helpful in forming a more cohesive case conceptualization that may initiate a more effective treatment plan. To assess which approach is best, the therapist should take into consideration how knowing private information about the client may impact the therapeutic relationship and dialogue with the client.

In this case, Amelia may be thinking about how knowing this information may impact the questions she asks Josie in session. For example, she may not feel comfortable asking questions directly related to blog content; therefore, Amelia may ignore important topics out of fear that Josie may figure out the origin of Amelia's questions. Amelia may also simply be tempted to read the blog to find out how Josie views therapy sessions. Moreover, knowing the information Josie puts on her blog may help Amelia gain a better understanding of what Josie finds helpful in therapy. In terms of case conceptualization, Amelia may also think that reading the blog will give her richer information to figure out what is driving Josie's anxiety and food-related issues. While Amelia's thought process may help her weigh the pros and cons of reading the blog, the following questions still remain: should Amelia have read the blog? How should Amelia respond to the parents? Should Amelia tell Josie what her parents are doing?

In cases such as this, psychologists should revisit the basic principles upon which they should build their professional work. That is, therapists should ensure that their actions minimize harm and are honest, fair, and respecting of clients' rights. By informing the client that their parents monitor their blog, the therapist may be causing the client additional harm, as this event may trigger the deletion of the blog, thus removing that client's main form of coping. As noted by Farber, Shafron, Hamadani, Wald, and Nitzburg (2012), communicating through social media forums may provide interpersonal distance as well as perceived anonymity, which in turn may promote a sense of safety. This sense of safety may then facilitate the quantity and quality of interpersonal disclosures. However, it is important to note that youth clients may overestimate the degree of anonymity provided in these media, and psychologists should ensure that their clients are aware of the limits of privacy in these contexts.

The additional problem of whether or not the therapist should tell the client that his/her parents monitor their blog still exists. In one scenario, the therapist may encourage the parents to tell their child that they have been monitoring the blog. While this may be a solution, is it the therapist's right to tell the parents how to proceed? By telling the parents to behave in a specific manner, the therapist may run the risk of offending the client's parents and hurting an important therapeutic relationship. Another potential scenario could be that the therapist informs the parents that she does not want to know any information and allows the parents to decide whether or not they wish to continue monitoring the blog. While ignoring the actions of the parents may seem like a solution, if the information about the parents' monitoring behaviors was ever revealed to the client, it would likely exacerbate any difficulties with trust that the client has with her parents and may bring about new conflict between the client and therapist. Another option would be to tell the client about the monitoring, as being truthful and transparent could be a way to maintain the integrity of the therapeutic services being provided. However, disclosing information to the client that the parents shared with the therapist may damage the relationship between the parents and the therapist. Maintaining a positive relationship with both the client and their parents is important as therapy relationships contribute to client success in treatment.

In this case, the therapist could have avoided these complications by being more explicit about how information from parents should be shared with the therapist. If the therapist had made it clear that all information should be shared with the client present and that it should be made clear to the client that the parents would like to speak with the therapist about an important issue, then discussions about the blog content could have occurred in a way that would minimize damage to the therapist/client relationship. Nonetheless, therapists often feel pressured to give parents the audience that they desire, especially new therapists working in a training environment.

Recommendations

When entering into multiple therapeutic relationships, psychologists are required to discuss the types of limits to confidentiality that can arise when treating minors (Standard 4.02, APA, 2010). Given that parents have a legal right to information regarding the treatment of their child, it is often the therapist who encourages parents to allow therapy to be a private experience for their child. Making session content private can help child and adolescent clients disclose more personal details related to their presenting problems. Limits relating to risk and potential harm must be disclosed, but what happens if a client is engaging in risky online behavior? Should parents be notified? To help safeguard the client/therapist relationship, children and adolescents must be informed of the information that the therapist is legally obligated to share with parents, and this should be extended into information found via social media. Similar to what is noted earlier in this chapter, educating young clients on the potential pitfalls of sharing intimate details online may prevent clients from entering into potentially harmful situations.

In the case of the blog example, it is recommended that the therapist educates the parents on the potential ramifications of their behavior and encourages the parents to talk to their child about the blog. By sharing intimate details online, the client is placed at increased risk for negative outcomes. For example, the client's public blog about personal information may place them at increased risk for being cyberbullied or bullied at school. Psychologists can help build clients' awareness of just how public their blogs and other social networking activities can be and the possible dangers that may accompany her involvement in social media. In fact, given the prevalence of frequent social media use among youths today, psychologists should consider inquiring about their clients' social media use in a similar fashion to their inquiries about social interactions/communications in general. It is important for psychologists to realize that there may be discrepancies between the quality and impact of web-based social behavior compared to face-to-face interactions.

As previously mentioned in this case, text-based electronic forms of communication (e.g., blogging, text messaging, Facebook messaging, etc.) may be used as a way to help clients cope with their problems. It is important for psychologists to consider the strengths and weaknesses of conducting psychotherapy services via social media and text-based communication strategies. While these forms of communication may increase anonymity and decrease feelings of stigma, they may also help to enable clients' avoidance behaviors. Overall, the psychologist should work together with the client and the parents to find a compromise that maintains the client's confidentiality and safety while maintaining treatment progress and positive rapport with both the client and their parents.

Given that the therapist is a graduate student, the ethical responsibilities of supervisors in relation to this situation must be discussed. In this specific case, as a supervisee, Amelia should consult with her supervisor regarding a future course of action and supervisors need to actively monitor the work of trainees. Supervisors must be able to help supervisees understand the potential ramifications of their decisions, as well as the ethical responsibilities of the therapist-in-training.

In training settings, it is imperative that supervisors are involved in difficult decision-making processes with their supervisees. It is also important that the parents are clearly informed (as part of the informed consent process) of the supervisory nature of the clinic setting, consistent with Standard 10.01c, and that the supervisee informs supervisors of issues that arise during the course of treatment. In this specific situation, Amelia would be encouraged to seek out additional supervision with her supervisor as needed to ensure that Amelia is taking the best course of action when dealing with her client, as well as the client's parents.

The Case of the Professional Facebook Page

Dr. Sanchez is not opposed to using self-disclosure in therapy when she feels it will enrich the client's experience and provide the client with a different perspective. Recently, Dr. Sanchez began treating a female adolescent, Stacey, and found that she can relate to Stacey's struggles with anxiety and public speaking. During a session, Dr. Sanchez spoke about her past experiences related to public speaking and the anxiety she would experience. Dr. Sanchez believed that disclosing this small piece of information might help Stacey see treatment as a more gradual process. Stacey appreciated Dr. Sanchez sharing this information and responded well to the session. Later that day, Dr. Sanchez saw a post on her professional Facebook page. The post was from Stacey. She had written about how she had appreciated Dr. Sanchez's self-disclosure in session and was excited to continue working with her in therapy. Dr. Sanchez, uncomfortable with the content of the posting, is now confronted with the dilemma of whether or not she should delete the comment.

In this case, the therapist is faced with multiple ethical issues in regard to both confidentiality and advertisement of services. As previously mentioned, as the use of social media increases, it may be particularly important for clinicians to consider whether they want to adopt social media policies within their practice. The case above mentions a professional page that a therapist has set up. This page was set up for advertisement in the hopes that the psychologist may have an easier way of providing updates related to the practice or sharing information related to mental health with clients and the general community. Although this type of social media page may have potential benefits for a clinician and potential clients, it also brings up potential ethical issues. For example, does a client "liking" a professional Facebook page put them at risk for their confidentiality to be violated? Although it is a client's responsibility to protect their own privacy, it is the therapist's responsibility to "take reasonable precautions to protect confidential information" (Standard 4.01, APA, 2010). Therefore, education is encouraged so that the therapist can discuss with a client how "liking" this type of professional page could suggest to others that they have a professional relationship with the provider. On a similar note, many psychologists have personal social media pages in which a client may want to be their "friend" or "follow" them. This particular situation can be very confusing for providers.

The APA Code states that a psychologist should refrain "from entering into a multiple relationship if the multiple relationship could reasonably be expected to impair the psychologist's objectivity, competence or effectiveness in performing his or her functions as a psychologist, or otherwise risks exploitation or harm to the person with whom the professional relationship exists" (Standard 3.05, APA, 2010). If a psychologist were to allow a client to "friend" them on a social media page, this may begin to form what could be considered a separate, unprofessional relationship with the client. The clinician would now have access to pictures, posts, and comments made by the client that could potentially affect the course of therapy. Ethical issues involving risk may come up, as the therapist may view a post that reveals a client's suicidal ideation or see a photo of the client engaging in high-risk behavior. Should the therapist bring this up in session? In the case of suicidal ideation, should they take immediate action? As a standard, information gathered about or given to the client should be relevant and useful to the therapeutic process. With an abundance of information now available on the Internet, a considerable amount of information may be obtained about a client from third-party Internet sources, such as information gathered from a general web search or by viewing the client's social media pages. Section H.6 of the American Counseling Association Code (American Counseling Association, 2014) provides information relevant to this issue and discusses the need for psychologists to have separate personal and professional presences on the Internet.

Referring back to the case example, the therapist is ultimately faced with the decision of whether or not to delete the comment. Being faced with such a decision may cause the treating psychologist to experience a myriad of emotions. For example, Dr. Sanchez may feel happy that her self-disclosure in session helped empower her client; however, she may also feel vulnerable now that her personal information has been displayed on a public forum. Moreover, Dr. Sanchez may feel upset or frustrated that her client posted something so personal on the Internet. Finally, Dr. Sanchez may also be concerned that other clients may start to post about their sessions on the Facebook page, leading to additional ethical decision-making problems. Psychologists who wish to not be faced with such a situation are encouraged to set privacy settings that make it impossible for others to post on the web page. Given that a professional page is a representation of the therapist, the therapist is responsible for all posts made on the page. Facebook and many other social media pages have settings that can prevent others from posting on the page or allow the page maker to approve all posts before they are made public on the page. However, if these settings were not already in place, the therapist is still faced with the decision of whether or not to delete the comment. Ultimately, the therapist has to decide what they are comfortable with and do their best to protect the client. It would not be inappropriate to delete the post if the reason for deleting the post was to protect the client's confidentiality as well as general well-being. Either way, a discussion should take place between the psychologist and client. It is best to have a discussion with the client directly to avoid any future confusion regarding boundaries in therapy. If the matter is not discussed, the client may be confused and feel rejected if their comment is suddenly deleted. This may cause unintentional harm to the client, hurt rapport, and halt the client's progress in therapy. Thus, a conversation between the psychologist and client is necessary. If the therapist decided to leave the post on the wall, it may still be appropriate to discuss with the client that the post made the therapist feel uncomfortable, and it may be appropriate to encourage the client to discuss their feelings in session rather than sharing them online.

Recommendations

In situations such as this one, where psychologists are forced to make decisions regarding Facebook comments, likes, tweets, etc., we suggest the following recommendations. First, psychologists should become familiarized with the available privacy settings within various social networking sites. Privacy settings are important because they allow psychologists to review comments and group requests before they are made public. It is recommended that psychologists who choose to have professional pages are educated about and actively manage privacy settings as a way to safeguard against potential ethical issues that may arise.

Some psychologists, in addition to using privacy settings, block client profiles. As Kolmes (2009) notes, blocking client profiles could be considered an invasion of privacy and a threat to the client's confidentiality. Psychologists have to search for the client on Facebook in order to block their profile. By searching a client's name, the psychologist is sharing information with Facebook about the type of relationship shared between the psychologist and client. Sharing a client's information, even unintentionally through searching for them on Facebook, may be viewed as a violation of the client's privacy. Thus, sharing information about the client with others, including social networking sites, should be discussed directly with the client or stated clearly in treatment contracts (see Guidelines 3 and 4, APA, 2013).

In this case, Dr. Sanchez should talk with her client about the potential ramifications of sharing personal information, including information about the client or the therapist, on social media. Specifically, it may be beneficial for Dr. Sanchez to talk about her preferences with regard to her professional Facebook page. In addition, Dr. Sanchez should consider implementing a social media policy to avoid situations like this one in the future. If Dr. Sanchez chooses to delete the comment, she would be strongly encouraged to talk about deleting the comment with the client prior to deleting the comment to retain the therapeutic relationship and minimize harm to the client.

The Case of Text Messaging

Dr. Jones is a licensed clinical psychologist and currently sees child and adolescent clients in her private practice. Dr. Jones prefers to use text messaging as a way to schedule and cancel appointments with her clients and their parents. Recently, Dr. Jones obtained feedback from her clients indicating they prefer using electronic modes of communication to schedule and/or cancel therapy appointments. In Dr. Jones's consent form, she specifically states that text messages, if used, should not include content related to therapy sessions because this form of communication is not completely secure or confidential. Moreover, Dr. Jones clarifies these important issues related to text messaging during the consent and assent processes. Dr. Jones has never before encountered any problems using text messaging with her clients; however, in the last few days, she has been confronted with an adolescent client and her mother who continue to send text messages that include information related to specific sessions. Moreover, the messages are being sent to Dr. Jones during nonbusiness hours. Dr. Jones spoke with the client and her mother about the appropriate use of text messaging; however, their inappropriate behavior continues. Further complicating the situation, this client has experienced recent suicidal ideation, as well as nonsuicidal self-harm behaviors. Given that this is a high-risk client, Dr. Jones is reluctant to terminate services, but grows frustrated with the family's lack of respect for therapeutic boundaries.

While instant forms of communication can ease some of the administrative frustrations that coincide with running a private practice, they can also bring about additional problems. Problems such as those highlighted in the case example above highlight whether or not psychologists should utilize instant electronic communication methods within practice and research settings. Clients who are unable to utilize electronic methods of communication in appropriate ways may compromise their confidentiality. Referring back to the social media and Internet policies outlined in the first case example, it is clear that more work can be done in terms of outlining for clients the limitations to their confidentiality when using electronic forms of communication. On the other hand, instant forms of communication (e.g., text messaging, Facebook messaging, or e-mail) can be particularly useful, inexpensive, and convenient tools for clinicians. In fact, one study examining the content of text messages shared between mental health providers and youths suggested that the number of clients who use text messaging in inappropriate ways is minimal (Furber et al., 2011).

In the last decade, many clinicians have attempted to integrate text messages into treatment protocols for eating disorders, obesity, diabetes management, and other conditions (Bauer, de Niet, Timman, & Kordy, 2010; Bauer, Okon, Meermann, & Kordy, 2012; Brown, Lustria, & Rankins, 2007). The flexibility of text-based communication methods allows for clients and clinicians to have immediate as well as delayed conversations. In addition, text-based communication strategies may decrease the amount of stigma involved with talking to a therapist directly face to face, thus possibly improving client response rates and session attendance (Sude, 2013). The popularity of text-based communication strategies may further decrease stigma around communications with therapists as clients may feel like they are behaving in typical and accepted social practices (given the popularity of text-based communications), rather than feeling like they stand out in the crowd when they leave the room to call their therapist.

While it is the therapist's duty to protect the confidentiality of their clients, the client is also seen as a responsible party, provided that the client is made fully aware of the potential risks involved in agreeing to communicate electronically with their therapist. Clinicians must decide whether or not they are comfortable and competent with regard to using text-based forms of communication with clients. Will the therapist use a personal cell phone or e-mail address or will they use a separate business cell phone and e-mail address? Kolmes (2010b) recommends that clinicians consider using digitally signed and encrypted forms of e-mail to offer clients additional privacy and security. Van Allen and Roberts (2011) present multiple ethical issues that can arise through the use of text-based communication between psychologists and clients. For example, accidental breaches to confidentiality can take place via forwarding client information via text message or e-mail to the wrong person. Therefore, when using electronic forms of communication with clients, psychologists need to consider additional security measures that may help protect against these types of accidental errors (see Guideline 5, APA, 2013).

In reference to this case, the therapist is forced to make a difficult decision regarding continuation of services. On one side, the client is clearly in need of services given her current risk level; however, on the other hand, the client and her mother's behavior is clearly impacting the therapist's views of the client. Being frequently frustrated with this client may inadvertently – through countertransference – lead to poor treatment and ultimately poor treatment outcomes for the client. Although the therapist provided information related to appropriate text messaging on consent forms and during the consent process (consistent with Standard 3.10), there were some clear negative consequences related to this form of communication that the therapist should consider for future clients.

Recommendations

Psychologists who choose to communicate with clients via text-based communications are advised to invest in a cell phone specifically for work. Phone numbers and e-mail addresses that are used for work purposes only allow psychologists to inform clients about specific limitations and boundaries concerning out-of-session communications. Specifically, psychologists are encouraged to inform clients that they cannot expect an immediate answer to text messages and that it is not the psychologist's obligation to provide such immediate responses. Rather, the therapist will respond when available and when the content of the message is consistent with the initial agreement established between the therapist and the client. Psychologists should engage in a frank, direct conversation with the client when they violate the previously established agreement related to text messaging. Furthermore, a psychologist should warn the client that services may be terminated (and a referral made to other sources of treatment) if they continue to violate the policy/ agreement or that, at the very least, the therapist will stop responding to text messages from the client altogether.

While it seems some of these communications have already taken place between the therapist and clients in this case example, more could be done to protect therapeutic boundaries. The therapist in this example is encouraged to get a work cell phone that is turned on only during working hours. This information should be provided to the client and her mother and an agreement regarding appropriate cell phone usage should be signed by all parties and documented. Furthermore, the therapist should also address that they will no longer respond to messages sent to the original number and will only respond to communications via their work cell phone. Again, documentation that the clients have received this information is strongly encouraged. If this does not change the clients' behaviors, a discussion regarding termination of services should take place to advise the clients about the consequences of ignoring therapeutic boundaries. Moreover, the therapist could consider allowing text messaging only to certain clients, perhaps after establishing a good working relationship, so that the therapist could be more confident that the abovementioned difficulties would not occur.

As previously mentioned, clients should be educated on the risks associated with sharing personal information via e-mail or text messaging. Clients may not fully grasp that text-based communication to their therapist will be documented in their client file. They may also not understand the limitations to confidentiality and privacy that could arise if the therapist's phone is stolen or lost. Policies like the one created by Kolmes (2010b), which outline how psychologists plan to navigate text-based communications with clients, are encouraged, as well as continued discussions about how clients can work with their therapist to help maintain the client's privacy.

The Case of the Client Photos

Angela, a 16-year-old female, was admitted to the hospital after she texted photos to her friend, Christina, suggesting she was suicidal. Angela texted Christina pictures of pills she had planned to take and a photo of what appears to be Angela's hand filled with pills. After receiving the photos, Christina called 911 and directed medical personnel to Angela's house, where Angela was picked up and taken to the hospital. At the hospital, psychological services were consulted to evaluate Angela for suicide risk and possible inpatient treatment. The psychologist consulting on the case, Dr. Harris, was informed that Angela's toxicological screening was negative, that Angela denied the interaction with Christina, and that Angela denied experiencing suicidal ideation. Christina and her family visited the hospital because they were concerned about Angela and Christina and her parents showed Dr. Harris the pictures on Christina's phone. Dr. Harris conducted a risk assessment. Angela continued to deny any suicidal ideation and denied ever taking the pictures. Given that there was no medical indication of having attempted suicide and that Angela denied suicidal ideation, Dr. Harris was unable to recommend inpatient services and provided the family with mental health resources prior to Angela's discharge from the hospital. Angela complained that this experience was an invasion of her privacy.

This case example highlights issues pertaining to minimizing intrusions to privacy, informed consent, avoiding harm, and third-party requests for services. While Christina did the right thing by calling 911 and getting help for her friend, was it appropriate for Dr. Harris to view the photos after Angela told the hospital staff that she had never sent the photos? Moreover, Angela denied having any suicidal ideation, yet the psychologist still viewed the photos on Christina's phone. Was this an invasion of privacy? Was it a violation of APA standards, guidelines, or principles? In addition, Angela's parents are likely concerned about this behavior and about the photos that were sent. They may be upset that Angela is not going to receive more intensive services at the hospital. How should Dr. Harris include the parents in decision-making?

As mentioned throughout this chapter, psychologists are expected to protect client information and minimize potential harm (e.g., Standards 3.04 and 4.01). Psychologists seeing clients on a weekly outclient basis are likely to have strong rapport and better understanding of their clients. Psychologists working in medical settings may not have the opportunity to build such rapport with clients and instead are often assessing and treating clients immediately after meeting them for the first time. In this case, it would be difficult for Dr. Harris to know if Angela was truly not experiencing any suicidal ideation. Making matters more complicated, Dr. Harris did look at Christina's phone and saw the pictures that Angela had supposedly sent. Although Dr. Harris may have substantial proof that Angela was engaging in risky behavior, there was no way to tell if her behaviors were true representations of actual risk versus attention-seeking behavior or a bizarre joke. Psychologists are encouraged to prepare themselves for situations (i.e., to develop sufficient competence) involving social media and instant electronic communications (APA Telepsychology Guideline #2). Given the triage nature of services provided in a hospital setting, it may not make sense for psychologists to have a social media policy delivered to all entering patients on admission. Of course, if the psychologist is to begin outpatient services with the client, a policy should be implemented; however, how should psychologists navigate social media issues with one-time consultation/liaison intervention services?

In the above scenario, Dr. Harris's actions can conceivably be justified both ethically and clinically. Given that Angela denied sending any pictures at all, how would looking at Christina's phone be an invasion of Angela's privacy? Dr. Harris did not call 911; therefore, Dr. Harris was doing her job by conducting a risk assessment. While it may not be an invasion of privacy, Dr. Harris clearly saw the photos and was faced with the ethical dilemma of whether the adolescent was actually suicidal. It is recommended that the psychologist attempts to build rapport and assess fully for potential risk. Psychologists in similar scenarios should take time to consider what to do with the client. Not taking enough time may lead to discharging a truly distressed adolescent; however, if the client continues to deny suicidal ideation, it would have been unethical to push Angela into inpatient services, as that would likely cause additional harm. In addition, Angela's parents may disagree with Dr. Harris's evaluation, particularly if they believe there is evidence of Angela's suicidality or if they believe that Angela is not being completely honest about her potential risk. It is important to consider the parents' opinions and their opinions on the accuracy of Angela's report.

Recommendations

Psychologists working in medical settings are required to adhere to psychological as well medical ethical standards. Does the psychologist have a duty to tell the parents about this? If similar situations like the case above arise, psychologists should consider a direct and honest discussion about pictures with the client. In reference to this case, the psychologist could inform the client that the friend showed them the picture and could follow up with the client by asking them about the pictures in light of their denial of suicidal ideation. If done sensitively, this may elicit more information from the client and more honesty.

Another key component in this case is the parents. As mentioned in the case of the blog, it is important for psychologists to maintain positive relationships with not only the client, but also the client's parent(s). In the case of the blog, the issue surrounded the parents providing information to the psychologist, whereas in this case, the psychologist is providing information to the parents. Consistent with Standard 3.10b, the psychologist must ensure that informed consent and assent are obtained and they should ensure that the parents and client understand how information can be shared with the therapist (and under what circumstances the psychologist must consider limits to confidentiality). If the parent is informed that their child may be suicidal, the psychologist should take additional time to help explain the situation to the parents. The psychologist would be expected to relay necessary information to the parents while simultaneously encouraging the client to feel safe and protected. Regardless of how the parents react, the psychologist should work with each family member to construct a plan for addressing the client's potential needs following hospital discharge. The psychologist may not have the grounds to order inpatient treatment for the client; however, it is their ethical and professional duty to provide resources to the family in hopes that the family will be able to acquire appropriate treatment for the child or adolescent.

Discussion

This chapter has offered information related to emerging and complex issues in the context of providing therapy to children and adolescents in an era of extensive social media use and instant electronic communication. The case examples presented represent common ethical challenges that we have experienced in this context and are issues that we believe will continue to challenge mental health professionals in the coming years. More specifically, ethical challenges related to multiple relationships, confidentiality and privacy, beneficence and nonmaleficence, boundaries, and therapeutic effectiveness were discussed. In addition, we have made some general recommendations for addressing such ethical challenges, but we acknowledge that these recommendations cannot be comprehensive or sufficient for the specific, individual cases that arise for other mental health professionals. Thus, our recommendations should be considered basic guidelines for common issues involved in cases within this context, but other complexities and challenges may require a different decision-making process or additional consultation with colleagues.

Of particular importance to this topic is the difficult challenge associated with striking a balance between the strengths and weaknesses of social media and instant communication. For example, inherent to this context are the intergenerational conflicts that often arise in systematic social change; namely, younger generations are much quicker than older generations to adopt technological advances, including applications of such advances as primary forms of social communication. These generational differences can create conflict, as the older generation's aversion and avoidance (often justified as an attempt to limit risk) are at odds with the perceived benefits of these changes in communication in the minds of the younger generation. Established psychologists from earlier generations should consider whether the benefits of social media and instant electronic communication could outweigh the potential risks in certain circumstances. In fact, these benefits could be realized by both the therapist and the client, and the therapist is encouraged to consider that the benefits to the client may be more important than the potential risks to the therapist. An evaluation of cost/benefit should not be considered for the client and/or therapist alone – it should be evaluated for all parties involved.

Therapists should also keep available research evidence in mind when designing practices and interventions that incorporate social media or instant electronic communication. For example, although the use of such media is likely to be very relevant to adolescents and young adults, there is also research indicating the potential negative outcomes that can be associated with an overreliance on these media. Thus, therapists who use social media or text messaging as their primary intervention media could be perpetuating a negative side effect even further. Therapists should seek to strike a balance between the conveniences of modern technology and the benefits of face-to-face therapy. For example, it may be the case that social media and instant electronic communication could help an adolescent feel more comfortable initiating therapy services and may help build rapport as a result, but solely relying on these media may enable avoidance in clients with anxiety or may not offer the initial behavioral activation of a face-to-face session that could be paramount to a client's recovery from depression.

On the other hand, it may be impractical – if not nearly impossible – for some clients to have face-to-face sessions with the therapist that can best treat their presenting concerns. Children and adolescents in rural areas of the country face considerable economic and logistical barriers to service provision. Therapy delivered via text messaging or web-based mechanisms may be much better solutions than what such children and adolescents have available to them locally. Nonetheless, these methods of intervention delivery limit the availability of nonverbal communication, as well as the progress (via momentum, behavioral activation, movement in stages of change, etc.) that can come from a client's efforts to attend face-to-face sessions. Although it does not solve all of the potential problems inherent in distance therapy, the use of videoconferencing (i.e., telemedicine or telemental health) may be preferred over therapy delivered via social media and/or instant electronic communication.

Admittedly, striking the right balance between technological adoption and traditional face-to-face services is daunting. At a minimum, therapists must be thoughtful about how they will use social media and instant electronic communication in their practice and how they will best address the challenges associated with therapy in this context. More specifically, therapists should establish specific policies related to social media and instant electronic communication and they may find that such policies prevent some ethical challenges in practice. For therapists who choose to develop specific policies, they must explain these policies to their child and adolescent clients and to the parents/caregivers. This is especially important for therapists who maintain an active presence in social media or who use text messaging and other instant messaging to communicate with clients. For therapists who do not communicate with clients using such media or who are not marketing themselves on social media, it is vital that they are aware of potential ethical issues that may still arise in their work with clients. For example, clients may describe frustrating interactions with others while using Facebook or may show their therapist text messages that are relevant to therapy. Being prepared for those situations can prevent future headaches and ensure the safety of clients. In general, educating clients on specific policies should be an ongoing process. That is, social media policies, client education, therapist education, and frank discussion surrounding the use of social media and the Internet should be addressed not just at the beginning of treatment or when a problem arises, but throughout the entire treatment process.

Despite the complexity of social media and instant electronic communication in the context of psychotherapy and clinical research, a number of benefits exist with these technologies and modes of communication and their adoption is ever growing. Therapists will need to be aware of issues pertaining to social media and electronic communication. It is not sufficient to consider these issues only after a problem surfaces; therapists should become familiar with these issues via continuing education and other trainings, so that they can develop competencies that will help them be prepared for ethical challenges before they occur and to more efficiently address those challenges in the moment. Although therapists may not be interested in using social media or other emerging forms of electronic communication in their own lives, they must be familiar with these topics if they are to work effectively with children and adolescents. Although psychologists cannot be expected to be experts in all aspects of social media or electronic communication, particularly given how fast things change and evolve in this area, they should continue educating themselves through conferences, workshops, and regional trainings and should consult with colleagues when difficulties arise. In a world with rapidly changing forms of communication, acknowledging the need for education and training is vital to our growth as competent and ethical therapists.

References

American Counseling Association (2014). *ACA Code of Ethics*. Alexandria, VA: American Counseling Association. Retrieved from www.counseling.org/resources/aca-code-of-ethics.pdf

American Psychological Association (2010). Ethical principles of psychologists and code of conduct. Retrieved from http://apa.org/ethics/code/index.aspx

American Psychological Association (2013). Guidelines for the practice of telepsychology. Retrieved from www.apa.org/practice/guidelines/telepsychology.aspx

Bauer, S., de Niet, J., Timman, R., & Kordy, H. (2010). Enhancement of care through self-monitoring and tailored feedback via text messaging and their use in the treatment of childhood overweight. *Patient Education and Counseling*, *79*, 315–319.

Bauer, S., Okon, E., Meermann, R., & Kordy, H. (2012). Technology-enhanced maintenance of treatment gains in eating disorders: Efficacy of an intervention delivered via text messaging. *Journal of Consulting and Clinical Psychology*, *80*, 700–706.

Brown, L. L., Lustria, M. L. A., & Rankins, J. (2007). A review of web-assisted interventions for diabetes management: Maximizing the potential for improving health outcomes. *Journal of Diabetes Science and Technology*, *1*, 892–902.

Farber, B. A., Shafron, G., Hamadani, J., Wald, E., & Nitzburg, G. (2012). Children, technology, problems, and preferences. *Journal of Clinical Psychology*, *68*, 1225–1229.

Furber, G. V., Crago, A. E., Meehan, K., et al. (2011). How adolescents use SMS (short message service) to micro-coordinate contact with youth mental health outreach services. *Journal of Adolescent Health*, *48*, 113–115.

Kolmes, K. (2009). Should mental health professionals block clients on Facebook? Retrieved from http://drkkolmes.com/2009/12/11/should-mental-health-professionals-block-clients-on-facebook

Kolmes, K. (2010a). My private social media policy. Retrieved from www.drkkolmes.com/docs/socmed.pdf

Kolmes, K. (2010b). Email tips for clinicians. Retrieved from http://drkkolmes.com/2010/04/28/email-tips-for-clinicians

Lenhart, A. (2015). Teens, social media & technology overview 2015. Retrieved from www.pewinternet.org/2015/04/09/teens-social-media-technology-2015

Lenhart, A., Purcell, K., Smith, A., & Zickuhr, K. (2010). Social media and young adults. Retrieved from www.pewinternet.org/2010/02/03/social-media-and-young-adults

McMinn, M. R., Bearse, J., Heyne, L. K., Smithberger, A., & Erb, A. L. (2011). Technology and independent practice: Survey findings and implications. *Professional Psychology: Research and Practice*, *42*, 176–184.

Sude, M. (2013). Text messaging and private practice: Ethical challenges and guidelines for developing personal best practices. *Journal of Mental Health Counseling*, *35*, 211–227.

Van Allen, J. & Roberts, M. C. (2011). Critical incidents in the marriage of psychology and technology: A discussion of potential ethical issues in practice, education, and policy. *Professional Psychology: Research and Practice*, *42*, 433–439.

31 Ethics and Ethical Decision-Making in Coaching

Four Case Scenarios

Sharon K. Anderson and Judy B. Smetana

Coaching as an activity to help another individual to develop and learn has its origins in the 1800s (Anderson, William, & Kramer, 2011). In the 1940s, businesses began to contract with individual consultants to improve the performance of individual employees, which is what we now call executive coaching (Anderson et al., 2011). By the mid-1990s, the coaching profession included different specializations such as executive coaching, life or personal coaching, career coaching, and leadership coaching (Anderson et al., 2011). In 1999, there were an estimated 2100 professional coaches (ICF, n.d.b). More recently, the number is estimated to be more than 47 000 professional coaches worldwide in practice, with cumulative annual revenue close to $2 billion (ICF, n.d.b).

According to the current literature, there are multiple definitions of the term "coaching" (Fillery-Travis & Passmore, 2011). Stober and Grant (2006) provide the following definition: ". . .a collaborative and egalitarian relationship between a coach, who is not necessarily a domain-specific specialist, and client, which involves a systematic process that focuses on collaborative goal setting to construct solutions and employ goal attainment process" (p. 2).

Note the clause that states the coach is not necessarily from a specific discipline or "a domain-specific specialist," which suggests that individuals with all different types and levels of training could call themselves coaches. This is, in and of itself, an ethical problem for the coaching profession (Sherman & Freas, 2004). This issue and related issues are the focuses of this chapter, in which case scenarios of individual and executive coaching illustrate decision-making processes.

Fundamental Questions, Ethical Standards, and Core Coaching Competencies

To frame our exploration and discussion of ethical issues and ethical decision-making in coaching, we present four fundamental questions: (a) Does the coach have a working knowledge or solid understanding of the evidence-based theories that support coaching? (b) Does the coach have a sound understanding of the ethical standards and can she competently demonstrate the core competencies as defined by associations such as the International Coach Federation (ICF)? (c) When an ethical dilemma or problem occurs, does the coach recognize there *is* an ethical issue and understand how to handle it in her role as the coach? (d) What framework might a coach use to guide her ethical choices and decision-making processes? We briefly discuss these questions before we move onto the four case scenarios.

Consider the first question, "Does the coach have a working knowledge or solid understanding of the evidence-based theories that support coaching?" Competent practice, a critical ethical foundation, begins with knowledge of the coaching literature. Competence is at the core of professional practice. Both the American Psychological Association (APA) and the American Counseling Association (ACA) ethical standards (ACA, 2014; APA, 2010) articulate the ethical importance of a psychologist or counselor knowing the boundaries of their professional competence. APA Standard 2.01, Boundaries of Competence, encourages psychologists to provide services (i.e., coaching) only if they have obtained the training or supervision to do so. There are similar standards for counselors to note in the ACA ethics code: Standards C.2.a and b. The general public and organizations that seek the services of coaches might assume that some minimum standards describe competence. The professional literature, professional coaching associations, and training institutions, however, suggest that the field has grappled with clarifying and defining what it means to be a competent coach. Sherman and Freas (2004) compared choosing an executive coach to the "Wild West of yesteryear," stating that "this frontier is chaotic, largely unexplored, and fraught with risk, yet immensely promising" (p. 1). The APA and ACA codes address this assumption to some extent by stating that education, training, and supervision are necessary when entering into a new practice area.

Several resources provide a good foundation for a working knowledge in coaching. *The handbook of knowledge-based coaching* (Wildflower & Brennan, 2011) presents a collection of theories coupled with coaching applications. The *Evidence based coaching handbook* (Stober & Grant, 2006) draws upon case examples to address a variety of coaching theories. *Coaching skills: A handbook* (Rogers, 2008) offers an introduction to and a discussion about the coaching profession.

The second question is, "Does the coach have a sound understanding of and commitment to the ethical standards and can she competently demonstrate the core competencies?" The ICF has an ethics code and a list of core competencies to support the profession of coaching (ICF, n.d.a). Wildflower and Brennan (in Cox, Bachkirova, & Clutterbuck, 2010) remind us that acting on these components is of utmost importance.

The four core ICF competencies that serve as the framework in a coaching relationship are:

(a) *Setting the foundation*. The coach strives to meet ethical guidelines and professional standards and the coaching contract is established.
(b) *Co-creating the relationship*. The coach establishes trust with the client and creates a safe, supportive environment by expressing moral virtues, ethical principles and maintaining the relationship boundaries.
(c) *Communicating effectively*. The coach communicates through active listening and powerful, thought-provoking questions, making sure the coaching agenda is what the client wants.

(d) *Facilitating learning environments.* Together, the coach and client design opportunities for ongoing learning and experimentation. This work is both cognitive and behavioral.

Coaching professionals who are psychologists, counselors, or other types of mental health professionals should use both the ICF ethics code and competencies in conjunction with their other professional ethics codes to guide them as they navigate ethical problems and dilemmas.

To answer the second question related to ethical codes and core competencies with a resounding "yes," the coach must have the foundation of knowledge previously discussed, together with other important elements and traits in place. Kitchener and Anderson (2011) have suggested that competence includes knowledge, skill (technical and clinical) to implement the knowledge, and ability, which is mental and behavioral. These three elements work together. Welfel (2016) has added diligence (giving priority to the client's needs and self-awareness) to knowledge and skill as a necessary component of competence. Anderson and Handelsman (2010) also have suggested two ethical virtues, humility and wisdom, as important traits of competence. Anderson (2015) draws the practitioner's attention to the importance of understanding oneself in the profession through developing a self-narrative as that of an ethical practitioner. This self-narrative can support the coach's general competence and self-management skills.

The third question is, "When an ethical dilemma or problem occurs, does the coach recognize there is an ethical issue and understand how to handle it?" Being able to identify that there is an ethical issue relates to ethical sensitivity. Rest (1984) suggested that ethical sensitivity is a capacity that enables a person to perceive a situation as having ethical dimensions and to identify how different courses of action might impact those involved.

Once the coach recognizes there is an ethical dilemma, the next step is the decision-making process. The fourth question is, "What framework might a coach use to guide her ethical choices and decision-making processes?" Passmore (2009) suggested that, as ethical decision-makers, coaches come to a decision on the continuum between two ethical positions: *deontological* and *consequential.* A deontological position is one in which a coach's behavior would be classified as either right or wrong and the right behavior would be to follow the rules, which is the coach's duty. A consequential position suggests that the right or ethical thing for a coach to do is to bring about the best outcome for the greatest number of people.

Passmore proposed that, in reality, the actions of coaches fall somewhere on a continuum between these two positions. This means that most coaches are "ethical pluralists, who hold to a few solid principles" (2009, p. 9), but they then consider the circumstances at hand and the motives of those involved as they decide what course of action to take. A concern comes to mind if, in fact, this is the case. One might say that this course of practice by coaches, in which circumstances and motivations influence outcomes, sounds like situational ethics. McDonald (2010) suggested that situational ethics describes a scenario in which the professional utterly disregards ethical standards when making decisions; the ethical perspective is one of, "If it works, it's OK … the end justifies the means" (p. 450). Obviously, this is not a position from which or the ethical lens through which a coach should work or operate. Although not foolproof, ethical decision-making models help to guard against such a position. Within the ACA Code of Ethics Purpose section, counselors are encouraged to recognize that "resolving ethical issues is a process" and that no one model is "always most effective." Choosing an appropriate model or process for the situation is imperative. The literature is overflowing with discussions of ethical decision-making models and processes and the factors that influence these processes (Anderson, Waggoner, & Moore, 2006; Duff & Passmore, 2010; Handelsman, Gottlieb, & Knapp, 2005; Kitchener & Anderson, 2011; Passmore, 2009; Rogerson, Gottlieb, Handelsman, Knapp, & Younggren, 2011). Below is a brief discussion of four models.

Ethical Choice-Making Process

Drawing upon Rest's four components of moral behavior, Anderson et al. (2006) created a model called the *ethical choice-making process*. The four components of Rest's model are: (a) ethical sensitivity; (b) formulation of an ethical plan; (c) ethical motivation and competing values; and (d) ethical follow-through. The choice-making model highlights the process as nonlinear and interactive (which fits with Rest's view of the components) through which new information can influence or impact one or more of the other components. The model also uses questions to help the professional access his thoughts, values, needs, motivations, and conflicts of interest, and also capture the client's input at appropriate times. The model pushes for perspective-taking by the professional.

ACTION Model

Duffy and Passmore (2010) developed a six-stage model (ACTION) from data collected in a focus group of experienced coaching psychologists. These stages include: (1) awareness; (2) classify; (3) time for reflection, support, and advice; (4) initiate; (5) option evaluation; and (6) novate. Although the stages are numbered chronologically, Duffy and Passmore advise that the conceptual model is meant to be nonlinear and offers iteration and flexibility.

SAD Formula

Day (2005) developed a model to build aspects of critical thinking into ethical reasoning. There are three stages: situation definition, analysis of the situation, and decision (Johnson, 2012, p. 206). The situation definition stage includes describing the facts, identifying ethical principles and ethical values, and stating the ethical issues or questions to be addressed. The analysis stage requires the ethical decision-maker – in our cases the coach – to weigh or assess competing ethical principles and values, consider external factors that impact the decision-making process, identify stakeholders and duties owed to them, and discuss the application of ethical theories such as utilitarian, categorical imperative, or justice that speak to ethical issues in the case. The final stage, decision, is where the decision-maker states their course of action to be taken.

Model for Ethical Decision-Making

Drawing upon the work of Kitchener (1984) and Kitchen and Anderson (2011), Welfel (2016) outlines a ten-step process. These steps include: develop ethical sensitivity; clarify facts, identify stakeholders, and consider the sociocultural context; identify the central ethical issues and possible courses of action; refer to ethical standards and relevant laws/regulations; review the ethics literature; apply ethical principles; consult with colleagues (including a supervisor); deliberate and decide; inform necessary individuals such as a supervisor and implement as well as document actions taken; and reflect on the above process and outcome.

As we move to the next section, we present four case scenarios. The cases include both ethical issues or problems and ethical dilemmas. An ethical issue or problem is when a situation arises that has ethical implications for the client, other stakeholders, or coach and the course of action is clear and supported by professional ethical codes and standards. For example, according to the ICF Code of Ethics, it is unethical for a coach to be romantically and sexually involved with a current client. When a coach oversteps that professional boundary, an ethical issue arises. An ethical dilemma describes the competing needs or demands that result when one is attempting to resolve an ethical problem. As examples, Kidder (1996) suggested that an ethical dilemma is a choice between two rights, while Kitchener (2000) defined an ethical dilemma as "a problem for which no choice seems completely satisfactory, since there are good but contradictory reasons to take conflicting and incompatible courses of action" (p. 2). The following cases address ethical issues and ethical dilemmas. We draw upon the models previously discussed as we work through each case.

Exploration of Ethical Issues through Case Scenarios

The first case appears to be a simple case of helping someone build their confidence to get back to work, but twists, turns, and surprises develop when the client reveals additional information and the coach's actions span two roles. The second case explores the areas of multicultural competence and differences, as well as contracting and confidentiality. The third case deals with similar issues to those in Case 2, but it goes into the dilemmas that arise when our personal biases come into play. The fourth case shows the complexities of entering different roles with a client and the potential conflicts that ensue. In working through these scenarios, we draw upon the discussion above and employ one or more ethical decision-making models.

The Case of What Role Am I In?

Part 1

Frank is a 53-year-old white male who has been on medical leave and wants to work on his self-confidence and ultimately get back to work. His work history is filled with multiple successes: he received a prestigious award for his creativity in work; he was successful at securing funding for special projects (which was no small feat); and several organizations sought him out to come work for them. About four months ago, he had what he called a "mild panic attack." Since then, he has experienced high anxiety as he anticipates the next attack. He is frustrated with himself and wants to "get his life together" and "and get to work again." A friend referred Frank to Susan, who practices as a life coach and psychologist. Susan identifies with and retains membership in both the APA and the ICF. The friend who referred Frank knew of Susan's work as a life coach from personal experience. Frank contacts Susan, and they agree to meet to assess their fit and a possible coaching relationship.

During the first visit, Susan takes time to address information about her training and her credentials as a coach and a psychologist. She discusses her approach in working with people. She and Frank discuss the focus of their work, the coaching process, the frequency of sessions, the nature and limits to confidentiality, and the roles, rights, and responsibilities of both parties. Frank appears engaged in the conversation. He identifies his goals: to be less anxious, to grow in his self-confidence, and to return to work. He is able to identify several strengths he has or did have before the panic attack. Susan probes further into the experience of the panic attack, wondering how Frank understands the term and whether or not it truly was a panic attack or something else. In addition, Susan asks questions in order to understand what "being less anxious" and "having greater self-confidence" would look like from Frank's view. Susan and Frank agree on the focus of the work. The two of them develop a coaching contract and decide to work together for the next four months. The contract includes the following aspects: (1) both Susan and Frank agree to be honest in how the coaching relationship is working; (2) Frank agrees to identify and discuss any interactions or experiences that hinder him accomplishing his goals; (3) Frank agrees to work on coaching assignments between sessions; (4) Frank agrees to pay the agreed-upon fee for service at the time of service; and (5) Susan agrees to help Frank identify hidden assets he can build on and to keep information confidential and private unless required by law.

Susan has done a good job of honoring several of the core competencies and aspects of Part 2 of the ICF Code of Ethics. For example, she honored Part 2, Sections 1 through 6 of the Code and also the ICF core competency of Setting the Foundation by (a) providing information to help Frank assess the match and (b) establishing a contract with Frank. Further, Susan (c) worked with Frank to co-create the working relationship, another core competency. In addition, Susan (d) clarified the responsibilities and rights of both Frank and herself, which are outlined in Part 3 of the ICF Code of Ethics, Sections 3 through 19. She also obtained what psychologists consider *informed consent*, which included addressing her training, her approach, limits to confidentiality, fees, and so on. In essence, she honored the following parts of the APA Ethics Code: Informed Consent (3.10), Maintaining Confidentiality (4.01), Limits of Confidentiality (4.02), and Fees and Financial Arrangements (6.04).

However, there is one ethical issue: since Susan is trained both as a psychologist and a life coach, does she need to speak to both of these professional roles? Has Susan clarified with Frank the distinction and the potential overlap, if she sees any, between these two roles when she is working with clients?

The roles and work of a life coach and psychologist can be overlapping; at the same time, there can be differences that have ethical implications for the focus of work with the client (Anderson, Williams, & Kramer, 2011; Sperry, 2004). Traditionally, psychologists have dealt with individuals in substantial emotional distress, many of whom have diagnosable mental illnesses. Most, though not all, of their training involves working with such clients. The focus for life coaches is on the client's strengths. In coaching, there is instruction and training, which means the coach is directive and the focus is forward-thinking.

In this case, Susan drew upon her training as a psychologist when she branched into the issue of psychopathology by asking for information about the panic attack and made an assessment about the information. Did she clarify with Frank that this might be what she does with clients because of her training as a psychologist? And if she did, is it an appropriate course of action to take depending on her role? Some literature would suggest that greater clarity is needed in this context for the client's benefit (McKelley & Rochlen, 2007; Peltier, 2001). The answers to these questions are addressed following Part 3 of this case.

Susan and Frank – Part 2

At the end of the second month, Susan and Frank do a mid-contract assessment. Frank reports that his confidence has been building. He has completed the agreed-upon assignments between coaching sessions. Susan notes that his self-descriptors have been more positive. Both Susan and Frank believe their work has been a successful endeavor thus far. At the end of the session, Frank mentions that he is on a new medication, lithium. Susan is surprised and enquires about this new development. Frank replies that he has been working with a psychotherapist who diagnosed him as *bipolar* based on his "highs and lows" and the psychotherapist spoke with Frank's physician to suggest medication.

This is the first that Susan has heard about Frank working with a psychotherapist. She has not seen or heard Frank mention anything about mood swings. She expresses her confusion about the highs and lows, the diagnosis, and the medication. In the initial meeting, Susan was not looking for mental illness since she is working in her role as a coach. She did explore the panic attacks to understand how Frank was using the term and because it was part of his reason for not being at work. Should she probe about this new diagnosis to clarify her thinking, similar to what she did in their first session regarding panic attacks?

Susan and Frank – Part 3

At their next meeting, Frank appears anxious and agitated and states that he is more tired than usual. Susan and Frank discuss his assignments from the previous weeks, which Frank did not complete. He is not clear about the reasons for his lack of follow-through and, following the core competency of co-creating, the two of them adjust the assignments for a greater likelihood of success. Susan asks for Frank's permission to contact the psychotherapist about their psychotherapy work, the diagnosis of bipolar disorder, and concerns about the medication's impact on Frank. Susan tries to contact the other professional the next day, based on Frank's verbal permission. The psychotherapist does not return Susan's call. In their next session, Frank appears to be less energized about his coaching progress and talks about his need for sleep. He apologizes for his lack of success. Susan addresses her concern about the bipolar disorder diagnosis and asks Frank a number of questions about symptoms. Frank looks puzzled and states, "I have paid you good money to help me be employed again. I don't need another shrink. Why are you asking me these questions?"

What Are the Ethical Issues?

Susan feels some frustration with Frank not sharing this information at an earlier point in their working together. She also recognizes Frank's frustration with her. She wonders how this emotion inside both of them might impact the work. On the objective or rational side, Susan knows there is no ethical mandate in the ICF Code that would suggest two professionals cannot work with the same client. In the APA Code of Ethics (Section 3.09, Cooperation with Other Professionals) (2010), psychologists are encouraged to work with other professionals, when appropriate, to serve the client effectively. So two professionals working with the same client is not necessarily an ethical issue. However, on the emotional side, Susan cannot deny her feelings of frustration nor Frank's feelings of irritation. She needs to draw upon her objectivity while not ignoring the emotions. Can she do this in an ethical way? Having an understanding of oneself and the profession and growing a self-narrative as that of an ethical practitioner (Anderson, 2015) support the coach's general competence and self-management skills.

Another ethical issue is how Susan manages her role with Frank. Initially, Susan started out in the role as coach, but became aware of psychopathology and asked questions about the panic attack. Now she has information about an additional diagnosis. At this juncture, would it be ethical for her to "cut bait and switch" to the role of psychologist? We would say *yes*, if by assessing psychopathology Susan could provide Frank with a good referral. In this case, however, someone else diagnosed the psychopathology. Susan has not seen or nor heard anything in their work that suggests Frank is dealing with a diagnosis of bipolar disorder.

Did she do the right thing as a life coach who is a psychologist by probing for more information, as she did the first time? Could she do more good by switching to the psychologist role and questioning the diagnosis, if in fact the diagnosis is wrong? Or would this strategy be an ethical misstep toward harm? We encourage Susan to draw upon the ethical choice-making process to think through her next steps. This model helps the professional tap into the different factors that contribute to the choice-making process. In addition, it encourages perspective-taking and client input at appropriate times.

(a) *Ethical sensitivity.* Susan can ask the following types of questions to raise her awareness of possible choices she could implement and the positive and negative impacts on Frank of those choices (we offer possible responses, from Susan's view, to each question):

- What strikes me as problematic in this situation with Frank?
  - There are multiple professionals with different views working with him. I see Frank as having strengths and a desire to get back to work. I have not seen or heard about symptoms that suggest bipolar disorder. The other view is that Frank is sick, he has a mental disorder, and he needs major medications.
  - I am concerned that Frank has been misdiagnosed and is therefore taking heavy-duty medication that is not necessary.
  - I did not clarify for Frank how I use my training as a psychologist when I work with coaching clients.
  - I know that Frank is irritated with my questioning about the highs and lows, but what if the diagnosis is wrong? Could I do more good by using my training as a psychologist to better understand these symptoms?
  - Do I not have an ethical obligation to offer information to Frank so he can make good choices? Am I honoring his autonomy to act on that information or not?

(b) *Formulating an ethical plan.* Susan can use these questions to begin developing her next steps:

- What are my possible courses of action and outcomes (Parts 2 and 3 of the ICF Code of Ethics)?
  - I can continue with Frank as is. Although I probably was not as clear as I needed to be, I did start out our work as a life coach, so I could maintain the coaching focus and finish out the contract as written, leaving the issue of the bipolar diagnosis alone.
  - I can discontinue with Frank, stating that, with my training as a psychologist, I seriously question the diagnosis of bipolar disorder. The diagnosis and medications to deal with the diagnosis appear to be incompatible with the goals we established.
  - I can ask Frank to choose between the coaching or the psychotherapy services because they seem incompatible.
  - I can ask Frank to renegotiate our contract or agreement, bringing in my role as a psychologist and my training to diagnose mental disorders as necessary.
  - If we renegotiate the agreement, I want to clarify my professional identity and the work that I do as a coach and a psychologist (Part 2 of the ICF Code of Ethics, Sections 1.5 and 1.6, and Boundaries of Competence and Informed Consent of the APA code).

- If I were Frank, what would I hope my coach would do and not do?
- Do any of the courses of action mentioned above violate the ICF Code of Ethics or the APA Ethical Principles of Psychologists and Code of Conduct?

(c) *Ethical motivation and competing values.* Susan can ask these questions to search out the heart of the matter and any conflicts between her values as a coach, a psychologist, and a person:
  - What are the conflicts inside me (Part 2 of the ICF Code of Ethics, Section 1.8)?
    - I do not like to be wrong. This differing view of Frank between myself and the other professional feels like a battle.
    - Is it possible that I am overlooking symptoms that are really there for Frank?
  - What else do I need to know?
    - Although I am still perplexed about the highs and lows and this diagnosis, I could ask Frank how this information and the medication will help or hinder our work and his getting back to work.
  - What did I do or not do as a professional that contributed to this scenario?

(d) *Ethical follow-through.* Susan can ask these questions to prompt implementation of the choice:
  - What do Frank and I need to discuss as I implement my choice?
  - What core values do I need to draw upon?

Going through the four-component decision-making process highlights what we believe are ethical next steps for Susan to take in this case and also ethical missteps for Susan to avoid with future clients. The first highlight is the recognition that Susan did not clarify how she used her training as a psychologist when she was working with a client in the role of a life coach. In essence, how does she define her practice to clients? This issue goes back to the informed consent process as addressed in the APA Code 3.10, Informed Consent. For a psychologist, informed consent is a key transaction and an important ethical issue between the client and professional to establish the basis for the relationship. However, the field of coaching has purposely chosen to steer away from the use of informed consent so as not to be confused with psychotherapy. We would encourage Susan and other life coaches to provide clients with information about their formal training in other fields that might influence the coaching process (Anderson et al., 2006).

The next highlight is that Susan has at least four possible courses of action. She needs to consider each course of action in light of the ethical codes, ethical principles, and virtue ethics. In addition, the process brings in Frank's view or perspective. We suggest that Susan: is honest with Frank; shares her ethical misstep of not clarifying her professional role and use of her training as a psychologist; gathers more information about the described highs and lows and then, if warranted, addresses her concern about the diagnosis of bipolar disorder; and finally, asks Frank whether he wants to renegotiate the contract, with her bringing in her training as a psychologist for diagnosis if necessary. If Frank wants to continue with the original coaching contract, we would encourage Susan to finish off her work with Frank in the role of a life coach as long as he is able to fulfill his responsibilities as initially constructed.

The last highlight from this process is the awareness that Susan gained. She realized that she was experiencing a feeling of competition with the other professional about Frank's mental health. She realized the need to have humility. She took the opportunity to ask herself what she did to contribute to the scenario. APA Code 3.04 encourages psychologists to take necessary steps to avoid harming clients and to minimize harm where it is foreseeable and unavoidable.

The Case of to Whom Do I Owe My Loyalty?

Part 1

The global human resources (HR) director of Audrey's soon-to-be client's company has contacted her. Audrey, who is an executive coach, is a trained HR professional with an MBA degree and a Ph.D. in industrial-organization psychology. She holds a professional certified coach credential from the ICF (ICF, n.d.c) and a certificate from Fielding Graduate University in evidence-based coaching. The company is a European venture that has a global presence in Europe, the Americas, and Asia. When Audrey receives Ruben's first 360-degree feedback assessment and anonymous feedback from peers, managers, and direct reports, his peers cited communication and relationship building as issues. Upon reading the feedback, Audrey understands his need for coaching. It is clear to Audrey and the HR director that Ruben is struggling with his people skills.

The HR director wants a quick fix. She wants Audrey to "fix Ruben" and to do so quickly because time is money in the business world. Audrey sets up an initial meeting with Ruben to go over what the sponsor/company thinks he needs and to determine whether he is willing to pursue this type of development. Ruben is very willing: he wants to pursue the coaching and is excited about the opportunity.

Audrey begins work with Ruben by drawing upon the ICF core competence of contracting and the APA informed consent standard (3.10), discussing the contracting questions and later discussing his 360-degree feedback assessment. For clarification, she asks Ruben the following questions (his responses follow in italics):

(a) What do you want to make sure you get from the coaching relationship? *Confidentiality, support, guidance, and expertise.*
(b) What do you want from me as a coach? *Clarity on the difference between a manager and an executive; support until I become a successful executive.*

During the first couple of meetings with Ruben, Audrey finds out he is a 30-something Israeli citizen living in the United States. As an Israeli, he is proud of his European/German ethnicity, which values education and cultivated behavior, and prides himself on being intellectually astute, as opposed to the Arabic ethnicity of some Israelis he looks down upon.

Regarding core competencies and the APA standards of informed consent and confidentiality, Audrey did a good job of building trust with Ruben and allowing him to set the pace for his professional development and awareness. However, there are multiple ethical issues and potential dilemmas for Audrey to address. We would encourage her to use the ACTION model in her ethical decision-making process. This approach offers the coach the opportunity to go through the stages in a flexible manner. As we work through the case using the ACTION model, we also highlight the pertinent ICF and APA ethical codes.

Stage 1: Awareness – Audrey knows that where her loyalty lies is extremely important. Audrey feels conflicted and confused – conflicted because she worries about doing the right thing and confused because she has two clients: one is the company who pays; the other is the client needing coaching. On the one hand, Audrey has a busy HR director who wants a quick fix. She wants Audrey to "fix Ruben." On the other hand, Ruben is the client and Audrey wants to help him develop at his own pace.

Stage 2: Classify – In this stage, Audrey identifies the ethical dilemmas. *The first ethical dilemma is: conflict of interest pertaining to confidentiality.* How much of what she covers with her client will she or should she report back to the HR director? Should Audrey be loyal to the sponsor/company or to the client? Audrey uses the ICF Code of Ethics as well as her own experience to think about how to address the question. The ICF Code of Ethics, Part 2, Section 2: Conflicts of Interest, Item 13 states that "[As a coach, I seek] to be conscious of any conflict or potential conflict of interest, openly disclose any such conflict and offer to remove myself when a conflict arises." APA Code 3.07 speaks to the importance of clarifying at the outset of the service the nature of the relationship with all individuals or organizations involved, an identification of who is the client, the probable uses of the services provided or the information obtained, and the fact that there may be limits to confidentiality. Other APA standards to consider are 3.05, Multiple Relationships and 4.02, Discussing the Limits of Confidentiality. Additionally, Kitchener (1988) points out that a professional should be aware of potential role conflicts and should curtail any possible harm (p. 220).

A second ethical dilemma could be differing goals between Ruben and his company. Ruben wants to be a successful executive. The company who is paying Audrey wants the coaching endeavor to help Ruben learn how to better communicate with his peers and subordinates. Again, this is a potential conflict of interest that the ethics code addresses.

Another ethical issue is cultural diversity and difference in gender. The coach and client are from two different parts of the world with different worldviews. How does Audrey deal with her own biases and values concerning gender and culture? The ICF Code of Ethics, Part 2, Section 1, Item 4 states the following: "Refrain from unlawful discrimination in occupational activities, including age, race, gender orientation, ethnicity, sexual orientation, religion, national origin or disability." APA Code 3.01 also highlights the importance of psychologists refraining from discrimination.

Ruben also has his biases. Through the initial visit with Ruben, Audrey became aware of his worldview. Ruben views his coworkers in much the same manner as he does Israelis with Arabic ethnicity. To him, they are less valuable as humans, not worthy of his respect. For Ruben, a white Euro-American culture is seen as desirable, superior, and normative. *How does Audrey work with Ruben in an honoring and ethical way?* This is another ethical issue. To impose her own value set on Ruben or to allow her bias to negatively affect the coaching relationship would be detrimental to the work. O'Hearne and Hamrick (2006) have pointed out that a coach should be familiar with their client's culture; otherwise, the coach risks an ethical predicament in the coaching relationship (p. 3). A coach should have an awareness of their own cultural lens because there is little if any place for ethnocentric perspectives (Sue & Sue, 2013).

Stage 3: Reflection – Throughout the other stages, Audrey became aware of language (how to articulate the ethical issues) and reflected on ways to think about and act on these ethical issues. For example, the relationship is really a triangle between the sponsor/company as payer for coaching services, Audrey as coach, and Ruben as client. The sponsor/company may feel that, since they are paying the coach, the coach's sole loyalty lies with them. However, Audrey reflects on this position as being unethical. She has a duty to also honor the coaching process as it relates to Ruben and should not cater to the "quick fix" solution of the sponsor/company. She clarifies for herself that her greater duty is to honor the client and his development through coaching. It is important for the coach to be aware of boundaries. According to Welfel (2016) "…boundaries provide structure for the process, safety for the client" (p. 225). Audrey thinks about her training as a psychologist as well as a coach, recalling how important trust is to a successful client–professional relationship. Ruben needs to feel he can trust Audrey. This trust occurs if the client feels the care and concern of the coach and if the coach creates and maintains a trustworthy and confidential space.

Stage 4: Initiate – With each dilemma, Audrey initiates action to address the ethical issues at hand.

Regarding the triangular relationship, Audrey clarifies the limits of confidentiality with Ruben. She reviews the coaching agreement and specifies that anything shared with the company will be with his permission. Audrey declares and acts on her dedication to Ruben's development and success.

Regarding the difference in goals, Audrey discusses with Ruben the potential difference in the definition of *success* between him and the sponsor/company. The ethical step here is to build Ruben's awareness. She reminds Ruben that she was hired by the sponsor/company, which has specific goals they would like him to achieve. Through the coaching process, his definition of success may reveal itself to be different from the company's definition. It will be up to Ruben to decide what to do with this information.

Stage 5: Option evaluation – Audrey evaluates the risks and benefits of different courses of action.

Audrey realizes that there is a cost to not sharing everything with the sponsor/company. The sponsor/company pays her and by holding back information about the client, they may feel as though Audrey is not worthy of her payment. This could result in a negative evaluation and missed opportunities for future work with the company.

Audrey also identifies the risks and negative impacts of if she decided to not address the cultural differences between herself and the client, as well as between the client and his peers and subordinates. A trusting and genuine relationship cannot be built without honesty and caring confrontation.

Stage 6: Novate – Audrey incorporates ethical experiences.

In this stage, Audrey takes time to explore in her coaching journal what she learned from the experience with the client and the company. The following could be some of the things she records.

First, her greater loyalty should remain with the client; otherwise, there is a risk of damaging the trust factor. When there is a triangular relationship, discuss this issue during the initial agreement. Second, always ask the client for permission to share particular information with the sponsor/company, making sure both parties understand what will be shared and what will be kept confidential. Third, checking in regularly with the client and the sponsor/company to make sure needs are being met in a manner acceptable to both parties is time well spent.

Both Pomerantz and Eiting (2003) and Wildflower and Brennan (in Cox et al., 2010) proffer several factors to keep in mind during the stage of contracting with a client. This discussion may be helpful for Audrey as the coach when dealing with a potential conflict of interest and deliberating about confidentiality. Pomerantz and Eiting (2003, pp. 3–4) have defined six ideas to discuss with the client before beginning an engagement: (1) discuss the differences between coaching and therapy; (2) identify who the stakeholders are and their roles; (3) understand the expectations of the stakeholders; (4) clarify boundaries; (5) understand the role of feedback; and (6) understand the exit or termination strategy.

The highlight for this case and for Audrey occurs in Stage 3 – Reflection. Taking the time to reflect and develop the language around the ethical issues brought greater clarity for Audrey. She was able to crystalize her ethical obligation/loyalty to Ruben, the client, in spite of clear risks with the company who hired her.

The Case of Who Is in the Room

Part 1

Company Y hires Sophia to coach a client, Isabel, in several areas, including leadership development, team building, and time management. Sophia holds an MA in counseling and a coaching certificate from ICF. Company Y is a company Sophia has worked for in the past as its HR director. Sophia was part of the search committee charged with hiring the position Isabel currently occupies. Isabel was not her first choice for the position, but because Isabel was related to a senior manager on staff, she was hired into the position. Isabel is related to Sophia's former boss. It is not Sophia's former boss who hired her as a coach, but rather the CEO of the company/sponsor.

Isabel is a 30-something white female. She works as the director of marketing for Company Y/the sponsor. According to Isabel's peers and subordinates, her strengths are her verbal skills and her commitment to the mission of the organization. Her weaknesses are her inconsistent work performance and excessive tardiness and absenteeism. Company Y has described Isabel's weaknesses as follows:

(a) Undependable – she often commits to meetings and then cancels at the last minute. Worse than that, she goes through cycles in which she is very good about attending and participating and then she goes through periods of the other extreme.

(b) Unpredictable – she goes through cycles in which she is not in the office on a regular basis. She has a reputation as a hypochondriac who cannot go more than two weeks without some sort of medical emergency.

(c) Intolerant/impatient – she is intolerant of others who do not see her priorities as their priorities.

Isabel sees herself as having given her all to the company. What she does not like and what she feels has worked against her are an inflexible schedule, her commute, and the boss's way of dealing with people. Her boss, the CEO, is ex-military.

The first ethical issue Sophia is faced with relates to her own biases. In this case, Sophia's upbringing and work ethic are different than those of her client. Sophia sees herself as being responsible, professional, and always on time. She has gotten jobs based on her experience and professionalism, not her connections. Isabel, Sophia's client, appears to have violated Sophia's idea of what is a good work ethic and getting a job based on merit.

To act consistently with the ICF and the ACA ethics codes, Sophia needs to recognize the personal bias that is driving her emotions and possible or potential choices. The ICF Code, Part 2, Section 1, Item 8 encourages the coach to recognize personal issues that impair or interfere with the coaching work or relationship. If there is a problem of this sort, the coach will take appropriate action. The ACA Ethics Code A.4.b encourages counselors to be aware of and avoid imposing their own values, attitudes, beliefs, and behaviors on clients.

Who Is in the Room – Part 2

Several months into the coaching process with Isabel, it becomes clear that Company Y will be terminating Isabel's employment. The CEO of the company tells Sophia that Isabel has not made the progress they expected and she will more than likely be asked to resign. The CEO/company hope the coaching will help Isabel develop professionally and address some of her weaknesses that, in turn, will help her land a next job or get the hint that she might be terminated and so resign.

The second ethical dilemma is, does Sophia tell Isabel about her conversation with the CEO? As the coach, where does her loyalty to the organization begin and end? The company still wants Sophia to work with Isabel to develop her skills, even though the company has no plans to keep Isabel as an employee. The ICF Code of Ethics section that speaks to this ethical dilemma is that on conflict of interest. In all cases, coaching engagement agreements should clearly establish the rights, roles, and responsibilities of both the client and the sponsor if the client and sponsor are different people. There are multiple ACA codes that Sophia can draw upon to guide her steps. First is the informed consent code A.2.a. Isabel needs the necessary information about Sophia and Sophia's role to determine whether she wants to work with her. Informed consent is an ongoing part of the working relationship. ACA code A.7.b, Confidentiality and Advocacy, clarifies the importance of determining limits of confidentiality. Does Sophia have an obligation to honor the confidentiality of the company who is paying for her services?

Regarding core competencies, Sophia did well in active listening and powerful questioning; however, she could have done better in fulfilling a couple of the ethical guidelines and establishing the coaching agreement. These issues are especially true after she becomes aware of the pending termination.

We would encourage Sophia to use the SAD model (Johnson, 2012, p. 206) to work through the ethical decision-making process. This model relies heavily on bringing critical thinking into the ethical reasoning process. The outline of the process is as given in the following.

Situation definition – there are at least two ethical situations. *Sophia identifies the first ethical issues as her bias toward Isabel.* Sophia recalls that she was not in favor of Isabel getting a job within the company. In addition, she taps into her feelings that are somewhat resentful because she does not understand how Isabel was able to get this far within the company. Sophia is challenged to be the unbiased coach. How can she handle these biases tugging on her? The ACA codes A.4.a and A.4.b speak to avoiding harm and imposing personal values, attitudes, beliefs, and behaviors.

The second situation Sophia identifies is the CEO's plan to terminate Isabel's employment even though the company hired her to help Isabel develop as a leader. This mixed message is confusing and violates her coaching principles. Why hire a coach to develop an employee when it appears there will be a pending termination?

Wildflower and Brennan (in Cox et al., 2010) discuss boundary management. They state that when coaches are brought into an organization, usually by who is identified as "the sponsor," they "face an added dimension of complexity around confidentiality" (p. 435). This perspective ties in nicely with Hannafey and Vitulano's (2012) article in which they discuss an agency-theory approach. They make a point of stating that "there is notable confusion about the nature of the obligations and duties coaches have to their clients and supporting organizations" (p. 600). They continue by saying that one should view the agency relation on two and possibly three levels, including the executive individual, the organization, and possibly the HR department (p. 600). Hannafey and Vitulano weigh into the ethical discussion by stating that "agency relation can serve as an important way to understand executive coaching practice and also its ethical dimensions" (p. 602).

Analysis

The analysis includes exploring the competing values, considering external factors that influence the ethical decision-making process, and contemplating different possible courses of action. On the one hand, Sophia recognizes her obligation to her client and her client's possible need to know the CEO's plans. On the other hand, Sophia has Company Y/the sponsor paying for her services and expecting confidentiality. Sophia recognizes that her former connections with the company and her view of Isabel are pressing on her decision-making process. Sophia ponders the different possible options: (1) she could tell Isabel about the CEO's plan to terminate her employment and see if Isabel still wants her service; (2) she could keep this information to herself, but still work with Isabel to help her develop some much-needed skills; or (3) she could end the coaching contract immediately and then decide whether or not to tell Isabel of the CEO's plans.

Decision

In the more perfect ethical world, Sophia decides her duty (a deontological approach) is to recontract with Company Y, explaining in greater clarity her moral and ethical obligation to the client, Isabel, and her moral and ethical obligation to the company who is paying for her service. In the recontracting process, Sophia draws upon the contracting question of Pomerantz and Eiting (2003). With this decision in place and action taken, Sophia adheres to the ICF Code of Ethics and navigates through the conflicts of interest. She clearly states with whom her allegiance exists.

Who Is (Really) in the Room – Part 3

We add this piece to the case as a "rest of the story," highlighting the reality of how an ethical decision-making process can be circumvented by conflicts of interests and unchallenged biases. In actuality, Sophia continues to work with Isabel, but she does not tell her about the impending termination. After some reflection, Sophia realizes that she does not tell Isabel because of her biases. There was a clear conflict of interest and as a result Sophia made an ethical error. Sophia's action was more intuitive than thought-out. She did not consciously decide not to tell Isabel about her upcoming termination. Rather, Sophia acted subconsciously from a place of her own bias concerning work ethic and merit. In this instance, Sophia lacked ethical sensitivity based on her own biases.

Although a decision-making model or process may tout critical thinking as a hallmark, the person using the model may have multiple nonrational and subconscious motivations that circumvent the process. As coaches, we need to guard against those circumstances when professional and personal values conflict. We do not come to the profession as blank slates (Welfel, 2016, p. 23). To guard against acting on our biases and conflicts of interest, Welfel (2016) encourages us to develop ethics of virtue, and Anderson (2015) reminds us to grow and encourages us to develop ethics of virtue and self-narratives that promote ethical practices.

The Case of Coach, Friend, or Referral

Part 1

Ron, a manager from Company X, contacts Lynn to help him with some coaching. Lynn has an MS in career counseling and is credentialed through the ICF as a coach.

Lynn was previously employed with Company X, where he served as the manager of HR. Ron, his former boss, trusts him and would like Lynn to help a certain staff member, Anne. According to the manager, Anne needs to become more of a people person if she wants to get promoted. Ron tells Lynn that Anne has become out of control and needs a reality check. Lynn agrees to see what he can do.

Lynn reaches out to Anne and sets up an appointment for an initial consult. During the meeting, he and Anne discuss some of the issues her boss cited, such as her being snappy, not following through with staff, and coming across as arrogant. In the course of an hour, Anne breaks down and tells Lynn she's going through a divorce and it is affecting her work. She wants to apply for a director position, but is afraid she will not get the job because of her lack of education and her current performance issues. They talk at length to clarify her coaching needs and goals. Anne decides to hire Lynn as a coach.

Part 2

The coaching goes on for a year. During this time, Lynn coaches Anne through the interviewing and on-boarding process. Once she is settled in her new position, he helps her transition into her role as a department director. In the final months of the coaching engagement, Lynn and Anne begin to have social conversations at the end of the coaching session. Lynn finds himself enjoying Anne's company.

Part 3

Within three to six months of ending his coaching agreement with Anne, she asks for his opinion about a certain staff member, Trudy. Anne is having some issues with Trudy concerning her time management and supervisory skills. Lynn coaches Anne through a particular scenario regarding Trudy. At subsequent social interactions, Anne continues to probe Lynn's expertise. This begins to feel uncomfortable for Lynn. He finally draws the line and states he cannot coach her on this issue because they have become friends and so coaching her would be unethical. Since the issues related to Trudy/the staff member revolve around supervising people, Lynn suggests that Anne refers Trudy to him for some coaching.

Lynn should be or could be congratulated on his good work with Anne for helping her successfully acquire the next position within the company. What prompted this positive outcome was good adherence to core competencies such as coaching presence, active listening, and designing action. Anne was the benefactor of Lynn's good coaching. However, an ethical issue develops. *The ethical issue is one of boundary crossings/violations or multiple relationships.* Lynn and Anne begin to move from coach–client to friend–friend and then back to coach–client. Lynn makes an ethical misstep when he decides to allow this role slippage (Welfel, 2016) to occur in the relationship. The ICF Ethics Code, Section 3: Professional Conduct with Clients #21 speaks to sexual and romantic relationships. It states, "As a coach, I avoid any sexual or romantic relationship with current clients or sponsor(s) or students, mentees or supervisees." However, the code does not address other types of boundary crossings or violations. The ACA Code, Managing and Maintaining Boundaries and Professional Relationships A.6, which Lynn is familiar with, speaks to the following codes: A.6.a, Previous Relationship; A.6.b, Extending Counseling Boundaries; and A.6.e, Nonprofessional Interactions or Relationships (other than sexual or romantic interactions or relationships). These parts of the ACA Code speak to the ethics of entering into another type of relationship with a client. If this occurs, it must be for the benefit of the client and not result in harm.

If Lynn had used a process to consider his thinking and behavior, such as Welfel's model for ethical decision-making, he might have steered clear of making an ethical misstep. We present the ten steps from Welfel's model for this case.

Step 1 – develop ethical sensitivity. Lynn could have and possibly did know or sense there was a possible ethical lapse occurring when the coaching sessions toward the end began to be more social in nature than professional. The sensitivity to recognize the ethical dimension of a situation is a key first step.

Step 2 – clarify facts, identify stakeholders, and consider the sociocultural context. The facts of the case are: good work is accomplished on the part of the coach and client, the client experiences success, a mutual appreciation develops over the one-year period, roles change, and this happens more than once. The stakeholders are Anne, Ron, and Trudy. The sociocultural context is the company where there are overlapping relationships from the beginning. Lynn was once an employee of the company he now is coaching for.

Step 3 – identify the central ethical issues and possible courses of action. As previously mentioned, the central ethical issue is multiple relationships. The possible courses of action include the following: (1) Lynn recognizes a developing pattern of coaching sessions turning into social interactions; (2) Lynn addresses the role slippage with Anne as well as anyone else who may be effected by it (i.e., Ron, the manager); (3) Lynn consults with other coaching professional to gain perspective; and (4) Lynn discusses with Anne the change in roles and possible negative outcomes.

Step 4 – refer to ethical standards and relevant laws/regulations. Lynn refers to both the ICF and ACA ethics code to evaluate the current scenario. As previously mentioned, the ICF Code would provide less guidance than the ACA Ethics Code. Lynn's task would be to assess whether the new role of friend is beneficial to the client or could it undo the good work done in the professional relationship.

Step 5 – review the ethics literature. The ethics literature in coaching and in counseling would speak to the pros and cons of adding another relationship to the professional relationship. The range of perspectives is large, with some authors encouraging the professional to not have boundary extensions or crossings with clients, to other authors encouraging just the opposite for the good of the client and the professional relationship.

Step 6 – apply ethical principles. To apply the ethical principles would be to assess how autonomy, beneficence, nonmaleficence, fidelity, and justice speak to the situation. Lynn can consider each principle. What would it mean to "do good," as the coaching is coming to an end and it appears that a friendship could ensue? How might harm be done or risked should a friendship develop? How should Lynn honor Anne's autonomy to choose? Would Lynn create or consider a friendship with other clients once coaching is done? Would Lynn see this friendship as fair if Lynn were another coach or client?

Step 7 – consult with colleagues. Lynn could and probably should contact other coaches to gain perspective. Have other coaches developed friendships with clients? How did these work out? If well, how come? If poorly, how come?

Step 8 – deliberate and decide. Lynn could consciously think about and decide what he will do regarding an additional role with Anne. Should Lynn decide that a friendship is not problematic and even potentially beneficial, he would likely want to clarify what this friendship really means for Anne. In the case as presented, it appears that the new role was not clear to Anne because she began to revert back to the client–coach relationship to get assistance regarding an employee.

Step 9 – inform necessary individuals and implement as well as document actions taken. Documentation of decisions made and actions taken is an important step for Lynn. At some time later, he may want to revisit his decision. This is better done when the decision is written down. This leads us to the next step.

Step 10 – reflect on the above process and outcome. The power of reflecting on a decision made cannot be overestimated. No matter whether it was "not adding another type of interaction/relationship" or "being friends and having a coaching relationship is fine," reflection on the decision-making process and the outcomes as currently understood provides opportunities for great learning.

Conclusion

In this chapter, we used four case scenarios to explore ethical issues and dilemmas while drawing upon the ICF, APA, and ACA ethics codes and decision-making models to suggest an ethical course of action. In conclusion, we believe the following points are helpful for coaches to consider when creating an ethical framework:

(a) Use some type of contracting method such as those outlined in the chapter to have a clear understanding of what each stakeholder expects.
(b) Draw upon evidence-based theories to enhance the coaching engagement.
(c) Remember the core competencies and the codes of ethics.
(d) Maintain the coaching role and address ethical issues and dilemmas as they come up.
(e) Draw upon ethical decision-making models that make sense for the scenario.
(f) Finally, remember the use of oneself in the coaching process, work to develop a self-narrative as that of an ethical practitioner, and reflect by journaling.

References

American Counseling Association (2014). ACA code of ethics. Retrieved from www
.counseling.org/resources/aca-code-of-ethics.pdf

American Psychological Association (2010). Ethical principles of psychologists and code of conduct. Retrieved from www.apa.org/ethics/code

Anderson, S. K. (2015). Morally sensitive professionals. In D. Mower, P. Vandenberg, & W. Robison (Eds.), *Developing moral sensitivity* (pp. 188–204). New York, NY: Routledge (Taylor and Francis Group).

Anderson, S. K. & Handelsman, M. (2010). *Ethics for psychotherapists and counselors: A proactive approach*. Malden, MA: Wiley/Blackwell.

Anderson, S. K., Waggoner, H., & Moore, G. K. (2006). Ethical choice: An outcome of being, blending, and doing. In P. Williams & S. K. Anderson (Eds.), *Law and ethics in coaching: How to solve and avoid difficult problems in your practice* (pp. 39–61). Hoboken, NJ: John Wiley & Sons.

Anderson, S. K., Williams, P., & Kramer, A. (2011). Life and executive coaching: Some ethical issues for consideration. In S. J. Knapp, M. M. Handelsman, M. C. Gottlieb, & L. D. VandeCreek (Eds.), *APA handbook of ethics in psychology: Practice, teaching, and research* (Vol. 2, pp. 169–181). Washington, DC: American Psychological Association.

Brennan, D. & Wildflower, L. (2010). Ethics in coaching. In E. Cox, T. Bachkirova, & D. Clutterbuck (Eds.), *The complete handbook of coaching* (pp. 369–380). London, UK: Sage.

Cavanagh, M. J. & Grant, A. M. (2014). The solution-focused approach to coaching. In E. Cox, T. Bachkirova, & D. Clutterbuck (Eds.), *The complete handbook of coaching* (2nd edn.) (pp. 51–64). London, UK: Sage.

Cox, E., Bachkirova, T., & Clutterbuck, D. A. (2010). *The complete handbook of coaching*. London, UK: Sage.

Day, L. (2005). *Ethics in media communications: Cases and controversies*. Belmont, CA: Cengage Learning.

Duffy, M. & Passmore, J. (2010). Ethics in coaching: An ethical decision making framework for coaching psychologists. *International Coaching Psychology Review, 5*, 140–151.

Fillery-Travis, A. & Passmore, J. (2011). A critical review of executive coaching research: A decade of progress and what's to come. *Coaching: An International Journal of Theory, Research and Practice, 4*, 70–88.

Frisch, M. H. (2008). Use of self in executive coaching. *i-Coach* Coaching Monograph Series 2008, No. 1, 1–23. Retrieved from http://icoachnewyork.com/wp-content/uploads/2015/09/Monograph.pdf

Handelsman, M. M., Gottlieb, M. C., & Knapp, S. (2005). Training ethical psychologists: An acculturation model. *Professional Psychology: Research and Practice, 36*, 59–65.

Hannafey, F.T. & Vitulano L.A. (2012). Ethics and executive coaching: An agency theory approach. *Springer Science+Business Media B.V.* Retrieved from DOI 10.1007/s10551-012-1442-z

International Coach Federation (n.d.a). Code of ethics. Retrieved from http://coachfederation.org/about/ethics.aspx?ItemNumber=854

International Coach Federation (n.d.b). FAQs: How has coaching grown? Retrieved from http://coachfederation.org/about/landing.cfm?ItemNumber=844&navItemNumber=617&navItemNumber=3745

International Coach Federation (n.d.c). Individual credentialing. Retrieved form http://coachfederation.org/credential/?navItemNumber=502

Johnson, C. E. (2012). *Meeting the ethical challenges of leadership* (5th edn.). Los Angeles, CA: Sage.

Kidder, R. M. (1996). *How good people make tough choices: Resolving the dilemmas of ethical living*. New York, NY: Simon & Schuster.

Kitchener, K. S. (1984). Intuition, critical evaluation and ethical principles: The foundation for ethical decisions in counseling psychology. *The Counseling Psychologist, 12*, 43–55.

Kitchener, K. S. (1988). Dual role relationships: What makes them so problematic? *Journal of Counseling and Development, 67*, 217–221.

Kitchener, K. S. (2000). *Foundations of ethical practice, research, and teaching in psychology*. Mahwah, NJ: Lawrence Erlbaum Associates.

Kitchener, K. S. & Anderson, S. K. (2011). *Foundations of ethical practice, research, and teaching in psychology and counseling* (2nd edn.). New York, NY: Routledge/Taylor & Francis Group.

McDonald, G. (2010). Ethical relativism vs absolutism: Research implications, *European Business Review, 22*, 446–464.

McKelley, R. A. & Rochlen, A. B. (2007). The practice of coaching: Exploring alternatives to therapy for counseling-resistant men. *Psychology of Men & Masculinity, 8*, 53–65.

O'Hearne, M. & Hamrick, C. (2006). The intersection of culture and ethics. In P. Williams & S. K. Anderson (Eds.), *Law and ethics in coaching: How to solve and avoid difficult problems in your practice* (pp. 215–244). Hoboken, NJ: John Wiley & Sons.

Passmore, J. (2009). Coaching ethics: Making ethical decisions – Novices and experts. *The Coaching Psychologist, 5*, 6–10.

Passmore, J., Peterson, D., & Freire, T. (2012). *The Wiley-Blackwell handbook of the psychology of coaching and mentoring*. Hoboken, NJ: John Wiley & Sons.

Peltier, B. (2001). *The psychology of executive coaching*. San Francisco, CA: Brunner-Routledge.

Pomerantz, S. & Eiting, J. (2003). Ethics in coaching, contracting, and confidentiality: Drawing lines in the sand. SHRM/Ethics Resource Center, Business Ethics Study (pp. 1–8). Retrieved from http://libraryofprofessionalcoaching.com/concepts/ethics/ethics-in-coaching-contracting-and-confidentiality-drawing-lines-in-the-sand

Rest, J. R. (1984). Research on moral development: Implications for training counseling psychologists. *Counseling Psychologist, 12*, 19–29.

Rogers, J. (2008). *Coaching skills: A handbook* (2nd edn.). Maidenhead, UK/New York, NY: McGraw Hill/Open University Press.

Rogerson, M. D., Gottlieb, M. C., Handelsman, M. M., Knapp, S., & Younggren, J. (2011). Nonrational processes in ethical decision making. *American Psychologist, 66*, 614–623.

Sherman, S. & Freas, A. (2004). The Wild West of executive coaching. *Harvard Business Review, 82*, 82–93.

Sperry, L. (2004). *Executive coaching: The essential guide for mental health professionals*. New York, NY: Brunner-Routledge.

Stober, D. R. & Grant, A. (2006). *Evidence based coaching handbook: Putting best practices to work for your clients*. Hoboken, NJ: John Wiley & Sons.

Sue, D. W. & Sue, D. (2013). *Counseling the culturally diverse: Theory and practice* (6th edn.). Hoboken, NJ: Wiley & Sons.

Webb, P. (2008). Coaching for wisdom, enabling wise decisions. In D. Drake, D. Brennan, & K. Gortz, *The philosophy and practice of coaching: Insights and issues for a new era* (pp. 161–175). West Sussex, UK: John Wiley & Sons, Ltd.

Welfel, E. R. (2016). *Ethics in counseling and psychotherapy: Standards, research, and emerging issues* (6th edn.). Pacific Grove, CA: Cengage.

Wildflower, L. & Brennan, D. (2011). *The handbook of knowledge-based coaching: From theory to practice*. San Francisco, CA: Jossey-Bass.

32 Ethical Issues in Prevention

Jonathan P. Schwartz, Sally M. Hage, and Christine Pao

Why Prevention Ethics Are Important

The utility of prevention has been well established in the literature (i.e., Kumpfer, Alvarado, Smith, & Bellamy, 2002; O'Connell, Boat, & Warner, 2009). Further, in addition to moral reasons of preventing suffering before it occurs, there is evidence that early prevention is more effective than remediation, as once problems are established, they are difficult to ameliorate (Prilleltensky, 2001). Prevention has also been identified as a key component to reducing mental health disparities, as well as the demand versus services gap for mental health treatment (Schwartz & Hage, 2009; Vera & Shin, 2006).

Although the efficacy and utility of prevention are well established (Prilleltensky, 2001), there is a lack of guidance on how to address ethical issues in prevention (Schwartz & Hage, 2009). The current ethical code for psychologists (American Psychological Association, 2010) does not adequately address the unique ethical issues that arise in prevention work. Most importantly, the core definition of prevention work is addressing problems before they occur. This obviously raises many ethical issues related to informed consent, confidentiality, and meaningful evaluation. In addition, prevention work involves working with communities, schools, and other groups, leading to substantial differences from individual therapy. By its nature, prevention includes the need to work within multiple systems and to impact those systems. For example, a focus on individual change without attention to social forces can unfairly blame individuals, sustaining social inequality (Prilleltensky, 1997; Vera & Reese, 2000).

The focus of this chapter will be on explicating a few of the core ethical issues that arise in prevention work. For each issue chosen – informed consent, cultural competency, competence, and evaluation – an illustrative case will be provided and discussed. The cases were written to emphasize the ethical challenges in prevention work and to offer suggestions for addressing these challenges.

The Case of a Community Intervention for Addressing Gun Violence

John Sumner is a white, male, middle-aged counseling psychologist who works as faculty at the local university and is known for his research on violence prevention. There has been a rash of gun violence in the community and he has been tasked by the mayor and city council with organizing and implementing a prevention program with a young population to avoid future violence. Dr. Sumner does not live in the targeted community and has little familiarity with the community context. The city that has hired Dr. Sumner as a consultant has geo-mapped the violence in the community and is asking him to create a prevention program for the community with the highest violence. The community identified is primarily African–American and Latino, is of low social economic status, and has a reputation as a highly gang-affiliated area. In addition, there is a history of university researchers coming into this community to gather data or doing an intervention often being funded by grants with little follow-up or sustainability. Thus, the community has a distrust of the local university. Dr. Sumner is planning to design a prevention program for all elementary school students in this community. The city manager who is in charge of supporting this project wants to see quick results and does not seem concerned with the rights of the participants. When Dr. Sumner tries to bring up informed consent, the city manager replies that they do not have time to worry about that because people are dying.

Discussion

The ethical challenges of intervening with a community as an outsider include a lack of understanding of the context for behavior, potential differences in worldview, and a lack of a trusting relationship, to name a few. For the purposes or this discussion, informed consent will be the focus. In this case, Dr. Sumner is obliged to obtain informed consent (Standard 3.10) from community leaders, from multiple school personnel, and from parents, regardless of the city manager's objections. The process is challenged by the need to address the stigmatizing issue of gun violence in a unique community context. The dilemma in the case could be categorized as primary or secondary prevention. The public health perspective defines different types of prevention. Primary prevention is focused on reducing the incidence of a problem before it develops (Conyne, 2004), so in this case, the focus is on preventing violence with a young population. Secondary prevention is focused on reducing the prevalence of an existing problem (Conyne, 2004). In this case, the community is suffering from violence, so intervention is focused on reducing future violence. The challenge in primary and secondary prevention in particular is that the intervention is designed to impact a whole population and often has secondary impacts on the ecological circles of the target population (Trickett, 1998). In addition, in contrast with typical therapy, there is a lack of a clearly defined client (i.e., individual, family), a circumstance that makes informed consent a sensitive and complicated process (Bloom, 1996; Schwartz & Hage, 2009). Additionally, the target population is not actively seeking help (Conyne, 2015). In this case, the targeted community might not only feel stigmatized by this intervention, as the originators of the intervention have identified them as a high-risk population for violence with no understanding of the community context, but the community members could also feel that racial bias is at play, as someone outside the community is attempting to intervene with no understanding of the community dynamics.

Further complicating this issue in informed consent is the power differential between the interventionists and the participants (Trickett, 1998). The imposed nature of prevention increases the already existing power differential. As the power differential grows, it becomes more difficult for participants to make fully autonomous decisions in the informed consent process (Schwartz & Hage, 2009; Trickett, 1998). What could be viewed as an isolated violence issue in a community may become an imposed identity with little choice offered to the participants in accepting that identity. Unforeseen results may become apparent during the course of an intervention (Durlak & Wells, 1997). For example, prevention of one problem – violence in this situation – in a specific context has the potential to create or exacerbate another (e.g., drug use).

To approach the issue of informed consent responsibly a first step is to involve the school, parents, students, and community leaders in the question of whether the intervention is needed and, if so, whether the approach Dr. Sumner advocates is the best. Understanding community attitudes is key not only to informed consent, but also to the success of interventions. In addition, Dr. Sumner must be transparent about his chosen intervention, what the empirical support is, whether it has been used with a similar population, and what the benefits versus risks are. He must also be clear as to how he will measure success and what precautions he will use against deleterious results. In this prevention program, a process rather than a one-time approach to consent appears most appropriate. A process approach to informed consent entails ongoing evaluation of the intervention and ensures that participants are informed of unforeseen or negative results of a prevention intervention. Ethical issues of maintaining autonomy and protecting participants from harm are relevant. The American Psychological Association (APA) Code has protecting participants from harm as one of its core principles and as one of its enforceable standards (Standard 3.10) (APA, 2010). Standard 3.10 on informed consent emphasizes participants' full understanding of what they are agreeing to, even when interventions are provided through organizations (Standard 3.07). The challenge for Dr. Sumner in this case is to balance real informed consent, including whether the intervention is desired by the community, with the pressure from the city to get the intervention underway and to see results. Ethical behavior, including guidance by the APA Code (APA, 2010), would view Dr. Sumner's role as a psychologist to involve putting the consent of participants as his priority. It is essential that participants at the individual, community, or systems (e.g., schools, agencies, government) levels are given the information necessary to make knowledgeable choices about involvement in a prevention intervention. In this case, the community school, parents, and children should be part of each process of the intervention, rather than having it imposed on them. Standard 3.10(b) also requires that the children are asked to give their assent to participation as well. In addition, the APA ethical principles of justice and respect for people's rights and dignity, along with Standards 3.01 on avoiding unfair discrimination and 2.01 on operating within one's boundaries of competence, all stress the importance of cultural competence if the intervention is conducted. Dr. Sumner must not simply use an intervention that has worked before, but must understand the demographics and context of previous empirical evidence. It is also important to have participants from the community involved in every stage of the prevention program (Hage & Schwartz, 2009). Dr. Sumner also has a responsibility to resist pressure from the city to shortcut a comprehensive consent process and must educate city officials about the value of such consent in ensuring that the intervention is successful. His own self-interest in directing the project and gaining experience, compensation, or any other benefit must be secondary to the rights of the participants, even if this ultimately results in his withdrawal from the project.

The Case of a Family-Based Drug Prevention Program

A group of psychologists is seeking to implement a culturally sound, family-based drug prevention program targeting substance use among middle school students in a diverse urban area. The psychologists on the team are all heterosexual, Caucasian, upper-middle-class individuals who were born and raised in the United States. The students and families of the students who attend the middle school are primarily Hispanic, African–American, and Southeast Asian and live in multigenerational households. The school's special education and English as a second language programs are filled to capacity, and the principal, staff, and teachers complain about the extensive behavioral issues and large numbers of disruptions during class time. A majority of students receive free or reduced lunches.

As the psychologists research existing preventive programs that have been used to target substance abuse prevention in schools, they come across several options that have substantial empirical support. The team ultimately selects a program developed originally for a primarily white, upper-middle-class sub-urban high school. Selection criteria are based largely on cost, availability of materials, and the fact that the original program developer was a previous colleague of one of the current psychologists. The program does have some evidence of initial empirical support.

The team plans to adapt the original prevention curriculum by editing the brochures and other marketing materials to including a more "diverse" representation of faces. They also decide that it would be helpful to separate the students by race during presentations and activities and to bring in speakers that match the racial backgrounds of each group of students. However, the language of the prevention program will remain completely in English because none of the psychologists speak any other languages. Once the intervention has been pilot tested for a few months, the psychologists will assess the program's effectiveness using the same evaluation criteria that the original developer proposed.

Discussion

As highlighted by the illustrative case above, the area of prevention poses a unique set of ethical challenges. The emerging importance of cultural competence in mental health care has been underscored by several trends. As population diversity continues to expand within the United States and internationally, clinicians are increasingly exposed to patients from a wide variety of backgrounds, demographic characteristics, and perceptions of mental health (Betancourt, Green, Carrillo, & Park, 2005). The combination of these diversity factors creates the potential for various types of cultural conflict in mental health care, particularly within the realm of prevention work. As such, cultural competence has become a necessity for psychologists in the provision of preventive interventions. In this case, the use of an intervention that is not validated on the target population violates the APA Code (2010) principles of justice (D) and respect for people's rights and dignity (E). It also violates Standard 2.01(b) because those involved do not appear to recognize the importance of understanding the cultural backgrounds of the participants. Specifically, not using an intervention validated on the target population does not provide equal access to quality treatment or take into account the elimination of cultural bias. The issue of cultural competence is more complex in prevention work.

The APA (2014) published a set of Guidelines for Prevention in Psychology to address the most important areas of prevention practice, research, and education. Guideline 2 highlights socially and culturally relevant preventive practices. Mental health professionals are encouraged to design, select, and implement culturally relevant preventive programs; a prevention intervention that is shown to be effective for one population and setting may not be as effective or applicable to another population and setting. Whenever possible, it is recommended that theory- and evidence-based preventive programs are selected based on the amount of empirical support for their efficacy in specific contexts and for specific program goals (Guideline 1, APA, 2014). This guideline was explicitly broken by the psychologists as they selected an intervention that was not validated on the population, only had initial empirical support, and may have been chosen because of a connection with the creator rather than because it was best for the population.

Cultural competence is an important ethical component of applied psychological preventive efforts. Multicultural differences between and within populations present a unique challenge to preventionists working at each stage of prevention intervention (i.e., design, implementation, and evaluation). The dangers of value imposition and ethnocentric interventions in individual therapy (Sue & Sue, 2012) also hold true for prevention work, as psychologists run the risk of imposing value-laden decisions at each stage of prevention (Danish, 1990). Prevention practitioners have the ethical responsibility of examining the intersections of their own cultural backgrounds, values, and biases with their prevention work (Sanson-Fisher & Turnbull, 1987; Sparks & Park, 2000). It is also essential for these beliefs to be communicated clearly with the target population. If left unaddressed, cultural values and biases may negatively impact the target population (Trickett, 1998; Trickett & Levin, 1990). Although the psychologists are attempting to address the context of the target population, their approach is based on superficial factors such as pictures on a marketing brochure. True cultural adaptation would address deeper between- and within-group differences such as acculturation, worldview, and ethnic identity.

Recent work by Reese and Vera (2007) also highlights the ethical obligation of preventionists to examine their own values and belief systems. Cultural relevance refers to the matching of values and beliefs between an intervention and the target population it intends to serve (Reese & Vera, 2007). The cultural relevance of a prevention program can influence participant participation, satisfaction, retention, and acceptance (Reese & Vera, 2007). Indeed, primary prevention can be viewed as an act of "premeditated intrusion into the lives and settings of individuals and groups" (Trickett & Levin, 1990, p. 9). Prevention psychologists should seek to establish collaborative partnerships with the target population by gaining familiarity with the culture of the community (Hage & Kenny, 2009). Reese and Vera (2007) provide suggestions to assist in this process, including: (a) developing positive working relationships with community members; and (b) developing and implementing programs that are valued by the community (p. 771).

The APA Code (2010) offers standards for professional practice regarding cultural competence. However, no specific guidelines exist to assist in the process of exploring cultural relevance, potential biases, and value imposition in prevention work. Pope (1990) and Trickett and Levin (1990) have also proposed some questions to help preventionists examine aspects of program development, implementation, and evaluation: what images do preventionists have of society? What images does society have of preventionists? What are the possibilities for direct harm to the people being treated and to those indirectly affected by prevention interventions (Pope, 1990; Trickett & Levin, 1990)? It is essential for prevention practitioners to engage in a continuous process of examination in order to minimize the cultural biases and potential harm that may inadvertently result from multicultural differences (Hage & Kenny, 2009; Reese & Vera, 2007). Further, examination of such differences between the preventionist and the target population may contribute to the development of a positive image of the preventionist as a multicultural and social change agent who is "strength-based, focuses on prevention, and empowerment, and proactively engages in creating social change by addressing community conditions through education, research, intervention, and political processes" (Hage & Kenny, 2009, p. 85). The APA Multicultural Guidelines (2003) were developed to provide psychologists with guidance regarding multicultural competency in all issues addressing multiculturalism and diversity. These recommendations aim to "articulate respect and inclusiveness for the national heritage of all cultural groups, recognition of cultural contexts as defining forces for individuals' and groups' lived experiences, and the role of external forces such as historical, economic, and sociopolitical events" (APA, 2003). In the case of this intervention, this would suggest a deeper understanding of the "lived experience" of the target population (APA, 2003). The challenge for these psychologists is to bridge cultural and perhaps other differences in order to utilize an approach that is effective.

In order to develop an understanding of the target population in primary prevention programs, it is necessary to conduct a large-scale needs assessment (Romano & Hage, 2000). Planning a prevention program without a thorough understanding of the context of behavior can lead to additional ethical concerns along the way; thus, there is an inherent risk involved when prevention psychologists do not develop competence in needs assessment (Sue, Arrendondo, & McDavis, 1992). Conducting a needs assessment may involve the use of both qualitative and quantitative research methods (D'Aunno & Price, 1985). However, this is a necessary practice in order to ensure adequate understanding of the multiple contexts informing the targeted problem behavior. All of these concerns are reflected in APA Standards 9.01 (Bases for Assessment) and 9.02 (Use of Assessments).

Hage and Kenny (2009) also recommend that ethical prevention efforts work to effect social change and reduce social inequities. The significance of social justice promotion through advocacy is often overlooked in psychology, particularly within the context of prevention efforts (Kenny & Hage, 2009). Because prevention work has the potential for large-scale societal impact, however, mental health professionals have an ethical responsibility to address issues of oppression and exploitation (Perry & Albee, 1994; Schwartz & Lindley, 2009) and to strive to be agents of social justice in the communities in which they work (Hage, 2005; Vera & Speight, 2003). Practitioners must aim to deal ethically with the complex interchange of social forces in prevention work, such as racism and poverty, in order to develop and maintain socially just prevention programs. Additionally, it has been suggested that ethical prevention practitioners must seek to balance power in their relationships with their target populations (Brabeck & Ting, 2000) while addressing systemic oppression.

Issues in Program Adaptation

Program adaptation refers to the modification of an intervention program's content to respond to the needs of a specific group (Castro, Barrera, & Martinez, 2004). Historically, most universal prevention programs were designed for mainstream American culture, and thus reflect European–American, middle-class values and methods (Kumpfer, Alvarado, Smith, & Bellamy, 2002). As a result, mental health professionals are tasked with the complex but necessary undertaking of revising preventive programs based on the needs, values, traditions, risk factors, and protective factors for the specific population at hand. Castro et al. (2004) recommend accounting for several different dimensions in order to guide program adaptation, including variations in (a) cognitive–information processing characteristics (e.g., age, developmental level, language), (b) affective–motivational characteristics (e.g., gender, religion, ethnicity, socioeconomic status), and (c) environmental characteristics (i.e., characteristics of the local physical environment). At the same time, adaptation of prevention programs must take into consideration the diversity that exists within cultural groups as well. Kumpfer et al. (2002) suggest that mental health professionals must be wary of within-group differences across a number of dimensions, including but not limited to race, ethnicity, social class, family income, gender, sexual orientation, geographical region, education, and acculturation level. Turner (2000) recommends that program modification takes into consideration the following cultural factors: (a) the degree of influence of specific cultural family risk and protective factors; (b) acculturation, lifestyle, and identity; (c) variations in the level of acculturation across family members that may produce conflict; (d) family relocation history; (e) the history of trauma, loss, and PTSD symptoms; (f) the levels of financial and work stress; and (g) language preferences and proficiency.

However, adaptation is not always as straightforward as simply revising existing evidence-based interventions to incorporate specific cultural values and needs. Program adaptation inherently conflicts with the concept of fidelity of implementation, which refers to the degree to which a manualized prevention program is delivered as prescribed by the program creator (Castro et al., 2004). Although the efficacy of prevention interventions depends largely on the successful adaptation of program content to match the needs and values of the specific population at hand, the core components of an empirically supported program should not be overlooked. It has been suggested that prevention programs seek to strike a balance between adaptation and fidelity by maintaining the original core components that account for the main effects, while also addressing the need for local adaptation (Backer, 2001; Castro et al., 2004).

Backer (2001) has proposed a set of guidelines for program implementation in order to maintain a balance between fidelity and adaptation while also maximizing program effectiveness. These six steps are: (1) identifying and understanding the theory behind a selected prevention program; (2) conducting an analysis of the core components of the program; (3) assessing fidelity and adaptation concerns for the target population; (4) consulting with the original program developers to review the preceding steps and how they have shaped a plan for implementing the program in a specific setting; (5) consulting and collaborating with the target population that the intervention will benefit; and (6) developing a comprehensive implementation plan based on all of the input received from the preceding steps.

In short, to act ethically in this case, the preventionists involved must take several additional steps in order to develop a program that is appropriate for the community, they must be more self-aware about their own cultural perspectives, and they should undertake any continuing education they need in order to become culturally competent. The following case further highlights these cultural competence issues.

The Case of Community Intervention and Prevention with an American Indian Tribe

Ellen, a white licensed psychologist, works in a small, rural community bordering an American Indian reservation. She has been invited to attend a meeting with other local leaders who have gathered to address an alarming statistic in their community. The suicide attempt rate among Indian youth aged 15–19 in this community is ten times the national average and three times the rate of similar rural communities across the state. The participants in this meeting include the mayor of Ellen's town, city council members, school officials, representatives of the local Indian Health Service (IHS), and tribal council members. Intense discussion quickly ensues as to the reasons for the escalating rate of suicide attempts among the community and how best to find a solution.

Representatives of the IHS cite a long history of trauma and racism against native peoples as being responsible for the incidents of self-harm. Town leaders cite family dynamics, particularly the involvement of alcohol among families. While there are disagreements about the cause of the high suicide rate, everyone present agrees that a solution needs to be found to reduce or eliminate teen suicides. Those gathered turn to Ellen, as the local expert in behavioral health, for guidance on how best to proceed with identifying contributing factors and reducing the incidence of adolescent suicides and suicide attempts in their community.

Competence for Prevention Work

Competence for prevention work necessitates specialized training to acquire the awareness, knowledge, and skills vital for competent and ethical practice. While little has been written on the specific competencies necessary for ethical prevention practice (Schwartz, Hage, & Gonzalez, 2013), the APA Guidelines for Prevention in Psychology (APA, 2014) encourage psychological practitioners to seek education and training in preventive approaches through course work and informal training opportunities. In addition, they outline a number of knowledge and skill domains that are important to engaging in ethical prevention practice, including: (a) understanding the difference between preventive and remedial approaches; (b) assessing community needs; (c) understanding systemic approaches that incorporate cultural and contextual factors; (d) collaborating with interdisciplinary teams; (e) promoting positive development across the life span; (f) empowering individuals and communities; (g) developing strength-based approaches that reduce risk and enhance resilience; (h) influencing policy decisions; and (i) evaluating preventive interventions (APA, 2014).

Discussion

The ethical considerations in this scenario are numerous. To begin, for Ellen to work effectively and competently to address the issue of teen suicide in this community, she needs to understand the Native American culture. The APA Multicultural Guidelines (2003) would be a good guide on competence with multicultural issues. The issue in need of prevention – teen suicide – exists within a cultural community with values, traditions, beliefs, and heritage that encompass every aspect of their lives. The native youth involved are part of a community that has a long history of oppression and discrimination. As APA Standard 2.01 indicates Ellen is not familiar with issues specific to Native American culture, she will need to begin by seeking out information and consultation to obtain the awareness, knowledge, and skills needed to work effectively in the community. Ellen needs to be aware that despite her best efforts, racial biases and prejudice may still be apparent in the effort to obtain cultural competency and to integrate native values and heritage into her prevention work (Sue & Sue, 2012). She will need to work diligently to avoid imposing her own values, worldview, cultural assumptions, and biases on the local community (Principle D: Justice, APA, 2010). Indeed, a first step for her may be stating these cultural assumptions and values in order to collaborate effectively with the native population in planning the intervention (Trickett, Barone, & Watts, 2000). Ellen may also be encouraged to invite ongoing discussion of privilege and power with those involved in the prevention intervention (APA, 2014).

In designing an effective psychological intervention to prevent teen suicide, Ellen needs to attend to the culture of youth within the context of this community and their families. An important step in this process will be for Ellen to consider the fit between her own assumptions, belief system, and expected process of change and those of the community. A danger in this situation is the possibility of "implicit imperialism," in which the prevention program is premised on cultural assumptions neither shared nor endorsed by the community and/or youth. As noted by Trickett et al. (2000), "...disregard for the cultural ecology of a setting may result in the arbitrary application of programs that are at best ineffective, and at worst disruptive or harmful" (p. 313). In addition, Ellen needs to recognize the importance of actively promoting and infusing diversity as a resource for the development of a preventive intervention, as well working collaboratively with the community to ensure clear, autonomous, and informed participation (APA, 2014). Ellen would be well advised to seek out consultation with other psychologists who may be more familiar with this population and who can help her evaluate her own cultural competence (Standard 2.01c).

Another sensitive contextual factor to which Ellen needs to attend is community-level political dynamics, which, while outside the immediate context of the prevention intervention, may present as powerful forces that impact and shape the efficacy of the helping relationship. For example, significant historical health care disparities exist among Indian people, and their health care status and the reasons for their illnesses differ from those of the general U.S. population (Willis, DeLeon, Haldane, & Heldring, 2014). American Indians experience some of the worst health conditions in the United States and these disparities have existed for 500 years, since the time colonists arrived in America (Jones, 2006). Any interventions that are developed need to take account of the fact that members of the Indian community tend to have lower incomes, with 55 percent of their incomes being 200 percent below the federal poverty level (Willis, 2000). Few reservations have on-site clinics that have the capacity to provide health care and prevention services to youth (Willis, 2000). Legislation and initiatives to provide funding at the federal level are sorely needed to address the "epidemic" of youth suicides in American Indian and Alaskan Native communities, the rate of which is 70 percent higher than the general population of the United States (Dorgan, 2010). In addition, one of the most important interventions Ellen can implement is to empower the community by creating sustainable change and giving voice to community members (APA, 2014).

A related issue is the importance of attending to the rural context of the prevention intervention. To begin, rural settings are distinguished from urban areas by the reduced availability of specialized resources. They often include fewer formalized roles and tend to rely more on informal skills and communication networks within the local community to accomplish necessary tasks. In addition, mental health professionals tend to be more visible and people in rural areas may initially place more importance on the personal qualities of the helping professional rather than, for example, her or his credentials. Some authors indicate that a more adaptive approach might be to focus on interpersonal interactions, especially during the preliminary stages of the consultation (Trickett et al., 2000).

Ellen also needs to attend to general issues of competence guided by Standard 2 in the APA Code (2010). She will need to make sure she pursues appropriate training and supervision for issues outside of her competence. Ellen may struggle with her worldview potentially differing from that of the community. Balancing the best evidence on appropriate interventions, cultural competency, and her own potential biases will be the challenge and the key to Ellen's success.

The Case of Health in the Rural Southwest

Sam, a Mexican–American psychologist, is working as a consultant for a rural county in the southwest United States. The county has recently been categorized as one of the top five counties in the United States for both obesity and diabetes. Sam has been asked to design a prevention program to address health in this county and to carefully evaluate the success of the prevention intervention. The county officials view these health issues as a crisis and want to ensure that the approach is well researched and evaluated. The county commissioner who is heading up the project believes that the residents are lazy and would like to limit access to unhealthy food if he could. He states that for the prevention intervention to be successful, Sam must prove people are less obese in the future and are eating less unhealthy food. The county commissioner believes the way to accomplish that is with an aggressive campaign that puts the full responsibility of obesity on the individual. The county has few resources and wants to ensure that the resources they spend are worth it. In addition, regarding the targets of the intervention – obesity and diabetes – the county also reports high rates of other health and mental health concerns, including substance abuse (high prescription drug abuse), as well as high rates of depression. The demographics of the county are 65 percent Latino, with parts of the county being primarily Spanish-speaking, and the county has large areas that have residents with low socioeconomic status. The psychologist must choose an appropriate intervention that is targeted at this community, as well as measure its efficacy.

Discussion

As is typical of the previous cases, there are many ethical issues raised here, especially the biased and uninformed attitudes of the county commissioner, but this discussion will focus on the unique ethical issues involved in responsible evaluation of prevention activities. Preventive interventions have an impact on the individual, the individual's immediate system, and the larger community (Albee, 1986; Durlak & Wells, 1997). Evaluation issues are complicated; the presence of numerous contexts may increase the potential for negative outcomes (Caplan & Caplan, 1994). Outcomes need to be evaluated at multiple levels, along with attention to unforeseen negative outcomes arising across multiple contexts. In this case, intervening with diet and exercise has the potential to create changes in the families and communities involved. Here, Sam is facing pressure to use a confrontational approach that does not take into account the context for behavior. He must find a responsible way to cope with this stress. Finally, the outcome of prevention programs may be dynamic over time, suggesting the importance of ongoing, long-term evaluation (Brown & Liao, 1999) and the danger of misinterpreting immediate results. A short-term intervention in this case, especially one that is confrontational, may provide immediate changes, but there may be a regression or even negative impact in terms of long-term outcomes. An emphasis on long-term evaluation must also be balanced in a responsible fashion with the importance of responding to the immediate need for prevention programs.

Prevention practitioners must also be alert to evidence related to context-specific prevention outcomes (Durlak & Wells, 1997). Subtle or unique differences in populations could make an effective prevention program in one population potentially harmful with a different population (Romano & Hage, 2000). In this case, it is important to consider whether the approaches used are validated with a similar population. For example, Sam should verify that the intervention has been normed in Spanish with a Latino population. Although the cultural relevance of therapeutic approaches is an important issue addressed by the Principle D: Justice of the APA Code (2010), it is particularly salient for prevention, which targets individual change as well as systemic and community change (Trickett, 1998). Caplan and Caplan (1994) point out the potential dangers of mass-produced prevention programs that do not address cultural relevance. For example, an intervention on healthy eating normed on white, teenage families would not be appropriate for a primarily older, Latino population.

Complicated issues in prevention program evaluation also bring up issues of professional competence (Standard 2.01, APA, 2010; Pope, 1990). In addition to general research competence, prevention practitioners must be competent in specific approaches relevant to evaluation in prevention such as needs assessment, formative and summative evaluation, and long-term follow-up (Romano & Hage, 2000). For example, knowledge of proper assessment regarding how a prevention program is administered throughout is vital to the ultimate conclusions of a program evaluation. Universal evaluation problems related to poor instrumentation, unclear target variables, infrequent assessment, no long-term outcomes, and researcher bias could contribute to misleading results. In this case, there is a real danger of stigmatizing a community. It would be very important for Sam to include members of the community in every aspect of the evaluation and communication of results, as Standard 3.07 indicates (APA, 2010). In this case, one of the challenges is balancing the needs of the community with pressure from the county to see results and to use a prescribed approach. Additionally, prevention researchers must be competent in methods to evaluate multiple ecological levels. Program evaluation that focuses on one ecological level (e.g., the individual) may only assess gains in knowledge, not behavior change. Finally, prevention focusing on social change often does not fit within a traditional quantitative research design (Prilleltensky & Nelson, 1997). Understanding the subjective experience of participants in order to understand the context of their behavior necessitates knowledge of qualitative methods. In the case of a community with multiple health issues, it is important to understand the context of behavior so as not to make the mistake of addressing one issue and exacerbating a different issue. For example, if unemployment is the root of health and mental health issues, it may be important to conduct a vocational intervention along with any health intervention.

Due to the large scope of typical preventive interventions, there may be multiple methods of service delivery. If a well-designed prevention program is not evaluated across each of these methods, the causative factors in the outcomes will be unclear and will not be able to be generalized. A lack of formative feedback reduces the replicability of the intervention and ultimately slows down the advancement of prevention science (Durlak & Wells, 1997; Guterman, 2004; Munoz, Mrazek, & Haggerty, 1996; Price, Cowen, Lorion, & Ramos-McKay, 1989; Waldo & Schwartz, 2003). Similarly, the lack of clear, summative evaluation poses multiple ethical dilemmas. Problems in research design, outcome measures, targets for evaluation, and/or a lack of long-term outcomes could lead to a misinterpretation of results. Specifically, misinterpretation of outcome data could raise ethical issues regarding the potential negative impact on a community and field (Bloom, 1996) and lead to deleterious effects such as stigmatizing a community or leading to unsuccessful follow-up programs. For instance, in this case, it might be appropriate to utilize community educators who are familiar with the community. It would be important to evaluate their training, the fidelity of the intervention, and outcomes during, after, and while following up the intervention. The health of the community is a dynamic process; for example, a parent who eats healthy foods and exercises will impact their children. Evaluation of prevention must consider the full context of behavior. To be successful, Sam must truly understand the community and advocate for the best approach that balances context and impact. If the county commissioner insists on an approach that is culturally insensitive, and thus ineffective, Sam would have an ethical responsibility (Standard 1.03.04; Conflict between Ethics and Organizational Demands, APA, 2010) to not participate in the prevention project.

APA Ethical Standards and Prevention

The APA Code (2010) has been criticized for failing to provide ethical guidelines that address the unique issues raised in both prevention and systems-oriented social change (Schwartz & Hage, 2009). Further, Serrano-Garcia (1994) argues that the APA ethical standards may be incompatible with the goals of action research and social change and may actually undermine the efforts of prevention-focused providers, unless the interactions between power and ethics are more clearly addressed.

However, the Preamble and General Principles of the APA Code of Ethics (2010) do offer general aspirational standards to those engaged in prevention. For example, the Preamble asserts the importance of "respecting and protecting human rights," as well as striving to "help the public in developing informed judgments and choices concerning human behavior" (p. 3). In addition, Principle E, Respect for People's

Rights and Dignity, states that psychologists must respect cultural differences and take such differences into account when working with diverse cultural and ethnic groups. The APA Code (2010) also introduces the principle of justice, affirming that all persons are entitled to "access to and benefit from the contributions of psychology and to equal quality in the processes, procedures, and services being conducted by psychologists" (p. 4). Furthermore, the APA Code (2010) urges psychologists to "take precautions to ensure that their potential biases, the boundaries of their competence, and the limitations of their expertise do not lead to or condone unjust practices" (p. 4) (Toporek & Williams, 2006).

In closing, while recognizing the importance of the aspirational guidelines found in the APA Code of Ethics (2010) in informing these cases, we propose that several key ethical issues in prevention need to be carefully addressed by collaboration with community leaders. These issues, briefly outlined below, include cultural diversity, informed consent, professional competency, and involving community partners in a focus on social change. Cultural relevance is particularly salient for competency in prevention, which addresses individual change as well as systemic and community change (Trickett, 1998).

Recently, there has been increasing attention given to addressing competent prevention practice (Hage et al., 2007; O'Neil & Britton, 2009), resulting in the APA Guidelines for Prevention in Psychology (2014). Psychologists are encouraged to obtain training in preventive approaches through a number of different avenues, including respecialization programs, postdoctoral fellowships, continuing education programs, self-study, conferences, and combinations of these. Those already in practice and unable to participate in concentrated, formal training programs may be able to utilize continuing education programs. Psychologists may also gain supervised experience and consultation by working with psychologists or other professionals who are skilled in prevention. Literature relevant to prevention is available through professional journals, including a growing number of applied journals in, for example, psychiatry, public health, and psychology. Several knowledge and skill domains important to psychologists engaging in prevention have been identified (Conyne, 2015; Hage et al., 2007; O'Neil & Britner, 2009). The domains include: (a) understanding distinctions between preventive and remedial approaches; (b) designing and implementing educational programs; (c) assessing community needs; (d) understanding systemic approaches that incorporate cultural and contextual factors into preventive interventions; (e) using group skills and approaches, when appropriate, in program design and implementation; (f) collaborating with interdisciplinary teams that include professionals and community leaders; (g) grant-writing and marketing skills to address the sustainability of preventive efforts; (h) promoting positive development across the life span; (i) empowering individuals and communities to work on their own behalf; (j) developing strength-based approaches that reduce risk and enhance resilience in individuals and communities; (k) influencing policy decisions and their impacts on preventive efforts; and (l) evaluating preventive interventions.

Conclusion

Although the efficacy and utility of prevention is well supported (i.e., Kumpfer, Alvarado, Smith, & Bellamy, 2002; O'Connell, Boat, & Warner, 2009), unfortunately training still lags behind. It is imperative that training programs provide real-world examples (such as the cases provided above) and experiences for psychologists in training. The implications of prevention on the individual as well as their dynamic ecological contexts are real and raise important ethical dilemmas. Further research is needed on the implications of prevention programs and how to best prepare competent prevention practitioners.

References

Albee, G. W. (1986). Toward a just society. Lessons from observations on the primary prevention of psychopathology. *American Psychologist, 41*, 891–898.

American Psychological Association (2003). Guidelines on Multicultural Education, Training, Research, Practice, and Organizational Change for Psychologists. *The American Psychologist, 58*, 377–402.

American Psychological Association (2010). Ethical principles of psychologists and code of conduct (2002, Amended June 1, 2010). Retrieved from www.apa.org/ethics/code/index.aspx

American Psychological Association (2014). Guidelines for prevention in psychology. *American Psychologist, 69*, 285–296.

Backer, T. E. (2001). *Finding the balance – Program fidelity and adaptation in substance abuse prevention: A state-of-the-art review.* Rockville, MD: Center for Substance Abuse Prevention.

Betancourt, J. R., Green, A. R., Carrillo, J. E., & Park, E. R. (2005). Cultural competence and health care disparities: Key perspectives and trends. *Health affairs, 24*, 499–505.

Bloom, M. (1996). *Prevention practices. Issues in children's and families lives* (Vol. 5). Thousand Oaks, CA: Sage Publications.

Brabeck, M. A. & Ting, K. (2000). Feminist ethics: Lenses for examining ethical and psychological practice. In Brabeck, M.M. (Ed.), *Practicing feminist ethics in psychology* (pp. 17–35). Washington, DC: American Psychological Association.

Brown, C. H. & Liao, J. (1999). Principles for designing randomized preventive trials in mental health: An emerging developmental epidemiology paradigm. *American Journal of Community Psychology, 27*, 673–710.

Caplan, G. & Caplan, R. B. (1994). The need for quality control in primary prevention. *Journal of Primary Prevention, 15*, 15–29.

Castro, F. G., Barrera Jr., M., & Martinez Jr., C. R. (2004). The cultural adaptation of prevention interventions: Resolving tensions between fidelity and fit. *Prevention Science, 5*, 41–45.

Conyne, R. K. (2004). *Preventive counseling: Helping people to become empowered in systems and settings.* New York, NY: Brunner-Routledge.

Conyne, R. K. (2015). *Counseling for wellness and prevention: Helping people become empowered in systems and settings* (3rd edn.). New York, NY: Brunner-Routledge.

D'Aunno, T. & Price, R. H. (1985). Organizational adaptation to changing environments: Community mental health and drug abuse services. *American Behavioral Scientist, 28*, 669–683.

Danish, S. J. (1990). Ethical considerations in the design, implementation, and evaluation of developmental interventions. In C. B. Fisher & W. W. Tryon (Eds.), *Ethics in applied developmental psychology: Emerging issues in an emerging field. Annual advances in applied developmental psychology* (Vol. 4, pp. 93–112). Westport, CT: Greenwood.

Dorgan, B. L. (2010). The tragedy of Native American youth suicide. *Psychological Services, 7*, 213–218.

Durlak, J. A. & Wells, A. M. (1997). Primary prevention mental health programs for children and adolescents: A meta-analytic review. *American Journal of Community Psychology, 25*, 115–152.

Guterman, N. B. (2004). Advancing prevention research on child abuse, youth violence, and domestic violence: Emerging strategies and issues. *Journal of Interpersonal Violence, 19*, 299–321.

Hage, S. M. (2005). Future considerations for fostering multicultural competence in mental health and educational settings: Social justice implications. In M. G. Constantine, D. Sue, M. G. Constantine, & D. Sue (Eds.), *Strategies for building multicultural competence in mental health and educational settings* (pp. 285–302). Hoboken, NJ: John Wiley & Sons, Inc.

Hage, S. M. & Kenny, M. E. (2009). Promoting a social justice approach to prevention: Future directions for training, practice, and research. *Journal of Primary Prevention, 30*, 75–87.

Hage, S. M., Romano, J. L., Conyne, R. K., Kenny, M., Matthews, C., Schwartz, J. P., & Waldo, M. (2007). Best practices guidelines on prevention practice, research, training, and social advocacy for psychologists. *The Counseling Psychologist, 35*, 493–566.

Jones, D. S. (2006). The persistence of American Indian health disparities. *American Journal of Public Health, 96*, 2122–2134.

Kenny, M. E. & Hage, S. M. (2009). The next frontier: Prevention as an instrument of social justice. *The Journal of Primary Prevention, 30*, 1–10.

Kumpfer, K. L., Alvarado, R., Smith, P., & Bellamy, N. (2002). Cultural sensitivity and adaptation in family-based prevention interventions. *Prevention Science, 3*, 241–246.

Muñoz, R. F., Mrazek, P. J., & Haggerty, R. J. (1996). Institute of Medicine report on prevention of mental disorders: Summary and commentary. *American Psychologist, 51*, 1116–1122.

O'Connell, M. E., Boat, T., & Warner, K. E. (2009). *Preventing mental, emotional, and behavioral disorders among young people: Progress and possibilities*. Washington, DC: National Academies Press.

O'Neil, J. M. & Britner, P. A. (2009). Training primary preventionists to make a difference in people's lives. In M. E. Kenny, A. M. Horne, P. Orpinas, et al. (Eds.), *Realizing social justice: The challenge of preventive interventions* (pp. 141–162). Washington, DC: American Psychological Association.

Perry, M. & Albee, G. W. (1994). On "The Science of Prevention." *American Psychologist, 49*, 1087–1088.

Pope, K. S. (1990). Identifying and implementing ethical standards for primary prevention. *Prevention in Human Services, 8*, 43–64.

Price, R. H., Cowen, E. L., Lorion, R. P., & Ramos-McKay, J. (1989). The search for effective prevention programs: What we learned along the way. *American Journal of Orthopsychiatry, 59,* 49–58.

Prilleltensky, I. (1997). Values, assumptions, and practices: Assessing the moral implications of psychological discourse and action. *American Psychologist, 52,* 517–535.

Trickett, E. J. & Levin, G. B. (1990). Paradigms for prevention: Providing a context for confronting ethical issues. *Prevention in Human Services, 8,* 3–21.

Prilleltensky, I. & Nelson, G. (1997). Community psychology: Reclaiming social justice. In D. Fox & I. Prilleltensky (Eds.), *Critical psychology: An introduction* (pp. 166–184). Thousand Oaks, CA: Sage.

Prilleltensky, I. (2001). Value-based praxis in community psychology: Moving toward social justice and social action. *American Journal of Community Psychology, 29,* 747–778.

Reese, L. E. & Vera, E. M. (2007). Culturally relevant prevention: The scientific and practical considerations of community-based programs. *The Counseling Psychologist, 35,* 763–778.

Romano, J. L. & Hage, S. M. (2000). Prevention and counseling psychology: Revitalizing commitments for the 21st century. *The Counseling Psychologist, 28,* 733–763.

Romano, J. & Hage, S. (2000). Prevention: A call to action. *The Counseling Psychologist, 28,* 854–856.

Sanson-Fisher, R. & Turnbull, D. (1987). "To do or not to do?": Ethical problems for behavioural medicine. In S. Fairbairn & G. Fairbairn (Eds.), *Psychology, ethics and change* (pp. 191–211). New York, NY: Routledge.

Schwartz, J. & Hage, S. M. (2009). Prevention: Ethics, responsibility, and commitment to public well-being. In M. E. Kenny, A. Horne, P. Orpinas, & L. E. Reese (Eds.), *Realizing social justice: The challenge of preventive interventions* (pp. 123–140). Washington, DC: American Psychological Association.

Schwartz, J., Hage, S. M., & Gonzalez, D. (2013). Ethical principles for the practice of prevention. In E. Vera (Ed.), *Handbook of prevention in counseling psychology* (pp. 65–75). Oxford, UK: Oxford University Press.

Schwartz, J. P. & Lindley, L. D. (2009). Impacting sexism through social justice prevention: Implications at the person and environmental levels. *The Journal of Primary Prevention, 30,* 27–41.

Serrano-Garcia, I. (1994). The ethics of the powerful and the power of ethics. *American Journal of Community Psychology, 22,* 1–20.

Sparks, E. E. & Park, A. H. (2000). The integration of feminism and multiculturalism: Ethical dilemmas at the border. In M. M. Brabeck (Ed.), *Practicing feminist ethics in psychology* (pp. 203–224). Washington, DC: American Psychological Association.

Sue, D. W., Arredondo, P., & McDavis, R. J. (1992). Multicultural counseling competencies and standards: A call to the profession. *Journal of Counseling & Development, 70,* 477–486.

Sue, D. W. & Sue, D. (2002). *Counseling the culturally diverse: Theory and practice.* Hoboken, NJ: John Wiley & Sons, Inc.

Sue, D. W. & Sue, D. (2012). *Counseling the culturally diverse: Theory and practice.* New York, NY: John Wiley & Sons.

Toporek, R. L. & Williams, R. A. (2006). Ethics and professional issues related to the practice of social justice in counseling psychology. In R. L. Toporek, L. Gerstein, N. Fouad, G. Roysircar, & T. Israel (Eds.), *Handbook for social justice in counseling psychology: Leadership, vision, and action* (pp. 17–34). Thousand Oaks, CA: Sage.

Trickett, E. J. (1998). Toward a framework for defining and resolving ethical issues in the protection of communities involved in primary prevention projects. *Ethics & Behavior*, *8*, 321–337.

Trickett, E. J., Barone, C. & Watts, R. (2000). Contextual influences in mental health consultation: Toward an ecological perspective on radiating change. In J. Rappaport & E. Seidman (Eds.), *Handbook of community psychology* (pp. 303–330). New York, NY: Kluwer Academic/Plenum Publishers.

Turner, W. (2000). Cultural considerations in family-based primary prevention programs in drug abuse. *Journal of Primary Prevention*, *21*, 285–303.

Vera, E. M. & Reese, L. E. (2000). Preventive interventions with school-age youth. In S. D. Brown & R. W. Lent (Eds.), *Handbook of counseling psychology* (pp. 411–434). New York, NY: Wiley.

Vera, E. M. & Speight, S. L. (2003). Multicultural competence, social justice, and counseling psychology: Expanding our roles. *The Counseling Psychologist*, *31*, 253–272.

Waldo, M. & Schwartz, J. P. (2003). Research competencies in prevention. Symposium conducted at the meeting of Prevention Competencies at the 111th Annual Convention of the American Psychological Association, Toronto, Ontario.

Willis, D. J. (2000). American Indians: The forgotten race. *The Clinical Psychology of Ethnic Minorities*, *8*, 1–2.

Willis, D. J., DeLeon, P. H., Haldane, S., & Heldring, M. B. (2014). Personal perspectives on the public policy process: Making a difference. *Professional Psychology: Research and Practice*, *45*, 143–151.

Vera, E. M. & Shin, R. Q. (2006). Promoting strengths in a socially toxic world: Supporting resiliency with systemic interventions. *The Counseling Psychologist*, *34*, 80–89.

33 Fostering Ethical Mental Health Practice across Diverse Settings and Populations

Concluding Thoughts

Elizabeth Reynolds Welfel and Mark M. Leach

As described in the preface, the purpose of this volume was to examine the ethical issues embedded in specific practice settings and with diverse populations. We planned the book to focus on complex and realistic ethical challenges that professionals face in these settings in order to expand the ethics scholarship in these areas. Did we succeed? Only the reader can judge that, of course, but we believe there are several clear messages from the book. The first is that the process of determining what ought to be done when ethical questions arise fully engages both the mind and the heart. Clinicians worry whether they will take an action that harms the client or ends treatment: they want to do what is right. They also sometimes worry about whether doing the right thing will jeopardize their own status or future in their organization. Ashton and Sullivan's chapter on issues in hospital settings highlights this experience of feeling caught between being a good citizen of the organization and an advocate for the welfare of the client/patient. Similarly, the chapter of ethical issues in college and university counseling centers by Covey and Keller illuminates the tension that clinicians experience when caught between the limits of program resources and the needs of the population they aim to serve. Such tensions are not limited to therapeutic work; Perry and Voight's contribution underscores the conflict between advancing one's career as a researcher and serving the needs of the research participants and participant organizations. That chapter also explores the ethical complications inherent in working with professionals from other careers such as educators and managers.

Taken together, these chapters also highlight a second issue that needs more attention in the professional literature. To date, this literature has centered largely on three components of ethical decision-making: (1) the knowledge base of standards, principles, and guidelines for practice; (2) models for decision-making; and (3) the attitudes mental health professionals need to resolve ethical questions. Clearly, these intellectual components are the foundation of responsible action. No one acts ethically without some level of thought behind the behavior. However, this cognitive and technical focus can leave the impression that concern about negative effects on our own careers from doing the right thing is either of minor consequence or in itself unwise or unethical. It suggests that even considering anything other than the welfare of the client(s) is ethically problematic. Such an interpretation of ethical duties is misguided and ultimately harmful. At its foundation, it ignores human nature. Instead of repressing feelings such as worrying about angering a boss, losing reimbursement from insurers, or alienating research sites, these reactions should be acknowledged without guilt. There is nothing unethical about these feelings and ethics education at all levels should more directly communicate this message. The absence of a conscious acknowledgment of the reality of such concerns increases the risk of making the very ethical errors the practitioner wants to avoid. Moreover, they can lead practitioners to be reluctant to seek consultation or supervision, fearing that they will be viewed as less ethical than other professionals. Pope and Vasquez (2016) echoed this view when they call for explicit discussion of feelings of attraction to clients during graduate training and practice. Psychologists, due to training or other reasons, tend to diminish the influence of emotions and other nonrational factors on ethical decision-making. The article by Rogerson and colleagues (2011) demonstrates the inevitable influences of "nonrational processes" on ethical decision-making. Acknowledging and normalizing these processes may lead to better decisions based on more robust information.

It follows, then, that this volume also reinforces the essential role of consultation and supervision in responsible work in applied psychology. Consultation is crucial because, as Johnson et al. (2012) noted, competence is best understood as a communal construct – the highest standards of practice derive not from isolated individual reasoning, but from individual thought supplemented by consultation with other mental health professionals, with ethics committees, and by reference to the wisdom in the broader psychological literature. These scholars posit that we need to begin to conceive of competence as a communal endeavor and that fully competent practice cannot be realized in the absence of the community. As implied previously, consultation and supervision have the advantage of reducing the emotional isolation that professionals facing tough ethical questions can experience.

This handbook also reinforces one other well-established recommendation in the literature: that ethical considerations in practice are intertwined with clinical and legal considerations. It is not possible to act ethically if professional practice is not clinically appropriate, as the chapters from Perez and Lee-Barber on therapy with LGBT clients and from Singer and Fuentes on working with immigrant clients so aptly demonstrate. These also highlight the fluid and dynamic nature of competence. The chapter from Van Allen and his colleagues is a clear example of that fact – no child therapist can currently provide optimal service to this population without the knowledge to appreciate the role of social media in young people's lives, the skill to implement online resources as appropriate, and the capacity to evaluate the ethical and legal dimensions of social media for psychotherapy practice. None of these influences on therapy were even conceived of as recently as a decade ago. Competent practice demands both honest evaluation of one's own capacity to work with specific clients and settings and openness to continual updating of one's knowledge and skills. Similarly, the ethical standards themselves are influenced by legal rulings and often contain both ethical and legal dimensions, as Benjamin and Beck describe so clearly in their chapter. Prior to the rulings in the Tarasoff case and the development of child abuse reporting statutes, mental health professions typically conceived of the confidentiality of therapeutic communications as absolute. Moreover, they did not conceive of duties to any persons outside of the therapeutic relationship and saw no duty to any third parties beyond notification of law enforcement of imminent dangers. The language regarding limits of confidentiality in the American Psychological Association Code, for example, only appeared subsequent to the Tarasoff ruling (APA, 1981).

Recommendations for Changes in Ethics Teaching and Scholarship

We view this handbook as a jumping-off point for more scholarship and more comprehensive ethics education. Specifically, we advocate for the following.

Recommendation 1: Ethics Education for the Real World – A Process, Not an Event

The limited research on the content of graduate education in ethics indicates that most applied psychology programs offer one single semester-long course devoted primarily to ethics education. Most instruction focuses on the Code, attending to both its standards and broader principles and including substantial time for class discussion (Rodriquez et al., 2014). These courses also tend to take place early in a student's graduate program, a sensible approach to helping the student develop both an understanding of professional standards and a commitment to them. Early placement helps them conceptualize their ethical ideals more explicitly and give attention to the fundamental ethical question of "What must I do to fulfill my ethical ideals?" (Knapp & VandeCreek, 2003). However, the disadvantage of this placement is the lack of experience students have with clinical, counseling, and research environments and their rudimentary level of professional skills. Many are also uncertain of the kind of professional practice they wish to undertake. Consequently, application of ethical standards and principles to any specific setting is difficult to realize under these circumstances. In the current system, additional ethics education tends to occur in practicum placements and internships, in clinical seminars, and in informal interactions with faculty and supervisors. Although all of these forms of ethics instruction are valuable, they lack a planned approach to the unique ethical issues in applied settings and can leave important gaps in students' readiness for the ethical dimensions of practice. In addition, the familiarity of supervisors and clinical instructors with current ethics research is likely to be variable since ethics scholarship is not their major interest. Thus, we call for active consideration of a more systematic approach to ethics education for advanced graduate students, especially in the year prior to internship and during internship. These are the most opportune times to translate the knowledge of the Code to application, especially since these are the times when students get their first meaningful exposure to the messy, complex ethical issues in practice. Such an approach may also address a rather troubling finding in the research: practitioners tend not to refer to the Code when facing an ethical question (Danzinger & Welfel, 2001). Instead, they turn to colleagues for help. Clearly, consultation is good, but ignoring the Code or relying on the memory of its contents from graduate school is risky.

Another potential benefit of systematic, ongoing ethics instruction is that it may assist with the "would versus should" problem. A number of analogue studies reveal that knowing what ethical standards require does not automatically translate into a decision to implement that action. For example, when students are presented with vignettes in which a professional or student acts unethically, they easily recognize that such actions would be unethical, but when asked whether they would select that choice, more than a third of those sampled indicated they would do less than the standards designate that they should do (e.g., Bernard & Jara, 1986; Betan & Stanton, 1999; O'Donnell, 2014). It is important to note that all such studies presented hypothetical ethical choices – and even in that circumstance, students did not choose the responsible option. Clearly, ethics training as currently designed in graduate school can do better than this.

Second, ethics education in continuing education (CE) programs must be as rigorous as ethics training during graduate school. Neimeyer and his colleagues have conducted a series of studies to explore psychologists' responses to ethics training that occurs after licensing and its impacts on professional practice (e.g., Neimeyer, Taylor, & Orwig, 2013). When queried about the value of CE programs, results indicate that psychologists generally find them helpful for their work (Neimeyer, Taylor, Zemansky, & Rothke, 2013). While such positive report measures are encouraging, self-report is an inadequate measure of success, especially when there are no data that mandated participation in ethics CE programs have reduced the number of disciplinary actions (Neimeyer, Taylor, & Orwig, 2013). CE programs for psychologists, social workers, counselors, and other mental health professionals have been mandated biannually by at least half of American states as a means of protecting the public and ensuring responsible practice. Thousands of these licensed professionals spend time and money on these workshops during their careers. It follows, then, that the profession owes a duty both to the public and to practitioners to ensure that these programs are effective and efficient means of increasing participants' ability to act responsibly. However, as Neimeyer et al. (2013) caution, in spite of the positive self-reporting regarding the value of these activities, the "behavioral outcomes of CE remain largely inconclusive" (p. 109). In an era of competency-based training in graduate school, it is crucial to extend this competency-based focus to CE.

Recommendation 2: Ethics When No One Is Looking

Some chapters in the book use cases that involve ethically problematic actions (e.g., see the chapters by Schwartz, Hage, and Pao or by Anderson and Smetana). These chapters discuss both the factors that caused the professional to make an unsatisfactory choice and the factors that render that choice irresponsible. The fictional psychologists depicted in these cases are not evil or motivated by what Keith-

Spiegel termed "willful disregard" of professional ethics (1977). Instead, their misconduct represents the ordinary failings to which all professionals are vulnerable. In fact, the ethics research teaches us that it is very unlikely for a mental health professional to go through a career without any ethical missteps, whether that misstep is an inadvertent violation of confidentiality, a minor distortion of a diagnosis to obtain reimbursement, or a brief period of incompetent practice either because of personal distress or illness. Surveys by Pope and Vetter (1992), for example, indicate that psychologists admit knowing about others' violations of confidentiality or making such ethical missteps themselves rather commonly. Similarly, research by Bourdreaux (2001) reveals that 96 percent of psychologists admitted discussing client data with life partners, often but not always protecting identifying information. In fact, 30 percent of the sample indicated they had disclosed identifying confidential client information to partners. Similarly, graduate students admitted googling clients or visiting their social media sites without permission, even though they agreed that those activities require informed consent (Harris & Kurpius, 2014). Some of the cases in the book show mental health professionals who made similar ethical errors, either from a lack of knowledge or experience or due to self-protection from perceived negative organizational fallout. Bazerman and Tenbrunsel (2012) refer to many of these as resulting from ethical "blind spots." They note that most individuals tend to overestimate their ability to follow through on their principles when confronted with ethical issues, though they tend to view themselves as more ethical than other people. The analysis of these cases provides excellent direction regarding what could or should have been done to prevent that misstep and thus they have enormous educative value. They spark consideration of what blinded the professional to the risks in the situation and what could have been done to prevent such actions.

It is also important to acknowledge that comprehensive, ongoing ethics education will never eradicate all ethical errors – after all, we are fallible humans. Consequently, in our view, ethics education must have three goals: to reduce misconduct to the fullest extent possible; to motivate mental health professionals to commit to the profession's ethical values and principles; and to offer guidance about what to do next when we fall short of that goal. To date, the profession has focused more attention on the first two goals than the last, but we assert that the goal of helping us deal with our own missteps has equal status and deserves a more central place in the ethics scholarship and our teaching. This need is especially strong since most unethical behaviors will never be reported to licensing boards or even become known to administrative supervisors, clinical directors, or colleagues. In these circumstances, it is the duty of the individual clinician to acknowledge and take action to remedy the error to the extent possible. Another way to phrase it comes from C. S. Lewis: "Integrity is doing the right thing even when no one is watching." Of course, it would be naive to expect that those professionals who commit egregious violations will take personal responsibility for them. In those situations, their misconduct can only be addressed through formal complaint channels. However, in the majority of circumstances, professional errors are best characterized as ethical missteps about which we feel remorseful.

Three steps are crucial to remediating the damage from these errors (Welfel, 2005, 2012). Needless to say, the first step is self-awareness. The professional must have the ability and willingness to acknowledge the misconduct. This awareness derives from both a person's character and their commitment to the profession's ethical values or, as Handelsman et al. (2005) would term it, taking personal responsibility for ethical errors stems from the development of a professional ethical identity that includes integration of personal and professional values. The second step is to assess and respond to any damage that has been caused to the client(s). Once again, consultation with a respected colleague may be vital here to help the clinician evaluate the harm that has occurred and to devise a plan for ameliorating that harm. In cases where the client is angry at the professional and unwilling to continue services, then that colleague may be able to act as an intermediary to determine what can be done. For instance, if a therapist has been inattentive, sarcastic, and generally insensitive in a session because of illness and stress, resulting in a client's refusal to return for any additional sessions, a colleague may be able to work out a satisfactory resolution. In addition to a refund of any cost of the unhelpful session, this mediation may involve arranging a meeting during which the therapist can apologize or a referral to another therapist. Clearly, though, to be consistent with the profession's ethical values and principles, clinicians have a responsibility to do more than simply admit to themselves that they erred.

The third step in the remediation process is to develop a rehabilitation plan. In the initial step, the professional has acknowledged the misconduct, but this step translates that acknowledgment into a fuller self-assessment of the cognitive errors and emotional problems that made him/her vulnerable to the violation. The goal is not to engender shame, but to build resoluteness for change. Specifically, this means a clear plan to alleviate the issues that caused the error in the first place and to increase resilience when similar ethical challenges arise in the future. Applied to the example above, the plan may include personal therapy for the clinician to better deal with stress, CE about self-care, or temporary supervision of her work until she is stable again. To reiterate, the time for the profession to attend more directly and comprehensively to the reality of human error and to provide more guidance to practitioners is overdue. Is this issue a topic of discussion in initial or CE in ethics? We do not know, but we encourage more research and, in the meantime, more attention.

Recommendation 3: More Charitable Attributions

> There but for fortune go you or I...
>
> J. Baez [recorded by Phil Ochs] (1964)

The ethics violations that get publicized are typically egregious violations of professional standards and ordinary human morality – the therapist who seduces clients who have previously suffered abuse; the researcher who exploits vulnerable populations and falsifies data; the forensic psychologist who acts as a hired gun and distorts facts for a paycheck; the psychologist who assists with cruel and inhuman treatment of prisoners. We share the public's outrage at such actions and endorse forceful and speedy sanctions against such violators. In our less noble moments, we feel superior to such people, believing we would never participate in such actions. And, indeed, there are few of us who would behave so outrageously. However, it is important that this feeling of moral superiority does not get generalized to all professional misconduct, because such an attitude may lead us to two negative outcomes: condemning all mental health professionals for even minor misconduct; and increasing the resistance we feel to dealing with our own ethical missteps when we inevitably make them. These negative judgments may also lead us to isolate ourselves when we feel at risk of violating a boundary or when we consider acceding to a superior's questionable directive, rather than seeking the support that we need to act responsibly.

Consequently, we call for what Krieshok (2009) terms "charitable attributions" when encountering the nonegregious violations of our colleagues. Attribution theory posits that in the face of ambiguous or incomplete information people tend to attribute motives to others' behavior. Assigning reasons to people's behavior helps us all make sense of the world and reduce its unpredictability. The attributions we give to the driver who cuts us off on the highway are typically uncharitable – she is an incompetent driver or, worse, an insensitive jerk, but it is quite possible that the driver was on her way to the hospital with a sick child in the back seat or was late for work because of caretaking duties with an aging relative. Note that the first attributions suggest that the driver's behavior is stable and continuous (it is the way she always drives), while the second attributions characterize the behavior as situational (in the absence of these circumstances she does not drive recklessly). Krieshok asks us to avoid impulsive and global negative attributions about the reasons people behave in ways that seem insensitive, irresponsible, or unethical. He reminds us that we do not really know what has motivated the other person to act so badly.

The application of the concept of the charitable attribution to ethical professional practice is helpful in several ways. First, it is consistent with the research that shows that minor incidents of misconduct are often atypical for clinicians – these ethical errors can be traced to high stress, personal problems, outside pressure, and the like. In other words, not all misconduct can be attributed to global characteristics of the practitioner. Clearly, this perspective should not be interpreted to excuse the behavior, eliminate the need for some level of professional sanction, or reduce the need for intervention to remedy the negative effects as fully as possible. It does, however, open up the potential for rehabilitation. Second, using charitable situational attributions as a starting point for understanding unethical practice may remind us all that we must be vigilant about circumstantial risks of misconduct. As Pope and Vasquez (2016) have highlighted so powerfully in their work, it is not just the character disordered who violate professional standards and values. Third, charitable attributions are, in essence, more consistent with the fundamental values of the profession than global negative judgments. After all, we are engaged in a profession that, at its foundation, embraces the concept of human potential for change.

In summary, we hope this volume offers assistance to practitioners working in diverse settings with diverse populations and that it stimulates us all to design more integrated and comprehensive ethics education.

References

American Psychological Association (APA) (1981). *Ethical principles of psychologists.* Washington, DC: American Psychological Association.

Baez, J. [Recorded by Ochs, P.] (1964). *There but for fortune.* New York, NY: Vanguard.

Bazerman, M. & Tenbrunsel, A. E. (2012). *Blind spots: Why we fail to do what is right and what to do about it.* Princeton, NJ: Princeton University Press.

Bernard, J. L. & Jara, C. S. (1986). The failure of clinical psychology graduate students to apply understood ethical principles. *Professional Psychology: Research and Practice, 17,* 313–315.

Betan, E. J. & Stanton, A. L. (1999). Fostering ethical willingness: Integrating emotional and contextual awareness with rational analysis. *Professional Psychology: Research and Practice, 30,* 295–301.

Bourdreaux, C. T. (2001). Psychologist disclosures of client information to significant others. *Dissertation Abstracts International: Section B, The Sciences and Engineering, 62,* 1566.

Danzinger, P. R. & Welfel, E. R. (2001). The impact of managed care on mental health counselors: A survey of perceptions, practices and compliance with ethical standards. *Journal of Mental Health Counseling, 23,* 137–150.

Handelsman, M. M., Gottlieb, M. C., & Knapp. S. J. (2005). Training ethical psychologists: An acculturation model. *Professional Psychology: Research and Practice, 26,* 59–65.

Harris, S. E. & Kurpius, S. E. (2014). Social networks and professional ethics: Client searches, informed consent, and disclosure. *Professional Psychology: Research and Practice, 45,* 11–19.

Johnson, W. B., Barnett, J. E., Ellman, N. S., Forrest, L., & Kaslow, N. J. (2012). The competent community: Toward a vital reformulation of professional ethics. *American Psychologist, 67,* 557–569.

Keith-Spiegel, P. (1977). Violation of ethical principles due to ignorance of professional judgment versus willful disregard. *Professional Psychology, 8,* 288–296.

Knapp, S. J. & VandeCreek, L. (2003). *A guide to the 2002 revision of the American Psychological Association's ethics code.* Sarasota, FL: Professional Resources Press.

Krieshok, T. (2009). Charitable attributions for student success and life success. Retrieved from www.people.ku.edu/~tkrieshok/attributions.htm

Neimeyer, G. J., Taylor, J. M., & Orwig, J. P. (2013). Do continuing education mandates matter? An exploratory study of the relationship between CE regulations and disciplinary actions. *Professional Psychology: Research and Practice, 44,* 99–104.

Neimeyer, G. J., Taylor, J. M., Zemansky, M., & Rothke, S. E. (2013). Do mandates matter? The impact of continuing education mandates on participation in continuing professional development activities. *Professional Psychology: Research and Practice, 44,* 105–111.

O'Donnell, D. (2014). Exploration of positive ethics factors and associations with ethical decision making (electronic thesis or dissertation). Retrieved from https://etd.ohiolink.edu

Pope, K. S. & Vasquez, M. J. T. (2016). *Ethics in psychotherapy and counseling* (5th edn.). Hoboken, NJ: Wiley.

Pope, K. S. & Vetter, V. A. (1992). Ethical dilemmas encountered by members of the American Psychological Association. *American Psychologist, 47,* 397–411.

Rodriguez, M., Domenech, M., Cornish, J. A. E., Thomas, J. T., Forrest, L., Anderson, A., & Bow, J. N. (2014). Ethics education in professional psychology: A survey of American Psychological Association Accredited Programs, *Training and Education in Professional Psychology*, *8*, 241–247.

Rogerson, M. D., Gottlieb, M. C., Handelsman, M. M., Knapp, S., & Younggren, J. (2011). Nonrational processes in ethical decision making. *American Psychologist*, *66*, 614–623.

Welfel, E. R. (2005). Accepting fallibility: A model for personal responsibility for nonegregious ethics violations. *Counseling and Values*, *49*, 120–131.

Welfel, E. R. (2012). Teaching ethics: Models, methods, and challenges. In S. J. Knapp, M. C. Gottlieb, M. M. Handelsman, & L. D. VandeCreek (Eds.), *APA handbook of ethics in psychology* (Vol. 2, pp. 277–305). Washington, DC: American Psychological Association.

Index

AAMFT standards
  1.2: Informed Consent 248
  1.3: Multiple Relationships 258
  1.7: Abuse of Therapeutic Relationship 258, 259, 260
  1.8: Client autonomy 240–241
  1.9: Relationship Beneficial 241, 242
  1.10: Referrals 251, 255
  2.1: Disclosing Confidentiality 245
  2.2: Client Information Release 241, 245–246
  3.4: Conflict of Interest 258
  3.6: New Skills 257
  3.10: Scope of Competence 241, 257
  7.2: Legal Testimony 258
  7.5: Avoiding Conflicts 258
  7.8: Professional Opinions 257
  8.4: Truthful Representation 243, 246–247
ACA Advocacy Competencies 314
ACA Code of Ethics
  Purpose 640
  Section 6: Managing and Maintaining Boundaries and Professional Relationships 654–655
  Section A2a: Informed consent 651–652
  Section A4b: Personal Values 651
  Section A7b: Confidentiality and Advocacy 651–652
  Section A9: Group Work 220, 231
  Section B: Confidentiality and Privacy 106
  Section B4: Groups and Families 220, 221–222
  Section C2a: Boundaries of Competence 233–234
  Section H6: Social Media 222, 626–627
Acculturation Model 386
ACTION model of decision-making 640, 648–650
addiction
  confidentiality issues 156–160, 173, 175
  decisional capacity 160–164, 175
  demographics 154
  informed consent issues 164–167, 175
  involuntary commitment 161, 163
  lack of ethical stance 155

  models of addiction 154–155
  prescription stimulants misuse 170–172
  stigmatization of addicts 167–169, 175
adolescents
  confidentiality 204–207, 622–626, 627–628
  genetic testing 578–579, 581–592
  parentification of immigrants 395
  social media use 617–618, 621, 631–633
  suicide intervention 631
advocacy 174, 274–275, 277–278
alienation strategies, in divorce 258–259
American Association for Marriage and Family Therapy *see* AAMFT
American Counselling Association *see* ACA
American Nurses Association 158, 168, 169
American Psychiatric Association, ED guidelines 200
American Psychologists Association *see* APA
APA Competencies for Psychology Practice in Primary Care 603, 606
APA Ethics Code *see* APA Principles; APA Standards; *individual ethical issues e.g.* competence
APA Guidelines
  Assessment and Intervention with Persons with Disabilities 290, 294, 297–298
  Child Custody Evaluations in Family Law Proceedings 463, 466–467, 468
  Clinical Supervision in Health Service Psychology 232, 523, 525, 527
  Ethnic, Linguistic and Cultural Diversity 98, 180, 252
  Multicultural Education, Training, Research, Practice and Organization Change 304, 307, 309, 312, 313, 385, 390–391, 395, 397, 569, 664
  Practice with Older Adults 331
  Practice of Telepsychology 618–620, 628, 632
  Prevention in Psychology 663, 672
  Psychological Evaluations in Child Protection Matters 454
  Psychological Practice with Lesbian Gay and Bisexual Clients 418–420
  Psychological Practice with Transgender and Gender Non-conforming People 333

Psychologists' Involvement in
    Pharmacological Issues 610–612
Specialty Guidelines for Forensic
    Psychologists 463, 466, 468
APA Ethics Code Principles
  A: Beneficence and non-maleficence
    benefits of screening 232–233
    bias of therapists 415–416, 418–419,
      423–424
    disability cases 296
    disclosure of information 56, 445
    eating disorders 202–203
    genetics testing 582, 585–586, 588–590
    immigrant clients 389–390
    legal conflicts 433, 445
    LGBT issues 273, 281, 333, 415–416, 420,
      423–424, 501–502
    multiple relationships 102–103
    older adults 281, 323–326, 328
    people of color 315–316
    personal issues 12, 52, 128–129
    preventative work 661
    in private practice 124
    research 349, 352, 354, 481–482, 496–498
    substance abuse cases 171
  B: Fidelity and Responsibility
    and confidentiality 120, 329
    eating disorders 273
    immigrants and refugees 385
    informed consent 73
    LGBT issues 281
    older adults 281, 328, 329
    personal issues 129
    private practice 124
    research 349, 354, 359, 481–482
    social media issues 221
    supervisors 538
  C: Integrity
    group contracts 223
    immigrants and refugees 385
    research projects 357–358, 359
    substance abuse cases 171–172
    supervisors 538–539
  D: Justice
    bias of therapists 415
    cultural competence 661–662, 663, 667
    immigrants and refugees 385
    LGBT research 503
    multiple relationships 225
    and people of color 316
    prevention work 667, 670
    and referrals 51–52
    and substance abuse cases 172
  E: Respect for People's Rights and Dignity
    bias of therapists 415, 418–419, 423–424
    in couples and family therapy 240–241
    cultural competence 304, 307, 663
    disability cases 286–287, 296

    and discrimination 390
    genetics testing 590–591
    in group psychotherapy 221, 223, 226
    immigrants and refugees 385
    LGBT clients 59, 273, 280, 281, 334–335,
      420, 423–424
    multiple relationships 103
    older adults 273, 277, 280, 323–326,
      328–329, 334–335
    online research of forums 476–477
    personal issues 129
    private practice 124
    research 476–477, 481–482, 483, 496
    sexual issues 277, 280
    and substance abuse 164
APA Skill Building Workshop 61
APA Ethics Code Standards
  Standard 1.02 14, 433
  Standard 1.03 14, 558, 608, 609–610, 671
  Standard 1.04 310, 517
  Standard 2.01
    cultural competence 87, 358–359, 496–498,
      569, 661–662, 663, 667, 668
    disability issues 286–287, 289
    eating disorders 200–201, 202–203
    emergency situations 96–97, 650
    group therapy 226
    language fluency 389
    LGBT clients 333, 418–420, 502, 523–525
    prevention work 663, 667, 668, 670
    primary care 610, 611–612
    psychological consultation 562, 566, 567
    psychological evaluations 457–458
    referrals 118, 393, 607–608
    refugee clients 393–394
    in research projects 362, 496–498, 502
    rural areas 94
    sexual violence 184–185
    and supervision 513
    training 119, 184–185, 202, 241
  Standard 2.02 96–97, 503
  Standard 2.03 130, 257, 280–281, 362, 393,
    419–420, 516, 569, 606
  Standard 2.04 457, 516
  Standard 2.05 393, 397, 502–503, 507, 513,
    522, 527
  Standard 2.06! 12, 129–130, 260, 287, 289,
    521, 527, 565
  Standard 3.01 125, 286–287, 304, 313,
    419–420, 648, 661–662
  Standard 3.03 286–287, 304
  Standard 3.04 181–182
    adolescents 620, 632
    cancellations 87
    coaching 647
    couples and family therapy 242, 259, 525
    cultural competence 255, 516–517
    and deception in research 480

APA Ethics Code Standards (cont.)
   eating disorders 200–201, 202–203
   group therapy 230
   hospital settings 632
   immigrant clients 389–390
   interrogation and torture 14
   legal conflicts 433
   LGBT issues 280, 415–416, 525
   misuse of data 558
   older adults 280, 329
   and patient autonomy 164
   personal issues 52, 126, 130, 394
   in psychological consultation 561
   sexual violence 184–185
   and substance abuse issues 171
   supervisee dilemmas 516–517
   supervisors 516–517, 527, 528
Standard 3.05
   boundary issues 307–308
   coaching 564, 648
   disability cases 287, 293
   group therapy 224–225
   legal cases 433
   primary care 608
   in research 479, 500
   rural areas 101
   supervision 513
Standard 3.06 129, 258, 564
Standard 3.07 560–561, 648, 670
Standard 3.08 126, 287–288, 496, 506
Standard 3.09 74, 241, 328, 644
Standard 3.10
   in coaching 647
   crisis situations 53
   decisional capacity 271, 287, 293–294
   genetics testing 582–584, 590
   minors 621
   preventative work 661
   refugee clients 394
   in research 480–481
   sexual violence cases 185
   social media 73
Standard 3.11 73, 328, 557–558, 561, 563,
   566
Standard 4.01
   elder abuse 328–329
   genetics testing 586, 590
   group therapy 225–226
   hospital settings 632
   international research 504–505
   primary care 606
   private practice 120
   research studies 479, 507
   rural areas 106
   social media 626
   suicide ideation 268–269
   transgender cases 333
   use of interpreters 393

Standard 4.02
   children 245
   coaching 648
   elder abuse 328–329
   genetics testing 584–585
   group therapy 222–226
   with immigrants 397–398
   informed consent 287
   sexual violence cases 185
   and social media 618–620, 622, 625
Standard 4.04 504–505
Standard 4.05 56, 400
   LGBT clients 334–335
   older adults 328–329, 334–335
   primary care 606
   private practice 120
   and protection from harm 164
   research projects 357–358
   and right to privacy 120
   suicidal clients 269
   working with minors and adolescents 205
Standard 4.06 251, 328–329, 361, 525, 606
Standard 5.01 51, 126, 566, 567
Standard 5.05 126
Standard 6.01 119, 268–269, 460
Standard 6.04 126, 243, 246–247, 401, 460
Standard 6.05! 125–126
Standard 7.04 528–529
Standard 7.06 418–420
Standard 8.01 478, 499, 503
Standard 8.02 483, 499–500, 506
Standard 8.03 487–488
Standard 8.05 353, 483, 506–507
Standard 8.07 477, 480
Standard 9.01 88, 259, 457, 466, 498, 507,
   664–665
Standard 9.02 466, 498, 507, 566, 665
Standard 9.03! 566, 582–584, 590
Standard 9.04 566
Standard 9.05 498
Standard 9.06 324, 359, 507, 566
Standard 9.07 498, 507, 566
Standard 9.10 508
Standard 10.01 87–88, 242, 245, 388, 394,
   399, 431, 513
Standard 10.02 240, 248, 257–258
Standard 10.03 219–220, 221–222, 394
Standard 10.04 120–121
Standard 10.10 120–121, 130, 522
ASGW Multicultural and Social Justice
   Competence Principles for Group
   Workers 229–230, 233–234, 516
at-risk clients, suicide assessment 54, 99,
   139–141, 142, 149, 212, 231
at-risk students 26–28, 54
Atkinson, Thompson and Grant model 398
autonomy of client
   see also APA Principles, E

children 204–205, 207–208, 212
end of life care 272
informed consent 168
involuntary commitment 161, 163, 209–211, 212
suicidal tendencies 143–145, 147–148, 150
avoidance of harm
    see also APA Principles, A; APA Standards, Standard 3.04
    conflicting ethical guidance 15, 16–17
    in couples and family therapy 252, 254
    crisis situations 84
    eating disorders therapy 200–201, 202–203, 206
    information release consent 56
    medical tourism 87
    multiple relationships 8
    protection of online researcher 486–488
    psychologist's health factors 52
    surgery 76

Barnett and Johnson model 497
Beauchamp and Childress model 84–85
behavioural problems (schools) 23–25, 28–35, 36–37
Belmont Report 493–494
beneficence see APA Principles, A; APA Standards, Standard 3.04
Berry's Model of Acculturation 386
bias (psychologists)
    see also cognitive development model
    and acculturation 397
    in coaching 653
    consultation for 335, 413–414, 416, 417, 420
    countertransference 367–368, 395–399, 415–416, 418–419
    cultural 664
    in forensic evaluations 460–465, 469–470
    LGBT clients 406, 410, 421–423
    referrals 411, 416, 419–420, 520, 522, 523
    self-awareness 310–311, 315, 326, 374, 406–407, 417, 682
    supervision for 61, 335, 371, 519–523
    unconscious bias 412
black people see people of color
blind spots (ethical errors) 681
boundaries 9, 105, 109–111, 543–544, 547
British Psychological Society internet guidelines 474–475
Bronfenbrenner's Ecological Model 385–386
bulldozer parenting 48
Burlingame, Fuhriman and Johnson, leadership model 234
business issues 118, 122–126, 127–131, 132, 626–628

Campbell and Gordon guidelines 104–105
Canadian Psychological Association Code of Ethics 180–181, 570
cancer, genetic testing 582–588
CBPA 341, 342–349, 350–359, 360–362
celebrity patients 85–89
charitable attributions 682–683
child abuse 184, 375–376, 434, 461–465
    mandated reporting 429–435
child protection 452–469
children
    see also adolescents; minors
    adult children and parents' end-of-life 271
    court testimony 464–465, 467
    in divorce cases 256–260
    domestic violence 431–432
    in family therapy 244–248, 252–256
    LGBT issues 252–256
    rights 39, 204–205
classification systems, diagnostic 22–23
classroom management 29–30
client identification
    see also multiple relationships
    couples and family therapy 240–241, 244–245, 249, 250, 253–254, 257–258
    prevention work 660
    psychological consultation 559–560, 561
clinical supervision
    competence of supervisors 515–518, 527–528
    complaints against supervisee 526–529
    cultural issues 515–525
    decision-making 514–515
    definitions 511–512
    ethical and legal issues 512–513
    supervisee value conflicts 518–523
coaching
    bias of coach 653
    boundary management 652
    confidentiality 648, 649, 650
    cultural competence 648–650
    decision-making 640–641
    definition 637
    differences from psychotherapy 643
    ethical standards and competencies 637–640
    framework 656
    multiple relationships 563–565, 641–656
    recontracting process 653
coercive interventions 36–37, 149, 166, 560–561
cognitive development model of ethical competence
    overview 407–409, 421
    preawareness 410–413, 421–422
    exploration and awareness 413–415, 421–423
    enactment and self-evaluation 415–417, 423
    personal commitment 423
    in supervision and training 417–420
college settings
    confidentiality and reports 54–57

college settings (cont.)
  demand on counseling services 48–52
  funding reduction 48
  higher education culture 47–48
  mental health severity 49, 52–54
  social media 62–65, 66, 67
  training for diversity 57–61
color-blind approach (cultural issues) 310
common couple violence 250
community based participatory action research
      see CBPA
compassion fatigue 11
competence
  see also APA Standards (Standard 2.01, 2.03);
      cognitive development model; cultural
      competence
  boundary violations 454–458, 652
  in couples and family therapy 241, 257–258,
      259, 288–291
  and currency 678
  disability issues 287, 289, 290, 299
  eating disorders cases 200–201, 205
  ethical competence 408
  in forensic evaluation 454–458
  in group psychotherapy 226, 230–236, 237
  healthcare settings 87, 89, 603, 610–612
  immigrant and refugee clients 392, 393
  and LGBT clients 331–335
  military settings 10–14
  and multiple relationships 224
  and personal problems 109–111, 127–130,
      131–132
  in prevention work 667
  private practice 116–121, 130
  psychological consultancy 565–567
  in RRICC model 369
  rural settings 94–100
  sexual violence scenarios 184–185
  of supervisors 515–529, 539–540, 548
competencies in primary care 603
complaints
  see also ethical violations
  court cases 433, 441, 446
  supervisor role 526–529, 535–546
confidentiality
  see also APA Standards (Standard 4.01, 4.02,
      4.05); informed consent
  abuse/sexual violence scenarios 185, 190, 191,
      327–331
  in addiction scenarios 156–160, 173, 175
  in care settings 274, 275
  consultancy 557–567
  and duty to warn 441
  end of life decisions 267–268
  in family therapy 241–242, 245–246, 250,
      254, 258
  genetics testing 584–585, 590
  in group therapy 219–224, 236, 618–620

in higher education 54–57
information sharing 54, 55–57, 116–121
and mandated reports 430–431, 432, 435, 446
of minors/dependents 204–207, 212, 254,
      430–431, 435, 623–624
multi-disciplinary teams 54, 55–57, 73–75
multiple relationships 5, 106–109, 158–159,
      246, 622–626
no secrets policy 248, 249, 250
in primary care 606
in psychological consulting 559–560, 561,
      565–566
religious issues 369
research studies 190, 191–192, 479, 504–505,
      506
in rural settings 105, 106–109
and social media 220–224, 618–620, 626–631,
      681
therapist's case discussion with partners 681
trainees 523, 528–529
conflicts of interest see AAMFT standards; APA
      Standards (Standards 1.02, 1.03, 2.06,
      3.06); multiple relationships; values
      conflicts
conscience clauses 518, 520–522
consultancy see psychological consultation
consultation with colleagues
  see also supervision
  addiction 173–174
  bias issues 413–414, 416, 417, 420
  in children's cases 207
  cultural issues 524–525, 668
  for decision-making 508
  dementia cases 269, 281
  disability issues 289–290
  eating disorders 201–202, 203, 213
  end of life situations 272
  financial advice for clients 589
  in forensic evaluation 469
  for immigrant and refugee clients 394, 402
  importance 678
  mediation for errors 682
  multiple relationships 105, 656
  religious areas 381
  risk assessment of client violence 441
  rural practice 99
  sexual abuse cases 188
  by supervisors 540, 549
continuing education
  see also consultation with colleagues;
      supervision
  for addiction work 155, 173
  for competence 420, 423, 669
  for disability issues 290
  efficacy 680
  for forensic work 458, 469
  for group psychotherapists 226, 235–236, 237
  for LGBT practice 421–422

for prevention work 672
for primary care 606
for private practice 126, 131, 132
for religious issues 381
for sexual violence work 187–188
for supervisors 529, 539
contracts 223, 558, 642
Corey, Corey and Callanan model 180
cost-benefit analyses, in schools 26–27, 28,
   35–36
counseling services
   in education 20, 48–52
   social media use 62–65, 66, 67
countertransference
   and bias 367–368, 395–399, 415–416,
      418–419
   in disability cases 294–295, 297
   in eating disorder cases 201, 203
   in forensic evaluation cases 459, 460
   with immigrant clients 396
   in multiple relationships 9, 110–111
   with older adults 294–295
   supervisors 545, 549
   and text messaging 630
couples and family therapy
   alienation strategies 258–259
   children 244–248, 252–260
   client identification 240–241, 244–245, 249,
      250, 253–254, 257–258
   competence 241, 257–258, 259, 288–291
   confidentiality 241–242, 245–246, 248–252,
      254, 258
   diagnosis of issues 243–244, 247, 255–256,
      260
   multicultural issues 523–525
   power relationships 242–244, 246, 251,
      254–255, 258–259, 260
   veracity 243, 246–247, 251–252, 255, 259
   whole family involvement 253
covert research 479–482
crisis situations 85, 78–80, 84, 85, 138
cultural competence
   in care settings 275
   consultancy 568–569
   for couples/family clients 255–256, 515–529
   disability cases 289
   ethical principles 87, 255, 304, 307, 315–317,
      358–359
   in group psychotherapy 229–230, 313–315
   language issues 95–96
   for LGBT clients 187, 333–334, 515–529
   for minority groups 303–316, 390, 399–401
   nursing staff 165
   preventative work 666–669
   program adaption 665–666
   religious issues 371, 377–378, 381
   research projects 355, 358–359
   rural settings 97, 669–671

sexual violence cases 187
supervisors 515–525, 534, 544
cultural differences
   collectivist cultures 494–495, 506
   color-blind approaches 310
   disability issues 292–293
   end of life care 271
   and genetics testing 587–588
   and group participation 229
   and informed consent 166–167
   language issues 94–98
      see also interpreters; translation
   religious cultures 370–371
   students in schools 35, 506

data storage/protection 484, 485, 489
deception
   see also APA Standards (Standard 5.01, 8.07)
   by client 168–169, 170–172
   by researcher 480
decision-making models
   ACTION model 640, 648–650
   Barnett and Johnson 497
   Corey, Corey and Callanan 180
   Fisher 328–330
   Karel's framework 322, 323–326, 328–330
   Knapp and VandeCreek 77
   Remley and Herlihy 198
   SAD formula 640–641, 652–653
   Welfel 641, 655–656
decisional capacity 160–164, 175, 210–211,
   276–281
dementia 266–269, 276–281
disability 288–298
   competence 288–291
   definition 286
   employment discrimination 295–298
   ethics codes 286–288
   evaluation 291–295
   guidelines 285–286
disadvantage see disability; LGBT clients; minority groups; people of color
disciplinary supervision
   avoiding therapist role 541–546
   benefits for supervisor 549
   definition 533
   monitoring supervisee 540–541, 547–548
   need for prior evaluation of cases 535–541
   recalibration following problems 546
   recommendations 547–549
   relationship 548
   supervisor's role 534–535, 545, 546
disclosure of information
   see also APA Standards, (Standard 4.05,
      7.04); confidentiality; informed consent;
      mandatory reporting
   addiction of nursing staff 157–158, 159–160
   multiple relationships 158–159

disclosure of information (cont.)
   sexual orientation 253, 254, 256, 272, 274
discrimination
   see also APA Standard, Standard 3.01
   disability 295–298
   and genetic predisposition to illness 586–587
   immigrants 398–399
   people of color 303, 326
   perception by client 280
   sexual orientation 272–276, 372–373
distributive justice 39
diversity
   see also cultural competence; cultural differ-
      ence; disability; LGBT clients; minority
      groups; people of color
   APA statement 58
divorce, non-normative 256–260
documentation *see* record-keeping; records
documentation of immigrants 398, 400
domestic violence *see* intimate partner violence;
   sexual violence
dual identity/relationships *see* multiple
   relationships
duty to warn 435–442, 584–585

eating disorders 197, 198–214
ecological model 385–386
education *see* college settings; school settings
education for ethics 679–682
elder abuse 279–280, 327–331
electronic health records 73–74, 432
eligibility for services, client awareness 53
email communication with clients 62
empathy failure 11–12
end of life issues 267–268, 269–272
Ethical Choice Making Process model 640,
   645–647
ethical codes *see* AAMFT standards; ACA Code
   of Ethics; APA Guidelines; APA
   Principles; APA Standards; NASW
ethical competence 408, 424
   see also cognitive development model; com-
      petence; disciplinary supervision
ethical principles 78, 158, 166, 219–220, 241,
   493–494, 603
ethical violations 310, 514–515, 517, 531–533,
   682–683
ethnic minorities 269–272, 306–308, 322–335
   see also cultural competence; people of color
ethnicity, definition 302–303
evidence-based interventions 40–42

Facebook use 59–61, 220–224, 626–628
fairness
   see also APA Principles, D
   school intervention issues 32, 37–39
false-positive diagnoses/screening 22–23, 26
family therapy *see* couples and family therapy

fertility preservation, genetics testing 588–592
financial issues
   private practice 121–126
   research project grants 347, 348, 349, 354
Fisher's decision-making model 328–330
forensic evaluations *see* psychological
   evaluations
forum research 476–482
frameworks 23–25, 305, 603–604
friendship issues 654–656

gender issues
   domestic violence 185, 187, 191, 252
   immigrants 400–401
   religious clients 370–371
genetic testing
   cancer testing 582–585
   counselling 582–592
   ethical issues 579
   psychologist's role 579–581, 582–583, 584,
      585–586, 588, 589, 592
   selective reproduction 591
   types 577–578
group psychotherapy
   competence 224–227, 230–236, 237
   confidentiality 219–224, 236, 618–620
   contracts 223
   cultural competence 229–230, 313–315
   different to coaching 643
   drop out 227–230, 234–235
   education of clients 621–622
   effectiveness 235
   ethical issues 219–220
   guidelines 235
   leadership skills 234
   preparation of members 230
   silent members 227–230
   and social media 617–622
   terminology 218
   voluntary participation 227–230
Guidelines *see* APA Guidelines

health insurance 73, 155–156, 586–587
health psychology
   see also hospital settings; primary care
   training 78–80
helicopter parenting 48
higher education *see* college settings
homosexuality 185, 187, 252–256, 272–276,
   372–374, 378–379, 501, 520–521
   see also LGBT clients
hospital settings
   ethical decision-making 77, 632
   high risk surgery 70–72
   holistic care 70
   international celebrity patients 85–89
   medical tourism 88, 89–90
   multidisciplinary working 70–72, 74–76, 78

suicide risk 632
supervision 81–85
hospitalization 161, 163, 209–211
human rights *see* APA Principles, E; children, rights

ICF, ethics code and competencies 638–639, 642–643, 644, 647, 648, 651, 654–655
immigrant and refugee clients 384
  see also interpreters; translation
  context for treatment 386–387, 391, 393–394, 395
  documentation 398, 400
  ethical issues 396–397
  language issues 252–256, 387–401
  models 385–386
information sharing 54, 223
  see also confidentiality; disclosure
informed consent
  see also APA Standards, (Standard 3.10, 8.02, 8.03, 9.03)
  addiction cases 164–167, 175
  APA Ethics Code 53
  and child abuse 435
  children 206, 248
  in coaching 646
  and confidentiality 557–561
  couples and family therapy 242–243, 248
  crisis appointments 53–54
  dementia cases 269
  disability cases 290
  eating disorders 206, 212
  genetics testing 582–584, 590
  in group psychotherapy 222
  international differences 494–495, 506
  language issues 87–88, 90, 99, 388, 399
  and legal incompetency 33
  and mandatory reporting 431, 439, 446
  in multidisciplinary scenarios 71, 72–73
  in multiple relationships 9
  in prevention work 659–662
  process approach 661
  in psychological consultation 559–560, 566
  in religious organisations 376
  in research studies 191, 353, 477, 478, 480–481, 483, 484, 494–495, 499–501, 506
  in sexual violence cases 185, 187, 191
  and social media 621–622
  in supervision 539–540, 541, 547
  for trainees 523
Integrative, Affirmative Supervision (ISA) model 420
integrity *see* APA Principles, C; competence
interdisciplinary consultation 99, 329
International Coach Federation *see* ICF
international ethical documents 494
international patients 85–89

international research
  competence 496–498
  cultural issues 495–508
  ethics codes and standards 493–494
  informed consent 494–495, 499–501
Internet 63, 64
  see also Facebook; social media
interpreters
  see also translation
  family members as 94–98, 252–256
  for immigrants/refugees 88, 387, 388–389, 392–393, 401, 402
  in rural settings 94–98
interprofessional teams *see* multidisciplinary teams
intimate partner violence (IPV) 182–187, 248–252
  see also sexual violence
  description 179
  identifying abuse 251–252
  patriarchal terrorism 250
involuntary commitment 161, 163, 209–211
IPV *see* intimate partner violence
ISA model 420

justice *see* APA Principles, D

Kanzler, Goodie, Hunter, Glotfelter and Bodart framework 603–604
Karel's decision-making framework 322, 323–326, 328–330
Knapp and VandeCreek's model 77
Kolmes' social media policy 621

labeling (diagnostic) 21–26, 35, 38
Lamb, Catanzaro and Moorman guidelines 103–104
language issues *see* interpreters; translation
leadership skills in group therapy 234
legal cases
  child abuse reporting 429–435
  protection from harm 435–442
  therapist-client privilege 443–446
legal issues
  addiction 155–156, 162
  capacity conflicts 162, 163–164
  coaching and therapy 564–565
  disclosure 55, 158–159, 430–431, 432, 435, 444
  LGBT discrimination 273
  mandatory reporting 397–398
  military service 5, 14–17
  online research 486, 488–489
  refusal of treatment 272
  sexual violence 185–186, 190–191
  suicidal clients 142
  supervision 186, 512–513
LGBT clients
  coming out to parents 252–256, 523–525

LGBT clients (cont.)
   counselor training 57–59
   discrimination 272–276, 372–373
   older adults 272–276, 331–335
   religious issues 57–61, 273, 372–380, 519–523
   sexual violence victims 182–187
   and therapist bias 406, 410, 421–423
   transgender issues 331–335, 415–417
LGBT research 501–506
Lowmans' taxonomy 564

mandatory reporting
   in child abuse cases 429–435
   and confidentiality 430–431
   duty to warn 435–436
   features 434
   legal requirements 435, 436, 437–438, 441
   and multiple relationships 433
   and therapeutic relationship 431–432
marginalized groups see disability; disadvan-
       tage; LGBT clients; minority groups;
       people of color
maternity leave, provisions for clients 122–126
MECA 386
medical tourism 88, 89–90
medication prescription 172, 610–612
military settings
   competence 10–14
   embedded assignments 5–6
   legal obligations 5, 14–17
   mixed agency issues 4–5
   recommendations 9–10, 13–14, 17
   traumatic impact on practitioners 10–14
   unique psychologist role 3–4
minority groups
   see also disability; LGBT clients; people of
       color
   cultural competence 303–316, 390, 399–401
   disability issues 288–298
   effect of IQ testing 35–36
   family therapy with immigrants 252–256
   increase in student populations 47
   language issues see interpreters; translation
   research with 340
   training for counselors 57–59
   victims of sexual violence 179, 185, 191
minors
   see also adolescents; parents
   autonomy 204–205, 207–208, 212
   confidentiality 204–207, 212, 254
   genetics testing 590, 591
   informed consent 206, 248
   recommendations for therapists 207–208
   social media issues 621, 628–633
misconduct see charitable attributions; ethical
       violations
misdiagnosis of medical conditions 22–23, 24
misuse of data 557–567

mixed agency, military service 4–5
mixed methods research 485–489
modification method 229
Multidimensional Ecosystemic Comparative
       Approach (MECA) 386
multidisciplinary teams 70–72, 74–76, 78, 213,
       608–612
multiple relationships
   see also APA Standards, Standard 3.05
   children and parents 254–255, 622–626
   coaching 563–565, 641–656
   confidentiality 5, 106–109, 158–159, 246,
       622–626
   consultation of colleagues 105, 656
   in couples therapy 257–258
   in evaluations 291–295, 458–461
   in group psychotherapy 224–227, 236
   with immigrant clients 254–255, 387–401
   informed consent 9
   Lamb, Cantanzaro and Moorman guidelines
       103–104
   and mandatory reporting 433
   military settings 4–5, 6–10
   Pomerantz and Eiting model 650
   psychological consultation 562–565
   and psychological evaluations 458–461
   research studies 191, 479
   rural settings 100–111
   supervision 535–546

NASW Code of Ethics (National Association of
       Social Workers) 101, 166
no secrets policy 248, 249, 250
nonmaleficence see APA Standards, standard
       3.04; avoidance of harm
nursing, ethical principles 158, 168, 169

older adults
   dementia 266–269, 276–281
   elder abuse 279–280, 327–331
   end of life care 267–268, 269–272
   ethical issues 321–322
   ethnic groups 269–272, 291–295,
       322–335
   LGBT adults 272–276, 331–335
   provision of psychological services 321
   sexuality issues 276–281
   suicide risk 266–269
online research
   avoiding counselor role 487
   domains 474
   mixed methods research 485–489
   protection of researcher 487–488
   qualitative research 476–489
   quantitative research 482–485
online surveys 482–485
Oregon Psychological Association model 180
organizational mirroring 559

palliative care, and suicide 144, 147
parental alienation syndrome (PAS) 464
parents
    see also minors
    confidentiality of children 204–207, 212,
        622–626
    consent in research study 353
    consultation 207, 212, 623, 632, 633
    relationship with therapists 623–624
    role in school screening 28
PAS 464
patriarchal terrorism 250
people of color 302–304
    cultural competence 303–306
    discrimination 303, 326
    ethical principles 315–317
    group description 302
Pomerantz and Eiting model 650
population-based care 600
post-traumatic stress disorder 15–16
power relationships
    couples and family therapy 242–244, 246,
        251, 254–255, 258–259, 260
    immigrant clients 391
    in research studies 360–361
    in supervision 533–534, 544
prevention work
    overview 659
    cultural competence 662–665, 666–669
    and ethical standards 671–672
    evaluation of programmes 669–671
    informed consent 659–662
    knowledge and skills 672
    planning process 664–665
    program adaptation 665–667
primary care settings
    culture 598, 600, 604–612
    ethics codes and competencies 603
    frameworks for ethical dilemmas 603–604
    models of care 599–602
privacy 62–65, 109–111, 627, 628
private practice
    characteristics 115–116
    competence 116–121, 130
    finance 121–126
    recommendations 132
    responsibility 116–121, 127–131
    rural areas 198–203
    self-care 127–131
    social media 628–631
procedural ethics 475, 477–478, 480–484,
        486–489
process ethics 475, 478–479, 482, 485,
        489
psychological consultation 552–553
    client identification 559–560, 561
    compared to professional collaboration
        555–556

compared to psychotherapy 555
    competence 565–567
    confidentiality 557–567
    cultural competence 567–569
    ethical issues 556–557
    ethical practice 569–571
    ethics codes and standards 556–557
    informed consent 557–567
    multiple relationships 562–565
    types 553–555
psychological evaluations
    bias of evaluators 460–465, 469–470
    ethical violations 453, 454–458, 461–465
    expertise required 452
    faulty methods 465–469
    multiple relationship conflicts 458–461
    in religious orders 372, 374–377
psychologists
    see also competence; countertransference;
        supervision
    acknowledgement of own emotions
        677–678
    bias see bias (psychologists)
    education role 274–275
    ethical violations 682–683
    fear of suicidal attempts 146
    forensic role and expertise 457–458
    personal issues 109–111, 183–184, 272,
        519–523
    secondary trauma 394
    self-care 10–14, 99, 100, 127–131, 132,
        289–290
psychopathology 22–25, 41
psychotherapeutic privilege 444
psychotherapy see group psychotherapy
punishment in schools 29–30, 38–39

qualitative research 476–482, 501–506
quantitative research 482–485

race, definition 303
racial issues see cultural competence; cultural
        differences; people of color
racism 303, 326, 398–399
reciprocal determinist framework 23–25
record-keeping
    of consultation with experts 174
    in couples and family therapy 242
    in disciplinary supervision 539–540,
        548–549
    multiple relationships 9–10, 656
    for protection in legal cases 446, 447
    rural scenarios 99
    violence threats to third parties 442
records, legal access and confidentiality 55
referrals
    bias issues 411, 416, 419–420, 520, 522, 523
    dementia and suicidal ideation 269

referrals (cont.)
  disability issues 290
  in forensic evaluation cases 458
  from primary care 607
  immigrant and refugee clients 393, 402
  and mandatory reporting 446–447
  students 50–52
  for translation needs 255
reflective practice 649, 650, 656
refugees 391–395
  see also immigrant and refugee clients
religious issues
  attitude to suicide 136
  challenges 367–368
  conscience clauses 518, 520–521
  ethical issues 369–371, 518
  mental illness 378
  RRICC model 368–369, 373–374, 375, 376,
    378, 379–380
  and sexual violence 182–187, 501
  and sexuality 57–59, 273, 370, 372–377,
    519–523
remediation for errors 682
Remley and Herlihy model 198
research
  see also international research; online
    research
  confidentiality 190, 191–192
  disability access 191
  ethical considerations 188–191
  guidelines 474
  informed consent 191, 353, 477, 478,
    480–481, 483, 484, 494–495, 499–501,
    506
  measurement instruments 498–499
research grants see CBPA
research-based interventions 40–42
resilience in immigrant populations 387
response to intervention (RtI) 25
risk assessments 440–441
RRICC model 368–369, 373–374, 375, 376, 378,
  379–380
rural settings
  competence 94–100, 669–671
  health issues 93–94
  multiple relationships 100–111
  preventative work 668
  privacy of psychologists 109–111

SAD formula for decision-making 640–641,
  652–653
safeguarding, victims of sexual violence 182,
  183–184, 187, 190–191
same-sex relationships see homosexuality;
  LGBT clients
school settings
  effective system change 42–43
  engagement in learning 31, 32

interventions 36–43
  labeling of students 21–26, 35
  nurturing environment 31
  resistance to counseling facilities 20
  screening for problems and risk 26–28
  social control strategies 28–35
  transformative approaches 42–43
science-based interventions 39–42, 43
screening
  for cancer 582–585, 586
  group therapy 220, 222, 232–233
  for religious ministries 372
  schools 26–28
secondary traumatic stress 11, 394
self-care 10–14, 99, 100, 127–131, 132,
  289–290
sexual harassment 179
sexual orientation
  see also homosexuality; LGBT clients
  disclosure of information 253, 254, 256, 272,
    274
  discrimination 272–276, 372–373
sexual violence
  allegations in divorce 256–260
  concerns in dementia 276–281
  cultural and religious issues 182–187,
    501
  ethical decision-making models 180–181
  legal issues 185–186, 190–191
  LGBT issues 185, 187
  personal values issues 183–184, 189, 256
  research 188–191
  safety issues 182, 434–435
  terminology 178–180
sexuality issues 276–281, 370, 379–380
short-term counseling 49–52, 105
silence, in group psychotherapy 228
situational ethics 639–640
social control strategies 28–35
social justice 665
social media
  see also telepsychology
  blogs 622–626
  and confidentiality 220–224, 618–620,
    626–631, 681
  counseling service use 65, 66, 67, 634
  education of clients 621–622, 625
  effect on children 616, 634
  ethical issues 617, 620
  Facebook 59–61, 220–224, 626–628
  images 631–633
  issues in counseling 62–65
  policies 65, 66, 67, 617–620, 621, 622, 630,
    635
  privacy 62–65, 627, 628
  text messaging 628–631
socialization interventions 32–34
stalking 179

standards *see* AAMFT standards; ACA Code of
    Ethics; APA Guidelines; APA Principles;
    APA Standards; NASW Code of Ethics
stepped care, integrated primary care
    601–602
stigmatization 167–169, 175, 629
stress, secondary traumatic stress 11
students *see* college settings; school settings
subpoenas 445–446
substance abuse 247
    see also addiction
suicidal clients
    assisted suicide 143–148, 266–269
    attitudes to 136–137, 146
    autonomy 143–148, 150
    and confidentiality 55–57, 628–631
    empathy towards 150
    ethical standards 137
    in group therapy 230–235
    legal issues 142
    responding to 62–65, 134–136, 138
    risk assessment 54, 99, 139–141, 142, 149, 231
    rural areas 93–99
    and social media 62–65, 628–633
suicidal ideation 135–136, 142–143, 627, 629
suicide
    attitudes to 135–137, 146
    community interventions 666–671
    and eating disorders 197
    and mental illness 136, 141–142, 149
    unsuccessful attempts 136–137
supervision
    see also disciplinary supervision
    for bias 59–61, 335, 371, 410–411, 417–420,
        519–523
    for countertransference 396
    for cultural sensitivity 50–52, 311–312,
        524–525, 534
    for eating disorders cases 202, 203, 214
    for group psychotherapy 233, 234–235
    hospital settings 80–85
    informed consent 539–540, 541, 547
    for legal issues 186, 512–513
    models 420
    for new counselors 50, 51–52
    online research 485
    for parent/minor cases 625–626
    role boundaries 543–544, 547
    for rural issues 99
    supervisor competence 515–529, 539–540,
        548
supervisors
    cultural competence 515–525, 534, 544

disciplinary supervision benefits 549
    power relationship 533–534, 544
    role 85, 232, 233, 234–235, 397, 419–420,
        486, 534–535, 543–544, 545, 546
survivors, definition 178

telepsychology 63, 97, 104
    see also social media
terminal illness, assisted suicide 144, 147
text-based communication 628–631
therapeutic relationship
    maintaining 143–144, 157, 169
    and mandatory reporting 431–432, 439, 442,
        446–447
torture, APA policies 14
training
    see also continuing education; supervision
    confidentiality of trainee 528–529
    ethical competence 420
    health care psychologists 78–80
    response to client issues 522–523
transgender issues 331–335, 415–417
translation (language) 86, 87–88, 253, 254–255,
    507
    see also interpreters
traumatised clients 393–394, 399–401
treatment refusal 271, 272
truthfulness 212–213, 243, 246–247, 251–252,
    255, 259
    see also APA Principles, B
    client-requested deceptions 168–169

universities *see* college settings

values conflicts
    LGBT clients 421–423, 519–523
    religious clients 370–371, 378–380
    sexual violence 183–184, 189, 256
victims, definition 178
violence
    see also child abuse; sexual violence
    threats from clients to third parties 435–442
voluntary participation in groups 227–230,
    236

Welfel's decision-making model 641, 655–656
Welfel's questioning process 416
Wilkins' capacity assessment model 277

young adults
    see also adolescents
    genetic testing 578–579, 582–592
    victims of sexual violence 184, 185